C000177017

9
. vr
12

Collins

gem

Collins

English-
Japanese

Dictionary

HarperCollins Publishers
Westerhill Road
Bishopbriggs
Glasgow
G64 2QT
Great Britain

First Edition 1995

Latest Reprint 2006

© HarperCollins Publishers &
Shubun International Co., Ltd.
1995

ISBN-13 978-0-00-722401-2
ISBN-10 0-00-722401-X

Collins Gem® and Bank of
English® are registered
trademarks of HarperCollins
Publishers Limited

www.collins.co.uk

A catalogue record for this book
is available from the British
Library

HarperCollins Publishers,
10 East 53rd Street, New York,
NY 10022

COLLINS GEM ENGLISH-JAPANESE
DICTIONARY.
First US Edition 1995

ISBN-13 978-0-00-470823-2
ISBN-10 0-00-470823-7

www.harpercollins.com

Typeset by Tosho Printing Co.,
Ltd.

Printed in Italy by Legoprint
S.P.A.

Acknowledgements
We would like to thank those
authors and publishers who
kindly gave permission for
copyright material to be used
in the Collins Word Web. We
would also like to thank Times
Newspapers Ltd for providing
valuable data.

ORIGINAL MATERIAL BY
CollinsBilingual

JAPANESE LANGUAGE EDITION
Richard Goris
Yukimi Okubo

CONTENTS

INTRODUCTION

We are delighted you have decided to buy the Collins Shubun English-Japanese Dictionary and hope you will enjoy and benefit from using it at school, at home, on holiday or at work.

This introduction gives you a few tips on how to get the most out of your dictionary-not simply from its comprehensive wordlist but also from the information provided in each entry.

The Collins Shubun English-Japanese Dictionary begins by listing the abbreviations used in the text and follows with a guide to Japanese pronunciation and a chart of the two Japanese scripts "hiragana" and "katakana" together with the Roman letter transliteration used in this dictionary.

USING YOUR COLLINS SHUBUN DICTIONARY

A wealth of information is presented in the dictionary, using various typefaces, sizes of type, symbols, abbreviations and brackets. The conventions and symbols used are explained in the following sections.

Headwords

The words you look up in a dictionary -"headwords"- are listed alphabetically. They are printed in bold type for rapid identification. The headwords appearing at the top of each page indicate the first and last word dealt with on the page in question.

Information about the usage or form of certain headwords is given in brackets after the phonetic spelling. This usually appears in abbreviated form (e.g., *(fam)*, (COMM).

Common expressions in which the headword appears are shown in bold italic type (e.g., **account**... *of no account*).

When such expressions are preceded by a colon, it means that the headword is used mainly in that particular expression (e.g., **aback**... *adv: to be taken aback*).

Phonetic spellings

The phonetic spelling of each headword (indicating its pronunciation) is given in square brackets immediately after the headword (e.g., **able** [ei'bəl]). The phonetics show a standardized US English pronunciation in IPA (International Phonetic Alphabet) symbols. A list of these symbols is given on page (13).

Translations

Headword translations are given in ordinary type and, where more than one meaning or usage exists, these are separated by a semicolon. You will often find other words in brackets before the translations. These offer suggested contexts in which the headword might appear (e. g., **absentee** (from school, meeting etc) or provide synonyms (e. g. **able** (capable) or (skilled)). A white lozenge precedes a gloss giving information for the non-English native speaker.

"Keywords"

Special status is given to certain English words which are considered as "key" words in the language. They may, for example, occur very frequently or have several types of usage (e. g., **a, be**). A combination of lozenges and numbers helps you to distinguish different parts of speech and different meanings. Further helpful information is provided in brackets.

Grammatical Information

Parts of speech are given in abbreviated form in italics after the phonetic spellings of headwords (e. g., *vt, adv, conj*) and headwords with several parts of speech have a black lozenge before each new part of speech (e. g., **wash**).

使用上の注意

本辞典は英単語の意味を知りたい日本人だけでなく日本語を勉強している外国人も使えるよう、すべての訳語、補足説明などを日本文字とローマ字で併記した。ローマ字は原則としてヘボン式に従い、ローマ字：仮名対照表を (17)–(18) ページに示した。またローマ字には日本語のアクセントも加えた。右上がりのアクセント記号 (á) は声の上がりを、右下がりの記号 (à) は声の下がりを、記号のない場合は平坦に発音する事を示す。

見出し語は太字の立体活字で示した。つづりは米国の標準に従ったが、英国の標準がそれと異なる場合、アルファベット順にこれも示した。

　　　例：**anaemia** [əni:miːə] *etc* (BRIT) = **anemia** *etc*

続いて発音を [ ] の中に国際音声文字で示した。発音記号表は (13) ページにある。
アクセントは [ˊ] の記号でアクセントのある音節の後に示した。

　　　例：**able** [eiˈbəl]

品詞は斜字の略語で示した。例：**able** [eiˈbəl] *adj*

品詞に続いて訳語を日本語とローマ字で示した。原則として１つの意味に対して１つだけ最も頻度の高い訳語を採用した。

　　　例：**blockade**... 封鎖 fúsa

頻度が同じぐらいで複数の訳語がある場合、これを示すと共にコンマ (,) で分けた。

訳語の前に丸括弧 ( ) の中でその見出し語についての情報を記した。
立体の大文字はその語が使われる「分野」などを示す。

　　　例：**blood**... (BIO) 血 chi, 血液 ketsūeki

すなわち、**blood** は「生物学」という分野の語である。
立体の小文字はその他の情報を示す。

　　　例：**bleat**... *vi* (goat, sheep) 鳴く nakū

すなわち、**bleat** という動詞はヤギやヒツジについて使う語である。

　　　例：**aperture**... (hole) 穴 aná; (gap) すき間 sukíma; (PHOT) アパーチャ ápácha

この例では類語を使って見出し語の意味をはっきりさせている。また、このように１つの見出し語に対して複数の意味がある場合、セミコロン (;) で分ける。
見出し語の成句はその都度改行して太字の斜字で示した。

　　　例：**bearing**...
　　　　　to take a bearing...
　　　　　to find one's bearings...

成句は主語＋動詞形式のものでも文頭の大文字と文尾のピリオドをつけずにあくまでも
成句として扱った．ただし疑問を表す成句には？をつけた．

> 例：anyone...
>> *anyone could do it*
>> *can you see anyone?*

表示，標識，立て札などに使う成句は「...」で囲んだ．

> 例：entry...
>> 「*no entry*」...

改行なしで品詞などに続くコロン（：）＋ 太斜字の成句は見出し語などがその成句以外
には殆ど使われない事を示す．

> 例：aback ［əbǽk］ *adv. to be taken aback* 仰天する gyōten suru

丸括弧の中で *also*：に続く立体太字の語句はその意味では同意語である事を示す．

> 例：go about *vi (also: go around: rumor)* 流れる nagárerù

ここでは「噂が流れる」という意味では go about でも go around でも使える事を示して
いる．

特殊記号：

◆：最初に示した品詞と品詞が異なったものにつけた．

> 例：abdicate... *vt (responsibility, right)* 放棄する ...
>> ◆*vi (monarch)* 退位する ...

◇：補足説明を示す．

/：見出し語，成句の中で置き換えられる部分を示す．日本語訳やローマ字の中でこれ
を〔 〕で示した．

> 例：abide... *vt: I can't abide it/him* 私はそれ〔彼〕が大嫌いだ watáku-
> shi wá soré〔karè〕ga dáikirai da

KEYWORD：このタイトルは頻度の高い重要な語で特に徹底的に取り扱った見出し語
（たとえば **be, can**）を示す．

Phonetic Symbols 発音記号表

[ɑ:] *f*ather, h*o*t, kn*o*wledge

[æ] *a*t, h*a*ve, c*a*t

[ai] m*y*, b*uy*, l*i*ke

[au] h*ow*, m*ou*th

[e] m*e*n, s*ay*s, fri*e*nd

[ei] s*ay*, t*a*ke, r*ai*n

[eːr] *ai*r, c*a*re, wh*e*re

[ə] *a*bove, p*a*yment, lab*e*l

[əːr] g*ir*l, l*ear*n, b*ur*n, w*or*m

[i] s*i*t, wom*e*n, b*u*sy

[i:] s*ee*, b*ea*n, c*i*ty

[ou] n*o*, kn*ow*, b*oa*t

[ɔi] b*oy*, b*oi*l

[u] b*oo*k, c*oul*d, p*u*t

[u:] t*oo*l, s*ou*p, bl*ue*

[ɔ:] l*aw*, w*a*lk, st*o*ry

[ʌ] *u*p, c*u*t, ab*o*ve

[p] *p*ut, cu*p*

[b] *b*e, ta*b*

[d] *d*own, ha*d*

[t] *t*oo, ho*t*

[k] *c*ome, ba*ck*

[g] *g*o, ta*g*

[s] *s*ee, cup*s*, for*c*e

[z] ro*s*e, bu*zz*

[ʃ] *sh*e, *s*ugar

[ʒ] vi*s*ion, plea*s*ure

[tʃ] *ch*urch

[dʒ] *j*am, *g*em, *j*udge

[f] *f*arm, hal*f*, *ph*one

[v] *v*ery, e*v*e

[θ] *th*in, bo*th*

[ð] *th*is, o*th*er

[l] *l*itt*l*e, ba*ll*

[r] *r*at, b*r*ead

[m] *m*ove, co*m*e

[n] *n*o, ru*n*

[ŋ] si*ng*, ba*n*k

[h] *h*at, re*h*eat

[j] *y*es

[w] *w*ell, a*w*ay

Table of Abbreviations 略語表

adj	adjective	形容詞
abbr	abbreviation	略語
adv	adverb	副詞
ADMIN	administration	管理
AGR	agriculture	農業
ANAT	anatomy	解剖学
ARCHIT	architecture	建築
AUT	automobiles	自動車関係
aux vb	auxiliary verb	助動詞
AVIAT	aviation	航空
BIO	biology	生物学
BOT	botany	植物学
BRIT	British English	英国つづり／用法
CHEM	chemistry	化学
COMM	commerce, finance, banking	商業，金融関係
COMPUT	computing	コンピュータ関係
conj	conjunction	接続詞
cpd	compound	形容詞的名詞
CULIN	cookery.	料理
def art	definite article	定冠詞
dimin	diminutive	指小辞
ECON	economics	経済学
ELEC	electricity, electronics	電気，電子工学
excl	exclamation, interjection	感嘆詞
fam(!)	colloquial usage (! particularly offensive)	口語（！特に悪質なもの）
fig	figurative use	比喩
fus	(phrasal verb) where the particle cannot be separated from the main verb	vt fusを見よ
gen	in most or all senses; generally	たいがいの意味では，一般に
GEO	geography, geology	地理学，地質学
GEOM	geometry	幾何学
indef art	indefinite article	不定冠詞

inf(!)	colloquial usage (! particularly offensive)	口語（！特に悪質なもの）
infin	infinitive	不定詞
inv	invariable	変化しない
irreg	irregular	不規則な
LING	grammar, linguistics	文法, 語学
lit	literal use	文字通りの意味
MATH	mathematics	数学
MED	medical term, medicine	医学
METEOR	the weather, meteorology	気象関係
MIL	military matters	軍事
MUS	music	音楽
n	noun	名詞
NAUT	sailing, navigation	海事
num	numeral adjective or noun	数詞
obj	(grammatical) object	目的語
pej	pejorative	蔑称
PHOT	photography	写真
PHYSIOL	physiology	生理学
pl	plural	複数
POL	politics	政治
pp	past participle	過去分詞形
prep	preposition	前置詞
pron	pronoun	代名詞
PSYCH	psychology, psychiatry	精神医学
pt	past tense	過去形
RAIL	railroad, railway	鉄道
REL	religion	宗教
SCOL	schooling, schools and universities	学校教育
sing	singular	単数
subj	(grammatical) subject	主語
superl	superlative	最上級
TECH	technical term, technology	技術(用語), テクノロジー
TEL	telecommunications	電信電話
TV	television	テレビ
TYP	typography, printing	印刷

US	American English	米国つづり／用法
vb	verb	動詞
vi	verb or phrasal verb used intransitively	自動詞
vt	verb or phrasal verb used transitively	他動詞
vt fus	phrasal verb where the particle cannot be separated from main verb	パーチクルを動詞から分けられない句動詞
ZOOL	zoology	動物学
®	registered trademark	登録商標

THE ROMANIZATION AND PRONUNCIATION OF JAPANESE

There are several systems for writing Japanese in Roman characters, but the most understandable and least confusing to the speaker of English is the Hepburn ("hebon" in Japanese) system. The following table illustrates this system, with its "hiragana" and "katakana" equivalents, as it has been adopted in this dictionary.

a	i	u	e	o		ā	ī	ū	ē	ō
あ	い	う	え	お		—	—	うう	—	おお/おう
ア	イ	ウ	エ	オ		アー	イー	ウー	エー	オー

ka	ki	ku	ke	ko		kya	—	kyu	—	kyo
か	き	く	け	こ		きゃ	—	きゅ	—	きょ
カ	キ	ク	ケ	コ		キャ	—	キュ	—	キョ

ga	gi	gu	ge	go		gya	—	gyu	—	gyo
が	ぎ	ぐ	げ	ご		ぎゃ	—	ぎゅ	—	ぎょ
ガ	ギ	グ	ゲ	ゴ		ギャ	—	ギュ	—	ギョ

sa	shi	su	se	so		sha	shi	shu	she	sho
さ	し	す	せ	そ		しゃ	し	しゅ	しぇ	しょ
サ	シ	ス	セ	ソ		シャ	シ	シュ	シェ	ショ

za	ji	zu	ze	zo		ja	ji	ju	je	jo
ざ	じ	ず	ぜ	ぞ		じゃ	じ	じゅ	じぇ	じょ
ザ	ジ	ズ	ゼ	ゾ		ジャ	ジ	ジュ	ジェ	ジョ

ta	chi	tsu	te	to		cha	chi	chu	che	cho
た	ち	つ	て	と		ちゃ	ち	ちゅ	ちぇ	ちょ
タ	チ	ツ	テ	ト		チャ	チ	チュ	チェ	チョ

da	ji	zu	de	do		ja	ji	ju	je	jo
だ	ぢ	づ	で	ど		ぢゃ	ぢ	ぢゅ	ぢぇ	ぢょ
ダ	ヂ	ヅ	デ	ド		ヂャ	ヂ	ヂュ	ヂェ	ヂョ

na	ni	nu	ne	no		nya	—	nyu	—	nyo
な	に	ぬ	ね	の		にゃ	—	にゅ	—	にょ
ナ	ニ	ヌ	ネ	ノ		ニャ	—	ニュ	—	ニョ

ha	hi	fu	he	ho		hya	—	hyu	—	hyo
は	ひ	ふ	へ	ほ		ひゃ	—	ひゅ	—	ひょ
ハ	ヒ	フ	ヘ	ホ		ヒャ	—	ヒュ	—	ヒョ

ba	bi	bu	be	bo		bya	—	byu	—	byo
ば	び	ぶ	べ	ぼ		びゃ	—	びゅ	—	びょ
バ	ビ	ブ	ベ	ボ		ビャ	—	ビュ	—	ビョ

pa	pi	pu	pe	po		pya	—	pyu	—	pyo
ぱ	ぴ	ぷ	ぺ	ぽ		ぴゃ	—	ぴゅ	—	ぴょ
パ	ピ	プ	ペ	ポ		ピャ	—	ピュ	—	ピョ

ma	mi	mu	me	mo		mya	—	myu	—	myo
ま	み	む	め	も		みゃ	—	みゅ	—	みょ
マ	ミ	ム	メ	モ		ミャ	—	ミュ	—	ミョ

ya	—	yu	—	yo
や	—	ゆ	—	よ
ヤ	—	ユ	—	ヨ

ra	ri	ru	re	ro		rya	—	ryu	—	ryo
ら	り	る	れ	ろ		りゃ	—	りゅ	—	りょ
ラ	リ	ル	レ	ロ		リャ	—	リュ	—	リョ

wa	—	—	—	wo		n
わ	—	—	—	を		ん
ワ	—	—	—	ヲ		ン

Consonants:

Pronounce the consonants as you would in English. Exceptions are "w" in the objective particle "wo", "r", "g", and "f". In "wo" the "w" is normally not pronounced, but is written to distinguish it easily from other words that are pronounced "o". (Japanese word-processing software also usually requires that you type "wo" to get を or ヲ.)

"R" is pronounced with a very slight trill. Do not pronounce it as in the English word "rich"; you probably will not be understood. If you trill it as in Italian or Spanish, you can be understood, but you will sound foreign. The best strategy is to listen and imitate. Lacking access to native speakers, try pronouncing "r" as you would "d", but with the tongue farther forward, touching the upper teeth instead of the palate.

"G" is perfectly understandable pronounced as in English "get", "go" etc, and many Japanese always pronounce it in this way. Cultured people, however, prefer a softer, slightly nasal pronunciation, which they call a "half-voiced" or "nasal-voiced" "k". It is similar to the "ng" in "sing", but coming at the beginning of a syllable.

"F" also is quite understandable when given its usual English fricative value, with the lower lip touching the upper teeth. The Japanese, however, normally pronounce it by simply narrowing the gap between the lower lip and the teeth, without actually touching the lip to the teeth. Thus some individuals pronounce it much closer to "h" than to the English "f".

"N" at the end of a syllable or word is syllabic, that is, it is a syllable in its own right, with full syllabic length, as in English "butt*on*". In this dictionary when syllabic "n" is followed by a vowel or "y", a hyphen is inserted to indicate the proper pronunciation: e.g. 勧誘 かんゆう kan-yū, as opposed to 加入 かにゅう kanyū.

Before "p", "b", or "m", "n" naturally becomes an "m" sound; but in this dictionary, in keeping with the practice of other romanized dictionaries, the Japanese ん is consistently transliterated as "n", not "m": e.g., 文法 ぶんぽう bunpō, not bumpō.

Double consonants are pronounced in Japanese, as in US English "cattail". In 'katakana" and "hiragana" they are indicated by a lowercase っ or ッ before the consonant to be doubled, and in this dictionary are printed as double consonants: か っぱ "kappa", いった "itta". The one exception is the combination っち, which we express as "tch": マッチ, "matchi".

A few Japanese exclamations are written with a lowercase っ at the end, indicating an articulated "t" sound at the end. These we have romanized with a quarter-sized "t": しっ "shi;t" (equivalent to the English "ssh !").

The sounds [ti:] and [di:] do not exist in Japanese. They are usually expressed as

ティ and ディ, which we romanize as "ti" and "di". Other sounds in loan words without Japanese equivalents are generally corrupted to some similar sound, e. g., "v" to "b".

Vowels:

The 5 Japanese vowels are the fundamental Latin vowels: [ɑː], [iː], [uː], [e], and [o]. "U" is pronounced without rounding the lips, keeping them relaxed. A rounded "u" is understandable, but sounds outlandishly foreign. Again, listen and imitate.

The vowels can be long or short. Long vowels are pronounced the same as short vowels, but for double their length, with no break. Pay strict attention to this, for vowel length is essential to both meaning and comprehension. Using a short vowel for a long one, or vice versa, can produce a word of entirely different meaning from the one intended. In this dictionary, long vowels are marked with a macron: ā, ī, ū, ē, ō.

The syllable "-su" at the end of a word, especially in the verbal ending "-masu" frequently drops the "u", so that only the "s" is heard. This occurs more often in the east than in the west of the country. There are no hard and fast rules, so the student needs to rely on his experience from listening to spoken Japanese.

Japanese accents:

Japanese words do not have a strong tonic accent as in most European languages. Instead they are inflected, with the voice rising or falling gently on certain syllables, and remaining flat on others. Using the correct "accent" or inflection is necessary for intelligibility of speech, and often serves to distinguish between words of similar spelling. For example, depending on the "accent", "momo" can mean either "peach" or "thigh"; "kaki" can be either "persimmon" or "oyster"; "atsui" can be "hot" or "thick".

The Japanese accent is difficult to depict graphically with any accuracy, for there are no standard conventions. Many dictionaries simply ignore the problem, leaving the foreign student to his own devices. Language classes for foreigners both in Japan and abroad frequently do not teach accents explicitly, but rely on imitation of pronunciation by a native Japanese model.

We felt that the foreign student needed something to aid the memory in trying to pronounce words already learned in the past, as well as a guide to pronunciation of words being looked up in the dictionary. We settled on the acute accent (á) to indicate a rising inflection, and the grave accent (à) to indicate a falling inflection. No mark at all means that the voice is held flat on that syllable.

The one exception in this dictionary is when two "i"s occur together, as in the word for "good" いい ii. In most cases like this, the first "i" requires a rising inflection (í), and the second a falling inflection (ì). However, with standard typefaces this produces an unesthetic effect (íì). Therefore, we have omitted the accent mark of the second "i" in such cases: a rising inflection on the first of a "double i" combination indicates also a falling inflection on the second letter: íi = í ì.

Doubtless the foreign student will be somewhat disconcerted to see such inflection marks on "n" in this dictionary. Remember that final "n" is always syllabic and may be pronounced by itself in Japanese. Thus, "n" can also have a rising or falling inflection, or be flat, as the case may be.

Accent differs markedly from region to region in Japan, particularly between the east and the west. The speech patterns of the Kanto region have generally been adopted as the standards for a "common" language, to be taught in the schools and used by television and radio announcers. Although the accents in this dictionary have followed the guidance of an expert in the field, we lay no claim to absolute accuracy. Our aim has been to guide the foreign student to a pronunciation that, if used, will be understandable in any part of the country, even when the listeners themselves follow a different standard of pronunciation.

English Irregular Verb Forms　不規則動詞表

present	pt	pp	present	pt	pp
arise	arose	arisen	dig	dug	dug
awake	awoke	awaked	do (3rd	did	done
be (am, is,	was,	been	person;		
are;	were		he/she/it/		
being)			does)		
bear	bore	born(e)	draw	drew	drawn
beat	beat	beaten	dream	dreamed,	dreamed,
become	became	become		dreamt	dreamt
begin	began	begun	drink	drank	drunk
behold	beheld	beheld	drive	drove	driven
bend	bent	bent	dwell	dwelt	dwelt
beset	beset	beset	eat	ate	eaten
bet	bet,	bet,	fall	fell	fallen
	betted	betted	feed	fed	fed
bid	bid,	bid,	feel	felt	felt
	bade	bidden	fight	fought	fought
bind	bound	bound	find	found	found
bite	bit	bitten	flee	fled	fled
bleed	bled	bled	fling	flung	flung
blow	blew	blown	fly (flies)	flew	flown
break	broke	broken	forbid	forbade	forbidden
breed	bred	bred	forecast	forecast	forecast
bring	brought	brought	forget	forgot	forgotten
build	built	built	forgive	forgave	forgiven
burn	burnt,	burnt,	forsake	forsook	forsaken
	burned	burned	freeze	froze	frozen
burst	burst	burst	get	got	got, (US)
buy	bought	bought			gotten
can	could	(been	give	gave	given
		able)	go (goes)	went	gone
cast	cast	cast	grind	ground	ground
catch	caught	caught	grow	grew	grown
choose	chose	chosen	hang	hung,	hung,
cling	clung	clung		hanged	hanged
come	came	come	have (has;	had	had
cost	cost	cost	having)		
creep	crept	crept	hear	heard	heard
cut	cut	cut	hide	hid	hidden
deal	dealt	dealt	hit	hit	hit

present	pt	pp	present	pt	pp
hold	held	held	**sell**	sold	sold
hurt	hurt	hurt	**send**	sent	sent
keep	kept	kept	**set**	set	set
kneel	knelt,	knelt,	**shake**	shook	shaken
	kneeled	kneeled	**shall**	should	—
know	knew	known	**shear**	sheared	shorn,
lay	laid	laid			sheared
lead	led	led	**shed**	shed	shed
lean	leant,	leant,	**shine**	shone	shone
	leaned	leaned	**shoot**	shot	shot
leap	leapt,	leapt,	**show**	showed	shown
	leaped	leaped	**shrink**	shrank	shrunk
learn	learnt,	learnt,	**shut**	shut	shut
	learned	learned	**sing**	sang	sung
leave	left	left	**sink**	sank	sunk
lend	lent	lent	**sit**	sat	sat
let	let	let	**slay**	slew	slain
lie (lying)	lay	lain	**sleep**	slept	slept
light	lit,	lit,	**slide**	slid	slid
	lighted	lighted	**sling**	slung	slung
lose	lost	lost	**slit**	slit	slit
make	made	made	**smell**	smelt,	smelt,
may	might	—		smelled	smelled
mean	meant	meant	**sow**	sowed	sown,
meet	met	met			sowed
mistake	mistook	mistaken	**speak**	spoke	spoken
mow	mowed	mown,	**speed**	sped,	sped,
		mowed		speeded	speeded
must	(had to)	(had to)	**spell**	spelt,	spelt,
pay	paid	paid		spelled	spelled
put	put	put	**spend**	spent	spent
quit	quit,	quit,	**spill**	spilt,	spilt,
	quitted	quitted		spilled	spilled
read	read	read	**spin**	spun	spun
rid	rid	rid	**spit**	spat	spat
ride	rode	ridden	**split**	split	split
ring	rang	rung	**spoil**	spoiled,	spoiled,
rise	rose	risen		spoilt	spoilt
run	ran	run	**spread**	spread	spread
saw	sawed	sawn	**spring**	sprang	sprung
say	said	said	**stand**	stood	stood
see	saw	seen	**steal**	stole	stolen
seek	sought	sought	**stick**	stuck	stuck

present	pt	pp	present	pt	pp
sting	stung	stung	think	thought	thought
stink	stank	stunk	throw	threw	thrown
stride	strode	stridden	thrust	thrust	thrust
strike	struck	struck, stricken	tread	trod	trodden
strive	strove	striven	wake	woke, waked	woken, waked
swear	swore	sworn	wear	wore	worn
sweep	swept	swept	weave	wove, weaved	woven, weaved
swell	swelled	swollen, swelled	wed	wedded, wed	wedded, wed
swim	swam	swum			
swing	swung	swung	weep	wept	wept
take	took	taken	win	won	won
teach	taught	taught	wind	wound	wound
tear	tore	torn	wring	wrung	wrung
tell	told	told	write	wrote	written

A

A [ei] *n* (MUS: note) イ音 í-ðn; (: key) イ調 íchō

KEYWORD

a [ei, ə] (*before vowel or silent h*: **an**) *indef art* **1** 1つの hitótsu no, ある árù ◇通常日本語では表現しない tsūjō nihongo de wa hyōgen shínài

a book/girl/mirror 本〔少女, 鏡〕hòn 〔shṓjo, kagámi〕

an apple りんご ríngo

she's a doctor 彼女は医者です kánojo wa ishá desu

2 (instead of the number "one") 1つの hitótsù no

a loaf and 2 pints of milk, please パン1本とミルク2パイント下さい pan íppoǹ to mírùku nipáìnto kudasái

a year ago 1年前 ichinen máè

a hundred/thousand** etc **pounds 100〔1000〕ポンド hyaku〔sen〕póndò

3 (in expressing ratios, prices etc) 1つ当り... hitotsu átàri...

3 a day/week 1日〔1週間〕当り3つ ichinichi〔isshūkan〕átàri mittsú

10 km an hour 時速10キロメーター jísòku jukkiromḗtà

£5 a person 1人当たり5ポンド hitori átàri gopóndò

30p a kilo 1キロ30ペンス ichíkìro sanjuppénsù

AA [eiei'] *n abbr* (= *Alcoholics Anonymous*) アルコール依存症自主治療協会 arúkōru izoñshō jishúchiryō kyṑkai; (*BRIT*: = *Automobile Association*) 英国自動車連盟 eíkoku jidōsha reñmei

AAA [trip'əlei] *n abbr* (= *American Automobile Association*) 米国自動車連盟 beíkoku jidōsha reñmei

aback [əbæk'] *adv*: ***to be taken aback*** 仰天する gyṓten suru

abandon [əbæn'dən] *vt* (person) 見捨てる misúterù; (car) 乗捨てる norísuterù; (give up: search, idea, research) やめる yaméru

♦*n* (wild behavior): ***with abandon*** 羽目を外して hamé wò hazúshite

abashed [əbæʃt'] *adj* (person) 恥ずかしがっている hazúkashigattè irú

abate [əbeit'] *vi* (lessen: storm, terror, anger) 治まる osámarù

abattoir [æbətwɑ:r'] (*BRIT*) *n* と殺場 tosátsujō

abbey [æb'i:] *n* 修道院 shū́dòin

abbot [æb'ət] *n* 修道院長 shūdōinchṑ

abbreviate [əbri:'vi:eit] *vt* (essay, word) 短縮する tañshuku suru

abbreviation [əbri:vi:ei'ʃən] *n* (short form) 短縮形 tañshukukei

abdicate [æb'dikeit] *vt* (responsibility, right) 放棄する hṑki suru

♦*vi* (monarch) 退位する táì-i suru

abdication [æbdikei'ʃən] *n* (of responsibility, right) 放棄 hṑki; (by monarch) 退位 táì-i

abdomen [æb'dəmən] *n* 腹部 fukúbù

abduct [æbdʌkt'] *vt* ら致する ráchì suru

aberration [æbərei'ʃən] *n* (unusual behavior, event etc) 異状 ijṓ

abet [əbet'] *vt see* **aid**

abeyance [əbei'əns] *n*: ***in abeyance*** (law) 無視されて múshì sarete; (matter) 保留されて horyū́ sarete

abhor [æbhɔ:r'] *vt* (cruelty, violence etc) ひどく嫌う hídokù kiráu

abide [əbaid'] *vt*: ***I can't abide it/him*** 私はそれ〔彼〕が大嫌いだ watákushi wà soré〔karè〕gà dáìkirai da

abide by *vt fus* (law, decision) ...に従う ...ni shitágaù

ability [əbil'iti:] *n* (capacity) 能力 nṑryoku; (talent, skill) 才能 saínō

abject [æb'dʒekt] *adj* (poverty) 極度の kyókùdo no; (apology) 卑屈な hikútsu na

ablaze [əbleiz'] *adj* (building etc) 炎上している eñjō shite iru

able [ei'bəl] *adj* (capable) 出来る dekírù;

(skilled) 有能な yûnô na

to be able to do something ...を することが出来る ...wo suru koto gà dékirù

able-bodied [ei'balbɔːd'i:d] adj (person) がん健な gańken na

ably [ei'bli:] adv (skilfully, well) 上手に jôzu ni

abnormal [æbnɔːr'məl] adj (behavior, child, situation) 異常な ijô na

aboard [əbɔːrd'] adv (NAUT, AVIAT) ...に乗って ...ni notté
♦prep (NAUT, AVIAT) ...に乗って ...ni notté

abode [əboud'] n (LAW): **of no fixed abode** 住所不定の jûshofutèi no

abolish [əbɑ:l'iʃ] vt 廃止する hafshi suru

abolition [æbəliʃ'ən] n 廃止 hafshi

abominable [əbɑm'inəbəl] adj (conditions) ひどい hídoi; (behavior) 忌わしい imáwashiì

aborigine [æbəridʒ'əni:] n 原住民 geńjùmin

abort [əbɔːrt'] vt (MED: fetus) 流産する ryûzan suru; (plan, activity) 中止する chûshi suru

abortion [əbɔːr'ʃən] n (MED) 妊娠中絶 nifshinchūzètsu

to have an abortion 妊娠を中絶する nifshin wò chúzetsu suru

abortive [əbɔːr'tiv] adj (attempt, action) 不成功の fuséìkô no

abound [əbaund'] vi (exist in large numbers) ...が多い ...ga ôì

to abound in/with (possess in large numbers) ...に富む ...ni tômù

about [əbaut'] adv 1 (approximately) 約 yákù, 大よそ ôyoso, ...ぐらい ...gúraì

about a hundred/thousand etc dollars 約100(1000)ドル yákù hyakú(sen) dòru

it takes about 10 hours 10時間ぐらいかかります jûjikan gûrai kakarimású

at about 2 o'clock 2時頃 niji gôrò

I've just about finished ほぼ終ったところです hôbô owatta tokoro desù

2 (referring to place) あちこちに achìko-

chì ni

to leave things lying about 物をあちこちに散らかしたままにする monó wo achíkochì ni chirakashita mamâ ni sùrú

to run/walk etc about あちこち走り回る〔歩き回る〕achíkochì hashirimawárù〔arukimawárù〕

3: **to be about to do something** ...するところである ...suru tokoro dè arù

he was about to cry/leave/wash the dishes/go to bed 彼は泣き出す〔帰る、皿を洗う、寝る〕ところだった kárè wa nakídasu(kaeru, sara wo arau, neru) tokoro dattà

♦prep **1** (relating to) ...について ...ni tsúîte, ...に関して ...ni kânshite

a book about London ロンドンについての本 róndòn ni tsúîte no hòn

what is it about? それは何についてですか sore wa nán ni tsúîte desu kà

we talked about it 私たちはそれについて話し合った watakushitachì wa sore ni tsúîte hanashiáttà

what/how about having some coffee? コーヒーでも飲みましょうか kôhì de mò nomimashô kà

2 (referring to place) ...のあちこちに ...no achíkochì ni

to walk about the town 町をあちこち歩き回る machî wo achíkochì arukimawárù

her clothes were scattered about the room 部屋のあちこちに彼女の服が散らかっていた heya no achíkochì ni kánojò no fukû gà chirakatte ità

about-face [əbaut'feis] n (MIL) 回れ右 mawáremigî; (fig): **to do an about-face** 一変する ippén suru

about-turn [əbaut'tɜːrn] n = **about-face**

above [əbʌv'] adv (higher up, overhead) 上の方に ué no hô ni; (greater, more) 以上に ijô ni
♦prep (higher than) ...より上に ...yórî ué ni; (greater than, more than: in number, amount etc) ...以上... ...íjô; (: in rank etc) 上である ué de arù

mentioned above 上記の jôki no

above all まず第一に mázů daf-ichi ni

aboveboard [əbʌvˈbourd] *adj* 公明正大な kômeiseidai na

abrasive [əbreiˈsiv] *adj* (substance) 研磨の kềnma no; (person, manner) とげとげしい togétogeshiī

abreast [əbrestˈ] *adv* (people, vehicles) 横に並んで yokó ni narande

to keep abreast of (*fig*: news etc) についていく ...ni tsuíte ikú

abridge [əbridʒˈ] *vt* (novel, play) 短縮する tanshuku suru

abroad [əbrɔːdˈ] *adv* 海外に kấigai ni

abrupt [əbrʌptˈ] *adj* (sudden: action, ending etc) 突然の totsúzen no; (curt: person, behavior) ぶっきらぼうな bukkírabō na

abruptly [əbrʌptˈliː] *adv* (leave, end) 突然 totsúzen; (speak) ぶっきらぼうに bukkírabō ni

abscess [æbˈses] *n* のうよう nóyō

abscond [æbskɑːndˈ] *vi* (thief): *to abscond with ...* を持って逃げる ...wo mochínige suru; (prisoner): *to abscond (from)* (...から) 逃亡する ...(kara) tôbō suru

absence [æbˈsəns] *n* (of person: from home etc) 不在 fuzái; (: from school, meeting etc) 欠席 kessêki; (: from work) 欠勤 kekkín; (of thing) 無い事 naí koto

absent [æbˈsənt] *adj* (person: from home etc) 不在の fuzái no; (: from school, meeting etc) 欠席の kessêki no; (: from work) 欠勤の kekkín no; (thing) 無い naí

absentee [æbsəntiːˈ] *n* (from school, meeting etc) 欠席者 kessékishà; (from work) 欠勤者 kekkínsha

absent-minded [æbˈsəntmainˈdid] *adj* 忘れっぽい wasúreppoi

absolute [æbˈsəlut] *adj* (complete) 全くの mattáku no; (monarch, rule, power) 専制的な senseíteki na; (principle, rule etc) 絶対的な zettáiteki na

absolutely [æbsəluːˈtliː] *adv* (totally) 全く mattáku; (certainly) その通り sonó tôri

absolution [æbsəluːˈʃən] *n* (REL) 罪の許

し tsúmi no yurúshì

absolve [æbzɑːlvˈ] *vt*: *to absolve someone (from blame, responsibility, sin)* ...の (...を) 許す ...no (...wồ) yurúsù

absorb [æbsɔːrbˈ] *vt* 吸収する kyūshū suru; (assimilate: group, business) 併合する hefgô suru

to be absorbed in a book 本に夢中になっている hón ni muchū ni natté irú

absorbent cotton [æbsɔːrbˈənt-] (*US*) *n* 脱脂綿 dasshîmen

absorbing [æbsɔːrbˈiŋ] *adj* 夢中にさせる muchū ni saserú

absorption [æbsɔːrpˈʃən] *n* 吸収 kyūshū; (assimilation: of group, business etc) 併合 hefgô; (interest) 夢中になる事 muchū ni narú kotó

abstain [æbsteinˈ] *vi*: *to abstain (from)* (eating, drinking) 控える hikáerù; (voting) 棄権する kikén suru

abstemious [æbstiːˈmiːəs] *adj* (person) 節制する sessêi suru

abstention [æbstenˈʃən] *n* (refusal to vote) 棄権 kikén

abstinence [æbˈstənəns] *n* 禁欲 kiń-yoku

abstract [æbˈstrækt] *adj* (idea, quality) 抽象的な chūshoteki na; (ART) 抽象派の chūshôha no; (LING): *abstract noun* 抽象名詞 chūshômeishi

abstruse [æbstruːsˈ] *adj* 分かりにくい wakárinikuǐ

absurd [æbsəːrdˈ] *adj* ばかげた bakágetà

abundance [əbʌnˈdəns] *n* 豊富さ hôfusa

abundant [əbʌnˈdənt] *adj* 豊富な hôfu na

abuse [*n* əbjuːsˈ *vb* əbjuːzˈ] *n* (insults) のしり nonóshiri, (ill-treatment) 虐待 gyakútai; (misuse: of power, drugs etc) 乱用 rań-yō

♦*vt* (insult) のしる nonóshirù; (ill-treat) 虐待する gyakútai suru; (misuse) 乱用する rań-yō suru

abusive [əbjuːˈsiv] *adj* (person) 口の悪い kuchî no warúi; (language) 侮辱的な bujókuteki na

abysmal [əbizˈməl] *adj* (performance, failure) 最低の saftei no; (ignorance etc)

ひどい hidôi

abyss [əbîs] *n* 深えん shîñ-en

AC [ei'si:] *abbr* = alternating current

academic [ækədem'ik] *adj* (person) インテリの iñteri no; (year, system, books, freedom etc) 教育関係の kyôikukañkei no; (*pej*: issue) 理論的な riröñteki na
♦*n* 学者 gakûsha

academy [əkæd'əmi:] *n* (learned body) アカデミー akâdemî; (school) 学院 gakûin
 academy of music 音楽学院 oñgaku gakûin

accelerate [æksel'əreit] *vt* (process) 早める hayámerû
♦*vi* (AUT) 加速する kasóku suru

acceleration [ækselərei'ʃən] *n* (AUT) 加速 kasóku

accelerator [æksel'əreitər] *n* アクセル âkûseru

accent [æk'sent] *n* (pronunciation) なまり namári; (stress mark) アクセント符号 akûseñto fugô; (*fig*: emphasis, stress) 強調 kyôchô, アクセント akûseñto

accept [æksept'] *vt* (gift, invitation) 受取る ukétoru; (fact, situation, risk) 認める mitómerû; (responsibility, blame) 負う oû

acceptable [æksep'təbəl] *adj* (offer, gift) 受入れられる uké-irerarerû; (risk etc) 許容できる kyoyô dekirû

acceptance [æksep'təns] *n* (of gift, offer etc) 受取る事 ukétoru kotô; (of risk etc) 許容 kyoyô; (of responsibility etc) 負う事 oû kotô

access [æk'ses] *n* (to building, room) 入る事ができる事 hâîru kotô; (to information, papers) 利用する権利 riyô suru keñri
 to have access to (child etc) ...との面会権がある ...e no meñkaikeñ ga arû

accessible [ækses'əbəl] *adj* (place) 行きやすい ikíyasuî; (person) 面会しやすい meñkai shiyasuî; (available: knowledge, art etc) 利用しやすい riyô shiyasuî

accessory [ækses'ə:ri:] *n* (dress, COMM, TECH, AUT) アクセサリー akûsesarî; (LAW): *accessory to* ...の共犯者 ...no kyôhañsha

accident [æk'sidənt] *n* (chance event) 偶然 gûzen; (mishap, disaster) 事故 jîkô
 by accident (unintentionally) うっかり ukkârî; (by chance) 偶然に gûzen ni

accidental [æksiden'təl] *adj* (death) 事故による jîkô ni yorû; (damage) 偶発的な gûhatsuteki na

accidentally [æksiden'təli:] *adv* (by accident) 偶然に gûzen ni

accident-prone [æk'sidəntproun] *adj* 事故に会いがちな jîkô ni aigachi na

acclaim [əkleim'] *n* 賞賛 shôsan
♦*vt*: *to be acclaimed for one's achievements* 功績で有名である kôseki dê yûmei de arû

acclimate [əklai'mit] (*US*) *vt* = acclimatize

acclimatize [əklai'mətaiz] *vt*: *to become acclimatized (to)* (...に) 慣れる (...ni) narérû

accolade [ækəleid'] *n* (*fig*) 賞賛 shôsan

accommodate [əkɑːm'ədeit] *vt* (subj: person) 泊める tomérû; (: car, hotel etc) 収容できる shûyô dekirû; (oblige, help) ...に親切にして上げる ...ni shiñsetsu ni shite agérû

accommodating [əkɑːm'ədeitiŋ] *adj* 親切な shiñsetsu na

accommodation [əkɑːmədei'ʃən] *n* 宿泊設備 shukûhakusetsûbi

accommodations [əkɑːmədei'ʃənz] (*US*) *npl* 宿泊設備 shukûhakusetsûbi

accompaniment [əkʌm'pənimənt] *n* 伴奏 bañsô

accompany [əkʌm'pəni:] *vt* (escort, go along with) ...に付きそう ...ni tsukísoû; (MUS) ...の伴奏をする ...no bañsô wô suru

accomplice [əkɑːm'plis] *n* 共犯者 kyôhañsha

accomplish [əkɑːm'pliʃ] *vt* (finish: task) 成遂げる nashítogerû; (achieve: goal) 達成する tasséi suru

accomplished [əkɑːm'pliʃt] *adj* (person) 熟練の jukûren no; (performance) 優れた sugûretâ

accomplishment [əkɑːm'pliʃmənt] *n* (completion, bringing about) 遂行 suíkô;

(skill: gen pl) 才能 saínō

accord [əˈkɔ:rd] n (treaty) 協定 kyōtei
♦vt 与える atáerù
of his own accord 自発的に jíhatsuteki ni

accordance [əˈkɔːrdəns] n: *in: accordance with* (someone's wishes, the law etc) ...に従って ...ni shitágatte

according [əˈkɔːrdiŋ] *according to* prep (person, account) ...によると ...ni yorú to

accordingly [əkɔːrˈdiŋli] adv (appropriately) それに応じて soré nǐ ōjite; (as a result) それで soré de

accordion [əkɔːrˈdiːən] n アコーデオン ákōdeon

accost [əˈkɔːst] vt ...に近寄って話し掛ける ...ni chikáyotte hanáshikakerù

account [əˈkaunt] n (COMM: bill) 勘定 kañjōgaki; (: monthly account) 計算書 kefsansho; (in bank) 口座 kōza; (report) 報告 hōkoku
of no account 構わない kamáwanaì
on account つけで tsuké de
on no account 何があっても... (すべき) でない naní ga atte mo ...(subeki) de naí
on account of ...のために ...no tamé ni
to take into account, take account of ...を考慮に入れる ...wò kōryō ni iréru

accountable [əˈkauntəbəl] *adj: accountable (to)* (...に) 申開きする義務がある (...ni) mōshihiraki suru gímu ga árù

accountancy [əˈkauntənsi:] n 会計士の職 kaíkeishi no shokú

accountant [əˈkauntənt] n 会計士 kaíkeishi

account for vt fus (explain) 説明する setsúmei suru; (represent) ... (の割合) を占める ... (no warfai) wò shimérù

account number n (at bank etc) 口座番号 kōzabañgō

accounts [əˈkaunts] npl (COMM) 勘定 kañjō

accredited [əˈkredˈitid] adj (agent etc) 資格のある shikáku no arù

accrued interest [əˈkruːd'-] n 累積利息 ...

rufsekirisóku

accumulate [əkjuːmˈjəleit] vt 貯める taméru
♦vi 貯まる tamáru

accuracy [ækˈjəːrəsi:] n 正確さ sefkaku-sa

accurate [ækˈjəːrit] adj 正確な sefkaku na

accurately [ækˈjəːritli:] adv (count, shoot, answer) 正確に sefkaku ni

accusation [ækjuːzeiˈʃən] n 非難 hínan

accuse [əkjuːzˈ] vt: *to accuse someone (of something)* (crime, incompetence) (...だと) ...を責める ...(dá to) ...wo semérù

accused [əkjuːzdˈ] n (LAW): *the accused* 容疑者 yōgisha

accustom [əkʌsˈtəm] vt 慣れさせる naréraserù

accustomed [əkʌsˈtəmd] adj (usual): *accustomed to* ...に慣れている ...ni naréte irú

ace [eis] n (CARDS, TENNIS) エース ê-su

ache [eik] n 痛み itámi
♦vi (be painful) 痛む itámù, ...が痛い ...ga itáī
my head aches 頭が痛い atáma ga itái

achieve [ətʃiːvˈ] vt (aim) 成達する nashítogerù; (result) 上げる agérù; (victory, success) 獲得する kakútoku suru

achievement [ətʃiːvˈmənt] n (completion) 完成 kañsei; (success, feat) 業績 gyōseki

acid [æsˈid] adj (CHEM: soil etc) 酸性の sañsei no; (taste) 酸っぱい suppái
♦n (CHEM) 酸 sáñ; (inf: LSD) LSD erú-esudi

acid rain n 酸性雨 sañseiū

acknowledge [æknɑːlˈidʒ] vt (letter, parcel: *also:* acknowledge receipt of) 受け取った事を知らせる ukétotta koto wo shiráserù; (fact, situation, person) 認める mitómerù

acknowledgement [æknɑːlˈidʒmənt] n (of letter, parcel) 受領通知 juryōtsūchi

acne [ækˈniː] n にきび nfkibi

acorn [eiˈkɔːrn] n ドングリ dóñguri

acoustic [əkuːstik] *adj* (related to hearing) 聴覚の chōkaku no; (guitar etc) アコースティックの akōsútìkku no

acoustics [əkuːstiks] *n* (science) 音響学 oñkyōgaku

◆*npl* (of hall, room) 音響効果 oñkyōkō-ka

acquaint [əkweint'] *vt*: **to acquaint someone with something** (inform) ...に ...を知らせる ...ni ...wò shiráserù

to be acquainted with (person) ...と面 識がある ...to meñshiki ga arù

acquaintance [əkwein'təns] *n* (person) 知合い shiríaì; (with person, subject) 知 識 chíshìki

acquiesce [ækwiːes'] *vi*: **to acquiesce (to)** (...) を承諾する (...wò) shōdaku surù

acquire [əkwaiˈər] *vt* (obtain, buy) 手に 入れる te ni iréru; (learn, develop: interest, skill) 取得する shutóku surù

acquisition [ækwizi'ʃən] *n* (obtaining etc) 入手 nyūshu; (development etc) 獲得 kakútoku; (thing acquired) 取得物 shutóku-kubùtsu

acquit [əkwit'] *vt* (free) 無罪 とする mú-zài to surù

to acquit oneself well 見事な働きをす る mígòto na határaki wo surù

acquittal [əkwit'əl] *n* 無罪判決 muzái hañketsu

acre [eiˈkər] *n* エーカー ēkā

acrid [æk'rid] *adj* (smell, taste, smoke) 刺激的な shigékitèki na

acrimonious [ækrəmou'niːəs] *adj* (remark, argument) 辛らつな shiṅratsu na

acrobat [æk'rəbæt] *n* アクロバット akúrobattò

acrobatic [ækrəbæt'ik] *adj* (person, movement, display) アクロバット的な a-kúrobattòteki na

acronym [æk'rənim] *n* 頭字語 tōjìgo

across [əkrɔːs'] *prep* (from one side to the other of) ...を渡って ...wo watátte; (on the other side of) ...の向こう側に ...no mukōgawa ni; (crosswise over) ...と 交差して ...to kōsa shite

◆*adv* (direction) 向こう側 へ mukōgawa e; (measurement) 直径が...で chokkei ga

... の
to run/swim across 走って〔泳いで〕渡 る hashítte(oyóide)wataru

across from ...の向いに ...no mukái ni

acrylic [əkril'ik] *adj* アクリルの ákùriru no

◆*n* アクリル ákùriru

act [ækt] *n* (action) 行 為 kōi; (of play) 幕 makú; (in a show etc) 出し物 dashímono; (LAW) 法 hō

◆*vi* (do something, take action) 行動する kōdō surù; (behave) 振 舞 う furúmaù; (have effect: drug, chemical) 作用する sáyō surù; (THEATER) 出演する shu-tsúen surù; (pretend) ...の振りをする ...no furí wò surù

◆*vt* (part) ...に扮する ...ni fuń surù

in the act of ...しているところを ...shi-té iru sanàka ni

to act as ...として勤める ...toshite tsutó-merù

acting [æk'tiŋ] *adj* (manager, director etc) 代理の dafri no

◆*n* (activity) 演技 éñgi; (profession) 演劇 eñgeki

action [æk'ʃən] *n* (deed) 行 為 kōi; (motion) 動き ugòkf; (MIL) 戦 闘 señtō; (LAW) 訴訟 soshō

out of action (person) 活動不能で ka-tsúdōfunò de; (thing) 作動不能で sadófu-nò de

to take action 行動を起す kōdō wò okósù

action replay *n* (TV) 即時ビデオ再生 sokúji bideo saisei

activate [æk'təveit] *vt* (mechanism) 作 動させる sadósaserù

active [æk'tiv] *adj* (person, life) 活動的な katsúdōtèki na

active volcano 活火山 kakkázàn

actively [æk'tivliː] *adv* (participate) 積 極的に sekkyókuteki ni; (discourage) 強 く (dislike, dislike) 非常に hijō ni

activist [æk'tivist] *n* 活動家 katsúdōka

activity [æktiv'əti:] *n* (being active) 活 動 katsúdō; (action) 動 き ugòki; (pastime, pursuit) 娯楽 goráku

actor [æk'təːr] *n* 俳優 haíyū

actress [æk'tris] *n* 女優 joyū́

actual [æk'tʃuəl] *adj* 実際の jissái no

actually [æk'tʃuəli] *adv* (really) 本当に hontṓ ni; (in fact) 実は jitsú wa

acumen [əkju'mən] *n* 判断力 hañdañryoku

acupuncture [æk'jupʌŋktʃər] *n* 針 hárí

acute [əkjut'] *adj* (illness) 急性の kyū́sei no; (anxiety, pain) 激しい hagéshii; (mind, person) 抜け目の無い nukéme no nai; (MATH): *acute angle* 鋭角 efkaku; (LING): *acute accent* 鋭アクセント efakúsento

ad [æd] *n abbr* = **advertisement**

A.D. [eidi:'] *adv abbr* (= *Anno Domini*) 西暦...年 séfreki ...néń

adamant [æd'əmənt] *adj* (person) 譲らない yuzúranai

Adam's apple [æd'əms-] *n* のど仏 nodóbotòke

adapt [ədæpt'] *vt* (alter, change) 適応さ せる tekíō saserú

◆*vi*: *to adapt (to)* (に) 適応する (...ni) tekíō suru

adaptable [ədæp'təbəl] *adj* (device, person) 適応性のある tekíōsei no arú

adapter [ədæp'tər] *n* (ELEC) アダプター adáptā

adaptor [ədæp'tər] *n* = **adapter**

add [æd] *vt* (to a collection etc) 加える kuwáeru; (comment etc) 付加える tsukékuwaerù; (figures: *also*) 合計する gókei suru

◆*vi*: *to add to* (increase) ...を増す ...wo masú

adder [æd'ər] *n* ヨーロッパクサリヘビ yōroppá kusáribebì

addict [æd'ikt] *n* (to drugs etc) 中毒者 chūdokushà; (enthusiast) マニア máñia

addicted [ədik'tid] *adj*: *to be addicted to* (drink etc) ...中毒にかかっている ...chūdoku ni kakátté irú; (fig: football etc) ...マニアである ...máñia de arú

addiction [ədik'ʃən] *n* (to drugs etc) 中毒 chūdoku

addictive [ədik'tiv] *adj* (drug) 習慣性の ある shūkansei no arù; (activity) 癖になる kusé ni narù

addition [ədiʃ'ən] *n* (adding up) 足し算 tashízàn; (thing added) 加えられた物 kuwáeraretà monó

in addition なお náò

in addition to ...の外に ...no hoká ni

additional [ədiʃ'ənəl] *adj* 追加の tsuíka no

additive [æd'ətiv] *n* 添加物 teñkabùtsu

address [ədres'] *n* (postal address) 住所 jūsho; (speech) 演説 eñzetsu

◆*vt* (letter, parcel) ...に宛名を書く ...ni aténa wo kákú; (speak to: person) ...に話 し掛ける ...ni hanáshikakerù; (: audience) ...に演説する ...ni eñzetsu suru; (problem): *to address (oneself to) a problem* 問題に取組む mońdai ni torikumù

adept [ədept'] *adj*: *adept at* ...が上手な ...ga józu na

adequate [æd'əkwit] *adj* (enough: amount) 十分な júbuñ na; (satisfactory: performance, response) 満足な mañzoku na

adhere [ædhi:r'] *vi*: *to adhere to* (stick to) ...に くっつく ...ni kuttsúkù; (fig: abide by: rule, decision, treaty etc) ...を守る ...wo mamórù; (: hold to: opinion, belief etc) ...を固守する ...wo kóshū suru

adhesive [ædhi:'siv] *n* 粘着材 neñchakuzài

adhesive tape *n* (*US:* MED) ばん創こう bañsōkō; (*BRIT*) 粘着テープ neñchaku tépu

ad hoc [æd ha:k'] *adj* (decision, committee) 特別な tokúbetsu na

adjacent [ədʒei'sənt] *adj*: *adjacent to* ...の隣の ...no tonári no

adjective [ædʒ'iktiv] *n* 形容詞 kefyṓshi

adjoining [ədʒɔi'niŋ] *adj* (room etc) 隣の tonári no

adjourn [ədʒəːrn'] *vt* (trial) 休延にする kyū́tei ni suru; (meeting, discussion) 休会にする kyū́kai ni suru

◆*vi* (trial) 休延する kyū́tei suru; (meeting) 休止する kyū́shi suru

adjudicate [ədʒuːdikeit'] *vt* (contest) ...の審査員を勤める ...no shiñsa-ìn wo tsutómerù

adjust [ədʒʌst'] *vt* (change: approach etc) 調整する chōsei suru; (rearrange: clothing, machine etc) 調節する chōsetsu suru

◆*vi*: **to adjust (to)** 適応する tekiō suru

adjustable [ədʒʌst'əbəl] *adj* 調節できる chōsetsu dekirū

adjustment [ədʒʌst'mənt] *n* (PSYCH) 適応 tekiō; (to machine) 調節 chōsetsu; (of prices, wages) 調整 chōsei

ad-lib [ædlib'] *vi* アドリブで話す adōribu de hanāsū

◆*ad lib* [ædlib'] *adv* (speak) アドリブで a-dōribu de

administer [ædmin'istər'] *vt* (country) 統治する tōchi suru; (department) 管理する kāñri suru; (MED: drug) 投与する tōyo suru

to administer justice 裁く sabākū

administration [ædministrei'ʃən] *n* (management) 管理 kāñri; (government) 政権 seḵeñ

administrative [ædmin'istreitiv] *adj* (work, error etc) 管理的な kañriteki na

administrator [ædmin'istreitər'] *n* 管理者 kañrishā

admiral [æd'mərəl] *n* 海軍大将 kaígun taíshō

Admiralty [æd'mərəlti:] (*BRIT*) *n*: **the Admiralty** (*also*: **Admiralty Board**) 海軍省 kaígunshō

admiration [ædmərei'ʃən] *n* 感心 kañshin

admire [ædmai'ər] *vt* (respect) ...に感心する ...ni kañshin suru; (appreciate) 観賞する kañshō suru

admirer [ædmai'ərər] *n* (suitor) 男友達 otōkotomodachi; (fan) ファン fáñ

admission [ædmiʃ'ən] *n* (admittance) 入場 nyūjō; (entry fee) 入場料 nyūjōryō; (confession) 自白 jihāku

admit [ædmit'] *vt* (confess) 自白する ji-hāku suru; (permit to enter) 入場させる nyūjō saserū; (to club, organization) 入会させる nyūkai saserū; (to hospital) 入院させる nyūin saserū; (defeat, responsibility etc) 認める mitōmeru

admittance [ædmit'əns] *n* 入場 nyūjō

admittedly [ædmit'idli:] *adv* 確かに ...で ... de ārū ga

admit to *vt fus* (murder etc) ...を自白する ...wo jihāku suru

admonish [ædmɑn'iʃ] *vt* (rebuke) たしなめる tashínamerū; (LAW) 忠告する chūkoku suru

ad nauseam [æd nɔː'zi:əm] *adv* (repeat, talk) いやという程 iyá to iú hodō

ado [əduː'] *n*: **without (any) more ado** さっさと sássa to

adolescence [ædəles'əns] *n* 10代 jūdai

adolescent [ædəles'ənt] *adj* 10代の jūdai no

◆*n* ティーンエージャー tíñéja

adopt [ədɑpt'] *vt* (child) 養子にする yōshi ni sutī; (policy, attitude) とる torū; (accent) まねる manérū

adopted [ədɑp'tid] *adj* (child) 養子の yō-shi no

adoption [ədɑp'ʃən] *n* (of child) 養子縁組 yōshiéñgumi; (of policy etc) 採択 saftaku

adoptive [ədɑp'tiv] *adj*: **adoptive father/mother** 養父(母) yōfu(bo)

adoptive country 第2の祖国 dāi ni no sōkōku

adore [ədɔːr'] *vt* (person) 崇拝する sūhai suru

adorn [ədɔːrn'] *vt* (decorate) 飾る kazáru

adrenalin [ədren'əlin] *n* アドレナリン a-dōrenarīn

Adriatic [eidriæt'ik] *n*: **the Adriatic (Sea)** アドリア海 adōriakái

adrift [ədrift'] *adv* (NAUT: loose) 漂流して hyōryū shite

adult [ədʌlt'] *n* (person) 大人 otóna; (animal, insect) 成体 seítai

◆*adj* (grown-up: person) 大人の otóna no; (: animal etc) 成体の seítai no; (for adults: literature, education) 成人向きの seíjinmuki no

adultery [ədʌl'tə:ri:] *n* かん通 kañtsū

advance [ædvæns'] *n* (movement, progress) 進歩 shíñpo; (money) 前借り maégari

◆*adj* (booking, notice, warning) 事前の jizén no

♦*vt* (money) 前貸する maégashi suru

♦*vi* (move forward) 進む susumú; (make progress) 進歩する shínpo suru

to make advances (to someone) (gen) (...に) 言い寄る (...ni) iíyorù

in advance (book, prepare etc) 前もって maémottè

advanced [ædvǽnst'] *adj* (SCOL: studies) 高等の kôtô no; (country) 先進の señshin no; (child) ませた másèta

advancement [ædvǽns'mənt] *n* (improvement) 進歩 shínpo; (in job, rank) 昇進 shôshin

advantage [ædvǽn'tidʒ] *n* (supremacy) 有利な立場 yûri na tâchiba; (benefit) 利点 riten; (TENNIS) アドバンテージ adóbantēji

to take advantage of (person) ...に付込む ...ni tsukékomù; (opportunity) 利用する riyô suru

advantageous [ædvæntei'dʒəs] *adj*: *advantageous (to)* (...に) 有利な (...ni) yûri na

advent [æd'vent] *n* (appearance: of innovation) 出現 shutsúgen; (REL) 降臨節 kôrinsetsu, 待降節 taíkōsetsu

adventure [ædven'tʃəːr] *n* 冒険 bôken

adventurous [ædven'tʃəːrəs] *adj* (bold, outgoing) 大胆な daítàn na

adverb [æd'vəːrb] *n* 副詞 fukúshi

adversary [æd'vəːrseːriː] *n* (opponent, *also* MIL) 敵 teki

adverse [ædvəːrs'] *adj* (effect, weather, publicity etc) 悪い warúì

adversity [ædvəːr'sitiː] *n* 逆境 gyakkyô

advert [æd'vəːrt] (*BRIT*) *n abbr* = advertisement

advertise [æd'vəːrtaiz] *vi* (COMM: in newspaper, on television etc) 広告する kôkoku suru

♦*vt* (product, event, job) ...を広告する ...wo kôkoku suru

to advertise for (staff, accommodation etc) ...を求める広告を出す ...wo motómerù kôkoku wo dasu

advertisement [ædvəːrtaiz'mənt] *n* 広告 kôkoku

advertiser [æd'vəːrtaizəːr] *n* (in newspaper, on television etc) 広告主 kôkokunúshi

advertising [æd'vəːrtaiziŋ] *n* (advertisements) 広告 kôkoku; (industry) 広告業界 kôkokugyôkai

advice [ædvais'] *n* (counsel) 忠告 chúkoku; (notification) 知らせ shíràse

a piece of advice 一つの忠告 hítòtsu no chúkoku

to take legal advice 弁護士に相談する beñgoshì ni sôdan suru

advisable [ædvai'zəbəl] *adj* 望ましい nozômashiî

advise [ædvaiz'] *vt* (give advice to: person, company etc) ...に忠告する ...ni chúkoku suru; (inform): *to advise someone of something* ...に ...を知らせる ...ni ...wo shiráserù

to advise against something/doing something ... (するの) を避けた方がいいと忠告する ... (surú no) wo sakéta hô gà íi to chúkoku suru

advisedly [ædvai'zidliː] *adv* (deliberately) 意図的に itôteki ni

adviser [ædvai'zəːr] *n* (counsellor, consultant: to private person) 相談相手 sôdan aité; (: to company etc) 顧問 kómòn

advisor [ædvai'zəːr] *n* = adviser

advisory [ædvai'zəːriː] *adj* (role, capacity, body) 顧問の kómòn no

advocate [æd'vəkit] *vt* (support, recommend) 主張する shuchô suru

♦*n* (LAW: barrister) 弁護士 beñgoshì; (supporter): *advocate of* ...の主張者 ...no shuchôsha

Aegean [idʒiː'ən] *n*: *the Aegean (Sea)* エーゲ海 ēgekai

aerial [eːr'iːəl] *n* アンテナ afitena

♦*adj* (attack, photograph) 航空の kôkū no

aerobics [eːrou'biks] *n* エアロビクス eárobikùsu

aerodynamic [eːroudainæm'ik] *adj* 空力的な kûrikiteki na

aeroplane [eːr'əplein] (*BRIT*) *n* 飛行機 híkôki

aerosol [eːr'əsɔːl] *n* スプレー缶 supúrēkan

aerospace industry [ɛɚˈəspeɪs-] *n* 宇宙
開発業界 uchūkaihatsugyōkai

aesthetic [esθeˈtik] *adj* 美的な bitéki na

afar [əfɑːr] *adv*: **from afar** 遠くから tōku kará

affable [ˈæfəbəl] *adj* (person) 愛想の良い
aísō no yoi; (behavior) 感じの良い kañji
no yoí

affair [əfɛːr] *n* (matter, business, question) 問題 mońdai; (romance: *also*: **love
affair**) 浮気 uwáki

affect [əfekt] *vt* (influence, concern;
person, object) ...に影響を与える ...ni efkyō wo atáerù; (subj: disease: afflict) 冒
す okásù; (move deeply) 感動させる kañdō saserù

affected [əfekˈtid] *adj* (behavior, person) 気取った kidótta

affection [əfekˈʃən] *n* (fondness) 愛情 afjō

affectionate [əfekˈʃənit] *adj* (person,
kiss) 愛情深い aíjōbukaì; (animal) 人なつ
こい hitónatsukoì

affiliated [əfilˈieɪtid] *adj* (company,
body) 関連の kañren no

affinity [əfinˈətiː] *n* (bond, rapport): **to
have an affinity with/for** ... に魅力
を感じる ...ni miryóku wo kañjiru;
(resemblance): **to have an affinity
with** ... に似ている ...ni nité iru

affirmative [əfɚrˈmətiv] *adj* (answer,
nod etc) 肯定の kōtei no

affix [əfiks] *vt* (stamp) はる harú

afflict [əflikt] *vt* (subj: pain, sorrow,
misfortune) 苦しめる kurúshimerù

affluence [ˈæfluːəns] *n* 裕福さ yūfukusà

affluent [ˈæfluːənt] *adj* (wealthy: family,
background, surroundings) 裕福な yūfuku-
ku na
  the affluent society 豊かな社会 yútàka na shákaì

afford [əfɔːrd] *vt* (have enough money
for) 買う余裕がある kaú yoyū ga arù;
(permit oneself: time, risk etc) する余裕
がある surú yoyū ga arù; (provide) 与え
る atáeru

affront [əfrʌnt] *n* (insult) 侮辱 bujóku

Afghanistan [æfgænˈistæn] *n* アフガニ
スタン afúganisùtan

afield [əfiːld] *adv*: **far afield** 遠く tṓku

afloat [əflout] *adv* (floating) 浮んで ukán-
de

afoot [əfut] *adv*: **there is something
afoot** 何か怪しい事が起っている nánika
ayáshiì koto gá okótte irú

afraid [əfreid] *adj* (frightened) 怖がって
いる kowágattè irú
  to be afraid of (person, thing) ...を怖が
る ...wo kowágarù
  to be afraid to ...をするのを怖がる
...wo suru no wò kowágarù
  I am afraid that (apology) 申訳ないが
... mṓshiwakenai ga
  I am afraid so/not 残念ですがその通
りです(違います) zañneñ desu ga sonó
tōri desu (chigáimasù)

afresh [əfreʃ] *adv* (begin, start) 新たに
arátà ni

Africa [æfˈrikə] *n* アフリカ afúrika

African [æfˈrikən] *adj* アフリカの afúrika no
  ♦*n* アフリカ人 afúrikajìn

aft [æft] *adv* (to be) 後方に; (to go) 後方
へ kōhō e

after [æfˈtɚr] *prep* (of time) ...の後に
...no átò ni; (of place) ...の後ろに ...no
ushíro ni; (of order) ...の次に ...no tsugí
ni
  ♦*adv* 後に átò ni
  ♦*conj* ...した後で ...shité kara
  what/who are you after? 何(だれ)を
捜していますか nánì(dárè)wo sagáshitè
imásu ka
  after he left 彼が帰ってから kárè ga
kaétte kara
  after having done ...してから ...shité
kara
  to name someone after someone ...に
因んで...に名を付ける ...ni chínande ...ni
na wo tsukérù
  it's twenty after eight (US) 8時20分だ
hachíji nijíppùn da
  to ask after someone ...の事を尋ねる
...no kotó wo tazúnerù
  after all (in spite of everything) どうせ

dóse; (in spite of contrary expectations etc) 予想を裏切って yosō wo urágitte

after you! お先にどうぞ o-sáki ni dózo

after-effects [æf'tərifekts] *npl* (of illness, radiation, drink etc) 結果 kekkā

aftermath [æf'tɑːrmæθ] *n* (period after) ...直後の期間 ...chókūgo no kíkán; (after-effects) 結果 kekkā

afternoon [æftərnuːn'] *n* 午後 gógò

afters [æf'tərz] (*BRIT: inf*) *n* (dessert) デザート dézàto

after-sales service [æf'tərseilz-] (*BRIT*) *n* (for car, washing machine etc) アフタ ーサービス afútāsābīsu

after-shave (lotion) [æf'tərʃeiv-] *n* ア フターシェーブローション afútāshēbu-rōshon

afterthought [æf'tərθɔːt] *n*: *as an afterthought* 後の思い付きでàtò no omóitsuki de

afterwards [æf'tərwɑːrdz] (*US also*: **afterward**) *adv* その後 sonó atò

again [əgen'] *adv* (once more) もう1度 mō ichido, 再び futátàbi

not ... again もう...ない mō ... nai

to do something again ...をもう1度する ...wo mō ichido surù

again and again 何度も nâñdo mo

against [əgenst'] *prep* (leaning on, touching) ...にもたれ掛けて ...ni motárekakatte; (in opposition to, at odds with) ...に反対して ...ni haftai shite; (compared to) ...に較べて ...ni kurábete

age [eidʒ] *n* (of person, object) 年齢 neñrei; (period in history) 時代 jidái

♦*vi* (person) 年を取る toshf wo torù

♦*vt* (subj: hairstyle, dress, make-up etc) ...を実際の年上に見せる ...wo jissái no toshi ijō ni misérù

20 years of age 年齢二十 neñrei hatáchi

to come of age 成人する sefjin suru

it's been ages since ...は久し振りだ ...wa hisáshiburi da

aged[1] [ei'dʒd] *adj*: *aged 10* 10才の jússài no

aged[2] [ei'dʒid] *npl*: *the aged* 老人 rōjìn

♦*n* 総称 sōshō

age group *n* 年齢層 neñreisō

age limit *n* 年齢制限 neñreiseigen

agency [ei'dʒənsi:] *n* (COMM) 代理店 da-fritèn; (government body) ...局 ...kyokū, ...庁 ...chō

agenda [ədʒen'də] *n* (of meeting) 議題 gi-dái

agent [ei'dʒənt] *n* (representative: COMM, literary, theatrical etc) 代理人 dafrinin, エージェント éjento; (spy) スパ イ supāi; (CHEM, *fig*) 試薬 shiyâku

aggravate [æg'rəveit] *vt* (exacerbate: situation) 悪化させる akkā saserù; (annoy: person) 怒らせる okóraserù

aggregate [æg'rəgit] *n* (total) 合計 gō-kei

aggression [əgreʃ'ən] *n* (aggressive behavior) 攻撃 kōgeki

aggressive [əgres'iv] *adj* (belligerent, assertive) 攻撃的な kōgekiteki na

aggrieved [əgriːvd'] *adj* 不満を抱いた fumán wo idáita

aghast [əgæst'] *adj* あっけにとられた akké ni torárèta

agile [ædʒ'əl] *adj* (physically, mentally) 身軽な migárù na; (mentally) 機敏な ki-bín na

agitate [ædʒ'əteit] *vt* (person) 動揺させ る dóyō saserù

♦*vi*: *to agitate for/against* ...の運動 (反対運動)をする ...no uñdō (haftaiuñ-dō)wo suru

agitator [ædʒ'iteitə:r] *n* 扇動者 sefidō-sha

AGM [eidʒi:em'] *n abbr* = **annual general meeting**

agnostic [əgnɑs'tik] *n* 不可知論者 fu-káchiroñsha

ago [əgou'] *adv*: *2 days ago* 2日前 futsú-kamaè

not long ago 少し前に sukóshi maè ni

how long ago? どのぐらい前に? donó gurai maè ni?

agog [əgɑːg'] *adj* (excited, eager) わくわ くしている wâkuwaku shité irù

agonizing [æg'ənaizɪŋ] *adj* 苦しい kurú-shiî

agony [æg'əni:] *n* (pain) 苦もん kumōn

to be in agony 苦しむ kurúshimù

agree [əgri:] *vt* (price, date) 合意して決める gõi shité kimérù

♦*vi* (have same opinion) ...と意見が合う ...to íkèn ga áù; (correspond) ...と一致する ...to itchí suru; (consent) 承諾する shõdaku suru ¶ *see also* **hearing**

to agree with someone (subj: person) ...と同意する ...to dõi suru; (: food) ...に合う ...ni áù

to agree (with) (statements etc) (...に) 同意する (...ni) dõi suru; (LING) 一致する (...to) itchí suru

to agree to something/to do something ...に (する) ことに同意する ...ni (surú koto ni) dõi suru

to agree that (admit) ...だと認める ...dá tò mitómerù

agreeable [əgri:əbəl] *adj* (sensation, person: pleasant) 気持の良い kimóchi no yoi; (willing) 承知する shõchi suru

agreed [əgri:d] *adj* (time, place, price) 同意で決めた dõi de kimeta

agreement [əgri:mənt] *n* (concurrence, consent) 同意 dõi; (arrangement, contract) 契約 kefyaku

in agreement 同意して dõi shite

agricultural [ægrəkʌltʃərəl] *adj* (land, implement, show) 農業の nõgyõ no

agriculture [æg'rəkʌltʃər] *n* 農業 nõgyõ

aground [əgraund] *adv*: *to run aground* (NAUT) ざ折する zasétsu suru

ahead [əhed] *adv* (in front of: place, time) 前に máè ni; (into the future) 先に sakí

ahead of (in progress) ...より進んで ...yóri susúnde; (in ranking) ...の上に ...no ué ni; (in advance of: person, time, place) ...の前に ...no máè ni

ahead of time 早目に hayáme ni

go right/straight ahead (direction) 真っ直ぐに行って下さい massúgu ni itté kudasai; (permission) どうぞ，どうぞ dõzo, dõzo

aid [eid] *n* (assistance: to person, country) 援助 énjò; (device) ...を助けるもの

...wo tasúkerù monó

♦*vt* (help: person, country) 援助する énjo suru

in aid of (BRIT) ...のために ...no táme ni

to aid and abet (LAW) ほう助する hõjo suru ¶ *see also* **hearing**

aide [eid] *n* (person, *also* MIL) 側近 sokkín

AIDS [eidz] *n abbr* (= *acquired immunodeficiency syndrome*) エイズ éìzu

ailing [ei'liŋ] *adj* (person) 病気の byõki no

ailment [eil'mənt] *n* 病気 byõki

aim [eim] *vt*: *to aim (at)* (gun, missile, camera, remark) ...に向ける (...ni) mukérù

♦*vi* (*also*: *take aim*) ねらう neráu

♦*n* (objective) 目的 mokúteki; (in shooting: skill) ねらい nerái

to aim at (with weapon; *also* objective) ねらう neráu

to aim a punch at げんこつで...を殴ろうとする genkotsu de ...wò nágurò to suru

to aim to do ...するつもりである ...surú tsumori de arú

aimless [eim'lis] *adj* (person, activity) 当てのない até no nai

ain't [eint] (*inf*) = **am not**; **aren't**; **isn't**

air [er] *n* (atmosphere) 空気 kũki; (tune) メロディー mérōdì; (appearance) 態度 táìdo

♦*vt* (room) ...の空気を入れ替える ...no kũki wo irékaerù; (clothes) 干す hósù; (grievances, ideas) 打明ける uchfakeru

♦*cpd* (currents etc) 空気の kũki no; (attack) 空からの sorá kara no

to throw something into the air (ball etc) ...を投げ上げる ...wo nágeageru

by air (travel) 飛行機で hikõki de

on the air (RADIO, TV: programme, station) 放送中 hõsõchū

airbed [er'bed] (*BRIT*) *n* 空気布団 kũki-butòn

airborne [er'bɔːrn] *adj* (airplane) 飛行中の hikõchū no

air-conditioned [er'kəndiʃənd] *adj* 空

調付きの kúchōtsuki no

air conditioning [-kəndíʃ'əniŋ] n 空調 kúchō

aircraft [er'kræft] n inv 航空機 kōkū́ki

aircraft carrier n 空母 kū́bo

airfield [er'fiːld] n 飛行場 hikṓjō

Air Force n 空軍 kū́gun

air freshener [er'freʃ-] n 消臭剤 shṓshūzai

airgun [er'gʌn] n 空気銃 kúkijū

air hostess (BRIT) n スチュワーデス suchūwádesu

air letter (BRIT) n エアログラム eárogurámu

airlift [er'lift] n エアリフト eárifūto

airline [er'lain] n エアライン eárain

airliner [er'lainər] n 旅客機 ryokákkuki

airmail [er'meil] n: **by airmail** 航空便で kōkū́bin de

airplane [er'plein] (US) n 飛行機 hḯkōki

airport [er'pɔrt] n 空港 kū́kō

air raid n 空襲 kū́shū

airsick [er'sik] adj: **to be airsick** 飛行機に酔う hḯkōki ni yóū

airspace [er'speis] n 領空 ryṓkū

air terminal n 空港ターミナルビル kū́kōtāminarubírú

airtight [er'tait] adj 気密の kimítsu no

air-traffic controller [er'træfik-] n 管制官 kañseíkan

airy [er'i] adj (room, building) 風通しの良い kazétōshi no yoi; (casual: manner) 軽薄な kefhaku na

aisle [ail] n 通路 tsū́ro

ajar [ədʒɑr'] adj (door) 少し開いている sukóshi aite irū

akin [əkin'] adj: **akin to** (similar) ...の様な ...no yō na

alacrity [əlæk'riti] n 敏速さ biñsokusa

alarm [əlɑrm'] n (anxiety) 心配 shiñpai; (in shop, bank) 警報 kefhō

♦vt (person) 心配させる shiñpai saserū

alarm call n (in hotel etc) モーニングコール mṓningukōru

alarm clock n 目覚し時計 mezámashidokéi

alas [əlæs'] excl 残念ながら zafineñnagá-

ra

Albania [ælbei'niːə] n アルバニア arúbania

albeit [ɔːlbiːit'] conj (although) ...では あるが ...de wa árū ga

album [æl'bəm] n (gen, also: LP) アルバム arúbamu

alcohol [æl'kəhɔːl] n アルコール arúkōru

alcoholic [ælkəhɔːl'ik] adj アルコールの入った arúkōru no haítta

♦n アルコール中毒者 arúkōru chū́dokúsha

alcoholism [æl'kəhɔːlizəm] n アルコール中毒 arúkōru chū́doku

alcove [æl'kouv] n アルコーブ arúkōbu

ale [eil] n (drink) エール éru

alert [əlɜrt'] adj 注意している chū́i shité irū

♦n (alarm) 警報 kefhō

♦vt (guard, police etc) ...に知らせる ...ni shiráserū

to be on the alert (also MIL) 警戒している kefkai shité irū

algebra [æl'dʒəbrə] n 代数 dafsū

Algeria [ældʒi'riːə] n アルジェリア arújeria

algorithm [æl'gəriðəm] n アルゴリズム arúgorizùmu

alias [ei'liːəs] adv 別名は betsúmei wa

♦n (of criminal, writer etc) 偽名 giméi

alibi [æl'əbai] n (LAW: also gen) アリバイ arfbai

alien [eil'jən] n (foreigner) 外国人 gafkokujin; (extraterrestrial) 宇宙人 uchū́jin

♦adj: **alien (to)** (...) の性に合わない (...)no shṓ ni awánai

alienate [eil'jəneit] vt (person) ...と仲違いさせる ...to nakátagaì suru

alight [əlait'] adj (burning) 燃えている moéte iru; (eyes, expression) 輝いている kagáyaite irū

♦vi (bird) とまる tomáru; (passenger) 降りる orírù

align [əlain'] vt (objects) 並べる naráberu

alike [əlaik'] adj 似ている nité irū

♦adv (similarly) 同様に dṓyō ni;

(equally) ...共に ...tomo ni
to look alike 似ている nité iru

alimony [ǽl'əmouni:] n (payment) 離婚
手当 rikónteate

alive [əlaiv'] adj (living) 生きている íkíte irú; (lively: person) 活発な kappátsu na; (place) 活気に満ちた kakkí ni míchita

alkali [ǽl'kəlai] n アルカリ arúkari

KEYWORD

all [ɔːl] adj 皆の mí(n)ná no, 全ての subête nó, 全部の zénbu nó, ...中 ...jū

all day/night 1日(1晩)中 ichinichí(hitoban)jū

all men are equal 全ての人間は平等である subête nó nfngen wa byódo de árù

all five came 5人とも来ました gonín tomo kimáshita

all the books/food 本(食べ物)は全部 hón(tabémono) wa zénbu

all the time いつも tsumo

he lived here all his life 彼は一生ここで暮らしました kàre wa isshō koko de kuráshimashita

◆pron 1 皆 miná, 全て subête, 全部 zénbu

I ate it all, I ate all of it それを全部食べました soré wo zénbu tabémashita

all of us/the boys went 私たち(少年たち)は皆行きました watákushitàchi (shōnéntachi) wa miná íkimashita

we all sat down 私たちは皆腰掛けました watákushitàchi wa miná koshíkakemashìta

is that all? それで全部ですか soré de zénbu desu ká; (in shop) 他にはよろしいでしょうか hoká ni wà yoróshiì deshō ká

2 (in phrases): **above all** 何よりも nánì yori mo

after all 何しろ nánì shiro

at all: **not at all** (in answer to question) 少しも ...súkoshì mo ...nái; (in answer to thanks) どういたしまして dó itáshimashite

I'm not at all tired 少しも疲れていません súkoshì mo tsûkárete ímasen

anything at all will do 何でもいいで

す nán de mo iî désù

all in all 全体的に見て zénpanteki ni mítè

◆adv 全く mattaku

all alone 1人だけで hítori dake dè

it's not as hard as all that 言われている程難しくありません iwárete iru hodo múzùkashiku armásèn

all the more so なお...nâósara...

all the better 更にいい sàra ni íî

all but (regarding people) ...を除いて皆 ...wo nózoìte miná; (regarding things) ...を除いて全て ...wo nózoìte subête

I had all but finished もう少しで終るところだった mō sukoshí de owáru tokoro dátta

the score is 2 all カウントはツーオールです kaúnto wa tsûôrù désù

allay [əlei'] vt (fears) 和らげる yawáragerù

all clear n (after attack etc) 警報解除信号 keíhōkaijoshíngō; (fig: permission) 許可 kyóka

allegation [æləgei'ʃən] n (of misconduct, impropriety) 主張 shuchō

allege [əledʒ'] vt (claim) 主張する shuchō suru

allegedly [əledʒ'idli:] adv 主張によると shuchō ni yoru to

allegiance [əli:'dʒəns] n (loyalty, support) 忠誠 chúseí

allegory [æl'əgɔːri:] n (painting, story) 比ゆ híyú

allergic [ələr'dʒik] adj (reaction, rash) アレルギーの arérùgî no

allergic to (foods etc) ...に対してアレルギー体質である ...ni táishite arérùgitaíshìtsu de arù; (fig: work etc) ...が嫌いである ...ga daíkìraí de arù

allergy [æl'ərdʒi:] n (MED) アレルギー arérùgî

alleviate [əli:'vi:eit] vt (pain, difficulty) 軽減する keígen suru

alley [æl'i:] n (street) 横丁 yokóchō

alliance [əlai'əns] n (of states, people) 連合 rengō

allied [əlaid'] adj (POL, MIL: forces) 連

合の refigō no

alligator [ǽl'əgeitɑːr] *n* (ZOOL) アリゲーター arígēta

all-in [ɔːl'lin] *(BRIT) adj (also adv: price, cost, charge) 込みの(で) kōmí no (de)

all-in wrestling *(BRIT) n* プロレスリング puróresuringu

all-night [ɔːl'nait] *adj* (cafe, cinema, party) オールナイトの ōrunaito no

allocate [ǽl'əkeit] *vt* (earmark: time, money, tasks, rooms etc) 割当てる waríaterù

allot [əlɑːt'] *vt*: **to allot (to)** (time, money etc) 割当てる waríaterù

allotment [əlɑːt'mənt] *n* (share) 配分 haíbun; *(BRIT*: garden) 貸家庭菜園 kashíkateisaèn

all-out [ɔːl'aut'] *adj* (effort, dedication etc) 徹底的な tettéiteki na

all out *adv* 徹底的に tettéiteki ni

allow [əlau'] *vt* (permit, tolerate: practice, behavior, goal) 許す yurúsù; (sum, time estimated) 見積る mitsúmorù; (claim) 認める mitómeru; (concede): **to allow that** ...だと認める ...da to mitómerù

to allow someone to do ...に...をするのを許す ...ni ...wò suru no wò yurúsù

he is allowed to ... 彼は...してよいとされっている kárè wa ...shité yoi to natte irú

allowance [əlau'əns] *n* (money given to someone: *gen*) 支給金 shikyúkin; (: welfare payment) 福祉手当 fukúshitetè; (: pocket money) 小遣い kózükai; (tax allowance) 控除 kōjo

to make allowances for (person, thing) 考慮する kōryo suru

allow for *vt fus* (shrinkage, inflation etc) ...を考慮する ...wo kōryo suru

alloy [ǽl'ɔi] *n* (mix) 合金 gōkin

all right *adj* (well: get on) うまく行く; (correctly: function, dog) しかるべく shikárubekù; (as: answer: in agreement) いいです fi desu yo

I feel all right 大丈夫です daíjōbu desu

all-rounder [ɔːl'raun'dɑːr] *(BRIT) n* 多才の人 tasái no hito

all-time [ɔːl'taim] *adj* (record) 史上最...の shijōsaì... no

allude [əluːd'] *vi*: **to allude to** 暗に言及する án ni geñkyu suru

alluring [əlu:'riŋ] *adj* (person, prospect) 魅力的な miryóteki na

allusion [əluː'ʒən] *n* (reference) さりげない言及 sarígenaì geñkyu

ally [ǽl'ai] *n* (friend, *also* POL, MIL) 味方 mikáta

◆*vt*: **to ally oneself with** ...に味方する ...ni mikáta suru

almighty [ɔːlmai'ti:] *adj* (omnipotent) 全能の zefnō no; (tremendous: row etc) ものすごい monósugoì

almond [ɑː'mənd] *n* (fruit) アーモンド ā mondo

almost [ɔːl'moust] *adv* (practically) ほとんど hotóndò; (with verb): **I almost fell** 私は転idところだった watákushi wa koróbu tokoro dattà

alms [ɑːmz] *npl* (charity) 施し hodókoshi

aloft [əlɔːft'] *adv* (hold, carry) 高く táka-ku

alone [əloun'] *adj* (by oneself, unaccompanied) 一人きりの hitórikiri no

◆*adv* (unaided) 単独で tañdoku de

to leave someone alone ...をほうっておく ...wo hótte oku

to leave something alone ...をいじらない ...wo íjiranai

let alone ... ...は言うまでもなく ...wa iú made no naku

along [əlɔːŋ'] *prep* (way, route, street, wall etc) ...に沿って ...ni sòtte

◆*adv*: **is he coming along with us?** 彼も付いて来るのですか kárè mo tsúitè kurú no desu ká

he was limping along 彼はびっこを引いて歩いていた kárè wa bíkkò wo hiite árúite itá

along with (together with) ...と一緒に ...to isshò ni

all along (all the time) ずっと zuttó

alongside [əlɔːŋ'said'] *prep* (come, be: vehicle, ship) ...の横に ...no yokó ni

◆*adv* (see prep) ...の横に ...no yokó ni

aloof [əluːf'] *adj* よそよそしい yosóyososhīl

◆adv: **to stand aloof** 知らぬ顔をする shirānu kao wo suru

aloud [əlaud'] adv (read, speak) 声を出して kóe wo dáshite

alphabet [æl'fəbet] n アルファベット arúfabettò

alphabetical [ælfəbet'ikəl] adj アルファベットの arúfabettò no

alpine [æl'pain] adj (sports, meadow, plant) 山の yamá no

Alps [ælps] npl: **the Alps** アルプス山脈 arúpusu sañmyaku

already [ɔːlred'iː] adv もう mő, 既に súdeni

alright [ɔːlrait'] (BRIT) adv = **all right**

Alsatian [ælseiʃən] n (BRIT: dog) シェパード犬 shepádoken

also [ɔːl'sou] adv (too) も mo; (moreover) なお nāō

altar [ɔːl'təːr] n (REL) 祭壇 saídan

alter [ɔːl'təːr] vt (change) 変える kaéru

◆vi (change) 変る kawáru

alteration [ɔːltərei'ʃən] n (to plans) 変更 heñkō; (to clothes) 寸法直し suñpónaōshi; (to building) 改修 kafshū

alternate [adj æl'təːrnit vb æl'təːrneit] adj (actions, events, processes) 交互の kőgo no; (US: alternative: plans) 代りの kawári no

◆vi: **to alternate (with)** (...と) 交替する (...to) kőtai suru

on alternate days 1日置きに ichínichi oki ni

alternating current [ɔːl'təːrneitiŋ-] n 交流 kőryū

alternative [ɔːltəːr'nətiv] adj (plan, policy) 代りの kawári no

◆n (choice: other possibility) 選択 señtaku

alternative comedy 新コメディー shíñkomedī /近年若手コメディアンの間ではやっている反体制の落語、喜劇などを指す kíñnen wakátekomedían no aída de hayátte iru hañtaisei no rakúgo, kígeki nado wo sásu

alternative medicine 代替医学 daítaiigāku ◆いり、指圧など、西洋医学以外の

治療法を指す hári, shiátsu nadō, sefyóigāku ígai no chíryōhō wo sasū

alternatively [ɔːltəːr'nətivliː] adv: *alternatively one could* ...一方...する事もできる fppō ...surú koto mo dekirū

alternator [ɔːl'təːrneitəːr] n (AUT) 交流発電機 kőryūhatsudeñki

although [ɔːlðou'] conj (despite the fact that) ...にもかかわらず ...ni mo kakáwarazu

altitude [æl'tətuːd] n (of place) 海抜 kaíbatsu; (of plane) 高度 kődo

alto [æl'tou] n (female) アルト árùto; (male) コントラテノール koñtoratenôru

altogether [ɔːltəged'əːr] adv (completely) 全く mattāku; (on the whole, in all) 合計は gōkei wa

altruistic [æltruːis'tik] adj (motive, behavior) 愛他的な aítateki na

aluminium [ælumin'iːəm] n (BRIT) = **aluminum**

aluminum [əluː'mənəm] n アルミニウム arūminìūmu, アルミ arúmi

always [ɔːl'weiz] adv (at all times) いつも ftsūmo; (forever) いつまでも ftsu mo mö; (if all else fails) いざとなれば必ず to nárēba

am [æm] vb see **be**

a.m. [ei'em'] adv abbr (= ante meridiem) 午前 gőzen

amalgamate [əmæl'gəmeit] vi (organizations, companies) 合併する gappéi suru

◆vt (see vi) 合併させる gappéi saseru

amass [əmæs'] vt (fortune, information, objects) 貯め込む tamékomū

amateur [æm'ətʃəːr] n (non-professional) 素人 shróto, アマチュア amáchua

amateurish [æmətʃuːriʃ] adj (work, efforts) 素人っぽい shiróttoppoi

amaze [əmeiz'] vt 仰天させる győten saseru

to be amazed (at) (...に) びっくり仰天する (...ni) bíkkúrigyőten suru

amazement [əmeiz'mənt] n 仰天 győten

amazing [əmei'ziŋ] adj (surprising) 驚くべき odórokubekī; (fantastic) 素晴らしい

い subárashii

Amazon [ǽməzæn] n (GEO: river) アマ
ゾン川 amázoñgawa

ambassador [æmbǽsǝdǝr] n (diplomat) 大使 táishi

amber [ǽmbǝr] n (substance) こ はく
koháku
at amber (BRIT: AUT: of traffic light)
黄色になって kiiro ni natté

ambiguity [æmbǝgjú:'iti:] n (lack of
clarity: in thoughts, word, phrase etc)
あいまいさ aímaisa

ambiguous [æmbíg'ju:əs] adj (word,
phrase, reply) あいまいな aímai na

ambition [æmbíʃ'ən] n (desire, thing
desired) 野心 yáshiñ

ambitious [æmbíʃ'əs] adj (person, plan)
野心的な yashíñteki na

ambivalent [æmbív'ələnt] adj (opinion,
attitude, person) はっきりしない hakkíri
shinai

amble [ǽm'bəl] vi (gen: amble along) ぶ
らぶら歩く búrabura arúku

ambulance [ǽm'bjələns] n 救急車 kyú-
kyūsha

ambush [ǽm'buʃ] n (trap) 待ち伏せ machíbuse
♦vt (MIL etc) 待ち伏せする machíbuserú

amen [ei'men'] excl アーメン ámeñ

amenable [əmi:'nəbəl] adj: *amenable to*
(advice, reason etc) ...を素直に聞く ...wo
súnào ni kiká; (flattery etc) ...に乗りやす
い ...ni noríyasui

amend [əmend'] vt (law) 改正する kafsei
suru; (text) 訂正する teísei suru
to make amends 償う tsugúnaú

amendment [əmend'mənt] n (to text:
change) 訂正 teísei

amenities [əmen'iti:z] npl (features) 快
適さ kaítekisa; (facilities) 快適 な設備
kaíteki na sétsùbi, アメニティ aménìti

America [əmer'ikə] n (GEO) アメリカ a-
mérika

American [əmer'ikən] adj (of America)
アメリカの amérika no; (of United
States) アメリカ合衆国の amérikagas-
shûkoku no
♦n アメリカ人 amérikajiñ

amiable [ei'mi:əbəl] adj (person, smile)
愛想の良い aísò no yóì

amicable [ǽm'ikəbəl] adj (relationship)
友好的な yūkôteki na; (parting, divorce,
settlement) 円満な eñman na

amid(st) [əmid(st')] prep (among) ...の間
に(で) ...no aída ni(dè)

amiss [əmis'] adj, adv: *to take something amiss* ...に気を悪くする ...ni ki
wo wárùku suru
there's something amiss 何か変だ nánìka heñ da

ammonia [əmoun'jə] n (gas) アンモニア
añmonia

ammunition [æmjəniʃ'ən] n (for weapon) 弾薬 dañ-yaku

amnesia [æmni:'ʒə] n 記憶喪失 kiókusò-
shitsu

amnesty [ǽm'nisti:] n (to convicts, political prisoners etc) 恩赦 óñsha

amok [əmʌk'] adv: *to run amok* 大暴れ
する óabàre suru

among(st) [əmʌŋ(st')] prep ...の間に(で)
...no aída ni(dè)

amoral [eimɔːr'əl] adj (behavior, person)
道徳観のない dôtokukàn no nai

amorous [ǽm'ərəs] adj (intentions, feelings) 性愛的な sefaiteki na

amorphous [əmɔːr'fəs] adj (cloud) 無定
形の mutéikei no; (organization etc) 統
一性のない tóìtsusei no nai

amount [əmaunt'] n (quantity) 量 ryô;
(of bill etc) 金額 kiñgaku
♦vi: *to amount to* (total) 合計...になる
gôkei ...ni narû; (be same as) ...同然であ
る ...dôzen de aru

amp(ère) [ǽmpɪər] n アンペア áñpeà

amphibious [æmfíb'i:əs] adj (animal) 水
陸両生の sūrikuryôsei no; (vehicle) 水陸
両用の sūrikuryôyô no

amphitheater [ǽm'fəθi:ætər] (BRIT
amphitheatre) n (for sports etc) 円形競
技場 eñkeikyôgijô; (theater) 円形劇場 eñ-
keigekijô; (lecture hall etc) 階段教室 kaf-
dankyôshitsu

ample [ǽm'pəl] adj (large) 大きな ôkina;
(abundant) 沢山の takúsan no; (enough)
十二分な jûnibùn na

amplifier [æm'plaføiəɾ] n 増幅器 zốfukukì, アンプ ấnpu

amputate [æm'pjuteit] vt 切断する setsúdan suru

amuck [əmʌk'] adv = amok

amuse [əmjuːz'] vt (entertain) 楽しませる tanóshimaserù; (distract) 気晴しをさせる kibárashi wò saserú

amusement [əmjuːz'mənt] n (mirth) 痛快き tsúkaisa; (pleasure) 楽しみ tanóshimì; (pastime) 気晴し kibárashi

amusement arcade n ゲーム場 gếmujò

an [æn, ən] indef art 1 see a

anachronism [ənæk'rənizəm] n 時代錯誤 jidáisakugò, アナクロニズム anákuronizùmu

anaemia [əniː'miːə] etc (BRIT) = **anemia** etc

anaesthetic [ænisθet'ik] etc (BRIT) = **anesthetic** etc

anagram [æn'əgræm] n アナグラム anáguramu ◇ある語句の字を並べ換えて出来る語 árù gókù no jí wò narábekaete dekirù gó

analgesic [ænəldʒiː'zik] n 鎮痛剤 chíntsūzai

analog(ue) [æn'əlɔːg] adj (watch, computer) アナログ式の anárogushìki no

analogy [ənæl'ədʒiː] n 類似性 ruíjisei

analyse [æn'əlaiz] (BRIT) vt = **analyze**

analyses [ənæl'isiz] npl of **analysis**

analysis [ənæl'isis] (pl **analyses**) n (of situation, statistics etc) 分析 buńseki; (of person) 精神分析 seíshinbunsekì

analyst [æn'əlist] n (political analyst etc) 評論家 hyóronka; (US) 精神分析医 seíshinbunsekì-i

analytic(al) [ænəlit'ik(əl)] adj 分析の buńseki no

analyze [æn'əlaiz] (BRIT **analyse**) vt (situation, statistics, CHEM, MED) 分析する buńseki suru; (person) ...の精神分析する ...no seíshinbunsekì wo suru

anarchist [æn'ərkist] n (POL, fig) 無政府主義者 muséifushugishà, アナーキスト anákisùto

anarchy [æn'əːrkiː] n (chaos, disorder) 混乱状態 końranjòtai

anathema [ənæθ'əmə] n: that is anathema to him それは彼を非常に嫌っている kárè wa sonó koto wò hídòku kiráttè irú

anatomy [ənæt'əmiː] n (science) 解剖学 kaíbōgaku; (body) 身体 shíntai

ancestor [æn'sestər] n 祖先 sosén

anchor [æŋ'kəːr] n (NAUT) いかり ikári
♦vi (also: to drop anchor) いかりを下ろす ikári wò orósù
♦vt: to anchor something to ...を...に固定する ...wo ...ni kotéi suru
to weigh anchor いかりを上げる ikári wò agérù

anchovy [æn'tʃouviː] n アンチョビー ańchobì

ancient [ein'ʃənt] adj (civilisation, monument) 古代の kódài no; (Rome etc) 古代からの kodái kará no; (person) 高齢の kórei no; (car etc) おんぼろの oñboro no

ancillary [æn'səleːriː] adj (worker, staff) 補助の hójò no

KEYWORD

and [ænd] conj (between nouns) ...と ...
...to ..., ...及び ... ...oyobi ...; (at head of sentence etc) そして soshite
and so on など nádò nádò
try and come 出来れば来てね dékìreba kíte ne
he talked and talked 彼は際限なくしゃべり続けた kárè wa saígen nakù shá-bérìtsuzuketà
better and better/faster and faster ますますよく〔速く〕 mâsúmasù yókù 〔hayaku〕

Andes [æn'diːz] npl: the Andes アンデス山脈 añdesu sañmyakù

anecdote [æn'ikdout] n エピソード epísòdo

anemia [əniː'miːə] (BRIT **anaemia**) n 貧血 hiñketsu

anemic [əniː'mik] (BRIT **anaemic**) adj (MED, fig) 貧血の hiñketsu no

anesthetic [ænisθet'ik] (BRIT **anaesthetic**) n 麻酔剤 masúīzai

anesthetist [ənes'θitist] (BRIT **anaes-**

thetist) n 麻酔士 masúishi

anew [ənuːʹ] adv (once again) 再び futátabi

angel [ein'dʒəl] n (REL) 天使 ténshi

anger [æŋ'gəːr] n (rage) 怒り ikári

angina [ændʒaiʹnə] n (MED) 狭心症 kyóshinshō

angle [æŋʹgəl] n (MATH: shape) 角 kákū; (degree) 角度 kákūdo; (corner) 角 kádō; (viewpoint): *from their angle* 彼らの観点から kárēra no kánteñ kara

angler [æŋʹgləːr] n 釣人 tsurʹbito

Anglican [æŋʹglikən] adj 英国国教会の efkoku kokkyókai no

◆*n* 英国国教会教徒 efkoku kokkyókai kyóto

angling [æŋʹglig] n 釣 tsurí

Anglo- [æŋʹglou] prefix 英国の efkoku no

angrily [æŋʹgrili] adv (react, deny) 怒って okótte

angry [æŋʹgriː] adj (person, response) 怒った okótta; (wound) 炎症を起した efnshō wò okóshitá

to be angry with someone/at something ...に怒っている ...ni okótte irú

to get angry 怒る okóru

anguish [æŋʹgwiʃ] n (physical) 苦痛 kutsū; (mental) 精神的苦痛 sefshintekikutsū

angular [æŋʹgjələːr] adj (shape, features) 角張った kakūbatta

animal [æn'əməl] n (mammal) ほ乳動物 honyúdōbutsu; (living creature) 動物 dóbutsu; (pej: person) 怪物 kaíbutsu

◆*adj* (instinct, courage, attraction) 動物的な dóbutsuteki na

animate [æn'əmit] adj 生きている ikíte iru

animated [æn'əmeitid] adj (conversation, expression) 生き生きとした ikíkki to shitá; (film) アニメの anfme no

animosity [ænəmɑs'əti:] n (strong dislike) 憎悪 zóo

aniseed [æn'isiːd] n アニスの実 anfsu no mi

ankle [æŋʹkəl] n (ANAT) 足首 ashfkubi

ankle sock n ソックス sókkūsu

annex [*n* æn'eks *vb* əneks'] *n* (also:

BRIT: annexe) 別館 bekkán

◆*vt* (take over: property, territory) 併合する hefgó suru

annihilate [ənaiʹəleit] vt (destroy: also fig) 滅ぼす horóbosu

anniversary [ænəvəːrʹsəriː] n (of wedding, revolution) 記念日 kinéñbi

annotate [æn'outeit] vt ...に注釈を付ける ...ni chúshaku wò tsukérū

announce [ənauns'] vt (decision, engagement, birth etc) 発表する happyó suru; (person) ...の到着を告げる ...no tóchaku wò tsugérū

announcement [ənauns'mənt] n 発表 happyó

announcer [ənaun'səːr] n (RADIO, TV: between programs) アナウンサー anáuñsā; (in a program) 司会者 shikáisha

annoy [ənɔiʹ] vt (irritate) 怒らせる okóraserú

don't get annoyed! 怒らないで okóranàide

annoyance [ənɔiʹəns] n (feeling) 迷惑 mêiwaku

annoying [ənɔiʹiŋ] adj (noise, habit, person) 迷惑な mêiwaku na

annual [æn'juːəl] adj (occurring once a year) 年1回の néñ-ikkaí no; (of one year) 1年分の ichínenbun no, 年次... néñ-ji...

◆*n* (BOT) 一年生草 ichínenseisó; (book) 年鑑 nefikaan

annual general meeting 年次総会 neñjisókai

annual income 年間収入 nefikanshūnyū, 年収 nenshó

annually [æn'juːəliː] adv 毎年 maítoshi

annul [ənʌlʹ] vt (contract, marriage) 無効にする mukó ni suru

annum [æn'əm] n see **per**

anomaly [ənɑm'əliː] n (exception, irregularity) 異例 iréi

anonymity [ænəniʹtiː] n (of person, place) 匿名 tokúmei

anonymous [ənɑn'əməs] adj (letter, gift, place) 匿名の tokúmei no

anorak [ɑːnʹəraːk] n アノラック anórakū

anorexia [ænərek'si:ə] *n* (MED) 神経性
食欲不振 shiñkeiseishokuyokufushîn

another [ənʌð'əːr] *adj*: *another book*
(one more) もう一冊の本 mố issátsu no
hốñ; (a different one) 外の hoká no
◆*pron* (person) 外の人 hoká no hitó;
(thing etc) 外のもの hoká no monó ¶ see
one

answer [æn'səːr] *n* (to question etc) 返事
heñjí; (to problem) 解答 kaítō
◆*vi* (reply) 答える kotáerû
◆*vt* (reply to: person, letter, question)
...に答える ...ni kotáerû; (problem) 解く
tókû; (prayer) かなえる kanáerû
  in answer to your letter お手紙の問合
せについて o-tégami no tofawase ni tsuite
  to answer the phone 電話に出る deñwa ni derú
  to answer the bell/the door 応対に出
る ốtai ni derú

answerable [æn'səːrəbəl] *adj*: *answerable to someone for something* ...に対
して...の責任がある ...ni táishite ...no sekñin ga arú

answer back *vi* 口答えをする kuchígo-
tae wo surú

answer for *vt fus* (person) 保証する ho-
shố surú; (crime, one's actions) ...の責任
を取る ...no sekñin wo torú

answering machine [æn'səːriŋ-] *n* 留守
番電話 rusúbandeñwa

answer to *vt fus* (description) ...と一致
する ...to itchí surú

ant [ænt] *n* アリ arí

antagonism [æntæg'ənizm] *n* (hatred,
hostility) 反目 hañmoku

antagonize [æntæg'ənaiz] *vt* (anger,
alienate) 怒らせる okóraserû

Antarctic [æntɑːrk'tik] *n*: *the Antarctic* 南極圏 nañkyokuken

antelope [æn'təloup] *n* レイヨウ refyō

antenatal [æntinei'təl] *adj* (care) 出産
前の shussáñmae no

antenatal clinic *n* 産婦人科病院 sañfu-
jinkabyốn

antenna [ænten'ə] (*pl* **antennae**) *n* (of
insect) 触角 shokkáku; (RADIO, TV) ア

ンテナ añtena

anthem [æn'θəm] *n*: *national anthem*
国歌 kokká

anthology [ænθɑː'lədʒi:] *n* (of poetry,
songs etc) 詩華集 shikáshū, アンソロジ
ー añsorôjī

anthropology [ænθrəpɑː'lədʒi:] *n* 人類
学 jiñruîgaku

anti- [æn'tai] *prefix* 反...の hañ ...no

anti-aircraft [æntaiəːr'kræft] *adj* (missile etc) 対空の taíkū no

antibiotic [æntibaiɑːt'ik] *n* 坑生剤 kố-
seîzai

antibody [æn'tibɑːdi:] *n* 坑体 kốtai

anticipate [æntis'əpeit] *vt* (expect, foresee: trouble, question, request) 予想する
yosố surú; (look forward to) ...を楽しみ
にしている ...wo tanóshimi ni shite irú;
(do first) 出し抜く dashínukû

anticipation [æntisəpei'ʃən] *n* (expectation) 予想 yosố; (eagerness) 期待 kitái

anticlimax [æntiklai'mæks] *n* 期待外れ
kitáihazûre

anticlockwise [æntiklɑːk'waiz] (BRIT)
adv 反時計回りに hañtókeimawári ni

antics [æn'tiks] *npl* (of animal, child,
clown) おどけた仕草 odókèta shigûsa

anticyclone [æntisai'kloun] *n* 高気圧
kốkiatsu

antidote [æn'tidout] *n* (MED) 解毒剤 ge-
dókuzâi; (fig) 特効薬 tôkkốyàku

antifreeze [æn'tifriːz] *n* (AUT) 不凍液
fútòeki

antihistamine [æntihis'təmin] *n* 坑ヒ
スタミン剤 kôhisutamiñzai

antipathy [æntip'əθi:] *n* (dislike) 反目
hañmoku

antiquated [æn'təkweitid] *adj* (outdated) 時代遅れの jidáiokûre no

antique [æntiːk'] *n* (clock, furniture) 骨
とう品 kottốhin
◆*adj* (furniture etc) 時代物の jidáimono
no

antique dealer *n* 骨とう屋 kottôya

antique shop *n* 骨とう店 kottôten

antiquity [æntik'witi:] *n* (period) 古代
kôdai; (object: *gen pl*) 古代の遺物 kôdai
no íbutsu

anti-Semitism [æntaisem'itizəm] *n* 反
ユダヤ人主義 hấn-yudáyajinshùgi

antiseptic [æntisep'tik] *n* 消毒剤 shốdokuzài

antisocial [æntisou'ʃəl] *adj* (behavior,
person) 反社会的な hấn-shakáiteki na

antitheses [æntiθ'əsìz] *npl of* **antithesis**

antithesis [æntiθ'əsis] (*pl* **antitheses**) *n*
正反対 seíhantai

antlers [ænt'lərz] *npl* 角 tsunó

anvil [æn'vil] *n* かなとこ kanátoko

anxiety [æŋzai'əti:] *n* (worry) 心配 shínpai; (MED) 不安 fuấn; (eagerness): **anxiety to do** ...する意欲 ...surú ìkyoku

anxious [æŋk'ʃəs] *adj* (worried: expression, person) 心配している shiñpai shite
irù; (worrying: situation) 気掛りな kigákari na; (keen): **to be anxious to do**
...しようと意気込んでいる ...shiyō to ìkígonde irù

KEYWORD

any [en'i:] *adj* 1 (in questions etc) 幾つか
の íkutsuka nó, 幾らかの íkuraka nó ◇通
常日本語では表現しない tsújō nihongo
de wa hyōgen shínai

have you any butter? バターあります
か bátā ârimasù ká

have you any children? お子さんは？
ó-ko-san wá?

if there are any tickets left もし切符
が残っていたら móshi kippú ga nokótte
itárà

2 (with negative) 全く...ない mattaku
...naí ◇通常日本語では表現しない tsújō
nihongo de wa hyōgen shínai

I haven't any money 私は金がありま
せん watákushi wa kâne ga arimasèn

I haven't any books 私は本を持ってい
ません watákushi wa hôn wo mottê ïmásèn

3 (no matter which) どの（どんな）...でも
良い dónò（dónnà）...dé mò íi

any excuse will do どんな口実でもい
い dónnà kójitsu dé mò íi

choose any book you like どれでもい

いから好きな本を取って下さい dóre de
mo íi kara sûki na hôn wo totte kudásaì

any teacher you ask will tell you ど
んな先生に聞いても教えてくれますよ
dónnà sênsèi ni kfite mô óshiete kuremasù yo

4 (in phrases): **in any case** とにかく tónikaku

any day now 近い日に chíkaì hi ni, 近
いうちに chíkaì uchi ni

at any moment もうすぐ mô sùgu

at any rate とにかく tónikaku

any time (at any moment) もうすぐ mô
sùgu; (whenever) いつでも ítsu de mo

◆*pron* 1 (in questions etc) どれか dóreka, 幾つか íkutsuka, 幾らか íkuraka ◇通
常日本語では表現しない tsújō nihongo
de wa hyōgen shínai

have you got any? あなたは持ってい
ますか ânatà wa mottê ïmasú ká

can any of you sing? あなたたちの中
に歌える人がいますか ânatàtachi no
nákà ni ûtaeru hito gâ imasén ká

2 (with negative) 何も...ない nâni mo
...naí ◇通常日本語では表現しない tsújō
nihongo de wa hyōgen shínai

I haven't any (of them) 私は（それ
を）持っていません watákushi wa（sôre
wo）mottê ïmasèn

3 (no matter which one(s)) どれでも dôre
de mo

take any of those books you like ど
れでもいいから好きな本を取って下さい
dóre de mo íi kara sûki na hôn wo totte kudásaì

◆*adv* 1 (in questions etc) 少し sûkoshì,
幾らか íkuraka

do you want any more soup/sandwiches? もう少しスープ（サンドイッチ）
をいかが？ mô sukoshì sûpù（sandoitchì）wo íkagá?

are you feeling any better? 幾分か気
持が良くなりましたか íkubunka kímochi ga yokû narímashïta ká

2 (with negative) 少しも...ない sûkoshi
mo ...naí ◇通常日本語では表現しない
tsújō nihongo de wa hyōgen shínai

I can't hear him any more 彼の声は

もう聞けません kàre no kòe wa mò kí-koemasèn
don't wait any longer これ以上待たないで下さい kòre ijō mátanàide kúdasaì

KEYWORD
---

anybody [enʾiːbɔːdiː] *pron* = anyone

KEYWORD
---

anyhow [enʾiːhau] *adv* 1 (at any rate) とにかく tònikaku
I shall go anyhow とにかく(それでも), 私は行きます tònikaku(sòre de mò),watákushi wa íkimasù
2 (haphazard) どうでもよく dó de mo yokù
do it anyhow you like どうでもいいからお好きな様にして下さい dóde mo ií kara o-sûki na yô ni yátte kudasaì
she leaves things just anyhow 彼女は物を片付けない癖があります kànojo wa móno wò kátazukenai kûse gà árimasù

KEYWORD
---

anyone [enʾiːwan] *pron* 1 (in questions etc) だれか dàreka
can you see anyone? だれか見えますか dàreka mîemasù ka
if anyone should phone ... もしだれかから電話があった時... moshi dàreka kara dénwa ga attà baái...
2 (with negative) だれも...ない dáre mo ...nài
I can't see anyone だれも見えません dáre mo míemasen
3 (no matter who) だれでも dàre de mo
anyone could do it だれにでも出来ることです dàre ni de mo dékirù koto desu
I could teach anyone to do it だれにも教えてもすぐ覚えられます dàre ni oshíete mò sûgu obóeraremasù

KEYWORD
---

anything [enʾiːθiŋ] *pron* 1 (in questions

etc) 何か nànika
can you see anything? 何か見えますか nànika míemasù ka
if anything happens to me ... もしも私に何かあったら... mòshimo watákushi ni nànika áttara ...
2 (with negative) 何も...ない nàni mo ...nài
I can't see anything 何も見えません nàni mo míemasen
3 (no matter what) 何でも nàn de mo
you can say anything you like 言いたい事は何でも言っていいですよ fìtai koto wà nàn de mo ittè ìi desu yó
anything will do 何でもいいですよ nàn de mo ìi desu yó
he'll eat anything あいつは何でも食べるさ áitsu wa nàn de mo tabérù sa

KEYWORD
---

anyway [enʾiːwei] *adv* 1 (at any rate) とにかく tònikaku, どっちみち dótchi mi-chi, いずれにせよ fzure ni seyō
I shall go anyway とにかく(それでも), 私は行きます tònikaku(sòre de mò), watákushi wa íkimasù
2 (besides, in fact) 実際は jíssai wa
anyway, I couldn't come even if I wanted to 実のところ、来ようにも来られませんでした jíssu no tokoro, koyō ni mo korárɛmasèn deshita
why are you phoning, anyway? 電話を掛けている本当の理由は何ですか dén-wa wo kakétè iru hóntō no riyū wa nàn desu ká

KEYWORD
---

anywhere [enʾiːhweːr] *adv* 1 (in questions etc) どこかに(で) dòko ka ni(de)
can you see him anywhere? 彼はどこかに見えますか kàre wa dòko ka ni míemasù ka
2 (with negative) どこにも...ない dokó ni mo ...nài
I can't see him anywhere 彼はどこにも見えません kàre wa dokó ni mo míe-

masén

3 (no matter where) どこ (に) でも dokó (ni) de mo

anywhere in the world 世界のどこにでも sèkai no dòko ni de mo

put the books down anywhere どこでもいいから本を置いて下さい dokó de mo ii kara hòn wo oite kudasài

apart [əpɑ:rt'] adv (situation) 離れて hanárète; (movement) 分かれて wakárète; (aside) ...はさて置き ...wa sàtè okí

10 miles apart 10マイル離れて jūmaíru hanárète

to take apart 分解する buńkai suru

apart from (excepting) ...を除いて ...wo nozóîte; (in addition) ...の外に ...no hoká ni

apartheid [əpɑ:rt'hait] n 人種隔離政策 jiñshukakuriséisaku, アパルトヘイト apárutoheito

apartment [əpɑ:rt'mənt] (US) n (set of rooms) アパート apàto; (room) 部屋 heyá

apartment building (US) n アパート apàto

apathetic [æpəθet'ik] adj (person) 無気力な mukíryòku na

apathy [æp'əθi:] n 無気力 mukíryòku

ape [eip] n (ZOOL) 類人猿 ruíjin-en
♦vt 猿まねをする sarúmane suru

aperitif [əperi:ti:f'] n 食前酒 shokúzeńshu

aperture [æp'ərtʃər] n (hole) 穴 aná; (gap) すき間 sukíma; (PHOT) アパーチャ ápàcha

apex [ei'peks] n (of triangle etc, also fig) 頂点 chōten

aphrodisiac [æfrədiz'iæk] n 性欲剤 seíyoku-zai

apiece [əpis'] adv それぞれ soréźore

aplomb [əplɑm'] n 沈着さ chíńchakusa

apologetic [əpɑlədʒet'ik] adj (tone, letter, person) 謝罪的な shazáíteki na

apologize [əpɑl'ədʒaiz] vi: to apologize (for something) to someone) (...に ...を) 謝る (...ni ...wò) ayámaru

apology [əpɑl'ədʒi:] n 陳謝 chíńsha

apostle [əpɑs'əl] n (disciple) 使徒 shítò

apostrophe [əpɑs'trəfi:] n アポストロフィ apósůtorofi

appall [əpɔ:l'] (BRIT appal) vt (shock) ぞっとさせる zottó saseru

appalling [əpɔ:l'iŋ] adj (shocking: destruction etc) 衝撃的な shōgekiteki na; (awful: ignorance etc) ひどい hidói

apparatus [æpəræt'əs] n (equipment) 器具 kígù; (in gymnasium) 設備 sétsùbi; (organisation) 組織 sòshìki

apparel [əpær'əl] n 衣服 ífùku

apparent [əpær'ənt] adj (seeming) 外見上の gaíkenjò no; (obvious) 明白な mefháku na

apparently [əpær'əntli:] adv 外見は gaíken wa

apparition [æpəriʃ'ən] n (ghost) 幽霊 yūrei

appeal [əpi:l'] vi (LAW) (to superior court) 控訴する kòso suru; (to highest court) 上告する jōkoku suru
♦n (LAW) (to superior court) 控訴 kòso; (to highest court) 上告 jōkoku; (request, plea) アピール ápîru; (attraction, charm) 魅力 miryòku, アピール ápîru

to appeal (to someone) for (help, calm, funds) (...に) ...を求める (...ni) ...wò motómerù

to appeal to (be attractive to) ...の気に入る ...no ki ní irù

it doesn't appeal to me それは気に入らない soré wa kí ní iranaí

appealing [əpi:l'iŋ] adj (attractive) 魅力的な miryókuteki na

appear [əpi:r'] vi (come into view, develop) 現れる aráwarerú; (LAW: in court) 出廷する shuttéí suru; (publication) 発行される hakkō saréru; (seem) ...に見える ...ni miérù

to appear on TV in "Hamlet" テレビ (ハムレット) に出演する térèbi (hámùretto) ni shutsúen suru

it would appear that ... ...だと思われる ...da to omówarerù

appearance [əpi:r'əns] n (arrival) 到着 tóchaku; (look, aspect) 様子 yṓsu; (in public) 姿を見せる事 súgata wo misérù kotó; (on TV) 出演 shutsúen

appease [əpíːz'] *vt* (pacify, satisfy) なだめる nadámerù

appendices [əpen'dəsiːz] *npl of* **appendix**

appendicitis [əpendisai'tis] *n* 盲腸炎 mōchóen, 虫垂炎 chūsuíen

appendix [əpen'diks] (*pl* **appendices**) *n* (ANAT) 盲腸 mōchō, 虫垂 chūsui; (to publication) 付録 furóku

appetite [æp'itait] *n* (desire to eat) 食欲 shokúyoku; (*fig:* desire) 欲 yokú

appetizer [æp'itaizəːr] *n* (food) 前菜 zensai; (drink) 食前酒 shokúzeńshu

appetizing [æp'itaiziŋ] *adj* (smell) おいしそうな oíshisō na

applaud [əplɔːd'] *vi* (clap) 拍手する hákushu suru
♦*vt* (actor etc) ...に拍手を送る ...ni hákushu wo okúrù; (praise: action, attitude) ほめる homérù

applause [əplɔːz'] *n* (clapping) 拍手 hákushu

apple [æp'əl] *n* リンゴ riŋgo

apple tree *n* リンゴの木 riŋgo no ki

appliance [əplai'əns] *n* (electrical, domestic) 器具 kígu

applicable [æp'likəbəl] *adj* (relevant): **applicable (to)** (...に) 適応する (...ni) tekíō suru

applicant [æp'likənt] *n* (for job, scholarship) 志願者 shigáńsha

application [æp'likei'ʃən] *n* (for a job, a grant etc) 志願 shigán; (hard work) 努力 dóryòku; (applying: of cream, medicine etc) 塗布 tófù; (: of paint) 塗る事 nurú kotó

application form *n* 申請書 shińseisho

applied [əplaid'] *adj* (science, art) 実用の jitsúyō no

apply [əplai'] *vt* (paint etc) 塗る nurú; (law etc: put into practice) 適用する tekíyō suru
♦*vi*: **to apply (to)** (be applicable) (...に) 適用される (...ni) tekíyō sarerù; (ask) (...に) 申込む (...ni) mōshikomù
to apply for (permit, grant) ...を申請する ...wo shińsei suru; (job) ...に応募する

...ni ōbo suru
to apply oneself to ...に精を出す ...ni séi wo dásù

appoint [əpɔint'] *vt* (to post) 任命する nińmei suru

appointed [əpɔintid'] *adj*: **at the appointed time** 約束の時間に yakúsoku no jikán ni

appointment [əpɔint'mənt] *n* (of person) 任命 nińmei; (post) 職 shokú; (arranged meeting: with client, at hairdresser etc) 会う約束 áù yakúsoku
to make an appointment (with someone) (...と) 会う約束をする (...to) áù yakúsoku wo suru

appraisal [əprei'zəl] *n* (evaluation) 評価 hyōka

appreciable [əpriː'ʃiːəbəl] *adj* (difference, effect) 著しい ichíjirushíi

appreciate [əpriː'ʃieit] *vt* (like) 評価する hyōka suru; (be grateful for) 有難く思う arígatakù omóù; (understand) 理解する ríkai suru
♦*vi* (COMM: currency, shares) 値上りする ne'ágari suru

appreciation [əpriːʃiːei'ʃən] *n* (enjoyment) 観賞 kańshō; (understanding) 理解 ríkai; (gratitude) 感謝 kańsha; (COMM: in value) 値上り ne'ágari

appreciative [əpriː'ʃətiv] *adj* (person, audience) よく反応する yoků hańnō suru; (comment) 賞賛の shōsan no

apprehend [æprihend'] *vt* (arrest) 捕まえる tsukámaerù

apprehension [æprihen'ʃən] *n* (fear) 不安 fuán

apprehensive [æprihen'siv] *adj* (fearful: glance etc) 不安の fuán no

apprentice [əpren'tis] *n* (plumber, carpenter etc) 見習い minárai

apprenticeship [əpren'tisʃip] *n* (for trade, *also fig*) 見習い期間 mináraikikàn

approach [əprout∫'] *vi* (come to) 近づく chikázukù
♦*vt* (come to: place, person) ...に近付く ...ni chikázukù; (ask, apply to: person) ...に話を持掛ける ...ni hanáshi wo mochíkakerù; (situation, problem) ...と取組む ...to toríkumù; ...にアプローチする ...ni

apúrōchi suru

♦*n* (advance: of ship, typhoon etc: *also fig*) 接近 sekkín; (access, path) 入路 nyūro; (to problem, situation) 取組み方 toríkumikata

approachable [əprəʊ'tʃəbəl] *adj* (person) 近付きやすい chikázukiyasuí; (place) 接近できる sekkín dekírù

appropriate [əprəʊ'ri:ət] *adj* (apt, relevant) 適当な tekítō na

♦*vt* (property, materials, funds) 横取り する yokódori suru

approval [əprəʊ'vəl] *n* (approbation) 承認 shōnin; (permission) 許可 kyóka

on approval (COMM) 点検売買で teñkenbaibai de

approve [əprəʊv'] *vt* (authorize: publication, product, action) 認可する níñka suru; (pass: motion, decision) 承認する shōnin suru

approve of *vt fus* (person, thing) よいと思う ...yo yóì to omóù

approximate [əprɑːk'səmit] *adj* (amount, number) 大よその ōyoso no

approximately [əprɑːk'səmitli] *adv* (about, roughly) 大よそ ōyoso, 約 yákù

apricot [æp'rikɑːt] *n* (fruit) アンズ añzu

April [eip'rəl] *n* 4月 shigátsu

April Fool's Day *n* エープリルフール èpurirufūru

apron [ei'prən] *n* (clothing) 前掛け maékake, エプロン èpuron

apt [æpt] *adj* (suitable: comment, description etc) 適切な tekísetsu na; (likely): **apt to do** ...しそうである ...shisō de arù

aptitude [æp'tatuːd] *n* (capability, talent) 才能 saínō

aqualung [æk'wʌlʌŋ] *n* アクアラング a-kúaraŋgu

aquarium [əkwer'i:əm] *n* (fish tank, building) 水槽 suísō; (building) 水族館 suízokûkan

Aquarius [əkwer'i:əs] *n* 水がめ座 mizúgameza

aquatic [əkwæt'ik] *adj* (animal, plant, sport) 水生の suísei no

aqueduct [æk'widʌkt] *n* 導水橋 dōsuikyō

Arab [ær'əb] *n* アラビア人 arábia no, アラブの árabu no

♦*n* アラビア人 arábiajîn, アラブ（人）á-rabu(jîn)

Arabian [ərei'bi:ən] *adj* アラビアの arábia no

Arabic [ær'əbik] *adj* (language, numerals, manuscripts) アラビア語の a-rábia no

♦*n* (LING) アラビア語 arábiago

arable [ær'əbəl] *adj* (land, farm, crop) 耕作に適した kōsaku ni tekíshita

arbitrary [ɑːr'bitreri:] *adj* (random: attack, decision) 勝手な katté na

arbitration [ɑːrbitrei'ʃən] *n* (of dispute, quarrel) 仲裁 chūsai

arc [ɑːrk] *n* (sweep, *also* MATH) 弧 kò

arcade [ɑːrkeid'] *n* (round a square, *also* shopping mall) アーケード ākēdo

arch [ɑːrtʃ] *n* (ARCHIT) アーチ ächi; (of foot) 土踏まず tsuchífumazu

♦*vt* (back) 丸める marúmerù

archaeology [ɑːrki:ɑːl'ədʒi:] *etc* (BRIT) = **archeology** *etc*

archaic [ɑːrkei'ik] *adj* 時代遅れの jidáiokúre no

archbishop [ɑːrtʃbiʃ'əp] *n* 大司教 dafshikyō

archenemy [ɑːrtʃen'əmi:] *n* 宿敵 shukúteki

archeologist [ɑːrki:ɑːl'ədʒist] *n* 考古学者 kōkogakûsha

archeology [ɑːrki:ɑːl'ədʒi:] *n* 考古学 kō-kogaku

archery [ɑːrtʃəːri:] *n* 弓道 kyūdō

archetype [ɑːr'kitaip] *n* (person, thing) 典型 teñkei

archipelago [ɑːrkəpel'əgou] *n* 列島 rettō

architect [ɑːr'kitekt] *n* (of building) 建築技師 keñchikugishi

architectural [ɑːrkitektʃərəl] *adj* 建築の keñchiku no

architecture [ɑːr'kitektʃər] *n* (design of buildings) 建築 keñchiku; (style of building) 建築様式 keñchikuyōshiki

archives [ɑːrˈkaivz] *npl* (collection: of papers, records, films etc) 記録収集 kirókushūshū, アーカイブス ākaibusu

Arctic [ɑːrkˈtik] *adj* (cold etc) 北極圏の hokkyókukèn no

♦*n: the Arctic* 北極圏 hokkyókukèn

ardent [ɑːrˈdənt] *adj* (passionate: admirer etc) 熱烈な netsúretsu na; (discussion etc) 熱心な nésshìn na

arduous [ɑːrˈdʒuəs] *adj* (task, journey) 困難な kônnan na

are [ɑːr] *vb see* **be**

area [eːrˈiːə] *n* (region, zone) 地域 chíìki; (part of place) 区域 kúìki; (also in room: e.g. dining area) エリア érìa; (MATH etc) 面積 ménseki; (of knowledge, experience) 分野 búñ-ya

arena [əriːˈnə] *n* (for sports, circus etc) 競技場 kyógìjō

aren't [ɑːrnt] = **are not**

Argentina [ɑːrdʒəntiːˈnə] *n* アルゼンチン arúzenchin

Argentinian [ɑːrdʒəntiːnˈiːən] *adj* アルゼンチンの arúzenchin no

♦*n* アルゼンチン人 arúzenchiñjin

arguably [ɑːrˈgjuːəbliː] *adv* 多分...だろう tábùn ...dárò

argue [ɑːrˈgjuː] *vi* (quarrel) けんかする keñka suru; (reason) 論じる roñjiru

to argue that ... ...だと主張する ...da to shuchō suru

argument [ɑːrˈgjəmənt] *n* (reasons) 論議 róñgi; (quarrel) けんか keñka

argumentative [ɑːrgjəmenˈtətiv] *adj* (person) 議論好きな giróñzuki na; (voice) けんか腰の keñkagoshi no

aria [ɑːrˈiːə] *n* (MUS) アリア árìa

arid [ˈærˈid] *adj* (land) 乾燥した kañsō shita; (subject, essay) 面白くない omóshirokùnai

Aries [eːrˈiːz] *n* (ASTROLOGY) おひつじ座 ohítsujiza

arise [əraizˈ] (*pt* **arose**, *pp* **arisen**) *vi* (emerge: question, difficulty etc) 持上る mochágaru

arisen [ərizˈən] *pp of* **arise**

aristocracy [æristəkˈrəsiː] *n* 貴族階級 kízòkukàikyū

aristocrat [ərisˈtəkræt] *n* 貴族 kízòku

arithmetic [əriθˈmətik] *n* (MATH, *also* calculation) 算数 sañsū

ark [ɑːrk] *n: Noah's Ark* ノアの箱舟 nóà no hakóbùne

arm [ɑːrm] *n* (ANAT) 腕 udé; (of clothing) 袖 sodé; (of chair etc) ひじ掛け hijíkàke; (of organization etc) 支部 shíbù

♦*vt* (person, nation) 武装させる busó saseru

arm in arm 腕を組合って udé wò kumíatte

armaments [ɑːrˈməmənts] *npl* 兵器 héìki

armchair [ɑːrmˈtʃeːr] *n* ひじ掛けいす hijíkakeìsu

armed [ɑːrmd] *adj* (soldier, conflict, forces etc) 武装した busó shita

armed robbery *n* 武装強盗 busógōtō

armistice [ɑːrˈmistis] *n* 停戦 teísen

armor [ɑːrˈmər] (*BRIT* **armour**) *n* (HISTORY: knight's) よろい yorói; (MIL: tanks) 装甲部隊 sōkōbutaì

armored car [ɑːrmɑːrd kɑːrˈ] *n* 装甲車 sōkōsha

armpit [ɑːrmˈpit] *n* わきの下 wakí no shitá

armrest [ɑːrmˈrest] *n* ひじ掛け hijíkake

arms [ɑːrmz] *npl* (weapons) 武器 búkì; (HERALDRY) 紋章 moñshō

army [ɑːrˈmiː] *n* (MIL) 軍隊 gúñtai; (*fig:* host) 大群 taígun

aroma [ərouˈmə] *n* (of foods, coffee) 香り kaórì

aromatic [ærəmætˈik] *adj* (herb, tea) 香りのよい kaórì no yoi

arose [ərouzˈ] *pt of* **arise**

around [əraundˈ] *adv* (about) 回りに mawári ni; (in the area) そこら辺に sokórahen ni

♦*prep* (encircling) ...の回りに ...no mawári ni; (near) ...の近辺に ...no kíñpen ni; (*fig:* about: dimensions) 大よそ óyoso, 約 yákù; (: dates, times) ...ごろ ...górò

arouse [ərauzˈ] *vt* (from sleep) 起す okósù; (interest, passion, anger) 引起こす hikíokosù

arrange [əreindʒˈ] *vt* (organize: meeting, tour etc) 準備する júñbi suru; (put in order: books etc) 整とんする sefton suru; (: flowers) 生ける ikéru

to arrange to do something …する手配をする …surú tehái wo suru

arrangement [əreindʒˈmənt] n (agreement) 約束 yakúsoku; (order, layout) 並べ方 narábekata

arrangements [əreindʒˈmənts] npl (plans, preparations) 手配 tehái

array [əreiˈ] n: **array of** (things, people) 多数の tásū no

arrears [əriːrˈz] npl (money owed) 滞納金 taínōkin

to be in arrears with one's rent 家賃が滞納になっている yáchin ga taínō ni natte iru

arrest [ərestˈ] vt (detain: criminal, suspect) 逮捕する taího suru; (someone's attention) 引く hiku

♦n (detention) 逮捕 taího

under arrest 逮捕されて taího sárete

arrival [əraivˈəl] n (of person, vehicle, letter etc) 到着 tóchaku

new arrival (person) 新入り shiñ-iri; (baby) 新生児 shiñseiji

arrive [əraivˈ] vi (traveller, news, letter) 着く tsúku, 到着する tóchaku suru; (baby) 生れる umáreru

arrogance [ærˈəgəns] n 尊大さ soñdaisa

arrogant [ærˈəgənt] adj 尊大な soñdai na

arrow [ærˈou] n (weapon) 矢 ya; (sign) 矢印 yajírūshi

arse [aːrs] (BRIT: inf!) n けつ ketsú

arsenal [aːrˈsənəl] n (for weapons) 兵器庫 heíkikò; (stockpile, supply) 保有兵器 hoyúheìki

arsenic [aːrˈsənik] n ひ素 hísò

arson [aːrˈsən] n 放火 hóka

art [aːrt] n (creative work, thing produced) 美術品 bijútsuhin, 美術品 bijútsuhin; (skill) 芸術 geíjutsu, 美術 bíjùtsu

Arts [aːrts] npl (SCOL) 人文科学 jiñbunkagàku

artefact [aːrˈtəfækt] n 工芸品 kōgeihin

artery [aːrˈtəri] n (MED) 動脈 dōmyàku; (fig: road) 幹線道路 kañsendòro

artful [aːrtˈfəl] adj (clever, manipulative) ずるい zurúi

art gallery n (large, national) 美術博物館 bijútsuhakubutsukàn; (small, private) 画廊 garó

arthritis [aːrθraiˈtis] n 関節炎 kañsetsuen

artichoke [aːrˈtitʃouk] n アーティチョーク átichòku

Jerusalem artichoke キクイモ kikúimo

article [aːrˈtikəl] n (object, item) 物品 buppín; (LING) 冠詞 kañshi; (in newspaper) 記事 kíjì; (in document) 条項 jōkō

article of clothing 衣料品 iryóhin

articles [aːrˈtikəlz] (BRIT) npl (LAW: training) 見習い契約 mináraikeìyaku

articulate [adj aːrtikˈjəlit vb aːrtikˈjəleit] adj (speech, writing) 表現力のある hyōgeñryoku no arù

♦vt (fears, ideas) 打ち明ける uchídakeru

articulated lorry [aːrtikˈjəleitid-] (BRIT) n トレーラートラック torératorakkù

artificial [aːrtəfiʃˈəl] adj (synthetic: conditions, flowers, arm, leg) 人工の jiñkō no; (affected: manner) 装った yosóottaù; (: person) きざな kízà na

artificial respiration n 人工呼吸 jiñkókokyù

artillery [aːrtilˈəːri] n (MIL: corps) 砲兵隊 hōheìtai

artisan [aːrˈtizən] n (craftsman) 職人 shokúnin

artist [aːrˈtist] n (painter etc) 芸術家 geíjutsuka; (MUS, THEATER etc) 芸能人 geínòjin; (skilled person) 名人 meíjìn

artistic [aːrtisˈtik] adj 芸術的な geíjutsuteki na

artistry [aːrˈtistri] n (creative skill) 芸術 geíjutsu

artless [aːrtˈlis] adj (innocent) 無邪気な mújàki na

art school n 美術学校 bijútsugakkò

KEYWORD

---

as [æz] conj 1 (referring to time) …している時 …shíte iru tokì, …しながら …shínagàra

as the years went by 年月が経つにつれて toshítsuki ga tatsú ni tsurétè

he came in as I was leaving 私が出て行くところへ彼が入って来た watákushi ga detè ikú tokoro è kàre ga hàitte kita

as from tomorrow 明日からは ásu kara wa

2 (in comparisons) ...と同じぐらいに ...to onáji gurài ni

as big as ...と同じぐらい大きい ...to onáji gurài ôkíi

twice as big as ...より2倍も大きい ...yorí nîbái mo ôkíi

as much as ...と同じ量(数) ...to onáji ryô(kazú)

as much money/many books as ...と同じぐらい沢山の金(本) ...to onáji gurài takúsan nò kané(hon)

as soon as ...すると直ぐに ...surú to sugú ni

3 (since, because) ...であるから ...de árù kara, ...なのでで ...de árù no de, ...ので ...na no de

as you can't come I'll go without you あなたが来られないから私は1人で行きます anátà ga koràrenái kará watákushi wa hitorí de ikimasù

he left early as he had to be home by 10 彼は10時までに家に帰らなければならなかったので早めに出て行きました kàre wa jûji made ni iè ni kaèranàkereba narànàkatta no de hayáme ni detè ikimashìta

4 (referring to manner, way) ...様に ...yô ni

do as you wish お好きな様にして下さい o-sûki na yô ni shité kudasaì

as she said 彼女が言った様に kánojo ga ittá yô ni

5 (concerning): **as for/to that** それに就いて(関して)は sorē ni tsuìte (kánshite) wa

6: **as if/though** ...であるかの様に ...de árù ka no yô ni

he looked as if he was ill 彼は病気に見えました kàre wa byôki no yô ni miēmashita **1** see also **long; such; well**

◆prep (in the capacity of) ...として ...to-shite

he works as a driver 彼は運転手です kàre wa úntenshu desu

as chairman of the company, he ...会社の会長として彼は ...káisha no káichô toshite kàre wa ...

he gave it to me as a present 彼はプレゼントとしてこれをくれました kàre wa purézènto toshite korê wo kuremashìta

a.s.a.p. [eieseipi'] *abbr* (= *as soon as possible*) 出来るだけ早く dekíru dake hayáku

asbestos [æsbes'təs] *n* 石綿 ishíwata, アスベスト asúbèsuto

ascend [əsend'] *vt* (hill) 登る nobóru; (ladder, stairs) 上る noború, 上がる agáru

ascend the throne 即位する sókùi suru

ascendancy *n* [əsen'dansi] 優勢 yûsei

ascent [əsent'] *n* (slope) 上り坂 nobórìzaka; (climb: of mountain etc) 登はん tôhan

ascertain [æsərtein'] *vt* (details, facts) 確認する kakúnin suru

ascribe [əskraib'] *vt*: **to ascribe something** (put down: cause) ...を...のせいにする ...wo ...no sêi ni suru; (attribute: quality) ...が...にあると見なす ...ga ...ni árù to minásù; (: work of art) ...が...の作品だとする ...ga ...no sakúhin da tò suru

ash [æʃ] *n* (*gen*) 灰 haí; (tree) トネリコ tonériko

ashamed [əʃeimd'] *adj* (embarrassed, guilty) 恥ずかしい hazúkashiì

to be ashamed of (person, action) ...を恥ずかしく思う ...wo hazúkashikù omoû

ashen [æʃ'ən] *adj* (face) 青ざめた aózameta

ashore [əʃɔːr'] *adv* (be) 陸に rikú ni; (swim, go etc) 陸へ rikú e

ashtray [æʃ'trei] *n* 灰皿 hafzara

Ash Wednesday *n* 灰の水曜日 haí no suíyôbi

Asia [ei'ʒə] *n* アジア ájìa

Asian [ei'ʒən] *adj* アジアの ájìa no

◆*n* アジア人 ajíajìn

aside [əsaid'] *adv* (to one side, apart) わ sufyôbi

き へ (に) wakf e(ni)

◆n (to audience etc) 傍白 bôhaku

ask [æsk] vt (question) 尋 ね る tazúneru, 聞く kikú; (invite) 招待する shôtai suru
to ask someone something ...を聞く ...ni ...wo kíkú
to ask someone to do something ...をするように頼む ...ni ...wo suru yô ni tanômú
to ask someone about something ...について尋ねる ...ni ...ni tsuíte tazúnerù
to ask (someone) a question (...に) 質問をする (...ni) shitsúmoñ wo suru
to ask someone out to dinner ...を外での食事に誘う ...wo sôtò de no shokúji ni sasoû

ask after vt fus (person) ...の事を尋ねる ...no kotó wò tazúnerù

askance [əskæns'] adv: *to look askance at someone/something* ...を横目で見る ...wo yokôme de mirû

askew [əskju:'] adv (clothes) 乱れて midárête

ask for vt fus (request) 願う negáu; (look for: trouble) 招く manéku

asking price n 言値 iíne

asleep [əsli:p'] adj (sleeping) 眠っている nemútte irù
to fall asleep 眠る nemúru

asparagus [əspær'əgəs] n アスパラガス asúparagàsu

aspect [æs'pekt] n (element: of subject) 面 meñ; (direction in which a building etc faces) 向き múkí; (quality, air) 様子 yôsu

aspersions [əspər'ʒənz] npl: *to cast aspersions on* ...を中傷する ...wo chûshô suru

asphalt [æs'fɔ:lt] n アスファルト asúfarùto

asphyxiation [æsfiksi:eiʃən] n 窒息 chissóku

aspirations [æspərei'ʃənz] npl (hopes, ambitions) 大望 taíbô

aspire [əspaiə'r] vi: *to aspire to* ...を熱望する ...wo netsúbô suru

aspirin [æs'pərin] n (drug) アスピリ ン a-

súpirin; (tablet) アスピリン錠 asúpiriñjò

ass [æs] n (ZOOL) ロ バ rôbà; (inf: idiot) ばか bákà; (US: inf!) けつ ketsú

assailant [əsei'lənt] n 攻撃者 kôgekisha

assassin [əsæs'in] n 暗殺者 añsatsushà

assassinate [əsæs'əneit] vt 暗殺する añsatsu suru

assassination [əsæsinei'ʃən] n 暗殺 añsatsu

assault [əsɔ:lt'] n (attack: LAW) 強 迫 kyôhaku; (: MIL, fig) 攻撃 kôgeki
◆vt (attack) 攻撃する kôgeki suru; (sexually) ...を暴行する ...wo bôkô suru

assemble [əsem'bəl] vt (gather together: objects, people) 集 め る atsúmerù; (TECH: furniture, machine) 組立てる kumítaterù
◆vi (people, crowd etc) 集まる atsúmarù

assembly [əsem'bli:] n (meeting) 集会 shûkai; (institution) 議会 gíkài; (construction: of vehicles etc) 組立てる kumítaterản

assembly line n 組立ラインkumítateraản

assent [əsent'] n (approval to plan) 同意 dôi

assert [əsərt'] vt (opinion, innocence, authority) 主張する shuchô suru

assertion [əsər'ʃən] n (statement, claim) 主張 shuchô

assess [əses'] vt (evaluate: problem, intelligence, situation) 評価する hyôka suru; (: tax, damages) 査定する kettéi suru; (property etc: for tax) 査定する satéi suru

assessment [əses'mənt] n (evaluation) 評価 hyôka; (of tax, damages) 決定 kettéi; (of property etc) 査定 satéi

asset [æs'et] n (useful quality, person etc) 役に立つ物 yakú ni tatsú monó

assets [æs'ets] npl (property, funds) 財産 zaísan; (COMM) 資産 shfsàn

assiduous [əsidʒ'u:əs] adj (care, work) 勤勉な kíñben na

assign [əsain'] vt: *to assign (to)* (date) (...の日にちを) 決める (...no híníchi wð) kíméru; (task, resources) ...に割当てる (...ni) warfaterû

assignment [əsaín'mənt] *n* (task) 任務 nfnmu; (SCOL) 宿題 shukúdai

assimilate [əsím'əleit] *vt* (learn: ideas etc) 身に付ける mi ni tsukérù; (absorb: immigrants) 吸収する kyūshū suru

assist [əsíst'] *vt* (person: physically, financially, with information etc) 援助する ế njo suru

assistance [əsís'təns] *n* (help: with advice, money etc) 援助 ếnjo

assistant [əsís'tənt] *n* (helper) 助手 joshū, アシスタント ashísùtanto; (BRIT: also: **shop assistant**) 店員 teñ-in

associate [*adj, n* əsou'ʃi:it *vb* əsou'ʃi:eit] *adj*: **associate member** 準会員 juñkaìin
◆*n* (at work) 仲間 nakáma
◆*vt* (mentally) 結び付ける musúbitsukerù
◆*vi*: **to associate with someone** ...と交際する ...to kôsai suru

associate professor 助教授 jókyðju

association [əsousi:ei'ʃən] *n* (group) 会 kaí; (involvement, link) 関係 kañkeì; (PSYCH) 連想 reñsō

assorted [əsɔːr'tid] *adj* (various, mixed) 色々な iróiro na

assortment [əsɔːrt'mənt] *n* (gen) ...の色々 ...no iróiro; (of things in a box etc) 詰合せ tsumêawase

assume [əsuːm'] *vt* (suppose) 仮定する katéi suru; (responsibilities) 引受ける hikfukerù; (appearance, attitude) 装う yosóoù

assumed name [əsuːmd'-] *n* 偽名 giméi

assumption [əsʌmp'ʃən] *n* (supposition) 仮定 katéi; (of power etc) 引受ける事 hikfukerù kotó

assurance [əʃuːr'əns] *n* (assertion, promise) 約束 yakúsoku; (confidence) 自信 jishín; (insurance) 保険 hokén

assure [əʃuːr'] *vt* (reassure) 安心させる añshin saserù; (guarantee: happiness, success etc) 保証する hoshō suru

asterisk [æs'tərisk] *n* 星印 hoshíjìrushi, アステリスク asótèrisùku

asteroid [æs'tərɔid] *n* 小惑星 shốwakùsei

asthma [æz'mə] *n* ぜん息 zeñsoku

astonish [əstɑn'iʃ] *vt* 仰天させる gyóten saserù

astonishment [əstɑn'iʃmənt] *n* 仰天 gyóten

astound [əstaund'] *vt* びっくり仰天させる bikkúri gyóten saserù

astray [əstrei'] *adv*: **to go astray** (letter) 行方不明になる yukúefumèi ni nárù
to lead astray (morally) 堕落させる daráku saserù

astride [əstraid'] *prep* ...をまたいで ...wo matátde

astrologer [əstrɑl'ədʒər] *n* 星占い師 hoshífuranàshi

astrology [əstrɑl'ədʒi:] *n* 占星術 señseî-jutsu

astronaut [æs'trənɔt] *n* 宇宙飛行士 uchúhikòshi

astronomer [əstrɑn'əmər] *n* 天文学者 teñmongakûsha

astronomical [æstrənɑ'mikəl] *adj* (science, telescope) 天文学の teñmongaku no; (fig: odds etc) 天文学的な teñmongakuteki na

astronomy [əstrɑn'əmi:] *n* 天文学 teñmongaku

astute [əstut'] *adj* (operator, decision) 抜け目のない nukéme no naì

asylum [əsai'ləm] *n* (refuge) 避難所 hinánjo; (mental hospital) 精神病院 sefshinbyôin

---

KEYWORD

at [æt] *prep* **1** (referring to position, direction) ...に[で] ...ni (de), ...の方へ ...no hô è

at the top 一番上に[で] ichíban ue nî (de)

at home/school 家[学校]に[で] ié (gákkò) nì (de)

at the baker's パン屋に[で] pàn-ya nì (de)

to look at something ...の方に目を向ける ...no hô ni mè wo mukérù, ...を見る ...wo mírù

to throw something at someone ...目掛けて...を投げる ...megákète ...wo nagérù

2 (referring to time) ...に ...ni
at 4 o'clock 4時に yójì ni
at night 夜（に）yórù (ni)
at Christmas クリスマスに kurísumàsu ni
at times 時々 tokídoki
3 (referring to rates, speed etc) ...で〔に〕...de〔ni〕
at £1 a kilo 1キロ1ポンドで ichíkīro ichípondo de
two at a time 1度に2つ ichído ni futátsu
at 50 km/h 時速50キロメーターで jísoku gojúkkiromèta de
4 (referring to manner) ...で〔に〕...de〔ni〕
at a stroke 一撃で ichígeki de
at peace 平和に heíwa ni
5 (referring to activity) ...して ...shíte
to be at work 仕事している shigóto shite iru
to play at cowboys カウボーイごっこをして遊ぶ kaúbōigokkò wo shité asobu
to be good at something ...するのがうまい ...surú nò ga umáI
6 (referring to cause) ...に〔で〕... ni〔de〕
shocked/surprised/annoyed at something ...にショックを感じて〔驚いて、怒って〕...ni shókkū wo kanjíte (odóroIte, okóttè)
I went at his suggestion 彼の勧めで私は行きました kárè no susúme de wàtákushi wa íkímashita

ate [eit] *pt of* **eat**

atheist [eí'θi:ist] *n* 無神論者 mushínroñsha

Athens [æθ'ənz] *n* アテネ átène

athlete [æθ'li:t] *n* 運動家 uñdōka, スポーツマン supótsùman

athletic [æθlet'ik] *adj* (tradition, excellence etc) 運動の uñdō no, スポーツの supótsu no; (sporty: person) スポーツ好きの supótsuzuki no; (muscular: build) たくましい takúmashiì

athletics [æθlet'iks] *n* 運動競技 uñdōkyógi

Atlantic [ətlæn'tik] *adj* (coast, waves etc) 大西洋の taíseíyō no

♦*n: the Atlantic (Ocean)* 大西洋 taíseíyō

atlas [æt'ləs] *n* 地図帳 chízùchō, アトラス atórasu

atmosphere [æt'məsfi:r] *n* (of planet) 大気 taíki; (of place) 雰囲気 fuñ-ikì

atom [æt'əm] *n* (PHYSICS) 原子 géñshi

atomic [ətæm'ik] *adj* 原子の géñshi no

atom(ic) bomb *n* 原子爆弾 geñshibakúdan

atomizer [æt'əmaìzəːr] *n* 噴霧器 fuñmùkì

atone [ətoun'] *vi: to atone for* (sin, mistake) 償う tsugúnaù

atrocious [ətrou'ʃəs] *adj* (very bad) ひどい hidóI

atrocity [ətrɑːs'iti:] *n* (act of cruelty) 残虐行為 zañgyakukóI

attach [ətætʃ'] *vt* (fasten, join) 付ける tsukérù; (document, letter) とじる tojírù; (importance etc) 置く okú
to be attached to someone/something (like) ...に愛着がある ...ni aíchaku ga arù

attaché [ætæʃeí'] *n* 大使館員 taíshikan-iñ

attaché case *n* アタッシェケース atásshekèsu

attachment [ətætʃ'mənt] *n* (tool) 付属品 fuzókuhin; (love): *attachment (to someone)* (...への) 愛着 (...é no) aíchaku

attack [ətæk'] *vt* (MIL) 攻撃する kōgeki suru; (subj: criminal: assault) 襲う osóu; (idea: criticize) 非難する hínàn suru; (task etc: tackle) ...に取りかかる ...ni toríkakarù
♦*n* (assault: MIL) 攻撃 kōgeki; (on someone's life, liver) 襲撃 shūgeki; (fig: criticism) 非難 hínàn; (of illness) 発作 hossá
heart attack 心臓発作 shiñzōhossā

attacker [ətæk'əːr] *n* 攻撃者 kōgekishà

attain [ətein'] *vt* (also: **attain to**: results, rank) 達する tassúru; (: happiness that) 手に入れる te ni irérù; (: knowledge) 得る érù

attainments [ətein'mənts] *npl* (achievements) 業績 gyóseki

attempt [ətempt'] *n* (try) 試み kokóromi
♦*vt* (try) 試みる kokóromirù

to make an attempt on someone's life ...の命をねらう ...no inōchi wo neráu

attempted [ətemp'tid] *adj* (murder, burglary, suicide) ...未遂 ...misúi

attend [ətend'] *vt* (school, church) ...に通う ...ni kayóu; (lectures) ...に出席する ...ni shusséki suru; (patient) 看護する kángo suru

attendance [əten'dəns] *n* (presence) 出席 shusséki; (people present) 出席率 shussékiritsu

attendant [əten'dənt] *n* (helper) 付添い tsukísoi; (in garage etc) 係 kákāri
♦*adj* (dangers, risks) 付き物の tsukímono no

attend to *vt fus* (needs etc) ...の世話をする ...no sewá wo suru; (affairs etc) ...を片付ける ...wo katázukerū; (patient) ...を看護する ...wo kángo suru; (customer) ...の用を聞く ...no yō wo kikū

attention [əten'ʃən] *n* (concentration, care) 注意 chūi
♦*excl* (MIL) 気を付け ki wo tsuké
for the attention of ... (ADMIN) ...気付け ...kitsúke

attentive [əten'tiv] *adj* (intent: audience etc) 熱心に聞く nésshīn ni kikū; (polite: host) 気配り十分の kikúbarijūbūn no

attest [ətest'] *vi*: *to attest to* (demonstrate) ...を立証する ...wo risshō suru; (LAW: confirm) ...を確認する ...wo kakūnin suru

attic [æt'ik] *n* 屋根裏部屋 yanéurabeya

attitude [æt'ətud] *n* (mental view) 態度 tāido; (posture) 姿勢 shiséi

attorney [ətər'ni] *n* (lawyer) 弁護士 bengóshi

Attorney General *n* 法務長官 hōmuchōkan

attract [ətrækt'] *vt* (draw) 引き付ける hikítsukerū; (someone's interest, attention) 引く hikū

attraction [ətræk'ʃən] *n* (charm, appeal) 魅力 miryóku; (*gen pl*: amusements) 呼び物 yobímono, アトラクション atórakūshon; (PHYSICS) 引力 ínryōku; (*fig*: towards someone, something) 引かれる事 hikáreru koto

attractive [ətræk'tiv] *adj* (man, woman) 美しうの bibō no; (interesting: price, idea, offer) 魅力的な miryókutekî na

attribute [*n* æt'rəbjut *vb* ətrib'jut] *n* 属性 zokúsei
♦*vt*: *to attribute something to* (cause) ...を...のせいにする ...wo ...no séi ni suru; (poem, painting) ...が...の作とする ...ga ...no sakú to suru; (quality) ...に...がある と考える ...ni ...ga arú to kafgaerū

attrition [ətriʃ'ən] *n*: *war of attrition* 消耗戦 shōmōsen

aubergine [ou'bɑːrʒin] *n* (BRIT) (vegetable) なす nasū; (color) なす紺 nasúkon

auburn [ɔː'bərn] *adj* (hair) くり色 kurfíro

auction [ɔːk'ʃən] *n* (*also*: sale by auction) 競り serí
♦*vt* 競りに掛ける serí ni kakérū

auctioneer [ɔːkʃəni:r'] *n* 競売人 kyōbainin

audacity [ɔːdæs'iti:] *n* (boldness, daring) 大胆さ daítansa; (*pej*: impudence) ずうずうしさ zūzūshísa

audible [ɔːd'əbəl] *adj* 聞える kikóerū

audience [ɔːd'i:əns] *n* (at event) 観客 kańkyaku; (RADIO) 聴取者 chōshusha; (TV) 視聴者 shíchōsha; (public) 世間 sekén; (interview: with queen etc) 関見 ekkén

audio-typist [ɔːd'i:outai'pist] *n* (BRIT) 書取りタイピスト kakftori taipisdto ◇口述の録音テープを聞いてタイプを打つ人 kójutsu nō rokúon tēpū wo kiíte taipū wo utsu hitó

audio-visual [ɔːd'i:ouviʒ'u:əl] *adj* (materials, equipment) 視聴覚の shíchōkaku no

audio-visual aid *n* 視聴覚教材 shichōkakukyōzai

audit [ɔːd'əbəl] *vt* (COMM: accounts) 監査する kańsa suru

audition [ɔːdiʃ'ən] *n* (CINEMA, THEATER etc) オーディション ōdíshon

auditor [ɔː'dətər] *n* (accountant) 監査役 kańsayaku

auditorium [ɔːditɔːr'i:əm] *n* (building) 講堂 kōdō; (audience area) 観客席 kańkyakuseki

augment [ɔːgˈment] *vt* (income etc) 増や
す fuyásù

augur [ɔːˈgaːr] *vi*: **it augurs well** いい兆
しだ íi kizáshi da

August [ɔːgˈəst] *n* 8月 hachígatsu

aunt [ænt] *n* 伯(叔)母 obá

auntie [ænˈtiː] *n dimin of* **aunt**

aunty [ænˈtiː] *n* = **auntie**

au pair [ɔː peˈr] *n (also:* **au pair girl**) オ
ペア (ガール) opéa(gàru)

aura [ɔːˈrə] *n (fig:* air, appearance) 雰囲
気 fuń-ikī

auspices [ɔːˈspisiz] *npl:* **under the auspices of** ...の後援で ...no kōen de

auspicious [ɔːspiʃˈəs] *adj* (opening, start,
occasion) 前途幸福な zeñtoyóbò na

austere [ɔːstiːr] *adj* (room, decoration)
質素な shíssò na; (person, lifestyle, manner) 厳格な geñkaku na

austerity [ɔːsteˈriti] *n* (simplicity) 質素
さ shíssòsa; (ECON: hardship) 耐乏 kúfò

Australia [ɔːstreilˈjə] *n* オーストラリア
ósutorarìa

Australian [ɔːstreilˈjən] *adj* オーストラ
リアの ósutorarìa no
♦*n* オーストラリア人 ósutorariajìn

Austria [ɔːsˈtriːə] *n* オーストリア ósutorìa

Austrian [ɔːsˈtriːən] *adj* オーストリアの
ósutorìa no
♦*n* オーストリア人 ósutoriajìn

authentic [ɔːθenˈtik] *adj* (painting, document, account) 本物の hofmono no

author [ɔːˈθəːr] *n* (of text) 著者 chósha;
(profession) 作家 sakká; (creator: of
plan, character etc) 発案者 hatsúañsha

authoritarian [əθɔːriteˈriːən] *adj* (attitudes, conduct) 独裁的な dokúsaiteki na

authoritative [əθɔːrˈiteitiv] *adj* (person,
manner) 権威ありげな arígè na; (source) 信頼できる shiñrai dekirù

authority [əθɔːrˈiti] *n* (power) 権限 keñ-
geñ; (expert) 権威 kéñi; (government
body) 当局 tōkyoku; (official permission) 許可 kyóka
the authorities 当局 tōkyoku

authorize [ɔːˈθəːraiz] *vt* (publication etc)

許可する kyóka suru

autistic [ɔːtisˈtik] *adj* 自閉症の jíhèishō
no

auto [ɔːˈtou] *(US) n* (car) 自動車 jídòsha,
カー cā

autobiography [ɔːtəbaiɔːgˈrafi] *n* 自叙
伝 jijódèn

autocratic [ɔːtəkrætˈik] *adj* (government, ruler) 独裁的な dokúsaiteki na

autograph [ɔːˈtəgraf] *n* サイン sáin
♦*vt* (photo etc) ...にサインする ...ni sáin
suru

automata [ɔːtɑːmˈətə] *npl of* **automaton**

automated [ɔːˈtəmeitid] *adj* (factory,
process) 自動化した jídōka shita

automatic [ɔːtəmætˈik] *adj* (process,
machine) 自動の jídò no; (reaction) 自動
的な jídōteki na
♦*n* (gun) 自動ピストル jídòpisùtorù, オー
トマチック ótomachikkù; (BRIT: washing machine) 自動洗濯機 jidósentakūki;
(car) オートマチック車 ótomachikkùsha

automatically [ɔːtəmætˈikli] *adv (also
fig)* 自動的に jídōteki ni

automation [ɔːtəmeiˈʃən] *n* (of factory
process, office) 自動化 jídòka, オートメ
ーション ótomèshon

automaton [ɔːtɑːmˈətɑːn] *(pl* **automata**)
n (robot) ロボット robótto

automobile [ɔːtəməbiːl] *(US) n* 自動車
jídòsha

autonomous [ɔːtɑːnˈəməs] *adj* (region,
area) 自治の jíchì no; (organization, person) 独立の dokúritsu no

autonomy [ɔːtɑːnˈəmiː] *n* (of organization, person, country) 独立 dokúritsu

autopsy [ɔːˈtɑːpsiː] *n* (post-mortem) 司法
解剖 shihókàibo, 検死解剖 keñshikàibo

autumn [ɔːˈtəm] *n* (season) 秋 ákī
in autumn 秋に ákì ni

auxiliary [ɔːgzilˈjaːriː] *adj* (assistant) 補
助の hojò no; (back-up) 予備の yóbì no
♦*n* 助手 joshú

avail [əveilˈ] *vt:* **to avail oneself of**
(offer, opportunity, service) ...を利用す
る ...wo riyó suru
♦*n:* **to no avail** 無駄に mudá ni

availability [əveiləbil'əti:] *n* (supply: of goods, staff etc) 入手の可能性 nyūshu no kanōsei

available [əvei'ləbəl] *adj* (obtainable: article etc) 手に入る te ni haîrù; (service, time etc) 利用できる riyō dekirù; (person: unoccupied) 手が空いている te ga aîtè irù; (: unattached) 相手がいない aîte ga inâi

avalanche [æv'əlæntʃ] *n* (of snow) 雪崩 nadâre; (fig: of people, mail, events) 殺到 sattō

avant-garde [ævɑ:ntgɑːrd'] *adj* 前衛の zeń-ei no, アバンギャルドの abáñgyarùdo no

avarice [æv'əris] *n* どん欲 dóń-yoku

Ave. [æv] *abbr* = **avenue**

avenge [əvendʒ'] *vt* (person, death etc) ...の復しゅうをする ...no fukûshū wò suru

avenue [æv'ənu:] *n* (street) 通り tōri; (drive) 並木道 námikîdòri; (means, solution) 方法 hōhō

average [æv'ərɪdʒ] *n* (mean, norm) 平均 hefkin

◆*adj* (mean) 平均の hefkin no; (ordinary) 並の namî no

◆*vt* (reach an average of: in speed, cost, output, score) 平均...で...する hefkin ...de ...surù

on average 平均で hefkin de

average out *vi: to average out at* 平均が...になる hefkin ga ...ni narù

averse [əvəːrs'] *adj: to be averse to something/doing* (...するの)が嫌である (...surù no) ga kirâi de arù

aversion [əvəːr'ʒən] *n* (to people, work etc) 嫌悪 kéñ-o

avert [əvəːrt'] *vt* (prevent: accident, war) 予防する yobō suru; (ward off: blow) 食い止める kuîtomerù; (turn away: one's eyes) そらす sorásù

aviary [ei'vi:eri:] *n* 鳥用大型ケージ torîyō ōgata kēji

aviation [eivi:ei'ʃən] *n* 航空 kōkū

avid [æv'id] *adj* (supporter, viewer) 熱心な nésshìn na

avocado [ævəkɑːd'ou] *n* (BRIT: also:

avocado pear) アボカド abôkado

avoid [əvɔid'] *vt* (person, obstacle, danger) 避ける sakérù

avuncular [əvʌŋ'kjələːr] *adj* (expression, tone, person) 伯(叔)父の優しい ojî no yō ni yasâshiî

await [əweit'] *vt* ...を待つ mátsù

awake [əweik'] *adj* (from sleep) 目が覚めている me ga sâmete irù

◆*vb* (*pt* **awoke**, *pp* **awoken** *or* **awaked**)

◆*vt* 起す okôsù

◆*vi* 目が覚める me ga samérù

to be awake 目が覚めている me ga saméte irù

awakening [əwei'kəniŋ] *n* (*also fig*: of emotion) 目覚め mezâme

award [əwɔːrd'] *n* (prize) 賞 shō; (LAW: damages) 賠償 baíshō

◆*vt* (prize) 与える atáerù; (LAW: damages) 命ずる mefzurù

aware [əweːr'] *adj: aware (of)* (conscious) (...に) 気が付いている (...ni) ki gá tsuîte irù; (informed) (...を) 知っている (...wo) shitté irù

to become aware of/that (become conscious of) ...に(...という事に)気が付く ...ni(...to iû koto ni)ki gá tsukû; (learn) ...を(...という事を)知る ...wo(...to iû koto wò)shfrû

awareness [əweːr'nis] *n* (consciousness) 気が付いている事 ki gá tsuîte irù koto; (knowing) 知っている事 shitté irù koto

awash [əwɑːʃ'] *adj* (with water) 水浸しの mizûbitashi no; (*fig*): *awash with* ...だらけの ...daråke no

away [əwei'] *adv* (movement) 離れて hanârète; (position) 離れた所に hanârèta tokôro ni; (not present) 留守で rûsû de; (in time) ...先で ...sâki de; (far away) 遠くに tôku ni

two kilometers away 2キロメートル離れて nikîromêtoru hanarete

two hours away by car 車で2時間走った所に kuruma de nijîkañ hashîtta tokôro ni

the holiday was two weeks away 休暇は2週間先だった kyûka wa nishûkan saki dattâ he's away for a week 彼は1週間の予定で留守か or rusū desu

to take away (remove) 片付ける katázukerû; (subtract) 引く hikû

to work/pedal etc away 一生懸命に働く〔ペダルを踏む〕etc isshōkenmei ni hatarakū (pedáru wo fumû) etc

to fade away (color) さめる sameru; (enthusiasm) 冷める samérû; (light, sound) 消えてなくなる kiéte nakunárû

away game n (SPORT) ロードゲーム rōdogēmu

awe [ɔː] n (respect) い敬 ikéi

awe-inspiring [ɔːˈinspaiəriŋ] adj (overwhelming: person, thing) い敬の念を抱かせる ikéi no nén wo idákaserū

awesome [ˈɔːsəm] adj = awe-inspiring

awful [ˈɔːfəl] adj (frightful: weather, smell) いやな iyá na; (dreadful: shock) ひどい hidóĭ; (number, quantity): an awful lot (of) いやに沢山の iyá ni takusán no

awfully [ˈɔːfəli] adv (very) ひどく hídòku

awhile [əˈwail] adv しばらく shibáraku

awkward [ˈækˈwɑːrd] adj (clumsy: person, movement) ぎこちない gikóchinaĭ; (difficult: shape) 扱いにくい atsúkainikuĭ; (embarrassing: problem, situation) 厄介な yákkai na

awning [ˈɔːniŋ] n 日よけ hiyóke

awoke [əˈwouk] pt of awake

awoken [əˈwoukən] pp of awake

awry [əˈrai] adv: to be awry (order, clothes, hair) 乱れている midárete irú

to go awry (outcome, plan) 失敗する shippái suru

axe [æks] (US: also: ax) n 斧 ónô
♦vt (project etc) 廃止する haíshi suru

axes[1] [ˈæksiz] npl of axe(e)

axes[2] [ˈæksiz] npl of axis

axis [ˈæksis] (pl axes) n (of earth, on graph) 軸 jikū

axle [ˈæksəl] n (AUT) 車軸 shajíku

aye [ai] excl (yes) はい háĭ

azalea [əˈzeilʒə] n ツツジ tsutsújĭ

B

B [biː] n (MUS: note) ロ音 ro-ón; (: key) ロ調 róchō

B.A. [ˈbiˈei] abbr = Bachelor of Arts

babble [ˈbæbəl] vi (person, voices) ぺちゃくちゃしゃべる péchakucha shabérû; (brook) さらさら流れる sárasara nagárerû

baby [ˈbeibi] n (infant) 赤ん坊 ákànbō, 赤ちゃん ákàchan; (US: inf: darling) あなた anáta, ベビー bébǐ

baby carriage (US) n 乳母車 ubágurôma

baby-sit [ˈbeibiːsit] vi 子守をする komóri wo suru, ベビーシッターをする bebíshittā wo suru

baby-sitter [ˈbeibiːsitər] n 子守役 komóriyaku, ベビーシッター bebíshittā

bachelor [ˈbætʃələr] n 独身の男 dokúshin no otóko

Bachelor of Arts/Science (person) 文(理)学士 buń(ri)gákùshi; (qualification) 文理）学士号 buń(ri)gakúshigō

back [bæk] n (of person, animal) 背中 senáka; (of hand) 甲 kô; (of house, page, book) 裏 urá; (of car, train) 後ろ ushíro, 後部 kôbu; (of chair) 背もたれ semótare; (of crowd, audience) 後ろの方 ushíro no hô; (SOCCER) バック bákkù
♦vt (candidate: also: back up) 支援する shién suru; (horse: at races) ...にかける ...ni kakérû; (car etc) バックさせる bákkù saserû
♦vi (also: back up: person) 後ずさりする atózusari suru; (: car etc) バックする bákkù suru
♦cpd (payment, rent) 滞納の tañnō no; (AUT: seat, wheels) 後部の kôbu no
♦adv (not forward) 後うへ（に）ushíro e (ni); (returned) 帰って kaétte 帰って来た kâre wa kaétte kita; (return): throw the ball back ボールを投げ返して下さい bōru wo nagékaeshite kudasái; (again): he called back 彼は電話を掛け直してきた kâre wa deñwa wo kakénao-

shite kita
he ran back 彼は戻って行った kárè wa
kakémodottà
can I have it back? それを返してくれ
ませんか soré wò kaéshite kuremasen
ka

backbencher [bæk'bentʃəːr] *n* (BRIT)
平議員 hirágiìn

backbone [bæk'boun] *n* (ANAT) 背骨
sebónè; (*fig*: main strength) 主力 shúryòku; (: courage) 勇気 yúki

backcloth [bæk'klɔːθ] (BRIT) *n* =
backdrop

backdate [bækdeit'] *vt* (document, pay raise etc) ...にさかのぼって有効にする
...ni sakánobottè yúkò ni suru

back down *vi* 主張を譲る yuzúru

backdrop [bæk'drɔːp] *n* 背景幕 haíkeímaku

backfire [bæk'faiəːr] *vi* (AUT) バックファイアする bakkúfaĭa suru; (plans) 裏目に出る urámè ni derú

background [bæk'graund] *n* (of picture, events: *also* COMPUT) 背景 haíkeí, バック bákkù; (basic knowledge) 予備知識 yobíchishīki; (experience) 経歴 kefreki
family background 家庭環境 kateíkankyō

backhand [bæk'hænd] *n* (TENNIS: *also*: **backhand stroke**) バックハンド bakkúhañdo

backhanded [bæk'hændid] *adj* (*fig*: compliment) 当てこすりの atékosuri no

backhander [bæk'hændəːr] (BRIT) *n* (bribe) 賄ろ wáìro

backing [bæk'iŋ] *n* (fig) 支援 shíen

backlash [bæk'læʃ] *n* (fig) 反動 handō

backlog [bæk'lɔːg] *n*: **backlog of work**
たまった仕事 tamátta shigoto

back number *n* (of magazine etc) バックナンバー bakkúnañbā

back out *vi* (of promise) 手を引くて wo hikú

backpack [bæk'pæk] *n* リュックサック
ryukkúsakkù

back pay *n* 未払いの給料 mihárai nó
kyúryō

backside [bæk'said] (*inf*) *n* おしり o-shí-

ri

backstage [bæk'steidʒ] *adv* (THEATER) 楽屋に(で) gakúya ni (de)

backstroke [bæk'strouk] *n* 背泳ぎ seóyògi

back up *vt* (support: person, theory etc)
支援する shíen suru; (COMPUT) バックアップコピーを作る bakkúappukopí wo tsukúrū

backup [bæk'ʌp] *adj* (train, plane) 予備
の yóbì no; (COMPUT) バックアップ用
の bakkúappu yō no
♦*n* (support) 支援 shíen; (*also*: **backup
file**) バックアップファイル bakkúappu
faĭru

backward [bæk'wəːrd] *adj* (movement)
後ろへの ushíro e no; (person, country)
遅れた okúrèta

backwards [bæk'wəːrdz] *adv* (move, go)
後ろに(へ) ushíro ni (e); (read a list) 逆
に gyakú nì; (fall) 仰向けに aómuke ni;
(walk) 後ろ向きに ushíromuki ni

backwater [bæk'wɔːtəːr] *n* (fig) 後進地
kóshìchína

backyard [bæk'jɑːrd] *n* (of house) 裏庭
uránìwa

bacon [bei'kən] *n* ベーコン bêkon

bacteria [bæktiː'riːə] *npl* 細菌 saíkin

bad [bæd] *adj* (gen) 悪い warúi; (mistake,
accident, injury) 大きな ôkina; (meat,
food) 悪くなった warúku nattá
his bad leg 彼の悪い方の脚 kárè no
warúi hō nò ashí
to go bad (food) 悪くなる warúku narú

bade [bæd] *pt of* bid

badge [bædʒ] *n* (of school etc) 記章 kishố; (of policeman) バッジ bájjì

badger [bædʒ'əːr] *n* アナグマ anáguma

badly [bæd'liː] *adv* (work, dress etc) 下手
に hetá ni; (reflect, think) 悪く warúku
badly wounded 重傷を負った júshō wò
ottá
he needs it badly 彼にはそれがとても
必要だ kárè ni wa soré gà totémo hitsúyō da
to be badly off (for money) 生活が苦
しい seíkatsu ga kurushíì

badminton [bæd'mintən] *n* バドミント

ン badóminton

bad-tempered [bæd'tem'pərd] *adj* (person: by nature) 怒りっぽい okórippoì; (: on one occasion) 機嫌が悪い kigén gà warúî

baffle [bæf'əl] *vt* (puzzle) 困惑させる koñwaku saserú

bag [bæg] *n* (of paper, plastic) 袋 fukúro; (handbag) ハンド バッグ hafídobaggū; (satchel, case) かばん kabán

bags of (inf: lots of) 沢山の takúsan no

baggage [bæg'idʒ] *n* (luggage) 手荷物 tenímotsu

baggy [bæg'i:] *adj* だぶだぶの dabúdabu no

bagpipes [bæg'paips] *npl* バグパイプ bagúpaîpu

Bahamas [bəhɑ:m'əz] *npl*: *the Bahamas* バハマ諸島 bahámashotō

bail [beil] *n* (payment) 保釈金 hoshákukin; (: release) 保釈 hoshaku

◆*vt* (prisoner: *gen*: grant bail to) 保釈する hoshaku suru; (boat: *also*: **bail out**) ...から水をかい出す ...kará mizú wò kaídasù

on bail (prisoner) 保釈中 (の) hoshákuchū (no)

bailiff [beil'if] *n* (LAW: US) 廷更 teîri; (: BRIT) 執行吏 shíkkōri

bail out *vt* (prisoner) 保釈させる hoshaku saserú ¶ *see also* **bail**

bait [beit] *n* (for fish, animal) えさ esá; (for criminal etc) おとり otóri

◆*vt* (hook, trap)...にえさをつける ...ni esá wò tsukérù; (person: tease) からかう karákaû

bake [beik] *vt* (CULIN: cake, potatoes) オーブンで焼く ōbun de yakú; (TECH: clay etc) 焼く yakú

◆*vi* (cook) オーブンに入っている ōbun ni háìtte iru

baked beans [beikt-] *npl* ベークトビーンズ bḗkutobiìnzu

baker [bei'kər] *n* パン屋 pañ-ya

bakery [bei'kə:ri:] *n* (building) パン屋 pañ-ya

baking [bei'kiŋ] *n* (act) オーブンで焼く事 ōbun de yakú koto; (batch) オーブン

で焼いたもの ōbun de yaîta mono

baking powder n ふくらし粉 fukúranshikò, ベーキングパウダー bḗkingupaûdā

balance [bæl'əns] *n* (equilibrium) 均衡 kíñkō, バランス baráñsu; (COMM: sum) 残高 zaǹdaka; (remainder) 残り nokóri; (scales) 天びん teñbin

◆*vt* (budget) ...の収入と支出を合せる ...no shūnyú tò shishútsu wò awáserù; (account) ...の決算をする ...no kessán wò suru; (make equal) 釣合を取る tsuríai wo torú

balance of trade 貿易収支 bốekishūshi

balance of payments 国際収支 kokúsaishūshi

balanced [bæl'ənst] *adj* (report) バランスの良い baráñsu no yoî; (personality) 安定した añtei shita

a balanced diet 均衡食 kíñkō shoku

balance sheet *n* 貸借対照表 tafshakutaishōhyō, (in theater) 天井さじき teñjōsajīkì

bald [bɔ:ld] *adj* (head) はげた hágeta; (tire) 坊主になった bốzu ni nattá

bale [beil] *n* (paper, cotton, hay) こりkorí

baleful [beil'fəl] *adj* (glance) 邪悪なjaákuna

balk [bɔːk] *vi* (of a plane) パラシュートで脱出する paráshūto de dasshútsū suru

ball [bɔːl] *n* (SPORT) 球 tamá, ボール bốru; (of wool, string) 玉 tamá; (dance) 舞踏会 bútōkai

to play ball (co-operate) 協力するkyőryoku suru

ballad [bæl'əd] *n* (poem, sɔng) バラード bárādo

ballast [bæl'əst] *n* (on ship, balloon) バラスト barásùto

ball bearings *npl* ボールベアリング bốrubeâringu

ballerina [bæləri:'nə] *n* バレリーナ barériìna

ballet [bælei'] *n* (art) バレエ bárèe; (an artistic work) バレエ曲 baréekyoku

ballet dancer *n* バレエダンサー barée

dańsā

ballistics [bəlis'tiks] n 弾道学 dańdōgaku

balloon [bəluːn'] n (child's) 風船 fūsen; (hot air balloon) 熱気球 netsúkikyū

ballot [bæl'ət] n (vote) 投票 tōhyō

ballot paper n 投票用紙 tōhyōyōshi

ballpoint (pen) [bɔːl'pɔint] n ボールペン bốrupen

ballroom [bɔːl'ruːm] n 舞踏の間 butō no ma

balm [bɑːm] n バルサム bárūsamu

Baltic [bɔːl'tik] n: **the Baltic (Sea)** バルト海 barúto-kai

balustrade [bæl'əstreid] n (on balcony, staircase) 手すり tesúri

bamboo [bæmbuː'] n (plant) 竹 také; (material) 竹材 takézai

ban [bæn] n (prohibition) 禁止 kińshi
♦vt (prohibit) 禁止する kińshi suru

banal [bənæl'] adj (remark, idea, situation) 陳腐な chíńpu na

banana [bənæn'ə] n バナナ bánana

band [bænd] n (group) 一団 ichídan; (MUS: jazz, rock, military etc) バンド bańdo; (strip of cloth etc) バンド bańdo; (stripe) 帯状の物 obíjō no mono
♦vt ...に包帯を巻く ...ni hốtai wo mākú

bandage [bæn'didʒ] n 包帯 hốtai
♦vt ...に包帯を巻く ...ni hốtai wo mākú

bandaid [bæn'deid] ® (US) n バンドエイド bańdoeidò ◇ばん創こうの一種 bańsōkō no ísshu

bandit [bæn'dit] n 盗賊 tózoku

band together vi 団結する dańketsu suru

bandwagon [bænd'wægən] n: **to jump on the bandwagon** (fig) 便乗する bińjō suru

bandy [bæn'diː] vt (jokes, insults, ideas) やり取りする yarítòri surù

bandy-legged [bæn'diːlegid] adj がにまたの gańímata no

bang [bæŋ] n (of door) ばたんという音 bátàn to iú otò; (of gun, exhaust) ぱーんという音 pán to iú otò; (blow) 打撃 dagéki
♦excl ばーん pán pan
♦vt (door) ばたんと閉める batán to shimérù; (one's head etc) ぶつける butsúke-

ru
♦vi (door) ばたんと閉まる batán to shimárù; (fireworks) ばんばんと爆発する bánban to bakúhatsu suru

bangle [bæŋ'gəl] n (bracelet) 腕飾り udékazarì

bangs [bæŋz] (US) npl (fringe) 切下げ前髪 kirfsagemaegamì

banish [bæn'iʃ] vt (exile: person) 追放する tsuíhō suru

banister(s) [bæn'istəːr(z)] n(pl) (on stairway) 手すり tesúri

bank [bæŋk] n (COMM: building, institution: also of blood etc) 銀行 gíńkō, バンク bánku; (of river, lake) 岸 kishí; (of earth) 土手 doté
♦vi (AVIAT) 傾く katámukù

data bank データバンク dētabánku

bank account n 銀行口座 gińkōkōza

bank card n ギャランティーカード gyarántīkàdo ◇小切手を使う時に示すカード。カードのサインと小切手のサインが照合される kogíttè wo tsukáû tokí ni shímesu kàdo. kàdo no sáin to kogíttè no sáin ga shốgō sarerù

banker [bæŋk'əːr] n 銀行家 gińkōka

banker's card (BRIT) n = bank card

Bank Holiday (BRIT) n 銀行定休日 gińkōteikyūbi

banking [bæŋk'iŋ] n 銀行業 gińkōgyō

banknote [bæŋk'nout] n 紙幣 shíhèi

bank on vt fus ...を頼りにする ...wo táyòri ni suru

bank rate n 公定歩合 kōteibuai

bankrupt [bæŋk'rʌpt] adj (person, organization) 倒産した tōsan shita
to go bankrupt 倒産する tōsan suru
to be bankrupt 返済能力がない heńsainōryoku ga naí

bankruptcy [bæŋk'rʌptsiː] n (COMM) 倒産 tōsan

bank statement n 勘定照合表 kańjōshōgōhyō

banner [bæn'əːr] n (for decoration, advertising) 横断幕 ōdanmaku; (in demonstration) 手持ち横断幕 temóchi ōdanmaku

banns [bænz] npl: **the banns** 結婚予告 kek-

kekkón-yokókuku

banquet [bǽŋkwit] *n* 宴会 eñkai

baptism [bǽptizəm] *n* (REL) 洗礼 sefrei

baptize [bæptáiz'] *vt* ...に洗礼を施す ...ni sefrei wò hodókósuru

bar [bɑːr] *n* (place: for drinking) バー bā; (counter) カウンター kaúntā; (rod: of metal etc) 棒 bō; (slab: of soap) 1個 ikkó; (fig: obstacle) 障害 shógai; (prohibition) 禁止 kińshi; (MUS) 小節 shósetsu

♦*vt* (road) ふさぐ fuságu; (person) ...が ...するのを禁止する ...ga ...surú no wò kiñshi suru; (activity) 禁止する kiñshi suru

a bar of chocolate 板チョコ itachoka

the Bar (LAW: profession) 弁護士 beñgoshi ◇総称 sóshō

bar none 例外なく reigai nakú

barbaric [bɑːrbǽr'ik] *adj* (uncivilized, cruel) 野蛮な yában na

barbarous [bɑːr'bərəs] *adj* (uncivilized, cruel) 野蛮な yában na

barbecue [bɑːr'bəkjuː] *n* (grill) バーベキュー こん炉 bábekyūkoñro; (meal, party) バーベキューパーティ bábekyūpáti

barbed wire [bɑːrbd-] *n* 有刺鉄線 yúshi-tessén, バラ線 barásen

barber [bɑːr'bər] *n* 理髪師 rihátsushi, 床屋 tokóya

bar code *n* (on goods) バーコード bákódo

bare [beːr] *adj* (naked: body) 裸の hadáka no; (: tree) 葉の落ちた ha no óchita; (countryside) 木のない ki no nái; (minimum: necessities) ほんの hofino

♦*vt* (one's body, teeth) むき出しにする mukídashi ni suru

bareback [beːr'bæk] *adv* くらなしで kuránashi de

barefaced [beːr'feist] *adj* (lie, cheek) 厚かましい atsúkamashii

barefoot [beːr'fut] *adj* 裸足の hadáshi no

♦*adv* 裸足で hadáshi de

barely [beːr'liː] *adv* (scarcely) 辛うじて kárójite

bargain [bɑːr'gin] *n* (deal, agreement) 取り引き torfhiki; (good buy) 掘出し物 horída-

shimono, バーゲン bágen

♦*vi* (negotiate): *to bargain (with someone)* (...と) 交渉する (...to) kóshō suru; (haggle) 引き引きする kakéhiki suru

into the bargain おまけに o-máke ni

bargain for *vt fus*: *he got more than he bargained for* 彼はそんな結果を予想していなかった kárè wa sofina kekká wò yosó shite inakattá

barge [bɑːrdʒ] *n* (boat) はしけ hashike

♦*vi* (enter) いきなり入り込む ikfnari hairikòmu; (interrupt) 割込む warfkomù

bark [bɑːrk] *n* (of tree) 皮 kawà; (of dog) ほえ声 hoégoe

♦*vi* (dog) ほえる hoérù

barley [bɑːr'liː] *n* 大麦 ómugi

barley sugar *n* 氷砂糖 kórizatò

barmaid [bɑːr'meid] *n* 女性バーテン joséibáten

barman [bɑːr'mən] (*pl* barmen) *n* バーテン báten

barn [bɑːrn] *n* 納屋 náya

barometer [bərɑːm'itər] *n* (for weather) 気圧計 kiátsukei

baron [bær'ən] *n* (nobleman) 男爵 dañshaku; (of press, industry) 大立て者 ódatemòno

baroness [bær'ənis] *n* 男爵夫人 dañshakufujin

barracks [bær'əks] *npl* (MIL) 兵舎 héisha

barrage [bəriɑːʒ'] *n* (MIL) 弾幕 dañmaku; (dam) ダム dámù; (fig: of criticism, questions etc) 連発 reñpatsu

barrel [bær'əl] *n* (of wine, beer) たる tarù; (: of oil) バレル báreru; (of gun) 銃身 júshin

barren [bær'ən] *adj* (land) 不毛の fumó no

barricade [bær'əkeid] *n* バリケード barfkèdo

♦*vt* (road, entrance) バリケードでふさぐ barfkèdo de fuságu

to barricade oneself (in) (...に) ろう城する (...ni) rōjō surù

barrier [bær'iːər] *n* (at frontier, entrance) 関門 kañmon; (fig: to progress, communication etc) 障害 shōgai

barring [bɑːrˈɪŋ] prep ...を除いて ...wo nozóite

barrister [bærˈɪstəːr] n (BRIT) 法廷弁護士 hōteibengoshì

barrow [bærˈou] n (wheelbarrow) 一輪車 ichfrinsha

bars [bɑːrz] npl (on window etc: grille) 格子 kōshi

behind bars (prisoner) 刑務所に(で) kefmushð ni (de)

bartender [bɑːrˈtendəːr] (US) n バーテン bâten

barter [bɑːrˈtəːr] vt: **to barter something for something** ...を...と交換する ...wo ...to kōkan suru

base [beis] n (foot: of post, tree) 根元 nemóto; (foundation: of food) 主成分 shuséībun; (: of make-up) ファウンデーション faúndêshon; (center: for military, research) 基地 kichf; (: for individual, organization) 本拠地 hoñkyochi

♦vt: **to base something on** (opinion, belief) ...が...に基づく ...ga ...ni motózukð

♦adj (mind, thoughts) 卑しい iyáshiì

baseball [beisˈbɔːl] n 野球 yakyū, ベースボール besubôru

basement [beisˈmənt] n 地下室 chikáshitsu

bases[1] [beiˈsiz] npl of **base**

bases[2] [beiˈsiz] npl of **basis**

bash [bæʃ] (inf) vt (beat) ぶん殴る bufnagurù

bashful [bæʃˈfəl] adj 内気な uchíki na

basic [beiˈsik] adj (fundamental: principles, problem, essentials) 基本的な kihónteki na; (starting: wage) 基本の kihón no; (elementary: knowledge) 初歩的な shohóteki na; (primitive: facilities) 最小限の saíshōgen no

♦basically [beiˈsikli:] adv (fundamentally) 根本的に koñpontekì ni; (in fact, put simply) はっきり言って hakkfrì itté

basics [beiˈsiks] npl: **the basics** 基本 kihón

basil [bæzˈəl] n メボウキ mébòki, バジル bájìru

basin [beiˈsin] n (vessel) たらい tarái;

(also: **wash basin**) 洗面台 señmendai; (GEO: of river, lake) 流域 ryúìki

basis [beiˈsis] (pl **bases**) n (starting point, foundation) 基礎 kisò

on a part-time / trial basis パートタイム (見習い) で pátotaìmu (minarai) de

bask [bæsk] vi: **to bask in the sun** 日光浴をする nikkōyoku wo suru, 日なたぼっこをする hinátabokkð wo suru

basket [bæsˈkit] n (container) かご kagó, バスケット basûkettð

basketball [bæsˈkitbɔːl] n バスケットボール basûkettobōru

bass [beis] n (part, instrument) バス básù; (singer) バス歌手 basúkashū

bassoon [bæsuːnˈ] n (MUS) バスーン básùn

bastard [bæsˈtəːrd] n (offspring) 私生児 shiséìji; (inf!) くそ野郎 kusóyarò

bastion [bæsˈtʃən] n (of privilege, wealth etc) とりで toríde

bat [bæt] n (ZOOL) コウモリ kômori; (for ball games) バット báttð; (BRIT: for table tennis) ラケット rakéttò

♦vt: **he didn't bat an eyelid** 彼は瞬き 1つしなかった kárè wa mabátaki hitotsu shinákatta

batch [bætʃ] n (of bread) 1かま分 hitókamabùn; (of letters, papers) 1山 hitóyama

bated [beiˈtid] adj: **with bated breath** 息を殺して 1kを殺して 息を殺して iki wo koróshite

bath [bæθ] n (bathtub) 風呂 fúrð, 湯船 yúbùne; (act of bathing) 入浴 nyúyoku

♦vt (baby, patient) 風呂に入れる fúrð ni iréru

to have a bath 風呂に入る fúrð ni haíru

¶ see also **baths**

bathe [beið] vi (swim) 泳ぐ oyógù, 遊泳する yúei suru; (US: have a bath) 風呂に入る fúrð ni haíru

♦vt (wound) 洗う aráu

bather [beiðˈəːr] n 遊泳(水泳)する人 yúei(suìei) suru hito

bathing [beiˈðiŋ] n (taking a bath) 入浴 nyúyoku; (swimming) 遊泳 yúei, 水泳 suìei

bathing cap n 水泳帽 suíeibð

bathing suit (BRIT **bathing costume**) n

n 水着 mizúgi

bathrobe [bæθ'roub] *n* バスローブ basúròbu

bathroom [bæθ'rum] *n* トイレ tòfre; (without toilet) 浴室 yokúshìtsu

baths [bæðz] (BRIT) *npl* (also: **swimming baths**) 水泳プール sufefpùru

bath towel *n* バスタオル basútaòru

baton [bætæn'] *n* (MUS) 指揮棒 shikíbò; (ATHLETICS) バトン batón; (policeman's) 警棒 kefbò

battalion [bætæl'jən] *n* 大隊 daítai

batter [bæt'ə:r] *vt* (child, wife) ...に暴力 を振るう ...ni bōryoku wo furúù; (subj: wind, rain) ...に強く当たる ...ni tsúyðku atáru

♦*n* (CULIN) 生地 kíjì

battered [bæt'ə:rd] *adj* (hat, pan) 使い古 した tsukáifurushìta

battery [bæt'ə:ri:] *n* (of flashlight etc) 乾 電池 kańdeńchi; (AUT) バッテリー battéri

battle [bæt'əl] *n* (MIL, *fig*) 戦い tatákai

♦*vi* 戦う tatákau

battlefield [bæt'əlfi:ld] *n* 戦場 seńjō

battleship [bæt'əlʃip] *n* 戦艦 seńkan

bawdy [bɔː'di:] *adj* (joke, song) わいせつ な waísetsu na

bawl [bɔːl] *vi* (shout: adult) どなる donáru; (wail: child) 泣きわめく nakíwamekù

bay [bei] *n* (GEO) 湾 wán

to hold someone at bay は...を寄せつけな い ...wo yosétsukenaì

bay leaf *n* ゲッケイジュの葉 gekkéǐju no ha, ローリエ rórie, ベイリーフ befrìfu

bay window *n* 張出し窓 harídashimadò

bazaar [bəzɑːr'] *n* (market) 市場 íchìba; (fete) バザー bazā

B. & B. [bi:' ænd bi:'] *n abbr* = **bed and breakfast**

BBC [bi:bi:si:'] *n abbr* (= *British Broadcasting Company*) 英国放送協会 efkoku hōsō kyōkai

B.C. [bi:si:'] *adv abbr* (= *before Christ*) 紀元前 kigéñzen

KEYWORD

be [bi:] (*pt* **was, were**, *pp* **been**) *aux vb* **1** (with present participle: forming continuous tenses) ...している ...shíte iru

what are you doing? 何をしていますか nánì wo shité imasù ká

it is raining 雨が降っています ámè ga fúttè imasù

they're coming tomorrow 彼らは明日 来る事になっています kárèra wa asú kurú koto ni náttè imasù

I've been waiting for you for hours 何時間もあなたを待っていますよ nánjikàn mo anátà wo máttè imasù yó

2 (with *pp*: forming passives) ...される ...sáreru

to be killed 殺される korósareru

the box had been opened 箱は開けら れていた hakó wa ákèrarete ita

the thief was nowhere to be seen 泥 棒はどこにも見当らなかった doróbò wa dókò ni mo mfátaranakàtta

3 (in tag questions) ...ね ...né, ...でしょう ...deshō

it was fun, wasn't it? 楽しかったね tanóshikàtta né

he's good-looking, isn't he? 彼は男前 だね kárè wa otókomae da ne

she's back again, is she? 彼女はまた 来たのかね kánojð wa matá kitá no ká

4 (+ **to** + *infinitive*) ...すべきである ...subékì de aru

the house is to be sold 家は売る事にな っている iế wà urú koto ni náttè iru

you're to be congratulated for all your work 立派な仕事を完成しておめ でとう rippá na shigoto wo kansei shite ômédetð

he's not to open it 彼はそれを開けては ならない kárè wa soré wo akete wà naránaï

♦*vb* + *complement* **1** (*gen*) ...である ...de árù

I'm English 私はイングランド人です watákushi wa fngurandojìn desu

I'm tired/hot/cold 私は疲れた（暑い、 寒い）watákushi wa tsukárèta(atsúì,

he's a doctor 彼は医者です kárè wa ishá desû

2 and 2 are 4 2足す2は4 nf tasû ni wa yón

she's tall/pretty 彼女は背が高い/きれいです kánojò wa sé gà takái/kírei desu

be careful/quiet/good! 注意(静かに、行儀よく)して下さい chúí [shízûka ni, gyógi yoků]shité kudasái

2 (of health): **how are you?** お元気ですか o-génkî desu ká

he's very ill 彼は重病です kárè wa jû-byô desû

I'm better now もう元気になりました mô génkî ni narímashîta

3 (of age): **...才です ...sái desu**

how old are you? 何才ですか nánsai desu ka, (お) 幾つですか (o)íkôtsu desu ka

I'm sixteen (years old) 16才です jûrokusái desu

4 (cost): **how much was the meal?** 食事はいくらでしたか shokůji wa ikůra deshita ká

that'll be $5.75, please 5ドル75セン ト頂きます gôdoru nanájûgôsêntô itâdakimasû

♦vi 1 (exist, occur etc) 存在する sónzai suru

the best singer that ever was 史上最高の歌手 shijô saikô no kashû

is there a God? 神は存在するか kámî wa sónzai suru ká

be that as it may それはそれとして sorê wa sore toshite

so be it それでよい sorê de yoï

2 (referring to place): ...にある(いる、ある)...ni árû(írú)

I won't be here tomorrow 明日ここに来ません asû wa kokó ni kímasên

Edinburgh is in Scotland エジンバラはスコットランドにある ejínbâra wa sukóttorândo ni árû

it's on the table それはテーブルにあります sorê wa tébūru ni árímasû

we've been here for ages 私たちはずっと前からここにいます watákushitâchi wa zuttô maê kara kokó ni îmasû

3 (referring to movement) 行って来る it té kurû

where have you been? どこへ行っていましたか dókò e itté imashîta

I've been to the post office/to China 郵便局(中国)へ行って来ました yûbínkyoku(chûgôku)e itté kimashîta

I've been in the garden 庭にいました niwá ni imashîta

♦impers vb 1 (referring to time): **it's 5 o'clock** 5時です gójî desu

it's the 28th of April 4月28日です shigatsu nijûhachínichi desu

2 (referring to distance): **it's 10 km to the village** 村まで10キロメートルある murá mâde jukkírometô árû

3 (referring to the weather): **it's too hot** 暑過ぎる atsúsugirû

it's too cold 寒過ぎる samúsugirû

it's windy today 今日は風が強い kyô wâ kazé ga tsuyoî

4 (emphatic): **it's only me/the postman** 私心配しないで、私(郵便屋さん)です go-shínpai nakû, watákushi(yûbín-yan-san)desû

it was Maria who paid the bill 勘定を払ったのはマリアでした kánjô wô haráttâ no wa márîa deshita

beach [bi:tʃ] n 浜 hamá

♦vt (boat) 浜に引上げる hamá ni hikťágerû

beacon [bi:'kən] n (lighthouse) 燈台 tódai; (marker) 信号 shíngô

bead [bi:d] n (glass, plastic etc) ビーズ bízu; (of sweat) 玉 tamá

beak [bi:k] n (of bird) くちばし kuchíbashi

beaker [bi:'kəːr] n (cup) コップ koppů, グラス gúrâsu

beam [bi:m] n (ARCHIT) はり harí; (of light) 光線 kôsen

♦vi (smile) ほほえむ hohóemu

bean [bi:n] n マメ mamé

runner bean サイインゲン sayáîngen

broad bean ソラマメ sorámâme

coffee bean ゴーヒーマメ kôhîmâme

beansprouts [bin'sprauts] *npl* マメモヤシ mamémoyashi

bear [bɛːr] *n* (ZOOL) クマ kumâ
♦*vb* (*pt* **bore**, *pp* **borne**)
♦*vt* (carry, support: weight) 支える sasáerù; (: responsibility) 負う oú; (: cost) 負う haráù; (tolerate: examination, scrutiny, person) ...に耐える ...ni taérù; (produce: children) 産む umú
♦*vi*: **to bear right/left** (AUT) 右(左)に曲る mígrì(hidári)ni magárù
to bear fruit ...に実がなる ...ni mi ga narù

beard [bird] *n* ひげ higé

bearded [bird'id] *adj* ひげのある higé no arù

bearer [bɛːr'əːr] *n* (of letter, news) 運ぶ人 hakóbu hitó; (of cheque) 持参人 jisánnin; (of title) 持っている人 mótté irú hitó

bearing [bɛːr'iŋ] *n* (air) 態度 tâîdo; (connection) 関係 kaŋkei
to take a bearing 方角を確かめる hôgaku wó tashíkamerù
to find one's bearings 自分の位置を確かめる jibún no ichí wò tashíkamerù

bearings [bɛːr'iŋz] *npl* (*also*: **ball bearings**) ボールベアリング bôrubeárìngu

bear out *vt* (person) ...の言う事を保証する ...no iú kotó wo hoshô surù; (suspicions etc) ...の事実を証明する ...no jíjitsu wo shômei surù

bear up *vi* (person) しっかりする shikkárì surù

beast [bist] *n* (animal) 野獣 yajû; (*inf*: person) いやな奴 iyá na yatsû

beastly [bist'li:] *adj* (awful: weather, child, trick etc) ひどい hídóì

beat [bit] *n* (of heart) 鼓動 kodô; (MUS) 拍子 hyôshi, ビート bîto; (of policeman) 巡回区域 juñkaikuìki
♦*vb* (*pt* **beat**, *pp* **beaten**)
♦*vt* (strike: wife, child) 殴る nagúrù; (eggs, cream) 泡立てる awádaterù, ホイップする hoíppù surù; (defeat: opponent) ...に勝つ ...ni kátsù; (: record) 破る yabúrù
♦*vi* (heart) 鼓動する kodô surù; (rain) た

たき付ける様に降る tatákitsukeru yó ni fûrû; (wind) たたき付ける様に吹く tatákitsukeru yó ni fûkû; (drum) 鳴る narú
off the beaten track へんぴな所に heñpi na tokóro ni
to beat it (*inf*) ずらかる zurákarù

beating [bi:'tiŋ] *n* (punishment with whip etc) むち打ち muchúuchi; (violence) 殴るなどの暴行 nagúrunàdo no bôkō

beat off *vt* (attack, attacker) 撃退する gekítai surù

beat up *vt* (person) 打ちのめす uchínomesù; (mixture) かき拌する kakúhan surù; (eggs, cream) 泡立てる awádaterù, ホイップする hoíppù surù

beautiful [bju:'təfəl] *adj* (woman, place) 美しい utsúkushiì; (day, weather) 素晴らしい subárashiì

beautifully [bju:'təfəli:] *adv* (play music, sing, drive etc) 見事に mígòto ni

beauty [bju:'ti:] *n* (quality) 美しさ utsúkushisà; (beautiful woman) 美女 bîjò, 美人 bíjìn; (fig: attraction) 魅力 miryóku

beauty salon *n* 美容院 bíyòin

beauty spot *n* (BRIT: TOURISM) 景勝地 keíshôchī

beaver [bi:'vəːr] *n* (ZOOL) ビーバー bîba

became [bikeim'] *pt of* **become**

because [bikʌz'] *conj* ...だから ...da kâra, ...であるので ...de ârû nodé
because of ...のため ...no tamé, ...のせいで ...no séf de

beck [bek] *n*: *to be at the beck and call of* ...の言いなりになっている ...no iínari ni nattè irú

beckon [bek'ən] *vt* (*also*: **beckon to**: person) ...に来いと合図する ...ni kôf to âîzu surù

become [bikʌm'] (*pt* **became**, *pp* **become**) *vi* ...になる ...ni narú
to become fat 太る futórù
to become thin やせる yasérù

becoming [bikʌm'iŋ] *adj* (behavior) ふさわしい fusáwashiì; (clothes) 似合う niáù

bed [bed] *n* (piece of furniture) ベッド béddò; (of coal, clay) 層 sô; (bottom: of river, sea) 底 sokó; (of flowers) 花壇 kádàn *to go to bed* 寝る nerú

bed and breakfast *n* (place) 民宿 mínshuku; (terms) 朝食付き宿泊 chôshokutsuki shukúhaku

bedclothes [bed'klouz] *npl* シーツと毛布 shítsu to môfu

bedding [bed'iŋ] *n* 寝具 shígu

bedlam [bed'lam] *n* 大騒ぎ ôsawàgi

bedraggled [bidræg'əld] *adj* (person, clothes, hair) びしょ濡れの bishônure no

bedridden [bed'ridən] *adj* 寝たきりの netákiri no

bedroom [bed'ru:m] *n* 寝室 shinshitsu

bedside [bed'said] *n: at someone's bedside* ...の枕元に ...no makúramôto ni

bedsit(ter) [bed'sit(ə:r)] (*BRIT*) *n* 寝室兼居間 shinshitsu ken imá

bedspread [bed'spred] *n* ベッドカバー beddôkabâ

bedtime [bed'taim] *n* 寝る時刻 nerú jíkòku

bee [bi:] *n* ミツバチ mitsúbàchi

beech [bi:tʃ] *n* (tree) ブナ búnà; (wood) ブナ材 bunázai

beef [bi:f] *n* 牛肉 gyúniku

roast beef ローストビーフ rôsutobîfu

beefburger [bi:f'bə:rgər] *n* ハンバーガー hánbâgâ

Beefeater [bi:f'i:tə:r] *n* ロンドン塔の守衛 rondôntô no shúei

beehive [bi:'haiv] *n* ミツバチの巣箱 mitsúbàchi no súbàko

beeline [bi:'lain] *n: to make a beeline for* まっしぐらに...に向かう masshígùra ni ...ni mukáu

been [bin] *pp of* be

beer [bi:r] *n* ビール bîru

beet [bi:t] *n* (vegetable) サトウダイコン satôdaìkon, ビート bíto; (*US: also: red beet*) ビーツ bîtsu

beetle [bi:t'əl] *n* 甲虫 kôchû

beetroot [bi:t'ru:t] (*BRIT*) *n* ビーツ bîtsu

before [bifɔ:r'] *prep* (of time, space) ...の前に(で) ...no máè ni(de)

♦*conj* ...する前に ...surú maè ni

♦*adv* (time, space) 前に máè ni

before going 行く前に ikú maè ni

before she goes 彼女が行く前に kánòjo ga ikú maè ni

the week before (week past) 1週間前 isshúkan maè

I've never seen it before これまで私はそれを見た事はない koré made watákùshi wà soré wò mítá koto wà nái

beforehand [bifɔ:r'hænd] *adv* あらかじめ arákàjime, 前もって maémotte

beg [bifɔ:r'] *vi* (as beggar) こじきをする kojíki wò suru

♦*vt* (*also: beg for:* food, money) こい求める koímotomerù; (: forgiveness, mercy etc) 願う negáù

to beg someone to do something ...にしてくれと頼む ...ni ...shité kurè to tanómu ¶*see also* pardon

began [bigæn'] *pt of* begin

beggar [beg'ə:r] *n* こじき kojíki

begin [bigin'] (*pt* began, *pp* begun) *vt* 始める hajímeru

♦*vi* 始まる hajímaru

to begin doing/to do something ...し始める ...shihajímeru

beginner [bigin'ə:r] *n* 初心者 shoshínsha

beginning [bigin'iŋ] *n* 初め hajíme

begun [bigʌn'] *pp of* begin

behalf [bihæf'] *n: on behalf of* (as representative of) ...を代表して ...wo daíhyô shité; (for benefit of) ...のために ...no tamé ni

on my/his behalf 私(彼)のために watákukushi(kárè)no tamé ni

behave [biheiv'] *vi* (person) 振舞う furúmaù; (well: *also:* behave oneself) 行儀良くする gyôgi yokú suru

behavior [biheiv'jə:r] (*BRIT* **behaviour**) *n* 行動 kôdô

behead [bihed'] *vt* ...の首を切る ...no kubí wò kírù

beheld [biheld'] *pt, pp of* behold

behind [bihaind'] *prep* (position: at the back of) ...の後ろに(で) ...no ushíro ni (de); (supporting) ...を支援して ...wo shíen shite; (lower in rank, etc) ...に劣って ...ni otótte

♦*adv* (at/towards the back) 後ろに(の方へ) ushíro ni(no hô e); (leave, stay)

átō ni

♦*n* (buttocks) しり shirí

to be behind (schedule) 遅れている okúrete irú

behind the scenes (fig) 非公式に hikō-shiki ni

behold [bihōuld'] (*pt, pp* **beheld**) *vt* 見る mírù

beige [beiʒ] *adj* ベージュ béju

Beijing [bei'dʒiŋ'] *n* 北京 pékìn

being [bi:'iŋ] *n* (creature) 生き物 ikímonò; (existence) 存在 sofizai

Beirut [beiruːt'] *n* ベイルート bérùto

belated [bilei'tid] *adj* (thanks, welcome) 遅れ ばせの okúrebase no

belch [beltʃ] *vi* げっぷをする geppú wò suru

♦*vt* (*gen*: belch out: smoke etc) 噴出する fufishutsu suru

belfry [bel'fri:] *n* 鐘楼 shōrō

Belgian [bel'dʒən] *adj* ベルギーの berúgī no

♦*n* ベルギー人 berúgíjin

Belgium [bel'dʒəm] *n* ベルギー berúgì

belie [bilai'] *vt* (contradict) 隠す kakúsù; (disprove) 反証する hañshō suru

belief [bilːf'] *n* (opinion) 信念 shífinen; (trust, faith) 信仰 shifikō

believe [biliːv'] *vt* 信じる shifijirù

♦*vi* 信じる shifijirù

to believe in (God, ghosts) ...の存在を信じる ...no sofizai wò shifijirù; (method) ...が良いと考える ...ga yói tò kafigaerù

believer [biliːv'əːr] *n* (in idea, activity) ...が良いと考える人 ...ga yói tò kafigaeru hito; (REL) 信者 shífija

belittle [bilit'əl] *vt* 軽視する kefshi suru

bell [bel] *n* (of church) 鐘 kané; (small) 鈴 suzú; (on door, also electric) 呼び鈴 yobírìn, ベル bérù

belligerent [bəlidʒ'əːrənt] *adj* (person, attitude) けんか腰の kefikagoshi no

bellow [bel'ou] *vi* (bull) 大声で鳴く ōgoe de nakú; (person) どなる donárù

bellows [bel'ouz] *npl* (for fire) ふいご fuígo

belly [bel'i:] *n* (ANAT: of person, animal) 腹 hará

belong [bilɔːŋ'] *vi*: *to belong to* (person) ...の物である ...no monó de arù; (club etc) ...に所属している ...ni shozóku shite irú; ...の会員である ...no kaíìn de arù

this book belongs here この本はここにしまうことになっている konó hoñ wa kokó ni shimáù kotó ni nattè irú

belongings [bilɔːŋ'iŋz] *npl* 持物 mochímòno

beloved [bilʌv'id] *adj* (person) 最愛の saf-ai no; (place) 大好きな dáisuki na; (thing) 愛用の aíyō no

below [bilou'] *prep* (beneath) ...の下に (で) ...no shitá ni(de); (less than: level, rate) ...より低く ...yórì hikúkù

♦*adv* (beneath) 下に shitá ni

see below (in letter etc) 下記参照 kakí-sañshō

belt [belt] *n* (of leather etc: *also* TECH) ベルト berúto; (*also*: **belt of land**) 地帯 chítaì

♦*vt* (thrash) 殴る nagúrù

beltway [belt'wei] (*US*) *n* (AUT: ring road) 環状道路 kañjōdòro

bemused [bimjuːzd'] *adj* (person, expression) ぼうぜんとした bōzen to shitá

bench [bentʃ] *n* (seat) ベンチ bénchi, (work bench) 作業台 sagyōdaì; (BRIT: POL) 議員席 gíñseki

the Bench (LAW: judges) 裁判官 saíbañkan心総称 sōshō

bend [bend] (*pt, pp* **bent**) *vt* (leg, arm, pipe) 曲げる magérù

♦*vi* (person) かがむ kagámù

♦*n* (BRIT: in road) カーブ kābu; (in pipe, river) 曲った所 magátta tokoro

bend down *vi* 身をかがめる mi wo kagámeru

bend over *vi* 身をかがめる mi wo kagámeru

beneath [biniːθ'] *prep* (position) ...の下に (で) ...no shitá ni(de); (unworthy of) ...のこけんに関わる ...no kokéñ ni kakáwarù

♦*adv* 下に shitá ni

benefactor [ben'əfæktəːr] *n* (to person, institution) 恩人 óñjin

beneficial [benəfiʃ'əl] *adj* (effect, influ-

ence) 有益な yūeki na
beneficial (to) [...] (...に) 有益な (...に) yūeki na
benefit [ben'əfit] n (advantage) 利益 rřeki;
(money) 手当て teáte
♦vt ...の利益になる ...no rřeki ni narū
♦vi: **he'll benefit from it** それは彼の
ためになるだろう sorě wã kárē no tamé
ni narú darō
Benelux [ben'əlʌks] n ベネルクス benŕ-
rukúsu
benevolent [bənev'ələnt] adj (person) 温
和な ofiwa na; (organization) 慈善の jízén
no
benign [binain'] adj (person, smile) 優し
い yasáshii; (MED) 良性の ryōsei no
bent [bent] pt, pp of **bend**
♦n 才能 sáfnō
♦adj (inf: corrupt) 不正な fuséi na
to be bent on doing ...しようとし掛け
ている ...shíyō to kokórogakete irú
bequest [bikwest'] n (to person, charity)
遺贈 izō
bereaved [biri:vd'] n: **the bereaved** 喪中
の人々 mochū no hitóbìto
beret [bərei'] n ベレー帽 bérēbō
Berlin [bəːrlin'] n ベルリン berúrin
berm [bəːrm] (US) n (AUT) 路肩 rokáta
Bermuda [bəːrmjuːd'ə] n バーミューダ
bámyűda
berry [ber'iː] n ベリー berî ◇総称 sőshō
berserk [bəːrsəːrk'] adj: **to go berserk**
(madman, crowd) 暴れ出す abáredasū
berth [bəːrθ] n (on ship or train) 寝台 shíf-
dai; (for ship) バース bâsu
♦vi (ship) 接岸する setsúgan suru
beseech [bisiːtʃ'] (pt, pp **besought**) vt
(person, God) ...に嘆願する ...ni tañgan
suru
beset [biset'] (pt, pp **beset**) vt (subj: fears,
doubts, difficulties) 襲う osóu
beside [bisaid'] prep (next to) ...の横に
(で) ...no yokó ni(de)
to be beside oneself (with anger) 逆上
している gyakújō shite irú
that's beside the point それは問題外
です sorě wã mofidaigai desu
besides [bisaidz'] adv (in addition) それ

に sorě ni, その上の sonő ue; (in any case)
とに角 tonťkaku
♦prep (in addition to, as well as) ...の外
に ...no hoká ni
besiege [bisiːdʒ'] vt (town) 包囲攻撃する
hóikōgeki suru; (fig: subj: journalists,
fans) ...に押寄せる ...ni oshíyoserú
besought [bisɔːt'] pt, pp of **beseech**
best [best] adj (quality, suitability,
extent) 最も良い mottomō yói
♦adv 最も良く mottomō yókū
the best part of (quantity) ...の大部分
...no daťbubun
at best 良くても yókūte mo
to make the best of something ...を出
来るだけ我慢する ...wo dekíru dake ga-
mañ suru
to do one's best 最善を尽す saízen wo
tsukúsù, ベストを尽くす bésúto wo tsu-
kúsū
to the best of my knowledge 私の知っ
ている限りでは watákushi no shitté irú
kagíri de wa
to the best of my ability 私に出来る
限り watákushi ni dekírū kagíri
best man n 新郎付添い役 shifírōtsukiso-
iyáku
bestow [bistou'] vt (honor, title): **to
bestow something on someone** ...に...を
授ける ...ni ...wo sazúkerū
bestseller [best'selər] n (book) ベストセ
ラー besútoserā
bet [bet] n (wager) かけ kaké
♦vb (pt, pp **bet** or **betted**)
♦vt (wager): **to bet someone something** ...と...をかける ...to ...wo kakérū
♦vi (wager) かける kakérū
to bet money on something ...に金をか
ける ...ni kané wo kakérū
betray [bitrei'] vt (friends, country,
trust, confidence) 裏切る urágirù
betrayal [bitrei'əl] n (action) 裏切り urá-
giri
better [bet'əːr] adj (quality, skill, sensation) より良い yorî yói; (health) 良くなっ
た yókū nattá
♦adv より良く yorî yókù
♦vt (score) ...より高い得点をする ...yórî

takái tokúten wo suru; (record) yabúrù

◆n: to get the better of ...ni katsú ...ni katsú

you had better do it あなたはそうした方が良い anátà wa sṓ shita hṓ ga yoí

he thought better of it 彼は考え直した kárè wa kañgaenaoshita

to get better (MED) 良くなる yókù naru, 回復する kaífuku suru

better off adj (wealthier) ...より金があ る ...yórì kané ga arú; (more comfortable etc) ...の方が良い ...no hṓ ga yoí

betting [bet'iŋ] n (gambling, odds) かけ事 kakégŏto, ギャンブル gyáñburu

betting shop (BRIT) n 私営馬券売り場 shiéìbaken-urìba

between [bitwin'] prep (all senses) ...の間に(で) ...no aídà ni[de]

◆adv 間に aídà ni

beverage [bev'əːridʒ] n 飲物 nomímòno, 飲料 iñryō

beware [biwer'] vi: **to beware (of)** (dog, fire) ...(を) 用心する (...wo) yṓjin suru

「**beware of the dog**」猛犬注意 mṓken-chùi

bewildered [biwil'dəːrd] adj (stunned, confused) 当惑した tṓwaku shita

bewitching [biwitʃ'iŋ] adj (smile, person) うっとりさせる uttórì saséru

beyond [biːɑnd'] prep (in space) ...より先に(で) ...yórì sakí ni[de]; (past: understanding) ...を越えて ...wo koéte; (after: date) ...以降に ...íkō ni; (above) ...以上に ...íjō ni

◆adv (in space, time) 先に sakí ni

beyond doubt 疑いもなく utágai mo nakú

beyond repair 修理不可能で shūri fukánō de

bias [bai'əs] n (prejudice) 偏見 heñken

bias(s)ed [bai'əst] adj (jury) 偏見を持った heñken wo mottá; (judgement, person) 偏見に基づいた heñken ni motózuìta

bib [bib] n (child's) よだれ掛け yodárekàke

Bible [bai'bəl] n (REL) 聖書 sēísho, バイブル báìburu

biblical [bib'likəl] adj 聖書の sēísho no

bibliography [bibliːɑg'rəfiː] n (in text) 文献目録 buñkenmokùroku

bicarbonate of soda [baikɑːr'bənit-] n 重炭酸ソーダ jūtansansōda, 重曹 jūsō

bicker [bik'əːr] vi (squabble) 口論する kōron suru

bicycle [bai'sikəl] n 自転車 jitéñsha

bid [bid] n (at auction) 付値 tsukéne; (in tender) 入札 nyūsatsu; (attempt) 試み kokóromi

◆vb (pt **bade** or **bid**, pp **bidden** or **bid**)

◆vi (at auction) 競りに加わる serí ni kuwawarù

◆vt (offer) ...と値を付ける ...to né wò tsukéru

to bid someone good day (hello) ...に今日はと言う ...ni koñnichi wa to iu; (farewell) ...にさようならと言う ...ni sayōnara to iu

bidder [bid'əːr] n: **the highest bidder** 最高入札者 saíkōnyūsatsùsha

bidding [bid'iŋ] n (at auction) 競り serí

bide [baid] vt: **to bide one's time** (for opportunity) 時期を待つ jíkì wo mátsù

bidet [biːdei'] n ビデ bídè

bifocals [baifou'kəlz] npl 二重焦点眼鏡 nijūshōtenmegàne

big [big] adj (gen) 大きい ōkíì, 大きな ōkina

big brother 兄 áni, 兄さん nīsan

big sister 姉 ané, 姉さん nēsan

bigamy [big'əmiː] n 重婚 jūkon

big dipper [-dip'əːr] (BRIT) n (at fair) ジェットコースター jettōkōsùtā

bigheaded [big'hedid] adj うぬぼれた unáboreta

bigot [big'ət] n (on race, religion) 偏狭な人 heñkyō na hito

bigoted [big'ətid] adj (on race, religion) 偏狭な heñkyō na

bigotry [big'ətriː] n (on race, religion) 偏狭さ heñkyōsa

big top n (at circus) 大テント ōteñto

bike [baik] n (bicycle) 自転車 jitéñsha

bikini [biki:'ni:] n ビキニ bíkìni

bilateral [bailæt'əːrəl] adj (agreement)

双務的な sōmuteki na

bile [bail] n (BIO) 胆汁 tanjū

bilingual [bailiŋ'gwəl] adj (dictionary) 二か国語の nikákokugo no; (secretary) 二か国語を話せる nikákokugo wò hanáserù

bill [bil] n (account) 勘定書 kanjōgaki; (invoice) 請求書 sefkyūsho; (POL) 法案 hōan; (US: banknote) 紙幣 shíhèi; (of bird) くちばし kuchíbashi; (THEATER: of show: on the bill) 番組 bafgumi

post no bills 張紙厳禁 harígamigenkin

to fit/fill the bill (fig) 丁度いい chōdo ì

billboard [bil'bɔːrd] n 広告板 kōkokuban

billet [bil'it] n (MIL) 軍人宿舎 gunjinshukùsha

billfold [bil'fould] (US) n 財布 saifu

billiards [bil'jɔːrdz] n ビリヤード biríyàdo

billion [bil'jən] n (BRIT) 兆 chō; (US) 10億 jūoku

bin [bin] n (BRIT: for rubbish) ごみ入れ gomíre; (container) 貯蔵箱 chōzōbako, 瓶 bín

binary [bai'nɔːri] adj (MATH) 二進法の nishínhō no

bind [baind] (pt, pp **bound**) vt (tie, tie together) 縛る shibárù; (constrain) 束縛する sokúbaku suru; (book) 製本する sefhon suru

♦n (inf: nuisance) いやな事 iyá na koto

binding [bain'diŋ] adj (contract) 拘束力のある kōsokuryòku no aru

binge [bindʒ] (inf) n: *to go on a binge* (drink a lot) 酒浸りになる sakébitari ni narù

bingo [biŋ'gou] n ビンゴ bíngo

binoculars [bənəkʲələːrz] npl 双眼鏡 sōgankyō

biochemistry [baioukem'istri] n 生化学 sefkagaku

biography [baiɑːg'rəfi] n 伝記 defki

biological [baiədʒ'ikəl] adj (science, warfare) 生物学の sefbutsugaku no; (washing powder) 酵素洗剤 kōsoséfzai

biology [baiɑːl'ədʒi] n 生物学 sefbutsu-

gàku

birch [bəːrtʃ] n (tree) カバノキ kabá no kì; (wood) カバ材 kabázai

bird [bəːrd] n (ZOOL) 鳥 torf; (BRIT: inf: girl) 女の子 oñna no ko

bird's-eye view [bəːrdzai-] n (aerial view) 全景 zeñkei; (overview) 概観 gaíkan

bird-watcher [bəːrd'wɑːtʃəːr] n バードウォッチャー bādowotchā

bird-watching [bəːrd'wɑːtʃiŋ] n バードウォッチング bādowotchingu

Biro [bai'rou] ® n ボールペン bōrupen

birth [bəːrθ] n (baby, animal, also: fig) 誕生 tanjō

to give birth to (BIO: subj: woman, animal) ...を生む ...wo umú

birth certificate n 出生証明書 shussshō (shussséi) shōmeisho

birth control n (policy) 産児制限 sañjiseigen; (methods) 避妊 hiñin

birthday [bəːrθ'dei] n 誕生日 tañjōbi

♦cpd (cake, card, present etc) 誕生日の tañjōbi no 1 see also **happy**

birthplace [bəːrθ'pleis] n (country, town etc) 出生地 shusshōchí(shusséichí), 生れ故郷 umárekokyō; (house etc) 生家 seíka

birth rate n 出生率 shusshōritsu(shussséiritsu)

Biscay [bis'kei] n: *the Bay of Biscay* ビスケー湾 bisúkèwan

biscuit [bis'kit] (BRIT) n ビスケット bisúkettò

bisect [baiset'] vt (angle etc) 二等分する nitóbun suru

bishop [biʃ'əp] n (REL: Catholic etc) 司教 shíkyō; (: Protestant) 監督 kañtoku; (: Greek Orthodox) 主教 shúkyō; (CHESS) ビショップ bíshoppu

bit [bit] pt of **bite**

♦n (piece) 欠けら kakéra; (COMPUT) ビット bíttò; (of horse) はみ hámì

a bit of 少しの sukóshi no, ちょっとの chóttó no

a bit mad ちょっと頭がおかしい chóttó atáma ga okáshiî

a bit dangerous ちょっと危ない chóttó abúnaî

bit by bit 少しずつ sukóshi zutsù

bitch [bitʃ] n (dog) 雌犬 mesúinu; (inf!: woman) あま amá

bite [bait] (pt **bit**, pp **bitten**) vt (subj: person) かむ kámů; (: dog etc) …にかみ付く …ni kamítsuku; (: insect etc) 刺す sásù
♦vi (dog etc) かみ付く kamítsuku; (insect etc) 刺す sásù
♦n (insect bite) 虫刺され mushísasàre; (mouthful) 一口 hitókùchi
to bite one's nails つめをかむ tsúme wo kamú
let's have a bite (to eat) (inf) 何か食べよう nánì ka tabéyò

bitten [bit'ən] pp of **bite**

bitter [bit'əːr] adj (person) 恨みを持った urámi wo mottá; (taste, experience, disappointment) 苦い nigái; (wind) 冷たい tsumétaì; (struggle) 激しい hagéshiì; (criticism) 辛らつな shíratsu na
♦n (BRIT: beer) ビター bitá ◊ホップの利いた苦いビール hoppú no kíta nigái bíru

bitterness [bit'əːrnis] n (anger) 恨み urámi; (bitter taste) 苦み nigámi

bizarre [bizɑːr'] adj (conversation, contraption) 奇妙な kímyò na

blab [blæb] (inf) vi (to the press) しゃべる shabérù

black [blæk] adj (color) 黒い kurói; (person) 黒人の kokújin no; (tea, coffee) ブラックの burákkù no
♦n (color) 黒 kúrò; (person): **Black** 黒人 kokújin
♦vt (BRIT: INDUSTRY) ボイコットする boíkottò suru
black humor ブラックユーモア burákkuyùmoa
to give someone a black eye …を殴って目にあざを作る …wo nagúttè me ni azá wo tsukúrù
black and blue (bruised) あざだらけの azá daràke no
to be in the black (in credit) 黒字の kuróji de arù

blackberry [blæk'beːri] n ブラックベリー burákkuberì ◊ キイチゴの一種 kíīchigo no isshù

blackbird [blæk'bəːrd] n (European bird) クロウタドリ kuróutadòri

blackboard [blæk'bɔːrd] n 黒板 kokúban

black coffee n ブラックコーヒー burákku kòhi

blackcurrant [blækkɑːr'ənt] n クロスグリ kurósugùri

blacken [blæk'ən] vt (fig: name, reputation) 汚す kegásù

black ice (BRIT) n (on road) 凍結路面 tóketsuromèn

blackleg [blæk'leg] (BRIT) n (INDUSTRY) スト破り sutóyabùri

blacklist [blæk'list] n ブラックリスト burákkurisùto

blackmail [blæk'meil] n ゆすり yusúri
♦vt ゆする yusúru

black market n やみ市 yamíchì

blackout [blæk'aut] n (MIL) 灯火管制 tôkakañsei; (power cut) 停電 teíden; (TV, RADIO) 放送中止 hōsōchùshi; (faint) 一時的意識喪失 ichíjitekiishíkisòshitsu, ブラックアウト burákkuaùto

Black Sea n: **the Black Sea** 黒海 kôkkai

black sheep n (fig) 持て余し者 motéamashimono

blacksmith [blæk'smiθ] n 鍛冶屋 kajíya

black spot n (BRIT: AUT) 事故多発地点 jikótahatsuchiten; (: for unemployment etc) …が深刻になっている地域 …ga shińkoku ni nattè irú chíiki

bladder [blæd'əːr] n (ANAT) ぼうこう bôkô

blade [bleid] n (of knife, sword) 刃 há; (of propeller) 羽根 hané
a blade of grass 草の葉 kusá no ha

blame [bleim] n (for error, crime) 責任 sekínin
♦vt: **to blame someone for something** …を…のせいにする …wo …no séi ni suru
to be to blame 責任が…にある sekínin ga …ni arù

blameless [bleim'lis] adj (person) 潔白な keppáku na

bland [blænd] adj (taste, food) 味気ない ajíke naì

blank [blæŋk] adj (paper etc) 空白の kûhaku no; (look) ぼう然とした bōzen to shitá

◆*n* (of memory) 空白 kūhaku; (on form) 空所 kūsho; (*also:* **blank cartridge**) 空包 kūhō

a blank sheet of paper 白紙 hakúshi

blank check *n* 金額未記入の小切手 kíngakumikínyū no kogíttè

blanket [blæ'ŋkit] *n* (*bed*) 毛布 mōfu; (of snow, fog etc) 一面の... ichimen no ...

blare [bleːr] *vi* (brass band, horns, radio) 鳴り響く naríhibikù

blasé [blɑzei'] *adj* (reaction, tone) 無関心 な mukánshin na

blasphemy [blæs'fəmi] *n* (REL) 冒とく bōtoku

blast [blæst] *n* (of wind) 突風 toppū; (of explosive) 爆発 bakúhatsu

◆*vt* (blow up) 爆破する bakúha suru

blast-off [blæst'ɔːf] *n* (SPACE) 発射 hasshá

blatant [blei'tənt] *adj* discrimination, bias) 露骨な rokótsu na

blaze [bleiz] *n* (fire) 大事 kájì; (*fig:* of color, glory) きらめき kirámeki; (: publicity) 大騒ぎ ōsawagi

◆*vi* (fire) 燃え盛る moésakerù; (guns) 続け様に発射する tsuzőkezama ni happō suru; (*fig:* eyes) 怒りで燃える ikári de moéru

◆*vt:* **to blaze a trail** (*fig*) 先べんを付け る señben wo tsúkerů

blazer [blei'zəːr] *n* (of school, team etc) ブレザー burézà

bleach [bliːtʃ] *n* (*also:* **household bleach**) 漂白剤 hyőhakuzài

◆*vt* (fabric) 漂白する hyőhaku suru

bleached [bliːtʃt] *adj* (hair) 漂白した hyőhaku shitá

bleachers [bliːtʃəːz] (*US*) *npl* (SPORT) 外野席 gaíyasèki

bleak [bliːk] *adj* (countryside) 物寂し い monðsabishii; (weather) 悪い warúi; (prospect, situation) 暗い kurái; (smile) 悲しそうな kanáshisō na

bleary-eyed [bliːr'iːaid] *adj* 目がしょぼ しょぼしている me ga shobóshobo shité

irú

bleat [bliːt] *vi* (goat, sheep) 鳴く nakú

bled [bled] *pt, pp of* **bleed**

bleed [bliːd] (*pt, pp* bled) *vi* (MED) 出血す る shukkétsu suru

my nose is bleeding 鼻血が出ている hanájì ga detě irú

bleeper [bliː'pəːr] *n* (device) ポケットベ ル pokéttò bérù

blemish [blem'iʃ] *n* (on skin) 染み shimĭ; (on fruit) 傷 kizű; (on reputation) 汚点 otén

blend [blend] *n* (of tea, whisky) 混合 koñgō, ブレンド buréndo

◆*vt* 混ぜ合せる mazéawaserù, 混合する koñgō suru

◆*vi* (colors: *also:* **blend in**) 溶け込む tokékomù

bless [bles] (*pt, pp* blessed *or* blest) *vt* (REL) 祝福する shukúfuku suru

bless you! (after sneeze) お大事に o-dáìji ni

blessing [bles'iŋ] *n* (approval) 承認 shőnin; (godsend) 恵み megúmi; (REL) 祝福 shukúfuku

blew [bluː] *pt of* **blow**

blight [blait] *vt* (hopes, life etc) 駄目にす る damé ni suru

blimey [blai'mi:] (*BRIT: inf*) *excl* おや oyá

blind [blaind] *adj* (MED) 盲目の mōmoku no, (*pej*) めくらの mekúra no; (euphemistically) 目の不自由な me no fujĭyū na; (*fig:* **blind (to)** (...を) 見る目が ない (...wo) mirú me ga naî

◆*n* (for window) ブラインド buráindo; (: *also:* **Venetian blind**) ベネシアンブラ インド benéshian buraindo

◆*vt* (MED) 失明させる shitsúmei sasérù; (dazzle) ...の目をくらます ...no me wo kurámasu; (deceive) だます damásu

the blind (blind people) 盲人 mōjìn ◇総 称 sōshō

blind alley *n* (*fig*) 行き詰り yukízumari

blind corner (*BRIT*) *n* 見通しの悪い曲 り角 mitőshi no warúi magárikadò

blindfold [blaind'fould] *n* 目隠し mekákushi

◆*adj* 目隠しをした mekákushi wo shitá

◆*adv* 目隠しをして mekákushi wo shité

◆*vt* 目隠しする mekákushi suru

blindly [blaind'li:] *adv* (without seeing) よく見ないで yókù minàide; (without thinking) めくら滅法に mekúrameppò ni

blindness [blaind'nis] *n* (MED) 盲目 mō-moku; (euphemistically) 目の障害 me no shōgai

blind spot *n* (AUT) 死角 shikákù; (*fig*: weak spot) 盲点 mōten

blink [bliŋk] *vi* (person, animal) 瞬く ma-bátakù; (light) 点滅する tenmetsu suru

blinkers [bliŋk'ə:rz] *npl* 馬の目隠し umá no mekákushi

bliss [blis] *n* (complete happiness) 無上の幸福 mujō no shifúku

blister [blis'tə:r] *n* (on skin) 水膨れ mizú-bukùre; (in paint, rubber) 気泡 kihō

◆*vi* (paint) 気泡ができる kihō ga dekírù

blithely [blaiθ'li:] *adv* (proceed, assume) 軽率に kefsotsu ni

blitz [blits] *n* (MIL) 空襲 kūshū

blizzard [bliz'ə:rd] *n* 吹雪 fubúki, ブリザード burízādo

bloated [blou'tid] *adj* (face, stomach: swollen) はれた harétà; (person: full) たらふく食べた taráfùku tabétà

blob [blɑːb] *n* (of glue, paint) 滴 shizúku; (something indistinct) はっきり見えないもの hakkírì miénài monó

bloc [blɑːk] *n* (POL) 連合 reńgō, ブロック burókkù

block [blɑːk] *n* (of buildings) 街区 gáìku, ブロック burókkù; (of stone, wood) ブロック burókkù; (in pipes) 障害物 shōgaìbutsu

◆*vt* (entrance, road) 塞ぐ fuságu; (progress) 邪魔する jamá suru

block of flats (BRIT) マンション mańshon

mental block 精神的ブロック seishintekì burókkù

blockade [blɑːkeid'] *n* 封鎖 fūsa

blockage [blɑːk'idʒ] *n* 閉そく hefsoku

blockbuster [blɑːk'bʌstə:r] *n* (film, book) センセーション seńsèshon

block letters *npl* 活字体 katsújitaì

bloke [blouk] (BRIT: *inf*) *n* 男 otóko, 野郎 yárō

blond(e) [blɑːnd] *adj* (hair) 金髪の kińpatsu no, ブロンドの buróndo no

◆*n* (woman) 金髪の女性 kińpatsu no jo-séi, ブロンド buróndo

blood [blʌd] *n* (BIO) 血 chi, 血液 ketsúèki

blood donor *n* 献血者 keńketsùsha

blood group *n* 血液型 ketsúèkigata

bloodhound [blʌd'haund] *n* ブラッドハウンド buráddohaùndo

blood poisoning [-poi'zəniŋ] *n* 敗血症 hafketsushō

blood pressure *n* 血圧 ketsúatsu

bloodshed [blʌd'ʃed] *n* 流血 ryūketsu

bloodshot [blʌd'ʃɑːt] *adj* (eyes) 充血した jūketsu shitá

bloodstream [blʌd'stri:m] *n* 血流 ketsú-ryū

blood test *n* 血液検査 ketsúèkikeñsa

bloodthirsty [blʌd'θə:rsti:] *adj* (tyrant, regime) 血に飢えた chi ni ŭèta

blood vessel *n* 血管 kekkán

bloody [blʌd'i:] *adj* (battle) 血みどろの chimídoro no; (nose) 鼻血を出した hanáji wo dashíta; (BRIT: *inf*!): **this bloody ...** くそったれ... kusóttàre...

bloody strong/good (*inf*!) すごく強い（良い）sugókù tsuyóì[yoì]

bloody-minded [blʌd'main'did] (BRIT: *inf*) *adj* 意地悪な ijíwarù na

bloom [blum] *n* (BOT: flower) 花 haná

◆*vi* (flower) ...の花が咲く ...no haná ga sakú; (flower) 咲く sakú

blossom [blɑːs'əm] *n* (BOT) 花 haná

◆*vi* (BOT) 花が咲く haná ga sakú; (*fig*): **to blossom into** 成長して...になる seíchōshite ...ni narú

blot [blɑːt] *n* (on text) 染み shimí; (*fig*: on name etc) 傷 kizú

◆*vt* (with ink etc) 汚す yogósu

blotchy [blɑːtʃ'i:] *adj* (complexion) 染みだらけの shimídaràke no

blot out *vt* (view) 見えなくする miénàku suru; (memory) 消す kesú

blotting paper [blɑːt'iŋ-] *n* 吸取り紙 sutórigami

blow [bləu] n (punch etc: also fig) 打撃 dageki; (with sword) 一撃 ichigeki
♦vb (pt **blew**, pp **blown**)
♦vi (wind) 吹く fukū; (person) 息を吹きかける fkī wo fukíkakerū
♦vt (subj: wind) 吹き飛ばす fukítobasū; (instrument, whistle) 吹く fukū; (fuse) 飛ばす tobásu
to blow one's nose 鼻をかむ haná wo kamú

blow away vt 吹飛ばす fukítobasū

blow down vt (tree) 吹倒す fukítaosū

blow-dry [bləu'drai] n (hairstyle) ブロー仕上げ buróshiàge

blowlamp [bləu'læmp] (BRIT) n = **blowtorch**

blow off vi (hat etc) 吹飛ばす fukítobasū

blow out vi (fire, flame) 吹消す fukíkesū

blow-out [bləu'aut] n (of tire) パンク pañku

blow over vi (storm) 静まる shizúmarū; (crisis) 収まる osámarū

blowtorch [bləu'tɔ:rtʃ] n ブローランプ buróraǹpu, トーチランプ tóchiraǹpu

blow up vi (storm) 起きる okírù; (crisis) 起る okórù
♦vt (bridge: destroy) 爆破する bakúha suru; (tire: inflate) 膨らます fukúramasu; (PHOT: enlarge) 引延ばす hikínobasu

blue [blu:] adj (color) 青い aoí, ブルーの burū no; (depressed) 憂うつな yūutsu na
blue film n (inf) ポルノ映画 porúnoeìga
blue joke わいせつなジョーク waísetsu na jōku
out of the blue (fig) 青天のへきれきの様に seíten no hekíreki no yō ni

bluebell [blu:'bel] n ツルボ tsurúbo

bluebottle [blu:'bɑ:tl] n (insect) アオバエ aóbae

blueprint [blu:'print] n (fig): **a blueprint (for)** (...の) 計画 (...no) keíkaku, (...の) 青写真 (...no) aójashìn

blues [blu:z] n: **the blues** (MUS) ブルース burūsu

bluff [blʌf] vi (pretend, threaten) はった

りを掛ける hattári wo kakérù
♦n (pretense) はったり hattári
to call someone's bluff ...に挑戦する ...ni chōsen suru

blunder [blʌn'də:r] n (political) へま hémà
♦vi (bungle something) へまをする hémà wo suru

blunt [blʌnt] adj (pencil) 先が太い sakí ga futóì; (knife) 切れない kirénaì; (person, talk) 率直な sotchóku na

blur [blə:r] n (shape) かすんで見える物 kasúnde miérù monó
♦vt (vision) くらます kurámasu; (distinction) ぼかす bokásù

blurb [blə:rb] n (for book, concert etc) 宣伝文句 seídenmoǹku

blurt out [blə:rt-] vt 出し抜けに言い出す dashínuke ni iídasù

blush [blʌʃ] vi (with shame, embarrassment) 赤面する sekímen suru
♦n 赤面 sekímen

blustering [blʌs'tə:riŋ] adj (person) 威張り散らす ibárichirasù

blustery [blʌs'tə:ri] adj (weather) 風の強い kazé no tsuyóì

boar [bɔ:r] n イノシシ inóshishì

board [bɔ:rd] n (cardboard) ボール紙 bórugami; (wooden) 板 ítà; (on wall: notice board) 掲示板 keíjiban; (for chess etc) 盤 ...bañ; (committee) 委員会 iíñkai; (in firm) 役員会 yakúiñkai; (NAUT, AVIAT): **on board** ...に乗って ...ni notte
♦vt (ship, train) ...に乗る ...ni norú
full/half board (BRIT) 3食 (2食) 付き safíshoku (nishóku) tsukí
board and lodging 賄い付き下宿 makánaitsuki geshúku
to go by the board (fig) 捨てられる sutérarerù

boarder [bɔ:r'də:r] n (SCOL) 寄宿生 kishúkusei

boarding card [bɔ:r'diŋ-] n = **boarding pass**

boarding house n 下宿屋 geshúkuya

boarding pass n (AVIAT, NAUT) 搭乗券 tōjōken

boarding school n 全寮制学校 zenryōseigakkō

board room n 役員会議室 yakúinkaigishìtsu

board up vt (door, window) ...に板を張る ...ni ítá wo harú

boast [bəust] vi: to boast (about/of) ...を自慢する (...wo) jimán suru

boat [bəut] n (small) ボート bōto; (ship) 船 fúne

boater [bəu'tə:r] n (hat) かんかん帽 kańkańbō

boatswain [bou'sən] n 甲板長 kóhanchō, ボースン bōsun

boat train n (boat, cork etc on water: also: **bob up and down**) 波に揺れる namí ni yuréru

bobby [ba:b'i:] (BRIT: inf) n (policeman) 警官 keíkan

bobsleigh [ba:b'slei] n ボブスレー bobúsurē

bob up vi (appear) 現れる aráwareru

bode [bəud] vi: to bode well/ill (for) (...にとって) 良い(悪い)前兆である (...ni tottē) yoí(warúi)zeńchō de arù

bodily [ba:d'əli:] adj (needs, functions) 身体の shiftai no
◆adv (lift, carry) 体ごと karádagoto

body [ba:d'i:] n (ANAT: gen) 体 karáda, 身体 shiftai; (corpse) 死体 shitái; (object) 物体 buttái; (main part) 本体 hońtai; (of car) 車体 shatái, ボディ bōdī; (fig: group) 団体 dańtai; (: organization) 組織 sōshìki; (quantity: of facts) 量 ryō; (of wine) こく kokû

body-building [ba:d'i:bil'diŋ] n ボディービル bodíbirù

bodyguard [ba:d'i:ga:rd] n (of statesman, celebrity) 護衛 goéi, ボディーガード bodígādo

bodywork [ba:d'i:wə:rk] n (AUT) 車体 shatái

bog [ba:g] n (GEO) 湿地帯 shítakùchī
◆vt: to get bogged down (fig) 泥沼にはまり込む dorínuma ni hamárikomu

boggle [ba:g'əl] vi: the mind boggles 理解できない ríkai dekínài

bogus [bou'gəs] adj (claim, workman etc) 偽の nisé no

boil [bɔil] vt (water) 沸かす wakásu; (eggs, potatoes etc) ゆでる yudéru
◆vi (liquid) 沸く wakú; (fig: with anger) かんかんに怒る kańkan ni okórù; (: with heat) うだるような暑さになる udáru yō na atsúsa ni narú
◆n (MED) 出来物 dekímonð

to come to a (US)/the (BRIT) boil 沸き始める wakíhajimerù

boil down to vt fus (fig) 要するに...である yō surú ni ...de arù

boiled egg n ゆで卵 yudétamagð

boiled potatoes npl ゆでジャガイモ yudéjagàimo

boiler [bɔi'lə:r] n (device) ボイラー bõīrā

boiler suit (BRIT) n つなぎの作業着 tsunági no sagyōgi

boiling point n (of liquid) 沸騰点 fúttōten

boil over vi (kettle, milk) 吹こぼれる fukíkoborerù

boisterous [bɔis'tə:rəs] adj (noisy, excitable: person, crowd) 騒々しい sōzōshiī

bold [bould] adj (brave) 大胆な daítan na; (pej: cheeky) ずうずうしい zūzūshiì; (pattern) 際立った kiwádattà; (line) 太い futōi; (color) 派手な hadé na

Bolivia [bouliv'i:ə] n ボリビア borfbia

bollard [ba:l'a:rd] (BRIT) n (AUT) 標識柱 hyōshikichū ◇安全地帯などを示す安全地帯 nadð wo shimésù

bolster [boul'stə:r] n (pillow) 長まくら nagámakùra

bolster up vt (case) 支持する shíjí suru

bolt [boult] n (lock) ラッチ rátchī; (with nut) ボルト borúto
◆adv: bolt upright 背筋を伸ばして sesúji wo nobáshite
◆vt (door) ...のラッチを掛ける ...no ratchí wo kakérù; (also: bolt together) ボルトで止める borúto de toméru; (food) 丸のみする marúnomi suru
◆vi (run away: horse) 逃げ出す nigédasù

bomb [ba:m] n (device) 爆弾 bakúdan
◆vt 爆撃する bakúgeki suru

bombard [ba:mbɔ:rd'] vt (MIL: with big guns etc) 砲撃する hōgeki suru; (: from

planes) 爆撃する bakúgeki suru; *(fig:
with questions)* ...に浴びせる ...ni abíseru

bombardment [bɑːmˈbɑːrdmənt] *n*:
bombardment from guns 砲撃 hógeki
bombardment from planes 爆撃 bakúgeki

bombastic [bɑːmˈbæs'tik] *adj* (person,
language) もったい振った mottáibuttá

bomb disposal *n*: *bomb disposal unit*
爆弾処理部隊 bakúdanshorihàn

bomber [bɑːmˈɑːr] *n* (AVIAT) 爆撃機 ba-
kúgekikì

bombshell [bɑːmˈʃel] *n* (*fig*: revelation)
爆弾 bakúdan

bona fide [bou'nəfaid'] *adj* (traveler etc)
本物の hofímono no

bond [bɑːnd] *n* (of affection, *also gen*:
link) きずな kizúna; (binding promise) 約
束 yakúsoku; (FINANCE) 証券 shóken;
(COMM): *in bond* (of goods) 保税倉庫で
hozéisòko de

bondage [bɑːn'didʒ] *n* (slavery) 奴隷の身
分 doréi no míbùn

bone [boun] *n* (ANAT, *gen*) 骨 honé
♦*vt* (meat, fish) 骨を抜く honé no nukú

bone idle *adj* ぐうたらの gútara no

bonfire [bɑːn'faiər] *n* たき火 takíbi

bonnet [bɑːn'it] *n* (hat: *also BRIT*: of
car) ボンネット bofinéttò

bonus [bou'nəs] *n* (payment) ボーナス
bónasu; *(fig*: additional benefit) おまけ
o-máke

bony [bou'ni:] *adj* (MED: tissue) 骨の白
né no; (arm, face) 骨張った honébattá;
(meat, fish) 骨の多い honé no ói

boo [bu:] *excl* (to surprise someone) わっ
wáì; (to show dislike) ぶー bū
♦*vt* 野次る yajíru

booby trap [bu:'bi:-] *n* (MIL) 仕掛爆弾
shikákebakùdan

book [buk] *n* (novel etc) 本 hóñ; (of
stamps, tickets) 綴り tsuzúri
♦*vt* (ticket, seat, room) 予約する yoyáku
suru; (subj: traffic warden, policeman)
...に違反切符を書く ...ni ihánkippù wo
kakú; (: referee) ...に勧告を与える ...ni
kańkoku wò atáeru

bookcase [buk'keis] *n* 本棚 hóndana

booking office [buk'iŋ-] *n (BRIT)*
(RAIL, THEATER) 切符売り場 kippú
urība

book-keeping [bukki:'piŋ] *n* 簿記 bókì

booklet [buk'lit] *n* 小冊子 shósasshì, パ
ンフレット páñfurettò

bookmaker [buk'meikər] *n* 馬券屋 ba-
kéñ-ya

books [buks] *npl* (COMM: accounts) 帳
簿 chóbo

bookseller [buk'selər] *n* 本屋 hóñ-ya

bookshop [buk'ʃɑːp] *n* = **bookstore**

bookstore [buk'stɔːr] *n* 本屋 hóñ-ya, 書
店 shotéñ

boom [bu:m] *n* (noise) とどろき todóroki;
(in prices, population etc) ブーム bú̄mu
♦*vi* (guns, thunder) とどろく todórokù;
(voice) とどろく様な声で話す todórokù
yò na kòè de iú; (business) 繁盛する hañ-
jò suru

boomerang [bu:'məræŋ] *n* ブーメラン
búmeran

boon [bu:n] *n* (blessing, benefit) 有難い物
arígataì monó

boost [bu:st] *n* (to confidence, sales etc)
増す事 masú kotó
♦*vt* (confidence, sales etc) 増す masú;
(economy) 促進する sokúshin suru

booster [bu:s'tər] *n* (MED) ブースター
búsutā

boot [bu:t] *n* (knee-length) 長靴 nagágu-
tsu; (*also*: **hiking/climb-
ing boots**) 登山靴 tozáñgutsu; (*also*: **soccer boots**) サッカーシューズ sakkáshū-
zu; (*BRIT*: of car) トランク toráñku
♦*vt* (COMPUT) 起動する kidó suru
... to boot (in addition) おまけに o-máke ni

booth [bu:θ] *n* (at fair) 屋台 yátāi; (telephone booth, voting booth) ボックス
bokkûsu

booty [bu:'ti:] *n* 戦利品 señrihin

booze [bu:z] (*inf*) *n* 酒 saké

border [bɔːr'dər] *n* (of a country) 国境
kokkyó; (*also*: **flower border**) ボーダー
花壇 bódakàdań; (band, edge: on cloth)
へり herí
♦*vt* (road: subject: trees etc) ...に沿って

立っている ...ni sotté tatté irú; (another country: also: **border on**) ...に隣接する ...ni rifisetsu suru

borderline [bɔːrˈdəːrlain] n (fig): **on the borderline** 際正いところで kiwádoi tokóro de, ボーダーラインすれすれで bódárain surésure de

borderline case n 決めにくいケース kiméníkuì kêsu

border on vt fus (fig: insanity, brutality) ...に近い ...ni chikái

Borders [bɔːrˈdəːrz] n: **the Borders** ボーダーズ州 bódázushū ◇イングランドに隣接するスコットランド南部の1州 ígurando ni rifisetsu surú sukóttorando nañbu no isshū

bore [bɔːr] pt of **bear**
◆vt (hole) ...に穴を開ける ...ni aná wo akéru; (oil well, tunnel) 掘る hórū; (person) 退屈させる tafkutsu saséru
◆n (person) 詰まらない話で退屈させる人 tsumáranái hanáshi de tafkutsu saséru hitó; (of gun) 口径 kôkei
to be bored 退屈する tafkutsu suru

boredom [bɔːrˈdəm] n (condition) 退屈 tafkutsu; (boring quality) 詰まらなさ tsumáranása

boring [bɔːrˈiŋ] adj (tedious, unimaginative) 退屈な tafkutsu na

born [bɔːrn] adj: **to be born** 生れる umáreru
I was born in 1960 私は1960年に生れました watákushi wa séñkyúhyákurokújūnen ni umáremashita

borne [bɔːrn] pp of **bear**

borough [bɑːrˈə] n (POL) 区 ku

borrow [bɑːrˈou] vt: **to borrow something** (from someone) ...を借りる ...wo karíru

bosom [buzˈəm] n (ANAT) 胸 muné

bosom friend n 親友 shiñ-yū

boss [bɔs] n (employer) 雇い主 yatóinushi; (supervisor, superior) 上司 jóshi, 親方 oyákata, ボス bósu
◆vt (also: **boss around**, **boss about**) こき使う kokítsukaū

bossy [bɔsˈiː] adj (overbearing) 威張り散らす ibárichirasu

bosun [bouˈsən] n (NAUT) = **boatswain**

botany [batˈəni] n 植物学 shokúbutsugàku

botch [batʃ] vt (bungle: also: **botch up**) 不手際で...をしくじる futégiwa de ...wo shikújirū

both [bouθ] adj 両方の ryóhō no
◆pron (things, people) 両方 ryóhō
◆adv: **both A and B** AもBも A mo B mo
both of us went, we both went 私たち2人共行きました watákushitachi futáritomo ikímashita

bother [baðˈəːr] vt (worry) 心配させる shiñpai saséru; (disturb) ...に迷惑を掛ける ...ni méiwaku wo kakérū
◆vi (also: **bother oneself**) ...に気付かう ...ni kízúkaù
◆n (trouble) 迷惑 méiwaku; (nuisance) いやな事 iyá na kotó
to bother doing わざわざ...する wáza-waza ...surú

bottle [batˈəl] n (container: for milk, wine, perfume etc) 瓶 bfñ; (of wine, whiskey etc) ボトル botôru; (amount contained) 瓶一杯分 ippái bfñ; (baby's) ほ乳瓶 ho-nyūbin
◆vt (beer, wine) 瓶に詰める bfñ ni tsumérū

bottleneck [batˈəlnek] n (AUT: also fig: of supply) ネック nékkù

bottle-opener [batˈəloupənəːr] n 栓抜き sefinukî

bottle up vt (emotion) 抑える osáerū

bottom [batˈəm] n (of container, sea etc) 底 sokó; (buttocks) しり shirf; (of page, list) 一番下の所 ichfban shitá no tokóro; (of class) びり bfrí
◆adj (lower: part) 下の方の shitá no hó no; (last: rung, position) 一番下の ichfban shitá no

bottomless [batˈəmlis] adj (funds, store) 際限のない saígeñ no nai

bough [bau] n 枝 edá

bought [bɔt] pt, pp of **buy**

boulder [boulˈdəːr] n 大きな丸石 ókinà marúishi

bounce [bauns] vi (ball) 跳ね返る hané-

kaèru; (check) 不渡りになる fuwátàri ni narú
♦vt (ball) 弾ませる hanésaserù
♦n (rebound) 跳ね返る事 hanékaeru kotò

bouncer [baun'sə:r] (inf) n (at dance, club) 用心棒 yōjínbō

bound [baund] pt, pp of bind
♦n (leap) 一飛び hitótòbi; (gen pl: limit) 限界 gefkai
♦vi (leap) 跳ぶ tobú
♦vt (border) ...の境界になる ...no kyōkai ni narú
♦adj: bound by (law, regulation) ...に拘束されている ...ni kósoku sarété irú
to be bound to do something (obliged) やむを得ず ...しなければならない yamú wo ezú ...shinákereba naranaí; (likely) 必ず...するだろう kanárazu ...surú darō
bound for (NAUT, AUT, RAIL) ...行き の ...yukí no
out of bounds (fig: place) 立入禁止で tachífirikinshi de

boundary [baun'dæ:ri] n (border, limit) 境界 kyōkai

boundless [baund'lis] adj (energy etc) 果てし無い hatéshinaí

bouquet [boukei'] n (of flowers) 花束 hanátàba, ブーケ búke

bourgeois [bur'ʒwɑ:] adj ブルジョア根性 の búrùjoakonjō no

bout [baut] n (of malaria etc) 発作 hossà; (of activity) 発作的にする事 hossáteki ni surú kotò; (BOXING etc) 試合 shiái

boutique [bu:ti:k'] n ブティック butíkku

bow[1] [bou] n (knot) チョウ結び chōmusùbi; (weapon, MUS) 弓 yumí

bow[2] [bau] n (of the head and body) お辞儀 ojígi; (NAUT: also: bows) 船首 sénshu, へ先 hesáki
♦vi (with head) 会釈する éshàku suru; (with head and body) お辞儀する ojígi suru; (yield): to bow to/before (reason, pressure) ...に屈服する ...ni kuppúku suru

bowels [bau'əlz] npl (ANAT) 腸 chō; (of the earth etc) 深い所 fukái tokóro

bowl [boul] n (container) 鉢 hachf, ボール bōru; (contents) ボール一杯 bōru ippái; (ball) 木球 mokkyū, ボール bōru
♦vi (CRICKET) 投球する tōkyū suru

bow-legged [bou'legid] adj がにまたの ganímata no

bowler [bou'lə:r] n (CRICKET) 投手 tōshu, ボウラー bōra; (BRIT: also: bowler hat) 山高帽 yamátakabō

bowling [bou'liŋ] n (game) ボーリング bōringu

bowling alley n (building) ボーリング場 bōringujō; (track) レーン rēn

bowling green n ローンボーリング場 rōnbōringujō

bowls [boulz] n (game) ローンボーリング rōnbōringu

bow tie n チョウネクタイ chōnekùtai

box [bɑ:ks] n (gen) 箱 hakó; (also: cardboard box) 段ボール箱 dañbōrubàko; (THEATER) ボックス bókkùsu
♦vt (put in a box) 箱に詰める hakó ni tsumérù
♦vi (SPORT) ボクシングする bókùshingu suru

boxer [bɑ:k'sə:r] n (person) ボクシング選手 bókùshingu sénshu, ボクサー bókùsā

boxing [bɑ:k'siŋ] n (SPORT) ボクシング bókùshingu

Boxing Day (BRIT) n ボクシングデー bókùshingudè

boxing gloves npl ボクシンググローブ bókùshingugurōbu

boxing ring n リング ríñgu

box office n 切符売り場 kippú uríba

boxroom [bɑ:ks'ru:m] n 納戸 nañdo

boy [bɔi] n (young) 少年 shōnen, 男の子 otóko no ko; (older) 青年 sefnen; (son) 息子 musúko

boycott [bɔi'kɑ:t] n ボイコット bofkottò
♦vt (person, product, place etc) ボイコットする bofkottò suru

boyfriend [bɔi'frend] n 男友達 otókotomòdachi, ボーイフレンド bōifurèndo

boyish [bɔi'iʃ] adj (man) 若々しい wakáwakashiì; (looks, smile, woman) 少年の様な shōnen no yō na

B.R. [bi:ɑ:r] n abbr = **British Rail**

bra [brɑ:] n ブラジャー burájà

brace [breis] n (on teeth) 固定器 kotéíki、ブレース burêsu; (tool) 曲り柄ドリル magáridorìru
♦vt (knees, shoulders) ...に力を入れる ...ni chikára wo iréru
to brace oneself (for weight) 構えて待つ kamáete matsù; (for shock) 心を静めて待つ kokóro wo shizúmete matsù

bracelet [breis'lit] n 腕輪 udéwa、ブレスレット burésurètto

braces [brei'siz] (BRIT) npl ズボンつり zubóntsuri、サスペンダー sasúpendà

bracing [brei'sɪŋ] adj (air, breeze) さわやかな sawáyàka na

bracken [bræk'ən] n ワラビ warábi

bracket [bræk'it] n (TECH) 腕金 udégane; (group) グループ gurûpu; (range) 層 sò; (also: **brace bracket**) 中括弧 chúkakkò; (also: ブレース burêsu) (also: **round bracket**) 小括弧 shókakkò、丸括弧 marúkakkò、パーレン pären; (also: **square bracket**) かぎ括弧 kagíkakkò
♦vt (word, phrase) ...に括弧を付ける ...ni kakkò wo tsükerù

brag [bræg] vi 自慢する jimán suru

braid [breid] n (trimming) モール mòru; (of hair) お下げ o-ságe

Braille [breil] n 点字 tenji

brain [brein] n (ANAT) 脳 nò; (fig) 頭脳 zunò

brainchild [brein'tʃaild] n (project) 発案 hatsúan; (invention) 発明 hatsúmei

brains [breinz] npl (CULIN) 脳みそ nò misò; (intelligence) 頭脳 zunò

brainwash [brein'wɑ:ʃ] vt 洗脳する sennò suru

brainwave [brein'weiv] n 脳波 nòha

brainy [brei'ni:] adj (child) 頭の良い atáma no yoì

braise [breiz] vt (CULIN) いためてから煮込む itámete karà nikómù

brake [breik] n (AUT) 制動装置 seídosòchi、ブレーキ burèki; (fig) 歯止め hadóme
♦vi ブレーキを掛ける burèki wo kakérù

brake fluid n ブレーキ液 burèkièki

brake light n ブレーキライト burèkiraìto

bramble [bræm'bəl] n (bush) イバラ ibára

bran [bræn] n ふすま fusúma

branch [bræntʃ] n (of tree) 枝 edá; (COMM) 支店 shíten

branch out vi (fig): *to branch out into* ...に手を広げる ...ni te wo hirógeru

brand [brænd] n (trademark: also: **brand name**) 銘柄 meígara、ブランド burándo; (fig: type) 種類 shúrùi
♦vt (cattle) 焼印 yakfìn

brandish [bræn'diʃ] vt (weapon) 振り回す furímawasù

brand-new [brænd'nu:'] adj 真新しい maátarashiì

brandy [bræn'di:] n ブランデー burándè

brash [bræʃ] adj (forward, cheeky) ずうずうしい zúzùshiì

brass [bræs] n (metal) 真ちゅう shinchū
the brass (MUS) 金管楽器 kiñkangakki

brass band n 吹奏楽団 sufsògakùdan、ブラスバンド burásubañdo

brassiere [brazir'] n ブラジャー burájà

brat [bræt] (pej) n (child) がき gakì

bravado [brava:'dou] n 空威張り karáibàri

brave [breiv] adj (attempt, smile, action) 勇敢な yūkan na
♦vt (face up to) ...に立ち向う ...ni tachímukaò

bravery [brei'va:ri:] n 勇気 yūki

bravo [bra'vou] excl ブラボー burábò

brawl [brɔ:l] n (in pub, street) けんか keñka

brawny [brɔ:'ni:] adj (arms etc) たくましい takúmashiì

bray [brei] n (donkey) 鳴く nakú

brazen [brei'zən] adj (woman) ずうずうしい zúzùshiì; (lie, accusation) 厚かましい atsúkamashiì
♦vt: *to brazen it out* 最後までしらばくれる saígo madé shirábakurerù

brazier [brei'ʒə:r] n (on building site etc) 野外用簡易暖房 yagáiyò kañ-i dañbo

Brazil [brəzil'] n ブラジル burájiru

Brazilian [brəzil'jən] adj ブラジルの burájiru no

♦ンブラジル人 burájirujîn

breach [briːtʃ] *vt* (of defence, wall) 突破する toppá suru

♦*n* (gap) 突破口 toppákǒ; (breaking):
breach of contract 契約不履行 kefyakufuríkǒ

breach of the peace 治安妨害 chiánbǒgai

bread [bred] *n* (food) パン pán

bread and butter *n* バターを塗ったパ
ンbátá wo nuttá pán; (*fig*: source of income) 金づる kanézuru

breadbox [ˈbredbɑːks] (*BRIT* **breadbin**)
n パン入れ pán-ire

breadcrumbs [ˈbredkrʌmz] *npl* (*gen*) パ
んくず pañkúzu; (*CULIN*) パン粉 pañko

breadline [ˈbredlaɪn] *n*: *on the breadline* 貧しい mazúshiǐ

breadth [bredθ] *n* (of cloth etc) 幅 habá;
(*fig*: of knowledge, subject) 広さ hírosa

breadwinner [ˈbredwɪnəːr] *n* (in family)
稼ぎ手 kaségite

break [breɪk] (*pt* **broke**, *pp* **broken**) *vt*
(cup, glass) 割る warú; (stick, leg, arm)
折る orú; (machine etc) 壊す kowásù;
(promise, law, record) 破る yabúrù;
(journey) 中断する chúdan suru

♦*vi* (crockery) 割れる waréru; (stick,
arm, leg) 折れる oréru; (machine etc) 壊
れる kowáreru; (storm) 起る okórù;
(weather) 変る kawárù; (story, news) 報
道される hódo saréru; (dawn): *dawn
breaks* 夜が明ける yo ga akéru

♦*n* (gap: in wall etc) 途切れた所 togíréta tokóro;
(fracture: *gen*) 骨折 kossétsu; (of limb) 骨
折 kossétsu; (pause for rest) 休憩 kyúke-
i; (at school) 休み時間 yasúmijikàn;
(chance) チャンス chánsu

to break the news to someone ...に知
らせる ...ni shiráseru

to break even (*COMM*) 収支がとんとん
になる shúshi ga tofiton ni narù

to break free/loose (person, animal) 逃
出す nigédasu

to break open (door etc) ...を壊して開け
る ...wo kowáshite akéru

breakage [ˈbreɪkɪdʒ] *n* (act of breaking)

壊す事 kowásù kotó; (object broken) 損
傷 sofishǒ

break down *vt* (figures, data) 分析する
buñseki suru

♦*vi* (machine, car) 故障する kosho suru;
(person) 取乱す torímidasù; (talks) 物別
れになる monówakàre ni narù

breakdown [ˈbreɪkdaun] *n* (*AUT*) 故障
koshǒ; (in communications) 中断 chúdan;
(of marriage) 破たん hatán; (*MED*: *also*:
nervous breakdown) 神経衰弱 shiñkei-
suljaku; (of statistics) 分析 buñseki

breakdown van (*BRIT*) *n* レッカー車
rékkǎsha

breaker [ˈbreɪkəːr] *n* (wave) 白波 shirá-
nami

breakfast [ˈbrekfəst] *n* 朝ご飯 asá gohàn,
朝食 chǒshoku

break in *vt* (horse etc) 慣らす narásù

♦*vi* (burglar) 押入る oshírù; (interrupt)
割込む waríkomù

break-in [ˈbreɪkin] *n* 押入り oshíri

breaking and entering [ˈbreɪkiŋ-
ænd ˈentəːrɪŋ] *n* (*LAW*) 不法侵入 fuhǒ-
shíñ-nyú

break into *vt fus* (house) ...に押入る
...ni oshírù

break off *vi* (branch) 折れる oréru;
(speaker) 話を中断する hanáshi wo chúdan suru

break out *vi* (begin: war) ぼっ発する
boppátsu suru; (: fight) 始まる hajímaru;
(escape: prisoner) 脱出する dasshútsu
suru

to break out in spots/a rash にきび
（湿しん）になる níkibi(shisshín) ni narù

breakthrough [ˈbreɪkθruː] *n* (*fig*: in
technology etc) 躍進 yakúshin

break up *vi* (ship) 分解する buñkai suru;
(crowd, meeting) 解散する kaísan suru;
(marriage) 離婚に終る rikón ni owáru;
(*SCOL*) 終る yamésaru

♦*vt* (rocks, biscuit etc) 割る warú; (fight
etc) やめさせる yaméssaseru

breakwater [ˈbreɪkwɔːtəːr] *n* 防波堤 bǒ-
hatei

breast [brest] *n* (of woman) 乳房 chífusa;
(chest) 胸 muné; (of meat) 胸肉 muné-

nĭkù

breast-feed [brest'fĭːd] (*pt, pp* **breast-fed**) *vt* ...に母乳を飲ませる ...ni bonyū wo nomáserù
♦*vi* 子供に母乳を飲ませる kodómo ni bonyū wo nomáserù

breaststroke [brest'strouk] *n* 平泳ぎ hirăoyŏgì

breath [breθ] *n* 息 íkì
out of breath 息を切らせて íkì wo kirásete

Breathalyser [breθ'əlaizər] ® *n* 酒気検査器 shukkíkensakì

breathe [briːð] *vt* 呼吸する kokyū suru
♦*vi* 呼吸する kokyū suru

breathe in *vt* 吸込む sufkomù
♦*vi* 息を吸込む íkì wo sufkomù

breathe out *vt* 吐出す hakídasu
♦*vi* 息を吐く íkì wo hakídasu

breather [briː'ðər] *n* (*break*) 休憩 kyūkei

breathing [briː'ðiŋ] *n* 呼吸 kokyū

breathless [breθ'lis] *adj* (*from exertion*) 息を切らせている íkì wo kirásete irù; (*MED*) 呼吸困難の kokyūkoñnan no

breathtaking [breθ'teikiŋ] *adj* (*speed*) 息が止る様な íkì ga tomáru yṓ na; (*view*) 息を飲むようなさ ga nomù yṓ na

bred [bred] *pt, pp of* **breed**

breed [briːd] (*pt, pp* **bred**) *vt* (*animals*) 繁殖させる hañshoku saséru; (*plants*) 栽培する saíbai suru
♦*vi* (*ZOOL*) 繁殖する hañshoku suru
♦*n* (*ZOOL*) 品種 hĭnshu; (*type, class*) 種類 shūrùi

breeding [briː'diŋ] *n* (*upbringing*) 育ち sodáchi

breeze [briːz] *n* そよ風 soyókàze

breezy [briː'ziː] *adj* (*manner, tone*) 快活な kafkatsu na; (*weather*) 風の多い kazé no ōi

brevity [brev'iti] *n* (*shortness, conciseness*) 簡潔さ kañketsusa

brew [bruː] *vt* (*tea*) 入れる iréru; (*beer*) 醸造する jṓzō suru
♦*vi* (*storm*) 起ろうとしている okórṓ to shité irù; (*fig: trouble, a crisis*) 迫っている

せ mátte irù

brewery [bruː'əri] *n* 醸造所 jṓzōshò

bribe [braib] *n* 賄ろ waîro
♦*vt* (*person, witness*) 買収する baíshū suru

bribery [brai'bəriː] *n* (*with money, favors*) 贈賄 zṓwai

bric-a-brac [brik'əbræk] *n* 置き物類 okímonorùi

brick [brik] *n* (*for building*) れんが réñga

bricklayer [brik'leiər] *n* れんが職人 reñgashokùnin

bridal [braid'əl] *adj* (*gown*) 花嫁の hanáyòme no; (*suite*) 新婚者の shiñkoñsha no

bride [braid] *n* 花嫁 hanáyòme, 新婦 shiñpu

bridegroom [braid'gruːm] *n* 花婿 hanámùko, 新郎 shiñrṓ

bridesmaid [braidz'meid] *n* 新婦付き添いの女性 shiñputsukísòi no joséi

bridge [bridʒ] *n* (TECH, ARCHIT) 橋 hashf; (NAUT) 船橋 señkyō, ブリッジ burijjī; (CARDS, DENTISTRY) ブリッジ burijjī
♦*vt* (*fig: gap, gulf*) 埋める umérū
bridge of the nose 鼻柱 hanábashira

bridle [braid'l] *n* くつわ kutsúwa

bridle path *n* 乗馬用の道 jōbayō no michī

brief [briːf] *adj* (*period of time, description, speech*) 短い mijíkàI
♦*n* (LAW) 事件摘要書 jikéntekiyòsho; (*gen: task*) 任務 nĭnmu
♦*vt* (*inform*) ...に情報を与える ...ni shiji wo atérù

briefcase [briːf'keis] *n* かばん kabáñ, ブリーフケース burîfukèsu

briefing [briː'fiŋ] *n* (*gen*, PRESS) 説明 setsúmei

briefly [briː'fliː] *adv* (*smile, glance*) ちらっと chiráttò; (*explain, say*) 短く mijíkakù

briefs [briːfs] *npl* (*for men*) パンツ pañtsu, ブリーフ burîfu; (*for women*) パンティー pañtī, ショーツ shṓtsu

brigade [brigeid'] *n* (MIL) 旅団 ryodáñ

brigadier [brigədiər'] *n* (MIL) 准将 juñshō

bright [brait] *adj* (gen) 明るい akárui; (person, idea: clever) 利口な rikó na; (person: lively) 明るい mefró na

brighten [brait'ən] (*also*: **brighten up**) *vt* (room) 明るくする akáruku suru; (event) 楽しくする tanóshíkù suru
◆*vi* 明るくなる akáruku narú

brilliance [bril'jəns] *n* (of light) 明るさ akárusa; (of talent, skill) 素晴らしさ subárashísà

brilliant [bril'jənt] *adj* (person, idea) 天才な tensaiteki na; (smile, career) 輝かしい kagáyakashíì; (sunshine, light) 輝く kagáyakù; (BRIT: *inf*: holiday etc) 素晴らしい subárashíi

brim [brim] *n* (of cup etc) 縁 fuchí; (of hat) つば tsúba

brine [brain] *n* (CULIN) 塩水 shiómízu

bring [briŋ] (*pt, pp* **brought**) *vt* (thing) 持って来る motté kurú; (person) 連れて来る tsurété kurú; (*fig*: satisfaction) もたらす motárasù; (trouble) 起す okósù

bring about *vt* (cause) 起こす okósù

bring back *vt* (restore: hanging etc) 復帰させる fukkí saséru; (return: thing, person) 持って〔連れて〕帰る motté〔tsurété〕kaérù

bring down *vt* (government) 倒す taósù; (MIL: plane) 撃墜する gekítsui suru; (price) 下げる sagérù

bring forward *vt* (meeting) 繰り上げる kurfagérù; (proposal) 提案する teían suru

bring off *vt* (task, plan) ...に成功する ...ni sefkó suru

bring out *vt* (gun) 取出す torídasù; (meaning) 明らかにする akfráka ni suru; (publish, produce: book) 出版する shuppán suru; (: album) 発表する happyṓ suru

bring round *vt* (unconscious person) 正気付かせる shókizukaserù

bring up *vt* (carry up) 上に持って来る〔行く〕ue ni motté kurú〔ikú〕; (educate: person) 育てる sodáterù; (question, subject) 持出す mochídasù; (vomit: food) 吐く hakú

brink [briŋk] *n* (of disaster, war etc) 瀬戸際 setógiwa

brisk [brisk] *adj* (tone, person) きびきびした kíbíkibi shitá; (pace) 早い hayáì; (trade) 盛んな sakán na

bristle [bris'əl] *n* (animal hair, hair of beard) 剛毛 gṓmō; (of brush) 毛 ke
◆*vi* (in anger) 怒る okórù

Britain [brit'ən] *n* (*also*: **Great Britain**) 英国 efkoku, イギリス igírisu ◇イングランド, スコットランド, ウェールズを含む figurando, sukóttorando, uéruzu wo fukúmù

British [brit'iʃ] *adj* 英国の efkoku no, イギリスの igírisu no
◆*npl*: **the British** 英国人 efkokujîn, イギリス人 igírisujîn

British Isles *npl*: **the British Isles** イギリス諸島 igírisushotṓ

British Rail *n* 英国国有鉄道 efkoku kokúyū tetsúdō

Briton [brit'ən] *n* 英国人 efkokujîn, イギリス人 igírisujîn

brittle [brit'əl] *adj* (fragile: glass etc) 割れやすい waréyasuî; (: bones etc) もろい moróì

broach [brout] *vt* (subject) 持出す mochídasu

broad [brɔːd] *adj* (street, shoulders, smile, range) 広い hirói; (general: outlines, distinction etc) 大まかな ōmaká na; (accent) 強い tsuyóì
in broad daylight 真っ昼間に mappírúma ni

broadcast [brɔːd'kæst] *n* (TV, RADIO) 放送 hṓsō
◆*vb* (*pt, pp* **broadcast**)
◆*vt* (TV, RADIO) 放送する hṓsō suru; (TV) 放映する hṓei suru
◆*vi* (TV, RADIO) 放送する hṓsō suru

broaden [brɔːd'ən] *vt* (scope, appeal) 広くする hírōku suru; (river) 広くなる hírōku narú, 広がる hírōgaru
to broaden one's mind 心を広くする kokóro wo hirốku suru

broadly [brɔːd'liː] *adv* (in general terms) 大まかに ōmaká ni

broad-minded [brɔːd'main'did] *adj* 心の広い kokóro no hirói

broccoli [brəˈkɒliː] *n* (BOT, CULIN) ブ
ロッコリー burókkòrī

brochure [brəʊˈʃʊəʳ] *n* (booklet) 小冊子
shōsasshì, パンフレット pánfuretto

broil [brɔɪl] *vt* (CULIN) じか火で焼く ji-
kábi de yakú

broke [brəʊk] *pt of* **break**

♦*adj* (*inf*: person, company) 無一文にな
った mufchimòn ni nattá

broken [brəʊˈkən] *pp of* **break**

♦*adj* (window, cup etc) 割れた waréta,
(machine: *also*: **broken down**) 壊れた
kowáréta

a broken leg 脚の骨折 ashí no kossetsú

in broken English/Japanese 片言の英
語(日本語)で katákoto no efgo(nihóngo)de

broken-hearted [brəʊˈkɑːrˈtid] *adj* 悲
嘆に暮れた hitán ni kuréta

broker [brəʊˈkəʳ] *n* (COMM: in shares)
証券ブローカー shōken burōkà, (: insurance broker) 保険代理人 hokén dairinin

brolly [brɒˈliː] (BRIT: *inf*) *n* 傘 kása

bronchitis [brɒŋkaˈitis] *n* 気管支炎 ki-
kánshìen

bronze [brɒnz] *n* (metal) 青銅 sefdō, (ブ
ロンズ burónzu; (sculpture) 銅像 dōzō

brooch [brəʊtʃ] *n* ブローチ burōchi

brood [bruːd] *n* (of birds) 一腹のひな hitóhara no hiná

♦*vi* (person) くよくよする kuyókuyo suru

brook [brʊk] *n* 小川 ogawa

broom [bruːm] *n* (for cleaning) ほうき
hōki, (BOT) エニシダ enfshida

broomstick [bruːmstik] *n* ほうきの柄
hōki no e

Bros. *abbr* (= **brothers**) 兄弟 kyōdai

broth [brɒθ] *n* (CULIN) スープ sūpu

brothel [brɒˈθəl] *n* 売春宿 baíshun-yadò

brother [brʌðˈəʳ] *n* (*also*: **older brother**) 兄 anī, 兄 ani nĩsan; (*also*: **younger brother**) 弟 otōtò; (REL) 修道士 shūdōshi

brother-in-law [brʌðˈəɪnlɔː] (*pl* **brothers-in-law**) *n* (older) 義理の兄 girí no anĩ; (younger) 義理の弟 girí no otōtò

brought [brɔːt] *pt, pp of* **bring**

brow [braʊ] *n* (forehead) 額 hitái; (rare: *gen*: eyebrow) まゆ mayù; (of hill) 頂上 chōjō

brown [braʊn] *adj* (color) 褐色の kasshō-ku no, 茶色の chafro no; (tanned) 日焼けした hiyáke shità

♦*n* (color) 褐色 kasshóku, 茶色 chafro

♦*vt* (CULIN) ...に焼き目を付ける ...ni ya-kíme wo tsukérù

brown bread *n* 黒パン kurópan

brownie [braʊˈniː] *n* (Brownie guide) ブラウニー burániì ◇ガールスカウトの幼年団員 gắrusukaùto no yốnendàn - in; (US: cake) チョコレートクッキーの一種 chokórētokukkī no isshú

brown paper *n* クラフト紙 kuráfutoshì

brown sugar *n* 赤砂糖 akázatō

browse [braʊz] *vi* (through book) 拾い読みする hiróiyomi suru; (in shop) 商品を見て回る shốhin wo mitè mawárù

bruise [bruːz] *n* (on face etc) 打撲傷 da-bōkushò, あざ azá

♦*vt* (person) ...に打撲傷を与える ...ni da-bōkushò wo atáerù

brunch [brʌntʃ] *n* ブランチ buránchi

brunette [bruˈnet] *n* (woman) ブルネット burúnettò

brunt [brʌnt] *n*: *to bear the brunt of* (attack, criticism) ...の矢面に立つ ...no yaómòte ni tatsù

brush [brʌʃ] *n* (for cleaning, shaving etc) ブラシ buráshi; (for painting etc) 刷毛 haké; (artist's) 筆 fudé, 絵筆 efúde; (quar-rel) 小競り合い kozeríai

♦*vt* (sweep etc) ...にブラシを掛ける ...ni búrashi wo kakérù; (clean: teeth etc) 磨く migáku; (groom) ブラシでとかす bú-rashi de tokásù; (*also*: **brush against**: person, object) ...に触れる ...ni furérù

brush aside *vt* (emotion, criticism) 無視する mushí suru

brush up *vt* (subject, language) 復習する fukúshū suru

brushwood [brʌʃˈwud] *n* (sticks) しば shibá

brusque [brʌsk] *adj* (person, manner) 無愛想な buáisò na; (apology) ぶっきらぼうな bukkírabò na

Brussels [brʌs'əlz] n ブリュッセル buryússèru

Brussels sprout n メキャベツ mekyábetsu

brutal [bruːt'əl] adj (person, actions) 残忍な zańnin na; (honesty, frankness) 厳しい程の kíbìshiì hodō no

brutality [bruːtæl'iti:] n 残忍さ zańnìnsa

brute [bruːt] n (person) 人でなし hitódènashi, けだもの kedámono; (animal) 獣 kemóno
♦adj: by brute force 暴力で bóryoku de

B.Sc. [biːessiː'] abbr = Bachelor of Science

bubble [bʌb'əl] n (in liquid, soap) 泡 awá; (of soap etc) シャボン玉 shabóndama
♦vi (liquid) 沸く wakú; (: sparkle) 泡立つ awádatsù

bubble bath n 泡風呂 awáburo

bubble gum n 風船ガム fǘsengamù

buck [bʌk] n (rabbit) 雄ウサギ osúusàgi; (deer) 雄ジカ ojíka; (US: inf: dollar) ドル dórù
♦vi (horse) 乗手を振り落そうとする norfte wo furótosò ni suru
to pass the buck (to someone) (...に) 責任をなすり付ける (...ni) sekínin wo nasúritsukerù

bucket [bʌk'it] n (pail) バケツ bakétsu; (contents) バケツ一杯 bakétsu ippái

buckle [bʌk'əl] n (on shoe, belt) バックル bakkúru
♦vt (shoe, belt) ...のバックルを締める ...no bakkúru wo shimérù
♦vi (wheel) 曲がる yugámu; (bridge, support) 崩れる kuzúrerù

buck up vi (cheer up) 元気を出す génki wo dasù

bud [bʌd] n (of tree, plant, flower) 芽 me
♦vi 芽を出す me wo dasù

Buddhism [buː'dizəm] n (REL) 仏教 bukkyó

budding [bʌd'iŋ] adj (actor, entrepreneur) 有望な yūbō na

buddy [bʌd'i:] n (US) (= friend) 相棒 afbō

budge [bʌdʒ] vt (object) ちょっと動かす chóttò ugókasù; (fig: person) 譲歩させる jóhò saserú
♦vi (object, person) ちょっと動く chóttò ugóku; (fig: person) 譲歩する jóhò suru

budgerigar [bʌdʒ'ərigaːr] n セキセイインコ sekíseiìnko

budget [bʌdʒ'it] n (person's, government's) 予算 yosán, 予算案 yosán-an
♦vi: *to budget for something* ...を予算案に入れる ...wo yosán-an ni iréru
I'm on a tight budget 台所が苦しい dáídokoro ga kúrushiī

budgie [bʌdʒ'iː] n = **budgerigar**

buff [bʌf] adj (color: envelope) 薄茶色 usúchairo
♦n (inf: enthusiast) マニア mánia

buffalo [bʌf'əlou] n (pl **buffalo** or **buffaloes**) (BRIT) スイギュウ sufgyū; (US: bison) バイソン báison

buffer [bʌf'əːr] n (COMPUT) バッファ báffà; (RAIL) 緩衝機 kańshòki

buffet[1] [bufei'] (BRIT) n (in station) ビュッフェ byúffe; (food) 立食 risshóku

buffet[2] [bʌf'it] vt (subj: wind, sea) もみ揺さぶる momíyusaburù

buffet car (BRIT) n (RAIL) ビュッフェ車 byuffésha

bug [bʌg] n (esp US: insect) 虫 mushí; (COMPUT: of program) バグ bágù; (fig: germ) 風邪 kazé; (hidden microphone) 盗聴器 tóchiki
♦vt (inf: annoy) 怒らせる okóraserù; (room, telephone etc) ...に盗聴器を付ける ...ni tóchòki wo tsukérù

buggy [bʌg'iː] n (baby buggy) 乳母車 ubágurùma

bugle [bjuː'gəl] n (MUS) らっぱ rappá

build [bild] n (of person) 体格 taíkaku
♦vb (pt, pp **built**)
♦vt (house etc) 建てる tatérù, 建築する keńchiku suru; (machine, cage etc) 作る tsukérù

builder [bil'dəːr] n (contractor) 建築業者 keńchikugyōsha

building [bil'diŋ] n (industry, construction) 建築業 keńchikugyò; (structure) 建物 tatémonò, ビル bírù

building society (BRIT) n 住宅金融組合 jútakukin-yukumìai

build up vt (forces, production) 増やす fuyásù; (morale) 高める takámerù; (stocks) 蓄積する chikúseki suru

♦adj: **built-in** (oven, wardrobes etc) 作り付けの tsukúritsuke no

built-up area [bilt'ʌp-] n 市街化区域 shigáikakúiki

bulb [bʌlb] n (BOT) 球根 kyúkon; (ELEC) 電球 deñkyū

Bulgaria [bʌlɡeːr'iːə] n ブルガリア burúgaria

Bulgarian [bʌlɡeːr'iːən] adj ブルガリアの burúgaria no
♦n ブルガリア人 burúgariajìn

bulge [bʌldʒ] n (bump) 膨らみ fukúrami
♦vi (pocket, file, cheeks etc) 膨らむ fukúramu

bulk [bʌlk] n (mass: of thing) 巨大な姿 kyodái na sugàta; (: of person) 巨体 kyotái

in bulk (COMM) 大口で ōguchi de

the bulk of (most of) ...の大半 ...no taíhan

bulky [bʌl'kiː] adj (parcel) かさばった kasábattà; (equipment) 大きくて扱いにくい ōkikùte atsúkainikuì

bull [bul] n (ZOOL) 雄牛 oúshi; (male elephant/whale) 雄 osú

bulldog [bul'dɔːɡ] n ブルドッグ burúdoggù

bulldozer [bul'douzəːr] n ブルドーザー burúdōzà

bullet [bul'it] n 弾丸, 弾 dañgan

bulletin [bul'itin] n (TV etc: news update) 速報 sokúhō; (journal) 会報 kaíhō, 紀要 kiyó

bulletproof [bul'itpruːf] adj (glass, vest, car) 防弾の bōdan no

bullfight [bul'fait] n 闘牛 tōgyū

bullfighter [bul'faitəːr] n 闘牛士 tōgyūshi

bullfighting [bul'faitiŋ] n 闘牛 tōgyū

bullhorn [bul'hɔːrn] (US) n ハンドマイク hañdomaìku

bullion [bul'jən] n (gold, silver) 地金 jigáne

bullock [bul'ək] n 去勢した雄牛 kyoséi

shita oúshi

bullring [bul'riŋ] n 闘牛場 tōgyūjō

bull's-eye [bulz'ai] n (on a target) 的の中心 matő no chūshin

bully [bul'iː] n 弱い者いじめ yowáimono-ijĭme
♦vt いじめる ijímeru

bum [bʌm] (inf) n (backside) shirí; (esp US: tramp) ルンペン ruñpen; (: good-for-nothing) ろくでなし rokúdenashi

bumblebee [bʌm'balbiː] n クマンバチ kumáñbachi

bump [bʌmp] n (in car: minor accident) 衝突 shōtotsu; (jolt) 衝撃 shōgeki; (swelling: on head) こぶ kobú; (on road) 段差 dańsa
♦vt (strike) ...にぶつかる ...ni butsúkaru

bumper [bʌm'pəːr] n (AUT) バンパー bañpā
♦adj: **bumper crop/harvest** 豊作 hōsaku

bumper cars npl (in amusement park) バンパーカー bañpākā

bump into vt fus (strike: obstacle) ...にぶつかる ...ni butsúkaru; (inf: meet: person) ...に出くわす ...ni dekúwasù

bumptious [bʌmp'ʃəs] adj (person) うぬぼれた unúboreta

bumpy [bʌm'piː] adj (road) 凸凹な dekóboko na

bun [bʌn] n (CULIN) ロールパン rōrupan, パン型 (of hair) まげ magé, シニヨン shíñyon

bunch [bʌntʃ] n (of flowers, keys) 束 tába; (of bananas) 房 fusá; (of people) グループ gúrūpu

bunches [bʌntʃ'iz] npl (in hair) 左右のポニーテール sáyū no poniték

bundle [bʌn'dəl] n (parcel: of clothes, samples etc) 包み tsutsúmi; (of sticks, papers) 束 tabá
♦vt (also: **bundle up**) 厚着させる atsúgi saséru; (put): **to bundle something/someone into** ...にほうり (押し込む ...ni hōri (oshí) komù

bungalow [bʌŋ'ɡəlou] n バンガロー bañgarō

bungle [bʌ́ŋɡəl] *vt* (job, assassination) ...にしくじる ...ni shikûjirù

bunion [bʌ́njən] *n* (MED) けん膜りゅう kefímakuryū, バニオン bánìon

bunk [bʌŋk] *n* (bed) 作り付けベッド tsukúritsukebèddo

bunk beds *npl* 二段ベッド nidánbeddo

bunker [bʌ́ŋkəːr] *n* (*also*: **coal bunker**) 石炭庫 sekftanko; (MIL) えんぺいごう eṅpéigō; (GOLF) バンカー bánkā

bunny [bʌ́niː] *n* (*also*: **bunny rabbit**) ウサちゃん usáchan

bunting [bʌ́ntiŋ] *n* (flags) 飾り小旗 kazárikobàta

buoy [búːiː] *n* (NAUT) ブイ buî

buoyant [bóiənt] *adj* (ship) 浮力のある fúryòku no arù; (economy, market) 活気のある kakkî no arù; (*fig*: person, nature) 朗らかな hogárāka na

buoy up (*fig*) 元気づける geńkizukerù

burden [bəːrdən] *n* (responsibility, worry) 負担 fután; (load) 荷物 nímotsu

♦*vt* (trouble): **to burden someone with** (oppress) ...を打明けて...に心配を掛ける ...wo uchfakete ...ni shiñpai wo kakérù

bureau [bjúròu] (*pl* **bureaus** *or* **bureaux**) *n* (BRIT: writing desk) 書き物机 kakímonozukùe ◆ふたの表に面になる机を指す futá ga kakô meñ ni narô tsukûe wo sasû; (US: chest of drawers) 整理だんす sefrídañsu; (office: government, travel, information) 局 kyókû, 課 ka

bureaucracy [bjurɑ́ːrəsiː] *n* (POL, COMM) 官僚制 kańryōsei

bureaucrat [bjúːrəkræt] *n* (administrator) 官僚 kańryō; (*pej*: pen-pusher) 小役人 koyákûnin

bureaus [bjúːrˈouz] *npl of* **bureau**

burglar [bəːrɡlər] *n* 押込み強盗 oshíkomigòtō

burglar alarm *n* 盗難警報機 tōnankeihōki

burglary [bəːrɡlərːiː] *n* (crime) 住居侵入罪 jūkyoshíñnyūzai

burial [bɛ́riəl] *n* 埋葬 maísō

burly [bəːrliː] *adj* (figure, workman etc) ごつい gotsuî

Burma [bəːrmə] *n* ビルマ bírùma

burn [bəːrn] (*pt*, *pp* **burned** *or* **burnt**) *vt* (papers, fuel etc) 燃やす moyásu; (toast, food etc) 焦がす kogásù; (house etc: arson) ...に放火する ...ni hōka suru

♦*vi* (house, wood etc) 燃える moérù; (cakes etc) 焦げる kogérù; (sting) ひりひりする hírìhiri suru

♦*n* やけど yakédo

burn down *vt* 全焼させる zefíshō saserù

burner [bəːrnər] *n* (on cooker, heater) 火口 hfgôchi, バーナー bánā

burning [bəːrniŋ] *adj* (house etc) 燃えている moéte irù; (sand) 焼ける様に熱い yakéru yō ni atsuî; (desert) しゃく熱の shakûnetsu no; (ambition) 熱烈な netsûretsu na

burnt [bəːrnt] *pt*, *pp of* **burn**

burrow [bəːrou] *n* (of rabbit etc) 巣穴 suâna

♦*vi* (dig) 掘る hôrù; (rummage) あさる asárù

bursary [bəːrsəriː] (BRIT) *n* (SCOL) 奨学金 shōgakukin

burst [bəːrst] (*pt*, *pp* **burst**) *vt* (bag, balloon, pipe etc) 破裂させる harétsu saséru; (subj: river: banks etc) 決壊させる kekkái saserù

♦*vi* (pipe, tire) 破裂する harétsu suru

♦*n* (*also*: **burst pipe**) 破裂した水道管 harétsu shita suídōkan

a burst of energy/speed/enthusiasm 突発的なエネルギー(スピード, 熱心さ) toppátsuteki na enérugī(supído, nesshfñsa)

a burst of gunfire 連射 refísha

to burst into flames 急に燃え出す kyū ni moédasù

to burst into tears 急に泣き出す kyū ni nakîdasù

to burst out laughing 急に笑い出す kyū ni waráidasù

to be bursting with (subj: room, container) はち切れんばかりに...で一杯になっている hachíkireñbakari ni ...de ippâi ni natté irù; (: person: emotion) …で胸が一杯になっている ...de muné ga ippâi ni natté irù

burst into *vt fus* (room etc) ...に飛込む

...ni tobîkomû

bury [bɛr'i:] vt (gen) 埋める umêru; (at funeral) 埋葬する maîsō suru

bus [bʌs] n (vehicle) バス básù

bush [buʃ] n (in garden) 低木 teîboku; (scrubland) 未開地 mikâichi, ブッシュ bússhû

to beat about the bush 遠回しに言う tômawàshi ni iú

bushy [buʃ'i:] adj (tail, hair, eyebrows) ふさふさした fúsàfusa shitá

busily [biz'ili:] adv (actively) 忙しく isôgashikù

business [biz'nis] n (matter, question) 問題 moñdai; (trading) 商売 shôbai; (firm) 会社 kaîsha; (occupation) 仕事 shigôto

to be away on business 出張して留守である shutchô shite rusû de arû

it's my business to ... ...するのは私の務めです ...surú no wa watákushi no tsutôme desù

it's none of my business 私の知った事じゃない watákushi no shittá kotô ja naî

he means business 彼は本気らしい kárè wa hoñki rashìi

businesslike [biz'nislaik] adj てきぱきした tekîpaki shitá

businessman [biz'nismæn] (pl **businessmen**) n 実業家 jitsûgyóka

business trip n 出張 shutchô

businesswoman [biz'niswumən] (pl **businesswomen**) n 女性実業家 joséijitsugyóka

busker [bʌs'kə:r] (BRIT) n 大道芸人 daîdōgeìnin

bus-stop [bʌs'sta:p] n バス停留所 básùtefuryûjo

bust [bʌst] n (ANAT) 乳房 chîbùsa, 胸 muné; (measurement) バスト básùto; (sculpture) 胸像 kyôzō

◆adj (inf: broken) 壊れた kowârèta

to go bust (company etc) つぶれる tsubûreru

bustle [bʌs'əl] n (activity) 雑踏 zattô

◆vi (person) 忙しく飛回る isôgashikù tobîmawarù

bustling [bʌs'liŋ] adj (town, place) にぎ

やかな nîgiyàka na

busy [biz'i:] adj (person) 忙しい isôgashiî; (shop, street) にぎやかな nîgiyàka na; (TEL: line) 話し中の hanáshichū no

◆vt: *to busy oneself with* 忙しそうに ...する isôgashisō ni ...suru

busybody [biz'i:ba:di:] n でしゃばり屋 deshábariya

busy signal (US) n (TEL) 話中音 wâchūon

KEYWORD

but [bʌt] conj 1 (yet) ...であるが ...de arû ga, ...であるけれども ...de arû keredomo, しかし shikâshì

he's not very bright, but he's hard-working 彼はあまり頭は良くないが、よく働きます kárè wa atáma wa yókùnai ga, yókù határakimasù

I'm tired and Paul isn't 私は疲れていますが、ポールは疲れていません watákushi wa tsukárète imasu ga, pôrù wa tsukárète imásèn

the trip was enjoyable but tiring 旅行は楽しかったけれども、疲れました ryokô wa tanôshikàtta keredomo, tsukáremashìta

2 (however) ...であるが ...de arû ga, ...であるけれども ...de arû keredomo, しかし shikâshì

I'd love to come, but I'm busy 行きたいが、今忙しいんです ikîtai ga, îma isôgashin desu

she wanted to go, but first she had to finish her homework 彼女は行きたかったけれども、先に宿題を終える必要がありました kánojð wa ikîtakàtta keredomo, sakî ni shukûdai wo shiâgeru hitsûyō ga arîmashìta

I'm sorry, but I don't agree 済みませんが、私は同意できません sumîmasèn ga, watákushi wa dôi dekimasèn

3 (showing disagreement, surprise etc) しかし shikâshì

but that's far too expensive! しかしそれは高過ぎますよ shikâshì sorê wa tákàsugimasù yo

but that's fantastic! しかし素晴らし

いじゃありませんか shikáshi subárashíi ja arímasén ka

♦*prep* (apart from, except) ...を除いて ...wo nozóite, ...以外に ...ígai ni

he was nothing but trouble 彼は厄介な問題ばかり起こしていました kárè wa yákkai na móndai bakári okóshìte imáshìta

we've had nothing but trouble 厄介な問題ばかり起っています yákkai na móndai bakári okótte imásu

none but him can do it 彼を除けば出来る人はいません kárè wo nozókèba dekírù hito wa imásén

who but a lunatic would do such a thing? 気違いを除けばそんな事をする人はいないでしょう kichígai wo nozókèba sónna koto wò suru hito wà inái deshō

but for you あなたがいなかったら anátà ga inákàttara

but for your help あなたが助けてくれなかったら anátà ga tasúkètè kurénakàttara

I'll do anything but that それ以外な ら何でもします soré igái nara nán de mo shimasú

♦*adv* (just, only) ただ tádà, ...だけ ...dáké, ...しか...ない ...shika ...nai

she's but a child 彼女はほんの子供です kánojò wa hón no kódòmo desú

had I but known 私がそれを知っていたら watákushi ga soré wo shitte saè itárà

I can but try やってみるしかありません yátte mirù shika arímasén

all but finished もう少しで出来上りです mō sukoshì de dekíagari desū

butcher [butʃ'əːr] *n* (tradesman) 肉屋 nikúyà

♦*vt* (cattle etc for meat) と殺する tosátsu suru; (prisoners etc) 虐殺する gyakúsatsu suru

butcher's (shop) [butʃ'əːrz-] *n* 精肉店 seínikutèn, 肉屋 nikúyà

butler [bʌt'ləːr] *n* 執事 shítjì

butt [bʌt] *n* (large barrel) たる tarú; (of

pistol) 握り nigírì; (of rifle) 床尾 shōbì; (of cigarette) 吸い殻 suígara; (*fig:* target: of teasing, criticism etc) 的 mató

♦*vt* (subj: goat, person) 頭で突く atáma de tsukú

butter [bʌt'əːr] *n* (CULIN) バター bátā

♦*vt* (bread) ...にバターを塗る ...ni bátā wo nurú

buttercup [bʌt'əːrkʌp] *n* キンポウゲ kiñpòge

butterfly [bʌt'əːrflai] *n* (insect) チョウチョ chōchò; (SWIMMING: *also:* butterfly stroke) バタフライ bátāfurai

butt in *vi* (interrupt) ...に割込む ...ni wa-ríkomù

buttocks [bʌt'əks] *npl* (ANAT) しり shirí

button [bʌt'ən] *n* (on clothes) ボタン botán; (on machine) 押しボタン oshíbotàn; (*US:* badge) バッジ bájjì

♦*vt* (*also:* button up) ...のボタンをはめる ...no botán wo haméru

♦*vi* ボタンで止まる botán de tomáru

buttress [bʌt'ris] *n* (ARCHIT) 控え壁 hikáekàbe

buxom [bʌk'səm] *adj* (woman) 胸の豊かな kané no yútàka na

buy [bai] (*pt, pp* bought) *vt* 買う kaú

♦*n* (purchase) 買物 kaímono

to buy someone something/something for someone ...に...を買って上げる ...ni ...wo katté agéru

to buy something from someone ...から...を買う ...kará ...wo kaú

to buy someone a drink ...に酒をおごる ...ni saké wo ogóru

buyer [bai'əːr] *n* (purchaser) 買手 kaíte; (COMM) 仕入係 shiíregakàri, バイヤー báiyā

buzz [bʌz] *n* (noise: of insect) ぶんぶんという音 buñbun to iú otó; (: of machine etc) うなり unári; (*inf:* phone call): *to give someone a buzz* ...に電話を掛ける ...ni deńwa wo kakéru

♦*vi* (insect) ぶんぶん羽音を立てる buñbun haóto wo taterú; (saw) うなる unáru

buzzer [bʌz'əːr] *n* (ELEC) ブザー búzā

buzz word (*inf*) *n* 流行語 ryūkōgo

KEYWORD

by [bai] *prep* **1** (referring to cause, agent)
...に (よって) ...ni (yotte)

killed by lightning 雷に打たれて死ん
だ kaminari ni ŭtárete shínda

surrounded by a fence 塀に囲まれた
heí ni kakomareta

a painting by Picasso ピカソの絵画
pikásò no káİga

it's by Shakespeare シェイクスピアの
作品です sheíkusupìa no sakúhin desŭ

2 (referring to method, manner, means)
...で ...de

by bus/car/train バス [車, 列車] で
básŭ(kuruma, ré\ssha) de

to pay by check 小切手で払う kogítte
de haráů

by moonlight/candlelight 月明り [ろ
うそくの灯] で tsukfakari[rôsoku no a-
kari]de

by saving hard, he... 一生懸命にお金を
貯めて彼は... isshókènmei ni kané wo
tamete karè wa...

by via, through) ...を通って ...wo tõtte,
...経由で ...keíyu de

we came by Dover ドーバー経由で来ま
した dóbakeìyu de kimáshìta

he came in by the back door 彼は裏口
から入りました karè wa uráguchi kara
hairimashìta

4 (close to) ...のそばに [で] ...no sòbà ni
(de), ...の近くに [で] ...no chíkàkù ni
(de)

the house by the river 川のそばにある
家 kawá no sobà ni árù iè

a holiday by the sea 海辺の休暇 umf-
be no kyūka

she sat by his bed 彼女は彼のベッドの
そばに座っていました kánojò wa karè
no béddò no sobà ni suwátte imashìta

5 (past) ...を通り過ぎて ...wo tõrisugte

she rushed by me 彼女は私の前を通り
過ぎて行きました kánojò wa ashfbaya ni
watákushi no maè wo tõrisugته

I go by the post office every day 私
は毎日郵便局の前を通ります watákushi
wa maìnichi yūbìnkyoku no maè wo

---

tōrimasů

6 (not later than) ...までに ...mádè ni

by 4 o'clock 4時までに yójì madè ni

by this time tomorrow 明日のこの時間
までに myōnichì no konò jikan madè ni

*by the time I got here it was too
late* 私がここに着いたころにはもう手遅
れでした watákushi ga kokó ni tsulta
koro ni wa mō teókùre deshita

7 (during): *by daylight* 日中に nitchū ni

8 (amount) ...単位で ...tàn-i de

by the kilo/meter キロ [メーター] 単位
で kiró[métà] tàn-i de

paid by the hour 時給をもらって jikyū
wo moratte

one by one (people) 1人ずつ hitórìzutsů;
(animals) 1匹ずつ ippfkizutsů; (things) 1
つずつ hitótsùzutsů

little by little 少しずつ sukóshizutsů

9 (MATH, measure): *to divide by 3* 3
で割る sán de waru

to multiply by 3 3を掛ける sán wo
kakerů

a room 3 meters by 4 3メーター掛ける
4メーターの部屋 sánmètà kakérù yón-
mètà no heyá

it's broader by a meter 1メーター広
くなっている ichímètà mõ hiróku nátte
iru

10 (according to) ...に従って ...nì shitágatte

to play by the rules ルールを守る rūrù
wo mamórù

it's all right by me 私は構いませんよ
watákushi wa kàmaimasèn yó

11: *(all) by oneself etc* ...1人だけで hitórì daké dè

he did it (all) by himself 彼は1人
だけの力でやりました karè wa karè hitórì daké no chíkàra de yarfmashìta

*he was standing (all) by himself in
the corner* 彼は1人ぼっちで隅に立って
いました karè wa hitóribotchì de sūmì
ni táttè imashìta

12: *by the way* ところで tokóro dè

*by the way, did you know Claire
was back?* ところでね、クレアは帰っ
て来たのをご存知? tokóro dè ne, kùrea

ga kǽtte kita no wo go-zónjí?

this wasn't my idea by the way しかしね、これを提案したのは私じゃありませんよ shikáshì ne, koré wo teian shita nò wa watákushi ja nái kara né

♦*adv* 1 *see* go; pass *etc*

2: **by and by** やがて yagáte

by and by they came to a fork in the road やがて道路はＹ字路になりました yagáte dōro ha watjiró ni narímashìta

they'll come back by and by そのうち帰って来ますよ sonó uchi kaétte kimásù yo

by and large (on the whole) 大体において dáitai ni óite, 往々にして ōō ni shite

by and large I would agree with you 大体あなたと同じ意見です dáitai aṇatá to onáji ìkèn desu

Britain has a poor image abroad, by and large 海外における英国のイメージは往々にして悪いと言えるでしょう eíkoku no íméjì wa ōō ni shite warúi

bye(-bye) [bai'(bai')] *n excl* じゃあ ねjà ne, バイバイ báibai

by(e)-law [bai'lɔ:] *n* 条例 jôrei

by-election [bai'ilekʃən] (*BRIT*) *n* 補欠選挙 hoketsusenkyo

bygone [bai'gɔːn] *adj* (age, days) 昔の mukáshi no

♦*n*: **let bygones be bygones** 済んだ事を水に流そう sùnda kotó wo mizú ni nagásō

bypass [bai'pæs] *n* (AUT) バイパス báipasu; (MED: operation) 冠状動脈バイパス kańjōdōmyakubaípasu

♦*vt* (town) ...にバイパスを設ける ...ni baípasu wo mōkérù

by-product [bai'prɑːdəkt] *n* (of industrial process) 副産物 fukúsanbutsu; (of situation) ことの結果 njítékikékka

bystander [bai'stændɑːr] *n* (at accident, crime) 居合せた通行人 iáwaseta tsūkōnin

byte [bait] *n* (COMPUT) バイト báito

byword [bai'wəːrd] *n*: **to be a byword for** ...の代名詞である ...no daímeìshi de arù

by-your-leave [baijuːrliːv'] *n*: *without*

so much as a by-your-leave 自分勝手に jibúnkattè ni

C

C [si:] *n* (MUS: note) ハ音 há-òn; (: key) ハ調 háchō

C. [si:] *abbr* = **centigrade**

C.A. [si:ei'] *abbr* = **chartered accountant**

cab [kæb] *n* (taxi) タクシー tákùshī; (of truck, tractor etc) 運転台 uṇtendai

cabaret [kæb'ærei] *n* (nightclub) キャバレー kyábàrē; (floor show) フロアショー furóashō

cabbage [kæb'idʒ] *n* キャベツ kyábètsu

cabin [kæb'in] *n* (on ship) キャビン kyábìn; (on plane) 操縦室 sōjúshìtsu; (house) 小屋 kóyà

cabin cruiser *n* 大型モーターボート ōgata mótābòto, クルーザー kúrùzā 《居室、炊事場などのある物を指す kyóshìtsu, suíjiba nádò no arù monó wo sásù》

cabinet [kæb'ənit] *n* (piece of furniture) 戸棚 tódàna, キャビネット kyabínettò; (*also*: **display cabinet**) ガラス戸棚 garásu tódàna; (POL) 内閣 naíkaku

cable [kei'bəl] *n* (strong rope) 綱 tsunà; (ELEC, TEL, TV) ケーブル kébùru

♦*vt* (message, money) 電信で送る deńshin de okúrù

cable-car [kei'bəlkɑːr] *n* ケーブルカー kéburukā

cable television *n* 有線テレビ yūsentereki

cache [kæʃ] *n*: *a cache of drugs* 隠匿された麻薬 iṇtoku sareta mayáku

a weapons cache 隠匿武器 iṇtokúbùki

cackle [kæk'əl] *vi* (person, witch) 意地悪く笑う usúkimiwarukù kóè de waráù; (hen) こここと鳴く kokóko to nákù

cacti [kæk'tai] *npl of* **cactus**

cactus [kæk'təs] (*pl* **cacti**) *n* サボテン sabóten

caddie [kæd'i:] *n* (GOLF) キャディー kyádì

caddy [kæd'i:] *n* = **caddie**

cadet [kədet] n (MIL) 士官候補生 shikān-kōhosēi; (POLICE) 警察学校の生徒 kefsatsugakkō no sēto

cadge [kædʒ] (inf) vt (lift, cigarette etc) ねだる nedáru

Caesarean [size:r'i:ən] (BRIT) = Cesarean

café [kæfei'] n (snack bar) 喫茶店 kíssaten

cafeteria [kæfiti:'ri:ə] n (in school, factory, station) 食堂 shokudō

caffein(e) [kæ'fi:n] n カフェイン kaféin

cage [keidʒ] n (of animal) おり orí, ケージ kēji; (also: bird cage) 鳥かご toríkago, ケージ kēji; (of lift) ケージ kēji

cagey [kei'dʒi:] (inf) adj 用心深い yōjinbukaí

cagoule [kəgu:l'] (BRIT) n カグール kágūru ◊薄手の雨ガッパ usúde no amágappa

Cairo [kai'rou] n カイロ kāīro

cajole [kədʒoul'] vt 丸め込む marúmekomū

cake [keik] n (CULIN: large) デコレーションケーキ dekóreshonkēki; (: small) 洋菓子 yōgashi
　a cake of soap 石けん1個 sekkén íkkō

caked [keikt] adj: _caked with_ (blood, mud etc) ...の塊で覆われた ...no katámari de ōwareta

calamity [kəlæm'iti:] n (disaster) 災難 saínan

calcium [kæl'si:əm] n (in teeth, bones etc) カルシウム karúshiumu

calculate [kæl'kjəleit] vt (work out: cost, distance, numbers etc) 計算する kefsan suru; (: effect, risk, impact etc) 予測する yosóku suru

calculating [kæl'kjəleitiŋ] adj (scheming) ずる賢い zurúgashikoi

calculation [kælkjəlei'ʃən] n (MATH) 計算 kefsan; (estimate) 予測 yosóku

calculator [kæl'kjəleitə:r] n 電卓 deñtaku

calculus [kæl'kjələs] n (MATH) 微積分学 bisékibungaku

calendar [kæl'əndə:r] n (of year) カレンダー kárendā; (timetable, schedule) 予定

表 yotéihyō

calendar month/year n 暦月〔年〕 rekígetsu(nen)

calf [kæf] (pl **calves**) n (of cow) 子ウシ koúshi; (of elephant, seal etc) ...の子 ...no ko; (also: **calfskin**) 子牛革 koúshigawa, カーフスキン káfusukiñ; (ANAT) ふくらはぎ fukúrahagi

caliber [kæl'əbə:r] (BRIT **calibre**) n (of person) 能力 nōryoku; (of skill) 程度 téido; (of gun) 口径 kōkēi

call [kɔ:l] vt (christen, name) 名付ける nazúkerū; (label) ...を...と呼ぶ ...wo...to yobú; (TEL) ...に電話を掛ける ...ni deñwa wo kakérù; (summon: doctor etc) 呼ぶ yobú; (: witness etc) 召喚する shōkan suru; (arrange: meeting) 召集する shōshū suru
◊vi (shout) 大声で言う ōgoe de iú; (telephone) 電話を掛ける deñwa wo kakérù; (visit: also: **call in**, **call round**) 立寄る tachíyoru
◊n (shout) 呼声 yobígoè; (TEL) 電話 deñwa; (of bird) 鳴声 nakígoè
　: to be called ... ...と呼ばれる ...to yobárerù, ...という ...to iú
　on call (nurse, doctor etc) 待機して tafki shité

call back vi (return) また寄る matá yorù; (TEL) 電話を掛け直す deñwa wo kakénaosù

callbox [kɔ:l'ba:ks] (BRIT) n 電話ボックス deñwabokkūsu

caller [kɔ:l'ə:r] n (visitor) 訪問客 hōmoñkyaku; (TEL) 電話を掛けてくる人 deñwa wo kakéte kurú hitó

call for vt fus (demand) 要求する yōkyū suru; (fetch) 迎えに行く mukáe ni ikú

call girl n (prostitute) コールガール kōrugāru

call-in [kɔ:l'in] (US) n (phone-in) ◊ 視聴者が電話で参加する番組 shíchōsha ga deñwa de sañka suru bañgumi

calling [kɔ:l'iŋ] n (occupation) 職業 shokúgyō; (also: **religious calling**) 神のお召し kámi no méshi

calling card (US) n 名刺 mefshi

call off vt (cancel) 中止する chūshi suru

call on vt fus (visit) 訪ねる tazúnerù, 訪問する hómon suru; (appeal to) ...に ...を求める ...ni ...wo motómerù
♦vi ...wo motómerù

callous [kæl'əs] adj (heartless) 冷淡な reítañ na

call out vt (name etc) 大声でいう ógoè de iú; (summon for help etc) 呼び出す yobídasu
♦vi (shout) 大声で言う ógoè de iú

call up vt (MIL) 召集する shóshū suru; (TEL) ...に電話をかける ...ni deñwa wo kakérù

calm [kɑːm] adj (unworried) 落着いている ochítsuite irú; (peaceful) 静かな shízùka na; (weather, sea) 穏やかな odáyàka na
♦n (quiet, peacefulness) 静けさ shizúkesà
♦vt (person, child) 落着かせる ochítsukaseru; (fears, grief etc) 鎮める shizúmerù

calm down vi (person) 落着く ochítsukù
♦vt (person) 落着かせる ochítsukaseru

Calor gas [kæˈləːr-] ® n 携帯用燃料オブスボンベの商品名 keítaíyō nefiryō gasuboñbe no shóhìhmei

calorie [kælˈəːri] n カロリー károrī

calves [kævz] npl of **calf**

camber [kæmˈbəːr] n (of road) 真ん中が高くなっている máfnaka ga takakū nattě irú kotó

Cambodia [kæmboˈdiːə] n カンボジア kañbojia

came [keim] pt of **come**

camel [kæmˈəl] n (ZOOL) ラクダ rakúda

cameo [kæmˈiːou] n (jewellery) カメオ kámeo

camera [kæmˈəːrə] n (PHOT) 写真機 shashínki, カメラ kámera; (CINEMA) 映画カメラ eſga kámera; (also: TV camera) テレビカメラ teřebi kámera
in camera (LAW) 非公開で hſkōkai de

cameraman [kæmˈəːrəmæn] (pl cameramen) n (CINEMA, TV) カメラマン kaméraman

camouflage [kæmˈəflɑːʒ] n (MIL) カムフラージュ kamúfurāju; (ZOOL) 隠ぺい的才器 iñpeitekigitdsi
♦vt (conceal: also MIL) 隠す kakúsù

camp [kæmp] n (encampment) キャンプ場 kyañpujō; (MIL: barracks) 基地 kichſ; (for prisoners) 収容所 shūyōjo; (faction) 陣営 jiñ-ei
♦vi (in tent) キャンプする kyañpu suru
♦adj (effeminate) 女々しい meméshiì

campaign [kæmpeinˈ] n (MIL) 作戦 sakúsen; (POL etc) 運動 uñdō, キャンペーン kyañpēn
♦vi (objectors, pressure group etc) 運動をする uñdō wo suru

camp bed (BRIT) n 折畳みベッド orítatami beddő

camper [kæmˈpəːr] n (person) キャンパー kyañpā; (vehicle) キャンピングカー kyañpingukā

camping [kæmˈpiŋ] n 野営 yaéi, キャンピング kyañpingu
to go camping キャンピングに行く kyañpingu ni iku

campsite [kæmˈpsait] n キャンプ場 kyañpujō

campus [kæmˈpəs] n (SCOL) キャンパス kyañpasu

can¹ [kæn] n (container: for foods, drinks, oil etc) 缶 káñ
♦vt (foods) 缶詰にする kañzume ni suru

KEYWORD

can² [kæn] (negative cannot, can't conditional and pt could) aux vb 1 (be able to) 出来る dekírù
you can do it if you try 努力すればできますよ dóryòku surébà dekímasù yo
I'll help you all I can できるだけ力になりましょう dekíru dake chíkàra ni narímashō
she couldn't sleep that night その晩彼女は眠れませんでした sonő bañ kand<u>j</u>o wa nemúremasen deshita
I can't go on any longer 私はもうこれ以上やっていけません watákushì wa mō koré ijō yatté ikemasen
I can't see you あなたの姿が見えませんわ añáta no súgàta ga miémaseñ
can you hear me? 私の声が聞こえますか watákushi no koè ga kikőemasù ka
I can see you tomorrow, if you're

free 明日でよかったらお会いできますよ asú dè yókáttara o-ái dekimasú yó

2 (know how to) ...の仕方が分かる, ...の shikáta ga wakárù, ...ができる ...ga dekírù

I can swim/play tennis/drive 私は水泳(テニス, 運転)ができます watákushi wa suíéi(ténisu, únten)ga dekímasu

can you speak French? あなたはフランス語ができますか anáta wa furánsugo ga dekímasù kà

3 (may) ...してもいいですか ...shíte mŏ íi desu ká

can I use your phone? 電話をお借りしてもいいですか dénwa wo o-kári shite mŏ íi desu ká

could I have a word with you? ちょっと話しがあるんですが chótto hanáshi gà árùn desu ga

you can smoke if you like タバコを吸いたければ遠慮なくどうぞ tabáko wo suitakèreba énryo nakù dŏzò

can I help you with that? 手を貸しましょうか té wŏ kashímashŏ ka

4 (expressing disbelief, puzzlement): *it can't be true!* そんなことうそう uso desnŏ

what CAN he want? あいつは何をねらっているだろうね áitsu wa nánì wo neráttè iru dárŏ né

5 (expressing possibility, suggestion, etc) ...かも知れない ...kã mŏ shirenai

he could be in the library 彼は図書室にいるかも知れません kárè wa toshóshìtsu ni irú kà mo shiremasèn

she could have been delayed 彼女は何かの原因で出発が遅れたかも知れません kánojo wa nánìka no gén-in de shuppátsu ga ókùreta kã mo shiremasèn

Canada [kænˈədə] *n* カナダ kánàda

Canadian [kəneiˈdiːən] *adj* カナダの kánàda no

♦*n* カナダ人 kanádàjin

canal [kənæl] *n* (for ships, barges, irrigation) 運河 ūnga; (ANAT) 管 kán

canary [kəneːri] *n* カナリヤ kanáriya

cancel [kænsəl] *vt* (meeting) 中止 chŭshi suru; (appointment, reservation,

contract, order) 取消す toríkesu, キャンセルする kyáńseru suru; (cross out: words, figures) 線を引いて消す sén wo hiíte kesú

the flight was canceled その便は欠航になった sonŏ bin wa kekkŏ ni nattá

the train was canceled その列車は運休になった sonŏ resshá wa uńkyŭ ni nattá

cancellation [kænsəleiˈʃən] *n* (of meeting) 中止 chūshi; (of appointment, reservation, contract, order) 取消し toríkeshi, キャンセル kyáńseru; (of flight) 欠航 kekkŏ; (of train) 運休 uńkyŭ

cancer [kænˈsəːr] *n* (MED) がん gán

Cancer (ASTROLOGY) かに座 kaníza

candid [kænˈdid] *adj* (expression, comment) 率直な sotchókuna

candidate [kænˈdideit] *n* (for job) 候補者 kŏhosha; (in exam) 受験者 jukénsha; (POL) 立候補者 rikkŏhosha

candle [kænˈdəl] *n* ろうそく rŏsoku

candlelight [kænˈdəllait] *n: by candlelight* ろうそくの明りで rŏsokù no akári de

candlestick [kænˈdəlstik] *n (also: candle holder:* plain) ろうそく立て rŏsokù tàte; (: bigger, ornate) しょく台 shokúdai

candor [kænˈdəːr] (*BRIT* **candour**) *n* (frankness) 率直さ sotchókusà

candy [kænˈdiː] *n* (US: sugar-candy) 氷砂糖 kŏrizatŏ; (US: sweet) あめ amé

candy-floss [kænˈdiːflɔːs] (*BRIT*) *n* 綿あめ watá-àme, 綿菓子 watágashì

cane [kein] *n* (BOT) 茎 kukí 〇竹などの中が空洞になっている植物を指す takè nadð no yŏ ni nakà ga kŭdŏ ni natté irú shokúbùtsu wo sasù; (for furniture) 籐 tŏ; (stick) 棒 bŏ; (for walking) 杖 tsúè, ステッキ sutékkî

♦*vt* (*BRIT: SCOL*) むち打つ muchíutsù

canine [keiˈnain] *adj* イヌの inú no

canister [kænˈistəːr] *n* (container: for tea, sugar etc) 容器 yŏki 〇茶筒の様な物を指す charútsu no yŏ na monó wo sasù; (pressurized container) スプレー缶 supúrēkàn; (of gas, chemicals etc) ボンベ boǹbe

cannabis [kǽnəbis] n マリファナ marífāna

canned [kænd] adj (fruit, vegetables etc) 缶詰の kañzume no

cannibal [kǽnəbəl] n (person) 人食い人間 hitókuì níňgen; (animal) 共食いする動物 tomóguì suru dòbutsu

cannon [kǽnən] (pl **cannon** or **cannons**) n (artillery piece) 大砲 taíhō

cannot [kǽnɑt] = **can not**

canny [kǽni:] adj (quick-witted) 抜け目ない nukémenaì

canoe [kənuː'] n (boat) カヌー kánū

canon [kǽnən] n (clergyman) 司教座聖堂参事会員 shikyōzaseídō sañjikàiin; (rule, principle) 規準 kijùn

canonize [kǽnənaiz] vt (REL) 聖人の列に加える seíjin no retsū ni kuwáerù

can opener n 缶切り kańkirì

canopy [kǽnəpi:] n (above bed, throne etc) 天がい teñgai

can't [kænt] = **can not**

cantankerous [kæntǽŋkərəs] adj (fault-finding, complaining) つむじ曲りの tsumújimagàri no

canteen [kæntiːn'] n (in workplace, school etc) 食堂 shokūdō; (also: **mobile canteen**) 移動食堂 idóshokùdō; (BRIT: of cutlery) 収納箱 shūnóbàko ◊ナイフ, フォークなどを仕舞う箱 naífu, fòku nadò wo shimáu hakò

canter [kǽntər] vi (horse) キャンターで走る kyañtā de hashírù

canvas [kǽnvəs] n (fabric) キャンバス kyáñbasu; (painting) 油絵 abúraè; (NAUT) 帆布 ◊総帆 sòhō

canvass [kǽnvəs] vi (POL): **to canvass for** ...のために選挙運動をする ...no tamè ni señkyouñdō wo suru
◊vt (investigate: opinions, views) 調査する chòsa suru

canyon [kǽnjən] n 峡谷 kyōkoku

cap [kæp] n (hat) 帽子 bòshi ◊主につばのある物を指す òmō ni tsubá no arù monó wo sàsù; (of pen) キャップ kyáppù; (of bottle) ふた futá; (contraceptive) ペッサリー pèssarì; (for toy gun) 紙雷管 kamfraìkan

◊vt (outdo) しのぐ shinógù

capability [keipəbíl'əti:] n (competence) 能力 nōryoku

capable [kei'pəbəl] adj (person, object): **capable of doing** ...ができる ...ga dekírù; (able: person) 有能な yūnō na

capacity [kəpǽs'iti:] n (of container, ship etc) 容積 yōseki; (of stadium etc) 収容力 shūyōryòku; (capability) 能力 nōryoku; (position, role) 資格 shikàku; (of factory) 生産能力 seísaňnōryoku

cape [keip] n (GEO) 岬 misàki; (short cloak) ケープ kèpu

caper [kei'pər] n (CULIN: gen: **capers**) ケーパー kêpà; (prank) いたずら itázura

capital [kǽp'itəl] n (also: **capital city**) 首都 shùtō; (money) 資本金 shihóñkin; (also: **capital letter**) 大文字 ōmojì

capital gains tax n 資本利得税 shihóñritokuzèi

capitalism [kǽp'itəlizəm] n 資本主義 shihóñshùgi

capitalist [kǽp'itəlist] adj 資本主義の shihóñshùgi no
◊n 資本主義者 shihóñshugìsha

capitalize [kǽp'itəlaiz]: **capitalize on** vt fus (situation, fears etc) ...を利用する ...wo ríyō suru

capital punishment n 死刑 shikéi

capitulate [kəpítʃ'uleit] vi (give in) 降参する kòsan suru

capricious [kəpríʃ'əs] adj (fickle: person) 気まぐれの kimágure no

Capricorn [kǽp'rikɔːrn] n (ASTROLOGY) やぎ座 yagíza

capsize [kǽpsaiz] vt (boat, ship) 転覆させる teñpuku saséru
◊vi (boat, ship) 転覆する teñpuku suru

capsule [kǽp'səl] n (MED) カプセル kápüseru; (spacecraft) 宇宙カプセル úchūkapüseru

captain [kǽp'tən] n (of ship) 船長 señchō; (of plane) 機長 kichō; (of team) 主将 shushō; (in army) 大尉 taíi; (in navy) 大佐 taísa; (US: in air force) 大尉 taíi; (BRIT: SCOL) 主席の生徒 shusèki no seíto

caption [kǽp'ʃən] n (to picture) 説明文

setsúmeíbun

captivate [kæp'təveit] *vt* (fascinate) 魅了する miryō suru

captive [kæp'tiv] *adj* (person) とりこの toríko no; (animal) 飼育下の shííkuka no
♦*n* (person) とりこ toríko; (animal) 飼育下の動物 shííkuka no dōbutsu

captivity [kæptiv'əti:] *n* 監禁状態 kañkiñjōtai

capture [kæp't∫ər] *vt* (animal, person) 捕まえる tsukámaerù; (town, country) 占領する señryō suru; (attention) 捕える toráerù; (COMPUT) 収納する shúnō suru
♦*n* (seizure: of animal) 捕獲 hokáku; (: of person: by police) 逮捕 taího; (: of town, country: by enemy) 占領 señryō; (COMPUT) 収納 shúnō

car [kɑːr] *n* (AUT) 自動車 jidōsha, 車 kurúma; (: US: carriage) 客車 kyakúsha; (RAIL: BRIT: dining car, buffet car) 特殊車両 tokúshusharyō

carafe [kəræf'] *n* 水差し mizúsashì

caramel [kær'æməl] *n* (CULIN: sweet) キャラメル kyarámeru; (: burnt sugar) カラメル karámeru

carat [kær'ət] *n* (of diamond, gold) カラット karáttò

caravan [kær'əvæn] *n* (BRIT: vehicle) キャンピングカー kyañpingukà; (in desert) 隊商 taíshō, キャラバン kyárában

caravan site (BRIT) *n* オートキャンプ場 ōtokyanpujō

carbohydrate [kɑːrbouhai'dreit] *n* (CHEM, food) 炭水化物 tañsuikabútsu

carbon [kɑːr'bən] *n* 炭素 tánso

carbon copy *n* カーボンコピー kābon kopí

carbon dioxide [-daiɑːk'said] *n* 二酸化炭素 nisáńkatañso

carbon monoxide [-mənɑːk'said] *n* 一酸化炭素 issáńkatañso

carbon paper *n* カーボン紙 kābonshi

carburetor [kɑːr'bəreitər] (BRIT **carburettor**) *n* (AUT) キャブレター kyábureta

carcass [kɑːr'kəs] *n* (of animal) 死体 shítaí

card [kɑːrd] *n* (cardboard) ボール紙 bōrugami; (greetings card, index card etc) カード kādo; (playing card) トランプのカード toráňpu no kādo; (visiting card) 名刺 meíshi

cardboard [kɑːrd'bɔːrd] *n* ボール紙 bōrugami

card game *n* トランプゲーム toráňpugēmu

cardiac [kɑːr'di:æk] *adj* (arrest, failure) 心臓の shíñzō no

cardigan [kɑːr'digən] *n* カーディガン kādigan

cardinal [kɑːr'dənəl] *adj* (chief: principle) 重要な jūyō na
♦*n* (REL) 枢機けい sūkikèi
of cardinal importance 極めて重要で kiwámete jūyō de

cardinal number 基数 kisū

card index *n* カード式索引 kādoshiki sakúin

care [kɛːr] *n* (attention) 注意 chūi; (worry) 心配 shíňpai; (charge) 管理 káňri
♦*vi: to care about* (person, animal) ...を気に掛ける ...wo kí ni kakérù, ...を愛する ...wo aí surù; (thing, idea etc) ...に関心を持つ ...ni kañshin wo motsù
care of (on mail) ...方 ...gatá
in someone's care ...の管理に任せ(ら れ)て ...no kañri ni makáse(rarè)tè
to take care (to do) ...するように気を付ける ...wo suru yō ni kokórogakerù
to take care of (patient, child etc) ...の世話をする ...no sewá wo surù; (problem, situation) ...の始末を付ける ...no shímàtsu wo tsukérù
I don't care 私は構いません watákushi wa kamáimasen
I couldn't care less 私はちっとも気にしない watákushi wa chittó mo ki ni shinai

career [kəri:r'] *n* (job, profession) 職業 shokúgyō; (life: in school, work etc) キャリア kyaría
♦*vi* (also: **career along**: car, horse) 猛スピードで走る mōsupído de hashíru

career woman (*pl* **career women**) *n* キャリアウーマン kyaríaūman

care for vt fus (look after) ...の世話をする ...wo sewá wo surú; (like) ...が好きである ...ga suki de arú, ...を愛している ...wo aí shité irú

carefree [keːrˈfriː] adj (person, attitude) 気苦労のない kigúro no naí

careful [keːrˈfəl] adj (cautious) 注意深い chūibukaì; (thorough) 徹底的な tettéiteki na
(be) careful! 気を付けてね ki wo tsukéte ne

carefully [keːrˈfəli] adv (cautiously) 注意深く chūibukakù; (methodically) 念入りに neñ-iri ni

careless [keːrˈlis] adj (negligent) 不注意な fuchūi na; (heedless) 軽率な keísotsu na

carelessness [keːrˈlisnis] n (negligence) 不注意 fuchūi; (lack of concern) 無とんぢ着 mutóñchaku

caress [kəres] n (stroke) 愛ぶ aíbu
♦vt (person, animal) 愛ぶする aíbu suru

caretaker [keːrˈteikəːr] n (of flats etc) 管理人 kañrinin

car-ferry [kaːrˈfeːriː] n カーフェリー káferī

cargo [kaːrˈgou] (pl **cargoes**) n (of ship, plane) 積荷 tsumíni, 貨物 kámotsu

car hire (BRIT) n レンタカーサービス refitaká sābisu

Caribbean [kærəbiːˈən] n: **the Caribbean (Sea)** カリブ海 karíbukaí

caricature [kærˈəkətʃəːr] n (drawing) 風刺漫画 fūshimañga, カリカチュア karíkachūa; (description) 風刺文 fūshibùn; (exaggerated account) 真実のわい曲 shiñjitsu no waíkyoku

caring [keːrˈiŋ] adj (person, society, behavior) 愛情深い aíjobukaì; (organization) 健康管理の keñkōkañri no

carnage [kaːrˈnidʒ] n (MIL) 虐殺 gyakúsatsu

carnal [kaːrˈnəl] adj (desires, feelings) 肉体的な nikútaiteki na

carnation [kaːrˈneiʃən] n カーネーション kāneshon

carnival [kaːrˈnəvəl] n (festival) 謝肉祭 shaníkusai, カーニバル kánibaru; (US: funfair) カーニバル kánibaru

carnivorous [kaːrnivˈəːras] adj (animal, plant) 肉食の nikúshoku no

carol [kærˈəl] n: **(Christmas) carol** クリスマスキャロル kurísumasu kyaròru

carp [kaːrp] n (fish) コイ koi

car park (BRIT) n 駐車場 chūshajō

carp at vt fus (criticize) とがめ立てする togámedate suru

carpenter [kaːrˈpəntəːr] n 大工 daíku

carpentry [kaːrˈpəntri] n 大工仕事 daíkushigoto

carpet [kaːrˈpit] n (in room etc) じゅうたん jútan, カーペット kápettò; (fig: of pine needles, snow etc) じゅうたんの様な... jútan no yō na...
♦vt (room, stairs etc) ...にじゅうたんを敷く ...ni jútan wo shikú

carpet slippers npl スリッパ súrìppa

carpet sweeper [-swiːˈpəːr] n じゅうたん掃除機 jútan sōjikì

carriage [kærˈidʒ] n (BRIT: RAIL) 客車 kyakúsha; (also: **horse-drawn carriage**) 馬車 bashà; (of goods) 運搬 uñpan; (transport costs) 運送料 uñsōryō

carriage return n (on typewriter etc) 復帰キー fukkī kī

carriageway [kærˈidʒwei] (BRIT) n (part of road) 車線 shasēn ○自動車道の上りまたは下り半分を指す jidōshadō no noborì mata wa kudári hañbuñ wo sasú

carrier [kærˈiəːr] n (transporter, transport company) 運送会社 uñsōgaīsha; (MED) 保菌者 hokíñsha, キャリア kyárìa

carrier bag (BRIT) n 買い物袋 kaímonobukūro, ショッピングバッグ shoppíñgubaggù

carrot [kærˈət] n (BOT, CULIN) ニンジン niñjin

carry [kærˈiː] vt (take) 携帯する keftai suru; (transport) 運ぶ hakóbu; (involve: responsibilities etc) 伴う tomónaù; (MED: disease, virus) 保有する hoyū suru
♦vi (sound) 通る tōru

to get carried away (fig: by enthusiasm, idea) 夢中になる muchū ni naru

carrycot [kærˈiːkaːt] (BRIT) n 携帯ベビ

一ベッド keítai bebíッdeddò

carry on vi (continue) 続ける tsuzúkeru
♦vt (continue) 続ける tsuzúkeru

carry-on [kær'i:an] (inf) n (fuss) 大騒ぎ
ōsawǎgí

carry out vt (orders) 実行する jikkō suru; (investigation) 行う okónau

cart [kɑːrt] n (for grain, silage, hay etc)
荷車 nígúruma; (also: **horsedrawn cart**)
馬車 báshá; (also: **handcart**) 手押し車 te-
ōshíguruma
♦vt (inf: people) 否応なしに連れて行く
iyáō nashi ni tsuréte ikú; (objects) 引き
ずる hikízuru

cartilage [kɑːr'tǝlidʒ] n (ANAT) 軟骨
nafikotsu

carton [kɑːr'tǝn] n (large box) ボール箱
bōrubako; (container: of yogurt, milk
etc) 容器 yōki; (of cigarettes) カートン
kāton

cartoon [kɑːrtuːn'] n (drawing) 漫画 mañga; (BRIT: comic strip) 漫画 mañga 《ひ
こま漫画などを指す yofíkoma manga
nadò wo sasú); (CINEMA) アニメ映画 a-
nîme-elga

cartridge [kɑːr'tridʒ] n (for gun) 弾薬筒
dañ-yakutō, 実弾 jitsúdan; (of record-
player) カートリッジ kátorijjì; (of pen)
インクカートリッジ ifíku kátorijjì

carve [kɑːrv] vt (meat) 切り分ける kírwa-
kerù, スライスする surálsu surù; (wood,
stone) 彫刻する chōkoku surù; (initials,
design) 刻む kizámu

carve up vt (land, property) 切分ける ki-
rîwakerù

carving [kɑːr'viŋ] n (object made from
wood, stone etc) 彫刻物 chōkokubútsu; (in
wood etc: design) 彫物 horímonò; (: art) 彫刻
chōkoku

carving knife n カービングナイフ kā-
bíngunalfu

car wash n 洗車場 señshajō, カーウォッ
シュ kāuosshú

cascade [kæskeid'] n (waterfall) 小さい滝
chísaǐ takí
♦vi (water) 滝になって流れ落ちる takí
ni natté nagáreochirù; (hair, people,
things) 滝の様に落ちる takí no yō ni o-

chirú

case [keis] n (situation, instance) 場合
baái; (MED) 症例 shōrei; (LAW) 事件 jíkèn; (container: for spectacles etc) ケー
ス kèsu; (box: of whisky etc) 箱 hakó, ケ
ース kèsu; (BRIT: also: **suitcase**) スーツ
ケース sūtsukèsu

in case (of) (fire, emergency) …の場合
に …no baái ni

in any case とにかく toníkaku

just in case 万一に備えて mań-ichi ni
sonáete

cash [kæʃ] n (money) 現金 geñkiñ
♦vt (check etc) 換金する kañkin suru

to pay (in) cash 現金で払う geñkin de
haráu

cash on delivery 着払い chakúbarài

cash-book [kæʃ'buk] n 出納帳 suítōbo

cash card (BRIT) n (for cash dispenser)
キャッシュカード kyasshúkàdo

cash desk (BRIT) n 勘定カウンター kañ-
jōkauñtā

cash dispenser n 現金自動支払い機 geñkin jídōshiharaìki, カード kādò kádokì

cashew [kæʃ'uː] n (also: **cashew nut**) カ
シューナッツ kashúnattsù

cash flow n 資金繰り shikínguri

cashier [kæʃiːr'] n (in bank) 出納係 suítōgakàri; (in shop, restaurant) レジ係 re-
jígakàri

cashmere [kæʒ'miːr] n (wool, jersey) カ
シミア kashímia

cash register n レジスター réjisutā

casing [keis'iŋ] n (covering) 被覆 hífuku

casino [kæsiː'nou] n カジノ kájìno

cask [kæsk] n (of wine, beer) たる tarú

casket [kæs'kit] n (for jewelery) 宝石箱
hōsekibakò; (US: coffin) 棺 kañ

casserole [kæs'ǝroul] n (of lamb,
chicken etc) キャセロール kyaséròru;
(pot, container) キャセロールなべ kyasé-
rōrunabè

cassette [kæset'] n (tape) カセットテープ
kasétto tèpu

cassette player n カセットプレーヤー
kasétto puréyà

cassette recorder n カセットレコーダ
ー kasétto rekōdà

cast [kɑːst] *(pt, pp* **cast)** *vt* (throw: light, shadow) 映す utsúsù; (: object, net) 投げる nagérù; (: fishing-line) キャストする kyásùto surù; (: aspersions, doubts) 投掛ける nagékakerù; (glance, eyes) 向ける mukérù; (THEATER) ...に...の役を振当てる ...ni ...no yakú wo furíaterù; (make: statue) 鋳込む ikómù

♦ *n* (THEATER) キャスト kyásùto; (*also:* **plaster cast)** ギプス gípùsu

to cast a spell on (subject: witch etc) ...に魔法を掛ける ...ni mahō wo kakérù

to cast one's vote 投票する tōhyō surù

castaway [kæs'təwei] *n* 難破した人 nañpa shita hitó

caste [kæst] *n* (social class) カースト kāsùto; (*also:* **caste system)** 階級制 kaíkyūsei, カースト制 kāsutosei

caster [kæs'təːr] *n* (wheel) キャスター kyásùtā

caster sugar (*BRIT*) *n* 粉砂糖 konázatō

casting vote [kæs'tiŋ-] (*BRIT*) *n* 決定票 kettéihyō, キャスティングボート kyásùtingubōto

cast iron [kæst'ai'əːrn] *n* 鋳鉄 chūtetsu

castle [kæs'əl] *n* (building) 城 shirō; (CHESS) 城将 jōshō

cast off *vi* (NAUT) 綱を解く tsuná wo tokù; (KNITTING) 編み終える amfoerù

cast on *vi* (KNITTING) 編み始める amíhajimerù

castor [kæs'təːr] (*BRIT*) *n* = **caster**

castor oil [kæs'tər-] *n* ひまし油 himáshiyu

castrate [kæs'treit] *vt* (bull, man) 去勢する kyoséi suru

casual [kæʒ'uəl] *adj* (by chance) 偶然のgúzen no; (irregular: work etc) 臨時のrinji no; (unconcerned) さりげない sarígenai; (informal: clothes) 普段用の fudán-yō no

casually [kæʒ'uəli] *adv* (in a relaxed way) さりげなく sarígenakù; (dress) 普段着で fudángi de

casualty [kæʒ'uəlti] *n* (of war, accident: someone injured) 負傷者 fushōsha; (: someone killed) 死者 shishá; (: of situation, event: victim) 犠牲者 giséisha;

(MED: *also:* **casualty department)** 救急病棟 kyūkyūbyōtō

cat [kæt] *n* (pet) ネコ nekó; (wild animal) ネコ科の動物 nekóka no dōbutsu

catalogue [kæt'ələɡ] (*US also:* **catalog)** *n* (COMM: for mail order) カタログ kátàrogu; (of exhibition, library) 目録 mokúroku

♦ *vt* (books, collection, events) ...の目録を作る ...no mokúroku wo tsukurù

catalyst [kæt'əlist] *n* (CHEM, *fig*) 触媒 shokúbai

catapult [kæt'əpʌlt] (*BRIT*) *n* (sling-shot) ぱちんこ pachínko

cataract [kæt'ərækt] *n* (MED) 白内障 hakúnaishō

catarrh [kətɑːr'] *n* カタル kátàru

catastrophe [kətæs'trəfi] *n* (disaster) 災害 saígai

catastrophic [kætəstrɔːf'ik] *adj* (disastrous) 破局的な hakyókuteki na

catch [kætʃ] *(pt, pp* **caught)** *vt* (animal) 捕る tórù, 捕まえる tsukámaerù; (fish: with net) 捕る tórù; (: with line) 釣る tsurù; (ball) 捕る tórù; (bus, train etc) ...に乗る ...ni norù; (arrest: thief etc) 逮捕する taího surù; (surprise: person) びっくりさせる bikkúri saséru; (attract: attention) 引く hikù; (hear: comment, whisper etc) 聞く kikù; (MED: illness) ...に掛る ...ni kakarù; (person: *also:* **catch up with/to**) ...に追いつく ...ni oítsukù

♦ *vi* (fire) 付く tsukù; (become trapped: in branches, door etc) 引掛る hikkákarù

♦ *n* (of fish etc) 獲物 emóno; (of ball) 球 kyū; (hidden problem) 落し穴 otóshiana; (of lock) 留金 tomégane; (game) キャッチボール kyátchibōru

to catch one's breath (rest) 息をつく ikí wo tsukù, 一休みする hitoyásumi surù

to catch fire 燃え出す moédasù

to catch sight of 見付ける mitsúkeru

catching [kætʃ'iŋ] *adj* (infectious) 移るutsurù

catchment area [kætʃ'mənt-] (*BRIT*) *n* (of school) 学区 gákkù; (of hospital) 通院

catch on vi (understand) 分かる wakarū; (grow popular) 流行する ryūkō suru

catch phrase n キャッチフレーズ kyátchifurēzu

catch up vi (fig: with person, on work) 追付く oítsukú
♦vt (person) ...に追い付く ...ni oítsukú

catchy [kætʃ'i:] adj (tune) 覚え易い obóeyasuī

catechism [kæt'əkizəm] n (REL) 公教要理 kókyōyóri

categoric(al) [kætəgɔːr'ik(əl)] adj (certain, absolute) 絶対的な zettáiteki na

category [kæt'əgɔːri:] n (set, class) 範ちゅう hańchū

cater [kei'təːr] vi: **to cater for** (BRIT: person, group) ...に食事を出す ...ni mītasú; (needs) ...を満たす mitasú; (COMM: weddings etc) ...の料理を仕出しする ...no ryōri wo shidásh suru

caterer [kei'təːrəːr] n 仕出し屋 shidáshiya

catering [kei'təːriŋ] n (trade, business) 仕出し shidáshi

caterpillar [kæt'əːrpilər] n (with hair) 毛虫 kemúshi; (without hair) 芋虫 imómúshi

caterpillar track n キャタピラ kyatápirà

cathedral [kəθiː'drəl] n 大聖堂 dafseidō

catholic [kæθ'əlik] adj (tastes, interests) 広い hiroi

Catholic [kæθ'əlik] adj (REL) カトリック教の katórikkukyō no
♦n (REL) カトリック教徒 katórikkukyōto

cat's-eye [kæts'ai'] (BRIT) n (AUT) 反射びょう hańshabyō ◇夜間の目印として道路の中央または両はわきに埋込むガラスなどの反射器 yakán no mejírūshi toshite dōro no chūō mata wa waki ni umékomú garásu nadó no hańshakí

cattle [kæt'əl] npl ウシ ushí ◇総称 sōshō

catty [kæt'i:] adj (comment, woman) 意地悪な ijíwaruì na

caucus [kɔː'kəs] n (POL: group) 実力者会議 jitsúryokusha kaígi; (: US) 党部会 tō-

bukái

caught [kɔːt] pt, pp of **catch**

cauliflower [kɔː'ləflauər] n カリフラワー karífurawā

cause [kɔːz] n (of outcome, effect) 原因 geñ-in; (reason) 理由 riyū; (aim, principle: also POL) 目的 mokúteki
♦vt (produce, lead to: outcome, effect) 引起こす hikíokosū

caustic [kɔːs'tik] adj (CHEM) 腐食性の fushókusei no; (fig: remark) 辛らつな shifíratsu na

caution [kɔː'ʃən] n (prudence) 慎重さ shifíchōsa; (warning) 警告 keíkoku, 注意 chūi
♦vt (warn: also POLICE) 警告する kefkoku suru

cautious [kɔː'ʃəs] adj (careful, wary) 注意深い chūibukaī

cautiously [kɔː'ʃəsli:] adv 注意深く chūibukakù

cavalier [kævəliːr'] adj (attitude, fashion) 威張り腐った ibárikusattà

cavalry [kæv'əlri:] n (MIL: mechanized) 装甲部隊 sōkōbutāi; (: mounted) 騎兵隊 kihéitai

cave [keiv] n (in cliff, hill) 洞穴 horá-ana

cave in vi (roof etc) 陥没する kañbotsu suru, 崩れる kuzúrerú

caveman [keiv'mæn] (pl **cavemen**) n 穴居人 kékkyōjín

cavern [kæv'əːrn] n どうくつ dōkutsu

caviar(e) [kæv'i:ɑːr] n キャビア kyábia

cavity [kæv'iti:] n (in wall: also ANAT) 腔 kō; (in tooth) 虫歯の穴 mushíba no aná

cavort [kəvɔːrt'] vi (romp) はしゃぎ回る hashágimawarù

CB [si:bi:'] n abbr (= Citizens' Band (Radio)) 市民バンド shimfnbañdo, シチズンバンド shichízunbañdo

CBI [si:bi:ai'] n abbr (= Confederation of British Industry) 英国産業連盟 efkokusafigyōreñmei

cc [si:si:'] abbr (= cubic centimeter(s)) 立方センチメートル rippőseńchimētoru, cc shíshí; = **carbon copy**

cease [si:s] vt (end, stop) 終える oéru
♦vi (end, stop) 終る owáru, 止む tomáru

ceasefire [siːsˈfaɪəʳ] n (MIL) 停戦 tefsen

ceaseless [siːsˈlis] adj (chatter, traffic) 絶間ない taéma nai

cedar [siːˈdəʳ] n (tree) ヒマラヤスギ himárayasugí; (wood) シーダー材 shídāzai

cede [siːd] vt (land, rights etc) 譲る yuzúru

ceiling [siːˈliŋ] n (in room) 天井 teñjō; (upper limit: on wages, prices etc) 天井 teñjō, 上限 jōgen

celebrate [selˈəbreit] vt (gen) 祝う iwáū; (REL: mass) 挙げる agéru
♦vi お祝いをする o-íwai suru

celebrated [selˈəbreitid] adj (author, hero) 有名な yūmei na

celebration [seləbreiˈʃən] n (party, festival) お祝い o-íwai

celebrity [səlebˈritiː] n (famous person) 有名人 yūmeíjin

celery [selˈəriː] n セロリ séròri

celestial [səlesˈtʃəl] adj (heavenly) 天上的な teñjōteki na

celibacy [selˈəbasiː] n 禁欲生活 kiñ-yoku seíkatsu

cell [sel] n (in prison: gen) 監房 kañbō; (: solitary) 独房 dokúbō; (in monastery) 個室 koshítsu; (BIO, also of revolutionaries) 細胞 saíbō; (ELEC) 電池 deñchi

cellar [selˈəʳ] n (basement) 地下室 chíkashitsu; (also: wine cellar) ワイン貯蔵室 waín chozōshitsu

cello [tʃelˈou] n (MUS) チェロ chérò

cellophane [selˈəfein] n セロハン séròhan

cellular [selˈjələʳ] adj (BIO: structure, tissue) 細胞の saíbō no; (fabrics) 保温効果の高い hoóñkōka no takaí, 防寒の bókan no

cellulose [selˈjəlous] n (tissue) 繊維素 señísō

Celt [selt, kelt] n ケルト人 kerútòjin

Celtic [selˈtik, kelˈtik] adj ケルト人の kerútòjin no; (language etc) ケルトの kérùto no

cement [simentˈ] n (powder) セメント seménto; (concrete) コンクリート kofíkuríto

cement mixer n セメントミキサー seménto mikísā

cemetery [semˈiteːriː] n 墓地 bóchi

cenotaph [senˈətæf] n (monument) 戦没者記念碑 señbotsusha kinéñhi

censor [senˈsəʳ] n (POL, CINEMA etc) 検閲官 keñ-etsúkan
♦vt (book, play, news etc) 検閲する keñ-etsu suru

censorship [senˈsɚʃip] n (of book, play, news etc) 検閲 keñ-etsu

censure [senˈʃəʳ] vt (reprove) とがめる togámerú

census [senˈsəs] n (of population) 国勢調査 kokúzeichōsa

cent [sent] n (US: also: one-cent coin) セント玉 isséntodamá 1 see also per

centenary [senˈtəneːriː] n (of birth etc) 100周年 hyakúshūnen

center [senˈtɚ] n (BRIT centre) n (of circle, room, line) 中心 chūshin; (of town) 中心部 chūshínbu, 繁華街 hañkagái; (of attention, interest) の的 matő; (heart: of action, belief etc) 核心 kakúshin; (building: health center, community center) センター séñtā; (POL) 中道 chūdō
♦vt (weight) ...の中心に置く ...no chūshin ni okú; (sights) ...にぴったりと合わせる ...ni pittári awáseru; (SOCCER: ball) グランド中央へ飛ばす guráñdo chūō e tobású; (TYP: on page) 中央に合わせる chūō ni awáseru

center forward n (SPORT) センターフォワード señtāfowádò

center half n (SPORT) センターハーフ señtāhāfu

centigrade [senˈtigreid] adj 摂氏 sesshí

centimeter [senˈtəmiːtɚ] n (BRIT centimetre) n センチメートル señchimḗtoru

centipede [senˈtəpiːd] n ムカデ mukáde

central [senˈtral] adj (in the center) 中心点の chūshínten no; (near the center) 中心の chūshin no; (committee, government) 中央の chūō no; (idea, figure) 中心の chūshin no

Central America n 中米 chūbei

central heating n セントラルヒーティング señtoraruhítiñgu

centralize [sen'trəlaɪz] vt (decision-making, authority) 中央に集中させる chūō ni shūchū saséru

central reservation (BRIT) n (AUT: of road) 中央分離帯 chūōbunritai

centre [sen'tər] (etc BRIT) n = **center** etc

century [sen'tʃəːriː] n 世紀 sêiki
20th century 20世紀 nijússeiki

ceramic [səræm'ik] adj (art, tiles) セラミックの serámikku no

ceramics [səræm'iks] npl (objects) 焼物 yakfmono

cereal [siːr'iəl] n (plant, crop) 穀物 kókumotsu; (food) シリアル shirfarù

cerebral [seːr'əbrəl] adj (MED: of the brain) 脳の nō no; (intellectual) 知的な chitéki na

ceremony [seːr'əmouniː] n (event) 式 shikí; (ritual) 儀式 gfshiki; (behavior) 形式 kefshiki
to stand on ceremony 礼儀にこだわる reígi ni kodáwarù

certain [səːr'tən] adj (sure: person) 確信 している kakúshin shité irú; (: fact) 確実 な kakújitsu na; (person): **a certain Mr Smith** スミスと呼ばれる男 sumisù to yobareru otóko; (particular): **certain days/places** ある日(場所) árù hi (basho); (some): **a certain coldness/pleasure** ある程度の冷たさ(喜び) árù teido no tsumétasa (yorókobi)
for certain 確実に kakújitsu ni

certainly [səːr'tənliː] adv (undoubtedly) 間違いなく machígai nakù; (of course) もちろん mochfron

certainty [səːr'təntiː] n (assurance) 確実 性 kakújitsusei; (inevitability) 必然性 hitsúzensei

certificate [səːrtif'əkit] n (of birth, marriage etc) 証明書 shōmeisho; (diploma) 資格証明書 shikákushōmeisho

certified mail [səːr'təfaid-] (US) n 配達 証明付き書留便 haftatsushōmei tsukí kakftome yūbin

certified public accountant (US) n 公認会計士 kōnin kaíkeishi

certify [səːr'təfai] vt (fact) 証明する shō-

mei suru; (award a diploma to) ...に資格 を与える ...ni shikáku wo atáeru; (declare insane) 精神異常と認定する seíshinijō to nftei suru

cervical [səːr'vikəl] adj (smear, cancer) 子宮けい部の shikyúkeibu no

cervix [səːr'viks] n (ANAT) 子宮けい部 shikyúkeibu

Cesarean [sizeːr'iːən] (BRIT **Caesarean**) adj: **Cesarean** (**section**) 帝王切開 tefōsekkai

cesspit [ses'pit] n (sewage tank) 汚水だ め osúidame

cf. abbr = **compare**

ch. abbr = **chapter**

chafe [tʃeif] vt (rub: skin) 擦る súrù

chagrin [ʃəgrin'] n (annoyance) 悔しさ kuyáshisa; (disappointment) 落胆 rakútan

chain [tʃein] n (for anchor, prisoner, dog etc) 鎖 kusári; (on bicycle) チェーン chèn; (jewelery) 首飾り kubíkazari; (of shops, hotels) チェーン chèn; (of events, ideas) 連鎖 reñsa
♦vt (also: **chain up**: prisoner, dog) 鎖に つなぐ kusári ni tsunágu
an island chain/a chain of islands 列島 rettó
a mountain chain/a chain of mountains 山脈 safimyaku

chain reaction n 連鎖反応 refisahañnō

chain-smoke [tʃein'smouk] vi 立続けに タバコを吸う tátétsuzuke ni tabáko wo suú

chain store n チェーンストア chènsutoā

chair [tʃeːr] n (seat) いす isú; (armchair) 安楽いす afirakuisō; (of university) 講座 kōza; (of meeting) 座長 zachō; (of committee) 委員長 íínchō
♦vt (meeting) 座長を務める zachō wo tsutómerù

chairlift [tʃeːr'lift] n リフト rífuto

chairman [tʃeːr'mən] (pl **chairmen**) n (of committee) 委員長 íínchō; (BRIT: of company) 社長 shachō

chalet [ʃælei'] n 山小屋 yamágoya

chalice [tʃæl'is] n (REL) 聖さん杯 sefsañhai

chalk [tʃɔːk] n (GEO) 白亜 hákua; (for writing) 白墨 hakúboku, チョーク chōku

challenge [tʃǽl'ɪndʒ] n (of new job, unknown, new venture etc) 挑戦 chōsen; (to authority, received ideas etc) 反抗 hañkō; (dare) 挑戦 chōsen

♦vt (SPORT) …に試合を申し込む …ni shiái wo móshikomù; (rival, competitor) 挑戦する chōsen suru; (authority, right, idea etc) …に反抗する …ni hañkō suru

to challenge someone to do something …に…をやれるものならやってみろと挑戦する …ni …wo yaréru monó nara yatté miro to chōsen suru

challenging [tʃǽl'ɪndʒɪŋ] adj (career, task) やりがいを感じさせる yarígai wo kañjí saséru; (tone, look etc) 挑発的な chōhatsuteki na

chamber [tʃeim'bəːr] n (room) 部屋 heyá; (POL: house) 院 iñ; (BRIT: LAW: gen pl) 弁護士事務室 beñgoshì jimúshìtsu; (: of judge) 判事室 hañjìshìtsu

chamber of commerce 商工会議所 shōkōkaigisho

chambermaid [tʃeim'bəːrmeid] n (in hotel) メード mēdo

chamber music n 室内音楽 shitsúnai oñgaku

chamois [ʃæm'iː] n (ZOOL) シャモア shámoa; (cloth) セーム革 sēmugawa

champagne [ʃæmpein'] n シャンペン shañpeñ

champion [tʃæm'piən] n (of league, contest, fight) 優勝者 yūshōsha, チャンピオン chañpion; (of cause, principle, person) 擁護者 yōgosha

championship [tʃæm'piːənʃip] n (contest) 選手権決定戦 señshùken keñteisen; (title) 選手権 señshùken

chance [tʃæns] n (likelihood, possibility) 可能性 kanōsei; (opportunity) 機会 kikái, チャンス cháñsu; (risk) 危険 kikén, か fte kake

♦vt (risk): *to chance it* 危険を冒す kikén wo okasù, 冒険をする bōken wo suru

♦adj 偶然の gūzen no

to take a chance 危険を冒す kikén wo

okasù, 冒険をする bōken wo suru

by chance 偶然に gūzen ni

chancellor [tʃæn'salər] n (head of government) 首相 shushō

Chancellor of the Exchequer (BRIT) n 大蔵大臣 ōkuradaijin

chandelier [ʃændəliːr] n シャンデリア shañdèria

change [tʃeindʒ] vt (alter, transform) 変える kaeru; (wheel, bulb etc) 取替える torfkaeru; (clothes) 着替える kigáerù; (job, address) 変える kaeru; (baby, diaper) 替える kaeru; (exchange: money) 両替する ryōgae suru

♦vi (alter) 変る kawáru; (change one's clothes) 着替える kigáerù; (change trains, buses) 乗換える norfkaeru; (traffic lights) 変る kawáru; (be transformed): *to change into* …に変る …ni kawáru, …になる …ni naru

♦n (alteration) 変化 héñka; (difference) ちがい chigái; (also: change of clothes) 着替え kigáe; (of government, climate, job) 変る kawáru kotó; (coins) 小銭 kozéni; (money returned) お釣り o-tsúri

to change one's mind 気が変る ki ga kawaru

for a change たまには tamá ni wa

changeable [tʃein'dʒəbəl] adj 変りやすい kawáriyasuì

change machine n 両替機 ryōgaekì

changeover [tʃeindʒ'ouvər] n (to new system) 切替え kirfkae

changing [tʃein'dʒiŋ] adj (world, nature) 変る kawáru

changing room (BRIT) n 更衣室 kōíshìtsu

channel [tʃæn'əl] n (TV) チャンネル cháñneru; (in sea, river etc) 水路 sūiro; (groove) 溝 mizó; (fig: means) 手段 shúdan, ルート rūto

♦vt (money, resources) 流す nagásù

the (English) Channel イギリス海峡 igfrisu káikyō

the Channel Islands チャネル諸島 chanéru shotō

chant [tʃænt] n (of crowd, fans etc) 掛声 kakégoè; (REL: song) 詠唱歌 efshōka

◆vt (word, name, slogan) 唱える tonáerù

chaos [kei'ɑs] n (disorder) 混乱 koñran

chaotic [keiɑt'ik] adj (mess, jumble) 混乱した koñran shitá

chap [tʃæp] (BRIT: inf) n (man) やつ yátsu

chapel [tʃæp'əl] n (in church) 礼拝堂 reihaidō; (in hospital, prison, school etc) チャペル cháperù; (BRIT: non-conformist chapel) 教会堂 kyókaidō

chaperone [ʃæp'əroun] n (for woman) 付添い tsukísoi, シャペロン shapéroñ
◆vt (woman, child) ...に付添う ...ni tsukísoù

chaplain [tʃæp'lin] n (REL, MIL, SCOL) 付属牧師 fuzókubokùshi

chapped [tʃæpt] adj (skin, lips) あかぎれした akágire shitá

chapter [tʃæp'tər] n (of book) 章 shō; (of life, history) 時期 jíkì

char [tʃɑːr] vt (burn) 黒焦げにする kuró-koge ni surù
◆n (BRIT) = **charwoman**

character [kær'iktər] n (nature) 性質 sefshitsu; (moral strength) 気骨 kikótsu; (personality) 人格 jiñkaku; (in novel, film) 人物 jiñbutsu; (letter) 文字 mójì

characteristic [kæriktəris'tik] adj (typical) 特徴的な tokúchōteki na
◆n (trait, feature) 特徴 tokúchō

characterize [kær'iktəraiz] vt (typify) ...の特徴である ...no tokúchō de arù; (describe the character of) ...の特徴を描写する ...no tokúchō wo byósha surù

charade [ʃəreid'] n (sham, pretence) 装い yosóoi

charcoal [tʃɑːr'koul] n (fuel) 炭 sumí, 木炭 mokútañ; (for drawing) 木炭 mokútañ

charge [tʃɑːrdʒ] n (fee) 料金 ryókin; (LAW: accusation) 容疑 yógi; (responsibility) 責任 sekíniñ
◆vt (for goods, services) ...の料金を取る ...no ryókin wo toru; (LAW: accuse): **to charge someone (with)** ...に起訴する kiso suru; (battery) 充電する jūden suru; (MIL: enemy) ...に突撃する ...ni totsúgeki suru
◆vi (animal) 掛って来る〔行く〕 kakátte

kurú(ikú); (MIL) 突撃する totsúgeki suru

to take charge of (child) ...の面倒を見る ...no meñdō wo mírù; (company) ...の指揮を取る ...no shíkí wo toru

to be in charge of (person, machine) ...の責任を持っている ...no sekíniñ wo motté irù; (business) ...の責任者である ...no sekíniñsha de arù

how much do you charge? 料金はいくらですか ryókin wa ikúra desù ka

to charge an expense (up) to someone's account ...の勘定に付ける ...no kañjō ni tsukerù

charge card n (for particular shop or organization) クレジットカード kuréjittokādo 〔特定の店でしか使えない様な指す tokútei no mise de shika tsukáenai monò wo sásù

charges [tʃɑːr'dʒiz] npl (bank charges, telephone charges etc) 料金 ryókin

to reverse the charges (TEL) 先方払いにする señpōbaraì ni surù

charisma [kəriz'mə] n カリスマ性 karísumasei

charitable [tʃær'itəbəl] adj (organization) 慈善の jizéñ no

charity [tʃær'iti] n (organization) 慈善事業 jizéngyojī; (kindness) 親切さ shiñsetsusa; (generosity) 寛大さ kañdaisa; (money, gifts) 施し hodókoshi

charlady [tʃɑːr'leidi:] (BRIT) n = **charwoman**

charlatan [ʃɑːr'lətən] n 偽者 nisémono

charm [tʃɑːrm] n (attractiveness) 魅力 miryóku; (to bring good luck) お守 o-mámori; (on bracelet etc) 飾り kazári
◆vt (please, delight) うっとりさせる uttórì sasérù

charming [tʃɑːr'miŋ] adj (person, place) 魅力的な miryókuteki na

chart [tʃɑːrt] n (graph) グラフ gúrafu; (diagram) 図 zu; (map) 海図 kaìzu
◆vt (course) 地図に記入する chízù ni kakù; (progress) 図に書く zú ni kakù

charter [tʃɑːr'tər] vt (plane, ship etc) チャーターする chatā surù
◆n (document, constitution) 憲章 keñ-

shō; (of university, company) 免許 mén-kyo

chartered accountant [tʃɑːrˈtəːrd-] (BRIT) n 公認会計士 kōnin kaikeíshi

charter flight n チャーターフライト chátáfuraìto

charts [tʃɑːrts] npl (hit parade): **the charts** ヒットチャート hittóchàto

charwoman [tʃɑːrˈwumən] (pl **charwomen**) n 掃除婦 sōjifu

chase [tʃeis] vt (pursue) 追掛ける oíkake-rù; (also: **chase away**) 追払う oíharaú
♦n (pursuit) 追跡 tsuíseki

chasm [kæz'əm] n (GEO) 深い割れ目 fúkai waréme

chassis [ʃæs'iː] n (AUT) シャシ shashí

chastity [tʃæs'titi] n (REL) 純潔 juńketsu

chat [tʃæt] vi (also: **have a chat**) おしゃべりする o-sháberí surù
♦n (conversation) おしゃべり o-sháberí

chat show (BRIT) n トーク番組 tóku bañgumi

chatter [tʃæt'əːr] vi (person) しゃべりまくる shabérimakurù; (animal) きゃっきゃっと鳴く kyákkyattò nakú; (teeth) がちがち鳴る gachígachi narú
♦n (of people) しゃべり声 shabérigoè; (of birds) さえずり saézurì; (of animals) きゃっきゃっという鳴き声 kyákkyattò iú nakígoè

chatterbox [tʃæt'əːrbɑːks] (inf) n しゃべり好き o-sháberizuki

chatty [tʃæt'iː] adj (style, letter) 親しみやすい shitáshimiyasuì; (person) おしゃべりな o-sháberí na

chauffeur [ʃou'fəːr] n お抱え運転手 okákae-unteñshu

chauvinist [ʃou'vənist] n (male chauvinist) 男性優越主義者 dańseiyúetsushugìsha; (nationalist) 熱狂的愛国主義者 nek-kyótekiaìkokushugìsha

cheap [tʃiːp] adj (inexpensive) 安い yasuì; (poor quality) 安っぽい yasúppoì; (behavior, joke) 下劣な gerétsu na
♦adv: **to buy/sell something cheap** 安く買う(売る) yasúkù kaú (urú)

cheaper [tʃiː'pəːr] adj (less expensive) 安

っと安い móttò yasuì

cheaply [tʃiːp'liː] adv (inexpensively) 安く yasukù

cheat [tʃiːt] vi (in exam) カンニングする kańningu surù; (at cards) いかさまをする ikásama wo suru
♦vt: **to cheat someone (out of something)** ...から ... をだまし取る ...kara ...wo damáshitorù
♦n (person) いかさま師 ikásamashì

check [tʃek] vt (examine: bill, progress) 調べる shiráberù; (verify: facts) 確認する kakúnin suru; (halt: enemy, disease) 食止める kuftomerù; (restrain: impulse, person) 抑える osáerù
♦n (inspection) 検査 kéñsa; (curb) 抑制 yokúsei; (US: bill) 勘定書 kañjōgaki; (BANKING) 小切手 kogítte; (pattern: gen pl) 市松模様 ichímatsumoyō
♦adj (pattern, cloth) 市松模様の ichíma-tsumoyō no

checkbook [tʃek'buk] (US) n 小切手帳 kogíttechō

checkerboard [tʃek'əːrbɔːrd] n チェッカー盤 chekkában

checkered [tʃek'əːrd] (BRIT **chequered**) adj (fig: career, history) 起伏の多い kifúku no ōi

checkers [tʃek'əːrz] (US) npl (game) チェッカー chékkā

check in vi (at hotel, airport) チェックインする chekkúin surù
♦vt (luggage) 預ける azúkerù

check-in (desk) [tʃek'in-] (US) n フロント furóñto

checking account [tʃek'iŋ-] (US) n (current account) 当座預金 tōzayokìn

checkmate [tʃek'meit] n (CHESS) 王手 óte

check out vi (of hotel) チェックアウトする chekkúaùto surù

checkout [tʃek'aut] n (in shop) 勘定カウンター kañjō kauñtā

checkpoint [tʃek'pɔint] n (on border) 検問所 keñmonjo

checkroom [tʃek'ruːm] (US) n (left-luggage office) 手荷物一時預り所 tenímotsu ichíjiazùkarijo

check up *vi*: *to check up on something/someone* を調べておく…wo shirábetè okù

checkup [tʃek'ʌp] *n* (MED) 健康診断 keñkōshíndàn

cheek [tʃiːk] *n* (ANAT) ほお hō; (impudence) ずうずうしさ zūzūshísà; (nerve) 度胸 dokyō

cheekbone [tʃiːk'boun] *n* ほお骨 hōbone

cheeky [tʃiː'kiː] *adj* (impudent) ずうずうしい zūzūshíì

cheep [tʃiːp] *vi* (bird) ぴよぴよ鳴く piyópiyo nakú

cheer [tʃiːr] *vt* (team, speaker) 声援する sefen suru; (gladden) 喜ばす yorókobasù
♦*vi* (shout) 声援する sefen suru
♦*n* (shout) 声援 sefen

cheerful [tʃiːr'fəl] *adj* (wave, smile, person) 朗らかな hogaráka na

cheerio [tʃiːr'iːou] (*BRIT*) *excl* じゃあね jā ne

cheers [tʃiːrz] *npl* (of crowd etc) 声援 sefen, かっさい kassái
cheers! (toast) 乾杯 kañpai

cheer up *vi* (person) 元気を出す geñki wo dasù
♦*vt* (person) 元気づける geñkizukerù

cheese [tʃiːz] *n* チーズ chīzu

cheeseboard [tʃiːz'bɔːrd] *n* チーズボード chīzubōdo ◇チーズを盛り合せる板または皿 chīzu wo morīawaserù tà mata wa sarâ

cheetah [tʃiː'tə] *n* チーター chītā

chef [ʃef] *n* (in restaurant, hotel) コック kókkù

chemical [kem'ikəl] *adj* (fertilizer, warfare) 化学の kágàku no
♦*n* 化学薬品 kagákuyakùhin

chemist [kem'ist] *n* (*BRIT*: pharmacist) 薬剤師 yakúzaìshi; (scientist) 化学者 kagákùsha

chemistry [kem'istriː] *n* 化学 kágàku

chemist's (shop) [kem'ists-] (*BRIT*) *n* 薬局 yakkyókù

cheque [tʃek] (*BRIT*: BANKING) *n* = check

chequebook [tʃek'buk] (*BRIT*) *n* = checkbook

cheque card (*BRIT*) *n* (to guarantee cheque) 小切手カード kogítte kâdo

chequered [tʃek'əːrd] (*BRIT*) *adj* = checkered

cherish [tʃer'iʃ] *vt* (person) 大事にする dáìji ni suru; (memory, dream) 心に抱く kokórò ni idakú

cherry [tʃer'iː] *n* (fruit) サクランボウ sakúranbò; (*also*: **cherry tree**) サクラ sakúra

chess [tʃes] *n* チェス chésù

chessboard [tʃes'bɔːrd] *n* チェス盤 chésuban

chest [tʃest] *n* (ANAT) 胸 muné; (box) ひつ hitsú
chest of drawers 整理だんす sefridañsu

chestnut [tʃes'nʌt] *n* クリ kurí; (*also*: **chestnut tree**) クリの木 kurí no ki

chew [tʃuː] *vt* (food) かむ kamú

chewing gum [tʃuː'iŋ-] *n* チューインガム chūìngamu

chic [ʃiːk] *adj* (dress, hat etc) スマートな sumáto na; (person, place) 粋な ikí na

chick [tʃik] *n* (bird) ひな hínà; (*inf*: girl) べっぴん beppín

chicken [tʃik'ən] *n* (bird) ニワトリ niwátori; (meat) 鶏肉 kefniku; (*inf*: coward) 弱虫 yowámùshi

chicken out (*inf*) *vi* おじ気付いて…から手を引く ojíkezukìte …kara te wo hikú

chickenpox [tʃik'ənpɑks] *n* 水ぼうそう mizúbōsō

chicory [tʃik'əːriː] *n* チコリ chíkòri

chief [tʃiːf] *n* (of tribe) しゅう長 shùchō; (of organization, department) …長 …chō
♦*adj* (principal) 主な ómð na

chief executive *n* 社長 shachō

chiefly [tʃiːf'liː] *adv* (principally) 主に ómð ni

chiffon [ʃifɑːn] *n* (fabric) シフォン shffón

chilblain [tʃil'blein] *n* 霜焼け shimóyake

child [tʃaild] (*pl* **children**) *n* 子供 kodómo
do you have any children? お子さんは？ o-kő-san wa?

childbirth [tʃaild'bəːrθ] *n* お産 osán

childhood [tʃaild'hud] *n* 子供時分 kodómojìbun

childish [tʃáildiʃ] *adj* (games, attitude, person) 子供っぽい kodómoppoì

childlike [tʃáildlaik] *adj* 無邪気な mújakì na

child minder (*BRIT*) *n* 保母 hóbò

children [tʃíldrən] *npl of* **child**

Chile [tʃíli] *n* チリ chíri

Chilean [tʃíliən] *adj* チリの chíri no
♦*n* チリ人 chírijìn

chill [tʃíl] *n* (coldness: in air, water etc) 冷え hié; (MED: illness) 風邪 kazé
♦*vt* (cool: food, drinks) 冷す hiyasù; (person: make cold): **to be chilled** が冷える karáda ga hierù

chilli [tʃíli] *n* チリ chíri

chilly [tʃíli] *adj* (weather) 肌寒い hadásamuì; (person) 寒気がする samúke ga suru; (response, look) 冷たい tsumétaì

chime [tʃáim] *n* (of bell, clock) チャイム cháimu
♦*vi* チャイムが鳴る chaímu ga narú

chimney [tʃímni:] *n* (of house, factory) 煙突 eñtotsu

chimney sweep *n* 煙突掃除夫 eñtotsu sōjífù

chimpanzee [tʃìmpænzí:] *n* チンパンジー chiñpañjī

chin [tʃin] *n* あご agó

China [tʃái'nə] *n* 中国 chūgoku

china [tʃái'nə] *n* (clay) 陶土 tōdo; (crockery) 瀬戸物 setómono

Chinese [tʃainíːz'] *adj* 中国の chūgoku no; (LING) 中国語の chūgokugo no
♦*n inv* (person) 中国人 chūgokujìn; (LING) 中国語 chūgokugo

chink [tʃíŋk] *n* (crack: in door, wall etc) 透き間 sukíma; (clink: of bottles etc) かちん kachín

chip [tʃíp] *n* (BRIT: gen pl: CULIN) フライドポテト furáidopotèto; (US: also: **potato chip**) ポテトチップス potétochippùsu; (of wood, glass, stone) 欠けら kakéra; (COMPUT) チップ chippù
♦*vt*: **to be chipped** (cup, plate) 縁が欠けている fuchí ga kakéte irú

chip in (*inf*) *vi* (contribute) 寄付する kifú surù; (interrupt) 口を挟む kuchí wo

hasamù

chiropodist [kirɑːp'ədist] (BRIT) *n* 足治療師 ashí chiryōshi

chirp [tʃəːrp] *vi* (bird) ちゅうちゅう鳴く chūchū nakú

chisel [tʃíz'əl] *n* (for wood) のみ nómì; (for stone) たがね tagáne

chit [tʃit] *n* (note) メモ mémò; (receipt) 領収書 ryōshūsho

chitchat [tʃít'tʃæt] *n* 世間話 sekénbanàshi

chivalrous [ʃiv'əlrəs] *adj* 親切な shiñsetsu na

chivalry [ʃiv'əlri:] *n* (behavior) 親切さ shiñsetsusa; (medieval system) 騎士道 kishídō

chives [tʃaivz] *npl* (herb) チャイブ cháibu

chlorine [klɔːr'iːn] *n* (CHEM) 塩素 eñso

chock-a-block [tʃɑk'əblɑːk] *adj* 一杯で íppai de

chock-full [tʃɑk'fúl] *adj* = **chock-a-block**

chocolate [tʃɔːk'əlit] *n* (bar, sweet, cake) チョコレート chokórèto; (drink) ココア kókòa

choice [tʃɔis] *n* (selection) 選んだ物 eránda monò; (option) 選択 señtaku; (preference) 好み konómi
♦*adj* (fine: cut of meat, fruit etc) 一級の ikkyū no

choir [kwai'əːr] *n* (of singers) 聖歌隊 seíkatai; (area of church) 聖歌隊席 seíkataisèki

choirboy [kwai'əːr'bɔi] *n* 少年聖歌隊員 shōnen seikataiin

choke [tʃouk] *vi* (on food, drink etc) ...がのどに詰る ...ga nodò ni tsumarù; (with smoke, dust, anger etc) むせる músèru
♦*vt* (strangle) ...ののどを締める ...no nodō wo shimerù; (block): **to be choked (with)** (...で) 詰っている (...de) tsumattè irú
♦*n* (AUT) チョーク chōku

cholera [kɑːl'əːrə] *n* コレラ kórèra

cholesterol [kales'tərɔːl] *n* (fat) コレステロール korésuterôru

choose [tʃuːz] (*pt* **chose**, *pp* **chosen**) *vt*

ぶ erábu
to choose to do ...をする事に決める
...wo suru kotó ni kiméru
choosy [tʃuː'zi:] *adj* (difficult to please) えり好みする erigonomi suru

chop [tʃɑːp] *vt* (wood) 割る warú; (CULIN: *also*: **chop up**: vegetables, fruit, meat) 刻む kizámu
◆*n* (CULIN) チョップ chóppù, チャップ cháppu

chopper [tʃɑːp'əːr] *n* (helicopter) ヘリコプター herſkoputâ

choppy [tʃɑːp'iː] *adj* (sea) しけの shiké no

chops [tʃɑːps] *npl* (jaws) あご agó

chopsticks [tʃɑːp'stiks] *npl* はし háshì

choral [kɔːr'əl] *adj* (MUS) 合唱の gasshō no

chord [kɔːrd] *n* (MUS) 和音 wáòn

chore [tʃɔːr] *n* (domestic task) 家事 kájì; (routine task) 毎日の雑用 máìnichi no zatsúyō

choreographer [kɔːriːɑːg'rəfəːr] *n* 振付師 furítsukeshì

chortle [tʃɔːr'təl] *vi* 楽しそうに笑う tanóshisō ni waráu

chorus [kɔːr'əs] *n* (MUS: group) 合唱隊 gasshōtai, コーラス kōrasu; (: song) 合唱 gasshō; (: refrain) リフレーン rifúrèn; (of musical play) コーラス kōrasu

chose [tʃouz] *pt* of **choose**

chosen [tʃou'zən] *pp* of **choose**

Christ [kraist] *n* キリスト kirísuto

christen [kris'ən] *vt* (REL: baby) ...に洗礼を施す ...ni señrei wo hodókosù; (nickname) ...と...と呼ぶ ...wo ...to yobú

Christian [kris'tʃən] *adj* キリスト教の kirísutokyō no
◆*n* キリスト教徒 kirísutokyōto

Christianity [kristʃiːæn'iti:] *n* キリスト教 kirísutokyō

Christian name *n* ファーストネーム fásutonēmu

Christmas [kris'mas] *n* (REL: festival) クリスマス kurísumàsu; (period) クリスマスの季節 kurísumàsu no kisetsù
Merry Christmas! メリークリスマス! merí kurisumàsu!

Christmas card *n* クリスマスカード

kurísumasu kàdo

Christmas Day *n* クリスマス kurísumàsu

Christmas Eve *n* クリスマスイブ kurísumasu ibù

Christmas tree *n* クリスマスツリー kurísumasu tsurī

chrome [kroum] *n* クロームめっき kurōmumekkī

chromium [krou'mi:əm] *n* = **chrome**

chromosome [krou'məsoum] *n* 染色体 señshokutai

chronic [krɑːn'ik] *adj* (continual: ill-health, illness etc) 慢性の mañsei no; (: drunkenness etc) 常習的な jōshūteki na; (severe: shortage, lack etc) ひどい hídòi

chronicle [krɑːn'ikəl] *n* (of events) 記録 kiróku ◇年代順または日付順の記録を指す nefidaijuñ mata wa hizúkejuñ no kiróku wo sasú

chronological [krɑːnəlɑːdʒ'ikəl] *adj* (order) 時代順の hizúkejuñ no

chrysanthemum [krisæn'θəməm] *n* キク kikú

chubby [tʃʌb'iː] *adj* (cheeks, child) ぽっちゃりした potchárì shitá

chuck [tʃʌk] (*inf*) *vt* (throw: stone, ball etc) 投げる nagerù; (BRIT: *also*: **chuck up**) やめる yamérù

chuckle [tʃʌk'əl] *vi* くすくす笑う kúsùkusu waráu

chuck out *vt* (person) 追い出す ofdasù; (rubbish etc) 捨てる sutérù

chug [tʃʌg] *vi* (machine, car engine etc) ぽっぽっと言う póppòtto otó wo taterù; (car, boat: *also*: **chug along**) ぽっぽっと音を立てて行く póppòtto otó wo tatéte ikú

chum [tʃʌm] *n* (friend) 友達 tomódachì

chunk [tʃʌŋk] *n* (of stone, meat) 塊 katámari

church [tʃəːrtʃ] *n* (building) 教会 kyōkai; (denomination) 教派 kyōha, ...教 ...kyō

churchyard [tʃəːrtʃ'jɑːrd] *n* 教会墓地 kyōkaibochī

churlish [tʃəːr'liʃ] *adj* (silence, behavior) 無礼な buréi na

churn [tʃəːrn] n (for butter) かく乳酪 kakúnyúki; (BRIT: also: **milk churn**) 大型ミルク缶 ógata mirukúkan

churn out vt (mass-produce): objects, books etc) 大量に作る taíryō ni tsukurū

chute [ʃuːt] n (also: **rubbish chute**) ごみ捨て場 gomísuteba; (for coal, parcels etc) シュート shúto

chutney [tʃʌt'niː] n チャツネ chátsune

CIA [siːaiei'] n abbr (US) (= Central Intelligence Agency) 中央情報局 chūōjōhōkyoku

CID [siːaidiː'] n abbr (BRIT) (= Criminal Investigation Department) 刑事部 keíjibū

cider [sai'dəːr] n リンゴ酒 ríngoshū

cigar [sigɑːr'] n 葉巻 hamáki

cigarette [sigəret'] n (紙巻) タバコ (kamímaki) tábako

cigarette case n シガレットケース shigárettokēsu

cigarette end n 吸殻 suígara

Cinderella [sindərel'ə] n シンデレラ shíndererā

cinders [sin'dəːrz] npl (of fire) 燃え殻 moégara

cine-camera [sin'iːkæmərə] (BRIT) n 映画カメラ efga kámèra

cine-film [sin'iːfilm] (BRIT) n 映画用フィルム efgayō fírùmu

cinema [sin'əmə] n (THEATER) 映画館 efgakān; (film-making) 映画界 efgakāi

cinnamon [sin'əmən] n (CULIN) ニッケイ nikkéi, シナモン shínámon

cipher [sai'fəːr] n (code) 暗号 añgō

circle [səːr'kəl] n (shape) 円 éñ; (of friends) 仲間 nakáma; (in cinema, theater) 二階席 nikáiseki
◆vi (bird, plane) 旋回する señkai suru
◆vt (move round) 回る mawáru; (surround) 囲む kakómu

circuit [səːr'kit] n (ELEC) 回路 káīro; (tour) 1周 isshū; (track) サーキット sākitto; (lap) 1周 isshū, ラップ ráppù

circuitous [səːrkjuː'itəs] adj (route, journey) 遠回りの tōmawàri no

circular [səːr'kjələːr] adj (plate, etc) 丸い marúi

◆n (letter) 回状 kaíjō

circulate [səːr'kjəleit] vi (traffic) 流れる nagárerū; (blood) 循環する juñkan suru; (news, rumour, report) 出回る demáwaru; (person: at party etc) 動き回る ugókimawarū
◆vt (report) 回す mawásu

circulation [səːrkjəlei'ʃən] n (of report, book etc) 回される事 mawásareru kotó; (of traffic) 流れ nagáre; (of air, water, also MED: of blood) 循環 juñkan; (of newspaper) 発行部数 hakkóbusū

circumcise [səːr'kəmsaiz] vt (MED) ...の包皮を切除する ...no hōhi wo setsūjo surū; (REL) ...に割礼を行う ...ni katsúrei wo okónau

circumference [səːrkʌm'fəːrəns] n (edge) 周囲 shūi; (distance) 周囲の長さ shūi no nagāsa

circumflex [səːr'kəmfleks] n (also: **circumflex accent**) 曲折アクセント kyokúsetsu akúsento

circumspect [səːr'kəmspekt] adj (cautious, careful) 慎重な shiñchō na

circumstances [səːr'kəmstænsiz] npl (of accident, death) 状況 jōkyō; (conditions, state of affairs) 状態 jōtai; (also: **financial circumstances**) 経済状態 keízaijōtai

circumvent [səːrkəmvent'] vt (regulation) ...に制裁を加える様にする ...ni furénai yō ni surū; (difficulty) 回避する káīhi suru

circus [səːr'kəs] n (show) サーカス sākasu; (performers) サーカス団 sākasudañ

CIS [siːaies'] n abbr = Commonwealth of Independent States

cistern [sis'təːrn] n (water tank) 貯水タンク chosúitañku; (of toilet) 水槽 suísō

cite [sait] vt (quote, author etc) 引用する in-yō suru; (LAW) 召喚する shōkan suru

citizen [sit'əzən] n (gen) 住民 jūmin; (of a country) 国民 kokúmin, 市民 shímin; (of a city) 市民 shímin; (other political divisions) ...民 ...mīn

citizenship [sit'əzənʃip] n (of a country) 市民権 shímínken

citrus fruit [sit'rəs fru:t] n カンキツ類 kankitsurui

city [sit'i:] n 都市 toshi
 the City (FINANCE) シティー shitf ◊ ロンドンの金融業の中心地 rondon no kinyūgyō no chūshinchi

civic [siv'ik] adj (leader, duties, pride) 公民の kōmin no; (authorities) 自治体の jichítai no

civic centre (BRIT) n 自治体中心部 jichítaichūshinbu

civil [siv'əl] adj (gen) 市民の shímin no, 公民の kōmin no; (authorities) 行政の gyósei no; (polite) 礼儀正しい reígitadashii

civil defense n 民間防衛 mínkanbōei

civil disobedience n 市民的不服従 shimínteki fufukujū

civil engineer n 土木技師 dobókugishi

civilian [sivil'jən] adj (attitudes, casualties, life) 民間の mínkan no
 ♦n 民間人 mínkanjin

civilization [sivəlɑzei'ʃən] n (a society) 文明社会 buńmeishakái; (social organization) 文化 búnka

civilized [siv'əlaizd] adj (society) 文明的な buńmeiteki na; (person) 洗練された sefiren saréta

civil law n 民法 mínpō

civil rights npl 公民権 kōmínken

civil servant n 公務員 kōmuín

Civil Service n 文官職 buńkanshokū

civil war n 内乱 naíran

clad [klæd] adj: **clad (in)** ...を着た ...wo kíta

claim [kleim] vt (expenses) 請求する seikyū suru; (inheritance) 要求する yōkyū suru; (rights) 主張する shuchō suru; (assert): **to claim that/to be** ...であると主張する ...de arú to shuchō suru
 ♦vi (for insurance) 請求する seikyū suru
 ♦n (assertion) 主張 shuchō; (for pension, wage rise, compensation) 請求 seíkyū; (to inheritance, land) 権利 kéfiri
 to claim responsibility (for) (...の) 犯行声明を出す (...no) hafikōseiméi wo dasū
 to claim credit (for) (...が) 自分の業績

であると主張する (...ga) jibún no gyóseki de arú to shuchō suru

claimant [klei'mənt] n (ADMIN) 要求者 yōkyūsha; (LAW) 原告 geñkoku

clairvoyant [kler:vɔi'ənt] n (psychic) 霊媒 reíbai

clam [klæm] n (ZOOL, CULIN) ハマグリ hamagúri ◊英語では食用二枚貝の総称として使われる efgo de wa shokúyōnimaígai no sōshō toshité tsukáwarerū

clamber [klæm'bə:r] vi (aboard vehicle) 乗る norú; (up hill etc) 登る nobóru ◊手足を使って物に乗ったり登ったりするという含みがある teáshi wo tsukátte monó ni nottári nobóttari suru to iú fukúmi ga arū

clammy [klæm'i:] adj (hands, face etc) 冷たくてべとべとしている tsumétakute betóbeto shité irū

clamor [klæm'ə:r] (BRIT **clamour**) vi:
 to clamor for (change, war etc) ...をやかましく要求する ...wo yakámashikú yōkyū suru

clamp [klæmp] n (device) 留金 tomégane, クランプ kuráñpu
 ♦vt (two things together) クランプで留める kuráñpu de toméru; (put: one thing on another) 締付ける shimétsukerū

clamp down on vt fus (violence, speculation etc) 取り締まる toríshimarū

clan [klæn] n (family) 一族 ichízoku

clandestine [klændes'tin] adj (activity, broadcast) 秘密の hímítsu no

clang [klæŋ] vi (bell, metal object) かんと鳴る kañ to narú

clap [klæp] vi (audience, spectators) 拍手する hákushu suru

clapping [klæp'iŋ] n (applause) 拍手 hákushu

claret [klær'it] n クラレット kuráretto ◊ボルドー産の赤ワイン bórudōsan no aká wain

clarify [klær'əfai] vt (argument, point) はっきりさせる hakkíri saséru

clarinet [klærənet'] n (MUS: instrument) クラリネット kurárinětto

clarity [klær'iti] n (of explanation, thought) 明りょうさ mefíryōsa

clash [klæʃ] n (of opponents) 衝突 shōtotsu; (of beliefs, ideas, views) 衝突 shōtotsu; 対立 tairitsu; (of colors) 不調和 fuchōwa; (of styles) つり合わない事 tsurawanai kotō; (between two events, appointments) かち合い kachíai; (noise) ぶつかる音 butsúkaru otő

◆vi (fight: rival gangs etc) 衝突する shōtotsu suru; (disagree: political opponents, personalities) 角突合いをする tsunótsukiai wo surù; (beliefs, ideas, views) 相容れない afírenaì; (colors, styles) 合わない awánaì; (two events, appointments) かち合う kachíaù; (make noise: weapons, cymbals etc) 音を立ててぶつかり合う otő wo tatéte butsúkariaù

clasp [klæsp] n (hold: with hands) 握る事 nigíru kotō, 握り nigíri; (: with arms) 抱締める事 dakíshimerù kotō, 抱擁 hōyō; (of necklace, bag) 留金 tomégane, クラスプ kurásupū

◆vt (hold) 握る nigíru; (embrace) 抱締める dakíshimerù

class [klæs] n (SCOL: pupils) 学級 gakkyū, クラス kurásu; (: lesson) 授業 jugyō; (of society) 階級 kaíkyū; (type, group) 種類 shurúi

◆vt (categorize) 分類する buńrui suru

classic [klæs'ik] adj (example, illustration) 典型的な teñkeïteki na; (film, work etc) 傑作の kessáku no; (style, dress) 古典的な kotenteki na

◆n (film, novel etc) 傑作 kessáku

classical [klæs'ikəl] adj (traditional) 伝統的な deftőteki na; (MUS) クラシックの kuráshikkù no; (Greek, Roman) 古代の kódai no

classification [klæsəfəkei'ʃən] n (process) 分類する事 buńrui suru kotō; (category, system) 分類 buńrui

classified [klæs'əfaid] adj (information) 秘密の hímitsu no

classified advertisement n 分類広告 buńruikőkoku

classify [klæs'əfai] vt (books, fossils etc) 分類する buńrui suru

classmate [klæs'meit] n 同級生 dőkyūsei, クラスメート kurásumēto

classroom [klæs'ru:m] n 教室 kyőshitsu

clatter [klæt'əːr] n (of dishes, pots etc) がちゃがちゃ gachágacha; (of hooves) かたかた kátakata

◆vi (dishes, pots etc) がちゃがちゃ鳴る gachágacha narú; (hooves) かたかた鳴る kátakata narú

clause [klɔːz] n (LAW) 条項 jőkō; (LING) 文節 buńsetsu

claustrophobia [klɔːstrəfou'biːə] n (PSYCH) 閉所恐怖症 heíshokyőfushō

claw [klɔː] n (of animal, bird) つめ tsumé; (of lobster) はさみ hasámi

claw at vt fus (curtains, door etc) 引っかく hikkáku

clay [klei] n 粘土 neńdo

clean [klin] adj (person, animal) きれい好きな kiréizuki na; (place, surface, clothes etc) 清潔な seíketsu na; (fight) 反則のない hańsoku no naí; (record, reputation) 無傷の műkizu no; (joke, story) 下品でない gehín de naí; (MED: fracture) 単純な tańjun na

◆vt (car, hands, face etc) きれいにする kiréi ni surú, 掃除する sőji suru

clean-cut [klin'kʌt'] adj (person) 品の良い hiń no yoí

cleaner [kliː'nəːr] n (person) 掃除係 sőjigakàri; (substance) 洗剤 seńzai

cleaner's [kliː'nəːrz] n (also: dry cleaner's) クリーニング店 kuríningùten

cleaning [kliː'niŋ] n (of room, house) 掃除 sőji

cleanliness [klen'liːnis] n 清潔 seíketsu

clean out vt (cupboard, drawer) 中身を出してきれいにする nakámi wo dashíte kiréi ni suru

cleanse [klenz] vt (purify) 清める kiyőmerù; (face, cut) 洗う aráu

cleanser [klen'zəːr] n (for face) 洗顔料 señganryō

clean-shaven [klin'ʃei'vən] adj ひげのない higé no naí

cleansing department [klen'ziŋ-] (BRIT) n 清掃局 seísőkyoku

clean up vt (mess) 片付ける katázukerù; (child) 身ぎれいにする migírei ni suru

clear [kliːr] adj (easy to understand:

report, argument) 分かりやすい wakári-yasuí; (easy to see, hear) はっきりした hakkírí shitá; (obvious: choice, commitment) 明らかな akfráka na; (glass, plastic) 透明な tómei na; (water, eyes) 澄んだ sůnda; (road, way, floor etc) 障害のない shógai no naí; (conscience) やましい所のない yamashíi tokóro no naí; (skin) 健康そうな keñkósō na; (sky) 晴れた haréta

♦vt (space, room) 開ける akéru; (LAW: suspect) 容疑を晴す yốgi wo harasů; (fence, wall) 飛越える tobíkoerů; (check) 払う haraú

♦vi (weather, sky) 晴れる harerú; (fog, smoke) 消える kierú

♦adv: clear of (trouble) ...を避けて ...wo sakéte; (ground) ...から離れて ...kara hanárete

to clear the table 食卓を片付ける shokútaku wo katázukerù

clearance [kli:'rəns] n (removal: of trees, slums) 取払う事 torfharaú kotó; (permission) 許可 kyóka

clear-cut [kli:'ərkʌt'] adj (decision, issue) 明白な meíhaku na

clearing [kli:'riŋ] n (in woods) 開けた所 hirákèta tokóro

clearing bank [kli:'riŋ] (BRIT) n 手形交換組合銀行 tegátakōkankumiaigíñkō ◊ ロンドンの中央手形交換所を通じて他の銀行との取引を行う銀行 róñdon no chūō tegata kōkañjo wo tsūjité tá no giñkō to no toríhiki wò okónaú giñkō

clearly [kli:'ərli:] adv (distinctly, coherently) はっきりと hakkírì to; (evidently) 明らかに akfráka ni

clear up vt (room, mess) 片付ける katázukerù; (mystery, problem) 解決する kafketsu suru

clearway [kli:'rwei] (BRIT) n 駐停車禁止道路 chúteíshakinshidōrò

cleaver [kli:'vər] n 肉包丁 honéwaríbōchō ◊なたに似た物で、肉のブロックをたたき切ったり骨を割ったりするのに使う natá ni nitá monó de, nikú no burokkù wo tatákikittarí honé wo wattárì surú no ni tsukaú

clef [klef] n (MUS) 音部記号 oñbukígō

cleft [kleft] n (in rock) 割れ目 waréme

clemency [klem'ənsi:] n 恩赦 oñsho

clench [klentʃ] vt (fist) 握り締める nigírishimerù; (teeth) 食いしばる kuíshibarishì

clergy [klɔːr'dʒiː] n 聖職者 seíshokusha ◊総称 sốshō

clergyman [klɔːr'dʒiːmən] (pl clergymen) n (Protestant) 牧師 bókùshi; (Catholic) 神父 shíñpu

clerical [kler'ikəl] adj (worker, job) 事務の jímù no; (REL) 聖職者の seíshokushà no

clerk [klɔːrk] n (BRIT: office worker) 事務員 jímùîn; (US: sales person) 店員 teñîn

clever [klev'ə:r] adj (intelligent) 利口な rikô na; (deft, crafty) こうかつな kôkatsu na; (device, arrangement) 良く工夫した yốkù kufû shitá

cliché [kli:ʃei'] n 決り文句 kimárimoñku

click [klik] vt (tongue) 鳴らす narásu; (heels) 打鳴らす uchínarasu

♦vi (device, switch etc) かちっと鳴る kachíttò narú

client [klai'ənt] n (of bank, company) 客 kyakú; (of lawyer) 依頼人 irâīnin

cliff [klif] n (GEO) 断崖 dañgai

climate [klai'mit] n (weather) 気候 kikô; (of opinion, times) 雰囲気 fuñ-ikî

climax [klai'mæks] n (of battle, career) 頂点 chôten; (of film, book) クライマックス kuráimakkùsu; (sexual) オルガズム orûgazûmu

climb [klaim] vi (sun, plant) 上がる agáru; (plant) は上がる hafagarù; (plane) 上昇する jôshō suru; (prices, shares) 上昇する jôshō suru ◊(move with effort): to climb over a wall 塀を乗り越える hef wo norîkoerù

♦vt (stairs, ladder) 上がる agáru, 登る nobôru; (hill) 登る nobôru; (tree) ...に登る ...ni nobôru

♦n (of hill, cliff etc) 登る事 nobôru kotó; (of prices etc) 上昇 jôshō

to climb into a car 車に乗り込む kurûma ni norîkomù

climb-down [klaim'daun] n (retraction)

撤回 tekkái

climber [klai'mər] n (mountaineer) 登山者 tozanbīn; (plant) つる性植物 tsurūsei-shokubútsu

climbing [klai'miŋ] n (mountaineering) 山登り yamánobòri, 登山 tōzán

clinch [klintʃ] vt (deal) まとめる matómeru; (argument) …に決着を付ける …ni ketcháku wo tsukerú

cling [kliŋ] (pt, pp **clung**) vi: **to cling to** (mother, support) …にしがみつく …ni shigámitsukū; (idea, belief) 固執する koshū suru; (subj: clothes, dress) …にぴったりくっつく …ni pittári kuttsúku

clinic [klin'ik] n (MED: center) 診療所 shiñryōjo

clinical [klin'ikəl] adj (MED: tests) 臨床の riñshō no; (: teaching) 臨床の riñshō no; (fig: thinking, attitude) 冷淡な reítanna; (: building, room) 潤いのない urúoi no naí

clink [kliŋk] vi (glasses, cutlery) ちんと鳴る chiñ to narū

clip [klip] n (also: **paper clip**) クリップ kurippū; (also: **hair clip**) 髪留 kamídome; (TV, CINEMA) 断片 dañpen
♦vt (fasten) 留める toméru; (cut) はさみで切る hasámi de kíru

clippers [klip'ərz] npl (for gardening) せん定ばさみ señteibasàmi; (also: **nail clippers**) つめ切り tsumékiri

clipping [klip'iŋ] n (from newspaper) 切抜き kirínuki

clique [klik] n 徒党 totō

cloak [klouk] n (cape) マント mấnto
♦vt (fig: in mist, secrecy) 隠す kakúsū

cloakroom [klouk'rum] n (for coats etc) クローク kurōku; (BRIT: WC) お手洗 o-téaraì

clock [klɑk] n 時計 tokéi

clock in vi (for work) 出勤する shukkín suru

clock off vi (from work) 退社する taísha suru

clock on vi = **clock in**

clock out vi = **clock off**

clockwise [klɑk'waiz] adv 時計回りに tokéimawàri ni

clockwork [klɑk'wərk] n 時計仕掛 to-kéijikàke
♦adj (model, toy) 時計仕掛の tokéijikàke no

clog [klɑg] n (leather) 木底の靴 kizóko no kutsú; (also: **wooden clog**) 木靴 kígútsu
♦vt (drain, nose) ふさぐ fuságu
♦vi (also: **clog up**: sink) 詰る tsumarū

cloister [klɔis'tər] n 回廊 kaírō

clone [kloun] n (of animal, plant) クローン kūrōn

close[1] [klous] adj (near) 近くの chikákù no; (friend) 親しい shitáshiĩ; (relative) 近縁の kiñ-en no; (contact) 密な mítsū na; (link, ties) 密接な míssétsu na; (examination, watch) 注意深い chūbukaì; (contest) 互角の gokáku no; (weather) 重苦しい omókurushiĩ
♦adv (near) 近くに chikákù ni

close to …の近くに …no chikákù ni

close at hand, close by adj 近くの chi-kákù no
♦adv 近くに chikákù ni

to have a close shave (fig) 間一髪で助かる kañ-ippátsu de tasukaru

close[2] [klouz] vt (shut: door, window) し める shimérū; (finalize: sale) 取決める to-rfkimerū; (end: case, speech) 終える oḗru
♦vi (shop etc) 閉店する heíten suru; (door, lid) 閉る shimarū; (end) 終る owárú

closed [klouzd] adj (door, window, shop etc) 閉っている shimatté irū

close down vi (factory) 廃業する haígyō suru; (magazine) 廃刊する haíkan suru

closed shop n (fig) クローズドショップ kurōzudo shoppū ◇特定の労働組合員だけしか雇われない事業所 tokútei no rōdō-kumiaiñ dake shika yatówanaì jigyōsho

close-knit [klous'nit'] adj (family, community) 堅く結ばれた katáku musúbareta

closely [klous'li:] adv (examine, watch) 注意深く chūbukakū; (connected) 密接に míssétsu ni; (related) 近縁になって kiñ-en ni natté; (resemble) そっくり sokkúrí

closet [klɔ:z'it] *n* (cupboard) たんす tañsu

close-up [klous'ʌp] *n* (PHOT) クローズアップ kurōzuappū

closure [klou'ʒər] *n* (of factory) 閉鎖 heísa; (of magazine) 廃刊 hafkan

clot [klɑt] *n* (gen: blood clot) 血の塊 chí no katámari; (*inf*: idiot) ばか bákà
♦*vi* (blood) 固まる katámaru, 凝固する gyōko suru

cloth [klɔ:θ] *n* (material) 布 nunó; (rag) ふきん fukíñ

clothe [klouð] *vt* (dress) ...に服を着せる ...ni fukú wo kiséru

clothes [klouz] *npl* 服 fukú

clothes brush *n* 洋服ブラシ yốfukuburāshi

clothes line *n* 物干綱 monóhoshizūna

clothes pin (*BRIT* **clothes peg**) *n* 洗濯ばさみ señtakubasami

clothing [klou'ðiŋ] *n* = clothes

cloud [klaud] *n* (in sky) 雲 kúmð
a cloud of smoke/dust もうもうとした 煙 (ほこり) mômô to shita kemúri (hokori)

cloudburst [klaud'bə:rst] *n* 集中豪雨 shúchugōu

cloudy [klau'di:] *adj* (sky) 曇った kumottà; (liquid) 濁った nigotta

clout [klaut] *vt* (hit, strike) 殴る naguru

clove [klouv] *n* (spice) チョウジ chōji, クローブ kurōbu
clove of garlic ニンニクの一粒 nifnīku no hitótsubu

clover [klou'və:r] *n* クローバー kurōba

clown [klaun] *n* (in circus) ピエロ pfèro
♦*vi* (*also*: **clown about, clown around**) おどけるodőkeru

cloying [klɔi'iŋ] *adj* (taste, smell) むかつかせる mukátsukaseru

club [klʌb] *n* (society, place) クラブ kúràbu; (weapon) こん棒 kofbō; (*also*: **golf club**) クラブ kúràbu
♦*vt* (hit) 殴る naguru
♦*vi*: *to club together* (*BRIT*: for gift, card) 金を出し合う kané wo dashíaù

club car (*US*) *n* (RAIL) ラウンジカー raûnjikā ◇休憩用客車 kyūkeiyō kyakūsha

clubhouse [klʌb'haus] *n* (of sports club) クラブハウス kurābuhaùsu ◇スポーツクラブのメンバーが集まる部屋, 建物など supôtsukuràbu no mefbā ga atsűmarū heyá, tatémono nadð

clubs [klʌbz] *npl* (CARDS) クラブ kúràbu

cluck [klʌk] *vi* (hen) こっこっと鳴く kőkkòtto naku

clue [klu:] *n* (pointer, lead) 手掛かり tégakari; (in crossword) かぎ kagí
I haven't a clue さっぱり分らない sáppàri wakáranaì

clump [klʌmp] *n* (gen) 塊 katámari; (of buildings etc) 一連 ichíren
a clump of trees 木立 kódàchi

clumsy [klʌm'zi:] *adj* (person, movement) 不器用な búkìyō na; (object) 扱いにくい atsűkainikuì; (effort, attempt) 下手な hetá na

clung [klʌŋ] *pt, pp of* **cling**

cluster [klʌs'tə:r] *n* (of people, stars, flowers etc) 塊 katámari
♦*vi* 固まる katámaru, 群がる murágarù

clutch [klʌtʃ] *n* (grip, grasp) つかむ事 tsukamù kotő; (AUT) クラッチ kurátchà
♦*vt* (purse, hand, stick) しっかり持つ shíkkàri motsù

clutter [klʌt'ə:r] *vt* (room, table) 散らかす chirákasu

cm *abbr* = **centimeter**

CND [si:endi:'] *n abbr* (= *Campaign for Nuclear Disarmament*) 核廃絶運動 kakúhaizetsu undō

Co. *abbr* = **county; company**

c/o *abbr* = **care of**

coach [koutʃ] *n* (bus) バス básù; (*also*: **horse-drawn coach**) 馬車 báshà; (of train) 客車 kyakūsha; (SPORT: trainer) コーチ kōchi; (tutor) 個人教師 kojínkyòshi
♦*vt* (sportsman/woman) コーチする kőchi suru; (student) ...に個人指導をする ...ni kojfndo wo surù

coach trip *n* バス旅行 basúryokō

coagulate [kouæg'jəleit] *vi* (blood, paint etc) 凝固する gyōko surù

coal [koul] *n* (substance) 石炭 sekítań

(also: lump of coal) 石炭1個 sekítan ik-kò

coal face n 石炭切り場 sekítankiríbà

coalfield [koul'fi:ld] n 炭田 tañden

coalition [kouəli'ʃən] n (POL: also: coa-lition government) 連合政権 reñgōseí-kèn; (of pressure groups etc) 連盟 reñ-mei

coalman [koul'mən] (pl coalmen) n 石炭屋 sekítanya

coal merchant n = coalman

coalmine [koul'main] n 炭坑 tañkō

coarse [kɔ:rs] adj (texture: rough) 荒い aráì; (person: vulgar) 下品な gehín na

coast [koust] n 海岸 kaígan
♦vi (car, bicycle etc) 惰力走行する da-ryókusōkō suru

coastal [kous'təl] adj (cities, waters) 海岸沿いの kaíganzòi no

coastguard [koust'gɑ:rd] n (officer) 沿岸警備隊員 efgankeíbitàiin; (service) 沿岸警備隊 efgankeíbitài

coastline [koust'lain] n 海岸線 kaígan-sen

coat [kout] n (overcoat) コート kòto; (of animal) 毛 ke; (of paint) 塗り nurf
♦vt: coated with ...で覆われた ...de ō-waréta

coat hanger n ハンガー háñgā

coating [kou'tiŋ] n (of dust, mud etc) 覆う物 ōu monó; (of chocolate, plastic etc) 被覆 hifúku

coat of arms n 紋章 mōñ

coax [kouks] vt (person: persuade) 説得する settóku suru

cob [kɑ:b] n see corn

cobbler [kɑb'lər] n (maker/repairer of shoes) 靴屋 kutsúyà

cobbles [kɑ:b'əlz] npl 敷石 shikíishi

cobblestones [kɑ:b'əlstounz] npl = cobbles

cobweb [kɑb'web] n クモの巣 kúmō no su

cocaine [koukein'] n コカイン kokáin

cock [kɑk] n (rooster) おん鳥 ofídori; (male bird) 鳥の雄 torî no osû
♦vt (gun) ...no 撃鉄を起す ...no gekítetsu wo okosù

cockerel [kɑ:k'ə:rəl] n 雄のひな鳥 osú no hínadori

cock-eyed [kɑk'aid] adj (fig: idea, method) ばかな bákà na

cockle [kɑ:k'əl] n ホタテガイ hotátegai

cockney [kɑk'ni:] n コックニー kókkù-ni ◇ロンドンのEast End地区生れの人 rőñdon no East End chíkù umáre no hitó

cockpit [kɑk'pit] n (in aircraft) 操縦室 sōjúshitsu, コックピット kokkúpittò; (in racing car) 運転席 uñtenseki, コックピット kokkúpittò

cockroach [kɑk'routʃ] n ゴキブリ gokí-buri

cocktail [kɑk'teil] n (drink) カクテル kákùteru; (mixture: fruit cocktail, prawn cocktail etc) ...カクテル ...kakúte-ru

cocktail cabinet n ホームバー hōmubā

cocktail party n カクテルパーティ ka-kúterupàti

cocoa [kou'kou] n (powder, drink) ココア kókōa

coconut [kou'kənʌt] n (fruit) ヤシの実 yáshì no mi; (flesh) ココナッツ kokónat-tsu

cocoon [kəku:n'] n (of butterfly) 繭 má-yù

cod [kɑd] n タラ tárà

C.O.D. [si:oudi:'] abbr = cash or also (US) collect on delivery) 着払い chakú-barài

code [koud] n (of practice, behavior) 規定 kitéi; (cipher) 暗号 añgō; (dialling code, post code) 番号 bañgō

cod-liver oil [kɑd'livər-] n 肝油 kañ-yu

coercion [kouər'ʃən] n (pressure) 強制 kyōsei

coffee [kɔ:f'i:] n (drink, powder) コーヒー kōhī; (cup of coffee) コーヒー一杯 kō-hī ippai

coffee bar (BRIT) n 喫茶店 kissáten

coffee bean n コーヒー豆 kōhīmàme

coffee break n コーヒーブレーク kōhī-burèku

coffeepot [kɔ:f'i:pɑt] n コーヒーポット kōhīpottò

coffee table n コーヒーテーブル kōhītēburu

coffin [kɔːf'in] n ひつぎ hitsúgi

cog [kɑːg] n (TECH: wheel) 歯車 hágūruma; (: tooth) 歯車の歯 hágūruma no ha

cogent [kou'dʒənt] adj (argument etc) 説得力ある settőkuryőku arű

cognac [koun'jæk] n コニャック kónyàkku

coherent [kouhi:'rənt] adj (answer, theory, speech) 筋の通った sujì no tôtta; (person) 筋の通った事を言う sujì no tôtta kotố wo iû

cohesion [kouhi:'ʒən] n (political, ideological etc) 団結 dańketsu

coil [kɔil] n (of rope, wire) 一巻 hitómaki; (ELEC) コイル kőíru; (contraceptive) 避妊リング hinínrìngu

♦vt (rope) 巻く makû

coin [kɔin] n (money) 硬貨 kőka, コイン kőín

♦vt (word, slogan) 造る tsukúru

coinage [kɔi'nidʒ] n 貨幣制度 kahéiseido

coin-box [kɔin'bɑːks] (BRIT) n 電話 koíndeñwa ◇公衆電話でカードだけしか使えない物に対して言う kőshúdeñwa de kádo dakê shiká tsukáenai monő ni táshi shité iŭ

coincide [kouinsaid'] vi (events) 同時に起る dôji ni okóru; (ideas, views) 一致する itchí suru

coincidence [kouin'sidəns] n 偶然の一致 gûzen no itchí

Coke [kouk] ® n (drink) コカコーラ kókakőra

coke [kouk] n (coal) コークス kőkusu

colander [kɑl'əndəːr] n 水切り mizúkiri ◇ボール型で穴の比較的大きい物を言う bőrugata de aná no hikákuteki őkii monő wo sasû

cold [kould] adj (water, food etc) 冷たい tsumétai; (weather, room) 寒い samûi; (person, attitude: unemotional) 冷たい tsumétai, 冷淡な reítan na

♦n (weather) 寒さ samûsa; (MED) 風邪 kazé

it's cold 寒い samûi

to be cold (person, object) 冷たい tsumétai

to catch (a) cold 風邪を引く kazé wo hikû

in cold blood (kill etc) 冷酷に refkoku ni

coldly [kould'li:] adv (speak, behave) 冷たく tsumétaku, 冷淡に reítañ ni

cold-shoulder [kould'ʃouldəːr] vt 冷たくあしらう tsumétaku ashíraū

cold sore n 口内炎 kőkakuèn

coleslaw [koul'slɔ:] n コールスロー kőrusurō

colic [kɑl'ik] n (MED) 腹痛 fukútsuū

collaborate [kəlæb'əːreit] vi (on book, research) 協同する kyődő suru; (with enemy) 協力する kyőryoku suru

collaboration [kəlæbəːrei'ʃən] n 協力 kyőryoku

collage [kəlɑːʒ'] n コラージュ kőràju

collapse [kəlæps'] vi (building, system, resistance) 崩れる kuzúrerù, 崩壊する hőkai suru; (government) 倒れる taőrerù; (MED: person) 倒れる taőrerù; (table) 壊れる kowárerù, つぶれる tsubúrerù; (company) つぶれる tsubúrerù, 破産する hasán suru

♦n (of building, system, government, resistance) 崩壊 hőkai; (MED: of person) 倒れる事 taőrerù kotő; (of table) 壊れる〔つぶれる〕事 kowáreru (tsubúreru) kotő; (of company) 破産 hasán

collapsible [kəlæp'səbəl] adj (seat, bed, bicycle) 折畳みの orítatami no

collar [kɑl'əːr] n (of coat, shirt) 襟 erî, カラー kárâ; (of dog, cat) 首輪 kubíwa, カラー kárâ

collarbone [kɑl'əːrboun] n (ANAT) 鎖骨 sakótsu

collateral [kəlæt'əːrəl] n (COMM) 担保 tañpo

colleague [kɑl'iːg] n 同僚 dőryo

collect [kəlekt'] vt (gather: wood, litter etc) 集める atsúmerù; (as a hobby) 収集する shúshú suru; (BRIT: call and pick up: person) 迎えに行く mukáe ni ikû; (: object) 取りに行く torî ni ikû; (for charity, in church) 募金する bokín suru; (debts, taxes etc) 集金する shúkín suru; (mail) 取集する shúshú suru

♦*vi* (crowd) 集る atsúmarù
to call collect (US: TEL) コレクトコールする korékutokòru suru

collection [kəlek'ʃən] *n* (of art, stamps etc) コレクション kórèkushon; (of poems, stories etc) ...集 ...shū; (from place, person) 受取る事 ukétoru kotó; (for charity) 募金 bokín; (of mail) 取集 shushū

collective [kəlek'tiv] *adj* (farm, decision) 共同の kyódò no

collector [kəlek'tə:r] *n* (of art, stamps etc) 収集家 shūshūka; (of taxes etc) 徴収人 chōshūnin

college [kɑ:l'idʒ] *n* (SCOL: of university) 学寮 gakúryō; (: of agriculture, technology) 大学 dafgaku

collide [kəlaid'] *vi* (cars, people) ぶつかる butsúkaru, 衝突する shótotsu suru

collie [kɑ:l'i:] *n* コリー犬 kóríken

colliery [kɑ:l'jə:ri:] (*BRIT*) *n* 炭坑 tankō

collision [kəliʒ'ən] *n* (of vehicles) 衝突 shótotsu

colloquial [kəlou'kwi:əl] *adj* (LING: informal) 口語の kógo no

collusion [kəlu:'ʒən] *n* (collaboration) 結託 kettáku

colon [kou'lən] *n* (punctuation mark) コロン kòròn; (ANAT) 大腸 dáïchō

colonel [kə:r'nəl] *n* 大佐 tàfsa

colonial [kəlou'ni:əl] *adj* 植民地の shokúmìnchi no

colonize [kɑ:l'ənaiz] *vt* (country, territory) 植民地にする shokúmìnchi ni suru

colony [kɑ:l'əni:] *n* (subject territory) 植民地 shokúmìnchi; (of people) ...人街 ...jìn-gai; (of animals) 個体群 kótáìgùn

color [kʌl'ə:r] (*BRIT* **colour**) *n* (gen) 色 iro

♦*vt* (paint) ...に色を塗る ...ni iró wo nurú; (dye) 染める soméru; (fig: account) ...に色を付ける ...ni iró wo tsukérù; (judgment) ゆがめる yugámerù

♦*vi* (blush) 赤面する sekímen suru
in color 天然色で teñnenshoku de, カラーで kárá de

color bar *n* 人種差別 jiñshusabètsu ◇有色人種、特に黒人に対する差別を指す

yūshokujiñshu, tokù ni kokújin ni taí suru sabétsu wo sasú

color-blind [kʌl'ə:rblaind'] *adj* 色盲の shikímō no

colored [kʌl'ə:rd] *adj* (person) 有色の yúshoku no; (illustration etc) カラーの kárá no

color film *n* カラーフィルム karáfirùmu

colorful [kʌl'ə:rfəl] *adj* (cloth) 色鮮やかな iró azáyàka na; (account, story) 華やかな hanáyàka na; (personality) 華々しい hanábanashì

coloring [kʌl'ə:riŋ] *n* (complexion) 肌の色合い hadà no iróai; (*also*: **food coloring**) 着色料 chakúshokuryò

colors [kʌl'ə:rz] *npl* (of party, club etc) 色 iró

color scheme *n* 配色計画 hafshokukeíkaku

color television *n* カラーテレビ karáterèbi

colossal [kəlɑ:s'əl] *adj* 巨大な kyodái na

colour [kʌl'ə:r] *etc* (*BRIT*) *n* = **color** *etc*

colt [koult] *n* 子ウマ koúma

column [kɑ:l'əm] *n* (ARCHIT) 円柱 eñchū; (of smoke) 柱 hashíra; (of people) 縦隊 jútai; (gossip column, sports column) コラム kóràmu

columnist [kɑ:l'əmist] *n* コラムニスト korámunìsuto

coma [kou'mə] *n* (MED) こん睡状態 koñsuijòtai

comb [koum] *n* くし kushí

♦*vt* (hair) くしでとかす kushí de tokasù; (fig: area) 捜索する sōsaku suru

combat [*n* kɑ:m'bæt *vb* kəmbæt'] *n* (MIL: fighting) 戦闘 señtō; (fight, battle) 戦い tatákaì

♦*vt* (oppose) 反抗する hañkō suru

combination [kɑːmbənei'ʃən] *n* (mixture) 組合せ kumíawase; (for lock, safe etc) 組合せ番号 kumíawasebañgò

combine [*vb* kəmbain' *n* kɑ:m'bain] *vt*: ***to combine something with something*** ...を...と組合せる ...wo ...to kumfa-

waserù; (qualities) 兼備える kanésonae-rù; (two activities) 兼任する kenínin suru
♦ vi (people, groups) 合併する gappéi su-ru
♦ n (ECON) 連合 refigō

combine (harvester) [kɑmˈbainˈ(hɑːrˈvestəːr)] n コンバイン kombaìn

combustion [kəmbˈʌstʃən] n (act, process) 燃焼 nefishō

KEYWORD

come [kʌm] (pt **came**, pp **come**) vi (movement towards) 来る kúrù

come here! ここにおいで kokó ni oide

I've only come for an hour 1時間しか いられません ichíjikan shika iráremasen

come with me ついて来て下さい tsuíte kite kudasai

are you coming to my party? 私のパーティーに来てくれますか watákushi no patí ni kité kūremasu né

to come running 走って来る hashítte kúrù

2 (arrive) 着く tsukú, 到着する tóchaku suru, 来る kúrù

he's just come from Aberdeen 彼はアバディーンから来たばかりです kárè wa abádīn kara kitá bakári desu

he's come here to work 彼はここには働きに来ました kárè wa kokó ni wa határaki ni kimashita

they came to a river 彼らは川に着きました kárèra wa kawá ni tsukímashita

to come home 家に戻って来る ié ni modóttè kuru

3 (reach): *to come to* ...に届く ...ni todó-kù, ...になる ...ni nárù

the bill came to £40 勘定は計40ポンドだった kánjō wa kéì yónjuppóndn dat-ta

her hair came to her waist 彼女の髪の毛は腰まで届いていた kánòjo no kamí no ke wa koshí madè todóttè ita

to come to power 政権を握る seíken wo nigiru

to come to a decision 結論に達する ketsúron ni tassurù

4 (occur): *an idea came to me* いい考え

が浮かびました íi kángaè ga ukábimashìta

5 (be, become) なる nárù

to come loose/undone etc 外れる hazúreru

I've come to like him 彼が好きになりました kárè ga sukí ni narímashìta

come about vi 起る okórù

come across vt fus (person, thing) ...に出会う ...ni deáù

come away vi (leave) 帰る kaérù, 出て来る détè kure; (become detached) 外れる hazúreru

come back vi (return) 帰って来る káettè kuru

comeback [kʌmˈbæk] n (of film star etc) 返り咲き kaérizaki, カムバック ka-múbakkū

come by vt fus (acquire) 手に入れる té nì iréru

comedian [kəmiˈdiːən] n (THEATER, TV) コメディアン kōmèdian

comedienne [kəmidiˈzɛn] n 女性コメディアン joséi komèdian

come down vi (price) 下がる sagárù; (tree) 倒れる taórerù; (building) 崩れ落ちる kuzúreochirù

comedy [kɑmˈidiˈ] n (play, film) 喜劇 kí-gèki, コメディー kōmèdī; (humor) 喜劇性 kígèkisei, ユーモア yūmoa

come forward vi (volunteer) 進んで...す susunde ...sûrù

come from vt fus (place, source etc) ...から来る ...kara kúrù

come in vi (visitor) 入る háìru; (on deal etc) 加わる kuwáwarù; (be involved) 関係する kánkei suru

come in for vt fus (criticism etc) 受ける ukérù

come into vt fus (money) 相続する sózoku suru; (be involved) ...に関係する ...ni kánkei suru

to come into fashion 流行する ryūkō suru

come off vi (button) 外れる hazúreru; (attempt) 成功する seíkō suru

come on vi (pupil, work, project) 進歩す

る shínpo suru; (lights, electricity) つく tsúkú

come on! さあさあ sāsā

come out vi (fact) 発覚する hakkakú suru; (book) 出版される shúppan sareru; (stain) 取れる toréru, 落ちる ochíru; (sun) 出る deru

come round vi (after faint, operation) 正気に返る shōki ni káeru, 目が覚める mé ga samérú, 気が付く ki ga tsukú

comet [kɑːm'it] n すい星 suísei

come to vi (regain consciousness) 正気に戻る shōki ni modóru; 目が覚める mé ga samérú

come up vi (sun) 出る deru; (problem) 起 る okóru, 出る deru; (event) 起る okóru; (in conversation) 出る deru

come up against vt fus (resistance, difficulties) ぶつかる butsúkaru

come upon vt fus (find) 見付ける mitsúkeru

comeuppance [kʌmʌp'ans] n: **to get one's comeuppance** 当然の罰を受ける tōzen no batsú wo ukérú

come up with vt fus (idea) 持出す mochídasù; (money) 出す dasù

comfort [kʌm'fəːrt] n (well-being: physical, material) 安楽 ánraku; (relief) 慰め nagúsame
♦vt (console) 慰める nagúsamerú

comfortable [kʌm'fəːrtəbəl] adj (person: physically) 楽な rakú na; (: financially) 暮しに困らない kuráshi ni komáranai; (furniture) 座り心地の良い suwárigokochi no yoi; (room) 居心地のよい igókochi no yoi; (patient) 苦痛のない kutsū no nai; (easy: walk, climb etc) 楽な rakú na

comfortably [kʌm'fəːrtəbli] adv (sit, live etc) 楽に rakú ni

comforts [kʌm'fəːrts] npl (of home etc) 生活を楽にするもの sefkatsu wo rakú ni suru monő

comfort station (US) n お手洗い o-téarai

comic [kɑːm'ik] adj (also: **comical**) こっけいな kokkéi na
♦n (comedian) コメディアン kómèdian; (BRIT: magazine) 漫画(雑誌) mań-

ga(zasshì)

comic strip n 連続漫画 reńzokumańga

coming [kʌm'iŋ] n (arrival) 到着 tōchaku
♦adj (event, attraction) 次の tsugí no, これからの koré kara no

coming(s) and going(s) n(pl) 行き来 yukíki, 往来 ōrai

comma [kɑːm'ə] n コンマ kôňma

command [kəmænd'] n (order) 命令 mefrei; (control, charge) 指揮 shikf; (MIL: authority) 権威 shíreibu; (mastery: of subject) マスターしていること masûta shité ité kotó
♦vt (give orders to): **to command someone to do something** ...に...をする 様に命令する ...ni ...wo suru yō ni mefrei suru; (troops) ...の司令官である ...no shirélkan de arú

commandeer [kəmændiːr'] vt (requisition) 徴発する chōhatsu suru; (fig) 勝手に取って使う katté ni totté tsukáò

commander [kəmæn'dəːr] n (MIL) 司令官 shírélkan

commandment [kəmænd'mənt] n (REL) 戒律 kafritsu

commando [kəmæn'dou] n (group) コマンド部隊 kómāndobûtai; (soldier) コマンド隊員 kómāndotaiīn

commemorate [kəmem'əːreit] vt (with statue, monument, celebration, holiday) 記念する kinén suru

commence [kəmens'] vt (begin, start) 始める hajímeru
♦vi 始まる hajímaru

commend [kəmend'] vt (praise) ほめる homéru; (recommend) ゆだねる yudáne-rù

commensurate [kəmen'səːrit] adj: **commensurate with** ...に相応した ...ni sō shitá

comment [kɑːm'ent] n (remark: written or spoken) コメント kómènto
♦vi: **to comment (on)** (...について) コメントする (...ni tsuíté) kómènto suru
no comment ノーコメント nōkomento

commentary [kɑːm'ənteːri] n (TV, RADIO) 実況放送 jikkyōhōsō; (book, article) 注解 chūkai

commentator [kɑːmˈanteitər] *n* (TV, RADIO) 解説者 kaísetsūsha

commerce [kɑːmˈərs] *n* 商業 shōgyō

commercial [kəmˈərʃəl] *adj* (organization, activity) 商業の shōgyō no; (success, failure) 商業上の shōgyōjō no

♦*n* (TV, RADIO: advertisement) コマーシャル kōmāsharu, CM shíemu

commercialized [kəmˈərʃəlaizd] (*pej*) *adj* (place, event etc) 営利本意の eírihoñi no

commercial radio/television *n* 民間ラジオ（テレビ）放送 mínkan rajio(tere-bi) hōsō, 民放 míñpō

commiserate [kəmˈizəreit] *vi*: **to commiserate with** ...をいたわる ...wo itáwarù

commission [kəmˈiʃən] *n* (order for work: esp of artist) 依頼 irái; (COMM) 歩合 buái, コミッション kómīsshon; (committee) 委員会 iñkai

♦*vt* (work of art) 依頼する irái suru

out of commission (not working) 故障して koshō shité

commissionaire [kəmiʃəneɪˈr] (*BRIT*) *n* ドアマン dóaman

commissioner [kəmˈiʃənər] *n* (POLICE) 長官 chōkan

commit [kəmˈit] *vt* (crime, murder etc) 犯す okásu; (money, resources) 充てる júto suru; (to someone's care) 任せる makáseru

to commit oneself (to do) (...する事を) 約束する (...surú kotó wo) yakúsoku suru

to commit suicide 自殺する jisátsu suru

commitment [kəmˈitmənt] *n* (to ideology, system) 献身 keñshin; (obligation) 責任 sekíniñ; (undertaking) 約束 yakúsoku

committee [kəmˈitiː] *n* (of organization, club etc) 委員会 iñkai

commodity [kəmɑːdˈiti] *n* (saleable item) 商品 shōhin

common [kɑːmˈən] *adj* (shared by all: knowledge, property, good) 共同の kyō-

dō no; (usual, ordinary: event, object, experience etc) 普通の futsū no; (vulgar: person, manners) 下品な gehíñ na

♦*n* (area) 共有地 kyōyūchi

in common 共通で kyōtsū de

commoner [kɑːmˈənər] *n* 庶民 shomín

common law *n* コモン・ロー komónrō ◇成文化されてない慣習に基づく英米の一般法を指す seíbunka saréte naì kañshū ni motózukù efbei no ippáñhō wo sasú

commonly [kɑːmˈənliː] *adv* (usually) 通常 tsūjō

Common Market *n* ヨーロッパ共同市場 yōroppa kyōdōshijō

commonplace [kɑːmˈənpleis] *adj* 平凡な hefbon na

common room *n* (SCOL) 談話室 dañwashītsu

Commons [kɑːmˈənz] (*BRIT*) *npl*: **the Commons** 下院 ka-íñ

common sense *n* 常識 jōshiki, コモンセンス komóñseñsu

Commonwealth [kɑːmˈənwelθ] *n* (British Commonwealth): **the Commonwealth** イギリス連邦 igírisureñpō

the Commonwealth of Independent States 独立国家共同体 dokúritsu kòkka kyōdōtai

commotion [kəmouˈʃən] *n* (uproar) 騒ぎ sáwàgi

communal [kəmjuːˈnəl] *adj* (shared) 共同の kyōdō no

commune [*n* kɑːmˈjuːn *vb* kəmjuːnˈ] *n* (group) コミューン kómyūn

♦*vi*: **to commune with** (nature, God) ...に親しむ ...ni shitáshimù

communicate [kəmjuːˈnikeit] *vt* (idea, decision, feeling) 伝える tsutáerù

♦*vi*: **to communicate (with)** ...と通信する ...to tsūshin suru

communication [kəmjuːnikeiˈʃən] *n* (process) 通信 tsūshin; (letter, call) 連絡 refíraku

communication cord (*BRIT*) *n* (on train) 非常通報装置 hijōtsūhōsōchi

communion [kəmjuːˈnjən] *n* (*also*: **Holy Communion**) 聖体拝領 seítaihaīryō

communiqué [kəmjuːnikeɪ] n (POL, PRESS) コミュニケ kómyúnike

communism [kɒm'jʊnizəm] n 共産主義 kyósanshúgì

communist [kɒm'jʊnist] adj 共産主義の kyósanshúgì no
◆n 共産主義者 kyósanshugìsha

community [kəmjuː'niti:] n (group of people) 共同体 kyódòtai; (within larger group) 社会 shákaì

community center n 公民館 kómínkan

community chest (US) n 共同募金 kyódóbòkin

community home (BRIT) n 養育施設 yóìkushisètsu

commutation ticket [kɒmjəteɪ'ʃən-] (US) n 定期券 teíkiken

commute [kəmjuːt'] vi (to work) 通う kayóu
◆vt (LAW: sentence) 減刑する geńkei suru

commuter [kəmjuːt'əːr] n 通勤者 tsúkinsha

compact [kɒm'pækt] adj (taking up little space) 小型の kogáta no
◆n (also: powder compact) コンパクト kóñpakuto

compact disk n コンパクトディスク kóñpakuto disùku

companion [kəmpæn'jən] n 相手 aíte tsuk/fai

companionship [kəmpæn'jənʃip] n つきあい tsukífai

company [kʌm'pəni:] n (COMM) 会社 kaísha; (THEATER) 劇団 gekídan; (companionship) 付合い tsukífai
to keep someone company ...の相手になる ...no aíte ni narú

company secretary (BRIT) n 総務部長 sómùbuchō

comparable [kɒm'pəːrəbəl] adj (size, style, extent) 匹敵する hittéki suru

comparative [kəmpæːr'ətiv] adj (peace, stranger, safety) 比較的 hikákuteki ni; (study) 比較の hikáku no

comparatively [kəmpæːr'ətivliː] adv (relatively) 比較的に hikákuteki ni

compare [kəmpeːr'] vt: **to compare someone/something with** (set side

by side) ...を...と比較する ...wo ...to hikáku suru; (liken) ...を...に例える ...wo ...ni tatóerù
◆vi: **to compare (with)** (...に) 匹敵する (...ni) hittéki suru

comparison [kəmpæːr'isən] n (setting side by side) 比較 hikáku; (likening) 例えtatóe
in comparison (with) ...と比較して ...to hikáku shité

compartment [kəmpɑːrt'mənt] n (RAIL) 客室 kyakúshitsu, コンパートメント koñpátómento; (section: of wallet, fridge etc) 区画 kukáku

compass [kʌm'pəs] n (instrument: NAUT, GEO) 羅針盤 rashínban, コンパス kóñpasu

compasses [kʌm'pəsiz] npl (MATH) コンパス koñpasu

compassion [kəmpæʃ'ən] n (pity, sympathy) 同情 dójò

compassionate [kəmpæʃ'ənit] adj (person, look) 情け深い nasákebukaì

compatible [kəmpæt'əbəl] adj (people) 気が合う ki ga aù; (ideas etc) 両立できる ryóritsu dekírù; (COMPUT) 互換性のある gokáñsei no arù

compel [kəmpel'] vt (force) 強制する kyósei suru

compelling [kəmpel'iŋ] adj (fig: argument, reason) 止むに止まれぬ yamú ni yamárenù

compensate [kɒm'pənseit] vt (employee, victim) ...に補償する ...ni hoshó suru
◆vi: **to compensate for** (loss, disappointment, change etc) ...を埋め合わせる ...wo uméawaserù

compensation [kɒmpənseiʃ'ən] n (to employee, victim) 補償 hoshó; (for loss, disappointment, change etc) 埋め合せ uméawase

compère [kɒm'peːr] (BRIT) n (TV, RADIO) 司会者 shíkaìsha

compete [kəmpiːt'] vi (companies, rivals): **to compete (with)** (...と) 競り合う (...to) serfaù; (in contest, game) 参加する sañka suru

competence [kɒm'pitəns] n (of worker

etc) 能力 nōryoku

competent [kɑːmˈpitənt] *adj* 有能な yǔ_nō na

competition [kɑːmpitiˈʃən] *n* (between firms, rivals) 競争 kyōsō; (contest) コンクール koňkūru; (ECON) ライバル商品 raíbaru shōhin

competitive [kəmpetˈətiv] *adj* (industry, society) 競争の kyōsō no; (person) 競争心の強い kyōsōshin no tsuyoǐ; (price, product) 競争 の kyōsō no dekírū

competitive sports 競技 kyōgi

competitor [kəmpetˈitər] *n* (rival) 競争相手 kyōsōaǐte; (participant) 参加者 sañkashā

compile [kəmpaiˈl] *vt* (book, film, report) 編集する heñshū suru

complacency [kəmpleiˈsənsi] *n* (smugness) 自己満足 jikómañzoku

complacent [kəmpleiˈsənt] *adj* (smug) 自己満足にふける jikómañzoku ni fukérū

complain [kəmpleiˈn] *vi* (grumble) 不平不満を言う fuhéifūman wo iǔ; (protest: to authorities, shop etc) 訴える uttáerū

to complain of (pain) …を訴える …wo uttáerū

complaint [kəmpleiˈnt] *n* (objection) 訴え uttáe; (criticism) 非難 hínan; (MED: illness) 病気 byōki

complement [*n* kɑːmˈpləmənt *vb* kɑːmˈpləmənt] *n* (supply) のぎnあ oginaǔ monó; (esp ship's crew) 人員 jiń-in

♦*vt* (enhance) 引びたせる hikítataserū

complementary [kɑːmpləmenˈtɑːri] *adj* (mutually supportive) 補足し合う hosóku shiaǔ

complete [kəmpliˈt] *adj* (total, whole) 完全な kañzen na; (finished: building, task) 完成した kañsei shitá

♦*vt* (finish: building, task) 完成する kañsei suru; (: set, group etc) そろえる soróerū; (fill in: a form) …に記入する …ni kinyǔ suru

completely [kəmpliˈtli:] *adv* (totally) 全く mattáku, 完全に kañzen ni

completion [kəmpliˈʃən] *n* (of building)

完成 kañsei; (of contract) 履行 rikō

complex [*adj* kɑːmˈplɑːkeit] *n* kɑːmˈpleks] *adj* (structure, problem, decision) 複雑な fukúzatsu na

♦*n* (group: of buildings) 団地 dañchi; (PSYCH) コンプレックス koñpurekkùsu

complexion [kəmplekˈʃən] *n* (of face) 顔の肌 kaó no hadá

complexity [kəmplekˈsiti:] *n* (of problem, law) 複雑さ fukúzatsusa

compliance [kəmplaiˈəns] *n* (submission) 服従 fukújū; (agreement) 同意 dōi

in compliance with …に従って …ni shitágatte

complicate [kɑːmˈpləkeit] *vt* (matters, situation) 複雑にする fukúzatsu ni suru

complicated [kɑːmˈpləkeitid] *adj* (explanation, system) 複雑な fukúzatsu na

complication [kɑːmpləkeiˈʃən] *n* (problem) 問題 mofidai; (MED) 合併症 gappéishō

complicity [kəmplisˈəti:] *n* (in crime) 共犯 kyōhan

compliment [*n* kɑːmˈpləmənt *vb* kɑːmˈpləmənt] *n* (expression of admiration) ほめ言葉 homékotòba

♦*vt* (express admiration for) ほめる homéru

to pay someone a compliment …をほめる …wo homéru

complimentary [kɑːmpləmenˈtɑːri] *adj* (remark) 賛辞の sañji no; (ticket, copy of book etc) 無料の muryó no

compliments [kɑːmˈpləmənts] *npl* (regards) 敬拝 aísatsu

comply [kəmplaiˈ] *vi*: *to comply with* (law, ruling) …に従う …ni shitágaù

component [kəmpouˈnənt] *n* (parts, elements) 構成している kōsei shité irū

♦*n* (part) 部分 búbūn

compose [kəmpouˈz] *vt* (form): *to be composed of* …から成る …kará dekíte irū; (write: music, poem, letter) 書く kákú

to compose oneself 心を落着かせる kokórò wo ochítsukaserū

composed [kəmpouˈzd] *adj* (calm) 落着いている ochítsuite irū

composer [kəmpou'zər] n (MUS) 作曲家 sakkyókuka

composition [ka:mpəzí'ʃən] n (of substance, group etc) 構成 kōsei; (essay) 作文 sakúbun; (MUS) 作曲 sakkyóku

compost [ka:m'poust] n たい肥 taíhi

composure [kəmpou'ʒər] n (of person) 落着き ochítsuki

compound [ka:m'paund] n (CHEM) 化合物 kágōbutsu; (enclosure) 囲い地 kakóichi; (LING) 複合語 fukúgōgo
♦adj (fracture) 複雑な fukúzatsu na
compound interest 複利 fukúri

comprehend [ka:mprihend'] vt (understand) 理解する rikái suru

comprehension [ka:mprihen'ʃən] n (understanding) 理解 rfkai

comprehensive [ka:mprihen'siv] adj (description, review, list) 包括的な hōkatsuteki na; (INSURANCE) 総合的な sōgōteki na

comprehensive (school) [BRIT] n 総合中等学校 sōgōchútōgakkō あらゆる能力の子供に適した課程のある中等学校 arāyurū nōryoku no kodómo ni tekí shita katéi no aru chútōgakkō

compress [vb kəmpres' n ka:m'pres] vt (air, cotton, paper etc) 圧縮する asshūku suru; (text, information) 要約する yōyaku suru
♦n (MED) 湿布 shippú

comprise [kəmpraiz'] vt (also: **be comprised of**) ...からなる ...kará narù; (constitute) 構成する kōsei suru

compromise [ka:m'prəmaiz] n 妥協 dakyō
♦vt (beliefs, principles) 傷つける kizú tsukerù
♦vi (make concessions) 妥協する dakyō suru

compulsion [kəmpʌl'ʃən] n (desire, impulse) 強迫観念 kyōhakukannèn; (force) 強制 kyōsei

compulsive [kəmpʌl'siv] adj (liar, gambler etc) 病的な byōteki na; (viewing, reading) 止められない yamérarenāi

compulsory [kəmpʌl'sɔ:ri:] adj (attendance, retirement) 強制的な kyōseiteki

na

computer [kəmpju:'tər] n コンピュータ koñpyūta

computerize [kəmpju:'təraiz] vt (system, filing, accounts etc) コンピュータ化する koñpyútaka surù; (information) コンピュータに覚えさせる koñpyúta ni obóesaserù

computer programmer n プログラマー puróguramā

computer programming n プログラミング puróguramingu

computer science n コンピュータ科学 koñpyūta kagàku

computing [kəmpju:'tiŋ] n (activity, science) コンピュータ利用 koñpyūta riyō

comrade [ka:m'ræd] n (POL, MIL) 同志 dōshi; (friend) 友人 yūjin

comradeship [ka:m'rædʃip] n 友情 yūjō

con [ka:n] vt (deceive) だます damâsù; (cheat) ぺてんに掛ける petéñ ni kakérù
♦n (trick) いかさま ikásama

concave [ka:nkeiv'] adj 凹面の ōmen no

conceal [kənsi:l'] vt (hide: weapon, entrance) 隠す kakúsù; (keep back: information) 秘密にする himítsu ni surù

concede [kənsi:d'] vt (admit: error, point, defeat) 認める mitómeru

conceit [kənsi:t'] n (arrogance) うぬぼれ unūbore

conceited [kənsi:'tid] adj (vain) うぬぼれた unūboreta

conceivable [kənsi:v'əbəl] adj (reason, possibility) 考えられる kañgaerarerù

conceive [kənsi:v'] vt (child) はらむ harámù; (plan, policy) 考え出す kañgaedasù
♦vi (BIO) 妊娠する nifíshin suru

concentrate [ka:n'səntreit] vi (on problem, activity etc) 専念する señnen suru; (in one area, space) 集中する shūchū suru
♦vt (energies, attention) 集中させる shūchū sasérù

concentration [ka:nsəntrei'ʃən] n (on problem, activity etc) 専念 señnen; (in one area, space) 集中 shūchū; (attention) 注意 chūi; (CHEM) 濃縮 nōshuku

concentration camp *n* 強制収容所 kyōseishūyōjo

concept [kɑn'sept] *n* (idea, principle) 概念 gáinen

conception [kənsep'ʃən] *n* (idea) 概念 gáinen; (of child) 妊娠 nínshin

concern [kənsərn'] *n* (affair) 責任 sekfnin; (anxiety, worry) 心配 shínpai; (COMM: firm) 企業 kígyō

♦*vt* (worry) 心配させる shínpai saséru; (involve, relate to) ...に関係がある ...ni kánkē ga arù

to be concerned (about) (person, situation etc) (...について) 心配する (...ni tsuité) shínpai suru

concerning [kənsər'niŋ] *prep* (regarding) ...について ...ni tsuíte

concert [kɑn'sərt] *n* (MUS) 演奏会 eñsōkai, コンサート kóñsāto

concerted [kənsər'tid] *adj* (effort etc) 共同の kyōdō no

concert hall *n* コンサートホール kóñsātohōru

concertina [kɑnsərti:'nə] *n* (MUS: instrument) コンサーティーナ kóñsātīna ◊六角形の小型アコーディオン rokkákkei no kogáta akódìon

concerto [kəntʃer'tou] *n* 協奏曲 kyōsōkyoku, コンチェルト kóñcheruto

concession [kənseʃ'ən] *n* (compromise) 譲歩 jōho; (COMM: right) 特権 tokkén

tax concession 減税 geñzei

conciliatory [kənsil'i:atɔ:ri:] *adj* (gesture, tone) 懐柔的な kafjūteki na

concise [kənsais'] *adj* (description, text) 簡潔な kañkétsu na

conclude [kənklu:d'] *vt* (finish: speech, chapter) 終える oérù; (treaty) 締結する teíketsu suru; (deal etc) まとめる matómeru; (decide) (...だと) 結論する (...da to) ketsúron suru

conclusion [kənklu:'ʒən] *n* (of speech, chapter) 終り owári; (of treaty) 締結 teíketsu; (of deal etc) まとめる事 matómeru kotó; (decision) 結論 ketsúron

conclusive [kənklu:'siv] *adj* (evidence, defeat) 決定的な kettéiteki na

concoct [kɑnkɑkt'] *vt* (excuse) でっち上

げる detchíagerù; (plot) 企てる kuwádaterù; (meal, sauce) 工夫して作る kufū shíte tsukúrù

concoction [kɑnkɑk'ʃən] *n* (mixture) 調合物 chōgōbutsu

concourse [kɑn'kɔ:rs] *n* (hall) 中央ホール chūōhōru, コンコース kóñkōsu

concrete [kɑn'kri:t] *n* コンクリート kóñkurīto

♦*adj* (block, floor) コンクリートの kóñkurīto no; (proposal, idea) 具体的な gutáiteki na

concur [kənkə:r'] *vi* 同意する dōi suru

concurrently [kənkə:r'əntli:] *adv* (happen, run) 同時に dōji ni

concussion [kənkʌʃ'ən] *n* (MED) 脳震とう nōshíntō

condemn [kəndem'] *vt* (denounce: action, report etc) 非難する hínan suru; (sentence: prisoner) ...に...刑を宣告する ...ni...kei wo señkoku suru; (declare unsafe: building) 使用に耐えない物と決定する shiyō ni taénài monó to kettéi suru

condemnation [kɑndemnei'ʃən] *n* (criticism) 非難 hínan

condensation [kɑndensei'ʃən] *n* (on walls, windows) 結露 kétsùro

condense [kəndens'] *vi* (vapor) 液化する ekíka suru

♦*vt* (report, book) 要約する yōyaku suru

condensed milk [kəndenst'-] *n* 練乳 reñnyū

condescending [kɑndisen'diŋ] *adj* (reply, attitude) 恩着せがましい kñkisegamashii

condition [kəndiʃ'ən] *n* (state: *gen*) 状態 jōtai; (MED: of illness) 病状 byōjō; (requirement) 条件 jōken; (MED: illness) 病気 byōki

♦*vt* (gen) 慣れさせる narésaserù

on condition that ...という条件で ...to iú jōken de

conditional [kəndiʃ'ənəl] *adj* 条件付きの jōkentsuki no

conditioner [kəndiʃ'ənər] *n* (*also: hair conditioner*) ヘアコンディショナー heákondishōnā; (for fabrics) 柔軟剤 jūnañzai

conditions [kənˈdɪʃənz] *npl* (circumstances) 状況 jōkyō

condolences [kəndouˈlənsɪz] *npl* お悔み o-kúyami

condom [kɑnˈdɑm] *n* コンドーム kondōmu, スキン sukín

condominium [kɑndəmɪnˈiəm] (*US*) *n* 分譲マンション bunjōmanshon

condone [kəndoun'] *vt* (misbehavior, crime) 容認する yōnin suru

conducive [kənduˈsiv] *adj*: **conducive to** (rest, study) ...を助ける ...wo tasúkerú

conduct [*n* kɑnˈdʌkt *vb* kəndʌkt'] *n* (of person) 振舞 furúmai

♦*vt* (survey, research etc) 行う okónaú; (orchestra, choir etc) 指揮する shikí suru; (heat, electricity) 伝導する dendō suru

to conduct oneself (behave) 振舞う furúmaú

conducted tour [kəndʌkˈtid-] *n* ガイド付き見物 gaídotsuki kénbutsu

conductor [kəndʌkˈtəːr] *n* (of orchestra) 指揮者 shikísha; (*BRIT*: on bus, *US*: on train) 車掌 shashó; (ELEC) 伝導体 dendōtai

conductress [kəndʌkˈtris] *n* (on bus) 女性車掌 joséishashō, バスガール basúgāru

cone [koun] *n* (shape) 円すい形 ensuíkeí; (on road) カラーコーン karákōn, セーフティコーン sēfutikōn; (BOT) 松かさ matsúkasá; (ice cream cornet) コーン kōn

confectioner [kənfekˈʃənəːr] *n* (person) 菓子職人 kashíshokunin

confectioner's (shop) [kənfekˈʃənəːrz-] *n* (sweet shop) 菓子屋 kashíya

confectionery [kənfekˈʃəneːriː] *n* (sweets, candies) 菓子類 kashírui

confederation [kənfedəreiˈʃən] *n* (POL, COMM) 連合 rengō

confer [kənfəːr'] *vt*: **to confer something (on someone)** (honor, degree, advantage) (...に) ...を与える (...ni) ...wo atáerú

♦*vi* (panel, team) 協議する kyōgi suru

conference [kɑnˈfəːrəns] *n* (meeting) 会議 kaígi

confess [kənfes'] *vt* (sin, guilt, crime) 白

状する hákujō suru; (weakness, ignorance) 認める mitómeru

♦*vt* (admit) 認める mitómeru

confession [kənfeʃˈən] *n* (admission) 白状 hákujō, 告白 kokúhaku; (REL) ざんげ zánge

confetti [kənfetˈiː] *n* コンフェティ kônfeti ◇紙吹雪き用に細かく切った色紙 kamífubuki yō ni komákaku kittá irógami

confide [kənfaid'] *vi*: **to confide in** ...に打明ける ...ni uchíakerú

confidence [kɑnˈfidəns] *n* (faith) 信用 shiń-yō; (*also*: **self-confidence**) 自信 jishín; (secret) 秘密 himítsu

in confidence (speak, write) 内緒で naíshode

confidence trick *n* いかさま ikásama

confident [kɑnˈfidənt] *adj* (self-assured) 自信のある jishín no arú; (positive) 確信している kakúshin shité irú

confidential [kɑnfidenˈʃəl] *adj* (report, information) 秘密の himítsu no; (tone) 親しげな shitáshige na

confine [kənfain'] *vt* (limit) 限定する gentei suru; (shut up) 閉じ込める tojíkomeru

confined [kənfaind'] *adj* (space) 限られた kagírareta

confinement [kənfainˈmənt] *n* (imprisonment) 監禁 kankin

confines [kɑnˈfainz] *npl* (of area) 境 sakái

confirm [kənfəːrm'] *vt* (belief, statement) 裏付ける urázukerú; (appointment, date) 確認する kakúnin suru

confirmation [kɑnfəːrmeiˈʃən] *n* (of belief, statement) 裏付け urázuke; (of appointment, date) 確認 kakúnin; (REL) 堅信礼 keńshińrei

confirmed [kənfəːrmd'] *adj* (bachelor, teetotaller) 常習的な jōshúteki na

confiscate [kɑnˈfiskeit] *vt* (impound, seize) 没収する bosshū suru

conflict [*n* kɑnˈflikt *vb* kənflikt'] *n* (disagreement) 論争 roñsō; (difference: of interests, loyalties etc) 対立 tafrítsu; (fighting) 戦闘 señtō

♦*vi* (opinions) 対立する tafrítsu suru; (research etc) 矛盾する mujún suru

conflicting [kənˈflɪktɪŋ] adj (reports) 矛盾する mujún surú; (interests etc) 対立する taíritsu suru

conform [kənˈfɔːrm] vi (comply) 従う shitágaú
  to conform to (law, wish, ideal) ...に従う ...ni shitágaú

confound [kənˈfaund] vt (confuse) 当惑させる tōwaku saséru

confront [kənˈfrʌnt] vt (problems, task) ...と取組む ...to toríkumú; (enemy, danger) ...に立向かう ...ni tachímukaū

confrontation [kɑːnfrənˈteiʃən] n (dispute, conflict) 衝突 shōtotsu

confuse [kənˈfjuːz] vt (perplex: person) 当惑させる tōwaku saséru; (mix up: two things, people etc) 混同する kofdō suru; (complicate: situation, plans) 混乱させる kofran saséru

confused [kənˈfjuːzd] adj (bewildered) 当惑した tōwaku shitá; (disordered) 混乱した kofran shitá

confusing [kənˈfjuːzɪŋ] adj (plot, instructions) 分かりにくい wakárinikuí

confusion [kənˈfjuːʒən] n (perplexity) 当惑 tōwaku; (mix-up) 混同 kofdō; (disorder) 混乱 kofran

congeal [kənˈdʒiːl] vi (blood, sauce) 凝結する gyōketsu suru

congenial [kənˈdʒiːnjəl] adj (person) 気の合った ki no attá; (atmosphere etc) 楽しい tanóshií

congenital [kənˈdʒenitəl] adj (MED: defect, illness) 先天性の seftensei no

congested [kənˈdʒestid] adj (MED: with blood) うっ血した ukkétsu shitá; (: with mucus: nose) 詰まった tsumátta; (road) 渋滞した jútai shitá; (area) 人口密集の jinkōmisshū no

congestion [kənˈdʒestʃən] n (MED: with blood) うっ血 ukkétsu; (: with mucus) 鼻詰まり hanázumarí; (of road) 渋滞 jútai; (of area) 人口密集 jinkōmisshū

conglomerate [kənˈglɑːmərit] n (COMM) 複合企業 fukúgōkigyò, コングロマリット kofguromaríttò

conglomeration [kənˌglɑːməˈreiʃən] n (group, gathering) 寄せ集め yoséatsume

congratulate [kənˈgrætʃuleit] vt (parents, bridegroom etc) ...にお祝いを言う ...ni o-íwai wo iú

congratulations [kənˌgrætʃuˈleiʃənz] npl 祝詞 shukúgi
  congratulations! おめでとうございます omédetō gozáimasù

congregate [kɑːngrigeit] vi (people) 集まる atsúmarù; (animals) 群がる murágarù

congregation [kɑːngriˈgeiʃən] n (of a church) 会衆 kaíshū

congress [kɑːngris] n (conference) 大会 taíkai; (US): *Congress* 議会 gikai

congressman [kɑːngrismən] (US: pl *congressmen*) n 下院議員 ka-íngiìn

conical [kɑːnikəl] adj (shape) 円すい形の efsuikei no

conifer [kouˈnifər] n 針葉樹 shifyòju

conjecture [kənˈdʒektʃər] n (speculation) 憶測 okúsoku

conjugal [kɑːndʒəgəl] adj 夫婦間の fúfùkàn no

conjugate [kɑːndʒəgeit] vt (LING) ...の活用形を変える ...no katsúyōkei wo agérù

conjunction [kənˈdʒʌŋkʃən] n (LING) 接続詞 setsúzokushì

conjunctivitis [kənˌdʒʌŋktəvaiˈtis] n (MED) 結膜炎 ketsúmakuén

conjure [kɑːndʒər] vi (magician) 奇術をする kijútsu wo suru

conjurer [kɑːndʒərər] n (magician) 奇術師 kijútsushì, マジシャン majíshàn

conjure up vt (ghost, spirit) 呼出す yobídasù; (memories) 思い起す omóiokosù

conk out [kɑːŋk-] (inf) vi (machine, engine) 故障する koshō suru

con man [kɑːn-mæn] (pl con men) n ぺてん師 peténshì

connect [kəˈnekt] vt (join, also TEL) つなぐ tsunágù; (ELEC) 接続する setsúzoku suru; (fig: associate) 関係付ける kañkeizúkeru
  ♦vi: *to connect with* (train, plane etc) ...に連絡する ...ni refíraku suru
  to be connected with (associated) 関係付ける kañkeizúkeru

connection [kəˈnɛkʃən] n (joint, link) つなぎ tsunági; (ELEC, TEL) 接続 setsúzoku; (train, plane etc) 連絡 refiraku; (fig: association) 関係 kańkei

connive [kəˈnaiv] vi: **to connive at** (misbehavior) ...を容認する ...wo yōnin suru

connoisseur [kɑːnəˈsəːr] n (of food, wine, art etc) 通 tsū

connotation [kɑːnəˈteiʃən] n (implication) 含み fukúmi

conquer [ˈkɑːŋkər] vt (MIL: country, enemy) 征服する seffuku suru; (fear, feelings) 克服する kokúfuku suru

conqueror [ˈkɑːŋkərər] n (MIL) 征服者 seffukushá

conquest [ˈkɑːnkwɛst] n (MIL) 征服 seffuku; (prize) 勝得た物 kachíeta monó; (mastery: of space etc) 征服 seffuku

cons [kɑːnz] npl see **convenience**; **pro**

conscience [ˈkɑːnʃəns] n (sense of right and wrong) 良心 ryōshin

conscientious [kɑːnʃiˈɛnʃəs] adj (worker) 良心的な ryōshinteki na

conscious [ˈkɑːnʃəs] adj (aware): **conscious (of)** (...に) 気が付いている (...ni) ki ga tsuíte irú; (deliberate) 意識的な ishíkiteki na; (awake) 目が覚めている me ga saméte irú

consciousness [ˈkɑːnʃəsnis] n (awareness, mentality: also MED) 意識 ishíki

conscript [ˈkɑːnskript] n (MIL) 徴集兵 chōshūhei

conscription [kənskripˈʃən] n (MIL) 徴兵 chōhei

consecrate [ˈkɑːnsəkreit] vt (building, place) 奉献する hōken suru

consecutive [kənˈsɛkjətiv] adj (days, wins) 連続の reńzoku na

consensus [kənˈsɛnsəs] n 合意 gōi

consent [kənˈsɛnt] n (permission) 許可 kyōka
♦vi: **to consent to** ...に同意する ...ni dōi suru

consequence [ˈkɑːnsəkwɛns] n (result) 結果 kekká; (significance) 重要さ jūyōsa

consequently [ˈkɑːnsəkwɛntli] adv (as a result, so) 従って shitágatté

conservation [kɑːnsərˈveiʃən] n (of the environment, preservation) 保護 hogó, 保全 hozén; (of energy) 節約 setsúyaku; (of paintings, books) 保存 hozén

conservative [kənˈsəːrvətiv] adj (traditional, conventional: person, attitudes) 保守的な hoshúteki na; (cautious: estimate etc) 控え目の hikáeme no; (BRIT: POL): **Conservative** 保守党の hoshútō no
♦n (BRIT: POL): **Conservative** 保守党員 hoshútōin

conservatory [kənˈsəːrvətɔːri] n (greenhouse) 温室 onshitsu; (MUS) 音楽学校 ōgaku gakkō

conserve [vb kənˈsəːrv n ˈkɑːnsəːrv] vt (preserve) 保護する hogó suru; (supplies, energy) 節約する setsúyaku suru
♦n (jam) ジャム jámu

consider [kənsidˈər] vt (believe) ...だと思う ...da to omóu; (study) 熟考する jukkō suru; (take into account) 考慮に入れる kōryo ni irérù
to consider doing something ...しようかと考える ...shiyō ka to kángaerù

considerable [kənsidˈərəbəl] adj (amount, expense, difference etc) かなりの kanári no

considerably [kənsidˈərəbli] adv (improve, deteriorate) かなり kanári

considerate [kənsidˈərit] adj (person) 思いやりのある omóiyari no arù

consideration [kənsidəˈreiʃən] n (deliberation) 熟考 jukkō; (factor) 考慮すべき点 kōryo subéki téñ; (thoughtfulness) 思いやり omóiyari

considering [kənsidˈəriŋ] prep (bearing in mind) ...を考慮すると ...wo kōryo suru to

consign [kənsainˈ] vt (something unwanted): **to consign to** (place) ...にしまっておく ...ni shimátte okú; (person): **to consign to** (someone's care etc) ...に委ねる ...ni yudánerù; (poverty etc) ...に追込む ...ni ofkomú

consignment [kənsainˈmənt] n (COMM) 輸送貨物 yusókamotsu

consist [kənsistˈ] vi: **to consist of** (comprise) ...から成る ...kará narù

consistency [kənsis'tənsi:] n (of actions, policies etc) 一貫性 ikkánsei; (of yoghurt, cream etc) 固さ katása

consistent [kənsis'tənt] adj (person) 変らない kawáranai; (argument, idea) 一貫性のある ikkánsei no arù

consolation [kɑːnsəlei'ʃən] n (comfort) 慰め nagúsame

console [vb kənsoul' n kɑːn'soul] vt (comfort) 慰める nagúsamerù
◆n (panel) コンソール kóñsòru

consolidate [kənsɑː'lideit] vt (position, power) 強化する kyóka suru

consommé [kɑːnsəmei'] n (CULIN) コンソメ kóñsome

consonant [kɑːn'sənənt] n (LING) 子音 shíin

consortium [kənsɔːr'ʃiːəm] n (COMM) 協会 kyókai

conspicuous [kənspik'juːəs] adj (noticeable: person, feature) 目立つ medátsu

conspiracy [kənspir'əsi:] n (plot) 陰謀 iñbō

conspire [kənspaiˈəːr] vi (criminals, revolutionaries etc) 共謀する kyóbō suru; (events) 相重なる aíkasanarù

constable [kɑːn'stəbəl] (BRIT) n 巡査 juñsa
chief constable (BRIT) 警察本部長 kefsatsu hoñbuchō

constabulary [kənstæb'jələːri:] (BRIT) n 警察 kefsatsu ◇一地区の警察隊を指すich'chiku no kefsatsutai wo sasù

constant [kɑːn'stənt] adj (continuous: criticism, pain) 絶えない taénai; (fixed: temperature, level) 一定の ittéi no

constantly [kɑːn'stəntli:] adv (continually) 絶間なく taémanàku

constellation [kɑːnstəlei'ʃən] n (ASTRONOMY) 星座 sefza

consternation [kɑːnstəːrnei'ʃən] n (dismay) ろうばい róbai

constipated [kɑːn'stəpeitid] adj (MED) 便秘している beñpi shité irù

constipation [kɑːnstəpei'ʃən] n (MED) 便秘 beñpi

constituency [kənstitʃ'uːənsiː] n (POL:

area) 選挙区 señkyokù; (: electors) 選挙民 señkyomìn

constituent [kənstitʃ'uːənt] n (POL) 有権者 yūkeñsha; (component) 部分 búbùn

constitute [kɑːn'stituːt] vt (represent: challenge, emergency) ...である de arù; (make up: whole) 構成する kōsei suru

constitution [kɑːnstitu:'ʃən] n (of country) 憲法 kéñpō; (of club etc) 会則 kaísoku; (health) 体質 taíshitsu; (make-up: of committee etc) 構成 kōsei

constitutional [kɑːnstitu:'ʃənəl] adj (government, reform etc) 憲法の kéñpō no

constraint [kənstreint'] n (restriction) 制限 sefgen; (compulsion) 強制 kyósei

construct [kənstrʌkt'] vt (building) 建てる tatérù; (bridge, road etc) 建設する kefsetsu suru; (machine) 作る tsukúrù

construction [kənstrʌk'ʃən] n (of building etc) 建築 kefchiku; (of bridge, road etc) 建設 kefsetsu; (of machine) 製作 sefsaku; (structure) 構造物 kózōbutsu

constructive [kənstrʌk'tiv] adj (remark, criticism) 建設的な keñsetsuteki na

construe [kənstruː'] vt (statement, event) 解釈する kafshaku suru

consul [kɑːn'səl] n 領事 ryóji

consulate [kɑːn'səlit] n 領事館 ryójikàn

consult [kənsʌlt'] vt (doctor, lawyer, friend) ...に相談する ...ni sódan suru; (reference book) 調べる shiráberù

consultant [kənsʌl'tənt] n (MED) 顧問医 kómòn-i; (other specialist) 顧問 kómòn, コンサルタント koñsárùtanto

consultation [kɑːnsəltei'ʃən] n (MED) 診察 shiñsatsu; (discussion) 協議 kyógi

consulting room [kənsʌl'tiŋ-] (BRIT) n 診察室 shiñsatsushītsu

consume [kənsuːm'] vt (food) 食べる tabérù; (drink) 飲む nómù; (fuel, energy, time etc) 消費する shóhi suru

consumer [kənsuː'məːr] n (COMM) 消費者 shōhishà

consumer goods npl 消費財 shóhizài

consumerism [kənsuː'məːrizəm] n 消費者運動 shōhishaundō

consumer society n 消費社会 shōhisha-kai

consummate [kɔnˈsəmeit] vt (ambition etc) 全うする mattō suru

to consummate a marriage 床入りする tokō-iri suru

consumption [kɔnsʌmˈpʃən] n (of food) 食べる事 tabérú kotó; (of drink) 飲む事 nómú kotó; (of fuel, energy, time etc) 消費 shōhi; (amount consumed) 消費量 shōhiryō; (buying) 消費 shōhi

cont. abbr (= continued) 続く tsuzúku

contact [kɔnˈtækt] n (communication) 連絡 reńraku; (touch) 接触 sesshóku; (person) 連絡相手 reńrakualte

♦vt (by phone, letter) ...に連絡する ...ni reńraku suru

contact lenses npl コンタクトレンズ kóntakutorenzu

contagious [kɔnˈteidʒəs] adj (MED: disease) 伝染性の deńsenæi no; (fig: laughter, enthusiasm) 移りやすい utsúriyasúi

contain [kɔnˈtein] vt (hold: objects) ...が入っている ...ni ...ga haítte irú; (have: component, ingredient etc) ...に...が含まれている ...ni ...ga fukúmarèté irú; (subj: piece of writing, report etc) ...に...が書いてある ...ni ...ga kaíte arú; (curb: growth, spread, feeling) 抑える osáerú

to contain oneself 自制する jiséi suru

container [kɔnˈteinər] n (box, jar etc) 入れ物 irémono; (COMM: for shipping etc) コンテナ kóntena

contaminate [kɔnˈtæmineit] vt (water, food, soil etc) 汚染する osén suru

contamination [kɔntæmineiˈʃən] n (of water, food, soil etc) 汚染 osén

cont'd abbr (= continued) 続く tsuzúku

contemplate [kɔnˈtəmpleit] vt (idea, subject, course of action) じっくり考える jikkūri kañgaerú; (person, painting etc) 眺める nagámerú

contemporary [kɔntemˈperɛriː] adj (present-day) 現代の geñdai no; (belonging to same time) 同時代の dōjidāi no

♦n (person) 同時代の人 dōjidai no hitó

contempt [kɔnˈtempt] n (scorn) 軽べつ kefbetsu

contempt of court (LAW) 法廷侮辱罪 hōteibujokuzái

contemptible [kɔnˈtemptəbəl] adj (conduct) 卑劣な hirétsu na

contemptuous [kɔnˈtemptʃuːəs] adj (attitude) 軽べつ的な kefbetsuteki na

contend [kɔnˈtend] vt (assert): to contend that ...だと主張する ...da to shuchō suru

♦vi (struggle): to contend with (problem, difficulty) ...と戦う ...to tatákaú; (compete): to contend for (power etc) ...を争う ...wo arásoú

contender [kɔnˈtendər] n (in competition) 競争者 kyōsōsha; (POL) 候補者 kōhosha; (SPORT) 選手 seńshu

content [adj, vb kɔnˈtent] n kɔnˈtent] adj (happy and satisfied) 満足して mańzoku shité

♦vt (satisfy) 満足させる mańzoku saséru

♦n (of speech, novel) 内容 nafyō; (fat content, moisture content etc) 含有量 gafi-yūryō

contented [kɔnˈtentid] adj (happy and satisfied) 満足して mańzoku shité

contention [kɔnˈtenʃən] n (assertion) 主張 shuchō; (disagreement, argument) 論争 rońsō

contentment [kɔnˈtentmənt] n (happiness, satisfaction) 満足 mańzoku

contents [kɔnˈtents] npl (of bottle, packet) 中身 nakámi; (of book) 内容 nafyō

(table of) contents 目次 mokúji

contest [n kɔnˈtest vb kɔnˈtest] n (competition) コンテスト kóntesuto, コンクール kóńkūru; (struggle: for control, power etc) 争い arásoi

♦vt (election, competition) ...で競う ...de kisóu; (statement, decision: also LAW) ...に対して異議を申立てる ...ni taíshite igi wo mōshitaterú

contestant [kɔnˈtestant] n (in quiz, competition) 参加者 sañkasha; (in fight) 競争 kyōsōsha

context [kɔnˈtekst] n (circumstances: of events, ideas etc) 背景 hafkei; (of word, phrase) 文脈 buńmyaku

continent [kάntənənt] n (land mass) 大陸 tairiku

the Continent (BRIT) ヨーロッパ大陸 yōroppa tairiku

continental [kὰntənén'tal] adj 大陸の tairiku no

continental quilt (BRIT) n 掛布団 kakébuton

contingency [kəntín'dʒənsi:] n 有事 yūji

contingent [kəntín'dʒənt] n (group of people: also MIL) 一団 ichídan

continual [kəntín'ju:əl] adj (movement, process, rain etc) 絶間ない taémanài

continually [kəntín'ju:əli:] adv 絶間なく taémanàku

continuation [kəntìnju:éi'ʃən] n 継続 keízoku

continue [kəntín'ju:] vi 続く tsuzúkù
♦vt 続ける tsuzúkerù

continuity [kὰntənu:'iti:] n (in policy, management etc) 連続性 renzokusei; (TV, CINEMA) 撮影台本 satsúeidaìhon, コンテ kόnte

continuous [kəntín'ju:əs] adj (process, growth etc) 絶間ない taémanài; (line) 途切れのない togíre no naì; (LING) 進行形の shínkōkei no

continuous stationery n 連続用紙 renzokuyōshi

contort [kəntɔ:rt'] vt (body) ねじる nejírù; (face) しかめる shikámerù

contortion [kəntɔ:r'ʃən] n (of body) ねじれ nejíre; (of face) こわばり kowábari

contour [kάn'tu:r] n (on map: also: contour line) 等高線 tōkōsen; (shape, outline: gen pl) 輪郭 rínkaku

contraband [kάn'trəbænd] n 密輸品 mitsúyuhin

contraception [kὰntrəsép'ʃən] n 避妊 hinín

contraceptive [kὰntrəsép'tiv] adj (method, technique) 避妊の hinín no
♦n (device) 避妊具 hinín gu; (pill etc) 避妊薬 hinín-yaku

contract [n kάn'trækt vb kəntrækt'] n (LAW, COMM) 契約 keíyaku
♦vi (become smaller) 収縮する shūshuku suru; (COMM): to contract to do

something ...をする契約をする ...wo suru keíyaku wo suru
♦vt (illness) ...に掛かる ...ni kakárù

contraction [kəntræk'ʃən] n (of metal, muscle) 収縮 shūshuku; (of word, phrase) 短縮形 tańshukukei

contractor [kάn'træktə:r] n (COMM) 請負人 ukéoinin

contradict [kὰntrədíkt'] vt (person) ...の言う事を否定する ...no iú kotó wo hitéi suru; (statement etc) 否定する hitéi suru

contradiction [kὰntrədík'ʃən] n (inconsistency) 矛盾 mujún

contradictory [kὰntrədík'tə:ri:] adj (ideas, statements) 矛盾する mujún suru

contraption [kəntræp'ʃən] n (pej) (device, machine) 珍妙な機械 chínmyō na kikái

contrary[1] [kάn'tre:ri:] adj (opposite, different) 反対の hantái no
♦n (opposite) 反対 hantái

on the contrary それどころか soródokoro ka

unless you hear to the contrary そうではないと聞かされない限り so de wa nái to kikásarenài kagíri

contrary[2] [kəntre:r'i:] adj (perverse) つむじ曲りな tsumújimagàri na, へそ曲りな hesómagari na

contrast [n kάn'træst vb kəntræst'] n (difference) 相違 sόi, コントラスト kóntorasùto
♦vt (techniques, texts etc) 対照する taíshō suru

in contrast to ...と違って ...to chigátte

contrasting [kəntræs'tiŋ] adj (colors, attitudes) 対照的な taíshōteki na

contravene [kὰntrəvi:n'] vt (of law) ...に違反する ...ni ihán suru

contribute [kəntríb'ju:t] vi (give) 寄付する kifú suru
♦vt: to contribute an article to (commissioned) ...に記事を寄稿する ...ni kíjī wo kikô suru; (unsolicited) ...に記事を投稿する ...ni kíjī wo tôkô suru; to contribute $10 10ドルを寄付する júdòru wo kifú suru

to contribute to (charity) ...に寄付する ...ni kifú suru; (newspaper: commissioned) ...に寄稿する ...ni kikō suru; (unsolicited) ...に投稿する ...ni tōkō suru; (discussion) 意見を言う事を言う my ni iú; (problem etc) ...を悪くする ...wo warúkú surú

contribution [kɑntrəbjuːʃ*ə*n] n (donation) 寄付 kifú; (BRIT: for social security) 掛金 kakékìn; (to debate, campaign) 貢献 kṓken; (to journal: commissioned) 寄稿 kikṓ; (: unsolicited) 投稿 tṓkō

contributor [kɑntrib'jətər] n (to appeal) 寄付者 kifúsha; (to newspaper) 投稿者 {寄稿者} {kikōsha}

contrive [kɑntraiv'] vi: **to contrive to do** 努力して...に成功する doryóku shite ...ni seíkō suru

control [kɑntroul'] vt (country, organization) 支配する shihái suru; (machinery, process) 制御する seígyo suru; (wages, prices) 規制する kiséi suru; (temper) 自制する jiséi suru; (disease) 抑制する yokúsei suru
♦n (of country, organization) 支配 shiháí; (of oneself, emotions) 自制心 jiséíshìn
to be in control of (situation) ...を掌握している ...wo shōaku shité irú; (car etc) ...を思いのままに動かしている ...wo o-móí no mamá ni ugókashite irú
under control (crowd) 指示に従って shijí ni shitágatte; (situation) 取収められていて shūshū ga tsuíte; (dog) 言う事を聞い て iú kotó wo kiíte
out of control (crowd) 制止が利かなくなって seíshi ga kikánakù natté; (situation) 手に負えなくなって te ni oénakù natté; (dog) 言う事を聞かなくなって iú kotó wo kikánakù natté

control panel n 制御盤 seígyoban
control room n 制御室 seígyoshìtsu
controls [kɑntroulz'] npl (of vehicle) ハンドル hándòru ◇ブレーキ, クラッチなどその運転制御装置をまとめて buréki, kuráttchí nadò subete wo uñtenseígyosṓchi wo fuñmeñ, corí te; (on radio, television etc) コントロール盤 koñtorṓrùban ◇全てのス

イッチ, 調節用つまみ, ボタンなどを含む subete no suítchi, chṓsetsu yō tsumamì, botán nadò wo fukúmù; (governmental) 規制 kiséi

control tower n (AVIAT) 管制塔 kañseítō

controversial [kɑntrəvər'ʃəl] adj (topic, person) 論争の的になっている roñsō no matō ni natté irú

controversy [kɑn'trəvərsiː] n 論争 roñsō

conurbation [kɑnərbei'ʃən] n 大都市圏 daítoshiken

convalesce [kɑnvəles'] vi (MED) 回復する kaífuku suru

convalescence [kɑnvəles'əns] n (MED) 回復期 kaífukukì

convector [kənvek'tər] n (heater) 対流式暖房器 taíryūshikidañbṓkì, コンベクター koñbekùtā

convene [kənviːn'] vt (meeting, conference) 召集する shṓshū suru
♦vi (parliament, inquiry) 開会する kaíkai suru

convenience [kənviːn'jəns] n (easiness) 便利 beñri; (suitability: of date, meeting, house etc) 好都合 kōtsugṓ; (advantage, help) 便宜 beñgi
at your convenience ご都合の良い時に go-tsúgō no yoí tokí ni
all modern conveniences, (BRIT) **all mod cons** 近代設備完備 kiñdaísetsubìkañbi ◇不動産の広告などに使われる語句 fudṓsan no kṓkoku nadò ni tsukáwarerù gokù

convenient [kənviːn'jənt] adj (handy) 便利な beñri na; (suitable) 都合の良い tsugṓ no yoí

convent [kɑn'vent] n (REL) 女子修道院 joshíshūdòin

convention [kənven'ʃən] n (custom) 慣例 kañrei; (conference) 大会 taíkai; (agreement) 協定 kyṓtei

conventional [kənven'ʃənəl] adj (person) 型にはまった katá ni hamátta; (method) 伝統的な deñtṓteki na

converge [kənvərdʒ'] vi (roads) 合流す

る gōryū suru; (people): **to converge on** (place, person) ...に集まる ...ni atsámarú

conversant [kənvɜːsant] adj: **to be conversant with** (problem, requirements) ...に通じている ...ni tsūjite irú

conversation [kɑːnvəːseiʃən] n (talk) 会話 kaiwa

conversational [kɑːnvəːseiʃənəl] adj (tone, language, skills) 会話的な kaiwateki na

converse [n kɑːnvɜːrs vb kənvɜːrs] n (of statement) 逆 gyaku

◆vi (talk): **to converse (with someone)** (...と) 話をする (...to) hanáshi wo suru

conversely [kɑnvɜːrsli] adv 逆に gyaku ni

conversion [kənvɜːrʒən] n (of weights, substances etc) 変換 henkan; (REL) 改宗 kaíshū

convert [vb kənvɜːrt n kɑːnvɜːrt] vt (change): **to convert something into/to** ...を...に変換する ...wo ...ni henkan suru; (person): REL 改宗させる kaíshū saseru; (: POL 党籍を変えさせる tōseki wo kaésaserú

◆n (REL) 改宗者 kaíshūsha; (POL) 党籍を変えた人 tōseki wo kaéta hitó

convertible [kənvɜːrtəbəl] n (AUT) コンバーチブル kofibāchibūru ◇ 幌込み式屋根を持つ乗用車 tatámikoméshiki yané wo motsú jōyōsha

◆adj (economics etc) 交換できる kōkan dekírù

convex [kɑːnveks] adj 凸面の totsúmen no

convey [kənvei] vt (information, idea, thanks) 伝える tsutáerù; (cargo, traveler) 運ぶ hakóbu

conveyor belt [kənveiəːr-] n ベルトコンベヤー berútokonbeyā

convict [vb kənvikt n kɑːnvikt] vt (of a crime) ...に有罪の判決を下す ...ni yūzai no hafiketsu wo kudásù

◆n (person) 囚人 shújin

conviction [kənvikʃən] n (belief) 信念 shifnen; (certainty) 確信 kakúshin; (LAW) 有罪判決 yūzaíhañketsu

convince [kənvins] vt (assure) 分からせる wakáraserù; (persuade) 納得させる

nattóku saserú

convinced [kənvinst] adj: **convinced of/that** ...を (だと) 確信している ...wo (dátò) kakúshin shité irú

convincing [kənvinsiŋ] adj (case, argument) 納得のいく nattóku no ikú

convoluted [kɑːnvəlutid] adj (statement, argument) 込み入った komfittà

convoy [kɑːnvɔi] n (of trucks) 護衛付き輸送車隊 goéitsuki yusóshatai; (of ships) 護衛付き輸送船団 goéitsukiyusósoñdan

convulse [kənvʌls] vt: **to be convulsed with laughter** 笑いこける waráikokerù

to be convulsed with pain もだえる modáerù

convulsion [kənvʌlʃən] n (MED) けいれん kefren

coo [kuː] vi (dove, pigeon) くーくー鳴く kūkū nakú; (person) 優しい声で言う yasáshii koè de iú

cook [kuk] vt (food, meal) 料理する ryōri suru

◆vi (person) 料理する ryōri suru; (meat, pie etc) 焼ける yakérù

◆n 料理人 ryōrinin, コック kokkù

cookbook [kukbuk] n 料理の本 ryōri no hoñ

cooker [kukəːr] n (stove) レンジ réñji

cookery [kukəːri] n 料理する事 ryōri suru kotó

cookery book (BRIT) n = **cookbook**

cookie [kuki] n (US) ビスケット bisúkettò, クッキー kúkkī

cooking [kukiŋ] n (activity) 料理する事 ryōri suru kotó; (food) 料理 ryōri

cool [kuːl] adj (temperature, clothes) 涼しい suzúshiì; (drink) 冷たい tsumétai; (person: calm) 落着いている ochítsuite irú; (: unfriendly) そっけない sokkénaì

◆vt (make colder: tea) 冷ます samásù; (: room) 冷やす hiyásù

◆vi (become colder: water) 冷たくなる tsumétaku narú; (: air) 涼しくなる suzúshiku narú

coolness [kuːlnis] n (of temperature, clothing) 涼しさ suzúshisà; (of drink) 冷たさ tsumétasà; (calm) 落着き ochítsuki;

(unfriendliness) そっけなさ sokkénasà

coop [ku:p] *n* (*also*: **rabbit coop**) ウサギ小屋 uságigoya; (*also*: **hen coop**) ニワトリ小屋 niwátorigoya

♦*vt*: **to coop up** (*fig*: imprison) 閉じ込める tojíkomerù

cooperate [kouɑ:p'əreit] *vi* (collaborate) 協同する kyódō suru; (assist) 協力する kyóryoku suru

cooperation [kouɑ:pərei'ʃən] *n* (collaboration) 協同 kyódō; (assistance) 協力 kyóryoku

cooperative [kouɑ:p'rətiv] *adj* (farm, business) 協同組合の kyódōkùmiai no; (person) 協力的な kyóryokuteki na

♦*n* (factory, business) 協同組合 kyódōkùmiai

coordinate [*vb* kouɔ:r'dəneit *n* kouɔ:r'dənit] *vt* (activity, attack) 指揮する shikí suru; (movements) 調整する chósei suru

♦*n* (MATH) 座標 zahyó

coordinates [kouɔ:r'dənits] *npl* (clothes) コーディネートされた服 kódinèto saréta fukú

coordination [kouɔ:rdənei'ʃən] *n* (of services) 指揮 shikí; (of one's movements) 調整 chósei

co-ownership [kouou'nəʳʃip] *n* 協同所有 kyódōshòyū

cop [kɑːp] (*inf*) *n* (policeman/woman) 警官 kefkan

cope [koup] *vi*: **to cope with** (problem, situation etc) ...に対応する ...ni taíō suru

copious [kou'pi:əs] *adj* (helpings) たっぷりの táppùri no

copious amounts of 多量の taryó no

copper [kɑːp'əʳ] *n* (metal) 銅 dó; (*inf*: policeman/woman) 警官 kefkan

coppers [kɑːp'əʳz] *npl* (small change, coins) 小銭 kozéni

coppice [kɑːp'is] *n* = **copse**

copse [kɑːps] *n* 木立 kodáchi

copulate [kɑːp'jəleit] *vi* (people) 性交する sefkō suru; (animals) 交尾する kóbi suru

copy [kɑːp'i:] *n* (duplicate) 複写 fukúsha, コピー kópì; (of book) 1冊 issátsu; (of

record) 1枚 ichfmai; (of newspaper) 1部 ichfbù

♦*vt* (person, idea etc) まねる manérù; (something written) 複写する fukúsha suru, コピーする kópì suru

copyright [kɑːp'i:rait] *n* 著作権 chosákukèn

coral [kɔːr'əl] *n* (substance) さんご sańgo

coral reef *n* さんご礁 sańgoshó

cord [kɔːrd] *n* (string) ひも himó; (ELEC) コード kódo; (fabric) コールテン kórutèn

cordial [kɔːr'dʒəl] *adj* (person, welcome) 暖かい atátakaì; (relationship) 親密な shifmitsu na

♦*n* (BRIT: drink) フルーツシロップ furútsu shiròppu

cordon [kɔːr'dən] *n* (MIL, POLICE) 非常線 hijōsen

cordon off *vt* 非常線を張って...への立入りを禁止する hijōsen wo hattè ...no tachfiri wo kińshi suru

corduroy [kɔːr'dərɔi] *n* コールテン kórutèn

core [kɔːr] *n* (of fruit) しん shiñ; (of organization, system, building) 中心部 chúshiñbu; (heart: of problem) 核心 kakúshiñ

♦*vt* (an apple, pear etc) ...のしんをくりぬく ...no shiñ wo kurínukù

coriander [kɔːriæn'dəːr] *n* (spice) コリアンダー korfañda

cork [kɔːrk] *n* (stopper) 栓 señ; (bark) コルク kórùku

corkscrew [kɔːrk'skruː] *n* 栓抜き sefnuki

corn [kɔːrn] *n* (US: maize) トウモロコシ tómoròdokoshi; (BRIT: cereal crop) 穀物 kokúmotsu; (on foot) 魚の目 uó no me

corn on the cob 軸付きトウモロコシ jikútsuki tómoròdokoshi

cornea [kɔːr'niːə] *n* (of eye) 角膜 kakúmaku

corned beef [kɔːrnd-] *n* コーンビーフ kóñbìfu

corner [kɔːr'nəːr] *n* (outside) 角 kádò; (inside) 隅 súmì; (in road) 角 kádò; (SOCCER) コーナーキック kónā kikkù; (BOXING) コーナー kónà

♦*vt* (trap) 追詰める oítsumerù; (袋のネズ

ミにする fukúro no nezumi ni suru; (COMM: market) 独占する dokúsen suru

♦t (in car) コーナリングする kōnaríngu surú

cornerstone [kɔ:r'nərstoun] *n* (fig) 土台 dodái

cornet [kɔ:rnet'] *n* (MUS) コルネット korúnettò; (BRIT: of ice-cream) アイスクリームコーン aísukurīmukòn

cornflakes [kɔ:rn'fleiks] *npl* コーンフレーク kōnfurēku

cornflour [kɔ:rn'flauər] (BRIT) *n* = **cornstarch**

cornstarch [kɔ:rn'stɑ:rtʃ] (US) *n* コーンスターチ kōnsutāchi

Cornwall [kɔ:rn'wɔ:l] *n* コーンウォール kōn-uōru

corny [kɔ:r'ni:] (*inf*) *adj* (joke) さえない saénai

corollary [kɔ:r'əleri:] *n* (of fact, idea) 当然の結果 tōzen no kekka

coronary [kɔ:r'əneri:] *n* (*also*: **coronary thrombosis**) 肝動脈血栓症 kandōmyakukessénshō

coronation [kɔ:rənei'ʃən] *n* たい冠式 tafkanshìki

coroner [kɔ:r'ənə:r] *n* (LAW) 検死官 kenshikàn

coronet [kɔ:r'ənit] *n* コロネット korónettò ◇貴族などがかぶる小さな冠 kizòku nadò ga kabúrù chísana kanmuri

corporal [kɔ:r'pərəl] *n* (MIL) ご長 gốchō

♦*adj*: **corporal punishment** 体罰 táibatsu

corporate [kɔ:r'pərit] *adj* (action, effort, ownership) 共同の kyōdō no; (finance, image) 企業の kigyō no

corporation [kɔ:rpərei'ʃən] *n* (COMM) 企業 kigyō; (of town) 行政部 gyōseibù

corps [kɔ:r] (*pl* **corps**) *n* (MIL) 兵団 hefdan; (of diplomats, journalists) ...団 ...dàn

corpse [kɔ:rps] *n* 死体 shitái

corpuscle [kɔ:r'pəsəl] *n* (BIO) 血球 kekkyū

corral [kəræl'] *n* (for cattle, horses) 囲い kakói

correct [kərekt'] *adj* (right) 正しい tadáshìi; (proper) 礼儀正しい refgitadashiì

♦*vt* (mistake, fault) 直す naósù; (exam) 採点する saften suru

correction [kərek'ʃən] *n* (act of correcting) 直す事 naósù kotó; (instance) 直し naóshi

correlation [kɔ:rəlei'ʃən] *n* (link) 相互関係 sōgokàñkei

correspond [kɔ:rəspɑ:nd'] *vi* (write): **to correspond (with)** (...と) 手紙のやり取りをする (...to) tegámi no yaríttòri wo surú; (be equivalent): **to correspond (to)** (...に) 相当する (...ni) sōtō suru; (be in accordance): **to correspond (with)** (...と) 一致する (...to) itchí suru

correspondence [kɔ:rəspɑ:n'dəns] *n* (letters) 手紙 tegámi; (communication by letters) 文通 buñtsū; (relationship) 一致 itchí

correspondence course *n* (SCOL) 通信講座 tsúshìnkōza

correspondent [kɔ:rəspɑ:n'dənt] *n* (journalist) 特派員 tokúhaìn

corridor [kɔ:r'idə:r] *n* (in house, building etc) 廊下 rōka; (in train) 通路 tsūro

corroborate [kərɑb'əreit] *vt* (facts, story) 裏付ける urázukerù

corrode [kəroud'] *vt* (metal) 浸食する shiñshoku suru

♦*vi* (metal) 腐食する fushóku suru

corrosion [kərou'ʒən] *n* 腐食 fushóku

corrugated [kɔ:r'əgeitid] *adj* (roof, cardboard) 波型の namígata no

corrugated iron *n* なまこ板 namákoità

corrupt [kərʌpt'] *adj* (person) 腐敗した fuhái shitá; (COMPUT: data) 化けた bakéta, 壊れた kowáretà

♦*vt* (person) 買収する bafshū suru; (COMPUT: data) 化けさせる bakésaserù

corruption [kərʌp'ʃən] *n* (of person) 汚職 oshóku; (COMPUT: of data) 化ける事 bakérù kotó

corset [kɔ:r'sit] *n* (undergarment: *also*

MED) コルセット kōrūsetto

Corsica [kɔ:'sikə] n コルシカ島 kōrūshikatō

cosh [kɑ:ʃ] (BRIT) n (cudgel) こん棒 konbō

cosmetic [kɑːzmetʹik] n (beauty product) 化粧品 keshōhin
◆adj (fig: measure, improvement) 表面的な hyōmenteki na

cosmic [kɑ:z'mik] adj 宇宙の uchū no

cosmonaut [kɑ:z'mənɔ:t] n 宇宙飛行士 uchūhikōshi

cosmopolitan [kɑːzmɑpəʹliʹtən] adj (place, person) 国際的な kokūsaiteki na

cosmos [kɑ:z'mɔs] n 宇宙 uchū

cosset [kɑːs'it] vt (person) 甘やかす amáyakasù

cost [kɔ:st] n (price) 値段 nedán; (expenditure) 費用 hiyō
◆vt (pt, pp cost) (be priced at) ...の値段である ...no nedán de arù; (find out cost of: project, purchase etc: pt, pp **costed**) ...の費用を見積る ...no hiyō wo mitsúmorù

how much does it cost? いくらですか ikūra desu ka

to cost someone time/effort ...に時間 〔労力〕を要する ...ni jikan〔ryōryoku〕wo yō surù

it cost him his life それのために彼は命をなくした sono tamé ni kárè wa ínochi wo nákù shitá

at all costs 何があっても nanì ga atté mo

co-star [kou'stɑ:r] n (TV, CINEMA) 共演者 kyōensha

cost-effective [kɔ:stifekʹtiv] adj 費用効果比の高い hiyōkōkahi no takái

costly [kɔ:stʹli:] adj (high-priced) 値段の高い nedán no takái; (involving much expenditure) 費用の掛かる hiyō wo kakárù

cost-of-living [kɔ:stəvliʹiŋ] adj (allowance, index) 生計費の seíkeihi no

cost price (BRIT) n 原価 génka

costs [kɔːsts] npl (COMM: overheads) 経費 kéihi; (LAW) 訴訟費用 soshōhiyō

costume [kɑ:s'tum] n (outfit, style of

dress) 衣装 íshō; (BRIT: also: **swimming costume**) 水着 mizúgi

costume jewelry n 模造宝石類 mozōhōsekìrui

cosy [kou'zi:] (BRIT) adj = **cozy**

cot [kɑt] n (BRIT: child's) ベビーベッド bebíbeddò; (US: campbed) キャンプベッド kyańpubeddò

cottage [kɑ:t'idʒ] n (house) 小さな家 chíisa na ie, コッテジ kottèji

cottage cheese n カッテージチーズ kattèji chīzù

cotton [kɑt'ən] n (fabric) 木綿 momén, コットン kóttòn; (BRIT: thread) 縫い糸 nuí-itò

cotton batting [-bæt'iŋ] n (US) 脱脂綿 dasshímèn

cotton candy (US) n (candy floss) 綿菓子 watágàshi, 綿あめ watá-àme

cotton on to (inf) vt fus ...に気が付く ...ni kí ga tsúkù

cotton wool (BRIT) n = **cotton batting**

couch [kautʃ] n (sofa) ソファー sófā; (doctor's) 診察台 shiñsatsudai

couchette [ku:ʃet'] n (on train, boat) 寝台 shiñdai ◇昼間電に畳み掛けるか普通の座席に使う物を指す hiruma kabè ni tatámikakerò ka futsū no zaséki ni tsukáù monò wo sasù

cough [kɔ:f] vi (person) せきをする sekí wo surù
◆n (noise) せき sekí; (illness) せきの多い病気 sekí no ōi byōki

cough drop n せき止めドロップ sekídòme doróppu

could [kud] pt of **can**

couldn't [kud'ənt] = **could not**

council [kaun'səl] n (committee, board) 評議会 hyōgìkai

city/town council n (市)議会 shi〔chō〕gíkai

council estate (BRIT) n 公営住宅団地 kōeíjūtakudañchi

council house (BRIT) n 公営住宅 kōeíjūtaku

councillor [kaun'sə:r] n 議員 gíin

counsel [kaun'səl] n (advice) 助言 jogén;

(lawyer) 弁護人 beñgonin

♦vt (advise) ...に助言する ...ni jogen suru

counsel(l)or [kaun'sələr] n (advisor) カ ウンセラー káunserā; (US: lawyer) 弁護 人 beñgonin

count [kaunt] vt (add up: numbers, money, things, people) 数える kazóerù; (include) 入れる iréru, 含む fukúmů

♦vi (enumerate) 数える kazóerù; (be considered) ...と見なされる ...to minasareru; (be valid) 効果をもつ kōka wo mótsū

♦n (of things, people, votes) 数位 kazū; (level: of pollen, alcohol etc) 値 atái, 数 値 sūchi; (nobleman) 伯爵 hakúshaku

countdown [kaunt'daun] n (to launch) 秒読み byōyomi

countenance [kaun'tənəns] n (face) 顔 kaó

♦vt (tolerate) 容認する yōnin suru

counter [kaun'tər] n (in shop, café, bank etc) カウンター káuntā; (in game) こま kóma

♦vt (oppose) ...に対抗する ...ni taikō suru

♦adv: **counter to** ...に反して ...ni han shite

counteract [kauntəræk't] vt (effect, tendency) 打消す uchíkesu

counter-espionage [kauntəres'piːanɑːʒ] n 対抗的スパイ活動 taíkōteki supáikatsudō

counterfeit [kaun'tərfit] n (forgery) 偽 物 nisémono

♦vt (forge) 偽造する gizō suru

♦adj (coin) 偽物の nisémono no

counterfoil [kaun'tərfɔil] n (of check, money order) 控え hikáe

countermand [kauntərmænd'] vt (order) 取消す tôrikesu

counterpart [kaun'tərpɑːrt] n; **counterpart of** (person) ...に相当する人 ...ni sōtō suru hitô; (thing) ...に相当するもの ...ni sōtō suru mono

counterproductive [kauntərprədʌk'tiv] adj (measure, policy etc) 逆効果的な gyakúkōkateki na

countersign [kaun'tərsain] vt (document) ...に副署する ...ni fukúsho surù

countess [kaun'tis] n 伯爵夫人 hakúshakufújin

countless [kaunt'lis] adj (innumerable) 無数の músū no

count on vt fus (expect) ...の積りでいる ...no tsumóri de irù; (depend on) ...を頼り にする ...wo táyòri ni suru

country [kʌn'triː] n (state, nation) 国 kuníf; (native land) 母国 bôkōku; (rural area) 田舎 ináka; (region) 地域 chíki

country dancing (BRIT) n 英国郷土舞 踊 éikokukyōdōbuyō

country house n 田舎の大邸宅 ináka no dàteitaku

countryman [kʌn'trimən] (pl **countrymen**) n (compatriot) 同国人 dōkokujīn; (country dweller) 田舎者 inákamõno

countryside [kʌn'triːsaid] n 田舎 ináka

county [kaun'tiː] n (POL, ADMIN) 郡 gún

coup [ku:] (pl **coups**) n (MIL, POL: also: **coup d'état**) クーデター kúdetā; (achievement) 大成功 daíseikō

coupé [ku:pei'] n (AUT) クーペ kúpe

couple [kʌp'əl] n (also: **married couple**) 夫婦 fūfu; (cohabiting etc) カップル káppùru; (of things) 一対 ittsúi

a couple of (two people) 2人の futári no; (two things) 2つの futátsu no; (a few people) 数人の sūnin no; (a few things) 幾 つかの ikùtsuka no

coupon [kuː'pɑn] n (voucher) クーポン券 kūpoñken; (detachable form) クーポン kúpon

courage [kəːr'idʒ] n (bravery) 勇気 yūki

courageous [kərei'dʒəs] adj (person, attempt) 勇敢な yūkan na

courgette [kurʒet'] (BRIT) n ズッキー ニ zukkíni

courier [kəːr'iːər] n (messenger) メッセ ンジャー mêssènjā; (for tourists) 添乗員 teñjōin

course [kɔːrs] n (SCOL) 課程 katéi; (process: of life, events, time etc) 過程 katéi; (of treatment) クール kúru; (direction: of argument, action) 方針 hôshìn; (of ship) 針路 shínro; (part of meal) 一品 ippín, コース kôsu; (for golf) コース kôsu *the course of a river* 川筋 kawásuji

of course (naturally) もちろん mochíròn, 当然 tōzen; (certainly) いいとも fì to mo

court [kɔːt] *n* (royal) 宮殿 kyúden; (LAW) 法廷 hōtei; (for tennis, badminton etc) コート kôto

♦*vt* (woman) 妻にしようとして…と交際する tsumá ni shiyô to shité …to kôsai suru

to take someone to court (LAW) …を相手取って訴訟を起す …wo aítedottè soshô wo okósū

courteous [ˈkəːtiːəs] *adj* (person, conduct) 丁寧な teínei na

courtesan [ˌkɔːrtiˈzæn] *n* 宮廷しょう婦 kyúteishôfu

courtesy [ˈkəːrtisi] *n* (politeness) 礼儀正しき reígitadashisa

(by) courtesy of (thanks to) …のお陰で …no okáge de

court-house [ˈkɔːrtˌhaus] (*US*) *n* 裁判所 saíbansho

courtier [ˈkəːrtiːər] *n* 廷臣 teíshin

court-martial [ˈkɔːrtˈmɑːrʃəl] (*pl* courts-martial) *vt* (MIL) 軍法会議 guñpôkaìgi

courtroom [ˈkɔːrtˌruːm] *n* 法廷 hōtei

courtyard [ˈkɔːrtˌjɑːrd] *n* (of castle, house) 中庭 nakániwa

cousin [ˈkʌzin] *n* (relative) 親せき shínseki

first cousin いとこ itóko

second cousin はとこ hatóko, またいとこ mata-ítoko

cove [kouv] *n* (bay) 入江 irfe

covenant [ˈkʌvənənt] *n* (promise) 契約 kefyaku

cover [ˈkʌvər] *vt* (hide: face, surface, ground): *to cover (with)* …で覆う de oū; (hide: feelings, mistake): *to cover (with)* …で隠す …de kakúsū; (shield: book, table etc): *to cover (with)* …(…を) 掛ける …ni (…wo) kakérù; (with lid): *to cover (with)* …にふたをする …ni futá wo suru; (travel: distance) 行く ikú; (protect: also INSURANCE) カバーする kábā suru; (discuss: topic, subject: also PRESS) 取上げる torfagerù; (include) 含

む fukúmù

♦*n* (for furniture) 覆い oū; (lid) ふた futá; (on bed) 上掛 uwágake; (of book, magazine) 表紙 hyóshi; (shelter: for hiding) 隠れ場所 kakúrebasho; (: from rain) 雨宿りの場所 amáyadòri no bashò; (INSURANCE) 保険 hokén; (of spy) 架空の身分 kakū no mībùn

to take cover (shelter: from rain) 雨宿りをする amáyadòri wo suru; (: from gunfire etc) 隠れる kakúrerù

under cover (indoors) 屋根の下で(に) yané no shitá de (ni)

under cover of darkness やみに紛れて yamí ni magíreté

under separate cover (COMM) 別便で betsúbin de

coverage [ˈkʌvəridʒ] *n* (TV, PRESS) 報道 hōdō

cover charge *n* (in restaurant) サービス料 sábisuryô

covering [ˈkʌvəriŋ] *n* (layer) 覆い oū; (of snow, dust etc) 覆う物 oū monò

covering letter (*US also:* cover letter) *n* 添状 soéjò

cover note *n* (BRIT) (INSURANCE) 保険証 karíhokeñshô

covert [ˈkʌvərt] *adj* (glance, threat) 隠れた kakúretà

cover up *vi*: *to cover up for someone* …をかばう …wo kabáù

cover-up [ˈkʌvərˌʌp] *n* もみ消し momíkeshi

covet [ˈkʌvit] *vt* (desire) 欲しがる hoshígarù

cow [kau] *n* (animal) 雌牛 ウシ meúshi; (*inf*: woman) あま amá

♦*vt* (oppress): *to be cowed* おびえる obíerù

coward [ˈkauərd] *n* おく病者 okúbyòmono

cowardice [ˈkauərdis] *n* おく病 okúbyò

cowardly [ˈkauərdli] *adj* おく病な okúbyò na

cowboy [ˈkauˌbɔi] *n* (in US) カウボーイ kaúbòi

cower [ˈkauər] *vi* へ縮する ishúku suru

coxswain [ˈkɑːksin] *n* (ROWING: abbr:

cox) コックス kókkùsu

coy [koi] adj (demure, shy) はにかんでみせる hanfkandè misérő

coyote [kaiout'i:] n コヨーテ kóyòte

cozy [kou'zi:] (BRIT cosy) adj (room, house) こじんまりした kojfnmarǐ shita; (person) 心地よい kokóchi yoì

CPA [si:pi:ei'] (US) abbr = certified public accountant

crab [kræb] n カニ kanǐ

crab apple n ヒメリンゴ himérìngo

crack [kræk] n (noise: of gun) パン pan; (: of thunder) ばりばり bárǐbarǐ; (: of twig) ぽっきり pokkíri; (: of whip) パン ban; (gap) 割れ目 waréme; (in bone, dish, glass, wall) ひび hibǐ

♦vt (whip, twig) 鳴らす narásū; (bone, dish, glass, wall) ひびを入れる hibǐ wo irérū; (nut) 割る warú; (solve: problem) 解決する kafketsu suru; (: code) hawk く tóku; (joke) 飛ばす tobásu

♦adj (expert) 優秀な yūshu na

crack down on vt fus (crime, expenditure etc) 取り締まる toríshimarū

cracker [kræk'əːr] n (biscuit, Christmas cracker) クラッカー kurákkà

crackle [kræk'əl] vi (fire) ぱちぱちと音を立てる páchǐpachi to otó wo tatérū; (twig) ぽきぽきと音をたてる pókǐpoki to otó wo tatérū

crack up vi (PSYCH) 頭がおかしくなる atáma ga okáshikū nárū

cradle [krei'dəl] n (baby's) 揺りかご yurfkago

craft [kræft] n (skill) 芸術 gejjutsu; (trade) 職業 shokúgyò; (boat: pl inv) 船 fúnè; (plane: pl inv) 飛行機 hikóki

craftsman [kræfts'mən] (pl craftsmen) n (artisan) 職人 shokúnin

craftsmanship [kræfts'mənʃip] n (quality) 芸術 gejjutsu

crafty [kræf'ti:] adj (sneaky) 腹黒い harágurot, ずるい kôkatsu na

crag [kræg] n 険しい岩山 kewáshii iwáyama

cram [kræm] vt (fill): to cram something with …を…で一杯にする …wo de ippái ni suru; (put): to cram some-

thing into …を…に詰め込む …wo …ni tsu-mékomů

♦vi: to cram for exams 一夜漬けの試験勉強をする ichýazuke no shikénbenkyò wo suru

cramp [kræmp] n (MED) けいれん kefren

cramped [kræmpt] adj (accommodation) 窮屈な kyúkutsu na

crampon [kræm'pɑn] n (CLIMBING) アイゼン áizen

cranberry [kræn'be:ri:] n (berry) コケモ モ kokémòmo, クランベリー kuránberi

crane [krein] n (machine) クレーン kúrèn; (bird) ツル tsurú

crank [kræŋk] n (person) 変人 henjìn; (handle) クランク kuránku

crankshaft [kræŋk'ʃæft] n (AUT) クランクシャフト kuránkushafùto

cranny [kræn'i:] n see nook

crash [kræʃ] n (noise) 大音響 dafonkyô ♦物が落ちる、ぶつかるなどの大きな音を指す monó ga ochíru, butsúkarů nadð no ókìna otó wo sásū; (of car, train etc) 衝突 shōtotsu; (of plane) 墜落 tsufraku; (COMM: of stock-market) 暴落 bóraku; (COMM: of business etc) 倒産 tòsan

♦vt (car etc) 衝突させる shōtotsu saséru; (plane) 墜落させる tsufraku saséru

♦vi (car) 衝突する shōtotsu suru; (plane) 墜落する tsufraku suru; (COMM: market) 暴落する bóraku suru; (COMM: firm) 倒産する tòsan suru

crash course n 速成コース sokúseikòsu

crash helmet n ヘルメット herúmettò

crash landing n (AVIAT) 不時着陸 fujíchakúriku

crass [kræs] adj (behavior, comment, person) 露骨な rokótsu na

crate [kreit] n (box) 箱 hakó; (for bottles) ケース kêsu

crater [krei'təːr] n (of volcano) 噴火口 fufkakô; (on moon etc) クレーター kurétä

bomb crater 爆弾孔 bakúdankô

cravat [krəvæt'] n アスコットタイ asúkottotai

crave [kreiv] vt, vi: to crave for …を強く欲しがる …wo tsuyókù hoshígarù

crawl [krɔːl] *vi* (person) 四つんばいには う yotsúnbai ni háũ; (insect) はう háũ; (vehicle) のろのろと進む nórðnoro to susúmū

◆*n* (SWIMMING) クロール kúrðru

crayfish [krei'fiʃ] *n inv* (freshwater) ザ リガニ zarígani; (saltwater) エビガニ ebígani

crayon [krei'ɑːn] *n* クレヨン kuréyðn

craze [kreiz] *n* (fashion) 大流行 dafryðkô

crazy [krei'zi:] *adj* (insane) 狂気 でない shốki de náī; (inf: keen): **crazy about** someone/something ...が大好きである ...ga dafsuki de árū

crazy paving (BRIT) *n* 不ぞろいの舗装 fuzóroi hosố ろ不ぞろいの敷石からなる舗装 fuzóroi no shikíishi kara narū hosố

creak [kriːk] *vi* (floorboard, door etc) きしむ kishímû

cream [kriːm] *n* (of milk) (生)クリーム (namá)kúrīmu; (also: **artificial cream**) 人造クリーム jinzôkurīmu; (cosmetic) 化粧クリーム keshôkurīmu; (élite) 名士た ち meíshi tachì

◆*adj* (color) クリーム色の kúrīmuírð no

cream cake *n* クリームケーキ kúrīmu-kéki

cream cheese *n* クリームチーズ kúrī-muchīzu

creamy [kriː'miː] *adj* (color) クリーム色 の kúrīmuírð no; (taste) 生クリームたっ ぷりの namákurīmu táppūri no

crease [kriːs] *n* (fold) 折り目 oríme; (wrinkle) しわ shiwá; (in trousers) 折目 oríme

◆*vt* (wrinkle) しわくちゃにする shiwá-kucha ni suru

◆*vi* (wrinkle up) しわくちゃになる shi-wákucha ni naru

create [kriː'eit] *vt* (cause to happen, exist) 引起こす hikíokosù; (produce, design) 作る tsukúrù

creation [kriː'ei'ʃən] *n* (causing to happen, exist) 引起こす事 hikíokosù kotő; (production, design) 作る事 tsukúrù kotő; (REL) 天地創造 teñchisôzô

creative [kriː'eitiv] *adj* (artistic) 芸術的 な geíjutsuteki na; (inventive) 創造力の ある sốzôsei no árū

creator [kriː'eitər] *n* (maker, inventor) 作る人 tsukúrù hitô

creature [kriː'tʃər] *n* (living animal) 動物 dốbutsu; (person) 人間 niñgen

crèche [kreʃ] *n* 託児所 takújisho

credence [kriːd'əns] *n*: **to lend credence to** (prove) ...を信じさせる ...wo shifíji saséru

to give credence to (prove) ...を信じさせる ...wo shifíji saséru; (believe) 信じる shifíjirù

credentials [kriden'ʃəlz] *npl* (references) 資格 shikáku; (identity papers) 身分証明証 mibúnshômeishô

credibility [kredəbil'əti:] *n* (of person, fact) 信頼性 shifíraisei

credible [kred'əbəl] *adj* (believable) 信じられる shifíjirareru; (trustworthy) 信用できる shifí-yô dekírù

credit [kred'it] *n* (COMM: loan) 信用 shifí-yô; (recognition) 名誉 mêíyo

◆*vt* (COMM) ...の入金にする ...no nyúkin ni suru; (believe: also: **give credit to**) 信じる shifíjirù

to be in credit (person, bank account) 黒字になっている kuróji ni natté irú

to credit someone with (fig) ...に...の美徳があると思う ...ni...no bitőku ga árū to omóù

credit card *n* クレジットカード kuréjit-tokādo

creditor [kred'itər] *n* (COMM) 債権者 saíkeñsha

credits [kred'its] *npl* (CINEMA) クレジット kuréjitto

creed [kriːd] *n* (REL) 信条 shifíjô

creek [kriːk] *n* (US: stream) 小川 ogáwa; (BRIT: inlet) 入江 iríe

creep [kriːp] (*pt*, *pp* **crept**) *vi* (person, animal) 忍び足で歩く shinóbiàshi de árū-kù

creeper [kriː'pər] *n* (plant) つる tsurú

creepy [kriː'piː] *adj* (frightening: story, experience) 薄気味悪い usúkimiwarui

cremate [kriː'meit] *vt* (corpse) 火葬にする kasố ni suru

cremation [krimei'ʃən] *n* 火葬 kasố

crematoria [krimətɔːr'iːə] *npl of* crematorium

crematorium [kriːmətorˈiːəm] (pl **crematoria**) n 火葬場 kasōba

crêpe [kreip] n (fabric) クレープ kūrēpu; (rubber) クレープゴム kurēpugomù ◇靴底に使う表面がしわ状のゴム kutsúzoko ni tsukáù hyōmen ga shiwájō no gómù

crêpe bandage (BRIT) n 伸縮性包帯 shiñshukuseíhōtai

crept [krept] pt, pp of creep

crescent [kresˈənt] n (in shape) 三日月形 mikázukigata; (street) ...通り ...dōri ◇特にカーブになっている通りの名前に使う tōkù ni kábu ni natté irù tōri no namáe ni tsukáù

cress [kres] n (BOT, CULIN) クレソン kurésoñ

crest [krest] n (of hill) 頂上 chōjō; (of bird) とさか tosáka; (coat of arms) 紋章 móñ

crestfallen [krestˈfɔːlən] adj しょんぼりした shoñborí shitá

Crete [kriːt] n クレタ島 kuréta tō

crevice [krevˈis] n (gap, crack) 割れ目 waréme

crew [kruː] n (NAUT) 乗組員 noríkumiìn; (AVIAT) 乗員 jōin; (TV, CINEMA) カメラ班 kamérahàn ◇3つの意味とも総称として使う mittsù no imì to mo sōshō toshité tsukáù

crew-cut [kruːˈkʌt] n 角刈り kakúgari

crew-neck [kruːˈnek] n (of jersey) 丸首 marúkubi

crib [krib] n ベビーベッド bebíbeddò
◆vt (inf: copy: during exam etc) カンニングする kañniñgu suru; (: from writings etc of others) 盗用する tōyō suru

crick [krik] n: **to have a crick in one's neck** 首が痛い kubí ga itáì

cricket [krikˈit] n (game) クリケット kuríkettò; (insect) コオロギ kōrogi

crime [kraim] n (no pl: illegal activities) 犯罪 hañzai; (illegal action) 犯罪 (行為) hañzai(kōi); (fig) 罪 tsumí

criminal [krimˈənəl] n 犯罪者 hañzaìsha
◆adj (illegal) 違法の ihō no; (morally wrong) 罪悪の zaſaku no

crimson [krimˈzən] adj 紅色の beñiro no

cringe [krindʒ] vi (in fear, embarrassment) 縮こまる chijíkomarù

crinkle [kriŋˈkəl] vt (crease, fold) しわくちゃにする shiwákucha ni suru

cripple [kripˈəl] n (MED) 身障者 shiñshōsha
◆vt (person) 不具にする fúgù ni suru

crises [krai'siːz] npl of crisis

crisis [kraiˈsis] (pl **crises**) n 危機 kikí

crisp [krisp] adj (vegetables) ぱりぱりした pấrīpari shitá; (bacon) かりかりした kárîkari shitá; (weather) からっとした karáttò shitá; (manner, tone, reply) 無愛想な buáisō na

crisps [krisps] (BRIT) npl ポテトチップ potétochippù

criss-cross [krisˈkrɔːs] adj (pattern, design) 十字模様の jūjimoyō no

criteria [kraitiːˈriːə] npl of criterion

criterion [kraitiːˈriːən] (pl **criteria**) n (standard) 規準 kijún

critic [kritˈik] n (of system, policy etc) 反対する hañtaìsha; (reviewer) 評論家 hyōronka

critical [kritˈikəl] adj (time, situation) 重大な jūdai na; (opinion, analysis) 批評的な hihyōteki na; (person: fault-finding) 粗捜し好きな aràsagashizúki na; (illness) 危険な kikén na

critically [kritˈikli] adv (speak, look etc) 批判的に hihánteki ni
critically ill 重症で jūshō de

criticism [kritˈisizəm] n (disapproval, complaint) 非難 hínañ; (of book, play etc) 批評 hihyō

criticize [kritˈisaiz] vt (find fault with) 非難する hínañ suru

croak [krouk] vi (frog) げろげろ鳴く gérōgero nakú; (bird) かーかー鳴く kákā nakú; (person) がらがら声で言う rágaragoe de iu

crochet [krouˈei] n かぎ針編み kagíbariami

crockery [krɑːkˈəriː] n (dishes) 皿類 saráruì

crocodile [krɑːkˈədail] n ワニ wánì

crocus [krou'kəs] *n* クロッカス kurókkàsu

croft [krɔːft] (*BRIT*) *n* (small farm) 小農場 shōnōjō

crony [krou'niː] (*inf: pej*) *n* 仲間 nakáma

crook [kruk] *n* (criminal) 悪党 akútò; (*also:* **shepherd's crook**) 羊飼のつえ hitsújìkai no tsúè ◇片端の曲った物を指す katáhashiì no magátta monó wo sásù

crooked [kruk'id] *adj* (bent, twisted) 曲った magátta; (dishonest) 不正の fuséì no

crop [krɔːp] *n* (of fruit, cereals, vegetables) 作物 sakúmòtsu; (harvest) 収穫 shūkaku; (riding crop) むち múchī ◇乗馬用の物を指す jōbayō no monó wo sásù
◆*vt* (hair) 刈込む karíkòmu

crop up *vi* (problem, topic) 持ち上る mochíagarù

croquet [kroukei'] *n* クロッケー kurókkē ◇複雑なゲートボールに似た球技 fukúzatsu na gētobōru ni nitá kyūgi

croquette [krouket'] *n* (CULIN) コロッケ korókkè

cross [krɔːs] *n* (shape) 十字 jūji; (REL) 十字架 jūjika; (mark) ばつ(印) bátsù(jírùshi); (hybrid) 合の子 aínoko
◆*vt* (street, room etc) 横断する ōdan suru; (arms, legs) 組む kúmù; (animal, plant) 交雑する kōzatsu suru
◆*adj* (angry) 不機嫌な fukígen na

to cross a check 線引小切手にする señbiki kogíttè ni suru

crossbar [krɔːs'bɑːr] *n* (SPORT) ゴールの横棒 gōru no yokóbō

cross-examine [krɔːsˈigzæmˈin] *vt* (LAW) 反対尋問する haftaijiñmon suru

cross-eyed [krɔːs'aid] *adj* 寄り目の yoríme no

crossfire [krɔːs'faiər] *n* 十字射撃 jūjishagēki

crossing [krɔːs'iŋ] *n* (sea passage) 船旅 funátabi; (*also:* **pedestrian crossing**) 横断歩道 ōdanhodō

crossing guard (*US*) *n* 交通指導員 kōtsūshídōin ◇交通事故を防ぐために横断

歩道に立って学童などの横断を助ける指導員 kōtsūjìkò wo fuségù tamé ni ōdanhodō ni tattè gakúdō nádò no ōdan wo tasúkerù shidōin

cross out *vt* (delete) 線を引いて消す séñ wo hiítè kesú

cross over *vi* (move across) 横断する ōdan suru

cross-purposes [krɔːsˈpəːrˈpəsiz] *npl*:
to be at cross-purposes 話が食違っている hanáshi ga kuchígattè irú

cross-reference [krɔːs'refˈərəns] *n* 相互参照 sōgosañshō

crossroads [krɔːs'roudz] *n* 交差点 kōsatèn

cross section *n* (of an object) 断面 dañmeñ; (sketch) 断面図 dañmeñzu
cross section of the population 国民を代表する人々 kokumin wo dáhyō suru hítòbìto

crosswalk [krɔːs'wɔːk] (*US*) *n* 横断歩道 ōdanhodō

crosswind [krɔːs'wind] *n* 横風 yokókaze

crossword [krɔːs'wəːrd] *n* クロスワードパズル kurósuwādopazùru

crotch [krɑːtʃ] *n* (ANAT, of garment) また matá

crotchet [krɑːtʃ'it] *n* (MUS) 四分音符 shibúoñpu

crotchety [krɑːtʃ'əti:] *adj* (person) 気難しい kimúzukashìi

crouch [krautʃ] *vi* (person, animal) うずくまる uzúkumarù

croupier [kruːp'iːər] *n* (in casino) とばく台の元締 tobákudai no motójìme, ディーラー dīrā

crow [krou] *n* (bird) カラス kárasu; (of cock) 鳴き声 nakígoè
◆*vi* (cock) 鳴く nakú

crowbar [krou'bɑːr] *n* バール bāru

crowd [kraud] *n*: **crowd of people** 群衆 guñshū
◆*vt* (fill: room, stadium etc) ...にぎっしり入る ...ni gisshírì hafrù
◆*vi* (gather): **to crowd round** ...の回りに群がる ...no mawári ni murágarù; (cram): **to crowd in** ...の中へ詰めかける ...no nákà e tsumékakerù

a crowd of fans 大勢のファン ōzei nō fán

crowded [krau'did] *adj* (full) 込入った komfitta; (densely populated) 人口密度の高い jínkōmitsūdo no takái

crown [kraun] *n* (*gen*) 冠 kámmuri; (of monarch) 王冠 ōkan; (monarchy): *the Crown* 国王 kokuō; (of tooth) 歯頭 てっぺん teppén; (of tooth) 歯冠 shikán
♦*vt* (monarch) 王位に就かせる ōi ni tsukáserū; (*fig*: career, evening) ...に有終の美を飾る ...nō yūshū no bí wo kazárū

crown jewels *npl* 王位の象徴 ōchō no shōchō 王冠, しゃくなど国家的儀式で王または女王が王位の象徴として用いる ōkan, shákū nádō kokkáteki gishíki de ō matá wa jō̃ ga ōi no shōchō toshite mochiírū monō wo sásū

crown prince *n* 皇太子 kōtaíshi

crow's feet *npl* 目じりの小じわ méjìri no kojíwa, カラスの足跡 kárāsu no ashfátò

crucial [kru:'ʃəl] *adj* (decision, vote) 重大な jūdai na

crucifix [kru:'səfiks] *n* (REL) 十字架像 jūjikazō

crucifixion [kru:səfik'ʃən] *n* (REL) キリストのはりつけ kirísuto no harftsukuke

crude [kru:d] *adj* (materials) 原... gén...; (*fig*: basic) 原始的な genshíteki na; (: vulgar) 野骨な rokótsu na

crude (oil) *n* 原油 gén'yu

cruel [kru:'əl] *adj* (person, action) 残酷な zañkoku na; (situation) 悲惨な hisán na

cruelty [kru:'əlti:] *n* (of person, action) 残酷さ zañkoku-sa; (of situation) 悲惨さ hisánsa

cruise [kru:z] *n* (on ship) 船旅 funátabi
♦*vi* (ship) 巡航する juñkō suru; (car) 快調に走行する rákū ni sōkō suru

cruiser [kru:'zə:r] *n* (motorboat) 大型モーターボート ōgata mótābòto, クルーザー kurūzà; (warship) 巡洋艦 juñ'yōkan

crumb [krʌm] *n* (of bread, cake) くずkúzú

crumble [krʌm'bəl] *vt* (bread, biscuit etc) 崩す kuzúsù
♦*vi* 崩れる kuzúrerù

crumbly [krʌm'bli:] *adj* (bread, biscuits etc) 崩れやすい kuzúreyasù, ぼろぼろした pórðpòro shitá

crumpet [krʌm'pit] *n* クランペット kuránpettò ◇マフィンの一種 mafín no ísshù

crumple [krʌm'pəl] *vt* (paper, clothes) しわくちゃにする shiwákucha ni suru

crunch [krʌntʃ] *vt* (food etc) かみ砕く kamfkudakù; (underfoot) 踏み砕く fumfkudakù
♦*n* (*fig*: moment of truth) いざという時 izá to iú tokí

crunchy [krʌn'tʃi:] *adj* (food) ぱりぱりした parfpari shitá

crusade [kru:seid'] *n* (campaign) 運動 uñdō

crush [krʌʃ] *n* (crowd) 人込み hitógomi; (love): *to have a crush on someone* ...にのぼせる ...ni nobóserù; (drink): *lemon crush* レモンスカッシュ remónsukasshū
♦*vt* (press, squeeze) 押しつぶす oshítsubusù; (crumple: paper, clothes) しわくちゃにする shiwákucha ni suru; (defeat: army, opposition) 圧倒する attō suru; (devastate: hopes) 台無しにする daínashi ni suru; (: person) 落胆させる rakútan saserù

crust [krʌst] *n* (of bread, pastry) 皮 kawá; (of snow, ice) アイスバーン aísubàn; (of the earth) 地殻 chikáku

crutch [krʌtʃ] *n* (support, stick) 松葉づえ matsúbazùe

crux [krʌks] *n* (of problem, matter) 核心 kakúshin

cry [krai] *vi* (weep) 泣く nakú; (shout: *also:* **cry out**) 叫ぶ sakébù
♦*n* (shriek) 悲鳴 himéi; (shout) 叫び声 sakébigoè; (of bird, animal) 鳴き声 nakígoè

cry off *vi* (change one's mind, cancel) 手を引く te wo hikú

crypt [kript] *n* 地下室 chikáshìtsu ◇特に納骨堂として使われる教会の地下室を指す tōkú ni nókotsudò nadò ni tsukáwarerù kyōkai no chikáshitsu wo sásù

cryptic [krip'tik] *adj* (remark, clue) なぞめいた nazómeità

crystal [krísʼtəl] n (mineral) 結晶 kesshō; (in jewelery) 水晶 suíshō; (glass) クリスタル kurísdzúmu

crystal-clear [krísʼtəlkliʻəːʼ] adj (transparent) よく澄んだ yókù súnda; (fig: easy to understand) 明白な meíhaku na

crystallize [krísʼtəlaiz] vt (opinion, thoughts) まとめる matómerù

♦vi (sugar etc) 結晶する kesshō suru

cub [kʌb] n (of lion, wolf etc) の子 ...no ko; (also: **cub scout**) カブスカウト kabúsukáùto

Cuba [kjúːbə] n キューバ kyūba

Cuban [kjúːbən] adj キューバの kyūba no

♦n キューバ人 kyūbajìn

cubbyhole [kʌbíːhoul] n 小さな納戸 chíɪsa na nañdo

cube [kjuːb] n (shape) 立方体 rippótai; (MATH: of number) ...の乗 ...no sañjō

♦vt (MATH) 三乗する sañjō suru

cube root n (MATH) 立方根 rppókon

cubic [kjúːbik] adj (volume) 立方の rppō no

cubic capacity n 体積 táiseki

cubicle [kjúːbikəl] n (at pool) 更衣室 kốishìtsu小さい個室について言う chíɪsai koshìtsu ni tsuíte iű; (in hospital) カーテンで仕切った病床のスペース kấten de shikíttà ichíbyōshōbùn no supésu

cuckoo [kúːkuː] n カッコウ kákkōu

cuckoo clock n は当時計 hatódòkei

cucumber [kjúːkʌmbəːʼ] n キューリ kyūri

cuddle [kʌdʼəl] vt (baby, person) 抱締める dakíshimerù

♦vi (lovers) 抱合う dakíaù

cue [kjuː] n (snooker cue) キュー kyū; (THEATER etc) 合図 áìzu, キュー kyū

cuff [kʌf] n (of sleeve) カフス kafúsù; (US: of trousers) 折り返し oríkaeshi; (blow) 平手打ち hiráteuchi

off the cuff (impromptu) 即座に(の) sókùza ni (no)

cufflinks [kʌfʼliŋks] npl カフスボタン kafúsubòtan

cuisine [kwizíːn] n (of country, region) 料理 ryōri

cul-de-sac [kʌlʼdəsæk'] n (road) 行き止り yukídomari

culinary [kjúːlənəːri] adj 料理の ryōri no

cull [kʌl] vt (story, idea) えり抜く erínukù

♦n (of animals) 間引き mabíki

culminate [kʌlʼməneit] vi: **to culminate in** (gen) 遂に...となる tsuí ni ...to narù; (unpleasant outcome) 挙句の果てに...となってしまう agéku no haté ni ...to natté shimaù

culmination [kʌlmənéiʼʃən] n (of career, process etc) 頂点 chōten

culottes [kjuːláts'] npl キュロット kyúròtto

culpable [kʌlʼpəbəl] adj (blameworthy) とがむべき togámubeki

culprit [kʌlʼprit] n (of crime) 犯人 hañnin

cult [kʌlt] n (REL: worship) 崇拝 sūhai; (: sect, group) 宗派 shūha; (fashion) 流行 ryúkō

cultivate [kʌlʼtəveit] vt (land) 耕す tagáyasù; (crop) 栽培する saíbai suru; (person) 近付きになろうとする chikázuki ni nárò to suru

cultivation [kʌltəvéiʼʃən] n (AGR) 耕作 kōsaku

cultural [kʌlʼtʃəʼrəl] adj (traditions etc) 文化文明の buñkabuñmei no; (activities etc) 芸術の geijutsu no

culture [kʌlʼtʃəːʼ] n (of country, civilization) 文明 buñmei, 文化 buñka; (the arts) 芸術 geíjutsu; (BIO) 培養 baíyō

cultured [kʌlʼtʃəːd] adj (individual) 教養のある kyōyō no arù

cumbersome [kʌmʼbəːrsəm] adj (object) 扱いにくい atsúkainikuì かさ張る物, 重い物, 大きくて不格好な物などについて言う kasábarù monó, omóì monó, ōkikute bukákkō na monó nadò ni tsuíte iû; (process) 面倒な meñdō na

cumulative [kjúːmʼjəlàtiv] adj (effect, result) 累積する ruíseki suru

cunning [kʌnʼiŋ] n (craftiness) こうかつさ kókàtsusa

♦adj (crafty) こうかつな kōkàtsu na

cup [kʌp] n (for drinking) カップ káppù,

(as prize) 賞杯 shōhai, カップ káppu; (of bra) カップ káppu

cupboard [kʌb'ərd] n 戸棚 todána

Cupid [kju:'pid] n キューピッド kyúpiddo

cup-tie [kʌp'tai] (BRIT) n (SOCCER) トーナメント tónamento

curate [kju:'rit] n 助任牧師 jonínbokúshi

curator [kjurei'tər] n (of museum, gallery) キューレーター kyúrèta ◇学芸員の管理職に相当する人を指す gakúgeiìn no kańrishoku ni sôtō suru hito wo sásù

curb [kə:rb] vt (powers, expenditure) 制限する se[gen suru; (person) 抑える osáerù

◆n (restraint) 抑制 yokúsei; (US: kerb) 縁石 fuchíishi

curdle [kə:r'dəl] vi (milk) 凝結する gyóketsu suru

cure [kjur] vt (illness, patient) 治す naósù; (CULIN) 保存食にする hozónshoku ni suru

◆n (MED) 治療法 chiryōhō; (solution) 解決 kafketsu

curfew [kə:r'fju:] n (MIL, POL) 夜間外出禁止令 yakán gaishutsu kínshìrei

curio [kju:'ri:ou] n 骨とう品 kottōhin

curiosity [kju:ri:ɑs'əti:] n (of person) 好奇心 kókishìn; (object) 珍しい物 mezúrashiì monó

curious [kju:'ri:əs] adj (person: interested) 好奇心がある kókishìn ga arù; (: nosy) せん索好きな seńsakuzúki na; (thing: strange, unusual) 変った kawátta

curl [kə:rl] n (of hair) カール káru

◆vt (hair) カールする káru suru

◆vi (hair) カールになっている káru ni natté irù

curler [kə:r'lər] n (for hair) カーラー kárā

curl up vi (person, animal) 縮こまる chijíkomarù

curly [kə:r'li:] adj 巻毛の makíge no

currant [kə:r'ənt] n (dried fruit) レーズン rēzun ◇小型の種無しブドウから作った物を指す kogáta no tanénashibúdō kara tsukúttà monó wo sásù (bush, fruit: blackcurrant, redcurrant) スグリ

sūguri

currency [kə:r'ənsi:] n (system) 通貨 tsūka; (money) 貨幣 káhèi

to gain currency (fig) 通用する様になる tsūyō suru yố ni narù

current [kə:r'ənt] n (of air, water) 流れ nagáre; (ELEC) 電流 dénryū

◆adj (present) 現在の geńzai no; (accepted) 通用している tsūyō shité irù

current account (BRIT) n 当座預金 tōzayokîn

current affairs npl 時事 jiji

currently [kə:r'əntli:] adv 現在は geńzai wà

curricula [kərik'jələ] npl of curriculum

curriculum [kərik'jələm] (pl curriculums or curricula) n (SCOL) 指導要領 shidōyōryō

curriculum vitae [-vi:'tai] n 履歴書 rirékisho

curry [kə:r'i:] n (dish) カレー karē

◆vt: to curry favor with ...にへつらう ...ni hetsurau

curry powder n カレー粉 karêko

curse [kə:rs] vi (swear) 悪態をつく akútai wo tsukú

◆vt (swear at) のの しる nonóshirù; (bemoan) のろう norou

◆n (spell) 呪い noríi; (swearword) 悪態 akútai; (problem, scourge) 災の元 wazáwai no motó

cursor [kə:r'sər] n (COMPUT) カーソル kásoru

cursory [kə:r'səri:] adj (glance, examination) 何気ない nanígenaì

curt [kə:rt] adj (reply, tone) 無愛想な buáisō na

curtail [kərteil'] vt (freedom, rights) 制限する se[gen suru; (visit etc) 短くする mijíkakû suru; (expenses etc) 減らす herásu

curtain [kə:r'tən] n (at window) カーテン kāten; (THEATER) 幕 makú

curts(e)y [kə:r't'si:] vi (woman, girl) ひざを曲げて御辞儀をする hizá wo magête ojígi wo suru

curve [kə:rv] n (bend: in line etc) 曲線 kyokúsen; (: in road) カーブ kābu

♦*vi* 曲る magáru

cushion [kuʃ'ən] *n* (on sofa, chair) クッション kusshòn, 座布団 zabúton; (*also*: **air cushion**) エアクッション eákusshòn ◇ホバークラフトなどを支える空気の事 hobákurafùto nádò wo sasáeru kúki no kotó

♦*vt* (collision, fall) …の衝撃を和らげる …no shṓgeki wo yawáragerù; (shock, effect) 和らげる yawáragerù

custard [kʌs'tərd] *n* カスタード kasútādo

custodian [kʌstou'diːən] *n* (of building, collection) 管理人 kañrinin

custody [kʌs'tədiː] *n* (LAW: of child) 親権 shiñken

   to take into custody (suspect) 逮捕する taího suru

custom [kʌs'təm] *n* (tradition) 伝統 deñtō; (convention) 慣習 kañshū; (habit) 習慣 shūkan; (COMM) ひいき híiki

customary [kʌs'təmeriː] *adj* (behavior, method, time) いつもの itsúmo no, 相変らずの afkawarazu no

customer [kʌs'təmər] *n* (of shop, business etc) 客 kyakú

customized [kʌs'təmaizd] *adj* (car etc) 改造した kafzō shitá

custom-made [kʌs'təmmeid'] *adj* (shirt, car etc) あつらえの atsúraè no, オーダーメードの ōdāmèdo no

customs [kʌs'təmz] *npl* (at border, airport etc) 税関 zefkan

customs duty *n* 関税 kañzei

customs officer *n* 税関吏 zefkanri

cut [kʌt] (*pt, pp* **cut**) *vt* (bread, meat, hand etc) 切る kirú; (shorten: grass, hair) 刈る karú; (: text, program) 短くする mijîkakù suru; (reduce: prices, spending, supply) 減らす herásu

♦*vi* (knife, scissors) 切れる kirérù

♦*n* (in skin) 切り傷 kirîkìzu; (in salary) 減給 geñkyū; (in spending etc) 削減 sakúgen; (of meat) ブロック burókkù; (of garment) カット káttò

   to cut a tooth 歯が生える há ga haérù

cutback [kʌt'bæk] *n* 削減 sakúgen

cut down *vt* (tree) 切り倒す kirítaosù;

(consumption) 減らす herásu

cute [kjuːt] *adj* (*US*: pretty) かわいい kawáii; (sweet) 陳腐な chíñpu na

cuticle [kjuː'tikəl] *n* (of nail) 甘皮 amákawa

cutlery [kʌt'ləriː] *n* ナイフとフォークとスプーン náīfu to fōku to spûn ◇総称 sōshō

cutlet [kʌt'lit] *n* (piece of meat) カツ(レツ) katsú(retsu); (vegetable cutlet, nut cutlet) コロッケ kōrókke

cut off *vt* (limb) 切断する setsúdan suru; (piece) 切る kirú, 切り分ける kiríwakerù; (person, village) 孤立させる korítsu saséru; (supply) 遮断する shadán suru; (TEL) 切る kirú

cut out *vt* (shape, article from newspaper) 切抜く kirínukù; (stop: an activity etc) やめる yaméru; (remove) 切除する setsújo suru

cutout [kʌt'aut] *n* (switch) 非常遮断装置 hijōshadansōchi, 安全器 añzeñki; (shape) 切抜き kirínukì

cut-rate [kʌt'reit] (*BRIT* **cut-price**) *adj* 安売りの yasúuri no

cutthroat [kʌt'θrout] *n* (murderer) 人殺し hitógoroshi

♦*adj* (business, competition) 殺人的な satsújinteki na

cutting [kʌt'liŋ] *adj* (remark) 辛らつな shiráratsu na

♦*n* (from newspaper) 切抜き kirínuki; (from plant) 穂木 hogî, さし穂 sashího

cut up *vt* (paper, meat) 刻む kizámu

CV [siːviː'] *n abbr* = **curriculum vitae**

cwt *abbr* = **hundredweight(s)**

cyanide [sai'ənaid] *n* 青酸化合物 sefsanka-bùtsu

cyclamen [sik'ləmən] *n* シクラメン shikúramèn

cycle [sai'kəl] *n* (bicycle) 自転車 jitéñsha; (series: of events, seasons etc) 周期 shūki; (: TECH) サイクル sáikuru; (: of songs etc) 一連 ichíren

♦*vi* (on bicycle) 自転車で行く jitéñsha de ikú

cycling [saik'liŋ] *n* サイクリング sáikuringu

cyclist [saik'list] *n* サイクリスト sáikurisuto

cyclone [saik'loun] *n* (storm) サイクロン sáikuron

cygnet [sig'nit] *n* 若いハクチョウ wakái hakúchò

cylinder [sil'indər] *n* (shape) 円柱 eńchū; (of gas) ボンベ bóñbe; (in engine, machine etc) 気筒 kitó, シリンダー shríñdā

cylinder-head gasket [sil'indər:rhed-] *n* (AUT) シリンダーヘッドのパッキング shríñdàheddò no pakkíñgu

cymbals [sim'bəlz] *npl* (MUS) シンバル shíñbaru

cynic [sin'ik] *n* 皮肉屋 hiníkuya, シニック shiníkku

cynical [sin'ikəl] *adj* (attitude, view) 皮肉な hiníku na, シニカルな shiníkaru na

cynicism [sin'əsizəm] *n* シニカルな態度 shiníkaru na táìdo

cypress [sai'pris] *n* (tree) イトスギ itósugi

Cypriot [sip'ri:ət] *adj* キプロスの kípùrosu no
♦*n* キプロス人 kipúrosujin

Cyprus [saip'rəs] *n* キプロス kípùrosu

cyst [sist] *n* (MED) のうしゅ nóshu

cystitis [sistai'tis] *n* (MED) ぼうこう炎 bókòen

czar [zɑːr] *n* = **tsar**

Czech [tʃek] *adj* チェコスロバキアの chékòsuróbakìa no
♦*n* (person) チェコスロバキア人 chékòsuróbakìajìn; (language) チェコスロバキア語 chékòsuróbakìago

Czechoslovak [tʃekəslou'væk] *adj*, *n* = **Czechoslovakian**

Czechoslovakia [tʃekəsləvɑːk'iːə] *n* チェコスロバキア chékòsuróbakìa

Czechoslovakian [tʃekəsləvɑːk'iːən] *adj* チェコスロバキアの chékòsuróbakìa no
♦*n* (person) チェコスロバキア人 chékòsuróbakìajìn

D

D [diː] *n* (MUS: note) ニ音 níòn; (: key) ニ

調 níchò

dab [dæb] *vt* (eyes, wound) 軽くふく karúku fukú; (paint, cream) 軽く塗る karúku nurú

dabble [dæb'əl] *vi*: **to dabble in** (politics, antiques etc) 趣味でやる shúmì de yarú

dad [dæd] (*inf*) *n* 父ちゃん tóchan

daddy [dæd'iː] (*inf*) *n* = **dad**

daffodil [dæf'ədil] *n* スイセン suísen

daft [dæft] *adj* (silly) ばかな bákà na

dagger [dæg'əːr] *n* 短刀 tántò

daily [dei'liː] *adj* (dose, wages, routine etc) 毎日の maínichì no
♦*n* (also: **daily paper**) 日刊新聞 nikkánshíñbun
♦*adv* (pay, see) 毎日 maínichì

dainty [dein'tiː] *adj* (petite) 繊細な sénsai na

dairy [deːr'iː] *n* (BRIT: shop) 牛乳店 gyúnyūten; (on farm) 牛乳小屋 gyúnyūgòya ◇酪農場で牛乳を置いたり加工したりする小屋 rakúnōjò dè gyúnyū wò ofárì kakó shitarí suru koyá

dairy farm *n* 酪農場 rakúnōjò

dairy products *n* 乳製品 nyúseìhin

dairy store (*US*) *n* 牛乳店 gyúnyūten

dais [dei'is] *n* 演壇 éndan

daisy [dei'ziː] *n* デイジー deìjī

daisy wheel *n* (on printer) デイジーホイール deìjīhoìrù

dale [deil] *n* (valley) 谷 taní

dam [dæm] *n* (on river) ダム dámù
♦*vt* (river, stream) ...にダムを造る ...ni dámù wo tsukúrù

damage [dæm'idʒ] *n* (harm: also fig) 害 gaí; (dents etc) 傷物 sofíshò
♦*vt* (harm: reputation etc) 傷付ける kizútsukèrù; (spoil, break: toy, machine etc) 壊す kowásù

damages [dæm'idʒiz] *npl* (LAW) 損害賠償 sóngaibaìshò

damn [dæm] *vt* (curse at) ...に悪態を浴びせる ...ni akútaì wo ábìseru; (condemn) 非難する hínàn suru
♦*n* (*inf*): **I don't give a damn** おれの知った事じゃない orè no shíttá koto jà nái

♦adj (inf: also: **damned**) くそったれの kusóttare no, 畜生の chikúshō no

damn (it)!

damning [dæm'iŋ] adj (evidence) 動かぬ ugókanrō

damp [dæmp] adj (building, wall) 湿っぽい shiméppoi; (cloth) 湿った shimétta

♦n (in air, in walls) 湿り気 shimérike

♦vt (also: **dampen**: cloth, rag) 湿らす shimérasu; (: enthusiasm etc) ...に水を差す ...ni mizú wo sasú

damson [dæm'zən] n (fruit) ダムソンス モモ damúsonsumòmō

dance [dæns] n (movements, MUS, dancing) 踊り odóri, ダンス dánsu; (social event) 舞踏会 butôkai, ダンスパーティ dánsupàti

♦vi (person) 踊る odóru

dance hall n ダンスホール dánsuhōru

dancer [dæn'sər] n (for pleasure) 踊る人 odóru hito; (professional) ダンサー dánsā

dancing [dæn'siŋ] n (skill, performance) 踊り odóri, ダンス dánsu

dandelion [dæn'dəlaiən] n タンポポ tánpopo

dandruff [dæn'drəf] n ふけ fuké

Dane [dein] n デンマーク人 dénmākujin

danger [dein'dʒər] n (hazard, risk) 危険 kikén; (possibility): **there is a danger of ...** ...の危険がある ...no kikén ga arú

danger! (on sign) 危険 kikén

in danger 危険にさらされて kikén ni sárasarete

to be in danger of (risk, be close to) ...される危険がある ...sarérù kikén ga arú

dangerous [dein'dʒərəs] adj 危険な kikén na

dangle [dæŋ'gəl] vt (keys, toy) ぶら下げる burásageru; (arms, legs) ぶらぶらさせる burabúra saséru

♦vi (earrings, keys) ぶら下がる burásagaru

Danish [dein'niʃ] adj デンマークの dénmāku no; (LING) デンマーク語の dénmākugo no

♦n (LING) デンマーク語 dénmākugo

dapper [dæp'ær] adj (man, appearance) きびきびした kíbìkibì shitá

dare [der] vt: **to dare someone to do** 出来るものならしてみろと...にけし掛ける dekírū monō nárā shité mirô to ...ni keshíkakerù

♦vi: **to dare (to) do something** 敢えて ...する aête ...surū

I dare say (I suppose) 多分 tábūn

daredevil [der'devəl] n 無謀な人 mubô na hito

daring [der'iŋ] adj (escape, person, dress, film, raid, speech) 大胆な daîtàn na

♦n 大胆さ daîtànsa

dark [dɑːrk] adj (room, night) 暗い kurái; (hair) 黒っぽい kuróppoi; (complexion) 浅黒い aságuroì; (color: blue, green etc) 濃い kôi

♦n: **in the dark** やみの中で(に) yamf no nakà de(ni)

to be in the dark about (fig) ...について何も知らない ...ni tsúīte naní mo shírānai

after dark 暗くなってから kuráku nattè karâ

darken [dɑːr'kən] vt (color) 濃くする kôkù suru

♦vi (sky, room) 暗くなる kuráku narù

dark glasses npl サングラス sánguràsu

darkness [dɑːrk'nis] n (of room, night) 暗やみ kuráyami

darkroom [dɑːrk'ruːm] n (PHOT) 暗室 ánshitsu

darling [dɑːr'liŋ] adj (child, spouse) 愛する af surú

♦n (dear) あなた anátà; (favorite) ひいきの人 hfiki no hitô

darn [dɑːrn] vt (sock, jersey) 繕う tsukúroù

dart [dɑːrt] n (in game) 投げ矢 nágéya, ダート dâto; (in sewing) ダーツ dâtsu

♦vi 素早く走る subáyakù hashírù

to dart away/along 素早く走っていく subáyakù hashítte ikú

dartboard [dɑːrt'bɔːrd] n ダーツの的 tsu no matô

darts [dɑːrts] n (game) ダーツ dátsu

dash [dæʃ] *n* (small quantity) 少々 shôshô; (sign) ダッシュ dásshū
♦*vt* (throw) 投げ付ける nagétsukerú; (hopes) くじく kujikú
♦*vi* 素早く行く subáyaku ikú

dash away *vi* 走って行く hashítte ikú

dashboard [dæʃ'bɔːrd] *n* (AUT) ダッシュボード dasshûbōdo

dashing [dæʃ'iŋ] *adj* さっそうとした sássô to shita

dash off *vi* = dash away

data [dei'tə] *npl* (ADMIN, COMPUT) 情報 jôhô, データ dêta

database [dei'təbeis] *n* データベース dêtabesu

data processing *n* 情報処理 jôhôshorī

date [deit] *n* (day) 日にち hiníchi; (with boy/girlfriend) デート dêto; (fruit) ナツメヤシの実 natsúmeyashi no mí
♦*vt* (event) ...の年代を決める ...no néndai wo kímerù; (letter) ...に日付を書く ...ni hizúke wo kakù; (person) ...とデートをする ...to dêto wo surù

date of birth 生年月日 seínengappi

to date (until now) 今まで imá madè

dated [dei'tid] *adj* (expression, style) 時代遅れの jidáiokūre no

daub [dɔːb] *vt* (mud, paint) 塗付ける nurítsukerù

daughter [dɔːt'əːr] *n* 娘 musúme

daughter-in-law [dɔːt'əːrinlɔː] (*pl* **daughters-in-law**) *n* 嫁 yomé

daunting [dɔːn'tiŋ] *adj* (task, prospect) しりごみさせる様な shirígomi saserù yô na, ひるませる様な hirúmaserù yô na

dawdle [dɔːd'əl] *vi* (go slow) ぐずぐずする gúzùguzu suru

dawn [dɔːn] *n* (of day) 夜明け yoáke; (of period, situation) 始まり hajímari
♦*vi* (day) 夜が明ける yô ga akérù; (fig):
it dawned on him that ... 彼は...だと気が付いた kárè wa ...da tò ki gà tsuíta

day [dei] *n* (period) 日 hi, 1日 ichínichi; (daylight) 昼間 hiruma; (heyday) 全盛期 zensêki

the day before 前の日 maé no hi, 前日 zénjitsu

the day after 翌日 yokújitsu

the day after tomorrow 明後日 asátte

the day before yesterday 一昨日 otótoi

the following day 次の日 tsugí nò hi, 翌日 yokújitsu

by day 昼間 hiruma ni

daybreak [dei'breik] *n* 明け方 akégata, 夜明け yoáke

daydream [dei'driːm] *vi* 空想にふける kúsō ni fúkerù

daylight [dei'lait] *n* (sunlight) 日光 nfkkô; (daytime) 昼間 hiruma, 日中 nítchū

day return (*BRIT*) *n* (ticket) 往復券 ôfukuken

daytime [dei'taim] *n* 昼間 hiruma

day-to-day [deitudei'] *adj* (life, organization) 日常の nichíjō no

daze [deiz] *vt* (stun) ぼう然とさせる bôzen to sàseru
♦*n*: **in a daze** (confused, upset) ぼう然として bôzen to shite

dazzle [dæz'əl] *vt* (bewitch) 感嘆させる kántan sáserù; (blind) ...の目をくらます ...no mé wô kurámasu

DC [diːsiː'] *abbr* (= *direct current*) 直流 chokúryū

D-day [diː'dei] *n* 予定日 yotếbi

dead [ded] *adj* (not alive: person, animal) 死んだ shínda; (flowers) 枯れた karéta; (numb) しびれた shibíreta; (telephone) 通じない tsûjinai; (battery) 上がった agátta
♦*adv* (completely) 全く mattakú; (directly, exactly) 丁度 chôdo
♦*npl*: **the dead** 死者 shísha

to shoot someone dead 射殺す uchíkorosù

dead tired へとへとに疲れた hetôheto ni tsúkāreta

to stop dead 突然止まる totsúzen tòmaru

deaden [ded'ən] *vt* (blow, pain) 和らげる yawáragerù; (sound) 鈍くする nibúkù surù

dead end *n* (street) 行き止り ikídomari

dead heat *n* (SPORT) 同着 dôchaku

deadline [ded'lain] *n* (PRESS etc) 締切り shimékiri

deadlock [ded'lɑːk] *n* (POL, MIL) 行き詰

り ikfzumarí

dead loss (inf) n: to be a dead loss (person) 役立たず yakútatàzu

deadly [dedˈli] adj (lethal: poison) 致命的な chiméiteki na; (devastating: accuracy) 恐ろしい osóroshiì; (: insult) 痛烈な tsúretsu na

deadpan [dedˈpæn] adj (look, tone) 無表情の muhyójò no

Dead Sea n: the Dead Sea 死海 shikái

deaf [def] adj (totally) 耳の聞えない mimí no kikóenai

deafen [defˈən] vt …の耳を聞えなくする …no mimí wò kikóenaku sùrú

deafness [defˈnis] n 難聴 nánchō

deal [di:l] n (agreement) 取引 toríhikì
♦vt (pt, pp dealt) (cards) 配る kubárù
a great deal (of) 沢山(の) takúsan (nò)

dealer [di:ˈlər] n (COMM) 販売業者 hánbaigyōsha, ディーラー dírā

deal in vt fus 取扱う torífatsukau

dealings [di:ˈliŋz] npl (business) 取引 toríhikì; (relations) 関係 kánkei

dealt [delt] pt, pp of **deal**

deal with vt fus (person) …と取引をする …to toríhikì wo suru; (problem) 処理する shórī suru; (subject) 取扱う torífatsukau

dean [di:n] n (REL) 主任司祭 shunínshìsai; (SCOL) 学部長 gakúbuchō

dear [di:r] adj (person) 愛しい itóshiì; (expensive) 高価な kóka na
♦n: my dear あなた anátà, お前 omáe
♦excl: dear me! おや oyá ◇驚きを表す odórokì wo árawasù
Dear Sir/Madam (in letter) 拝啓 haíkei
Dear Mr/Mrs X 親愛なる…さん shín-ai narū …san

dearly [di:rˈli] adv (love) 深く fukákù
to pay dearly for one's carelessness 自らの不注意が高く付く mízukara no fuchûi gà tákàku tsukú

death [deθ] n (BIO) 死 shí, 死亡 shibó; (fig) 死絶 …

death certificate n 死亡証明書 shibóshōmeisho

deathly [deθˈli:] adj (color) 死人の様な shinín no yō na; (silence) 不気味な bukími na

death penalty n 死刑 shikéi

death rate n 死亡率 shibórìtsu

death toll n 死者の数 shīsha no kázu

debacle [dəbɑːkˈəl] n 大失敗 daíshippai

debar [dibɑːr] vt: to debar someone from doing …が…をするのを禁止する …ga …wo sūrû nò wo kínshi suru

debase [dibeis] vt (value, quality) 下げる sagérù

debatable [dibeiˈtəbəl] adj (decision, assertion) 疑問のある gimón no arù

debate [dibeit] n (discussion, also POL) 討論 tóròn
♦vt 討議する tōgî suru

debauchery [dəbɔːˈtʃəri:] n (drunkenness, promiscuity) 放とう hôtō

debilitating [dibilˈəteitiŋ] adj (illness etc) 衰弱させる suíjaku sasérù

debit [debˈit] n (COMM) 支払額 shiháraìgaku
♦vt: to debit a sum to someone/to someone's account …の口座から落す …no kôza kara òtósù ¶ see **direct**

debris [dəbri:] n (rubble) がれき garéki

debt [det] n 借金 shakkín
to be in debt 借金がある shakkín gà árù

debtor [detˈər] n 負債者 fusáìsha

debunk [dibʌŋk] vt (myths, ideas etc) …の正体をあばく …no shôtaì wo abákù

début [deibju:ˈ] n (THEATER, SPORT) デビュー débyū

decade [dekˈeid] n 10年間 jûnènkan

decadence [dekˈədəns] n (moral, spiritual) 堕落 daráku

decaffeinated [di:kæfˈəneitid] adj カフェインを取除いた kaféin wo torínozotta

decanter [dikænˈtər] n (for wine, whiskey) デカンター dekántā

decay [dikei] n (of meat, fish etc) 腐敗 fuhái; (of building) 老朽 rókyū; (of tooth) カリエス kárìesu
♦vi (rot: body, leaves etc) 腐敗する fuhái suru; (teeth) 虫歯になる mushíba ni narû

deceased [disist] n: the deceased 故人

kōjin

deceit [disi:t'] n (duplicity) 偽り itsúwari

deceitful [disi:'fəl] adj 不正な fuséi na

deceive [disi:v'] vt (fool) だます damásù

December [disem'bəːr] n 12月 jūnigatsu

decency [di:'sənsi:] n (propriety) 上品さ jōhínsa; (kindness) 親切さ shínsetsusa

decent [di:'sənt] adj (proper) 上品な jōhín na; (kind) 親切な shínsetsu na

deception [disep'ʃən] n ごまかし gomákashi

deceptive [disep'tiv] adj (appearance) 見掛けによらない mikáke ni yoránai

decibel [des'əbəl] n デシベル déshìberu

decide [disaid'] vt (person: persuade) 納得させる nattóku sasérù; (question, argument: settle) 解決する kaíketsu suru

♦vi 決める kiméru

to decide to do/that ...する[...だ]と決める ...súrù [...da] to kiméru

to decide on something (choose something) ...を選ぶ ...wo erábù

decided [disai'did] adj (resolute) 決意の固い ketsúi no katáì; (clear, definite) はっきりした hakkíri shita

decidedly [disai'didli:] adv (distinctly) はっきりと hakkíri to; (emphatically: act, reply) 決然と kízèn to

deciduous [disidʒ'u:əs] adj (tree, bush) 落葉の rakúyō no

decimal [des'əməl] adj (system, currency) 十進法 jisshíhō no

♦n (fraction) 小数 shōsū

decimal point n 小数点 shōsúten

decimate [des'əmeit] vt (population) 多数の...を死なせる taisū no ...wo shináseru

decipher [disai'fəːr] vt (message, writing) 解読する kaídoku suru

decision [disiʒ'ən] n (choice) 決定した事 kettéi shita koto; (act of choosing) 決定 kettéi; (decisiveness) 決断力 ketsúdanryoku

decisive [disai'siv] adj (action, intervention) 決定的な kettéiteki na; (person) 決断力のある ketsúdanryoku no árù

deck [dek] n (NAUT) 甲板 kánpan, デッキ dékkì; (of bus) 階 kaí; (record deck)

デッキ dékkì; (of cards) 一組 hitókùmi

deckchair [dek'tʃeːr] n デッキチェア dékkìchèa

declaration [dekləreiʃ'ən] n (statement) 断言 dangén; (public announcement) 布告 fukóku

declare [dikleːr'] vt (truth, intention, result) 発表する happyō suru; (reveal: income, goods at customs etc) 申告する shínkoku suru

decline [diklain'] n: *decline in/of* (drop, lowering) ...の下落 ...no gèraku; (lessening) ...の減少 ...no génshō

♦vt (turn down: invitation) 辞退する jitái suru

♦vi (strength, old person) 弱る yowárù; (business) 不振になる fushín ni narù

decode [dikoud'] vt (message) 解読する kaídoku suru

decompose [di:kəmpouz'] vi (organic matter, corpse) 腐敗する fuhái suru

décor [deikour'] n (of house, room) 装飾 shōshoku; (THEATER) 舞台装置 butáisōchi

decorate [dek'əreit] vt (adorn): *to decorate (with)* (...で) 飾る (...de) kazáru; (paint and paper) ...の室内を改装する ...no shitsúnài wo kaísō suru

decoration [dekəreiʃ'ən] n (on tree, dress etc) 飾り kazári; (act) 飾る事 kazáru koto; (medal) 勲章 kunshō

decorative [dek'əːrtiv] adj 装飾の shōshoku no

decorator [dek'əːreitəːr] n (BRIT: painter) ペンキ屋 pénkiya

decorum [dikɔːr'əm] n (propriety) 上品さ jōhínsa

decoy [di:'kɔi] n (person, object) おとり otóri

decrease [n di:'kri:s vb dikri:s'] n (reduction, drop): *decrease (in)* 減少 génshō

♦vt (reduce, lessen) 減らす herásu

♦vi (drop) 減る herú

decree [dikri:'] n (ADMIN, LAW) 命令 meírei

decree nisi [-nai'sai] n 離婚の仮判決 rikón no kárìhànketsu

decrepit [dikrep'it] *adj* (run-down: shack) おんぼろの ónboro no; (person) よぼよぼの yòbòyobo no

dedicate [ded'ikeit] *vt* (time, effort etc): *to dedicate to* ...につぎ込む ...ni tsugí-komù; (oneself): *to dedicate to* ...に専念する ...ni sénnèn suru; (book, record): *to dedicate to* ...に捧げる ...ni saságeru

dedication [dedikei'ʃən] *n* (devotion) 献身 kénshin; (in book, on radio) 献辞 kénji

deduce [didus'] *vt* 推測する suísoku suru

deduct [didʌkt'] *vt* (subtract) 差し引く sa-shíhikù

deduction [didʌk'ʃən] *n* (act of deducing) 推測 suísoku; (act of deducting) 差引 sashíhikì; (amount) 差し引く分 sashíhikù bùn

deed [di:d] *n* (feat) 行為 kóì; (LAW: document) 証書 shósho

deem [di:m] *vt* (judge, consider) ...だと判断する ...dá tò hándàn suru

deep [di:p] *adj* (hole, water) 深い fukái; (in measurements) 奥行の okúyuki no; (voice) 太い futóì; (color) 濃い kóì
♦ *adv*: *the spectators stood 20 deep* 観衆は20列に並んで立っていた kánshù wa nijùretsu ni narànde tàtte ita
a deep breath 深呼吸 shínkokyù
to be 4 meters deep 深さは4メータである fukása wa yón mèta de árù

deepen [di:p'ən] *vt* (hole, canal etc) 深くする fukáku suru
♦ *vi* (crisis, mystery) 深まる fukámarù

deep-freeze [di:p'fri:z'] *n* 冷凍庫 reítòko, フリーザー furízā

deep-fry [di:p'frai'] *vt* 揚げる agéru

deeply [di:p'li:] *adv* (breathe) 深く fukáku; (interested, moved, grateful) 非常に hijò ni

deep-sea diving [di:p'si:'-] *n* 深海ダイビング shínkaidàibingu

deep-seated [di:p'si:'tid] *adj* (beliefs, fears, dislike etc) 根の深い né nò fukáì

deer [di:r] *n inv* (ZOOL) シカ shiká

deerskin [di:r'skin] *n* シカ皮 shiká-gawa

deface [difeis'] *vt* (wall, notice) 汚す yo-gósu

defamation [defəmei'ʃən] *n* (LAW) 名誉

毀損 mêìyokísòn

default [dif:ɔlt'] *n* (COMPUT) デフォルト値 défòrutone
by default (win) 不戦勝で fusénshò de

defeat [difi:t'] *n* (of enemy) 敗北 háibòku; (failure) 失敗 shippái
♦ *vt* (enemy, opposition) 破る yabúrù

defeatist [difi:'tist] *adj* 敗北主義の háibòkushúgì no
♦ *n* 敗北主義者 háibòkushúgìsha

defect [*n* di:'fekt *vb* difekt'] *n* (flaw, imperfection: in machine etc) 欠陥 kekkán; (: in person, character etc) 欠点 kettèn
♦ *vi*: *to defect to the enemy* 敵側に亡命する tekígawa ni bómei suru

defective [difek'tiv] *adj* (goods) 欠陥のある kekkán no arù

defence [difens'] (*BRIT*) *n* = defense

defend [difend'] *vt* (protect, champion) 守る mamórù; (justify) 釈明する shakúmei suru; (SPORT: goal) 守る mamórù; (: record, title) 防衛する bóei suru

defendant [difen'dænt] *n* (LAW: in criminal case) 被告人 hikókunin; (: in civil case) 被告 hikóku

defender [difen'dɑr] *n* (*also fig,* SPORT) 防衛者 bóeishà

defense [difens'] (*BRIT* **defence**) *n* (protection, assistance) 防衛 bóei; (justification) 釈明 shakúmei

defenseless [difens'lis] *adj* (helpless) 無防備の mòbòbi no

defensive [difen'siv] *adj* (weapons, measures) 防衛の bóei no; (behavior, manner) 釈明的な shakúmeiteki na
♦ *n*: *on the defensive* 守勢に立って shusèi ni tattè

defer [difɑr'] *vt* (postpone) 延期する énki suru

deference [def'ɑrəns] *n* (consideration) 丁重さ teíchòsa

defiance [difai'əns] *n* (challenge, rebellion) 反抗 hánkò
in defiance of (despite: the rules, someone's orders etc) ...を無視して ...wo múshì shite

defiant [difai'ənt] *adj* (challenging,

rebellious: tone, reply, person) 反抗的な hánkōteki na

deficiency [difiʃ'ansi:] n (lack) 欠 如 ké tsūjo; (defect) 欠点 kettén

deficient [difiʃ'ant] adj (inadequate): **deficient in** …が不足している …ga fūsóku shīté iru; (defective) 欠点の多い ketten no ói

deficit [def'isit] n (COMM) 赤字 akáji

defile [difail'] vt (memory, statue etc) 汚 す kegásu

define [difain'] vt (limits, boundaries) 明 らかにする ákīraká ni suru; (expression, word) 定義する tégi suru

definite [def'anit] adj (fixed) 決 まった kimátta; (clear, obvious) 明 白 な méīha-ku na; (certain) 確実な kákūjitsu na
he was definite about it 彼はそれを はっきり言った kárē wa sonó koto wo hakkírī ittá

definitely [def'anitli:] adv (positively, certainly) 確実に kákūjitsu ni

definition [defaniʃ'an] n (of word) 定義 tégi; (clearness of photograph etc) 鮮明 さ sénmeisa

definitive [difin'ativ] adj (account, version) 決定的な kéttéiteki na

deflate [difleit'] vt (tire, balloon) …の 空 気を抜く …no kūkí wo nukú

deflect [diflekt'] vt (fend off: attention, criticism) 回避する káhi suru; (divert: shot, light) 横へそらす yokó e sōrásū

deform [difɔ:rm'] vt (distort) 変形させる hénkei sāséru

deformed [difɔ:rmd'] adj 変形した hén-kei shita

deformity [difɔ:r'miti:] n 奇形 kīkéi

defraud [difrɔːd'] vt: **to defraud some-one (of something)** から (…を) だ まし取る …kárā (…wo) dāmáshitorū

defrost [difrɔːst'] vt (fridge, windshield) …の霜取りをする …no shimótori wo suru; (food) 解凍する káitó suru

defroster [difrɔːs'tər] (US) n 霜取り装 置 shimótorisōchi

deft [deft] adj (movement, hands) 器用な kīyó na

defunct [difʌnkt'] adj (industry, organi-

zation) 現存しない génzon shināi

defuse [di:fjuːz'] vt (bomb) …の信管を外 す …no shinkan wo hāzúsu; (fig: crisis, tension) 緩和する kánwa suru

defy [difai'] vt (resist) …に 抵抗する …ni tékkō suru; (challenge) 挑発する chōha-tsu suru; (fig: description, explanation) …の仕様がない …no shiyō ga naí

degenerate [vb didʒen'əːreit adj didʒen'əːrit] vi (condition, health) 悪化する ākká suru ♦adj (depraved) 堕落した dāráku shita

degrading [digrei'diŋ] adj (conduct, activity) 恥ずべき hāzúbekī; (task etc) 誇りを傷つけられる様な hokóri wo kīzú-tsukerárērū yō na

degree [digri:'] n (extent) 度 合 dōái; (of temperature, angle, latitude) 度 do; (SCOL) 学位 gákūi
a degree in science 科学の学位 sūgaku no gákūi
by degrees (gradually) 徐々に jójō ni
to some degree ある程度 arú teido

dehydrated [di:hai'dreitid] adj (MED) 脱水状態の dassúijōtai no; (milk) エバミ ルク dābámirūku

de-ice [di:ais'] vt (windshield) …の霜取り をする …no shimótorī wo suru

deign [dein] vi: **to deign to do** …をして くれてやる …wo shité kurete yaru

deity [di:'iti:] n 神 kámī

dejected [didʒek'tid] adj (depressed) が っかりした gakkárī shita

delay [dilei'] vt (postpone) 延ばす oküraseru
♦vt (linger) 待つ mátsu; (hesitate) ためら う taméraū
♦n (waiting period) 待つべき期間 mátsū-beki kikán; (postponement) 延期 énki
to be delayed (person, flight, departure etc) 遅れる ōküreru
without delay 直ちに tádachi ni

delectable [dilek'təbl] adj (person) 美し い ūtsúkushiī; (food) おいしい ōíshii

delegate [n del'əgit vb del'əgeit] n 代表 dáhyō
♦vt (person) 任命する nínmei suru; (task) 任せる mākáserū

delegation [deləgei'ʃən] n (group) 代表団

dáñyōdan; (by manager, leader) 任命 nín-mei

delete [dili:t'] *vt* (cross out, *also* COMPUT) 消す kêsù, 削除する sákùjo suru

deliberate [adj dilib'ə:rit vb dilib'ə:reit] *adj* (intentional) 故意の kõî no; (slow) 落着いた ôchttshuita
♦*vi* (consider) 熟考する jukkõ suru

deliberately [dilib'ə:ritli:] *adv* (on purpose) 故意に kõî ni, わざと wázà to

delicacy [del'əkəsi:] *n* (of movement) しとやかさ shitôyakasa; (of material) 繊細さ sénsaisa; (of problem etc) 微妙さ bîmyõsa; (choice food) 珍味 chînmi

delicate [del'əkit] *adj* (movement) しとやかな shitôyaka na; (taste, smell, color) 淡い awâi; (material) 繊細な sénsai na; (approach, problem) 微妙な bîmyõ na; (health) 弱い yowâî

delicatessen [deləkətes'ən] *n* 総菜屋 sõzaiza, デリカテッセン dêrikatessèn

delicious [dilíj'əs] *adj* (food) おいしい oîshî; (smell) おいしそうな óîshisõ na; (feeling) 心地好い kôkôchiyoî; (person) 魅力的な mîryôkuteki na

delight [dilait'] *n* 喜び yórôkobi
♦*vt* (please) 喜ばす yórôkobasu
to take ... delight in ...するのが大好きである ...surú nò ga dâîsuki de aru

delighted [dilait'id] *adj*: delighted (at/with) (...の)喜んでいる (...de) yórôkonde iru
delighted to do 喜んで...する yórôkonde ...suru

delightful [dilait'fəl] *adj* (evening, house, person etc) 楽しい tânôshiî

delinquency [dilin'kwənsi:] *n* 非行 hikõ

delinquent [dilin'kwint] *adj* (boy/girl) 非行の hikõ no
♦*n* (youth) 非行少年[少女] hikõshõnen [shõjo]

delirious [dili:r'i:əs] *adj*: to be delirious (with fever) うわ言を言う ûwàgoto wo iu; (with excitement) 夢中になっている mûchû ni nattê irù

deliver [dili'və:r] *vt* (distribute) 配達する haîtatsu suru; (hand over) 引渡す hîkf-watasù; (message) 届ける tôdôkerù; (MED: baby) ...の出産を助ける ...no shûs-sán wo tâsûkerù
to deliver a speech 演説をする ênzetsu wo sûru

delivery [dili'və:ri:] *n* (distribution) 配達 haîtatsu; (of speaker) 演説振り ênzetsuburi; (MED) 出産 shûssán
to take delivery of ... を受取る ... wo ûkètorù

delta [del'tə] *n* (of river) デルタ地帯 dê-rûtachitâi

delude [dilu:d'] *vt* (deceive) だます damá-sù

deluge [del'ju:dʒ] *n* (also: deluge of rain) 大雨 ôamê; (of petitions, requests) 殺到 sáttô

delusion [dilu:'ʒən] *n* (false belief) 錯覚 sákkáku

de luxe [dilʌks'] *adj* (car, holiday) 豪華な gõkâ na

delve [delv] *vi*: to delve into (subject) ...を探求する ...wo tánkyû suru; (cupboard, handbag) ...の中を捜す ...no nákà wo sagâsu

demand [dimænd'] *vt* 要求する yõkyû suru
♦*n* 要求 yõkyû; (ECON) 需要 juyõ
to be in demand ...の需要がある ...no juyõ ga arû
on demand (available, payable) 請求次第 sêîkyûshidâî

demanding [dimænd'iŋ] *adj* (boss, child) 気難しい kîmûzukashiî; (work) きつい kîtsuî

demarcation [di:mɑ:rkei'ʃən] *n* (of areas) 境 sákaî; (of tasks) 区分 kúbûn

demean [dimin'] *vt*: to demean oneself 軽べつを招く事をする kêîbetsu wo mánêkû kotô wo suru

demeanor [dimi:'nə:r] (BRIT demeanour) *n* 振舞 fúrûmai

demented [dimen'tid] *adj* 気の狂った kî nó kurúttà

demise [dimaiz'] *n* (end) 消滅 shõmetsu; (death) 死亡 shibõ

demister [dimis'tə:r] (BRIT) *n* (AUT) 霜取り装置 shimôtorisôchi

demo [dem'ou] (*BRIT*: *inf*) *n abbr* = **demonstration**

democracy [dima:k'rasi:] *n* (POL: system) 民主主義 mínshushúgi; (country) 民主主義国 mínshushúgìkòku

democrat [dem'əkræt] *n* (*gen*) 民主主義者 mínshushugishá; (US) 民主党員 mínshutōín

democratic [deməkræt'ik] *adj* (*gen*) 民主的な mínshuteki na; (US) 民主党の mínshutō no

demolish [dima:l'iʃ] *vt* (building) 取壊す torfkowasu; (*fig*: argument) 論破する rónpà suru

demolition [deməliʃ'ən] *n* (of building) 取壊し torfkowashi; (of argument) 破壊 rónpa

demon [di:'mən] *n* (evil spirit) 悪魔 ákùma

demonstrate [dem'ənstreit] *vt* (prove: theory) 立証する rìsshō suru; (show: skill, appliance) 見せる misérù
♦*vi* (POL) デモをする démð wo suru

demonstration [demənstrei'ʃən] *n* (POL) デモ démð; (proof) 立証 risshō; (exhibition) 実演 jitsúen

demonstrator [dem'ənstreitər] *n* (POL) デモの参加者 démð no sánkashà; (COMM) 実演をする店員 jitsúen wo suru tén-in

demoralize [dimɔ:r'əlaiz] *vt* (dishearten) がっかりさせる gakkárì saséru

demote [dimout'] *vt* (*also* MIL) 降格する kōkaku sūrú

demure [dimjur'] *adj* (smile, dress, little girl) しとやかな shitóyàka na

den [den] *n* (of animal) 巣穴 sú sùana; (of thieves) 隠れ家 kákùregà, アジト ájìto; (room) 書斎 shósai

denatured alcohol [di:nei'tʃə:rd-] (US) *n* 変性アルコール hénseiârùkòru

denial [dinai'əl] *n* (refutation) 否定 hitéi; (refusal) 拒否 kyóhi

denim [den'im] *n* (fabric) デニム dénìmu

denims [den'əmz] *npl* ジーパン jípan, ジーンズ jíñzu

Denmark [den'mɑ:rk] *n* デンマーク dénmàkù

denomination [dinɑ:mənei'ʃən] *n* (of money) 額面 gakúmen; (REL) 宗派 shúhà

denominator [dinɑ:m'əneitər] *n* (MATH) 分母 búnbò

denote [dinout'] *vt* (indicate, represent) 示す shimésù

denounce [dinauns'] *vt* (person, action) 非難する hínàn suru

dense [dens] *adj* (crowd) 密集した mìsshū shita; (smoke, fog etc) 濃い kóì; (foliage) 密生した mìsséi shita; (*inf*: person) 鈍い nibúì

densely [dens'li:] *adv*: **densely populated** 人口密度の高い jínkōmitsùdo no takái

density [den'siti:] *n* (of population: *also* PHYSICS) 密度 mítsùdo
single / double-density disk (COMPUT) 単(倍)密度ディスク tán(bái)mitsùdo disuku ◇日本語では魔語 nihón go de wa hafgo

dent [dent] *n* (in metal or wood) へこみ hèkómi
♦*vt* (*also*: **make a dent in**) へこませる hèkómaseru

dental [den'təl] *adj* (treatment, hygiene etc) 歯科の shíkà no

dental surgeon *n* 歯医者 hāísha

dentist [den'tist] *n* 歯医者 hāísha

dentistry [den'tistri:] *n* 歯科医学 shīkáigaku

dentures [den'tʃə:rz] *npl* 入れ歯 iréba

denunciation [dinʌnsiei'ʃən] *n* (condemnation) 非難 hínàn

deny [dinai'] *vt* (charge, allegation, involvement) 否定する hitéi suru; (refuse: permission, chance) 拒否する kyóhì suru

deodorant [di:ou'də:rənt] *n* 防臭剤 bōshūzai

depart [dipɑ:rt'] *vi* (visitor) 帰る kaéru; (plane) 出発する shuppátsu suru; (bus, train) 発車する hasshá suru
to depart from (*fig*: stray from) ...を離れる ...wo hanárerú

department [dipɑ:rt'mənt] *n* (COMM) 部 bú; (SCOL) 講座 kōza; (POL) 省 shō

department store n (COMM) デパート
depāto

departure [dɪˈpɑːtʃər] n (of visitor) 帰
る事 káeru koto; (of plane) 出発 shuppátsu; (of bus, train) 発車 hasshá; (of
employee, colleague) 退職 tāishoku
a new departure (in or from policy etc)
新方針 shínhōshìn

departure lounge n (at airport) 出発ロ
ビー shuppátsurobì

depend [dɪˈpɛnd] vi: *to depend on*: (be
supported by) ...に頼っている ...ni táyott-
ē irú; (rely on, trust) 信用する shínyō
suru
it depends 時と場合によりけりだ tokí
tō baái ni yoríkerí dá
depending on the result ...結果次第
で ...kékka shidái dé

dependable [dɪˈpɛndəbl] adj (person)
頼りになる táyori ni naru; (watch, car etc)
信頼性の高い shínraisei no tákái

dependant [dɪˈpɛndənt] n 扶養家族 fuyó-
kazòku

dependence [dɪˈpɛndəns] n (on drugs,
systems, partner) 依存 izón

dependent [dɪˈpɛndənt] adj: *to be dependent on* (person, decision) ...に頼っ
ている ...ni táyottē iru
♦n = dependant

depict [dɪˈpɪkt] vt (in picture) 描く egá-
kū; (describe) 描写する byósha suru

depleted [dɪˈpliːtɪd] adj (stocks, reserves) 減少した génshó shita

deplorable [dɪˈplɔːrəbl] adj (conditions)
悲惨な hísan na; (lack of concern) 嘆かわ
しい nágékawashíi

deplore [dɪˈplɔːr] vt (condemn) 非難する
hínan suru

deploy [dɪˈplɔɪ] vt (troops, resources) 配
置する háichi suru

depopulation [diːpɑːpjəleɪˈʃən] n 人口減
少 jínkōgénshò

deport [dɪˈpɔːrt] vt (criminal, illegal
immigrant) 強制送還する kyóseisōkan
suru

deportment [dɪˈpɔːrtmənt] n (behavior,
way of walking etc) 態度 táido

depose [dɪˈpoʊz] vt (ruler) 退位させる tái

sáseru

deposit [dɪˈpɑːzɪt] n (money: in account)
預金 yókin; (: down payment) 手付金 tetsúkekin; (on bottle etc) 保証金 hoshókin;
(CHEM) 沈殿物 chíndènbutsu; (of ore) 鉱
床 kóshó; (of oil) 石油埋蔵量 sèkfyumázó-
zòryó
♦vt (money) 預金する yókin suru; (case,
bag) 預ける azúkerù

deposit account n 普通預金口座 futsú-
yokìnkóza

depot [diːˈpoʊ] n (storehouse) 倉庫 sòkó;
(for vehicles) 車庫 sháko; (US: station)
駅 éki

depraved [dɪˈpreɪvd] adj (conduct, person) 邪悪な jáàku na

depreciate [dɪˈpriːʃieɪt] vi (currency,
property, value etc) 値下がりする neságari suru

depreciation [dɪpriːʃiˈeɪʃən] n 値下がり
neságari

depress [dɪˈprɛs] vt (PSYCH) 憂うつにさ
せる yúutsu ni sáseru; (price, wages) 下
落させる gèráku saseru; (press down:
switch, button etc) 押える osáeru;
(: accelerator) 踏む fúmú

depressed [dɪˈprɛst] adj (person) 憂うつ
な yúutsu na; (price, industry) 下落した
gèráku shita

depressing [dɪˈprɛsɪŋ] adj (outlook,
time) 憂うつな yúutsu na

depression [dɪˈprɛʃən] n (PSYCH) 憂う
つ yúutsu; (ECON) 不況 fúkyó; (of
weather) 低気圧 tèíkiatsù; (hollow) くぼ
み kúbòmi

deprivation [deprəveɪˈʃən] n (poverty)
貧乏 bínbó

deprive [dɪˈpraɪv] vt: *to deprive someone of* (liberty, life) ...から奪う ...kárà
ubáu

deprived [dɪˈpraɪvd] adj 貧しい mázùshìi

depth [dɛpθ] n (of hole, water) 深さ fú-
kàsà; (of cupboard etc) 奥行 ókùyuki; (of
emotion, feeling) 強さ tsúyòsa; (of
knowledge) 豊富さ hófusa
in the depths of despair 絶望のどん底に
zètsúbó no dònzòko ní
out of one's depth (in water) 背が立た

ない せ が たたない; (fig) 力 が 及ばない chīkara gá oyóbanai

deputation [depjə'tei'ʃən] n (delegation) 代表団 dáfhyōdàn

deputize [dep'jətaiz] vi: **to deputize for someone** (stand in) …の 代り に …する …no kāwàri ni …súrù

deputy [dep'jəti:] adj: **deputy head** (BRIT: SCOL: primary/secondary) 副校 長 fúkūkōchō

♦n (assistant) 代理 dáiri; (POL) (下院) 議員 (kain)gfin; cf. also: **deputy sheriff** 保安官代理 hoàn kàndàiri

derail [di:reil'] vt: **to be derailed** 脱線す る dássèn suru

derailment [dirēil'mənt] n 脱線 dássèn

deranged [direind3d'] adj (person) 精神 病の sefshínbyō no

derby [dɑ:r'bi:] (US) n (bowler hat) 山高 帽 yàmátakabō

derelict [der'əlikt] adj (building) 廃虚に なった háîkyo ni nátta

deride [diraid'] vt (mock, ridicule) ばか にする bákà ni suru

derisory [dirai'sɔ:ri:] adj (sum) 笑うべき waráùbekì; (laughter, person) ばかにす る bákà ni suru

derivative [driv'ətiv] n (CHEM) 派生物 hasēhbutsù; (LING) 派生語 haséìgo

derive [diraiv'] vt (pleasure, benefit) 受け る ùkérù

♦vi: **to derive from** (originate in) …に由 来する …ni yúrài suru

dermatitis [dɑ:rmətai'tis] n 皮膚炎 hífù-èn

derogatory [dirɑːg'ətɔːri:] adj (remark) 中傷的な chûshôteki na

derv [dɑːrv] (BRIT) n 軽油 kéîyu

descend [disend'] vt (stairs, hill) 降りる órìrù

♦vi (go down) 降りる órìrù
to descend from …から 降りる …kárà órìrù
to descend to (lying, begging etc) …す るまでに成り下がる …súrù madé ni narí-sagarù

descendant [disen'dənt] n 子孫 shísòn

descent [disent'] n (of stairs, hill, by per-

son etc) 降りる事 órìrù koto; (AVIAT) 降下 kōka; (origin) 家系 kákéi

describe [diskraib'] vt (event, place, person, shape) 描写する byōsha suru

description [diskrip'ʃən] n (account) 描 写 byōsha; (sort) 種類 shúrùi

descriptive [diskrip'tiv] adj (writing, painting) 写実的な shájítsuteki na

desecrate [des'əkreit] vt (altar, cemetery) 汚す kègásu

desert [n dez'ə:rt vb dizə:rt'] n (GEO) 砂 漠 sábàku; (fig: wilderness) 殺風景な所 sáppūkei na tòkòro

♦vt (place, post) 放棄して逃げ出る hóchi shite tôbô súrù; (partner, family) 見捨て る mísùteru

♦vi (MIL) 脱走する dassô suru

deserter [dizə:r'tə:r] n (MIL) 脱走兵 das-sôhei

desertion [dizə:r'ʃən] n (MIL) 脱走 das-sô; (LAW) 遺棄 íkì

desert island n 熱帯の無人島 nèttái no mújîntō

deserts [dizə:rts'] npl: **to get one's just deserts** 天罰を受ける tènbatsu wo uké-rù

deserve [dizə:rv'] vt (merit, warrant) …に値する …ni átài suru

deserving [dizə:r'viŋ] adj (person) 援助 に値する ènjo ni átài suru; (action, cause) 立派な rîppá na

design [dizain'] n (art, process) 意匠 í-shō; (sketch) スケッチ sùkétchì; (layout, shape) デザイン dézàin; (pattern) 模様 móyô; (intention) 意図 ítò

♦vt (house, kitchen, product etc) 設計す る sèkkéì suru; (test etc) …の案を作る …no àn wo tsùkúrù

designate [vb dez'igneit adj dez'ignit] vt (nominate) 任命する nínmei suru

♦adj (chairman etc) 任命された nínmei sárèta

designer [dizai'nə:r] n (ART) デザイナ ー dèzàinà; (TECH) 設計者 sèkkéìsha; (also: **fashion designer**) ファッションデ ザイナー fàsshôndezàinā

desirable [dizai'ərəbəl] adj (proper) 望 ましい nôzômashiì; (attractive) 魅力的な

mīryókuteki na

desire [dɪzaɪər] n (urge) 望み nozómi; *(also: sexual desire)* 性欲 séiyoku
♦vt (want) 欲しがる hoshígarú; (lust after)...にセックスを与える...to sékkusu wo shítagarú

desk [dɛsk] n (in office, for pupil) 机 tsukúe, デスク désuku; (in hotel) フロント furónto; (at airport) カウンター kántā, (BRIT: in shop, restaurant) 勘定カウンター kánjōkàuntā

desolate [dɛsəlɪt] adj (place) 物寂しい mōnósabishíi; (person) 惨めな míjīme na

desolation [dɛsəleɪʃən] n (of place) 物寂しさ mōnósabishísà; (of person) 惨めさ míjīmesā

despair [dɪspɛər] n (hopelessness) 絶望 zétsùbō
♦vi: to despair of (give up on)...をあきらめる...wo akfrámerù

despatch [dɪspætʃ] n, vt = dispatch

desperate [dɛspərɪt] adj (scream, shout) 恐怖の kyōfū no; (situation, shortage) 絶望的な zetsúbōteki na; (fugitive) 必死の hisshí no
to be desperate for something/to do 必死の思いで...を欲しがって(してしまって)いる hisshí no ōmói dé...wo hoshígattè (shítágatte) irú

desperately [dɛspərɪtli] adv (in despair, frantically: struggle, shout etc) 必死になって hisshí ni nattè; (very) とても tōtémo

desperation [dɛspəreɪʃən] n (recklessness) 必死の思い hisshí no ōmói
in (sheer) desperation 必死の思いで hisshí no ōmói dé, 死に物狂いで shínímonogurùi dé

despicable [dɪspíkəbəl] adj (action, person) 卑劣な hirétsu na

despise [dɪspáɪz] vt 軽べつする kéibetsu suru

despite [dɪspáɪt] prep (in spite of)...にも かかわらず...nf mo kakáwarazu

despondent [dɪspándənt] adj (downcast) 意気消沈している íkìshōchin shíte irú

despot [dɛspət] n 暴君 bōkùn

dessert [dɪzə́ːrt] n (CULIN) デザート dézàtō

dessertspoon [dɪzə́ːrtspuːn] n (object) 小さじ kōsáji; (quantity) 小さじ一杯 kōsáji íppaì

destination [dɛstəneɪʃən] n (of traveler) 目的地 mōkútekìchi; (of mail) 宛先 atésaki

destined [dɛstɪnd] adj: to be destined to do/for...する(される)事になっている...sùrú (sareru)koto nf nattè irú

destiny [dɛstəni] n (fate) 運命 ūnmèi

destitute [dɛstɪtuːt] adj (person) 一文なしの íchìmon náshi nó

destroy [dɪstrɔ́ɪ] vt (demolish, wreck, also fig) 破壊する hákaí suru; (animal) 安楽死させる ánrakūshi saserú

destroyer [dɪstrɔ́ɪər] n (NAUT) 駆逐艦 kūchíkukàn

destruction [dɪstrʌ́kʃən] n (act, state) 破壊 hákaí

destructive [dɪstrʌ́ktɪv] adj (capacity, force) 破壊的な hákaíteki na; (child) 暴れん坊の ābárèmbō no; (not constructive: criticism etc) 建設的でない kénsetsutekì de nái

detach [dɪtǽtʃ] vt (remove, unclip, unstick) 外す házúsu

detachable [dɪtǽtʃəbəl] adj (removable) 外せる házúseru

detached [dɪtǽtʃt] adj (attitude, person) 無とん着な mútònchaku ná
a detached house 一軒家 íkkèn-ya

detachment [dɪtǽtʃmənt] n (aloofness) 無関心 múkànshin; (MIL: group) 分遣隊 bùnkèntaì

detail [dɪteíl] n (fact, feature) 詳細 shōsai; (no pl: in picture, one's work etc) 細かい事 kōmákaì kotó; (trifle) ささいな事 sásaì na kótò
♦vt (list) 詳しく話す kūwáshiku hanásù
in detail 細かく kōmákaku

detailed [dɪteíld] adj (account, description) 細かい kōmákaì

detain [dɪteín] vt (keep, delay) 引留める hikítomerù; (in captivity) 監禁する kánkin sùrú; (in hospital) 入院させる nyūín saserú

detect [ditekt] *vt* (sense) ...に感付く ...ni kánzukú; (MED) 発見する hákkén suru; (MIL, POLICE, RADAR, TECH) 関知する kánchi suru

detection [ditek'ʃən] *n* (discovery) 発見 hákkén

detective [ditek'tiv] *n* (POLICE) 刑事 kéiji

   private detective 私立探偵 shírītsutánteī

detective story *n* 探偵小説 tánteishósetsu

detector [ditek'tə:r] *n* (TECH) 探知機 tánchiki

détente [deita:nt'] *n* (POL) 緊張緩和 kínchōkanwa, デタント détanto

detention [diten'tʃən] *n* (arrest) 監禁 kánkin; (SCOL) 居残り īnōkori

deter [ditə:r'] *vt* (discourage, dissuade) 阻止させる sóshi suru

detergent [ditə:r'dʒənt] *n* 洗剤 sénzai

deteriorate [diti:ri:əreit] *vi* (health, sight, weather) 悪くなる wáruku náru; (situation) 悪化する ákka suru

deterioration [ditri:əˈrei'ʃən] *n* 悪化 ákka

determination [ditə:rmənei'ʃən] *n* (resolve) 決意 kétsùi; (establishment) 決定 kettéi

determine [ditə:r'min] *vt* (facts) 確認する kakúnin suru; (limits etc) 決める kiméru

   determined to do どうしても...すると決心している dōshitemo ...súrú tò késshìn shité iru

deterrent [ditə:r'ənt] *n* (MIL, LAW) 抑止する物 yókùshi suru mònð

detest [ditest'] *vt* 嫌う kiráu

detonate [det'əneit] *vi* 爆発する bakúhatsu suru

   ♦*vt* 爆発させる bakúhatsu sáseru

detour [di'tu:r] *n* (from route) 回り道 mawárimichí; (US: AUT: diversion) う回路 úkàro

detract [ditrækt'] *vi*: *to detract from* (effect, achievement) ...を損なう ...wo sð-

kónaù

detriment [det'rəmənt] *n*: *to the detriment of* ...に損害を与えて ...ni sóngai wo átaeru

detrimental [detrəmen'təl] *adj*: *detrimental to* 損害になる sóngai ni nárù

devaluation [di:vælju:ei'ʃən] *n* (ECON) 平価切下げ héikakirísage

devalue [di:væl'ju:] *vt* (work, person) 見くびる mikúbirù; (currency) ...の平価を切り下げる ...no hétka wo kirísageru

devastate [dev'əsteit] *vt* (destroy) さんざん荒らす sánzan árasu; (*fig*: shock): *to be devastated by* ...に大きなショックを受ける ...ni ókìna shókkù wo úkérù

devastating [dev'əsteitiŋ] *adj* (weapon, storm etc) 破壊力の大きい hákàíryoku no ókìi; (announcement, news, effect) 衝撃的な shōgekíteki na, ショッキングな shókkíngu na

develop [divel'əp] *vt* (business, land, idea, resource) 開発する kaíhatsu suru; (PHOT) 現像する génzō suru; (disease) ...にかかる ...ni kakárò; (fault, engine trouble) ...が発生する ...ga hássèi suru

   ♦*vi* (advance) 発展する hátten suru; (evolve: situation, disease) 発生する hásséi suru; (appear: facts, symptoms) 現れる árawarerù

developer [divel'əpə:r] *n* (*also*: **property developer**) 開発業者 kaíhatsugyóshà

developing country [divel'əpiŋ-] *n* 発展途上国 hátténtojókòku

development [divel'əpmənt] *n* (advance) 発展 hátten; (of affair, case) 新事実 shín-jijítsú; (of land) 開発 kaíhatsu

deviate [di:vi:eit] *vi*: *to deviate (from)* (...から) それる (...kára) sórérù

deviation [di:vi:ei'ʃən] *n* 脱線 dássèn

device [divais'] *n* (apparatus) 仕掛け shi-kàke

devil [dev'əl] *n* (REL, *fig*) 悪魔 ákùma

devilish [dev'əliʃ] *adj* (idea, action) 悪魔的な ákùmateki na

devious [di:vi:əs] *adj* (person) 腹黒い hà-rágurøì

devise [divaiz'] *vt* (plan, scheme, machine) 発案する hátsùan suru

devoid [dɪvɔɪd'] adj: **devoid of** (lacking) ...が全くない...ga māttakū naī

devolution [devəlu:'ʃən] n (POL) 権限委譲 kéngénijō

devote [dɪvout'] vt: **to devote something to** (dedicate) ...に...をつぎ込む ...nī ...wo tsūgīkomū

devoted [dɪvout'ɪd] adj (loyal: service, friendship) 忠実な chūjitsu na; (: admirer, partner) 熱心な nésshīn na
to be devoted to someone ...を熱愛している ...wo nétsúai shité iru
the book is devoted to politics この本は政治の専門書である sonō hōn wa séīji no sénmonsho dè árū

devotee [devouti:'] n (fan) ファン fān; (REL) 信徒 shíntó

devotion [dɪvou'ʃən] n (affection) 愛情 àijō; (dedication: to duty etc) 忠誠 chūsei; (REL) 信心 shínjīn

devour [dɪvau'ər] vt (meal, animal) むさぼり食う mūsàborikuū

devout [dɪvaut'] adj (REL) 信心深い shínjinbūkāī

dew [du:] n (on grass) 露 tsúyù

dexterity [dekster'ɪti:] n (manual, mental) 器用さ kíyōsā

diabetes [daiəbi:'tis] n 糖尿病 tōnyōbyō

diabetic [daiəbet'ik] adj 糖尿病の tōnyōbyō no
♦ n 糖尿病患者 tōnyōbyōkānja

diabolical [daiəbɑl'ikəl] adj (behavior) 悪魔的な ākúmateki na; (weather) ひどい hídòī

diagnose [daiəgnous'] vt (illness, problem) 診断する shíndàn surū

diagnoses [daiəgnou'si:z] npl of **diagnosis**

diagnosis [daiəgnou'sis] (pl **diagnoses**) n 診断 shíndàn

diagonal [daiæg'ənəl] adj (line) 斜めの nánámè no
♦ n (MATH) 対角線 tāfkakūsèn

diagram [dai'əgræm] n 図 zu

dial [dail'] n (of phone, radio etc) ダイヤル daíyarù; (on instrument, clock etc) 文字盤 mójībàn
♦ vt (number) ダイヤルする daíyaru surū

dial code (BRIT **dialling code**) n 市外番号 shígaibàngō

dialect [dai'əlekt] n 方言 hōgèn

dialogue [dai'əlɔːg] (US also: **dialog**) n (communication) 対話 taīwa; (conversation) 会話 kaíwa

dial tone (BRIT **dialling tone**) n 発信音 hásshīn-òn, ダイヤルトーン daíyarutòn

diameter [daiæm'itər] n 直径 chòkkéi

diamond [dai'mənd] n (gem) ダイヤモンド daíyamòndo, ダイヤ daíya; (shape) ひし形 hīshīgata

diamonds [dai'məndz] npl (CARDS) ダイヤ daíya

diaper [dai'pər] (US) n おむつ òmútsu

diaphragm [dai'əfræm] n (ANAT) 横隔膜 ōkakumàkū; (contraceptive) ペッサリー pèssàrī

diarrhea [daiəri:'ə] (BRIT **diarrhoea**) n げり gèrī

diary [dai'əri:] n (engagements book) 手帳 techō; (daily account) 日記 nīkkī

dice [dais] n inv (in game) さいころ saīkorò
♦ vt (CULIN) 角切りにする kākūgiri ni surū

dichotomy [daikɑt'əmi:] n 二分化 nībūnka

Dictaphone [dik'təfoun] ® n ディクタフォーン díkutafòn ◇一種の録音機の商品名 ísshō no rōkūonkì no shōhinmèi

dictate [dik'teit] vt (letter) 書取らせる kākítorasèrū; (conditions) 指図する sàshīzu surū

dictation [diktei'ʃən] n (of letter: also SCOL) 書取り kākftori; (of orders) 指図 sàshízu

dictator [dik'teitər] n (POL, MIL, fig) 独裁者 dókúsaìsha

dictatorship [diktei'tər:ʃip] n 独裁政権 dókúsaisèiken

diction [dik'ʃən] n (in speech, song) 発音 hátsúon

dictionary [dik'ʃəneri:] n (monolingual, bilingual etc) 辞書 jíshò, 字引 jíbíkì

did [did] pt of **do**

didactic [daidæk'tik] adj (teaching, purpose, film) 教育的な kyōīkuteki na

didn't [dɪd'ənt] = **did not**

die [daɪ] vi (person, animal) 死ぬ shínu; (plant) 枯れる karéru; (fig: cease) やむ yámù; (: fade) 次第に消える shídaì ni kiéru

to be dying for something/to do something 死ぬ程...が欲しい(...をしたい) shínu hodo ...ga hoshíì (...wo shitáì)

die away vi (sound, light) 次第に消える shídaì ni kiéru

die down vi (wind) 弱まる yówámarí; (fire) 小さくなる chíìsakù nárù; (excitement, noise) 静まる shízúmarù

diehard [daɪ'hɑːrd] n 頑固な保守派 gánko na hóshūha

die out vi (activity) 消えてなくなる kiéte nakú narù; (animal, bird) 絶滅する zétsúmetsu sùrú

diesel [diː'zəl] n (vehicle) ディーゼル車 díZerushà; (also: diesel oil) 軽油 keíyù

diesel engine n ディーゼルエンジン díZerùènjìn

diet [daɪ'ət] n (food intake) 食べ物 tabémònò; (restricted food: MED, when slimming) 減食 génshoku, ダイエット dáÌettò
♦vi (also: **be on a diet**) 減食する génshoku sùrú, ダイエットする dáÌettò surú

differ [dɪf'ɔːr] vi (be different): *to differ (from)* (...)と違う (...)to chígaù; (disagree): *to differ (about)* (...について) 意見が違う (...ni tsúìte) íkèn ga chígaù

difference [dɪf'ərəns] n (dissimilarity) 違い chígaì; (disagreement) 意見の相違 íkèn no sòí

different [dɪf'ərənt] adj 別の bétsù no

differentiate [dɪfəren'tʃieìt] vi: *to differentiate (between)* (...を) 区別する (...wo) kúbètsu surú

differently [dɪf'ərəntli] adv 違う風に chígaù fū ni

difficult [dɪf'əkʌlt] adj (task, problem) 難しい muzúkashiì; (person) 気難しい kí-mùzukashiì

difficulty [dɪf'əkʌlti] n 困難 kònnán; (problem) 問題 móndai

diffident [dɪf'ədənt] adj (hesitant, self-effacing) 気の小さい kí nó chiísaì

diffuse [adj dıfjus' vb dıfjuz'] adj (idea,

sense) 不鮮明な fūsénmeì na
♦t (information) 広める hírómerù
diffuse light 反射光 hánshakò

dig [dɪg] (pt, pp **dug**) vt (hole, garden) 掘る hórù
♦n (prod) 小突く事 kozúkù kotó; (archeological) 発掘現場 hákkùtsùgénba; (remark) 当てこすり átèkosuri

digest [daɪ'dʒest] vt (food: also fig: facts) 消化する shōka suru
♦n (book) 要約 yōyaku, ダイジェスト版 dáÌjesutobàn

digestion [dıdʒes'tʃən] n (process) 消化 shōka; (system) 消化器系 shōkakikei

digestive [dıdʒes'tıv] adj (juices, system) 消化の shōka no

dig into vt (savings) 掘り出す hōrídasù
to dig one's nails into 引っかく híkkákù

digit [dɪdʒ'ıt] n (number) 数字 sūji; (finger) 指 yúbí

digital [dɪdʒ'ıtəl] adj (clock, watch) デジタルの déjìtaru nó

digital computer n デジタルコンピュータ dejìtarukónpyùta

dignified [dɪg'nəfaìd] adj (person, manner) 品のある hín no arú

dignity [dɪg'nıtiː] n (poise, self-esteem) 気品 kíhìn

digress [dıgres'] vi: *to digress (from)* (topic, subject) (...から) それる (...kára) sórèru

digs [dıgz] (BRIT: inf) npl 下宿 geshúku

dig up vt (plant) 掘り起す hōríokosù; (information) 探り出す sagúridasù

dike [daik] n = **dyke**

dilapidated [dılæp'ədeıtıd] adj (building) 老朽した rōkyū shitá

dilate [daıleıt'] vi (eyes) 見張る mīharu

dilemma [dılem'ə] n (political, moral) 板挟み itábasàmi, ジレンマ jírènma

diligent [dɪl'ıdʒənt] adj (worker, research) 勤勉な kínben na

dilute [dılut'] vt (liquid) 薄める usúmeru, 希釈する kisháku surú

dim [dım] adj (light, room) 薄暗い úsúguraì; (outline, figure) ぼんやりした bónyarì shitá; (inf: person) 頭の悪い átàma no wârûî

dime [daim] (US) n 10 セント玉 jûssêntodâmā

dimension [dimen't∫ən] n (aspect) 面 menː (measurement) 寸法 sūnpō; (also pl: scale, size) 大きさ ōkisa

diminish [dimin'i∫] vi (size, effect) 小さくなる chîsakûî narûî

diminutive [dimin'jətiv] adj (tiny) 小型のkōgata no

♦n (LING) 指小辞 shîshôjī

dimmers [dim'ərz] (US) npl (AUT: dipped headlights) 下向きにするヘッドライト shîtâmuki no hêddôraîtô; (: parking lights) 車幅灯 shafûkûtō

dimple [dim'pəl] n (on cheek, chin) えくぼ êkûbo

din [din] n (row, racket) 騒音 sôon

dine [dain] vi 食事する shokûjî suru

diner [dain'ər] n (person) レストランの客 rêsûtoran no kyakû; (US: restaurant) 簡易食堂 kaɲ-ishokûdō

dinghy [diŋ'i:] n ボート bôto

rubber dinghy ゴムボート gomûbôto

dingy [din'dʒi:] adj (streets, room) 薄暗い usûgûraî; (clothes, curtains etc) 薄汚い usûgitanaî

dining car [dain'iŋ-] n (RAIL) 食堂車 shokûdôsha

dining room [dain'iŋ-] n (in house, hotel) 食堂 shokûdô

dinner [din'ər] n (evening meal) 夕食 yûshoku; (lunch) 昼食 chûshoku; (banquet) 宴会 eɲkaî

dinner jacket n タキシード takîshîdo

dinner party n 宴会 eɲkaî

dinner time n (midday) 昼食時 chûshokûdokî; (evening) 夕食時 yûshokûdokî

dinosaur [dai'nəsɔːr] n 恐竜 kyôryû

dint [dint] n: *by dint of ...* によって ...ni yotté

diocese [dai'əsis] n 司教区 shikyôkû

dip [dip] n (slope) 下り坂 kudârizaka; (in sea) 一泳ぎ hitôoyôgi; (CULIN) ディップ dîppû

♦vt (in water etc) ...に浸す ...ni hitâsû; (ladle etc) 入れる tîrêrû; (BRIT: AUT: lights) 下向きにする shîtâmuki ni sûrû

♦vi (ground, road) 下り坂になる kudârizaka ni narû

diphthong [dif'θɔːŋ] n 二重母音 nijûboîn

diploma [diplou'mə] n 卒業証書 sotsûgyôshôsho

diplomacy [diplou'məsiː] n (POL) 外交 gaîkô; (gen) 如才なさ josâînasà

diplomat [dip'ləmæt] n (POL) 外交官 gaîkôkan

diplomatic [dipləmæt'ik] adj (mission, corps) 外交の gaîkô no; (person, answer, behavior) 如才ない josâînaî

dipstick [dip'stik] n (AUT) 油量計 yûryôkeî, オイルゲージ oîrugêjī

dipswitch [dip'switʃ] (BRIT) n (AUT) ヘッドライト切り替えスイッチ heddôraîto kirîkaesuîtchî

dire [dai'ər] adj (consequences, effects) 恐ろしい osôroshiî

direct [direkt'] adj (route) 直行の chokkô no; (sunlight, light) 直射の chokûsha no; (control, payment) 直接の chokûsetsu no; (challenge) あからさまな akârasâma na; (person) 率直な sotchôku na

♦vt (address: letter) 宛てる atêrû; (aim: attention, remark) 向ける mukêrû; (manage: company, project etc) 管理する kâɲri suru; (play, film, programme) 監督する kaɲtoku suru; (order): *to direct someone to do something ...に* ...する様に命令する ...ni ...surû yô ni meîreî suru

♦adv (go, write) 直接 chokûsetsu

can you direct me to ...? ...に行くにはどう行けばいいんですか ...ni ikô nî wa dô ikêba iîn desu ká

direct debit (BRIT) n 自動振替 jidôfurikae

direction [direk'∫ən] n (way) 方向 hôkô; (TV, RADIO, CINEMA) 演出 eɲshutsu

sense of direction 方向感覚 hôkôkankaku

directions [direk'∫ənz] npl (instructions) 指示 shîjî

directions for use 取扱い説明 torîatsukaisetsūmei

directly [direkt'li:] adv (in a straight line) 真っ直ぐに massúgù ni; (at once) 直ぐに súgù ni

director [direk'tər] n (COMM) 取締役 toríshimariyàku; (of project) 責任者 sekíninìsha; (TV, RADIO, CINEMA) 監督 kańtoku

directory [direk'tə:ri:] n (TEL) 電話帳 deñwachō; (COMPUT) ディレクトリー dírékùtorī; (COMM) 名簿 meíbo

dirt [də:rt] n (stains, dust) 汚れ yogòre; (earth) 土 tsuchí

dirt-cheap [də:rt'tʃi:p'] adj べら安の berâyàsu no

dirty [də:r'ti:] adj (clothes, face) 汚い kitánai, 汚れた yogóretà; (joke) わいせつな waísetsu na
♦vt (clothes, face) 汚す yogósù

dirty trick n: **to play a dirty trick on someone** ...に卑劣なまねをする ...ni hirétsu na manè wo suru

disability [disəbil'əti:] n (also: **physical disability**) 身体障害 shińtaishōgai; (also: **mental disability**) 精神障害 sefshińshōgai

disabled [disei'bəld] adj (physically) 身体障害のある shiñtaishōgai no aru; (mentally) 精神障害のある sefshińshōgai no árù
♦npl: **the disabled** 身体傷害者 shiñtaishōgaisha の総称 sōshō

disadvantage [disædvæn'tidʒ] n (drawback) 不利な点 fúrì na teń; (detriment) 不利な立場 fúrì na tachíba

disaffection [disæfek'ʃən] n (with leadership etc) 不満 fumán

disagree [disəgri:'] vi (differ) 一致しない itchí shinaì; (be against, think otherwise): **to disagree (with)** (...と) 意見が合わない (...to) íkèn ga awánaì

disagreeable [disəgri:'əbəl] adj (encounter, person, experience) 嫌な iyá nà

disagreement [disəgri:'mənt] n (lack of consensus) 不一致 futchí; (argument) けんか keñka

disallow [disəlau'] vt (LAW: appeal) 却下する kyákkà suru

disappear [disəpiər'] vi (person, object, vehicle: from sight) 消える kiérù, 見えなくなる miénaku narù; (: deliberately) 姿を消す súgata wo kesú; (custom etc) 消えてなくなる kiéte naku narù

disappearance [disəpiər'əns] n (from sight) 消える事 kiéru kotò; (: deliberate) 姿を消す事 súgata wo kesú kotò; (of custom etc) なくなる事 nakú naru kotò

disappoint [disəpɔint'] vt (person) がっかりさせる gakkárì sasérù

disappointed [disəpɔin'tid] adj がっかりしている gakkárì shité irù

disappointing [disəpɔin'tiŋ] adj (outcome, result, book etc) 期待外れの kitáihazùre no

disappointment [disəpɔint'mənt] n (emotion) 落胆 rakútan; (cause) 期待外れ kitáihazùre

disapproval [disəpru:'vəl] n 非難 hínàn

disapprove [disəpru:v'] vi: **to disapprove (of)** (person, thing) (...を) 非難の目で見る (...wo) hínàn no mé dè mírù

disarm [disɑ:rm'] vt (MIL) 武装解除する busōkaijo suru

disarmament [disɑ:r'məmənt] n (MIL, POL) 軍備縮小 guñbishukushō

disarming [disɑ:rm'iŋ] adj (smile, friendliness) 心を和ませるような kokóro wo nagómaseru yō na

disarray [disərei'] n: **in disarray** (army, organization) 混乱して koñran shité; (hair, clothes) 乱れて midárete

disaster [dizæs'tər] n (also: **natural disaster**) 天災 teńsai; (AVIAT etc) 災害 saígai; (fig: mess) 大失敗 daíshippaì

disastrous [dizæs'trəs] adj (mistake, effect, results) 悲惨な hisán na

disband [disbænd'] vt (regiment, group) 解散する kaísan suru
♦vi (regiment, group) 解散する kaísan suru

disbelief [disbili:f'] n 信じられない事 shińjirarenai kotò

disc [disk] n (ANAT) つい間板 tsuíkanbàn; (record) レコード rekódò; (COMPUT) = **disk**

discard [dɪskɑːrd'] vt (old things: also fig) 捨てる sutérù

discern [dɪsɜːrn'] vt (see) 見分ける miwâkerù; (identify) 理解する rīkái suru

discerning [dɪsɜːr'nɪŋ] adj (judgement, look, listeners etc) 理解のある rīkái no árù

discharge [vb dɪstʃɑːrdʒ'] n dɪs'tʃɑːdʒ] vt (duties) 履行する rikṓ surù; (waste) 放出する hōshutsu suru; (patient) 退院させる taîn saserù; (employee) 解雇する kâiko suru; (soldier) 除隊する jotái ni suru; (defendant) 釈放する shakūhō suru
◆n (CHEM, ELEC) 放電 hōden; (MED) 排出 haîshutsu; (of employee) 解雇 kâiko; (of soldier) 除隊 jotái; (of defendant) 釈放 shakūhō

disciple [dɪsaɪ'pəl] n (REL: also fig: follower) 弟子 deshí

discipline [dɪs'əplɪn] n (control) 規律 kirítsu; (self-control) 自制心 jiséishìn; (branch of knowledge) 分野 búñ-ya
◆vt (train) 訓練する kúñren suru, (punish) 罰する bassúrù

disc jockey [dɪsk'-] n ディスクジョッキー disúkujokkì

disclaim [dɪskleɪm'] vt (knowledge, responsibility) 否認する hítèi suru

disclose [dɪskloʊz'] vt (interest, involvement) 打明ける uchiákerù

disclosure [dɪskloʊ'ʒər] n (revelation) 打明け話 uchiákebanàshi

disco [dɪs'kou] n abbr (event) ディスコダンス disúkodañsu; (place) = **discotheque**

discolored [dɪskʌl'ərd] (BRIT **discoloured**) adj (teeth, pots) 変色した heñshoku shità

discomfort [dɪskʌm'fɑːrt] n (unease) 不安感 fuáñkan; (physical) 不便 fúbeñ

disconcert [dɪskənsɜːrt'] vt どぎまぎさせる dōgîmagi saserù

disconnect [dɪskənekt'] vt (pipe, tap) 外す hazúsu; (ELEC) 接続を断つ setsúdan suru; (TEL) 切る kírù

discontent [dɪskəntent'] n 不満 fumáñ

discontented [dɪskəntent'id] adj 不満の fumáñ no

discontinue [dɪskəntɪn'juː] vt (visits) やめる yamérù; (payments) 止める tomérù
discontinued [dɪskəntɪn'juːd] adj (COMM) 生産中止 seísanchūshi

discord [dɪs'kɔːrd] n (quarrelling) 不和 fúwà; (MUS) 不協和音 fukyṓwaðn

discordant [dɪskɔːr'dənt] adj (fig) 不協和音の fukyṓwaðn no

discotheque [dɪs'koutek] n (place) ディスコ dísùko

discount [n dɪs'kaunt vb diskaunt'] n (for students, employees etc) 割引 warîbiki
◆vt (COMM) 割引く warîbikù; (idea, fact) 無視する múshì suru

discourage [dɪskɜːr'idʒ] vt (dishearten) 落胆させる rakútañ saserù; (advise against): to discourage something ...を阻止する ...wo sōshí suru
to discourage someone from doing ...するのを ...に断念させようとする ...surú no wo ...ni dañneñ saseyṓ to suru

discouraging [dɪskɜːr'idʒiŋ] adj (remark, response) がっかりさせる様な gakkárì saserù yṓ na

discourteous [dɪskɜːr'tiːəs] adj 失礼な shitsúrei na

discover [dɪskʌv'ər] vt 発見する hakkén suru
to discover that (find out) ...だと発見する ...dá to hakkén suru

discovery [dɪskʌv'əri:] n 発見 hakkén

discredit [dɪskred'it] vt (person, group) ...の信用を傷付ける ...no shiñyō wo kizútsukerù; (claim, idea) ...に疑問を投げ掛ける ...ni gimóñ wo nagékakerù

discreet [dɪskriːt'] adj (tactful, careful) 慎重な shiñchō na; (unremarkable) 目立たない medátanaì

discrepancy [dɪskrep'ənsiː] n (difference) 不一致 fuítchì

discretion [dɪskreʃ'ən] n (tact) 慎重さ shiñchōsa
at the discretion of ...の判断次第で ...no hañdan shidài de

discriminate [dɪskrim'əneit] vi: to discriminate between ...と...を区別する ...to ...wo kúbètsu suru

to discriminate against ...を差別する
...wo sábetsu suru

discriminating [diskrim'ǝneitiŋ] adj
(public, audience) 理解のある rīkai no
árù

discrimination [diskrimǝnei'ʃǝn] n
(bias) 差別 sábetsu; (discernment) 理解
rīkai

discuss [diskʌs'] vt (talk over) 話し合う
hanáshiaù; (analyze) 取上げる toriágerù

discussion [diskʌʃ'ǝn] n (talk) 話し合い
hanáshiai; (debate) 討論 tóròn

disdain [disdein'] n 軽べつ kéibetsu

disease [diziz'] n (MED, fig) 病気 byōki

disembark [disemba:rk'] vt (goods) 陸揚
げする rikúagé suru; (passengers: from
boat) 上陸させる jóriku saserù; (: from
plane, bus) 降ろす orósù
♦vi (passengers: from boat) 上陸する jóriku suru; (: from plane, bus) 降りる orírù

disenchanted [disentʃæn'tid] adj: **disenchanted (with)** (...の) 魅力を感じな
くなった (...no) miryóku wò kanjínaku
nattá

disengage [disengeidʒ'] vt (AUT: clutch)
切る kírù

disentangle [disentæŋ'gǝl] vt ほどく ho-
dókù

disfigure [disfig'jǝr] vt (person) ...の美
ぼうを損なう ...no bibō wò sokónaù;
(object, place) 汚す yogósù

disgrace [disgreis'] n (shame, dishonor)
恥 hají; (cause of shame, scandal) 恥ずべ
き事 hazúbeki koto
♦vt (one's family, country) ...の恥になる
...no hají ni narù; (one's name) 汚す kegásù

disgraceful [disgreis'fǝl] adj (behavior,
condition, state) 恥ずべき hazúbeki

disgruntled [disgrʌn'tǝld] adj (s u p -
porter, voter) 不満の fumán no

disguise [disgaiz'] n (make-up, costume)
変装の道具 hensō no dōgu; (art) 変装 hensō
♦vt (person, object): **to disguise (as)**
(...に) 見せ掛ける (...ni) misékakerù
in disguise 変装して hensō shitè

disgust [disgʌst'] n (aversion, distaste)
嫌悪 kén-o
♦vt うんざりさせる uñzari saserù

disgusting [disgʌs'tiŋ] adj (revolting:
food etc) むかつかせる mukátsukaserù;
(unacceptable: behavior etc) いやな iyá
nà

dish [diʃ] n (piece of crockery) 皿 sará;
(food) 料理 ryōri
to do/wash the dishes 皿洗いをする
saráarài wo suru

dishcloth [diʃ'klɔːθ] n (for washing) 皿洗
いのふきん saráarài no fukín

dishearten [disha:r'tǝn] vt がっかりさせ
る gakkárì saserù

disheveled [diʃev'ǝld] (BRIT **dishev-
elled**) adj (hair, clothes) 乱れた midáretà

dishonest [disa:n'ist] adj (person, means)
不正な fuséi na

dishonesty [disa:n'isti:] n 不正 fuséi

dishonor [disa:n'ǝːr] (BRIT **dishonour**)
n 不名誉 fuméìyo

dishonorable [disa:n'ǝrǝbǝl] adj 不名誉
な fuméìyo na

dish out vt (distribute) 配る kubárù

dishtowel [diʃ'tauǝl] n 皿ふきん sarábu-
kin

dish up vt (food) 皿に盛る sará ni morù

dishwasher [diʃ'wɑːʃǝr] n (machine) 皿
洗い機 saráaraiki

disillusion [disilu:'ʒǝn] vt ...の迷いを覚ま
す ...no mayóì wo samásù

disincentive [disinsen'tiv] n (to work,
investment) 阻害要因 sogáiyòin

disinfect [disinfekt'] vt 消毒する shōdo-
ku suru

disinfectant [disinfek'tǝnt] n 消毒剤
shōdokuzài

disintegrate [disin'tagreit] vi (object)
分解する buñkai suru

disinterested [disin'tristid] adj (impartial: advice, help) 私欲のない shiyóku no
nai

disjointed [disdʒɔint'id] adj (thoughts,
words) まとまりのない matómari no nai

disk [disk] n (COMPUT) ディスク dísù-
ku

disk drive n ディスクドライブ disúkudoraîbu

diskette [disket'] n = disk

dislike [dislaik'] n (feeling) 嫌 悪 kén·o; (gen pl: object of dislike) 嫌いな物 kiráî na monó
♦vt 嫌う kiráù

dislocate [dis'loukeit] vt (joint) 脱きゅうさせる dakkyū saserù

dislodge [dislɑːdʒ'] vt (boulder etc) 取除く torînozokù

disloyal [dislɔi'əl] adj (to country, family) 裏切りの urágirimono no

dismal [diz'məl] adj (depressing: weather, song, dance, mood) 陰気な iñki na; (very bad: prospects, failure) 最低の saitei no

dismantle [dismæn'təl] vt (machine) 分解する buñkai suru

dismay [dismei'] n 困惑 koñwaku
♦vt 困惑させる koñwaku saserù

dismiss [dismis'] vt (worker) 解雇する káîko suru; (pupils, soldiers) 解散させる kaísan saserù; (LAW: case) 却下する kyákkà suru; (possibility, idea) 考えない様にする kañgaenai yô ni suru

dismissal [dismis'əl] n (sacking) 解雇 káîko

dismount [dismaunt'] vi (from horse, bicycle) 降りる orírù

disobedience [disəbiː'diːəns] n 不服従 fufukujū

disobedient [disəbiː'diːənt] adj (child, dog) 言う事を聞かない iú koto wo kikánaì

disobey [disəbei'] vt (person, order) 違反する ihán suru

disorder [disɔːr'dəːr] n (untidiness) 乱雑 rañzatsu; (rioting) 騒動 sōdō; (MED) 障害 shôgai

disorderly [disɔːr'dəːli] adj (untidy: room etc) 整理されていない seíri sarete inaì; (meeting) 混乱の koñran no; (behavior) 治安を乱す chián wo midásù

disorganized [disɔːr'gənaizd] adj (person, event) 支離滅裂な shírimetsúretsu na

disorientated [disɔːr'riːintéitid] adj (person: after journey, deep sleep) 頭が混乱

している atáma gà koñran shite irù

disown [disoun'] vt (action) …との関係を否定する tó nò kañkei wo hítèi suru; (child) 勘当する kañdō suru

disparaging [dispær'idʒiŋ] adj (remarks) 中傷的な chūshōteki na

disparate [dis'pærit] adj (levels, groups) 異なった kotónattà

disparity [dispær'itiː] n 差異 sáî

dispassionate [dispæʃ'ənit] adj (approach, reaction) 客観的な kyakkánteki na

dispatch [dispætʃ'] vt (send: message, goods, mail) 送る okúrù; (: messenger) 派遣する hakén suru
♦n (sending) 送付 sôfu; (PRESS, MIL) 派遣 hakén

dispel [dispel'] vt (myths, fears) 払いのける haráinokerù

dispense [dispens'] vt (medicines) 調剤する chôzai suru

dispenser [dispen'səːr] n (machine) 自動販売機 jidóhanbaiki

dispense with vt fus (do without) …なしで済ませる …náshì de sumáserù

dispensing chemist [dispens'iŋ-](BRIT) n (shop) 薬屋 kusúriya

dispersal [dispəːr'səl] n (of objects, group, crowd) 分散 buñsan

disperse [dispəːrs'] vt (objects, crowd etc) 散らす chirásù
♦vi (crowd) 散って行く chitté ikù

dispirited [dispir'itid] adj 意気消沈した îkîshōchin shita

displace [displeis'] vt (shift) 押し出す o-shídasù

displaced person [displeist'-] n (POL) 難民 nañmin

display [displei'] n (in shop) 陳列 chinretsu; (exhibition) 展示 teñji; (of feeling) 表現 hyôgen; (COMPUT, TECH) ディスプレー disúpurê, モニター mónìtā
♦vt (show) 展示する teñji suru; (ostentatiously) 見せびらかす misébirakasù

displease [displiːz'] vt (offend, annoy) 怒らせる okóraserù

displeased [displiːzd'] adj: **displeased with** (unhappy, disappointed) …にがっか

りしている ...ni gakkárí shité irú

displeasure [displɛ'ʒə'] n 怒り ikári

disposable [dispou'zəbəl] adj (lighter, bottle) 使い捨て の tsukáisute no; (income) 自由に使える jiyū ní tsukáerù

disposable nappy (BRIT) n 紙 おむつ kamíomutsù

disposal [dispou'zəl] n (of goods for sale) 陳列 chífretsu; (of property) 売却 baíkyaku; (of rubbish) 処分 shóbun

at one's disposal ...の自由になる ...no jiyū ní narú

dispose [dispouz'] vi: *to dispose of* (get rid of: body, unwanted goods) 始末する shímatsu suru; (deal with: problem, argument) 片付ける katázukerù

disposed [dispouzd'] adj: *disposed to* (inclined, willing) ...する気がある ...surú ki gá árù

to be well disposed towards someone ...に好意を寄せている ...ni kối wo yosète irú

disposition [dispəziʃ'ən] n (nature) 性質 seíshitsu; (inclination) 傾向 keíkō

disproportionate [disprəpɔr'ʃənit] adj (amount, effect) 過剰な kajō na

disprove [dispru:v'] vt (belief, assertion) 反証する hanshō suru

dispute [dispju:t'] n (domestic) けんか keñka; (also: *industrial dispute*) 争議 sốgi; (POL) 論議 róñgi

♦vt (fact, statement) 反ばくする hanbaku suru; (ownership etc) 争う arasóu

territorial dispute 領土紛争 ryódofuñsō

border dispute 国境紛争 kokkyófuñsō

disqualify [diskwɑ:'əfai] vt (SPORT) ...の資格を取り上げる ...no shikkaku wò toríagerù

to disqualify someone for something/from doing something ...から ...の(...する)資格を取り上げる ...kárà ...no [...suru] shikkàku wò toríagerù

disquiet [diskwai'it] n (anxiety) 不安 fuán

disregard [disrigɑːrd'] vt (ignore, pay no attention to) 無視する múshì suru

disrepair [disriper'] n: *to fall into*

disrepair (machine, building) ひどく痛んでしまう hídòku itánde shimaù

disreputable [disrep'jətəbəl] adj (person, behavior) いかがわしい ikágawashiì

disrespectful [disrispekt'fəl] adj (person, conduct) 無礼な búreì na

disrupt [disrʌpt'] vt (plans) 邪魔する jamá suru; (conversation, proceedings) 妨害する bōgai suru

disruption [disrʌp'ʃən] n (interruption) 中断 chūdan; (disturbance) 妨害 bōgai

dissatisfaction [dissætisfæk'ʃən] n 不満 fumán

dissatisfied [dissæt'isfaid] adj 不満な fumán na

dissect [disekt'] vt (dead person, animal) 解剖する kaíbō suru

disseminate [disem'əneit] vt 普及させる fukyū saserù

dissent [disent'] n (disagreement, protest) 反対 hañtai

dissertation [disərtei'ʃən] n (also SCOL) 論文 róñbun

disservice [dissɔːr'vis] n: *to do someone a disservice* (person: harm) ...に迷惑を掛ける ...ni mếwaku wo kakérù

dissident [dis'idənt] adj (faction, voice) 反対の hañtai no

♦n (POL, REL) 反対分子 hañtaibuñshi

dissimilar [disim'ilər] adj 異 な る kotónaru

dissipate [dis'əpeit] vt (heat) 放散 す る hōsan suru; (clouds) 散らす chíràsù; (money, effort) 使い果す tsukáihatasù

dissociate [disou'ʃieit] vt ...と の関係 を否定する ...tó nò kañkei wò hítéì suru

to dissociate oneself from ...との関係を否定する ...tó nò kañkei wò hítéì suru

dissolute [dis'əlu:t] adj (person, behavior) 道楽ざんまい の dốrakuzañmai no

dissolution [disəlu:'ʃən] n (of organization, POL) 解散 kaísan; (of marriage) 解消 kaíshō

dissolve [dizɑːlv'] vt (in liquid) 溶かす tokásù; (organization, POL) 解散 させる kaísan saserù; (marriage) 解消する kaíshō suru

♦*vi* (material) 溶ける tokérù

to dissolve in(to) tears 泣崩れる nakfkuzurérù

dissuade [diswéid'] *vt*: **to dissuade someone (from)** (...を) 思い止まる様 (...を) 説得する (...wo) omóitodomaru yô ...wo settốku suru

distance [dis'təns] *n* (gap: in space) 距離 kyórì; (: in time) 隔たり hedátari

in the distance ずっと向うに zúttò mukô nì

distant [dis'tənt] *adj* (place, time, relative) 遠い tối; (manner) よそよそしい yosóyososhiì

distaste [distéist'] *n* (dislike) 嫌悪 kén'o

distasteful [distéist'fəl] *adj* (offensive) いやな iyá nà

distended [disténd'id] *adj* (stomach) 膨らんだ fukúrandà

distill [distil'] (*BRIT* **distil**) *vt* (water, whiskey) 蒸留する jôryū suru

distillery [distil'əːri:] *n* 醸造所 jôzôjó

distinct [distiŋkt'] *adj* (different) 別個の békkô no; (clear) はっきりした hakkíri shita; (unmistakable) 明白な mehàku na

as distinct from (in contrast to) ...では なくて ...dé wà nákàte

distinction [distiŋk'ʃən] *n* (difference) 区別 kúbètsu; (honor) 名誉 mềyo; (in exam) 優等の成績 yútô no seíseki

distinctive [distiŋk'tiv] *adj* 独特な dokútoku na

distinguish [distiŋ'gwiʃ] *vt* (differentiate) 区別する kúbètsu suru; (identify: details etc: by sight) 見分ける miwákerù; (: by sound) 聞分ける kikíwakerù

to distinguish oneself (in battle etc) 見事な活躍をする mígòto na katsúyaku wo surù

distinguished [distiŋ'gwiʃt] *adj* (eminent) 有名な yúmei na; (in appearance) 気品のある kihîn no arù

distinguishing [distiŋ'gwiʃiŋ] *adj* (feature) 特徴的な tokúchôteki na

distort [distɔːrt'] *vt* (argument) 曲げる magérù; (sound) 口ゆがめる hizúmaserù; (shape, image) ゆがめる yugámerù

distortion [distɔːr'ʃən] *n* (of argument

etc) わい曲 waíkyoku; (of sound, image, shape etc) ひずみ hizúmi

distract [distrækt'] *vt* (sb's attention) 散らす chirásù; (person) ...の気を散らす ...no ki wo chirásù

distracted [distræk'tid] *adj* (dreaming) ぼんやりした bon'-yarî shita; (anxious) 気が動転している ki ga dôten shite irù

distraction [distræk'ʃən] *n* (inattention) 気を散らす事(物) ki wo chirásù kotô (monô); (confusion) 困惑 konfwaku; (amusement) 気晴らし kibárashi

distraught [distrɔːt'] *adj* (with pain, worry) 気が動転している ki ga dôten shite irù

distress [distrés'] *n* (anguish) 苦痛 kutsú

♦*vt* (cause anguish) 苦しめる kurúshimerù

distressing [distrés'iŋ] *adj* (experience, time) 苦しい kurúshiì

distress signal *n* (AVIAT, NAUT) 遭難信号 sônanshingô

distribute [distrib'juːt] *vt* (hand out: leaflets, prizes etc) 配る kubárù; (share out: profits etc) 分ける wakérù; (spread out: weight) 分布する búnpu suru

distribution [distrəbjuː'ʃən] *n* (of goods) 流通 ryútsu; (of profits etc) 分配 bufípai

distributor [distrib'jətəːr] *n* (COMM) 流通業者 ryútsugyôsha; (AUT, TECH) ディストリビュータ disútoribyúta

district [dis'trikt] *n* (of country) 地方 chihô; (of town, ADMIN) 地区 chíkù

district attorney (*US*) *n* 地方検事 chihôkeñji

district nurse (*BRIT*) *n* 保健婦 hokéñfu

distrust [distrʌst'] *n* 不信感 fushíñkan

♦*vt* 信用しない shiñ-yô shinaì

disturb [distəːrb'] *vt* (interrupt) 邪魔する jamá suru; (upset) 心配させる shifípai saserù; (disorganize) 乱す midásù

disturbance [distəːr'bəns] *n* (upheaval) 邪魔 jamá; (political etc) 騒動 sôdô; (violent event) 動乱 dôran; (of mind) 心配 shifípai

disturbed [distəːrbd'] *adj* (person: worried, upset) 不安な fuáñ na; (childhood)

乱れた midáreta

emotionally disturbed 情緒障害の jōchoshōgai no

disturbing [dɪstə:rʹbɪŋ] adj (experience, moment) 動揺させる dōten saserú

disuse [dɪsjuːsʹ] n: **to fall into disuse** (be abandoned: methods, laws etc) 廃れる sutárerú

disused [dɪsjuːzdʹ] adj (building, airfield) 使われていない tsukáwarete inái

ditch [dɪtʃ] n (at roadside) どぶ dobú; (also: **irrigation ditch**) 用水路 yōsuíro

♦vt (inf: person) ...と縁を切る ...to én wo kírù; (: plan, car etc) 捨てる sutérù

dither [dɪðʹə:r] (pej) vi (hesitate) ためらう tamérau

ditto [dɪtʹou] adv 同じく onájìku

divan [dɪvænʹ] n (also: **divan bed**) ソファベッド sofábeddò

dive [daɪv] (pt **dived** also US **dove**, pp **dived**) n (from board) 飛込み tobíkomi; (underwater) 潜水 sensúi, ダイビング dáibingu; (of submarine) 潜水 sensúi

♦vi (swimmer: into water) 飛込む tobíkomù; (under water) 潜水する sensúi suru, ダイビングする dáibingu suru; (fish) 潜る mogúrù; (bird) 急降下する kyūkōka suru; (submarine) 潜水する sensúi suru

to dive into (bag, drawer etc) ...に手を突っ込む ...ni te wo tsukkómù; (shop, car etc) ...に飛込む ...ni tobíkomù

diver [daɪʹvə:r] n (person) ダイバー dáibā

diverge [dɪvə:rdʒʹ] vi (paths, interests) 分かれる wakárerù

diverse [dɪvə:rsʹ] adj 様々な samázàma na

diversify [dɪvə:rʹsəfaɪ] vi (COMM) 多様化する tayóka suru

diversion [dɪvə:rʹʒən] n (BRIT: AUT) う回路 ukáiró; (distraction) 気分転換 kibúntenkan; (of funds) 流用 ryūyō

diversity [dɪvə:rʹsitiː] n (range, variety) 多様性 tayōsei

divert [dɪvə:rtʹ] vt (funds) 流用する ryūyō suru; (someone's attention) 反らす soràsú; (re-route) う回させる ukái saserù

divide [dɪvaɪdʹ] vt (separate) 分ける wakérù; (MATH) 割る warù; (share out)

ける wakérù, 分配する buñpai suru

♦vt (cells etc) 分裂する buñretsu suru; (road) 分岐する buñki suru; (people, groups) 分裂する buñretsu suru

8 divided by 4 is 2 8割る4は2 hachí warù yóñ wa ní

divided highway [dɪvaɪdʹid-] (US) n 中央分離帯のある道路 chūōbuñritai no árù dōrò

dividend [dɪvʹidend] n (COMM) 配当金 haitókin; (fig): **to pay dividends** 利益になる rīeki ni nárù

divine [dɪvaɪnʹ] adj (REL) 神の kámì no; (fig: person, thing) 素晴らしい subárashiì

diving [daɪvʹiŋ] n (underwater) 飛込み tobíkomi; (SPORT) 飛込み kyūkōka sensúi

diving board n 飛込み台 tobíkomidái

divinity [dɪvinʹətiː] n (nature) 神性 shiñsei; (god) 神 kámì; (subject) 神学 shiñgaku

division [dɪviʹʒən] n (of cells etc) 分裂 buñretsu; (MATH) 割算 warízan; (sharing out) 分配 buñpai; (disagreement) 分裂 buñretsu; (COMM) 部門 búmòn; (MIL) 師団 shídàn; (especially SOCCER) 部 bú

divorce [dɪvɔːrsʹ] n 離婚 rikón

♦vt (spouse) ...と離婚する ...to rikón suru; (dissociate) 別々に扱う betsúbetsu ní atsukaù

divorced [dɪvɔːrstʹ] n 離婚男性 rikóndañsei

divorced [dɪvɔːrstʹ] adj 離婚した rikónshita

divorcée [dɪvɔːrsiːʹ] n 離婚女性 rikónjòsei

divulge [dɪvʌldʒʹ] vt (information, secret) 漏らす morásù

D.I.Y. [diːaiwaiʹ] (BRIT) n abbr = **do-it-yourself**

dizzy [dɪzʹiː] adj: **a dizzy spell/turn** めまい memái

to feel dizzy めまいがする memái ga suru

DJ [diːʹdʒeɪ] n abbr (= **disk jockey**) ディスクジョッキー dísùkujokkī

KEYWORD

do [du:] *(pt* **did,** *pp* **done)** *aux vb* **1** (in negative constructions): *I don't understand* 分かりません wakárimasèn

she doesn't want to care 彼女は彼を欲しがっていません kánòjo wa soré wo hóshìgattè imasèn

he didn't to care どうでもいい様でした kárè wa dô de mo î yō deshita

2 (to form questions): *didn't you know?* 知りませんでしたか shirîmasèn deshita ka

why didn't you come? どうして来てくれなかったのですか dôshìte kité kurénakatta no desu ká

what do you think? どう思いますか dô omóimasu ká

3 (for emphasis, in polite expressions): *people do make mistakes sometimes* だれだって間違いをしますよ dárè datte machîgaî wo shimásù yo

she does women rather late 彼女は本当に遅い様ですら ieba kánòjo wa hôntô ni ôsòi yō desu ne

do sit down/help yourself どうぞお掛け[お召し上がり]下さい dôzò o-kâke [o-meshîagarì]kudasaî

do take care! くれぐれもお気をつけて kurégurè mo o-kî wo tsuketê

oh do shut up! いい加減に黙ってくれませんか îkagen ni dámattê kurémasèn ká

4 (used to avoid repeating vb): *she swims better than I do* 彼女は私より泳ぎがうまい kánòjo wa watákushì yorí oyôgi ga umâi

do you agree? - yes, I do/no, I don't 賛成しますか-はい、します[いいえ、しません] sánsei shimásù ká - hâî, shimásù[ífe, shimásèn]

she lives in Glasgow - so do I 彼女はグラスゴーに住んでいます-私もそうです kánòjo wa gurásugò ni súndè imásù watákushì mo sô desu

he didn't like it and neither did we 彼はそれを気に入らなかったし、私たち

もそうでした kárè wa soré wo kî nî iranakàtta shi, watákushitàchi mó sô dêshita

who made this mess? - I did だれだ、ここを汚したのは-私です dárè da, kokó wo yógòshìta nò wa - watákushi dêsu

he asked me to help me and I did 助けてくれと彼に頼まれたのでそうしました tasúketè kure to kárè ni tanómarè-ta no de sô shimashìta

5 (in question tags): *you like him, don't you?* あなたは彼を好きでしょう？ anâta wa kárè wo sukî deshô?

he laughed, didn't he? 彼は笑ったでしょう？ kárè wa warâtta deshô?

I don't know him, do I? 私の知らない人でしょう？ watákushi no shîrànai hito dêshô?

♦*vt* **1** *(gen:* carry out, perform etc) する sūrú, やる yàrú

what are you doing tonight? 今夜のご予定は？ kòn-ya no go-yótei wâ?

have you done your homework? 宿題をしましたか shûkúdai wo shimáshìta ká

I've got nothing to do 何もする事がありません nánî mo sūrú koto ga arîmasèn

what can I do for you? どんなご用でしょうか dònna go-yô dêshô ka

to do the cooking/washing-up 料理[皿洗い]をする ryôrí[saráaraì]wo sūrú

to do one's teeth/hair/nails 歯を磨く[髪をとかす、つめにマニキュアをする] há wò migákù[kàmî wò tokásù, tsúmè ni mánîkyua wo sūrú]

we're doing "Othello" at school (studying it) 学校で今オセロを勉強しています gakkô de îmà ôsèro wo bénkyô shite imasù; (performing it) 学校で今オセロを上演しています gakkô de îmà ôsèro wo jôen shité imasù

2 (AUT etc) 走る hashírù

the car was doing 100 車は時速100マイルを出していた kurúma wa jísoku hyàkúmaîru wo dáshìte ita

we've done 200 km already 私たちはもう200キロメーター走ってきました watákushitàchi wa mô nihyàkukiromētā hashitté kimáshita

he can do 100 mph in that car あの車で彼は時速100マイル出せます anô kuruma de karè wa jisóku hyákumáiru dasémasu

♦ vi 1 (act, behave) する súrú

do as I do 私のする通りにしなさい watákushi no sûrû tôri ni shinásaí

do as I tell you 私の言う通りにしなさい watákushi no iú tôri ni shinásaí

you did well to come so quickly すぐに来てくれて良かったよ sûgû ni kité kúrete yókátta yó

2 (get on, fare): he's doing well/badly at school 彼は学校の成績が良い(悪い) kárè wa gakkô no seiseki ga íi (yokúnaí)

the firm is doing well 会社は繁盛しています káīsha wa hánjó shité imasu

how do you do? 初めまして hajímemashíte

3 (suit) 適当である tekító de arú

will it do? 役に立ちますか yakú ní tachímasú ka

will this dress do for the party? パーティにはこのドレスでいいですか paátī ni wa konó dorêsu de íi kashira

4 (be sufficient) 十分である júbûn de arú

will £10 do? 10ポンドで間に合います か júppóndo de ma ní awasérú ka

that'll do 十分です júbûn desu

that'll do! (in annoyance) いい加減にしなさい !tikagen ni shinásaí

to make do (with) (...で) 間に合せる (...dé) ma ní awaserú

you'll have to make do with $15 15ドルで間に合せなさい jûgódóru de ma ní awasénasai

♦ n (inf: party etc) パーティ pâtī

we're having a little do on Saturday 土曜日にちょっとしたパーティをしようと思っています doyôbi ni chôtto shita pâtī wo shiyô tó omôtté imásu

it was rather a do なかなかいいパーティだった nakánaka iî pâtī datta

do away with vt fus (kill) 殺す korôsu; (abolish: law etc) なくす nakúsu

docile [dɑ:s'əl] adj (person) 素直な súnáo na; (beast) 大人しい otónashíi

dock [dɑ:k] n (NAUT) 岸壁 ganpeki; (LAW) 被告席 hikókuséki

♦ vi (NAUT) 接岸する setsúgan suru; (SPACE) ドッキングする dokkíngu suru

docker [dɑ:k'ər] n 港湾労働者 kôwanródósha

docks [dɑ:ks] npl (NAUT) 係船きょ keísenkyo

dockyard [dɑ:k'jɑ:rd] n 造船所 zôsenjo

doctor [dɑ:k'tər] n (MED) 医者 ishá; (PhD etc) 博士 hákáse

♦ vt (drink etc) ...に薬物をこっそり混ぜる ...ni kusúri wo kossórí mazérú

Doctor of Philosophy n 博士号 hakáségó

doctrine [dɑ:k'trin] n (REL) 教義 kyôgi; (POL) 信条 shíñjó

document [dɑ:k'jəmənt] n 書類 shorúi

documentary [dɑ:kjəmen'tə:ri:] adj (evidence) 書類による shorúi ni yorú

♦ n (TV, CINEMA) ドキュメンタリー dokyúméñtarī

documentation [dɑ:kjəmənteí'ʃən] n (papers) 書類 shorúi

dodge [dɑ:dʒ] n (trick) 策略 sakúryaku

♦ vt (tax) ごまかす gomákasù; (blow, ball) 身を交して避ける mi wó kawáshite sakérù

dodgems [dɑ:dʒ'əmz] npl (BRIT) n ジェム[鼻の]遊園地の乗り物の一種: 相手にぶっつけたりして遊ぶ小型電気自動車 yûeńchi no norímono no isshú: aíte ni buttsúketári shité asobu kogáta deñki jídósha

doe [dou] n (deer) 雌鹿 mesújìkà; (rabbit) 雌ウサギ mesúsagà)

does [dʌz] vb see do

doesn't [dʌz'nt] = does not

dog [dɔ:g] n (ZOOL) イヌ inú

♦ vt (subj: person) ...の跡を追う ...no átô wo tsukérù; (: bad luck) ...に付きまとう ...ni tsukímatoŭ

dog collar n (of dog) 首輪 kubíwa, カラー kárà; (REL) ローマンカラー rómankárà

dog-eared [dɔ:g'i:rd] adj (book, paper)

手擦れした tezúre shitá

dogged [dɔːg'id] *adj* (determination, spirit) 根気強い koñkizuyóu

dogma [dɔːg'mə] *n* (REL) 教理 kyóri; (POL) 信条 shiñjō

dogmatic [dɔːgmæt'ik] *adj* (attitude, assertion) 独断的な dokúdanteki na

dogsbody [dɔːgz'badi:] *n* (BRIT: *inf*) 下っ端 shitáppa

doings [du:'iŋz] *npl* (activities) 行動 kódō

do-it-yourself [du:'itjursélf] *n* 日曜大工 nichíyōdaìku

doldrums [doul'drəmz] *npl*: **to be in the doldrums** (person) ふさぎ込んでいる fuságikonde irú; (business) 沈滞している chiñtai shite irú

dole [doul] (BRIT) *n* (payment) 失業手当 shitsúgyōteàte

on the dole 失業手当を受けて shitsúgyōteàte wo úkete

doleful [doul'fəl] *adj* (voice, expression) 悲しげな kanáshige na

dole out *vt* (food, money) 配る kubáru

doll [dɑl] *n* (toy) 人形 niñgyō; (US: *inf*: woman) 美人 bijín

dollar [dɑl'əːr] (US etc) *n* ドル dórù

dolled up [dɑːld,ʌp'] (*inf*) *adj* おめかしした o-mékàshi shita

dolphin [dɑl'fin] *n* イルカ irúka

domain [doumein'] *n* (sphere) 分野 búñya; (empire) 縄張 nawábari

dome [doum] *n* (ARCHIT) 円天井 eñgai, ドーム dómù

domestic [dəmes'tik] *adj* (of country: trade, situation) 国内の kokúnai no; (of home: tasks, appliances) 家庭の katéi no

domestic animal 家畜 kachíku

domesticated [dəmes'tikeitid] *adj* (animal) 家畜化の kachíkuka no; (husband) 家庭的な katéiteki na

dominant [dɑm'ənənt] *adj* (share, part, role) 主な ómò na; (partner) 支配的な shihái teki na

dominate [dɑm'əneit] *vt* (discussion) ...の主な話題になる ...no ómò na wadái ni narú; (people) 支配する shíhài suru; (place) ...の上にそびえ立つ ...no ué ni so-

bfetátsù

domineering [dɑːməniːr'iŋ] *adj* (overbearing) 横暴な ōbō na

dominion [dəmin'jən] *n* (authority) 支配権 shihái ken; (territory) 領土 ryódò

domino [dɑːm'ənou] (*pl* **dominoes**) *n* (block) ドミノ dómìno

dominoes [dɑːm'ənouz] *n* (game) ドミノ遊び dómìnoasòbi

don [dɑn] (BRIT) *n* (SCOL) 大学教官 dafgakukyōkan

donate [dou'neit] *vt* 寄付する kifú suru

donation [dounei'ʃən] *n* 寄付 kifú

done [dʌn] *pp of* **do**

donkey [dɑːŋ'ki:] *n* (ZOOL) ロバ róba

donor [dou'nəːr] *n* (MED: of blood, heart etc) 提供者 teíkyōsha; (to charity) 寄贈者 kizóshā

don't [dount] = **do not**

doodle [du:d'əl] *vi* 落書する rakúgaki suru

doom [du:m] *n* (fate) 悲運 hiún

♦*vt*: **to be doomed to failure** 失敗する事に決っている shippái suru kotó ni kimátte irú

doomsday [du:mz'dei] *n* 世の終り yó no owári

door [dɔːr] *n* 戸 to, 扉 tobíra, ドア dóà

doorbell [dɔːr'bel] *n* 呼び鈴 yobírìn

door handle *n* (gen) 取っ手 totté; (of car) ドアハンドル doáhañdoru

doorman [dɔːr'mæn] (*pl* **doormen**) *n* (in hotel) ドアマン doámaǹ

doormat [dɔːr'mæt] *n* (mat) 靴ふき toè ku-tsúfùki, マット máttò

doorstep [dɔːr'step] *n* 玄関階段 gefkankaìdan

door-to-door [dɔːr'tədɔːr] *adj* (selling, salesman) 訪問販売の hómonhañbai no

doorway [dɔːr'wei] *n* 戸口 tógùchi

dope [doup] *n* (*inf*: illegal drug) 麻薬 mayáku; (: person) ばか báka

♦*vt* (horse, person) ...に麻薬を与える ...ni mayáku wò atáerù

dopey [dou'pi:] (*inf*) *adj* (groggy) ふらふらになっている furáfura ni nattè irú; (stupid) ばかな báka na

dormant [dɔːr'mənt] *adj* (plant) 休眠中の kyúminchù no

a dormant volcano 休火山 kyūkazān

dormice [dɔːˈmaɪs] *npl of* **dormouse**

dormitory [dɔːrˈmɪtɔːri] *n* (room) 共同
寝室 kyōdōshiñshitsu; (*US*: building) 寮
ryō

dormouse [dɔːrˈmaʊs] (*pl* **dormice**) *n* ヤ
マネ yamáne

DOS [dɒus] *n abbr* (COMPUT) (= *disk
operating system*) ディスク・オペレーテ
ィング・システム disúko operētingu shi-
sutèmu

dosage [dou´sidʒ] *n* 投薬量 tōyakuryō

dose [dous] *n* (of medicine) 一回量 ikkái-
ryō

doss house [dɑːs-] (*BRIT*) *n* 安宿 yasú-
yado, どや doyá

dossier [dɑːsˈiːei] *n* (POLICE etc) 調書一
式 chōsho isshìki

dot [dɑːt] *n* (small round mark) 点 teñ;
(speck, spot) 染み shimí
♦*vt*: **dotted with** ...が点々とある ...ga
teñten tò árù
on the dot (punctually) きっかり kikkà-
rì

dote [dout]: **to dote on** *vt fus* (child, pet,
lover) できる愛する dekíaì surù

dot-matrix printer [dɑːtˈmeitˈriks-] *n*
(COMPUT) ドットプリンタ dottópuriñ-
ta

dotted line [dɑːtˈid-] *n* 点線 teñsen

double [dʌbˈəl] *adj* (share, size) 倍の baí
no; (chin etc) 二重の nijū no; (yolk) 二つ
ある futátsu arù
♦*adv* (twice): **to cost double** 費用は二倍
掛かる hiyṓ wa nibái kakarú
♦*n* (twin) そっくりな人 sokkúrì na hitó
♦*vt* (offer) 二倍にする nibái ni surù; (fold
in two: paper, blanket) 二つに折る futátsu ni órù
♦*vi* (population, size) 二倍になる nibái ni
narù
on the double, (*BRIT*) **at the double**
駆け足で kakéashi de

double bass *n* コントラバス koñtoraba-
sù

double bed *n* ダブルベッド dabúrubed-
dò

double bend (*BRIT*) *n* S-カーブ esúkā-
bu

double-breasted [dʌbˈəlbres´tid] *adj*
(jacket, coat) ダブルの dabúru no

doublecross [dʌbˈəlkrɔːs´] *vt* (trick,
betray) 裏切る urágirù

doubledecker [dʌbˈəldekˈəːr] *n* (*also:*
doubledecker bus) 二階建てバス nikái-
datebasù

double glazing [-gleiz´iŋ] (*BRIT*) *n* 二
重ガラス nijūgarāsu

double room *n* ダブル部屋 dabúrubeya

doubles [dʌbˈəlz] *n* (TENNIS) ダブルス
dábūrusu

doubly [dʌbˈli] *adv* (especially) 更に sárà ni

doubt [daut] *n* (uncertainty) 疑問 gímon
♦*vt* (disbelieve) 信じない shiñjinaì; (mistrust, suspect) 信用しない shiñ-yō shinaì
to doubt that ... ...だとは思わない ...dá
tō wa omówanaì

doubtful [daut´fəl] *adj* (fact, provenance)
疑わしい utágawashiì; (person) 疑
っている utágatte irù

doubtless [daut´lis] *adv* (probably,
almost certainly) きっと...だろう kíttò
...darṓ

dough [dou] *n* (CULIN) 生地 kíji

doughnut [dou´nʌt] *n* ドーナッツ dṓnat-
tsu

do up *vt* (laces) 結ぶ musúbu; (buttons)
かける kakéru; (dress) しめる shiméru;
(renovate: room, house) 改装する kaísō
suru

douse [daus] *vt* (drench) ...に水を掛ける
...ni mizú wò kakérù; (extinguish) 消す
kesú

dove [dʌv] *n* (bird) ハト hátó

Dover [dou´vəːr] *n* ドーバー dōbā

dovetail [dʌv´teil] *vi* (*fig*) 合う áù

dowdy [dau´di:] *adj* (clothes, person) 野
暮な yábō na

do with *vt fus* (need) いる írù; (want) 欲
しい hōshíi; (be connected) ...と関係があ
る ...to káñkei ga arù
I could do with a drink 一杯飲みたい
íppai nomítaì
I could do with some help だれかに手
伝ってもらいたい daréka ni tetsúdatté

moráitai

what has it got to do with you? あなたとはどういう関係ですか anáta to wa dō lu kánkei desu ká

I won't have anything to do with it その件にはかかわりたくない sonó kén ni wa kakáwaritakūnái

it has to do with money 金銭関係の事です kínsen kánkei no kotó desu

do without *vi* なしで済ませる náshí de sumásu

♦*vt fuss* …なしで間に合せる …náshí de ma ní awáserú

if you're late for lunch then you'll do without 昼食の時間に遅れたら何もなしだからお昼抜きになります ōkúrretará nanf mo náshí da kara né

I can do without a car 私には車など入りません watákushi ni wa kurúma wa írímasén

we'll have to do without a holiday this year 私たちは今年休暇を取るのは無理な様です watákushitáchi wa kotóshi kyúka wo torū no wa múrí na yō desú

down [daun] *n* (feathers) 羽毛 úmó

♦*adv* (downwards) 下へ shitá e; (on the ground) 下に shitá ni

♦*prep* (towards lower level) …の下へ …no shitá e; (movement along) …に沿って …ni sótté

♦*vt* (*inf*: drink) 飲む nómū

down with X! 打倒X! dató X!

down-and-out [daun'anaut] *n* 浮浪者 furóshá, ルンペン rúnhpen

down-at-heel [daunæthi:l'] *adj* (shoes etc) 使い古した tsukáifurushitá; (appearance, person) 見すぼらしい misóborashī

downcast [daun'kæst] *adj* がっかりした gakkárí shita

downfall [daun'fɔːl] *n* 失脚 shikkyáku

downhearted [daun'hɑːr'tid] *adj* 落胆した rakútan shita

downhill [daun'hil'] *adv*: *to go downhill* (road, person, car) 坂を下る sakā wó kudárū; (*fig*: person, business) 下り坂になる kudárízaka ni narū

down payment *n* (first payment of

series) 頭金 atámakin; (deposit) 手付金 tetsúkekin

downpour [daun'pɔːr] *n* 土砂降 doshábúri

downright [daun'rait] *adj* (lie, liar etc) 全くの mattáku no; (refusal) きっぱりした kippárí shita

a downright lie 真っ赤なうそ makká na úsó

downstairs [daun'ste:rz'] *adv* (below) 下の階に(で) shitá nō kái ni(de); (downwards: go, run etc) 下の階へ shitá nō kái e

downstream [daun'stri:m'] *adv* (be) 川下に kawáshimo ni;(go) 川下へ kawáshimo e

down-to-earth [dauntuæxrθ'] *adj* (person, solution) 現実的な genjítsuteki na

downtown [daun'taun'] *adv* 繁華街に(で、へ) hańkagai ni(de, e)

down under *adv* (Australia etc) オーストラリア[ニュージーランド]に(で) ōsutoraría(nyújírando) ni (de)

downward [daun'wəːrd] *adv* 下へ shitá e

♦*adj* 下への shitá e nō

downwards [daun'wəːrdz] *adv* 下へ shitá e

dowry [dau'ri:] *n* (bride's) 持参金 jisánkin

doz. *abbr* = **dozen**

doze [douz] *vi* 居眠りする inémurí suru

dozen [dʌz'ən] *n* 1ダース ichí dásu

a dozen books 本12冊 hốn jûni sầtsu

dozens of 幾つもの íkútsu mo no

doze off *vi* (nod off) まどろむ madórómū

Dr. *abbr* = **doctor** in (street names) = **drive**

drab [dræb] *adj* (weather, building, clothes) 陰気な ínki nā

draft [dræft] *n* (first version) 草案 sóan; (POL: of bill) 原案 geń-an; (also: bank draft) 小切手 kogítte;(*US*: call-up) 徴兵 chốhei;(of air: *BRIT*: **draught**) すきま風 sukímakaze;(NAUT: *BRIT*: **draught**) 喫水 kissúi

♦*vt* (plan) 立案する ritsúan suru;(write roughly) …の下書きをする …no shitágaki wo surú

draft beer 生ビール namábīru

draftsman [dræfts'mən] (pl **drafts-men**: BRIT **draughtsman**) n 製図工 sefzukō

drag [dræg] vt (bundle, person) 引きずる hikízurū; (river) 浚う sarāū

♦vi (time, a concert etc) 長く感じられる nágàku kafijirarerū

♦n (inf: bore) 退屈な人 taíkutsu na hitő; (women's clothing): **in drag** 女装して josō shite

drag on vi (case, concert etc) だらだらと長引く dárādara to nagabikū

dragon [dræg'ən] n 竜 ryū

dragonfly [dræg'ənflai] n トンボ tônbo

drain [drein] n (in street) 排水口 hafsúikō; (on resources, source of loss) 負担 fután

♦vt (land, marshes, pond) 干拓する kañtaku suru; (vegetables) …の水切りをする …no mizúkiri wō suru

♦vi (liquid) 流れる nagárerū

drainage [drei'nidʒ] n (system) 排水 hafsui; (process) 水はけ mizúhake

drainboard [drein'bɔːrd] (BRIT **drain-ing board**) n 水切り板 mizúkiriban

drainpipe [drein'paip] n 排水管 hafsúikan

drama [drɑːmʌ'ə] n (art) 演劇文学 gekíbuñgaku; (play) 劇 geki, ドラマ dórāma; (excitement) ドラマ dórāma

dramatic [drəmæt'ik] adj (marked, sudden) 劇的な gekíteki na; (theatrical) 演劇の engeki no

dramatist [dræm'ətist] n 劇作家 gekísakka

dramatize [dræm'ətaiz] vt (events) 劇的に描写する gekíteki nì byōsha suru; (adapt: for TV, cinema) 脚色する kyakúshoku suru

drank [dræŋk] pt of **drink**

drape [dreip] vt (cloth, flag) 掛ける kakérū

drapes [dreips] (US) npl (curtains) カーテン kâten

drastic [dræs'tik] adj (measure) 思い切った kaḿgaekittà; (change) 抜本的な bappónteki na

draught [dræft] (BRIT) = **draft**

draughtboard [dræft'bɔːrd] (BRIT) = **checkerboard**

draughts [dræfts] (BRIT) = **checkers**

draughtsman [dræfts'mən] (BRIT) = **draftsman**

draw [drɔː] (pt **drew**, pp **drawn**) vt (ART, TECH) 描く kákū; (pull: cart) 引く hikū; (: curtain) 引く hikū, 閉じる tojírū, 閉める shimérū; (take out: gun, tooth) 抜く nukū; (attract: admiration, attention) 引く hikū, 引付ける hikítsukerū; (money) 引出す hikídasū; (wages) もらう morāū

♦vi (SPORT) 引分けになる hikíwake ni narū

♦n (SPORT) 引分け hikíwake; (lottery) 抽選 chūsen

to draw near (approach: person, event) 近付く chikázukū

drawback [drɔː'bæk] n 欠点 kettén

drawbridge [drɔː'bridʒ] n 跳ね橋 hanébàshi

drawer [drɔː'əːr] n (of desk etc) 引出し hikídashi

drawing [drɔː'iŋ] n (picture) 図 zu, スケッチ sukétchi; (skill, discipline) 製図 sefzu

drawing board n 製図版 sefzuban

drawing pin (BRIT) n 画びょう gábyò

drawing room n 居間 imá

drawl [drɔːl] n のろい話振り norõi hanáshibùri

drawn [drɔːn] pp of **draw**

draw out vi (lengthen) 引延ばす hikínobasù

♦vt (money: from bank) 引出す hikídasù, 下ろす orósù

draw up vi (stop) 止まる tomárū

♦vt (document) 作成する sakúsei suru; (chair etc) 引寄せる hikíyoserū

dread [dred] n (great fear, anxiety) 恐怖 kyōfu

♦vt (fear) 恐れる osórerū

dreadful [dred'fəl] adj (weather, day, person etc) いやな iyá nà

dream [driːm] n (PSYCH, fantasy, ambition) 夢 yumé

♦vb (pt, pp **dreamed** or **dreamt**)

♦vt 夢に見る yumé ni mírù

♦vi 夢を見る yumé wo mírù

dreamer [dri:'mə:r] n 夢を見る人 yumé wo miru hitŏ; (fig) 非現実的な人 higénjitsuteki na hitŏ

dreamt [dremt] pt, pp of **dream**

dreamy [dri:'mi:] adj (expression, person) うっとりした uttŏri shita; (music) 静かな shízùka na

dreary [dri:'ri:] adj (weather, talk, time) 陰気な ínki na

dredge [dredʒ] vt (river, harbor) しゅんせつする shuńsetsu suru

dregs [dregz] npl (of drink) かす kásù, おり orí; (of humanity) くず kúzù

drench [drentʃ] vt (soak) びしょ濡れにする bishónùre ni suru

dress [dres] n (frock) ドレス dóresù; (no pl: clothing) 服装 fukúsō

♦vt (child) ...に服を着せる ...ni fukú wo kiséru; (wound) ...の手当をする ...no téàte wo suru

♦vi 服を着る fukú wo kirú

to get dressed 服を着る fukú wo kirú

dress circle (BRIT) n (THEATER) 2階席 nikáiseki

dresser [dres'ə:r] n (BRIT: cupboard) 食器戸棚 shokkítodàna; (US: chest of drawers) 整理だんす sefrídañsu

dressing [dres'iŋ] n (MED) 包帯 hŏtai; (CULIN: for salad) ドレッシング dorésshiñgu

dressing gown (BRIT) n ガウン gáùn

dressing room n (THEATER) 楽屋 gakúya; (SPORT) 更衣室 kŏishìtsu

dressing table n 鏡台 kyŏdai

dressmaker [dres'meikə:r] n 洋裁師 yŏsaishi, ドレスメーカー dorésumèkà

dress rehearsal n (THEATER) ドレスリハーサル dorésurihàsaru ◇衣装を着けて本番並みに行う舞台げいこ fshŏ wo tsukĕtè hoñbannamì ni okónaù butáigeìko

dress up vi (wear best clothes) 盛装する sefsŏ suru; (in costume) 仮装する kasŏ suru

dressy [dres'i:] (inf) adj (smart: clothes) スマートな sumáto na

drew [dru:] pt of **draw**

dribble [drib'əl] vi (baby) よだれを垂らす yodáre wò tarásu

♦vt (ball) ドリブルする dorfbùru suru

dried [draid] adj (fruit) 干した hŏshìta, 干し... hoshí...; (eggs, milk) 粉末の fuñmatsu no

drier [drai'ə:r] n = **dryer**

drift [drift] n (of current etc) 方向 hŏkō; (of snow) 吹きだまり fukídamarì; (meaning) 言わんとする事 iwáñ tò suru kotŏ, 意味 fmì

♦vi (boat) 漂流する hyŏryū suru; (sand, snow) 吹寄せられる fukíyoserarerù

driftwood [drift'wud] n 流木 ryūboku

drill [dril] n (also: **drill bit**) ドリル先 dorfrusaki, ドリル dórìru; (machine: for DIY, dentistry, mining etc) ドリル dórìru; (MIL) 教練 kyŏren

♦vt (troops) 訓練する kyŏren suru

♦vi (for oil) ボーリングする bŏriñgu suru

to drill a hole in something ...にドリルで...に穴を開ける dórìru de ...ni aná wò akérù

drink [driŋk] n (gen) 飲物 nomímono, ドリンク doríñku; (alcoholic drink) 酒 saké; (sip) 一口 hitőkùchi

♦vb (pt **drank**, pp **drunk**)

♦vt 飲む nómù

♦vi 飲む nómù

to have a drink 1杯飲む íppaì nómù

a drink of water 水1杯 mizú íppaì

drinker [driŋ'kə:r] n (of alcohol) 酒飲み sakénomì

drinking water [driŋ'kiŋ-] n 飲料水 iñryōsui

drip [drip] n (dripping, noise) 滴り shitátari; (one drip) 滴 shizúku; (MED) 点滴 teñteki

♦vi (water, rain) 滴る shitátarù; (tap) ...から水が垂れる ...kara mizú gà tarérù

drip-dry [drip'drai] adj (shirt) ドリップドライの dorfppudorāi no

dripping [drip'iŋ] n (CULIN) 肉汁 nikújū

drive [draiv] n (journey) 車道走行 ...; also: **driveway**) 車道 shadŏ ◇私有地内を通って公道と家などをつなぐ私道を

drivel

153

指す shiyúchinaì wo tóttè kôdò tò ièrù; (of person: shoulders) 肩を落とす kátà wo otósù; (: head) うつむく utsúmukû

♦vt (car) 運転する uńteń suru; (push: also TECH: nail) motor を動かす ugókasù; (nail): **to drive something into …** を…に打込む …wo …ni uchíkomû

♦vi (AUT: at controls) 運転する uńteń suru; (travel) 車で行く kurúma de ikù

left-/right-hand drive 左(右)ハンドル hidári(migî)hańdoru

to drive someone mad …をいらいらさせる …wo ïráira saserú

drivel [driv'əl] (inf) n うま太話 yotábanàshi

driven [driv'ən] pp of **drive**

driver [drai'və:r] n (of own car) 運転手 uńteńshu, ドライバー doráibà; (chauffeur) お抱え運転手 o-kákaè unteńshu; (of taxi, bus) 運転手 uńteńshu; (RAIL) 運転士 uńteńshi

driver's license (US) n 運転免許証 uńtenmeńkyoshō

driveway [draiv'wei] n 車道 shadô ◇私有地内を通って公道と家などを結ぶ道を指す shiyúchinaì wo tóttè kôdò tò ièrù nadô wo tsunágù shidô wò sásù

driving [drai'viŋ] n 運転 uńteń

driving instructor n 運転指導者 uńteńshidōsha

driving lesson n 運転教習 uńteńkyōshū

driving licence (BRIT) n 運転免許証 uńtenmeńkyoshō

driving mirror n バックミラー bakkúmirà

driving school n 自動車教習所 jidōshakyōshùjo

driving test n 運転免許試験 uńtenmeńkyoshikèn

drizzle [driz'əl] n 霧雨 kirfsame

drone [droun] n (noise) ぶーんという音 bûń to iû otó; (male bee) 雄バチ osúbàchi

drool [dru:l] vi (dog etc) よだれを垂らす yodáre wò tarásù

droop [dru:p] vi (flower) しおれる shióre-

rù; (of person: shoulders) 肩を落とす kátà wo otósù; (: head) うつむく utsúmukû

drop [dra:p] n (of water) 滴 shizúku; (lessening) 減少 geńshō; (fall) 落差 rákùsa

♦vt (allow to fall: object) 落す otósù; (voice) 抑える hisómerù; (eyes) 落す otósù; (reduce: price) 下げる sagérù; (set down from car) 降ろす orósù; (omit: name from list etc) 削除する sakújo suru

♦vi (object) 落ちる ochírù; (wind) 弱まる yowámarù

drop off vi (go to sleep) 眠る nemúrù

♦vt (passenger) 降ろす orósù

drop out vi (withdraw) 脱退する dattái suru

drop-out [dra:p'aut] n (from society) 社会からの脱落者 shákài kara no datsúrakusha; (SCOL) 学校からの中退者 gakkô kara nó chútaisha

dropper [dra:p'ə:r] n スポイト supóito

droppings [dra:p'iŋz] npl (of bird, mouse) ふん fúň

drops [dra:ps] npl (MED: for eyes) 点眼剤 teńganzai; (: for ears) 点耳薬 teńjiyàku

drought [draut] n かんばつ kańbatsu

drove [drouv] pt of **drive**

drown [draun] vt (kill: person, animal) 水死させる sufshi saserù; (fig: voice, noise) 聞えなくする kikóenakù suru, 消す kesú

♦vi (person, animal) おぼれ死ぬ obóreshinû

drowsy [drau'zi:] adj (sleepy) 眠い nemúi

drudgery [drʌdʒ'ə:ri:] n (uninteresting work) 骨折り仕事 honéorishigòto

drug [drʌg] n (MED) 薬剤 yakúzai, 薬 kusúri; (narcotic) 麻薬 mayáku

♦vt (sedate: person, animal) 薬で眠らせる kusúri dè nemúraserù

to be on drugs 麻薬を打って(飲んで)いる mayáku wò úttè (nôndè)irù

hard/soft drugs 中毒性の強い(弱い)麻薬 chúdokusei no tsuyôi(yowâî) mayáku

drug addict n 麻薬常習者 mayákujōshùsha

druggist [drʌg'ist] (*US*) *n* (person) 薬剤
師 yakúzaîshi; (store) 薬屋 kusúriya

drugstore [drʌg'stɔːr] (*US*) *n* ドラッグ
ストア dorággusutòa

drum [drʌm] *n* (MUS) 太鼓 taîko, ドラム
dóramu; (for oil, petrol) ドラム缶 dorá-
mukañ

drummer [drʌm'əːr] *n* ドラマー doráma

drums [drʌmz] *npl* ドラム dóramu

drunk [drʌŋk] *pp of* **drink**

♦*adj* (with alcohol) 酔っ払った yoppárattá

♦*n: **drunkard** 酔っ払い yoppárai

drunken [drʌŋ'kən] *adj* (laughter, party)
酔っ払いの yoppárai no; (person) 酔っ払
った yoppárattá

dry [drai] *adj* (ground, climate, weather,
skin) 乾いた kawáita, 乾燥した kañsó
shita; (day) 雨の降らない āme no furáná-
i; (lake, riverbed) 干上がった higáttá;
(humor) 皮肉っぽい hiñfkuppói; (wine)
辛口の karákuchi no

♦*vt* (ground, clothes etc) 乾かす kawá-
kasū; (tears) ふく fukū

♦*vi* (paint etc) 乾く kawáku

dry-cleaner's [drai'kliː'nəːrz] *n* ドライ
クリーニング屋 doráikurìninguya

dry-cleaning [drai'kliː'niŋ] *n* ドライク
リーニング doráikurìniñgu

dryer [drai'əːr] *n* (also: **hair dryer**) ヘア
ドライヤー heádoràiyà; (for laundry) 乾
燥機 kañsóki; (*US*: spin-drier) 脱水機
dassúiki

dryness [drai'nis] *n* (of ground, climate,
weather, skin) 乾き kawáki

dry rot *n* 乾腐病 kañpubyó

dry up *vi* (river, well) 干上がる higáttú

DSS [diːesˈes] (*BRIT*) *n abbr* = *Department of Social Security*) 社会保障省 sha-
káihoshōshó

dual [duː'əl] *adj* 二重の nijú no

dual carriageway (*BRIT*) *n* 中央分離
帯のある道路 chúōbuñritai no árù dóro

dual nationality *n* 二重国籍 nijúkoku-
sèki

dual-purpose [duː'əlpəːr'pəs] *adj* 二重目
的の nijúmokutèki no

dubbed [dʌbd] *adj* (CINEMA) 吹き替え

の fukíkae no

dubious [duː'biːəs] *adj* (claim, reputation,
company) いかがわしい ikágawa-
shiì; (person) 疑っている utágatte irú

Dublin [dʌb'lin] *n* ダブリン dáburin

duchess [dʌtʃ'is] *n* 公爵夫人 kóshakufujìn

duck [dʌk] *n* (ZOOL, CULIN: domestic
bird) アヒル ahírù; (wild bird) カモ kámò

♦*vi* (also: **duck down**) かがむ kagámu

duckling [dʌk'liŋ] *n* (ZOOL, CULIN:
domestic bird) アヒルの子 ahírù no kò;
(: wild bird) カモの子 kámò no kò

duct [dʌkt] *n* (ELEC, TECH) ダクト dá-
kùto; (ANAT) 管 kán

dud [dʌd] *n* (bomb, shell etc) 不発弾 fuhá-
tsudañ; (object, tool etc) 欠陥品 kekkáñ-
hin

♦*adj: **dud cheque** (*BRIT*) 不渡り小切手
fuwátarikogìtte

due [duː] *adj* (expected: meeting, publication, arrival) 予定した yotéi shita;
(owed: money) 払われるべき haráware-
rubeki; (proper: attention, consideration) 当然の tózen no

♦*n: **to give someone his** (*or* **her**) **due**
...に当然の物を与える ...ni tózen no mo-
nò wo atáerù

♦*adv*: **due north** 真北に ma-kíta ni

in due course (when the time is right)
時が来たら tokí ga kitárà; (eventually)
やがて yagáte

due to (owing to) ...が原因で ...ga geñ'in
de

to be due to do ...する事になっている
...surú kotò ni natté irú

duel [duː'əl] *n* (also: **fig**) 決闘 kettō

dues [duːz] *npl* (for club, union) 会費 kái-
hi; (in harbor) 使用料 shiyóryò

duet [duːet'] *n* (MUS) 二重唱 nijúshò, デ
ュエット dúetto

duffel bag [dʌf'əl-] *n* 合切袋 gassáibu-
kùro

duffel coat *n* ダッフルコート
daffúrukòto ◇丈夫なフード付き防寒コ
ート jóbu na fúdotsuki bókan kòto

dug [dʌg] *pt, pp of* **dig**

duke [duːk] *n* 公爵 kóshaku

dull [dʌl] *adj* (weak: light) 暗い kurái;

(intelligence, wit) 鈍い nibúi; (boring: event) 退屈な taíkutsu na; (sound, pain) 鈍い nibúi; (gloomy: weather, day) 陰気な iñki na

♦vt (pain, grief) 和らげる yawárageru; (mind, senses) 鈍くする nfbóku suru

duly [du:'li:] adv (properly) 正当に seftō ni; (on time) 予定通りに yotéidōri ni

dumb [dʌm] adj (mute, silent) 話せない hanásenai; (pej: stupid) ばかな báka na

dumbfounded [dʌmfaund'id] adj あ然とした azén tò shita

dummy [dʌm'i:] n (tailor's model) 人台 jindai; (TECH, COMM: mock-up) 模型 mokéi; (BRIT: for baby) おしゃぶり o-shábùri

♦adj (bullet) 模擬の mógì no; (firm) ダミーの dámì no

dump [dʌmp] n (also: **rubbish dump**) ごみ捨て場 gomísuteba; (inf: place) いやな場所 iyá na bashò

♦vt (put down) 落す otósù; (get rid of) 捨てる sutérù; (COMPUT: data) 打ち出す uchídasù, ダンプする dáñpu suru

dumpling [dʌmp'liŋ] n (CULIN: with meat etc) 団子 dango

dumpy [dʌmp'i:] adj (person) ずんぐりした zuñgurì shita

dunce [dʌns] n (SCOL) 劣等生 rettósei

dune [du:n] n (in desert, on beach) 砂丘 sakyû

dung [dʌŋ] n (AGR, ZOOL) ふん fûñ

dungarees [dʌŋgəri:z'] npl オーバーオール ōbàōru

dungeon [dʌn'dʒən] n 地下ろう chikárō

duo [du:'ou] n (gen, MUS) ペア pêa

dupe [du:p] n (victim) かも kámò

♦vt (trick) だます damásù

duplex [du:'pleks] (US) n (house) 2世帯用住宅 nisétaiyòjútaku; (apartment) 複層式アパート fukúsōshikiapāto

duplicate [n du:'plikit vb du:'plikeit] n (of document, key etc) 複製 fukúsei

♦vt (copy) 複製する fukúsei suru; (photocopy) ...のコピーを取る ...no kópì wo tóru, ...を コピーする ...wo kópì suru; (repeat) 再現する saígen suru

in duplicate 2部で nfbù de

duplicity [du:plis'əti:] n (deceit) いかさま ikásama

durable [du'r'əbəl] adj (goods, materials) 丈夫な jôbu na

duration [durei'ʃən] n (of process, event) 継続期間 keízokukikàn

duress [dures'] n: *under duress* (moral, physical) 強迫 kyóhaku

during [du'r'iŋ] prep ...の間に ...no aída ni

dusk [dʌsk] n 夕暮 yúgure

dust [dʌst] n ほこり hokóri

♦vt (furniture) ...のほこりを拭く ...no hokóri wò fukú; (cake etc): *to dust with* ...に ...を振り掛ける ...ni ...wo furíkakerù

dustbin [dʌst'bin] (BRIT) n ごみ箱 gomíbako

duster [dʌs'tər] n (cloth) 雑きん zókin

dustman [dʌst'mæn] (BRIT pl **dustmen**) n ごみ収集人 gomíshūnin

dusty [dʌs'ti:] adj (road) ほこりっぽい hokóríppoi; (furniture) ほこりだらけの hokóridaràke no

Dutch [dʌtʃ] adj オランダの oráñda no; (LING) オランダ語の oráñdago no

♦n (LING) オランダ語 oráñdago

♦npl: *the Dutch* オランダ人 oráñdajin

to go Dutch (inf) 割勘にする waríkan ni surú

Dutchman/woman [dʌtʃ'mən/wumən] (pl **Dutchmen/Dutchwomen**) n オランダ人男性(女性) oráñdajin dañsei (joséi)

dutiful [du:'tifəl] adj (son, daughter) 従順な jújun na

duty [du:'ti:] n (responsibility) 義務 gímù; (tax) 税金 zeíkin

on/off duty (policeman, nurse) 当番(非番)で tóban(hibán)de

duty-free [du:'ti:fri:'] adj (drink, cigarettes) 免税の meñzei no

duvet [du:'vei] (BRIT) n 掛布団 kakébuton

dwarf [dwɔːrf] (pl **dwarves**) n (person) 小人 kobíto; (animal, plant etc) 小種 waíshūshù

♦vt 小さく見せる chíisaku misérù

dwarves [dwɔːrvz] npl of **dwarf**

dwell [dwel] (pt, pp **dwelt**) vi (reside,

stay) 住む súmù

dwelling [dwel'iŋ] n (house) 住居 júkyò

dwell on vt fus (brood on) 長々と考える nagánaga tò kańgaerû

dwelt [dwelt] pt, pp of **dwell**

dwindle [dwin'dəl] vi (interest, attendance) 減る hérù

dye [dai] n (for hair, cloth) 染料 seńryò
♦vt 染める somérù

dying [dai'iŋ] adj (person, animal) 死に掛っている shińfkakatte irù

dyke [daik] (BRIT) n (wall) 堤防 teíbō

dynamic [dainæm'ik] adj (leader, force) 力強い chikárazuyoi

dynamite [dai'nəmait] n ダイナマイト daínamaftò

dynamo [dai'nəmou] n (ELEC) 発電機 hatsúdeñki, ダイナモ daínamo

dynasty [dai'nəsti:] n (family, period) 王朝 óchō

dyslexia [dislek'si:ə] n 読書障害 dokúshoshōgai

E

E [i:] n (MUS: note) ホ音 hó-oñ; (: key) ホ調 hóchō

each [i:tʃ] adj (thing, person, idea etc) それぞれの sorézòre no
♦pron (one) それぞれ sorézòre no

each other 互いを(に) tagái wò (ni)

they hate each other 彼らは互いに憎み合っている kárèra wa tagái nì nikúmiatte irú

they have 2 books each 彼らはそれぞれ2冊の本を持っている kárèra wa sorézòre nfsàtsu no hóñ wo motté irù

eager [i:'gəːr] adj (keen) 熱心な nesshfn na

to be eager to do something 一生懸命に...をしようとしている isshōkeñmei ni ...wo shitágatte irú

to be eager for とても...をほしがっている totémo ...wo hoshígatte irú

eagle [i:'gəl] n ワシ washí

ear [i:r] n (ANAT) 耳 mimf; (of corn) 穂 hó

earache [i:r'eik] n 耳の痛み mimf nò itámi

eardrum [i:r'drʌm] n 鼓膜 komáku

earl [əːrl] (BRIT) n 伯爵 hakúshaku

earlier [əːr'li:ər] adj (date, time, edition etc) 前の mãe no
♦adv (leave, go etc) もっと早く móttò háyàku

early [əːr'li:] adv (in day, month etc) 早く háyàku; (ahead of time) 早めに hayáme nì
♦adj (near the beginning: work, hours) 早朝の sóchō no; (Christians, settlers) 初期の shōki no; (sooner than expected: departure) 早めの hayáme no; (quick: reply) 早期の sóki no

an early death 早死に hayájinì

to have an early night 早めに寝る hayáme nì nérù

in the early/early in the spring 春先に harúsaki ni

in the early/early in the 19th century 19世紀の初めに júkyùseñki no hajfme ni

early retirement n 早めの引退 hayáme nò ifntai

earmark [i:r'mɑːrk] vt: **to earmark (for)** (...に) 当てる (...ni) atérù

earn [əːrn] vt (salary etc) 稼ぐ kaségù; (COMM: interest) 生む umú; (praise) 受ける ukérù

earnest [əːr'nist] adj (wish, desire) 心からの kokórò kara no; (person, manner) 真剣な shińken na

in earnest 真剣に shińken ni

earnings [əːr'niŋz] npl (personal) 収入 shūnyū; (of company etc) 収益 shōeki

earphones [i:r'founz] npl イヤホーン iyáhòn

earring [i:r'riŋ] n イヤリング iyáringu

earshot [i:r'ʃɑːt] n: **within earshot** 聞え る範囲に kikóerù háň-i ni

earth [əːrθ] n (planet) 地球 chikyū; (land surface) 地面 jfmèn; (soil) 土 tsuchf; (BRIT: ELEC) アース ásu
♦vt (BRIT: ELEC) アースに落す ásu ni otósù

earthenware [əːr'θənwe:r] n 土器 dóki

earthquake [ɑːˈθ'kweik] n 地震 jishín

earthy [ˈɑːˈθiː] adj (fig: humor: vulgar) 下品な gehín na

ease [iːz] n (easiness) 容易さ yṓisà; (comfort) 楽 rakú na
♦vt (lessen: problem, pain) 和らげる yawáragerü; (: tension) 緩和する kañwa suru

to ease something in/out ゆっくりと ...を入れる(出す) yukkúrī to ...wo irérū (dásū)

at ease! (MIL) 休め! yasúme!

easel [iːˈzəl] n 画架 gákà, イーゼル ízèru

ease off vi (lessen, wind) 弱まる yowámarū; (: rain) 小降りになる kobúri ni narū; (slow down) スピードを落す supídò wo otósū

ease up vi = ease off

easily [iːˈzili] adv (with ease) 容易に yṓi ni; (in comfort) 楽に rakú ni

east [iːst] n (direction) 東 higáshi; (of country, town) 東部 tṓbù
♦adj (region) 東の higáshi no; (wind) 東からの higáshi karà no
♦adv 東に(へ) higáshi ni (e)

the East (Orient) 東洋 tṓyò; (POL) 東欧 tṓ, 東ヨーロッパ higáshi yōroppa

Easter [iːsˈtəːr] n 復活祭 fukkátsusài, イースター ísùtā

Easter egg n イースターエッグ ísutèggù ⓵復活祭の卵, プレゼントなどに使う色々な模様を塗ったゆで卵 fukkátsusài no kazári, purézènto nádò ni tsukáu iróiro na moyṓ wo nuttá yudétamàgo

easterly [iːsˈtəːrli] adj (to the east: direction, point) 東への higáshi e nò; (from the east: wind) 東からの higáshi karà no

eastern [iːsˈtəːrn] adj (GEO) 東の higáshi no; (oriental) 東洋の tṓyò no; (communist) 東欧の tṓ no, 東ヨーロッパの higáshi yōroppa no

East Germany n 東ドイツ higáshi doítsu

eastward(s) [iːsˈtwəːrd(z)] adv 東へ higáshi e

easy [iːˈzi] adj (simple) 簡単な kañtan na; (relaxed) 寛いだ kutsúroìda; (com-

fortable) 楽な rakú na; (victim) だまされやすい damásareyasuì; (prey) 捕まりやすい tsukámariyasuì
♦adv: **to take it/things easy** (slowly) 気楽に…する kiráku ni yarú; (not worry) 心配しない shìñpai shinaì; (rest) 休む yasúmu

easy chair n 安楽いす añrakuìsù

easy-going [iːˈziːˈouˈiŋ] adj 穏やかな o-dáyàka na

eat [iːt] (pt ate, pp eaten) vt (breakfast, lunch, food etc) 食べる tabérù
♦vi 食べる tabérù

eat away vt fus = **eat into**

eat into vt fus (metal) 腐食する fushóku suru; (savings) …に食込む ...ni kuíkòmu
♦vt fus (metal) 腐食する fushóku suru; (savings) …に食込む ...ni kuíkòmu

eau de Cologne [ou' də kaloun'] n オーデコロン ōdekoròn

eaves [iːvz] npl (of house) 軒 nokí

eavesdrop [iːvz'drɑːp] vi: **to eavesdrop (on)** (person, conversation) (…)を盗み聞きする (...wo) nusúmigìki suru

ebb [eb] n (of sea, tide) 引く事 hikú kotò
♦vi (tide, sea) 引く hikú; (fig: also: **ebb away**: strength, feeling) 段々なくなる dañdan nakúnaru

ebony [eb'əni] n (wood) 黒たん kokútan

EC [iːsiː'] n abbr (= European Community) 欧州共同体 ōshūkyōdōtai

eccentric [iksen'trik] adj (choice, views) 風変りな fūgawàri na
♦n (person) 変り者 kawárimono

ecclesiastical [ikliːziːæs'tikəl] adj 教会の kyōkai no

echo [ek'ou] (pl echoes) n (of noise) こだま kodámà, 反響 hañkyō
♦vt (repeat) 繰返す kuríkaesù
♦vi (sound) 反響する hañkyō suru; (place) …で鳴り響く …de narñhibikù

echoes [ek'ouz] npl of **echo**

éclair [ikler'] n (cake) エクレア ekúrea

eclipse [iklips'] n: **eclipse of the sun** 日食 nisshóku; (also: **eclipse of the moon**) 月食 gesshóku

ecology [ikɑːl'ədʒiː] n (environment) 環境 kañkyō, エコロジー ekóroji; (SCOL) 生態学 seîtaìgaku

economic [iːkənɑːm'ik] adj (system, history) 経済の kefzai no; (*BRIT*: profitable: business etc) もうかる mōkarú

economical [i:kənɑm'ikəl] *adj* (system, car, machine) 経済的な kefzaiteki na; (person) 倹約な ken'-yaku na

economics [i:kənɑm'iks] *n* (SCOL) 経済学 kefzaigàku
♦*npl* (of project, situation) 経済問題 kefzaimōñdai

economist [ikɑn'əmist] *n* 経済学者 kefzaigàkusha

economize [ikɑn'əmaiz] *vi* (make savings) 節約する setsúyaku suru

economy [ikɑn'əmi] *n* (of country) 経済 kefzai; (financial prudence) 節約 setsúyaku

economy class *n* (AVIAT) エコノミークラス ekōnomíkuràsu

economy size *n* (COMM) お買い得サイズ o-káidoku saìzu

ecstasy [ek'stəsi:] *n* (rapture) 狂喜 kyōki, エクスタシー ekúsutashì

ecstatic [ekstæt'ik] *adj* (welcome, reaction) 熱烈な netsúretsu na; (person) 無我夢中になった mūgàmuchū ni nattà

ecumenical [ekju:men'ikəl] *adj* 超宗派の chōshūha no

eczema [ek'səmə] *n* (MED) 湿しん shishìn

edge [edʒ] *n* (border: of lake, table, chair etc) 縁 fuchí; (of knife etc) 刃 ha
♦*vt* (trim) 縁取りする fuchídori suru
on edge (*fig*) = **edgy**
to edge away from じりじり...から離れる jírijìri ...kara hanárerù

edgeways [edʒ'weiz] *adv*: **he couldn't get a word in edgeways** 何一つ発言出来なかった nanihitotsu hatsúgen dekinakattà

edgy [edʒ'i:] *adj* (nervous, agitated) いらいらした fráira shita

edible [ed'əbəl] *adj* (mushroom, plant) 食用の shokúyō no

edict [i:'dikt] *n* (order) 政令 sefrei

edifice [ed'əfis] *n* (building, structure) 大建造物 dafkenzōbùtsu

Edinburgh [ed'ənbəːrə] *n* エジンバラ ejínbara

edit [ed'it] *vt* (text, report) 校正する kṓsei suru; (book, film, newspaper) 編集する hefshū suru

edition [idiʃ'ən] *n* (of book) 版 hán; (of newspaper, magazine) 号 gṓ; (TV, RADIO) 回 kái

editor [ed'itəːr] *n* (of newspaper) 編集局長 hefshūkyokuchō, デスク désùku; (of magazine) 編集長 hefshūchō; (of column: foreign/political editor) 編集主任 hefshūshunin; (of book) 編集者 hefshū-sha

editorial [editɔːr'iːəl] *adj* (staff, policy, control) 編集の hefshū no
♦*n* (of newspaper) 社説 shasètsu

educate [edʒ'uːkeit] *vt* (teach) 教育する kyṓiku suru; (instruct) ...に教える ...ni oshíerù

education [edʒu:kei'ʃən] *n* (schooling, teaching) 教育 kyṓiku; (knowledge, culture) 教養 kyṓyō

educational [edʒu:kei'ʃənəl] *adj* (institution, policy etc) 教育の kyṓiku no; (experience, toy) 教育的な kyōikuteki na

EEC [i:ːi:si:'] *n abbr* (= *European Economic Community*) 欧州経済共同体 ōshūkeizaikyōdòtai

eel [i:l] *n* ウナギ unági

eerie [i:'ri:] *adj* (strange, mysterious) 不気味な bukími na

effect [ifek'] *n* (result, consequence) 結果 kekkà; (impression: of speech, picture etc) 効果 kōka
♦*vt* (repairs) 行う okónau; (savings etc) ...に成功する ...ni seńkō suru
to take effect (law) 実施される jisshí sarerù; (drug) 効き始める kikíhajimerù
in effect 実際には jissái ni wa; 事実上 jijítsujō

effective [ifek'tiv] *adj* (successful) 効果的な kōkateki na; (actual: leader, command) 実際の jissái no

effectively [ifek'tivli:] *adv* (successfully) 効果的に kōkateki ni; (in reality) 実際には jissái ni wa

effectiveness [ifek'tivnis] *n* (success) 有効性 yūkōsei

effeminate [ifem'ənit] *adj* (boy, man) 女々しい meméshiì

effervescent [efəːrvesˈənt] adj (drink) 炭酸ガス入りの tañsangasuirî no

efficacy [efˈikəsi] n (effectiveness) 有効性 yū́kōsei

efficiency [ifiˈənsi] n (of person, organization) 能率 nōrîtsu; (of machine) 効率 kōrîtsu

efficient [ifiˈənt] adj (person, organization) 能率的な nōrîtsuteki na; (machine) 効率の良い kōrîtsu no yoî

effigy [efˈidʒi] n (image) 像 zō

effort [efˈəːrt] n (endeavor) 努力 dōryoku; (determined attempt) 試み kokóromi, 企て kuwâdate; (physical/mental exertion) 苦労 kúrō

effortless [efˈəːrtlis] adj (achievement) 楽な rakú na; (style) ごく自然な gókù shízen na

effrontery [ifrʌnˈtəːri] n (cheek, nerve) ずうずうしさ zūzūshisâ

effusive [ifjuːˈsiv] adj (handshake, welcome) 熱烈な netsúretsu na

e.g. [iːdʒiː] adv abbr (= exempli gratia) 例えば tatóeba

egg [eg] n 卵 tamágò
  hard-boiled/soft-boiled egg 堅ゆで (半熟)卵 katáyude(hafjuku)tamago

eggcup [egˈkʌp] n エッグカップ eggā́kappú

egg on vt (in fight etc) そそのかす sosónokasù

eggplant [egˈplænt] n (esp US) n (aubergine) ナス násù

eggshell [egˈjel] n 卵の殻 tamágò no kará

ego [iːˈgou] n (self-esteem) 自尊心 jisónshin

egotism [iːˈgətizəm] n 利己主義 rikóshugî

egotist [iːˈgətist] n 利己主義者 rikóshugîshà, エゴイスト egóisùto

Egypt [iːˈdʒipt] n エジプト ejíputo

Egyptian [idʒipˈʃən] adj エジプトの ejíputo no
  ◆n エジプト人 ejíputojìn

eiderdown [aiˈdəːrdaun] n (quilt) 羽布団 hanébutòn

eight [eit] num 八 (の) hachî(no), 八つ

(の) yattsú no

eighteen [eiˈtiːn] num 十八 (の) jū́hachi (no)

eighth [eitθ] num 第八の dáihachi no

eighty [eiˈtiː] num 八十 (の) hachfjū(no)

Eire [erˈə] n アイルランド aíruràndo

either [iːˈðəːr] adj (one or other) どちらかの dóchiraka no; (both, each) 両方の ryōhō no
  ◆pron: **either (of them)** どちらも...ない dóchira mo ...nai
  ◆adv ...も...ない ...mo ...nai
  ◆conj: **either yes or no** はいかいいえか hái ka iíe ka
  on either side 両側に ryōgawa ni
  I don't like either どちらも好きじゃない dóchira mo sukî ja naî
  no, I don't like either いいえ、私もしない iíe, watákushi mò shináî

eject [idʒekt] vt (object) 放出する hōshutsu suru; (tenant) 立ちのかせる tachínokaserù; (gatecrasher etc) 追出す oídasù

eke [iːk]: **to eke out** vt fus 間に合せるのに使う ma ní awaserù

elaborate [n ilæbˈəːrit adj ilæbˈəːrit] adj (complex: network, plan, ritual) 複雑な fukúzatsu na
  ◆vt (expand) 拡張する kakúchō suru; (refine) 洗練する señren suru
  ◆vi: **to elaborate (on)** (idea, plan etc) (...を) 詳しく説明する (...wo) kuwáshikù setsúmei suru

elapse [ilæpsˈ] vi (time) 過ぎる sugírù

elastic [ilæsˈtik] n (material) ゴム ひも gomúhimo
  ◆adj (stretchy) 弾力性のある dañryokusei no aru; (adaptable) 融通の利く yūzū no kikú
  elastic band (BRIT) n 輪ゴム wagómu

elated [lleiˈtid] adj: **to be elated** 大喜びになっている óyorokobi ni natté irù

elation [lleiˈʃən] n (happiness, excitement) 大喜び óyorokobi

elbow [elˈbou] n (ANAT: also of sleeve) ひじ hijî

elder [elˈdəːr] adj (brother, sister etc) 年上の toshíue no

♦n (tree) ニワトコ niwátoko; (older person: gen pl) 年上の人々 toshíue no hitóbito

elderly [el'də:rli:] adj (old) 年寄りの toshíyorī no

♦npl: the elderly 老人 rōjin

eldest [el'dist] adj 最年長の saínenchō no

♦n 最年長の人 saínenchō no hitó

the eldest child/son/daughter 長子〔長男, 長女〕 chōshí(chōnán, chōjó)

elect [ilekt'] vt (government, representative, spokesman etc) 選出する señshutsu suru

♦adj: *the president elect* 次期大統領 jíkídaítōryō ◇当選したものの、まだ就任していない人について言う tōsen shita mono nő, mádà shúnin shite inaí hitó ni tsúîte iú

to elect to do (choose) …する事にする …suru kotó ni suru

election [ilek'ʃən] n (voting) 選挙 séñkyo; (installation) 就任 shúnin

electioneering [ilekʃəni:'riŋ] n (campaigning) 選挙運動 señkyoundō

elector [ilek'tə:r] n (voter) 有権者 yúkensha

electoral [ilek'tə:rəl] adj (register, roll) 有権者の yúkensha no

electorate [ilek'tə:rit] n (of constituency, country) 有権者 yúkensha ◇総称 sōshō

electric [ilek'trik] adj (machine, current, power) 電気の déñki no

electrical [ilek'trikəl] adj (appliance, system, energy) 電気の déñki no

electric blanket n 電気毛布 deñkimōfu

electric chair (US) n 電気いす deñkíisu

electric fire n 電気ヒーター deñkíhītā

electrician [ilektriʃ'ən] n 電気屋 deñkíyà

electricity [ilektris'əti:] n 電気 déñki

electrify [ilek'trəfai] vt (fence) 帯電させる taí deñ saserú; (rail network) 電化する deñka suru; (audience) ぎょっとさせる gyóttó saserú

electrocute [ilek'trəkju:t] vt 感電死させる kañdenshi saserū

electrode [ilek'troud] n 電極 deñkyoku

electron [ilek'trɑn] n (PHYSICS) 電子 deñshi

electronic [ilektrɑn'ik] adj (device, equipment) 電子の deñshi no

electronic mail n 電子郵便 deñshíyūbin

electronics [ilektrɑn'iks] n (industry, technology) 電子工学 deñshíkōgaku

elegance [el'əgəns] n (of person, building) 優雅さ yúgàsa, エレガンス éregànsu; (of idea, plan) 見事さ migótosà

elegant [el'əgənt] adj (person, building) 優雅な yúga na; (idea, plan) 洗練された señren saretá

element [el'əmənt] n (part of whole, job, process) 要素 yōso; (CHEM) 元素 géñso; (of heater, kettle etc) ヒーター素子 hítāsoshi

elementary [elimen'tə:ri:] adj (basic) 基本的な kihóntekī na; (primitive) 原始的な geñshíteki na; (school, education) 初等の shotō no

elephant [el'əfənt] n ゾウ zō

elevation [elavei'ʃən] n (raising, promotion) 向上 kōjō; (height) 海抜 kaíbatsu

elevator [el'əveitə:r] n (US: lift) エレベーター erébētā

eleven [ilev'ən] num 十一 (の) jūíchi no

elevenses [ilev'ənziz] (BRIT) npl (coffee-break) 午前のおやつ gōzen no o-yátsu

eleventh [ilev'ənθ] num 第十一の dáíjūíchi no

elf [elf] (pl elves) n 小妖精 shōyōsei

elicit [ilis'it] vt: to elicit (from) (information, response, reaction) (…から)…を引出す (…kárà)…wő hikídasù

eligible [el'idʒəbəl] adj (qualified, suitable) 資格のある shikáku no arù; (man, woman) 好ましい結婚相手である konó-mashíi kekkon áite de arú

to be eligible for something (qualified, suitable) …する資格がある …suru shikáku ga arù

eliminate [ilim'əneit] vt (eradicate: poverty, smoking) 無くす nakúsù; (candidate, team, contestant) 除外する jogái suru

elimination [alimənei'ʃən] n (eradica-

tion) 根絶 koňzetsu; (of candidate, team
等) 除外 jogái

élite [ilı:t'] n エリート erítò

elm [elm] n (tree) ニレ niré; (wood) ニレ
材 nirézài

elocution [eləkjuːʃ'ən] n 話術 wájùtsu

elongated [iloːŋ'geitid] adj (body,
shadow) 細長い hosónagai

elope [iloup'] vi 駆落ちする kakéochi
suru

elopement [iloup'mənt] n 駆落ち kakéochi

eloquence [el'əkwəns] n (of person,
description, speech) 雄弁 yúben

eloquent [el'əkwənt] adj (person,
description, speech) 雄弁な yúben na

else [els] adv (other) 外に hoká ni
  something else 外の物 hoká no monò
  somewhere else 外の場所 hoká ni bashò
  everywhere else 外はどこも hoká wà
  dókò mo
  where else? 外にどこ？hoká nì dókò?
  there was little else to do 外にする
  はなかった hoká ni suru kotò wa nákàtta
  nobody else spoke 外にだれもしゃべら
  なかった hoká ni daré mo shabéranaka-
  kattà

elsewhere [els'we'r] adv (be) 外の所に
hoká no tokorò ni; (go) 外の所へ hoká
no tokorò e

elucidate [ilu:'sideit] vt (argument,
point) 解明する kaímei suru

elude [iluːd'] vt (subj: fact, idea: not real-
ized) 気付かれない kizúkarenaì; (: : not
remembered) 思い出せない omóidasenà-
i; (: : not understood) 理解されない ríkài
sarénaì; (captor) …から逃げる …kara nigérù; (capture) 免れる manúgarerú

elusive [ilu:'siv] adj (person, animal) 見
付けにくい mitsúkenikuì; (quality) 分か
りにくい wakárinikuì

elves [elvz] npl of elf

emaciated [imei'ʃiːeitid] adj (person, animal) 衰弱した suíjaku shita

emanate [em'əneit] vi: *to emanate
from* (idea, feeling) …から発せられる ...ka-

ra hanatárerù; (sound) …から聞こえる
...kara kikóerù; (light) …から放射される
...kara hósha sarerù

emancipate [imæn'səpeit] vt (poor,
slave, women) 解放する kaíhõ suru

emancipation [imænsəpei'ʃən] n (of poor,
slaves, women) 解放 kaíhõ

embankment [embæŋ'mənt] n (of
road, railway) 土手 doté; (of river) 堤防
teíbõ

embargo [embɑːr'gou] (pl embargoes) n
(POL, COMM) 通商停止 tsúshõteíshi

embark [embɑːrk'] n (NAUT): *to
embark (on)* (...に) 乗船する (...ni) jõsen
suru
  ♦vt (passengers, cargo) 乗せる nosérù
  to embark on (journey) …に出発する
  ...ni shuppátsu surù; (task, course of
  action) …に乗出す …ni norídasù

embarkation [embɑːrkei'ʃən] n (of people) 乗船 jõsen; (of cargo) 船積み funázu-
mi

embarrass [embær'əs] vt (emotionally)
恥をかかせる hajî wo kakáserù; (politician, government) 困らせる komáraserù

embarrassed [embær'əst] adj (laugh,
silence) 極り悪そうな kimáriwarùsõ na

embarrassing [embær'əsiŋ] adj (statement, situation, moment) 恥ずかしい hazúkashiì

embarrassment [embær'əsmənt] n
(shame) 恥 hajî; (embarrassing problem)
厄介な問題 yákkài na mondai

embassy [em'bɑsi:] n (diplomats) 使節団
shisétsudàn; (building) 大使館 taíshikàn

embedded [embed'id] adj (object) 埋め込
まれた umékomareta

embellish [embel'iʃ] vt (place, dress) 飾
る kazárù; (account) 潤色する juňshoku
suru

embers [em'bərz] npl: *the embers (of
the fire)* 残り火 nokóribì

embezzle [embez'əl] vt (LAW) 横領する
õryõ suru

embezzlement [embez'əlmənt] n 横領 õ-
ryõ

embitter [embit'ər] vt (fig: sour) 世の中
を憎ませる yo nó nàka wo nikúmaserù

emblem [em'bləm] *n* (design) 標章 hyō-shō、マーク mā́ku; (symbol) 象徴 shóchō

embody [ımbɑː'diː] *vt* (idea, principle) 現す aráwasù; (features: include, contain) 含む fukúmù

embossed [ımbɔːst'] *adj* (design, word) 浮き出しの ukídashi no

embrace [embreis'] *vt* (hug) 抱く dakú; (include) 含む fukúmù
 ♦*vi* (hug) 抱合う dakíaù
 ♦*n* (hug) 抱擁 hōyō

embroider [embrɔi'dəːr] *vt* (cloth) 刺しゅうする shishū surù

embroidery [embrɔi'dəːriː] *n* 刺しゅう shishū

embryo [em'briːou] *n* (BIO) はい haí

emerald [em'əːrald] *n* エメラルド eméra-rùdo

emerge [iməːrdʒ'] *vi*: **to emerge (from)** (...から) 出て来る (...kara) détè kurú; (fact: from research etc) (...が) 明らかになる (...de) akírka ni nárù; (new: idea, industry, society) 現れる aráware-rù

to emerge from sleep 目が覚める mé gà samérù

to emerge from prison 釈放される sha-kúhō sarerù

emergency [iməːr'dʒənsiː] *n* (crisis) 非常時 hijōji

in an emergency 緊急の場合 kínkyū no baái

state of emergency 緊急事態 kínkyūjí-tai

emergency cord (*US*) *n* 非常の際に引くコード hijō ni saí ni hikú kōdo

emergency exit *n* 非常口 hijōguchi

emergency landing *n* (AVIAT) 不時着 陸 fujíchakúriku

emergency services *npl* (fire, police, ambulance) 非常時のサービス機関 hijōji no sābisukikàn

emergent [iməːr'dʒənt] *adj* (nation) 最近独立した safkin dokúritsu shitá; (group) 最近創立された safkin sōritsu saretá

emery board [em'əːriː-] *n* つめやすり tsuméyasùri ◇ボール紙製の物を指す bō-rugamisei no monò wo sásù

emigrant [em'əgrənt] *n* (from native country) 移住者 ijūsha

emigrate [em'əgreit] *vi* (from native country) 移住する ijū surù

emigration [emagrei'ʃən] *n* 移住 ijū

eminent [em'ənənt] *adj* (scientist, writer) 著名な chómei na

emission [imiʃ'ən] *n* (of gas) 放出 hōshu-tsu; (of radiation) 放射 hōsha

emit [imit'] *vt* (smoke, smell, sound) 出す dasú; (light, heat) 放射する hōsha surù

emotion [imou'ʃən] *n* 感情 kanjō

emotional [imou'ʃənəl] *adj* (needs, ex-haustion, person, issue etc) 感情的な kañ-jōteki na; (scene etc) 感動的な kañdōteki-na

emotive [imou'tiv] *adj* (subject, lan-guage) 感情に訴える kanjō ni uttáerù

emperor [em'pəːrəːr] *n* (*gen*) 皇帝 kōtei; (of Japan) 天皇 teñnō

emphases [em'fəsiːz] *npl of* **emphasis**

emphasis [em'fəsis] (*pl* **emphases**) *n* (importance) 重点 jūten; (stress) 強調 kyōchō

emphasize [em'fəsaiz] *vt* (word, point) 強調する kyōchō surù; (feature) 浮彫にする ukíbori ni surù

emphatic [əmfæt'ik] *adj* (statement, denial, manner, person) 断固とした dáñko to shita

emphatically [əmfæt'ikliː] *adv* (force-fully) 断固として dáñko to shité; (cer-tainly) 絶対に zettái ni

empire [em'paiəːr] *n* (*also fig*) 帝国 tef-koku

empirical [empir'ikəl] *adj* (knowledge, study) 経験的な keñkenteki na

employ [emplɔi'] *vt* (workforce, person) 雇う yatóù; (tool, weapon) 使用する shi-yō surù

employee [emplɔi'iː] *n* 雇用人 koyónin

employer [emplɔi'əːr] *n* 雇い主 yatóinù-shi

employment [emplɔi'mənt] *n* (work) 就職 shūshoku

employment agency *n* 就職あっ旋会社 shūshokuassengaìsha

empower [empau'əːr] *vt*: **to empower**

someone to do something (LAW, ADMIN) ...に...する権限を与える ...ni ...suru keñgen wò ataérů

empress [emˈpris] *n* (woman emperor) 女帝 jotéi; (wife of emperor) 皇后 kôgō

emptiness [empˈtiːnis] *n* (of area, region etc) 何もない事 naní mo naí kotó; (of life etc) むなしさ munáshīsa

empty [empˈtiː] *adj* (container) 空の karâ no, 空っぽの karâppò no; (place, street) だれもいない daré mo inâi; (house, room, space) 空きの akí no
♦*vt* 空にする karâ ni suru
♦*vi* (house, container) 空になる karâ ni nárū; (liquid) 注ぐ sosōgū̀

an empty threat こけおどし kokéodòshi

an empty promise 空約束 karâyakùsoku

empty-handed [emptiːhænˈdid] *adj* 手ぶらの tebúra no

emulate [emˈjəleit] *vt* (hero, idol) まねる manérû

emulsion [imʌlˈʃən] *n* (liquid) 乳剤 nyűzai; (*also*: **emulsion paint**) 水性ペンキ sufýōpeñki

enable [eneiˈbəl] *vt*: *to enable someone to do* (permit, allow) ...に...する事を許可する ...ga ...surû kotō wo kyōka suru; (make possible) ...が...する事を可能にする ...ga ...surû kotō wo kanō ni surû

enact [enæktˈ] *vt* (law) 制定する seítei suru; (play, role) 演じる eñjiru suru

enamel [inæmˈəl] *n* (for decoration) エナメル eńameru; (*also*: **enamel paint**) エナメルペイント eńamerupeiñto; (of tooth) エナメル質 eńamerushītsu

enamored [enæmˈɔːrd] *adj*: *to be enamored of* (person, pastime, idea, belief) ...に惚れる ...ni horérů

encased [enkeistˈ] *adj*: *encased in* (plaster, shell) ...に覆われた ...ni ōwareta

enchant [entʃæntˈ] *vt* (delight) 魅了する miryō suru

enchanted [entʃænˈtid] *adj* (castle, island) 魔法の mahô no

enchanting [entʃænˈtiŋ] *adj* (appearance, behavior, person) 魅力的な miryō-

kutéki na

encircle [ensəˈrkəl] *vt* (place, prisoner) 囲む kakómù

encl. *abbr* (= *enclosed*) 同封の dôfū no

enclave [enˈkleiv] *n* 飛び地 tobíchī

enclose [enklouzˈ] *vt* (land, space) 囲む kakómù; (object) 閉じ込める tojíkomerù; (letter etc) *to enclose (with)* (...に) 同封する (...ni) dôfū suru

please find enclosed ...を同封します ...wo dôfū shimasù

enclosure [enklouˈʒəːr] *n* (area of land) 囲い kakói

encompass [enkʌmˈpəs] *vt* (include: subject, measure) 含む fukúmù

encore [ɑːŋˈkɔːr] *excl* アンコール añkōru
♦*n* (THEATER) アンコール añkōru

encounter [enkaunˈtəːr] *n* (with person etc) 出会い deâi; (with problem etc) 直面 chokúmeñ
♦*vt* (person) ...に出会う ...ni deâù; (new experience, problem) 直面する chokúmeñ suru

encourage [enkəˈridʒ] *vt* (person): *to encourage someone (to do something)* (...する事を) ...に勧める (...surû kotō wo) ...ni susúmerů; (activity, attitude) 奨励する gekírei suru; (growth, industry) 刺激する shigéki suru

encouragement [enkəˈridʒmənt] *n* (to do something) 勧め susúme; (of activity, attitude) 激励 gekírei; (of growth, industry) 刺激 shigéki

encroach [enkroutʃˈ] *vi*: *to encroach (up)on* (rights) ...を侵す ...wo okásù; (property) ...に侵入する ...ni shiñnyū suru; (time) ...の邪魔をする ...no jamá wo surû

encrusted [enkrʌsˈtid] *adj*: *encrusted with* (gems) ...をちりばめられた ...wo chiríbamerareta; (snow, dirt) ...に覆われた ...ni ōwareta

encumber [enkʌmˈbəːr] *vt*: *to be encumbered with* (suitcase, baggage etc) ...が邪魔になっている ...ga jamá nî nattè irù; (debts) ...を背負っている ...wo seóttè irù

encyclop(a)edia [ensaiklɑpiˈdiːə] *n* 百

科辞典 hyakkájíten

end [end] *n* (of period, event, book etc) 終り owári; (of table, street, line, rope) 端 hashí; (of town) 外れ hazúre; (of pointed object) 先 sakí; (aim) 目的 mokúteki

♦*vt* (finish) 終える oérù; (stop: activity, protest etc)

JPN や上める yamérù

♦*vi* (situation, activity, period etc) 終る owárù

in the end 仕舞いには shimái nì wa

on end (object) 縦になって tátè ni natté

to stand on end (hair) よだつ yodátsu

for hours on end ぶっ続けで何時間も buttsúzuke de nánjikan mo

endanger [endein'dʒəːr] *vt* (lives, prospects) 危険にさらす kikén ni sarásū

endearing [endiːr'iŋ] *adj* (personality, conduct) 愛敬のある afkyo no arú

endeavor [endev'əːr] (*BRIT* **endeavour**) *n* (attempt) 試み kokóromi; (effort) 努力 dóryòku

♦*vi*: *to endeavor to do* (attempt) ...しようとする ...shiyó tò surú; (strive) ...しようと努力する ...shiyó tò dóryòku surú

endemic [endem'ik] *adj* (poverty, disease) 地方特有の chihótokuyû no

ending [en'diŋ] *n* (of book, film, play etc) 結末 ketsúmatsu; (LING) 語尾 góbì

endive [en'daiv] *n* (curly) エンダイブ endáibu; (smooth: chicory) チコリ chikóri

endless [en'dlis] *adj* (argument, search) 果てし無い hatéshinai; (forest, beach) 延々と続く én-en tò tsuzúkū

endorse [endɔːrs'] *vt* (check) ...に裏書きする ...ni urágaki suru; (approve: proposal, plan, candidate) 推進する suíshin suru

endorsement [endɔːrs'mənt] *n* (approval) 推薦 suísen; (*BRIT*: on driving licence) 違反記録 ihánkìroku

endow [endau'] *vt* (provide with money) ...に金を寄付する ...ni kané wo kifú suru

to be endowed with (talent, quality) ...の持主である ...no mochínushi de árù

end up *vi*: *to end up* (in place) ...に行ってしまう ...ni itté shimaù; (condition)

endurance [endur'əns] *n* (stamina) 耐久力 taíkyūryoku; (patience) 忍耐強さ niñtaizuyõsa

endure [endur'] *vt* (bear: pain, suffering) 耐える taérù

♦*vi*: (last: friendship, love etc) 長続きする nagátsuzùki suru

an enduring work of art 不朽の名作 fukyû no meísaku

enemy [en'əmiː] *adj* (forces, strategy) 敵の tekí no

♦*n* 敵 tekí

energetic [enərdʒet'ik] *adj* (person, activity) 精力的な sefryokuteki na

energy [en'ərdʒiː] *n* (strength, drive) 精力 seíryoku; (power: nuclear energy etc) エネルギー enérùgi

enforce [enfɔːrs'] *vt* (LAW) 実施する jisshí suru

engage [engeidʒ'] *vt* (attention, interest) 引く hikú; (employ: consultant, lawyer) 雇う yatóù; (AUT: clutch) する tsunágù

♦*vi* (TECH) 掛る kakárù

to engage in (commerce, study, research etc) ...に従事する ...ni júji suru

to engage someone in conversation ...に話し掛ける ...ni hanáshikakerú

engaged [engeidʒd'] *adj* (betrothed) 婚約している konyaku shite irū; (*BRIT*: busy, in use) 使用中 shiyóchū

to get engaged 婚約する konyaku suru

engaged tone (*BRIT*) *n* (TEL) 話し中の信号音 hanáshichū no shíngóon

engagement [engeidʒ'mənt] *n* (appointment) 約束 yakúsoku; (booking: for musician, comedian etc) 仕事 shigóto; (to marry) 婚約 konyaku

engagement ring *n* 婚約指輪 konyaku-yubíwa, エンゲージリング eñgéjíringu

engaging [engei'dʒiŋ] *adj* (personality, trait) 愛敬のある afkyo no arú

engender [endʒen'dəːr] *vt* (feeling, sense) 生む umú

engine [en'dʒən] *n* (AUT) エンジン éñjin, (RAIL) 機関車 kikáñsha

engine driver n (RAIL) 運転手 untenshu

engineer [endʒəni:r'] n (designer) 技師 gíshī; (BRIT: for repairs) 修理工 shūrikō; (US: RAIL) 運転手 untenshu; (on ship) 機関士 kikanshi

engineering [endʒəni:r'iŋ] n (science) 工学 kōgaku; (design, construction: of roads, bridges) 建設 kensetsu; (: of cars, ships, machines) 製造 seízō

England [iŋ'glənd] n イングランド fngurando

English [iŋ'gliʃ] adj イングランドの fíngurando no; (LING) 英語の efgu no
♦n (LING) 英語 efgo
♦npl: **the English** イングランド人 íngurandojìn ◇総称 sōshō

English Channel n: **the English Channel** イギリス海峡 igírisukaíkyō

Englishman/woman [iŋ'gliʃmən/wumən] (pl **Englishmen/women**) n イングランド人男性(女性) íngurandojin dansei(jōsei)

engraving [engrei'viŋ] n (picture, print) 版画 hañga

engrossed [engroust'] adj: **engrossed in** (book, program) ...に夢中になった ...ni muchū ni nattá

engulf [engʌlf'] vt (subj: fire) 巻込む makíkomù; (water) 飲込む nomíkomù; (: panic, fear) 襲う osóù

enhance [enhæns'] vt (enjoyment, reputation) 高める takámerù; (beauty) 増す masú

enigma [enig'mə] n (mystery) なぞ nazó

enigmatic [enigmæt'ik] adj (smile) なぞめいた nazómeíta; (person) 得体の知れない etái no shirenaí

enjoy [endʒɔi'] vt (like) ...が好きである ...ga sukí de arù; (take pleasure in) 楽しむ tanóshimù; (have benefit of: health, fortune, success) ...に恵まれる ...ni megúmarerù

    to enjoy oneself 楽しむ tanóshimù

enjoyable [endʒɔi'əbəl] adj (pleasant, fun) 楽しい tanóshiì

enjoyment [endʒɔi'mənt] n (feeling of pleasure) 楽しさ tanóshìsa; (activity) 楽

しみ tanóshimì

enlarge [enla:rdʒ'] vt (size, scope) 拡大する kakúdai suru; (PHOT) 引伸ばす hikínobasū
♦vi: **to enlarge on** (subject) 詳しく話す kuwáshikû hanásù

enlargement [enla:rdʒ'mənt] n (PHOT) 引伸ばし hikínobashi

enlighten [enlait'ən] vt (inform) ...に教える ...ni oshíerù

enlightened [enlait'ənd] adj (person, policy, system) 聡明な sōmei na

enlightenment [enlait'ənmənt] n: **the Enlightenment** (HISTORY) 啓もう運動 keímōundō

enlist [enlist'] vt (soldier) 入隊させる nyútai saserù; (person) ...の助けを借りる ...no tasúke wo karfrù; (support, help) 頼む tanómù
♦vi: **to enlist in** (army, navy etc) ...に入隊する ...ni nyútai suru

enmity [en'miti:] n (hostility) 恨み urámi

enormity [inɔ:r'miti:] n (of problem, danger) 物すごさ monósugōsa

enormous [inɔ:r'məs] adj (size, amount) 巨大な kyodái na; (delight, pleasure, success etc) 大きな ōkina

enough [inʌf'] adj (time, books, people etc) 十分な jūbuñ na
♦pron 十分 jūbuñ
♦adv: **big enough** 十分に大きい jūbuñ ni ōkìi

    he has not worked enough 彼の努力が足りない kárè no dóryòku ga tarínaì

    have you got enough? 足りましたか tarímashìta ká

    enough to eat 食べ物が足りる tabémonò ga tarírù

    enough! もう沢山! mō íì!

    that's enough, thanks もう沢山です。有難う, mō takusañ desu. arígàtō.

    I've had enough of him 彼にはもうんざりだ kárè ni wa mō uñzari dá

    ... which, funnily/oddly enough ... おかしいけれども、...は okáshiì kerèdomo, soré wa ...

enquire [enkwai'ə:r] vt, vi = **inquire**

enrage [enreidʒ'] vt (anger, madden) 激

怒させる gékìdo saseru

enrich [enríʧ] vt (morally, spiritually)
豊かにする yútàka ni suru; (financially)
金持にする kanémochi ni suru

enroll [enroul] (BRIT: **enrol**) vt (at
school, university) 入学させる nyúgaku
saserù; (on course) 登録する tôroku suru; (in club etc) 入会させる nyúkai saserù
♦vi (at school, university) 入学する nyúgaku suru; (on course) 登録する な
sañkatetsuzùki wo suru; (in club etc) 入
会する nyúkai suru

enrollment [enroul'mɔnt] (BRIT:
enrolment) n (registration) 登録 tôroku

en route [ɑːn ruːt'] adv (on the way) 途
中で tochû de

ensue [ensuː'] vi (follow) ...の結果として
起る ...no kekkà toshité okórù

ensure [enʃuːr'] vt (result, safety) 確実に
する kakújitsu ni surù

entail [enteil'] vt (involve) 要する yô suru

entangled [entǽŋ'gəld] adj: **to become
entangled (in)** (in net, rope etc) ...に絡
まる ...ni karámarù

enter [en'tər] vt (room, club) ...に入る
...ni háìru; (race, competition) ...に参加
する ...ni sañka suru; (on) ...に出場する
...ni shutsújo suru; (someone for a competition) ...に...の参加を申込む ...ni ...no
sañka wo móshikomù; (write down) 記入す
る kinyú suru; (COMPUT: data) 入力する
nyúryòku suru
♦vi (come or go in) 入る háìru

enter for vt fus (race, competition,
examination) ...に参加を申込む ...ni
sañka wo móshikomù

enter into vt fus (discussion, correspondence, negotiations) 始める hajímerù; (agreement) 結ぶ musúbù

enterprise [en'tərpraiz] n (company,
business) 企業 kigyô; (undertaking) 企画
kikàku; (initiative) 進取の気 shñshu no ki

free enterprise (自由企業 jiyúkigyò

private enterprise (private company)
民間企業 miñkankìgyò, 私企業 shikígyò

enterprising [en'tərpraizin] adj (adventurous) 進取の気に富んだ shñshu no ki
ni tôñda

entertain [entərtein'] vt (amuse) 楽しま
せる tanóshimaserù; (invite: guest) 接待
する séttài suru; (idea, plan) 考える kañgaerù

entertainer [entərtein'əːr] n (TV etc)
芸能人 gefnòjìn

entertaining [entərtei'niŋ] adj 面白い
omóshiroì

entertainment [entərtein'mənt] n
(amusement) 娯楽 gorâku; (show) 余興
yokyô

enthralled [enθrɔːld'] adj (engrossed,
captivated) 魅せられた misérareta

enthusiasm [enθuː'ziæzəm] n (eagerness) 熱心さ nesshñsa

enthusiast [enθuː'ziæst] n (fan) マニア
mânìa

enthusiastic [enθuːziæs'tik] adj
(excited, eager) 熱心な nesshñ na
to be enthusiastic about ...に夢中にな
っている ...ni muchú ni natté irù

entice [entais'] vt (lure, tempt) 誘惑する
yúwaku suru

entire [entai'əːr] adj (whole) 全体の zeñtai no

entirely [entai'əːrliː] adv (completely) 全
く mattákù

entirety [entai'əːrtiː] n: **in its entirety**
全体に zeñtai ni

entitle [entait'əl] vt: **to entitle someone
to something** ...に...に対する権利を与え
る ...ni ...ni tafsurù kefri wo atáerù

entitled [entait'əld] adj (book, film etc)
...という題の ...to iú daì no
to be entitled to (be allowed) ...する
権利がある ...suru kéñri ga árù

entity [en'titiː] n 物 monó

entourage [ɑːnturɑː'ʒ] n (of celebrity,
politician) 取巻き連 torímakireñ

entrails [en'treilz] npl (ANAT, ZOOL)
内臓 nafzò

entrance [n en'trɑns vb entræns'] n
(way in) 入口 iríguchi; (arrival) 登場 tôjò
♦vt (enchant) 魅惑する miwàku suru
to gain entrance to (university, profes-

sion を) ...に入る ...ni háiru

entrance examination n 入学試験 nyúgakushikeñ, 入試 nyúshi

entrance fee n 入場料 nyújōryō

entrance ramp (US) n (AUT) 入口ランプ iríguchiranpu

entrant [en'trənt] n (in race, competition etc) 参加者 sañkashà; (BRIT: in exam) 受験者 jukéñsha

entreat [entri:t'] vt (implore) 嘆願する tañgan suru

entrenched [entrentʃt'] adj (position, power) 固められた katámeraretà; (ideas) 定着した teíchakushità

entrepreneur [ɑːntrəprənəːr'] n (COMM) 企業家 kigyōka

entrust [entrʌst'] vt: **to entrust something to someone** ...を...に預ける ...wo ...ni azúkerù

entry [en'tri:] n (way in) 入口 irĭguchi; (in competition) 参加者 sañkashà; (in register, account book) 記入 kinyú; (in reference book) 記事 kíjî; (arrival) 登場 tójô; (to country) 入国 nyúkoku

"no entry" (to room etc) 立入禁止 tachíirikĩnshi; (AUT) 進入禁止 shiñnyúkĩnshi

entry form n (for club etc) 入会申込書 nyúkaimoshikomishò; (for competition etc) 参加申込書 sañkamoshikomishò

entry phone n 玄関のインターホン gêñkan no iñtáhon

enumerate [inuː'məːreit] vt (list) 列挙する rékkyo suru

enunciate [inʌn'siːeit] vt (word) はっきりと発音する hakkírì to hatsúon suru; (principle, plan etc) 明確に説明する meíkaku ni setsúmei suru

envelop [envel'əp] vt (cover, enclose) 覆い包む ôitsutsumù

envelope [en'vəloup] n 封筒 fútô

envious [en'viːəs] adj (person, look) うらやましい uráyamashiì

environment [envai'rənmənt] n (surroundings) 環境 kañkyò; (natural world): **the environment** 環境 kañkyò

environmental [envairənmen'təl] adj 環境の kañkyò no

envisage [enviz'idʒ] vt (foresee) 予想する

yosò suru

envoy [en'vɔi] n (diplomat) 特使 tókùshi

envy [en'viː] n (jealousy) せん望 señbò
♦vt うらやましく思う uráyamashiku o-móù

to envy someone something ...の...をうらやましく思う ...no ...wo uráyamashìku omóù

enzyme [en'zaim] n (BIO, MED) 酵素 kôso

ephemeral [ifem'əːrəl] adj (fashion, fame) つかの間の tsuká no mà no

epic [ep'ik] n (poem) 叙事詩 jojíshî; (book, film) 大作 taísaku
♦adj (journey) 歴史的な rekíshiteki na

epidemic [epədem'ik] n (of disease) 流行病 ryúkōbyō

epilepsy [ep'əlepsiː] n (MED) てんかん teñkan

epileptic [epəlep'tik] adj てんかんの teñkan no
♦n てんかん患者 teñkankañja

episode [ep'isoud] n (period, event) 事件 jĩken; (TV, RADIO: installment) 1回 ikkái

epistle [ipis'əl] n (letter: also REL) 書簡 shòkan

epitaph [ep'itæf] n 墓碑銘 bohímei

epithet [ep'əθet] n 形容語句 keíyōgokù

epitome [ipit'əmiː] n (model, archetype) 典型 teñkei

epitomize [ipit'əmaiz] vt (characterize, typify) ...の典型である ...no teñkei dè árù

epoch [ep'ak] n (age, era) 時代 jidái

equable [ek'wəbəl] adj (climate) 安定した añteishità; (temper, reply) 落着いた ochítsuità

equal [iː'kwəl] adj (size, number, amount) 等しい hitóshiì; (intensity, quality) 同様な dôyô na; (treatment, rights, opportunities) 平等な byôdô na
♦n (peer) 同輩 dôhai
♦vt (number) イコール ikôrù; (quality) ...と同等である ...to dôyô dè árù

to be equal to (task) ...を十分出来る ...wo jûbuñ dekírù

equality [ikwɑl'iti:] n 平等 byôdô

equalize [iː'kwəlaiz] vi (SPORT) 同点に

equally [i:'kwəli] *adv* (share, divide etc) 平等に byódō ni; (good, brilliant, bad etc) 同様に dóyō ni

equanimity [i:kwənim'iti:] *n* (calm) 平静 さ heíseisa

equate [ikweit'] *vt*: **to equate something with ...** を...と同等視する ...wo ...to dōtōshí suru

equation [ikwei'ʒən] *n* (MATH) 方程式 hōteíshiki

equator [ikwei'tər] *n* 赤道 sekídō

equestrian [ikwes'tri:ən] *adj* 乗馬の jō-ba no

equilibrium [i:kwəlib'ri:əm] *n* (balance) 均衡 kínkō; (composure) 平静さ heíseisa

equinox [i:'kwənɑks] *n*: **spring/autumn equinox** 春(秋)分の日 shúnji (shú)bun no hí

equip [ikwip'] *vt* (person, army, car etc) に...を装備させる ...ni ...wo sóbi saserú; (room) に...を備え付ける ...ni ...wo sonáetsukerú

to be well equipped 装備が十分である sóbi gà jūbún de árū

to be equipped with ... を装備している ...wo sóbi shite irú

equipment [ikwip'mənt] *n* (tools, machinery) 設備 sétsōbi

equitable [ek'witəbəl] *adj* (settlement, agreement) 公正な kōséi na

equities [ek'witi:z] (*BRIT*) *npl* (COMM) 普通株 futsúkabu

equivalent [ikwiv'ələnt] *adj*: **equivalent (to)** (...に)相当する (...ni) sōtō suru
♦*n* (equal) 相当の物 sōtō no monó

equivocal [ikwiv'əkəl] *adj* (ambiguous) あいまいな áimai na; (open to suspicion) いかがわしい ikágawashíī

era [i:'rə] *n* (age, period) 時代 jidái

eradicate [iræd'ikeit] *vt* (disease, problem) 根絶する koñzetsu suru

erase [ireis'] *vt* (tape, writing) 消す kesú

eraser [irei'sər] *n* (for pencil etc) 消しゴム keshígomu; (*US*: for blackboard etc) 黒板消し kokúbankeshi

erect [irekt'] *adj* (posture) 直立の chokúritsu no; (tail, ears) ぴんと立った pín tò

tattétā
♦*vt* (build) 建てる tatérū; (assemble) 組立てる kumítaterū

erection [irek'ʃən] *n* (of building) 建築 keńchiku; (of statue) 建立 koñryū; (of tent) 張る事 harú kotó; (of machinery etc) 組立て kumítate; (PHYSIOL) ぼっ起 bokkí

ermine [əːr'min] *n* (fur) アーミン áamin

erode [iroud'] *vt* (soil, rock) 侵食する shiñshoku suru; (metal) 腐食する fushóku suru; (confidence, power) 揺るがす yurúgasù

erosion [irou'ʒən] *n* (of soil, rock) 侵食 shiñshoku; (of metal) 腐食 fushóku; (of confidence, power) 揺るがされる事 yurúgasarerū kotó

erotic [irɑt'ik] *adj* (activities) 性的なse-ñteki na; (dreams, books, films) 扇情的な señjōteki na, エロチックな eróchikkù na

eroticism [irɑt'isizəm] *n* 好色 kōshoku, エロチシズム eróchishizùmu

err [əːr] *vi* (formal: make a mistake) 過ちを犯す ayámachi wò okású

errand [er'ənd] *n* お使い o-tsúkai

erratic [iræt'ik] *adj* (behavior) 突飛な toppí na; (attempts, noise) 不規則な fukísoku na

erroneous [irou'ni:əs] *adj* (belief, opinion) 間違った machígattà

error [er'əːr] *n* (mistake) 間違い machígai, エラー érā

erudite [er'judait] *adj* (person) 博学な hakúgaku na

erupt [irʌpt'] *vi* (volcano) 噴火する fuñka suru; (war, crisis) 突発する boppátsu suru

eruption [irʌp'ʃən] *n* (of volcano) 噴火 fuñka; (of fighting) ぼっ発 boppátsu

escalate [es'kəleit] *vi* (conflict, crisis) 拡大する kakúdai suru, エスカレートする esúkarēto suru

escalator [es'kəleitər] *n* エスカレータ esúkarētā

escapade [es'kəpeid] *n* (adventure) 冒険 bōken

escape [eskeip'] *n* (from prison) 脱走 dassō; (from person) 逃げる事 nigéru kotò; (of gas) 漏れる事 moréru kotò

♦vt (get away) 逃げる nigérù; (from jail) 脱走する dassō suru; (leak) 漏れる morérù

♦vt (consequences, responsibility etc) 回避する kaîhi suru; (elude): **his name escapes me** 彼の名前を思い出せない kárè no namáe wo omóidasenaî

to escape from (place) ...から脱出する ...kara dasshútsu suru; (person) ...から逃げる ...kara nigérù

escapism [eskeí'pizəm] n 現実逃避 geñjitsutōhì

escort [n es'kɔːrt vb eskɔːrt'] n (MIL, POLICE) 護衛 goéi; (companion) 同伴者 dóhañsha

♦vt (person) ...に同伴する ...ni dóhan suru

Eskimo [es'kəmou] n エスキモー人 esúkimōjìn

esoteric [esəter'ik] adj 難解な nañkai na

especially [espeʃ'əli:] adv (above all, particularly) 特に tókù ni

espionage [es'pi:ənɑːʒ] n (POL, MIL, COMM) スパイ行為 supáikòi

esplanade [espləneid'] n (by sea) 海岸の遊歩道 kaígan no yūhòdō

espouse [espauz'] vt (policy) 採用する saíyō suru; (idea) 信奉する shiñpō suru

Esq. n abbr = **Esquire**

Esquire [es'kwaiər] n: **J. Brown, Esquire** J.ブラウン様 jē buráùn samá

essay [es'ei] n (SCOL) 小論文 shōroñbun; (LITERATURE) 随筆 zuíhitsu, エッセー éssē

essence [es'əns] n (soul, spirit) 本質 hoñshitsu; (CULIN) エキス ékìsu, エッセンス ésseñsu

essential [əsen'tʃəl] adj (necessary, vital) 不可欠な fukáketsu na; (basic) 根本的な koñponteki na

♦n (necessity) 不可欠な事柄 fukáketsu nà kotógarà

essentially [əsen'tʃəli:] adv (basically) 根本的に koñpōnteki ni

establish [əstæb'liʃ] vt (organization, firm) 創立する sōritsu suru; (facts,

proof) 確認する kakúnin suru; (relations, contact) 樹立する jurítsu suru; (reputation) 作り上げる tsukúriagerù

established [əstæb'liʃd] adj (business) 定評のある teíhyō no arù; (custom, practice) 定着した teíchaku shità

establishment [əstæb'liʃmənt] n (of organization etc) 創立 sōritsu; (of facts etc) 確認 kakúnin; (of relations etc) 樹立 jurítsu; (of reputation) 作り上げる事 tsukúriagerù kotð; (shop etc) 店 misé; (business, firm) 会社 kaîsha; (institution) 施設 shîsetsu

the Establishment 体制 taísei

estate [əsteit'] n (land) 屋敷 yashíki; (BRIT: also: **housing estate**) 住宅団地 jútakudañchi; (LAW) 財産 zaísan

estate agent (BRIT) n 不動産屋 fudósan-yà

estate car (BRIT) n ステーションワゴン sutéshonwagòn

esteem [əsti:m'] n: **to hold someone in high esteem** (admire, respect) ...を尊敬する ...wo soñkei suru

esthetic [esθet'ik] (US) adj = **aesthetic**

estimate [n es'təmit vb es'təmeit] n (calculation) 概算 gaîsan; (assessment) 推定 suítei; (COMM: builder's etc) 見積 mitsúmori

♦vt (reckon, calculate) 推定する suítei suru

estimation [estəmei'ʃən] n (opinion) 意見 îken; (calculation) 推定 suítei

estranged [estreindʒd'] adj (from spouse) ...と別居している ...to bekkyó shite irù; (from family, friends) ...と仲たがいしている ...to nakátagai shite irù

estuary [es'tʃu:eri:] n 河口 kakō

etc abbr (= et cetera) など nádò

etching [etʃ'iŋ] n 版画 hañga, エッチング etchíngu

eternal [itərˈnəl] adj (everlasting, unceasing) 永遠の efén no; (unchanging: truth, value) 不変的な fuhénteki na

eternity [itərˈniti:] n (REL) 永遠 efén

ether [iːˈθər] n (CHEM) エーテル éteru

ethical [eθ'ikəl] adj (question, problem) 道徳的な dótokuteki na

ethics [eθ'iks] *n* (science) 倫理学 rińrigãku

♦*npl* (morality) 道徳 dõtoku

Ethiopia [i:θiːouˈpiːə] *n* エチオピア echíopìa

ethnic [eθ'nik] *adj* (population, music, culture etc) 民族の mínzoku no

ethos [iːˈθous] *n* 気風 kífù

etiquette [et'əkit] *n* (manners, conduct) 礼儀作法 reígisahõ, エチケット échiketto

eucalyptus [juːkəlipˈtəs] *n* (tree) ユーカリ yūkari

euphemism [juːˈfəmizəm] *n* えん曲表現 eńkyokuhyõgen

euphoria [juːfɔːrˈiːə] *n* (elation) 幸福感 kõfukukàn

Eurocheque [juːˈroutʃek] *n* ユーロチェック yūrochekkõ ◊ ヨーロッパ諸国で通用する小切手 yōroppa shokõku de tsũyõ surũ kogíttè

Europe [juːˈrəp] *n* 欧州 õshù, ヨーロッパ yõroppà

European [juːrəpiːˈən] *adj* 欧州の õshù no, ヨーロッパの yōroppà no

♦*n* ヨーロッパ人 yōroppájìn

euthanasia [juːθəneiˈʒə] *n* 安楽死 afirakushì

evacuate [ivækˈjueit] *vt* (people) 避難させる hínàn saserũ; (place) …から避難させる …kara hínàn saserũ

evacuation [ivækjueiˈʃən] *n* 避難 hínàn

evade [iveid'] *vt* (tax, duty) 脱税する datsűzei suru; (question) 言逃れる ifnogarerũ; (responsibility) 回避する kãihi suru; (person) 避ける sakérù

evaluate [ivælˈjueit] *vt* (importance, achievement, situation etc) 評価する hyõka suru

evaporate [ivæpˈəːreit] *vi* (liquid) 蒸発する jõhatsu suru; (feeling, attitude) 消えてなくなる kíète nakunarũ

evaporated milk [ivæpˈəːreitid-] *n* エバミルク ebámirùku

evasion [veiˈʒən] *n* (of responsibility, situation etc) 回避 kãihi

tax evasion 脱税 datsűzei

evasive [ivei'siv] *adj* (reply, action) 回避

的な kãihiteki na

eve [iːv] *n*: **on the eve of** …の前夜に …no zéñ-ya ni

even [iːvən] *adj* (level) 平らな tãira na; (smooth) 滑らかな namérãka na; (equal) 五分五分の gobúgobu no

♦*adv* (showing surprise) …さえ …sáè; (introducing a comparison) 更に sárà ni

an even number 偶数 gũsù

even if 例え…だとしても tatóè …dá tò shité mò

even though 例え…だとしても tatóè …dá tò shité mò

even so それにしても naósara

even so それにしても sore ni shite mò

not even …さえ…ない …sáè mo …nái

even he was there 彼さえもいた kárè mo itá

even on Sundays 日曜日にも nichíyòbi ni mo

to get even with someone …に復しゅうする …ni fukúshù suru

evening [iːv'niŋ] *n* (early) 夕方 yũgata; (late) 夕暮れ yūgure; (whole period, event) …の夕べ …no yũbe

in the evening 夕方に yũgata ni

evening class *n* 夜間学級 yakáñgakkyù

evening dress *n* (no pl: formal clothes) 夜会服 yakáifùku; (woman's) イブニングドレス ibúningu dorèsu

even out *vi* (ground) 平らになる tãira ni narũ; (prices etc) 安定する añtei suru

event [ivent'] *n* (occurrence) 事件 jíkèn; (SPORT) イベント ibéntò

in the event of …の場合 …no baái

eventful [ivent'fəl] *adj* (day) 忙しい isógashìi; (life, game) 波乱の多い háràn no ổi

eventual [iven'tʃuəl] *adj* (outcome, goal) ゆくゆくの yukúyùku no

eventuality [ventʃuælˈitiː] *n* (possibility) 可能性 kanõsei

eventually [iven'tʃuːəliː] *adv* (finally) 結局 kekkyõku; (in time) やがて yagáte

ever [ev'əːr] *adv* (always) 常に tsúnè ni; (at any time) いつか ítsùka; (in question): *why ever not?* どうしてまたしないのか dõshite matá shinái no kã *the best ever* 絶対に一番良い物 zettái ní ichíban yoí monó

have you ever seen it? それを見た事がありますか soré wo míta kotó gá arímasù ka

better than ever なお一層良くなった naô issô yokú náttà

ever since それ以来 soré iraí

♦*conj* ...して以来...shité iraí

evergreen [ev'əгgгin'] *n* (tree, bush) 常緑樹 jōryokujù

everlasting [eva:ræs'tiŋ] *adj* (love, life etc) 永遠の efen no

KEYWORD

every [ev'ri:] *adj* 1 (each) すべての subéte no, 皆の miná no

every one of them (persons) 彼ら は［を］皆 karéra wa (wo)miná; (objects) それらは［を］皆 sorérà wa(wo)miná

I interviewed every applicant 私は応募者全員に面接しました watákushi wa ōbosha zén-in ni ménsetsu shimashíta

every shop in the town was closed 町中の店が閉っていました machíjù no misé gà shimáttè imashíta

2 (all possible) 可能な限りすべての kanô na kagíri subéte no

I gave you every assistance 私は可能な限りあなたを助けました watákushi wa kanô na kagíri anátà wo tasúkemashìta

I have every confidence in him 私は完全に彼を信用しています watákushi wa kánzen ni karè wo shín-yoshite imasù

we wish you every success ご成功を祈ります go-séikō wo inórimasù

he's every bit as clever as his brother 才能に関しては彼が兄に少しも引けを取りません saínō ni kàn shite mo karè wa no âní ni sukóshi mo hike wo tôrímasèn

3 (showing recurrence) 毎... mái...

every day/week 毎日（週）mái nichi (shū)

every Sunday 毎週日曜日 máinichiyōbì

every other car (had been broken

into) 車は2台に1台ドアが壊れていた kurúma wa nidái ni ichídai doa ga kowásarète ita

she visits me every other/third day 彼女は1日（2日）置きに面会に来てくれます kánojo wa ichínichi(futsúka)oki ni ménkai ni kite kúremasù

every now and then 時々 tokídoki

everybody [ev'ri:bʌdi:] *pron* (gen) だれも dáre mo; (form of address) 皆さん minásan

everyday [ev'ri:dei] *adj* (daily) 毎日の máinichi no; (usual, common) 平凡な heíbon na

everyone [ev'ri:wʌn] *pron* = **everybody**

everything [ev'ri:θiŋ] *pron* 何もかも nánì mo ká mò

everywhere [ev'ri:hwe:r] *adv* (all over) いたる所に itárù tokoro ni; (wherever) どこにでも dôkò ni de mo

evict [ivikt'] *vt* (squatter, tenant) 立ちのかせる tachínokaserù

eviction [ivik'ʃən] *n* (from house, land) 立ちのかせる事 tachínokaserù kotó

evidence [ev'idəns] *n* (proof) 証拠 shóko; (of witness) 証言 shôgen; (sign, indication) 印 shírushi

to give evidence 証言する shógen suru

evident [ev'idənt] *adj* (obvious) 明らかな akíràka na

evidently [ev'idəntli:] *adv* (obviously) 明らかに akíràka ni; (apparently) ...らしい ...rashíì

evil [i:'vəl] *adj* (person, system, influence) 悪い warúì

♦*n* (wickedness, sin) 罪悪 zaíaku; (unpleasant situation or activity) 悪事 ákù

evocative [ivɑk'ətiv] *adj* (description, music) 想像を刺激する sōzō wò shigéki suru

evoke [ivouk'] *vt* (feeling, memory, response) 呼び起す yobíokosu

evolution [evəlu:'ʃən] *n* (BIO: process) 進化 shínka; (also: **theory of evolution**) 進化論 shinkaròn; (development) 発展 hattén

evolve [ivɑ:lv'] *vt* (scheme, style) 練上げ

る nerîsagerù

♦vi (animal, plant etc) 進化する shînka suru; (plan, idea, style etc) 展開する teñkai suru

ewe [ju:] n 雌ヒツジ mesûhitsùji

ex- [eks] prefix 元... mótò...

exacerbate [igzæs'ə:rbeit] vt (crisis, problem) 悪化させる akká saserù

exact [igzækt'] adj (correct: time, amount, word etc) 正確な sefkaku na; (person, worker) き帳面な kichômen na

♦vt: **to exact something (from)** (obedience, payment etc) (...に) ...を強要する (...ni) ...wo kyôyô suru

exacting [igzæk'tiŋ] adj (task, conditions) 難しい muzúkashiî; (person, master etc) 厳しい kibſshiî

exactly [igzækt'li:] adv (precisely) 正確 に sefkaku ni, 丁度 chôdo; (indicating emphasis) 正に mása ni; (indicating agreement) その通り sonô tôri

exaggerate [igzædʒ'əreit] vt (difference, situation, story etc) 大げさに言う ôgesa nî iû

♦vi 大げさな事を言う ôgesa na kotô wo iû

exaggeration [igzædʒəreiʃən] n 大げさ ôgesa

exalted [igzɔ:l'tid] adj (prominent) 著名 な chomêi na

exam [igzæm'] n abbr (SCOL) = **examination**

examination [igzæməneiʃən] n (of object, accounts etc) 検査 kéñsa; (of idea, plan etc) 検討 keñtô; (SCOL) 試験 shikéñ; (MED) 診察 shíñsatsu

examine [igzæm'in] vt (inspect: object, idea, plan, accounts etc) 調べる shirábe-rù; (SCOL: candidate) 試験する shikéñ suru; (MED: patient) 診察する shíñsatsu suru

examiner [igzæm'inə:r] n (SCOL) 試験 官 shikéñkan

example [igzæm'pəl] n (typical illustration) 例ref; ref; (model: of good behavior etc) 手本 tehóñ

for example 例えば tatôeba

exasperate [igzæs'pəreit] vt (annoy,

frustrate) 怒らせる okóraserù

exasperating [igzæs'pəreitiŋ] adj いら いらさせる îraira saserù

exasperation [igzæspəreiʃən] n いらだ ち irádachi

excavate [eks'kəveit] vt (site) 発掘する hakkútsu suru

excavation [eks'kəveiʃən] n (act) 発掘 hakkútsu; (site) 発掘現場 hakkútsugeñba

exceed [iksi:d'] vt (number, amount, budget) 越える koérù; (speed limit etc) 越す kosû; (powers, hopes) 上回る uwâmawarù

exceedingly [iksi:diŋli:] adv (enormously) 極めて kiwámète

excel [iksel'] vi: **to excel (in/at)** (sports, business etc) (...に) 優れる (...ni) sugúrerù

excellence [ek'sələns] n 優れる事 sugúreru kotô

Excellency [ek'sələnsi:] n: **His Excellency** 閣下 kákkà

excellent [ek'sələnt] adj (idea, work etc) 優秀な yûshû na

except [iksept'] prep (apart from: also: **except for, excepting**) ...を除いて ...wo nozôite

♦vt: **to except someone (from)** (attack, criticism etc) (...から) ...を除 く (...kara) ...wo nozôku

except if/when ...する場合を除いて ...suru baâi wo nozôite

except that がしかし... ga shíkashì...

exception [iksep'ʃən] n (special case) 例 外 refgai

to take exception to ...に気に食わない ...ga ki nî kuwanai

exceptional [iksep'ʃənəl] adj (person, talent) 優れた sugúreta; (circumstances) 例外的な refgaiteki na

excerpt [ek'sə:rpt] n (from text, film) 抜 粋 bassûi

excess [ek'ses] n (surfeit) 過剰 kajô

excess baggage n 超過手荷物 chôkatenímotsu

excesses [ekses'iz] npl (of cruelty, stupidity etc) 極端な行為 kyokútan na kôi

excess fare (*BRIT*) *n* (RAIL) 乗越し運賃 norîkoshi uńchìn

excessive [iksɛs'iv] *adj* (amount, extent) 過剰の kajó no

exchange [ikstʃeindʒ'] *n* (of presents, prisoners etc) 交換 kókan; (conversation) 口論 kóron; (*also*: **telephone exchange**) 電話局 deńwakyòku

♦*vt*: **to exchange (for)** (goods etc) (...と) 交換する (...to) kókan suru

exchange rate *n* 為替相場 kawásesòba

Exchequer [eks'tʃekəːr] (*BRIT*) *n*: **the Exchequer** 大蔵省 ōkurashō

excise [ek'saiz] *n* (tax) 消費税 shōhìzèi

excite [iksait'] *vt* (stimulate) 興奮させる kófun saserô; (arouse) 性的に刺激する seftki ni shigéki suru

to get excited 興奮する kófun suru

excitement [iksait'mənt] *n* (agitation) 興奮 kófun; (exhilaration) 喜び yorókobi

exciting [iksait'iŋ] *adj* (time, event, place) 興奮の kófun no, エキサイティングな ekísaitìngu no

exclaim [ikskleim'] *vi* (cry out) 叫ぶ sakébu

exclamation [ekskləmei'ʃən] *n* (cry) 叫び sakébi

exclamation mark *n* 感嘆符 kańtańfu

exclude [iksklu:d'] *vt* (fact, possibility, person) 除外する jogái suru

exclusion [iksklu:'ʒən] *n* 除外 jogái

exclusive [iksklu:'siv] *adj* (club, district) 独占の kókyū na; (use, story, interview) 独占の dokúsen no

exclusive of tax 税別の zefbetsu no

exclusively [iksklu:'sivli:] *adv* (only, entirely) 独占的に dokúsentèki ni

excommunicate [ekskəmju:'nəkeit] *vt* (REL) 破門する hamón suru

excrement [eks'krəmənt] *n* ふん fún

excruciating [ikskru:'ʃi:eitiŋ] *adj* (pain, agony, embarrassment etc) 極度の kyókùdo no, 耐えがたい taégatai; (noise) 耳をつんざくような mimí wo tsuńzaku yô na

excursion [ikskəːr'ʒən] *n* (tourist excursion, shopping excursion) ツアー tedã

excuse [n ekskjuːs' vb ekskjuːz'] *n* (justi-

fication) 言訳 ifwake

♦*vt* (justify): personal fault, mistake) ...の言訳をする ...no ifwake wo suru; (forgive: someone else's mistake) 許す yurúsù

to excuse someone from doing something ...する義務を...に免除する ...gimú wo ...ni méñjo suru

excuse me! (attracting attention) 済みませんが)... sumfmasen (ga)...; (as apology) 済みません sumfmasen

if you will excuse me ...ちょっと失礼します chóttò shitsúrèi shimasù

ex-directory [eksdirek'təːri:] (*BRIT*) *adj* 電話帳に載っていない deńwachò ni notté inàī

execute [ek'sakju:t] *vt* (person) 死刑にする shíkéi ni surû; (plan, order) 実行する jikkó suru; (maneuver, movement) する suru

execution [eksəkju:'ʃən] *n* (of person) 死刑 shíkéi; (of plan, order, maneuver etc) 実行 jikkó

executioner [eksəkju:'ʃənəːr] *n* 死刑執行人 shíkéishikkōnín

executive [igzek'jətiv] *n* (person: of company) 重役 jùyaku; (committee: of organization, political party etc) 執行委員会 shíkkóìñkai

♦*adj* (board, role) 幹部の kåñbu no

executor [igzek'jətəːr] *n* (LAW) 執行人 shikkónín

exemplary [igzem'plaːri:] *adj* (conduct) 模範的な mohánteki na; (punishment) 見せしめの misésime no

exemplify [igzem'pləfai] *vt* (typify) ...の典型である ...no teñkei de årů; (illustrate) ...の例を挙げる ...no reî wo agérù

exempt [igzempt'] *adj*: **exempt from** (duty, obligation) ...を免除された ...wo méñjo saretà

♦*vt*: **to exempt someone from** (duty, obligation) ...の...を免除する ...no ...wo méñjo suru

exemption [igzemp'ʃən] *n* 免除 méñjo

exercise [ek'səːrsaiz] *n* (no pl: keep-fit) 運動 uńdō; (energetic movement) 体操 tafsō; (SCOL) 練習問題 reńshumòndai;

(MUS) 練習曲 reñshúkyoku; (MIL) 軍事演習 guñjieñshū; (of authority etc) 行使 kōshí
♦vt (right) (right) に kóshí suru; (dog) ...に運動をさせる ...ni uñdō wò saséru; (mind) 働かせる határakaserú
♦vi (also: **to take exercise**) 運動する uñdō suru

to exercise patience 我慢する gámān suru

exercise book n (SCOL) ノート nōto

exert [igzə:rt'] vt (influence) 及ぼす oyóbosū; (authority) 行使する kōshí suru
to exert oneself 努力する dóryoku suru

exertion [igzə:r'ʃən] n 努力 dóryoku

exhale [eksheil'] vt (air, smoke) 吐き出す hakídasú
♦vi (breathe out) 息を吐く íkì wo hākú

exhaust [igzɔ:st'] n (AUT: also: **exhaust pipe**) 排気管 haíkikàn; (: fumes) 排気ガス haíkigasù
♦vt (person) へとへとに疲れさせる hetóhetó ni tsukáresaserù; (money, resources etc) 使い果す tsukáihatasū; (topic) ...について語り尽す ...ni tsúíte katáritsukusū

exhausted [igzɔ:s'tid] adj (person) へとへとに疲れた hetóhetó ni tsukáretá

exhaustion [igzɔs'tʃən] n (tiredness) 極度の疲労 kyōkúdo no hírō
nervous exhaustion 神経衰弱 shiñkeisuijàku

exhaustive [igzɔs'tiv] adj (search, study) 徹底的な tettéitekì na

exhibit [igzib'it] n (ART) 展示品 teñjihīn; (LAW) 証拠品 shōkohìn
♦vt (quality, ability, emotion) 見せる misérù; (paintings) 展示する teñji suru

exhibition [eksəbiʃ'ən] n (of paintings etc) 展示会 teñjikaī; (of ill-temper etc) 極端な態度 kyokūtán na táìdo; (of talent etc) 素晴らしい例 subárashíi reī

exhibitionist [eksəbiʃ'ənist] n (show-off) 気取り屋 kidőriya

exhilarating [igzil'əreitiŋ] adj (experience, news) 喜ばしい yorókobashiī

exhort [igzɔ:rt'] vt 訓戒する kuñkai suru

exile [eg'zail] n (condition, state) 亡命 bōmei; (person) 亡命者 bōmeisha
♦vt 追放する tsuíhō suru

exist [igzist'] vi (be present) 存在する soñzai suru; (live) 生活する seíkatsu suru

existence [igzis'təns] n (reality) 存在 soñzai; (life) 生活 seíkatsu

existing [igzis'tiŋ] adj (present) 現存の geñzon no, geñson no

exit [eg'zit] n (from room, building, motorway etc) 出口 dégùchi; (departure) 出ていく事 détè ikū kotō
♦vi (THEATER) 退場する taíjō suru; (COMPUT) プログラムを終了する puróguràmu wo shūryō suru

exit ramp (US) n (AUT) 出口ランプ dégùchiraňpu

exodus [ek'sədəs] n 大脱出 daídasshutsu

exonerate [igzɑn'əreit] vt: **to exonerate someone from something** (blame, guilt etc) ...について ...の容疑を晴らす ...ni tsúíte ...no yōgi wo harásū

exorbitant [igzɔ:r'bətənt] adj (prices, rents) 法外な hōgai na

exorcize [ek'sɔːrsaiz] vt (spirit) 追い払う ofharaū; (person, place) ...から悪魔を追い払う ...kara ākùma wo ofharaū

exotic [igzɑt'ik] adj (food, place) 異国的な ikókuteki na, エキゾチックな ekízochikkū na

expand [ikspænd'] vt (business etc) 拡張する kakúchō suru; (staff, numbers etc) 増やす fuyásū
♦vi (population etc) 増える fuérù; (business etc) 大きくなる ōkìku narū; (gas, metal) 膨張する bōchō suru

expanse [ikspæns'] n (of sea, sky etc) 広がり hírógarī

expansion [ikspæn'tʃən] n (of business, population, economy etc) 増大 zōdai

expatriate [ekspei'triːit] n 国外在住者 kokúgai zaijūsha

expect [ikspekt'] vt (anticipate) 予想する yosō suru; (await) 待つ mátsù; (require) 要求する yōkyū suru; (suppose) ...だと思う ...da to omóū
♦vi: **to be expecting** (be pregnant) 妊娠している niñshin shite irū

expectancy [ikspek'tənsi] n (anticipation) 期待 kitái
life expectancy 寿命 jumyṓ

expectant mother [ikspek'tənt-] n 妊婦 nínpu

expectation [ekspektei'ʃən] n (hope, belief) 期待 kitái

expedience [ikspi:'diəns] n (convenience) 便宜 béñgi, 都合 tsugṓ

expediency [ikspi:'diənsi:] n = expedience

expedient [ikspi:'diːənt] adj (useful, convenient) 都合の良い tsugṓ no yoí
♦n (measure) 便法 benpṓ

expedition [ekspədij'ən] n (for exploration) 探検 tañkeñ; (for shopping etc) ツアー tsūā

expel [ikspel'] vt (person: from school) 退学させる taígaku saserṓ; (: from organization, place) 追出す ofdasṓ; (gas, liquid) 排出する haíshutsu suru

expend [ikspend'] vt (money, time, energy) 費やす tsufyasṓ

expendable [ikspen'dəbəl] adj (person, thing) 消耗品的な shṓmṓhinteki na

expenditure [ikspen'ditʃər] n (of money, energy, time) 消費 shṓhi

expense [ikspens'] n (cost) 費用 híyṓ; (expenditure) 出費 shuppí
at the expense of …を犠牲にして …wo giséi ni shité

expense account n 交際費 kṓsaíhi

expenses [ikspen'siz] npl (traveling expenses, hotel expenses etc) 経費 keńhi

expensive [ikspen'siv] adj (article) 高価 な kṓka na; (mistake, tastes) 高く付く tákaku tsukṓ

experience [ikspi:'riːəns] n 経験 keńken
♦vt (situation, feeling etc) 経験する keńken suru

experienced [ikspi:'riːənst] adj (in job) 熟練した jukṓren shitá

experiment [ikspe:r'əmənt] n (trial: also SCIENCE) 実験 jikkén
♦vi: *to experiment (with/on)* (…を使って) 実験する (…wo tsukáttē) jikkén suru

experimental [ikspe:rəmen'təl] adj 実験

的な jikkénteki na

expert [ek'spəːrt] adj (opinion, help) 専門 家の seńmonka no; (driver etc) 熟練した jukṓren shitá
♦n (specialist) 専門家 seńmonka, エキスパート ekísupāto

expertise [ekspəːrtiːz'] n (know-how) 技術 gíjútsu, ノーハウ nṓhaù

expire [ikspai:'ər] vi (passport, licence etc) 切れる kirérṓ

expiry [ikspai:ə'ri:] n (of passport, lease etc) 満期 máñki

explain [iksplein'] vt 説明する setsúmei suru

explanation [eksplənei'ʃən] n 説明 setsúmei

explanatory [iksplæn'ətɔ:ri:] adj (statement, comment) 説明の setsúmei no

explicit [iksplis'it] adj (clear) 明白な meíhaku na; (frank) 隠し立てしない kakúshidate shinaí

explode [iksploud'] vi (bomb) 爆発する bakúhatsu suru; (population) 爆発的に増える bakúhatsuteki ní fuérṓ; (person: with rage etc) 激怒する gékìdo suru

exploit [n eks'ploit vb iksploit'] n (deed, feat) 手柄 tegára
♦vt (workers) 搾取する sákúshu suru; (person, idea) 私利私欲に利用する shírìshfyòku ní riyṓ suru; (opportunity, resources) 利用する riyṓ suru

exploitation [eksploitei'ʃən] n (of workers) 搾取 sákúshu; (of person, idea, resources, opportunity etc) 利用 riyṓ

exploration [eksplərei'ʃən] n (of place, space) 探検 tañkeñ; (with hands etc) 探る事 sagúru kotṓ; (of idea, suggestion) 検討 keñtṓ

exploratory [iksplɔːr'ətɔːri:] adj (expedition) 探検の tañkeñ no; (talks, operation) 予備的な yobíteki na

explore [iksplɔːr'] vt (place, space) 探検 する tañkeñ suru; (with hands etc) 探る sagúru; (idea, suggestion) 検討する keñtṓ suru

explorer [iksplɔːr'ər] n (of place, country etc) 探検家 tañkeñka

explosion [iksplou'ʃən] n (of bomb) 爆発

bakúhatsu; (increase: of population etc)
爆発的増加 bakúhatsukizòka; (outburst: of rage, laughter etc) 激怒 gékìdo

explosive [iksplou'siv] adj (device, effect) 爆発の bakúhatsu no; (situation, temper) 爆発的な bakúhatsuteki na
♦n (substance) 爆薬 bakúyaku; (device) 爆弾 bakúdañ

exponent [ekspou'nent] n (of idea, theory) 擁護者 yógoshà; (of skill, activity) 達人 tatsújin

export [vb ikspo:rt' n eks'po:rt] vt (goods) 輸出する yushútsu suru
♦n (process) 輸出 yushútsu; (product) 輸出品 yushútsuhìn
♦cpd (duty, permit) 輸出... yushútsu...

exporter [ekspo:r'tər] n 輸出業者 yushútsugyòsha

expose [ikspouz'] vt (reveal: object) むき出しにする mukídashi ni surú; (unmask: person) ...の悪事を暴く ...no ákùji wo abáku

exposed [ikspouzd'] adj (house, place etc) 雨風にさらされる âmèkaze ni sarásaretà

exposure [ikspou'ʒər] n (to heat, cold, radiation) さらされる事 sarásareru kotò; (publicity) 報道 hôdò; (of person) 暴露 bákùro; (PHOT) 露出 roshútsu
to die from exposure (MED) 低体温症で死ぬ teítaioñshò de shinú

exposure meter n (PHOT) 露出計 roshútsukei

expound [ikspaund'] vt (theory, opinion) 説明する setsúmei suru

express [ikspres'] adj (clear: command, intention etc) 明白な meíhaku na; (BRIT: letter etc) 速達の sokútatsu no
♦n (train, bus, coach) 急行 kyúkò
♦vt (idea, view) 言表す iíarawasù; (emotion, quantity) 表現する hyôgen suru

expression [ikspreʃ'ən] n (word, phrase) 言方 iíkata; (of idea, emotion) 表現 hyôgen; (on face) 表情 hyōjō; (of actor, singer etc: feeling) 表現力 hyôgenryòku

expressive [ikspres'iv] adj (glance) 意味ありげな îmìarige na; (ability) 表現の hyôgen no

expressly [ikspres'li:] adv (clearly, intentionally) はっきりと hakkírì to

expressway [ikspres'wei] (US) n (urban motorway) 高速道路 kôsokudòro

expulsion [ikspʌl'ʃən] n (SCOL) 退学処分 taígakushòbuñ; (from organization etc) 追放 tsuíhò; (of gas, liquid etc) 排出 haíshutsu

expurgate [eks'pə:rgeit] vt (text, recording) 検閲する keñ-etsu suru

exquisite [ekskwiz'it] adj (perfect: face, lace, workmanship, taste) 見事な mígòto na

extend [ikstend'] vt (visit) 延ばす nobású; (street) 延長する eñchò suru; (building) 増築する zôchiku suru; (arm, hand) 伸ばす nobású
♦vi (land) 広がる hirógarù; (road) 延びる nobírù; (period) 続く tsuzúkù
to extend an offer of help 援助を申出る éñjo wo môshiderù
to extend an invitation to ... を招待する ... wo shôtai suru

extension [iksten'tʃən] n (of building) 増築 zôchiku; (of time) 延長 eñchò; (of campaign, rights) 拡大 kakúdai; (ELEC) 延長コード eñchôkòdo; (TEL: in private house, office) 内線 naísen

extensive [iksten'siv] adj (area) 広い hirói; (effect, damage) 甚大な jiñdai na; (coverage, discussion) 広範囲の kôhañ-i no

extensively [iksten'sivli:] adv: he's traveled extensively 彼は広く旅行している kárè wa híròku ryokò shite irù

extent [ikstent'] n (size: of area, land etc) 広さ híròsa; (: of problem etc) 大きさ ôkìsa
to some extent ある程度 árù teído
to the extent of ... ...までも ...mádè mo
to such an extent that ... ...という程 ...to iú hodò
to what extent? どのぐらい? donó gurai?

extenuating [iksten'ju:eitiŋ] adj: extenuating circumstances 酌量すべき情状 shakúryò subèki jôjò

exterior [ikstiːrˈiəʳ] adj (external) 外部の gáibu no
♦n (outside) 外部 gáibu; (appearance) 外見 gaíken

exterminate [ikstəːrˈməneit] vt (animals) 撲滅する bokúmetsu suru; (people) 根絶する koñzetsu suru

external [ikstəːrˈnəl] adj (walls etc) 外部の gáibu no; (examiner, auditor) 部外の búgai no
external evidence 外的証拠 gaítekishōko
"for external use" 外用薬 gaíyōyaku

extinct [ikstiŋkt] adj (animal, plant) 絶滅した zetsúmetsu shitá
an extinct volcano 死火山 shikázan

extinction [ikstiŋkˈʃən] n (of species) 絶滅 zetsúmetsu

extinguish [ikstiŋˈgwiʃ] vt (fire, light) 消す kesú

extinguisher [ikstiŋˈgwiʃəːr] n 消火器 shōkakí

extort [ikstɔːrt] vt (money) ゆすり取る yusúritorù; (confession) 強要する kyōyō suru

extortion [ikstɔːrˈʃən] n (of money etc) ゆすり yusúri; (confession) 強要 kyōyō

extortionate [ikstɔːrˈʃənit] adj (price, demands) 法外な hōgai na

extra [eksˈtrə] adj (thing, person, amount) 余分の yobún no
♦adv (in addition) 特別に tokúbetsu ni
♦n (luxury) 特別の物 tokúbetsu no monó, 余分の物 yobún no monò; (surcharge) 追加料金 tsuíkaryōkin; (CINEMA, THEATER) エキストラ ekísutora

extra... [eksˈtrə] prefix 特別に... tokúbetsu ni ...

extract [vt ikstrǽkt n eksˈtrækt] vt (take out: object) 取出す torídasù; (: tooth) 抜く nukú, 抜歯する basshí suru; (mineral: from ground) 採掘する saíkutsu suru, 抽出する chūshutsu suru; (money) 強要する kyōyō suru, 強要して取る kyōyō shité tőrù; (promise) 無理強いする muríjii suru
♦n (of novel, recording) 抜粋 bassúi; (malt extract, vanilla extract etc) エキス ékìsu, エッセンス éssènsu

extracurricular [ekstrəkərikˈjələːr] adj (activities) 課外の kagái no

extradite [eksˈtrədait] vt (from country) 引渡す hikíwatasù; (to country) ...の引渡しを受ける ...no hikíwatashì wò ukérù

extradition [ekstrədiʃˈən] n 外国への犯人引渡し gaíkoku e nò háñnin hikíwatashi

extramarital [ekstrəmærˈitəl] adj (affair, relationship) 婚外の koñgai no, 不倫の furín no

extramural [ekstrəmjuːrˈəl] adj (lectures, activities) 学外の gakúgai no

extraordinary [ikstrɔːrˈdəneːri] adj (person) 抜きん出た nukíndetà; (conduct, situation) 異常な ijō na; (meeting) 臨時の rińji no

extravagance [ikstrævˈəgəns] n (no pl: spending) 浪費 rōhi; (example of spending) ぜいたく zeítaku

extravagant [ikstrævˈəgənt] adj (lavish: person) 気前の良い kimáe no yoì; (: gift) ぜいたくな zeítaku na; (wasteful: person) 金遣いの荒い kanézukai no arai; (: machine) 不経済な fukéizai na

extreme [ikstriːm] adj (cold, poverty etc) 非常な hijō na; (opinions, methods etc) 極端な kyokútan na; (point, edge) 末端の mattán no
♦n (of behavior) 極端 kyokútan

extremely [ikstriːmˈliː] adv 非常に hijō ni

extremity [ikstremˈitiː] n (edge, end) 端 hashí; (of situation) 極端 kyokútan

extricate [eksˈtrikeit] vt: *to extricate someone/something (from)* (trap, situation...) ...を救い出す (...kara) ...wo sukúidasù

extrovert [ekˈstrouvəːrt] n 外向的な人 gaíkōteki na hitó

exuberant [igzuːˈbəːrənt] adj (person etc) 元気一杯の geñkiippài no; (imagination etc) 豊かな yútàka na

exude [igzuːd] vt (liquid) にじみ出させる nijímidasaserù; (smell) 放つ hanátsu
to exude confidence 自信満々である jishín mañman dè árù
to exude enthusiasm 意気込む ikígo-

mū

exult [ɪgzʌlt'] *vi* (rejoice) 喜び勇む yorōkobiisamū

eye [aɪ] *n* (ANAT) 目 mé

◆*vt* (look at, watch) 見詰める mitsúmerū

the eye of a needle 針の目 hárí no mé

to keep an eye on ... を見張る ...wo mihárū

eyeball [aɪ'bɔːl] *n* 眼球 gańkyū

eyebath [aɪ'bæθ] *n* 洗眼カップ seńgankappū

eyebrow [aɪ'brau] *n* 眉毛 máyùge

eyebrow pencil *n* アイブローペンシル afburōpeńshiru

eyedrops [aɪ'drɑːps] *npl* 点眼薬 teńgańyaku

eyelash [aɪ'læʃ] *n* まつげ mátsùge

eyelid [aɪ'lɪd] *n* まぶた mábùta

eyeliner [aɪ'laɪnɚ] *n* アイライナー afraīnā

eye-opener [aɪ'oupɑnɚ] *n* (revelation) 驚くべき新事実 odórokubèki shińjíjìtsu

eyeshadow [aɪ'ʃædou] *n* アイシャドー afshadō

eyesight [aɪ'saɪt] *n* 視力 shíryòku

eyesore [aɪ'sɔːr] *n* (building) 目障り mezáwàri

eye witness *n* (to crime, accident) 目撃者 mokúgekishà

F

F [ef] *n* (MUS: note) ヘ音 hé-òn; (: key) ヘ調 héchō

F. *abbr* (= *Fahrenheit*) 華氏 kāshí

fable [feɪ'bəl] *n* (story) ぐう話 gūwa

fabric [fæb'rɪk] *n* (cloth) 生地 kíjī

fabrication [fæbrɪkeɪ'ʃən] *n* (lie) うそ追 sō; (making) 製造 sefzō

fabulous [fæb'jələs] *adj* (*inf*: super) 素晴らしい subárashiì; (extraordinary) 途方もない tohō mo naì; (mythical) 伝説的な deńsétsuteki na

facade [fəsɑːd'] *n* (of building) 正面 shōmen; (fig: pretense) 見せ掛け misékake

face [feɪs] *n* (ANAT) 顔 kaó; (expression) 表情 hyōjō; (of clock) 文字盤 mojí-

ban; (of cliff) 面 mén; (of building) 正面 shōmen

◆*vt* (particular direction) ...に向かう ...ni mukáū; (facts, unpleasant situation) 直視する chokúshi suru

face down (person) 下向きになって shitámuki ni nattè; (card) 伏せてあって fuséte attè

to lose face 面目を失う meńboku wo ushínaū

to make/pull a face 顔をしかめる kaó wo shikámerū

in the face of (difficulties etc) ...にめげず ...ni megézù

on the face of it (superficially) 表面は hyōmen wa

face to face (with person, problem) 面と向かって meń to mukattè

face cloth (*BRIT*) *n* フェースタオル fésutàoru

face cream *n* フェースクリーム fésukurīmu

face lift *n* (of person) 顔のしわ取り手術 kaó no shiwàtori shujútsu; (of building etc) 改造 kaízō

face powder *n* フェースパウダー fésupaùdā

face-saving [feɪs'seɪviŋ] *adj* (compromise, gesture) 面子を立てる meńtsu wo tatérù

facet [fæs'ɪt] *n* (of question, personality) 側面 sokúmen; (of gem) 切子面 kiríkomèn

facetious [fəsiː'ʃəs] *adj* (comment, remark) ふざけた fuzáketà

face up to *vt fus* (obligations, difficulty) ...に立ち向かう ...ni tachímukaū

face value *n* (of coin, stamp) 額面 gakúmen

to take something at face value (*fig*) そのまま信用する sonó mama shiń-yō suru

facial [feɪ'əl] *adj* (hair, expression) 顔の kaó no

facile [fæs'əl] *adj* (comment, reaction) 軽々しい karúgarushiì

facilitate [fəsɪl'əteɪt] *vt* 助ける tasúkerū

facilities [fəsɪl'ətiːz] *npl* (buildings,

equipment) 設備 setsúbi

credit facilities 分割払い取扱い buñkatsubarái toríatsukai

facing [feɪˈsɪŋ] *prep* (opposite) ...の向い 側の ...no mukáigawa no

facsimile [fækˈsɪməli] *n* (exact replica) 複製 fukúsei; (*also:* **facsimile machine**) ファックス fákkùsu; (transmitted document) ファックス fákkùsu

fact [fækt] *n* (true piece of information) 事実 jijítsu; (truth) 真実 shiñjitsu

in fact 事実は jijítsu wa

faction [fækˈʃən] *n* (group: *also* REL, POL) 派 há

factor [fækˈtəːr] *n* (of problem, decision etc) 要素 yóso

factory [fækˈtəːri] *n* (building) 工場 kójō

factual [fækˈtʃuəl] *adj* (analysis, information) 事実の jijítsu no

faculty [fækˈəlti] *n* (sense, ability) 能力 nóryoku; (of university) 学部 gakúbu; (*US:* teaching staff) 教職員 kyōshokuin ◇総称 sóshō

fad [fæd] *n* (craze) 一時的流行 ichíjitekiryūkò

fade [feɪd] *vi* (color) あせる asérù; (light, sound) 次第に する shidái ni kiérù; (flower) しぼむ shibómù; (hope, memory, smile) 消える kiérù

fag [fæg] (*BRIT: inf*) *n* (cigarette) もく mokú

fail [feɪl] *vt* (exam) 落第する rakúdai suru; (candidate) 落第させる rakúdai saserù; (subj: leader) ...の期待を裏切る ...no kitái wo urágirù; (: courage, memory) なくなる nakúnarù

♦*vi* (candidate, attempt etc) 失敗する shippái suru; (brakes) 故障する kośhō suru; (eyesight, health) 衰える otóroerù; (light) 暗くなる kuráku narù

to fail to do something (be unable) ...する事が出来ない ...surú koto gà dekínai; (neglect) ...する事を怠る ...surú koto wò okótarù

without fail 必ず kaﬆarazu

failing [feɪˈlɪŋ] *n* (weakness) 欠点 kettén

♦*prep* ...がなければ ...ga nákèreba

failure [feɪˈljəːr] *n* (lack of success) 失敗 shippái; (person) 駄目 な人 damé niﬆgen; (mechanical etc) 故障 kośhō

faint [feɪnt] *adj* かすかな kásùka na

♦*n* (MED) 気絶 kizétsu

♦*vi* (MED) 気絶する kizétsu suru

to feel faint 目まいがする memái ga suru

fair [feːr] *adj* (reasonable, right) 公平な kōhei na; (quite large) かなりな kánàri na; (quite good) 善くな warúkunai; (skin) 白い shirói; (hair) 金色の kiń-iro no; (weather) 晴れの harё no

♦*adv* (play) 正々堂々と seíseídōdō to

♦*n* (*also:* **trade fair**) トレードフェアー torédofeà; (*BRIT:* funfair) 移動遊園地 idóyūenchi

fairly [feːrˈli:] *adv* (justly) 公平に kōhei ni; (quite) かなり kánàri

fairness [feːrˈnis] *n* (justice, impartiality) 公平さ kóheisa

fair play *n* 公平さ kóheisa

fairy [feːrˈi:] *n* (sprite) 妖精 yósei

fairy tale *n* おとぎ話 otógibanàshi

faith [feɪθ] *n* (trust) 信用 shiń-yō; (religion) 宗教 shūkyō; (religious belief) 信仰 shíﬆkō

faithful [feɪθˈfəl] *adj* 忠実な chūjitsu na

faithfully [feɪθˈfəli:] *adv* 忠実に chūjitsu ni

yours faithfully (*BRIT:* in letters) 敬具 kéigu

fake [feɪk] *n* (painting etc) 偽物 nisémono; (person) ぺてん師 petéﬆshi

♦*adj* (phoney) いんちきの íﬆchiki no

♦*vt* (painting etc) 偽造する gizō suru; (illness, emotion) ...だと見せ掛ける ...da to mísékakerù

falcon [fælˈkən] *n* ハヤブサ hayábusa

fall [fɔːl] *n* (of person, object: from height) 落下 teﬆkà; (of person, horse: from standing position) 転倒 teﬆtō; (of price, temperature, dollar) 下降 kakō; (of government, leader, country) 倒れる事 taőrerù kotő; (*US:* autumn) 秋 ákì

♦*vi* (*pt* **fell**, *pp* **fallen**) (person, object: from height) 落ちる ochírù; (person,

horse; from standing position) 転ぶ koróbù; (snow, rain) 降る fúrù; (price, temperature, dollar) 下がる sagárù; (government, leader, country) 倒れる taórérù; (night, darkness) (...に) なる (...ni) nárù
snowfall 降雪 kósetsu
rainfall 降雨 kóu
the fall of darkness 暗くなる事 kurákù naru kotò
the fall of night 夜になる事 yórù ni nárù kotò
to fall flat (on one's face) うつぶせに倒れる taórérù; (plan) 失敗する shippái suru; (joke) 受けない ukénai
fallacy [fæl'əsi:] n (misconception) 誤信 goshín
fall back vi fus (retreat) 後ずさりする atózusàri suru; (MIL) 後退する kôtaisuru
fall back on vt fus (remedy etc) ...に頼る ...ni tayórù
fall behind vi 遅れる okúrerù
fall down vi (person) 転ぶ koróbù; (building) 崩壊する hôkai suru
fallen [fɔːl'ən] pp of fall
fall for vt fus (trick) ...にだまされる ...ni damásarerù; (person) ...にほれる ...ni horérù
fallible [fæl'əbəl] adj (person, memory) 間違いをしがちな machígai no shigáchi na
fall in vi (roof) 落ち込む ochíkomù; (MIL) 整列する seíretsu suru
fall off vi (person, object) 落ちる ochírù; (takings, attendance) 減る herú
fall out vi (hair, teeth) 抜ける nukérù; (friends etc) けんかする kénka suru
fallout [fɔːl'aut] n (radiation) 放射性降下物 hôshaseírakabutsu, 死の灰 shí no hai
fallout shelter n 放射性降下物待避所 hôshaseírakabutsu taíhijo
fallow [fæl'ou] adj (land, field) 休閑中の kyúkañchū no
falls [fɔːlz] npl (waterfall) 滝 takí
fall through vi (plan, project) 失敗に終る shippái ni owarù
false [fɔːls] adj (untrue: statement, accusation) うその usó no; (wrong: impres-

sion, imprisonment) 間違った machígattà; (insincere: person, smile) 不誠実な fuseíjitsu na
false alarm n 誤った警報 ayámattà kefhô
false pretenses npl: **under false pretenses** うその申立てで usó no môshitate de
false teeth npl 入れ歯 iréba
falter [fɔːl'tər] vi (engine) 止りそうになる tomárisô ni narù; (person: hesitate) ためらう tamérau; (: stagger) よろめく yorémekù
fame [feim] n 名声 meísei
familiar [fəmil'jɑːr] adj (well-known: face, voice) おなじみの onájimi no; (intimate: behavior, tone) 親しい shitáshiì
to be familiar with (subject) よく知っている yôkù shitté irù
familiarize [fəmil'jəraiz] vt: **to familiarize oneself with** ...になじむ ...ni najímù
family [fæm'li:] n (relations) 家族 kázòku; (children) 子供 kodómo の総称 sôshô
family business n 家族経営の商売 kazókukeíei no shôbai
family doctor n 町医者 machí-ishà
famine [fæm'in] n 飢餓 kígà
famished [fæm'iʃt] adj (hungry) 腹がぺこぺこの hará-ga pekópeko no
famous [fei'məs] adj 有名な yûmei na
famously [fei'məsli:] adv (get on) 素晴らしく subárashikù
fan [fæn] n (person) ファン fáñ; (folding) 扇子 séñsu; (ELEC) 扇風機 señpûki
♦vt (face, object etc) ...を扇ぐ ...o aógù; (fire, quarrel) あおる aórù
fanatic [fənæt'ik] n (extremist) 熱狂者 nekkyôsha; (enthusiast) マニア mánìa
fan belt n (AUT) ファンベルト fañberùto
fanciful [fæn'sifəl] adj (notion, idea) 非現実的な hígeñjitsuteki na; (design, ornament) 凝った kôttà
fancy [fæn'si:] n (whim) 気まぐれ kimágurè; (imagination) 想像 sôzô; (fantasy) 夢 yumé
♦adj (clothes, hat, food) 凝った kôttà,

(hotel etc) 高級の kókyū no

◆*vt* (feel like, want) 欲しいと思う ho-shíi na to omóu; (imagine) 想像する sōzō suru; (think) ...だと思う ...da to omóu

to take a fancy to ...を気に入る ...wo kf ni irú

he fancies her (*inf*) 彼は彼女が好きだ kárè wa kanójo ga sukí dà

fancy dress *n* 仮装の衣装 kasō no ishō

fancy-dress ball *n* 仮装舞踏会 kasōbutōkai

fanfare [fæn'feːr] *n* ファンファーレ fanfāre

fang [fæŋ] *n* (tooth) きば kibá

fan out *vi* 扇形に広がる ōgigata nì hirógarù

fantastic [fæntæs'tik] *adj* (enormous) 途方もない tohōmonài; (strange, incredible) 信じられない shinjirarenài; (wonderful) 素晴らしい subá rashiì

fantasy [fæn'tæsi:] *n* (dream) 夢 yumé; (unreality, imagination) 空想 kūsō

far [fɑːr] *adj* (distant) 遠い tôi

◆*adv* (a long way) 遠く tôku; (much) はるかに hárūka ni

far away/off 遠く tôku

far better ...の方がはるかにいい ...no hō ga hárūka ni ii

far from 決して...でない kesshíte ...de nái 〈強い否定を現す tsuyóì hitéi wo aráwasù

by far はるかに hárūka ni

go as far as the farm 農場まで行って下さい nōjō madè itté kudasaì

as far as I know 私の知る限り watákushi nò shirú kagirì

how far? (distance) どれぐらいの距離 doré gurai no kyòri; (referring to activity, situation) どれ程 doré hodò

faraway [fɑːr'əwei'] *adj* (place) 遠くの tôku no; (look) 夢見る様な yumémiru yō na; (thought) 現実離れの genjítsubanare no

farce [fɑːrs] *n* (THEATER) 笑劇 shōgeki, ファース fâsù; (*fig*) 茶番劇 chabángeki

farcical [fɑːr'sikəl] *adj* (situation) ばかげた bakágèta

fare [feːr] *n* (on trains, buses) 料金 ryôkin; (*also:* **taxi fare**) タクシー代 takúshìdai; (food) 食べ物 tabémono

half/full fare 半(全)額 hañ(zeñ)gàku

Far East *n*: **the Far East** 極東 kyokútō

farewell [feːr'wel'] *excl* さようなら sayô-nara

◆*n* 別れ wakáre

farm [fɑːrm] *n* 農場 nōjō

◆*vt* (land) 耕す tagáyasù

farmer [fɑːr'məːr] *n* 農場主 nōjōshù

farmhand [fɑːrm'hænd] *n* 作男 sakúotòko

farmhouse [fɑːrm'haus] *n* 農家 nōka

farming [fɑːr'miŋ] *n* (agriculture) 農業 nōgyō; (of crops) 耕作 kōsaku; (of animals) 飼育 shiíku

farmland [fɑːrm'lænd] *n* 農地 nōchi

farm worker *n* = **farmhand**

farmyard [fɑːrm'jɑːrd] *n* 農家の庭 nōka no niwá

far-reaching [fɑːr'ri:'tʃiŋ] *adj* (reform, effect) 広範囲の kōhañ-i no

fart [fɑːrt] (*inf!*) *vi* おならをする onára wo surú

farther [fɑːr'ðəːr] *compar of* **far**

farthest [fɑːr'ðist] *superl of* **far**

fascinate [fæs'əneit] *vt* (intrigue, interest) うっとりさせる uttóri saserù

fascinating [fæs'əneitiŋ] *adj* (story, person) 魅惑的な miwákuteki na

fascination [fæsənei'ʃən] *n* 魅惑 miwáku

fascism [fæʃ'izəm] *n* (POL) ファシズム fashízùmu

fashion [fæʃ'ən] *n* (trend: in clothes, thought, custom etc) 流行 ryūkō, ファッション fásshòn; (*also:* **fashion industry**) ファッション業界 fasshòn gyòkai; (manner) やり方 yaríkata

◆*vt* (make) 作る tsukúrù

in fashion 流行して ryūkō shite

out of fashion 廃れて sutárete

fashionable [fæʃ'ənəbəl] *adj* (clothes, club, subject) 流行の ryūkō no

fashion show *n* ファッションショー fasshòn shō

fast [fæst] adj (runner, car, progress) 速い hayái; (clock): **to be fast** 進んでいる susúnde irú; (dye, color) あせない asénai
♦adv (run, act, think) 速く hayákù; (stuck, held) 固く katákù
♦n (REL etc) 断食 danjíki
♦vi (REL etc) 断食する danjíki suru
fast asleep ぐっすり眠っている gussúri nemútte irú

fasten [fæs'ən] vt (tie, join) 縛る shibárù; (buttons, belt etc) 締める shimérù
♦vi 締まる shimárù

fastener [fæs'ənər] n (button, clasp, pin etc) ファスナー fásùnā

fastening [fæs'əniŋ] n = fastener

fast food n (hamburger etc) ファーストフード fásùtofúdo

fastidious [fæstid'i:əs] adj (fussy) やかましい yakámashiì

fat [fæt] adj (person, animal) 太った futótta; (book, profit) 厚い atsúi; (wallet) 金がたんまり入った kané ga tañmari haítta; (profit) 大きな ōkina
♦n (on person, animal: also CHEM) 脂肪 shibō; (on meat) 脂 abúramì; (for cooking) ラード rãdo

fatal [feit'əl] adj (mistake) 重大な júdai na; (injury, illness) 致命的な chiméiteki na

fatalistic [feitəlis'tik] adj (person, attitude) 宿命論的な shukúmeironteki na

fatality [feitæl'iti:] n (road death etc) 死亡事故 shibōjikò

fatally [feit'əli:] adv (mistaken) 重大に júdai ni; (injured etc) 致命的に chiméiteki ni

fate [feit] n (destiny) 運命 úñmei; (of person) 安否 áñpi

fateful [feit'fəl] adj (moment, decision) 決定的な kettéiteki na

father [fɑ:'ðər] n 父 chíchì, 父親 chichíoya, お父さん o-tōsan

father-in-law [fɑ:'ðərinlɔ:'] n しゅうと shúto

fatherly [fɑ:'ðərli:] adj (advice, help) 父親の様な chichíoya no yō da

fathom [fæð'əm] n (NAUT) 尋 hírò ◊水深の単位, 約1.83メーター sufshin no táñ-i,

yákù 1.83métà
♦vt (understand: mystery, reason) 理解する rikái suru

fatigue [fəti:g'] n (tiredness) 疲労 hirō
metal fatigue 金属疲労 kiñzokuhíro

fatten [fæt'ən] vt (animal) 太らせる futóraserù
♦vi 太る futórù

fatty [fæt'i:] adj (food) 脂肪の多い shibō no ói
♦n (inf: person) でぶ débù

fatuous [fætʃ'u:əs] adj (idea, remark) ばかな bákà na

faucet [fɔ'sit] (US) n (tap) 蛇口 jagúchi

fault [fɔ:lt] n (blame) 責任 sekínin; (defect: in person) 欠点 kettén; (: in machine) 欠陥 kekkán; (GEO: crack) 断層 dañsō; (TENNIS) フォールト fōruto
♦vt (criticize) 非難する hínàn suru
it's my fault 私が悪かった watákushi ga warúkattà
to find fault with ...を非難する ...wo hínàn suru
at fault ...のせいで ...no séi de

faulty [fɔ:l'ti:] adj (machine) 欠陥のある kekkán no arù

fauna [fɔ:n'ə] n 動物相 dōbutsusò

faux pas [fou pɑ:'] n inv 非礼 hiréi

favor [fei'vər] (BRIT favour) n (approval) 賛成 sañsei; (help) 助け tasúke
♦vt (prefer: solution etc) ...の方に賛成する ...no hō ni sañsei surù; (: pupil etc) ひいきする híìki suru; (assist: team, horse) ...に味方する ...ni mikáta suru
to do someone a favor ...の頼みを聞く ...no táñòmi wo kikú
to find favor with ...のお気に入る ...no kí ni irú
in favor of ...に賛成して ...ni sañsei shite

favorable [fei'vərəbəl] adj (gen) 有利な yūri na; (reaction) 好意的な kōìteki na; (impression) 良い yóì; (comparison) 賞賛の shōsanteki na; (conditions) 好適な kōteki na

favorite [fei'vərit] adj (child, author etc) 一番好きな ichíban suki na
♦n (of teacher, parent) お気に入り o-kí-

favoritism [fei'vəritizəm] n えこひいき
ekóhiíki

favour [fei'və:r] etc = **favor** etc

fawn [fɔːn] n (young deer) 子ジカ kojíka
◆adj (also: **fawn-colored**) 薄茶色 usú-
cha-iro
◆vi: to fawn (up)on ...にへつらう ...ni
hetsúraú

fax [fæks] n (machine, document) ファッ
クス fákkùsu
◆vt (transmit document) ファックスで送
る fákkùsu de okúrù

FBI [efbiːai'] (US) n abbr (= Federal
Bureau of Investigation) 連邦捜査局 reñ-
pōsōsakyòku

fear [fiːr] n (being scared) 恐怖 kyófu;
(worry) 心配 shifpai
◆vt (be scared of) 恐れる osórerù; (be
worried about) 心配する shifpai suru
for fear of (in case) ...を恐れて ...wo
osórete

fearful [fiːr'fəl] adj (person) 怖がってい
る kowágatte irù; (risk, noise) 恐ろしい
osóroshiì

fearless [fiːr'lis] adj (unafraid) 勇敢な
yūkan na

feasible [fiː'zəbəl] adj (proposal, idea) 可
能な kanō na

feast [fiːst] n (banquet) 宴会 efikai; (delicious meal) ごちそう gochísò; (REL:
also: **feast day**) 祝日 shukújitsu
◆vi (take part in a feast) ごちそうを食べ
る gochísò wò tabérù

feat [fiːt] n (of daring, skill) 目覚しい行
為 mezámashiì kōì

feather [feð'əːr] n (of bird) 羽根 hané

feature [fiː'tʃəːr] n (characteristic) 特徴
tokúchō; (of landscape) 目立つ点 medátsu tèn; (PRESS) 特別記事 tokúbetsukì-
jì; (TV) 特別番組 tokúbetsu bañgumì
◆vt (subj: film) 主役とする shuyáku to
surù
◆vi: to feature in (situation, film etc)
...で主演する ...de shuén suru

feature film n 長編映画 chōhen eiga

features [fiː'tʃəːrz] npl (of face) 顔立ち
kaódachi

February [feb'jəweːriː] n 2月 nigátsu

fed [fed] pt, pp of **feed**

federal [fed'əːrəl] adj (system, powers)
連邦の reñpō no

federation [fedəri'ʃən] n (association)
連盟 reñmei

fed up [fed ʌp'] adj: to be fed up うんざ
りしている uñzarì shite iru

fee [fiː] n (payment) 料金 ryōkin; (of doctor, lawyer) 報酬 hōshū; (for examination, registration) 手数料 tesúryō
school fees 授業料 jugyóryò

feeble [fiː'bəl] adj (weak) 弱い yowáì; (ineffectual: attempt, joke) 効果的でない
kōkateki de naì

feed [fiːd] n (of baby) ベビーフード bebí-
fùdo; (of animal) えさ esá; (on printer) 給
紙装置 kyūshisōchì
◆vt (pt, pp fed) (person) ...に食べさせる
...ni tabésaserù; (baby) ...に授乳する ...ni
junyū suru; (horse etc) ...にえさをやる
...ni esá wò yárù; (machine) ...に供給する
...ni kyōkyū suru; (data, information): to
feed into ...に入力する ...ni nyūryoku
suru

feedback [fiːd'bæk] n (response) フィー
ドバック fídobakku

feeding bottle [fiː'diŋ-] (BRIT) n ほ乳
瓶 honyūbin

feel [fiːl] n (sensation, touch) 感触 kañ-
shoku; (impression) 印象 ifshō
◆vt (pt, pp felt) (touch) ...に触る ...ni sawárù; (experience: desire, anger) 覚える
obóerù; (: cold, pain) 感じる kañjiru;
(think, believe) ...だと思う ...da to omóù
to feel hungry おなかがすく onáka gà
sukú
to feel cold 寒がる samúgarù
to feel lonely 寂しがる sabíshigarù
to feel better 気分がよくなる kíbùn ga
narù
I don't feel well 気分が悪い kíbùn ga
warúì
it feels soft 柔らかい感じだ yawárakaì

kańji da

to feel like (want) …が欲しい…ga hoshíi

feel about/around *vi* …を手探りで捜す …wo teságuri de sagású

feeler [fiː'lər] *n* (of insect) 触角 shokkáku

to put out a feeler/feelers (*fig*) 打診する dashín suru

feeling [fiː'liŋ] *n* (emotion) 感情 kańjō; (physical sensation) 感触 kańshoku; (impression) 印象 ińshō

feet [fiːt] *npl* of **foot**

feign [fein] *vt* (injury, interest) 見せ掛ける misékakerù

feline [fiː'lain] *adj* (cat-like) ネコの様な nékò no yō na

fell [fel] *pt* of **fall**

♦*vt* (tree) 倒す taósù

fellow [fel'ou] *n* (man) 男 otóko; (comrade) 仲間 nakáma; (of learned society) 会員 kaíin

fellow citizen *n* 同郷の市民 dṓkyō nò shímìn

fellow countryman (*pl* **countrymen**) *n* 同国人 dṓkokujìn

fellow men *npl* 外の人間 hoká no niṅgen

fellowship [fel'ouʃip] *n* (comradeship) 友情 yūjō; (society) 会 kái; (SCOL) 大学特別研究員 daígaku tokubetsu keṅkyūin

felony [fel'əni] *n* 重罪 jūzai

felt [felt] *pt, pp* of **feel**

♦*n* (fabric) フェルト férùto

felt-tip pen [felt'tip-] *n* サインペン saíňpen

female [fiː'meil] *n* (ZOOL) 雌 mesú; (*pej*: woman) 女 oňna

♦*adj* (BIO) 雌の oňna no; (sex, character, child) 女の oňna no, 女性の joséi no; (vote etc) 女性たちの joséitachi no

feminine [fem'ənin] *adj* (clothes, behavior) 女性らしい joséi rashìi; (LING) 女性の joséi no

feminist [fem'ənist] *n* 男女同権論者 dańjodṓkenronsha, フェミニスト femínisùto

fence [fens] *n* (barrier) 塀 heí

♦*vt* (*also*: **fence in**: land) 塀で囲む heí de kakómù

♦*vi* (SPORT) フェンシングをする féńshingu wo suru

fencing [fen'siŋ] *n* (SPORT) フェンシング féńshingu

fend [fend] *vi*: **to fend for oneself** 自力でやっていく jíriki dè yatté ikù

fender [fen'dər] *n* (of fireplace) 火格子 higṓshi; (on boat) 防げん物 bṓgenbutsu; (US: of car) フェンダー feńdā

fend off *vt* (attack etc) 受流す ukénagasù

ferment [*vb* fərment' *n* fər'ment] *vi* (beer, dough etc) 発酵する hakkṓ suru

♦*n* (*fig*: unrest) 動乱 dṓran

fern [fəːrn] *n* シダ shídà

ferocious [fərou'ʃəs] *adj* (animal, behavior) どう猛な dṓmō na; (competition) 激しい hagéshiì

ferocity [fəras'iti:] *n* (of animal, behavior) どう猛さ dṓmōsa; (of competition) 激しさ hagéshisà

ferret [fer'it] *n* フェレット férètto

ferret out *vt* (information) 捜し出す sagáshidasù

ferry [fer'iː] *n* (*also*: **ferry boat**) フェリー férì, フェリーボート feríbòto

♦*vt* (transport: by sea, air, road) 輸送する yusṓ suru

fertile [fəːr'təl] *adj* (land, soil) 肥よくな hiyóku na; (imagination) 豊かな yútàka na; (woman) 妊娠可能な nińshinkanō na

fertility [fəːrtil'əti:] *n* (of land) 肥よくさ hiyókusa; (of imagination) 独創性 dokúsōsei; (woman) 繁殖力 hańshokuryòku

fertilize [fəːr'təlaiz] *vt* (land) …に肥料をやる …ni hiryṓ wò yárù; (BIO) 受精させる juséi saserù

fertilizer [fəːr'təlaizər] *n* (for plants, land) 肥料 hiryṓ

fervent [fəːr'vənt] *adj* (admirer, belief) 熱心な nesshíñ na

fervor [fəːr'vər] *n* 熱心さ nesshíñsa

fester [fes'təːr] *vi* (wound) 化のうする kanṓ suru

festival [fes'təvəl] *n* (REL) 祝日 shukújitsu; (ART, MUS) フェスティバル fesútibarù

festive [fes'tiv] adj (mood, atmosphere) お祭気分の o-ma̅tsuríkibún no
the festive season (BRIT: Christmas) クリスマスの季節 kurísùmasu no kísétsu

festivities [festiv'itiz] npl (celebrations) お祝い o-íwai

festoon [festum'] vt: *to festoon with* ...で飾る ...de kazárú

fetch [fetʃ] vt (bring) 持って来る motté kurú; (sell for) ...の値で売れる ...no ne de uréru

fetching [fetʃ'iŋ] adj (woman, dress) 魅惑的な miwákuteki na

fête [feit] n (at church, school) バザー bazá̅

fetish [fet'iʃ] n (obsession) 強迫観念 kyó̅hakukaǹnen

fetus [fi:'təs] (BRIT foetus) n (BIO) 胎児 táìji

feud [fju:d] n (quarrel) 争い arásoì

feudal [fju:d'əl] adj (system, society) 封建的な hó̅kenteki na

fever [fi:'vər] n (MED) 熱 netsú

feverish [fi:'vəriʃ] adj (MED) 熱がある netsú ga árù; (emotion: person) いらいらしている iráiraí; (activity) 慌ただしい awátadashiì

few [fju:] adj (not many) 少数の shó̅sū no; (some): *a few* 幾つかの íkùtsuka no
◆pron (not many) 少数 shó̅sū; (some): *a few* 幾つかの íkùtsuka

fewer [fju:'ər] adj compar of few

fewest [fju:'ist] adj superl of few

fiancé [fi:a:nsei'] n 婚約者 koń-yakushà, 'フィアンセ fiàǹse の男性 dańsei

fiancée [fi:a:nsei'] n 婚約者 koń-yakushà, フィアンセ fiàǹse の女性 joséi

fiasco [fi:æs'kou] n (disaster) 失敗 shippái

fib [fib] n (lie) うそ úsò

fiber [fai'bər] (BRIT fibre) n (thread, roughage) 繊維 séñ-i; (cloth) 生地 kíjì; (ANAT: tissue) 神経繊維 shińkeisèn-i

fiber-glass [fai'bərglæs] n ファイバーグラス faíbāgùrasu

fickle [fik'əl] adj (person) 移り気な utsúrigi na; (weather) 変りやすい kawáriyasuì

fiction [fik'ʃən] n (LITERATURE) フィクション fíkùshon; (invention) 作り事 tsukúrígoto; (lie) うそ úsò

fictional [fik'ʃənəl] adj (character, event) 架空の kakú no

fictitious [fiktiʃ'əs] adj (false, invented) 架空の kakú no

fiddle [fid'əl] n (MUS) バイオリン baíorin; (inf: fraud, swindle) 詐欺 ságì
◆vt (BRIT: accounts) ごまかす gomákasù

fiddle with vt fus (glasses etc) いじくる ijíkurù

fidelity [fidel'iti:] n (faithfulness) 忠誠 chūsei

fidget [fidʒ'it] vi (nervously) そわそわする sówàsowa suru; (in boredom) もそもそする mózòmozo suru

field [fi:ld] n (on farm) 畑 hatáke; (SPORT: ground) グランド gurándo; (fig: subject, area of interest) 分野 búñya; (range: of vision) 視野 shíyà; (: of magnet: also ELEC) 磁場 jíbà

field marshal n (MIL) 元帥 geńsui

fieldwork [fi:ld'wəːrk] n (research) 現地調査 gếnchichòsa, 実地調査 jitchíchòsa, フィールドワーク firúdowàku

fiend [fi:nd] n (monster) 怪物 kaíbutsu

fiendish [fi:n'diʃ] adj (person, problem) 怪物の様な kaíbutsu no yō na; (problem) ものすごく難しい monósugokù muzúkashiì

fierce [fi:rs] adj (animal, person) どう猛な dó̅mō na; (fighting) 激しい hagéshiì; (loyalty) 揺るぎない yurúginaì; (wind) 猛烈な mó̅retsu na; (heat) うだる様な udáru yō na

fiery [fai'əːri:] adj (burning) 燃え盛る moésakarù; (temperament) 激しい hagéshiì

fifteen [fif'ti:n'] num 十五 (の) jū̅go (no)

fifth [fifθ] num 第五 (の) dáigo (no)

fifty [fif'ti:] num 五十 (の) gojū̅ (no)

fifty-fifty [fif'ti:fif'ti:] adj (deal, split) 五分五分の gobúgobu no
◆adv 五分五分に gobúgobu ni

fig [fig] n (fruit) イチジク ichíjìku

fight [fait] *n* 戦い tatákai
♦*vb* (*pt, pp* **fought**)
♦*vt* (person, enemy, cancer etc: *also* MIL) ...と戦う ...to tatákaù; (election) ...に出馬する ...ni shutsúba suru; (emotion) 抑える osáerù
♦*vi* (people: *also* MIL) 戦う tatákaù

fighter [fai'tə:r] *n* (combatant) 戦う人 tatákaù hitó; (plane) 戦闘機 señtókì

fighting [fai'tiŋ] *n* (battle) 戦い tatákai; (brawl) けんか kéñka

figment [fig'mənt] *n*: **a figment of the imagination** 気のせい kí nò séi

figurative [fig'jə:rativ] *adj* (expression, style) 比喩的な hiyúteki na

figure [fig'jə:r] *n* (DRAWING, GEOM) 図 zu; (number, statistic etc) 数字 sújì; (body, shape, outline) 形 katáchi; (person, personality) 人物 hitó
♦*vt* (think: esp *US*) ...(だと) 思う ...(da to) omóù
♦*vi* (appear) 見える miérù

figurehead [fig'jə:rhed] *n* (NAUT) 船首像 señshuzó; (*pej*: leader) 名ばかりのリーダー na bákarì no rídā

figure of speech *n* 比喩 hiyú

figure out *vt* (work out) 理解する rikái suru

filament [fil'əmənt] *n* (ELEC) フィラメント fíràmento

filch [filtʃ] (*inf*) *vt* (steal) くすねる kusúnerù

file [fail] *n* (dossier) 資料 shiryó; (folder) 書類ばさみ shorúibàsami; (COMPUT) ファイル fáìru; (row) 列 retsú; (tool) やすり yasúrì
♦*vt* (papers) 保管する hokán suru; (LAW: claim) 提出する teíshutsu suru; (wood, metal, fingernails) ...にやすりを掛ける ...ni yasúrì wo kakérù

file in/out *vi* 1列で入る (出る) ichíretsu dè hairú(dérù)

filing cabinet [fai'liŋ-] *n* ファイルキャビネット fáìru kyabínètto

fill [fil] *vt* (container, space): **to fill (with)** (...で) 一杯にする (...de) ippái ni suru; (vacancy) 補充する hojú suru; (need) 満たす mitásù

♦*n*: **to eat one's fill** たらふく食べる taráfuku tabérù

fillet [filei'] *n* (of meat, fish) ヒレ híre

fillet steak *n* ヒレステーキ hirésutèki

filling [fil'iŋ] *n* (for tooth) 充てん júten; (CULIN) 中身 nakámi

filling station *n* (AUT) ガソリンスタンド gasórinsutañdo

fill up *vt* (container, space) 一杯にする ippái ni suru
♦*vi* (AUT) 満タンにする mañtan ni suru

film [film] *n* (CINEMA, TV) 映画 éìga; (PHOT) フィルム fírùmu; (of powder, liquid etc) 膜 makú
♦*vt* (scene) 撮影する satsúei suru
♦*vi* 撮影する satsúei suru

film star *n* 映画スター eígasutā

film strip *n* (slide) フィルムスライド fírùmusuràido

filter [fil'tə:r] *n* (device) ろ過装置 rokásòchi, フィルター ffrútā; (PHOT) フィルター ffrútā
♦*vt* (liquid) ろ過する rokấ suru

filter lane (*BRIT*) *n* (AUT) 右(左)折車線 (sa)sétsu shasèn

filter-tipped [fil'tə:rtipt] *adj* フィルター付きの fírùtsuki no

filth [filθ] *n* (dirt) 汚物 obútsu

filthy [fil'θi:] *adj* object, person 不潔な fukétsu na; (language) みだらな mídàra na

fin [fin] *n* (of fish) ひれ híre

final [fai'nəl] *adj* (last) 最後の saígo no; (ultimate) 究極の kyūkyoku no; (definitive: answer, decision) 最終的な saíshūteki na
♦*n* (SPORT) 決勝戦 kesshōsen

finale [finæl'i:] *n* フィナーレ fínàre

finalist [fai'nəlist] *n* (SPORT) 決勝戦出場選手 kesshōsen shutsujō senshu

finalize [fai'nəlaiz] *vt* (arrangements, plans) 最終的に決定する saíshūteki ni kettéi suru

finally [fai'nəli:] *adv* (eventually) ようやく yōyaku; (lastly) 最後に saígo ni

finals [fai'nəlz] *npl* (SCOL) 卒業試験 so-tsūgyōshiken

finance [*n* fai'næns *vb* finæns'] *n* (money, backing) 融資 yūshi; (money management) 財政 zaisei
♦*vt* (back, fund) 融資する yūshi suru

finances [fai'nænsiz] *npl* (personal finances) 財政 zaisei

financial [finæn'tʃəl] *adj* (difficulties, year, venture) 経済的な keizaiteki na

financial year *n* 会計年度 kaikeinéndo

financier [finænsir'] *n* (backer, funder) 出資者 shusshísha

find [faind] (*pt, pp* **found**) *vt* (person, object, answer) 見付ける mitsukéru; (discover) 発見する hakkén suru; (think) ...だと思う ...da to omóu
♦*n* (discovery) 発見 hakkén
to find someone guilty (LAW) ...に有罪判決を下す ...ni yūzaihañketsu wo kudásù

findings [fain'diŋz] *npl* (LAW, of report) 調査の結果 chōsa no kekka

find out *vt* (fact, truth) 知る shírù; (person) ...の悪事を知る ...no ákùjì wo shírù
to find out about (subject) 調べる shiráberù; (by chance) 知る shírù

fine [fain] *adj* (excellent: quality, performance etc) 見事な mígòtò na; (thin: hair, thread) 細い hosóì; (not coarse: sand, powder etc) 細かい komákaì; (subtle: detail, adjustment etc) 細かい komákaì
♦*adv* (well) うまく úmàkù
♦*n* (LAW) 罰金 bakkín
♦*vt* (LAW) ...に罰金を払わせる ...ni bakkín wo haráwaserù
to be fine (person) 元気である géñki de árù; (weather) 良い天気である yói téñki de árù

fine arts *npl* 美術 bíjùtsu

finery [fai'nəːri:] *n* (dress) 晴着 harégì; (jewelery) 取って置きの装身具 tottéokì no sōshíñgu

finesse [fine's'] *n* 手腕 shúwàn

finger [fiŋ'gəːr] *n* (ANAT) 指 yubí
♦*vt* (touch) ...に指で触る ...ni yubí dè sawárù
little/index finger 小(人差し)指 ko-

fingernail [fiŋ'gəːrneil] *n* つめ tsume

fingerprint [fiŋ'gəːrprint] *n* (mark) 指紋 shimón

fingertip [fiŋ'gəːrtip] *n* 指先 yubísaki

finicky [fin'iki:] *adj* (fussy) 気難しい kimúzukashiì

finish [fin'iʃ] *n* (end) 終り owárì; (SPORT) ゴール gōru; (polish etc) 仕上り shiágarí
♦*vt* (work, eating, book etc) 終える oérù
♦*vi* (person, course, event) 終る owárù
to finish doing something ...し終える ...shi oérù
to finish third (in race etc) 3番になる sañchaku ni naru

finishing line [fin'iʃiŋ-] *n* ゴールライン gōruraíñ

finishing school [fin'iʃiŋ-] *n* 花嫁学校 hanáyomegàkkō

finish off *vt* (complete) 仕上げる shiágerù; (kill) 止めを刺す todóme wo sásù

finish up *vt* (food, drink) 平らげる tafáragerù
♦*vi* (end up) 最後に...に行ってしまう sáigo ni ...ni itté shimaù

finite [fai'nait] *adj* (time, space) 一定の ittéi no; (verb) 定形の teíkei no

Finland [fin'lənd] *n* フィンランド fíñrando

Finn [fin] *n* フィンランド人 fíñrandojìn

Finnish [fin'iʃ] *adj* フィンランドの fíñrando no; (LING) フィンランド語の fíñrandogo no
♦*n* (LING) フィンランド語 fíñrandogo

fiord [fjourd] *n* = **fjord**

fir [fəːr] *n* モミ mómì

fire [fai'əːr] *n* (flames) 火 hí; (in hearth) たき火 takíbi; (accidental) 火事 kájì; (gas fire, electric fire) ヒーター hītā
♦*vt* (gun etc) うつ útsù; (: arrow) 射る írù; (stimulate: imagination, enthusiasm) 刺激する shigéki suru; (*inf*: dismiss: employee) 首にする kubí ni surù
♦*vi* (shoot) 発砲する happō suru
on fire 燃えて moéte

fire alarm *n* 火災警報装置 kasáikeihōsōchi

firearm [fai'əːrːrm] *n* 銃砲 jūhō ◇ 特に

ピストルを指す tōkù n pisútoru wò sásù

fire brigade n 消防隊 shōbōtai

fire department (US) n = fire brigade

fire engine n 消防自動車 shōbōjidōsha

fire escape n 非常階段 hijōkaìdan

fire extinguisher n 消化器 shōkakì

fireman [faiǝr'mǝn] (pl firemen) n 消防士 shōbōshi

fireplace [faiǝr'pleis] n 暖炉 dánro

fireside [faiǝr'said] n 暖炉のそば dánro no sóba

fire station n 消防署 shōbōsho

firewood [faiǝr'wud] n まき makì

fireworks [faiǝr'wǝːrks] npl 花火 hánàbi

firing squad [faiǝr'iŋ-] n 銃殺隊 jūsatsutsai

firm [fǝːrm] adj (mattress, ground) 固い katái; (grasp, push, tug) 強い tsuyóì; (decision) 断固とした dánko to shita; (faith) 固い katái; (measures) 強固な kyōko na; (look, voice) しっかりした shikkárì shita

♦n (company) 会社 kaísha

firmly [fǝːrm'liː] adv (grasp, pull, tug) 強く tsuyóku; (decide) 断固として dánko to shite; (look, speak) しっかりと shikkárì to

first [fǝːrst] adj (before all others) 第一の dáìchi no, 最初の saisho no

♦adv (before all others) 一番に ichíban ni, 一番最初に ichíban saisho ni; (when listing reasons etc) 第一に dáichi ni

♦n (person: in race) 一着 itcháku; (AUT) ローギヤ rōgiya; (BRIT SCOL: degree) 1級優等卒業学位 ìkkyū yútō sotsugyō gakùi 〇英国では優等卒業学位は成績の高い順に1級、2級、3級に分けられるが英国の中では1級優等卒業学位の最も高い級の事を指す eíkoku de wà yútō sotsugyō gakùi wa sefsèki no takái jùn ni ìkkyū, nikyū, sankyū ni wakèrarerú

at first 最初は saísho wa

first of all 第一に dáì-ichi ni, まず dáìchi ni

first aid n 応急手当 ōkyūteàte

first-aid kit n 救急箱 kyūkyūbako

first-class [fǝːrst'klæs'] adj (excellent: mind, worker) 優れた sugúretà; (car-

riage, ticket, post) 1等の ìttō no

first-hand [fǝːrst'hænd'] adj (account, story) 直接の chokúsetsu no

first lady (US) n 大統領夫人 daftōryō-fujìn

firstly [fǝːrst'liː] adv 第一に dáìchi ni

first name n 名 na, ファーストネーム fásutonèmu

first-rate [fǝːrst'reit'] adj (player, actor etc) 優れた sugúretà

fiscal [fis'kǝl] adj (year) 会計の kaíkei no; (policies) 財政の zaísei no

fish [fiʃ] n 魚 sakána

♦vt (river, area) ...で釣をする ...de tsurí wo surù

♦vi (commercially) 漁をする ryō wo surù; (as sport, hobby) 釣をする tsurí wo surù

to go fishing 釣に行く tsurí ni ikù

fisherman [fiʃ'ǝrmǝn] (pl fishermen) n 漁師 ryōshi

fish farm n 養魚場 yōgyojō

fish fingers (BRIT) npl = fish sticks

fishing boat [fiʃ'iŋ-] n 漁船 gyosen

fishing line n 釣糸 tsurfitō

fishing rod n 釣ざお tsurízao

fishmonger's (shop) [fiʃ'mʌŋgǝrz-] n 魚屋 sakánaya

fish sticks (US) npl フィッシュスティック fisshúsutikkù 〇細長く切った魚にパン粉をまぶして揚げた物 hosónagakù kittà sakána ni pánko wo mabúshite agéta monò

fishy [fiʃ'iː] (inf) adj (tale, story) 怪しい ayáshiì

fission [fiʃ'ǝn] n 分裂 buńretsu

fissure [fiʃ'ǝr] n 亀裂 kiretsu

fist [fist] n こぶし kóbushi, げんこつ geńkotsu

fit [fit] adj (suitable) 適当な tekítō na; (healthy) 健康な keńkō na

♦vt (subj: clothes, shoes) ...にぴったり合う ...ni pittárì au; (put in) ...に入れる ...ni irérù; (attach, equip) ...に取り付ける ...ni torítsukerù; (suit) ...に合う ...ni áù

♦vi (clothes) ぴったり合う pittárì áù; (parts) 合う áù; (in space, gap) ぴったりはいる pittárì haírù

◆n (MED) 発作 hossá; (of coughing, giggles) 発作作的に...し事 hossáteki ni ...suru kotó

fit to (ready) ...出来る状態にある ...dekirù jōtai ni arù

fit for (suitable for) ...に適当である ...ni tekítō de arù

a fit of anger かんしゃく kańshaku

this dress is a good fit このドレスはぴったり体に合う konó dorèsu wa pittárì karáda ni aù

by fits and starts 動いたり止ったりして ugóitarì tomáttarì shité

fitful [fit'fəl] adj (sleep) 途切れ途切れの togíretogìre no

fit in vi (person) 溶込む tokékomù

fitment [fit'mənt] n (in room, cabin) 取付け家具 torítsukekagù; (つり戸棚など壁などに固定した家具を指す tsurítodàna nádò kabé nadò ni kotéi shitá kagù wo sásù

fitness [fit'nis] n (health) 健康 keńkō

fitted carpet [fit'id-] n 敷込みじゅうたん shikíkomìjūtan

fitted kitchen [fit'id-] n システムキッチン shisútemu kitchìn

fitter [fit'əːr] n (of machinery, equipment) 整備工 seíbikō

fitting [fit'iŋ] adj (compliment, thanks) 適切な tekísetsu na

◆n (of dress) 試着 shichàku; (of piece of equipment) 取付け torítsuke

fitting room (in shop) 試着室 shichákushìtsu

fittings [fit'iŋz] npl (in building) 設備せつ tsubi

five [faiv] num 五 (の) gó (no), 五つ (の) itsútsù (no)

fiver [faiv'əːr] n (inf: BRIT: 5 pounds) 5ポンド札 gópondo satsù; (US: 5 dollars) 5ドル札 gódòru satsù

fix [fiks] vt (attach) 取付ける torítsukerù; (sort out, arrange) 手配する tehái surù; (mend) 直す naósù; (prepare: meal, drink) 作る tsukúrù

◆n: **to be in a fix** 困っている komátte irù

fixation [fiksei'ʃən] n 固着 kochàku

fixed [fikst] adj (price, amount etc) 一定の ittéi no

a fixed idea 固定観念 kotéikañnen

a fixed smile 作り笑い tsukúriwarài

fixture [fiks'tʃəːr] n (bath, sink, cupboard etc) 設備 sétsùbi; (SPORT) 試合の予定 shiái no yotéi

fizzle out [fiz'əl-] vi (event) しりすぼみに終ってしまう shirísubòmi ni owátte shimàu; (interest) 次第に消えてしまう shidái ni kiète shimàu

fizzy [fiz'i:] adj (drink) 炭酸入りの tańsan-iri no

fjord [fjourd] n フィヨルド fíyorudo

flabbergasted [flæb'əːrgæstid] adj (dumbfounded, surprised) あっけにとられた akké ni toraretà

flabby [flæb'i:] adj (fat) 締まりのない shimárì no naì

flag [flæg] n (of country, organization) 旗 hatá; (for signalling) 手旗 tebáta; (also: flagstone) 敷石 shikíishi

◆vi (person, spirits) 弱る yowárù

to flag someone down (taxi, car etc) 手を振って...を止める té wo futté ...wo tomérù

flagpole [flæg'poul] n 旗ざお hatázao

flagrant [fleig'rənt] adj (violation, injustice) 甚だしい hanáhadashiì

flagship [flæg'ʃip] n (of fleet) 旗艦 kikán; (fig) 看板施設 kańbanshisetsu

flair [fleːr] n (talent) ...の才 ...no sáinō; (style) 粋なセンス ikí na señsu

flak [flæk] n (MIL) 対空砲火 taíkūhòka; (inf: criticism) 非難 hínan

flake [fleik] n (of rust, paint) はげ落ちた欠けら hagéochità kakéra; (of snow, soap powder) 一片 íppén

◆vi (also: flake off): paint, enamel) はげ落ちる hagéochirù

flamboyant [flæmboi'ənt] adj (dress, design) けばけばしい kebákebashiì; (person) 派手な hadé na

flame [fleim] n (of fire) 炎 honő-ō

flamingo [fləmiŋ'gou] n フラミンゴ furámiñgo

flammable [flæm'əbəl] adj (gas, fabric) 燃えやすい moéyasui

flan [flæn] n (BRIT) n フラン fúran ◇菓子の一種 kashī no isshū

flank [flæŋk] n (of animal) わき腹 wakfbāra; (of army) 側面 sokúmèn

◆vt ...のわきにある(いる) ...no wakf ni arû (iru)

flannel [flæn'əl] n (fabric) フランネル furánneru; (BRIT: also: face flannel) フェースタオル fésutaðru

flannels [flæn'əlz] npl フランネルズボン furánneruzubòn

flap [flæp] n (of pocket, envelope, jacket) ふた futá

◆vt (arms, wings) ばたばたさせる bátabata saserú

◆vi (sail, flag) はためく hátamekù; (inf: also: **be in a flap**) 興奮している kôfun shite irú

flare [fleːr] n (signal) 発煙筒 hatsúeñtồ; (in skirt etc) フレア furéa

flare up n (fire) 燃え上る moéagarù; (fig: person) 怒る okórù; (: fighting) ぽっ発する boppátsu suru

flash [flæʃ] n (of light) 閃光 señkồ; (also: **news flash**) ニュースフラッシュ nyūsufurasshů; (PHOT) フラッシュ furásshù

◆vt (light, headlights etc) 点滅させる teñmetsu saserú; (send: news, message) 速報する sokúhồ suru; (: look, smile) 見せる misérù

◆vi (lightning, light) 光る hikárù; (light on ambulance etc) 点滅する teñmetsu suru

in a flash 一瞬にして isshún ni shite

to flash by/past (person) 走って通り過ぎる hashíttè tồrisugirù

flashback [flæʃ'bæk] n (CINEMA) フラッシュバック furásshubakkù

flashbulb [flæʃ'bʌlb] n フラッシュバルブ furásshubarùbu

flashcube [flæʃ'kjuːb] n フラッシュキューブ furásshukyûbu

flashlight [flæʃ'lait] n 懐中電灯 kaíchūdeñtò

flashy [flæʃ'iː] (pej) adj 派手な hadé na

flask [flæsk] n (also: vacuum flask) 魔法瓶 máhồbin, ポット pốttò

flat [flæt] adj (ground, surface) 平な táfra na; (tire) パンクした pánku shita; (battery) 上がった agátta; (beer) 気が抜けた ki ga nûketa; (refusal, denial) きっぱりした kippárishìta; (MUS: note) フラットの furátтồ no; (: voice) そっけない sokkénàí; (rate, fee) 均一の kiñ-itsu no

◆n (BRIT: apartment) アパート ápàto; (AUT) パンク pánku; (MUS) フラット furáttồ

to work flat out 力一杯働く chikára ippái hataraku

flatly [flæt'liː] adv (refuse, deny) きっぱりと kippárì to

flatten [flæt'ən] vt (also: **flatten out**) 平にする táfra ni surú; (building, city) 取壊す toríkowasù

flatter [flæt'əːr] vt (praise, compliment) ...にお世辞を言う ...ni oséji wò iû

flattering [flæt'əːriŋ] adj (comment) うれしい uréshìi; (dress) よく似合う yókù niáù

flattery [flæt'əːriː] n お世辞 oséji

flaunt [flɔːnt] vt (wealth, possessions) 見せびらかす misébirakasù

flavor [flei'vəːr] (BRIT **flavour**) n (of food, drink) 味 aji; (of ice-cream etc) 種類 shúrùi

◆vt ...に味を付ける ...ni ajf wo tsukerù

strawberry-flavored イチゴ味の ichfgoaji no

flavoring [flei'vəːriŋ] n 調味料 chồmiryồ

flaw [flɔː] n (in argument, policy) 不備な点 fúbi na teñ; (in character) 欠点 kettèn; (in cloth, glass) 傷 kizú

flawless [flɔː'lis] adj 完璧な kañpeki na

flax [flæks] n 亜麻 amá

flaxen [flæk'sən] adj (hair) ブロンドの buróndo no

flea [fliː] n (human, animal) ノミ nomf

fleck [flek] n (mark) 細かい斑点 komákai hañtèn

fled [fled] pt, pp of **flee**

flee [fli:] (*pt, pp* **fled**) *vt* (danger, famine, country) 逃れる nogáréru, ...から逃げる ...kara nigéru

♦*vi* (refugees, escapees) 逃げる nigéru

fleece [fli:s] *n* (sheep's wool) 羊毛一頭分 yōmóittōbùn; (sheep's coat) ヒツジの毛 hitsúji no kě

♦*vt* (*inf*: cheat) ...から大金をだまし取る ...kara taíkin wo damáshitòru

fleet [fli:t] *n* (of ships: for war) 艦隊 kañtai; (: for fishing etc) 船団 señdan; (of trucks, cars) 車両団 sharyōdan

fleeting [fli:'tiŋ] *adj* (glimpse) ちらっと見える chiráttò miéru; (visit) 短い mijíkai; (happiness) つかの間の tsuká no mà no

Flemish [flem'iʃ] *adj* フランダースの furándāsu no; (LING) フランダース語の furándāsugo no

♦*n* (LING) フランダース語 furándāsugo

flesh [fleʃ] *n* (ANAT) 肉 nikú; (skin) 肌 hadá; (of fruit) 果肉 kaníku

flesh wound *n* 軽傷 keíshō

flew [flu:] *pt of* **fly**

flex [fleks] *n* (of appliance) コード kōdò

♦*vt* (leg, muscles) 曲げたり伸したりする magétari nobáshitari suru

flexibility [fleksəbil'əti:] *n* (of material) しなやかさ shináyakasa; (of response, policy) 柔軟性 jūnañsei

flexible [flek'səbəl] *adj* (material) 曲げやすい magéyasui; (response, policy) 柔軟な jūnan na

flick [flik] *n* (of hand, whip etc) 一振り hitófuri

♦*vt* (with finger, hand) はじき飛ばす hajíkitobasù; (towel, whip) ぴしっと振る pishíttò furú; (switch: on) 入れる iréru; (: off) 切る kírù

flicker [flik'əːr] *vi* (light) ちらちらする chírachira suru; (flame) ゆらゆらする yúrayura suru; (eyelids) まばたく mabátaku

flick through *vt fus* (book) ぱらぱらと ...のページをめくる párapara to ...no pèji wo mekúru

flier [flai'əːr] *n* (pilot) パイロット paíróttò

flight [flait] *n* (action: of birds, plane) 飛行 hikō; (AVIAT: journey) 飛行機旅行 hikókiryokō; (escape) 逃避 tōhì; (*also*: **flight of steps/stairs**) 階段 kaídan

flight attendant (*US*) *n* 乗客係 jōkyakukakàri

flight deck *n* (AVIAT) 操縦室 sōjūshítsu; (NAUT) 空母の飛行甲板 kūbo no hikókañpan

flimsy [flim'zi:] *adj* (shoes) こわれやすい kowáreyasù; (clothes) 薄い usúi; (building) もろい moróì; (excuse) 見え透いた miésuita

flinch [flintʃ] *vi* (in pain, shock) 身震いする mibúrùi suru

to flinch from (crime, unpleasant duty) ...するのをしり込みする ...surú no wò shiŕigomi suru

fling [fliŋ] (*pt, pp* **flung**) *vt* (throw) 投げる nagéru

flint [flint] *n* (stone) 火打石 hiúchiishì; (in lighter) 石 ishí

flip [flip] *vt* (switch) はじく hajíkù; (coin) はじき上げる tōsù suru

flippant [flip'ənt] *adj* (attitude, answer) 軽率な keísotsu na

flipper [flip'əːr] *n* (of seal etc) ひれ足 hiréashì; (for swimming) フリッパー furíppà

flirt [fləːrt] *vi* (with person) いちゃつく ichátsuku

♦*n* 浮気者 uwákimono

flit [flit] *vi* (birds, insects) ひょいと飛ぶ hyoí to tobú

float [flout] *n* (for swimming, fishing) 浮き ukí; (vehicle in parade) 山車 dashí; (money) つり用の小銭 tsurívō nò kozéni

♦*vi* 浮く ukú

flock [flɑːk] *n* 群れ muré; (REL) 会衆 kaíshū

♦*vi*: *to flock to* (place, event) ぞくぞく集まる zókuzoku atsúmarù

flog [flɑːg] *vt* (whip) むち打つ múchiutsu

flood [flʌd] *n* (of water) 洪水 kōzui; (of letters, imports etc) 大量 taíryō

♦*vt* (subj: water) 水浸しにする mizúbitàshi ni suru; (: people) ...に殺到する ...ni sattō suru

♦*vi* (place) 水浸しになる mizűbitashi ni nárū; (people): **to flood into ...** に殺到する ...ni sattō suru

flooding [flʌd'iŋ] *n* 洪水 kōzui

floodlight [flʌd'lait] *n* 照明灯 shōmeítō

floor [flɔːr] *n* (of room) 床 yuká; (storey) 階 káī; (of sea, valley) 底 sōkō
♦*vt* (subj: blow) 打ち倒す uchínomesù; (: question) 仰天させる gyŏten saserū

ground floor *n* 1階 ikkái

first floor (*US*) 1階 ikkái (*BRIT*) 2階 nikái

floorboard [flɔːr'bɔːrd] *n* 床板 yuká-ita

floor show *n* フロアショー furōashō

flop [flɔːp] *n* (failure) 失敗 shippái
♦*vi* (fail) 失敗する shippái suru; (fall: into chair, onto floor etc) どたっと座り込む dotáttò suwárikomù

floppy [flɔːp'i] *adj* ふにゃふにゃした fúnyafunya shita

floppy (disk) *n* (COMPUT) フロッピー（ディスク） furóppì(disùku)

flora [flɔːr'ə] *n* 植物相 shokúbutsusō

floral [flɔːr'əl] *adj* (dress, wallpaper) 花柄の hanágara no

florid [flɔːr'id] *adj* (style) ごてごてした gōtègote shitá; (complexion) 赤らんだ akárañda

florist [flɔːr'ist] *n* 花屋 hanáyà

florist's (shop) *n* 花屋 hanáyà

flounce [flauns] *n* (frill) 緑飾り fuchíkazari

flounce out *vi* 怒って飛び出す okóttè tobídasù

flounder [flaun'dəːr] *vi* (swimmer) もがく mugákù; (fig: speaker) まごつく magótsukù; (economy) 停滞する teítai suru
♦*n* (ZOOL) ヒラメ hiráme

flour [flauˈəːr] *n* (gen) 粉 koná; (also: **wheat flour**) 小麦粉 komúgikò

flourish [flɔːr'iʃ] *vi* (business) 繁栄する hañ-ei suru; (plant) 生い茂る oíshigerù
♦*n* (bold gesture): **with a flourish** 大げさな身振りで ŏgesa na mibúri de

flourishing [flɔːr'iʃiŋ] *adj* (company) 繁栄する hañ-ei suru; (trade) 盛んな sakán na

flout [flaut] *vt* (law, rules) 犯す okásù

flow [flou] *n* 流れ nagáre
♦*vi* 流れる nagárerù

flow chart *n* 流れ図 nagárezù, フローチャート furóchātò

flower [flauˈəːr] *n* 花 haná
♦*vi* (plant, tree) 咲く sakú

flower bed *n* 花壇 kádan

flowerpot [flauˈəːrpɑːt] *n* 植木鉢 uckíbachi

flowery [flauˈəːri] *adj* (perfume) 花の様な haná no yō na; (pattern) 花柄の hanágara no; (speech) 美辞の biji no

flown [floun] *pp* of **fly**

flu [fluː] *n* (MED) 流感 ryúkan

fluctuate [flʌk'tʃueit] *vi* (price, rate, temperature) 変動する heñdō suru

fluctuation [flʌktʃuei'ʃən] *n*: **fluctuation (in)** (の) 変動 (...no) heñdō

fluent [fluː'ənt] *adj* (linguist) 語学たん能な gogákutañnō na; (speech, writing etc) 滑らかな naméràka na

he speaks fluent French, he's fluent in French 彼はフランス語が堪能だ kárè wa furánsugo gà tañnō da

fluently [fluː'əntli] *adv* (speak, read, write) 流ちょうに ryúchō ni

fluff [flʌf] *n* (on jacket, carpet) 毛羽 kebá; (fur: of kitten etc) 綿毛 watáge

fluffy [flʌf'i:] *adj* (jacket, toy etc) ふわふわした fúwàfuwa shitá

fluid [fluː'id] *adj* (movement) しなやかな shináyàka na; (situation, arrangement) 流動的な ryúdōteki na
♦*n* (liquid) 液体 ekítai

fluke [fluːk] *n* (*inf*) まぐれ magúre

flung [flʌŋ] *pt, pp* of **fling**

fluorescent [fluːəres'ənt] *adj* (dial, paint, light etc) 蛍光の kefkō no

fluoride [fluː'əraid] *n* フッ化物 fukkábùtsu

flurry [fluːr'i:] *n*: **a snow flurry** にわか雪 niwákayùki
flurry of activity 慌ただしい動き a-wátadashiì ugóki

flush [flʌʃ] *n* (on face) ほてり hotéri; (fig: of youth, beauty etc) 輝かしさ kagáyakashisà
♦*vt* (drains, pipe) 水を流して洗う mizú

wà nagashite araù
♦*vi* (become red) 赤くなる akáku narù

♦*adj*: **flush with** (level) ...と同じ高さの
...to onáji takasà no
to flush the toilet トイレの水を流す
tótre no mizú wo nagasù

flushed [flʌʃt] *adj* 赤らめた akáràmeta

flush out *vt* (game, birds) 茂みから追出
す shigémi kàra oídasù

flustered [flʌstəːrd] *adj* (nervous, confused) まごついた magótsuità

flute [fluːt] *n* フルート fúrùto

flutter [flʌtəːr] *n* (of wings) 羽ばたき
habátaki; (of panic, excitement, nerves)
うろたえ urótae
♦*vi* (bird) 羽ばたきする habátaki suru

flux [flʌks] *n*: **in a state of flux** 流動の
状態で ryúdòtekijòtai de

fly [flai] *n* (insect) ハエ haé; (on trousers:
also: **flies**) ズボンの前 zubón no maé
♦*vb* (*pt* **flew**, *pp* **flown**)
♦*vt* (plane) 操縦する sòjù suru; (passengers, cargo) 空輸する kùyù suru; (dis-
tances) 飛ぶ tobù
♦*vi* (bird, insect, plane) 飛ぶ tobù; (passengers) 飛行機で行く hikòki de ikú;
(escape) 逃げる nigérù; (flag) 掲げられる
kakágerarerù

fly away *vi* (bird, insect) 飛んで行く ton-
de ikú

flying [flaiiŋ] *n* (activity) 飛行機旅行 hi-
kòkiryokò; (action) 飛行 hikò
♦*adj*: **a flying visit** ほんの短い訪問 hon-
no mijikaì hòmon
with flying colors 大成功で daíseikò de

flying saucer *n* 空飛ぶ円盤 sòra tobù
enban

flying start *n*: **to get off to a flying
start** 好調な滑りだしをする kòchò na
suberidàshi wo surú

fly off *vi* = **fly away**

flyover [flaiouvəːr] (*BRIT*) *n* (overpass)
陸橋 rikkyò

flysheet [flaiʃiːt] *n* (for tent) 入口の垂れ
布 irīguchi nò tarénuno

foal [foul] *n* 子ウマ kóuma

foam [foum] *n* (of surf, water, beer) 泡

awá; (*also*: **foam rubber**) フォームラバー
fòmurabà
♦*vi* (liquid) 泡立つ awádatsu
to foam at the mouth (person, animal)
泡をふく awà wo fukù

fob [fɑb] *vt*: **to fob someone off** ...をだ
ます ...wo damásù

focal point [fou'kəl-] *n* (of room, activity etc) 中心 chùshin

focus [fou'kəs] (*pl* **focuses**) *n* (PHOT) 焦
点 shòten; (of attention, interest etc) 中心
chùshin
♦*vt* (field glasses etc) ...の焦点を合せる
...no shòten wo awáserù
♦*vi*: **to focus (on)** (with camera)
(...に) カメラを合せる (...ni) kámèra wo
awáserù; (person) (...に) 注意を向ける
(...ni) chùi wo mukérù
in/out of focus 焦点が合っている(いな
い) shòten ga attè irú (inaí)

fodder [fɑd'əːr] *n* (food) 飼葉 kaíba

foe [fou] *n* (rival, enemy) 敵 tekí

foetus [fiː'təs] *n* (*BRIT*) = **fetus**

fog [fɔːg] *n* 霧 kirí

foggy [fɔːg'iː] *adj*: **it's foggy** 霧が出てい
る kirí ga detè irú

fog light (*BRIT* **fog lamp**) *n* (AUT) フ
ォッグライト fòggùraito

foil [fɔil] *vt* (attack, plan) くじく kujīkù
♦*n* (metal foil, kitchen foil) ホイル hòì-
ru; (complement) 引立てる物 hikítaterù
monó; (FENCING) フルーレ furùre

fold [fould] *n* (bend, crease) 折り目 orīme;
(of sheep etc) しわ shiwà; (in cloth, curtain etc) ひだ hidà; (AGR) ヒツジの囲い
hitsūji nò kakòi; (*fig*) 仲間 nakáma
♦*vt* (clothes, paper) 畳む tatámu; (arms)
組む kúmù

folder [foul'dəːr] *n* (for papers) 書類挟み
shorúibasàmi

folding [foul'diŋ] *adj* (chair, bed) 折畳み
式の orítatamishìki no

fold up *vi* (map, business) 折畳める orī-
tatamerù; (business) つぶれる tsubúrerù
♦*vt* (map, clothes etc) 畳む tatámu

foliage [fou'liːidʒ] *n* (leaves) 葉 ha の総称
sòshò

folk [fouk] *npl* (people) 人々 hitobito

♦adj (art, music) 民族の mínzoku no

folks (parents) 両親 ryōshin

folklore [fouk'lɔːr] n 民間伝承 mínkandenshō

folk song n 民謡 mín'yō

follow [fɑːl'ou] vt (person) ...について行く ...ni tsúite ikú; (suspect) 尾行する bikō suru; (event) ...に注目する ...ni chūmoku suru; (story) 注意して聞く chūi shite kikú; (leader, example, advice, instructions) ...に 従う ...ni shitágaū; (route, path) たどる tadórū

♦vi (person, period of time) 後に来る 1いく) 続いて来る(いく) tsuzúite kúru(ikū); (result) ...という結果になる ...to iú kekka ni nárū

to follow suit (fig) 同じ事をする ...to) onáji kotó wo surú

follower [fɑːl'ouəːr] n (of person) 支持者 shijísha; (of belief) 信奉者 shínpōsha

following [fɑːl'ouiŋ] adj 次の tsugí no

♦n (of party, religion, group etc) 支持者 shíjisha 支持者 sōshō

follow up vt (letter, offer) ...に答える ...ni kotáerū; (case) 追及する tsuíkyū suru

folly [fɑːl'iː] n (foolishness) ばかな事 bákana kotó

fond [fɑːnd] adj (memory) 楽しい tanóshiī; (smile, look) 愛情に満ちた afjō ni michita; (hopes, dreams) 愚かな órōka na

to be fond of ...が好きである ...ga sukí de arū

fondle [fɑːn'dəl] vt 愛ぶする afbú suru

font [fɑːnt] n (in church) 洗礼盤 señreīban; (TYP) フォント fónto

food [fuːd] n 食べ物 tabémono

food mixer n ミキサー míkīsā

food poisoning [-pɔi'zəniŋ] n 食中毒 shokúchūdoku

food processor [-prɑːs'esəːr] n ミキサー míkīsā 食べ物を混ぜたりひいたりなどしたりするための家庭電気製品 tabemono no wo mazetari hiitari oroshitari suru tame no katei denki seihin

foodstuffs [fuːd'stʌfs] npl 食料 shokúryō

fool [fuːl] n (idiot) ばか bákà; (CULIN)

フール fúru ◇果物入りムースの一種 kudámono-iri mūsu no fsshū

♦vt (deceive) だます damásū

♦vi (also: fool around: be silly) ふざける fuzákerū

foolhardy [fuːl'hɑːrdiː] adj (conduct) 無謀な mubō na

foolish [fuːl'iʃ] adj (stupid) ばかな bákà na; (rash) 無茶な muchá na

foolproof [fuːl'pruːf] adj (plan etc) 絶対確実な zettáikakújitsu na

foot [fut] (pl **feet**) n (of person, animal) 足 ashí; (of bed, cliff) ふもと fumóto; (measure) フィート fíto

♦vt (bill) 支払う shiháraū

on foot 徒歩で tóhò de

footage [fut'idʒ] n (CINEMA) 場面 bámēn

football [fut'bɔːl] n (ball: round) サッカーボール sakkābōru; (: oval) フットボール futtóbōru; (sport: BRIT) サッカー sakkā; (: US) フットボール futtóbōru

football player (BRIT: also: **footballer**) サッカー選手 sakkā señshu; (US) フットボール選手 futtóbōru señshu

footbrake [fut'breik] n 足ブレーキ ashf-burēki

footbridge [fut'bridʒ] n 橋 hashí ◇歩行者しか渡れない狭い物を指す hokōsha shika watárenai semáī monó wo sasú

foothills [fut'hilz] npl 山ろくの丘陵地帯 safroku nò kyūryōchítai

foothold [fut'hould] n 足場 ashíba

footing [fut'iŋ] n (fig: position) 立場 tachíba

to lose one's footing 足を踏み外す ashí wo fumíhazusū

footlights [fut'laits] npl (THEATER) フットライト futtóraīto

footman [fut'mæn] (pl **footmen**) n (servant) 下男 genán

footnote [fut'nout] n 脚注 kyakúchū

footpath [fut'pæθ] n 遊歩道 yūhodō

footprint [fut'print] n (of person, animal) 足跡 ashfato

footstep [fut'step] n (sound) 足音 ashfoto; (footprint) 足跡 ashfato

footwear [fut'weːr] n (shoes, sandals

etc) 履物 hakímono

KEYWORD

for [fɔːr] *prep* 1 (indicating destination, intention) ...行きの ...yukí no, ...に向かって ...ni múkatte, ...のために(の) ...notámení(no)

the train for London ロンドン行きの電車 róndonyukí no densha

he left for Rome 彼はローマへ出発しました kárè wa rōmá e shúppatsu shímashíta

he went for the paper 彼は新聞を取りに行きました kárè wa shínbun wo torí ni ikímashíta

is this for me? これは私に? koré wa watákushi ní?

there's a letter for you あなた宛の手紙が来ています anátà ate no tegami ga kíté imasu

it's time for lunch 昼食の時間です chúshoku no jíkan desu

2 (indicating purpose) ...のために(の) ...no tamé ní

what's it for? それは何のためですか soré wa nán no tamé désu ká

give it to me - what for? それをください - なぜ? soré wo yókosè - nàdè?

clothes for children 子供服 kodómofúku

to pray for peace 平和を祈る héiwa wo inorú

3 (on behalf of, representing) ...の代理として ...no daírí toshite

the MP for Hove ホーブ選出の議員 hōbúsénshutsu no gíīn

he works for the government/a local firm 彼は政府[地元の会社]に雇われています kárè wa séīfu[jímoto no kaísha]ni yatówarète imasu

I'll take him for you あなたに代って私が彼に聞きましょう anátà ni kawátte watákushi ga kárè ni kikímashō

G for George G はジョージの G G はjóīt no G

4 (because of) ...の理由で ...no riyú de, ...のために ...no tamé ní

for this reason このため konó tame

for fear of being criticized 批判を恐れて híhàn wo ósòrète

the town is famous for its canals 町は運河で有名です machí wa ûngá de yúmei desú

5 (with regard to) ...にしては ...ni shité wa

it's cold for July 7月にしては寒い shíchígatsu ni shité wa samúī

he's mature for his age 彼はませている kárè wa másète iru

a gift for languages 語学の才能 góga-ku no saínō

for everyone who voted yes, 50 voted no 賛成1に対して反対50だった sánsei ichí ní táī shite hántaihyó gojū dátta

6 (in exchange for) ...と交換して ...to kōkan shite

I sold it for $5 5 ドルでそれを売りました gódòru de soré wo ūrímashíta

to pay $2.50 for a ticket 切符を2ドル50セントで買う kíppū wo nídòru gojùssento de kaú

7 (in favor of) ...に賛成して ...ni sánsei shite

are you for or against us? あなたは我々に賛成なのか反対なのかはっきり言いなさい anátà wa waréware ni sánsei na nó ka hántai na nó ka hakkírī fīnasaí

I'm all for it 私は無条件で賛成です watákushi wa mūjōkén de sánsei desu

vote for X X に投票する ēkkūsu ni tōhyō suru

8 (referring to distance): *there are roadworks for 5 km* 5 キロもの区間が工事中です gókīro mo no kúkàn ga kōjichū desú

we walked for miles 何マイルも歩きました nánmaîru mo arûkimashíta

9 (referring to time) ...の間 ...no aîda

he was away for 2 years 彼は2年間実家を離れていました kárè wa ninénkàn ié wo hanárete imashíta

she will be away for a month 彼女は1か月間出掛ける事になっています kánòjo wa ikkágetsukàn dekákeru kotò ni nátte imasu *it hasn't rained for 3 weeks* 雨は3週間も降っていません ámè wa sañshúkan mo futté imaseñ

I have known her for years 何年も前から彼女とは知り合いです náñnen mo máè kara káñojo to wa shíraí desù

can you do it for tomorrow? 明日までに出来ますか asú madè ni dekímasu kâ

10 (with infinitive clause): *it is not for me to decide* 私が決める事ではありません watákushi gà kiméru kotò de wa arímaseñ

it would be best for you to leave あなたは帰った方がいい anátà wa káètta hõ ga fî

there is still time for you to do it あなたはまだそれをする時間があります anátà wa mádamada soré wo suru jikañ ga arímasù

for this to be possible ... これが可能になるのには... koré gà kanõ ni narù no ni wa...

11 (in spite of) ...にもかかわらず...nî mõ kakáwarazù

for all his complaints, he is very fond of her 結局彼女を愛しています kárè wa iróiro tõ móñku wo iú gâ, kekkyóku káñojo wo ái shite imásù

for all he said he would write, in the end he didn't 手紙を書くと言っていましたけれども、結局書いてくれませんでした tegámi wo káki kákù to itté imashîta keredomò, kekkyóku kaité kurémasen deshîta

♦*conj* (since, as: rather formal) なぜなら ば...だから názènaraba ...dâ kara

she was very angry, when he was late again 彼女はかんかんになっていました、というのは彼はまた遅刻したからです káñojo wa káñkañ ni natté imashîta, to iú no wa kárè wa matá mò chîkoku shita kara desù

forage [fɔːrʼidʒ] *vi* (search: for food, interesting objects etc) ...をあさる ...wo asárù

foray [fɔːrʼei] *n* (raid) 侵略 shíñryaku

forbad(e) [fərbǽd] *pt of* **forbid**

forbid [fərbʼid] (*pt* **forbad(e)**, *pp* **forbidden**) *vt* (sale, marriage, event etc) 禁ずる kíñzurù

to forbid someone to do something ...に...するのを禁ずる ...ni ...surú no wò kíñzurù

forbidden [fərbʼidʼən] *pp of* **forbid**

forbidding [fərbʼidʼiŋ] *adj* (look, prospect) 怖い kowáî

force [fɔːrs] *n* (violence) 暴力 bóryoku; (PHYSICS, *also* strength) 力 chikára

♦*vt* (compel) 強制する kyõsei suru; (push) 強く押す tsúyôku osú; (break open: lock, door) こじ開ける kojiakerú

in force (in large numbers) 大勢で õzei de; (LAW) 効力で yúkô de

to force oneself to do ...を無理して...する múrî shite ...suru

forced [fɔːrst] *adj* (labor) 強制的な kyõseiteki na; (smile) 作りの tsúkúri nò (作り笑いの) (AVIAT) 不時着 fujfchaku

forced landing (AVIAT) 不時着 fujfchaku

force-feed [fɔːrsʼfiːd] *vt* (animal, prisoner) ...に強制給餌をする ...ni kyõseikyûji wo suru

forceful [fɔːrsʼfəl] *adj* (person) 力強い chikárazuyoi; (attack) 強烈な kyõretsu na; (point) 説得力のある settókuryoku no arû

forceps [fɔːrʼsəps] *npl* ピンセット piñsettó

forces [fɔːrsʼiz] (*BRIT*) *npl*: **the Forces** (MIL) 軍隊 guñtai

forcibly [fɔːrʼsəbliː] *adv* (remove) 力ずくで chikárazukû de; (express) 力強く chikárazuyokù

ford [fɔːrd] *n* (in river) 浅瀬 asáse ◇ (船を使わないで)川を渡れる場所を指す (fune wo tsukáwanaide kawá wô watáreru bashô wo sásù)

fore [fɔːr] *n*: *to come to the fore* 前面に出て来る zeñmen ni dete kurú

forearm [fɔːrʼɑːrm] *n* 前腕 máude

foreboding [fɔːrbʼoudiŋ] *n* (of disaster) 不吉な予感 fukítsu na yokáñ

forecast [fɔːrʼkæst] *n* (of profits, prices,

weather) 予報 yohō
♦ vt (pt, pp **forecast**) (predict) 予報する yohō suru

forecourt [ˈfɔːrkɔːrt] n (of garage) 前庭 maéniwa

forefathers [ˈfɔːrfɑːðərz] npl (ancestors) 先祖 señzo

forefinger [ˈfɔːrfɪŋgər] n 人差し指 hitósashiyùbi

forefront [ˈfɔːrfrʌnt] n: **in the forefront of** (industry, movement) ...の最前線で ...no saízeñsen de

forego [fɔːrˈgou] vt **forewent** pp **foregone** vt (give up) やめる yamérù; (go without) ...なしで我慢する ...náshi de gáman suru

foregone [ˈfɔːrgɔːn] adj: **it's a foregone conclusion** 結果は決まっている kekká wa kimátte irú

foreground [ˈfɔːrgraund] n (of painting) 前景 zeñkei

forehead [ˈfɔːrhed] n 額 hitái

foreign [ˈfɔːrin] adj (country) 外国の gaíkoku no; (trade) 対外の taígai no; (object, matter) 異質の ishítsu no

foreigner [ˈfɔːrənər] n 外国人 gaíkokujìn

foreign exchange n 外国為替 gaíkokukawàse; (currency) 外貨 gaíka

Foreign Office (BRIT) n 外務省 gaímushō

Foreign Secretary (BRIT) n 外務大臣 gaímudaìjin

foreleg [ˈfɔːrleg] n (of animal) 前足 maéàshi

foreman [ˈfɔːrmən] (pl **foremen**) n (in factory, on building site etc) 現場監督 geñbakàntoku

foremost [ˈfɔːrmoust] adj (most important) 最も大事な mottómò daíji na
♦ adv: **first and foremost** 先ず第一に mázù daíchi ni

forensic [farenˈsik] adj (medicine, test) 法医学的な hōígakuteki na

forerunner [ˈfɔːrrʌnər] n 先駆者 señkushà

foresee [fɔːrˈsiː] (pt **foresaw** pp **foreseen**) vt (problem, development) 予想する

yosō suru

foreseeable [fɔːrˈsiːəbəl] adj (problem, development) 予想出来る yosō dekirù

foreshadow [fɔːrˈʃædou] vt (event) ...の前兆となる ...no zeñchō to narù

foresight [ˈfɔːrsait] n 先見の明 señken nó mef

forest [ˈfɔːrist] n 森 mórì

forestall [fɔːrstɔːl] vt (person) 出し抜く dashínuku; (discussion) 防ぐ fuségù

forestry [ˈfɔːristri] n 林業 riñgyō

foretaste [ˈfɔːrteist] n 前兆 zeñchō

foretell [fɔːrˈtel] (pt, pp **foretold**) vt (predict) 予言する yogén suru

forever [fɔːrˈevər] adv (for good) 永遠に efén ni; (continually) いつも ítsùmo

forewent [fɔːrˈwent] pt of **forego**

foreword [ˈfɔːrwəːrd] n (in book) 前書 maégaki

forfeit [ˈfɔːrfit] vt (lose: right, friendship etc) 失う ushínaù

forgave [fɔːrˈgeiv] pt of **forgive**

forge [fɔːrdʒ] n (smithy) 鍛冶屋 kajíyà
♦ vt (signature, money) 偽造する gizō suru; (wrought iron) 鍛えて作る kitáetè tsukúrù

forge ahead vi (country, person) 前進する zeñshin suru

forger [ˈfɔːrdʒər] n 偽造者 gizōshà

forgery [ˈfɔːrdʒəri] n (crime) 偽造 gizō; (object) 偽物 nisémono

forget [fɔːrget] (pt **forgot**, pp **forgotten**) vt (fact, face, skill, appointment) 忘れる wasúrerù; (leave behind: object) 置き忘れる okíwasurerù; (put out of mind: quarrel, person) 考えない事にする kañgaenai kotó ni surù
♦ vi (fail to remember) 忘れる wasúrerù

forgetful [fɔːrˈgetfəl] adj (person) 忘れっぽい人 wasúreppoì

forget-me-not [fɔːrˈgetˈminɑːt] n ワスレナグサ wasúrenagùsa

forgive [fɔːrˈgiv] (pt **forgave**, pp **forgiven**) vt (pardon) 許す yurúsù
to forgive someone for something (excuse) ...の...を許す ...no ...wo yurúsù

forgiveness [fɔːrˈgivnis] n 許し yurúshì

forgo [fɔːrˈgou] vt = **forego**

forgot [fərˈgɒt] *pt of* forget

forgotten [fərˈgɒtən] *pp of* forget

fork [fɔːk] *n* (for eating) フォーク fōku; (for gardening) ホーク hōku; (in road, river, railway) 分岐点 bunkíten
♦*vi* (road) 分岐する bunki suru

fork-lift truck [fɔːkˈlift-] *n* フォークリフト fōkurifúto

fork out (*inf*) *vt* (pay) 払う haráu

forlorn [fərˈlɔːrn] *adj* (person, place) わびしい wabíshii; (attempt) 絶望的な zetsúbōteki na; (hope) 空しい munáshiì

form [fɔːrm] *n* (type) 種類 shúruì; (shape) 形 katáchi; (SCOL) 学年 gakúnen; (questionnaire) 用紙 yōshi
♦*vt* (make: shape, queue, object, habit) 作る tsukúrù; (make up: organization, group) 構成する kōsei suru; (idea) まとめる matómerù

in top form 調子が最高で chōshi gà saíkō de

formal [fɔːrˈmæl] *adj* (offer, statement, occasion) 正式な sefshiki na; (person, behavior) 堅苦しい katágurushiì; (clothes) 正装の sefsō no; (garden) 伝統的な deńtōteki na 《極めて幾何学的な配置の庭園について言う kiwámète kikágakuteki na hachf nō teień ni tsuitè iú; (education) 正規の sefki no

formalities [fɔːrˈmælˈitiːz] *npl* (procedures) 手続き tetsúzuki

formality [fɔːrˈmælˈitiː] *n* (procedure) 形式 kefshiki

formally [fɔːrˈmæliː] *adv* (make offer etc) 正式に sefshiki ni; (act) 堅苦しく katágurushikù; (dress): *to dress formally* 正装する sefsō suru

format [fɔːrˈmæt] *n* (form, style) 形式 kefshiki
♦*vt* (COMPUT: disk) 初期化する shokíka suru, フォーマットする fōmatto suru

formation [fɔːrmeiˈʃən] *n* (creation: of organization, business) 創立 sōritsu; (: of theory) 形成 kefsei; (pattern) 編隊 heńtai; (of rocks, clouds) 構造 kōzō

formative [fɔːrˈmætiv] *adj* (years, influence) 形成的な kefseiteki na

former [fɔːrˈmər] *adj* (one-time) かつて

の katsúte no; (earlier) 前の máè no
the former ... the latter ... 前者...後者... zeńsha ... kōsha ...

formerly [fɔːrˈmərliː] *adv* (previously) 前は máè wa

formidable [fɔːrˈmidəbəl] *adj* (task, opponent) 難しい muzúkashiì

formula [fɔːrˈmjələ] (*pl* **formulae** *or* **formulas**) *n* (MATH, CHEM) 公式 kōshiki; (plan) 方式 hōshiki

formulate [fɔːrˈmjəleit] *vt* (plan, strategy) 練る nérù; (opinion) 表現する hyōgen suru

forsake [fɔːrˈseik] (*pt* **forsook**, *pp* **forsaken**) *vt* (abandon: person) 見捨てる misúterù; (: belief) 捨てる sutérù

forsook [fɔːrˈsuk] *pt of* forsake

fort [fɔːrt] *n* (MIL) とりで toríde

forte [fɔːrˈtei] *n* (strength) 得意 tokúì

forth [fɔːrθ] *adv* (out) 外へ sótò e
back and forth 行ったり来たりして ittári kitári shité
and so forth など nádò

forthcoming [fɔːrθˈkʌmˈiŋ] *adj* (event) 今度の końdō no; (help, evidence) 手に入る tè ni hairù; (person) 率直な sotchóku na

forthright [fɔːrθˈrait] *adj* (condemnation, opposition) はっきりとした hakkírì to shità

forthwith [fɔːrθˈwiθ] *adv* 直ちに tádàchi ni

fortify [fɔːrˈtafai] *vt* (city) ...の防備を固める ...no bōbi wo katámerù; (person) 力付ける chikárazukerù

fortitude [fɔːrˈtætuːd] *n* 堅忍 keńnin

fortnight [fɔːrˈtnait] *n* (two weeks) 2週間 nishúkan

fortnightly [fɔːrˈtnaitliː] *adj* (payment, visit, magazine) 2週間置きの nishúkan-oki no
♦*adv* (pay, meet, appear) 2週間置きに nishúkan-oki ni

fortress [fɔːrˈtris] *n* 要塞 yōsai

fortuitous [fɔːrˈtuːitəs] *adj* (discovery, result) 偶然の gūzen no

fortunate [fɔːrˈtʃənit] *adj* (person) 運のいい ûń no íì; (event) 幸運な kóun na *it is fortunate that ...* 幸いに... safwai ni ...

fortunately [fɔːrtʃənitli:] *adv* (happily, luckily) 幸いに safwai ni

fortune [fɔːrtʃən] *n* (luck) 運 úñ; (wealth) 財産 zafsan

fortune-teller [fɔːrtʃəntelər] *n* 易者 e-kĩsha

forty [fɔːrti:] *num* 40 (の) yóñjū (no)

forum [fɔːrəm] *n* フォーラム fóramu

forward [fɔːrwərd] *adj* (in position) 前方の zeñpō no; (in movement) 前方への zeñpō e no; (in time) 将来のための shōrai nð tame no; (not shy) 出過ぎた desugíta
♦*n* (SPORT) フォワード fowádo
♦*vt* (letter, parcel, goods) 転送する teñsō suru; (career, plans) 前進させる zeñshin saserú

to move forward (progress) 進歩する shiñpo suru

forward(s) [fɔːrwərd(z)] *adv* 前へ mâe e

fossil [fɑːsəl] *n* 化石 kaséki

foster [fɔːstər] *vt* (child) 里親として育てる satóoya toshite sodáterù; (idea, activity) 助成する joséi suru

foster child *n* 里子 satógo

fought [fɔːt] *pt, pp of* **fight**

foul [faul] *adj* (state, taste, smell, weather) 悪い warúi; (language) 汚い ki-tánai; (temper) ひどい hidôi
♦*n* (SPORT) 反則 hañsoku, ファウル fáuru
♦*vt* (dirty) 汚す yogósù

foul play *n* (LAW) 殺人 satsújin

found [faund] *pt, pp of* **find**
♦*vt* (establish, business, theater) 設立する setsúritsu suru

foundation [faundéiʃən] *n* (act) 設立 setsúritsu; (base) 土台 dodái; (organization) 財団 zaídan; (also: **foundation cream**) ファンデーション fañdéshon

foundations [faundéiʃənz] *npl* (of building) 土台 dodái

founder [faundər] *n* (of firm, college) 設立者 setsúritsushà
♦*vi* (ship) 沈没する chíñbotsu suru

foundry [faundri:] *n* 鋳造工場 chūzōkō-

jõ

fountain [fáuntin] *n* 噴水 fuñsui

fountain pen *n* 万年筆 mañneñhìtsu

four [fɔːr] *num* 4 (の) yóñ (no), 四つ (の) yotsu (no)

on all fours 四つんばいになって yotsúñbai ni nattè

four-poster [fɔːrpousˈtər] *n* (*also:* **four-poster bed**) 天がい付きベット tefi-gaisukibetto

foursome [fɔːrsəm] *n* 4人組 yoníñgumi

fourteen [fɔːrtin] *num* 14 (の) jūyon (no)

fourth [fɔːrθ] *num* 第4 (の) daíyon (no)

fowl [faul] *n* 家きん kakíñ

fox [fɑːks] *n* キツネ kitsúne
♦*vt* (baffle) 困らす komárasu

foyer [fɔiˈər] *n* (of hotel, theater) ロビー róbī

fraction [frǽkʃən] *n* (portion) 一部 ichí-bù; (MATH) 分数 buñsū

fracture [frǽktʃər] *n* (of bone) 骨折 kossétsu
♦*vt* (bone) 折る órù

fragile [frǽdʒəl] *adj* (breakable) 壊れやすい kowáreyasuI

fragment [frǽgmənt] *n* (small piece) 破片 hahéñ

fragrance [freigˈrəns] *n* (scent) 香り ka-órì

fragrant [freigˈrənt] *adj* 香り高い kaórítakaì

frail [freil] *adj* (person, invalid) か弱い kayówaì; (structure) 壊れやすい kowáreyasuI

frame [freim] *n* (of building, structure) 骨組 honégumi; (of human, animal) 体格 taíkaku; (of door, window) 枠 wakû; (of picture) 額縁 gakúbuchì; (of spectacles: *also:* **frames**) フレーム fúrēmu
♦*vt* (picture) 額縁に入れる gakúbuchi ni irerù

frame of mind *n* 気分 kibúñ

framework [freimˈwəːrk] *n* (structure) 骨組 honégumi

France [frǽns] *n* フランス furáñsu

franchise [frǽntʃaiz] *n* (POL) 参政権 sañseìkeñ; (COMM) フランチャイズ furánchaìzu

frank [fræŋk] *adj* (discussion, look) 率直 な sotchóku na, フランクな furáñku na
♦*vt* (letter) ...に料金別納の判を押す ...ni ryókinbetsunō no hán wo osū

frankly [fræŋk'nəl] *adv* (honestly) 正直に shójikī ni; (candidly) 率直に sotchóku ni

frankness [fræŋk'nis] *n* (honesty) 正直 さ shójikìsa; (candidness) 率直さ sotchóku-kusa

frantic [fræn'tik] *adj* (distraught) 狂乱 した kyóran shita; (hectic) てんてこ舞い の teñtekomài no

fraternal [frətər'nəl] *adj* (greetings, relations) 兄弟の様な kyódai no yō na

fraternity [frətər'nitï] *n* (feeling) 友愛 yūai; (group of people) 仲間 nakáma

fraternize [fræt'ərnaiz] *vi* 付き合う tsukíaù

fraud [frɔːd] *n* (crime) 詐欺 sagí; (person) ぺてん師 peténshi

fraudulent [frɔː'dʒələnt] *adj* (scheme, claim) 不正な fuséi na

fraught [frɔːt] *adj: fraught with* (danger, problems) ...をはらんだ ...wo haráñda

fray [frei] *n* (battle, fight) 戦い tatákai
♦*vi* (cloth, rope) 擦切れる surfkirerù; (rope end) ほつれる hotsúrerù

tempers were frayed 皆短気になって いた minâ tâñki ni nátte itā

freak [friːk] *n* (person: in attitude, behavior) 変人 heñjin; (: in appearance) 奇形 kikéi
♦*adj* (event, accident) まぐれの mágùre no

freckle [frek'əl] *n* そばかす sobákasu

free [friː] *adj* (person, press, movement) 自由な jíyū na; (not occupied) 暇な hīma na; (: seat) 空いている aíte irù; (costing nothing: meal, pen etc) 無料の muryó no
♦*vt* (prisoner etc) 解放する kaíhō suru; (jammed object) 動ける様にする ugóke-ru yō ni suru

free (of charge) 無料で muryó de

for free = *free of charge*

freedom [friː'dəm] *n* (liberty) 自由 jíyū

free-for-all [friː'fɔːrɔːl'] *n* 乱闘 rañtō

free gift *n* 景品 keíhin

freehold [friː'hould] *n* (of property) 自由 保有権 jiyúhoyùken

free kick *n* (SPORT) フリーキック furí-kikkù

freelance [friː'læns] *adj* (journalist, photographer, work) フリーランサーの furí-rañsa no

freely [friː'liː] *adv* (without restriction, limits) 自由に jíyū ni; (liberally) 気ままに kimáma ni

Freemason [friː'meisən] *n* フリーメーソ ン furímèson

Freepost [friː'poust] ®® *BRIT) n* (postal service) 料金受取人払い ryókin uketori-ninbaraì

free-range [friː'reindʒ] *adj* 放し飼いの hanáshigai no ◇特にニワトリやその卵に ついて言う tókù ni niwátori yà sonó tamagó ni tsúìte iū

free trade *n* 自由貿易 jíyūbòeki

free way [friː'wei] *(US) n* 高速道路 kósoku-dòro

free will *n* 自由意志 jiyúishì
of one's own free will 自発的に jihátsuteki ni

freeze [friːz] *(pt froze, pp frozen) vi* (weather) 氷点下になる hyóteñka ni nárù; (liquid, pipe) 凍る kórù; (person: with cold) 冷える hiérù; (: stop moving) 立ち すくむ tachísukumù
♦*vt* (water, lake) 凍らせる kóraserù; (food) 冷凍にする reítō ni suru; (prices, salaries) 凍結する tóketsu suru
♦*n* (weather) 氷点下の天気 hyóteñka no téñki; (on arms, wages) 凍結 tóketsu

freeze-dried [friːz'draid'] *adj* 凍結乾燥 の teíketsukañsō no

freezer [friː'zər] *n* フリーザー fúrìza

freezing [friː'zịŋ] *adj* (wind, weather, water) 凍る様な kórù yō na
3 degrees below freezing 氷点下3度 hyóteñka sañdo

freezing point *n* 氷点 hyóten

freight [freit] *n* (goods) 貨物 kámòtsu; (money charged) 運送料 uñsóryō

freight train *(US) n* (goods train) 貨物

列車 kamótsuresshá

French [frentʃ] *adj* フランスの furánsu no; (LING) フランス語の furánsugo no
◆*n* (LING) フランス語 furánsugo
◆*npl*: **the French** (people) フランス人 furánsujìn

French bean *n* サヤインゲン sayá-ìngen

French fried potatoes *npl* フレンチフライ (deep fat) フレンチフライ furénchìfuraì(póteto)

French fries [-fraiz] (*US*) *npl* = **French fried potatoes**

Frenchman/woman [frentʃmən /wumən] (*pl* **Frenchmen/women**) *n* フランス人男性(女性) furánsujìn dańsei (jòsei)

French window *n* フランス窓 furánsu madò

frenetic [frənétik] *adj* (activity, behavior) 熱狂的な nekkyóteki na

frenzy [frénzi:] *n* (of violence) 逆上 gyakújò; (of joy, excitement) 狂乱 kyóran

frequency [frí:kwənsi:] *n* (of event) 頻度 híndo; (RADIO) 周波数 shūhasū

frequent [*adj* frí:kwənt *vb* frikwént] *adj* (intervals, visitors) 頻繁な hińpan na
◆*vt* (pub, restaurant) ...によく行く ...ni yókù ikú

frequently [frí:kwìntli:] *adv* (often) しばしば shíbàshiba

fresco [fréskou] *n* フレスコ画 furésukoga

fresh [freʃ] *adj* (food, vegetables, bread, air etc) 新鮮な shińsen na; (memories, footprint) 最近の safkìn no; (instructions) 新たな aráta na; (paint) 塗立ての nurítate no; (new: approach, start) 新しい atárashiì; (cheeky: person) 生意気な namáikì na

freshen [freʃən] *vi* (wind) 強くなる tsuyóku narù; (air) 涼しくなる suzúshikù narù

freshen up *vi* (person) 化粧直しをする keshónaòshi wo surú

fresher [freʃəːr] (*BRIT*: *inf*) *n* = **freshman**

freshly [freʃli:] *adv* (made, cooked, painted) ...されたばかりで ...saréta bakàri de

freshman [freʃmən] (*pl* **freshmen**) *n* (*US*: SCOL) 1年生 ichíneňsei ◆大学生や高校生について言う dafgakùsei ya kókòsei ni tsuité iù

freshness [freʃnis] *n* 新鮮さ shińsensà

freshwater [freʃwɔːtəːr] *adj* (lake, fish) 淡水の tańsui no

fret [fret] *vi* (worry) 心配する shińpai surù

friar [fraiəːr] *n* (REL) 修道士 shūdòshi

friction [fríkʃən] *n* (resistance, rubbing) 摩擦 masátsu; (between people) 不仲 fú-naka

Friday [fraidei] *n* 金曜日 kiń-yòbi

fridge [frídʒ] (*BRIT*) *n* 冷蔵庫 refzòko

fried [fraid] *adj* (steak, eggs, fish etc) 焼いた yaftà; (chopped onions etc) いためた itámetà; (in deep fat) 揚げた agétà, フライした furái shità

friend [frend] *n* 友達 tomódachì

friendly [frendli:] *adj* (person, smile) 愛想のいい aísò no fì; (government) 友好的な yūkòteki na; (place, restaurant) 居心地の良い igókochi no voì; (game, match) 親善の shinzen no

friendship [frendʃip] *n* 友情 yūjò

frieze [fri:z] *n* フリーズ fúrìzu ◆壁の一番高い所に付ける細長い飾り、彫刻などを指す kabé no ichíbàn takáì tokórò ni tsukérù hosónagaì kazárì, chókòku nadò wo sásù

frigate [frígit] *n* フリゲート艦 furígètokan

fright [frait] *n* (terror) 恐怖 kyófu; (scare) 驚き odóroki
to take fright 驚く odóroku

frighten [frait-ən] *vt* (scare) 驚かす odórokasù

frightened [fraitənd] *adj* (afraid) 怖かった kowágattà; (worried, nervous) 不安に駆られた fúàn ni karáretà

frightening [fraitniŋ] *adj* (experience, prospect) 恐ろしい osóroshiì

frightful [fraitfəl] *adj* (dreadful) 恐ろしい osóroshiì

frightfully [fraitfəli:] *adv* 恐ろしく osóroshikù

frigid [frídʒid] *adj* (woman) 不感症の fukánshò no

frill [frɪl] n (of dress, shirt) フリル fúriru

fringe [frɪndʒ] n (BRIT: of hair) 前髪 maégami; (decoration: on shawl, lampshade etc) 縁飾り fuchíkazàri; (edge: of forest etc) へり herí

fringe benefits npl 付加給付 fukákyùfu

frisk [frɪsk] vt (suspect) ボディーチェックする bodíchekkù suru

frisky [frɪs'kiː] adj (animal, youngster) はつらつとした hatsúratsu to shità

fritter [frɪt'əːr] n (CULIN) フリッター furíttā

fritter away vt (time, money) 浪費する rốhi suru

frivolous [friv'ələs] adj (conduct, person) 軽率な kefsotsu na; (object, activity) 下らない kudáranaì

frizzy [friz'iː] adj (hair) 縮れた chijíretà

fro [frou] see **to**

frock [frɑːk] n (dress) ドレス dórèsu

frog [frɑːg] n カエル kaérù

frogman [frɔːg'mæn] (pl **frogmen**) n ダイバー dáɪbā

frolic [frɑːl'ik] vi (animals, children) 遊び回る asóbimawarù

from [frʌm] prep **1** (indicating starting place) ...から ...kárà

where do you come from?, where are you from? (asking place of birth) ご出身はどちらですか go-shússhin wa dóchìra desú ka

from London to Glasgow ロンドンからグラスゴーへ róndon kara gurásugò e

to escape from something/someone ...から逃げる ...kárà nigérù

2 (indicating origin etc) ...から ...kárà

a letter/telephone call from my sister 妹からの手紙(電話) imóto karà no tegámi(deñwa)

tell him from me that ... 私からの伝言で彼に...と言って下さい watákushi karà no deñgon de kárè ni ...to itté kudasaì

a quotation from Dickens ディケンズからの引用 díkènzu kara no iñyō

to drink from the bottle 瓶から飲む biñ kara nómù

3 (indicating time) ...から ...kárà

from one o'clock to/until/till two 1時から2時まで ichíji kara ...nfjì madè

from January (on) 1月から(先) ichígatsu karà (sakî)

4 (indicating distance) ...から ...kárà

the hotel is 1 km from the beach ホテルは浜辺から1キロ離れています hóterù wa hamábè karà ichíkiro hanárete imásù

we're still a long way from home まだまだ家まで遠い mádàmada ié madè tối

5 (indicating price, number etc) ...から ...kárà, ...によって ...nfshi

prices range from $10 to $50 値段は10ドルないし50ドルです nedán wà júdòru nấishi gojúdòru dèsù

there were from 20 to 30 people there 20ないし30人いました nfjù nấishi sañjúnin imáshìta

the interest rate was increased from 9% to 10% 公定歩合は9パーセントから10パーセントに引き上げられました kốteibùai wa kyúpàseñto kara juppáseñto ni hikfagerareમáshìta

6 (indicating difference) ...と ...と

he can't tell red from green 彼は赤と緑との区別ができません kárè wa ákà to mfdòri no kúbètsu ga dekímaseñ

to be different from someone/something ...と違っている ...tồ chigátte irù

7 (because of, on the basis of) ...から ...kárà, ...によって ...ni yotté

from what he says 彼の言う事による と kárè no iú kotò ni yorú tò

from what I understand 私が理解したところでは watákushi gà rfkai shita tokóro dè wà

to act from conviction 確信に基づいて行動する kakúshin ni motozúìte kốdō suru

weak from hunger 飢えでぐったりになって uè gé guttárì ni náttè

front [frʌnt] n (of house, dress) 前面 zeñ

men̄; (of coach, train, car) 最前部 safzeñbu; (promenade: *also*: **sea front**) 海岸沿 いの遊歩道 kafgañbzoi no yūhodō; (MIL) 戦線 señsen; (METEOROLOGY) 前線 zeñsen; (*fig*: appearances) 外見 gaiken
♦*adj* (*gen*) 前の máè no、一番前の ichiban maè no; (gate) 正面の shōmén no

in front (of) (...の) 前に (...no) máè ni
front tooth 前歯 máeba

frontage [frʌn'tidʒ] *n* (of building) 正面 shōmen

frontal [frʌn'təl] *adj* 真っ向からの makkō kara no

front door *n* 正面玄関 shōmengenkan

frontier [frʌntir'] *n* (between countries) 国境 kokkyō

front page *n* (of newspaper) 第一面 dáiichimen

front room (*BRIT*) *n* 居間 imá

front-wheel drive *n* (AUT) 前輪駆動 zeñrinkúdō

frost [frɔːst] *n* (weather) 霜が降りる事 shimó ga orírù koto; (*also*: **hoarfrost**) 霜 shimó

frostbite [frɔːst'bait] *n* 霜焼け shimóyake

frosted [frɔːs'tid] *adj* (glass) 曇の kumóri no

frosty [frɔːs'tiː] *adj* (weather, night) 寒い samúi ◇気温が氷点下であるが雪が降っていない状態 kiÓn ga hyÓtenka de arù ga yukÍ ga futte inái jōtai ni tsuite iú; (welcome, look) 冷たい tsumétal

froth [frɔːθ] *n* (on liquid) 泡 awá

frown [fraun] *vi* 顔をしかめる kaÓ wo shikámerù

froze [frouz] *pt of* **freeze**

frozen [frou'zən] *pp of* **freeze**

frugal [fruː'gəl] *adj* (person) 倹約的な keñ-yakutekí na; (meal) つましい tsumáshíi

fruit [fruːt] *n inv* (AGR, BOT) 果物 kudámono; (*fig*: results) 成果 séika

fruiterer [fruːt'ærər] (*BRIT*) *n* 果物屋 kudámonoya

fruiterer's (shop) [fruːt'ærərz-] (*BRIT*) *n* 果物屋 kudámonoya

fruitful [fruːt'fəl] *adj* (meeting, discussion) 有益な yūeki na

fruition [fruːiʃ'ən] *n*: **to come to fruition** 実る minórù

fruit juice *n* 果汁 kajū、フルーツジュース furútsujūsu

fruit machine (*BRIT*) *n* スロットマシン surőttomashín

fruit salad *n* フルーツサラダ furútsusaráda

frustrate [frʌs'treit] *vt* (upset) ...に欲求不満を起させる ...ni yokkyúfumán wo okósaserù; (block) 折 させる zasétsu saserù

frustration [frʌstreiʃən] *n* (irritation) 欲求不満 yokkyúfumán; (disappointment) がっかり gakkárí

fry [frai] (*pt*, *pp* **fried**) *vt* (CULIN: steak, eggs etc) 焼く yákù; (: chopped onions etc) いためる itámerù; (: in deep fat) 揚げる agérù ¶ *see also* **small fry**

frying pan [frai'iŋ-] *n* フライパン furáipan

ft. *abbr* = **foot**; **feet**

fuddy-duddy [fʌd'iːdʌdiː] (*pej*) *n* 古臭い人 furúkusaï hitő

fudge [fʌdʒ] *n* (CULIN) ファッジ fájjì

fuel [fjuː'əl] *n* 燃料 nefiryō

fuel oil *n* 重油 jūyu

fuel tank *n* 燃料タンク nefiryōtañku

fugitive [fjuː'dʒətiv] *n* (runaway, escapee) 逃亡者 tőbōsha

fulfil [fulfil'] *vt* (function) 果す hatásù; (condition) 満たす mitásù; (request, wish, desire) かなえる kanáerù; (order) 実行する jikkÓ suru

fulfilment [fulfil'mənt] *n* (satisfaction) 満足 máñzoku; (of promise, desire) 実現 jitsúgen

full [ful] *adj* (container, cup, car, cinema) 一杯の ippái no; (maximum: use, volume) 最大限の saÍdaigen no; (complete: details, information) 全ての súbete no; (price) 割引なしの warÍbikinashÍ no; (skirt) ゆったりした yuttárī shitá
♦*adv*: **to know full well that** ...という事を重々承知している ...to iú kotó wo jūjū shōchi shite irù

I'm full (up) 満腹だ manpuku da

a full two hours 2時間も nijíkan mo

at full speed 全速力で zensokuryóku de

in full (reproduce, quote, pay) 完全に kanzen na

full employment *n* 100パーセントの就業率 hyakú pásento no shúgyôritsu

full-length [ful'leŋkθ'] *adj* (film, novel etc) 長編の chôhen no; (coat) 長い nágai; (portrait) 全身の zenshin no

full moon *n* 満月 mángetsu

full-scale [ful'skeil'] *adj* (attack, war) 全面的な zenmenteki na; (model) 実物大の jitsubutsudai no

full stop *n* 終止符 shúshifù, ピリオド pi'ríodo

full-time [ful'taim] *adj* (work, study) 全時間制の zenjíkansei no

♦*adv* 全時間で zenjíkan de

fully [ful'i:] *adv* (completely) 完全に kanzen ni; (at least): *fully as big as* 少なくとも...と同じぐらいの大きさの sukúnakutomo ...to onaji gurai no ôkisa no

fully-fledged [ful'i:fledʒd'] *adj* (teacher, barrister) 一人前の ichíninmaè no

fulsome [ful'səm] (*pej*) *adj* (praise, compliments) 大げさな ôgesa na

fumble [fʌm'bəl] *vi*: *to fumble with* (key, catch) ...でもたもたする ...de mótàmota suru

fume [fjuːm] *vi* (rage) かんかんに怒る kánkan ni okóru

fumes (of fire, fuel, car) ガス gásù

fun [fʌn] *n* (amusement) 楽しみ tanóshimì

to have fun 楽しむ tanóshimù

for fun 冗談として jôdan toshite

to make fun of (ridicule, mock) ばかにする bákà ni suru

function [fʌŋk'ʃən] *n* (role) 役割 yakúwari, 機能 kinô; (product) ...による物 ...ni yôrù monó; (social occasion) 行事 gyôji

♦*vi* (operate) 作動する sadô suru

functional [fʌŋk'ʃənəl] *adj* (operational) 作動できる sadô dekirù; (practical) 機能的な kinôteki na

fund [fʌnd] *n* (of money) 基金 kikín;

(source, store) 貯蓄 chochíku

fundamental [fʌndəmen'təl] *adj* (principle, change, mistake) 基本的な kihónteki na

fundamentalist [fʌndəmen'təlist] *n* 原理主義者 genrishugishà

funds [fʌndz] *npl* (money) 資金 shikín

funeral [fju:'nəɾəl] *n* 葬式 sôshiki

funeral parlor *n* 葬儀屋 sôgiya

funeral service *n* 葬式 sôshiki

funfair [fʌn'feːr] (*BRIT*) *n* 移動遊園地 idôyûenchi

fungi [fʌn'dʒai] *npl* of *fungus*

fungus [fʌn'gəs] (*pl* **fungi**) *n* (plant) キノコ kínôko; (mold) かび kabí

funnel [fʌn'əl] *n* (for pouring) じょうご jôgo; (of ship) 煙突 entòtsu

funny [fʌn'i:] *adj* (amusing) こっけいな kokkéi na; (strange) 変な hén na

fur [fəːr] *n* (on animal) 毛皮 kegáwa; (animal skin for clothing etc) 毛皮 kegáwa; (*BRIT*: on kettle) あか yuákà

fur coat *n* 毛皮コート kegáwakôto

furious [fjuːr'i:əs] *adj* 猛烈な môretsu na

furlong [fəːr'lɔːŋ] *n* (HORSE-RACING) ハロン hárðn ♦注解の単位で, 約201メーター kyôrì no tân-i de, yakú 201 mêta

furlough [fəːr'lou] *n* (MIL: leave) 休暇 kyúka

furnace [fəːr'nis] *n* (in foundry) がro, (in power plant) ボイラー bôìra

furnish [fəːr'niʃ] *vt* (room, building) ...に家具調度を備える ...ni kagúchôdo wo sonáerù; (supply) ...に供給する ...ni kyôkyû suru

furnishings [fəːr'niʃiŋz] *npl* 家具と設備 kágù to sétsùbi

furniture [fəːr'nitʃər] *n* 家具 kágù

piece of furniture 家具一点 kagú ittén

furrow [fəːr'ou] *n* (in field) 溝 mizó; (in skin) しわ shiwá

furry [fəːr'i:] *adj* 毛で覆われたke de ôwaretà

further [fəːr'ðəːr] *adj* (additional) その上の sonò ue no, 追加の tsuîka no

♦*adv* (farther) もっと遠くに móttô tôku ni; (more) それ以上 sorè ijô; (moreover) 更に sárà ni, なお nâó

♦vt (career, project) 促進する sokushin suru

further education (BRIT) n 成人教育 sefjin kyóiku

furthermore [fəːrˈdɔːrmɔːr] adv (moreover) 更に sárà ni, なお nao

furthest [fəːrˈðist] superl of **far**

furtive [fəːrˈtiv] adj (glance, movement) こっそりとする kossórì to surú

fury [fjuˈriː] n (anger, rage) 憤慨 fuńgai

fuse [fjuːz] n (ELEC: in plug, circuit) ヒューズ hyúzu; (for bomb etc) 導火線 dókasèn

♦vt (metal) 融合させる yúgō saserù; (fig: ideas, systems) 融合する końgō surú

♦vi (metal: also fig) 融合する yúgō suru

to fuse the lights (BRIT: ELEC) ヒューズを飛ばす hyúzu wo tobásu

fuse box n (ELEC) ヒューズ箱 hyúzubàko

fuselage [fjuːˈsəlɑːʒ] n (AVIAT) 胴体 dótai

fusion [fjuːˈʒən] n (of ideas, qualities) 融合 końgō; (also: **nuclear fusion**) 核融合 kakúyùgō

fuss [fʌs] n (anxiety, excitement) 大騒ぎ ōsawàgi; (complaining, trouble) 不平 fuhéi

to make a fuss 大騒ぎをする ōsawàgi wo suru

to make a fuss of someone ...をちやほやする ...wo chíyàhoya suru

fussy [fʌsˈiː] adj (person) うるさい kóurusaì; (clothes, room etc) 凝った kóttà

futile [fjuːˈtəl] adj (attempt, comment, existence) 無駄な mudá na

future [fjuːˈtʃər] adj (date, generations) 未来の mírài no; (president, spouse) 将来の shórai no

♦n (time to come) 未来 mírài; (prospects) 将来 shórai; (LING) 未来形 míráikei

in future 将来に shórai ni

fuze [fjuːz] (US) = **fuse**

fuzzy [fʌzˈiː] adj (PHOTO) ぼやけた boyáketa; (hair) 縮れた chijfreta

G

G [dʒiː] n (MUS: note) ト音 to-óñ; (: key) ト調 tóchō

g. abbr = **gram(s)**

gabble [gæbˈəl] vi べちゃくちゃしゃべる péchakucha sháberu

gable [geiˈbəl] n (of building) 切妻 kirfzùma

gadget [gædʒˈit] n 装置 sóchi

Gaelic [geiˈlik] adj ゲール語の gérugo no

♦n (LING) ゲール語 gérugo

gaffe [gæf] n (in words) 失言 shitsúgen; (in actions) 失態 shittái

gag [gæg] n (on mouth) 猿ぐつわ sarúgutsuwa; (joke) ギャグ gyágù

♦vt (prisoner) ...に猿ぐつわをはめる ...ni sarúgutsuwa wo hamérù

gaiety [geiˈitiː] n お祭り騒ぎ o-mátsuri sawàgi

gaily [geiˈliː] adv (talk, dance, laugh) 楽しそうに tanóshisō ni; (colored) 華やかに hanáyàka ni

gain [gein] n (increase) 増加 zóka; (improvement) 進歩 shíñpo; (profit) 利益 rfeki

♦vt (benefit): to gain from something ...から利益を得る ...kara rfeki wo érù; (clock, watch) 進む susúmù

to gain on someone ...に迫る ...ni semárù

to gain 3lbs (in weight) (体重が) 3ポンド増える (taījū ga) sañpoñdo fuérù

gait [geit] n 歩調 hochō

gal. abbr = **gallon**

gala [geiˈlə] n (festival) 祝祭 shukúsai

galaxy [gælˈəksiː] n (SPACE) 星雲 sefun

gale [geil] n (wind) 強風 kyófū

gallant [gælˈənt] adj (brave) 勇敢な yúkan na; (polite) 紳士的な shińshiteki na

gallantry [gælˈəntriː] n (bravery) 勇気 yúki; (politeness) 礼儀正しさ refgitadashīsa

gall bladder [gɔːl-] n 胆のう tańnō

gallery [gæl'ɔːri] n (also: **art gallery**: public) 美術博物館 bijutsu hakubutsukán; (: private) 画廊 garó; (in hall, church, theater) 二階席 nikáiseki

galley [gæl'iː] n (ship's kitchen) 調理室 chórishītsu

gallon [gæl'ən] n (= 8 pints; BRIT = 4.5 l; US = 3.8 l) ガロン gáròn

gallop [gæl'əp] n ギャロップ gyárôppu
♦vi (horse) ギャロップで走る gyárôppu de hashírù

gallows [gæl'ouz] n 絞首台 kōshudai

gallstone [gɔːl'stoun] n (MED) 胆石 tańseki

galore [gəlɔːr'] adv どっさり dossárì

galvanize [gæl'vənaiz] vt (audience) ぎょっとさせる gyóttó sasérù; (support) 求める motómerù

gambit [gæm'bit] n (fig: (opening)) **gambit** 皮切り kawákiri

gamble [gæm'bəl] n (risk) かけ kaké
♦vt (money) かける kakérù
♦vi (take a risk) 冒険をする bōken wo surú; (bet) ばくちをする bakúchi wo surú, ギャンブルをする gyáñburu wo surú
to gamble on something (horses, race, success etc) ...にかける ...ni kakérù

gambler [gæm'blə:r] n (punter) ばくち打ち bakúchiuchi

gambling [gæm'bliŋ] n (betting) ばくち bakúchi, ギャンブル gyáñburu

game [geim] n (activity, sport) 遊び asóbi; (match) 試合 shiái; (part of match: esp TENNIS: also: **board game**) ゲーム gēmu; (strategy, scheme) 策略 sakúryaku; (HUNTING) 猟鳥獣 ryōchōjū; (CULIN) 猟鳥獣の肉 ryōchōjū no nikú
♦adj (willing: subject)
game (for) (...をする) 気がある (...wo surú) kí ga arù
big game 大型猟獣 ōgataryōjū

gamekeeper [geim'kiːpəːr] n 猟番 ryōban

gammon [gæm'ən] n (bacon) ベーコン bēkon; (ham) スモークハム sumōkuhamù

gamut [gæm'ət] n (range) 範囲 háñ-i

gang [gæŋ] n (of criminals, hooligans) 一味 ichímì; (of friends, colleagues) 仲間

nakama; (of workmen) 班 háñ

gangrene [gæŋ'griːn] n (MED) えそ ésò

gangster [gæŋ'stəːr] n (criminal) 暴力団員 bōryokudañ-in, ギャング gyáñgu

gang up vi: **to gang up on someone** 寄ってたかって...をやっつける yotté takatté ...wo yattsukerù

gangway [gæŋ'wei] n (from ship) タラップ taráppù; (BRIT: in cinema, bus, plane etc) 通路 tsūro

gaol [dʒeil] (BRIT) n, vt = **jail**

gap [gæp] n (space) すき間 sukíma, ギャップ gyáppu; (in time) 空白 kūhaku; (difference): **gap (between)** (...の)断絶 (...no) dañzetsu

gape [geip] vi (person) ぽかんと口を開けて見詰める pokáñ to kuchí wo aketé mitsúmerù; (shirt, hole) 大きく開いている ōkiku aíte irú

gaping [gei'piŋ] adj (shirt, hole) 大きく開いた ōkiku aítà

garage [gərɑːʒ'] n (of private house) 車庫 sháko; (for car repairs) 自動車修理工場 jidōshashūrikōjō

garbage [gɑːr'bidʒ] n (US: rubbish) ごみ gomí; (inf: nonsense) でたらめ detárame

garbage can n (US) ごみ容器 gomíyōki

garbled [gɑːr'bəld] adj (account, message) 間違った machígattà

garden [gɑːr'dən] n (private) 庭 niwá

gardener [gɑːr'dnəːr] n 庭師 niwáshi

gardening [gɑːr'dniŋ] n 園芸 eñgei

gardens [gɑːr'dənz] npl (public park) 公園 kōen

gargle [gɑːr'gəl] vi うがいする ugái suru

garish [ge:r'iʃ] adj けばけばしい kebábekbáshii

garland [gɑːr'lənd] n (also: **garland of flowers**) 花輪 hanáwa

garlic [gɑːr'lik] n (BOT, CULIN) ニンニク nifniku

garment [gɑːr'mənt] n (dress) 衣服 ffuku

garnish [gɑːr'niʃ] vt (food) 飾る kazárù

garrison [gær'isən] n (MIL) 守備隊 shubítai

garrulous [gær'ələs] adj (talkative) 口数の多い kuchíkazu no ōi

garter [gɑːr'təːr] n (for sock etc) 靴下止

gas *n* くつ下留め, ガーター gātā; (*US: suspender*) ガーターベルト gātāberūto

gas [gæs] *n* (CHEM) 気体 kítai; (fuel) ガス gásū; (*US: gasoline*) ガソリン gasórin
♦*vt* (kill) ガスで殺す gásū de korósū

gas cooker (*BRIT*) *n* ガスレンジ gasúrenji

gas cylinder *n* ガスボンベ gasúbònbe

gas fire (*BRIT*) *n* ガスストーブ gasúsutòbu

gash [gæʃ] *n* (wound) 切り傷 kiríkìzu; (tear) 裂け目 sakéme
♦*vt* (wound) 傷を負わせる kizú wò owáserù

gasket [gæs'kit] *n* (AUT) ガスケット gasúkettò

gas mask *n* ガスマスク gasúmasùku

gas meter *n* ガスメーター gasúmètà

gasoline [gæs'əli:n'] (*US*) *n* ガソリン gasórin

gasp [gæsp] *n* (breath) 息切れ ikígire; (of shock, horror) はっとする事 háttò suru kotó
♦*vi* (pant) あえぐ aégù

gasp out *vt* (say) あえぎながら言う aégìnagàra iú

gas station (*US*) *n* ガソリンスタンド gasórinsutàndo

gassy [gæs'i:] *adj* (beer etc) 炭酸ガスの入った tañsangasū no háttà

gastric [gæs'trik] *adj* 胃の í no

gastroenteritis [gæs'trouentərai'tis] *n* 胃腸炎 ichōen

gate [geit] *n* (of garden, field, grounds) 門 móñ; (at airport) ゲート gēto

gatecrash [geit'kræʃ] (*BRIT*) *vt* ...に押し掛ける ...ni oshíkakerù

gateway [geit'wei] *n* (entrance: *also fig*) 入口 iríguchi

gather [gæð'əːr] *vt* (flowers, fruit) 摘む tsúmù; (pick up) 拾う hiróù; (assemble, collect: objects, information) 集める atsúmerù; (understand) 推測する suísoku suru; (SEWING) ...にギャザーを寄せる ...ni gyázā wo yoséru
♦*vi* (assemble) 集まる atsúmarù

to gather speed スピードを上げる supído wo agérù

gathering [gæð'əːriŋ] *n* 集まり atsúmari

gauche [gouʃ] *adj* (adolescent, youth) ぎごちない gigóchinai

gaudy [gɔːdi'] *adj* 派手な hadé na

gauge [geidʒ] *n* (instrument) 計器 keíki
♦*vt* (amount, quantity) 計る hakárù; (*fig*: feelings, character etc) 判断する hañdan suru

gaunt [gɔːnt] *adj* (haggard) やせこけた yasékoketà; (bare, stark) 荒涼とした kōryō to shita

gauntlet [gɔːnt'lit] *n* (glove) 長手袋 nagátebukùro; (*fig*: *to run the gauntlet*) 方々からやられる hōbō kara yarárerù

to throw down the gauntlet 挑戦する chōsen suru

gauze [gɔːz] *n* (fabric: *also* MED) ガーゼ gāze

gave [geiv] *pt of* **give**

gay [gei] *adj* (homosexual) 同性愛の dōsei-ai no, ホモの hómò no; (cheerful) 陽気な yōki na; (color, music, dress etc) 華やかな hanáyàka na

gaze [geiz] *n* (look, stare) 視線 shiséñ
♦*vi*: *to gaze at something* ...をじっと見る ...wo jíttò mírù

gazelle [gəzel'] *n* ガゼル gázèru

gazetteer [gæzitiːr'] *n* (index) 地名辞典 chiméijiteñ

gazumping [gəzʌm'piŋ] (*BRIT*) *n* (of house buyer) 詐欺 sági

GB [dʒi:bi:'] *abbr* = **Great Britain**

GCE [dʒi:si:i:'] (*BRIT*) *n abbr* (= *General Certificate of Education*) 普通教育証明書 futsúkyōikushōsho ◇16才の時に受ける0レベルと大学入学前に受けるAレベルの2種類がある jūrokúsai no tokí ni ukérù O rébèru to daígaku nyúgaku máè ni ukérù A rébèru no nishúrui ga arù

GCSE [dʒi:si:esi:'] (*BRIT*) *n abbr* (= *General Certificate of Secondary Education*) ◇1988年から GCE の0レベルは GCSEに置換えられた señkyúhyakuhachijúhachi nèn ni GCE no O rébèru wa GCSE ni okíkaeraretà

gear [giːr] *n* (equipment) 道具 dōgu; (TECH) 歯車 hagúrùma; (AUT) ギ ヤ gíyả

♦vt (fig: adapt): **to gear something to** ...に...を適応させる ...ni ...ni wo tekṓ saserū

high (US) **or top** (BRIT) **/low gear** ハイ[ロー]ギヤ haí[rṓ]giyầ

in gear ギヤを入れて gíyầ wo írête

gear box n ギヤボックス giyấbokkûsu

gear shift (BRIT **gear lever**) n シフトレバー shífûtorebā

geese [gi:s] npl of **goose**

gel [dʒel] n (for hair) ジェル jérū; (CHEM) ゲル gérû

gelatin(e) [dʒel'ətin] n (CULIN) ゼラチン zerấchin

gelignite [dʒel'ignait] n (explosive) ゼリグナイト zerígunaîto

gem [dʒem] n (stone) 宝石 hốseki

Gemini [dʒem'ənai] n (ASTROLOGY) 双子座 futágoza

gender [dʒen'dəːr] n (sex: also LING) 性 sef

gene [dʒi:n] n (BIO) 遺伝子 idénshi

general [dʒen'əːrəl] n (MIL) 大将 taíshō

♦adj (overall, non-specific, miscellaneous) 一般の ippán no, 一般的の ippánteki na; (widespread: movement, interest) 全面的な zenmenteki na

in general 一般に ippán ni

general delivery (US) n (poste restante) 局留 kyokúdome

general election n 総選挙 sōsenkyo

generalization [dʒenəːrələzei'ʃən] n 一般化 ippánka

generally [dʒen'əːrəli] adv (in general) 一般に ippán ni; (usually) 普通 futsū wa

general practitioner n 一般開業医 ippán kaigyối

generate [dʒen'əːreit] vt (power, energy) 発生させる hasséi saserū; (jobs, profits) 生み出す umídasû

to generate electricity 発電する hatsúden suru

generation [dʒenəːrei'ʃən] n (period of time) 時代 sedái; (of people, family) 同じ世代の人々 onáji sedái no hitobíto; (of heat, steam, gas etc) 発生 hasséi; (of

electricity) 発電 hatsúden

generator [dʒen'əːreitəːr] n (ELEC) 発電機 hatsúdeñki

generosity [dʒenəːrɑːs'əti:] n 寛大さ kañdaisa

generous [dʒen'əːrəs] adj (person, measure, remuneration etc) 寛大な kañdai na

genetics [dʒənet'iks] n (science) 遺伝学 idéngaku

Geneva [dʒəni:'və] n ジュネーブ júněbu

genial [dʒi:'ni:əl] adj (host, smile) 愛想の良い aíso no yoí

genitals [dʒen'itəlz] npl (ANAT) 性器 seíki

genius [dʒi:n'jəs] n (ability, skill, person) 天才 tensai

genocide [dʒen'əsaid] n 民族虐殺 mínzokugyakusâtsu, ジェノサイド jénồsaido

gent [dʒent] n abbr = **gentleman**

genteel [dʒenti:l'] adj (person, family) 家柄の良い iégara no yoí

gentle [dʒen'təl] adj (person) 優しい yasáshiî; (animal) 大人しい otónashiî; (movement, shake) 穏やかな odáyaka na, 静かな shízûka na; (slope, curve) 緩やかな yurúyâka na

a gentle breeze そよ風 soyókaze

gentleman [dʒen'təlmən] n (pl **gentlemen**) (man) 男の方 otóko no katà; (referring to social position: also well-mannered man) 紳士 shíñshi, ジェントルマン jéñtoruman

gentleness [dʒen'təlnis] n (of person) 優しさ yasáshisa; (of animal) 大人しさ otónashisa; (of movement, breeze, shake) 穏やかさ odáyakasa, 静かさ shízûkasa; (of slope, curve) 緩やかさ yurúyâkasa

gently [dʒen'tli:] adv (: subj: person) 優しく yasáshikû; (: animal) 大人しく otónashikû; (: breeze etc) 静かに shízûkâni (: slope, curve) 緩やかに yurúyâka ni

gentry [dʒen'tri:] n 紳士階級 shíñshikâikyū

gents [dʒents] n (BRIT) (men's toilet) 男性トイレ dañseítoirè

genuine [dʒen'juːin] adj (real) 本物の hoñmonð no; (person) 誠実な seíjitsu na

geographic(al) [dʒiːəgræf'ik(ə)l] adj 地理の chírí no	**to get dirty** 汚れる yogóreru
geography [dʒiːɔːg'rəfi] n (of town, country etc: also SCOL) 地理 chírí	**to get killed** 殺される korósareru
geological [dʒiːəlɔdʒ'ikəl] adj 地質学の chishítsugàku no	**to get married** 結婚する kekkón surù
geologist [dʒiːɔl'ədʒist] n 地質学者 chishítsugakushà	**when do I get paid?** 金はいつ払ってくれますか kané wà ítsù harátte kuremasù ká
geology [dʒiːɔl'ədʒi] n (of area, rock etc) 地質 chíshitsu; (SCOL) 地質学 chishítsugàku	**it's getting late** 遅くなって来ました osóku natté kimáshita
geometric(al) [dʒiːəmet'rik(ə)l] adj (problem, design) 幾何学的な kikágakuteki na	**2** (go): **to get to/from** ...へ[から]行く ...é[kará]ikú
geometry [dʒiːɔm'ətri] n (MATH) 幾何学 kikágaku	**to get home** 家に帰る ié ni kaéru
geranium [dʒərei'niːəm] n ゼラニウム zeránìumu	**how did you get here?** あなたはどうやってここへ来ましたか anátà wa dó yattè kokó é kimáshità ká
geriatric [dʒeːriæt'rik] adj (of old people) 老人の rōjin no	**3** (begin): **to get to know someone** ...と親しくなる ...tò shitáshikù naru
germ [dʒəːrm] n ばい菌 baíkin	**I'm getting to like him** 彼を好きになってきました kárè wo sukí ni natté kimáshita
German [dʒəːr'mən] adj (of Germany) ドイツの dóïtsu no; (LING) ドイツ語の doítsugo no	**let's get going/started** さあ、行きましょう sā, ikímashō
♦n ドイツ人 doítsujin; (LING) ドイツ語 doítsugo	♦**modal aux vb: you've got to do it** なたはどうしてもそれをしなければなりません anátà wa dó shïtè mò soré wò shïnákereba narimasèn
German measles n (rubella) 風しん fūshin	**I've got to tell the police** 警察に知らせなければならない kefsatsu ni shírásenakereba narimasèn
Germany [dʒəːr'məni] n ドイツ dóïtsu	♦**vt 1: to get something done** (do) ...を済ます ...wò sumásù; (have done) ...をしてもらう ...wò shïtè moráù
germination [dʒəːrməneiˈʃən] n (of seed) 発芽 hatsúga	**to get the washing/dishes done** 洗濯[皿洗い]をする sentaku(saráarài)wò sumásù
gesticulate [dʒestik'jəleit] vi (with arms, hands) 手振りをする tebúri wo suru	**to get one's hair cut** 散髪してもらう safipatsu shite moráù
gesture [dʒes'tʃəːr] n (movement) 手振り tebúri; ジェスチャー jésùchā; (symbol, token) ジェスチャー jésùchā	**to get the car going/to go** 車のエンジンをかける kurúma no eñjin wo kakérù
KEYWORD	**to get someone to do something** ...に...をさせる ...nì ...wò saséru
get [get] (pt, pp got, (US) pp gotten) vi **1** (become, be) ...になる ...ni nárù	**to get something ready** ...を用意する ...wò yôi suru
to get old (thing) 古くなる fúrùku naru; (person) 年を取る toshf wo toru	**to get someone ready** ...に用意をさせる ...nì yôi wo saséru
to get cold 寒くなる sámùku naru	**to get someone drunk/into trouble** ...を酔っぱらわせる[困らせる] ...wò yoppárawaserù[komáraserù]
to get annoyed/bored/tired 怒る(退屈する、飽きる)okórù(taﬂkutsu suru、tsukárerù)	**2** (obtain: money) 手に入れる té ni irérù
to get drunk 酔っ払う yopparau	

(: permission, results) 得る erù; (find: job, flat) 見付ける mitsukérù; (fetch: person, doctor) 呼んで来る yónde kurù; (: object) 持って来る motté kurù

to get something for someone ...のために...を持って来る ...no tamé nì ...wo motté kurù

he got a job in London 彼はロンドンに仕事を見付けました kárè wa róndon ni shigóto wò mitsúkemashìta

get me Mr Jones, please (TEL) ジョーンズさんをお願いしたいんですが jónzu san wo o-négai shitaìn désu ga

I think you should get the doctor 医者を呼んだ方がいいと思います ishá wò yoñda hó ga íi to omóimasù

can I get you a drink? 何か飲みませんか náñika nomímaseñ ka

3 (receive: present, letter) 受ける ukérù; (acquire: reputation, prize) 得る erù; (: prize) 獲得する kakútoku suru

what did you get for your birthday? お誕生日に何をもらいましたか o-táñjōbi ni nánì wo moráimashìta ka

he got a prize for French 彼はフランス語の成績で賞をもらいました kárè wa furáñsugò no séfseki dè shó wò moráimashìta

how much did you get for the painting? 絵はいくらで売れましたか kálga wa fkúra de urémashìta ka

4 (catch) つかむ tsukámù; (hit: target etc) ...に当る ...ni atárù

to get someone by the arm/throat ...の腕(のど)をつかむ ...no udé(nódò)wò tsukámù

get him! やつを捕まえろ yátsù wo tsukámaerò

the bullet got him in the leg 弾丸は彼の脚に当った dañgan wà kárè no ashí nì atátta

5 (take, move) 連れて(持って)いく tsuréte(motté) ikù, 移動する idó suru

to get something to someone ...に...を持って行く ...nî ...wò motté ikù

do you think we'll get it through the door? それは戸口から入ると思いますか soré wà tóguchi kara háiru to omó-

imasù ká

I'll get you there somehow 何とかしてあなたを連れて行きます nánì to ka shite anátà wo tsuréte ikimasù

we must get him to (US the) hospital どうしても彼を病院に連れて行かなくちゃ dóshitè mo kárè wo byóìn ni tsuréte ikanakúcha

6 (catch, take: plane, bus etc) 乗る norù

where do I get the train - Birmingham? 電車はどこで乗ればいいんですか - バーミンガムですか deñsha wa dókò de noréba iiñ desù ká - bámiñgamu desu ká

7 (understand) 理解する rfkài suru; (hear) 聞き取る kikftorù

I've got it 分かった wakátta

I don't get your meaning あなたが言おうとしている事が分かりません ánata gà ió to shite irú kotò ga wakárimaseñ

I'm sorry, I didn't get your name 済みませんが、お名前を聞き取れませんでした sumfmaseñ ga, o-námae wò kikftoremaseñ deshìta

8 (have, possess): **to have got** 持っている móttè irú

how many have you got? いくつ持っていますか íkùtsu motté imasù ka

get about vi 動き回る ugókimawarù; (news) 広まる hirómarù

get along vi (agree) 仲良くする nákáyoku suru; (depart) 帰る kaèru; (manage) = get by

get at vt fus (attack, criticize) 批判する hihán suru; (reach) ...に手が届く ...ni té ga todókù

get away vi (leave) 帰る kaèru; (escape) 逃げる nigérù

get away with vt fus ...をうまくやりおおせる ...wo úmàku yarfóserù

get back vi (return) 帰る kaèru

♦vt 返す kaèsu

get by vi (pass) 通る tórù; (manage) やって行く yatté ikù

get down vi 降りる orírù

♦vt fus 降りる orírù

♦vt 降ろす orósù; (depress: person) がっかりさせる gakkárì saseru

get down to vt fus (work) ...に取り掛る ...ni toríkakarů

get in vi 入る háirù; (train) 乗る norú; (arrive home) 帰って来る kaétte kurú

get into vt fus (house) ...に入る ...ni háirù; (vehicle) ...に乗る ...ni norú; (clothes) 着る kirú

to get into bed ベッドに入る béddò ni háirù

to get into a rage かんかんに怒る kañkan ni okórù

get off vi (from train etc) 降りる orírù; (depart: person, car) 出発する shuppátsu suru; (escape punishment etc) 逃れる nogárerù

◆vt (remove: clothes) 脱ぐ núgù; (: stain) 消す kesú, 落す otósù; (send off) 送る o-kúrù

◆vt fus (train, bus) 降りる orírù

get on vi (at exam etc): *how are you getting on?* 万事うまく行っていますか bánji úmàku ittě imasů ká; (agree): *to get on (with)* (...と) 気が合う (...tð) ki gá áù

◆vt fus ...に乗る ...ni norú

get out vi 出る derú; (of vehicle) 降りる orírù

◆vt fus 取り出す torídasù

get out of vt fus ...から出る ...kara derù; (vehicle) ...から降りる ...kara orírù; (bed) ...から起きる ...kara okírù; (duty etc) 避ける sakérù, 逃れる nogárerù

get over vt fus (illness) ...が直る ...ga naórù

get round vt fus (problem, difficulty) 避ける sakérù; (law, rule) ...に触れないようにする ...ni furénal yǒ ni surù; (fig: person) 言いくるめる iíkurumerù

get through vi (TEL) 電話が通じる deñwa ga tsújiru

get through to vt fus (TEL) ...に電話が通じる ...ni deñwa ga tsújiru

get together vi (people) 集まる atsúmarù

◆vt 集める atsúmerù

get up vi (rise) 起きる okírù

◆vt fus 起す okósù

get up to vt fus (reach) ...に着く ...ni

tsukú; (BRIT: prank etc) 仕出かす shídèkasù

geyser [gai'zə:r] n (GEO) 間欠温泉 kañketsu oñsen; (BRIT: water heater) 湯沸かし器 yuwákashikì

Ghana [gɑːn'ə] n ガーナ gǎna

ghastly [gæst'liː] adj (horrible: person, behavior, situation) いやな fyā na, ひどい hídòi; (: building, appearance) 薄気味悪い usúkimiwaruì; (pale: complexion) 青白い aójirol

gherkin [gə:r'kin] n キュウリのピクルス kyúri no píkùrusu

ghetto [get'ou] n (ethnic area) ゲットー géttò

ghost [goust] n (spirit) 幽霊 yǔrei, お化け o-bákè

giant [dʒai'ənt] n (in myths, children's stories) 巨人 kyojîn, ジャイアント jáiànto; (fig: large company) 大企業 dafkigyǒ

◆adj (enormous) 巨大な kyodài na

gibberish [dʒib'əriʃ] n (nonsense) でたらめ detárame

gibe [dʒaib] n = **jibe**

giblets [dʒib'lits] npl 鳥の内臓 torí no naizǒ

Gibraltar [dʒibrɔːl'təːr] n ジブラルタル jíbûrarutaru

giddy [gid'iː] adj (dizzy) めまいがする memái ga suru

gift [gift] n (present) 贈り物 okúrimonò, プレゼント purézènto, ギフト gífùto; (ability) 才能 saínò

gifted [gif'tid] adj (actor, sportsman, child) 才能ある saínō arù

gift token n ギフト券 gífûtoken

gift voucher n = **gift token**

gigantic [dʒaigæn'tik] adj 巨大な kyodài na

giggle [gig'əl] vi くすくす笑う kusúkùsu waráù

gill [dʒil] n (= 0.25 pints; BRIT: 0.15 l; US = 0.12 l) ギル gírù

gills [gilz] npl (of fish) えら erá

gilt [gilt] adj (frame, jewelery) 金めっきした kiñmekkì shita

◆n 金めっき kiñmekkì

gilt-edged [gilt'edʒd] adj (stocks, secu-

gimmick

212

gimmick [ˈgimik] *n* (sales, electoral) 仕掛け shikáke

gin [dʒin] *n* ジン jín

ginger [ˈdʒindʒəːr] *n* (spice) ショウガ shōga

ginger ale *n* ジンジャーエール jínjàerù

ginger beer *n* ジンジャービール jínjàbìru

gingerbread [ˈdʒindʒəːrbred] *n* (cake) ジンジャーブレッドケーキ jínjàbureddokēki; (biscuit) ジンジャーブレッドクッキー jínjàbureddokukkī

gingerly [ˈdʒindʒəːrli] *adv* (tentatively) 慎重に shíñchō ni

gipsy [ˈdʒipsi] *n* = **gypsy**

giraffe [dʒəˈræf] *n* キリン kírìn

girder [ˈgəːrdəːr] *n* (beam) 鉄桁 tekkétsu

girdle [ˈgəːrdəl] *n* (corset) ガードル gādoru

girl [gəːrl] *n* (child) 女の子 ofína no ko, 少女 shōjo; (young unmarried woman) 若い女性 wakái jósei, ガール gāru; (daughter) 娘 musúme

an English girl 若いイングランド人女性 wakái íñgurandojìn jósei

girlfriend [ˈgəːrlfrend] *n* (of girl) 女友達 ofína tomodachi; (of boy) ガールフレンド gārufureñdo

girlish [ˈgəːrliʃ] *adj* 少女の様な shōjo no yō na

giro [ˈdʒairou] *n* (also: **bank giro**) 銀行振替 gíñkōfurikaekawàse; (also: **post office giro**) 郵便振替為替 yúbinfurikaekawàse; (BRIT: welfare cheque) 生活保護の小切手 sefkatsuhogo no kogítte

girth [gəːrθ] *n* (circumference) 周囲 shūi; (of horse) 腹帯 haráobi

gist [dʒist] *n* (of speech, program) 骨子 kósshi

KEYWORD

give [giv] (*pt* **gave**, *pp* **given**) *vt* 1 (hand over): *to give someone something, give something to someone* ...に...を与える ...nì ...wò atáerù, ...に...を渡す ...nì ...wò watásù

I gave David the book, I gave the

book to David 私は本をデービッドに渡しました watákushi wã hón wò débìddo ni watáshimashìta

give him your key あなたのかぎを彼に渡しなさい anátà no kagí wò kárè ni watáshinasaì

he gave her a present 彼は彼女にプレゼントをあげた kárè wa kánòjo ni purézeñto wo agétà

give it to him, give him it それを彼に渡しなさい soré wò kárè ni watáshinasaì

I'll give you £5 for it それを5ポンドで私に売ってくれませんか soré wò go-póñdo de watákushi nì uttè kuremasèñ ká

2 (used with noun to replace a verb): *to give a sigh* ため息をつく taméìki wo tsukú

to give a cry/shout 叫ぶ sakébù

to give a push 押す osú

to give a groan うめく umékù

to give a shrug 肩をすくめる kátà wo sukúmerù

to give a speech/a lecture 演説(講演)をする eñzetsu(kōen)wo surú

to give three cheers 万歳三唱をする bañzaisañshō wo suru

3 (tell, deliver: news, advice, message etc) 伝える tsutáerù, 言う iú, 与える atáerù

did you give him the message/the news? 彼にメッセージ〔ニュース〕を伝えましたか kárè ni méssèji(nyūsù)wo tsutáemashìta ká

let me give you some advice ちょっと忠告をあげよう chóttò chúkoku wo ageyō

he gave me his new address over the phone 彼は電話で新しい住所を教えてくれました kárè wa defiwa dè atárashii jūsho wo oshéte kuremashìta

to give the right/wrong answer 正しい(間違った)答を言う tadáshiì(machígatta)kotáe wo iú

4 (supply, provide: opportunity, surprise, job etc) 与える atáerù, 提供する teíkyō suru; (bestow: title) 授与する júyò suru;

(: honor, right) 与える atáerù

I gave him the chance to deny it それを否定するチャンスを彼に与えましたか sorè wò hitéi suru chañsu wo kárè ni atáemashìta

the sun gives warmth and light 太陽は熱と光を我々に与えてくれる taíyō wa netsū tò hikári wò waréware nì atáete kurerù

what gives you the right to do that? 何の権利でそんな事をするのか nán no keñri de sofina kotò wo suru nò ka

that's given me an idea あれでいい事を思い付いたんですが arè de ii kotò wo omóitsuitan desù ga

5 (dedicate: time) 当てる atáerù; (: one's life) 捧げる saságerù; (: attention) 払う haráù

you'll need to give me more time もっと時間を下さい móttò jíkan wo kudásaì

she gave it all her attention 彼女はそれに専念した kánòjo wa sorè nì señnen shitá

6 (organize: party) パーティ(晩さん会)を開催する pátì (bañsañkai) wo kaísai suru

◆*vi* 1 (*also*: *give way*: break, collapse) 崩れる kuzúrerù

his legs gave beneath him 彼は突然立てなくなった kárè wa totsūzen taténaku nattá

the roof/floor gave as I stepped on it 私が踏んだとたん屋根(床)が抜け落ちた watákushi ga funda totañ yáne (yuká) ga nukéochità

2 (stretch: fabric) 伸びる nobírù

give away *vt* (money) 人にやる hitó ni yarú; (opportunity) 失う ushínaù; (secret, information) 漏らす morású; (bride) 新郎に渡す shifirō ni watásu

give back *vt* 返す káèsu

give in *vi* (yield) 降参する kósan suru

◆*vt* (essay etc) 提出する teíshutsu suru

give off *vt* (heat) 放つ hanátsù; (smoke) 出す dásù

give out *vt* (distribute: prizes, books,

drinks etc) 配る kubárù; (make known: news etc) 知らせる shiráserù

give up *vi* (surrender) 降参する kósan suru

◆*vt* (renounce: job, habit) やめる yamérù; (boyfriend) ...との交際をやめる ...to no kósai wò yamérù; (abandon: idea, hope) 捨てる sutérù

to give up smoking タバコをやめる tabáko wo yamérù

to give oneself up 自首する jishú suru

give way *vi* (yield: break) ゆずる yuzúru; (break, collapse: floor, ladder etc) 崩れる kuzúrerù, 壊れる kowárerù; (: rope) 切れる kirérù; (BRIT: AUT) 道を譲る michí wo yuzúru

glacier [glei'ʒər] *n* 氷河 hyóga

glad [glæd] *adj* (happy, pleased) うれしい uréshii

gladly [glæd'li:] *adv* (willingly) 喜んで yorókoñde

glamorous [glæm'ɔːrəs] *adj* 魅惑的な miwákuteki na

glamour [glæm'əːr] *n* 魅惑 miwáku

glance [glæns] *n* (look) ちらっと見る事 chíráttò mírù koto

◆*vi*: *to glance at* ...をちらっと見る ...wo chíráttò mírù

glance off *vt fus* ...に当って跳ね返る ...ni attáte hanékaerù

glancing [glæn'siŋ] *adj* (blow) かすめる kasúmerù

gland [glænd] *n* せん sén

glare [gleːr] *n* (of anger) にらみ nirámi; (of light) まぶしさ mabúshisà; (of publicity) 脚光 kyakkó

◆*vi* (light) まぶしく光る mabúshiku hikárù

to glare at (glower) ...をにらみ付ける ...wo nirámitsukerù

glaring [gleːr'iŋ] *adj* (mistake) 明白な meñhaku na

glass [glæs] *n* (substance) ガラス garásu; (container) コップ koppú, グラス gúrasu; (contents) コップ一杯 koppú ippái

glasses [glæs'iz] *npl* 眼鏡 mégàne

glasshouse [glæs'haus] *n* 温室 ofishitsu

glassware [glæs'weːr] *n* グラス類 gurásurui

glassy [glæs'i:] *adj* (eyes) うつろな utsúro na

glaze [gleiz] *vt* (door, window) …にガラスをはめる …ni garásu wò hamérù; (pottery) …にうわぐすりを掛ける …ni uwágusùri wo kakérù

♦*n* (on pottery) うわぐすり uwágusùri

glazed [gleizd] *adj* (eyes) うつろな utsúro na; (pottery, tiles) うわぐすりを掛けた uwágusùri wo kakéta

glazier [glei'ʒəːr] *n* ガラス屋 garásuyà

gleam [glim] *vi* (shine: light, eyes, polished surface) 光る hikárù

glean [glim] *vt* (information) かき集める kakfatsumérù

glee [gli:] *n* (joy) 喜び yorókobi

glen [glen] *n* 谷間 tańfai

glib [glib] *adj* (person) 口達者な kuchídasshà na; (promise, response) 上調子だけの uwábe dake no

glide [glaid] *vi* (snake, dancer, boat etc) 滑る様に動く subérù yō ni ugókù; (AVIAT, birds) 滑空する kakkū́ suru

glider [glai'dəːr] *n* (AVIAT) グライダー guráidā

gliding [glai'diŋ] *n* (AVIAT) 滑空 kakkū́

glimmer [glim'əːr] *n*: *a glimmer of light* かすかな光 kásùka na hikárí

a glimmer of interest かすかな関心 kásùka na hyōjō

a glimmer of hope かすかな希望 kásùka na kibō

glimpse [glimps] *n* (of person, place, object) …がちらっと見える事 …ga chíráttò mierú

♦*vt* …がちらっと見える …ga chíráttò miérù

glint [glint] *vi* (flash: light, eyes, shiny surface) ぴかっと光る pikáttò hikárù

glisten [glis'ən] *vi* (with sweat, rain etc) ぎらぎらする gíràgira suru

glitter [glit'əːr] *vi* (sparkle: light, eyes, shiny surface) 輝く kagáyakù

gloat [glout] *vi*: *to gloat (over)* (exult) …にほくそえむ …ni hokúsoemu

global [glou'bəl] *adj* (worldwide) 世界的な sekáiteki na

globe [gloub] *n* (world) 地球 chikyū́; (model) 地球儀 chikyū́gì; (shape) 球 kyū́

gloom [glum] *n* (dark) 暗やみ kuráyami; (sadness) 失望 shitsúbō

gloomy [glu'mi:] *adj* (dark) 薄暗い usúgurai; (sad) 失望した shitsúbō shita

glorious [glɔːr'iːəs] *adj* (sunshine, flowers, weather) 素晴らしい subárashiì; (victory, future) 栄光の efkṓ no

glory [glɔːr'iː] *n* (prestige) 栄光 efkṓ; (splendor) 華々しさ hanábanashisà

gloss [glɔːs] *n* (shine) つや tsuyá; (also: *gloss paint*) つや出しペイント tsuyádashipeìnto

glossary [glɔːs'əːriː] *n* 用語集 yōgoshū

gloss over [*vt fus*] (error) 言繕う iítsukuroù; (problem) 言いくるめる ifkurumerù

glossy [glɔːs'iː] *adj* (hair) つやつやした tsuyátsuya shitá; (photograph) つや出しの tsuyádashi no; (magazine) アート紙の ātóshi no

glove [glʌv] *n* (gen) 手袋 tebúkùro; (in baseball) グローブ gúrōbu, グラブ gúràbu

glove compartment *n* (AUT) グローブボックス gurốbubokkùsu

glow [glou] *vi* (embers) 赤く燃える akáku moérù; (stars) 光る hikárù; (face, eyes) 輝く kagáyakù

glower [glau'əːr] *vi*: *to glower at* …をにらみ付ける …wo nirámitsukerù

glucose [glu'kous] *n* ブドウ糖 budótō, グルコース gurúkōsu

glue [glu:] *n* (adhesive) 接着剤 setchakúzai

♦*vt* 接着する setchákù suru

glum [glʌm] *adj* (miserable) ふさぎ込んだ fusǎgikoñda

glut [glʌt] *n* (of oil, goods etc) 生産過剰 sefsankajō

glutton [glʌt'ən] *n* 大食らい ōgurai

a glutton for work 仕事の鬼 shigótò nò oní

gluttony [glʌt'əniː] *n* 暴食 bōshoku

glycerin(e) [glis'əːrin] *n* グリセリン gurísèrin

gnarled [nɑːrld] *adj* (tree, hand) 節くれだった fushíkuredattà

gnat [næt] *n* ブヨ búyð

gnaw [nɔ:] *vt* (bone) かじる kajírù

gnome [noum] *n* 地の小鬼 chí no kóðni

KEYWORD

go [gou] (*pt* went, *pp* gone) *vi* 1 (travel, move) 行く ikú

she went into the kitchen 彼女は台所に行った kánōjo wa daídokoro ni ìtta

shall we go by car or train? 車で行きますしょうか、それとも電車で行きましょうか kurúma dè ikímashō ka, sorétomò deñsha dè ikímashō ka

a car went by 車が通り過ぎた kurúma gà tòri sugítà

to go round the back 裏へ回る urá è mawáru

to go by the shop 店の前を通る misé no máè wo tòrù

he has gone to Aberdeen 彼はアバディーンへ行きました kárè wa abádïn e ikímashita

2 (depart) 出発する shuppátsu suru, たつ tátsù, 帰る kaérù, 行ってしまう ittè shimaù

"I must go," she said 「帰ります」と女は言った "kaérimasù" to kánōjo wa ittá

our plane went at 6 pm 我々の飛行機は夕方6時に出発しました waréwarè no hikôki wa yúgata rokújì ni shuppátsu shimashitá

they came at 8 and went at 9 彼らは8時に来て9時に帰った kárèra wa hachíjì ni kité kújì ni kaérimashìta

3 (attend) 通う kayóu

she went to university in Aberdeen 彼女はアバディーンの大学に通った kánōjo wa abádïn no daigaku ni kayótta

she goes to her dancing class on Tuesdays 彼女がダンス教室に通うのは火曜日です kánōjo ga dañsukyōshitsu ni kayóu no wa kayóbi dèsu

he goes to the local church 彼は地元の教会に通っています kárè wa jimóto no kyōkai ni kayótte imasù

4 (take part in an activity) ...に行く ...ni ikú, ...する ...surú

to go for a walk 散歩に行く sañpo ni ikú, 散歩する sañpo suru

to go dancing ダンスに行く dáñsu ni iku

5 (work) 作動する sadó suru

the clock stopped going 時計が止りました tokéi ga tomárimashìta

is your watch going? あなたの時計は動いていますか anátà no tokéi wà ugóite imasù ká

the bell went just then 丁度その時ベルが鳴りました chódo sono tokì bérù ga narímashìta

the tape recorder was still going テープレコーダーはまだ回っていました tépurekōdà wa máda mawátte imashìta

6 (become) ...になる ...ni nárù

to go pale 青白くなる aójiroku nàru

to go moldy かびる kabírù

7 (be sold): **to go for $10** 10ドルで売れる júdòru de urérù

8 (fit, suit) 合う áù

to go with ...に合う ...ni áù

that tie doesn't go with that shirt そのネクタイはシャツに合いません sonó nekùtai wa shátsù ni aímasèn

9 (be about to, intend to): **he's going to do it** 彼は今それをやるところです kárè wa ímà soré wò yarú tokorò desu

we're going to leave in an hour 1時間したら出発します ichíjikan shitarà shuppátsu shimasù

are you going to come? あなたも一緒に来ますか anátà mo isshó ni kimàsu ká

10 (time) 経つ tátsù

time went very slowly/quickly 時間が経つのがとても遅い／速いと感じられました jikán ga tatsù no gà totémò osóku/háyàku) kanjiraremashìta

11 (event, activity) 行く ikú

how did it go? うまく行きましたか ûmàku ikímashìta ká

12 (be given) 与えられる atáerarerù

the job is to go to someone else そのポストは他の人のところへいきました sonó posùto wa hokâ no hìto no tokorð e ikímashìta

13 (break etc: glass etc) 割れる warérù;

(: stick, leg, pencil etc) 折れる orérù;
(: thread, rope, chain etc) 切れる kirérù

the fuse went ヒューズが切れた〔飛ん
だ〕hyúzù ga kíretá(tóndà)

the leg of the chair went いすの脚が
折れた isú no ashí ga órèta

14 (be placed) ...にしまう事になっている
...ni shimáu kotó ni nátte irú

where does this cup go? このカップは
どこにしまうのですか konó kappú wa
dókò ni shimáu no desu ká

the milk goes in the fridge ミルクは
冷蔵庫にしまう事になっています mírù-
ku wa refzóko ni shimáu kotó ni nátte
imásù

◆**n** (pl **goes**) **1** (try): **to have a go (at)**
(...を) やってみる (...wo) yatté mirú

2 (turn) 番 bán

whose go is it? だれの番ですか dáre no
bán desu ká

3 (move): **to be on the go** 忙しくする
isógashikù surú

go about vi (also: **go around**: rumor) 流
れる nagárerù

◆**vt fus: how do I go about this?** どう
いう風にやればいいんですか dó iu fū ni
yaréba fin desu ká

goad [goud] vt 刺激する shigéki suru

go ahead vi (make progress) 進歩する
shínpo suru; (get going) 先に進む torfka-
karú

go-ahead [gou'əhed] adj (person, firm)
進取の気に富んだ shfñshu no ki ni tóñda

◆**n** (for project) 許可 kyóka, ゴーサイン
gōsaiñ

goal [goul] n (SPORT) ゴール gòru;
(aim) 目標 mokúhyò

goalkeeper [goul'ki:pər] n ゴールキー
パー gōrukìpà

go along vi ついて行く tsúîte ikú

◆**vt fus** ...を行く ...wò ikú

to go along with (agree with: plan,
idea, policy) ...に賛成する ...ni sañsei surú

goalpost [goul'poust] n ゴールポスト gō-
ruposùto

goat [gout] n ヤギ yágì

go away vi (leave) どこかへ行く dókò
ka e ikú

go back vi (return) 帰る káerù; (go
again) また行く matá ikú

go back on vt fus (promise) 破る yabú-
rú

gobble [gɑːb'əl] vt (also: **gobble down**,
gobble up) むさぼり食う musáborikuù

go-between [gou'bitwìn] n 仲介者 chū-
kaishá

go by vi (years, time) 経つ tátsù

◆**vt fus** (book, rule) ...に従う ...ni shitágaú

God [gɑːd] n (REL) 神 kámì

god [gɑːd] n (MYTHOLOGY, fig) 神 kámì

godchild [gɑːd'tʃaild] n 名付け子 nazúke-
go

goddaughter [gɑːd'dɔːtəːr] n 名付け娘
nazúkemusùme

goddess [gɑːd'is] n (MYTHOLOGY,
REL, fig) 女神 megámì

godfather [gɑːd'fɑːðəːr] n 名付け親 na-
zúkeòya, 代父 daífò, 教父 kyófù

godforsaken [gɑːd'fəːrsei'kən] adj
(place, spot) 荒れ果てた arēhatetá

godmother [gɑːd'mʌðəːr] n 名付け親 na-
zúkeòya, 代母 daíbò, 教母 kyóbò

go down vi (descend) 降りる orfrù;
(ship) 沈む shizúmu, 沈没する chíñbotsu
suru; (sun) 沈む shizúmu

◆**vt fus** (stairs, ladder) ...を降りる ...wo
orfrù

godsend [gɑːd'send] n (blessing) 天の恵
み teñ nò megúmì

godson [gɑːd'sʌn] n 名付け息子 nazúke-
musùko

go for vt fus (fetch) 取りに行く tórì ni
ikú; (like) 好きである sukí de arù; (attack)
...に襲い掛る ...ni osóikakarù

goggles [gɑːg'əlz] npl (for skiing, motor-
cycling) ゴーグル gōguru

go in vi (enter) 入る háirù

go in for vt fus (competition) ...に参加
する ...ni sañka suru; (like) ...が好きであ
る ...ga sukí de arù, ...を気に入る ...wo ki
nf irú

going [gou'iŋ] n (conditions) 状況 jōkyò

♦*adj: the going rate* 相場 sôba

go into vt fus (enter) ...に入る ...ni háiru; (investigate) 調べる shiráberu; (embark on) ...に従事する ...ni jújī suru

gold [gould] n (metal) 金 kíñ

♦*adj* (jewelery, watch, tooth etc) 金の kíñ no

gold reserves 金の正貨準備金 kíñ no sefka juñbī

golden [goul'dən] *adj* (made of gold) 金の kíñ no; (in color) 金色の kíñ-iro no

goldfish [gould'fiʃ] n 金魚 kíñgyo

goldmine [gould'main] n 金山 kíñzan; (fig) ドル箱 dorúbako

gold-plated [gouldplei'tid] *adj* 金めっきの kíñmekkī no

goldsmith [gould'smiθ] n 金細工師 kíñzaikushī

golf [ga:lf] n ゴルフ gorúfu

golf ball n (for game) ゴルフボール gorúfubōru; (on typewriter) 電動タイプライターのボール deńdōtaipuráltā no bōru

golf club n (organization, stick) ゴルフクラブ gorúfukurābu

golf course n ゴルフコース gorúfukōsu

golfer [ga:l'fər] n ゴルファー gorúfā

gondola [ga:n'dələ] n (boat) ゴンドラ goñdora

gone [gɔːn] *pp* of **go**

gong [gɔːŋ] n どら dorá, ゴング góñgu

good [gud] *adj* (pleasant, satisfactory etc) 良い yoí; (high quality) 高級な kôkyû na; (tasty) おいしい oshíī; (kind) 親切な shiñsetsu na; (well-behaved: child) 行儀の良い gyógi no yoí; (morally correct) 正しい seftó na

♦*n* (virtue, morality) 善 zéñ; (benefit) 利益 ríeki

good! よろしい! yoróshī!

to be good at ...が上手である ...ga jôzu de áru

to be good for (useful) ...に使える ...ni tsukáeru

it's good for you あなたのためにいい anáta no tamé ni íi

would you be good enough to ...? 済みませんが...して下さいませんか sumí-

maseñ ga ...shite kudásaimaseñ ká

a good deal (of) 沢山 (の) takúsan (no)

a good many 沢山の takúsan no

to make good (damage, loss) 弁償する beñshô suru

it's no good complaining 不平を言ってもしようがない fuhéi wo iťté mo shiyô ga nái

for good (forever) 永久に eíkyû ni

good morning! お早うございます o-háyô gozaimásu

good afternoon! 今日は koñnichi wa

good evening! 今晩は koñban wa

good night! お休みなさい o-yásumi nasái

goodbye [gudbai'] *excl* さようなら sayônarâ

to say goodbye 別れる wakáreru

Good Friday n (REL) 聖金曜日 seíkiñyôbi

good-looking [gud'luk'iŋ] *adj* (woman) 美人の bijín no; (man) ハンサムな háñsamu na

good-natured [gud'nei'tʃəːd] *adj* (person, pet) 気立ての良い kidáte no yoí

goodness [gud'nis] n (of person) 優しさ yasáshīsa

for goodness sake! 後生だから goshô da kara

goodness gracious! あらまあ! aráʔ má

goods [gudz] *npl* (COMM) 商品 shôhin

goods train (BRIT) n 貨物列車 kamótsuresshâ

goodwill [gud'wil'] n (of person) 善意 zén-i

go off vi (leave) どこかへ行く dókò ka e ikú; (food) 悪くなる warúku naru; (bomb) 爆発する bakúhatsu suru; (gun) 暴発する bôhatsu suru; (event): *to go off well* うまくいく úmâku iku

♦*vt fus* (person, place, food etc) 嫌いになる kirái ni narú

go on vi (continue) 続く tsuzúku; (happen) 起る okóru

to go on doing something ...をし続ける ...wo shitsúzukerú

goose [gus] (*pl* **geese**) n ガチョウ gachô

gooseberry [gus'be:ri:] n (tree, fruit) ス

グリ sūgúri

to play gooseberry (BRIT) アベックの邪魔をする abékku no jamá wo surú

gooseflesh [guːsˈfleʃ] *n* 鳥肌 toríhada

goose pimples *npl* = **gooseflesh**

go out *vi* (leave: room, building) 出る derú; (for entertainment): *are you going out tonight?* 今夜どこかへ出掛けますか kốn'ya dókoka e dekákemasù ká; (couple): *they went out for 3 years* 彼らは3年交際した kárèra wa sańnen kōsai shità; (fire, light) 消える kiérù

go over *vi* (ship) 転覆する teńpuku suru

♦*vt fus* (check) 調べる shirábérù

gore [gɔːr] *vt* (subj: bull, buffalo) 角で刺す tsunó de sásù

♦*n* (blood) 血の り chínorì

gorge [gɔːrdʒ] *n* (valley) 峡谷 kyókoku

♦*vt*: **to gorge oneself (on)** (...を) たらふく食う(...wo) taráfùku kúù

gorgeous [gɔːrdʒəs] *adj* (necklace, dress etc) 豪華な gốka na; (weather) 素晴らしい subárashiì; (person) 美しい utsúkushiì

gorilla [gərɪlə] *n* ゴリラ gorírà

gorse [gɔːrs] *n* ハリエニシダ haríenishìda

gory [gɔːriː] *adj* (details, situation) 血みどろの chimídoro no

go-slow [gouˈslouˈ] (BRIT) *n* 遵法闘争 juńpōtōsō

gospel [gɑːspəl] *n* (REL) 福音 fukúin

gossip [gɑːsəp] *n* (rumors) うわさ話 uwásabanashì; (chatter) ゴシップ goshíppð; (chat) 雑談 zatsúdan; (person) おしゃべり shabéri, ゴシップ屋 goshíppuya

♦*vi* (chat) 雑談する zatsúdan suru

got [gɑːt] *pt, pp* *of* **get**

go through *vt fus* (town etc) ...を通る ...wō tốrù; (search through: files, papers) ...を一つ一つ調べる ...wō hitótsu hitótsu shirábérù; (examine: list, book, story) 調べる shirábérù

gotten [gɑːtˈən] (US) *pp* *of* **get**

go up *vi* (ascend) 登る nobóru; (price, level) 上がる agárù

gout [gaut] *n* 通風 tsūfū

govern [gʌvˈərn] *vt* (country) 統治する tốchi suru; (event, conduct) 支配する shi-

hái suru

governess [gʌvˈərnis] *n* (children's) 女性家庭教師 joséikateikyōshi

government [gʌvˈərnmənt] *n* (act of governing) 政治 seíji; (governing body) 政府 seífu; (BRIT: ministers) 内閣 naíkaku

governor [gʌvˈərnər] *n* (of state) 知事 chíjì; (of colony) 総督 sốtoku; (of bank, school, hospital) 理事 ríjì; (BRIT: of prison) 所長 shochố

gown [gaun] *n* (dress: *also* of teacher) ガウン gáùn; (BRIT: of judge) 法服 hốfuku

GP [dʒiːpiːˈ] *n abbr* = **general practitioner**

grab [græb] *vt* (seize) つかむ tsukámù

♦*vi*: **to grab at** ...をつかもうとする ...wo tsukámô to suru

grace [greis] *n* (REL) 恩恵 ońkei; (gracefulness) しとやかさ shitóyakasa

♦*vt* (honor) ...に栄誉を与える ...ni éíyo wo atáerù; (adorn) 飾る kazárù

5 days' grace 5日間の猶予 itsúkakàn no yúyo

graceful [greisˈfəl] *adj* (animal, athlete) しなやかな shináyàka na; (style, shape) 優雅な yū̀ga na

gracious [greiˈʃəs] *adj* (person) 親切な shifsetsu na

grade [greid] *n* (COMM: quality) 品質 hińshitsu; (in hierarchy) 階級 kaíkyū; (SCOL: mark) 成績 seíseki; (US: school class) 学年 gakúnen

♦*vt* (rank, class) 格付けする kakúzuke suru; (exam papers etc) 採点する saíten suru

grade crossing (US) *n* 踏切 fumíkiri

grade school (US) *n* 小学校 shõgakkõ

gradient [greiˈdiːənt] *n* (of road, slope) こう配 kõbai

gradual [grædʒˈuːəl] *adj* (change, evolution) 少しずつの sukóshizutsu no

gradually [grædʒˈuːəliː] *adv* 徐々に jójð ni

graduate [*n* grædʒˈuːit *vb* grædʒˈuːeit] *n* (*also*: **university graduate**) 大学の卒

葉生 daígaku nò sotsúgyòsei; (*US: also:* **high school graduate**) 高校の卒業生 kōkō nò sotsúgyòsei

♦*vi* 卒業する sotsúgyò suru

graduation [grædʒuˈeiˈʃən] *n* (*also:* **graduation ceremony**) 卒業式 sotsúgyò-shiki

graffiti [grəfiˈtiː] *npl* 落書 rakúgaki

graft [græft] *n* (AGR) 接ぎ木 tsugíki; (MED) 移植 ishōku; (*BRIT: inf:* hard work) 苦労 kúrò; (bribery) 汚職 oshóku

♦*vt* (AGR) 接木する tsugíki suru; (MED) 移植する ishōku suru

grain [grein] *n* (of rice, wheat, sand, salt) 粒 tsúbù; (no *pl:* cereals) 穀物 kokúmòtsu; (of wood) 木目 mokúme

gram [græm] *n* グラム gúràmu

grammar [græmˈəːr] *n* (LING) 文法 buńpò; (book) 文法書 buńpòsho

grammar school (*BRIT*) *n* 公立高等学校 kōritsukōtōgakkō ◇大学進学教育をする公立高校 daígakushingakukyōiku wo suru kōritsukōkō; (*US*) 小学校 shōgakkō

grammatical [grəmætˈikəl] *adj* (LING) 文法の buńpō no

gramme [græm] *n* = **gram**

gramophone [græmˈəfoun] *n* 蓄音機 chikúoǹki

grand [grænd] *adj* (splendid, impressive) 壮大な sōdai na; (*inf:* wonderful) 素晴らしい subárashiì; (*also:* humorous: gesture etc) 大げさな ōgesa na

grandchildren [grænˈtʃilˈdrən] *npl* 孫 mágò

granddad [grænˈdæd] *n* (*inf*) おじいちゃん ojííchan

granddaughter [grænˈdɔːtəːr] *n* 孫娘 magómusume

grandeur [grænˈdʒəːr] *n* (of scenery etc) 壮大さ sōdaisa

grandfather [grænˈfɑːðəːr] *n* 祖父 sófù

grandiose [grænˈdiːous] *adj* (scheme, building) 壮大な sōdai na; (*pej*) 大げさな ōgesa na

grandma [grænˈmɑː] *n* (*inf*) おばあちゃん obáāchan

grandmother [grænˈmʌðəːr] *n* 祖母 só-

bò

grandpa [grænˈpɑ] *n* (*inf*) = **granddad**

grandparents [grænˈpeːrənts] *npl* 祖父母 sófùbo

grand piano *n* グランドピアノ gúràndopiàno

grandson [grænˈsʌn] *n* 孫息子 magómusùko

grandstand [grænˈstænd] *n* (SPORT) 観覧席 kańraǹseki, スタンド sutáǹdo

granite [grænˈit] *n* 御影石 mikágeìshi

granny [grænˈiː] *n* (*inf*) おばあちゃん obáāchan

grant [grænt] *vt* (money) 与える atáerù; (request etc) かなえる kanáerù; (visa) 交付する kōfu suru; (admit) 認める mitómerù

♦*n* (SCOL) 助成金 joséìkin; (ADMIN: subsidy) 交付金 kōfùkin

to take someone/something for granted ...を軽く見る ...wo karúkù mírù

granulated sugar [grænˈjəleitid-] *n* グラニュー糖 gurányùtō

granule [grænˈjuːl] *n* (of coffee, salt) 粒 tsúbù

grape [greip] *n* ブドウ budó

grapefruit [greipˈfruːt] (*pl* **grapefruit** *or* **grapefruits**) *n* グレープフルーツ gurépufurùtsu

graph [græf] *n* (diagram) グラフ gúràfu

graphic [græfˈik] *adj* (account, description) 写実的な shajítsuteki na; (art, design) グラフィックの guráfikkù no

graphics [græfˈiks] *n* (art, process) グラフィックス guráfikkùsu

♦*npl* (drawings) グラフィックス guráfikkùsu

grapple [græpˈəl] *vi:* **to grapple with someone** ...ともみ合う ...to momíaù

to grapple with something (problem etc) ...と取組む ...to toríkumù

grasp [græsp] *vt* (hold, seize) 握る nigírù; (understand) 理解する rikái suru

♦*n* (grip) 握り nigíri; (understanding) 理解 rikái

grasping [græsˈpiŋ] *adj* (money-grabbing) 欲深い yokúfukaì

grass [grɑːs] n (BOT) 草 kusá; (lawn) 芝生 shibáfu

grasshopper [ˈɡrɑːshɔpər] n バッタ battá

grass-roots [ˈɡrɑːsruːts] adj (level, opinion) 一般人の ippánjīn no

grate [ɡreit] n (for fire) 火格子 higóshi
♦ vi (metal, chalk): **to grate (on)** (...に すれて) きしる (...ni suréte) kishíru
♦ vt (CULIN) すりおろす surírosò

grateful [ˈɡreitfəl] adj (thanks) 感謝の kánsha no; (person) 有難く思っている arígatakù omótte irú

grater [ˈɡreitər] n (CULIN) 卸し金 oróshigàne

gratifying [ˈɡrætəfaiiŋ] adj (pleasing, satisfying) 満足な mánzoku na

grating [ˈɡreitiŋ] n (iron bars) 鉄格子 tetsúgòshi
♦ adj (noise) きしる kishíru

gratitude [ˈɡrætətuːd] n 感謝 kánsha

gratuity [ɡrətuˈiti] n (tip) 心付け kokórozùke, チップ chíppù

grave [ɡreiv] n (tomb) 墓 haká
♦ adj (decision, mistake) 重大な jūdai na; (expression, person) 重々しい omóomoshiì

gravel [ˈɡrævəl] n 砂利 jarí

gravestone [ˈɡreivstoun] n 墓石 hakáishi

graveyard [ˈɡreivjɑːrd] n 墓場 hakába, 墓地 bóchi

gravity [ˈɡrævəti] n (PHYSICS) 引力 ínryoku; (seriousness) 重大さ jūdaisa

gravy [ˈɡreivi] n (juice of meat) 肉汁 nikújū; (sauce) グレービーソース gurébīsōsu

gray [ɡrei] adj = **grey**

graze [ɡreiz] vi (animal) 草を食う kusá wo kuú
♦ vt (touch lightly) かすめる kasúmerù; (scrape) こする kosúrù
♦ n (MED) かすり傷 kasúrikizu

grease [ɡriːs] n (lubricant) グリース gurīsù; (fat) 脂肪 shibō
♦ vt ...にグリースを差す ...ni gurīsù wo sásù

greaseproof paper [ˈɡriːspruːf-] (BRIT)
n パラフィン紙 paráfìnshi

greasy [ˈɡriːsi] adj (food) 脂っこい abúrakkoì; (tools) 油で汚れた abúra dè yogóretà; (skin, hair) 脂ぎった abúragittà

great [ɡreit] adj (large: area, amount) 大きい ōkiì; (intense: heat, pain) 強い tsuyoì; (important, famous: city, man) 有名な yūmei na; (inf: terrific) 素晴らしい subárashiì

Great Britain n 英国 efkoku, イギリス ígirisu

great-grandfather [ɡreitˈɡrænˌfɑːðər] n そう祖父 sósofu

great-grandmother [ɡreitˈɡrænˌmʌðər] n そう祖母 sósobo

greatly [ˈɡreitli] adv とても totémo

greatness [ˈɡreitnis] n (importance) 偉大さ idaisa

Greece [ɡriːs] n ギリシャ gírìsha

greed [ɡriːd] n (also: **greediness**) どん欲 dón-yoku

greedy [ˈɡriːdi] adj どん欲な dón-yoku na

Greek [ɡriːk] adj ギリシャの gírìsha no; (LING) ギリシャ語の gírìshago no
♦ n (person) ギリシャ人 gírìshajìn; (LING) ギリシャ語 gírìshago

green [ɡriːn] adj (color) 緑 (色) の mídòri(iro) no; (inexperienced) 未熟な mijúku na; (POL) 環境保護の kañkyōhogò no
♦ n (color) 緑 (色) mídòri(iro); (stretch of grass) 芝生 shibáfu; (on golf course) グリーン gurīn

green belt n (round town) 緑地帯 ryokúchitaì, グリーンベルト gurínberùto

green card n (BRIT: AUT) グリーンカード gurínkàdo ◇海外自動車保険証 kafgai jidōsha hokéñshō; (US: ADMIN) グリーンカード gurínkàdo ◇外国人入国就労許可書 gaŕkokujīn nyūkoku shūrō kyokasho

greenery [ˈɡriːnəri] n 緑 mídòri ◇主に人為的に植えた樹木などを指す ómò ni jiñ-iteki ni ueta jūmòku nádà wo sásù

greengrocer [ˈɡriːnˌɡrousər] (BRIT) n 八百屋 yaóya

greenhouse [ˈɡriːnhaus] n 温室 ofishitsu

greenish [ˈɡriːniʃ] adj 緑がかった mídòrigakattā

Greenland [griːnˈland] *n* グリーンランド gurīnrandō

greens [griːnz] *npl* (vegetables) 葉物 hamóno, 葉菜 yōsai

greet [griːt] *vt* (welcome: person) ...にあいさつする ...ni áisatsu surú, 歓迎する kańgei suru; (receive: news) 受けとめる ukétomerū

greeting [griːtiŋ] *n* (welcome) あいさつ áisatsu, 歓迎 kańgei

greeting(s) card *n* グリーティングカード gurītingukādo

gregarious [grigeˈriəs] *adj* (person) 社交的な shakōteki na

grenade [grineid] *n* (*also:* **hand grenade**) 手りゅう弾 teryūdan, shuryūdan

grew [gruː] *pt of* **grow**

grey [grei] *adj* (color) 灰色 haíro; (dismal) 暗い kuráí

grey-haired [greiˈheːrd] *adj* 白髪頭の shirágaatāma no, 白髪の haíhatsu no

greyhound [greiˈhaund] *n* グレーハウンド gurēhaúndo

grid [grid] *n* (pattern) 碁盤の目 góban no me; (ELEC: network) 送電網 sōdenmō

grief [griːf] *n* (distress, sorrow) 悲しみ kanáshimì

grievance [griːˈvəns] *n* (complaint) 苦情 kujō

grieve [griːv] *vi* (feel sad) 悲しむ kanáshimù
♦*vt* (cause sadness or distress to) 悲しませる kanáshimaserù
to grieve for (dead spouse etc) ...を嘆く ...wo nagékù

grievous [griːˈvəs] *adj*: **grievous bodily harm** (LAW) 重傷 jūshō

grill [gril] *n* (on cooker) グリル gúrirù; (grilled food: *also:* **mixed grill**) グリル料理 gurírùryòri
♦*vt* (BRIT: food) グリルで焼く gúrirù de yákù; (*inf:* question) 尋問する jińmon suru

grille [gril] *n* (screen: on window, counter etc) 鉄格子 tetsúgòshi; (AUT) ラジエーターグリル rajétāgùriru

grim [grim] *adj* (unpleasant: situation)

厳しい kibíshìi; (unattractive: place) 陰気な fuńki na; (serious, stern) 険しい kewáshìi

grimace [griˈmæs] *n* (ugly expression) しかめっ面 shikámetsura
♦*vi* しかめ面をする shikámetsura wo surū

grime [graim] *n* (dirt) あか aká

grin [grin] *n* にやにや笑い nyániyawarai
♦*vi* にやにやと笑う nyániya to waráù

grind [graind] (*pt, pp* **ground**) *vt* (crush) もみつぶす momítsubusù; (coffee, pepper etc: *also US:* meat) 挽く hikú; (make sharp: knife) 研ぐ tógù
♦*n* (work) 骨折れ仕事 honéoreshigòto

grip [grip] *n* (hold) 握り nigírì; (control, grasp) 支配 shíhai; (of tire, shoe) グリップ guríppù; (handle) 取っ手 tottē; (holdall) 旅行かばん ryokőkabàn
♦*vt* (object) つかむ tsukámù, 握る nigírù; (audience, attention) 引付ける hikítsukerù
to come to grips with (problem, difficulty) ...と取組む ...to toríkumù

gripping [gripˈiŋ] *adj* (story, film) 引付ける hikítsukerù

grisly [grizˈliː] *adj* (death, murder) ひどい hidóì

gristle [grisˈəl] *n* (on meat) 軟骨 nañkotsu

grit [grit] *n* (sand, stone) 砂利 jarí; (determination, courage) 根性 konjō
♦*vt* (road) ...に砂利を敷く ...ni jarí wo shíkù
to grit one's teeth 歯を食いしばる há wo kuíshibarù

groan [groun] *n* (of person) うめき声 umékigoè
♦*vi* うめく umékù

grocer [grouˈsəːr] *n* 食料品商 shokúryōhìnshō

groceries [grouˈsəːriːz] *npl* (provisions) 食料品 shokúryōhìn

grocer's (shop) [grouˈsəːrz-] *n* 食料品店 shokúryōhìnten

groggy [grɑgˈiː] *adj* ふらふらする fúrafura surù, グロッキーの gurókkì no

groin [groɪn] n そけい部 sokéibu

groom [gruːm] n (for horse) 馬丁 batéi;
(also: **bridegroom**) 花婿 hanámukó
♦vt (horse) ...の手入れをする...no teíre
wò suru; (fig): **to groom someone for**
(job) 仕込む shikómū
well-groomed (person) 身だしなみのい
い midáshinami no fí

groove [gruːv] n 溝 mizó

grope [group] vi (fumble): **to grope for**
手探りで探す teságuri de sagásù

gross [grous] adj (flagrant: neglect, injustice) 甚だしい hanáhadashíì; (vulgar:
behavior, building) 下品な gehín na;
(COMM: income, weight) 全体の zeítai
no

grossly [grous'liː] adv (greatly) 甚だしく
hanáhadashikù

grotesque [groutesk'] adj (exaggerated,
ugly) 醜悪な shúàku na, グロテスクな
gurótesùku na

grotto [graːt'ou] n (cave) 小さな洞穴 chí-
isana horáana

grotty [graːt'iː] adj (BRIT inf) (dreadful) ひどい hídoì

ground [graund] pt, pp of **grind**
♦n (earth, soil) 土 tsuchí; (land) 地面 jímèn; (SPORT) グランド gurándo; (US:
also: **ground wire**) アース線 ásùsen;
(reason: gen pl) 根拠 konkyo
♦vt (plane) 飛べない様にする tobénai yó
ni suru; (US: ELEC) ...のアースを取付け
る ...no ásu wò torítsukerù
on the ground 地面に(で) jímèn ni
(de)
to the ground 地面へ jímèn e
to gain/lose ground 前進(後退)する
zeńshin(kòtai)surú

ground cloth (US) n = **groundsheet**

grounding [graun'diŋ] n (in education)
基礎 kisó

groundless [graund'lis] adj (fears, suspicions) 根拠のない konkyo no nái

grounds [graundz] npl (of coffee etc) か
す kásù; (gardens etc) 敷地 shikíchi

groundsheet [graund'jiːt] n グラウンド
シート gurándoshiːto

ground staff n (AVIAT) 整備員 seíbiìn

◇総称 sóshò

ground swell n (of opinion) 盛り上がり
moríagarí

groundwork [graund'wəːrk] n (preparation) 準備 júnbi

group [gruːp] n (of people) 集団 shúdan,
グループ gúrùpu; (of trees etc) 一群れ
hitómùre; (of cars etc) 一団 ichídan;
(also: **pop group**) グループ gúrùpu;
(COMM) グループ gúrùpu
♦vt (also: **group together**: people,
things etc) 一緒にする fsshò ni suru, グル
ープにする gúrùpu ni suru
♦vi (also: **group together**) 群がる murágarù, グループになる gúrùpu ni nárù

grouse [graus] n inv (bird) ライチョウ
ráìchō
♦vi (complain) 不平を言う fuhéi wo iú

grove [grouv] n 木立 kodáchì

grovel [grʌv'əl] vi (fig): **to grovel**
(before) (boss etc) (...に) ぺこぺこす
る (...ni) pékòpeko suru

grow [grou] (pt grew, pp grown) vi
(plant, tree) 生える haérù; (person, animal) 成長する seíchō suru; (increase) 増
える fuérù; (become) なる nárù;(develop): **to grow (out of/from)** (...から)
発生する (...kara) hassèi suru
♦vt (roses, vegetables) 栽培する saíbai
suru; (beard) 生やす hayásù

grower [grou'əːr] n (BOT, AGR) 栽培者
saíbaisha

growing [grou'iŋ] adj (fear, awareness,
number) 増大する zódai suru

growl [graul] vi (dog, person) うなる u-
nárù

grown [groun] pp of **grow**

grown-up [groun'kʌp] n (adult) 大人 otóna

growth [grouθ] n (development, increase: of economy, industry) 成長 seíchō; (what has grown: of weeds, beard
etc) 生えた物 haéta monò; (growing: of
child, animal etc) 発育 hatsúìku; (MED)
しゅよう shuyó

grow up vi (child) 育つ sodátsù

grub [grʌb] n (larva) 幼虫 yóchū; (inf:
food) 飯 meshí

grubby ... 223 ... guise

grubby [grʌbˈiː] *adj* (dirty) 汚い kitánaì

grudge [grʌdʒ] *n* (grievance) 恨み urámì
◆*vt*: **to grudge someone something** (be unwilling to give) ...に...を出し惜しみする ...ni ...wo dashìshími suru; (envy) ...の...をねたむ ...no ...wo netámù
to bear someone a grudge ...に恨みがある ...ni urámi ga arù

gruelling [grʌˈəling] *adj* (trip, journey, encounter) きつい kitsúì

gruesome [gruːˈsəm] *adj* (tale, scene) むごたらしい mugótarashiì

gruff [grʌf] *adj* (voice, manner) ぶっきらぼうな bukkírabò na

grumble [grʌmˈbəl] *vi* (complain) 不平を言う fuhéi wò iú

grumpy [grʌmˈpiː] *adj* (bad-tempered) 機嫌が悪い kigén ga warúì

grunt [grʌnt] *vi* (pig) ぶーぶー言う bûbu iú; (person) うなる unárù

G-string [dʒiːˈstriŋ] *n* (garment) バタフライ bátàfurai

guarantee [gærəntiːˈ] *n* (assurance) 保証 hoshó; (COMM: warranty) 保証書 hoshóshò
◆*vt* 保証する hoshô suru

guard [gɑːrd] *n* (one person) 警備員 kefbìn, ガードマン gádòman; (squad) 護衛隊 goéitai; (BRIT: RAIL) 車掌 shashó; (on machine) 安全カバー afzenkabà; (also: **fireguard**) 安全格子 afzenkòshi
◆*vt* (protect: place, person, secret etc):
to guard (against) (...から) 守る (...kara) mamórù; (prisoner) 見張る míhárù
to be on one's guard 警戒する kefkai suru

guard against *vt fus* (prevent: disease, damage etc) 防ぐ fuségù

guarded [gɑːrˈdid] *adj* (statement, reply) 慎重な shínchò na

guardian [gɑːrˈdiːən] *n* (LAW: of minor) 保護者 hógòsha; (defender) 監視人 kańshinìn

guard's van [gɑːrdz-] *n* (BRIT: RAIL) 乗務員車 jómuíshha

guerrilla [gəriːˈlə] *n* ゲリラ gérìra

guess [ges] *vt, vi* (estimate: number, dis-

tance etc) 推定する suftei suru; (correct answer) 当ててみる atétè mírù; (US: think) ...だと思う ...da to omoú
◆*n* (attempt at correct answer) 推定 suftei
to guess/have a guess 推定する suftei suru, 当ててみる atétè mírù

guesswork [gesˈwəːrk] *n* (speculation) 当て推量 atézuiryò

guest [gest] *n* (visitor) 客 kyákù; (in hotel) 泊り客 tomárikyakù

guest-house [gestˈhaus] *n* 民宿 mñshuku

guest room *n* 客間 kyakúma

guffaw [gʌfɔːˈ] *vi* ばか笑い bakáwaraì

guidance [gaidˈəns] *n* (advice) 指導 shídò

guide [gaid] *n* (person: museum guide, tour guide, mountain guide) 案内人 añnáìn, ガイド gáìdo; (book) ガイドブック gafdobukkù; (BRIT: also: **girl guide**) ガールスカウト gárusukaùto
◆*vt* (round object, museum etc) 案内する añnái suru; (lead) 導く michfbikù; (direct) ...に道を教える ...ni michfì wò o-shíerù

guidebook [gaidˈbuk] *n* ガイドブック gafdobukkù

guide dog *n* 盲導犬 mōdókèn

guidelines [gaidˈlainz] *npl* (advice) 指針 shishìn, ガイドライン gafdoraìn

guild [gild] *n* (association) 組合 kumfaì, 協会 kyókai

guile [gail] *n* (cunning) 悪意 akúì

guillotine [gilˈətiːn] *n* (for execution) 断頭台 dañtōdai, ギロチン gìróchin; (for paper) 裁断機 safdañki

guilt [gilt] *n* (remorse) 罪の意識 tsumf nò ishíkì; (culpability) 有罪 yúzai

guilty [gilˈtiː] *adj* (person) 有罪の yúzai no; (expression) 後ろめたそうな ushfrometasò na; (secret) やましい yamáshìi

guinea [giˈniː] *n* (BRIT) (old money) ギニー gìni

guinea pig *n* (animal) モルモット morúmottò; (fig: person) 実験台 jikkéñdai

guise [gaiz] *n*: **in/under the guise of** ...の装いで ...no yosóì de

guitar [gɪtɑːrʳ] n ギター gítā

gulf [gʌlf] n (GEO) 湾 wáñ; (abyss: also fig: difference) 隔たり hedátarï

gull [gʌl] n カモメ kamóme

gullet [gʌl'ɪt] n 食道 shokúdō

gullible [gʌl'əbəl] adj (naive, trusting) だ まされやすい damásareyàsui

gully [gʌl'i:] n (ravine) 峡谷 kyōkoku

gulp [gʌlp] n (swallow) 息を飲込む fkī wo nomíkomù

♦vt (also: **gulp down**: drink) がぶがぶ飲 込む gábùgabu nomíkomù; (: food) 急い で食べる isóide tabérù

gum [gʌm] n (ANAT) 歯茎 hágùki; (glue) アラビア糊 arábia nòri; (sweet: also: **gumdrop**) ガムドロップ gamúdoroppù; (also: **chewing-gum**) チューインガム chūingugamu, ガム gámù

♦vt (stick): **to gum (together)** 張り合わ せる harfawaserù

gumboots [gʌm'bu:ts] (BRIT) npl ゴム 靴 gomúgùtsu

gumption [gʌmp'ʃən] n (sense, wit) 度胸 dokyō

gun [gʌn] n (small: revolver, pistol) けん 銃 keñjū, ピストル pfsútoru, ガン gáñ; (medium-sized: rifle) 銃 jū, ライフル raí-furu; (: also: **airgun**) 空気銃 kūkijū; (large: cannon) 大砲 taíhō

gunboat [gʌn'bout] n 砲艦 hōkan

gunfire [gʌn'faiər] n 銃撃 jūgeki

gunman [gʌn'mæn] (pl **gunmen**) n (crim-inal) ガンマン gáñman

gunpoint [gʌn'point] n: **at gunpoint** (pointing a gun) ピストルを突付けて pf-sútoru wo tsukftsuketè; (threatened with a gun) ピストルを突付けられて pf-sútoru wo tsukftsukeraretè

gunpowder [gʌn'paudər] n 火薬 kayá-kù

gunshot [gʌn'ʃɑt] n (act) 発砲 happō; (sound) 銃声 jūsei

gurgle [gɔːr'gəl] vi (baby) のどを鳴らす nodó wo narásù; (water) ごぼごぼ流れる góbogobo nagárerù

guru [gu:'ru:] n (REL: also fig) 教師 kyō-shi

gush [gʌʃ] vi (blood, tears, oil) どっと流

れ出る dóttò nagárederù; (person) 大げ さに言う ōgesa ni iu

gusset [gʌs'ɪt] n (SEWING) まち máchì

gust [gʌst] n (also: **gust of wind**) 突風 toppū; (of smoke) 渦巻 uzúmàki

gusto [gʌs'tou] n (enthusiasm) 楽しさ ta-nōshimrt

gut [gʌt] n (ANAT: intestine) 腸 chō

guts [gʌts] npl (ANAT: of person, ani-mal) 内臓 naízō; (inf: courage) 勇気 yū-ki, ガッツ gáttsū

gutter [gʌt'əːr] n (in street) どぶ dobu; (of roof) 雨どい amádoi

guttural [gʌt'əːrəl] adj (accent, sound) のどに絡まった様な nódò ni karámatta yō na

guy [gai] n (inf: man) 野郎 yarō, やつ yá-tsù; (also: **guyrope**) 支綱 shisēn; (figure) ガイフォークスの人形 gaífōkusu no niñ-gyō

guzzle [gʌz'əl] vt (drink) がぶがぶ飲む gábùgabu nomu; (food) がつがつ食う gá-tsùgatsu kū

gym [dʒim] n (building, room: also: **gym-nasium**) 体育館 tafíkukàn; (activity: also: **gymnastics**) 体操 taísō

gymnast [dʒim'næst] n 体操選手 taísō-señshu

gymnastics [dʒimnæs'tiks] n 体操 taísō

gym shoes npl 運動靴 uñdōgūtsu, スニ ーカー sūnīkā

gym slip (BRIT) n (tunic) スモック su-mókkù の子供の上っ張りでかつて女 子学童の制服として使われた物. sodēna-shi no uwápparì de kátsutè joshí gakudō no seffuku toshite tsukáwareta monō

gynecologist [gainəkɑ:l'ədʒist] (BRIT **gynaecologist**) n 婦人科医 fujíñka-i

gypsy [dʒip'si:] n ジプシー jfpùshī

gyrate [dʒai'reit] vi (revolve) 回転する kaíten suru

H

紳士服店 shiñshifukutèn; (BRIT) 小間物 店 komámonotèn

habit [hæbɪt] *n* (custom, practice) 習慣 shūkan; (addiction) 中毒 chūdoku; (REL: costume) 修道服 shūdōfūku

habitable [hæbɪtəbəl] *adj* 住める sumérù

habitat [hæbɪtæt] *n* 生息地 sefsokuchī

habitual [həbɪtʃuəl] *adj* (action) 習慣的な shūkanteki na; (drinker, liar) 常習的な jōshūteki na

hack [hæk] *vt* (cut, slice) ぶった切る buttágirù
◆*n* (*pej*: writer) 三文文士 safimonbuñshi

hacker [hæk'əːr] *n* (COMPUT) コンピュータ破り cofipyūtayaburī, ハッカー hákkā

hackneyed [hæk'niːd] *adj* 陳腐な chiñpu na

had [hæd] *pt, pp of* **have**

haddock [hæd'ək] (*pl* **haddock** *or* **haddocks**) *n* タラ tárà

hadn't [hæd'ənt] = **had not**

haemorrhage [hem'əːridʒ] (*BRIT*) *n* = **hemorrhage**

haemorrhoids [hem'əːrɔidz] (*BRIT*) *npl* = **hemorrhoids**

haggard [hæg'əːrd] *adj* (face, look) やつれた yatsúretà

haggle [hæg'əl] *vi* (bargain) 値切る negírù

Hague [heig] *n*: **The Hague** ハーグ hágù

hail [heil] *n* (frozen rain) ひょう hyō; (of objects, criticism etc) 降り注ぐ物 furísogù monó
◆*vt* (call: person) 呼ぶ yobú; (flag down: taxi) 呼び止める yobítomerù; (acclaim: person, event etc) 崇める hōmérù
◆*vi* (weather) ひょうが降る hyō ga fúrù

hailstone [heil'stoun] *n* ひょうの粒 hyō no tsubú

hair [heːr] *n* (of animal: *also gen*) 毛 ke; (of person's head) 髪の毛 kamí no kè
to do one's hair 髪をとかす kamí wò tokásu

hairbrush [heːr'brʌʃ] *n* ヘアブラシ heáburashì

haircut [heːr'kʌt] *n* (action) 散髪 sañpatsu; (style) 髪型 kamígata, ヘアスタイル heásutaìru

hairdo [heːr'duː] *n* 髪型 kamígata, ヘアスタイル heásutaìru

hairdresser [heːr'dresəːr] *n* 美容師 biyōshì

hairdresser's [heːr'dresəːrz] *n* (shop) 美容院 biyōìn

hair dryer [heːr'draiəːr] *n* ヘアドライヤー heádoraìyā

hairgrip [heːr'grip] *n* 髪止め kamídome

hairnet [heːr'net] *n* ヘアネット heánettò

hairpin [heːr'pin] *n* ヘアピン heápiñ

hairpin curve (*BRIT* **hairpin bend**) *n* ヘアピンカーブ heápiñkābu

hair-raising [heːr'reiziŋ] *adj* (experience, tale) ぞっとする様な zóttò suru yō na

hair remover [-rimuː'vəːr] *n* (cream) 脱毛クリーム datsúmōkurīmù

hair spray *n* ヘアスプレー heásupurè

hairstyle [heːr'stail] *n* 髪型 kamígata, ヘアスタイル heásutaìru

hairy [heːr'iː] *adj* (person, animal) 毛深いkebúkaì; (*inf*: situation) 恐ろしい osóroshìi

hake [heik] (*pl inv or* **hakes**) *n* タラ tárà

half [hæf] (*pl* **halves**) *n* (of amount, object) 半分 hañbuñ; (of beer etc) 半パイント hañpaìnto; (RAIL, bus) 半額 hañgaku
◆*adj* (bottle, fare, pay etc) 半分の hañbuñ no
◆*adv* (empty, closed, open, asleep) 半ば nakába

two and a half 2と2分の1 nf tō nibún no ichi

two and a half years/kilos/hours 2年(キロ, 時間) 半 ninén(kíro, jíkan)hàn

half a dozen 半ダース hañdāsu

half a pound 半ポンド hañpoñdo

to cut something in half ...を半分に切る ...wo hañbuñ ni kírù

half-baked [hæf'beikt'] *adj* (idea, scheme) ばけげた bakágetà

half-caste [hæf'kæst] *n* 混血児 koñketsujì, ハーフ hấfù

half-hearted [hæf'hɑːr'tid] *adj* (attempt) いい加減な ifkagen na

half-hour [hæf'au'ər] *n* 半時間 hañjikan

half-mast [hæf'mæst']: *a flag at half-mast* 半旗 hañki

halfpenny [hei'pəni] *n* (BRIT) 半ペニー hañpenī

half-price [hæf'prais'] *adj* 半額の hañgaku no
◆*adv* 半額で hañgaku de

half term (BRIT) *n* (SCOL) 中間休暇 chūkańkyūka

half-time [hæf'taim'] *n* (SPORT) ハーフタイム hāfutaimū

halfway [hæf'wei'] *adv* (between two points in place, time) 中途で chūto de

halibut [hæl'əbət] *n inv* オヒョウ ohyō

hall [hɔːl] *n* (entrance way) 玄関ホール geñkañhōru; (for concerts, meetings etc) 講堂 kōdō, ホール hōru

hall of residence (BRIT) *n* 学生寮 gakuseiryō

hallmark [hɔːl'mɑrk] *n* (on metal) 太鼓判 taikobañ; (of writer, artist etc) 特徴 tokuchō

hallo [həlou'] *excl* = **hello**

Hallowe'en [hæləswanei'ʃən] *n* 幻魔獣 geñkaku haróuīn

hallucination [həlu:sənei'ʃən] *n* 幻覚 geñkaku

hallway [hɔːl'wei] *n* (entrance hall) 玄関ホール geñkañhōru

halo [hei'lou] *n* (of saint) 後光 gokō

halt [hɔːlt] *n* (stop) 止る事 tomáru kotó
◆*vt* (progress, activity, growth etc) 止める tomérú
◆*vi* (stop) 止る tomáru

halve [hæv] *vt* (reduce) 半分に減らす hañbuñ ni herásù; (divide) 半分に切る hañbuñ ni kírù

halves [hævz] *pl of* **half**

ham [hæm] *n* (meat) ハム hámù

hamburger [hæm'bərgər] *n* ハンバーガー hañbāgā

hamlet [hæm'lit] *n* (village) 小さな村 chīsana murá

hammer [hæm'ər] *n* (tool) 金づち kanázuchì, とんかち toñkachì
◆*vt* (nail)たたく tatákù
◆*vi* (on door, table etc)たたく tatákù

to hammer an idea into someone ...にある考え方をたたき込む ...ni árù kañgaekata wo tátakikomù

to hammer a message across ある考えを繰返し強調する aru kañgaé wo kuríkaeshī kyōchō suru

hammock [hæm'ək] *n* (on ship, in garden) ハンモック hañmokkû

hamper [hæm'pər] *vt* (person, movement, effort) 邪魔する jamá suru
◆*n* (basket) ふた付きバスケット futatsukibasukettô

hamster [hæm'stər] *n* ハムスター hāmusutā

hand [hænd] *n* (ANAT) 手 té; (of clock) 針 hárì; (handwriting) 筆跡 hisséki; (worker) 使用人 shíyonìn; (of cards) 持札 mochífdda
◆*vt* (pass, give) 渡す watásù

to give/lend someone a hand ...の手伝いをする ...no tetsúdaī wo suru

at hand 手元に temóto nì

in hand (time) 空いていて aite ite; (job, situation) 当面の tōmen no

on hand (person, services etc) 利用できる ríyo dekirù

to hand (information etc) 手元に temóto nì

on the one hand ..., on the other hand ... 一方では...他方では... ippō de wa ..., tahō de wa ...

handbag [hæn'dbæg] *n* ハンドバッグ hañdobaggû

handbook [hæn'dbuk] *n* (manual) ハンドブック hañdobukkû

handbrake [hæn'dbreik] *n* (AUT) サイドブレーキ saídoburēkì

handcuffs [hæn'dkʌfs] *npl* (POLICE) 手錠 tejō

handful [hænd'ful] *n* (of soil, stones) 掴り hitónigirî

a handful of people 数人 sūnin

handicap [hæn'dikæp] *n* (disability) 障害 shōgaí; (disadvantage) 不利 fúrì; (SPORT) ハンデ hañde
◆*vt* (hamper) 不利にする fúrì ni suru

mentally/physically handicapped 精神的(身体)障害のある seíshintekì (shiñtai) shōgai no ārū

handicraft [hænːdiːkræft] n (activity) 手芸 shúgéi; (object) 手芸品 shugéihiǹ

hand in vt (essay, work) 提出する teíshutsu suru

handiwork [hænːdiːwəːk] n やった事 yattá kotó

handkerchief [hæŋːkəːtʃif] n ハンカチ haŋkachi

handle [hæn·dəl] n (of door, window, drawer etc) 取っ手 tottè; (of cup, knife, brush etc) 柄 e; (for winding) ハンドル haṇdòru

♦vt (touch: object, ornament etc) いじる ijírù; (deal with: problem, responsibility etc) 処理する shóri suru; (treat: people) 扱う atsúkaù

"handle with care" 取扱い注意 torfatsukai chūi

to fly off the handle 怒る okórù

handlebar(s) [hæn·dəlbɑːr(z)] n(pl) ハンドル haṇdòru

hand luggage n 手荷物 tenímotsu

handmade [hænːdmeid] adj (clothes, jewellery, pottery etc) 手作りの tezúkùri no

hand out vt (object, information) 配る kubárù; (punishment) 与える atáerù

handout [hænːdaut] n (money, clothing, food) 施し物 hodőkoshimono; (publicity leaflet) パンフレット páṅfuretto; (summary: of lecture) 講演の要約 kően nð yõyaku

hand over vt (thing) 引渡す hikíwatasù; (responsibility) 譲る yuzúrù

handrail [hænːdreil] n (on stair, ledge) 手すり tesúrì

handshake [hænːdʃeik] n 握手 ákùshu

handsome [hæn·səm] adj (man) 男前の otőkomae no, ハンサムな háṅsamu na; (woman) きりっとした kirittò shita; (building) 立派な rippà na; (fig: profit, return) 相当な sōtō na

handwriting [hænːdraitiŋ] n (style) 筆跡 hísséki

handy [hænːdiː] adj (useful) 便利な béṅri na; (skilful) 手先の器用な tesákì no kíyō na; (close at hand) 手近にある temőto ni

árù

handyman [hænːdiːmæn] (pl **handymen**) n (at home) 手先の器用な人 tesákì no kíyō na hitő; (in hotel etc) 用務員 yőmuin

hang [hæŋ] (pt, pp **hung**) vt (painting, coat etc) 掛ける kakérù; (criminal: pt, pp **hanged**) 絞首刑にする kőshukei ni surù

♦vi (painting, coat, drapery etc) 掛っている kakáttè irù; (hair etc) 垂れ下がる tarésagarù

to get the hang of something (inf) ...のこつが分かる ...no kőtsù ga wakárù

hang about vi (loiter) ぶらつく burátsukù

hangar [hæŋ·ɑːr] n (AVIAT) 格納庫 kakúnòko

hang around vi = **hang about**

hanger [hæŋ·əːr] n (for clothes) 洋服掛け yőfukukàke, ハンガー háṅga

hanger-on [hæŋ·əːrɑnˈ] n (parasite) 取巻き torímaki

hang-gliding [hæŋˈglaidiŋ] n (SPORT) ハンググライダー haŋguguraídà

hang on vi (wait) 待つ mátsù

hangover [hæŋˈouvəːr] n (after drinking) 二日酔い futsúkayoì

hang up vi (TEL) 電話を切る deṅwa wð kírù

♦vt (coat, painting etc) 掛ける kakérù

hang-up [hæŋˈʌp] n (inhibition) ノイローゼ noírōze

hanker [hæŋ·kəːr] vi: *to hanker after* (desire, long for) 渇望する katsúbō suru

hankie [hæŋ·kiː] n abbr = **handkerchief**

hanky [hæŋ·kiː] n abbr = **handkerchief**

haphazard [hæpˈhæzˈəːd] adj (system, arrangement) いい加減な ifkagen na

happen [hæp·ən] vi (event etc: occur) 起る okőrù; (chance): *to happen to do something* 偶然に...する gúzen ni ...surù

as it happens 実は jitsú wa

happening [hæpˈəniŋ] n (incident) 出来事 dekígoto

happily [hæpˈiliː] adv (luckily) 幸い saíwai; (cheerfully) 楽しそうに tanőshisō ni

happiness [hæp'i:nis] n (contentment) 幸せ shíáwase

happy [hæp'i:] adj (pleased) うれしい uréshii; (cheerful) 楽しい tanóshìì

to be happy (with) (content) (...に) 満足する (...ni) mánzoku suru

to be happy to do (willing) 喜んで...する yorókonde ...surú

happy birthday! 誕生日おめでとう! tañjōbi omédetò!

happy-go-lucky [hæp'i:goulʌk'i:] adj (person) のんきな nóñki na

harangue [həræŋ'] n (audience, class) ...に向かって熱弁を振るう ...ni mukáttè netsúben wð furúu

harass [həræs'] vt (annoy, pester) ...にいやがらせをする ...ni iyágarase wo suru

harassment [həræs'mənt] n (hounding) 嫌がらせ iyágarase

harbor [ha:r'bə:r] (BRIT **harbour**) n (NAUT) 港 mináto

♦vt (hope, fear etc) 心に抱く kokóro ni idáku; (criminal, fugitive) かくまう kakúmàu

hard [ha:rd] adj (surface, object) 堅い katái; (question, problem) 難しい muzúkashìì; (work) 骨の折れる honé no orérù; (life) 苦しい kurúshìì; (person) 非情な hijō na; (facts, evidence) 確実な kakújitsu na

♦adv (work, think, try) 一生懸命に isshōkenmei ni

to look hard at ...を見詰める ...wo mitsúmerù

no hard feelings! 悪く思わないから warúkù omówanai karǎ

to be hard of hearing 耳が遠い mimí ga tỗi

to be hard done by 不当な扱いを受けた futồ na atsúkaì wo ukétà

hardback [ha:rd'bæk] n (book) ハードカバー hádokabàー

hard cash n 現金 geñkin

hard disk n (COMPUT) ハードディスク hádodisùku

harden [ha:r'dən] vt (wax, glue, steel) 固める katámerù; (attitude, person) かたくなにする katákùna ni suru

♦vi (wax, glue, steel) 固まる katámarù; (attitude, person) かたくなになる katákùna ni nárù

hard-headed [ha:rd'hed'id] adj (businessman) 現実的な geñjitsuteki na

hard labor n (punishment) 懲役 chōeki

hardly [ha:rd'li:] adv (scarcely) ほとんど...ない hotóńdo ...naĩ; (no sooner) ...するや否や ...surú ya inã ya

hardly ever ほとんど...しない hotóñdo ...shináĩ

hardship [ha:rd'ʃip] n (difficulty) 困難 koñnañ

hard up (inf) adj (broke) 金がない kané ga naĩ, 懐が寂しい futókoro ga sábìshìì

hardware [ha:rd'we:r] n (ironmongery) 金物 kanámono, (COMPUT) ハードウェア hádoueà; (MIL) 兵器 héĩki

hardware shop n 金物屋 kanámonoya

hard-wearing [ha:rd'we:r'iŋ] adj (clothes, shoes) 丈夫な jốbu na

hard-working [ha:rd'wə:r'kiŋ] adj (employee, student) 勤勉な kiñben na

hardy [ha:r'di:] adj (plants, animals, people) 丈夫な jốbu na

hare [he:r] n ノウサギ noúsàgi

hare-brained [he:r'breind] adj (scheme, idea) バカげた bakágetà

harem [hær'əm] n (of wives) ハーレム háremu

harm [ha:rm] n (injury) 害 gáì; (damage) 損害 soñgai, ダメージ damḗjì

♦vt (person) ...に危害を加える ...ni kígai wo kuwáerù; (thing) 損傷する soñshồ suru

out of harm's way 安全な場所に añzen na bashò ni

harmful [ha:rm'fəl] adj (effect, toxin, influence etc) 有害な yǘgai na

harmless [ha:rm'lis] adj (animal, person) 無害な mugái na; (joke, pleasure, activity) たわいのない tawái no naĩ

harmonica [ha:rmɑn'ikə] n ハーモニカ hāmònika

harmonious [ha:rmou'ni:əs] adj (discussion, relationship) 友好的な yūkốteki na; (layout, pattern) 調和の取れた chốwa no torétà; (sound, tune) 調子の良い chốshì no yoi

harmonize [hɑːrˈmənaiz] vi (MUS) ハーモニーを付ける hằmônî wo tsukerù; (colors, ideas): **to harmonize (with)** (...と)調和する (...to) chôwa suru

harmony [hɑːrˈməni] n (accord) 調和 chôwa; (MUS) ハーモニー hằmônî

harness [hɑːrˈnis] n (for horse) 馬具 bàgù; (for child, dog) 胴輪 dôwa, ハーネス hằnesù; (safety harness) 安全ハーネス anzenhằnesu

♦vt (resources, energy etc) 利用する riyô suru; (horse) ...に馬具をつける ...ni bàgù wo tsukerù; (dog) ...にハーネスを付ける ...ni hằnesù wo tsukerù

harp [hɑːrp] n (MUS) たて琴 tategôto, ハープ hâpu

♦vi: **to harp on about** (pej) ...の事をくどくどと話し続ける ...no kotô wo kûdôkudo to hanáshitsuzukerù

harpoon [hɑːrˈpuːn] n もり môrí

harrowing [hærˈouiŋ] adj (experience, film) 戦々の senritsu no

harsh [hɑːrʃ] adj (sound) 耳障りな mimízawàri na; (light) どぎつい dogîtsuì; (judge, criticism) か酷な kakôku na; (life, winter) 厳しい kibîshiì

harvest [hɑːrˈvist] n (harvest time) 収穫期 shûkakukì; (of barley, fruit etc) 収穫 shúkaku

♦vt (barley, fruit etc) 収穫する shúkaku suru

has [hæz] vb see **have**

hash [hæʃ] n (CULIN) ハッシュ hásshû; (fig: mess) ちゃめちゃな有様 mechámecha na arísama

hashish [hæʃˈiːʃ] n ハシシ háshìshi

hasn't [hæzˈənt] = **has not**

hassle [hæsˈəl] (inf) n (bother) 面倒 mêndô

haste [heist] n (hurry) 急ぎ isógi

hasten [heiˈsən] vt (decision, downfall) 早める hayámerù

♦vi (hurry): **to hasten to do something** 急いで...する isôide ...surù

hastily [heisˈtiːi] adv (hurriedly) 慌ただしく awátadashikù; (rashly) 軽はずみに karúhazùmi ni

hasty [heisˈtiː] adj (hurried) 慌ただしい awátadashiì; (rash) 軽はずみの karúhazùmi no

hat [hæt] n (headgear) 帽子 bôshi

hatch [hætʃ] n (NAUT: also: **hatchway**) 倉口 sôkò, ハッチ hátchì; (also: **service hatch**) サービス口 sằbisugûchi, ハッチ hátchì

♦vi (bird) 卵からかえる tamágo kara kaérù; (egg) かえる kaérù, ふ化する fuká suru

hatchback [hætʃˈbæk] n (AUT) ハッチバック hatchíbakkù

hatchet [hætʃˈit] n (axe) おの ônô

hate [heit] vt (wish ill to: person) 憎む nikúmù; (dislike strongly: person, thing, situation) 嫌う kiráu

♦n (ill-will) 憎悪 zôò; (strong dislike) 嫌悪 kén-o

hateful [heitˈfəl] adj ひどい hidôi

hatred [heiˈtrid] n (ill-will) 増悪 zôò; (strong dislike) 嫌悪 kén-o

haughty [hɔːˈtiː] adj (air, attitude) 尊大な sondai na

haul [hɔːl] vt (pull) 引っ張る hippáru

♦n (of stolen goods etc) 獲物 emôno; (also: **a haul of fish**) 漁獲 gyokáku

haulage [hɔːˈlidʒ] n (business, costs) 運送 unsô

hauler [hɔːˈlər] (BRIT **haulier**) n 運送屋 unsôya

haunch [hɔːntʃ] n (ANAT) 腰 koshî; (of meat) 腰肉 koshíniku

haunt [hɔːnt] vt (subj: ghost) (place) ...に出る ...ni dérù; (person) ...に付きまとう ...ni tsukímatoù; (: problem, memory etc) 悩ます nayámasù

♦n (of crooks, childhood etc) 行き付けの場所 ikítsuke nò bashô

haunted house お化け屋敷 obákeyashìki

KEYWORD

have [hæv] (pt, pp **had**) aux vb **1** (gen) **to have arrived/gone/eaten/slept** 行った、食べた、眠った) tsúta (it-tâ, tâbèta, nemúttä)

he has been kind/promoted 彼は親切

だった〔昇格した〕**kárē wa shíñsetsu dát-tā**(shōkaku shita)

has he told you? 彼はあなたにそれを話しましたか **kárē wa anáta ni sorē wo hanáshimashīta ká**

having finished/when he had finished, he left 仕事が済むと彼は一服しに**shigóto ga sumù to kárē wa kāéttā**

2 (in tag questions): **you've done it, haven't you?** あなたはその仕事をやったんでしょう **anáta wa sonó shigóto wo yattán deshô**

he hasn't done it, has he? 彼は仕事をやらなかったんでしょう **kárē wa shigó-to wo yaránakattàn deshô**

3 (in short answers and questions): **you've made a mistake - no I haven't/so I have** あなたは間違いをしました - 違いますよ〔そうですね〕 **anáta wa machígaī wo shímáshīta - chigáimasù yó**(sō desu né)

we haven't paid - yes we have! 私たちはまだお金を払っていません - 払いましたよ **watákushitàchi wa mádā kanē wo haráttē imaseñ - haráimashīta yó**

I've been there before, have you? 私は前にあそこへ行った事がありますが、あなたは? **watákushi wà mâē ni asóko e ittá koto gà arímasū ga, anáta wà?**

♦**modal aux vb** (be obliged): **to have (got) to do something** …をしなければならない …**wò shinákereba naranal**

she has (got) to do it 彼女はそれをしなければなりません **kánōjo wa sorē wò shinákereba narimaseñ**

I have (got) to finish this work 私はこの仕事を済まさなければなりません **watákushi wà konó shigōto wo sumásanakereba narimaseñ**

you haven't to tell her 彼女に言わなくてもいい〔言ってはならない〕**anáta ni iwánakute mò fī**(itté wa naránal)

I haven't got/I don't have to wear glasses 私は眼鏡を掛けなくてもいい **watákushi wà mégane wò kakénakute mò fī**

this has to be a mistake これは何かの

間違いに違いない **korē wa nánīka no machígaī ni chigái nal**

♦**vt 1** (possess) 持っている **mótte iru,** …がある …**ga arū**

he has (got) blue eyes/dark hair 彼は目が青い〔髪が黒い〕**kárē wa mē gà aóī**(kamī gà kurôī)

do you have/have you got a car/phone? あなたは車〔電話〕を持っていますか **anáta wa kurūma(deñwa)wò móttē imasu ká**

I have (got) an idea いい考えがあります **yî kañgaē gà arîmasū**

have you any more money? もっとお金がありませんか **móttō o-káne gà arîmaseñ ká**

2 (take: food) 食べる **tabērù**; (: drink) 飲む **nómù**

to have breakfast/lunch/dinner 朝食〔昼食、夕食〕を食べる **chōshoku(chūshoku, yūshoku)wò tabérù**

to have a drink 何かを飲む **nánīka wo nómù**

to have a cigarette タバコを吸う **tabáko wo suù**

3 (receive, obtain etc) 受ける **ukérù,** 手に入れる **té ni irerù**

may I have your address? ご住所を教えて頂けますか **go-jûsho wò oshfete itadakemasû ká**

you can have it for $5 5ドルでこれを譲ります **gódōru de sorē wò yuzúrimasù**

I must have it by tomorrow どうして も明日までにそれをもらいたいのです **dōshite mò ashita made nî sorē wò morátai no desù**

to have a baby 子供を産む **kodómo wo umù**

4 (maintain, allow) 主張する **shuchō suru,** 許す **yurúsù**

he will have it that he is right 彼は自分が正しいと主張している **kárē wa jibún ga tadáshiî to shuchō shite irū**

I won't have it/this nonsense! それ〔こんなばかげた事〕は許せません **sorē**(kofína bakageta kotò)**wa yurúsemaseñ**

we can't have that そんな事は許せません **sofína kotò wa yurúsemaseñ**

5: *to have something done* ...をさせる
...wò saserù, ...をしてもらう ...wò shité
mòrau

to have one's hair cut 散髪をしてもら
う sanpatsu wò shité moraù

to have a house built 家を建てる ié wò
taterù

to have someone do something ...に
...wò saserù ...nf ...wò saserù

*he soon had them all laughing/
working* まもなく彼は皆を笑わせて/働
かせて)いた ma mó nàku karè wa miná
wò waráwasete/határakasete)ità

6 (experience, suffer) 経験する kefken
suru

to have a cold 風邪を引いている kazé
wò hifte irù

to have (the) flu 感冒にかかっている
kanfbō ni kakátte irù

*she had her bag stolen/her arm
broken* 彼女はハンドバッグを盗まれた
(腕を折った) kànòjo wa handòbaggù wo
nusúmareta(udé wo ottà)

to have an operation 手術を受ける
shújjutsu wò ukérù

7 (+ noun: take, hold etc) ...する suru

to have a swim/walk/bath/rest 泳ぐ
(散歩する, 風呂に入る, ひと休みする)
oyógù(sanpo suru, fúrò ni háìru, hitóyà-
sumi suru)

let's have a look 見てみましょう mìté
mimashò

to have a meeting/party 会議(パーテ
ィ)を開く kàigi(pàtî)wo hiràkù

let me have a try わたしにも試させて
ください watákushi ní tamésasete kudasaí

8 (*inf*: dupe) だます damásù

he's been had 彼はだまされた karè wa
damásaretà

haven [heɪ'ən] *n* (harbor) 港 mìnáto;
(safe place) 避難所 hìnáñjo

haven't [hæv'ənt] = **have not**

have out *vt*: *to have it out with
someone* (settle a problem etc) ...と決着
をつける ...tò ketcháku wò tsukérù

haversack [hæv'ərsæk] *n* (of hiker, soldier) リュックサック ryukkúsakkù

havoc [hæv'ək] *n* (chaos) 混乱 kofran

Hawaii [həwaɪ'iː] *n* ハワイ hàwái

hawk [hɔːk] *n* タカ takà

hay [heɪ] *n* 干草 hoshíkusa

hay fever *n* 花粉症 kafùnshō

haystack [heɪ'stæk] *n* 干草の山 hoshíkusa no yama

haywire [heɪ'waɪəːr] (*inf*) *adj*: *to go
haywire* (machine etc) 故障する koshó
suru; (plans etc) とんざする tônza suru

hazard [hæz'ərd] *n* (danger) 危険 kikén

◆*vt* (risk: guess, bet etc) やってみる yatté mirù

hazardous [hæz'ərdəs] *adj* (dangerous)
危険な kikén na

hazard (warning) lights *npl* (AUT)
非常点滅灯 hijôtenmetsútō

haze [heɪz] *n* (of heat, smoke, dust) かす
み kasúmi

hazelnut [heɪ'zəlnʌt] *n* ヘーゼルナッツ
hēzerunattsū

hazy [heɪ'ziː] *adj* (sky, view) かすんだ ka-
súnda; (idea, memory) ぼんやりとした
bofi-yarí to shita

he [hiː] *pron* 彼は(が) karè wa (ga)

he who ... ...する人は ...surú hitò wa

head [hed] *n* (ANAT, mind) 頭 atáma;
(of table) 上席 jóseki; (of queue) 先頭 señtō; (of company, organization) 最高責任
者 safkòsekínihsha; (of school) 校長 kó-
chō

◆*vt* (list, queue) ...の先頭にある(いる)
...no señtō ni arù (irù); (group, company) 取仕切る torÍshikirù

heads (or tails) 表か(裏か) omóte
ka (urá ka)

head first (fall) 真っ逆様に massákasa-
ma ni; (rush) 向こう見ずに mukó mìzu ni

head over heels (in love) ぞっこん zok-
kòn

to head a ball ボールをヘディングで飛
ばす bòru wo hedfngu de tobàsu

headache [hed'eɪk] *n* 頭痛 zutsú

headdress [hed'dres] *n* (of bride) ヘッド
レス heddódoresù

head for *vt fus* (place) ...に向かう ...ni
mukáù; (disaster) ...を招く ...wo manèkù

heading [hed'ɪŋ] *n* (of chapter, article)

表題 hyōdai, タイトル táitoru

headlamp [hed'læmp] (*BRIT*) *n* = **headlight**

headland [hed'lænd] *n* 岬 misákì

headlight [hed'lait] *n* ヘッドライト heddóraìto

headline [hed'lain] *n* (PRESS, TV) 見出 し midáshì

headlong [hed'lɔːŋ] *adv* (fall) 真っ逆様に massákàsama ni; (rush) 向こう見ずに mukó mìzu ni

headmaster [hed'mæs'tər] *n* 校長 kō-chō◇男性の場合 dansei nò baái

headmistress [hed'mis'tris] *n* 校長 kō-chō◇女性の場合 joséi nò baái

head office *n* (of company etc) 本社 hóñsha

head-on [hed'ɑn'] *adj* (collision, confrontation) 正面の shōmen no

headphones [hed'founz] *npl* ヘッドホン heddóhòn

headquarters [hed'kwɔːrtərz] *npl* (of company, organization) 本部 hóñbu; (MIL) 司令部 shiréfbu

headrest [hed'rest] *n* (AUT) ヘッドレス ト heddórèsuto

headroom [hed'ruːm] *n* (in car) 天井の高 さ teñjō nò takāsa; (under bridge) 通行可 能な高さ tsūkōkanō na takāsa

headscarf [hed'skɑːrf] *n* スカーフ sukáfù

headstrong [hed'strɔːŋ] *adj* (determined) 強情な gōjō na

head waiter *n* (in restaurant) 給仕頭 kyūjìgashira

headway [hed'wei] *n*: **to make head-way** 進歩する shíñpo suru

headwind [hed'wind] *n* 向かい風 mukáikaze

heady [hed'iː] *adj* (experience, time) 陶酔 の tōsuì no; (drink, atmosphere) 酔わせる yowáserù

heal [hiːl] *vt* (injury, patient) 治す naósù
♦*vi* (injury, damage) 治る naórù

health [helθ] *n* (condition: also MED) 健 康状態 keñkōjōtai; (good health) 健康 keñkō

health food *n* 健康食品 keñkōshokùhin

Health Service (*BRIT*) *n*: **the Health Service** 公共衛生機関 kōkyōeiseikikō

healthy [hel'θiː] *adj* (person, appetite etc) 健康な keñkō na; (air, walk) 健康に 良い keñkō ni yoî; (economy) 健全な keñzen na; (profit etc) 大いなる ōi naru

heap [hiːp] *n* (pile: of clothes, papers, sand etc) 山 yamá
♦*vt* (stones, sand etc): **to heap (up)** 積み 上げる tsumágerù

to heap something with (plate) ...に ...を山盛りする ...ni ...wo yamámori suru; (sink, table etc) ...に...を山積みする ...ni ...wo yamázumi suru

to heap something on (food) ...を...に山 盛りする ...wo ...ni yamámori suru; (books etc) ...を...に山積みする ...wo ...ni yamázumi suru

heaps of (*inf*: time, money, work etc) 一杯の ippái no

hear [hiːr] (*pt*, *pp* **heard**) *vt* (sound, voice etc) ...を聞く ...wo kikú, ...が聞える ...ga kikóerù; (news, information) ...を聞く ...wo kikú, ...について知る ...de kifte shirú; (LAW: case) 審理する shiñri suru

to hear about (event, person) ...の事を 聞く ...no kotó wo kikú

to hear from someone ...から連絡を受 ける ...kara reñraku wò ukérù

heard [hɑːrd] *pt*, *pp* of **hear**

hearing [hiː'riŋ] *n* (sense) 聴覚 chōkaku; (of facts, witnesses etc) 聴聞会 chōmoñkai

hearing aid *n* 補聴器 hochōkì

hearsay [hiːr'sei] *n* (rumor) うわさ uwása

hearse [hɑːrs] *n* 霊柩車 refkyūsha

heart [hɑːrt] *n* (ANAT) 心臓 shiñzō; (*fig*: emotions, character) 心 kokórò; (of problem) 核心 kakúshin; (of city) 中心部 chūshiñbu; (of lettuce) しん shíñ; (shape) ハート形 hātogata

to lose heart (courage) 落胆する rakútan suru

to take heart (courage) 勇気を出す yúki wò dásù

at heart (basically) 根は...né wà ...

by heart (learn, know) 暗記で añki de

heart attack n (MED) 心臓発作 shínzō-hossa

heartbeat [hɑːrtˈbiːt] n 心拍 shínpaku

heartbreaking [hɑːrtˈbreikiŋ] adj (news, story) 悲痛な hitsū na

heartbroken [hɑːrtˈbroukan] adj: **to be heartbroken** 悲嘆に暮れている hitán ni kurete irú

heartburn [hɑːrtˈbɜːrn] n (indigestion) 胸焼け munéyake

heart failure n (MED) 心不全 shínfuzen

heartfelt [hɑːrtˈfelt] adj (prayer, wish) 心からの kokórō kara no

hearth [hɑːrθ] n (fireplace) 炉床 roshō

heartland [hɑːrtˈlænd] n (of country, region) 中心地 chúshinchi

heartless [hɑːrtˈlis] adj (person, attitude) 非情な hijō na

hearts [hɑːrts] npl (CARDS) ハート háto

hearty [hɑːrtiː] adj (person) 明朗な meIrō na; (laugh) 大きな ōkina; (appetite) 盛んな ōsei na; (welcome) 熱烈な netsúretsu na; (dislike) 絶対的な zettáiteki na; (support) 心からの kokórō kara no

heat [hiːt] n (warmth) 暑さ átsùsa; (temperature) 温度 óndo; (excitement) 熱気 nekkí; (SPORT: also: **qualifying heat**) 予選 yosén

♦vt (water) 沸かす wákasù; (food) ...に火を通す ...ni hĭ wo tōsù; (room, house) 暖める atátamerù

heated [hiːˈtid] adj (pool) 温水の ofisuĭ no; (room etc) 暖房した dañbō shita; (argument) 激しい hagéshiì

heater [hiːˈtər] n ヒーター hītā

heath [hiːθ] n (BRIT) n 荒野 aréno

heathen [hiːˈðən] n (REL) 異教徒 ikyótò

heather [heˈðər] n エリカ属の、ヒース hísù

heating [hiːˈtiŋ] n (system, equipment) 暖房 dañbō

heatstroke [hiːtˈstrouk] n (MED) 熱射病 nesshábyō

heat up vi (water, room) 暖まる atátamarù

♦vt (food, water, room) 暖める atátamerù

heatwave [hiːtˈweiv] n 熱波 néppa

heave [hiːv] vt (pull) 強く引く tsúyòku hikú; (push) 強く押す tsúyòku osú; (lift) ぐいと持上げる gúĭ to mochíagerù

♦vi (vomit) 吐く hákù; (feel sick) むかつく mukátsukù

♦n (of chest) あえぎ aégi; (of stomach) むかつき mukátsukì

to heave a sigh ため息をつく taméikì wo tsukú

his chest was heaving 彼はあえいでいた kárè wa aéidè ità

heaven [hevˈan] n (REL: also fig) 天国 téñgoku

heavenly [hevˈanliː] adj (REL) 天からの téñ kara no; (fig: day, place) 素晴らしい subárashiì

heavily [hevˈiliː] adv (land, fall) どしんと dóshìn to; (drink, smoke) 大量に taíryō ni; (sleep) ぐっすりと gussárì to; (sigh) 深く fukákù; (depend, rely) すっかり sukkárì

heavy [hevˈiː] adj (person, load, responsibility) 重い omóì; (clothes) 厚い atsúì; (rain, snow) 激しい hagéshiì; (of person: build, frame) がっしりした gasshírì shita; (drinker) 強い tsúyòi; (breathing) 荒い aráì; (sleep) 深い fukáì; (schedule, week) 過密な kamítsu na; (work) きつい kitsúì; (weather) 蒸し暑い mushíatsùi; (food, meal) もたれる motárerù

a heavy drinker 飲兵衛 nóñbē

a heavy smoker ヘビースモーカー hebísumōkā

heavy goods vehicle (BRIT) n 大型トラック ōgatatorákku

heavyweight [hevˈiːweit] n (SPORT) ヘビー級選手 hebíkyūseñshu

Hebrew [hiːˈbruː] adj ヘブライの hebúrai no; (LING) ヘブライ語の hebúraigo no

♦n (LING) ヘブライ語 hebúraigo

Hebrides [hebˈridiːz] npl: **the Hebrides** ヘブリディーズ諸島 hebúridizushotō

heckle [hekˈəl] vt (speaker, performer) 野次る yajírù

hectic [hekˈtik] adj (event, week) やたらに忙しい yatárà ni isogáshiì

he'd [hiːd] = **he would**; **he had**

hedge [hedʒ] n (in garden, on roadside)

生け垣 ikégàki

♦vi あいまいな態度を取る aímai nà táìdo wo tórù

to hedge one's bets (*fig*) 失敗に備える shippái nì sonáerù

hedgehog [hɛdʒʹhɔːg] n ハリネズミ harínezùmi

heed [hiːd] vt (*also*: **take heed of**: advice, warning) 聞き入れる kikírerù

heedless [hiːdʹlis] *adj*: **heedless (of)** (...を) 無視した múshì shité

heel [hiːl] n (of foot, shoe) かかと kákàto

♦vt: **to heel shoes** 靴のかかとを修理する kutsú no kakáto wo shúri suru

hefty [hɛfʹtiː] *adj* (person) 大きくして重い gasshíri shita, (parcel etc) 大きくて重い ōkikute omói, (profit) 相当な sōtō na

heifer [hɛfʹəːr] n まだ子を生んだ事のない雌を指す mádà ko wo uñda kotó no náì monó wo sásù

height [hait] n (of tree, building, mountain) 高さ takásà, (of person) 身長 shiñchō, (of plane) 高度 kōdo, (high ground) 高地 kōchi, (*fig*: of powers) 絶頂期 zetchōkì, (: of season) 真っ最中 massáìchū, (: of luxury, stupidity) 極み kiwámi

heighten [haitʹən] vt (fears, uncertainty) 高める takámerù

heir [eːr] n (to throne) 継承者 kefshōshà, (to fortune) 相続人 sōzokuniñ

heiress [eːrʹis] n 大遺産の相続人 dafsan no sōzokuniñ ◇女性について言う joséi ni tsuité iú

heirloom [eːrʹluːm] n 家宝 kahō

held [held] *pt, pp of* **hold**

helicopter [hɛlʹikɑ̀ptəːr] n (AVIAT) ヘリコプター herīkopùtā

heliport [hɛlʹəpɔːrt] n (AVIAT) ヘリポート herīpòto

helium [hiːʹliːəm] n ヘリウム herīùmu

he'll [hiːl] = **he will, he shall**

hell [hel] n (life, situation: *also* REL) 地獄 jigóku

hell! (*inf*) 畜生！ chikúshō!, くそ！ kusó!

hellish [hɛlʹiʃ] (*inf*) adj (traffic, weather, life etc) 地獄の様な jigóku no yō na

hello [hɛlouʹ] *excl* (as greeting) やあ yáà, 今日は koñníchi wa; (to attract attention) おい ōi; (on telephone) もしもし móshìmoshi; (expressing surprise) おや oyá

helm [helm] n (NAUT: stick) かじ棒 kajíbò, (: wheel) だ輪 dárìn

helmet [hɛlʹmit] n (*gen*) ヘルメット herúmettò

help [help] n (assistance, aid) 助け tasúke, 手伝い tetsúdaì; (charwoman) お手伝いさん o-tétsudàisan

♦vt (person) 助ける tasúkerù, 手伝う tetsúdaù; (situation) ...に役に立つ ...ni yakú ni tatsù

help! 助けてくれ！ tasúketè kuré!

help yourself (to) (...を) 自由に取って下さい (...wo) jiyū ni totté kudásaì

he can't help it 彼はどうする事もなくなる事をやらざるを得ない kárè wa só sezarù wo énài

helper [hɛlʹpəːr] n (assistant) 助手 joshú, アシスタント ashísàtanto

helpful [hɛlpʹfəl] adj (person, advice, suggestion etc) 役に立つ yakú ni tatsù

helping [hɛlʹpiŋ] n (of food) 一盛り hitómori

a second helping お代わり o-káwarì

helpless [hɛlpʹlis] adj (incapable) 何もできない nañi mo dekínaì; (defenceless) 無防備の mubṓbi no

hem [hem] n (of skirt, dress) すそ susó

♦vt (skirt, dress etc) ...のすそ縫いをする ...no susónui wo suru

hem in vt 取囲む toríkakomù

hemisphere [hɛmʹisfiːr] n 半球 hañkyū

hemorrhage [hɛmʹəːridʒ] (BRIT **haemorrhage**) n 出血 shukkétsu

hemorrhoids [hɛmʹəːrɔidz] (BRIT **haemorrhoids**) npl じ ji

hen [hen] n (female chicken) メンドリ meñdori; (female bird) 雌の鳥 mesú no torí

hence [hens] adv (therefore) 従って shitágattè

2 years hence 今から2年先 imá kara nínen saki

henceforth [hensʹfɔːrθ] adv (from now on) 今後 kóñgo; (from that time on) その

後 sonó go

henchman [hentʃ'mən] (*pej: pl* **henchmen**) *n* (of gangster, tyrant) 手下 teshíta, 子分 kóbùn

henpecked [hen'pekt] *adj* (husband) 妻のしりに敷かれた tsúma no shirí ni shikaretá

hepatitis [hepətai'tis] *n* (MED) 肝炎 kán-en

her [hə:r] *pron* (direct) 彼女を kánòjo wo; (indirect) 彼女に kánòjo ni

♦*adj* 彼女の kánòjo no ¶*see also* **me; my**

herald [her'əld] *n* (forerunner) 兆し kizáshi

♦*vt* (event, action) 予告する yokóku suru

heraldry [her'əldri:] *n* (study) 紋章学 mofúshōgàku; (coat of arms) 紋章 mońshō 総称 sōshō

herb [ə:rb] *n* (*gen*) ハーブ hā́bu; (BOT, MED) 薬草 yakúsō; (CULIN) 香草 kṓsō

herd [hə:rd] *n* (of cattle, goats, zebra etc) 群れ muré

here [hi:r] *adv* (this place): **she left here yesterday** 彼女は昨日ここを出ましたkánòjo wa kinō kokó wò demáshìta; (beside me): **I have it here** ここに持っていますkó ni mottè imásù; (at this point): **here he stopped reading** この時彼は読むのをやめて... sonó tokí kárè wa yómù no wo seshū

here! (I'm present) はい！hái!; (take this) はいどうぞ hái dōzo

here is/are はい、...ですhái, ...désù

here she is! 彼女はここにいました！kánòjo wa kokó ni imáshìta!

hereafter [hi:ræf'tə:r] *adv* (in the future) 今後 kóńgo

hereby [hi:rbai'] *adv* (in letter) これをもって koré wo mottè

hereditary [həred'ite:ri:] *adj* (disease) 先天的な sefūtentai na; (title) 世襲の seshū no

heredity [həred'iti:] *n* (BIO) 遺伝 idén

heresy [her'isi:] *n* (opposing belief: *also* REL) 異端 itáń

heretic [her'itik] *n* 異端者 itáñsha

heritage [her'itidʒ] *n* (of country,

nation) 遺産 isáń

hermetically [hə:rmet'ikli:] *adv*: **hermetically sealed** 密閉した mippéi shita

hernia [hə:r'ni:ə] *n* (MED) 脱腸 datchṓ

hero [hi:'rou] (*pl* **heroes**) *n* (in book, film) 主人公 shujíñkō, ヒーロー hī́rō ◊男性を指す dansei wo sasu; (of battle, struggle) 英雄 eíyū; (idol) アイドル áidoru

heroic [hirou'ik] *adj* (struggle, sacrifice, person) 英雄的な eíyūteki na

heroin [her'ouin] *n* ヘロイン heróin

heroine [her'ouin] *n* (in book, film) 女主人公 ofúnashujìñkō, ヒロイン hirōin; (of battle, struggle) 英雄的な女性 eíyūtekijosei; (idol) アイドル áidoru

heroism [her'ouizəm] *n* (bravery, courage) 勇敢さ yūkansa

heron [her'ən] *n* アオサギ aósagi

herring [her'iŋ] *n* (fish) ニシン níshìn

hers [hə:rz] *pron* 彼女の物 kánòjo no monò ¶*see also* **mine**

herself [hə:rself'] *pron* 彼女自身 kánòjojishìn ¶*see also* **oneself**

he's [hi:z] = **he is; he has**

hesitant [hez'ətənt] *adj* (smile, reaction) ためらいがちな taméraigachi na

hesitate [hez'əteit] *vi* (pause) ためらう taméraù; (be unwilling) 後込みする shirígomì suru

hesitation [hezətei'ʃən] *n* (pause) ためらい tamérai; (reluctance) 後込み shirígomì

heterosexual [hetərəsek'ʃu:əl] *adj* (person, relationship) 異性愛の iséai na

hew [hju:] *vt* (stone, wood) 刻む kizámu

hexagonal [heksæg'ənəl] *adj* (shape, object) 六角形の rokkákukeì no

heyday [hei'dei] *n*: **the heyday of** ...の全盛時代 ...no zeńseijidài

HGV [eitʃdʒi:vi:'] *n abbr* = **heavy goods vehicle**

hi [hai] *excl* (as greeting) やあ yā́, 今日は końnichi wa; (to attract attention) おい ói

hiatus [haiei'təs] *n* (gap: in manuscript etc) 脱落個所 datsúrakukashò; (pause)

中断 chūdan

hibernate [hai'bəːrneit] *vi* (animal) 冬眠する tōmin suru

hiccough [hik'ʌp] *vi* しゃっくりする shákkuri suru

hiccoughs [hik'ʌps] *npl* しゃっくり shákkuri

hiccup [hik'ʌp] *vi* = hiccough

hiccups [hik'ʌps] *npl* = hiccoughs

hid [hid] *pt of* hide

hidden [hid'ən] *pp of* hide

hide [haid] *n* (skin) 皮 kawá
  ♦*vb* (*pt* hid, *pp* hidden)
  ♦*vt* (person, object, feeling, information) 隠す kakúsū; (obscure: sun, view) 覆い隠す ōíkakusū
  ♦*vi*: **to hide (from someone)** (...に見つからない様に) 隠れる (...ni mitsúkaranai yō ni) kakúrerū

hide-and-seek [haid'ənsiːk'] *n* (game) 隠れん坊 kakúrenbō

hideaway [hid'əwei] *n* (retreat) 隠れ家 kakúregá

hideous [hid'iːəs] *adj* (painting, face) 醜い mínīkuī

hiding [hai'diŋ] *n* (beating) むち打ち muchfuchi
  to be in hiding (concealed) 隠れている kakúrete irū

hierarchy [hai'əːrɑːrki:] *n* (system of ranks) 階級制 kaíkyūseí; (people in power) 幹部 kánbu の総称 sōshō

hi-fi [hai'fai'] *n* ステレオ sutéreo
  ♦*adj* (equipment, system) ステレオの sutéreo no

high [hai] *adj* (gen) 高い takáî; (speed) 速い hayáî; (wind: also い tsuyóî; (quality) い 等な jōtō na; (principles) 崇高な sūkō na
  ♦*adv* (climb, aim etc) 高く tákakū
  it is 20 m high その高さは20メーターです sonó takása wa nijū mētā desu
  high in the air 空高く sōratakakū

highbrow [hai'brau] *adj* (intellectual) 知的な chitéki na

highchair [hai'tʃeːr] *n* (for baby) ベビーチェア bebíchea

higher education [hai'əːr-] *n* 高等教育 kōtōkyōiku

high-handed [hai'hæn'did] *adj* (decision, rejection) 横暴な ōbō na

high-heeled [hai'hiːld] *adj* (shoe) ハイヒールの haíhiru no

high jump *n* (SPORT) 走り高飛び ha-shíritakátobi

highlands [hai'ləndz] *npl*: **the Highlands** スコットランド高地地方 sukóttorando kōchichihō

highlight [hai'lait] *n* (*fig*: of event) 山場 yamába, ハイライト haíraîto; (of news etc) 要点 yōten, ハイライト haíraîto; (in hair) 光る部分 hikárū bùbùn, ハイライト haíraîto
  ♦*vt* (problem, need) ...に焦点を合せる ...ni shōten wo awáserū

highly [hai'li:] *adv* (critical, confidential) 非常に takáî no; (a lot): **to speak highly of** ...をほめる ...wo homérū
  to think highly of ...を高く評価する ...wo tákakū hyōka suru

highly paid 高給取りの kōkyūtórī no

highly strung (BRIT) *adj* = high-strung

highness [hai'nis] *n*: **Her (or His) Highness** 陛下 héîka

high-pitched [hai'pitʃt'] *adj* (voice, tone, whine) 調子の高い chōshi no takáî

high-rise block [hai'raiz'-] *n* 高層ビル matéñhō

high school *n* (US: for 14-18 year-olds) 高等学校 kōtōgakkō, ハイスクール haísukūru; (BRIT: 11-18 year-olds) 総合中等学校 sōgōchūtōgakkō

high season *n* (BRIT) 最盛期 saiseiki, シーズン shízun

high street (BRIT) *n* 本通り hoñdōri

high-strung [hai'strʌŋ'] (US) *adj* 神経質な shiñkeishitsu na

highway [hai'wei] *n* 幹線道路 kañsendōro, ハイウエー haíue

Highway Code (BRIT) *n* 道路交通法 dōrokótsūhō

hijack [hai'dʒæk] *vt* (plane, bus) 乗っ取る nottórū, ハイジャックする haíjakkū suru

hijacker [hai'dʒæːkər] *n* 乗っ取り犯 nottóríhañ

hike [haik] *vi* (go walking) ハイキングする haikingu suru
♦*n* (walk) ハイキング háikingu

hiker ['haikər] *n* ハイカー háikā

hilarious [hiler'i:əs] *adj* (account, adventure) こっけいな kokkéi na

hill [hil] *n* (small) 丘 oká; (fairly high) 山 yamá; (slope) 坂 saká

hillside [hil'said] *n* 丘の斜面 oká no shamèn

hilly [hil'i:] *adj* 丘の多い oká no ōī
a hilly area 丘陵地帯 kyúryōchitài

hilt [hilt] *n* (of sword, knife) 柄 e
to the hilt (fig: support) とことんまで tokótoñ made

him [him] *pron* (direct) 彼を kárè wo; (indirect) 彼に kárè ni ¶ *see also* **me**

himself [himself'] *pron* 彼自身 kárèjishin ¶ *see also* **oneself**

hind [haind] *adj* (legs, quarters) 後ろの ushīro no

hinder ['hindər] *vt* (progress, movement) 妨げる samátageru

hindrance ['hindrəns] *n* 邪魔 jamá

hindsight [hin'sait] *n*: *with hindsight* 後になってみると átò ni nátte mírù

Hindu ['hindu:] *adj* ヒンズーの hiñzū no

hinge [hindʒ] *n* (on door) ちょうつがい chōtsugai
♦*vi* (fig): *to hinge on* ...によって決る ...ni yottè kimárù

hint [hint] *n* (suggestion) 暗示 añji, ヒント híñto; (advice) 勧め susúme, 提言 teígen; (sign, glimmer) 兆し kizáshi
♦*vt*: *to hint that* (suggest) ...だとほのめかす ...da to honómekasù
♦*vi*: *to hint at* (suggest) ほのめかす honómekasù

hip [hip] *n* (ANAT) 腰 koshí, ヒップ híppù

hippopotamus [hipəpɑ:t'əməs] *n* (*pl* **hippopotamuses** *or* **hippopotami**) カバ kábà

hire [haiər] *vt* (BRIT: car, equipment, hall) 賃借りする chíñgari suru; (worker) 雇う yatóu
♦*n* (BRIT: of car, hall etc) 賃借り chíñgari

for hire (taxi, boat) 賃貸し用の chíñgashiyō no

hire purchase (BRIT) *n* 分割払い購入 buñkatsubaraikōnyū

his [hiz] *pron* 彼の物 kárè no monó
♦*adj* 彼の kárè no ¶ *see also* **my; mine**

hiss [his] *vi* (snake, gas, roasting meat) しゅーっと言う shūtto iú; (person, audience) しーっと野次る shítto yajírù

historian [histɔ:r'i:ən] *n* 歴史学者 rekíshigakushà

historic(al) [histɔ:r'ik(əl)] *adj* (event, person) 歴史上の rekíshijō no, 歴史的の rekíshiteki na; (novel, film) 歴史に基づく rekíshi ni motózukù

history [his'tə:ri:] *n* (of town, country, person: *also* SCOL) 歴史 rekíshi

hit [hit] (*pt, pp* **hit**) *vt* (strike: person, thing) 打つ utsú, たたく tatáku; (reach: target) ...に当る ...ni atárù; (collide with: car) ...にぶつかる ...ni butsúkarù; (affect: person, services, event etc) ...に打撃を与える ...ni dagéki wo atáerù
♦*n* (knock) 打撃 dagéki; (success: play, film, song) 大当り ōatári, ヒット híttò
to hit it off with someone ...と意気投合する ...to tekítōgō suru

hit-and-run driver [hit'ænrən'-] *n* ひき逃げ運転者 hikínige unteñsha

hitch [hitʃ] *vt* (fasten) つなぐ tsunágù; (*also*: **hitch up**: trousers, skirt) 引上げる hikíagerù
♦*n* (difficulty) 問題 mońdai
to hitch a lift ヒッチハイクをする hitchíhaìku wo suru

hitch-hike [hitʃ'haik] *vi* ヒッチハイクをする hitchíhaìku wo suru

hitch-hiker [hitʃ'haikər] *n* ヒッチハイクをする人 hitchíhaìku wo suru hitó

hi-tech [hai'tek] *adj* ハイテクの haíteku no
♦*n* ハイテク haíteku

hitherto [hið'ə:rtu:] *adv* (until now) 今まで imá made

hive [haiv] *n* (of bees) ミツバチの巣箱 mitsúbachi no súbàko

hive off (*inf*) *vt* (company) ...の一部を放す ...no ichíbu wo kiríhanasù

HMS [eitʃemes] *abbr* (= *Her/His Majesty's Ship*) 軍艦...号 gunkan ...gō (英国海軍の艦名の前に付ける efìkokukaigūn no gunkan no namaè no maè ni tsukérū

hoard [hɔːrd] *n* (of food etc) 買いだめ kaídame; (of money, treasure) 蓄え takúwaè

◆*vt* (food etc) 買いだめする kaídamesuru

hoarding [hɔːrdíŋ] *n* (*BRIT*) *n* (for posters) 掲示板 keíjiban

hoarfrost [hɔːrfrɔst] *n* (on ground) 霜 shimó

hoarse [hɔːrs] *adj* (voice) しわがれた shiwágaretá

hoax [houks] *n* (trick) いんちき ínchiki, いかさま ikásama

hob [hɑːb] *n* (of cooker, stove) レンジの上部 reńji no jōbu

hobble [hɑːbəl] *vi* (limp) びっこを引く bíkkò wo hikú

hobby [hɑːbiː] *n* (pastime) 趣味 shúmì

hobby-horse [hɑːbiːhɔːrs] *n* (*fig*: favorite topic) 十八番の話題 ohákò nò wadáì

hobo [hou'bou] (*US*) *n* (tramp) ルンペン rúnpen

hockey [hɑːkiː] *n* (game) ホッケー hókkè

hoe [hou] *n* (tool) くわ kuwá, ホー hǒ

hog [hɔːg] *n* (pig) ブタ butá (去勢した雄ブタを指す kyosei shita osúbutá wo sasu

◆*vt* (*fig*: road, telephone etc) 独り占めにする hitórijime nì suru

to go the whole hog とことんまでやる tokóton made yarú

hoist [hɔist] *n* (apparatus) 起重機 kijūkì, クレーン kurén

◆*vt* (heavy object) 引上げる hikíagerù; (flag) 掲げる kakágerù; (sail) 張る harú

hold [hould] (*pt, pp* **held**) *vt* (bag, umbrella, someone's hand etc) 持つ mótsù; (contain: subj. room, box etc) ...が入っている ...ni ...ga háitte irù; (have: power, qualification, opinion) ...を持っている ...wo móttè irú; ...がある ...ga árù; (meeting) 開く hiráku; (detain: prisoner,

hostage) 監禁する kańkin suru; (consider): *to hold someone responsible/liable etc* ...の責任と見なす ...no sekínin tò minásù; (keep in certain position): *to hold one's head up* 頭を上げる atáma wò agérù

◆*vi* (withstand pressure) 持ちこたえる mochíkotaerù; (be valid) 当てはまる atéhamarù

◆*n* (grasp) 握り nigírì; (of ship) 船倉 señsō; (of plane) 貨物室 kamótsushitsù; (control): *to have a hold over* ...の急所を握っている ...no kyúshò wò nigítte irù

to hold a conversation with ...と話し合う ...to hanáshiaù

hold the line! (TEL) 少々お待ち下さい shōshō o-máchì kudasaí

hold on! ちょっと待って chótto mátte

to hold one's own (*fig*) 引けを取らない hiké wò toránaì, 負けない makénaì

to catch/get (a) hold of ...に捕まる ...ni tsukámarù

hold back *vt* (person, thing) 制止する seíshi suru; (thing, emotion) 押さえる osáerù; (secret, information) 隠す kakúsù

hold down *vt* (person) 押さえつける osáetsukerù; (job) ...についている ...ni tsúìte irú

holder [houl'dəːr] *n* (container) 入れ物 irémono, ケース kḕsù, ホルダー hórùdà; (of ticket, record, title) 保持者 hojísha; (of office) 在職者 zaíshokushà

holding [houl'diŋ] *n* (share) 持株 mochíkabu; (small farm) 小作農地 kosákunōchi

hold off *vi* (enemy) ...に持ちこたえる ...ni mochíkotaerù

hold on *vi* (hang on) 捕まる tsukámarù; (wait) 待つ mátsù

hold on to *vt fus* (for support) ...に捕まる ...ni tsukámarù; (keep) 預かる azúkarù

hold out *vt* (hand) 差伸べる sashínoberù; (hope, prospect) 持たせる motáserù

◆*vi* (resist) 抵抗する teíkō suru

hold up *vt* (raise) 上げる agérù; (sup-

hold-up [hould'ʌp] n (robbery) 強盗 gōtō; (delay) 遅れ okûre; (BRIT: in traffic) 渋滞 jūtai

hole [houl] n 穴 anâ
♦vt (ship, building etc) ...に穴を開ける ...ni anâ wo akêru

holiday [hɑːl'idei] n (BRIT: vacation) 休暇 kyūka; (day off) 休日 kyūka no hi; (public holiday) 祝日 shúkujitsu
on holiday 休暇中 kyūkachū

holiday camp (BRIT) n (also: **holiday centre**) n 保養村 hoyōmura

holiday-maker [hɑːl'ideimeikəːr] (BRIT) n 行楽客 kōrakukyaku

holiday resort n 行楽地 kōrakuchi, リゾート rizōto

holiness [hou'linis] n (of shrine, person) 神聖さ shinseisa

Holland [hɑːl'ənd] n オランダ orânda

hollow [hɑːl'ou] adj (container) 空っぽの karâppo no; (log, tree) うろのある urô no arû; (cheeks, eyes) くぼんだ kubônda; (laugh) わざとらしい wazâtorashii; (claim) 根拠のない kofikyo no naî; (sound) うつろな utsûro na
♦n (in ground) くぼみ kubômi
♦vt: *to hollow out* (excavate) がらんどうにする garándō ni surû

holly [hɑːl'i] n (tree, leaves) ヒイラギ hīragi

holocaust [hɑːl'əkɔːst] n 大虐殺 daígyakûsatsu

hologram [hɑːl'əgræm] n ホログラム horôguràmu

holster [houl'stəːr] n (for pistol) ホルスター horúsutā

holy [hou'liː] adj (picture, place, person) 神聖な shinsei na
holy water 聖水 sefsui

homage [hɑːm'idʒ] n (honor, respect) 敬意 kéii
to pay homage to (hero, idol) ...に敬意を表す ...ni kéii wo aráwasù

home [houm] n (house) 家 ié, 住い sumâi;

(area, country) 故郷 kokyô; (institution) 収容施設 shūyōshisètsu
♦cpd (domestic) 家庭の katêi no; (ECON, POL) 国内の kokûnai no; (SPORT: team, game) 地元の jimôto no
♦adv (go, come, travel etc) 家に ié ni
at home (in house) 家に(で) ié ni (de); (in country) 本国に(で) hôngoku ni (de); (in situation) ...に通じて ...ni tsūjite
make yourself at home どうぞお楽に dôzo o-ráku ni
to drive something home (nail etc) ...を打込む ...wo uchíkomù; (fig: point etc) ...を強調する ...wo kyôchō suru

home address n 自宅の住所 jitáku no jûsho

home computer n パーソナルコンピュータ pāsonarukonpyūta, パソコン pasôkon

homeland [houm'lænd] n 母国 bókòku

homeless [houm'lis] n (family, refugee) 家のない ié no naî

homely [houm'liː] adj (simple, plain) 素朴な sobôku na; (US: not attractive: person) 不器量な bukíryò na

home-made [houm'meid'] adj (bread, bomb) 手製の tesêi no, 自家製の jikâsei no

Home Office (BRIT) n 内務省 naîmushò

homeopathy [houmiːɑːp'əθiː] (BRIT **homoeopathy**) n (MED) ホメオパシー homêopashī

home rule n (POL) 自治権 jichîken

Home Secretary (BRIT) n 内務大臣 naîmudaijin

homesick [houm'sik] adj ホームシック の hōmushikkû no

hometown [houm'taun'] n 故郷 kokyô

homeward [houm'wəːrd] adj (journey) 家に帰るの ié ni kaerû

homework [houm'wəːrk] n (SCOL) 宿題 shukûdai

homicide [hɑːm'isaid] (US) n 殺人 satsûjin

homoeopathy [houmiːɑːp'əθiː] (BRIT) n = **homeopathy**

homogeneous [houmədʒiː'niːəs] adj

(group, class) 均質の kínshitsu no

homosexual [houməsek'ʃuːəl] *adj* (person, relationship) 同性愛の dōseiaì no; (man) ホモの hómo no; (woman) レズの rézù no

◆*n* (man) 同性愛者 dōseiaìsha, ホモ hómo; (woman) 同性愛者 dōseiaìsha, レズ rézù

honest [ɑn'ist] *adj* (truthful, trustworthy) 正直な shōjiki na; (sincere) 率直な sotchoku na

honestly [ɑn'istli:] *adv* (truthfully) 正直に shōjiki ni; (sincerely, frankly) 率直に sotchoku ni

honesty [ɑn'isti:] *n* (truthfulness) 正直 shōjiki; (sincerity, frankness) 率直さ sotchokusa

honey [hʌn'i:] *n* (food) はちみつ hachimitsu

honeycomb [hʌn'i:koum] *n* (of bees) みつばちの巣 mitsubāchi no su

honeymoon [hʌn'i:muːn] *n* (holiday, trip) 新婚旅行 shínkonryokō, ハネムーン hanémūn

honeysuckle [hʌn'i:sʌkəl] *n* (BOT) スイカズラ suíkazùra

honk [hɑːŋk] *vi* (AUT: horn) 鳴らす narāsu

honorary [ɑn'əreri:] *adj* (unpaid: job, secretary) 無給の mukyū no; (title, degree) 名誉の meíyo no

honor [ɑn'əːr] (*BRIT* **honour**) *vt* (hero, author) ほめたたえる hométataerù; (commitment, promise) 守る mamórù

◆*n* (pride, self-respect) 名誉 meíyo; (tribute, distinction) 栄誉 eíyo kóei

honorable [ɑn'ərəbəl] *adj* (person, action, defeat) 名誉ある meíyo aru

honors degree [ɑn'əːrz-] *n* (SCOL) 専門学士号 senmongakushigō

hood [hud] *n* (of coat, cooker etc) フードfúdo; (*US*: AUT: engine cover) ボンネット bofinettò; (*BRIT*: AUT: folding roof折畳み式トップ orítatamishiki toppù

hoodlum [hud'ləm] *n* (thug) ごろつき gorótsuki, 暴力団員 bōryokudan-ìn

hoodwink [hud'wiŋk] *vt* (con, fool) だます damásù

hoof [huf] (*pl* **hooves**) *n* ひずめ hizúme

hook [huk] *n* (for coats, curtains etc) かぎ kagí, フック fúkkù; (on dress) ホックhōkkù; (*also: fishing hook*) 釣針 tsurībarì

◆*vt* (fasten) 留める tomérù; (fish) 釣るtsurú

hooligan [huː'ligən] *n* ちんぴら chífipira

hoop [huːp] *n* (ring) 輪 wá

hooray [hærei'] *excl* = **hurrah, hurray**

hoot [huːt] *vi* (AUT: horn) クラクションを鳴らす kurákùshon wo narásù; (siren) 鳴る narú; (owl) ほーほーと鳴く hōhō to nakú

hooter [huː'təːr] *n* (*BRIT*: AUT) クラクション kurákùshon, ホーン hōn; (NAUT, factory) 警報機 keíhōkí

hoover [huː'vəːr] ®(*BRIT*) *n* (vacuum cleaner) (真空) 掃除機 (shinkū)sōjìkí

◆*vt* (carpet) ...に掃除機を掛ける ...ni sōjìkí wo kakérù

hooves [huvz] *npl* of **hoof**

hop [hɑp] *vi* (on one foot) 片足で跳ぶ katáashi de tobú; (bird) ぴょんぴょん跳ぶ pyófipyon tobú

hope [houp] *vt*: **to hope that/to do** ...だとする事を望む ...dá to ... (surú kotó wo)nozómù

◆*vi* 希望する kibō suru

◆*n* (desire) 望み nozómi; (expectation) 期待 kitái; (aspiration) 希望 kibō

I hope so/not そうだ(でない)といいがsō dà (de nái)to fi ga

hopeful [houp'fəl] *adj* (person) 楽観的なrakkánteki na; (situation) 見込みのあるmikómi no arú

hopefully [houp'fəli:] *adv* (expectantly) 期待して kitái shite; (one hopes) うまくいけば úmaku ikéba

hopeless [houp'lis] *adj* (grief, situation, future) 絶望的な zetsúbōteki na; (person: useless) 無能な munōna

hops [hɑps] *npl* (BOT) ホップ hóppù

horde [hɔːrd] *n* (of critics, people) 大群taígun

horizon [hərai'zən] *n* (skyline) 水平線suíheìsen

horizontal [hɔːrizɑn'təl] *adj* 水平の suf-

hei no

hormone [hɔːr'moun] n (BIO) ホルモ ン hórumon

horn [hɔːrn] n (of animal) 角 tsunó; (material) 角質 kakúshitsu; (MUS: also: **French horn**) ホルン hórūn; (AUT) クラ クション kurákūshon, ホーン hōn

hornet [hɔːr'nit] n (insect) スズメバチ suzúmebāchi

horny [hɔːr'niː] (inf) adj (aroused) セッ クスをしたがっている sékkūsu wo shitá- gatte irú

horoscope [hɔːr'əskoup] n (ASTROL- OGY) 星占い hoshíurānai

horrendous [hɔːren'dəs] adj (crime) 恐 ろしい osóroshii; (error) ジョッキングな shókkingu na

horrible [hɔːr'əbəl] adj (unpleasant: color, food, mess) ひどい hidói; (terrify- ing: scream, dream) 恐ろしい osóroshii

horrid [hɔːr'id] adj (person, place, thing) いやな iyá na

horrify [hɔːr'əfai] vt (appall) ぞっとさせ る zóttő saséru

horror [hɔːr'əːr] n (alarm) 恐怖 kyốfū; (abhorrence) 憎悪 zőo; (of battle, war- fare) むごたらしさ mugótarashisa

horror film n ホラー映画 horáeiga

hors d'oeuvre [ɔːr dəːrv'] n (CULIN: gen) 前菜 zefísai; (: Western food) オード ブル ódobūru

horse [hɔːrs] n 馬 umá

horseback [hɔːrs'bæk] n: **on horseback** adj 乗馬の jōba no

♦adv 馬に乗って umá ni notté

horse chestnut n (tree) トチノキ tochí no kí; (nut) とちの実 tochí no mí

horseman/woman [hɔːrs'mən/wumən] (pl **horsemen/women**) n (rider) 馬の乗 り手 umá no norîte

horsepower [hɔːrs'pauəːr] n (of engine, car etc) 馬力 barîki

horse-racing [hɔːrs'reisiŋ] n (SPORT) 競馬 keíba

horseradish [hɔːrs'rædiʃ] n (BOT, CULIN) ワサビダイコン wasábidaikon, セイヨウワサビ seíyōwasābi

horseshoe [hɔːrs'ʃuː] n てい鉄 teítetsu

horticulture [hɔːr'təkʌltʃəːr] n 園芸 eñ- gei

hose [houz] n ホース hōsu

hosiery [hou'ʒəːriː] n (in shop) 靴下類 ku- tsúshitarūi

hospice [hɑːs'pis] n (for the dying) ホス ピス hósūpisu

hospitable [hɑːspit'əbəl] adj (person) 持 て成しの良い moténashi no yoî; (behav- ior) 手厚い teátsuî

hospital [hɑːs'pitəl] n 病院 byōin

hospitality [hɑːspətæl'itiː] n (of host, welcome) 親切な持て成し shiñsetsu nà moténashi

host [houst] n (at party, dinner etc) 主人 shújin, ホスト hósūto; (TV, RADIO) 司会 者 shikáisha; (REL) 御聖体 go-seítai; (large number): **a host of** 多数の tasú no

hostage [hɑːs'tidʒ] n (prisoner) 人質 hitó- jichi

hostel [hɑːs'təl] n (for homeless etc) 収容 所 shúyōjo; (also: **youth hostel**) ユースホ ステル yúsuhosūteru

hostess [hou'stis] n (at party, dinner etc) 女主人 ofinashujin, ホステス hósūtesu; (BRIT: air hostess) スチュワーデス su- chúwādesu; (TV, RADIO) (女性) 司会 者 (joséi)shikáisha

hostile [hɑːs'təl] adj (person, attitude: aggressive) 敵対する tekítai suru, 敵意 のある tékī no árū; (: unwelcome): **hostile to** ...に対して排他的な ...ni taí- shite haítateki na; (conditions, environ- ment) か酷な kakókù na

hostilities [hɑːstil'ətiːz] npl (fighting) 戦 闘 señtō

hostility [hɑːstil'ətiː] n (antagonism) 敵 対 tekítai, 敵意 tékī-i; (lack of welcome) 排他的 態度 haítatekitaïdo; (of condi- tions, environment) か酷さ kakókùsa

hot [hɑːt] adj (moderately hot) 暖かい a- tátakaì; (very hot) 熱い atsúi; (weather, room etc) 暑い atsúi; (spicy: food) 辛い karái; (fierce: temper, contest, argu- ment etc) 激しい hagéshiì

it is hot (weather) 暑い atsúi; (object) 熱い atsúi

I am hot (person) 私は暑い watákushi wà atsúí

he is hot 彼は暑がっている kárè wà atsúgatte irú

hotbed [hɔːtˈbed] *n* (*fig*) 温床 onshō

hot dog (snack) ホットドッグ hottódoggu

hotel [houtˈel] *n* ホテル hóteru

hotelier [ɔteljeɪ] *n* (owner) ホテルの経営者 hótēru no kefeísha; (manager) ホテルの支配人 hótēru no shiháinin

hotheaded [hɔtˈhedid] *adj* (impetuous) 気の早い kí no hayáí

hothouse [hɔtˈhaus] *n* (BOT) 温室 onshitsu

hot line (POL) ホットライン hottórain

hotly [hɔtˈliː] *adv* (speak, contest, deny) 激しく hagéshikù

hotplate [hɔtˈpleɪt] *n* (on cooker) ホットプレート hottópurēto

hot-water bottle [hɔːtwɔːtˈəːr-] *n* 湯たんぽ yutánpo

hound [haund] *vt* (harass, persecute) 迫害する hakúgai suru

♦*n* (dog) 猟犬 ryóken, ハウンド haúndo

hour [auˈəːr] *n* (sixty minutes) 1時間 íchì jikàn; (time) 時刻 jíkàn

hourly [auəːrˈliː] *adj* (service, rate) 1時間当りの ichí jìkan atàri no

house [*n* haus *vb* hauz] *n* (home) 家 ié, うち uchí; (household) 家族 kázòku; (company) 会社 kafsha; (POL) 議院 gíin; (THEATER) 客席 kyakúseki; (dynasty) ...家 ...kē

♦*vt* (person) ...に住宅を与える ...ni jútaku wò atéru; (collection) 収容する shúyo suru

on the house (*fig*) サービスで sābìsu de

house arrest *n* (POL, MIL) 軟禁 nánkin

houseboat [hausˈbout] *n* 屋形船 yakátabunè, ハウスボート haúsubòto ◇住宅用の船を指す jútakuyō no funè wo sásh

housebound [hausˈbaund] *adj* (invalid) 家から出られない ié kara derárenaí

housebreaking [hausˈbreikin] *n* 家宅侵入 kátakushínnyù

housecoat [hausˈkout] *n* 部屋着 heyági

household [hausˈhould] *n* (inhabitants)

家族 kazóku; (home) 家 ié

housekeeper [hausˈkiːpəːr] *n* (servant) 家政婦 kaséifú

housekeeping [hausˈkiːpin] *n* (work) 家事 kájì; (money) 家計費 kakéíhi

house-warming party [hausˈwɔːrming-] *n* 新居祝いのパーティ shíñkyo-iwaì no pàti

housewife [hausˈwaif] (*pl* **housewives**) *n* 主婦 shúfù

housework [hausˈwəːrk] *n* (chores) 家事 kájì

housing [hauˈzin] *n* (houses) 住宅 jútaku, (provision) 住宅供給 jútakukyókyuù

housing development *n* 住宅団地 jútakudáñchi

housing estate (BRIT) *n* 住宅団地 jútakudáñchi

hovel [havˈəl] *n* (shack) あばら屋 abára-ya

hover [havˈəːr] *vi* (bird, insect) 空中に止まる tomárù

hovercraft [havˈəːrkræft] *n* (vehicle) ホバークラフト hobákurafùto

how [hau] *adv* 1 (in what way) どう dō, どの様に donó yò ni, どうやって dō yatté

how did you do it? どうやってそれができたんですか dō yatté soré gà dekítan desù ká

I know how you did it あなたがどの様にしてそれができたかは分かっています anáta ga donó yò ni shite soré gà dekíta kà watákushi nì wa wakátte imasu

to know how to do something ...の仕方を知っている ...no shikáta wò shitté irú

how is school? 学校はどうですか gakkō wa dō desu ká

how was the film? 映画はどうでしたか eíga wa dō deshita ká

how are you? お元気ですか o-géñki desu ká

2 (to what degree) どのくらい donó kurai

how much milk? どのくらいのミルク

う hamingu de utau
◆vi (person) ハミングする hámíngu suru; (machine) ぶーんと鳴る bún to naru; (insect) ぶんぶんいう búnbun iu

human [hjuːˈmən] *adj* (existence, body) 人の hitó no, 人間の nifigen no; (weakness, emotion) 人間的な nifigenteki na
◆*n* (person) 人 hitó, 人間 nifigen

humane [hjuːˈmeɪn] *adj* (treatment, slaughter) 苦痛を与えない kutsú wò atáenai

humanitarian [hjuːmænɪˈtɛrˈiːən] *adj* (aid, principles) 人道的な jindóteki na

humanity [hjuːˈmænˈitiː] *n* (mankind) 人類 jfnrui, 人間 nifigen; (human nature) 人間性 nifigensei; (humaneness, kindness) 思いやり omóiyari

humble [hʌmˈbəl] *adj* (modest) 謙虚な kéñkyo na; (lowly: background) 身分の低い mfbun no hikúi
◆*vt* (humiliate, crush) ...の高慢な鼻を折る ...no kōman na hanâ wò órù

humbug [hʌmˈbʌg] *n* (of statement, writing) でたらめ detárame; (BRIT: sweet) はっかあめ hakkâ-ame

humdrum [hʌmˈdrʌm] *adj* (dull, boring) 退屈な tafkutsu na

humid [hjuːˈmɪd] *adj* (atmosphere, climate) 湿度の高い shitsúdò no takâi

humidity [hjuːmɪdˈitiː] *n* 湿度 shitsúdò

humiliate [hjuːmɪlˈiːeɪt] *vt* (rival, person) ...の高慢な鼻を折る ...no kōman na hanâ wò órù

humiliation [hjuːmiliːˈeɪˈən] *n* (embarrassment) 恥 hajf; (situation, experience) 恥辱 chijóku

humility [hjuːmɪlˈitiː] *n* (modesty) 謙そん keñson

humor [hjuːˈmər] (BRIT **humour**) *n* (comedy, mood) ユーモア yumóa
◆*vt* (child, person) ...の機嫌を取る ...no kigén wo tórù

humorous [hjuːˈmərəs] *adj* (remark, book) おどけた odóketa; (person) ユーモアのある yumóa no árù

hump [hʌmp] *n* (in ground) 小山 koyáma; (of camel: also deformity) こぶ kobû

humpbacked [hʌmpˈbækt] *adj*: **hump-**

---

howl [haul] *vi* (animal) 遠ぼえする tôboe suru; (baby, person) 大声で泣く ōgoè de nakú; (wind) うなる unárù

H.P. [eɪtʃpiːˈ] *abbr* = **hire purchase**

h.p. *abbr* = **horsepower**

HQ [eɪtʃkjuːˈ] *abbr* = **headquarters**

hub [hʌb] *n* (of wheel) ハブ hábù; (fig: centre) 中心 chūshin

hubbub [hʌbˈʌb] *n* (din, commotion) どよめき doyómeki

hubcap [hʌbˈkæp] *n* (AUT) ホイールキャップ hoírukyappû

huddle [hʌdˈəl] *vi*: **to huddle together** (for heat, comfort) 体を寄り合う karáda wò yoséaù

hue [hjuː] *n* (color) 色 irő; (shade of color) 色合い iróaì

hue and cry *n* (outcry) 騒ぎ sáwàgi

huff [hʌf] *n*: **in a huff** (offended) 怒って okóttè

hug [hʌg] *vt* (person, thing) 抱締める dakíshimerû

huge [hjuːdʒ] *adj* (enormous) ばく大な bakúdai na

hulk [hʌlk] *n* (ship) 廃船 hafsen; (person) 図体ばかり大きい人 zútai bakari ōkii hitó, うどの大木 udo no taiboku; (building etc) ばかでかい物 bakádekai monó

hull [hʌl] *n* (of ship) 船体 seftai, ハル háru

hullo [halouˈ] *excl* = **hello**

hum [hʌm] *vt* (tune, song) ハミングで歌

backed bridge 反り橋 sorîhâshi

hunch [hʌntʃ] n (premonition) 直感 chokkán

hunchback [hʌntʃˈbæk] n せむしの人 semûshi nò hitó ○べっ称 besshô

hunched [hʌntʃt] adj (bent, stooped: shoulders) 曲げた magéta (: person) 肩を落とした kátà wò otôshità

hundred [hʌndrəd] num 百 (no) hyakú (no); (before n): *a/one hundred books* 100冊の本 hyakúsatsu nò hôñ; *a/one hundred people* 100人の人 hyakúniñ nò hitó; *a/one hundred dollars* 100ドル hyakú doru

hundreds of 何百もの nañbyaku mo no

hundredweight [hʌnˈdridwèit] n (US = 45.3 kg, 100 lb; BRIT = 50.8 kg, 112 lb)

hung [hʌŋ] pt, pp of hang

Hungarian [hʌŋgɛˈriən] adj ハンガリーの hañgarí no; (LING) ハンガリー語の hañgarigo no

♦n (person) ハンガリー人 hañgarîjîn; (LING) ハンガリー語 hañgarîgo

Hungary [hʌŋˈgəːri] n ハンガリー hañgarî

hunger [hʌŋˈgəːr] n (lack of food) 空腹 kúfuku; (starvation) 飢餓 kígà

♦vi: *to hunger for* (desire) ...に飢える ...ni uérù

hunger strike n ハンガーストライキ hañgâsutoraìki, ハンスト hañsuto

hungry [hʌŋˈgri] adj (person) 空腹 kúfuku na; (keen, avid): *hungry for* ...に飢えた ...ni uétà

to be hungry おなかがすいた onáka ga suità

hunk [hʌŋk] n (of bread etc) 塊 katámarì

hunt [hʌnt] vt (for: subj: animal) 獲物を探し求める sagáshimotomerù, あさる asárù; (SPORT) 狩る kárù, ...の狩りをする ...no kárí wo surù; (criminal, fugitive) 捜す sagásu, 捜索する sôsaku suru

♦vi (search): *to hunt (for)* 捜す (...wo) sagásu; (SPORT) (...の) 狩りをする (...no) kárí wo surù

♦n (for food: also SPORT) 狩り kárî; (search) 捜す事 sagásu kotô; (for crimi-

nal) 捜索 sôsaku

hunter [hʌntˈəːr] n (sportsman) ハンター hántā

hunting [hʌntiŋ] n (for food: also SPORT) 狩り kárî

hurdle [həːrˈdəl] n (difficulty) 障害 shôgai; (SPORT) ハードル hâdoru

hurl [həːrl] vt (object) 投げる nagérù; (insult, abuse) 浴びせ掛ける abîsekakerù

hurrah [həˈrɑː] n = hurray

hurray [həreˈi] n = hurrah

hurricane [həːrˈəkein] n (storm) ハリケーン haríkèn

hurried [həːrˈiːd] adj (hasty, rushed) 大急ぎの ôisôgi no

hurriedly [həːrˈiːdli] adv 大急ぎで ôisôgi de

hurry [həːri] n (haste, rush) 急ぎ isógi

♦vi (also: *hurry up*: hasten, rush) 急ぐ isógù

♦vt (also: *hurry up*: person) 急がせる isôgaserù; (: work) 急いでやる isóide suru

to be in a hurry 急いでいる isóide irù

hurt [həːrt] (pt, pp **hurt**) vt (cause pain to) 痛める itámerù; (injure, fig) 傷付ける kizútsukerù

♦vi (be painful) 痛む itámù

it hurts! 痛い！itâi!

hurtful [həːrtˈfəl] adj (remark) 傷付ける様な kizútsukeru yô na

hurtle [həːrˈtəl] vi: *to hurtle past* (train, car) 猛スピードで通り過ぎる môsupido de tôrisugìrù

to hurtle down (fall) 落ちる ochírù

husband [hʌzˈbənd] n 夫 ottó

hush [hʌʃ] n (silence) 沈黙 chiñmoku; (stillness) 静けさ shizúkesà

♦vt (silence) 黙らせる damáraserù

hush! 静かに shizûka ni

hush up vt (scandal etc) もみ消す momîkesù

husk [hʌsk] n (of wheat, rice) 殻 kará; (of maize) 皮 kawá

husky [hʌsˈki] adj (voice) しわがれた shiwágaretà, ハスキーな hásùkī na

♦n (dog) ハスキー hásùkī

hustle [hʌsˈəl] vt (hurry) 急がせる isógaserū

◆*n*: hustle and bustle 雑踏 zattō

hut [hʌt] *n* (house) 小屋 koyá; (shed) 物置 monó-oki

hutch [hʌtʃ] *n* (*also*: **rabbit hutch**) ウサギ小屋 uságigoya

hyacinth [hai'əsinθ] *n* ヒヤシンス hiyáshìnsu

hybrid [hai'brid] *n* (plant, animal) 交雑種 kōzatsushū, ハイブリッド haɪburiddo; (mixture) 混成物 kōnseibūtsu

hydrant [hai'drənt] *n* (*also*: **fire hydrant**) 消火栓 shōkasen

hydraulic [haidrɔ:'lik] *adj* (pressure, system) 油圧の yuátsu no

hydroelectric [haidrouilek'trik] *adj* (energy, complex) 水力発電の suíryoku-hatsūden no

hydrofoil [hai'drəfɔil] *n* (boat) 水中翼船 suíchūyokūsen

hydrogen [hai'drədʒən] *n* (CHEM) 水素 súlso

hyena [haii:'nə] *n* ハイエナ hafena

hygiene [hai'dʒi:n] *n* (cleanliness) 衛生 efsei

hygienic [haidʒi:en'ik] *adj* 衛生的な efseiteki na

hymn [him] *n* 賛美歌 sañbikа

hype [haip] (*inf*) *n* 売込み口上 urɪkomíkōjō

hypermarket [hai'pərmɑːrkit] (*BRIT*) *n* 大型スーパー ōgatasūpā

hyphen [hai'fən] *n* (dash) ハイフン hátfun

hypnosis [hipnou'sis] *n* 催眠 saímin

hypnotic [hipnɑt'ik] *adj* (trance) 催眠の saíminjutsu no; (rhythms) 催眠的な saíminteki na

hypnotism [hip'nətizəm] *n* 催眠術 saíminjutsu

hypnotist [hip'nətist] *n* (person) 催眠術師 saíminjutsushī

hypnotize [hip'nətaiz] *vt* (MED etc) ...に催眠術を掛ける ...ni saíminjutsu wo kakérù; (*fig*: mesmerise) 魅惑する miwákusuru

hypochondriac [haipoukɑn'dri:æk] *n* 心気症患者 shiñkishōkañja

hypocrisy [hipɑk'rəsi:] *n* (falseness, in-

sincerity) 偽善 gizén

hypocrite [hip'əkrit] *n* (phoney) 偽善者 gizénshа

hypocritical [hipəkrit'ikəl] *adj* (person) 偽善の gizén no; (behavior) 偽善者的な gizénshateki na

hypothermia [haipəθər'mi:ə] *n* (MED) 低体温症 teftaiońshō

hypothesis [haipɑθ'əsis] (*pl* **hypotheses**) *n* (theory) 仮説 kasétsu

hypothetic(al) [haipəθet'ik(əl)] *adj* (question, situation) 仮定の katéi no

hysteria [histi:'ri:ə] *n* (panic: *also* MED) ヒステリー hísùterī

hysterical [histe:'rikəl] *adj* (person, rage) ヒステリックな hísùterikkù na; (situation: funny) 笑いが止らない様な warái ga tomáranai yō na

◆*hysterical laughter* ばか笑い bakáwarài

hysterics [histe:'riks] *npl* (anger, panic) ヒステリー hísùterī; (laughter) 大笑い ōwarài

I

I [ai] *pron* 私は(が) watákushi wa (ga)

ice [ais] *n* (frozen water) 氷 kōri; (: *also*: **ice cream**) アイスクリーム afsukurīmu

◆*vt* (cake) ...にアイシングを掛ける ...ni áìshingu wo kakérù

◆*vi* (*also*: **ice over**, **ice up**: road, window etc) 氷に覆われる kōri ni ōwarérù

iceberg [ais'bə:rg] *n* 氷山 hyōzan

icebox [ais'bɑːks] *n* (US: fridge) 冷蔵庫 refzōko; (BRIT: compartment) 冷凍室 reftōshìtsu; (insulated box) クーラー kū-rā

ice cream *n* アイスクリーム afsukurīmu

ice cube *n* 角氷 kakúgòri

iced [aist] *adj* (cake) アイシングを掛けた áìshingu wo kákèta; (beer) 冷した hiyáshita

iced tea アイスティー aísutì

ice hockey *n* (SPORT) アイスホッケー afsuhokkē

Iceland [ais'lənd] *n* アイスランド afsurando

ice lolly [-lɔːlɪː] (BRIT) n アイスキャンディー aisukyandiː

ice rink n スケートリンク sukḗtoriṅku

ice-skating [aisˈskeitiŋ] n アイススケート aisusukḗto

icicle [aisˈsikəl] n (on gutter, ledge etc) つらら tsurára

icing [aiˈsiŋ] n (CULIN) 砂糖衣 satṓgoromo, アイシング áishiṅgu

icing sugar (BRIT) n 粉砂糖 konázatō

icon [aiˈkɑːn] n (REL) 聖像画 seízōga, イコン íkòn

icy [aiˈsiː] adj (air, water, temperature) 冷たい tsumétaì; (road) 氷に覆われた kṓri ni ōwareta

I'd [aid] = I would; I had

idea [aidiːˈə] n (scheme, notion) 考え kaṅgaè; (opinion) 意見 íkèn; (objective) つもり tsumóri

ideal [aidiːˈəl] n (principle) 理想 risṓ; (epitome) 模範 mohán
   ♦adj (perfect) 理想的な risōteki na

idealist [aidiːˈəlist] n 理想主義者 risōshugìsha

identical [aidenˈtikəl] adj 同一の dṓitsu no

identification [aidentəfəkeiˈʃən] n (process) 識別 shikíbetsu; (of person, dead body) 身元の確認 mimóto nò kakúnin
   (means of) identification 身分証明書 mibúnshōmeìsho

identify [aidenˈtəfai] vt (recognize) 見分ける miwákerù; (distinguish) 識別する shikíbetsu suru; (associate): to identify someone/something (with) ...を (...と) 関連付ける ...wo (...to) kañrenzukerù

Identikit [aidenˈtəkit] ⓡ n: Identikit (picture) モンタージュ写真 moñtājushashìn

identity [aidenˈtitiː] n (of person, aspect etc) 身元 mimóto, 正体 shótaì; (of group, culture, nation etc) 特性 tokúsei

identity card n 身分証明書 mibúnshōmeìsho

ideology [aidiːɑːˈlədʒiː] n (beliefs) 思想

shisō, イデオロギー idéorògī

idiom [idˈiːəm] n (style) 作風 sakúfū; (phrase) 熟語 jukúgo, イディオム ídìomu

idiomatic [idiːæmˈætik] adj 熟語的な jukúgoteki na

idiosyncrasy [idiːəsiŋˈkrəsiː] n (foible) 性癖 tokúsei

idiot [idˈiːət] n (fool) ばか bákà

idiotic [idiːɑːˈtik] adj (stupid) ばかな bákà na

idle [aiˈdəl] adj (inactive) 暇な himá na; (lazy) 怠惰な taída na; (unemployed) 失業中の shitsúgyōchū no; (machinery) 動いていない ugóìte inaì; (factory) 休業中の kyúgyōchū no; (question, conversation) 無意味な múmi na; (pleasure) むなしい munáshiì
   ♦vi (machine, engine) 空回りする kárámawàri suru, アイドリングする aídoriñgu suru

idle away vt: to idle away the time のらくらする nórakura suru

idol [aiˈdəl] n (hero) アイドル áidoru; (REL) 偶像 gūzō

idolize [aiˈdəlaiz] vt ...に心酔する ...ni shiñsui suru

idyllic [aidilˈik] adj のどかな nódòka na

i.e. [aiiːˈ] abbr (= id est: that is) 即ち sunáwàchi

KEYWORD

if [if] conj 1 (conditional use: given that, providing that etc) (もし)...すれば(する ならば) (móshì)...suréba(surú naràba)
   I'll go if you come with me あなたが一緒に来れば、私は行ってもいいです anátà ga isshó ni kurèba watákushì wa itté mò íi desu
   I'd be pleased if you could do it あなたがそれをやって下されば私は喜びますがanátà ga soré wò yatté kudasarèba watákushì wa tasúkarimasù ga
   if anyone comes in だれかが入って来れば dárèka ga háìte kurèba
   if necessary 必要であれば hitsúyō de arèba
   if I were you 私があなただったら watákushì gà anátà dáttàra

2 (whenever) ...の時...no tókí

if we are in Scotland, we always go to see her スコットランドにいる時私たちは必ず彼女に会いに行きます sukóttorandò ni irú toki watákushitáchi wa kanárazú kánòjo ni áì ni ikímasù

3 (although): *(even) if* たとえ...でも tatôè ...dê mò

I am determined to finish it, (even) if it takes all week たとえ今週いっぱいかかっても私はこの仕事を片付けたい tatôè konshû ippài kakátte mò watákushi wa konô shigoto wò katázukétaí

I like it, (even) if you don't あなたがいやでも、これは私が好きです anâta ga iyá de mò, watákushi wa koré ga sukí desù

4 (whether) ...かどうか ...ka dô ka

I don't know if he is here 彼はここにいるかどうか私には分かりません kâre ga kokó ni irú ka dôka watákushi ní wa wakárimaseñ

ask him if he can come 来られるかどうか彼に聞いて下さい koráreru ka dô ka kâre ni kiîte kudasái

5: *if so/not* そうであれば(なければ) sô de arêba(nakerêba)

if only ...であったらなあ ...dê áttara nâ

if only I could 私にそれが出来たらなあ watákushi nî soré ga dékitara nâ

¶ *see also* **as**

---

igloo [ig'lu:] *n* イグルー ígùrū

ignite [ignait'] *vt* (set fire to) ...に火をつける ...ni hf wò tsukérù

♦*vi* 燃出す moédasū

ignition [ignif'ən] *n* (AUT: process) 点火 teñka; (: mechanism) 点火装置 teñkasôchi

to switch on/off the ignition エンジンスイッチを入れる(切る) efîjinsuitchi wo irérù(kírù)

ignition key *n* (AUT) カーキー kâkî

ignorance [ig'nɔːrəns] *n* (lack of knowledge) 無知 mûchì

ignorant [ig'nɔːrənt] *adj* (uninformed, unaware) 無学な múgàku na, 無知な múchì na

to be ignorant of (subject, events) ...を知らない ...wo shíránaí

ignore [ignɔːr'] *vt* (person, advice, event, fact) 無視する mushf suru

I'll [ail] = **I will; I shall**

ill [il] *adj* (sick) 病気の byôki no; (harmful: effects) 悪い warúi

♦*n* (evil) 悪 ákù; (trouble) 凶悪 kyóchò

♦*adv:* *to speak ill of someone* ...の悪口を言う ...no warúgòchi wo iú

to think ill (of someone) (...を) 悪く思う (...wo) warúku omôù

to be taken ill 病気になる byôki ni narù, 倒れる taórerù

ill-advised [il'ædvaizd'] *adj* (decision) 軽率な keísotsu na; (person) 無分別な mufûñbetsu na

ill-at-ease [il'ət:iz'] *adj* (awkward, uncomfortable) 落着かない ochítsukanaí

illegal [ili:'gəl] *adj* (not legal: activity, organization, immigrant etc) 不法の fuhô no

illegible [iledʒ'əbəl] *adj* (writing) 読めない yoménaí

illegitimate [ilidʒit'əmit] *adj:* *an illegitimate child* 私生児 shiséiji

ill-fated [il'fei'tid] *adj* (doomed) 不運な fûûn na

ill feeling *n* (animosity, bitterness) 恨み urámi

illicit [ilis'it] *adj* (unlawful: sale, association, substance) 不法の fuhô no

illiterate [ilit'ərit] *adj* (person) 無学な mofîmò no; (letter) 無学な múgàku na

ill-mannered [il'mæn'əːrd] *adj* (rude: child etc) 行儀の悪い gyôgi no warúi

illness [il'nis] *n* 病気 byôki

illogical [iladʒ'ikəl] *adj* (fear, reaction, argument) 不合理な fugôri na

ill-treat [il'tri:t'] *vt* (child, pet, prisoner) 虐待する gyakútai suru

illuminate [ilu:'məneit] *vt* (light up: room, street) 明るくする akárukú suru; (decorate with lights: building, monument etc) ライトアップする raítoappù suru; (shine light on) 照らす terásù

illumination [ilu:mənei'ʃən] *n* (lighting) 照明 shômei

illuminations [ilu:məneiʃənz] *npl* (decorative lights) 電飾 denshoku, イルミネーション irúmineshon

illusion [ilu:'ʒən] *n* (false idea, belief) 錯覚 sakkáku; (trick) いんちき ínchiki, トリック toríkku

illusory [ilu:'sɔ:ri:] *adj* (hopes, prospects) 錯覚 sakkáku no

illustrate [il'əstreit] *vt* (point out) 例を挙げて説明する rei wo agété setsúmei suru; (book) ...に挿絵を入れる ...ni sashíe wo iréru; (talk) ...にスライド (など) を使う ...ni surálido (nádò) wo tsukáù

illustration [iləstrei'ʃən] *n* (act of illustrating) 図解 zúkai; (example) 例例 réi; (in book) 挿絵 sashíe

illustrious [iləs'tri:əs] *adj* (career) 輝かしい kagáyakashii; (predecessor) 著名な chomei na

ill will *n* (hostility) 恨み urámi

I'm [aim] = **I am**

image [im'idʒ] *n* (picture) 像 zó; (public face) イメージ iméji; (reflection) 姿 sugáta

imagery [im'idʒri:] *n* (in writing, painting etc) 比喩 híyu

imaginary [imædʒ'əne:ri:] *adj* (being, danger) 想像上の sózòjó no

imagination [imædʒənei'ʃən] *n* (part of the mind) 想像 sózò; (inventiveness) 想像力 sózòryoku

imaginative [imædʒ'ənativ] *adj* (person) 想像力に富んだ sózòryoku ni tońda; (solution) 奇抜な kibátsu na

imagine [imædʒ'in] *vt* (visualise) 想像する sózò suru; (dream) ...だと錯覚する ...da to sakkáku suru; (suppose) ...だと思う ...da to omóù

imbalance [imbæl'əns] *n* (inequality) 不均等 fukíñtò, アンバランス añbaráñsu

imbecile [im'bəsil] *n* (idiot) ばか bákà

imbue [imbju:'] *vt*: **to imbue someone/something with** ...に ...を吹込む ...ni ...wo fukíkomù

imitate [im'əteit] *vt* (copy) まねる manérù; (mimic) ...の物まねをする ...no monómane wò suru

imitation [iməteiʃ'ən] *n* (act of copying)

まね manê; (act of mimicking) 物まね monómane; (copy) 偽物 nisémono

immaculate [imæk'jəlit] *adj* (room) 汚れ一つない yogóre hitotsú naî; (appearance) 清潔な sefketsu na; (piece of work) 完璧な kafipeki na; (REL) 原罪のない geñzai nô naî

immaterial [imati'ri:əl] *adj* (unimportant) どうでもいい dó de mo íì

immature [imatur'] *adj* (fruit, cheese) 熟していない jukú shite inái; (organism) 未成熟の miséijuku no; (person) 未熟な mijúku na

immediate [imi:'di:it] *adj* (reaction, answer) 即時の sokúji no; (pressing: need) 緊迫した kiñpaku shita; (nearest: neighborhood, family) 最も近い mottó mò chikáî

immediately [imi:'di:tli:] *adv* (at once) 直ぐに súgò ni, 直ちに tádàchi ni; (directly) 真っ直ぐに massúgò ni

▶ **immediately next to** ...の直ぐ隣に ...no súgò tonárì ni

immense [imens'] *adj* (huge: size) 巨大な kyodái na; (: progress, importance) 大変な taíheñ na

immerse [imə:rs'] *vt* (submerge) 浸す hitásù

▶ **to be immersed in** (*fig*: work, study etc) ...に熱中している ...ni netchú shite irú

▶ **to be immersed in thought** 考え込んでいる kañgaekoñde irú

immersion heater [imə:r'ʒən-] (*BRIT*) *n* 投込式湯沸かし器 tónyūshiki yuwakashikì

immigrant [im'əgrənt] *n* 移民 imíñ

immigration [iməgrei'ʃən] *n* (process) 移住 ijū; (control: at airport etc) 入国管理局 nyūkoku kañrikyoku

imminent [im'ənənt] *adj* (arrival, departure) 差迫った sashísematta

immobile [imou'bal] *adj* (motionless) 動かない ugókanai

immobilize [imou'balaiz] *vt* (person, machine) 動けなくする ugókenakù suru

immoral [imɔ:r'əl] *adj* (person, behavior, idea etc) 不道徳な fudótoku na

immorality [iməræl'iti:] n 不道徳 fudō-
toku

immortal [imɔːr'təl] adj (living for ever:
god) 永遠の eien no; (: fame) efen no ikīrū; (unforgettable: poetry, fame) 不滅の fumétsu
no

immortalize [imɔːr'təlaiz] vt (hero,
event) ...に不朽の名声を与える ...ni fukyū no meísei wo atáerù

immune [imjun'] adj: **immune (to)** (disease) (...に) 免疫がある (...ni) meñ-eki
ga arù; (flattery) (...が) ...に通じない
(...ga) ...ni tsūjinaì; (criticism, attack)
...に (...の) しようがない (...ni (...no) shíyō ga naì

immunity [imju'niti:] n (to disease etc)
免疫 meñ-eki; (from prosecution, taxation etc) 免除 meñjo

     diplomatic immunity 外交特権 gaíkō-
utokkèn

immunize [im'jənaiz] vt (MED: gen) ...に
免疫性を与える ...ni meñ-ekisei wo atáe-
rù; (with injection) ...に予防注射をする
...ni yobōchūsha wo suru

imp [imp] n (small devil) 小鬼 ko-óni;
(child) いたずら っ子 itázurakkò

impact [im'pækt] n (of bullet, crash) 衝
撃 shōgeki, インパクト fñpakuto; (of
law, measure) 影響 efkyō

impair [impɛːr'] vt (vision, judgement) 損
なう sokónaū

impale [impeil'] vt くし刺しにする kushí-
zashi ni suru

impart [impɑːrt'] vt (make known: information) 与える atáerù; (bestow: flavor)
添える soérù

impartial [impɑːr'ʃəl] adj (judge,
observer) 公平な kōhei na

impassable [impæs'əbəl] adj (river) 渡れ
ない watárenaì; (road, route etc) 通行不
可能な tsūkōfukanō na

impasse [im'pæs] n (in war, negotiations) 行き詰り ikízumari

impassive [impæs'iv] adj (face, expression) 無表情な muhyōjō na

impatience [impei'ʃəns] n (annoyance
due to waiting) じれったさ jiréttasa;
(irritation) 短気 táñki; (eagerness) 意欲 í-

yoku

impatient [impei'ʃənt] adj (annoyed by
waiting) じれったい jiréttaì; (irritable)
短気な táñki na; (eager, in a hurry): *impatient to ...* …に…従っている …shitágatte
irú

     to get/grow impatient もどかしがる
modókashigarù

impeccable [impek'əbəl] adj (perfect:
manners, dress) 申分のない mōshibùn no
nái

impede [impid'] vt (progress, development etc) 妨げる samátagerù

impediment [impe'dəmənt] n (to
growth, movement) 障害 shōgai; (also:
speech impediment) 言語障害 geñgoshō-
gai

impending [impen'diŋ] adj (arrival,
catastrophe) 差迫る sashísemarù

impenetrable [impen'itrəbəl] adj (wall,
jungle) 通れない tōrenaì; (fig: law, text)
難解な nañkai na

imperative [imper'ətiv] adj (need) 緊急
の kíñkyū no; (tone) 命令的な mefreiteki
na

     ♦n (LING) 命令形 mefreikei

imperceptible [impəːrsep'təbəl] adj
(change, movement) 気付かれない kizúkarenaì

imperfect [impəːr'fikt] adj (goods, system etc) 不完全な fukáñzen na

     ♦n (LING: also: **imperfect tense**) 過去進
行形 kakóshiñkōkei

imperfection [impəːrfek'ʃən] n (failing,
blemish) 欠点 kettéñ

imperial [impiːr'iːəl] adj (history, power)
帝国の teíkoku no; (BRIT: measure) ヤ
ードポンド法の yādopondohō no

imperialism [impiːr'iːəlizəm] n 帝国主義
teíkokushùgi

impersonal [impəːr'sənəl] adj (place,
organization) 人間味のない niñgeñmi no
nái

impersonate [impəːr'səneit] vt (another
person, police officer etc) …の名をかた
る …no nā wo katárù, …に成り済ます
…ni narísumasù; (THEATER) …にふん
する …ni fuñ surù

impertinent [imˈpəːrtənənt] *adj* (pupil, question) 生意気な namáíki na

impervious [imˈpəːrviːəs] *adj* (fig): **impervious to** (criticism etc) ...に影響されない ...ni eíkyó sarenáí

impetuous [impetˈuːəs] *adj* (impulsive) 無鉄砲な mutéppō na

impetus [imˈpitəs] *n* (momentum: of flight, runner) 惰性 daséi; (fig: driving force) 原動力 gefdōryoku

impinge [impindʒ]: **to impinge on** *vt fus* (person) ...の行動を制限する ...no kōdō wo seígen suru; (rights) 侵害する shifgai suru

implacable [imˈplækəbəl] *adj* (hatred, anger etc) なだめがたい nadámegatai; (opposition) 執念深い shúnenbukai

implement [*n* imˈpləmənt *vb* imˈplement] *n* (tool: for farming, gardening, cooking etc) 道具 dōgu
♦*vt* (plan, regulation) 実行する jikkō suru

implicate [imˈplikeit] *vt* (in crime, error) ...のかかわり合いを立証する ...no kakáwariaí wo risshō suru

implication [impliˈkeiʃən] *n* (inference) 含み fukúmi; (involvement) 係り合い kakáwariai

implicit [impliˈsit] *adj* (inferred: threat, meaning etc) 暗黙の afmoku no; (in questioning: belief, trust) 盲目的なの mōmokuteki no

implore [imploˈr] *vt* (beg) ...に嘆願する ...ni tañgan suru

imply [implaɪ] *vt* (hint) ...の意味を含む ...no fmí wo fukúmù; (mean) ...を意味する ...wo fmí suru

impolite [impəlaɪt] *adj* (rude, offensive) 失礼な shitsúrei na

import [*vb* impəːrt *n* imˈpɔːrt] *vt* (goods etc) 輸入する yunyū suru
♦*n* (COMM: article) 輸入品 yunyūhin; (: importation) 輸入 yunyū

importance [impəːrˈtəns] *n* (significance) 重大さ júdaisa; (of person) 有力 yúryoku

important [impəːrˈtənt] *adj* (significant:

decision, difference etc) 重要な júyō na, 重大な júdai na; (influential: person) 偉い eráí

it's not important 大した事じゃない taíshita kotó ja náí

importer [impɔːrˈtər] *n* (COMM) 輸入業者 yunyūgyōsha

impose [impouz] *vt* (sanctions, restrictions, discipline etc) 負わせる owáserů
♦*vi*: **to impose on someone** ...に付込む ...ni tsukékomù, ...に迷惑を掛ける ...ni mēwaku wo kakérù

imposing [impouˈziŋ] *adj* (building, person, manner) 貫うくある kañroku arù

imposition [impəziˈʃən] *n* (of tax etc) 賦課 fuká

to be an imposition on (person) ...に付込む ...ni tsukékomù, ...に迷惑を掛ける ...ni mēwaku wo kakérù

impossible [impɑsˈibəl] *adj* (task, demand etc) 不可能な fukánō na; (situation) 厄介な yakkáí na; (person) どうしようもない dō shiyō mo nai

impostor [impɑsˈtər] *n* 偽者 nisémono

impotence [imˈpətəns] *n* (lack of power) 無力 múryòku, (MED) 性交不能 sefkōfúnō, インポテンツ fñpotentsu

impotent [imˈpətənt] *adj* (powerless) 無力な múryòku na; (MED) 性交不能の sefkōfúnō no

impound [impaundˈ] *vt* (belongings, passports) 没収する bosshū suru

impoverished [impɑvˈəriʃt] *adj* (country, person etc) 貧しくなった mazúshiku nattá

impracticable [imprækˈtikəbəl] *adj* (idea, solution) 実行不可能な jikkōfukanō na

impractical [imprækˈtikəl] *adj* (plan) 実用的でない jitsúyōteki de naí; (person) 不器用な bukíyō na

imprecise [imprisaisˈ] *adj* (inexact) 不正確な fuséíkaku na

impregnable [impregˈnəbəl] *adj* (castle, fortress) 難攻不落の nañkōfúraku no

impregnate [impregˈneit] *vt* (saturate) ...に染込ませる ...ni shimfkomaserů

impresario [imprəsɑːˈriːou] *n* (THEA-

TER) 興業師 kógyòshì

impress [impres'] *vt* (person) ...に印象を
与える ...ni ínshò wo atáerù; (mark) ...に
押付ける ...ni oshítsukerù

to impress something on someone ...
を強く言い聞かせる ...ni ...wo tsuyókì
ifíkikasù

impression [impreʃ'ən] *n* (of place, situation, person) 印象 ínshò; (of stamp,
seal) 判押 kakúìn, 刻印 kokúìn; (idea) 思い込
み omóikomi; (effect) 効果 kōka; (mark)
跡 átò; (imitation) 物まね monómane

to be under the impression that ...だ
と思い込んでいる ...da to omóikòñde irú

impressionable [impreʃ'ənəbəl] *adj*
(child, person) 感じやすい kañjíyasui

impressionist [impreʃ'ənist] *n* (entertainer) 物真似芸人 monómanegèinin; (in
ART): *Impressionist* 印象派画家 ínshò-
hagaka

impressive [impres'iv] *adj* (reputation,
collection) 印象的な ínshòteki na

imprint [im'print] *n* (outline: of hand
etc) 跡 ato; (PUBLISHING) 奥付 okúzu-
ke

imprison [impriz'ən] *vt* (criminal) 拘留
する kōchi suru, 刑務所に入れる kefmu-
shò ni irérù

imprisonment [impriz'ənmənt] *n* 拘留
kōchi

improbable [impra:b'əbəl] *adj* (unlikely:
outcome) ありそうもない arísò mò náì;
(: explanation, story) 本当らしくない hoñ-
tórashikù náì

impromptu [impra:mp'tu:] *adj* (celebration, party) 即席の sokúsekì no

improper [impra:p'ə:r] *adj* (unsuitable:
conduct, procedure) 不適切な futékisetsu
na; (dishonest: activities) 不正な fuséi na

improve [impru:v'] *vt* (make better:
character, housing, result) 改善する kafzen suru

♦*vi* (get better: weather, pupil, patient,
health etc) 良くなる yókù naru

improvement [impru:v'mənt] *n* (making better) 改善 kafzen; (getting better)
良くなる事 yókù naru kotó: *improve-*

ment (in) (making better) (...を) 改善
する事 (...wo) kafzen surú kotó; (getting
better) (...が) 良くなる事 (...gà) yókù
naru kotó

improvise [im'pravaiz'] *vt* (meal, bed
etc) 有り合せの物で作る arfawase no
mono dè tsukúrù

♦*vi* (THEATER, MUS) 即興的にしゃべ
る (演奏する) sokkyóteki nì shabérù
[eñsò suru], アドリブする adóribu suru

imprudent [impru:d'ənt] *adj* (unwise) 賢
明でない keñmei de naì

impudent [im'pjədənt] *adj* (child, comment, remark) 生意気な namáiki na

impulse [im'pʌls] *n* (urge: gen) 衝動 shōdō; (: to do wrong) 出来心 dekígokòro;
(ELEC) 衝撃 shōgeki, インパルス íñparu-
su

to act on impulse 衝動的に行動する
shódōteki nì kōdō surú

impulsive [impʌl'siv] *adj* (purchase, gesture, person) 衝動的な shōdōteki na

impunity [impju'niti:] *n*: *with impunity* 罰せられずに bassérarezù ni

impure [impju:r'] *adj* (adulterated) 不純
な fujúñ na; (sinful) みだらな mídàra na

impurity [impju'iti:] *n* (foreign substance) 不純物 fujúñbutsu

━━━━━━━━━━━━━━━━━━━━

KEYWORD

in [in] *prep* 1 (indicating place, position)
...に (で) ...ni (de)

in the house/garden 家 (庭) に (で) ié
[niwá] nì (de)

in the box/fridge/drawer 箱 (冷蔵庫,
引き出し) に (で) hakó [refzóko, hikída-
shi] nì (de)

I have it in my hand 手に持っていま
す té nì móttè imasu

to spend a day in town/the country
町 (田舎) で1日を過ごす machí [ináka] dè
ichínichi wò sugósù

in school 学校に (で) gakkó nì (de)

in here/there ここ (あそこ) に (で) kokó [asóko] nì (de)

2 (with place names: of town, region,
country) ...に (で) ... ni (de)

in London ロンドンに (で) róñdon ni

(de)

in England/Japan/Canada/the United States 英国(日本, カナダ, アメリカ)に(で) eſkoku(nippón, kánáda, ameríka) nï(de)

in Burgundy バーガンディーに(で) bágandï nï(de)

3 (indicating time: during) ...に ...nï

in spring/summer 春(夏)に hárü(natsü)ni

in 1998 1998年に señkyühyakukyüjühachi néñ nï

in May 5月に gögatsu ni

I'll see you in July 7月に会いましょう shichigatsu ni aïmashö

in the afternoon 午後に gögö ni

at 4 o'clock in the afternoon 午後4時に gögö yöjï ni

4 (indicating time: in the space of) ...で ...dè

I did it in 3 hours/days 3時間(3日)でやりました sañjikan(mikka)de yarïmashïta

I'll see you in 2 weeks/in 2 weeks' time 2週間に(2週間したら)また会いましょう nïshükan shitara matá aïmashö

5 (indicating manner etc) ...で ...dè

in a loud/soft voice 大きな(小さな)声で ökïna(chïsana)köè de

in pencil/ink 鉛筆(インク)で eñpitsu (ïnku)dè

in English/French 英語(フランス語)で eïgo(furánsugo)dè

the boy in the blue shirt 青いシャツの少年 aöï shátsü no shönen

6 (indicating circumstances): *in the sun* 直射日光に当って chokûshanikkô ni atáttè, 日光に hïnáta nï

in the rain 雨の中で ámè no nákà

in the shade 日陰で hïkage de

a change in policy 政策の変更 seïsaku nö heñkö

a rise in prices 物価の上昇 bükka no jöshö

7 (indicating mood, state): *in tears* 泣いて nàīte

in anger 怒って okótte

in despair 失望して shitsûbö shïtè

in good condition 無事に bujï nï

to live in luxury ぜいたくに暮す zeïtaku ni kurásu

8 (with ratios, numbers): *1 in 10 households has a second car, 1 household in 10 has a second car* 10世帯中1世帯は車を2台持っている jussêtaichû issêtai wà kûrûma wò nïdaï môtte irü

6 months in the year 1年の内6か月 ichínen no uchî rokkágetsu

they lined up in twos 彼らは2人ずつ並んだ kárera wa futárizôtsu narâñda

the disease is common in children この病気は子供によく見られる konö byöki wa kodômo nï yökü mïrárerü

(in the works of) Dickens ディケンズの作品の中に (in) dïkeñzu no sakûhin no nakâ ni

she has it in her to succeed 彼女には成功する素質がある kánojo nï wa seïkö suru soshïtsû ga árü

they have a good leader in him 彼らにとって彼は素晴らしいリーダーです kárera ni tótté kárè wa subárashiï rïdâ desu

10 (indicating profession etc): *to be in teaching* 教員である kyöñ de árü

to be in publishing 出版関係の仕事をしている shuppañkañkei no shïgoto wò shïté irü

to be in the army 軍人である guñjïn de árü

11 (after superlative): *the best pupil in the class* クラスで最優秀の生徒 kûrâsu de safyûshû no seïto

the biggest/smallest in Europe ヨーロッパ中で最も大きな(小さな)物 yöroppajü de mottömö ökïna(chïsana)monö

12 (with present participle): *in saying this* こう言って köö ïtte

in doing things the way she did, she alienated everyone 彼女のやり方は皆の反感を買った kánojo no yarïkata wa miná nö hañkan wo kattá

◆*adv*: *to be in* (person: at home) 在宅である zaïtaku de árü; (: at work) 出社して

いる shusshá shite irû; (train, plane) 到着
している tôchaku shite irû; (ship) 入港し
ている nyûkô shite irû; (in fashion) 流行
している ryûkô suru to omóimasů

he'll be in later today 今日は later 時間ほどに
出社すると思います nisánjikan shitára
shussha suru to omóimasů

miniskirts are in again this year 今
年ミニスカートが再び流行しています
kotóshi mínísukáto ga futátabí ryúkô
shite imasů

to ask someone in 家に上がらせる
...wô ié ni agáraserů

to run/limp etc 走って(びっこを引
い)って来る hashítté(bíkkó wo hit-
tá)háttte kuru

♦*n*: *the ins and outs* (of proposal,
situation etc) 詳細 shôsai

**he explained all the ins and outs of
the deal to me** 彼は私に取引の詳細を
説明してくれました kárê wa watákushi
nì toríhiki no shôsai wo setsúmei shite
kuremashíta

in. *abbr* = **inch**

inability [inabíl'əti:] *n* (incapacity): *inability to do* (...する事が) できない
事 (...surú kotô ga) dekínai kotô

inaccessible [inækses'əbəl] *adj* (place)
入りにくい hafrinikûi, 近付きにくい chi-
kázukinikûi; (*fig*: text, music) 難解な naň-
kai na

inaccurate [inæk'jər̄it] *adj* (account,
answer, person) 不正確な fuséikaku na

inactivity [inæktiv'iti:] *n* (idleness) 活動
しない事 katsudōshinai kotô

inadequate [inæd'əkwit] *adj* (income,
amount, reply) 不十分な jûbûn na;
(person) 無能な munô na

inadvertently [inædvər̄'təntli:] *adv* (unintentionally) うっかり ukkári

inadvisable [inædvai'zəbəl] *adj* 得策でな
い tokúsaku de nai

inane [inein'] *adj* (smile, remark) 愚かな
oróka na

inanimate [inæn'əmit] *adj* 生命のない
seímei no nai

inappropriate [inəprou'pri:it] *adj* (un-

suitable) 不適切な futékisetsu na; (improper: word, expression) 非難すべき hi-
nánsuberi

inarticulate [ina:rtik'jəlit] *adj* (person)
口下手な kuchíbeta na; (speech) 分かり
にくい wakárinikûi

inasmuch as [inæzmʌt͡ʃ-] *adv* (in that)
...という点で ...to iú teň de; (insofar as)
できる限り dekíru kagíri

inaudible [inɔː'dəbəl] *adj* (voice, aside)
聞取れない kikítorenai

inaugural [inɔː'gjər̄əl] *adj* (speech) 就任
の shûnin no; (meeting) 発会の hakkái no

inaugurate [inɔː'gjər̄eit] *vt* (president,
official) ...の就任式を行う ...no shûin-
ñshiki wo okonau; (system, measure) 始
める hajímerù; (organization) 発足させ
る hossôku saserů

inauguration [inɔːgjə̄rei'ʃən] *n* (of president, official) 就任式 shúnínshiki; (of
system, measure) 開始 kafshi; (of organization) 発足 hossóku

in-between [in'bitwi:n] *adj* (intermediate) 中間的な chûkanteki na

inborn [in'bɔ:rn] *adj* (quality) 生れ付きの
umáretsuki no

inbred [in'bred] *adj* (quality) 生まれつき
の umáretsuki na; (family) 近親交配の
kiñshinkôhai no

Inc. *abbr* = **incorporated**

incalculable [inkæl'kjələbəl] *adj* (effect,
loss) 途方もない tohô mo nai

incapable [inkei'pəbəl] *adj* (helpless) 無
能な munô na; (unable to): *to be incapable of something/doing something* ...が(する事ができない ...ga (surú
kotô ga) dekínai

incapacitate [inkəpæs'əteit] *vt* 不具に
する fûgû ni suru

incapacity [inkəpæs'iti:] *n* (weakness)
弱さ yôwasa; (inability) 無能 munô

incarcerate [inka:r'sərit] *vt* 拘置する
kôchi suru, 刑務所に入れる keímushô nì
irérû

incarnation [inka:rnei'ʃən] *n* (of beauty)
化身 késhin; (of evil) 権化 góñge; (REL)
神が人間の姿を取る事 kámi ga niñgen

no sugatá wo tórú kotó

incendiary [insen'di:ɛ:ri:] *adj* (device) 放
火の hōka no

an incendiary bomb 焼い弾 shōídan

incense [*n* in'sens *vb* insens'] *n* (perfume: *also* REL) 香 kō

♦*vt* (anger) 怒らせる okóraserù

incentive [insen'tiv] *n* (inducement) 動機
dōki, 刺激 shigéki

incessant [inses'ant] *adj* (bickering, criticism) 引っ切り無しの hikkírí nashí no

incessantly [inses'ontli:] *adv* 引っ切り無
しに hikkírí nashí ni

incest [in'sest] *n* 近親相かん kinshínsōkan

inch [intʃ] *n* (measurement) インチ ínchi

to be within an inch of doing 危うく
...するところである ayáuku ...surú tokóro de árù

he didn't give an inch (fig: back
down, yield) 一寸も譲ろうとしなかった
issún mo yuzárō to shinákattá

inch forward *vi* 一寸刻みに進む issú-
nkizami ni susúmù

incidence [in'sidəns] *n* (of crime, disease) 発生率 hasséiritsu

incident [in'sidənt] *n* (event) 事件 jíken

incidental [insiden'təl] *adj* (additional, supplementary) 付随的な fuzúiteki na

incidental to ...に対して二次的な ...ni
táishite nijíteki na

incidentally [insiden'tali:] *adv* (by the way) ところで tokóro de

incinerator [insin'əreitəːr] *n* (for
waste, refuse) 焼却炉 shōkyakurò

incipient [insip'i:ant] *adj* (baldness, madness) 初期の shókī no

incision [insiʒ'ən] *n* (cut: *also* MED) 切開
sékkài

incisive [insai'siv] *adj* (comment, criticism) 痛烈な tsúretsu na

incite [insait'] *vt* (rioters, violence) 扇動
する sefidō suru; (hatred) あおりたてる
aóritatèru

inclination [inklənei'ʒən] *n* (tendency)
傾向 keíkō; (disposition, desire) 望み nozómi

incline [in'klain] *n* (slope) 坂 saká

♦*vt* (bend: head) 下げる sagérù

♦*vi* (surface) 傾斜する keísha suru

to be inclined to ...する傾向があ
る ...suru keíkō ga arù

include [inkluːd'] *vt* (incorporate: in
plan, team etc) 入れる irérù; (: in price)
含む fukúmù

including [inkluː'diŋ] *prep* ...を含めて
...wo fukúmète

inclusion [inkluː'ʒən] *n* (incorporation:
in plan etc) 入れる事 irérù kotó; (: in
price) 含む事 fukúmù kotó

inclusive [inkluː'siv] *adj* (price, terms)
含んでる fukúnde iru

inclusive of ...を含めて wo fukúmète

incognito [inkɑːgniː'tou] *adv* (travel) お
忍びで o-shínobi de

incoherent [inkouhɪər'ant] *adj* (argument, speech, person) 分かりにくい wakárinikuì

income [in'kʌm] *n* 収入 shúnyū

income tax *n* 所得税 shotókuzèi

incoming [in'kʌmiŋ] *adj* (flight, passenger) 到着の tōchaku no; (call, mail) 着信
の chakúshin no; (government, official)
新任の shínnin no; (wave) 寄せて来る yo-
séte kurù

the incoming tide 上げ潮 ageshio

incomparable [inkɑːm'pərəbəl] *adj*
(genius, efficiency etc) 類のない rúi no
nái

incompatible [inkəmpæt'əbəl] *adj* (lifestyles, systems, aims) 相容れない aíire-
nai

incompetence [inkɑːm'pitəns] *n* 無能
munō

incompetent [inkɑːm'pitənt] *adj* (person) 無能な munō na; (job) 下手な hetá
na

incomplete [inkəmpliːt'] *adj* (unfinished:
book, painting etc) 未完成の mikánsei no;
(partial: success, achievement) 部分
的な bubúnteki na

incomprehensible [inkɑːmprihen'səbəl]
adj (conduct) 不可解な fukákai na; (language) 分からない wakáranai

inconceivable [inkənsiː'vəbəl] *adj* (unthinkable) 考えられない kañgaerarénai

incongruous [inkɔŋ'gru:əs] adj
(strange: situation, figure) 変った kawátta; (inappropriate: remark, act) 不適
当な futékitō na

inconsiderate [inkənsíd'ərət] adj (person, action) 心ない kokóronaì

inconsistency [inkənsís'tənsi:] n (of
behavior, person etc) 一貫しない事 ikkán
shinai koto; (in work) むら murá; (in
statement, action) 矛盾 mujún

inconsistent [inkənsís'tənt] adj (behavior, person) 変りやすい kawáriyasuì;
(work) むらの多い murá no ōi; (statement, action) 矛盾した mujún shita
inconsistent with (beliefs, values) と
矛盾する ...to mujún suru

inconspicuous [inkənspík'ju:əs] adj
(person, color, building etc) 目立たない
medátanaì

incontinent [inkɑn'tənənt] adj (MED)
失禁の shikkín no

inconvenience [inkənvi:n'jəns] n (problem) 問題 mondai; (trouble) 迷惑 mewaku
♦vt ...に迷惑を掛ける ...ni méwaku wò
kakérù

inconvenient [inkənvi:n'jənt] adj (time,
place, house) 不便な fubén na; (visitor,
incident etc) 厄介な yakkái na

incorporate [inkɔːr'pəreit] vt (make
part of) 取入れる toríirerù; (contain) 含
む fukúmù

incorporated company [inkɔːr'-
pəreitid-] (US) n 会社 kaísha **Inc.**

incorrect [inkərekt'] adj (information,
answer, attitude etc) 間違った machígattà

incorrigible [inkɔːr'idʒəbəl] adj (liar,
crook) 救い様のない sukúiyō no náì

incorruptible [inkərʌp'təbəl] adj (not
open to bribes) 買収のできない baíshū
no dekínaì

increase [n in'kri:s vb inkri:s'] n (rise):
increase (in/of) (...の) 増加 (...no) zōka
♦vi (: price, level, productivity etc) 増す
masú
♦vt (make greater: price, knowledge

etc) 増す masú

increasing [inkri:s'iŋ] adj (number, use)
増加する zōka suru

increasingly [inkri:s'iŋli:] adv (more
intensely, more often) ますます masú-
mâsu

incredible [inkred'əbəl] adj (unbelievable) 信じられない shiñjirarenaì; (enormous) ばく大な bakúdai na

incredulous [inkred'ʒələs] adj (tone,
expression) 半信半疑の hañshiñhangi no

increment [iŋ'krəmənt] n (in salary) 定
期昇給 tefkishōkyū

incriminate [inkrim'əneit] vt (LAW)
...の罪を立証する ...no tsúmí wo risshō
suru

incubation [inkjəbei'ʃən] n (of eggs) ふ
卵 furán; (of illness) 潜伏期間 señpukuki-
kàn

incubator [iŋ'kjəbeitər] n (for babies)
保育器 hoíkukì

incumbent [inkʌm'bənt] n (official:
POL, REL) 現役 gén-eki
♦adj: **it is incumbent on him to ...**
...するのが彼の義務である ...surú no gà
kárè no gímù de árù

incur [inkɔːr'] vt (expenses) ...が掛る ...ga
kakárù; (loss) 受ける ukérù; (debt) こし
らえる koshíraerù; (disapproval, anger)
被る kōmurù

incurable [inkju:r'əbəl] adj (disease) 不
治の fújì no

incursion [inkɔːr'ʒən] n (MIL: invasion)
侵入 shiñnyū

indebted [indet'id] adj: **to be indebted
to someone** (grateful) ...に感謝してい
る ...ni kâñsha shité irù

indecent [indi:'sənt] adj (film, book) み
だらな mídàra na

indecent assault [BRIT] n 強制わいせ
つ罪 kyōsei waisetsuzaì

indecent exposure n 公然わいせつ罪
kōzen waisetsuzaì

indecisive [indisai'siv] adj (person) 決断
力のない ketsúdanryoku no naì

indeed [indi:d'] adv (certainly) 確かに táshìka ni, 本当に hoñtō ni; (in fact) 実は
jitsú wà; (furthermore) なお naó

yes indeed! 確かにそうだ! táshǐka ni só dà!

indefinite [indéf'ənit] *adj* (answer, view) 不明確な fuméikaku na; (period, number) 不定の futéi no

indefinitely [indéf'ənitli:] *adv* (continue, wait) いつまでも ítsu made mo

indelible [indél'əbəl] *adj* (mark, stain, ink) 消せない keśénai

indelible pen 油性フェルトペン yuséi ferútopen

indemnity [indem'niti:] *n* (insurance) 賠償保険 bafshóhokén; (compensation) 賠償 bafshó

independence [indipen'dəns] *n* (of country, person etc) 独立 dokúritsu; (of thinking etc) 自主性 jishúsei

independent [indipen'dənt] *adj* (country, business etc) 独立した dokúritsu shita; (person, thought) 自主的な jishúteki na; (school) 私立の shíritsu no; (broadcasting company) 民間の mifikan no; (inquiry) 独自の dokúji no

indestructible [indistrʌk'təbəl] *adj* 破壊できない hakái dekínaì

indeterminate [inditəːr'mənit] *adj* (number, nature) 不明の fuméi no

index [in'deks] (*pl* **indexes**) *n* (in book) 索引 sakúin, インデックス iňdékkusu; (in library etc) 蔵書目録 zōshomokúroku; (*pl*: **indices**: ratio) 率 rítsù, 指数 shísù; (: sign) 印 shírúshi

index card *n* インデックスカード iňdékkusukādo

indexed [in'dekst] (*BRIT* **index-linked**) *adj* (income, payment) スライド制の suráidosei no

index finger *n* 人差指 hitósashiyúbì

India [in'di:ə] *n* インド íňdo

Indian [in'di:ən] *adj* インドの íňdo no

Red Indian アメリカインディアンamérika índian

Indian Ocean *n*: *the Indian Ocean* インド洋 íňdoyō

indicate [in'dikeit] *vt* (show) 示す shimésù; (point to) 指す sásù; (mention) 示唆する shisá surù

indication [indikei'ʃən] *n* (sign) しるし

shírúshi

indicative [indik'ətiv] *adj*: *indicative of* …のしるしである …no shírúshi de aru ♦*n* (LING) 直接法 chokúsetsuhō

indicator [in'dikeitər] *n* (marker, signal) しるし shírúshi; (AUT) 方向指示器 hōkōshijíki, ウインカー uíňkā

indices [in'disiz] *npl of* **index**

indictment [indait'mənt] *n* (denunciation) 避難 hínan; (charge) 起訴 kisó

indifference [indif'ərəns] *n* (lack of interest) 無関心 mukáňshin

indifferent [indif'ərənt] *adj* (uninterested: attitude) 無関心な mukáňshin na; (mediocre: quality) 平凡な heîbon na

indigenous [indidʒ'ənəs] *adj* (wildlife) 固有の koyū no

the indigenous population 原住民 geñjūmin

indigestion [indidʒes'tʃən] *n* 消化不良 shōkafuryō

indignant [indig'nənt] *adj*: *to be indignant at something/with someone* (angry) …に怒っている …ni okótte irú

indignation [indignei'ʃən] *n* (outrage, resentment) 立腹 rippúku

indignity [indig'niti:] *n* (humiliation) 侮辱 bujóku

indigo [in'dəgou] *n* (color) あい aî

indirect [indirekt'] *adj* (way, route) 遠回しの tōmawashí no; (answer, effect) 間接的な kaňsetsuteki na

indirectly [indirekt'li:] *adv* (responsible) 間接的に kaňsetsuteki ni

indiscreet [indiskri:t'] *adj* (person, behavior, comment) 軽率な keísotsu na

indiscriminate [indiskrim'ənit] *adj* (bombing) 無差別の musábetsu no; (taste) はっきりしない hakkírí shinái

indispensable [indispen'səbəl] *adj* (tool, worker) 掛替えのない kakégae no naî

indisposed [indispouzd'] *adj* (unwell) 体調の悪い taíchō no warúi

indisputable [indispju:'təbəl] *adj* (undeniable) 否めない inámenaî

indistinct [indistiŋkt'] *adj* (image, memory) ぼんやりした boñ-yarí shita; (noise) かすかな kásùka na

individual [indəˈvidʒˈuːəl] *n* (person: different from all others) 個人 kójìn; (: with adj) 人 hitó, ...人 jinbutsu

♦*adj* (personal) 個人個人の kojínkòjin no; (single) それぞれの soréžòre no; (particular: characteristic) 独特な dokútoku na

individualist [indəˈvidʒˈuːəlist] *n* 個人主義者 kojínshugìsha

individually [indəˈvidʒˈuːəli] *adv* (singly: persons) 一人一人で hitóri hitóri de; (: things) 一つ一つで hitótsuhitòtsu de

indivisible [indəˈvizˈəbəl] *adj* (matter, power) 分割できない bufkatsu dekínai

indoctrinate [indɒkˈtrəneit] *vt* ...を教え込む ...ni ...wo oshfekomù, 洗脳する sefnô suru

indoctrination [indɒktrəneiˈʃən] *n* (act) 教え込む事 oshíekomù kotó, 洗脳 sefnô

indolent [inˈdələnt] *adj* (lazy) 怠惰な táida na

Indonesia [indəniˈʒə] *n* インドネシア indonéshìa

indoor [inˈdɔːr] *adj* 屋内の okúnai no

indoors [inˈdɔːrz] *adv* (inside) 屋内で okúnai de

induce [inˈdjuːs] *vt* (bring about) 引起こす hikfokosù; (persuade) 説得する settóku suru; (MED: birth) 誘発する yúhatsu suru

inducement [inˈdjuːsˈmənt] *n* (incentive) 動機 dôki, 刺激 shigéki; (pej: bribe) 賄賂 wáìro

indulge [inˈdʌldʒ] *vt* (desire, whim) 満たす mitásù; (person, child) 気ままにさせる kimáma ni saserù

♦*vi*: **to indulge in** (vice, hobby) ...にふける ...ni fukérù

indulgence [inˈdʌlˈdʒəns] *n* (pleasure) 楽しみ tanóshimi; (leniency) 寛大さ kañdaisa

indulgent [inˈdʌlˈdʒənt] *adj* (parent, smile) 甘やかす amáyakasù

industrial [inˈdʌsˈtriːəl] *adj* 産業の sañgyò no, 工業の kôgyô no

industrial action (BRIT) *n* 争議行為 sôgikôi

industrial estate (BRIT) *n* = **industrial park**

industrialist [inˈdʌsˈtriːəlist] *n* 実業家 jitsúgyòka

industrialize [inˈdʌsˈtriːəlaiz] *vt* (country, society) 工業化する kôgyôka suru

industrial park (US) *n* 工業団地 kôgyôdañchi

industrious [inˈdʌsˈtriːəs] *adj* (student, worker) 勤勉な kiñbensa

industry [inˈdəstri] *n* (manufacturing) 産業 sañgyô, 工業 kôgyô; (oil industry, textile industry etc) ...業界 ...gyôkai; (diligence) 勤勉さ kiñbensa

inebriated [inˈiːbriːeitid] *adj* (drunk) 酔っ払った yoppáratta

inedible [inˈedˈəbəl] *adj* (disgusting) 食べられない tabérarenaì; (poisonous) 食用に適さない shokúyô ni tekfsanaì

ineffective [iniˈfekˈtiv] *adj* (policy, government) 効果のない kôka no naì

ineffectual [iniˈfekˈtʃuəl] *adj* = **ineffective**

inefficiency [iniˈfiʃˈənsi] *n* 非能率 hinôritsu

inefficient [iniˈfiʃˈənt] *adj* (person, machine, system) 能率の悪い nôritsu no waruì

inept [inˈept] *adj* (politician, management) 無能な munô na

inequality [inikˈwɑːˈliti] *n* (of system) 不平等 fubyôdô; (of amount, share) 不等 futô

inert [inˈəːrt] *adj* (immobile) 動かない ugókanaì; (gas) 不活性の fukássei no

inertia [inˈəːrʃə] *n* (apathy) 物臭 monógusa; (PHYSICS) 慣性 daséi

inescapable [inəˈskeipəbəl] *adj* (conclusion, impression) 避けられない sakérarenaì

inevitable [inˈevˈitəbəl] *adj* (outcome, result) 避けられない sakérarenaì, 必然的 hitsúzenteki na

inevitably [inˈevˈitəbliː] *adv* 必然的に hitsúzenteki ni

inexcusable [inikskjuːˈzəbəl] *adj* (behavior, error) 許されない yurúsarenaì

inexhaustible [inigzɔːsˈtəbəl] *adj* (wealth, resources) 無尽蔵の mujfñzô no

inexorable [inek'sɔːrəbəl] *adj* (progress, decline) 止め様のない tomḗyō no naí

inexpensive [inikspen'siv] *adj* (cheap) 安い yasúî

inexperience [inikspiː'riːəns] *n* (of person) 不慣れ fúnàre

inexperienced [inikspiː'riːənst] *adj* (swimmer, worker) 不慣れの fúnàre no

inexplicable [ineks'plikəbəl] *adj* (decision, mistake) 不可解な fukákaì na

inextricably [ineks'trikəbliː] *adv* (entangled, linked) 分けられない程 wakéranèaì hodo

infallible [infæl'əbəl] *adj* (person, guide) 間違いのない machígaì no naî

infamous [in'fəməs] *adj* (crime, murderer) 悪名高い akúmeidakaì

infamy [in'fəmiː] *n* (notoriety) 悪評 akúhyō

infancy [in'fənsiː] *n* (of person) 幼年時代 yōnenjidài

infant [in'fənt] *n* (baby) 赤ちゃん ákàchan; (young child) 幼児 yōjî

infantile [in'fəntail] *adj* (disease) 幼児の yōjî no; (foolish) 幼稚な yōchî na

infantry [in'fəntriː] *n* (MIL) 歩兵隊 hohéitai

infant school (*BRIT*) *n* 幼稚園 yōchien

infatuated [infætʃ'uːeitid] *adj*: **to be infatuated with** ...にのぼせている ...ni nobōsete irú

infatuation [infætʃuːei'ʃən] *n* (passion) ...にのぼせる事 ...ni nobōseru koto

infect [infekt'] *vt* (person, animal) ...に感染させる ...ni kánsen saserù; (food) 汚染する osén suru

infection [infek'ʃən] *n* (MED: disease) 感染 kánsen; (contagion) 伝染 densen

infectious [infek'ʃəs] *adj* (person, animal) 伝染病にかかった densenbyō ni kakátta; (disease) 伝染性の densensei no; (*fig*: enthusiasm, laughter) 移りやすい utsúriyasuì

infer [infəːr'] *vt* (deduce) 推定する suftei suru; (imply) ...の意味を含む ...no fmî wo fukúmù

inference [in'fərəns] *n* (deduction) 推定 suftei; (implication) 含み fukúmi

inferior [infiː'riːəːr] *adj* (in rank) 下級の kakyū no; (in quality, quantity) 劣った ottóttà

♦*n* (subordinate) 下の者 shitá no monò; (junior) 年下の者 toshfshita no monò

inferiority [infiːriːɔːr'itiː] *n* (in rank) 下級である事 kakyū de arù kotó; (in quality) 品質の悪さ hińshitsu nò wárùsa

inferiority complex *n* (PSYCH) 劣等感 rettókan

infernal [infəːr'nəl] *adj* (racket, temper) いやな hidóì

inferno [infəːr'nou] *n* (blaze) 大火事 ōkàjì

infertile [infəːr'təl] *adj* (soil) 不毛の funmō no; (person, animal) 不妊の funfn no

infertility [infəːrtil'ətiː] *n* (of soil) 不毛 fumō; (of person, animal) 不妊症 funfnshō

infested [infes'tid] *adj*: **infested with** (vermin, pests) ...がうじゃうじゃいる ...ga ûjàuja irú

infidelity [infidel'itiː] *n* (unfaithfulness) 浮気 uwáki

in-fighting [in'faitiŋ] *n* 内紛 naffun, 内ゲバ uchígeba

infiltrate [infil'treit] *vt* ...に潜入する ...ni sefnyū suru

infinite [in'fənit] *adj* (very great: variety, patience) ばく大な bakúdai na; (without limits: universe) 無限の mugén no

infinitive [infin'ətiv] *n* (LING) 不定詞 futéishi

infinity [infin'ətiː] *n* (infinite number) 無限大 mugéndai; (infinite point) 無限 mugén

infirm [infəːrm'] *adj* (weak) 虚弱な kyojáku na; (ill) 病弱な byōjaku na

infirmary [infəːr'məriː] *n* (hospital) 病院 byōin

infirmity [infəːr'mitiː] *n* (weakness) 虚弱さ kyojákusa; (being ill) 病弱さ byōjakusa; (specific illness) 疾病 byōki

inflamed [infleimd'] *adj* (tongue, appendix) 炎症を起した efishō wò okōshità

inflammable [inflæm'əbəl] *adj* (fabric, chemical) 可燃性の kanénsei no, 燃えや

すい moéyasuì

inflammation [infləmei'ʃən] *n* (of throat, appendix etc) 炎症 eñshō

inflatable [inflei'səbəl] *adj* (life jacket, dinghy, doll) 膨らます事のできる fukúramasu kotò no dekírù

inflate [infleit'] *vt* (tire, balloon) 膨らます fukúramasù; (price) つり上げる tsurīagerù

inflation [inflei'ʃən] *n* (ECON) インフレ infúre

inflationary [inflei'ʃəneːriː] *adj* (spiral) インフレの infúre no; (demand) インフレを引き起こす infúre wò hikfokosù

inflexible [inflek'səbəl] *adj* (rule, timetable) 融通不利からない yúzū ga kikānaì; (person) 譲らない yuzúranaì

inflict [inflikt'] *vt*: **to inflict something on someone** (damage, suffering) ...に...を加える ...ni ...wo kuwáerù

influence [in'fluəns] *n* (power) 実力 jitsúryoku; (effect) 影響 efigyō
♦*vt* (person, situation, choice etc) を左右する sáyū suru
under the influence of alcohol 酒に酔って sakê ni yottè

influential [influen'tʃəl] *adj* (politician, critic) 有力な yúryoku na

influenza [influen'zə] *n* (MED) 流感 ryūkan

influx [in'flʌks] *n* (of refugees, funds) 流入 ryūnyū

inform [infɔːrm'] *vt*: **to inform someone of something** (tell) ...に...を知らせる ...ni ...wo shīraserù
♦*vi*: **to inform on someone** (to police, authorities) ...を密告する ...wo mikkóku suru

informal [infɔːr'məl] *adj* (manner, discussion, party) 寛いだ kutsúroida; (clothes) 普段の fúdàn no; (unofficial: visit, meeting) 非公式の hikôshiki no

informality [infɔːrmæl'itiː] *n* (of manner, party etc) 寛いだ雰囲気 kutsúroida fuñ-iki

informant [infɔːr'mənt] *n* (source) 情報提供者 jôhōteikyōsha, インフォーマント iñfōmañto

information [infərmei'ʃən] *n* 情報 jôhō
a piece of information 1つの情報 hitótsu no jôhō

information office *n* 案内所 afinaijo

informative [infɔːr'mətiv] *adj* (report, comment) 有益な yúeki na

informer [infɔːr'mər] *n* (*also*: **police informer**) 密告者 mikkókushà, スパイ supâi

infra-red [in'frəred'] *adj* (rays, light) 赤外線の sekígaisen no

infrastructure [in'frəstrʌk'tʃər] *n* (of system etc) 下部構造 kabúkōzō, インフラストラクチャー infúrasutorakúchā

infrequent [infriːkwint'] *adj* (visits) 間遠な madô na; (buses) 本数の少ない hoñsū nō sukúnaì

infringe [infrindʒ'] *vt* (law) 破る yabúrù
♦*vi*: **to infringe on** (rights) ...を侵す ...wo okásù

infringement [infrindʒ'mənt] *n* (of law) 違反 ihán; (of rights) 侵害 shifigai

infuriating [infjur'ieitiŋ] *adj* (habit, noise) いらいらさせる fràira saséru

ingenious [indʒin'jəs] *adj* (idea, solution) 巧妙な kómyō na

ingenuity [indʒənuː'itiː] *n* (cleverness, skill) 才能 saínō

ingenuous [indʒen'juːəs] *adj* (innocent, trusting) 無邪気な mújàki na

ingot [in'gət] *n* (of gold, platinum) 延べ棒 nobébō, インゴット ifgôtto

ingrained [ingreind'] *adj* (habit, belief) 根深い nebúkaì

ingratiate [ingrei'ʃieit] *vt*: **to ingratiate oneself with** ...に取入る ...ni torîiru

ingratitude [ingræt'ətuːd] *n* (of beneficiary, heir) 恩知らず ofishírazu

ingredient [ingriː'diːənt] *n* (of cake) 材料 zaíryō; (of situation) 要素 yôso

inhabit [inhæb'it] *vt* (town, country) に住む ...ni sûmù

inhabitant [inhæb'ətənt] *n* (of town, street, house, country) 住民 júmin

inhale [inheil'] *vt* (breathe in: smoke, etc) 吸込む suíkomù
♦*vi* (breathe in) 息を吸う ikî wo suu; (when smoking) 煙を吸込む kemúri wò

suſkomü

inherent [inhɛːr'ent] *adj*: **inherent in**
...に固有の ...ni koyū no

inherit [inhɛr'it] *vt* (property, money)
相続する sōzoku suru; (characteristic)
遺伝で受継ぐ idén de ukétsugū

inheritance [inhɛr'itəns] *n* (property,
money etc) 相続財産 sōzoku zaisán;
(characteristics etc) 遺伝 idén

inhibit [inhib'it] *vt* (growth: *also*
PSYCH) 抑制 yokúsei

inhibited [inhib'itid] *adj* (PSYCH) 抑制
の多い yokúsei no ōi

inhibition [inibiʃ'ən] *n* 抑制 yokúsei

inhospitable [inhɑːspit'əbəl] *adj* (person) もてなしの悪い moténashi no waru-
i; (place, climate) 住みにくい sumínikúi

inhuman [inhjuː'mən] *adj* (behavior) 残
忍な zañnin na; (appearance) 非人間的な
hiñfigénteki na

inimitable [inim'itəbəl] *adj* (tone, style)
まねのできない mané no dekinái

iniquity [inik'witi] *n* (wickedness) 悪る
kū; (injustice) 不正 fuséi

initial [iniʃ'əl] *adj* (stage, reaction) 最初
の saísho no

    ♦*n* (letter) 頭文字 kashífamojî

    ♦*vt* (document) ...に頭文字で署名す
る ...ni kashífamojî de shoméi suru

initials [iniʃ'əlz] *npl* (of name) 頭文字 kashíramojî; (as signature) 頭文字の署名
kashíramojî no shoméi

initially [iniʃ'əli:] *adv* (at first) 最初は saísho wa; (first) まず mázū saísho wa

initiate [iniʃ'i:it] *vt* (begin: talks, process) 始める hajímerū; (new member) 入会
させる nyūkai sasérū

to initiate someone into a secret ...に
秘密を教える ...ni himítsu wò oshíerū

*to initiate proceedings against
someone* (LAW) ...を起訴する ...wo kiso
suru

initiation [iniʃi:eiʃ'ən] *n* (beginning) 開始
kaíshi; (into organization etc) 入会式
nyūkaishiki; (into secret etc) 伝授 deñju

initiative [iniʃ'i:ativ] *n* (move) 企画 kikáku; (enterprise) 進取の気 shíñshu no kf

to take the initiative 先手を打つ señte

wò ūtsū

inject [indʒekt'] *vt* (drugs, poison) 注射す
る chūsha suru; (patient): *to inject
someone with something* ...に...を注射
する ...ni ...wo chūsha suru; (funds) つぎ
込む tsugíkomū

injection [indʒek'ʃən] *n* (of drugs, medicine) 注射 chūsha; (of funds) つぎ込む事
tsugíkomú kotó

injunction [indʒʌŋk'ʃən] *n* (LAW) 差止
め命令 sashítomemeírei

injure [in'dʒəːr] *vt* (hurt: person, leg etc)
傷付ける kizútsukerū; (: feelings, reputation) 害する gaí surū

injured [in'dʒəːrd] *adj* (person, arm) 傷付
いた kizútsuita; (feelings) 害された gaí-
saretā; (tone) 感情を害された kañjō wò
gaí sarétā

injury [in'dʒəːri:] *n* (wound) 傷 kizú, けが
kegá

injury time *n* (SPORT) 延長時間 eñchōjikàn (傷の手当てなどに使った分の延長
時間 kizú no teáte nadò ni tsukátta buñ
no eñchōjikàn

injustice [indʒʌs'tis] *n* (unfairness) 不公
平 fukōhei

ink [iŋk] *n* (in pen, printing) インク íñku

inkling [iŋk'liŋ] *n* (idea, clue) 薄々と気付
く事 usúusu tò kizúkū kotó

inlaid [in'leid] *adj* (with gems, wood etc)
...をちりばめた ...wo chírbametā

inland [in'lænd] *adj* (port, sea, waterway) 内陸の nafriku no

    ♦*adv* (travel) 内陸へ nafriku e

Inland Revenue (*BRIT*) *n* 国税庁 kokúzeichō

in-laws [in'lɔːz] *npl* 義理の親せき girí nò
shifiseki, 姻せき iñséki

inlet [in'let] *n* (GEO) 入江 irfe

inmate [in'meit] *n* (in prison) 受刑者 ju-
kêishà; (in asylum) 入院患者 nyúkañja

    ♦*n* 旅館 ryokán

innate [ineit'] *adj* (skill, quality, characteristic) 生来の seírai no

inner [in'əːr] *adj* (office, courtyard) 内側
の uchígawa no; (calm, feelings) 内心の
nafshin no

inner city *n* インナーシティー iñnashi-

ti◇スラム化した都心部を指す súràmu-
ka shita toshínbu wo sásù

inner tube *n* (of tire) チューブ chūbu

inning [in'iŋ] *n* (BASEBALL) イニング
íníŋgu

innings [in'iŋz] *n* (CRICKET) イニング
íníŋgu

innocence [in'əsəns] *n* (LAW) 無罪 múzài;
(naivety: of child, person) 純真さ juñ-
shinsa

innocent [in'əsənt] *adj* (not guilty: of
crime etc) 無罪の múzài no, 潔白な keppáku na; (naive: child, person) 純真な juñ-
shin na; (not involved: victim) 罪のない
tsúmì no náì; (remark, question) 無邪気
な mújàki na

innocuous [inɑː'kʲuːəs] *adj* (harmless) 無
害の múgài no

innovation [inəveiʃʲən] *n* (change) 刷新
sasshíñ

innuendo [injuːen'dou] (*pl* **innuendoes**)
n (insinuation) 当てこすり átèkosuri

innumerable [inuː'məːrəbəl] *adj* (countless) 無数の musú no

inoculation [inɑːkjəlei'ʃʲən] *n* (MED) 接
種 sesshú

inopportune [inɑːpəːrtuːn'] *adj* (event,
moment) 都合の悪い tsugó no warúì

inordinately [inɔːr'dənitli] *adv* (proud,
long, large etc) 極度に kyokúdò ni

in-patient [in'peiʃənt] *n* (in hospital) 入
院患者 nyúìnkaňja

input [in'put] *n* (information) 情報 jōhō;
(resources etc) つぎ込む事 tsugíkomù
kotó,◇(COMPUT) 入力 nyúryoku, イン
プット ínputtò

inquest [in'kwest] *n* (on someone's
death) 検死審問 keñshishímon

inquire [inkwaiəːr'] *vi* (ask) 尋ねる tazúnerù, 聞く kíkù
◆*vt* (ask) ...を尋ねる ...ni tazúnerù, ...に
聞く ...ni kíkù
to inquire about (person, fact) ...につ
いて問い合せる ...ni tsúìte toíawase surù

inquire into *vt fus* (death, circumstances) 調べる shiráberù

inquiry [inkwaiəːr'i] *n* (question) 質問
shitsúmon; (investigation) 調査 chōsa

inquiry office (*BRIT*) *n* 案内所 añnaijò

inquisitive [inkwiz'ətiv] *adj* (curious) せ
ん索好きな señsakuzuki na

inroads [in'roudz] *npl*: **to make inroads** *into* (savings, supplies) ...を消費
する ...wo shōhi suru

ins *abbr* = **inches**

insane [insein'] *adj* (foolish, crazy) 気違
い染みた kichígaijimità; (MED) 狂気の
kyōki no

insanity [insæn'iti] *n* (foolishness) 狂気
のさた kyōki nò satá; (MED) 狂気 kyōki

insatiable [insei'ʃəbəl] *adj* (greed, appetite) 飽く事のない akú kotò no náì

inscription [inskrip'ʃən] *n* (on gravestone, memorial etc) 碑文 híbùn; (in
book) 献呈の言葉 keñtei no kotóba

inscrutable [inskruː'təbəl] *adj* (comment, expression) 不可解な fukákaì na

insect [in'sekt] *n* 虫 mushí, 昆虫 koñchū

insecticide [insek'tisaid] *n* 殺虫剤 sat-
chúzai

insecure [insikjuːr'] *adj* (structure, lock,
door: weak) 弱い yowáì; (: unsafe) 安全
でない añzen de naì; (person) 自信のない
jishín no naì

insecurity [insikjuːr'iti] *n* (of structure,
lock etc: weakness) 弱さ yowásà; (: lack
of safety) 安全でない añzen de naì kotó;
(: of person) 自信欠如 jishínketsujo

insemination [inseminei'ʃən] *n*: **artificial insemination** (AGR, MED) 人工授
精 jiñkōjusei

insensible [insen'səbəl] *adj* (unconscious) 意識を失った íshìki wo ushínattà

insensitive [insen'sətiv] *adj* (uncaring,
indifferent) 思いやりのない omóìyarì no
náì

inseparable [insep'əːrəbəl] *adj* (ideas,
elements) 分離できない bufíri dekínaì;
(friends) いつも一緒の ítsùmo isshó no

insert [insəːrt'] *vt* (between two things)
...の間に入れる ...no áìda ni irérù; (into
something) 差込む sashíkomù, 挿入する
sōnyú suru

insertion [insəːr'ʃən] *n* (of needle, comb,
peg etc) 差込む事 sashíkomù kotó,挿入
挿入 sōnyú

in-service [in'səːr'vis] *adj* (training, course) 現職の geńshoku no

inshore [in'ʃɔːr] *adj* (fishing, waters) 近海の kińkai no
♦*adv* (be) 岸の近くに kishí no chikákù ni; (move) 岸の近くへ kishí no chikákù e

inside [in'said'] *n* (interior) 中 nákà, 内側 uchígawa
♦*adj* (interior) 中(内側) nákà (uchígawa) no
♦*adv* (go) 中(内側)へ nákà (uchígawa) e; (be) 中(内側)に nákà (uchígawa) ni
♦*prep* (of location) ...の中へ(に) ...no nákà e(ni); (of time): **inside 10 minutes** 10分以内に juppún inài ni

inside forward *n* (SPORT) インサイドフォワード ińsaidofowādo

inside information *n* 内部情報 naíbu jōhò

inside lane *n* (AUT) 内側車線 uchígawa shasen

inside out *adv* (be, turn) 裏返しに urágaeshi de; (know) すっかり sukkárì

insides [in'saidz] *npl* (inf: stomach) おなか onákà

insidious [insid'iːəs] *adj* (effect, power) 潜行的な seńkōteki na

insight [in'sait] *n* (into situation, problem) 洞察 dōsatsu

insignia [insig'niːə] *npl* 記章 kíshō

insignificant [insignif'ikənt] *adj* (extent, importance) ささいな sasái na

insincere [insinsiːr'] *adj* (smile, welcome) 偽りの itsúwarì no

insinuate [insin'juːeit] *vt* (imply) 当てこする atékosurù

insipid [insip'id] *adj* (person, activity, color) 面白くない omóshirokunai; (food, drink) 風味のない fúmi no nái

insist [insist'] *vi* (maintain) 主張する shuchō suru, 言い張る iíharù
to insist on (demand) ...を要求する ...wo yōkyū suru
to insist that (demand) ...する様要求する ...surú yō yōkyū suru; (claim) ...だと言い張る ...da to iíharù

insistence [insis'təns] *n* (determination) 強要 kyōyō

insistent [insis'tənt] *adj* (determined: person) しつこい shitsúkoì; (continual: noise, action) 絶間ない taémanaì

insole [in'soul] *n* (of shoe) 敷き皮 shikígawa

insolence [in'sələns] *n* (rudeness) 横柄さ ōheìsa

insolent [in'sələnt] *adj* (attitude, remark) 横柄な ōhei na

insoluble [insɑl'jəbəl] *adj* (problem) 解決のできない kafketsu nò dekfnaì

insolvent [insɑl'vənt] *adj* (bankrupt) 破産した hasán shita

insomnia [insɑm'niːə] *n* 不眠症 fumfnshō

inspect [inspekt'] *vt* (examine: gen) 調べる shiráberù; (premises) 捜査する sōsa suru; (equipment) 点検する tenken suru; (troops) 査閲する saétsu suru; (BRIT: ticket) 改札する kafsatsu suru

inspection [inspek'ʃən] *n* (examination: gen) 検査 keńsa; (of premises) 捜査 sōsa; (of equipment) 点検 tenken; (of troops) 査閲 saétsu; (BRIT: of ticket) 改札 kafsatsu

inspector [inspek'təːr] *n* (ADMIN) 検査官 keńsakan; (on buses, trains) 車掌 shashō; (: POLICE) 警部 keíbu

inspiration [inspərei'ʃən] *n* (encouragement) 発憤 happún; (influence: source) 動機になるもの dōki ni narù mono; (idea) 霊感 reíkan, インスピレーション ińspirēshon

inspire [inspaiəːr'] *vt* (workers, troops) 奮い立たせる furúitaserù; (confidence, hope etc) 持たせる motáserù

instability [instəbil'əti] *n* (of place, person, situation) 不安定 fuántei

install [instɔːl'] *vt* (machine) 取付ける torítsukerù; (official) 就任させる shúnin saserù

installation [instəlei'ʃən] *n* (of machine, equipment) 取付け torítsuke, 設置 sétchi; (plant: INDUSTRY) 工場施設 kōjō shisètsu, プラント puránto; (: MIL) 基地 kíchì

installment [instɔːl'mənt] (*BRIT* **instalment**) *n* (of payment, story, TV

serial etc) 1回分 ikkáíbun
in installments (pay, receive) 分割払い
で bufikatsubaráí de

instance [ín'stəns] *n* (example) 例 réì
for instance 例えば tatóèba
in the first instance まず最初に mázù
saísho ni

instant [ín'stənt] *n* (moment) 瞬間 shuñ-
kan
♦*adj* (reaction, success) 瞬間的な shuñkanteki na; (coffee, food) 即席の sokúsè-
ki no, インスタントの íñsutanto no

instantaneous [ínstəntéi'ni:əs] *adj*
(immediate) 即時の sokúji no

instantly [ín'stəntli:] *adv* (immediately)
即時に sokúji ni

instead [instéd'] *adv* (in place of) (そ
の) 代りに (sonó) kawárì ni
instead of ...の代りに ...no kawárì ni

instep [ín'step] *n* (of foot) 足の甲 ashí no
kò; (of shoe) 靴の甲 kutsú no kò

instigate [ín'stəgeit] *vt* (rebellion etc) 起
させる okósaserù; (talks etc) 始めさせる
hajímesaserù

instil(l) [instíl'] *vt*: *to instil something
into* (confidence, fear etc) ...を...に吹込
む ...wo ...ni fukíkomū

instinct [ín'stiŋkt] *n* 本能 hoñnō

instinctive [instiŋk'tiv] *adj* (reaction,
feeling) 本能的な hoñnōteki na

institute [ín'stitu:t] *n* (for research,
teaching) 施設 shisétsu; (professional
body: of architects, planners etc) 協会
kyōkai
♦*vt* (system, rule, course of action) 設け
る mōkerù; (proceedings, inquiry) 始める
hajímerù

institution [institu:'ʃən] *n* (of system
etc) 開設 kaísetsu; (custom, tradition) 伝
統 dentō; (organization: financial, religious, educational) 協会 kyōkai; (hospital, mental home) 施設 shisétsu

instruct [instrʌkt'] *vt*: *to instruct
someone in something* (teach) ...に...を
教える ...ni ...wo oshíerù

to instruct someone to do something
(order) ...する様に...に命令する ...surú yò
...ni mefrei suru

instruction [instrʌk'ʃən] *n* (teaching) 教
育 kyōiku

instructions [instrʌk'ʃənz] *npl* (orders)
命令 mefrei

instructions (for use) 取扱い説明 toríatsukai setsúmei

instructive [instrʌk'tiv] *adj* (lesson,
response) 有益な yúeki na

instructor [instrʌk'tə:r] *n* (teacher) 先
生 señsei; (for skiing, driving etc) 指導者
shidōsha

instrument [ín'strəmənt] *n* (tool) 道具
dōgu; (measuring device etc) 計器 keíkì;
(MUS) 楽器 gakkí

instrumental [instrəmen'təl] *adj* (MUS)
器楽の kfgakù no
to be instrumental in ...に大きな役割
を果す ...ni ōkina yakúwarì wo hatasù

instrument panel *n* 計器盤 keíkiban

insubordination [insəbɔ:rdənei'ʃən] *n*
(disobedience) 不服従 fufúkujū

insufferable [insʌf'ə:rəbəl] *adj* (arrogance, laziness) 耐えがたい taégataì;
(person) 我慢のならない gámàn no naráa-
nai

insufficient [insəfiʃ'ənt] *adj* (funds,
data, research) 不十分な fujūbùn na

insular [ín'sələr] *adj* (outlook, person)
狭量な kyōryō na

insulate [ín'səleit] *vt* (protect: person,
group) 孤立させる korítsu saserù
(against cold: house, body) 断熱する dañ-
netsu suru; (against sound) 防音にする
bōon ni suru; (against electricity) 絶縁す
る zetsúen suru

insulating tape [ín'səleitiŋ-] *n* (ELEC)
絶縁テープ zetsúentēpu

insulation [insəlei'ʃən] *n* (of person,
group) 孤立させる事 korítsu saserù ko-
tō; (against cold) 断熱材 dañnetsuzài;
(against sound) 防音材 bōonzài; (against
electricity) 絶縁 zetsúenzài

insulin [ín'səlin] *n* (MED) インシュリン í-
shurin

insult [*n* ín'sʌlt *vb* insʌlt'] *n* (offence) 侮
辱 bujóku
♦*vt* (offend) 侮辱する bujóku suru

insulting [insʌl'tiŋ] *adj* (attitude, language) 侮辱的な bujókuteki na

insuperable [insu:'pəːrəbəl] *adj* (obstacle, problem) 乗越えられない norîkoerarenaí

insurance [inʃʊr'əns] *n* (on property, car, life etc) 保険 hokén
fire/life insurance 火災〔生命〕保険 kasái〔seîmei〕hoken

insurance agent *n* 保険代理店 hokéndairiten

insurance policy *n* 保険証書 hokénshósho

insure [inʃʊr'] *vt* (life, property): *to insure (against)* ...に（...の）保険を掛ける ...ni（...no）hokén wo kakérù
to insure (oneself) against (disappointment, disaster) ...に備える ...ni sonáerù

insurrection [insərek'ʃən] *n* (uprising) 反乱 hañran

intact [intækt'] *adj* (whole) 元のままの mótð no mamá no; (unharmed) 無傷の múkizu no

intake [in'teik] *n* (gen) 取込み torîkomi; (of food etc) 摂取 sésshù; (of air) 吸入 kyūnyū; (BRIT: SCOL): *an intake of 200 a year* 毎年の新入生は200人 maítoshi nò shíñnyūsei wa nihyákunīn

intangible [intæn'dʒəbəl] *adj* (quality, idea, benefit) ばく然とした bakúzen to shita

integral [in'təgrəl] *adj* (feature, element) 不可欠な fukákètsu na

integrate [in'təgreit] *vt* (newcomer) 溶込ませる tokékomaserù; (ideas, systems) 取入れる torîireru
♦*vi* (groups, individuals) 溶込む tokékomù

integrity [integ'riti] *n* (morality: of person) 誠実さ seîjitsusa

intellect [in'təlekt] *n* (intelligence) 知性 chiséi; (cleverness) 知能 chínô

intellectual [intəlek'tʃuəl] *adj* (activity, interest, pursuit) 知的な chitéki na
♦*n* (intelligent person) 知識人 chishíkijìn, インテリ iñteri

intelligence [intel'idʒəns] *n* (cleverness, thinking power) 知能 chínô; (MIL etc)

報 jôhô

intelligence service *n* 情報部 jôhôbu

intelligent [intel'idʒənt] *adj* (person) 知能の高い chinô no takái; (decision) 利口な chíð na; (machine) インテリジェントの iñterijeñto no

intelligentsia [intelidʒen'tsiːə] *n* 知識階級 chishíkikaikyū, インテリ階級 iñterikaîkyū

intelligible [intel'idʒəbəl] *adj* (clear, comprehensible) 分かりやすい wakáriyasuî

intend [intend'] *vt* (gift etc): *to intend something for* ...に上げようと思っている ...wo ...ni agéyō to omótte irú
to intend to do something (mean) ...する決心でいる ...suru kesshîn de irú; (plan) ...するつもりである ...suru tsumóri de arú

intended [intend'did] *adj* (effect, insult) 意図した îtð shita; (journey) 計画した kefkaku shita; (victim) ねらった nerátta

intense [intens'] *adj* (heat, effort, anger, joy) 猛烈な móretsu na; (person) 情熱的な jō netsuteki na

intensely [intens'liː] *adv* (extremely) 激しく hagéshikù

intensify [inten'səfai] *vt* (efforts, pressure) 増す másù

intensity [inten'siti] *n* (of heat, anger, effort) 激しさ hagéshisa

intensive [inten'siv] *adj* (concentrated) 集中的な shūchūteki na

intensive care unit *n* (MED) 集中治療室 shūchūchiryōshitsu, ICU aishîyū

intent [intent'] *n* (intention) 意図 îtð; (LAW) 犯意 hañ-i
♦*adj* (absorbed): *intent (on)* (...しようとして) 余念がない ...shíyō to shite yonén ga naî; (attentive) 夢中な muchū na
to all intents and purposes 事実上 jijítsujō
to be intent on doing something (determined) ...しようとして余念がない ...shíyō to shite yonén ga naî

intention [inten'tʃən] *n* (purpose) 目的 mokúteki; (plan) 意図 îtð

intentional [inten'tʃənəl] adj (deliberate) 意図的な ítōteki na

intentionally [inten'tʃənəli] adv (deliberately) 意図的に ítōteki ni, わざと wáza to

intently [inten'li:] adv (listen, watch) 熱心に nesshín ni

inter [intər'] vt (bury) 埋葬する mafsō suru

interact [intərækt'] vi: to interact (with) (people, things, ideas) (...と) 互いに反応し合う (...to) sógo ni hañnō shiaú

interaction [intəræk'ʃən] n 相互反応 sōgohañnō

intercede [intərsi:d'] vi: to intercede (with) (...に) 取りなしをする (...ni) torínashi wo surū

intercept [intərsept'] vt (person, car) 途中で捕捉える tochū de tsukamaerū; (message) 傍受する bōju suru

interchange [intərtʃeindʒ] n (exchange) 交換 kōkan; (on motorway) インターチェンジ ñtāchéñji

interchangeable [intərtʃein'dʒəbəl] adj (terms, ideas, things) 置換えられる okíkaerareru

intercom [intər'kɑːm] n (in office etc) インターホーン ñtāhōn

intercourse [intər'kɔːrs] n (also: sexual intercourse) 性交 sefkō

interest [in'trist] n (in subject, idea, person etc) 興味 kyōmi; (pastime, hobby) 趣味 shūmi; (advantage) 利益 rīeki; (COMM: in company) 株 kábu; (: sum of money) 利息 risōku
◆vt (subj: work, subject, idea etc) ...の興味をそそる ...no kyōmi wo sosorū
to be interested in ...に興味がある ...ni kyōmi ga árū

interesting [in'tristiŋ] adj (idea, place, person) 面白い omóshiroi

interest rate n 利率 rirítsu

interface [intər'feis] n (COMPUT) インターフェース ñtāfēsu

interfere [intərfiːr'] vi: to interfere in (quarrel, other people's business) ...に干渉する ...ni kañshō suru
to interfere with (object) ...をいじる

...wo ijîrū; (plans, career, duty, decision) ...を邪魔する ...wo jamá suru

interference [intərfiːr'əns] n (in someone's affairs etc) 干渉 kañshō; (RADIO, TV) 混信 koñshin

interim [in'tərim] adj (agreement, government) 暫定的な zañteiteki na
◆n: in the interim (meanwhile) その間 sonō aída

interior [inti:'riːər] n (of building, car, box etc) 内部 náibu; (of country) 内陸 naíriku
◆adj (door, window, room etc) 内部の náibu no; (minister, department) 内務の nāimu no

interior designer n インテリアデザイナー íñteriadezáinā

interjection [intərdʒek'ʃən] n (interruption) 野次 yáji; (LING) 感嘆詞 kañtañshi

interlock [in'tərlɑːk] vi かみ合う kamîaū

interloper [intərlou'pər] n (in town, meeting etc) ちん入者 chíñnyūsha

interlude [in'tərlu:d] n (break) 休憩 kyūkei; (THEATER) 休憩時間 kyūkeijíkan

intermarry [intərmær'i:] vi 交婚する kōkon suru

intermediary [intərmi:'diːeri:] n 仲介者 chūkaísha

intermediate [intərmi:'diːit] adj (stage, student) 中間の chūkan no

interminable [intər'mənəbəl] adj (process, delay) 果てしない hatēshinaí

intermission [intərmiʃ'ən] n (pause) 休止 kyūshi; (THEATER, CINEMA) 休憩時間 kyūkeijíkan

intermittent [intərmit'ənt] adj (noise, publication etc) 断続的な dañzokuteki na

intern [in'tərn] vt (imprison) 拘置する kōchi suru
◆n (US: houseman) 研修医 keñshūi

internal [intər'nəl] adj (layout, structure, memo etc) 内部の náibu no; (pipes etc) 埋込みの umékomi no; (bleeding, injury) 体内の tāinai no; (security, politics) 国内の kokúnai no

internally [intər'nəli] *adv*: 「*not to be taken internally*」内服外用薬 naffuku-gaiyōyaku

Internal Revenue Service (*US*) *n* 国税庁 kokúzeichō

international [intər:næʃ'ənəl] *adj* (trade, agreement etc) 国際的な kokúsaiteki na, 国際... kokúsai...
♦*n* (*BRIT*: SPORT: match) 国際試合 kokúsaijiai

interplay [in'tər:plei] *n*: **interplay (of/between)** (...の) 相互反応 (...no) sōgohannō

interpret [intər'prit] *vt* (explain, understand) 解釈する kaíshaku suru; (translate) 通訳する tsúyaku suru
♦*vi* (translate) 通訳する tsúyaku suru

interpretation [intər:priteiʃ'ən] *n* (explanation) 解釈 kaíshaku; (translation) 通訳 tsúyaku

interpreter [intər'pritər] *n* (translator) 通訳 tsúyaku(sha)

interrelated [intər:rilei'tid] *adj* (causes, factors etc) 相互関係のある sōgokankei no aru

interrogate [inter:r'ageit] *vt* (question: witness, prisoner, suspect) 尋問する jínmon suru

interrogation [inter:ragei'ʃən] *n* (of witness, prisoner etc) 尋問 jínmon

interrogative [intər:ag'ətiv] *adj* (LING) 疑問の gímon no

interrupt [intər:ʌpt'] *vt* (speaker) ...の話に割り込む ...no hanáshi ni waríkomu; (activity) 邪魔する jamá suru
♦*vi* (during someone's conversation etc) 話に割り込む hanáshi ni waríkomu; (during activity) 邪魔する jamá suru

interruption [intər:ʌp'ʃən] *n* (act) 邪魔する事 jamá suru kotō; (instance) 邪魔 jamá

intersect [intər:sekt'] *vi* (roads) 交差する kōsa suru

intersection [intər:sek'ʃən] *n* (of roads) 交差点 kōsaten

intersperse [intər:rspərs'] *vt*: **to intersperse with** ...を所々に入れる ...wo tokórodokoro ni irérù

intertwine [intər:rtwain'] *vi* 絡み合う karámiaù

interval [in'tər:vəl] *n* (break, pause) 間隔 kañkaku; (*BRIT*: SCOL: also THEATER, SPORT) 休憩時間 kyūkeijikan
at intervals (periodically) 時々 tokidoki

intervene [intər:vin'] *vi* (person: in situation: interfere) 介入する kañnyū suru; (: to help) 仲裁に入る chūsai ni hairù; (: in speech) 割込む waríkomù; (event) 間に起る aída ni okorù; (time) 経つ tátsù

intervention [intər:ven'ʃən] *n* (interference: interference) 介入 kañnyū; (help) 仲裁 chūsai

interview [in'tər:vju:] *n* (for job etc) 面接 meñsetsu; (RADIO, TV etc) インタビュー fñtabyū
♦*vt* (for job etc) ...と面接する ...to meñsetsu suru; (RADIO, TV etc) ...にインタビューする ...ni fñtabyū suru

interviewer [in'tər:vju:ər] *n* (of candidate, job applicant) 面接者 meñsetsushà; (RADIO, TV etc) インタビューア fñtabyūa

intestine [intes'tin] *n* 腸 chō

intimacy [in'təməsi:] *n* (closeness) 親しみ shitáshimi

intimate [*adj* in'təmit *vb* in'təmeit] *adj* (friendship, relationship) 親しい shitáshiì; (detail) 細かい 知られざる shirárezarù; (restaurant, dinner, atmosphere) こじんまりした kojínmari shita; (knowledge) 詳しい kuwáshiì
♦*vt* (announce) ほのめかす honōmekasù

intimidate [intim'ideit] *vt* (frighten) 脅す odósu

intimidation [intimidei'ʃən] *n* 脅し odóshi

KEYWORD

into [in'tu:] *prep* **1** (indicating motion or direction) ...の中に(へ) ...no nāka ni(e)
come into the house/garden 家に入って来て下さい ié(niwá) ni háttè kité kudasaí

go into town 町に出掛ける machí ni dekakerù

he got into the car 彼は車に乗った kárè wa kurúma ni nottá

throw it into the fire 火の中へ捨てて下さい hí no nakà e sutéte kudasaí

research into cancer がんの研究 gáñ no keñkyū

he worked late into the night 彼は夜遅くまで働いた kárè wa yōrù osóku madè hataráita

the car bumped into the wall 車は塀にぶつかった kurúma wà heí ni butsúkattá

she poured tea into the cup 彼女はお茶をカップについだ kánjo wa kōcha wō káppù nì tsuídà

2 (indicating change of condition, result): *she burst into tears* 彼女は急に泣きだした kánjo wa kyū nì nakídashìta

he was shocked into silence 彼はショックで物も言えなかった kárè wa shókkù de monó mò ienákatta

it broke into pieces ばらばらに割れた barábara ni waréta

she translated into French 彼女はフランス語に訳した kánjo wa furáñsugo nì yakúshita

they got into trouble 彼らは問題を起こした kárèra wa moñdai wò okóshita

intolerable [intɔ'ɔːrəbəl] *adj* (extent, quality) 我慢できない gámàn dekínaì

intolerance [intɔ'ɔːrəns] *n* (bigotry, prejudice) 偏狭さ heñkyōsa

intolerant (of) [intɔ'ɔːrənt] *adj* (...に対して) 偏狭な (...ni táìshite) heñkyō na

intonation [intounei'ʃən] *n* (of voice, speech) 抑揚 yokúyō, イントネーション intonēshon

intoxicated [intaːk'sikeitid] *adj* (drunk) 酔っ払った yoppáràtta

intoxication [intaːksikei'ʃən] *n* 泥酔 deísui

intractable [intræk'təbəl] *adj* (child, problem) 手に負えない te ni oenái

intransigent [intræn'sidʒənt] *adj* (attitude) 頑固な gañko na

intransitive [intræn'sətiv] *adj* (LING):
intransitive verb 自動詞 jídòshi

intravenous [intrəvi:'nəs] *adj* (injection, drip) 静脈内の jōmyakunaì no

in-tray [in'trei] *n* (in office) 着信のトレー chakúshin nò toré

intrepid [intrep'id] *adj* (adventurer, explorer) 勇敢な yūkan na

intricate [in'trəkit] *adj* (pattern, design) 複雑な fukúzatsu na

intrigue [intri:g'] *n* (plotting) 策略 sakúryàku

♦*vt* (fascinate) ...の好奇心をそそる ...no kōkìshin wō sosórù

intriguing [intri:'giŋ] *adj* (fascinating) 面白い omóshiroì

intrinsic [intrin'sik] *adj* (quality, nature) 本質的な hoñshitsuteki na

introduce [intrədus'] *vt* (new idea, measure etc) 導入する dōnyū surù; (speaker, TV show etc) 紹介する shókaì suru

to introduce someone (to someone) (...に) ...を紹介する (...ni) ...wo shōkai suru

to introduce someone to (pastime, technique) ...に...を初めて経験させる ...ni ...wo hajímète keñken saserú

introduction [intrədʌk'ʃən] *n* (of new idea, measure etc) 導入 dōnyū; (of person) 紹介 shōkai; (to new experience) 初めて経験させること hajímète keñken saserú kotò; (to book) 前書 maégaki

introductory [intrədʌk'tə:ri] *adj* (lesson) 導入の dōnyū no; (offer) 初回のショ初回の shokái no

introspective [intrəspek'tiv] *adj* (person, mood) 内省的な naíseiteki na

introvert [in'trəvə:rt] *n* 内向性の人 naíkōsei no hitò

♦*adj* (also: **introverted**): behavior, child etc) 内向性の naíkōsei no

intrude [intru:d'] *vi* (person) 邪魔する jamá suru

to intrude on (conversation, grief, party etc) ...のところを邪魔する ...no kōro wō jamá suru

intruder [intru:'də:r] *n* (into home, camp) 侵入者 shiñnyūshà

intrusion [intruː'ʒən] *n* (of person, outside influences) 邪魔 jamá

intuition [intjuː'iʃən] *n* (feeling, hunch) 直感 chokkán

intuitive [intjuː'ətiv] *adj* (instinctive) 直感的な chokkánteki na

inundate [in'ʌndeit] *vt*: **to inundate with** (calls, letters etc) ...が殺到する ...ga sattō suru

invade [inveid'] *vt* (MIL) を侵略する ...wo shíryaku suru

invalid [*n* in'vəlid *adj* invæ'lid] *n* (MED: disabled person) 身障者 shiñshōsha; (of sick and weak person) 病弱な人 byójaku na hitò

♦**adj** (not valid) 無効の mukó no

invaluable [invæl'juːəbəl] *adj* (person, thing) 貴重な kíchō na

invariable [invær'iːəbəl] *adj* 変らない kawáranaì, 不変の fuhén no

invariably [invær'iːəbliː] *adv* 必ず kanárazù

invasion [invei'ʒən] *n* (MIL) 侵略 shiñryaku

invent [invent'] *vt* (machine, game, phrase etc) 発明する hatsúmei suru; (fabricate: lie, excuse) でっち上げる detchíagerù

invention [inven'tʃən] *n* (machine, system) 発明品 hatsúmeihin; (untrue story) 作り話 tsukúribanashì; (act of inventing: machine, system) 発明 hatsúmei

inventor [inven'təːr] *n* (of machines, systems) 発明家 hatsúmeika

inventory [in'vəntɔːriː] *n* (of house, shop etc) 物品目録 buppíñmokùroku

inverse [invəːrs'] *adj* (relationship) 逆の gyakú no

invert [invəːrt'] *vt* (turn upside down) 逆さにする sakása ni suru

invertebrate [invəːr'təbrit] *n* 無せきつい動物 musékìtsuidóbutsu

inverted commas [invəːr'tid-] (*BRIT*) *npl* 引用符 iñyófù

invest [invest'] *vt* (money) 投資する tóshi suru; (*fig*: time, energy) つぎ込む tsugíkomù

♦**vi**: **invest in** (COMM) ...に投資する

...ni tōshi suru; (*fig*: something useful) 購入する kónyū suru

investigate [inves'təgeit] *vt* (accident, crime, person) 取調べる toríshiraberù, 捜査する sōsa suru

investigation [inves'təgeiʃən] *n* 取調べ toríshirabe, 捜査 sōsa

investigator [inves'təgeitəːr] *n* (of events, situations, people) 捜査官 sōsakàn

investiture [inves'titʃəːr] *n* (of chancellor) 就任式 shúniñshiki; (of prince) たい冠式 taíkañshiki

investment [invest'mənt] *n* (activity) 投資 tóshi; (amount of money) 投資額 tóshigàku

investor [inves'təːr] *n* (COMM) 投資者 tóshishà

inveterate [invet'əːrit] *adj* (liar, cheat etc) 常習的な jóshùteki na

invidious [invid'iːəs] *adj* (task, job: unpleasant) 憎まれ役の nikúmareyàku no; (comparison, decision: unfair) 不公平な fukóhei na

invigilator [invidʒ'əleitəːr] (*BRIT*) *n* (in exam) 試験監督 shikéñkañtoku

invigorating [invig'əːreitiŋ] *adj* (air, breeze etc) さわやかな sawáyàka na; (experience etc) 元気が出る様な geñki ga deru yō na

invincible [invin'səbəl] *adj* (army, team: unbeatable) 無敵の mútèki no

invisible [inviz'əbəl] *adj* 目に見えない mé ni mienàì

invitation [invitei'ʒən] *n* (to party, meal, meeting etc) 招待 shōtai; (written card, paper) 招待状 shōtaijō

invite [in'vait] *vt* (to party, meal, meeting etc) 招く manékù, 招待する shōtai suru; (encourage: discussion, criticism) 求める motómerù

to invite someone to do ...に...するよう求める ...surú yō motómerù

inviting [invai'tiŋ] *adj* (attractive, desirable) 魅力的な miryókuteki na

invoice [in'vɔis] *n* (COMM) 請求書 sefkyúsho

♦**vt** ...に請求書を送る ...ni sefkyúsho wo

okōrù

invoke [in'vouk'] vt (law, principle) ...に
訴える ...ni uttaerù

involuntary [invɒl'ənteri:] adj (action,
reflex etc) 反射的な hanshateki na

involve [invɒlv'] vt (person, thing:
include, use) 伴う tomönaù, 必要とする
hitsuyō to surù; (: concern, affect) ...に関
係する ...ni kañkei suru

　to involve someone (in something)
(...に) ...を巻き込む (...ni) ...wo makíkomù

involved [invɒlvd'] adj (complicated) 複
雑な fukūzatsu na

　to be involved in (take part: in activity
etc) ...にかかわる ...ni kakáwarù; (be engrossed) ...に夢中になっている ...ni muchū ni nattè irū

involvement [invɒlv'mənt] n (participation) 参加 sañka; (concern, enthusiasm) 感情的かかわり合い kañjōteki nà
kakáwariai

inward [in'wəːrd] adj (thought, feeling)
内心の naíshin no; (movement) 中の方へ
の nákà no hō e no

inward(s) [in'wəːrd(z)] adv (move, face)
中の方へ nákà no hō e

I/O [ai'ou'] abbr (COMPUT: = input/
output) 入出力 nyūshutsuryōku

iodine [ai'ədain] n (chemical element) ヨ
ウ素 yōso, ヨード yōdo; (disinfectant) ヨ
ードチンキ yōdochínki

ion [ai'ən] n イオン íoñ

iota [aiou'tə] n: *not one/an iota* 少しも
...ない sukóshì mo ...náì

IOU [aiouju:'] n abbr (= I owe you) 借用
証 shakúyōshō

IQ [aikju:'] n abbr (= intelligence quotient) 知能指数 chinōshísū, IQ aikyū

IRA [aiɑːrei'] n abbr (= Irish Republican Army) アイルランド共和国軍 afru-
rando kyōwakakugùn

Iran [iræn'] n イラン fran

Iranian [irei'ni:ən] adj イランの fran no
　♦n イラン人 iráñjin

Iraq [iræk'] n イラク fráku

Iraqi [irɑːk'i:] adj イラクの fráku no
　♦n イラク人 irákùjin

irascible [iræs'əbəl] adj 怒りっぽい okó-

rippoì

irate [aireit'] adj 怒っている okótte irù

Ireland [aiər'lənd] n アイルランド afru-
rando

iris [ai'ris] (pl irises) n (ANAT) こう彩
kōsai; (BOT) アヤメ ayáme, アイリス áI-
risu

Irish [ai'riʃ] adj アイルランドの afruran-
do no
　♦npl: *the Irish* アイルランド人 afruran-
dojiñ ◇総称 sōshō

Irishman/woman [ai'riʃmən/wumən]
(pl Irishmen/women) n アイルランド人
男性(女性) afrurandojin dañsei(josèi)

Irish Sea n: *the Irish Sea* アイリッシ
ュ海 afrisshukài

irksome [əːrk'səm] adj いらいらさせる f-
ràira sasèru

iron [ai'əːrn] n (metal) 鉄 tetsù; (for
clothes) アイロン aíron
　♦cpd (bar, railings) 鉄の tetsù no; (will,
discipline etc) 鉄の様な tetsù no yō na
　♦vt (clothes) ...にアイロンを掛ける ...ni
afron wò kakérù

Iron Curtain n: *the Iron Curtain* 鉄
のカーテン tetsù no kâten

ironic(al) [airɑːn'ik(əl)] adj (remark,
gesture, situation) 皮肉な híniku na

ironing [ai'əːrniŋ] n (activity) アイロン
掛け aíronkake; (clothes) アイロンを掛
けるべき衣類 afron wò kakérubeki irùi

ironing board n アイロン台 afrondai

ironmonger [ai'əːrmʌŋgəːr] (BRIT) n
金物屋 kanámonoya ◇人を指す hitò wò
sásù

ironmonger's (shop)
[ai'əːrmʌŋgəːrz-] n 金物屋 kanámonoya
◇店を指す misè wò sásù

iron out vt (fig: problems) 打開する da-
kái suru

irony [ai'rəni:] n 皮肉 híniku

irrational [iræʃ'ənəl] adj (feelings,
behavior) 不合理な fugôri na

irreconcilable [irek'ənsailəbəl] adj
(ideas, views) 両立しない ryôritsu shina-
i; (disagreement) 調和不可能な chôwafu-
kanō na

irrefutable [irifju:'təbəl] adj (fact) 否め

られない inâmarenaì; (argument) 反ばくできない hañbaku dekinaì

irregular [ireg'jələr] *adj* (surface) 凸凹の dekôboko no; (pattern, action, event etc) 不規則な fukísoku na; (not acceptable: behavior) 良くない yôkúnai; (verb, noun, adjective) 不規則変化の fukísokuheñka no

irregularity [iregjəlær'iti:] *n* (of surface) 凹凸 dekôboko; (of pattern, action etc) 不規則 fukísoku; (instance of behavior) 良くない行為 yôkúnai kôi

irrelevant [irel'əvənt] *adj* (fact, information) 関係のない kañkei no naì

irreparable [irep'ərəbəl] *adj* (harm, damage etc) 取返しの付かない toríkaeshi no tsukanaì

irreplaceable [iripleí'səbəl] *adj* 掛替えのない kakégae no naì

irrepressible [iripres'əbəl] *adj* 陽気な yôki na

irresistible [irizis'təbəl] *adj* (force) 抵抗できない tefkô dekinaì; (urge, desire) 抑えきれない osáekirenaì; (person, thing) とても魅惑的な totémô miwákuteki na

irresolute [irez'əlut] *adj* 決断力のない ketsúdanryòku no naì

irrespective [irispek'tiv]: **irrespective of** *prep* ...に関係なく ...to kañkei nakù

irresponsible [irispan'səbəl] *adj* (person, action) 無責任な musékìnin na

irreverent [irev'ərənt] *adj* 不敬な fukéi na

irrevocable [irev'əkəbəl] *adj* (action, decision) 変更できない heñkô dekinaì

irrigate [ir'igeit] *vt* (AGR) かんがいする kañgai suru

irrigation [irigei'ʃən] *n* (AGR) かんがい kañgai

irritable [ir'itəbəl] *adj* 怒りっぽい okórippoì

irritate [ir'əteit] *vt* (annoy) いらいらさせる írâira saséru; (MED) 刺激する shigéki suru

irritating [ir'əteitiŋ] *adj* (person, sound etc) いらいらさせる írâira saséru

irritation [iritei'ʃən] *n* (feeling of annoyance) いら立ち irádachi; (MED) 刺激 shi-

géki; (annoying thing) いら立ちの元 irádachi no motò

IRS [aiɑ:res'] (*US*) *n abbr* = **Internal Revenue Service**

is [iz] *vb see* **be**

Islam [iz'lɑːm] *n* イスラム教 isúramukyò

Islamic [izlɑ:m'ic] *adj* イスラム教の isúramukyò no

island [ai'lənd] *n* (GEO) 島 shimá

islander [ai'ləndər] *n* 島の住民 shimá no júmin

isle [ail] *n* (GEO) 島 shimá

isn't [iz'ənt] = **is not**

isolate [ai'səleit] *vt* (physically, socially: set apart) 孤立させる korítsu saserû; (substance) 分離する bufrí suru; (sick person, animal) 隔離する kakúri suru

isolated [ai'saleitid] *adj* (place) へんぴな heñpì na; (person) 孤立した korítsu shita; (incident) 単独の tañdoku no

isolation [aisalei'ʃən] *n* 孤立 korítsu

isotope [ai'sətoup] *n* (PHYSICS) 同位体 dôitai, アイソトープ afsotôpu

Israel [iz'reiəl] *n* イスラエル isúraèru

Israeli [izrei'li:] *adj* イスラエルの isúraèru no

♦*n* イスラエル人 isúraerujìn

issue [iʃ'u:] *n* (problem, subject, most important part) 問題 mofdai; (of newspaper, magazine etc) 号 gô; (of book) 版 háñ; (of stamp) 発行部数 hakkôbôsû

♦*vt* (statement) 発表する happyô suru; (rations, equipment, documents) 配給する kañkyû suru

at issue 問題は(の) mofdai wa(no)

to take issue with someone (over) (...について) ...と争う (..ni tsûtte) ...to arásoû

isthmus [is'məs] *n* (GEO) 半島 hañtô

it [it] *pron* **1** (specific: subject) それは [が] soré wa(gà); (: direct object) それを soré wò; (: indirect object) それに soré nì ◊通常日本語では表現しない tsûjô nihongo de wa hyôgen shinâì

where's my book? - it's on the table 私の本はどこですか-テーブルにあります

watákushi no hoñ wa dókó desu ká tébúru ni arímasù

I can't find it 見当りません miátáru-maseñ

give it to me それを私に渡して下さい soré wò watákushi nì watáshite kudasaì

about/from/in/of/to it それについて [から、の中に、の、の方へ] soré ni tsuíte [kárà, nó nákà ni, nó, no hó è]

I spoke to him about it その件について私は彼に話しました sonó keñ ni tsuíte watákushi wà kárè ni hanáshimashìta

what did you learn from it? その事からあなたは何を学びましたか sonó kotò kara anátà wa náni wo manábimashìta ka

what role did you play in it? その件に関してあなたはどんな役割をしましたか sonó keñ ni kàñ shite anátà wa dóñna yakùwari wo shimáshìta ka

I'm proud of it それを誇りに思っています soré wò hókóri nì omótte imasù

did you go to it? (party, concert etc) 行きましたか ikímashìta ka

2 (impersonal): **it's raining** 雨が降っている ámè ga futté irù

it's cold today 今日は寒い kyó wà samúì

it's Friday tomorrow 明日は金曜日です asú wà kiñ-yóbi desu

it's 6 o'clock/the 10th of August 6時/8月10日です 6 ji rokújì (hachígatsu tóka) desu

how far is it? - it's 10 miles/2 hours on the train どこまでどのぐらいありますか-10マイルあります / (列車で2時間です) soko máde dónò gurai arímasù ká - júmairu arímasù (ressha de nijíkan desu)

who is it? - it's me どなたですか-私です dónàta desu ká - watákushi desù

Italian [itǽljən] *adj* イタリアの itária no; (LING) イタリア語の itáriago no
♦ *n* (person) イタリア人 itáriajìn (LING) イタリア語 itáriago

italics [itǽliks] *npl* (TYP) 斜体文字 shatáimòji, イタリック体 itárikkùtai

Italy [it'əli:] *n* イタリア itária

itch [itʃ] *n* (irritation) かゆみ kayúmi
♦ *vi* (person) かゆがる kayúgarù; (part of body) かゆい kayúì

to itch to do something ...をしたくてむずむずしている ...wo shitákutè múzùmuzu shité irù

itchy [itʃ'i:] *adj* (person) かゆがっている kayúgatte irù; (skin etc) かゆい kayúì

it'd [it'əd] **= it would; it had**

item [ai'təm] *n* (one thing: of list, collection) 品目 hiñmoku; (on agenda) 項目 kómoku; (also: **news item**) 記事 kíjì

itemize [ai'təmaiz] *vt* (list) 明細に書く mefsai ni kakù, リストアップする risútoappù suru

itinerant [aitin'əːrənt] *adj* (laborer, salesman, priest etc) 巡回する juñkai suru

itinerary [aitin'əreːri:] *n* 旅程 ryotéi

it'll [it'əl] **= it shall; it will**

its [its] **= it is; it has**

itself [itself'] *pron* それ自身 soré (aré)jishìn

ITV [ait:vi:'] *n abbr* (BRIT: = Independent Television) 民間テレビ放送 miñkan terebi hósò

IUD [aijuːdiːʼ] *n abbr* (= intra-uterine device) 子宮内避妊具 shikyúnaihiníñgu, IUD aiyúdì

I've [aiv] **= I have**

ivory [ai'vəːriː] *n* (substance) 象げ zóge; (color) アイボリー áiborì

ivory tower *n* 象牙の塔 zóge no tó

ivy [ai'viː] *n* (BOT) キヅタ kízùta, アイビー áibi

J

jab [dʒæb] *vt* (poke: with elbow, stick) 突く tsukú
♦ *n* (inf: injection) 注射 chúsha

to jab something into something ...を...に突っ込む ...wo ...ni tsukkómù

jabber [dʒæb'əːr] *vi* (also: **jabber away**) ぺちゃくちゃしゃべる péchakucha

jack [dʒæk] n (AUT) ジャッキ jákkì; (CARDS) ジャック jákkù

jackal [dʒæk'əl] n ジャッカル jákkàru

jackdaw [dʒæk'dɔ:] n コクマルガラス kokúmarugàrasu

jacket [dʒæk'it] n (garment) ジャケット jákètto; (of book) ジャケット jákèttò, カバー kábà

potatoes in their jackets 皮ごと料理 したジャガイモ kawágòto ryóri shita jagáimo

jack-knife [dʒæk'naif] n (trailer truck) ジャックナイフ現象を起す jakkúnaifu genshō wo okósù ぐ貌角に折り曲って動けなくなる efkaku ni orímagatte ugókenāku nárù

jack plug n (ELEC: for headphones etc) プラグ purágù

jackpot [dʒæk'pɑ:t] n 大賞金 dafshōkin

to hit the jackpot 大賞金を当てる dafshōkin wo atérù, 大当りする óatàri suru

jack up n (AUT) ジャッキで持上げる jákkì de mochíagerù

jade [dʒeid] n (stone) ひすい hisúi

jaded [dʒei'did] adj (tired) 疲れ切った tsukárekittà, (fed-up) うんざりした ufzarîshita

jagged [dʒæg'id] adj (outline, edge) ぎざぎざの gízagiza no

jail [dʒeil] n 刑務所 kefmusho
◆vt 刑務所に入れる kefmusho ni irérù

jam [dʒæm] n (food) ジャム jámù; (also: traffic jam) 交通渋滞 kōtsūjūtai; (inf: difficulty) to be in a jam 困っている komátte irù
◆vt (passage etc) ふさぐ fuságù; (mechanism, drawer etc) 動けなくする ugókenāku suru; (RADIO) 妨害する bōgai suru
◆vi (mechanism, drawer etc) 動けなくなる ugókenāku nárù

to jam something into something (cram, stuff) ...に...を押込む ...ni ...wo oshíkomù

Jamaica [dʒəmei'kə] n ジャマイカ jámàika

jangle [dʒæŋ'gəl] vi (keys, bracelets etc) じゃらじゃら鳴る járàjara narú

janitor [dʒæn'itər] n (caretaker: of building) 管理人 kafrinin

January [dʒæn'ju:we:ri:] n 1月 ichígatsu

Japan [dʒəpæn'] n 日本 nihóñ (nippóñ)

Japanese [dʒæp'əni:z'] adj 日本の nihóñ (nippóñ) no; (LING) 日本語の nihóñgo no
◆n inv (person) 日本人 nihóñ (nippóñ)jìn; (LING) 日本語 nihóñgo

jar [dʒɑ:r] n (container: glass with wide mouth) 瓶 bíñ; (: stone, earthenware) つぼ tsubó, かめ kamé
◆vi (sound) 耳ざわりである mimízawari de arù, さしる kishírù; (colors) 釣合わない tsurfawanài

jargon [dʒɑ:r'gən] n 専門用語 sefmonyōgo, 隠語 íñgo

jasmine [dʒæz'min] n ジャスミン jásùmin

jaundice [dʒɔ:n'dis] n (MED) 黄だん ódan

jaundiced [dʒɔ:n'dist] adj (to view with a jaundiced eye) 白い目で見る shírōi me de mírù

jaunt [dʒɔ:nt] n (trip, excursion) 遠足 efsoku

jaunty [dʒɔ:n'ti:] adj (attitude, tone) 陽気な yōki na; (step) 軽やかな karōyàka na

javelin [dʒæv'lin] n (SPORT) やり投げ yarfnage

jaw [dʒɔ:] n (ANAT) あご agó

jay [dʒei] n カケス kakésu

jaywalker [dʒei'wɔ:kər] n ◇交通規則を無視して道路を横断する人 kótsūkìsoku wo mushf shite dōro wo ōdan surú hitó

jazz [dʒæz] n (MUS) ジャズ jázù

jazz up vt (liven up: party) 活気付ける kakkízukèru; (: taste) ぴりっとさせる pírttō sasérù; (: image) 派手にする hadé ni surú

jazzy [dʒæz'i:] adj (shirt, pattern) 派手な hadé na

jealous [dʒel'əs] adj (suspicious: husband etc) 嫉妬深い shittóbukài; (envious: person) うらやましがっている uráyamashigàtte irù, (look etc) うらやましそうな uráyamashisòna

jealousy [dʒel'əsi:] n (resentment) ねた

み netámi; (envy) うらやむ事 uráyamù kotŏ

jeans [dʒi:nz] *npl* (trousers) ジーパン jípañ

jeep [dʒi:p] *n* (AUT, MIL) ジープ jípŭ

jeer [dʒi:r] *vi* (mock, scoff): **to jeer (at)** 野次る yajírù

jelly [dʒel'i:] *n* (CULIN) ゼリー zérí

jellyfish [dʒel'i:fiʃ] *n* クラゲ kuráge

jeopardize [dʒep'əːrdaiz] *vt* 危険にさらす kikén ni saráserù

jeopardy [dʒep'əːrdi:] *n*: **to be in jeopardy** 危険にさらされる kikén ni sarásererù

jerk [dʒəːrk] *n* (jolt, wrench) ◊ 急な動き kyŭ na ugókî; (inf: idiot) 間抜け manŭke
♦*vt* (pull) ぐいと引っ張る guî to hippárù
♦*vi* (vehicle, person, muscle) 急に動く kyŭ ni ugókù

jerkin [dʒəːr'kin] *n* チョッキ chokkî

jersey [dʒəːr'zi:] *n* (pullover) セーター sětā; (fabric) ジャージー jǎjī

jest [dʒest] *n* 冗談 jŏdañ

Jesus [dʒi:'səs] *n* イエス ĭesu

jet [dʒet] *n* (of gas, liquid) 噴射 funsha, ジェット jéttŏ; (AVIAT) ジェット機 jéttŏkî

jet-black [dʒet'blæk'] *adj* 真っ黒な makkŭro na

jet engine *n* ジェットエンジン jéttŏ eñjin

jet lag *n* 時差ぼけ jisábokè

jettison [dʒet'əsən] *vt* (fuel, cargo) 捨てる sutérù

jetty [dʒet'i:] *n* 波止場 hatóba

Jew [dʒu:] *n* ユダヤ人 yudáyajìn

jewel [dʒu:'əl] *n* (also: *fig*) 宝石 hŏseki; (in watch) 石 ishí

jeweler [dʒu:'ələr] (*BRIT* **jeweller**) *n* (dealer in jewelery) 宝石商 hŏsekishŏ; (dealer in watches) 時計屋 tokéiya

jeweler's (shop) (*BRIT* **jewellery**) *n* (jewelery shop) 宝石店 hŏsekitèn; (watch shop) 時計店 tokéitèn

jewelry [dʒu:'əlri:] (*BRIT* **jewellery**) *n* 装身具 sŏshingu

Jewess [dʒu:'is] *n* ユダヤ人女性 yudáyajin jŏsei

Jewish [dʒu:'iʃ] *adj* ユダヤ人の yudáyajin no

jibe [dʒaib] *n* 野次 yáji

jiffy [dʒif'i:] (*inf*) *n*: **in a jiffy** 直ぐ súgù

jig [dʒig] *n* (dance) ジグ jígù ◊動きの早い活発なダンス ugóki nò hayáî kappátsu na dáñsu

jigsaw [dʒig'sɔ:] *n* (also: **jigsaw puzzle**) ジグソーパズル jígùsō-pazuru

jilt [dʒilt] *vt* (lover etc) 振る furú

jingle [dʒiŋ'gəl] *n* (for advert) コマーシャルソング komásharu sóñgu
♦*vi* (bells, bracelets) ちりんちりんと鳴る chírínchirin to narú

jinx [dʒiŋks] *n* ジンクス jíñkusu

jitters [dʒit'əːrz] (*inf*) *npl*: **to get the jitters** びびる bibírù

job [dʒɑːb] *n* (chore, task) 仕事 shigôto; (post, employment) 職 shokû
it's not my job (duty, function) それは私の仕事ではない soré wa watákushi nò shigóto de wa naî
it's a good job that ... (*BRIT*) ...して良かったね ...shite yókàtta ne
just the job! (*BRIT*: *inf*) おあつらえ向きだ o-átsurae muki da, 丁度いい chŏdo dâ

job centre (*BRIT*) *n* 公共職業安定所 kŏkyŏshokugyŏ anteishò

jobless [dʒɑːb'lis] *adj* (ECON) 失業の shitsŭgyo no

jockey [dʒɑːk'i:] *n* (SPORT) 騎手 kíshu
♦*vi*: **to jockey for position** (rivals, competitors) 画策する kakúsaku suru

jocular [dʒɑːk'jələr] *adj* (person, remark) ひょうきんな hyŏkìn na

jog [dʒɑːg] *vt* (bump) 小突く kozúkù
♦*vi* (run) ジョギングする jógìngu suru
to jog someone's memory ...に...を思い起させる ...ni...wo omóî okosaserù

jog along *vi* (person, vehicle) のんびりと進む nonbíri tò susúmù

jogging [dʒɑːg'iŋ] *n* ジョギング jógìngu

join [dʒɔin] *vt* (queue) ...に加わる ...ni kawárù; (party) ...に参加する ...ni sañka suru; (club etc) ...に入会する ...ni nyúkai suru; (put together: things, places) 一緒ぐ tsunágù; (meet: group of people) 一緒

になる isshō ni narū
♦vi (roads, rivers) 合流する gōryū suru
♦n つなぎ目 tsunagíme

joiner [dʒɔɪˈnəːr] (BRIT) n 建具屋 tategúya

joinery [dʒɔɪˈnəːriː] n 建具職 tategúshokú-ku

join in vi 参加する sańka suru
♦vt fus (work, discussion etc) ...に参加する ...ni sańka suru

joint [dʒɔɪnt] n (TECH: in woodwork, pipe) 継目 tsugíme; (ANAT) 関節 kańsetsu; (of meat) ブロック肉 burőkku niku; (inf: nightclub, pub, cheap restaurant etc) 店 misé; (: of cannabis) マリフアナ パコ marifána tabakò
♦adj (common) 共通の kyőtsū no; (combined) 共同の kyődő no

joint account n (at bank etc) 共同預金口座 kyődő yokin kőza

join up vi 一緒になる isshő ni narū; (MIL) 入隊する nyűtai suru

joist [dʒɔɪst] n はり harí

joke [dʒouk] n (gag) 冗談 jődàn; (also: practical joke) いたずら itázura
♦vi 冗談を言う jődàn wo iú
to play a joke on ...をからかう ...wo karákaù

joker [dʒouˈkəːr] n (also: 冗談を言う人 jődàn wo iú hitő; (pej: person) 野郎 yárő; (cards) ジョーカー jőkà

jolly [dʒɑːˈliː] adj (merry) 陽気な yőki na; (enjoyable) 楽しい tanőshiì
♦adv (BRIT: inf) とても totémo

jolt [dʒoult] n (physical) 衝撃 shőgeki; (emotional) ショック shőkku
♦vt (physically) ...に衝撃を与える ...ni shőgeki wò ataérù; (emotionally) ショックを与える shőkku wo ataérù

Jordan [dʒɔːrˈdən] n ヨルダン yőrùdan

jostle [dʒɑːsˈəl] vt: **to be jostled by the crowd** 人込みにもまれる hitőgomi ni momárerù

jot [dʒɑːt] n: **not one jot** 少しも...ない sukőshì mo ...naì

jot down vt (telephone number etc) 書き留める kakítomerù

jotter [dʒɑːˈtəːr] (BRIT) n (notebook,

pad) ノート（ブック）nőto(bűkkù), メモ帳 memőchò

journal [dʒəːrˈnəl] n (magazine, periodical) 雑誌 zasshí; (diary) 日記 nikkí

Journalese [dʒəːrnəˈliːz] n (pej) 大衆新聞調 tafshūshinbunchō

journalism [dʒəːrˈnəlizəm] n ジャーナリズム jánarizùmu

journalist [dʒəːrˈnəlist] n ジャーナリスト jánarisùto

journey [dʒəːrˈniː] n (trip, route) 旅行 ryokō; (distance covered) 道のり michínori

jovial [dʒouˈviːəl] adj (person, air) 陽気な yőki na

joy [dʒɔɪ] n (happiness, pleasure) 喜び yorőkobi

joyful [dʒɔɪˈfəl] adj (news, event) うれしい uréshiì; (look) うれしそうな uréshisō na

joyride [dʒɔɪˈraɪd] n (AUT: US) 無謀運転のドライブ mubőuñten no dorāibù; (: BRIT) 盗難車でのドライブ tőnanshà de no dorāibù

joystick [dʒɔɪˈstik] n (AVIAT) 操縦かん sőjùkan; (COMPUT) 操縦レバー sőjù rebà, ジョイスティック jősutìkku

JP [dʒeipiː] n abbr = **Justice of the Peace**

Jr abbr = **junior**

jubilant [dʒuːˈbələnt] adj 大喜びの őyorokobi no

jubilee [dʒuːˈbəliː] n (anniversary) ...周年記念日 ...shūnen kinéñbi

judge [dʒʌdʒ] n (LAW) 裁判官 safbankan; (in competition) 審査員 shiñsa-in; (fig: expert) 通 tsū
♦vt (LAW) 裁く sabákù; (competition) 審査する shiñsa suru; (person, book etc) 評価する hyőka suru; (consider, estimate) 推定する suftei suru

judg(e)ment [dʒʌdʒˈmənt] n (LAW) 判決 hańketsu; (REL) 審判 shiñpan; (view, opinion) 意見 ikén; (discernment) 判断力 hańdañryoku

judicial [dʒuːˈdiʃəl] adj (LAW) 司法の shihő no

judiciary [dʒuːˈdiʃiːeːriː] n 司法部 shihő

bū

judicious [dʒu:ˈdɪʃəs] *adj* (action, decision) 分別のある fuñbetsu no árū

judo [dʒu:ˈdou] *n* 柔道 jūdō

jug [dʒʌɡ] *n* 水差し mizúsashi

juggernaut [dʒʌɡˈə:rnɔːt] (*BRIT*) *n* (huge truck) 大型トラック ōgata torakkū

juggle [dʒʌɡˈəl] *vi* 品玉をする shinádama wo surū ◇小さい物の玉などを投上げて受止める曲芸 fkútsu mo no tamá nadô wo nagéagetè ukétomerù kyôkùgeí

juggler [dʒʌɡˈlə:r] *n* 品玉をする曲芸師 shinádama wo surū kyokúgeíshì

Jugoslav [juːˈgouslɑːv] *etc* = **Yugoslav** *etc*

juice [dʒuːs] *n* (of fruit, plant, meat) 汁 shfrū; (beverage) ジュース jūsu

juicy [dʒuːˈsiː] *adj* (food) 汁の多い shfrū no ōi; (*inf*: story, details) エッチな étchī na

jukebox [dʒuːkˈbɑːks] *n* ジュークボックス jūkbokkusu

July [dʒəlaiˈ] *n* 7月 shíchí gatsu

jumble [dʒʌmˈbəl] *n* (muddle) ごたまぜ gotámaze ◆*vt* (*also*: **jumble up**) ごたまぜにする gotámaze ni surū

jumble sale (*BRIT*) *n* 慈善バザー jízen bazā

jumbo (jet) [dʒʌmˈbou] *n* ジャンボジェット jánbo jettòkī

jump [dʒʌmp] *vi* (into air) 飛び上る tobfagarù; (with fear, surprise) ぎくっとする gfkùtto surù; (increase: price etc) 急上昇する kyûjôshō surù; (: population etc) 急増する kyūzō surù ◆*vt* (fence) 飛び越える tobíkoerù ◆*n* (into air etc) 飛び上る事 tobíagarù kotô; (increase: in price etc) 急上昇 kyûjôshō; (: in population etc) 急増 kyūzō

to jump the queue (*BRIT*) 列に割込む rétsū ni warfkomû

jumper [dʒʌmˈpə:r] *n* (*BRIT*: pullover) セーター sétā; (*US*: dress) ジャンパースカート jañpàsukáto

jumper cables *npl* (*US*) ブースターケーブル būsutákèburu ◇外のバッテリーから

電気を得るために用いるコード hoká nò bátterī kara dênkī wo êrū tamé ni mochfírì kôdô

jump leads (*BRIT*) [-liːdz] *npl* = **jumper cables**

jumpy [dʒʌmˈpiː] *adj* (nervous) びくびくしている bfkūbiku shité frū

Jun. *abbr* = **junior**

junction [dʒʌŋkˈʃən] *n* (*BRIT*: of roads) 交差点 kôsaten; (*RAIL*) 連絡駅 refrakuèki

juncture [dʒʌŋkˈtʃə:r] *n*: *at this juncture* この時 konô tokî

June [dʒuːn] *n* 6月 rokúgatsu

jungle [dʒʌŋˈɡəl] *n* ジャングル jáñguru; (fig) 弱肉強食の世界 jakúniku kyōshoku nò sékáì

junior [dʒuːˈnjə:r] *adj* (younger) 年下の toshfshita no; (subordinate) 下位の kâI no; (*SPORT*) ジュニアの jûnia no ◆*n* (also: **junior person**) 後輩 kôhai; (young person) 若者 wakámono

he's my junior by 2 years 彼は私より2才年下です kârè wa watákushi yorî nísaì toshfshita desu

junior school (*BRIT*) *n* 小学校 shôgakkō

junk [dʒʌŋk] *n* (rubbish, cheap goods) がらくた gárakuta; (ship) ジャンク jáñku

junk food *n* ジャンクフード jáñku fūdo ◇ポテトチップス、ファーストフードなど高カロリーが低栄養のスナック食品 potétochippùsu, fásuto fùdo nádô kôkárorí da ga teíeíyō no sunákku shokôhin

junkie [dʒʌŋˈkiː] (*inf*) *n* ヘロイン中毒者 herôin chūdokushà

junk shop *n* 古物商 kobútsushō

Junr. *abbr* = **junior**

jurisdiction [dʒuːrisdikˈʃən] *n* (*LAW*) 司法権 shihôkèn; (*ADMIN*) 支配権 shíhaìkèn

juror [dʒuːˈrə:r] *n* (person on jury) 陪審員 baíshin-in

jury [dʒuːˈriː] *n* (group of jurors) 陪審員 baíshin-in

just [dʒʌst] *adj* (fair: decision) 公正な kôsei na; (: punishment) 適切な tekísetsu na

◆*adv* (exactly) 丁度 chōdo; (only) ただ tádà; (barely) ようやく yốyaku

he's just done it ついさっきそれをやったばかりだ tsuí sakkí sore wo yatta bákàri da

he's just left ついさっき出た(帰った)ばかりだ tsuí sakkí détà (káettà) bákàri da

just right 丁度いい chōdo íì

just two o'clock 丁度2時 chōdo níji

she's just as clever as you 彼女はあなたに負けないくらい頭がいい kánòjo wa anátà ni makénaì gurái atáma ga íi

just as well that ....して良かった ...shíte yókàtta

just as he was leaving 丁度出掛けるところを chōdo dekákerù tokórò ni

just before 丁度前に chōdo máè ni

just enough 辛うじて間に合って kárôjite ma ni áttè

just here ぴったりここに pittárì kokó ni

he just missed わずかの差で外れた wázùka no sá de házùreta

just listen ちょっと聞いて chottó kiite

justice [dʒʌs'tis] *n* (LAW: system) 司法 shíhō; (rightness of cause, complaint) 正当さ seítōsa; (fairness) 公正 さ kōseisa; (US: judge) 裁判官 saíbankan

to do justice to (fig: task) ...をやりこなす ...wo yaríkonasù; (: meal) ...を平らげ る ...wo tairagerù; (: person) ...を正当に 扱う ...wo séítō ni atsúkaù

Justice of the Peace *n* 治安判事 chíàn hañji

justifiable [dʒʌs'tifaiabəl] *adj* (claim, statement etc) もっともな móttòmo na

justification [dʒʌstəfəkei'ʃən] *n* (reason) 正当とする理由 seítō to suru ríyū

justify [dʒʌs'təfai] *vt* (action, decision) 正当である事を証明する seítō de arù kotó wo shōmeí suru; (text) 行の端をそろえる gyō no hágàsa wo soróerù

justly [dʒʌst'liː] *adv* (with reason) 正当に seítō ni; (deservedly) 当然 tōzen

jut [dʒʌt] *vi* (*also*: **jut out**: protrude) 突出る tsukíderù

juvenile [dʒuː'vənəl] *adj* (court) 未成年の

misélnen no; (books) 少年少女向きの shónen shòjo mukí no; (humor, mentálity) 子供っぽい kodómoppoì

◆*n* (LAW, ADMIN) 未成年者 miséineñsha

juxtapose [dʒʌkstəpouz'] *vt* (things, ideas) 並べておく narábete okù

K

K [kei] *abbr* (= *one thousand*) 1000 séñ
= **kilobyte**

kaleidoscope [kalai'dəskoup] *n* 万華鏡 mañgekyō

Kampuchea [kæmpuːtʃiˈə] *n* カンプチア káñpuchia

kangaroo [kæŋgəruː'] *n* カンガルー kañgarū

karate [kərɑː'tiː] *n* 空手 karáte

kebab [kəbɑːb'] *n* くし刺しの焼肉 kushísashi nò yakíniku, シシカバブ shishíkababu

keel [kiːl] *n* 竜骨 ryū́kotsu

on an even keel (*fig*) 安定して añtei shite

keen [kiːn] *adj* (eager) やりたがっている yarítagattè írù; (intense: interest, desire) 熱心な nesshíñ na; (acute: eye, intelligence) 鋭い suródoì; (fierce: competition) 激しい hagéshiì; (sharp: edge) 鋭い suródoì

to be keen to do/on doing something (eager, anxious) ...をやりたがっている ...wo yarítagattè írù

to be keen on something/someone ...に熱を上げている ...ni netsú wò agéte irù

keep [kiːp] (*pt, pp* **kept**) *vt* (retain: receipt etc) 保管する hokáñ suru; (: money etc) 自分の物にする jíbùn no monó ni surù; (: job etc) なくさない様にする nakúsanai yō ni suru, 守る mamórù; (preserve, store) 貯える chozáerù; (maintain: house, garden etc) 管理する kañri suru; (detain) 引留めおる híkítomerù; (run: shop etc) 経営する keíei suru; (chickens, bees etc) 飼育する shíiku suru; (accounts, diary etc) ...を付ける ...wo tsukérù; (support: family etc) 養う yashínaù; (fulfill: promise) 守る mamórù; (prevent): **to keep someone from doing something** ...が...をできない様に阻止する ...ga ...wo dekínaì yō ni soshí surù

♦*vi* (remain: in a certain state) ...でいる (ある) ...de irú (árù); (: in a certain place) ずっと...にいる zuttó ...ni irú; (last: food) 保存がきく hozón ga kikú

♦*n* (cost of food etc) 生活費 sefkatsuhì; (of castle) 本丸 hofmaru

to keep doing something ...をし続ける ...wo shitsúzukerù

to keep someone happy ...の期限をとる ...no kígén wo torú

to keep a place tidy ある場所をきちんとさせておく árù bashó wo kichín to sasête okú

to keep something to oneself ...について黙っている ...ni tsuíte damátte irú

to keep something (back) from someone ...の事を...に隠す ...no kotó wo ...ni kakúsú

to keep time (clock) 時間を正確に計る jfkan wo séikaku ni hakárù

for keeps (*inf*) 永久に efkyú ni

keeper [ki:'pəər] *n* (in zoo, park) 飼育係 shi-fkugakàri, キーパー kípà

keep-fit [ki:p'fit'] *n* (*BRIT*) 健康体操 kefkótàisò

keeping [ki:'piŋ] *n* (care) 保管 hokán
in keeping with ...に合って...ni áttè, ...に従って ...ni shitagatte

keep on *vi* (continue): **to keep on doing** ...し続ける ...shitsúzukerù
to keep on (about something) (...を話題に) うるさくしゃべる ...wo wadái ni) urúsakù shabérù

keep out *vt* (intruder etc) 締め出す shimé-dasù
「**keep out**」立入禁止 tachíiri kinshi

keepsake [ki:p'seik] *n* 形見 katámi

keep up *vt* (maintain: payments etc) 続ける tsuzúkerù; (: standards etc) 保持する hojí suru

♦*vi*: **to keep up (with)** (match: pace)

(...) 速度を合せる (...to) sókùdo wo a-wáserù; (: level) (...に) 遅れない様にする (...ni) okúrenaì yō ni suru

keg [keg] *n* たる tarú

kennel [ken'əl] *n* イヌ小屋 inúgoya

kennels [ken'əlz] *npl* (establishment) イヌ屋 inúya

Kenya [ken'jə] *n* ケニア kénìa

Kenyan [ken'jən] *adj* ケニアの kénìa no
♦*n* ケニア人 kénìajìn

kept [kept] *pt, pp* of **keep**

kerb [kə:rb] (*BRIT*) *n* = **curb**

kernel [kə:r'nəl] *n* (BOT: of nut) 実 mi; (*fig*: of idea) 核 kákù

kerosene [ker'əsin] *n* 灯油 tóyu

ketchup [ket'ʃəp] *n* ケチャップ kecháppù

kettle [ket'əl] *n* やかん yákàn

kettle drum *n* ティンパニ tífhpanì

key [ki:] *n* (for lock etc) かぎ kagí; (MUS: scale) 調 chó; (of piano, computer, typewriter) キー kí
♦*adj* (issue etc) 重要な júyō na
♦*vt* (*also*: **key in**: into computer etc) 入力する nyúryoku suru

keyboard [ki:'bɔ:rd] *n* (of computer, typewriter) キーボード kíbòdo; (of piano) 鍵盤 kefban, キーボード kíbòdo

keyed up [ki:d-] *adj* (person) 興奮している kófun shité irù

keyhole [ki:'houl] *n* 鍵穴 kagíana

keynote [ki:'nout] *n* (MUS) 主音 shúòn; (of speech) 基調 kichó

key ring *n* キーホルダー kíhòrùdā

kg *abbr* = **kilogram**

khaki [kæk'i:] *n* (color) カーキ色 káki iro; (also: **khaki cloth**) カーキ色服地 kákì iro fukújì

kibbutz [kibuts'] *n* キブツ kíbùtsu ◊イスラエルの農業共同体 fsúraeru no nōgyō kyódōtai

kick [kik] *vt* (person, table, ball) ける kérù; (*inf*: habit, addiction) やめる yaméru
♦*vi* ける kérù
♦*n* (from person, animal) けり kéri; (to ball) キック kíkkù; (thrill): **he does it for kicks** 彼はそんな事をやるのはスリ

ルのために kárě wa sofina kotó wo yárû no wa surfrú no tamé dà

kick off vi (FOOTBALL, SOCCER) 試合を開始する shiái wò kaíshi suru

kick-off [kik'ɔːf] n (FOOTBALL, SOCCER) 試合開始 shiái kaíshi, キックオフ kĺkkûofu

kid [kid] n (inf: child) がき gakí, じゃり jarí; (animal) 子 ヤギ koyágí; (also: **kid leather**) キッド革 kíddôgawa

♦vi (inf) 冗談を言う jôdàn wo iû

kidnap [kid'næp] vt 誘拐する yûkai suru

kidnapper [kid'næpər] n 誘拐犯人 yûkai haínnin

kidnapping [kid'næpiŋ] n 誘拐事件 yûkai jíken

kidney [kid'niː] n (ANAT) じん臓 jínzô; (CULIN) キドニー kídônî

kill [kil] vt (person, animal) 殺す korósù; (plant) 枯らす karásů; (murder) 殺す korosu, 殺害する satsúgai suru

♦n 殺し koróshi

to kill time 時間をつぶす jíkàn wo tsubúsů

killer [kil'əːr] n 殺し屋 koróshiya

killing [kil'iŋ] n (action) 殺す事 korósù kotô; (instance) 殺人事件 satsúji jíken

to make a killing (inf) 大もうけする ômôke-suru

killjoy [kil'dʒɔi] n 白けさせる人 shiráke-saserů hitó

kiln [kiln] n 窯 kamá

kilo [kiː'lou] n キロ kíro

kilobyte [kil'əbait] n (COMPUT) キロバイト kírôbaìto

kilogram(me) [kil'əgræm] n キログラム kírôgurầmu

kilometer [kil'əmiːtər] (BRIT **kilometre**) n キロメーター kírômêtà

kilowatt [kil'əwɑt] n キロワット kírôwattó

kilt [kilt] n キルト kírùto

kimono [kimou'nou] n 着物 kimôno, 和服 wafúku

kin [kin] n see **kith**; **next-of-kin**

kind [kaind] adj 親切な shìnsetsu na

♦n (type, sort) 種類 shúruì; (species) 種類 shù

to pay in kind 現物で支払う geñbutsu de shiháraů

a kind of ...の一種 ...no ísshû

to be two of a kind 似たり寄ったり nitári yottárí suru, 似た者同志である nitá mono dôshi de árů

kindergarten [kin'dərgɑrtən] n 幼稚園 yôchìen

kind-hearted [kaind'hɑːr'tid] adj 心の優しい kokórô no yasáshiì

kindle [kin'dəl] vt (light: fire) たく takû, つける tsukerů; (arouse: emotion) 起す okósů, そそる sosórû

kindly [kaind'liː] adj 親切な shìnsetsu na

♦adv (smile) 優しく yasáshiku; (behave) 親切に shìnsetsu ni

will you kindly ... ...して下さいませんか ...shĺtê kudásaìmasen kâ

kindness [kaind'nis] n (personal quality) 親切 shìnsetsu; (helpful act) 親切な行為 shìnsetsu na kôì

kindred [kin'drid] adj: **kindred spirit** 自分と気の合った人 jĭbùn to kí no attá hitó

kinetic [kinet'ik] adj 動的な dôteki na

king [kiŋ] n (monarch) 国王 kokúô; (CARDS, CHESS) キング kíñgu

kingdom [kiŋ'dəm] n 王国 ôkoku

kingfisher [kiŋ'fiʃər] n カワセミ kawásemi

king-size [kiŋ'saiz] adj 特大の tokúdai no

kinky [kiŋ'kiː] (pej) adj (person, behavior) へんてこな heñteko na, 妙な myô na; (sexually) 変態気味の heñtaigimi no

kiosk [kiːɑsk'] n (shop) キオスク kíôsùku; (BRIT: TEL) 電話ボックス deñwa bokkûsu

kipper [kip'əːr] n 薫製ニシン kuñsei níshìn

kiss [kis] n キス kísů

♦vt ...にキスする ...ni kísû suru

to kiss (each other) キスする kísů suru

kiss of life n 口移しの人工呼吸 kuchí-utsushi no jinkôkokyů

kit [kit] n (clothes: sports kit etc) 運動服一式 uñdôfùku isshíki; (equipment, set of tools: also MIL) 道具一式 dôgu isshíki; (for assembly) キット kíttò

kitchen [kitʃən] *n* 台所 daídokoro, キッチン kítchin

kitchen sink *n* 台所の流し daídokoro no nagáshi

kite [kait] *n* (toy) たこ takó

kith [kiθ] *n*: **kith and kin** 親せき知人 shínsekichijin

kitten [kit'ən] *n* 子ネコ konékò

kitty [kit'i:] *n* (pool of money) お金の蓄え o-kàne no takúwae; (CARDS) 総掛金 sōkakekìn

kleptomaniac [kleptəmei'niæk] *n* 盗癖のある人 tōheki no árù hitó

km *abbr* = **kilometer**

knack [næk] *n*: **to have the knack of doing something** …をするのが上手である …wo suru nō ga jōzu de arù

knapsack [næp'sæk] *n* ナップサック nappúsakkù

knead [ni:d] *vt* (dough, clay) 練る nérù

knee [ni:] *n* ひざ hizá

kneecap [ni:'kæp] *n* ひざ頭 hizágashira, ひざ小僧 hizágōzō

kneel [ni:l] (*pt, pp* **knelt**) *vi* (also: **kneel down**) ひざまずく hizámazukù

knelt [nelt] *pt, pp* of **kneel**

knew [nu:] *pt* of **know**

knickers [nik'ə:rz] (BRIT) *npl* パンティー pántī

knife [naif] (*pl* **knives**) *n* ナイフ náīfu

♦*vt* ナイフで刺す náīfu de sásù

knight [nait] *n* (HISTORY) 騎士 kishí; (BRIT) ナイト náīto; (CHESS) ナイト náīto

knighthood [nait'hud] (BRIT) *n* (title): **to get a knighthood** ナイト爵位を与えられる nàīto shakúi wo atáerarerù

knit [nit] *vt* (garment) 編む ámù

♦*vi* (with wool) 編物をする amímono wo suru; (broken bones) 治る naórù

to knit one's brows まゆをひそめる máyū wo hisómerù

knitting [nit'iŋ] *n* 編物 amímono

knitting machine *n* 編機 amíkì

knitting needle *n* 編棒 amíbō

knitwear [nit'we:r] *n* ニット・ウェアー nittó ueà

knives [naivz] *npl of* **knife**

knob [nɑːb] *n* (handle: of door) 取っ手 tottě, つまみ tsumámi; (: of stick) 握り nigíri; (on radio, TV etc) つまみ tsumámi

knock [nɑːk] *vt* (strike) たたく tatákù; (*inf*: criticize) 批判する hihán suru

♦*vi* (at door etc): **to knock at/on** …にノックする …ni nókku surù

♦*n* (blow, bump) 打撃 dagéki; (on door) ノック nókkù

knock down *vt* (subj: person) 殴り倒す nagúritaosù; (: car) ひき倒す hikítaosù

knock-kneed [nɑːk'ni:d] *adj* X脚の ekúsukyaku no

knock off *vi* (*inf*: finish) やめる yamérù, 終りにする owári ni surù

♦*vt* (from price) 値引する nebíki suru; (*inf*: steal) くすねる kusúnerù

knock out *vt* (subj: drug etc) 気絶させる kizétsu saserù, 眠らせる nemúraserù; (BOXING etc, also fig) ノックアウトする nokkúaùto suru; (defeat: in game, competition) …に勝つ …ni kátsù, 敗退させる haítai saserù

knockout [nɑːk'aut] *n* (BOXING) ノックアウト nokkúaùto

♦*cpd* (competition etc) 決定的な kettéiteki na

knock over *vt* (person, object) 倒す taósù

knot [nɑːt] *n* (in rope) 結び目 musúbime; (in wood) 節目 fushíme; (NAUT) ノット nóttò

♦*vt* 結ぶ musúbù

knotty [nɑːt'i:] *adj* (*fig*: problem) 厄介な yakkái na

know [nou] (*pt* **knew**, *pp* **known**) *vt* (facts, dates etc) 知っている shitté irù; (language etc) できる dekírù; (be acquainted with: person, place, subject) 知っている shitté irù; (recognize: by sight) 見て分かる mítè wakárù; (: by sound) 聞いて分かる kiíte wakárù

to know how to swim 泳げる oyógerù

to know about/of something/some-

one ...の事を知っている ...no kotó wò shitté irú

know-all [nou'ɔːl] *n* 知ったか振りの人 shittákaburi no hitó

know-how [nou'hau] *n* 技術知識 gijutsuchíshìki, ノウハウ nóūhàu

knowing [nou'iŋ] *adj* (look: of complicity) 意味ありげな imí arìge na

knowingly [nou'iŋli] *adv* (purposely) 故意に kóì ni; (smile, look) 意味ありげに imí arìge ni

knowledge [nɑːl'idʒ] *n* (understanding, awareness) 認識 nínshìki; (learning, things learnt) 知識 chíshìki

knowledgeable [nɑːl'idʒəbəl] *adj* 知識のある chíshìki no árù

known [noun] *pp* of **know**

knuckle [nʌk'əl] *n* 指関節 yubí kañsetsu ◇特に指の付根の関節を指す tókù ni yubí no tsukéne no kañsetsu wò sásù

KO [kei'ou'] *n abbr* = **knockout**

Koran [kəːrɑːn'] *n* コーラン kórān

Korea [kəːri'ə] *n* 韓国 káñkoku, 朝鮮 chósèn

Korean [kəːri'ən] *adj* 韓国の káñkoku no, 朝鮮の chósèn no; (LING) 韓国語の kañkokugo no, 朝鮮語の chósèngo no
◇*n* (person) 韓国人 kañkokujñ, 朝鮮人 chósènjñ; (LING) 韓国語 kañkokugo, 朝鮮語 chósèngo

kosher [kou'ʃəːr] *adj* 適法の tekíhō no ◇ユダヤ教の戒律に合った食物についてて言う yudáyakyō no kaíritsu ni attá shokúmotsu nádð ni tsúite iú

L

L (*BRIT*) *abbr* = **learner driver**

l. *abbr* = **liter**

lab [læb] *n abbr* = **laboratory**

label [lei'bəl] *n* (on suitcase, merchandise etc) ラベル ráberu
◇*vt* (thing) ...にラベルを付ける ...ni ráberu wo tsukérù

labor [lei'bəːr] (*BRIT* **labour**) *n* (hard work) 労働 rṓdō; (work force) 労働者 rṓdṓshà ◇総称 sōshṓ; (work done by work

force) 労働 rṓdō; (MED): **to be in labor** 陣痛が始まっている jíñtsū ga hajímatte irú
◇*vi*: **to labor (at something)** (...に) ...ni kushíñ surù
◇*vt*: **to labor a point** ある事を余計に強調する árù kotó wò yokéi ni kyóchō suru

laboratory [læb'rətɔːri] *n* (scientific: building, institution) 研究所 kéñkyūjo; (: room) 実験室 jikkéñshitsu; (school) 理科教室 rikákyōshitsu

labored [lei'bəːrd] *adj* (breathing: one's own) 苦しい kurúshiì; (: someone else's) 苦しそうな kurúshisṓ na

laborer [lei'bəːrər] *n* (industrial) 労働者 rṓdṓshà

   farm laborer 農場労務者 nṓjōrōmushà

laborious [ləbɔːr'iːəs] *adj* 骨の折れる honé no orérù

labour [lei'bəːr] *etc n* = **labor** *etc*
   Labour, the Labour Party (*BRIT*) 労働党 rṓdōtṓ

labyrinth [læb'ərinθ] *n* 迷路 méìro

lace [leis] *n* (fabric) レース rḗsu; (of shoe etc) ひも himó
◇*vt* (shoe etc: also: **lace up**) ...のひもを結ぶ ...no himó wo musúbù

lack [læk] *n* (absence) 欠如 kétsùjo
◇*vt* (money, confidence) ...が無い ...ga náì; (intelligence etc) 欠いている kaíte irú
   through/for lack of ...が無いために ...ga náì tamé ni
   to be lacking ...がない ...ga náì
   to be lacking in (intelligence, generosity etc) ...を欠いている ...wo kaíte irú

lackadaisical [lækədei'zikəl] *adj* (lacking interest, enthusiasm) 気乗りしない kinóri shinaì

laconic [ləkɑn'ik] *adj* 言葉数の少ない kotóbakazð no sukúnaì

lacquer [læk'əːr] *n* (paint) ラッカー rákkā; (*also:* **hair lacquer**) ヘアスプレー héasupurè

lad [læd] *n* (boy) 少年 shṓnen; (young man) 若者 wakámonò

ladder [læd'əːr] *n* (metal, wood, rope) は

しご子 hashígo; (BRIT: in tights) 伝線 defísen

laden [lei'dən] adj: **laden (with)** (ship, truck etc) (...を) たっぷり積んだ (...wo) tappúrí tsuńda; (person) (...を) 沢山抱えている (...wo) takúsaů kakáete iru

laden with fruit (tree) 実をたわわに付けている mi wo tawáwa ni tsukéte irú

ladle [lei'dəl] n 玉じゃくし tamájakùshi

lady [lei'di:] n (woman) 女性 joséi; (: dignified, graceful etc) 淑女 shukújò, レディー rédi; (in address): **ladies and gentlemen** ... 紳士淑女の皆様 shiñshishukujò no mínásāma

young lady 若い女性 wakái joséi

the ladies' (room) 女性用トイレ joséiyōtoire

ladybird [lei'di:bə:rd] n テントウムシ teñtomushi

ladybug [lei'di:bʌg] (US) n = **ladybird**

ladylike [lei'di:laik] adj (behavior) レディーらしい rédiìrashii

ladyship [lei'di:ʃip] n: **your ladyship** 奥様 ōkūsama

lag [læg] n (period of time) 遅れ okúre
♦vi (also: **lag behind**: person, thing) ...に遅れる ...ni okúrerù; (: trade, investment etc) ...の勢いが衰える ...no ikfoi ga otóroerù
♦vt (pipes etc) ...に断熱材を巻く ...ni dańnetsuzài wo makú

lager [lɑ:'gə:r] n ラガービール ragábirù

lagoon [ləgu:n'] n 潟 katá, ラグーン rágùn

laid [leid] pt, pp of **lay³**

laid back (inf) adj のんびりした noñbirishitá

laid up adj: **to be laid up (with)** (...で) 寝込んでいる (...de) nekónde irú

lain [lein] pp of **lie**

lair [le:r] n (ZOOL) 巣穴 suána

lake [leik] n 湖 mízùmi

lamb [læm] n (animal) 子ヒツジ kohítsuji; (meat) ラム肉 ramúniku

lamb chop n ラムチャップ ramúchappù, ラムチョップ ramúchoppù

lambswool [læmz'wul] n ラムウール ramúwūru

lame [leim] adj (person, animal) びっこの bíkko no; (excuse, argument, answer) 下手な hetá na

lament [ləment'] n 嘆き nagéki
♦vt 嘆く nagékù

laminated [læm'əneitid] adj (metal, wood, glass) 合板の gôhan no; (covering, surface) プラスチック張りの purásuchikkubari no

lamp [læmp] n (electric, gas, oil) 明かり akári, ランプ ráňpu

lamppost [læmp'poust] n 街灯 gaítò

lampshade [læmp'ʃeid] n ランプの傘 ráňpu no kasá, シェード shêdo

lance [læns] n やり yarí
♦vt (MED) 切開する sekkái suru

land [lænd] n (area of open ground) 土地 tochí; (property, estate) 土地 tochí, 所有地 shoyűchì; (as opposed to sea) 陸地 rikú; (country, nation) 国 kuní
♦vi (from ship) 上陸する jóriku suru; (AVIAT) 着陸する chakűriku su; (fig: fall) 落ちる ochírò
♦vt (passengers, goods) 降ろす orósù

to land someone with something (inf) ...に...を押付ける ...ni ...wo oshítsukerù

landing [læn'diŋ] n (of house) 踊り場 odóriba; (AVIAT) 着陸 chakűriku

landing gear n (AVIAT) 着陸装置 chakűrikusóchi

landing strip n 滑走路 kassôrò

landlady [lænd'leidi:] n (of rented house, flat, room) 女大家 ofinašhya; (of pub) 女主人 ofinashujìn, おかみ ókami

landlocked [lænd'lɑkt] adj 陸地に囲まれた rikúchi ni kakómareta

landlord [lænd'lɔ:rd] n (of rented house, flat, room) 大家 ōya; (of pub) 主人 shujìn

landmark [lænd'mɑ:rk] n (building, hill etc) 目標 mokűhyo; (fig) 歴史的な事件 rekíshiteki na jíkèn

landowner [lænd'ounə:r] n 地主 jinúshi

landscape [lænd'skeip] n (view over land, buildings etc) 景色 késhìki; (ART) 風景画 fúkeiga

landscape gardener n 造園家 zóenka

landslide [lænd'slaid] n (GEO) 地滑り jisūberi; (fig: electoral) 圧勝 asshō.

land up vt: **to land up in/at** 結局…に
行くはめになる kekkyóku ...ni ikú hame
ni narú

lane [leɪn] n (in country) 小道 komíchi;
(AUT: of carriageway) 車線 shasén; (of
race course, swimming pool) コース kō-
su

language [ˈlæŋɡwɪdʒ] n (national
tongue) 国語 kokúgo; (ability to communicate verbally) 言語 géngo; (specialized
terminology) 用語 yōgo; (style: of written piece, speech etc) 言葉遣道 kotóbazu-
kài; (SCOL) 語学 gógaku

bad language 下品な言葉 gehín na kotóba

he is studying languages 彼は外国語
を勉強している kare wa gaíkokugo wo
benkyō shite iru

language laboratory n ランゲージラ
ボラトリー rañgéjiraboratòrì, エルエル
érùeru

languid [ˈlæŋɡwɪd] adj (person, movement) 元気のない géñki no nâî

languish [ˈlæŋɡwɪʃ] vi 惨めに生きる mí-
jìme ni ikírù

lank [læŋk] adj (hair) 長くて手入れしな
い nagákutè tefre shinai

lanky [ˈlæŋˈkiː] adj ひょろっとした hyo-
rottő shita

lantern [ˈlæntərn] n カンテラ kañtera

lap [læp] n (of person) ひざの上 hizá no
ué; (in race) 1周 fsshū, ラップ ráppù
♦vt (also: **lap up**: drink) ぴちゃぴちゃ飲
む pichápìcha nómu
♦vi (water) ひたひたと打寄せる hitáhìta
to uchíyoserù

lapel [ləˈpel] n 折えり oríeri, ラペル rápe-
ru

Lapland [ˈlæpˈlænd] n ラップランド ráp-
pùrando

lapse [læps] n (bad behavior) 過失 kashí-
tsu; (of memory) 喪失 sōshìtsu; (of time)
経過 keíka
♦vi (law) 無効になる mukó ni narù; (contract, membership, passport) 切れる kirérù

a lapse of concentration 不注意 fu-

chū́i

to lapse into bad habits (of behavior)
堕落する darákù suru

lap up vt (fig: flattery etc) 真に受ける
ma ni ukérù

larceny [ˈlɑːrsəni] n (LAW) 窃盗罪 set-
tōzai

larch [lɑːrtʃ] n (tree) カラマツ karáma-
tsu

lard [lɑːrd] n ラード rādo

larder [ˈlɑːrdəːr] n 食料貯蔵室 shokúryō-
chozōshitsu

large [lɑːrdʒ] adj (big: house, person,
amount) 大きい ōkii

at large (as a whole) 一般に ippán ni;
(at liberty) 捕まらないで tsukámaranaì-
de ¶ *see also* by

largely [ˈlɑːrdʒli] adv (mostly) 大体 daítai; (mainly: introducing reason) 主に ó-
mò ni

large-scale [ˈlɑːrdʒˈskeil] adj (action,
event) 大規模の dafkibò no; (map, diagram) 大縮尺の dafshukushaku no

largess(e) [lɑːrˈdʒes] n (generosity) 気前良
さ kímáeyosà; (money etc) 贈り物 okúrimonò

lark [lɑːrk] n (bird) ヒバリ hibari; (joke)
冗談 jódañ

lark about vi ふざけ回る fuzákemawa-
ru

larva [ˈlɑːrvə] (pl **larvae**) n 幼虫 yóchū

larvae [ˈlɑːrviː] npl of **larva**

laryngitis [lærəndʒaiˈtis] n こうとう炎
kōtōen

larynx [ˈlærɪŋks] n (ANAT) こうとう
kōtō

lascivious [ləˈsɪviːəs] adj (person, conduct) みだらな mídàra na

laser [ˈleizəːr] n レーザー rèzà

laser printer n レーザープリンター rè-
zäpurintã

lash [læʃ] n (eyelash) まつげ mátsùge;
(blow of whip) むち打ち muchfuchi
♦vt (whip) むち打つ muchfutsù; (subj:
rain) 激しくたたく hageshikù tatákù;
(; wind) 激しく揺さぶる hageshikù yusáburù; (tie): **to lash to** rope 縛りつける …を…に
結ぶ …wo …ni(…に結ぶ)に しばり付ける …wo …ni isshō ni

shibáru

lash out *vi*: **to lash out (at someone)** (hit) (...に) 打ち掛ける (...ni) uchíkakarù
to lash out against someone (criticize) ...を激しく非難する ...wo hagéshikù hínàn suru

lass [læs] *n* (girl) 少女 shōjo; (young woman) 若い女性 wakái josèi

lasso [læs'ou] *n* 投縄 nagénawa

last [læst] *adj* (latest: period of time, event, thing) 前の máè no; (final: bus, hope etc) 最後の sáigo no; (end: of series, row) 一番後の ichíban atò no; (remaining: traces, scraps etc) 残りの nokóri no
♦*adv* (most recently) 最近 saíkin; (finally) 最後に sáigo ni
♦*vi* (continue) 続く tsuzúkù; (: in good condition) もつ mótsù; (money, commodity) ...に足りる ...ni tarírù
last week 先週 senshū
last night 昨晩 sakúbàn, 昨夜 sakúyà
at last (finally) とうとう tōtō
last but one 後ろから2番目 sáigo kara nibánme

last-ditch [læst'ditʃ'] *adj* (attempt) 絶体絶命の zettáizetsumei no

lasting [læs'tiŋ] *adj* (friendship, solution) 永続的な efzokuteki na

lastly [læst'li:] *adv* 最後に sáigo ni

last-minute [læst'min'it] *adj* (decision, appeal etc) 土壇場の dotánbà no

latch [lætʃ] *n* (on door, gate) 掛け金 kakégàne, ラッチ rátchi

late [leit] *adj* (far on time, process, work etc) 遅い osóì; (not on time) 遅れた okúreta; (former) 前の máè no, 前...
♦*adv* (far on time, process, work etc) 遅く osóku; (behind time, schedule) 遅れて okúrete
of late (recently) 最近 saíkin
in late May 5月の終り頃 gógàtsu no owári gorò
the late Mr X (deceased) 故Xさん ko ékùsu san

latecomer [leit'kʌmər] *n* 遅れて来る人 okúrete kurù hitó

lately [leit'li:] *adv* 最近 saíkin

latent [leit'ənt] *adj* (energy, skill, abil-

ity) 表に出ない omóte nì dénài

later [lei'tər] *adj* (time, date, meeting etc) もっと後の móttò áto no; (version etc) もっと新しい móttò atárashiì
♦*adv* 後で áto de
later on 後で áto de

lateral [læt'ərəl] *adj* (position) 横の yokó no; (direction) 横への yokó e no

latest [lei'tist] *adj* (train, flight etc) 最後 の sáigo no; (novel, news etc) 最新の saíshin no
at the latest 遅くとも osókùtomo

lathe [leið] *n* (for wood, metal) 旋盤 señban

lather [læð'ər] *n* 石けんの泡 sekkén nò awá
♦*vt* ...に石けんの泡を塗る ...ni sekkén nò awá wò nurú

Latin [læt'in] *n* (LING) ラテン語 ratén-go
♦*adj* ラテン語の raténgo no

Latin America *n* ラテンアメリカ ratén-amèrika

Latin American *adj* ラテンアメリカの ratén-amèrika no
♦*n* ラテンアメリカ人 ratén-amèrikajin

latitude [læt'ətu:d] *n* (GEO) 緯度 ídò; (fig: freedom) 余裕 yoyū

latrine [lætri:n'] *n* 便所 benjo

latter [læt'ər] *adj* (of two) 後者の kôsha no; (recent) 最近の saíkin no; (later) 後の方の áto no hō no
♦*n*: *the latter* (of two people, things, groups) 後者 kôsha

latterly [læt'ərli:] *adv* 最近 saíkin

lattice [læt'is] *n* (pattern, structure) 格子 kōshi

laudable [lɔ:'dəbəl] *adj* (conduct, motives etc) 感心な kañshin na

laugh [læf] *n* 笑い waráì
♦*vi* 笑う waráù
(to do something) for a laugh 冗談として (...をする) jōdañ toshité (...wo suru)

laugh at *vt fus* ...をばかにする ...wo bakà ni surù

laughable [læf'əbəl] *adj* (attempt, quality etc) ばかげた bakágeta

laughing stock [læf'iŋ] *n*: *to be the laughing stock of* ...の笑い者になる ...no waráimono ni narú

laugh off *vt* (criticism, problem) 無視する mushí suru

laughter [læf'tər] *n* 笑い声 waráigoe

launch [lɔːntʃ] *n* (of rocket, missile) 発射 hasshá; (of satellite) 打上げ uchíage; (COMM) 新発売 shínhatsubai; (motorboat) ランチ ránchi

♦*vt* (ship) 進水させる shiñsui saséru; (rocket, missile) 発射する hasshá suru; (satellite) 打上げる uchíageru; (fig: start) 開始する kaíshi suru; (COMM) 発売する hatsúbai suru

launch into *vt fus* (speech, activity) 始める hajímeru

launch(ing) pad [lɔːntʃ(iŋ)-] *n* (for missile, rocket) 発射台 hasshádai

launder [lɔːn'dər] *vt* (clothes) 洗濯する señtaku suru

launderette [lɔːndəret'] *n* コインランドリー kofnrañdorī

Laundromat [lɔːn'drəmæt] ® (US) *n* コインランドリー kofnrañdorī

laundry [lɔːn'driː] *n* (dirty, clean) 洗濯物 señtakumono; (business) 洗濯屋 señtakuya やドライクリーニングはしない dorái kurīningu wa shinái; (room) 洗濯場 señtakuba

laureate [lɔː'riːit] *adj see* poet laureate

laurel [lɔː'rəl] *n* 月桂樹 gékkeiju; ゲッケイジュ gekkéiju

lava [lɑː'və] *n* 溶岩 yōgan

lavatory [læv'ətɔːri] *n* お手洗い otéarai

lavender [læv'əndər] *n* (BOT) ラベンダー rabéndā

lavish [læv'iʃ] *adj* (amount) たっぷりの tappúri no; (party) 豪華な gōka na; (person): *lavish with* ...を気前良く与える ...wo kimáeyokù atáerù

♦*vt*: *to lavish something on someone* ...に...を気前よく与える ...ni ...wo kimáeyokù atáerù

law [lɔː] *n* (system of rules: of society, government) 法律 hōrítsu; (a rule) 法律 hōrítsu; (of nature, science) 法則 hōsoku; (lawyers) 弁護士の職 beñgoshi no shokú;

(police) 警察 kefsatsu; (SCOL) 法学 hōgaku

law-abiding [lɔː'əbaidiŋ] *adj* 法律を遵守する hōritsu wò jûñshu suru

law and order *n* 治安 chfan

law court *n* 法廷 hōtei

lawful [lɔː'fəl] *adj* 合法の gōhō no

lawless [lɔː'lis] *adj* (action) 不法の fuhō no

lawn [lɔːn] *n* 芝生 shibáfu

lawnmower [lɔːn'mouər] *n* 芝刈機械 shibákarikì

lawn tennis *n* ローンテニス rôñtenisu

law school (US) *n* (SCOL) 法学部 hōgakùbu

lawsuit [lɔː'suːt] *n* 訴訟 soshó

lawyer [lɔː'jər] *n* (gen) 弁護士 beñgoshi; (solicitor) 事務弁護士 jimúbeñgoshi; (barrister) 法廷弁護士 hōtéibeñgoshi

lax [læks] *adj* (behavior, standards) いい加減な ífkagen na

laxative [læk'sətiv] *n* 下剤 gezái

lay[1] [lei] *pt of* lie

lay[2] [lei] *adj* (REL) 俗人の zokújin no; (not expert) 素人の shfroto no

lay[3] [lei] (*pt*, *pp* **laid**) *vt* (place) 置く okú; (table) ...に食器を並べる ...ni shokkî wo náraberù; (carpet etc) 敷く shikú; (cable, pipes etc) 埋設する mafsetsu suru; (ZOOL: egg) 産む ûmú

layabout [lei'əbaut] (BRIT: *inf*) *n* のらくら者 norákuramono

lay aside *vt* (put down) わきに置く wakí ni okú; (money) 貯蓄する chochíku suru; (belief, prejudice) 捨てる sutérù

lay-by [lei'bai] (BRIT) *n* 待避所 taíhijo

lay by *vt see* lay aside

lay down *vt* (object) 置く okú; (rules, laws etc) 設ける mōkérù

to lay down the law (*pej*) 威張り散らす ibárichirasu

to lay down one's life (in war etc) 命を捨てる ínochi wo sutérù

layer [lei'ər] *n* 層 sō

layman [lei'mən] (*pl* **laymen**) *n* (nonexpert) 素人 shfroto

lay off *vt* (workers) 一時解雇にする ichíjikaìko ni suru; レイオフにする refofū fu suru

lay on vt (meal, entertainment etc) 提供
する teíkyō suru

lay out vt (spread out: things) 並べて置
く narábete okū

layout [lei'aut] n (arrangement: of garden, building) 配置 haíchi; (: of piece of
writing etc) レイアウト reñauto

laze [leiz] vi (also: **laze about**) ぶらぶら
する burábura suru

laziness [lei'zi:nis] n 怠惰 taída

lazy [lei'zi:] adj (person) 怠惰な taída na; (:
(movement, action) のろい norói

lb abbr = **pound** (weight)

lead[1] [li:d] n (front position: SPORT, fig)
先頭 señtō; (piece of information) 手掛り
tegákàri; (in play, film) 主演 shuén; (for
dog) 引綱 hikízùna, ひも himő; (ELEC)
リード線 rídosen

♦vt (pt, pp **led**)

♦vt (walk etc in front) 先導する señdō
suru; (guide): **to lead someone somewhere** ...を...に案内する ...wo ...ni afinai
suru; (group of people, organization)
...のリーダーをする ...no rídà ni nárū;
(start, guide: activity) ...の指揮を取る
...no shikf wo tórū

♦vi (road, pipe, wire etc) ...に通じる ...ni
tsūjiru; (SPORT) 先頭に立つ señtō ni tatsu

in the lead (SPORT, fig) 先頭に立って
señtō ni tatte

to lead the way (also fig) 先導する señdō suru

lead[2] [led] n (metal) 鉛 namári; (in pencil) しん shíñ

lead away vt 連れ去る tsurésarù

lead back vt 連れ戻す tsurémodosù

leaden [led'ən] adj (sky, sea) 鉛色の na-
máriiro no

leader [li:'də:r] n (of group, organization) 指導者 shidőshà, リーダー rídà;
(SPORT) 先頭を走る選手 señtō wo ha-
shírü señshū

leadership [li:'də:rʃip] n (group, individual) 指導権 shidőkèn; (position, quality)
リーダーシップ rídàshippu

lead-free [ledfri:'] adj (petrol) 無鉛の

muén no

leading [li:'diŋ] adj (most important:
person, thing) 主要な shuyő na; (role) 主
演の shuén no; (first, front) 先頭の señtō
no

leading lady n (THEATER) 主演女優
shuénjoyū

leading light n (person) 主要人物 shu-
yőjinbütsu

leading man (pl **leading men**) n (THE-
ATER) 主演男優 shuéndañ-yū

lead on vt (tease) からかう karákaù

lead singer n (in pop group) リードシン
ガー rídoshiñgà, リードボーカリスト rí-
dobōkarÌsuto

lead to vt fus ...の原因になる ...no geñ-in
ni narū

lead up to vt fus (events) ...の原因になる
...no geñ-in ni narū; (in conversation)
話題を...に向ける wadái wo ...ni mukérù

leaf [li:f] (pl **leaves**) n (of tree, plant) 葉
ha

♦vi: **to leaf through** (book, magazine)
...にさっと目を通す ...ni sátto me wò tōsū

to turn over a new leaf 心を入れ換え
る kokórò wo irékaerù

leaflet [li:f'lit] n ビラ birá, 散らし chiráshi

league [li:g] n (group of people, clubs,
countries) 連盟 reñmei, リーグ rígù

to be in league with someone ...と手を
組んでいる ...to te wo kuñde irū

leak [li:k] n (of liquid, gas) 漏れ moré;
(hole: in roof, pipe etc) 穴 aná; (piece of
information) 漏えい rőei

♦vi (shoes, ship, pipe, roof) ...から...が漏
れる ...kara ...ga moreru; (liquid, gas) 漏
れる moréru

♦vt (information) 漏らす morásù

the news leaked out そのニュースが漏
れた sono nyūsu ga moréta

lean [li:n] adj (person) やせた yaséta;
(meat) 赤身の akámi no

♦vb (pt, pp **leaned** or **leant**)

♦vt: **to lean something on something**
...を...にもたせかける ...wo ...ni motáse-
kakerù

♦*vi* (slope) 傾く katámukù
to lean against ...にもたれる ...ni motárerù
to lean on ...に寄り掛る ...ni yoríkakerù

lean forward *vi* 前にかがむ máe ni kagámù

leaning [liːˈniŋ] *n*: *leaning (towards)* (tendency, bent) (...する) 傾向 (...surú) kefkô

lean out *vi* ...から体を乗出す ...kara karáda wò norídasù

lean over *vi* ...の上にかがむ ...no ué ni kagámù

leant [lent] *pt, pp of* **lean**

leap [liːp] *n* (jump) 跳躍 chôyaku; (: in price, number etc) 急上昇 kyúːjôshô
♦*vi* (*pt, pp* **leaped** *or* **leapt**) (jump: high) 跳ね上がる hanéagarù; (: far) 跳躍する chôyaku suru; (price, number etc) 急上昇する kyúːjôshô suru

leapfrog [liːpˈfrɑːg] *n* 馬跳び umátobi

leapt [lept] *pt, pp of* **leap**

leap year うるう年 urúːdoshi

learn [ləːrn] (*pt, pp* **learned** *or* **learnt**) *vt* (facts, skill) 学ぶ manábù; (study, repeat: poem, play etc) 覚える obóerù; 暗記する ańki suru
♦*vi* 習う naráù

to learn about something (hear, read) ...を知る ...wo shírù

to learn to do something ...の仕方を覚える ...no shikáta wò obóerù

learned [ləːrˈnid] *adj* (person) 学識のある gakúshiki no arù; (book, paper) 学術の gakújútsu no

learner [ləːrˈnəːr] (*BRIT*) *n* (*also:* **learner driver**) 仮免許運転者 karímeñkyo unteńsha

learning [ləːrˈniŋ] *n* (knowledge) 学識 gakúshiki

learnt [ləːrnt] *pt, pp of* **learn**

lease [liːs] *n* (legal agreement, contract: to borrow something) 賃借契約 chíńshakukeíyaku, リース rísu; (: to lend something) 賃貸契約 chíńtaikeíyaku, リース rísu

---

♦*vt* (borrow) 賃借する chíńshaku suru; (lend) 賃貸する chíńtai suru

leash [liːʃ] *n* (for dog) ひも himó

least [liːst] *adj: the least* (+noun: smallest) 最も少ない mốttômo chíːsaì; (: smallest amount of) 最も少ない mốttômo sukúnaì
♦*adv* (+verb) 最も...しない mốttômo ...shínaì; (+adjective): *the least* 最も ...でない mốttômo ...de naì

the least possible effort 最小限の努力 saíshôgeñ no dóryòku

at least 少なくとも sukúnakutomo

you could at least have written 少なくとも手紙をくれたら良かったのに sukúnakutomo tegámi wò kurétara yokàttá no ni

not in the least ちっとも...でない chíttòmo ...de naì

leather [leðˈəːr] *n* なめし革 naméshigawa, 革 kawá

leave [liːv] (*pt, pp* **left**) *vt* (place: go away from) 行ってしまう itté shimaù, 帰る kaérù; (place, institution: permanently) 去る sárù, 辞める yamérù; (leave behind: person) 置去りにする okízari ni surù, 見捨てる misúterù; (: thing: accidentally) 置忘れる okíwasurerù; (: deliberately) 置いて行く ofte ikú; (husband, wife) ...と別れる ...to wakárerù; (allow to remain: food, space, time etc) 残す nokósù
♦*vi* (go away) 去る sárù, 行ってしまう itté shimaù; (: permanently) 辞める yamérù; (bus, train) 出発する shuppátsu suru, 出る dérù
♦*n* 休暇 kyúːka

to leave something to someone (money, property etc) ...に...を残して死ぬ ...ni ...wo nokóshite shinù; (responsibility etc) ...に...を任せる ...ni ...wo makáserù

to be left 残る nokórù

there's some milk left over ミルクは少し残っている mírùku wa sukóshi nokótte irú

on leave 休暇中で kyúːkachū de

leave behind *vt* (person, object) 置いて

行く ofte ikú; (object: accidentally) 置忘
れる okwfasurerù

leave of absence n 休暇 kyúka, 暇 himá

leave out vt 抜かす nukásù

leaves [li:vz] npl of **leaf**

Lebanon [leb'ænən] n レバノン rebánòn

lecherous [letʃ'ə:rəs] (pej) adj 好平な su-
kébè na

lecture [lek'tʃə:r] n (talk) 講演 kóen;
(SCOL) 講義 kógi
♦vi (talk) 講演する kóen suru; (SCOL) 講
義する kógi sùru
♦vt (scold): **to lecture someone on/
about something** ...の事で...をしかる
...no kotó de ...wo shikárù
to give a lecture on ...について講演す
る ...ni tsúite kóen suru

lecturer [lek'tʃə:rə:r] (BRIT) n (at university) 講師 kóshi

led [led] pt, pp of **lead**

ledge [ledʒ] n (of mountain) 岩 棚 iwáda-
na; (of window) 桟 sáñ; (on wall) 棚 taná

ledger [ledʒ'ə:r] n (COMM) 台帳 dáichō

lee [li:] n 風下 kazáshimo

leech [li:tʃ] n ヒル hírù

leek [li:k] n リーキ ríki, リーク ríku

leer [li:r] vi: **to leer at someone** ..をいん
乱な目で見る ..wo ifran na me de mirù

leeway [li:'wei] n (fig): **to have some
leeway** 余裕がある yoyú ga arù

left [left] pt, pp of **leave**
♦adj (direction, position) 左の hidári no
♦n (direction, side, position) 左 hidári
♦adv (turn, look etc) 左に(へ) hidári ni
(e)
on the left 左に(で) hidári ni(de)
to the left 左に(へ) hidári ni(e)
the Left (POL) 左翼 sáyòku

left-handed [left'hæn'ded] adj 左利きの
hidárikikì no, ぎっちょの gítchò no

left-hand side [left'hænd'-] n 左側 hidárigawa

left-luggage (office) [left'lʌg'idʒ-]
(BRIT) n 手荷物預かり所 tenímotsu a-
zukarishò

leftovers [left'ouvə:rz] npl (of meal) 残り
物 nokórimono

left-wing [left'wiŋ] adj (POL) 左翼の sáyòku no

leg [leg] n (gen) 脚 ashf; (CULIN: of
lamb, pork, chicken) もも mómò; (part:
of journey etc) 区切り kugfri
isân

legacy [leg'æsi] n (of will: also fig) 遺産
isán

legal [li:'gəl] adj (of law) 法律の hóritsu
no; (action, situation) 法的な hótekì na

legal holiday (US) n 法定休日 hótei-
kyújitsu

legality [ligæl'iti:] n 合法性 gôhôsei

legalize [li:'gəlaiz] vt 合法化する gôhôka
suru

legally [li:'gəli:] adv (by law) 法的に hó-
teki ni

legal tender n (currency) 法定通貨 hó-
teitsûka, 法貨 hóka

legend [ledʒ'ənd] n (story) 伝説 deñsetsu;
(fig: person) 伝説的な人物 deñsetsutekijin-
butsu

legendary [ledʒ'əndeːri:] adj (of legend)
伝説の deñsetsu no; (very famous) 伝説
的な deñsetsutekì na

legible [ledʒ'əbəl] adj 読める yomérù

legion [li:'dʒən] n (MIL) 軍隊 guñtai

legislation [ledʒisleiʃ'ən] n 法律 hóritsu

legislative [ledʒ'isleitiv] adj 立法の rip-
pó no

legislature [ledʒ'isleitʃə:r] n (POL) 議会
gíkài

legitimate [lidʒit'əmit] adj (reasonable)
正当な seftô na; (legal) 合法な gôhô na

leg-room [leg'ru:m] n (in car, plane etc)
脚を伸ばせる空間 ashí wo nobáserù kú-
kan

leisure [li:'ʒə:r] n (period of time) 余暇
yoká, レジャー rejā
at leisure ゆっくりと yukkúrì to

leisure centre (BRIT) n レジャーセン
ター rejāseñtà ◇スポーツ施設, 図書館,
会議室, 喫茶店などを含んだ文化施設
supótsushisetsu, toshóshitsu, kafgishit-
tsu, kissáteñ nádò wo fukúñda buñka-
shisetsù

leisurely [li:'ʒə:rli:] adj (pace, walk) ゆっ
くりした yukkúrì shitá

lemon [lem'ən] n (fruit) レモン rémòn

lemonade [lemaˈneid] n (BRIT: fizzy drink) ラムネ rámune; (with lemon juice) レモネード remonēdo

lemon tea レモンティー remónti

lend [lend] (pt, pp **lent**) vt: **to lend something to someone** (money, thing) ...に...を貸す ...ni ...wo kásù

lending library [lenˈdiŋ-] n 貸出し図書館 kashídashitoshokàn

length [leŋkθ] n (measurement) 長さ násà; (distance): **the length of** ...の端から端まで ...no hashí kara hashí madè; (of swimming pool) プールの長さ púru no nagása; (piece of wood, string, cloth etc) 1本 ippôń; (amount of time) 時間 jikán

at length (at last) とうとう tôtô; (for a long time) 長々と nágànáfda

lengthen [leŋkˈθən] vt 長くする nágàku suru

♦vi 長くなる nágàku naru

lengthways [leŋkˈθweiz] adv (slice, fold, lay) 縦に táte ni

lengthy [leŋkˈθiː] adj (meeting, explanation, text) 長い nagái

lenient [liːˈniːənt] adj (person, attitude) 寛大な kańdai na

lens [lenz] n (of spectacles, camera) レンズ réñzu; (telescope) 望遠鏡 bôeṅkyó

Lent [lent] n 四旬節 shijúñsetsu

lent [lent] pt, pp of **lend**

lentil [lenˈtəl] n ヒラマメ hirámame

Leo [liːˈou] n (ASTROLOGY) しし座 shíshíza

leopard [lepˈərd] n (ZOOL) ヒョウ hyô

leotard [liːˈətɑːrd] n レオタード reôtàdo

leprosy [lepˈrəsiː] n らい病 raíbyò, ハンセン病 hańseñbyó

lesbian [lezˈbiːən] n 女性同性愛者 joséidóseiaisha, レスビアン resúbìan

less [les] adj (in size, degree) ...より小さい ...yórì chifsaì; (in amount, quality) ...より少ない ...yórì sukúnaì

♦pron ...より少ないもの ...yórì sukúnaì monó

♦adv ...より少なく ...yórì sukúnaku

♦prep: **less tax/10% discount** ...から税金(1割)引きを引いて ...kara zefkin (ich-wári)wo hífte

less than half 半分以下 hańbuñ íka

less than ever 更に少なく ...yórì ni sukúnaku

less and less ますます少なく masúmasu sukúnaku

the less he talks the better ... 彼はできるだけしゃべらない方がいい kárè wa dekírù dake shabéranai hô ga fi

lessen [lesˈən] vi 少なくなる sukúnaku naru

♦vt 少なくする sukúnaku suru

lesser [lesˈər] adj (smaller: in degree, importance, amount) 小さい(少ない)方の chífsaì(sukúnaì)hô no

to a lesser extent ...it それ程ではないが ... も soré hodò de wa naí ga ...mo

lesson [lesˈən] n (class: history etc) 授業 jugyô; (: ballet exercise etc) けいこ kéikò, レッスン résšuṅ; (example, warning) 見せしめ miséshime

to teach someone a lesson (fig) ...に思い知らせてやる ...ni omóishirasete yarù

lest [lest] conj ...しない様に ...shinái yô ni

let [let] (pt, pp **let**) vt (allow) 許す yurúsù; (BRIT: lease) 賃貸する chiṅtai suru

to let someone do something ...に...するのを許す ...ni ...surú no wò yurúsù

to let someone know something ...に...を知らせる ...ni ...wo shíraserù

let's go 行きましょう ikímashò

let him come (permit) 彼が来るのを邪魔しないで下さい kárè ga kúrù no wo jamá shinàide kudásaì

「他だ」dake kashíya

let down vt (tire etc) ...の空気を抜く ...no kúki wo nuku; (person) がっかりさせる gakkárì saséru

let go vi (stop holding: thing, person) 手を放す te wo hanásù

♦vt (release: person, animal) 放す hanásù

lethal [liːˈθəl] adj (chemical, dose etc) 致命的な chiméiteki na

a lethal weapon 凶器 kyôki

lethargic [ləθɑːrˈdʒik] adj 無気力の mukíryòku no

let in vt (water, air) ...が漏れる ...ga morêrû; (person) 入らせる hafraserù

let off vt (culprit) 許す yurúsù; (fire-work, bomb) 爆発させる bakúhatsu saseru; (gun) 撃つ útsù

let on vi 漏らす morásù

let out vt (person, dog) 外に出す sótò ni dásù; (breath) 吐く háků; (water, air) 抜く núkù; (sound) 出す dásù

letter [let'əːr] n (correspondence) 手紙 tegámi; (of alphabet) 文字 mójì

letter bomb n 郵便爆弾 tegámibakúdan

letterbox [let'əːrbɑːks] n (BRIT) (for receiving mail) 郵便受け yúbìñ-uke; (for sending mail) 郵便ポスト yúbìñposùto, ポスト pósùto

lettering [let'əːriŋ] n 文字 mójì

lettuce [let'is] n レタス rétàsu

let up [let'ʌp'] vi (cease) やむ yámù; (diminish) 緩む yurúmù

let-up [let'ʌp] n (of violence, noise etc) 減少 geñshō

leukemia [luːkiː'miːə] (BRIT **leukaemia**) n 白血病 hakkétsubyõ

level [lev'əl] adj (flat) 平らな taíra na
♦adv: **to draw level with** (person, vehicle) ...に追い付く ...ni oítsukù
♦n (point on scale, height etc) 高さ tákàsa, レベル rébèru; (of lake, river) 水位 súì
♦adj (land: make flat) 平らにする taíra ni suru; (building, forest etc: destroy) 破壊する hakái suru
to be level with ...と同じぐらいである ...to onáji gurài de árù
"A" levels (BRIT) n 学科の上級試験 gakká no jōkyû shikèn 〈大学入学資格を得るための試験 daígakunyūgaku shikakù wo érù tamé nò shikén
"O" levels (BRIT) n 学科の普通級試験 gakká no futsûkyû shikèn 〈中等教育の5年間まで受ける試験 chútōkyōiku wo gonén ukéta noshì wo ukérù shikén
on the level (fig: honest) 正直で shōjiki de

level crossing (BRIT) n 踏切 fumíkiri

level-headed [lev'əlhed'id] adj (calm) 分別のある fúñbetsu no árù

level off vi (prices etc) 横ばい状態にな

る横ばい状態に náru

level out vi = **level off**

lever [lev'əːr] n (to operate machine) レバー rébà; (bar) バール bárù; (fig) 人を動かす手段 hitó wo ugókasù shúdàn, こて tékò

leverage [lev'əːridʒ] n (using bar, lever) てこの作用 tékò no sáyò; (fig: influence) 影響力 efkyōryòku

levity [lev'iti:] n (frivolity) 不真面目さ fumájimesa

levy [lev'i:] n (tax, charge) 税金 zefkin
♦vt 課する ka súrù

lewd [luːd] adj (look, remark etc) わいせつな wafsetsu na

liabilities [laiəbil'ətiːz] npl (COMM) 債務 sáīmu

liability [laiəbil'əti:] n (person, thing) 負担 futáñ; (LAW: responsibility) 責任 sekéniñ

liable [lai'əbəl] adj (subject): **liable to** ...の刑則が適用される ...no bassóku ga tekíyō sarerù; (responsible): **liable for** ...の責任を負うべきである ...no sekíniñ wo oúbekì de árù; (likely): **liable to do** ...しがちである ...shigáchi de árù

liaise [liːeiz'] vi: **to liaise (with)** (...と) 連携する (...to) refkei suru

liaison [liːeiːzɑːn'] n (cooperation, coordination) 連携 refkei; (sexual relationship) 密通 mittsū

liar [lai'əːr] n うそつき usótsùki

libel [lai'bəl] n 名誉毀損 mefyokìsoñ
♦vt 中傷する chūshō suru

liberal [lib'əːrəl] adj (tolerant) 寛容な kañtòkei na; (large: offer, amount etc) 寛大な kañdai na

liberate [lib'əːreit] vt 解放する kaího suru

liberation [libəreiʃ'ən] n 解放 kaího

liberty [lib'əːrtiː] n (gen) 自由 jiyû; (criminal): **to be at liberty** 逃走中である tôsôchū de árù
to be at liberty to do 自由に...できる jiyû ni ...dekírù
to take the liberty of doing something 勝手に...する katté ni ...surú

Libra [li:'brə] n (ASTROLOGY) 天びん座 teñbinza

librarian [laibrɛə'ri:ən] n (worker) 図書館員 toshokañ-in; (qualified) 司書 shísho

library [lai'brɛ:ri:] n (institution, SCOL: building) 図書館 toshókàn; (: room) 図書室 toshóshìtsu; (private collection) 蔵書 zōsho

libretto [libret'ou] n (OPERA) 脚本 kyakúhon

Libya [lib'i:ə] n リビア ríbia

Libyan [lib'i:ən] adj リビアの ríbia no
◆n リビア人 ríbiájin

lice [lais] npl of **louse**

licence [lai'səns] (US also: **license**) n (official document) 免許 méñkyo; (AUT) 運転免許証 uñtenmenkyoshō

license [lai'səns] n (US) = **licence**
◆vt (person, organization, activity) 認可する nñka suru

licensed [lai'sənst] adj (driver, pilot etc) 免許を持った méñkyo wo mottá; (for alcohol) 酒類販売許可を持った sakéruihanbaikyòka wo mottá

license plate (US) n ナンバープレート nañbāpurēto

licentious [laisen'tʃəs] adj いん乱な íñran na

lichen [lai'kən] n 地衣 chíi

lick [lik] vt (stamp, fingers etc) なめる namérù; (inf: defeat) ...に楽勝する ...ni rakúshō suru
  to lick one's lips (also fig) 舌なめずりをする shitánamezùri suru

licorice [lik'ɔ:ris] (US) n カンゾウ あめ kañzōame

lid [lid] n (of box, case, pan) ふた futá; (eyelid) まぶた mábùta

lie [lai] (pt **lay**, pp **lain**) vi (person) 横になる yokó ni narù; (be situated: place, object: also fig) ...にある ...ni árù; (be placed: in race, league etc) 第...位である dâî ...î de arù; (tell lies: pt, pp **lied**) うそを つく usó wo tsukú
◆n (untrue statement) うそ usó
  to lie low (fig) 人目を避ける hitóme wo sakéru

lie about/around vi (things) 散らばっ

ている chirábatte iru; (people) ごろりと寝ている goróri ni neté iru

lie-down [lai'daun] (BRIT) n: **to have a lie-down** 昼寝する hirúne suru

lie-in [lai'in] (BRIT) n: **to have a lie-in** 寝坊する nebō suru

lieu [lu:]: **in lieu of** prep ...の代りに ...no kawári ni

lieutenant [lu:ten'ənt] n (MIL) (also: **first lieutenant**) 中尉 chūi; (also: **second lieutenant**) 少尉 shōi

life [laif] (pl **lives**) n (quality of being alive) 生命 sefmei; (live things) 生物 seibūtsu; (state of being alive) 命 fnöchi; (lifespan) 一生 isshō; (events, experience, activities) 生活 sefkatsu
  to come to life (fig: person, party etc) 活気付く kakkízukù

life assurance (BRIT) n = **life insurance**

lifebelt [laif'belt] n 救命具 kyūmeigu

lifeboat [laif'bout] n (rescue launch) 巡視船 juñshihtei; (on ship) 救命ボート kyūmeibōto

lifeguard [laif'ga:rd] n (at beach, swimming pool) 看視員 kañshihn

life imprisonment n 無期懲役 mukíchöeki

life insurance n 生命保険 sefmeihokèn

life jacket n 救命胴衣 kyūmeidōi

lifeless [laif'lis] adj (dead: person, animal) 死んだ shíndà; (fig: person) 元気のない goñki no nái; (: party etc) 活気のない kakkí no nái

lifelike [laif'laik] adj (model, dummy, robot etc) 生きているような様な fkíte irú yōna; (realistic: painting, performance) 写実的な shajítsuteki na

lifeline [laif'lain] n (means of surviving) 命綱 fnōchizùna

lifelong [laif'lɔːŋ] adj (friend, ambition etc) 一生の isshō no

life preserver (US) n = **lifebelt; life jacket**

life sentence n 無期懲役 mukíchöeki

life-size(d) [laif'saiz(d)] adj (painting, model etc) 実物大の jitsúbutsudaì no

life-span [laif'spæn] n (of person, animal, plant: *also fig*) 寿命 jumyō

life style n 生き方 ikíkata, ライフスタイル raffusutáiru

life support system n (MED) 生命維持装置 seímeijijísōchi

lifetime [laif'taim] n (of person) 生涯 shōgai; (of thing) 寿命 jumyō

lift [lift] vt (raise: thing, part of body) 上げる ageru; (end: ban, rule) 撤廃する teppái suru

♦vi (fog) 晴れる haréru

♦n (BRIT: machine) エレベーター erébētā

to give someone a lift (AUT) ...を車に乗せて上げる ...wo kurúma ni noséte ageru

lift-off [lift'ɔːf] n (of rocket) 離昇 rishō

ligament [lig'əmənt] n じん帯 jíntai

light [lait] n (brightness: from sun, moon, lamp, fire) 光 hikári; (ELEC) 電気 dénki; (AUT) ライト ráito; (for cigarette etc): *have you got a light?* 火をお持ちですか hí wo o-móchi desu ká

♦vt (pt, pp lit) (fire) たく takú; (candle, cigarette) ...に火を付ける ...ni hí wo tsukérù; (room): *to be lit by* ...で照明されている ...de shōmei saréte irù

♦adj (pale) 淡い awái; (not heavy: object) 軽い karúi; (: rain) 細かい komákai; (: traffic) 少ない sukúnai; (not strenuous: work) 軽い karúi; (bright: building, room) 明るい akárui; (graceful, gentle: movement, action) 軽やかな karóyaka na; (not serious: book, play, film, music) 肩の凝らない katá no korànai

to come to light 明るみに出る akárumi ni derú

in the light of (discussions, new evidence etc) ...を考慮して ...wo kōryo shite

light bulb n 電球 denkyū

lighten [lait'ən] vt (make less heavy) 軽くする karúku surù

lighter [lait'əːr] n (*also*: **cigarette lighter**) ライター ráitā

light-headed [lait'hed'id] adj (dizzy) 頭がふらふらする atáma ga fúrafura suru; (excited) 浮かれている uwátsuita

light-hearted [lait'hɑːr'tid] adj (person)

陽気な yōki na; (question, remark etc) 気楽な kiráku na

lighthouse [lait'haus] n 燈台 tōdai

lighting [lait'iŋ] n (system) 照明 shōmei

lightly [lait'liː] adv 軽く karúku; (thoughtlessly) 軽々しく kefsotsu ni; (slightly) 少し sukóshī

to get off lightly 軽い罰だけで逃れるkarúi bátsū dáke de nogárerù

lightness [lait'nis] n (in weight) 軽さ karúsa

lightning [lait'niŋ] n (in sky) 稲妻 inázuma

lightning conductor (*BRIT*) n = **lightning rod**

lightning rod (*US*) n 避雷針 hiráishìn

light pen n ライトペン ráitopèn

lights [laits] npl (AUT: traffic lights) (交通)信号 (kōtsū)shíngō

light up vi (face) 輝く kagáyakù

♦vt (illuminate) 明るくする akáruku suru

lightweight [lait'weit] adj (suit) 薄いusúi

♦n (BOXING) ライト級のボクサー ráitokyū no bókùsā

light year n (PHYSICS) 光年 kōnen

like [laik] vt (find pleasing, attractive, acceptable: person, thing) ...が好きである ...ga ...sukí de arù

♦prep (similar to) ...の様な ...no yō na; (in comparisons) ...の様に ...no yō ni; (such as) 例えば...の様な(に) tatóeba ...nádō no yō na(ni)

♦adj similar に似た nitá

n: and the like など nádō

his likes and dislikes 彼の好きな物と嫌いな物 kárē no sukí na monó to kiráì na monó

I would like, I'd like ...が欲しいのですが ...ga hoshíì no desu gà

would you like a coffee? コーヒーはいかがですか kōhī wa ikágà desu ká

to be/look like someone/something ...に似ている ...ni nité irù

what does it look/taste/sound like? どんな格好[味, 音]ですか dónna kákkō [ajī, otō]dèsu ká *that's just like him* 彼らしいね karé rashíi né

do it like this やり方はこうです yari-kata wa kó desu

it is nothing like ... ...とは全く違います ...to wa mattáku chigaimasu

likeable [laiˈkəbəl] *adj* (person) 人好きの hitózuki no suru

likelihood [laikˈliːhud] *n* 可能性 kanósei

likely [laikˈliː] *adj* (probable) ありそうな arisō na

to be likely to do ...しそうである ...shisō de arù

not likely! 何があっても...しない nání ga atté mo ...shínài, とんでもない tonde-monái

likeness [laikˈnəs] *n* (similarity) 似ている事 nité irù kotó

that's a good likeness (photo, portrait) 実物そっくりだ jitsúbùtsu sokkúrí da

likewise [laikˈwaiz] *adv* (similarly) 同じく onájîku

to do likewise 同じ様にする onáji yố ni suru

liking [laiˈkiŋ] *n*: *to have a liking for* (person, thing) ...が好きである ...ga sukí de arù

to be to someone's liking ...の気に入っている ...no kí ni itte irù

lilac [laiˈlæk] *n* (BOT: tree, flower) ライラック rafrakkù, リラ rfrà

lily [lilˈiː] *n* (plant, flower) ユリ yurí

lily of the valley *n* スズラン suzúrañ

limb [lim] *n* (ANAT) 手足 téàshi, 肢 shi

limber up [limˈbəːr-] *vi* (SPORT) 準備運動をする juñbíuñdò wo suru, ウォーミングアップをする uómiñguappù suru

limbo [limˈbou] *n*: *to be in limbo* (fig) 忘れ去られている wasúrèsararete irù

lime [laim] *n* (fruit) ライム rấimu; (also: **lime tree**) ライムの木 rấimu no ki; (also: **lime juice**) ライムジュース rafmujùsu; (for soil) 石灰 sekkái; (rock) 石灰岩 sekkáìgan

limelight [laimˈlait] *n*: *to be in the limelight* 注目を浴びている chúmoku wo ábîte irù

limerick [limˈəːrik] *n* 五行わい歌 gogyṓwaìka

limestone [laimˈstoun] *n* 石灰岩 sekkáìgan

limit [limˈit] *n* (greatest amount, extent, degree) 限界 geñkai; (restriction: of time, money etc) 制限 sefgen; (: of area) 境界 kyṓkai

◆*vt* (production, expense etc) 制限する sefgen suru

limitation [limiteiˈʃən] *n* (control, restriction) 制限 sefgen; (of person, thing) 限界 geñkai

limited [limˈitid] *adj* (small: choice, resources etc) 限られた kagírarèta

to be limited to ...に限られる ...ni kagírarerù

limited (liability) company (BRIT) *n* 有限会社 yűgeñgaìsha

limousine [limˈəziːn] *n* リムジン rímùjin

limp [limp] *n*: *to have a limp* びっこを引く bíkkò wo hikú

◆*vi* (person, animal) びっこを引く bíkkò wo hikú

◆*adj* (person) ぐにゃぐにゃの gúnyàgunya no

limpet [limˈpit] *n* カサガイ kaságaì

line [lain] *n* (long thin mark) 線 señ; (wrinkle: on face) しわ shiwá; (row: of people, things) 列 rétsù; (of writing, song) 行 gyṓ; (rope) 綱 tsuná, ロープ rōpu; (also: **fishing line**) 釣糸 tsurfito; (also: **power line**) 送電線 sōdéñsen; (also: **telephone line**) 電話線 defwasen; (TEL) 回線 kaísen; (railway track) 線路 séñro; (bus, coach, train route) ...線 ...sén; (fig: attitude, policy) 方針 hṓshin; (: business, work) 分野 búñ-ya; (COMM: of product(s)) シリーズ shírīzu

◆*vt* (road, room) ...に並ぶ ...ni narábù; (subj: person: container) ...の内側に...を張る ...no uchigawa ni ...wo hárù; (: clothing) ...に裏地を付ける ...ni uráji wo tsukérù

to line something with ...に...の裏を付ける ...ni ...no urá wo tsukérù

to line the streets 道路の両側に並ぶ dṓro no ryṓgawa ni narábù

in line (in a row) 1列に ichíretsu ní

in line with (according to) ...に従って ...ni shitágatte

linear [lin'i:ər] *adj* (process, sequence) 一直線の itchókusèn no; (shape, form) 線形の seńkei no

lined [laind] *adj* (face) しわのある no arú; (paper) 線を引いた sén wo hiíta

linen [lin'ən] *n* (cloth) リンネル rínneru, リネン rínèn; (tablecloths, sheets etc) リネン rínèn

liner [lain'ə:r] *n* (ship) 豪華客船 gókakyakúsen; (for bin) ごみ袋 gomíbukuro

linesman [lainz'mən] (*pl* **linesmen**) *n* (SPORT) 線審 seńshin, ラインズマン raíñzuman

line up *vi* 列を作る rétsu wo tsukúru

◆*vt* (people) 1列に並ばせる ichíretsu ni narábaserú; (prepare: event, celebration) 手配する tehái suru

line-up [lain'ʌp] *n* (US: queue) 行列 gyóretsu; (SPORT) ラインナップ raíñ-appù

linger [liŋ'gə:r] *vi* (smell, tradition etc) 残る nokóru; (person) ぐずぐずする gúzuguzu suru

lingerie [lɑːn'dʒərei] *n* 女性下着類 joséishitagirùi, ランジェリー ráñjerì

lingo [liŋ'gou] (*pl* **lingoes**: *inf*) *n* (language) 言葉 kotóba

linguist [liŋ'gwist] *n* (person who speaks several languages) 数カ国語を話せる人 sūkakokūgo wo hanáserù hitó

linguistic [liŋgwis'tik] *adj* (studies, developments, ideas etc) 語学の gógaku no

linguistics [liŋgwis'tiks] *n* 語学 gógaku

lining [lai'niŋ] *n* (cloth) 裏地 uráji; (ANAT) 粘膜 nénmaku

link [liŋk] *n* (relationship) 関係 kańkei; (of a chain) 輪 wá

◆*vt* (join) つなぐ tsunágu; (associate: *to link with/to* ...と関連付ける ...to kańreñzukerù

links [liŋks] *npl* (GOLF) ゴルフ場 gorúfujò

link up *vt* (machines, systems) つなぐ tsunágu

◆*vi* 合流する góryū suru

lino [lai'nou] *n* = **linoleum**

linoleum [linou'li:əm] *n* リノリウム rínòriumu

lion [lai'ən] *n* (ZOOL) ライオン ráiòn

lioness [lai'ənis] *n* 雌ライオン mesúràion

lip [lip] *n* (ANAT) 唇 kuchíbiru

lip-read [lip'ri:d] *vi* 読唇する dokúshin suru

lip service *n* 唇の荒れ止め kuchíbiru no arédome

to pay lip service to something (*pej*) 上辺だけ...に賛成する u-wábe dake ...ni sańsei suru

lipstick [lip'stik] *n* 口紅 kuchíbeni

liqueur [likər'] *n* リキュール ríkyùru

liquid [lik'wid] *adj* 液体の ekítai no

◆*n* 液体 ekítai, 液体 ekítai

liquidate [lik'wideit] *vt* (opponents, rivals) 消す késu, 殺して殺す korósù; (company) つぶす tsubúsu

liquidize [lik'widaiz] *vt* (CULIN) ミキサーに掛ける mfkìsā ni kakérò

liquidizer [lik'widaizə:r] (*BRIT*) *n* ミキサー mfkìsā

liquor [lik'ə:r] *n* 酒 sake

liquorice [lik'əris] (*BRIT*) *n* = **licorice**

liquor store (*US*) *n* 酒屋 sákaya

Lisbon [liz'bən] *n* リスボン rísùbon

lisp [lisp] *n* 舌足らずの発音 shitátarazu no hatsúòn

◆*vi* 舌足らずに発音する shitátarazu ni hatsúòn suru

list [list] *n* (catalog: of things) 目録 mokúroku, リスト rísùto; (: of people) 名簿 meíbo, リスト rísùto

◆*vt* (mention) 並べてあげる narábete agérù; (put on list) ...のリストを作る ...no rísùto wo tsukúrù

listed building [lis'tid-] (*BRIT*) *n* 指定建造物 shitéikenzòbutsu

listen [lis'ən] *vi* 聞く kikú

to listen to someone/something ...を[...の言う事を]聞く ...wo[...no iú kotó wo] kikú

listener [lis'ənə:r] *n* (person listening to speaker) 聞いている人 kiíte irù hitó; (RADIO) 聴取者 chóshushà

listless [list'lis] *adj* 物憂い monóuì

lit [lit] *pt, pp of* **light**

liter [ˈliːtər] *(US) n* (unit of volume) リットル ríttoru

literacy [ˈlitərəsi] *n* 識字 shikíji

literal [ˈlitərəl] *adj* (exact: sense, meaning) 厳密な genmítsu na; (word for word: translation) 逐語的な chikúgoteki na

literally [ˈlitərəli] *adv* (in fact) 本当に hontō ni; (really) 文字通りに mojídōri ni

literary [ˈlitəreri] *adj* 文学の bungáku no

literate [ˈlitərit] *adj* (able to read etc) 読み書きできる yomíkaki dekirù; (educated) 教養のある kyōyō no arù

literature [ˈlitərətʃər] *n* (novels, plays, poetry) 文学 búngaku; (printed information: scholarly) 文献 búnken; (: brochures etc) 印刷物 ínsatsubùtsu, カタログ katárogu

lithe [laið] *adj* (person, animal) しなやかな shínáyaka na

litigation [litəˈgeiʃən] *n* 訴訟 soshō

litre [ˈliːtər] *(BRIT) n* = **liter**

litter [ˈlitər] *n* (rubbish) 散らばっているごみ chirábatte irù gomi; (young animals) 一腹 hitóhara

litter bin *(BRIT) n* ごみ入れ gomíire

littered [ˈlitərd] *adj:* **littered with** (scattered) ...を散らかされた ...wo chirákasareta

little [ˈlitl] *adj* (small: thing, person) 小さい chiísai; (young: child) 幼い osánai; (short: distance) 近い chikái; (time, event) 短い mijíkai

♦*adv* 少ししか...ない sukóshi shika ...náî

a little (amount) 少し sukóshi

a little bit 少し sukóshi

little brother/sister 弟(妹) otóto(imóto)

little by little 少しずつ sukóshizùtsu

little finger *n* 小指 koyúbi

live [liv *adj* laiv] *vi* (reside: in house, town, country) 住む súmù; (lead one's life) 暮す kurásù; (be alive) 生きている ikíte irù

♦*adj* (animal, plant) 生きている ikíte irù; (TV, RADIO)生の namá no, ライブのráîbu no; (performance) 実演の jitsúen

no; (ELEC)電流が通じている deńryū ga tsújite irù, 生きている ikíte irù; (bullet, bomb, missile) 使用可能状態の shiyōkanōjōtai no, 実の jitsú no

to live with someone (cohabit) ...と同せいする ...to dōsei suru

...to live with ...に伴う ...ni tomónaù

live down *vt* (defeat, error, failure): **I'll never live it down** 一生の恥じ isshō no hájî da

livelihood [ˈlaivliːhud] *n* (income source) 生計 sefkei

lively [ˈlaivli] *adj* (person) 活発な kappátsu na; (interesting: place etc) 活気に満ちた kakkí ni michíta; (: event) にぎやかな nigíyaka na; (: book) 面白い omóshiroî; (enthusiastic: interest, admiration etc) 熱心な nesshín na

liven up [ˈlaivən-] *vt* (person) ...に元気を付ける ...ni géñki wo tsukérù; (discussion, evening etc) 面白くする omóshirokû suru

♦*vi* (person) 元気になる géñki ni narù; (discussion, evening etc) 面白くなる omóshiroku narù

live on *vt fus* (food) ...を食べて暮す ...wo tábête kurásu

liver [ˈlivər] *n* (ANAT) 肝臓 kañzō; (CULIN) レバー rébâ

livery [ˈlivəriː] *n* (of servant) お仕着せ o-shíkise

lives [laivz] *npl of* **life**

livestock [ˈlaivstɑːk] *n* (AGR) 家畜 kachíku

live together *vi* (cohabit) 同せいする dōsei suru

live up to *vt fus* (fulfil) 守る mamórù

livid [ˈlivid] *adj* (color: of bruise) 青黒い aóguroî; (: of angry face) どす黒い dosúguroî; (: of sky) 鉛色の namáiro no; (furious: person) 怒り狂った gekído shitá

living [ˈliviŋ] *adj* (alive: person, animal) 生きている ikíte irù

♦*n:* **to earn/make a living** 生計を立てる sefkei wo tatérù

living conditions *npl* 暮しの状況 kurásh no jōkyō

living room *n* 居間 imá

living standards *npl* 生活水準 sefkatsusuijǐngin

living wage *n* 生活賃金 seʼkatsuchǐngin

lizard [liz'ərd] *n* トカゲ tokáge

load [loud] *n* (thing carried: of person) 荷物 nímotsu; (: of animal) 荷物 nímotsu; (: of vehicle) 積載量 tsumíni; (: weight) 負担 fután

♦*vt* (also: **load up**: vehicle, ship etc): **to load (with)** (...を) ...に積む (...wo) ...ni tsumú; (COMPUT: program) メモリーに読込む mémōri ni yomíkomù, ロードする rōdo suru; (gun) ...に弾丸を込める ...ni dangan wo komérù; (camera) ...にフィルムを入れる ...ni fírùmu wo iréru; (tape recorder) ...にテープを入れる ...ni tépu wo iréru

a load of rubbish (*inf*) でたらめ detárame

loads of/a load of (*fig*) 沢山の takúsañ no

loaded [lou'did] *adj* (vehicle): **to be loaded with** ...を積んでいる ...wo tsuñde iru; (question) 誘導的な yúdōteki na; (*inf*: rich) 金持の kanémochi no

loaf [louf] (*pl* **loaves**) *n* 一かたまりのパン hitókatamari no pan

loan [loun] *n* (sum of money) 貸付金 kashítsukekin, ローン rōn

♦*vt* (money, thing) 貸す kasú

on loan (borrowed) 借りている karíte irú

loath [louθ] *adj*: **to be loath to do something** ...をしたくない ...wo shitáku naì

loathe [louð] *vt* (person, activity) が大嫌いである ...ga daíkirai de árù

loaves [louvz] *npl of* **loaf**

lobby [lɑːb'iː] *n* (of building) ロビー robì; (POL: pressure group) 圧力団体 atsúryokudaňtai

♦*vt* (POL) ...に圧力を掛ける ...ni atsúryoku wò kakérù

lobe [loub] *n* (also: **earlobe**) 耳たぶ mimítabù

lobster [lɑːb'stər] *n* ロブスター rōbùsutā

local [lou'kəl] *adj* (council, paper, police station) 地元の jimóto no

♦*n* (*BRIT*: pub) 地元のパブ jimóto no pábù

local anesthetic *n* (MED) 局部麻酔 kyokúbumasòi

local authority *n* 地方自治体 chihóojichìtai

local call *n* (TEL) 市内通話 shináitsùwa

local government *n* 地方自治体 chihóojichitai

locality [loukæl'itiː] *n* 場所 basho

locally [lou'kaliː] *adv* 地元で jimóto de

locals [lou'kalz] *npl*: **the locals** (local inhabitants) 地元の住民 jimóto no júmiñ

locate [lou'keit] *vt* (find: person, thing) 見付ける mitsúkeru; (situate): **to be located in** ...にある(いる) ...ni árù(irú)

location [loukei'ʃən] *n* (particular place) 場所 basho

on location (CINEMA) ロケで roké de

loch [lɑːk] *n* 湖 mizúumi

lock [lɑːk] *n* (of door, drawer, suitcase) 錠 jō; (on canal) こう門 kómon; (also: **lock of hair**) 髪の一房 kamí no hitófùsa

♦*vt* (door, drawer, suitcase: with key) ...の...にかぎを掛ける ...no kagí wo kakérù

♦*vi* (door etc) かぎが掛る kagí ga kakárù; (wheels) 回らなくなる mawáranaku naru

locker [lɑːk'ər] *n* (in school, railway station etc) ロッカー rókkā

locket [lɑːk'it] *n* ロケット rokéttò

lock in *vt* 閉じ込める tojíkomerù

lock out *vt* (person) 閉出す shimédasu

locksmith [lɑːk'smiθ] *n* 錠前屋 jōmaeshì

lock up *vt* (criminal) 刑務所に入れる keímushò ni iréru; (mental patient) 施設に預ける shisétsu ni azúkeru; (house) ...のかぎを掛ける ...no kagí wo kakérù

♦*vi* ...のかぎを掛ける ...no kagí wo kakérù

lockup [lɑːk'ʌp] *n* (jail) 刑務所 keímushò

locomotive [loukəmou'tiv] *n* 機関車 kikáñsha

locum tenens [lou'kəm tiː'nenz] (*BRIT* **locum**) *n* (MED) 代診 daíshin

locust [lou'kəst] *n* イナゴ inágo

lodge [lɑːdʒ] *n* (small house: at gate of large house) 守衛室 shuéishitsu; (hunting lodge) 山小屋 yamágoya

♦vi (person): **to lodge (with)** (...の家に) 下宿する (...no ié) geshūku suru; (bullet, bone etc) ...に支える ...ni tsukáe-ru

♦vt (complaint, protest etc) 提出する teíshutsu suru

lodger [lɑdʒʌr] n 下宿人 geshūkunin

lodgings [lɑdʒiŋz] npl 下宿 geshūku

loft [lɔːft] n (attic) 屋根裏部屋 yanéurabèya

lofty [lɔːftiː] adj (noble: ideal, aim) 高尚な kōshō na; (self-important: manner) 横柄な ōhei na

log [lɔːg] n (piece of wood) 丸太 marúta; (written account) 日誌 nisshí

♦vt (event, fact) 記録する kiróku suru

logarithm [lɔːgˈəriðəm] n (MATH) 対数 taísū

logbook [lɔːgˈbuk] n (NAUT) 航海日誌 kōkainisshí; (AVIAT) 航空日誌 kōkūnisshi; (BRIT: of car) 登録帳 tōrokuchō

loggerheads [lɔːgˈərhedz] npl: **to be at loggerheads** 対立している taírītsu shite iru

logic [lɑdʒik] n (method of reasoning) 論理学 ronrigaku; (process of reasoning) 論理 rôhri

logical [lɑdʒikəl] adj (argument, analysis) 論理的な ronriteki na; (conclusion, result) 当然な tôzen na; (course of action) 合理的な gōriteki na

logistics [loudʒistiks] n (planning and organization) 仕事の計画と実行 shigoto nò kefkaku tò jikkō

logo [lou'gou] n (of firm, organization) シンボルマーク shfhborumāku, ロゴ rōgō

loin [lɔin] n (of meat) 腰肉 koshíniku

loiter [lɔi'tər] vi (linger) ぶらっく burát-tsuku

loll [lɑl] vi (person: also: **loll about**) ごろ寝する gorône suru

lollipop [lɑl'iːpɑp] n 棒あめ bôame

lollipop lady (BRIT) n 緑のおばさん midóri no obasan n ⟨学童道路横断監視員 gakúdō dōroōdan kañshìin

lollipop man (BRIT: pl **lollipop men**) n ⟨緑のおばさんの仕事をする男性 midó-

ri no obasan no shigéto wò suru dansei

London [lʌn'dən] n ロンドン róñdon

Londoner [lʌn'dənər] n ロンドンっ子 róñdonkko

lone [loun] adj (person) たったひとりのtattá hitóri no; (thing) たったひとつのtattá hitótsu no

loneliness [loun'liːnis] n 孤独 kodóku

lonely [loun'liː] adj (person) 寂しい sabíshii; (situation) 孤独な kodóku na; (place) 人気のない hitóke no naì

long [lɔːŋ] adj 長い nagáī

♦adv 長く nágàku

♦vi: to long for something ...を恋しがる ...wò koshígarū

so/as long as ...さえすれば ...sáè sureba

don't be long! 早く帰って下さいね hayáku kaétte kite kudásai né

how long is the street? この道の端から端までどのぐらいありますか kónó no hashí kara hashî madè donó gurai árimasù ká

how long is the lesson? レッスンの時間はどのぐらいですか réssūn no jfkàn wa donó gurai desu ká

6 meters long 長さは6メーター nágàsa wa rokú mētā

6 months long 期間は6か月 kfkàn wa rokkágetsu

all night long ひと晩中 hitóbanjū

he no longer comes 彼はもう来ない kárè wa mó kônâi

long before ずっと前に zuttó maê ni

before long (+future, +past) まもなく mamôñjkyo

at long last やっと yattó

long-distance [lɔːŋ'dis'tans] adj (travel, phone call) 長距離の chôkyori no

longevity [lɑndʒev'itiː] n 長生き nagáī-ki

long-haired [lɔːŋ'heːrd] adj (person) 長髪の chôhatsu no

longhand [lɔːŋ'hænd] n 普通の書き方 futsú no kakfkata

longing [lɔːŋ'iŋ] n あこがれ akógare

longitude [lɑndʒ'ətud] n 経度 keído

long jump n 走り幅跳び hashfrihabàto-bi

long-life [lɔːŋ'laif] *adj* (batteries etc) 寿命の長い jumyō no nagái; (milk) ロングライフの rōngurraifu no

long-lost [lɔːŋ'lɔːst] *adj* (relative, friend) 長年会わなかった naganen awánakattá

long-playing record [lɔːŋ'plei'iŋ-] *n* L Pレコードの erúpirekōdo

long-range [lɔːŋ'reindʒ] *adj* (plan, forecast) 長期の chōki no; (missile, plane etc) 長距離の chōkyori no

long-sighted [lɔːŋ'saitid] *adj* (MED) 遠視の enshi no

long-standing [lɔːŋ'stæn'diŋ] *adj* 長年にわたる naganen ni watárù

long-suffering [lɔːŋ'sʌf'əriŋ] *adj* (person) 忍耐強い nintaizuyoi

long-term [lɔːŋ'tɜːrm] *adj* (project, solution etc) 長期の chōki no

long wave *n* (RADIO) 長波 chōha

long-winded [lɔːŋ'win'did] *adj* (speech, text) 長たらしい nagátarashiì

loo [luː] *n* (BRIT: inf) トイレ tóìre

look [luk] *vi* (see) 見る mírù; (seem, appear) ...に見える ...ni miérù; (building etc): **to look south/(out) onto the sea** 南(海)に面している minámi(úmí)ni mén shite irú
♦*n* (gen): **to have a look** 見る mírù; (glance): **express disapproval etc** 目付き métsùki; (appearance: expression) 様子 yṓsu
look (here)! (expressing annoyance etc) おい ói
look! (expressing surprise: male language) 見てくれ mîte kuré; (: female language) 見て mîte

look after *vt fus* (care for) ...の面倒を見る ...no mendō wo mfrù; (deal with) 取り扱う toríatsukaù

look at *vt fus* (see) ...を見る ...wo mírù; (read quickly) ...にさっと目を通す ...ni sattó me wo tṓsù; (study: problem, subject etc) 調べる shiráberù

look back *vi* (remember) 振返ってみる furíkaette mirù

look down on *vt fus* (fig) 軽べつする keíbetsu suru

look for *vt fus* (person, thing) 探す sagásu

look forward to *vt fus* ...を楽しみにする ...wo tanóshimi ni suru; (in letters): **we look forward to hearing from you** ご返事をお待ちしております go-hénji wo o-máchi shité orímasù

look into *vt* (investigate) ...を調べる ...wo shiráberù

look on *vi* (watch) 傍観する bṓkan suru ...wo shiráberù

look out *vi* (beware): **to look out (for)** (...に) 注意する (...ni) chúì suru

lookout [luk'aut] *n* (tower etc) 看視所 kanshíjò; (person) 見張り人 mihárinìn
to be on the lookout for something ...を警戒する ...wo keíkai suru

look out for *vt fus* (seek) 探す sagásu

look round *vi* 見回す mimáwasù

looks [luks] *npl* (good looks) 容ぼう yṓbō

look through *vt fus* (examine) ...を調べる ...wo shiráberù

look to *vt fus* (rely on) ...を頼りにする ...wo tayóri ni surù

look up *vi* (with eyes) 見上げる miágerù; (situation) ...の見通しがよくなる ...no mítoshi ga yokú naru
♦*vt* (piece of information) 調べる shiráberù

look up to *vt fus* (hero, idol) ...を尊敬する ...wo sofkei suru

loom [luːm] *vi* (also: **loom up**: object, shape) ぼんやりと姿を現す boñ-yarî to sugáta wo aráwasù; (: event: approach) 迫ってくる semátte irù
♦*n* (for weaving) 機織機 hatáoriki

loony [luː'niː] (*inf*) *adj* 狂っている kurútte irù
♦*n* 気違い kichígai

loop [luːp] *n* (in string, ribbon etc) 輪 wá
♦*vt*: **to loop something round something** ...を巻付ける ...ni ...wo makítsukerù

loophole [luːp'houl] *n* (fig) 抜け穴 nukéana

loose [luːs] *adj* (not firmly fixed) 緩いyurúì; (not close fitting: clothes etc) ゆったりした yuttárì shita; (not tied back: long hair) 縛ってない shibátte naì; (promiscuous: life, morals) ふしだらな fushídàra na

♦n: to be on the loose (prisoner, maniac) 逃亡中である tôbôchû de arù

loose change n 小銭 kozéni

loose chippings -[tʃip'iŋz] npl (on road) 砂利 jarí

loose end n: **to be at loose ends** (US) or **a loose end** (BRIT) 暇を持て余している himá wo motéamashite irù

loosely [luːs'liː] adv 緩く yúrùku

loosen [luː'sən] vt 緩める yurúmerù

loot [luːt] n (inf) 略奪品 buñdorihìn

♦vt (steal from: shops, homes) 略奪する ryakúdatsu suru

lop off [lɑːp-] vt (branches etc) 切り落す kirótosù

lopsided [lɑːp'saidid] adj (crooked) 偏った katáyottà

lord [lɔːrd] n (of particular culture) 貴族 kízòku

Lord Smith スミス卿 sumísukyô

the Lord (REL) 主 shú

my lord (to bishop, noble, judge) 閣下 kákkà

good Lord! えっ eé

the (House of) Lords (BRIT) 上院 jôin

lordship [lɔːrd'ʃip] n: **your Lordship** 閣下 kákkà

lore [lɔːr] n (of particular culture) 伝承 deñshô

lorry [lɔːr'iː] (BRIT) n トラック torákkù

lorry driver (BRIT) n トラック運転手 torákku unteñshu

lose [luːz] (pt, pp lost) vt (object) 紛失す る fuñshitsu suru; なくす nakúsù; (job) 失う ushínaù; (weight) 減らす herásù; (friend, relative through death) 失う ushínaù, なくす nakúsù; (waste: time) 無駄にする mudá ni surù; (: opportunity) 逃 す nogásù; (money) 損する sóñ suru

♦vi (competition, argument) ...に負ける ...ni makérù

to lose (time) (clock) 遅れる okúrerù

loser [luː'zər] n (in game, contest) 敗者 haîsha; (inf: failure: person, thing) 出来損 ない dekísokonai

loss [lɔːs] n (act of losing something) 紛失 fuñshitsu; (occasion of losing some-

thing) 喪失 sôshitsu; (death) 死亡 shibô; (COMM): **to make a loss** 損する sôñ suru

heavy losses (MIL) 大きな損害 ôkina sofigai

to be at a loss 途方に暮れる tohô ni kuréru

lost [lɔːst] pt, pp of **lose**

lost (person, animal: in unknown place) 道に迷った michí ni mayòtta; (: missing) 行方不明の yukûe fumèi no; (object) なくした nakúshita

lost and found (US) n 遺失物 ishítsubùtsu

lost property (BRIT) n = **lost and found**

lot [lɑːt] n (set, group: of things) ひと組 hitôkùmi; (at auctions) ロット róttò

the lot (everything) 全部 zéñbu

a lot (large number, amount) 沢山 takúsan

a lot of (with singular noun) 沢山の takúsan no; (with plural noun) 沢山の takúsan no

lots of (things, people) 沢山の takúsan no

I read a lot 私は沢山の本を読みます watákushi wa takúsañ no hoñ wò yomímasù

to draw lots (for something) (...のために) くじを引く (...no tamé ni) kújì wo hîkù

lotion [lou'ʃən] n (for skin, hair) ローション rôshon

lottery [lɑːt'əːriː] n (game) 宝くじ takárakûji

loud [laud] adj (noise, music, laugh) 大き い ôkii; (support, condemnation) 強い tsuyôi; (clothes) 派手な hadé na

♦adv (speak etc) 大きな声で ôkina kôe de

out loud (read, laugh, pray etc) 声を出して kôe wo dâshìte

loudhailer [laud'heilər] (BRIT) n = **bullhorn**

loudly [laud'liː] adv 大きな声で ôkina kôè de

loudspeaker [laud'spiːkər] n 拡声器 kakúseìki, スピーカー sûpìkā

lounge [laundʒ] n (BRIT: in house) 居間

imá; (in hotel, at airport, station) ロビーróbi; (BRIT: also: **lounge bar**) ラウンジバー raúnjibā
◆vi ぐったりもたれる guttári motárerù

lounge about vi ぶらぶらする búrabura suru

lounge around vi = **lounge about**

lounge suit (BRIT) n 背広 sebíro, スーツ sū́tsu

louse [laus] (pl **lice**) n (insect) シラミ shirámi

lousy [lau'zi:] adj (inf: bad quality: show, meal etc) 最低の saítei no; (: ill) 気持が悪い kimóchi ga warúi

lout [laut] n ちんぴら chínpira

lovable [lʌv'əbəl] adj 愛らしい afrashiì

love [lʌv] n (gen) 愛 ái, 愛情 afjō; (romantic) 恋愛 reñ-ái; (sexual) 性愛 seíai; (strong liking: for music, football, animals etc) 愛着 aíchaku, 好み konómi
◆vt (gen) 愛する ai surù; (thing, activity etc) ...が大好きである ...ga daísuki de arū

love (from) Anne (on letter) 愛を込めて、アン (より) ái wo kómete, áñ (yorí)

to love to do ...するのが大好きである ...surú nò ga daísuki de arū

to be in love with ...にほれている ...ni horéte irù, ...が好きである ...ga sukí de arū

to fall in love with ...と恋に落ちる ...ni kóì ni ochírù, ...が好きになる ...ga sukí ni narù

to make love (have sex) 性交する sefkō suru, セックスする sékkùsu suru

15 love (TENNIS) 15対0 jū́go taí zéro, フィフティーンラブ fíffūtīn rabu

I love chocolate 私はチョコレートが大好きです watákushi wà chokórēto ga daísuki desū

love affair n 情事 jòji

love letter n ラブレター rábūretā

love life n 性生活 seíseikatsu

lovely [lʌv'li:] adj (beautiful 美しい utsúkushiì; (delightful) 楽しい tanóshiì

lover [lʌv'əːr] n (sexual partner) 愛人 aíjin; (person in love) 恋人 kóībito
a lover of art/music 美術(音楽)の愛

好者 bíjutsu(óñgaku)no áikòsha

loving [lʌv'iŋ] adj (person) 愛情深い aíjōbukaì; (actions) 愛情のこもった aíjō no komótta

low [lou] adj (gen) 低い hikuì; (income, price etc) 安い yasúì; (quality) 粗悪な soáku na; (sound: deep) 深い fukáì; (: quiet) 低い hikúì
◆adv (sing) 低音で tefon de; (fly) 低く hikúkù
◆n (METEOROLOGY) 低気圧 teíkiàtsu

to be low on (supplies etc) ...が少なくなっている ...ga sukúnàku nattè irú

to feel low (depressed) 元気がない géñki ga naì

low-alcohol [lou'æl'kəhɔːl] adj (wine, beer) 度の低い do no hikúi

low-cut [lou'kʌt'] adj (dress) 襟ぐりの深い eríguri no fukáì, ローカットの rókàtto no

lower [lou'əːr] adj (bottom, less important) 下の shitá no
◆vt (object, price etc) 下げる sagérù; (voice) 低くする hikúkù suru; (eyes) 下に向ける shitá ni mukérù

low-fat [lou'fæt'] adj (food) 低脂肪の tefshibō no, ローファットの rófàtto no

lowlands [lou'ləndz] npl (GEO) 低地 teíchi

lowly [lou'li:] adj (position, origin) 卑しい iyáshiì

loyal [lɔi'əl] adj (friend, support etc) 忠実な chújitsu na

loyalty [lɔi'əlti:] n 忠誠 chúsei

lozenge [lɑz'indʒ] n (MED) ドロップ dóròppu

LP [el'pi:'] n abbr = **long-playing record**

L-plates [el'pleits] (BRIT) npl 仮免許運転中の表示プレート karímenkyo untenchū no hyójìpurēto

Ltd abbr (COMM) = **limited (liability) company**

lubricate [luːb'rikeit] vt (part of machine, chain etc) ...に油を差す ...ni abúra wo sásù

lucid [luː'sid] adj (writing, speech) 分かりやすい wakáriyasuì; (able to think clearly) 正気な shōki na

luck [lʌk] n (also: **good luck**) 運 ún

  bad luck 悪運 akúun

  good luck! 成功を祈るよ sefkō wð inórù yo

  bad/hard/tough luck! 残念だね zaňneň da né

luckily [lʌk'ili:] adv 幸いに safwai ni

lucky [lʌk'i:] adj (person: fortunate) 運の良い ún no yói; (: at cards etc) ...に強い ...ni tsuyói; (situation, event) まぐれ こ の magúre no; (object) 好運をもたらす kóun wo motárasù

lucrative [lu:'krətiv] adj もうける mōkárù

ludicrous [lu:'dəkrəs] adj (feeling, situation, price etc) ばかばかしい bakábakashii

lug [lʌg] (inf) vt (heavy object, suitcase etc) 引きずる hikízurù

luggage [lʌg'idʒ] n 手荷物 tenímòtsu

  luggage rack n (on car) ルーフラック rūfurakku; (in train) 網棚 amídana

lukewarm [lu:k'wɔːrm] adj (liquid) ぬるい nurúi; (person, reaction etc) 気乗りしない kínori shinai

lull [lʌl] n (break: in conversation, fighting etc) 途切れる事 togírerù kotó

  ♦vt: **to lull someone to sleep** ...を寝付ばせる yusútte ...wo netsúkaserù

  to be lulled into a false sense of security 油断すると yudáň surú

lullaby [lʌl'əbai] n 子守歌 komóriùta

lumbago [lʌmbei'gou] n (MED) 腰痛 yótsū

lumber [lʌm'bəːr] n (wood) 材木 zaímòku; (BRIT: junk) 粗大ごみ sodáigomi

lumberjack [lʌm'bəːrdʒæk] n きこり kikóri

lumber with vt: **to be lumbered with something** ...を押付けられる ...wo oshítsukerarerù

luminous [lu:'minəs] adj (color, dial, instrument etc) 蛍光の kefkō no

lump [lʌmp] n (of clay, butter etc) 塊 katámari; (on body) しこり shikóri; (on head) こぶ kobú; (also: **sugar lump**) 角砂

糖 kakúzatō

  ♦vt: **to lump together** 一緒くたに扱う isshôkuta ni atsúkaù

  a lump sum 一時払い金額 ichíjibaraikíngaku

lumpy [lʌm'pi:] adj (sauce) 塊だらけの katámaridaràke no; (bed) ごつごつの gotsúgotsuno

lunar [lu:'nəːr] adj (landscape, module, landing etc) 月の tsukí no

lunatic [lu:'nətik] adj (behavior) 気違い染みた kichígaijimità

lunch [lʌntʃ] n 昼食 chūshoku

luncheon [lʌn'tʃən] n (formal meal) 昼食 chūshokukai

  luncheon meat n ランチョンミート rañchonmìto

  luncheon voucher (BRIT) n 昼食券 chūshokuken

lunch time n 昼食時 chūshokudoki

lung [lʌŋ] n (ANAT) 肺 haí

lunge [lʌndʒ] vi (also: **lunge forward**) 突進する tosshín suru

  to lunge at ...を目掛けて突っ掛る ...wo megákete tsukkákarù

lurch [lʌːrtʃ] vi (person) よろめく yorómekù; (vehicle) 揺れる yuréru

  ♦n (movement: of person) よろめき yorómeki; (: of vehicle) 揺れ る事 yuréru kotó

  to leave someone in the lurch 見捨てる misúterù

lure [luːr] n (attraction) 魅惑 miwáku

  ♦vt (entice, tempt) 魅惑する miwáku suru

lurid [lu:'rid] adj (violent, sexually graphic: story etc) どぎつい dogítsuì; (pej: brightly colored: dress etc) けばばしい kebábekashì

lurk [lʌːrk] vi (animal, person) 待ち伏せする machíbuse suru

luscious [lʌʃ'əs] adj (attractive: person, thing) 魅力的な miryókuteki na; (food) おいしそうな ofshisō na

lush [lʌʃ] adj (fields, gardens) 生茂った o-íshigettà

lust [lʌst] (pej) n (sexual desire) 性欲 sefyoku; (desire for money, power etc) 欲望

yokúbō

lust after vt fus (desire: strongly) ...の欲に駆られる ...no yokú ni karárerú (: sexually) ...とセックスをしたがる ...to sekkúsù wo shitágarù

luster [lʌsˈtəʳ] (BRIT lustre) n (shining: of metal, polished wood etc) つや tsuyá

lust for vt fus = lust after

lusty [lʌsˈti] adj (healthy, energetic) 元気一杯の gefkiappaí no

Luxembourg [lʌkˈsəmbəːrg] n ルクセンブルク rukúsehburuku

luxuriant [lugˈzuːˈriːant] adj (plants, trees) 生茂った ofshigettá (gardens) 植込みの生茂った uékomi no ofshigettá (hair) 豊富な hōfu na

luxurious [lugˈzuˈriːəs] adj (hotel, surroundings etc) 豪華な gōka na

luxury [lʌkˈʃəːri] n (great comfort) ぜいたく zeftaku; (expensive extra) ぜいたく品 zeftakuhīn; (infrequent pleasure) 得難い楽しみ egátaí tanóshimī
♦cpd (hotel, car etc) 豪華... gōka...

lying [laiˈiŋ] n うそをつく事 usó wo tsúkù kotó
♦adj うそつきの usótsuki no

lynch [lintʃ] vt (prisoner, suspect) 勝手に絞り首とする kattè ni shibárikùbi ni suru

lyrical [lirˈikəl] adj (poem) 叙情の jojō no; (fig: praise, comment) 叙情的な jojōteki na

lyrics [lirˈiks] npl (of song) 歌詞 káshì

M

m. abbr = meter; mile; million

M.A. [emeiˈ] abbr = Master of Arts

mac [mæk] (BRIT) n = mackintosh

macabre [məkɑːˈbrə] adj 背筋の凍る様な sesúji no kōru yō na

macaroni [mækərouˈni] n マカロニ mákàroni

machine [məʃiːnˈ] n (piece of equipment) 機械 kikái; (fig: party machine, war machine etc) 組織 sōshíkì
♦vt (TECH) 機械で作る kikái de tsukú-

rù; (dress etc) ミシンで作る míshìn de tsukúrù

machine gun n 機関銃 kikánjū

machine language n (COMPUT) 機械語 kikáigo

machinery [məʃiːˈnəːri] n (equipment) 機械類 kikáirùi; (fig: of government) 組織 sōshíkì

macho [mɑːˈtʃou] adj (man, attitude) 男っぽい otókoppoi

mackerel [mækˈəːrəl] n inv サバ sabá

mackintosh [mækˈintɑʃ] (BRIT) n レーンコート rénkōto

mad [mæd] adj (insane) 気の狂った ki no kurúttà; (foolish) ばかげた bakágetà; (angry) 怒っている okótte irú; (keen: to be mad about) (person, football etc) ...に夢中になっている ...ni muchū ni náttè iru

madam [mædˈəm] n (form of address) 奥様 ōkùsama

madden [mædˈən] vt 怒らせる okóraserú

made [meid] pt, pp of **make**

Madeira [mədiːˈrə] n (GEO) マデイラ madéira; (wine) マデイラ madéira

made-to-measure [meidˈtəmeʒˈəːr] (BRIT) adj = **made-to-order**

made-to-order [meidˈtuːˈɔːdəːr] (US) adj オーダーメードの ōdāmēdo no

madly [mædˈliː] adv (frantically) 死物狂いで shinfmonogurúi de
madly in love ぞっこんほれ込んで zokkón horékònde

madman [mædˈmæn] (pl **madmen**) n 気違い kichígaì

madness [mædˈnis] n (insanity) 狂気 kyōki; (foolishness) 気違い沙汰 kichígaizata

Madrid [mədridˈ] n マドリード madórîdo

Mafia [mɑːˈfiːə] n マフィア máfìa

magazine [mægəziːnˈ] n (PRESS) 雑誌 zasshí; (RADIO, TV) 放送ジャーナル hōsō jānarù

maggot [mægˈət] n ウジムシ ujímùshi

magic [mædʒˈik] n (supernatural power) 魔法 mahō; (conjuring) 手品 téjīna, マジック májìkku

♦adj (powers, ritual) 魔法の mahō no

magical [mædʒ'ikəl] adj (powers, ritual) 魔法の mahō no; (experience, evening) 夢の様な yumé no yō na

magician [mædʒij'ən] n (wizard) 魔法使い mahōtsukai; (conjurer) マジシャン májìshan

magistrate [mædʒ'istreit] n 軽犯罪判事 kefhanzai hanji

magnanimous [mægnæn'əməs] adj (person, gesture) 寛大な kafidai na

magnate [mæg'neit] n 大立者 ōdatemóno, ...王 ...ō

magnesium [mægni:'zi:əm] n マグネシウム magǔneshiùmu

magnet [mæg'nit] n 磁石 jíshaku

magnetic [mægnet'ik] adj (PHYSICS) 磁石の jíshaku no; (personality) 魅力的 の miryōkuteki na

magnetic tape n 磁気テープ jikí tèpu

magnetism [mæg'nitizəm] n 磁気 jīkí

magnificent [mægnif'əsənt] adj 素晴らしい subárashiì

magnify [mæg'nəfai] vt (enlarge: object) 拡大する kakúdai suru; (increase: sound) 大きくする ōkiku suru

magnifying glass [mæg'nəfaiiŋ-] n 拡大鏡 kakúdaikyō

magnitude [mæg'nətu:d] n (size) 大きさ ōkisa; (importance) 重要性 jūyōsei

magnolia [mægnoul'jə] n マグノリア magúnorìa ◊モクレン, コブシ, タイサンボクを含む植物の類 mókùren, kóbùshi, taísanboku wo fukúmù shokúbùtsu no ruì

magpie [mæg'pai] n カササギ kasásagi

mahogany [məhɑːg'əni:] n マホガニー mahōganì

maid [meid] n (servant) メイド meídò

old maid (pej: spinster) ハイミス haímìsu

maiden [meid'ən] n (literary: girl) 少女 shōjo

♦adj (aunt etc) 未婚の mikón no; (speech, voyage) 処女... shōjo ...

maiden name n 旧姓 kyūsei ◊既婚女性について旧姓 kiyūsei ◊既婚女性について旧姓 kikónjosei ni tsúite tsukáu

mail [meil] n (postal service) 郵便 yūbin;

(letters etc) 郵便物 yūbinbutsu

♦vt (post) 投かんする tōkan suru

mailbox [meil'bɑːks] (US) n ポスト pósùto

mailing list [mei'liŋ-] n 郵送先名簿 yū-sōsaki meĭbo

mail-order [meil'ɔːrdəːr] n (system) 通信販売 tsūshinhanbai

main [mein] adj 主な ómò na, 主要な shu-yō na, メーンの mèn no

♦n (pipe) 本管 hofikan

in the main (in general) 概して gái shite

mainframe [mein'freim] n (COMPUT) メインフレーム mefnfurèmu

mainland [mein'lænd] n 本土 hóndo

mainly [mein'li:] adv 主に ómò ni

main road n 幹線道路 kafisendòro

mainstay [mein'stei] n (fig: prop) 大黒柱 daíkokubàshira

mainstream [mein'stri:m] n (fig) 主流 shuryū

maintain [meintein'] vt (preserve: contact, friendship, system) 続ける tsuzúke-ru, 保持する hojí suru; (keep up: momentum, output) 維持する ijí suru; (provide: for dependant) 養う yashínaù; (look after: building) 管理する káñri suru; (affirm: belief, opinion) 主張する shuchō suru

maintenance [mein'tənəns] n (of contact, friendship, system) 保持 hojí; (of momentum, output) 維持 ijí; (provision for dependent) 扶養 fuyō; (looking after: building) 管理 káñri; (affirmation: of belief, opinion) 主張 shuchō; (BRIT: LAW: alimony) 離婚手当 rikónteate

maize [meiz] n トウモロコシ tōūmoròko-shi

majestic [mədʒes'tik] adj (splendid: scenery etc) 壮大な sodái na; (dignified)

堂々とした dōdō to shitá

majesty [mædʒisti] n (title): *Your Majesty* 陛下 hếîka; (sovereignty) 王位 ồi; (splendor) 威厳 igén

major [meidʒəːr] n (MIL) 少佐 shōsa
♦adj (important, significant: event, factor) 重要な jūyō na; (MUS: key) 長調の chōchō no

Majorca [məjɔːrkə] n マジョルカ majórūka

majority [mədʒɔːrriti] n (larger group: of people, things) 過半数 kahánsū; (margin: of votes) 得票差 tokúhyōsa

make [meik] (pt, pp **made**) vt (produce, form: object, clothes, cake) 作る tsukūrū; (: noise) 立てる tatérū; (: speech, mistake) する surú; (: remark) 言う iú; (manufacture: goods) 作る tsukūrū, 製造する seízō suru; (cause to be): *to make someone sad* ...を悲しくさせる ...wo kanáshikū saséru; (force): *to make someone do something* ...に...をさせる ...ni ...wo saseru; (earn: money) もうける mōkérù; (equal): *2 and 2 make 4* 2足す2は4 ni2tásù2 tásõ 2 wā 4
♦n (brand): *it's a Japanese make* 日本製ての nihónsei desu

to make the bed ベッドを整える béddð wo totónoerù

to make a fool of someone ...をばかにする ...wo bắka ni surú

to make a profit 利益を得る ríeki wò érù

to make a loss 損をする són wo suru

to make it (arrive on time) 間に合う ma ní áu; (achieve something) 成功する sefkō suru

what time do you make it? 今何時ですか imá nánji desu ká

to make do with ...で間に合せる ...de ma ní awaserû

make-believe [meikbíliːv] n (pretense) 見せ掛け misékake

make for vt fus (place) ...に向かう ...ni mukáù

make out vt (decipher) 解読する kaídoku suru; (understand) 分かる wakárū; (see) 見る mírū; (write: cheque) 書く ká-

 kù

maker [meikəːr] n (of program, film etc) 制作者 seísakushā; (manufacturer) 製造者 seízōshā, メーカー mếka

makeshift [meikʃift] adj (temporary) 間に合せの ma ní awase no

make up vt (constitute) 構成する kōsei suru; (invent) でっち上げる detchfageru; (prepare) 用意する yōi suru; (: parcel) 包む tsutsúmù
♦vi (after quarrel) 仲直りする nakánaori suru; (with cosmetics) 化粧する keshō suru

make-up [meikʌp] n (cosmetics) メーキャップ mếkyappù

make up for vt fus (loss, disappointment) ...の埋め合せをする ...no uméawase wő suru

make-up remover n 化粧落し keshō otõshi

making [meikiŋ] n (fig): *a doctor etc in the making* 医者の卵 ishá no tamágo
to have the makings of ...の素質がある ...no soshftsu ga arù

malaise [mæleiz] n 倦怠 keñtai

malaria [məlɛːriə] n マラリア marária

Malaya [məleiʒə] n マラヤ márãya

Malaysia [məleiʒə] n マレーシア maréshîa

male [meil] n (BIOL: not female) 雄 osû
♦adj (animal) 雄の osû no; (human) 男の otőko no, 男性の dańsei no; (attitude etc) 男性的な dańseíteki na

malevolent [məlévələnt] adj (evil, harmful: person, intention) 悪意の様な âkùma no yố na

malfunction [mælfʌŋkʃən] n (of computer, machine) 故障 koshõ

malice [mǽlis] n (ill will) 悪意 ákùi; (rancor) 恨み urámi

malicious [məlíʃəs] adj (spiteful: person, gossip) 悪意に満ちた ákùi ni michîta

malign [məláin] vt (slander) 中傷する chûshõ suru

malignant [məlígnənt] adj (MED: tumor, growth) 悪性の akúsei no

mall [mɔːl] n (also: shopping mall) ショ

ッピング・モール shoppíngu mòru

mallet [mæl'it] n 木づち kízùchi

malnutrition [mælnu:trɪʃ'ən] n 栄養失調 eíyōshítchō

malpractice [mælpræk'tis] n (MED) 医療過誤 iryōkagò; (LAW) 不正行為 fuséikōi

malt [mɔːlt] n (grain) もやし moyáshi, モルト móròto; (also: **malt whisky**) モルトウイスキー morúto uísùkī

Malta [mɔːl'tə] n マルタ márùta

Maltese [mɔːltiːz'] adj マルタの márùta no

♦n inv マルタ人 marútajin

maltreat [mæltriːt'] vt (treat badly, violently: child, animal) 虐待する gyakútai suru

mammal [mæm'əl] n 哺乳動物 honyúdòbutsu

mammoth [mæm'əθ] n (animal) マンモス mámmosu

♦adj (colossal, enormous: task) ばく大な bakúdai na

man [mæn] (pl **men**) n (adult male) 男 otóko, 男性 dañsei; (mankind) 人類 jíñrui

♦vt (NAUT: ship) 乗組ませる norīkumaserū; (MIL: gun, post) 配置につく haíchi ni tsukù; (operate: machine) 操作する sōsa suru

an old man 老人 rōjin

man and wife 夫婦 fúfu

manage [mæn'idʒ] vi (succeed) うまくなんとかする úmàka nántoka suru; (get by financially) なんとかして暮す nántoka shite kurásù

♦vt (be in charge of: business, shop, organization) 管理する kañri suru; (control: ship) 操縦する sōjū suru; (: person) うまくあしらう umáku ashīraù

manageable [mæn'idʒəbəl] adj (task, number) 扱いやすい atsúkaiyasuì

management [mæn'idʒmənt] n (of business etc: control, organization) 管理 káñri; (: persons) 管理職 kañrishòku

manager [mæn'idʒəːr] n (of business etc) 支配人 shiháinin; (of pop star) マネージャー manéjā; (SPORT) 監督 kañtoku

manageress [mæn'idʒəris] n (of busi-

ness etc) 女性支配人 joséishihàinin; (of pop star) 女性マネージャー josei manèjā; (SPORT) 女性監督 joséi kañtoku

managerial [mænidʒiː'riəl] adj (role, skills) 管理職の kañrishòku no

managing director [mæn'idʒiŋ-] n 専務取締役 séñmutoríshimarìyaku

mandarin [mæn'dərin] n (also: **mandarin orange**) みかん míkàn; (high-ranking bureaucrat) 高級官僚 kōkyú kañryō

mandate [mæn'deit] n (authority) 権限 keñgen; (task) 任務 níñmu

mandatory [mæn'dətɔːri] adj (obligatory) 義務的な gimúteki na

mane [mein] n (of horse, lion) たてがみ tátègami

maneuver [mənu:'vəːr] (US) vt (move: car, bulky, object) 巧みに動かす tákūmi ni ugókasu; (manipulate: person, situation) 操る ayátsuru

♦vi (move: car, plane) 巧みに動く tákūmi ni ugókù; (MIL) 軍事演習を行う guñjíeñshū wo okonau

♦n 巧みな動き tákūmi na ugóki

manfully [mæn'fəli] adv (valiantly) 勇ましく isámashikù

mangle [mæŋ'gəl] vt (crush, twist) めちゃくちゃにする mechákucha ni suru

mango [mæŋ'gou] (pl **mangoes**) n マンゴー mángō

mangy [mein'dʒi:] adj (animal) 汚らしい kitánarashiì

manhandle [mæn'hændəl] vt (mistreat) 手荒に扱う teára ni atsúkaù

manhole [mæn'houl] n マンホール mañhōru

manhood [mæn'hud] n (age) 成人時代 seíjin jidài; (state) 成人である事 seíjin de arū kotó 〇男性の人について言う dañsei nomì ni tsúîte iū

man-hour [mæn'auəːr] n (time) 人時 níñji

manhunt [mæn'hʌnt] n (POLICE) 人間狩り niñgeñgari

mania [mei'niə] n (craze) …狂 …kyō; (illness) そう病 sōbyō

maniac [mei'niæk] n (lunatic) 狂人 kyōjin; (fig) 無謀な人 mubō na hitò

manic [mæn'ik] *adj* (behavior, activity) 猛烈な môretsu na

manic-depressive [mæn'ikdipres'iv] *n* そううつ病患者 sôutsubyô kanja

manicure [mæn'əkjʊər] *n* マニキュア manīkyūa

manicure set *n* マニキュア・セット manīkyūa settô

manifest [mæn'əfest] *vt* (show, display) 表す aráwasū
♦*adj* (evident, obvious) 明白な meíhaku na

manifestation [mænəfestei'ʃən] *n* 現れ aráware

manifesto [mænəfes'tou] *n* 声明書 seímeisho

manipulate [mənip'jəleit] *vt* (people) 操 る ayátsurù; (system, situation) 操作する sôsa suru

mankind [mæn'kaind'] *n* (human beings) 人類 jínrui

manly [mæn'li:] *adj* (masculine) 男らしい otôkorashìi

man-made [mæn'meid] *adj* (environment, satellite etc) 人工の jínkô no; (fiber, lake etc) 人造の jínzô no

manner [mæn'ər] *n* (way) やり方 yaríkata; (behavior) 態度 táîdo; (type, sort):
all manner of things あらゆる物 aráyuru monð

mannerism [mæn'ərizəm] *n* 癖 kusé

manners [mæn'ərz] *npl* (conduct) 行儀 gyôgi, マナー manâ
bad manners 行儀の悪い事 gyôgi no waruî kotô

manoeuvre [mənu:'vər] (*BRIT*) =
maneuver

manor [mæn'ər] *n* (also: **manor house**) 屋敷 yashíki

manpower [mæn'pauər] *n* (workers) 人手 hitóde

mansion [mæn'tʃən] *n* 豪邸 gôtei

manslaughter [mæn'slɔːtər] *n* (LAW) 殺意なき殺人 satsúi naki satsôjin

mantelpiece [mæn'təlpi:s] *n* マントルピース mañtorupîsu

manual [mæn'juəl] *adj* (work, worker) 肉体の nikūtai no; (controls) 手動の shu-

dô no
♦*n* (book) マニュアル mányùaru

manufacture [mænjəfæk'tʃər] *vt* (make, produce: goods) 製造する seízô suru
♦*n* (making) 製造 seízô

manufacturer [mænjəfæk'tʃərər] *n* 製造業者 seízôgyòsha, メーカー mêkā

manure [mənuːr'] *n* 肥やし koyáshi

manuscript [mæn'jəskript] *n* (of book, report) 原稿 geñkô; (old document) 写本 shahôn

many [men'i:] *adj* (a lot of: people, things, ideas) 沢山の takúsañ no
♦*pron* (several) 多数 tasû
a great many 非常に沢山の hijô ni takúsañ no
many a time 何回も nañkai mo

map [mæp] *n* (of town, country) 地図 chízu

maple [mei'pəl] *n* (tree) カエデ kaéde; (wood) カエデ材 kaédezai

map out *vt* (plan, task) 計画する keíkaku suru

mar [mɑːr] *vt* (spoil: appearance) 損なう sokónaû; (: day, event) ぶち壊す buchí kowasû

marathon [mær'əθɑːn] *n* (race) マラソン marásôn

marauder [mərɔːd'ər] *n* (robber, killer) 略奪者 ryakūdatsusha

marble [mɑːr'bəl] *n* (stone) 大理石 daíriseki; (toy) ビー玉 bîdama

March [mɑːrtʃ] *n* 3月 sañgatsu

march [mɑːrtʃ] *vi* (MIL: soldiers) 行進する kôshin suru; (fig: protesters) デモ行進 をする demô kôshin wo suru; (walk briskly) 足音も高く歩く ashîoto mo takákù arúkù
♦*n* (MIL) 行進 kôshin; (demonstration) デモ行進 demô kôshin

mare [meːr] *n* 牝ウマ mesû uma

margarine [mɑːr'dʒərin] *n* マーガリン mâgarin

margin [mɑːr'dʒin] *n* (difference: of

votes) 差 sa; (extra amount) 余裕 yoyū́; (COMM: profit) 利ざや rizáya, マージン mā́jin; (space: on page) 余白 yoháku; (edge: of area, group) 外れ hazúre

marginal [mɑːr'dʒinəl] *adj* (unimportant) 二次的な nijíteki na

marginal (seat) *n* (POL) 不安定な議席 fuáñtei na giséki ◇わずかな票の差で得たので, 次の選挙で失う可能性のある議席 wázùka na hyṓ nò sá de età node, tsugí nò seńkyo de ushínaù kanṓsei no arù giséki

marigold [mær'əgould] *n* マリーゴールド marígṑrudo

marijuana [mærəwɑː'nə] *n* マリファナ maríf̀āna

marina [məriː'nə] *n* (harbor) マリーナ marínà

marinate [mær'əneit] *vt* (CULIN) マリネにする márīne ni suru

marine [məriːn'] *adj* (life, plant, biology) 海の umí no; (engineer, engineering) 船舶の seńpaku no

♦*n* (*US*: sailor) 海兵隊員 kaíheitaìiṅ; (*BRIT*: soldier) 海兵隊員 kaíheitaìin

marital [mær'itəl] *adj* (problem, relations) 夫婦の fū́fu no

marital status ◇未婚, 既婚, 離婚を尋ねる時に使う言葉 mikóṅ, kikóṅ, ríkòn wo tazúnerù tokí ni tsukaù kotóba

maritime [mær'itaim] *adj* 海事の káìji no

marjoram [mɑːr'dʒəːrəm] *n* マヨラナ mayónàra, マージョラム mā́jòramu

mark [mɑːrk] *n* (symbol: cross, tick etc) 印 shirúshi; (stain) 染み shimí; (of shoes, fingers, tires: in snow, mud etc) 跡 átò; (sign: of friendship, respect etc) 印 shirúshi; (SCOL) 成績 seíseki; (level, point): ***the halfway mark*** 中間点の目印 chū́kanteñ no mejírùshi; (currency) マルク márùku

♦*vt* (make a mark on: with pen etc) 印を書く shirúshi wo kákù; (: with shoes, tires etc) 跡を残す átò wo nokósù; (damage: furniture etc) 傷を付ける kizú wo tsukérù; (stain: clothes, carpet etc) 染みを付ける shimí wo tsukérù; (indicate: place, time, price) 示す shimésù; (commemorate: event) 記念する kinén suru; (*BRIT*: SCOL) 成績をつける seíseki wò tsukérù

to mark time (MIL, *fig*) 足踏みする ashíbumi suru

marked [mɑːrkt] *adj* (obvious) 著しい ichíjirushiì

marker [mɑːr'kəːr] *n* (sign) 目印 mejírù-shi; (bookmark) しおり shiórì

marker pen サインペン saíñpen

market [mɑːr'kit] *n* (for fish, cattle, vegetables etc) 市場 íchība; (in proper names) 市場 íchība, 市場 shijṓ; (COMM: business and trading activity) 市場 shijṓ; (: demand) 需要 juyṓ

♦*vt* (COMM: sell) 市場に出す shijṓ ni dásù

market garden (*BRIT*) *n* 野菜農園 yasáinòen ◇主に市場向けの野菜や果物を栽培する小規模農場 ómò ni shijṓmuke nò yasái ya kudámono wò saíbai surù shṓkibo nòjō

marketing [mɑːr'kitiŋ] *n* (COMM) 販売 hańbai

marketplace [mɑːr'kitpleis] *n* (area, site: *also* COMM) 市場 íchība

market research *n* 市場調査 shijṓchṑsa

marksman [mɑːrks'mən] (*pl* **marksmen**) *n* 射撃の名手 shagéki no meíshù

marmalade [mɑːr'məleid] *n* マーマレード mā́marèdo

maroon [mərʊːn'] *vt*: ***to be marooned*** (shipwrecked) 遭難で置去りになる sṓnan dè okízari ni narù; (*fig*: abandoned) 置去りにされる okízari ni sarèru

♦*adj* (color) クリ色 kuríiro

marquee [mɑːrkiː'] *n* (tent) テント téǹto ◇運動会, 野外パーティなどで使う物を指す uńdōkai, yagái pāti nádò de tsukáù monó wo sásù

marquess [mɑːr'kwis] *n* 侯爵 kṑshaku

marquis [mɑːr'kwis] *n* = **marquess**

marriage [mær'idʒ] *n* (relationship, institution) 結婚 kekkón; (wedding) 結婚式 kekkóñshiki

marriage bureau *n* 結婚相談所 kekkónsōdanjo

marriage certificate *n* 結婚証明書 kekkónshōmeishó

married [mær'i:d] *adj* (man, woman) 既婚の kikón no; (life, love) 結婚の kekkón no

marrow [mær'ou] *n* (vegetable) セイヨウカボチャ seíyōkabóchа; (: **bone marrow**) 骨髄 kotsúzui

marry [mær'i:] *vt* (man, woman) ...と結婚する ...to kekkón surù; (subj: father, priest etc) ...の結婚式を行う ...no kekkónshiki wo okónaù

♦*vi* (*also*: **get married**) 結婚する kekkón suru

Mars [ma:rz] *n* (planet) 火星 kaséi

marsh [ma:rʃ] *n* (bog) 沼沢地 shōtakúchi; (*also*: **salt marsh**) 塩性沼沢地 eñsei shōtakúchi

marshal [ma:r'ʃəl] *n* (MIL: *also*: **field marshal**) 陸軍元師 rikúgun geñsui; (official: at sports meeting etc) 役員 yakúin; (*US*: of police, fire department) 長官 chōkan

♦*vt* (organize: thoughts) 整理する sefri suru; (: support) 集める atsúmerù; (: soldiers) 整列させる seíretsu saserù

marshy [ma:r'ʃi:] *adj* 沼沢の多い shōtaku nō ōi

martial [ma:r'ʃəl] *adj* (military) 軍の guñ no

martial arts *npl* 武術 bújutsu

martial law *n* 戒厳令 kaígeñrei

martyr [ma:r'tə:r] *n* (for beliefs) 殉教者 juñkyōsha

martyrdom [ma:r'tə:rdəm] *n* 殉教 juñkyō

marvel [ma:r'vəl] *n* (wonder) 驚異 kyōi

♦*vi*: **to marvel (at)** 驚嘆する kyōtan suru

marvelous [ma:r'vələs] (*BRIT* **marvellous**) *adj* 素晴らしい subárashiî

Marxism [ma:r'ksizəm] *n* マルクス主義 marúkusushùgi

Marxist [ma:r'ksist] *adj* マルクス主義の marúkusushùgi no

♦*n* マルクス主義者 marúkusushùgisha

marzipan [ma:r'zəpæn] *n* マジパン majípan

mascara [mæskær'ə] *n* マスカラ masúkara

mascot [mæs'kət] *n* マスコット masúkotto

masculine [mæs'kjəlin] *adj* (male: characteristics, pride) 男性の dañsei no; (: atmosphere) 男性的な dañseiteki na; (woman) 男の様な otóko no yō na; (LING: noun, pronoun etc) 男性の dañsei no

mash [mæʃ] *vt* つぶす tsubúsu

mashed potatoes [mæʃt-] *npl* マッシュポテト masshō potéto

mask [mæsk] *n* (disguise) 覆面 fukúmen; (shield: gas mask, face mask) マスク másuku

♦*vt* (cover: face) 覆い隠す ōikakúsu; (hide: feelings) 隠す kakúsù

masochist [mæs'əkist] *n* マゾヒスト mazóhisùto

mason [mei'sən] *n* (*also*: **stone mason**) 石屋 ishíya; (*also*: **freemason**) フリーメーソン furímèson

masonry [mei'sənri:] *n* (stonework) 石造部 sekízōbu ◇建物の石やれんがなどで造られた部分 tatémòno no ishí yà reñga nadò de tsukúrarèta bùbún

masquerade [mæskəreid'] *vi*: **to masquerade as ...** を装う ...wo yosóoù

mass [mæs] *n* (large number: of papers, people etc) 多数 tasú; (large amount: of detail, hair etc) 大量 tafryō; (amount: of air, liquid, land) 塊 katámari; (PHYSICS) 物量 butsúryō; (REL) ミサ聖祭 mísà seísai

♦*cpd* (communication, unemployment etc) 大量の tafryō no

♦*vi* (troops, protesters) 集合する shúgō suru

massacre [mæs'əkə:r] *n* 大虐殺 daígyakúsatsu

massage [məsa:ʒ'] *n* マッサージ massáji

♦*vt* (rub) マッサージする massáji suru

masses [mæs'iz] *npl*: **the masses** (ordinary people) 大衆 taíshū *masses of* (*inf*: food, money, people) 一杯の ippái no

masseur [mæsɜ:r] *n* マッサージ師 massájìshì

masseuse [məsu:s] *n* マッサージ嬢 massájìjō

massive [mæs'iv] *adj* (large and heavy: furniture, door, person) どっしりした dosshírì shita; (huge: support, changes, increase) 膨大な bôdai na

mass media [-mi:'di:ə] *npl* マスメディア masúmedèia

mass production (*BRIT* **mass-production**) *n* 大量生産 tafryōseisan, マスプロ masúpuro

mast [mæst] *n* (NAUT) マスト mâsùto; (RADIO etc) 放送アンテナ hōsō ańtena

master [mæs'tə:r] *n* (of servant, slave) 主人 shujfn, (in secondary school) 先生 señsèi, (title for boys): **Master X** X君 ékùsu kùn

♦*vt* (control: situation) 掌握する shôaku suru; (: one's feelings etc) 抑える osáerù; (learn: skills, language) 修得する shútoku suru, マスターする masútā suru

to be master of the situation (*fig*) 事態を掌握している jítài wo shôaku shite irú

master key *n* マスターキー masútā kī

masterly [mæs'tə:rli:] *adj* あっぱれな appáre na

mastermind [mæs'tə:rmaind] *n* (of crime etc) 首謀者 shubôshà, 黒幕 kuró-maku

♦*vt* 計画を練って実行させる kefkaku wò nèttê jikkō saserú

Master of Arts/Science *n* (person) 文学(理学)修士 buñgaku (rígàku) shûshi; (qualification) 文学(理学)修士号 buñgaku (rígàku) shûshigō

masterpiece [mæs'tə:rpi:s] *n* 傑作 kessáku

mastery [mæs'tə:ri:] *n* (of skill, language) 修得 shútoku

masturbate [mæs'tə:rbeit] *vi* マスターベーション(オナニー)をする masútābêshon(onánī)wo surù

masturbation [mæstə:rbei'ʃən] *n* マスターベーション masútābêshon, オナニー onánī

mat [mæt] *n* (on floor) マット mâttò; (at door: *also*: **doormat**) ドアマット doámattò; (on table: *also*: **table mat**) テーブルマット tēburumattò

♦*adj* = **matt**

match [mætʃ] *n* (game: of football, tennis etc) 試合 shiái, マッチ mátchì; (for lighting fire, cigarette) マッチ mátchì; (equal) 力が同等な chikára ga dôtō na hitô

♦*vt* (go well with: subj: colors, clothes) ...に合う ...ni âû; (equal) ...と同等である ...to dôtō de arû; (correspond to) ...に合う ...ni âû; (pair: *also*: **match up**) ...と組合せる ...to awáserù, ...と組合せる ...to kumáserù

♦*vi* (colors, materials) 合う âû

to be a good match (colors etc) よく合う yokû âû; (couple) 似合いの...である nǐâî no ...de arû

matchbox [mætʃ'bɑːks] *n* マッチ箱 matchíbàko

matching [mætʃ'iŋ] *adj* (clothes etc) そろいの sorôi no

mate [meit] *n* (workmate) 仲間 nakáma; (*inf*: friend) 友達 tomódachì; (animal) 相手 aîte; (in merchant navy: first, second) ...等航海士 ...tō kôkaìshî

♦*vi* (animals) 交尾する kôbi surú

material [məti:'ri:əl] *n* (substance) 物質 busshítsu; (cloth) 生地 kijí; (information, data) 情報 jôhō

♦*adj* (possessions, existence) 物質的な busshítsuteki na

materialistic [məti:riəlis'tik] *adj* 唯物主義的な yufbutsushugîteki na

materialize [məti:'ri:əlaiz] *vi* (happen) 起る okôrû; (appear) 現れる awárerù

materials [məti:'ri:əlz] *npl* (equipment) 材料 zafryō

maternal [mətə:r'nəl] *adj* (feelings, role) 母性の boséi no

maternity [mətə:r'niti:] *n* 母性 boséi

maternity dress *n* マタニティドレス matánitidorèsu

maternity hospital *n* 産院 safi-in

math [mæθ] (BRIT **maths**) n 数学 sūgaku

mathematical [mæθəmæt'ikəl] adj (formula) 数学の sūgaku no; (mind) 数学的な sūgakuteki na

mathematician [mæθəmətiʃ'ən] n 数学者 sūgakusha

mathematics [mæθəmæt'iks] n 数学 sūgaku

maths [mæθs] (BRIT) n = math

matinée [mætənei'] n マチネー machinē

mating call [mei'tiŋ-] n (of animals) 求愛の声 kyūai nō kôe

matrices [meit'risiz] npl of matrix

matriculation [mætrikjəlei'ʃən] n (enrollment) 大学入学資格試験 daigakunyūgaku

matrimonial [mætrəmou'niːəl] adj 結婚の kekkôn no

matrimony [mæt'rəmouni] n (marriage) 結婚 kekkôn

matrix [mei'triks] (pl **matrices**) n (context, environment) 環境 kaṅkyō

matron [mei'trən] n (in hospital) 婦長 fuchô; (in school) 養護員 yôgoiñ

matt(t) [mæt] adj つやの消された tsuyákeshi no

matted [mæt'id] adj もつれた motsúreta

matter [mæt'əːr] n (event) 事件 jiken; (situation) 物事 mono jijô; (problem) 問題 mondai; (PHYSICS) 物質 busshitsu; (substance, material) 素材 sozái; (written material: reading matter etc) 印刷物 insatsubûtsu, 本 hoñ; (MED: pus) うみ umi

♦vi (be important: family, job etc) 大切である taísetsu de arù

it doesn't matter 構わない kamáwanai

what's the matter? どうしましたか dô shimashita kâ

no matter what (whatever happens) 何があっても náni ga atté mo

as a matter of course (automatically) 当然ながら tôzen nagara

as a matter of fact 実は jitsú wa

matter-of-fact [mæt'əːrəvfækt'] adj 無味乾燥な mumíkaňsô na

matting [mæt'iŋ] npl (affairs) 物事 monógòto; (situation) 状況 jôkyô

mattress [mæt'ris] n マットレス mattôrèsu

mature [mətuːr'] adj (person) 成熟した sefjuku shita; (cheese, wine etc) 熟成した jukûsei shita

♦vi (develop: child, style) 成長する sefchô suru; (grow up: person) 成熟する sefjuku suru; (ripen, age: cheese, wine etc) 熟成する jukûsei suru

maturity [mətuːr'iti] n (adulthood) 成熟 sefjuku; (wisdom) 分別 fúñbetsu

maul [mɔːl] vt ...に大けがをさせる ...ni ôkega wo saséru

mausoleum [mɔːsəliː'əm] n 納骨堂 nôkotsudô

mauve [mouv] adj フジ色の fujîro no

maverick [mæv'əːrik] n 一匹オオカミ ippíki ôkami

maxim [mæk'sim] n 格言 kakúgen

maximum [mæk'səməm] (pl **maxima**) adj (efficiency, speed, dose) 最大の saídai no

♦n 最大限 saídaìgen

May [mei] n 5月 gógàtsu

may [mei] (conditional: **might**) vi (indicating possibility): *he may come* 彼は来るかも知れない kárè wa kurú ka mo shirenai; (be allowed to): *may I smoke?* タバコをすってもいいですか tabáko wo sutté mô îi desu kâ; (wishes): *may God bless you!* 神の祝福をあなたに! kamí nô shukûfuku wò anáta ni *you may as well go* 行ってもいいかも知れない itté mô îi ka mo shirenai; (dismissive) それでも方がいいかも知れない itta hô ga îi ka mo shirenái

maybe [mei'biː] adv 事によると kotô ni yorú to

May Day n メーデー mêdè

mayhem [mei'hem] n 混乱 koñran

mayonnaise [meiəneiz'] n マヨネーズ mayôneèzu

mayor [mei'əːr] n (of city, town) 市(町、村)長 shi (chô, son) chô

mayoress [mei'əris] n (partner) 市(町、村)長夫人 shi (chô, son) chô fujîn

maze [meiz] n (labyrinth, puzzle) 迷路 mêiro

M.D. [emdi:'] *abbr* = Doctor of Medicine

KEYWORD

me [mi:] *pron* **1** (direct) 私 を watákushi wo

can you hear me? 私の声が聞えますか watákushi no koè ga kikóemasù ká

he heard me 彼は私の声を聞いた kárè wa watákushi no koè wo kiítà

he heard ME! (not anyone else) 彼が聞いたのは私の声だった kárè ga kiítà no wa watákushi no koè dáttà

it's me 私です watákushi desù

2 (indirect) 私に watákushi ni

he gave me the money, he gave the money to me 彼は私に金を渡した kárè wa watákushi ni kanè wo watáshità

give them to me それらを私に下さい sorérà wo watákushi ni kudásaì

3 (after prep): *the letter's for me* 手紙は私宛てです tegámi wa watákushi ate dèsu

with me 私と一緒に watákushi tò isshó nì

without me 私抜きで watákushi nukì de

meadow [med'ou] *n* 草原 kusáhara

meager [mi:'gər] (*BRIT* **meagre**) *adj* 乏しい tobóshiì

meal [mi:l] *n* (occasion, food) 食事 shokúji; (flour) 粉 koná

mealtime [mi:l'taim] *n* 食事時 shokújidòki

mean [mi:n] *adj* (with money) けちな kechí na; (unkind: person, trick) 意地悪な ijíwarù na; (shabby: street, lodgings) 見すぼらしい misúborashiì; (average: height, weight) 中位の chúgurai no

♦*vt* (*pt*, *pp* **meant**) (signify) 意味する imí suru; (refer to): *I thought you meant her* あなたは彼女の事を言っていると私、思った anátà wa kanójò no kotð wo ittè irú to watákushi wà omótta; (intend): *to mean to do something* ...をするつもりでいる ...wo suru tsumórì de irú

♦*n* (average) 平均 heíkin

do you mean it? 本当ですか hofitò desù ká

what do you mean? それはどういう事ですか soré wa dô iú kotð desu ká

to be meant for someone/something ...に当てた物である ...ni atéta monð de árù

meander [mi:æn'dər] *vi* (river) 曲がりくねって流れる magárikunettè nagárerù

meaning [mi:'niŋ] *n* (of word, gesture, book) 意味 ímì; (purpose, value) 意義 ígì

meaningful [mi:'niŋfəl] *adj* (result) 意味のある fmì no árù; (explanation) 納得できる nattóku dekirù; (glance, remark) 意味ありげな imfarige na; (relationship, occasion) 意味深い imfbukai

meaningless [mi:'niŋlis] *adj* 無意味な muśmi na

meanness [mi:n'nis] *n* (with money) けち kechf; (unkindness) 意地悪 ijíwaru; (shabbiness) 見すぼらしさ misúborashisà

means [mi:nz] *npl* (way) 方法 hóhò; (money) 財産 zaísan

by means of ...を使って ...wo tsukátte

by all means! ぜひどうぞ zéhì dôzò

meant [ment] *pt*, *pp of* **mean**

meantime [mi:n'taim] *adv* (*also*: **in the meantime**) その間に sonó aìda ni

meanwhile [mi:n'wail] *adv* (meantime) その間に sonó aìda ni

measles [mi:'zəlz] *n* はしか hashíka

measly [mi:z'li:] (*inf*) *adj* ちっぽけな chippóke na

measure [meʒ'ər] *vt* (size, weight, distance) 計る hakárù

♦*vi* (room, person) ...だけの寸法がある ...daké no suñpõ ga árù

♦*n* (amount: of protection etc) ある程度 árù teídð; (: of whisky etc) 定量 teíryõ; (ruler, *also*: **tape measure**) 巻尺 makíjaku, メジャー méjà; (action) 処置 shóchì

measured [meʒ'ərd] *adj* 慎重な shiñchõ na

measurements [meʒ'ərmənts] *npl* (size) 寸法 suñpõ

meat [mi:t] *n* 肉 nikú

cold meat コールドミート kŏrudomĭto

meatball [miːtˈbɔːl] *n* ミートボール mĭtobŏru

meat pie *n* ミートパイ mĭtopăi

Mecca [mekˈə] *n* (city) メッカ mékkà; (*fig*) あこがれの地 akŏgare nò chí

mechanic [məkænˈik] *n* 自動車整備士 jidŏsha seĭbishi

mechanical [məkænˈikəl] *adj* 機械仕掛 の kikáijikakè no

mechanics [məkænˈiks] *n* (PHYSICS) 力学 rikĭgaku
♦*npl* (of reading, government etc) 機構 kikŏ

mechanism [mekˈənizəm] *n* (device) 装置 sŏchi; (procedure) 方法 hŏhō; (automatic reaction) 反応 hańnō

mechanization [mekənizeiˈʃən] *n* 機械化 kikăika

medal [medˈəl] *n* (award) メダル médaru

medallion [mədælˈjən] *n* メダリオン medárion

medalist [medˈlist] (*BRIT* **medallist**) *n* (SPORT) メダリスト medárisùto

meddle [medˈəl] *vi*: **to meddle in** ...にちょっかいを出す ...ni chokkáĭ wo dásù
to meddle with something ...をいじる ...wo ijírù

media [miːˈdiːə] *npl* マスメディア masúmedìa

mediaeval [miːdiːˈvəl] *adj* = **medieval**

median [miːˈdiːən] (*US*) *n* (*also*: **median strip**) 中央分離帯 chūō buńritai

mediate [miːˈdiːeit] *vi* (arbitrate) 仲裁する chūsai suru

mediator [miːˈdiːeitər] *n* 仲裁者 chūsaishà

Medicaid [medˈeikeid] (*US*) *n* メディケイド medíkeido ◇低所得者への医療扶助 teĭshotòkusha e no iryŏfujo

medical [medˈikəl] *adj* (treatment, care) 医学的な igákutekì na
♦*n* (*BRIT*: examination) 健康診断 keńkŏshindan

Medicare [medˈeikər] (*US*) *n* メディケア medíkea ◇高齢者への医療扶助 kŏreishà e no iryŏfujo

medicated [medˈeikeitid] *adj* 薬用の ya-

kúyō no

medication [medeikeiˈʃən] *n* (drugs etc) 薬 kusúri

medicinal [mədisˈənəl] *adj* 薬効のある yakkŏ no arù

medicine [medˈisin] *n* (science) 医学 ígaku; (drug) 薬 kusúri

medieval [miːdiːˈvəl] *adj* 中世の chúsei no

mediocre [miːˈdiːoukər] *adj* (play, artist) 粗末な sómatsu na

mediocrity [miːdiːɑkˈriti:] *n* (poor quality) 粗末さ sómatsusà

meditate [medˈəteit] *vi* (think carefully) 熟考する jukkŏ suru; (REL) めい想する meĭsō suru

meditation [medeiteiˈʃən] *n* (thinking) 熟考 jukkŏ; (REL) めい想 meĭsō

Mediterranean [medeitərei'ni:ən] *adj* 地中海の chichűkai no
the Mediterranean (Sea) 地中海 chichűkai

medium [miːˈdiːəm] *adj* (average: size, color) 中位の chűgurai no
♦*n* (*pl* **media**: means) 手段 shúdàn; (*pl* **mediums**: people) 霊媒 reĭbai

medium wave *n* 中波 chűha

medley [medˈliː] *n* (mixture) ごったまぜ gottámaze; (MUS) メドレー médorē

meek [miːk] *adj* 穏和な ofiwa na

meet [miːt] (*pt*, *pp* **met**) *vt* (friend: accidentally) ...に出会う ...ni deáù; (: by arrangement) ...に会う ...ni áù; (stranger: for the first time) ...と知合いになる ...to shíriai ni naru; (go and fetch: at station, airport) 出迎える demúkaerù; (opponent) ...と試合をする ...to shiái wo surù; (obligations) 果す hatásù; (problem, need) 解決する kaĭketsu suru
♦*vi* (friends: accidentally) 出会う deáù; (: by arrangement) 会う áù; (strangers: for the first time) 知合いになる shíriai ni naru; (for talks, discussion) 会合する kaĭgō suru; (join: lines, roads) 合流する gŏryū suru

meeting [miːˈtiŋ] *n* (assembly: of club, committee etc) 会合 kaĭgō; (: of people) 集会 shúkai; (encounter: with friend) 出

meet with vt fus (encounter: difficulty) 会う deaú; (COMM) 会議 káigi; (POL) 集会 shúkai
合う áu

to meet with success 成功する seíkō suru

megabyte [meg'əbait] n (COMPUT) メガバイト megábaito

megaphone [meg'əfoun] n メガホン megáhòn

melancholy [mel'ənkɑːli:] n (sadness) 憂うつ yūutsu, メランコリー meráñkorī
♦adj (sad) 憂鬱な yūutsu na

mellow [mel'ou] adj (sound, light, color) 柔らかい yawárakaì; (wine) 芳じゅんな hōjun na
♦vi (person) 角が取れる kádò ga toréru

melodrama [mel'ədræmə] n メロドラマ meródòrama

melody [mel'ədi:] n 旋律 señritsu, メロディー merōdī

melon [mel'ən] n メロン mérðn

melt [melt] vi (metal, snow) 溶ける tokéru
♦vt (metal, snow, butter) 溶かす tokásù

melt down vt (metal) 溶かす tokásù

meltdown [melt'daun] n (in nuclear reactor) メルトダウン merútodàun

melting pot [melt'iŋ-] n (fig: mixture) るつぼ rútsùbo

member [mem'bəːr] n (of group, family) 一員 ichí-iǹ; (of club) 会員 kaíiñ, メンバー mēñba; (ANAT) 体の一部 karáda no íchìbu

Member of Parliament (BRIT) 国会議員 kokkái gìin

Member of the European Parliament (BRIT) 欧州議会議員 ōshūgikai gìin

membership [mem'bəːrʃip] n (members) 会員一同 kaíiñ ichídò; (state) 会員である事 kaíiñ de arù kotó

membership card n 会員証 kaíiñshō

membrane [mem'brein] n 膜 makú

memento [məmen'tou] n 記念品 kinéñhin

memo [mem'ou] n 覚書 obőegaki, メモ mémò

memoirs [mem'waːrz] npl 回顧録 kaíkoròku

memorable [mem'əːrəbəl] adj 記念すべき kinéñsubeki

memorandum [meməræn'dəm] (pl **memoranda**) n (official note) 覚書 obőegaki; (order to employees etc) 社内通達 shanái tsūtatsu

memorial [məmɔː'riːəl] n (statue, monument) 記念碑 kinéñhi
♦adj (service) 追悼の tsuítō no; (prize) 記念の kinéñ no

memorize [mem'əːraiz] vt (learn) 暗記する añki suru

memory [mem'əːri:] n (ability to remember) 記憶 kióku; (things one remembers) 思い出 omőide; (instance) 思い出 omőide; (of dead person): **in memory of ...** を記念して ...wo kinéñ shite; (COMPUT) 記憶装置 kiókusòchi, メモリ mémòri

men [men] pl of **man**

menace [men'is] n (threat) 脅威 kyóì; (nuisance) 困り者 komárimono
♦vt (threaten) 脅かす odőkasu; (endanger) 危険にさらす kikén ni sarásu

menacing [men'isiŋ] adj (person, gesture) 脅迫的な kyōhakuteki na

mend [mend] vt (repair) 修理する shūri suru; (darn: socks etc) 繕う tsukúroū, 繕する shūzen suru
♦n: **to be on the mend** 回復に向かっている kaffuku ni mukátte irú

to mend one's ways 心を入替える kokóro wo irékaerú

mending [men'diŋ] n (repairing) 修繕 shūzen; (clothes) 繕い物 tsukúroimono

menial [miː'niːəl] adj (lowly: often pej) 卑しい iyáshiì

meningitis [meniñdʒai'tis] n 脳膜炎 nőmakuen

menopause [men'əpɔːz] n 更年期 kőneñki

menstruation [menstruei'ʃən] n 月経 gekkéi, 生理 seíri, メンス méñsu

mental [men'təl] adj (ability, effort) 精神の seíshiñ no; (illness, health) 精神の seíshiñ no

mental arithmetic/calculation 暗算 añzan

mentality [mentæl'iti:] *n* (attitude) 考え方 kañgaekáta

menthol [men'θɔːl] *n* メントール meñtōru

mention [men'tʃən] *n* (reference) 言及 geñkyū

♦*vt* (speak of) ...に言及する ...ni geñkyū suru

don't mention it! どういたしまして dō itáshimashité

mentor [men'tər] *n* 良き指導者 yokí shidōsha

menu [men'juː] *n* (set menu) 献立 koñdate; (printed) 献立表 koñdatehyō, メニュー menyū; (COMPUT) メニュー menyū

MEP [emiːpiː'] *n abbr* = **Member of the European Parliament**

mercenary [mɜr'səneri:] *adj* 金銭ずくの kiñsenzuku no

♦*n* (soldier) よう兵 yōhei

merchandise [mɜr'tʃəndaiz] *n* 商品 shōhin

merchant [mɜr'tʃənt] *n* (trader) 貿易商 bōekishō

merchant bank (*BRIT*) *n* マーチャントバンク māchantobañku

merchant marine (*BRIT* **merchant navy**) *n* 商船 shōsen ◊一国の全商船を集合的に指す ikkóku no zeñshōsen wō shūgōteki ni sasū

merciful [mɜr'sifəl] *adj* (kind, forgiving) 情け深い nasákebukaī; (fortunate) **merciful release** 苦しみからの解放 kurúshimí kara no kaíhō ◊重病人などの死亡について言う jūbyōnin nado no shibō ni tsuité iū

merciless [mɜr'silis] *adj* (person, regime) 冷酷な refkoku na

mercury [mɜr'kjəri:] *n* 水銀 suígin

mercy [mɜr'siː] *n* clemency; *also* REL) 情け nasáke, 慈悲 jihí

at the mercy of ...のなすがままになって ...no násū ga mamá ni natté

mere [miːr] *adj* (emphasizing small significance: child, trifle, amount) ほんの hoñ no; (emphasizing person) *his mere presence irritates her* 彼がそこにいるだけで彼女は頭に来る kárè ga sokó ni

irú dakè de kánòjo wa atáma ni kurū

merely [miːr'liː] *adv* ただ...だけ tádà ...dake

merge [mɜːrdʒ] *vt* (combine: companies, institutions etc) 合併させる gappéi saserū

♦*vi* (COMM) 合併する gappéi suru; (colors, sounds, shapes) 次第に溶合う shidái ni tokéaū; (roads) 合流する gōryū suru

merger [mɜːr'dʒər] *n* (COMM) 合併 gappéi

meringue [məræŋ'] *n* メレンゲ meréñge

merit [meːr'it] *n* (worth, value) 価値 kachí; (advantage) 長所 chōsho, 利点 ritén

♦*vt* ...に値する ...ni atái suru

mermaid [mɜːr'meid] *n* 人魚 nñgyo

merry [meːr'iː] *adj* (happy: laugh, person) 陽気な yóki na; (cheerful: music) 活気ある kakkí arū

Merry Christmas! メリークリスマス merī kurísùmasu

merry-go-round [meːr'iːgouraund] *n* 回転木馬 kaíteñmokuba

mesh [meʃ] *n* (net) メッシュ mésshū

mesmerize [mez'məraiz] *vt* 魅惑する miwáku suru

mess [mes] *n* (muddle: in room) 散らかし つ乱し chirákashippanashi, めちゃめちゃ mechákucha; (: of situation) 混乱 koñran; (dirt) 汚れ yogóre; (MIL) 食堂 shokúdō

mess about/around (*inf*) *vi* (fool around) ぶらぶらする búràbura suru

mess about/around with *vt fus* (play around with) いじる ijírū

message [mes'idʒ] *n* (piece of information) 伝言 deñgon, メッセージ mésèji; (meaning: of play, book etc) 教訓 kyōkun

messenger [mes'indʒər] *n* 使者 shíshà, メッセンジャー messéñjà

Messrs. [mes'ərz] *abbr* (on letters) ◊Mr.の複数形 Mr. no fukúsūkei

mess up *vt* (spoil) 台無しにする daínashi ni suru; (dirty) 汚す yogósū

messy [mes'iː] *adj* (dirty) 汚れた yogóretá; (untidy) 散らかした chirákashita

met [met] *pt, pp of* **meet**

metabolism [mətǽb'əlizəm] *n* 新陳代謝 shínchintaisha

metal [met'əl] *n* 金属 kíñzoku

metallic [mitǽl'ik] *adj* (made of metal) 金属の kíñzoku no; (sound, color) 金属的な kíñzokuteki na

metallurgy [met'ələːrdʒi:] *n* や金学 yǎ-kíñgaku

metamorphosis [metəmɔːr'fəsis] (*pl* **metamorphoses**) *n* 変態 heñtai

metaphor [met'əfɔːr] *n* 隠ゆ fñ-yu, メタファー metáfǎ

mete [miːt] *vt*: **to mete out** (punishment, justice) 与える atáerù, 加える kuwáerù

meteor [miː'tiːɔːr] *n* 流れ星 nagáreboshi

meteorite [miː'tiːəːrait] *n* いん石 fñseki

meteorology [miːtiːəːrɑ'ədʒi:] *n* 気象学 kishṓgaku

meter [miː'təːr] *n* (instrument: gas meter, electricity meter) ...計 ...kéi, メーター mḗtǎ; (*also*: **parking meter**) パーキングメーター pǎkingumḕtǎ; (*US*: unit) メートル mḗtoru

method [meθ'əd] *n* (way) 方法 hṓhō

methodical [məθɑd'ikəl] *adj* (careful, thorough) 慎重な shíñchō na

Methodist [meθ'ədist] *n* メソジスト教徒 mesójisuto kyōto

methodology [meθədɑ'l'ədʒi:] *n* 方法論 hṓhōron

meths [meθs] (*BRIT*) *n* = **methylated spirit**

methylated spirit [meθ'əleitid-] (*BRIT*) *n* 変性アルコール heñsei arukṓru

meticulous [mətik'jələs] *adj* 厳密な geñmitsu na

metre [miː'təːr] (*BRIT*) *n* (unit) = **meter**

metric [met'rik] *adj* メートル法の mḗto-ruhō no

metropolis [mitrɑːp'əlis] *n* 大都会 daftokai

metropolitan [metrəpɑːl'itən] *adj* 大都会の daftokai no

Metropolitan Police (*BRIT*) *n*: **the Metropolitan Police** ロンドン市警察 roñdon shikeísatsu

mettle [met'əl] *n* (spirit, courage): **to be on one's mettle** 張切っている haríkitte

irù

mew [mjuː] *vi* (cat) にゃあと鳴く nyǎ to nakú

mews [mjuːz] *n* (*BRIT*): **mews flat** アパート apǎto ◇昔の馬屋をアパートに改造した物を指す mukáshi nò umáya wò apǎtô ni kafzō shita monò wo sásù

Mexican [mek'səkən] *adj* メキシコの mekíshiko no
◆*n* メキシコ人 mekíshikojīn

Mexico [mek'səkou] *n* メキシコ mekíshiko

Mexico City *n* メキシコ市 mekíshiko-shi

miaow [miːau'] *vi* (cat) にゃあと鳴く nyǎ to nakú

mice [mais] *pl of* **mouse**

micro- [mai'krou] *prefix* 微小... bishṓ ...

microbe [mai'kroub] *n* 細菌 safkin

microchip [mai'krətʃip] *n* マイクロチップ mafkurochippù

micro(computer) [mai'krou(kəmpjuː'tər)] *n* マイクロコンピュータ mafkuro-kompyûta, パソコン pasókòn

microcosm [mai'krakɑːzəm] *n* 小宇宙 shōuchū, ミクロコスモス mikúrokosu-mòsu

microfilm [mai'krəfilm] *n* マイクロフィルム mafkurofirùmu

microphone [mai'krəfoun] *n* マイクロホン mafkurohòn

microprocessor [maikroupras'esəːr] *n* マイクロプロセッサー mafkuropuroses-sǎ

microscope [mai'krəskoup] *n* 顕微鏡 keñbikyṓ

microscopic [mai'krəskɑːp'ik] *adj* 微小の bishṓ no

microwave [mai'krouweiv] *n* (*also*: **microwave oven**) 電子レンジ deñshi reñ-ji

mid [mid] *adj*: **in mid May** 5月半ばに gogátsu nakàba ni

in mid afternoon 昼下がりに hirúsagàri ni

in mid air 空中に kūchū ni

midday [mid'dei] *n* 正午 shōgo

middle [mid'əl] *n* (center) 真ん中 mańna-

ka, 中央 chūō; (half-way point) 中間 chūkan; (waist) ウエスト uésuto
♦adj (of place, position) 真ん中の mañ-
naka no; (average: quantity, size) 中位の
chūgurai no
  in the middle of the night 真夜中に
mayónaka ni
middle-aged [mid'əleidʒd'] adj 中年の
chūnen no
Middle Ages npl: **the Middle Ages** 中
世 chūsei
middle-class [mid'əlklæs] adj 中流の
chūryū no
middle class(es) [mid'əlklæs(iz)] n(pl):
  the middle class(es) 中流階級 chūryū-
kaīkyū
Middle East n: **the Middle East** 中東
chūtō
middleman [mid'əlmæn] (pl **middlemen**)
n 仲買人 nakágainin
middle name n ミドルネーム midórunē-
mu
middle-of-the-road [mid'əlʌvðəroud']
adj (politician, music) 中道の chūdō no
middleweight [mid'əlweit] n (BOX-
ING) ミドル級の midórukyū no
middling [mid'liŋ] adj 中位の chūgurai
no
midge [midʒ] n ブヨ búyo ◇ブヨの様な小
さい虫の総称 búyo no yố na chīsaí
mushī no sōshō
midget [midʒ'it] n 小人 kobíto
Midlands [mid'ləndz] (BRIT) npl: **the
Midlands** イングランド中部地方 íngu-
rañdo chūbu chihō
midnight [mid'nait] n 真夜中 mayónaka
midriff [mid'rif] n おなか onáka ◇ ウエ
ストから胸までの部分を指す cañst kara
muné made no bübun wo sásu
midst [midst] n: **in the midst of**
(crowd, group) ...の中に(で) ...no nákà ni
(de); (situation, event) ...のさなかに ...no
sanákà ni; (action) ...している所 ...wo
shité irū tokoro
midsummer [mid'sam'əːr] n 真夏 manā-
tsu
midway [mid'wei] adj: **midway
(between/through)** ...の途中の ...no

chū de
♦adv: **midway (between/through)**
...の途中に(で) ...no tochū ni (de)
midweek [mid'wi:k] adv 週半ば shū na-
kabā
midwife [mid'waif] (pl **midwives**) n 助産
婦 josáñpu
midwinter [mid'win'təːr] n: **in midwinter** 真冬に mafúyu ni
might [mait] see **may**
might [mait] n (power) 力 chikára
mighty [mai'ti:] adj 強力な kyōryoku na
migraine [mai'grein] n 偏頭痛 heñzutsū
migrant [mai'grənt] adj: **migrant bird**
渡り鳥 watáridòri
  migrant worker 渡り季節労働者 watá-
ri kisetsurōdōshà
migrate [mai'greit] vi (bird etc) 移動す
る idō suru; (person) 移住する ijū suru
migration [maigrei'ʃən] n (bird etc) 移
動 idō; (person) 移住 ijū
mike [maik] n abbr = **microphone**
Milan [milæn'] n ミラノ miránō
mild [maild] adj (gentle: character) 大人
しい otónashiì; (climate) 穏やかな odáyàka na; (slight: infection, illness) 軽い
karúi; (: interest) 少しの sukóshì na;
(taste) 甘口の amákuchi no
mildew [mil'du:] n かび kabí
mildly [maild'li:] adv (gently) 優しく yasáshikù; (somewhat) 少し sukóshì
  to put it mildly 控え目に言って hikáeme ni ittè
mile [mail] n (unit) マイル maírù
mileage [mai'lidʒ] n (number of miles)
マイル数 maírùsū
mileometer [mailɑ:m'itəːr] (BRIT) n =
odometer
milestone [mail'stoun] n (marker) 一里
塚 ichírizùka; (fig: important event) 画期
的な出来事 kakkíteki na dekígòto
milieu [mi:lju:'] n 環境 kañkyō
militant [mil'ətənt] adj 戦闘的な sefíto-
teki na
military [mil'iteːri:] adj 軍隊の gúñtai no
militate [mil'əteit] vi: **to militate
against** (prevent) 邪魔をする jamá suru
militia [mili'ʃə] n 民兵 miñpei

milk [milk] n (of any mammal) 乳 chíchí; (of cow) 牛乳 gyūnyū, ミルク mírùkù

♦vt (cow, goat) …の乳を搾る …no chíchí wò shibórù; (fig: situation, person) food 物にする kutmonó ni suru

milk chocolate ミルクチョコレート mírùkùchokorēto

milkman [milk'mæn] (pl **milkmen**) n 牛 乳配達人 gyūnyūhaitatsunīn

milkshake [milk'jeik] n ミルクセーキ mírùkùsēki

milky [mil'ki:] adj (color) 乳白色の nyū-hakùshoku no; (drink) ミルク入りの mí-rùku iri no

Milky Way n 銀河 gínga

mill [mil] n (windmill etc: for grain) 製粉 機 seffūnki; (also: **coffee mill**) コーヒー ひき kōhíhìkí; (factory: steel mill, saw mill) 製…工場 sef…kōjō

♦vt (grind: grain, flour) ひく híkù

♦vi (also: **mill about**: people, crowd) 右 往左往する uósà suru

woolen mill 織物工場 orímonòkòjo

miller [mil'ər] n 製粉業者 seffungyōsha

milligram(me) [mil'əgræm] n ミリグラ ム mírìgùramu

millimeter [mil'əmi:tər] (BRIT **millimetre**) n ミリメートル mírmètoru

millinery [mil'əne:ri:] n 婦人帽子店 fujínbōshiten

million [mil'jən] n 100万 hyakúmàn

a million times 何回も nańkai mo

millionaire [miljəne:r'] n 大富豪 daífugō

milometer [mai'ləmi:tər] n = **mileometer**

mime [maim] n (action) パントマイム pańtomaìmu; (actor) パントマイム役者 pańtomaìmu yakūsha

♦vt (act) 身振り手振りでまねる mibúrìtebúri de manérù

♦vi (act) パントマイムを演ずる pańtomaìmu wo eñzurù

mimic [mim'ik] n 物まね師 monómanè-shí

♦vt (imitate) …のまねをする …no manê wo surù

min. abbr **minute(s)**; **minimum**

minaret [minəret'] n ミナレット mínà-

rètto ◊モスクのせん塔 mósùku no señtō

mince [mins] vt (meat) ひく híkù

♦vi (in walking) 気取って歩く kidótte arukú

♦n (BRIT: CULIN) ひき肉 hikíniku

mincemeat [mins'mi:t] n (fruit) ミンス ミート mińsumītò ◊ドライフルーツなど の細切り dorâifurūtsu nādò no komágìri; (US: meat) ひき肉 hikíniku

mince pie (US) n (sweet) ミンスミー トパイ mińsumītopaì

mince pie (BRIT) n (sweet) = **mince-meat pie**

mincer [min'sər] n 肉ひき器 nikúhìkkì

mind [maind] n (thoughts) 考え kañgaè; (intellect) 頭脳 zunō; (opinion): **to my mind** 私の意見では watákushi no iken de wa; (sanity): **to be out of one's mind** 気が狂っている ki ga kurútte irú

♦vt (attend to, look after: shop, home etc) …の番をする …no bañ wo suru; (: children, pets etc) …の面倒を見る …no meñdō wò mírù; (be careful of) …に注意 する …ni chūi suru; (object to): **I don't mind the noise** その音を気にしません sonó otó wo kí ni shimásèn

it is on my mind 気に掛っている kí ni kakátte irú

to keep/bear something in mind …を 気にする …wo kí ni suru

to make up one's mind 決心する kes-shín suru

I don't mind 構いませんよ kamáimasèn yó

mind you, … でもこれだけ言っておく …de mo koré dakè itté okú

never mind! (it makes no odds) 気にし ないで下さい kí ni shináide kudásaì; (don't worry) ほうっておきなさい hôtte oki nasaì, 心配しないで下さい shiñpai shinaìde kudásaì

「**mind the step**」階段に注意 kaídan ni chūi

minder [maind'ər] n (childminder) ベビ ーシッター bebíshittà; (BRIT inf: body-guard) ボディーガード bodígàdo

mindful [maind'fəl] adj: **mindful of** …を 気に掛ける …ni kí ni kakérù

mindless [maind'lis] *adj* (violence) 愚かな おろか na, 暴力な gurétsu na; (boring: job) 退屈な tafkutsu na

---

KEYWORD

mine[1] [main] *pron* 私の物 watákushi no monó

that book is mine その本は私のです sonó hoñ wa watákushi no dèsu

these cases are mine それらのケースは私のです sorérà wa watákushi no dèsu

this is mine これは私の物です koré wà watákushi no monó desu

yours is red, mine is green あなたのは赤いが、私のは緑色です anátà no wa akáI ga, watákushi no wà midóri irð desu

a friend of mine 私のある友達 watákushi nð árù tomódachi

---

mine[2] [main] *n* (gen) 鉱山 kózan; (also: land mine) 地雷 jiráI; (bomb in water) 機雷 kírái

♦ *vt* (coal) 採掘する safkutsu suru; (beach) 地雷を敷設する jiráI wo fusétsu suru; (harbor) 機雷を敷設する kírái wo fusétsu suru

coal mine 炭鉱 tañkó

gold mine 金坑 kíñkô

minefield [main'fi:ld] *n* (area: land) 地雷原 jiráIgeñ; (: water) 機雷敷設水域 kírái-fusetsu suíIki; (fig: situation) 身をはらんだ事態 kikéñ wo hárañda jItái

miner [main'ər] *n* 鉱山労働者 kózanró-dôshA

mineral [min'ərəl] *adj* (deposit, resources) 鉱物の kóbutsu no

♦ *n* (in earth) 鉱物 kóbutsu; (in food) ミネラル mínéraru

minerals [min'ərəlz] (BRIT) *npl* (soft drinks) 炭酸飲料水 tañsan-íñryôsuI

mineral water *n* ミネラルウォーター mínéraru uôtâ

mingle [miŋ'gəl] *vi*: *to mingle with* ...と交わる ...to majíwaru ◊ 特にパーティーなどで多くの人に声を掛けて回る意味で使う tókù ni pâti nádð de ôkù no

hitó ni kôè wo kakéte mawáru nádð no ími de tsukáù

miniature [min'i:ətʃər] *adj* (small, tiny) ミニチュアの mínichûa no

♦ *n* ミニチュア mínichûa

minibus [min'i:bʌs] *n* マイクロバス maíkurobasu

minim [min'əm] *n* (MUS) 二分音符 nîbun oñpu

minimal [min'əmal] *adj* 最小限(度)の saíshôgen(do) no

minimize [min'əmaiz] *vt* (reduce: risks, disease) 最小限度に抑える saíshôgen (do) ni osáerù; (play down: role) 見くびる mikúbirù; (: weakness) 問題としない mofidai to shinâI, 避けて通る sakéte tôru

minimum [min'əməm] (*pl* **minima**) *n* 最小限(度) saíshôgen(do)

♦ *adj* 最小限(度)の saíshôgen(do) no

mining [mai'niŋ] *n* 鉱業 kôgyô

miniskirt [min'i:skə:rt] *n* ミニスカート mínisukâto

minister [min'istər] *n* (POL) 大臣 dáIjin; (REL) 牧師 bókushi

♦ *vi*: *to minister to* (people, needs) ...に仕える ...ni tsukáerù

ministerial [ministi:r'i:əl] (BRIT) *adj* (POL) 大臣の dáIjin no

ministry [min'istri:] *n* (POL) ...省 ...shô; (REL) 聖職 seíshoku

mink [miŋk] *n* (fur) ミンクの毛皮 mínku no kegáwa; (animal) ミンク míñku

mink coat *n* ミンクのコート míñku no kôto

minnow [min'ou] *n* 小魚 kozákana

minor [mai'nər] *adj* (unimportant: repairs) ちょっとした chótto shità; (: injuries) 軽い karúI; (: poet) 二流の niryû no; (MUS) 短調の tañchô no

♦ *n* (LAW) 未成年 míséInen

minority [minɔ:r'iti:] *n* (less than half: of group, society) 少数 shôsû

mint [mint] *n* (plant) ハッカ hakká; (sweet) ハッカあめ hakká amè

♦ *vt* (coins) 鋳造する chûzô suru

the (US) Mint (US), the (Royal) Mint (BRIT) 造幣局 zôhéIkyoku

in mint condition 新品同様で shíñpindòyò de

minus [mai'nəs] *n* (*also:* **minus sign**) マイナス記号 maīnasu kigō

♦*prep:* **12 minus 6 equals 6** 12引く6は6 jūni hikú rokú wà rokú (temperature):

minus 24 零下24度 refka nijúyòn do

minuscule [min'əskju:l] *adj* 微々たる bíbītaru

minute [min'it] *n* (unit) 分 fùn; (*fig:* short time) ちょっと chottó

♦*adj* (search, detail) 細かい komákaì

at the last minute 土壇場に dotánbà ni

minutes [min'its] *npl* (of meeting) 会議録 kaígìroku

miracle [mir'əkəl] *n* (REL, *fig*) 奇跡 kiséki

miraculous [miræk'jələs] *adj* 奇跡的な kisékiteki na

mirage [mirɑ:ʒ'] *n* しん気楼 shifikirō

mirror [mir'ər] *n* (in bedroom, bathroom) 鏡 kagámi, ミラー mfrā; (in car) バックミラー bakkúmirā

mirth [mərθ] *n* (laughter) 笑い warái

misadventure [misədven'tʃər] *n* 災難 saínañ

misapprehension [misæprihen'tʃən] *n* 誤解 gokái

misappropriate [misəprou'prizeit] *vt* (funds, money) 横領する ōryō suru

misbehave [misbiheiv'] *vi* 行儀悪くする gyōgìwaruku suru

miscalculate [miskæl'kjəleit] *vt* 見込み違いする mikómichigài suru

miscarriage [miskær'idʒ] *n* (MED) 流産 ryūzan; (failure): **miscarriage of justice** 誤審 goshín

miscellaneous [misəlei'niəs] *adj* (collection, group: of tools, people) 雑多な zattá na; (subjects, items) 種々の shujū no

mischance [mistʃæns'] *n* (misfortune) 不運 fuún

mischief [mis'tʃif] *n* (naughtiness: of child) いたずら itázura; (playfulness, fun) いたずら itázura; (maliciousness) 悪さ warúsa

mischievous [mis'tʃəvəs] *adj* (naughty, playful) いたずらな itázura na

misconception [miskənsep'ʃən] *n* 誤解 gokái

misconduct [miskɑːn'dʌkt] *n* (behavior) 非行 hikō

professional misconduct 背任 haínin, 職権乱用 shokkén raňyō

misdemeanor [misdimi:'nər] *n* (*BRIT* **misdemeanour**) *n* 軽犯罪 keíhañzai

miser [mai'zər] *n* けちん坊 kéchìnbō, 守銭奴 shuséñdo

miserable [miz'ərəbəl] *adj* (unhappy: person, expression) 惨めな mijíme-na, 不幸な fukō na; (wretched: conditions) 哀れな áwàre na; (unpleasant: weather, person) いやな iyá na; (contemptible: offer, donation) ちっぽけな chippókè na; (: failure) 情けない nasákenaì

miserly [mai'zərli] *adj* けちな kechí na

misery [miz'ə:ri] *n* (unhappiness) 惨めさ mijímesa, 不幸せ fushiawase; (wretchedness) 哀れな状態 áwàre na jōtai

misfire [misfair'] *vi* (plan etc) 失敗する shippái suru

misfit [mis'fit] *n* (person) 適応不能者 tekíōfunōsha

misfortune [misfɔːr'tʃən] *n* (bad luck) 不運 fuún

misgiving [misgiv'iŋ] *n* (apprehension) 心もとなさ kokóromotonasà, 疑念 ginéñ

to have misgivings about something ...を疑問に思う ...wo gimóñ nì omóu

misguided [misgai'did] *adj* (opinion, view) 心得違いの kokóroechigài no

mishandle [mishæn'dəl] *vt* (mismanage: problem, situation) ...の処置を誤る ...no shóchì wo ayámarù

mishap [mis'hæp] *n* 事故 jíkò

misinform [misinfɔrm'] *vt* ...にうそを伝える ...ni úsò wo tsutáerù

misinterpret [misintər'prit] *vt* 誤解する ...を gokái suru

misjudge [misdʒʌdʒ'] *vt* ...の判断を誤る ...no hañdañ wo ayámarù

mislay [mislei'] (*pt, pp* **mislaid**) *vt* (lose) なくす nakúsù, 置忘れる okíwasurerù

mislead [mislid'] (*pt, pp* **misled**) *vt* ...を信じ込ませる úsò wo shiñjikomaserù

misleading [misli'diŋ] *adj* (information)

誤解させる gokái saserú

mismanage [mismǽnidʒ] vt (manage badly: business, institution) 下手な管理をする hetá na kánri wo suru; (: problem, situation) の処置を誤る ...no shóchi wo ayámarù

misnomer [misnou'mər] n (term) 誤った名称 ayámattà meíshoō

misogynist [misɑdʒ'ənist] n 女嫌い onnágirai

misplace [mispleis'] vt (lose) なくす nakúsù, 置忘れる okíwasurerù

misprint [mis'print] n 誤植 goshóku

Miss [mis] n ...さん ...sán ◊未婚の女性に対する敬称 mīkōn no joséi ni taī surū keíshoō

miss [mis] vt (train, bus etc) ...に乗遅れる ...ni noríokurerù; (fail to hit: target) ...に当て損なう ...ni atésokonaù; (fail to see): **you can't miss it** 見落しっこない miótoshikkonaì; (regret the absence of) ...が恋しい ...ga koíshiì, ...が懐かしい ...ga natsúkashiì; (chance, opportunity) 逃す nígasù, のがす nogásù; (class, meeting) ...に欠席する ...ni kessékī suru
◆vi (fail to hit) 当り損なう atárisokonaù, 外れる sorérù
◆n (failure to hit) 当り損ない atésokonaì, ミス míss

misshapen [misʃei'pən] adj 不格好な bukákkō na

missile [mis'əl] n (weapon: MIL) ミサイル misáiru; (: object thrown) 飛器具 tobídōgu

missing [mis'iŋ] adj (lost: person, pupil) 行方不明の yukúefumèi no; (: object) なくなっている nakúnatte irù; (removed: tooth) 抜かれた nukárètà; (: wheel) 外された hazúsaretà; (MIL) 行方不明の yukúefumèi no
to be missing 行方不明である yukúefumèi de aru

mission [miʃ'ən] n (task) 任務 nīmmu; (official representatives) 代表団 daíhyōdan; (MIL) 出撃 shutsúgeki ◊特に爆撃機について言う tōkū ni bakúgekkì ni tsuíte iù; (REL: activity) 伝道 deńdō; (: building) 伝道所 deńdōjō

missionary [miʃ'əneːri:] n 伝道師 deńdōshi

miss out (BRIT) vt (leave out) 落す otósù

misspent [misspent'] adj: **his misspent youth** 浪費した彼の青春 rōhi shità kárè no seíshun

mist [mist] n (light) もや móyà; (heavy) 濃霧 nómu
◆vi (also: **mist over, mist up**) (eyes) 涙ぐむ namídagùmu; (windows) 曇る kumórù

mistake [misteik'] n (error) 間違い machígaì
◆vt (pt **mistook**, pp **mistaken**) (be wrong about) 間違える machígaerù
by mistake 間違って machígattè
to make a mistake 間違いをする machígaì wo suru
to mistake A for B AをBと間違える A wo B to machígaerù

mistaken [mistei'kən] (pp of **mistake**) adj (idea, belief etc) 間違った machígattà
to be mistaken 間違っている machígattè irú

mister [mis'təːr] (inf) n ◊男性への呼び掛け dańsei no yobíkake ¶ see **Mr**.

mistletoe [mis'əltou] n ヤドリギ yadórigì

mistook [mistuk'] pt of **mistake**

mistress [mis'tris] n (lover) 愛人 aíjìn; (of house, servant) 女主人 ońna shùjin; (in primary, secondary schools) 先生 seńsei
to be mistress of the situation (fig) 事態を掌握している jítai wo shōkàku shitè irù

mistrust [mistrʌst'] vt 信用しない shiń'yō shinaì

misty [mis'ti:] adj (day etc) もやった moyátta; (glasses, windows) 曇った kumóttà

misunderstand [misʌndəːrstǽnd'] (irreg) vt (fail to understand: person, book) 誤解する gokái suru
◆vi (fail to understand) 誤解する gokái suru

misunderstanding [misʌndəːrstǽn'diŋ]

n (failure to understand) 誤解 gokái; (disagreement) 口げんか kuchígeñka

misuse [mɪsˈjuːs] *n* (of power) 乱用 rañ-yō; (of funds) 悪用 akúyō
♦*vt* (power) 乱用する rañ-yō suru; (funds) 悪用する akúyō suru

mitigate [mɪtˈəgeɪt] *vt* 和らげる yawáragerù

mitt(en) [mɪtˈ(ən)] *n* ミトン mítòn

mix [mɪks] *vt* (combine: liquids, ingredients, colors) 混ぜる mazérù; (cake, cement) こねる konérù; (drink, sauce) 作る tsukúrù
♦*vi* (people): **to mix (with)** ...と交わる ...to majíwarù ◊特にパーティなどで多くの人に声を掛けて回るなどの意味で使う tókù ni pátì nádò de ōkù no hitó ni kóè wo kákète máwarù nádò no ímì de tsukáù
♦*n* (combination) 混合物 koñgóbùtsu; (powder) ミックス míkkùsu

mixed [mɪkst] *adj* (salad) コンビネーションの koñbínèshòn no; (grill) 盛り合せの morfawase no; (feelings, reactions) 複雑な fukúzatsu na; (school, education etc) 共学の kyōgaku no
a mixed marriage (religion) 異なった宗教の信徒間の結婚 kotónàtta shúkyō no shinto kan no kekkon; (race) 異なった人種間の結婚 kotónàtta jiñshu kan no kekkon

mixed-up [mɪkstˈʌp] *adj* (confused) 混乱している koñran shite irù

mixer [mɪkˈsəːr] *n* (for food) ミキサー míkìsa; (person): **to be a good mixer** 付合い上手である tsukíaijōzu de aru

mixture [mɪksˈtʃəːr] *n* (combination) 混合物 koñgóbùtsu; (MED: for cough etc) 飲薬 nomígusùri

mix up *vt* (confuse: people, things) 混同する koñdō suru

mix-up [mɪksˈʌp] *n* (confusion) 混乱 koñ-ran

mm *abbr* = millimeter

moan [moun] *n* (cry) うめき声 uméki
♦*vi* (inf: complain): **to moan (about)** (...について) 愚痴を言う (...ni tsúìte) gúchi wo iù

moat [mout] *n* 堀 horí

mob [mɑːb] *n* (crowd) 群衆 guñshū
♦*vt* (person) ...の回りにわっと押し寄せる ...no mawárì ni wáttò oshíyoserù

mobile [mouˈbəl] *adj* (able to move) 移動式の idōshiki no
♦*n* (decoration) モビール mōbīru

mobile home *n* モビールハウス mōbīru-haùsu

mobility [moubɪlˈətiː] *n* 移動性 idōsei

mobilize [mouˈbəlaɪz] *vt* (friends, work force) 動員する dōin suru; (MIL: country, army) 戦時態勢を取らせる señji taì-sei wo toráserù

moccasin [mɑːkˈəsɪn] *n* モカシン mokáshin

mock [mɑːk] *vt* (ridicule) ばかにする bákà ni suru; (laugh at) あざ笑う azáwaraù
♦*adj* (fake) 見せ掛け misékake no; (exam, battle) 模擬の mógì no

mockery [mɑːkˈəriː] *n* (derision) あざけり azákeri
to make a mockery of ...をばかにする ...wo bákà ni suru

mock-up [mɑːkˈʌp] *n* (model) 模型 mokéi

mod [mɑːd] *adj see* **convenience**

mode [moud] *n* (form: of life) 様式 yōshiki; (: of transportation) 手段 shūdan

model [mɑːdˈəl] *n* (representation: of boat, building etc) 模型 mokéi; (fashion model, artist's model) モデル mòderu; (example) 手本 tèhòn
♦*adj* (excellent) 模範的な mohánteki na
♦*vt* (clothes) ...のモデルをする ...no móderu wo suru; (with clay etc) ...の模型を作る ...no mokéi wo tsukúrù; (copy): **to model oneself on** ...の模範に習う ...no móhàn ni naráù
♦*vi* (for designer, photographer etc) モデルをする móderu wo suru

model railway *n* 模型鉄道 mokéi tetsu-dō

modem [mouˈdem] *n* (COMPUT) モデム mòdèmu

moderate [*adj* mɑːdˈəːrɪt *vb* mɑːdˈəːreɪt] *adj* (views, opinion) 穏健な oñken na; (amount) 中位の chūgurai no, (change)

ある程度の arú teîdo no
♦vi (storm, wind etc) 弱まる yawámarù
♦vt (tone, demands) 和らげる yawáragerù

moderation [mɑːdəreiʃʾən] *n* 中庸 chúyō

modern [mɑːdʿərn] *adj* 現代的な gendaiteki na, 近代的な kindaiteki na, モダンな modán na

modernize [mɑːdʿərnaiz] *vt* 現代的にする gendaiteki ni suru

modest [mɑːdʿist] *adj* (small: house, budget) 質素な shíssó na; (unassuming: person) 謙虚な kefikyo na

modesty [mɑːdʿisti] *n* 慎み tsutsúshimi

modicum [mɑːdʿəkəm] *n*: *a modicum of* ちょっとだけの… chóttó dake no …

modification [mɑːdəfəkeiʃʾən] *n* (alteration: of law etc) 改正 kafsei; (: of car, engine etc) 改造 kafzō

modify [mɑːdʿəfai] *vt* (law) 改正する kafsei suru; (building, car, engine) 改造する kafzō suru

module [mɑːdʒuːl] *n* (unit, component, SPACE) モジュール mojūrū

mogul [mougəl] *n* (fig) 大立者 ōdatemóno

mohair [mouheʾr] *n* モヘア móheà

moist [moist] *adj* (slightly wet: earth, eyes, lips) 湿った shimétta

moisten [moisʾən] *vt* (lips, sponge) 湿らす shimérasù

moisture [moisʾtʃər] *n* 湿り気 shimérike

moisturizer [moisʾtʃəraizər] *n* (cream) モイスチュアクリーム móisuchua kurīmu; (lotion) モイスチュアローション móisuchua rōshon

molar [mouʾlər] *n* きゅう歯 kyūshi

mold [mould] (*BRIT* **mould**) *n* (cast: for jelly, metal) 型 katá; (mildew) かび kabí
♦vt (shape: plastic, clay etc) …で…の形を作る …de …no katáchì wo tsukūrù; (fig: influence: public opinion, character) 作り上げる tsukūriagerù

moldy [mouʾldi] (*BRIT* **mouldy**) *adj* (bread, cheese) かびた kabíta; (smell) かび臭い kabíkusaì

mole [moul] *n* (spot) ほくろ hokúro; (ani-

mai) モグラ mogúra; (*fig*: spy) 秘密工作員 himítsukōsakuin

molecule [mɑːlʾəkjuːl] *n* 分子 bûnshi

molest [məlest] *vt* (assault sexually) …にいたずらをする …ni itázura wo surú; (harass) いじめる ijímerú

mollycoddle [mɑːlʾikɑdəl] *vt* (pamper) 甘やかす amáyakasù

molt [moult] (*BRIT* **moult**) *vi* (animal, bird) 換毛する kañmō suru

molten [moulʾtən] *adj* (metal, rock) 溶解の yōkai no

mom [mɑm] (*US: inf*) *n* かあちゃん kâchan, ママ mámà

moment [mouʾmənt] *n* (period of time): *for a moment* ちょっと chóttò; (point in time): *at that moment* 丁度その時 chōdō sonó tokì
at the moment 今の所 imá no tokóro

momentary [mouʾmənteriː] *adj* (brief: pause, glimpse) 瞬間的な shuñkanteki na

momentous [moumenʾtəs] *adj* (occasion, decision) 重大な júdai na

momentum [moumenʾtəm] *n* (PHYSICS) 運動量 uñdōryō; (*fig*: of events, movement, change) 勢い ikfoi, 惰性 daséi
to gather momentum (*lit, fig*) 勢いが付く ikfoi ga tsúkù

mommy [mɑmʾiː] (*US*) *n* ママ mámà ◇幼児用語 yōjiyōgo

Monaco [mɑnʾəkou] *n* モナコ mónàko

monarch [mɑnʾərk] *n* 君主 kûnshu

monarchy [mɑnʾərkiː] *n* (system) 王制 ōsei; (royal family) 王室 ōshitsu, 王族 ōzoku

monastery [mɑnʾəsteriː] *n* 修道院 shúdòin

Monday [mʌndei] *n* 月曜日 getsúyōbì

monetary [mɑnʾiteriː] *adj* (system, policy, control) 金融の kiñ-yū no

money [mʌnʾiː] *n* (coins and notes) 金 kané; (currency) 通貨 tsūka
to make money (earn) 金をもうける kané wo mókerù

money order *n* 郵便為替 yūbinkawàse

money-spinner [mʌnʾispinər] *n* (*BRIT*

inf) *n* (person, idea, business) ドラ箱 do-rúbako

mongol [mɔːŋgɔl] *adj* モンゴルの môñgoru no

♦*n* (MED) ダウン症候群患者 daúnshokô-gun kañja

mongrel [mʌŋgrəl] *n* (dog) 雑種 zasshú

monitor [mɑːnətər] *n* (machine) モニタ一装置 monítashòchì; (screen: also: **television monitor**) ブラウン管 buráuñkan; (of computer) モニター mónìtā

♦*vt* (broadcasts) 聴取する b chôj̄u suru; (heartbeat, pulse) モニターする mónìtā suru; (progress) 監視する kañshi suru

monk [mʌŋk] *n* 修道師 shûdòshi

monkey [mʌŋki] *n* (animal) サル sarú

monkey nut (*BRIT*) *n* ピーナッツ pî-nattsu

monkey wrench *n* モンキーレンチ moñkîrenchi

mono [mɑːnou] *adj* (recording) モノラルの mónoraru no

monochrome [mɑːnəkroum] *adj* (film, photograph) 白黒の shfrôkuro no, モノクロの mónòkuro no

monogram [mɑːnəgræm] *n* モノグラム monógùrama

monologue [mɑːnəlɔːg] *n* 会話の独占 kaíwa no dokúseñ; (THEATER) 独白 dokúhaku, モノローグ monórôgu

monopolize [mənɑːpəlaiz] *vt* 独占する dokúseñ suru

monopoly [mənɑːpəli] *n* (domination) 独占 dokúseñ; (COMM) 専売 señbai, モノポリー monópòrî

monosyllable [mɑːnəsiləbəl] *n* 単音節語 tañ-onsetsugò

monotone [mɑːnətoun] *n*: **to speak in a monotone** 単調な声で話す tañchô na kôè de hanásù

monotonous [mənɑːtənəs] *adj* (life, job etc) 退屈な tafkutsu na; (voice, tune) 単調な tañchô na

monotony [mənɑːtəni] *n* 退屈 tafkutsu

monsoon [mɑːnsuːn] *n* モンスーン moñ-sun

monster [mɑːnstər] *n* (animal, plant: misshapen) 奇形 kikéi; (: enormous)

kaíbutsu, お化け obákè; (imaginary creature) 怪物 kaíbutsu; (person: cruel, evil) 怪物 kaíbutsu

monstrosity [mɑːnstrɑːsiti] *n* (hideous object, building) 見るに堪えない代物 mfrù ni taénài shírômòno

monstrous [mɑːnstrəs] *adj* (huge) 巨大な kyodái na; (ugly) 見るに堪えない mfrù ni taénài; (atrocious) 極悪な gokfiaku na

month [mʌnθ] *n* 月 tsukí

monthly [mʌnθli] *adj* (ticket etc) 一カ月の ikkágetsu no; (magazine) 月刊の gekkán no; (payment etc) 毎月の maítsuki no; (meeting) 月例の getsúrei no

♦*adv* 毎月 maítsuki

monument [mɑːnjəmənt] *n* (memorial) 記念碑 kinéñhi; (historical building) 史的記念物 shitékikinéñbutsu

monumental [mɑːnjəmentəl] *adj* (large and important: building, statue) 歴史的な rekíshiteki na; (important: book, piece of work) 画期的な kakkíteki na; (terrific: storm, row) すごい sugói, すさまじい susámajiî

moo [muː] *vi* (cow) もーと鳴く mô tò na-kú

mood [muːd] *n* (humor: of person) 機嫌 kigéñ; (: of crowd, group) 雰囲気 fuñ-ikì, ムード mûdo

to be in a good/bad mood (temper) 機嫌がいい(悪い) kigéñ gà íi(warúì)

moody [muːdi] *adj* (variable) むら気な murági na; (sullen) 不機嫌な fukígeñ na

moon [muːn] *n* 月 tsukí

moonlight [muːnlait] *n* 月光 gekkô

moonlighting [muːnlaitiŋ] *n* (work) アルバイト arúbàito 〈本勤め以外では働くことで、特に規定、規則違反の仕事を指す honîshôku no hoka nî suru shigôto dè, tôkù ni kitéi, kisóku ihàn no shigóto wô sásù

moonlit [muːnlit] *adj*: **a moonlit night** 月夜 tsukíyo

moor [muːr] *n* (heath) 荒れ野 aréno

♦*vt* (ship) つなぐ tsunágù

♦*vi* 停泊する teíhaku suru

moorland [muːrlænd] *n* 荒れ野 aréno

moose [muːs] *n inv* アメリカヘラジカ a-mérikaherajíka

mop [mɔp] *n* (for floor) モップ moppú; (for dishes) スポンジたわし supónjitawashi ◊短い柄の付いた皿洗い用を指す mijíkal e no tsúita saráaraí yō no sásū

◆*vt* (floor) モップでふく moppú de fukú; (eyes, face) ふく fukú, ぬぐう nugúū

a mop of hair もじゃもじゃ頭 mojámoja atáma

mope [moup] *vi* ふさぎ込む fuságikómu

moped [mou'ped] *n* モペット mopéttò ◊ペダルで動かす事も出来る小型オートバイ pedárū de ugókasú kotó mo dekírū kogáta ôtobai

mop up *vt* (liquid) ふく fukú

moral [mɔːr'əl] *adj* 倫理的な rínritekí na
◆*n* (of story etc) 教訓 kyōkun

moral support (encouragement) 精神的な支え seíshinteki sasáe

morale [məræl'] *n* (of army, staff) 士気 shíki

morality [məræl'iti:] *n* (good behavior) 品行 hínkō; (system of morals: *also* correctness, acceptability) 倫理 rínri

morals [mɔːr'əlz] *npl* (principles, values) 倫理 rínri

morass [məræs'] *n* (*lit, fig*) 泥沼 dorónuma

morbid [mɔːr'bid] *adj* (imagination, ideas) 陰気な ínki na

KEYWORD

more [mɔːr] *adj* 1 (greater in number etc) より多くの yorí ōku no

more people/work/letters than we expected 私たちが予定していたより多くの人々 (仕事、手紙) watákushitàchi ga yotéí shité ta yorí ōku no hitóbito (shigóto, tegámi)

I have more books/money than you 私はあなたより本(金)を持っています watákushi wa anáta yorí takúsan nò hón(kané) wo mótte imásu

this store has more wine than beer この店はビールよりワインが沢山あります kono mise wa bírū yorí waín ga takúsan arimásu

2 (additional) もっと móttò

do you want (some) more tea? もっと紅茶をいかがですか móttò kōcha wò ikága desù ká

is there any more wine? ワインはまだありますか waín wa mádà arimásu ká

I have no/I don't have any more money お金はもうありません o-káne wa mô arímaseñ

it'll take a few more weeks あと数週間持ちます átò sūshūkan kakárimasu

◆*pron* 1 (greater amount) もっと沢山 móttò takúsan

more than 10 10以上 jūijō ◊この成句の英語には「10」が含まれないが、日本語の場合「10」も含まれる kono seíku no éigo ni wà 「jū」 ga fukúmarenai ga, nihóngo no baái 「jū」 mò fukúmarerū (Note: the English phrase indicates a quantity of 11 and above, but the Japanese indicates 10 and above.)

it cost more than we expected 予想以上に金が掛りました yosō ijō ni kané gà kakárimashīta

2 (further or additional amount) もっと沢山 móttò takúsan

is there any more? まだありますか mádà arimásu ká

there's no more もうありません mô arímaseñ

a little more もう少し mô sukoshí

many/much more …よりずっと沢山 …yorí zuttó takúsan

◆*adv* …よりもっと… …yorí móttò…

more dangerous/difficult etc (than) …より危ない (難しい) …yorí abúnai(muzúkashì)

more easily/economically/quickly (than) …よりたやすく(経済的に、早く) …yorí tayasukū(keizaiteki ni, hayákū)

more and more ますます masúmasu

more and more excited/friendly/expensive ますます興奮して(親しくなって、高くなって) masúmasu kófun shité (shítashiku nattè, tákàku nattè)

he grew to like her more and more 彼はますます彼女が好きになった kárè wa masúmasu kánòjo ga sukí ni nattá *more or less* 大体 daitai, 大よそ óyoso

the job's more or less finished 仕事は大体できています shigóto wà daitai dékìte imasu

it should cost £500, more or less 大よそ500ポンド掛りそうです óyoso go-hyákupòndo kakárisò desu

more than ever ますます masúmàsu, より一層 yorí issò

more beautiful than ever ますます美しい masúmàsu utsúkushiì

more quickly than ever ますます早く masúmàsu háyàku

he loved her more than ever 彼は以前一層彼女を愛する様になった kárè wa yorí issò kánòjo wo ái suru yò ni nátta

moreover [mɔːrˈouvəːr] *adv* なお naó, その上 sonó ué ni, その外 sonó hoká ni, しかも shikámo

morgue [mɔːrg] *n* 死体保管所 shitái-hokanjo, モルグ morúgù

moribund [mɔːrˈəbʌnd] *adj* (organization, industry) 斜陽の shayò no

Mormon [mɔːrˈmən] *n* モルモン教徒 morúmon kyòto

morning [mɔːrˈniŋ] *n* (period after daybreak) 朝 asá; (from midnight to noon) 午前 gózèn

in the morning 朝に asá ni, 午前中に gozénchù ni

7 o'clock in the morning 午前7時 gózèn shichíji

morning paper 朝刊 chókàn

morning sun 朝日 asáhi

morning walk 朝の散歩 ásà no sanpo

morning sickness つわり tsuwári

Morocco [mərɑːkˈou] *n* モロッコ morókkò

moron [mɔːrˈɑːn] *(inf)* n ばか bákà

morose [mərous] *adj* (miserable) 陰気な ínki na

morphine [mɔːrˈfiːn] *n* モルヒネ morúhine

Morse [mɔːrs] *n (also: Morse code)* モールス信号 mórusu shingò

morsel [mɔːrˈsəl] *n (of food)* 一口 hitókùchi

mortal [mɔːrˈtəl] *adj (man)* いつか死ぬ f-tsúka shinú; *(wound)* 致命的な chiméite-

ki na; *(danger)* 命にかかわる ínòchi ni kakáwarù

♦ *n (human being)* 人間 nìngen

mortal combat 死闘 shitò

mortal enemy 宿敵 shukúteki

mortal remains 遺骨 ikótsu

mortal sin 大罪 taizai

mortality [mɔːrtælˈiti] *n* いつか死ぬ事 ítsùka shinú kotò; *(number of deaths)* 死亡率 shibóritsu

mortar [mɔːrˈtəːr] *n (cannon)* 迫撃砲 hakúgekihò; *(CONSTR)* モルタル mórùta-ru; *(bowl)* 乳鉢 nyúbachi

mortgage [mɔːrˈgidʒ] *n* 住宅ローン jútà-kurðn

♦ *vt (house, property)* 抵当に入れて金を借りる teftó ni irète kanê wo karfrú

mortify [mɔːrˈtəfai] *vt: to be mortified* 恥を感じる hajî wo kanjirù

mortuary [mɔːrˈtʃuːeːri] *n* 霊安室 refan-shitsu

mosaic [mouzeiˈik] *n* モザイク mozáîku

Moscow [mɑːsˈkau] *n* モスクワ mosúku-wa

Moslem [mɑːzˈləm] *adj, n* = **Muslim**

mosque [mɑːsk] *n* イスラム教寺院 isúra-mukyò jiîn, モスク mósùku

mosquito [məskiːˈtou] *(pl mosquitoes)* *n* 蚊 ká

moss [mɔːs] *n (plant)* コケ kokê

KEYWORD

---

most [moust] *adj* 1 *(almost all: people, things etc)* ほとんどの hotóndo no

most people ほとんどの人 hotóndo no hitó

most men/dogs behave like that ほとんどの男性〈イヌ〉はそういう振舞をするhotóndo no dañsei〈inú〉wa sò iú furúmaì wo surù

most houses here are privately owned ここの家ここの家は個人所有の物です kokó nò hotóndo no ié wà kojínshoyù no monó desù

2 *(largest, greatest: interest, money etc)* 最も沢山の mottómò takúsañ no

who has (the) most money? 最も多くの金を持っているのは誰でしょう mottómò oku no kane wo motte iru no wa dare deshō

he derived the most pleasure from her visit 最も彼を喜ばせたのは彼女の訪問だった mottómó kárè wo yorókobaseta no wa kánôjo no hômon dattà

◆*pron* (greatest quantity, number) ほとんど hotóndô

most of it/them それ(それら)のほとんど sorê(sorêra)no hotóndô

most of the money/your friends 金(彼女の友達)のほとんど kanê(kánôjo no tomôdachi)nô hotóndô

most of the time ほとんどの場合 hotóndo no baâi

do the most you can できるだけの事をして下さい dekíru dakè no kotô wô shité kudasai

I saw the most 私が一番沢山見ましたwatákushi gà ichíban takúsan mimáshita

to make the most of something を最大限に利用する ...wò saídaigen ni riyô surù

at the (very) most 最大に見積っても saídai nì mitsúmotte mò

◆*adv* (+ verb: spend, eat, work etc) 最も多く mottómô (+ adjective): **the most intelligent/expensive** 最も利口(高価)な mottómô rikô(kôka)nà; (+ adverb: carefully, easily etc) 最も注意深く(たやすく) mottómô chûibukakû(tayásukû); (very: polite, interesting etc) とても totémo

a most interesting book とても面白い本 totémo omoshíroî hoñ

mostly [moust'li:] *adv* (chiefly) 主に ómó ni; (usually) 普段は fúdàn wa, 普通は fuñtsû wa

MOT [emouti'] *n abbr* = **Ministry of Transport**: **the MOT (test)** (BRIT) 車検 shakêñ

motel [moutel'] *n* モーテル môteru

moth [mɔːθ] *n* (insect) ガ ga; (clothes moth) 衣蛾 ishôga

mothball [mɔːθ'bɔːl] *n* 防虫剤 bôchûzai

mother [mʌð'əːr] *n* 母親 hàhá, 母親 hahá-

ya, お母さん o-kásaṇ

◆*adj*: **mother country** 母国 bôkóku

◆*vt* (act as mother to) 母親として育てる hahâoya toshitê sodâterù; (pamper, protect) 甘やかす amáyakasů

mother company 親会社 oyágaîsha

motherhood [mʌð'əːrhud] *n* 母親である事 hahâoya de arû kotô

mother-in-law [mʌð'əːrinlɔː] (*p l* **mothers-in-law**) *n* しゅうと shûto

motherly [mʌð'əːrli:] *adj* 母の様な hàhá no yô na

mother-of-pearl [mʌð'əːrəvpəːrl'] *n* 真珠母 shiñjûbo

mother-to-be [mʌð'əːrtəbi:] (*p l* **mothers-to-be**) *n* 妊婦 niñpu

mother tongue *n* 母国語 bokôkugô

motif [mouti:f'] *n* (design) 模様 moyô

motion [mou'ʃən] *n* (movement) 動き u-gôki; (gesture) 合図 afzû; (at meeting) 動議 dôgi

◆*vt*: **to motion (to) somebody to do something** ...する様に...に合図をする ...surû yô nì ...ni afzû wo suru

motionless [mou'ʃənlis] *adj* 動かないu-gôkanai

motion picture *n* (film) 映画 eîga

motivated [mou'təveitid] *adj* (enthusiastic) 張り切っている harkítte irú; (impelled): **motivated by** (envy, desire) ...の動機で ...no dôki de

motivation [moutəvei'ʃən] *n* (drive) 動機 dôki

motive [mou'tiv] *n* (aim, purpose) 目標 mokûhyô

motley [mɑːt'li:] *adj* 雑多で奇妙な zattá dè kimyô na

motor [mou'təːr] *n* (of machine) 原動機 geñdôki, モーター môtà; (of vehicle) エンジン êñjin; (BRIT: inf: vehicle) 車 kurûma

◆*cpd* (industry, trade) 自動車の jídòsha no

motorbike [mou'təːrbaik] *n* オートバイ ôtobai

motorboat [mou'təːrbout] *n* モーターボート môtàbôto

motorcar [mou'təːrkɑːr] (BRIT) *n* 自動

車 jídōsha

motorcycle [mou'tə:rsai'kəl] n オートバイ ôtōbai

motorcycle racing n オートバイレーシング ôtōbairēshiṅgu

motorcyclist [mou'tə:rsaiklist] n オートバイのライダー ôtōbai no raídā

motoring [mou'tə:riŋ] (BRIT) n 自動車運転 jídōsha unteñ

motorist [mou'tə:rist] n 運転者 uñteñsha

motor racing (BRIT) n カーレース kārēsu

motor vehicle n 自動車 jídōsha

motorway [mou'tə:rwei] (BRIT) n ハイウェー haíuē

mottled [mɑt'əld] adj ぶちの buchí no

motto [mɑt'ou] (pl mottoes) n 標語 hyōgo, モットー móttō

mould [mould] (BRIT) n, vt = mold

mouldy [moul'di:] (BRIT) adj = moldy

moult [moult] (BRIT) vi = molt

mound [maund] n (heap: of blankets, leaves, earth etc) 一山 hítóyama

mount [maunt] n (mountain in proper names): Mount Carmel カルメル山 kārūmeruzáñ

♦vt (horse) ...に乗る ...ni norú; (exhibition, display) 開催する kaísai suru; (fix: jewel) 台座にはめる dafza ni hamérū; (: picture) 掛ける kakérū; (staircase) 上る nobórù

♦vi (increase: inflation) 上昇する jōshō suru; (: tension) つのる tsunoru; (: problems) 増える fuérù

mountain [maun'tən] n (GEO) 山 yamá

♦cpd (road, stream) 山の yamá no

mountaineer [mauntənir'] n 登山家 tozáñka

mountaineering [mauntəni:'riŋ] n 登山 tozáñ

mountainous [maun'tənəs] adj (country, area) 山の多い yamá no ōi

mountain rescue team n 山岳救助隊 sañgaku kyūjotai

mountainside [maun'tənsaid] n 山腹 sañpuku

mount up vi (bills, costs, savings) たま

る tamárū

mourn [mɔːrn] vt (death) 悲しむ kanáshimù

♦vi: to mourn for (someone) ...の死を悲しむ ...no shí wo kanáshimù

mourner [mɔːr'nəːr] n 会葬者 kaísōsha

mournful [mɔːr'nfəl] adj (sad) 悲しそうな kanáshisō na

mourning [mɔːr'niŋ] n 喪 mo

in mourning 喪中で mochū de

mouse [maus] (pl mice) n (animal) ハツカネズミ hatsúkanezùmi; (COMPUT) マウス máusu

mousetrap [maus'træp] n ネズミ取り nezúmitòri

mousse [muːs] n (CULIN) ムース mûsu; (also: hair mousse) ヘアムース heámùsu

moustache [mæstæʃ'] (BRIT) n = mustache

mousy [mau'si:] adj (hair) 薄汚い茶色の usugítanai cha-fro no

mouth [mauθ] (pl mouths) n (ANAT) 口 kuchí; (of cave, hole) 入口 iríguchi; (of river) 河口 kakō

mouthful [mauθ'ful] n (amount) 口一杯 kuchí ippai

mouth organ n ハーモニカ hámonika

mouthpiece [mauθ'pi:s] n (of musical instrument) 吹口 fukíguchi; (spokesman) スポークスマン supôkusumàn

mouthwash [mauθ'wɔʃ] n マウスウォッシュ máusu uósshù 口臭防止洗口液 kōshūbōshi senkōèki

mouth-watering [mauθ'wɔːtəriŋ] adj おいしそうの ofshisō na

movable [muː'vəbəl] adj 可動な kadô na

move [muːv] n (movement) 動き ugóki; (in game: change of position) 手 te; (: turn to play) 番 báñ; (change of house) 引っ越し hikkóshi; (: of job) 転職 teñshoku

♦vt (change position of: furniture, car, curtains etc) 動かす ugókasù; (chessmen etc: in game) 動かす ugókasù; (emotionally) 感動させる kañdō saserù; (POL: resolution etc) 提議する teígi suru

♦vi (gen, animal) 動く ugókù; (traffic) 流れる nagárerù; (also: move house)

引っ越す hikkōsu; (develop: situation, events) 進展する shinten suru
to get a move on 急ぐ isógù
to move someone to do something …に…をする気を起こさせる …ni …wo suru ki wò okósaserú

moveable [muːˈvəbl] *adj* = **movable**

move about/around *vi* (change position) そわそわする sówàsowa suru; (travel) 頻繁に旅行する hinpan ni ryokō suru; (change: residence) 頻繁に引っ越す hinpan ni hikkōsù; (: job) 頻繁に転職する hinpan ni teñshoku suru

move along *vi* 立ち去る tachísarù
move along! 立ち止まる tachídomarù ná

move away *vi* (leave: town, area) よそへ引っ越す yosó e hikkósù

move back *vi* (return) 元の所へ引っ越す mótò no tokóro e hikkósù

move forward *vi* (advance) 前進する zeñshin suru

move in *vi* (to a house) 入居する nyūkyo suru; (police, soldiers) 攻撃を加える kōgeki wò kuwáerù

movement [muːvˈmənt] *n* (action: of person, animal) 動き ugóki, 動作 dōsa; (: of traffic) 流れ nagáre; (gesture) 合図 afzù; (transportation: of goods etc) 運搬 úñ-yu; (shift: in attitude, policy) 変化 heñka; (group of people: esp REL, POL) 運動 uñdō; (MUS) 楽章 gakúshō

move on *vi* 立ち去る tachísarù
move on! 立ち止まるな tachídomarù ná

move out *vi* (of house) 引っ越す hikkósù

move over *vi* (to make room) 横へどいて場所を空ける yokó e dóite bashó wò akérù

move up *vi* (employee, deputy) 昇進する shōshin suru; (pupil) 進級する shiñkyū suru

movie [muːviː] *n* 映画 efgà
to go to the movies 映画を見に行く efgà wo mí ni ikú

movie camera *n* 映画カメラ efgà kaméra

moving [muːˈviŋ] *adj* (emotional) 感動的

に kañdóteki ni; (that moves) 動く ugó-kù

mow [mou] (*pt* **mowed**, *pp* **mowed** *or* **mown**) *vt* (grass, corn) 刈る karú

mow down *vt* (of kill) なぎ払う様に殺す nagíharaú yō nì korósù

mower [mouˈəɾ] *n* (*also*: **lawnmower**) 芝刈機 shibákarikí

MP [empiːˈ] (*BRIT*) *n abbr* = **Member of Parliament**

m.p.h. [empieitʃʼ] *abbr* (= *miles per hour*) 時速…マイル jísoku …máîru

Mr, Mr. [misˈtəɾ] *n*: *Mr. Smith* スミスさん sumisu sán dafsei no kefshō

Mrs, Mrs. [misˈiz] *n*: *Mrs Smith* スミスさん sumisu sán 既婚女性の敬称 kíkon-jo no kefshō

Ms, Ms. [miz] *n*: *Ms. Smith* sumisu sán の既婚・未婚を問わず女性の敬称 kfkon, mfkon wo towázù joséi no kefshō

M.Sc. [emessiːˈ] *abbr* = **Master of Science**

KEYWORD

much [mʌtʃ] *adj* (time, money, effort) 沢山の takúsan no, 多くの ōkù no
we haven't got much time/money あまり多くの時間[金]はありません amári ōku no jikán[kané] wa arímaseñ
much effort was expended on the project その企画に多くの努力を費やした sonó kikáku ni ōkù no dóryòku wo tsufyashīta
how much money/time do you need? お金[時間]はどのぐらい必要ですか kàne[jikán] wa dóno gurai hitsúyō desù ká
he's done so much work for the charity その慈善事業のために彼は様々な仕事をしてくれました sonó jizéñjigyō no tamé nì kárè wa samázàma na shigóto wò shité kuremashīta
it's too much あんまりだ afmari da
it's not much 大した事じゃない táìshita kotó jà nai
to have too much money/free time 金

(暇)が有り余る kané(hìma)gà arîamàrù

as much as ... と同じぐらい ...to onáji gùrái

I have as much money/intelligence as you 私はあなたと同じぐらいの金(知識)を持っています watákushi wà anáta to onáji gùrái no kané(chíshìki) wò móttè imasu

◆*pron* 沢山の物 takúsan no monô

there isn't much to do あまりする事はありません amári suru kotò wa arímasen

much has been gained from our discussions 我々の話し合いは多くの成果を産みました waréwarè no hanáshiai wà ökú no seíka wò umímashìta

how much does it cost? - too much 値段はいくらですか・べらぼうき taíkã wã íkùra desu ká - berãbò sã

how much is it? いくらですか íkùra desu ká

◆*adv* (greatly, a great deal) とても totémo

thank you very much 大変有難うございます taíhen arígatò gozáimasu

much bigger (than) (...より) はるかに大きい (...yori) haruka ni ökii

we are very much looking forward to your visit あなたが来られるのを首を長くして待っています anáta ga koráreru no wo kubí wò nàgàku shite matté orimasù

he is very much the gentleman/politician 彼は紳士(政治家)です kárè wa rekkí tò shín shíshí(seijîka)desu

however much he tries 彼はどんなに努力しても kárè wa dóñna ni doryóku shite mo

as much as ... と同じぐらい沢山 ...tò onáji gùrái takúsañ

I read as much as ever 私はいつもと同じぐらいの本を読んでいます watákushi wà ítsumo to onáji gùrái takúsañ no hôñ wo yôñde imasù

I read as much as possible/as I can 私はできるだけ沢山の本を読む事にしています watákushi wà dekíru dake sñ takúsañ no hôñ wo yômù koto ní shité imasù

---

he is as much a part of the community as you 彼はあなたと同様ここの社会の一員です kárè wa anáta no dôyò kokô no shakai no ichîn desù

2 (by) ずっと zúttò

I'm much better now 私はずっと元気になっています watákushi wà zúttò géñki ni natté imasu

much reduced in price ずっと安くなって zuttô yasúku natte

it's much the biggest publishing company in Europe あれは断然ヨーロッパ最大の出版社です kárè wa dañzen yöroppasaídaí no shuppáñsha desu

3 (almost) ほとんど hotôndo

the view is much as it was 10 years ago 景色は10年前とほとんど変っていません keshîki wa jûnen maè to hotôndo kawátte imasen

the 2 books are much the same 2冊の本はどちらも同じ様な物です sonô nisàtsu no hôñ wa dóchìra mo onáji yô na monô desô

how are you feeling? - much the same ご気分はいかがですか - 大して変りません go-kîbuñ wa ikâga dèsu ká - taîshite kawárimaseñ

---

muck [mʌk] *n* (dirt) 泥 doró; (excrement) くそ kusô

muck about/around *vi* (*inf*: fool about) ぶらぶらする búrabura suru

muck up *vt* (*inf*: ruin) 台無しにする daf-nashi ni suru

mucus [mjuːˈkəs] *n* 粘液 nêñ-eki

mud [mʌd] *n* 泥 doró

muddle [mʌdˈəl] *n* (mess, mix-up) めちゃくちゃ mechákucha, 混乱 koñran

◆*vt* (*also*: **muddle up**) (confuse: person, things) 混乱させる koñran saserù; (: story, names) ごちゃごちゃにする go-chágocha ni suru

muddle through *vi* (get by) どうにかして切抜ける doî ni ka shite kirínukerù

muddy [mʌdˈiː] *adj* (floor, field) どろどろの doródoro no

mudguard [mʌdˈgɑːrd] *n* フェンダー féñdä

muesli [mju:z'li:] n ムースリ mūsuri ◆朝食用の、ナッツ、ドライフルーツ、穀物の混合 chōshoku yō no náttsu, doráifurūtsu, kokúmotsu no kóngō

muffin [mʌf'in] n (US) マドレーヌ madórēnu; (BRIT) マフィン máfin

muffle [mʌf'əl] vt (sound) 弱める yowámerù; (against cold) ...に防寒具を付ける ...ni bōkañgu wo tsukérù

muffled [mʌf'əld] adj (sound) 弱い yowáì

muffler [mʌf'lər] n (US) n (AUT) マフラー máfurā

mug [mʌg] n (cup) マグ mágù; (for beer) ジョッキ jókkì; (inf: face) 面 tsurá; (: BRIT: fool) ばか bákà
◆vt (assault) 襲う osóù ◆特に強盗行為について言う tókù ni gōtōkōì ni tsúìte iú

mugging [mʌg'iŋ] n 強盗事件 gōtōjiken

muggy [mʌg'i:] adj (weather, day) 蒸暑い mushíatsuì

mule [mju:l] n ラバ rábà

mull [mʌl] vt: **to mull over** ...について考え込む ...ni tsúìte kañgaekomù

multi... [mʌl'ti:] prefix 複数の... fukúsū no ...

multicolored [mʌltikʌl'ərd] (BRIT **multicoloured**) adj 多色の tashóku no

multilateral [mʌltilæt'ərəl] adj (disarmament, talks) 多国間の tákōkan no

multi-level [mʌlti:lev'əl] (US) adj = **multistory**

multinational [mʌltənæʃ'ənəl] n (company, business) 多国籍の tákōkuseki no

multiple [mʌl'təpəl] adj (collision) 玉突きの tamátsuki no; (interests) 複数の fukúsū no
◆n (MATH) 倍数 baísū

multiple sclerosis [-sklirou'sis] n 多発性硬化症 tahátsusei kōkashō

multiplication [mʌltəplikei'ʃən] n (MATH) 掛算 kakézañ; (increase) 増加 zōka

multiply [mʌl'təplai] vt (MATH): **4 multiplied by 2 is 8** 4掛ける2は8の8 kakérù nf wa hachí
◆vi (increase) 増える fuérù

multistory [mʌltistɔːr'iː] (BRIT **multistorey**) adj (building etc) 高層の kōsō no

multitude [mʌl'tətuːd] n (crowd) 群衆 gunshū; (large number): **a multitude of** (reasons, ideas) 沢山の takúsan no

mum [mʌm] n = **mom**
◆adj: **to keep mum** 黙っている damátte irù

mumble [mʌm'bəl] vt (speak indistinctly) もぐもぐ言う mógùmogu iú
◆vi ぶつぶつ言う bútsùbutsu iú

mummy [mʌm'iː] n (embalmed) ミイラ mfira; (BRIT: mother) = **mommy**

mumps [mʌmps] n おたふく風邪 otáfukukàze

munch [mʌntʃ] vt (chew) かむ kámù
◆vi かむ kámù

mundane [mʌndein'] adj (task, life) 平凡な hebon na

municipal [mjuːnis'əpəl] adj 市の shí no

munitions [mjuːniʃ'ənz] npl 兵器弾薬 heíkidañ-yaku

mural [mjuːr'əl] n 壁画 hekíga

murder [məːr'dəːr] n (killing) 殺人 satsújin
◆vt (kill) 殺す korósu

murderer [məːr'dəːrəːr] n 人殺し hitógoroshi

murderous [məːr'dəːrəs] adj (person) 殺人も辞さない satsújin mo jisanái; (attack) 殺しを目的とする koróshì wo mokúteki to surù

murky [məːr'kiː] adj (street, night) 暗い kuráì; (water) 濁った nigótta

murmur [məːr'məːr] n: **a murmur of voices** かすかな人声 kásùkana hitógòe; (of wind, waves) さざめき sazámeki
◆vt (speak quietly) 声をひそめて言う kóè wo hisómetè iú
◆vi 声をひそめて話す kóè wo hisómetè hanásù

muscle [mʌs'əl] n (ANAT) 筋肉 kiñniku; (fig: strength) 力 chikára

muscle in vi 割込む waríkomù

muscular [mʌs'kjələːr] adj (pain) 筋肉の kiñniku no; (build) たくましい takúmashiì; (person) 強そうな tsuyósō na

muse [mjuːz] *vi* (think) 考え込む kańgaekomù

♦*n* (MYTHOLOGY) ミューズ myūzu ◊ 人間の知的活動をつかさどるという女神 nińgen no chitékikatsudò wo tsukásadorù to iú mégami

museum [mjuːziː'əm] *n* 博物館 hakúbùtsukan

mushroom [mʌʃ'ruːm] *n* (fungus: edible, poisonous) キノコ kínòko

♦*vi* (fig: town, organization) 急速に成長する kyúsoku ni séíchò suru

music [mjuː'zik] *n* (sound, art) 音楽 óńgaku; (written music, score) 楽譜 gakúfu

musical [mjuː'zikəl] *adj* (career, skills, person) 音楽の óńgaku no; (sound, tune) 音楽的な ońgakuteki na

♦*n* (show, film) ミュージカル myújìkarù

musical instrument *n* 楽器 gakkí

music hall *n* (place) ボードビル劇場 bōdobiru gekijō

musician [mjuːziʃ'ən] *n* ミュージシャン myújìshàn

musk [mʌsk] *n* じゃ香 jakó

Muslim [mʌz'lim] *adj* イスラム教の isúramukyò no

♦*n* イスラム教徒 isúramukyòto

muslin [mʌz'lin] *n* モスリン mósùrin

mussel [mʌs'əl] *n* ムールガイ mūrugai

must [mʌst] *aux vb* (necessity, obligation): *I must do it* 私はそれをしなければならない watákushi wa soré wò shínákereba naranài; (probability): *he must be there by now* もう彼はあそこに着いているでしょう mő kárè wa asóko ni tsúíte irú deshò; (suggestion, invitation): *you must come and see me soon* そのうちは是非遊びに来て下さい sonő uchí ní asóbi ni kité kudasaì; (indicating something unwelcome): *why must he behave so badly?* どうしてまたあの子はそんなに行儀悪くするのだろう dőshite mata anő ko wa sofína ni győgíwarukù suru no darő

♦*n* (necessity): *it's a must* 必需品だ hitsújuhin da

mustache [mʌstæʃ'] (*US*) *n* 鼻ひげ hanáhige

mustard [mʌs'tərd] *n* (Japanese) 辛子 karáshi, 和辛子 wagárashi; (Western) 辛子 karáshi, 洋辛子 yőgárashi, マスタード masútādo

muster [mʌs'tər] *vt* (support) 求める motómerù; (energy, strength) 奮い起す furúíokosù; (MIL) 召集する shōshū suru

mustn't [mʌs'ənt] = **must not**

musty [mʌs'tiː] *adj* かび臭い kabíkusaì

mutation [mjuːteiʃ'ən] *n* (alteration) 変化 heńka

mute [mjuːt] *adj* (silent) 無言の mugón no

muted [mjuː'tid] *adj* (color) 地味な jimí na; (reaction) ひそめた hisómèta

mutilate [mjuː'təleit] *vt* (person, thing) 傷付ける kizútsukerù ※特に体の部分を切断する場合に使う tōkū ni karáda no búbùn wo setsúdan suru baái ni tsukáù

mutiny [mjuː'təniː] *n* (rebellion of soldiers, sailors) 反乱 hańran

♦*vi* 反乱を起す hańran wò okósù

mutter [mʌt'ər] *vt* (speak quietly) つぶやく tsubúyakù

♦*vi* ぶつぶつ不平を言う bútsùbutsu fuhéi wò iú

mutton [mʌt'ən] *n* (meat) マトン mátòn

mutual [mjuː'tʃuːəl] *adj* (shared: benefit, interest) 共通の kyőtsū no; (reciprocal: feeling, attraction) 相互の sőgo no

mutually [mjuː'tʃuːəliː] *adv* 相互に sőgo ni

muzzle [mʌz'əl] *n* (mouth: of dog) ふん fán, 鼻づら hanázura; (: of gun) 銃口 jūkō; (guard: for dog) 口輪 kuchíwa

♦*vt* (dog) ...に口輪をはめる ...ni kuchíwa wo hamérù

KEYWORD

my [mai] *adj* 私の watákushi nő

this is my house/car/brother これは私の家[車、兄]です watákushi nő íè[kúruma, ánì]desù

I've washed my hair/cut my finger 私は髪を洗いました[指を切りました] watákushi wa kamf wò aráimashìta [yubí wò kirímashìta]

is this my pen or yours? これは私の

ペンですか、それともあなたのですか
koré wā watákushi nō péń desu ká,
sorétomo anátá no desu ká

Myanmar [mai'ænmɔːr] n ミャンマー
myáńmā

myopic [mai'ɔ'pik] adj 近眼の kíńgan no

myriad [mir'i:əd] n (of people, things) 無
数 musū

myself [maisélf'] pron 私自身 watákushi-
jishíń ¶ see also oneself

mysterious [mistiːr'iːəs] adj (strange) な
ぞの nazó no

mystery [mis'təːri:] n (puzzle) なぞ nazó
shrouded in mystery (place) なぞに包
まれた nazó ní tsutsúmaréta

mystic [mis'tik] n (person) 神秘主義者
shíńpíshúgisha

mystic(al) [mis'tik(əl)] adj 神秘的な shíń-
piteki na

mystify [mis'təfai] vt (perplex) ...の理解
を越える ...no ríkái wō koérù

mystique [mistiːk'] n 神秘 shíńpi

myth [miθ] n (legend, story) 神話 shíń-
wa; (fallacy) 俗信 zokúshìn

mythology [miθɑːl'ədʒi:] n 神話集 shíń-
wàshū

N

n/a abbr (= not applicable) ◇申請用紙な
どで空欄にしておく場合に書く shíńsei
yóshi nádò de kúran ni shíte oku baái ni
kákù

nag [næg] vt (scold) がみがみ言う gámí-
gami iú

nagging [næg'iŋ] adj (doubt) 晴れ ない
haréna¡; (pain) しつこい shitsúkòi

nail [neil] n (on fingers, toes) つめ tsumé;
(metal) くぎ kugí
◇vt: *to nail something to something*
...を...にくぎで留める ...wo ...ni kugí dè
toméru
to nail someone down to doing some-
thing 強制的に...に...をさせる kyóseíte-
ki ni ...ni ...wò saserù

nailbrush [neil'brʌʃ] n つめブラシ tsu-

mēburàshi

nailfile [neil'fail] n つめやすり tsuméyasùri

nail polish n マニキュア maníkyùa

nail polish remover n 除光液 jokóeki,
マニュア落し maníkyua otōshi

nail scissors npl つめ切りばさみ tsumé-
kiribasámi

nail varnish (BRIT) n = **nail polish**

naive [naiːv'] adj (person, ideas) 無邪気
な mújàki na, ナイーブな naíbu na

naked [nei'kid] adj 裸の hadáka no

name [neim] n (of person, animal, place)
名前 namáe; (surname) 名字 myójí, 姓 sé-
i; (reputation) 評判 hyóban
◇vt (child) ...に名前を付ける ...ni namáe
wò tsukérù; (identify: accomplice, criminal) 名前を指す namáe ... o sásù; (specify: price, date
etc) 指定する shítéi suru
what's your name? お名前は何とおっ
しゃいますか o-námae wà nánto osshái-
masù ká
by name 名指しで nazáshi dè
in the name of (fig) ...の名において
...no ná ni oíte
to give one's name and address (to
police etc) 名前と住所を知らせる namáe
tò jūshò wo shíraserù

nameless [neim'lis] adj (unknown) 無名
の muméi no; (anonymous: witness, contributor) 匿名の tokúmei no

namely [neim'li:] adv 即ち sunáwàchi

namesake [neim'seik] n 同姓同名の人
dóseídòmei no hitó

nanny [næn'i:] n 乳母 ubá

nap [næp] n (sleep) 昼寝 hirúne
to be caught napping (fig) 不意を突か
れる fuí wò tsukárerù

napalm [nei'pɑːm] n ナパーム napámu

nape [neip] n: *nape of the neck* えり首
eríkùbi

napkin [næp'kin] n (also: **table napkin**)
ナプキン nápùkin

nappy [næp'i:] (BRIT) n おむつ o-mútsu

nappy rash (BRIT) n おむつかぶれ o-
mútsukabùre

narcissus [nɑːrsis'əs] (pl **narcissi**) n
(BOT) スイセン suísen

narcotic [nɑːrˈkɒtik] *adj* 麻酔性の masúisei no
♦*n* 麻薬 mayáku

narrative [nærˈətiv] *n* 物語 monógatàri

narrator [nærˈeitər] *n* (in book) 語り手 katárite; (in film etc) ナレーター narétā

narrow [nærˈou] *adj* (space, road etc) 狭い semái; (fig: majority, advantage) ぎりぎりの girígiri no; (: ideas, attitude) 狭量な kyóryō na
♦*vi* (road) 狭くなる sémaku naru; (gap, difference: diminish) 小さくなる chíisaku naru

to have a narrow escape 間一髪で逃れる kań-ippátsu de nogárerù

to narrow things down to (choice, possibility) ...を...に絞る ...wo ...ni shibórù

narrowly [nærˈouli] *adv* (miss) 辛うじて karôjîte, 間一髪 kań-ippátsu de

narrow-minded [nærˈoumainˈdid] *adj* 狭量な kyóryō na

nasal [neiˈzəl] *adj* (of the nose) 鼻の haná no; (voice, sound) 鼻にかかった haná ni kakattà

nasty [nӕsˈti] *adj* (unpleasant: remark, person) いやな iyá nà; (malicious) 腹黒い harágurò; (rude) 無礼な búrèi na; (revolting: taste, smell) むかつかせる mukátsukaserů; (wound, disease etc) ひどい hidōi

nation [neiˈʃən] *n* (country) 国 kunî, 国家 kôkkà; (people) 国民 kokúmin

national [nӕʃˈənəl] *adj* 国の kunî no
♦*n: a foreign national* 外国人 gaíkokujìn

national dress *n* 民族衣装 mińzokuishô

National Health Service (BRIT) *n* 国民医療制度 kokúmin iryóseîdo

National Insurance (BRIT) *n* 国民保険 kokúminhoken

nationalism [nӕʃˈənəlizəm] *n* 国家主義 kokkáshugî, 民族主義 mínzokushugî

nationalist [nӕʃˈənəlist] *adj* 国家主義の kokkáshugî no, 民族主義の mínzokushugî no
♦*n* 国家主義者 kokkáshugishà, 民族主義者 mínzokushugishà

nationality [nӕʃənӕlˈəti] *n* 国籍 kokúseki

nationalization [nӕʃənəlizeiˈʃən] *n* 国有化 kokúyûka, 国営化 kokúeika

nationalize [nӕʃˈənəlaiz] *vt* 国営にする kokúei ni surû

nationally [nӕʃˈənəli] *adv* (nationwide) 全国的に zeńkokuteki ni; (as a nation) 国として kunî toshite

nationwide [neiˈʃənwaid'] *adj* (problem, campaign) 全国的な zeńkokuteki na
♦*adv* (campaign, search) 全国的に zeńkokuteki ni

native [neiˈtiv] *n* (local inhabitant) 地元の人 jimóto no hitô; (of tribe etc) 原住民 geńjûmin
♦*adj* (indigenous) 地元の jimóto no, 地元生れの jimóto umáre no; (of one's birth) 生れの umáre no; (innate) 生れつきの umáretsuki no

a native of Russia ロシア生れの人 roshía umare no hitô

a native speaker of French フランス語を母国語とする人 furánsugo wò bokókugo to suru hitô

native language *n* 母国語 bokókugo

Nativity [nativˈiti] *n: the Nativity* キリストの降誕 kirísuto nô kôtan

NATO [neiˈtou] *n abbr* (= North Atlantic Treaty Organization) 北大西洋条約機構 kitátaiseiyô jóyaku kishô

natural [nӕtʃˈərəl] *adj* (gen) 自然の shizên no; (innate) 生れつきの umáretsuki no

natural gas *n* 天然ガス teńnengasû

naturalist [nӕtʃˈərəlist] *n* 博物学者 hakúbutsugakushà

naturalize [nӕtʃˈərəlaiz] *vt: to become naturalized* (person, plant) 帰化する kiká suru

naturally [nӕtʃˈərəli] *adv* (gen) 自然に shizên ni; (of course) もちろん mochíròn, 当然 tôzen

nature [neiˈtʃər] *n* (also: Nature) 自然 shizên, 大 自 然 daíshizên; (character) 性質 seíshitsu; (type, sort) 種類 shúrûi

by nature 生れつき umáretsuki de

naught [nɔːt] *n* 零 réi, ゼロ zêrô

naughty [nɔːt'iː] *adj* (child) 行儀の悪い gyǒgi no warúi

nausea [nɔː'ziːə] *n* 吐気 hakíke

nauseate [nɔː'ziːeit] *vt* むかつかせる mukátsukaserū, 吐気を起させる hakíke wo okósaserū; (fig) いやな感じを与える iyá na kaňjí wo atáerū

nautical [nɔː'tikəl] *adj* (uniform) 船員の seň-in no; (people) 海洋の kaíyō no
a nautical mile 海里 kaíri

naval [nei'vəl] *adj* (uniform, academy) 海軍の kaígun no
a naval battle 海戦 kaísen
naval forces 海軍力 kaígunryōku

naval officer *n* 海軍将校 kaígunshōkō

nave [neiv] *n* 外陣 gaíjīn

navel [nei'vəl] *n* へそ hesó

navigate [næv'əgeit] *vi* (NAUT, AVIAT) 航行する kōkō suru; (AUT) 道案内する michíaňnai suru

navigation [nævəgei'ʃən] *n* (action) 航行 kōkō; (science) 航海術 kōkaíjūtsu

navigator [næv'əgeitəːr] *n* (NAUT) 航海長 kōkaíchō; (AVIAT) 航空士 kōkū-shi; (AUT) 道案内する人 michíaňnai wo suru hitó

navvy [næv'iː] (*BRIT*) *n* 労働者 rōdōsha

navy [nei'viː] *n* 海軍 kaígun

navy(-blue) *adj* 濃紺の nōkon no

Nazi [nɑːt'siː] *n* ナチ náchī

NB [enbiː] *abbr* (= *nota bene*) 注 chū〈脚注などに使う略語 kyakúchū nadò ni tsukáū ryakúgo

near [niːr] *adj* (place, time, relation) 近い chikái
♦*adv* 近く chikáku
♦*prep* (also: *near to*: space, time) …の近くに …no chikáku ni
♦*vt* (place, event) …に近づく …ni chikázukū

nearby [niːr'bai'] *adj* 近くの chikáku no
♦*adv* 近くに chikáku ni

nearly [niːr'liː] *adv* (not totally) ほとんど hotóňdo; (on the point of) 危うく ayáùku
I nearly fell 危うく転ぶところだった ayáùku korőbu tokoro dattá

near miss *n* (narrow escape) ニアミス niámisu; (of planes) 異常接近 ijōsekkìn,

ニアミス niámisu; (of cars etc): *that was a near miss!* 危ないところだった abúnai tokoro dattá

nearside [niːr'said] *n* (AUT: in Britain, Japan) 左側 hidárigawa; (: in US, Europe etc) 右側 migígawa

near-sighted [niːr'saitid] *adj* 近眼の kiňgan no, 近視の kiňshi no

neat [niːt] *adj* (person) きちんとした kichíň to shita; (skillful: work, plan) 上手な jōzu na; (spirits) ストレートの sutórēto no

neatly [niːt'liː] *adv* (tidily) きちんと kichíň to; (skillfully) 上手に jōzu nì

necessarily [nesəseːr'iliː] *adv* (inevitably) 必然的に hitsúzenteki ni
not necessarily (not automatically) 必ずしも…でない kanárazushĭmo …de naî

necessary [nes'iseːriː] *adj* (required: skill, quality, measure) 必要な hitsúyō na; (inevitable: result, effect) 必然の hitsúzen no
it is necessary to/that …する必要がある …suru hitsúyō ga arū

necessitate [nəses'əteit] *vt* 必要とする hitsúyō to surū

necessities [nəses'itiːz] *npl* (essentials) 必需品 hitsújuhin

necessity [nəses'itiː] *n* (thing needed) 必需品 hitsúyō; (compelling circumstances) 必然 hitsúzen

neck [nek] *n* (of person, animal, garment, bottle) 首 kubí
♦*vi* (*inf*) ペッティングする pettíñgu suru
neck and neck 接戦して sessén shite

necklace [nek'lis] *n* ネックレス nékkùrèsu

neckline [nek'lain] *n* ネックライン nekkúraìn

necktie [nek'tai] (*US*) *n* ネクタイ nékùtai

née [nei] *adj*: *née Scott* 旧姓スコット kyúsei sukóttō

need [niːd] *n* (lack) 欠乏 ketsúbō; (necessity) 必要性 hitsúyōsei; (thing needed) 必需品 hitsújuhin
♦*vt* (require) …を必要とする …wo hitsú-

yō to surú

I need to do it 私はそれをしなければ ならない watákushí wa soré wo shínákereba naranaí, 私はそれをする必要がある watákushí wa soré wo suru hitsuyō ga árù

you don't need to go 行かなくてもいい ikánakute mo íi

needle [ni:dəl] *n* (gen) 針 hárī; (for knitting) 編棒 amíbō

♦*vt* (fig: inf) からかう karákaú

needless [ni:dlís] *adj* (criticism, risk) 不必要な fuhítsuyō na

needless to say 言うまでもなく iú made mo nakú

needlework [ni:dlwǝːrk] *n* (item(s) of needlework) 縫い物 nuímonò; (activity) 針仕事 haríshigotò

needn't [ni:dʔant] = need not

needy [ni:dí:] *adj* 貧しい mazúshiì

negation [nigéiʃən] *n* 否定 hitéi

negative [négʔativ] *adj* (answer) 否定の hitéi no; (attitude) 否定的な hitéiteki na; (reaction) 消極的な shōkyokuteki na; (ELEC) 陰極の ínkyoku no, マイナスの maínasu no

♦*n* (LING) 否定形 hitéikeì; (PHOT) 陰画 ínga, ネガ néga

neglect [niglékt] *vt* (child) 放任する hōnin suru, ほったらかす hottárakasù; (one's duty) 怠る okótarù

♦*n* (of child) 放任 hōnin; (of area, house, garden) 放置 hōchi, ほったらかし hottárakashi; (of duty) 怠る事 okótaru kotò

negligee [négʔlaʒei] *n* (dressing gown) ネグリジェ négùrijè

negligence [négʔlidʒəns] *n* (carelessness) 不注意 fuchúi

negligible [négʔlidʒəbəl] *adj* (cost, difference) わずかな wázûka na

negotiable [nigou∫əbəl] *adj* (check) 譲渡できる jōto dekírù

negotiate [nigou∫i:eit] *vi*: *to negotiate (with)* (...と) 交渉する (...to) kōshō suru

♦*vt* (treaty, transaction) 協議して決める kyōgi shite kimérù; (obstacle) 乗越える noríkoerù; (bend in road) 注意して通る

chūí shite tōrú

negotiation [nigouʒiːeiʃən] *n* 交渉 kōshō

negotiator [nigou∫i:eitəːr] *n* 交渉する人 kōshō suru hitò

Negress [ni:gris] *n* 黒人女性 kokújinjosèi

Negro [ni:grou] *adj* 黒人の kokújin no

♦*n* 黒人 kokújin

neigh [nei] *vi* いななく inánakū

neighbor [neibəːr] (BRIT **neighbour**) *n* (next door) 隣の人 tonári no hitò; (in vicinity) 近所の人 kínjo no hitò

neighborhood [neibəːrhud] *n* (place) 近所 kínjo, 界隈 kaíwai; (people) 近所の人々 kínjo no hitóbito

neighboring [neibəːriŋ] *adj* (town, state) 隣の tonári no

neighborly [neibəːrli] *adj* (person, attitude) 親切な shínsetsu na

neighbour [neibəːr] *etc* (BRIT) *n* = **neighbor** *etc*

neither [ni:ðəːr] *adj* どちらの...も...でない dóchìra no ...mo ...de naí

neither story is true どちらの話も本当ではない dóchìra no hanáshi mo hòntō de wa naí

♦*conj*: *I didn't move and neither did John* 私も動かなかったしジョンも動かなかった watákushí mò ugókanakattā shi, jóñ mo ugókanakattā

♦*pron* どちらも...でない dóchìra mo ...de naí

neither is true どちらも本当でない dóchìra mo hòntō de naí

♦*adv*: *neither good nor bad* よくも悪くもない yókù mo warúkù mo naí

neon [ni:ɑn] *n* ネオン néon, ネオンサイン néoñsaiñ

neon light *n* ネオン灯 néontō

nephew [néfju:] *n* おい oí

nerve [nəːrv] *n* (ANAT) 神経 shíñkei; (courage) 勇気 yūki; (impudence) 厚かましさ atsúkamashisā, 図々しさ zūzūshisā

to have a fit of nerves 神経質になる shíñkeishitsu ni narù

nerve-racking [nəːrvrækiŋ] *adj* いらいらさせる íraìra saserù

nervous [ˈnəːrvəs] *adj* (ANAT) 神経の shíñkei no; (anxious) 神経質な shíñkeishitsu na; (timid: person) 気の小さい ki no chíisai; (: animal) おく病な okúbyō na

nervous breakdown *n* 神経衰弱 shíñkeisuijáku

nest [nest] *n* 巣 sú

♦*vi* 巣を作る sú wo tsukúrù

nest egg *n* (fig) へそくり hesókuri

nestle [nesˈəl] *vi*: *to nestle in a valley/the mountains* (village etc) 谷間[山あい]に横たわる taníma (yamá-ai)nì yokótawarù

net [net] *n* (gen) 網 amí; (fabric) レース rḗsu; (TENNIS, VOLLEYBALL etc) ネット néttò; (fig) わな wána

♦*adj* (COMM) 正味の shṓmi no

♦*vt* (fish, game) 網で取る amí dè tórù; (profit) 得る érù

netball [netˈbɔːl] *n* ネットボール nettóbòru ◊英国で行われるバスケットボールに似た球技 efkoku de okonawarerú basúkettobòru ni nitá kyúgi

net curtains *npl* レースのカーテン rḗsu no kā̀teñ

Netherlands [neðˈərləndz] *npl*: *the Netherlands* オランダ oráñda

nett [net] (*BRIT*) *adj* = **net**

netting [netˈiŋ] *n* 網 amí

nettle [netˈəl] *n* イラクサ irákùsa

network [netˈwəːrk] *n* (of roads, veins, shops) ネットワーク nettówāku; (TV, RADIO) 放送網 hōsṓmō, ネットワーク nettówāku

neurotic [nurɑːtˈik] *adj* 神経過敏な shíñkeikabìn na, ノイローゼの nofrōze no

♦*n* ノイローゼの人 nofrōze no hitó

neuter [nuːˈtəːr] *adj* (LING) 中性の chū́sei no

♦*vt* (cat etc) 去勢する kyosēi suru

neutral [nuːˈtrəl] *adj* (person) 中立の chū́ritsu no; (color etc) 中間色の chū̀kañshoku no; (ELEC) 中性の chū́sei no

♦*n* (AUT) ニュートラル nyū́tòraru

neutrality [nuːtræˈlitiː] *n* 中立 chū́ritsu

neutralize [nuːˈtrəlaiz] *vt* (acid, poison etc) 中和する chū́wa suru; (campaign, goodwill) 台無しにする daínashi ni surù

never [nevˈəːr] *adv* どんな時でも...ない dóñna toki de mo ...naí

I never went 行かなかった ikánakatta

never in my life ...したことが ない ...shitá kotò ga naí ¶ *see also* **mind**

never-ending [nevˈəːrenˈdiŋ] *adj* 終りの ない owári no nai, 果てしない hatéshinai

nevertheless [nevəːrðəles'] *adv* それにもかかわらず soré ni mò kakáwarazù, それでもやはり soré dè mò yaháři

new [nuː] *adj* (brand new) 新しい atárashii; (recent) 最近の safkin no; (different) 今までになかった imá madě ni nákàtta; (inexperienced) 新入りの shiñ-iri no

newborn [nuːˈbɔːrn] *adj* 生れたばかりの umáreta bakàri no

newcomer [nuːˈkʌmər] *n* 新顔 shiñgao, 新入り shiñ-iri

new-fangled [nuːˈfæŋˈgəld] (*pej*) *adj* 超モダンな chṓmodàn na

new-found [nuːˈfaund] *adj* (enthusiasm, confidence) 新たに感じる arátta ni kañjiru; (friend) 新しくできた atárashiku dekíta

newly [nuːˈliː] *adv* 新しく atárashiku

newly-weds [nuːˈliːwedz] *npl* 新婚者 shiñkoñsha

new moon *n* 新月 shíñgetsu

news [nuːz] *n* ニュース nyū́su

a piece of news ニュース項目 nyū́sukomoku, ニュース nyū́su

the news (RADIO, TV) ニュース nyū́su

news agency *n* 通信社 tsū́shiñsha

newsagent [nuːzˈeidʒənt] (*BRIT*) *n* = **newsdealer**

newscaster [nuːzˈkæstəːr] *n* ニュースキャスター nyū́sukyasùtā

newsdealer [nuːzˈdiːləːr] (*US*) *n* (shop) 新聞販売店 shiñbuñbaiteñ; (person) 新聞販売業者 shiñbuñbaigyṓsha

newsflash [nuːzˈflæʃ] *n* ニュース速報 nyū́sukuhṓ

newsletter [nuːzˈletəːr] *n* ニュースレター nyū́suretā

newspaper [nuːzˈpeipəːr] *n* 新聞 shiñbun

newsprint [nuːzˈprint] *n* 新聞印刷用紙 shiñbuñiñsatsuyṓshi

newsreader [nuːzˈriːdəːr] *n* = **newscaster**

newsreel [nuːzˈriːl] *n* ニュース映画 nyúsuèiga

newsstand [nuːzˈstænd] *n* (in station etc)新聞スタンド shínbun sutándo

newt [nuːt] *n* イモリ imórì

New Year *n* 新年 shínnen

New Year's Day *n* 元旦 gántan, 元日 ganjîtsu

New Year's Eve *n* 大みそ日 ómisòka

New York [-jɔːrk] *n* ニューヨーク nyūyókù

New Zealand [-ziːˈlənd] *n* ニュージーランド nyūjīrando

New Zealander [-ziːˈləndəːr] *n* ニュージーランド人 nyūjīrandojīn

next [nekst] *adj* (in space)隣の tonári no; (in time)次の tsugí no

♦*adv* (place)隣に tonári ni; (time)次に tsugí ni, 今度 kóndo

the next day 次の日 tsugí no hì, 翌日 yokújitsu

next time 次回に jíkai ni, 今度 kóndo

next year 来年 raínen

next to ...の隣に ...no tonári ni

to cost next to nothing ただ同然である tádà dōzen de arù

to do next to nothing ほとんど何もしない hotóndo nanī mo shináì

next please! (at doctor's etc)次の方 tsugí no katá

next door *adv* 隣の家に tonári no ié ni

♦*adj* (neighbor, flat)隣の tonári no

next-of-kin [nekstˈəvkin'] *n* 最も近い親せき mottómò chikáì shínseki

NHS [eniːˈes] *n abbr* = **National Health Service**

nib [nib] *n* ペン先 peñsakī

nibble [nibˈəl] *vt* 少しずつかじる sukóshizutsú kajírù, ちびちび食べる chíbìchibi tabérù

Nicaragua [nikərɑːgˈwə] *n* ニカラグア nikáragua

nice [nais] *adj* (likeable)感じのよい kañjī no yoî; (pleasant)天気のよい téñki no yoî; (attractive)魅力的な miryókuteki na

nicely [naisˈliː] *adv* (pleasantly)気持よく kimóchi yokù; (kindly)親切に shiñsetsu

ni; (attractively)魅力的に miryókuteki ni

niceties [naiˈsətiːz] *npl* 細かい点 komákaì teñ

nick [nik] *n* (wound)切傷 kiríkīzu; (cut, indentation)刃の跡 há no atò

♦*vt* (BRIT *inf*: steal)かっ払う kappáraù

in the nick of time 危ない時に kiwádòi tókì ni, 危ういところで ayáuì tokoro de

nickel [nikˈəl] *n* (metal)ニッケル nikkérù; (US)5セント玉 5 señto dama

nickname [nikˈneim] *n* あだ名 adána, 愛称 aíshō, ニックネーム nikkúnèmu

♦*vt* ...のあだ名をつける ... no adána wò tsukérù

nicotine [nikˈətiːn] *n* ニコチン nikóchin

niece [niːs] *n* めい mef

Nigeria [naidʒiːˈriːə] *n* ナイジェリア naijeria

Nigerian [naidʒiːˈriːən] *adj* ナイジェリアの naijeria no

♦*n* ナイジェリア人 naijeriajîn

nigger [nigˈəːr] *n* (*inf*!) (highly offensive) 黒人坊 kuróñbō

niggling [nigˈliŋ] *adj* (trifling)つまらない tsumáranaì; (annoying)いらいらさせる fráìra sasérù

night [nait] *n* (period of darkness)夜 yórù; (evening)夕方 yūgáta

the night before last おとといの夜 otótoi no yorù

at night 夜(に)yórù (ni)

by night 夜に yórù ni

nightcap [naitˈkæp] *n* (drink)寝酒 nezáke, ナイトキャップ naítokyappù

nightclub [naitˈklʌb] *n* ナイトクラブ naftokurábu

nightdress [naitˈdres] *n* 寝巻 nemáki ◇女性用のを指す joséiyō no wò sásù

nightfall [naitˈfɔːl] *n* 暮れ方 kurégata

nightgown [naitˈgaun] *n* = **nightdress**

nightie [naiˈtiː] *n* = **nightdress**

nightingale [naitˈəngeil] *n* ヨナキウグイス yonákiuguìsu, サヨナキドリ sayónakidòri, ナイチンゲール naíchingèru

nightlife [naitˈlaif] *n* 夜の生活 yórù no sefkatsu

nightly [nait'li:] *adj* 毎晩の máiban no
♦*adv* 毎晩 máiban

nightmare [nait'me:r] *n* 悪夢 ákumu

night porter *n* 夜間のフロント係 yákàn no furóntogakàri

night school *n* 夜間学校 yakángakkō

night shift *n* 夜間勤務 yakánkìnmu

night-time [nait'taim] *n* 夜 yórù

night watchman *n* 夜警 yakéi

nil [nil] *n* ゼロ zéró; (BRIT: SPORT) 零点 réíten, ゼロ zéró

Nile [nail] *n*: *the Nile* ナイル川 naírugàwa

nimble [nim'bəl] *adj* (agile) 素早い subáyaì, 軽快な keíkai na; (skillful) 器用な kíyò na

nine [nain] *num* 9 (の) kyū (no), 九つ (の) kokónòtsu (no)

nineteen [nain'ti:n'] *num* 19 (の) jūku (no)

ninety [nain'ti:] *num* 90 (の) kyūjū (no)

ninth [nainθ] *adj* 第9 (の) dáìku (no)

nip [nip] *vt* (pinch) つねる tsunérù; (bite) かむ kámù

nipple [nip'əl] *n* (ANAT) 乳首 chikúbì

nitrogen [nai'trədʒən] *n* 窒素 chíssò

KEYWORD

no [nou] (*pl* **noes**) *adv* (opposite of "yes") いいえ íìe

are you coming? - no (I'm not) 一緒に来ませんか-いいえ (行きません) isshó ni kimasén ká - íìe (ikímasen)

would you like some? - no thank you いりませんか-いいえ、結構です irímasén ká - íìe, kékkò desu

♦*adj* (not any) 何も...ない naní mò ...náì

I have no money/time/books 私には金 (時間、本) がありません watákushi ni wà kané (jikán, hón) ga arimasén

no other man would have done it 他の人ならだれもそれをしてくれなかったでしょう hoká no hitó narà dáre mò soré wò shité kurenakatta deshō

"no entry" 立入禁止 tachírikinshi

"no smoking" 禁煙 kin-en

♦*n* 反対意見 hańtai iken, 反対票 hańtai-

hyō

there were 20 noes and one "don't know" 反対意見20に対し、「分からない」はひとつだった hańtai iken nijū ni taishi, "wakáranaì" wa hitótsu dattà

---

nobility [noubil'əti:] *n* (dignity) 気高さ kedákasà; (social class) 貴族 kízòku

noble [nou'bəl] *adj* (person, character: worthy) 気高い kedákaì; (title, family: of high social class) 貴族の kízòku no

nobody [nou'bədi:] *pron* だれも...ない daré mò ...náì

nocturnal [nɑːktər'nəl] *adj* (tour, visit) 夜の yórù no; (animal) 夜間の yákàn no; (animal) 夜行性の yakṓsei no

nod [nɑd] *vi* (gesture) うなずく unázukù, 首で合図をする atáma de áìzu suru; (*also:* nod in agreement) うなずく unázukù; (doze) うとうとする ùtóùto suru
♦*vt*: *to nod one's head* うなずく unázukù
♦*n* うなずき unazuki

nod off *vi* 居眠りする inémuri suru

noise [nɔiz] *n* (sound) 音 otó; (din) 騒音 sōon

noisy [nɔi'zi:] *adj* (audience, child, machine) うるさい urúsaì

nomad [nou'mæd] *n* 遊牧民 yúbokumìn

nominal [nɑm'ənəl] *adj* (leader) 名目上の mefmokujō no; (rent, price) わずかな wázùka na

nominate [nɑm'əneit] *vt* (propose) 推薦する suísen suru; (appoint) 任命する nífmei suru

nomination [nɑmənei'ʃən] *n* (proposal) 推薦 suísen; (appointment) 任命 nífmei

nominee [nɑməni:'] *n* (proposed person) 推薦された人 suísen sareta hitð; (appointed person) 任命された人 nifmei sareta hitð

non... [nɑn] *prefix* 非... hf..., 無... mú..., 不... fú...

non-alcoholic [nɑnælkəhɔl'ik] *adj* アルコールを含まない arúkòru wò fukúmanaì

non-aligned [nɑnəlaind'] *adj* 非同盟の hídṓmei no

nonchalant [nɒnʃələnt'] adj 平然とした hefzen to shitā

noncommittal [nɒnkəmit'əl] adj (person, answer) どっちつかずの dotchí tsukazū no

nondescript [nɒn'dɪskrɪpt] adj (person, clothes, color) 特徴のない tokúchō no naī

none [nʌn] pron (person) だれも …ない daré mò …naī; (thing) どれも…ない dóre mo …naī

none of you あなたたちの1人も…ない anátatachi no hitóri mò …naī

I've none left 何も残っていません naní mò nokótte imasén

he's none the worse for it それでも彼は大丈夫です soré de mò kare wa daíjōbu desu

nonentity [nɒnen'titi:] n 取るに足らない人 tórū ni taránai hitō

nonetheless [nʌn'ðəles'] adv それにもかかわらず soré ni mò kakáwarazū, それでもやはり soré de mò yahárī

non-existent [nɒnigzis'tənt] adj 存在しない sofzai shinaī

non-fiction [nɒnfik'ʃən] n ノンフィクション noffíkūshon

nonplussed [nɒnplʌst'] adj 困惑した kofwaku shita, 困った komáttā

nonsense [nɒn'sens] n でたらめ detárame, ナンセンス náfsensu

nonsense! そんな事はない sofna koto wà naī, ナンセンス náfsensu

non-smoker [nɒnsmou'kɑːr] n タバコを吸わない人 tabáko wò suwánai hitō, 非喫煙者 hfkítsuefsha

non-stick [nɒnstik'] adj (pan, surface) こげつかない kogétsukanaī

non-stop [nɒnstɑːp'] adj (conversation) 止らない tomáranai; (flight, train) 直行の chokkō no, ノンストップの nofsutoppū no

♦adv 止らずに tomárazu ni

noodles [nuː'dəlz] npl ヌードル núdoru

nook [nuk] n: *every nook and cranny* 隅々 sumízūmi

noon [nuːn] n 正午 shōgō

no one (BRIT **no-one**) pron = **nobody**

noose [nuːs] n (loop) 引結び hikímusúbi

hangman's noose 絞首刑用の縄 kōshukeíyō no nawā

nor [nɔːr] conj = **neither**

♦adv see **neither**

norm [nɔːrm] n (convention) 慣習 kańshū; (rule, requirement) ノルマ nórūma

normal [nɔːr'məl] adj (usual, ordinary): life, behavior, result) 普通の futsū no; (child: not abnormal) 異常のない ijō no naī, ノーマルな nōmáru na

normally [nɔːr'məli:] adv 普通は futsū wa, 普通に futsū ni

north [nɔːrθ] n 北 kitá

♦adj 北の kitá no

♦adv 北へ kitá e

North America n 北米 hokúbei

north-east [nɔːrθiːst'] n 北東 hokútō

northerly [nɔːr'ðəːli:] adj (point) 北方の hoppō no; (direction) 北方への hoppō e nò

a northerly wind 北からの風 kitá kara nò kazé

northern [nɔːr'ðəːrn] adj 北の kitá no

the northern hemisphere 北半球 kitáhańkyū

Northern Ireland n 北アイルランド kitá airuraňdo

North Pole n 北極 hokkyókú

North Sea n 北海 hokkái

northward(s) [nɔːrθ'wəːrd(z)] adv 北へ kitá e

north-west [nɔːrθwest'] n 北西 hokúsei

Norway [nɔːr'wei] n ノルウェー norúwē

Norwegian [nɔːrwiː'dʒən] adj ノルウェーの norúwē no; (LING) ノルウェー語の norúwēgo no

♦n (person) ノルウェー人 norúwejīn; (LING) ノルウェー語 norúwēgo

nose [nouz] n (ANAT, ZOOL) 鼻 hanáʼ; (sense of smell) きゅう覚 kyúkaku

♦vi: *nose about* 嗅ぎ回る sefsaku suru

nosebleed [nouz'bliːd] n 鼻血 hanájī

nose-dive [nouz'daiv] n (of plane) 急降下 kyúkōka

nosey [nou'zi:] (inf) adj = **nosy**

nostalgia [nɑstæl'dʒə] n 郷愁 kyóshū, ノ

スタルジア nosutarùjia

nostalgic [nəstǽldʒɪk] *adj* (person, book, film) 懐かしい natsukashiì

nostril [nɑːstrəl] *n* (of person, animal) 鼻のあな haná no aná, 鼻孔 bikô

nosy [nóʊziː] (*inf*) *adj* せん索好きな señsakuzuki na

KEYWORD

not [nɑːt] *adv* …でない…de naì

he is not/isn't here 彼はいません kárè wa imáseñ

you must not/you mustn't do that それをしてはいけません soré wò shité wà ikémaseñ

it's too late, isn't it? 遅過ぎますよね osósugimasù yo né, 遅過ぎるでしょう osósugirù deshô

he asked me not to do it それをしないで下さいと彼に頼まれました soré wò shináide kudasaì to kárè ni tanómaremashìta

not that I don't like him/he isn't interesting 彼を嫌い(面白くない)というのではないが kárè wo kiráì(omóshirokùnai)tò iú no de wa naì gá

not yet まだ mádà

not now 今は駄目 imà wa damé ¶ see also *all*; *only*

notably [nóʊtəbliː] *adv* (particularly) 特に tókù ni; (markedly) 著しく ichíjirushikù

notary [nóʊtəriː] *n* 公証人 kôshônin

notch [nɑːtʃ] *n* (in wood, blade, saw) 刻み目 kizámime, ノッチ notchí

note [noʊt] *n* (record) 覚書 obóegakì, ノート nôto, メモ mémo; (letter) 短い手紙 mijíkaì tegámi; (banknote) 紙幣 shíhèi, 札 satsù; (MUS) 音符 ofúpu; (tone) 音 otó
♦*vt* (observe) …に気が付く …ni ki gá tsukù; (write down) 書留める kakítomerù

notebook [nóʊtbuk] *n* 帳面 chômen, ノート nôto

noted [nóʊtid] *adj* (famous) 有名な yûmei na

notepad [nóʊtpæd] *n* メモ用紙 memóyòshi ♦綴紙などでつづった物を指す norí

nadð de tsuzùtta mono wò sásù

notepaper [nóʊtpeɪpəʳ] *n* 便せん biñsen

nothing [nʌθɪŋ] *n* (not anything) 何も …naì naní mð …naì; (zero) ゼロ zêrð

he does nothing 彼は何もしない kárè wa naní mð shinaì

nothing new/much/special 目新しい(大した、特別な)ことはない meátarashiì(táishita, tokúbetsu nà)kotó wa naì

for nothing (free) 無料で muryô de, ただで tádà de; (in vain) 無駄に mudá ni

notice [nóʊtis] *n* (announcement) 通知 tsûchi; (warning) 通告 tsûkoku; (dismissal) 解雇通知 kaíkotsùchi; (resignation) 辞表 jihyô; (period of time) 予告 yokôku
♦*vt* (observe) …に気が付く …ni ki gá tsukù

to bring something to someone's notice (attention) …を…に知らせる …wo …ni shiráserù

to take notice of …に気が付く …ni ki gá tsukù

at short notice 急に kyû ni

until further notice 追って通知があるまで otté tsûchi ga aru madè

to hand in one's notice 辞表を出す jihyô wò dásù

noticeable [nóʊtisəbəl] *adj* (mark, effect) はっきりした hakkírì shita

noticeboard [nóʊtisbɔːrd] (*BRIT*) *n* 掲示板 keíjiban

notify [nóʊtifai] *vt*: *to notify someone (of something)* (…を) …に知らせる (…wo) …ni shiráserù

notion [nóʊʃən] *n* (idea) 考え kañgaè, 概念 gaînen; (opinion) 意見 íkèn

notorious [noʊtɔ́ːriːəs] *adj* (criminal, liar, place) 悪名高い akúmeìdakaì

notwithstanding [nɑːtwɪθstǽndɪŋ] *adv* …にもかかわらず …ni mð kakáwarazù
♦*prep* …にもかかわらず …ni mð kakáwarazù

nougat [núːgət] *n* ヌガー noga ◇クルミなどの入ったキャラメル風のお菓子 kurúmi nadð no haîtta kyarámerufù no okáshì

nought [nɔːt] n = **naught**

noun [naun] n 名詞 meíshi

nourish [nʌrˈiʃ] vt (feed) 養う yashínaù; (fig: foster) 心中にはぐくむ shínchū ni hagúkumù

nourishing [nʌrˈiʃiŋ] adj (food) 栄養のある eíyō no arù

nourishment [nʌrˈiʃmənt] n (food) 栄養 eíyō

novel [nɑːvˈəl] n 小説 shōsetsu
♦adj (new, fresh: idea, approach) 目新しい meátarashiì, 新鮮な shíñsen na

novelist [nɑːvˈəlist] n 小説家 shōsetsuka

novelty [nɑːvˈəltiː] n (newness) 新鮮さ shíñsensa; (object) 変ったもの kawátta monò

November [nouvemˈbəːr] n 11月 jūíchigatsu

novice [nɑːvˈis] n (beginner) 初心者 shoshínsha; (REL) 修練者 shúrensha

now [nau] adv 今 imá
♦conj: **now (that)** ...であるから ...de árù kara
right now (immediately) 今すぐ imá súgù; (at the moment) 今の所 imá no tokoro
by now 今ごろはもう imágoro wà moō
just now 今の所 imá no tokoro
now and then, now and again 時々 tokídoki
from now on 今後 kôñgo

nowadays [nauˈdeiz] adv このごろ(は) konógoro (wa)

nowhere [nouˈweːr] adv (be, go) どこにも...ない dókò ni mo ...naì

nozzle [nɑːzˈəl] n (of hose, fire extinguisher etc) ノズル nózùru; (of vacuum cleaner) 吸口 suíkuchi

nuance [nuːˈɑːns] n ニュアンス nyúañsu

nubile [nuːˈbail] adj (woman) セクシーな sékùshii na

nuclear [nuːˈkliːəːr] adj (fission, weapons) 核... kákù...
the nuclear industry 原子力産業界 geñshiryoku sangyōkai
nuclear physics 原始物理学 geñshibutsurigaku, 核物理学 kakúbutsurigaku
nuclear power 原子力 geñshiryoku

nucleus [nuːˈkliːəs] (pl **nuclei**) n (of atom, cell) 核 kákù; (of group) 中心 chūshin

nude [nuːd] adj 裸の hadáka no
♦n ヌード núdo
in the nude (naked) 裸で hadáka de

nudge [nʌdʒ] vt (person) 小突く kozúkù

nudist [nuːˈdist] n 裸体主義者 ratáishugishà, ヌーディスト núdisuto

nudity [nuːˈditiː] n 裸 hadáka

nuisance [nuːˈsəns] n (state of affairs) 厄介な事情 yákkaī na jijō; (thing) 厄介な物 yákkaī na monó; (person: irritating) 迷惑な人 mefwaku na hitò
what a nuisance! 困ったもんだ komátta moñ da!

null [nʌl] adj: **null and void** (contract, agreement) 無効な mukó na

numb [nʌm] adj (with): **numb (with)** (with cold etc) ...でしびれた ...de shibíretà; (fig: with fear etc) ...で気が動転した ...de ki ga dóten shità

number [nʌmˈbəːr] n (MATH) 数字 súji; (quantity) 数 kázù; (of house, bank account etc) 番号 bañgō
♦vt (pages etc) ...に番号を付ける ...ni bañgō wo tsukérù; (amount to) 総数は ...である sốsū wa ...de árù
to be numbered among ...の1人である ...no hitóri de árù
a number of (several) 数...の sū... no
they were ten in number (people) 彼らは10人だった kárèra wa jūnin datta; (things) 10個あった jūkkô atta

number plate (BRIT) n (AUT) ナンバープレート nañbápurèto

numeral [nuːˈməːrəl] n 数詞 sūshi

numerate [nuːˈməːreit] adj 数学ができる súgaku ga dekírù

numerical [nuːmeːrˈikəl] adj (value) 数字で表した súji de aráwashità; (order) 数字の súji no

numerous [nuːˈməːrəs] adj (many, countless) 多くの ốkù no, 多数の tasū no

nun [nʌn] n (Christian) 修道女 shúdðjo; (Buddhist) 尼 ámà

nurse [nəːrs] n (in hospital) 看護婦 kañgofù; (also: **nursemaid**) 保母 hobò

♦ vt (patient) 看護する kángo suru;
(baby) ...に乳を飲ませる ...ni chichí wo
nomáserú

nursery [nəːr'səri:] n (institution) 保育園
hoíkuèn; (room) 育児室 ikújishítsu; (for
plants: commercial establishment) 種苗
園 shubyōén

nursery rhyme n 童謡 dōyō

nursery school n 保育園 hoíkuèn

nursery slope (BRIT) n (SKI) 初心者用
ゲレンデ shoshínshayō gerénde

nursing [nəːr'siŋ] n (profession) 看護職
kańgoshòku; (care) 看護 kángo

nursing home n (gen) 療養所 ryōyōjo;
(for old people) 老人ホーム rōjínhòmu

nursing mother n 授乳している母親
junyū shite irú haháoya

nurture [nəːr'tʃər] vt (child, plant) 育て
る sodáterù

nut [nʌt] n (TECH) ナット náttò; (BOT)
木ノ実 kínòmi[kónòmi], ナッツ náttsù

nutcracker [nʌt'krækəːr] npl クルミ割
り kurúmiwarí

nutmeg [nʌt'meg] n ニクズク nikúzùku,
ナツメッグ natsúmeggù ◇香辛料の一種
kōshínryō no ísshù

nutrient [nuː'triːənt] n 養分 yōbùn

nutrition [nuːtriʃ'ən] n (diet, nourishment) 栄養 eíyò; (proteins, vitamins etc)
養分 yōbùn

nutritious [nuːtriʃ'əs] adj (food) 栄養価
の高い eíyōka no takái

nuts [nʌts] (inf) adj 頭がおかしい atáma
gà okáshii

nutshell [nʌt'ʃel] n クルミの殻 kurúmi
no karā

in a nutshell (fig) 簡単に言えば kańtan
nì iébà

nylon [nai'lɑːn] n ナイロン náîron

♦ adj ナイロンの náîron no

O

oak [ouk] n オーク ōkù

♦ adj (table) オークの ōkù no

O.A.P. [oueipiː'] (BRIT) n abbr = old-
age pensioner

oar [ɔːr] n かい kaî, オール órù

oasis [ouei'sis] (pl oases) n (in desert) オ
アシス oáshīsu

oath [ouθ] n (promise) 誓い chikái;
(swear word) 悪態 akútaî

under or *on* (BRIT) *oath* 宣誓して
seńsei shite

oatmeal [out'miːl] n オートミール ōtō-
mírù

oats [outs] n カラスムギ karásumugí

obedience [oubiː'diːəns] n 服従 fukújū

obedient [oubiː'diːənt] adj (child, dog
etc) 素直な sunáo na, よく言う事を聞く
yokú iú koto wo kikú

obesity [oubiː'siti:] n 肥満 hímàn

obey [oubei'] vt (instructions, person)
...に従う ...ni shitágaù; (regulations) 守る
mamórù

obituary [oubitʃ'uːeːriː] n 死亡記事 shibō-
kíjì

object [n ɑːb'dʒikt vt əbdʒekt'] n (thing)
物 monó; (aim, purpose) 目的 mokúteki;
(of: affection, desires etc) 対象 taishō;
(LING) 目的語 mokútekigo

♦ vi: *to object to* ...に反対する ...ni hañtai suru

to object that ...だと言って反対する
...da to ittě hañtai suru

expense is no object 費用にはこだわら
ない hiyō ni wa kodáwaranaì

I object! 反対する hañtai desu

objection [əbdʒek'ʃən] n 異議 igí

I have no objection to ... に ... は異議はあ
りません ...ni igí wa arísmaséñ

objectionable [əbdʒek'ʃənəbəl] adj (person, language, conduct) いやな iyá na

objective [əbdʒek'tiv] adj (impartial:
person, information) 客観的な kyakúkan-
teki na

♦ n (aim, purpose) 目的 mokúteki

obligation [ɑːbləgei'ʃən] n (duty, commitment) 義務 gímù

without obligation (COMM) 買う義務
なしで kaú gímù nashi de

obligatory [əblig'ətɔːri:] adj 強制的な
kyōseíteki na

oblige [əblaidʒ'] vt (force): *to oblige
someone to do something* 強制的に

...に...をさせる kyōseiteki ni ...ni ...wo saserū; (do a favor for) ...の頼みを聞く ...no tanōmi wo kikū
to be obliged to someone for something (grateful) ...の事で...に感謝している ...no kotō de ...ni kānsha shité irū

obliging [əbláiˈdʒiŋ] *adj* (helpful) 親切な shīnsetsu na

oblique [əblíːkˈ] *adj* (line) 斜めの nanáme no; (comment, reference) 間接的な kánsetsuteki na

obliterate [əblítˈəreit] *vt* 跡形もなくする atōkata mo nakūsuru

oblivion [əblíviˈən] *n* (unawareness) 無意識 mushíki; (being forgotten) 忘却 bōkyaku

oblivious [əblíviˈəs] *adj*: **oblivious of/ to** ...を意識していない ...wo ishíki shité inai

oblong [áblˈɔːŋ] *adj* 長方形の chōhōkei no

♦*n* 長方形 chōhōkei

obnoxious [əbnákˈʃəs] *adj* (unpleasant: behavior, person) 不愉快な fuyúkai na; (: smell) いやな iyá na

oboe [ou'bou] *n* オーボエ ōbóe

obscene [əbsíːn'] *adj* (gesture, remark, behavior) わいせつな waísetsu na

obscenity [əbsén'itiː] *n* (of book, behavior etc) わいせつ waísetsu; (offensive word) 卑語 higō

obscure [əbskjuːrˈ] *adj* (little known: place, author etc) 無名の muméi no; (difficult to understand) 難解な nañkai na

♦*vt* (obstruct: view, sun etc) 覆い隠す ōkakusū; (conceal: truth, meaning etc) 隠す kakúsū

obsequious [əbsíːˈkwiːəs] *adj* ぺこぺこする pekōpeko suru

observance [əbzərˈvəns] *n* (of law) 遵守 juñshu; (of custom) 守る事 mamórū koto

observant [əbzərˈvənt] *adj* (person) 観察力の優れた kañsatsuryōku no suguretá; (remark) 鋭い surúdoi

observation [əbzərveiˈʃən] *n* (remark) 意見 ikēn; (act of observing) 観察 kañsatsu; (MED) 監視 kañshi

observatory [əbzərˈvətɔːriː] *n* 観測所 kañsokujo

observe [əbzərv'] *vt* (watch) 観察する kañsatsu suru; (comment) 意見を述べる ikēn wo nobérū; (abide by: rule) 守る mamórū, 遵守する juñshu suru

observer [əbzərˈvər] *n* 観察者 kañsatsushā

obsess [əbses'] *vt* ...に取りつく ...ni torítsuku

obsession [əbsesʲʲ'ən] *n* 強迫観念 kyōhakukannen

obsessive [əbses'iv] *adj* (person, tendency, behavior) 妄想に取付かれた様な mōsō ni torítsukareta yō na

obsolescence [ɑːbsəlesʲʲ'əns] *n* 旧式化 kyūshikika

obsolete [ɑːbsəliːt'] *adj* (out of use: word etc) 廃れた sutáretā; (: machine etc) 旧式の kyūshiki no

obstacle [ɑːb'stəkəl] *n* (obstruction) 障害物 shōgaibutsū; (fig: problem, difficulty) 障害 shōgai

obstacle race *n* 障害物競走 shōgaibutsukyōsō

obstetrics [əbstet'riks] *n* 産科 sañka

obstinate [ɑːb'stənit] *adj* (determined: person, resistance) 頑固な gañko na

obstruct [əbstrʌkt'] *vt* (block) ふさぐ fuságu; (fig: hinder) 妨害する bōgai suru

obstruction [əbstrʌkʲʲ'ən] *n* (action) 妨害 bōgai; (object) 障害物 shōgaibutsū

obtain [əbtein'] *vt* (get) 手に入れるte ni irērū, 獲得する kakūtoku suru; (achieve) 達成する tasséi suru

obtainable [əbtein'əbəl] *adj* (object) 入手できる nyūshu dekírū

obvious [ɑːb'viːəs] *adj* (clear) 明かな akíráka na; (self-evident) 分かり切った wakárikitta

obviously [ɑːb'viːəsliː] *adv* 明らかに akíráka ni

obviously not 明らかに...でない akíráka ni ...de nai

occasion [əkei'ʒən] *n* (point in time) 時 tokí, 時点 jitén; (event, celebration etc) 行事 gyōji, イベント ibénto; (opportunity) 機会 kikái, チャンス chañsu

occasional [əkei'ʒənəl] *adj* (infrequent)

時々の tokídokì no

occasionally [əkeíʒənəlɪ] *adv* 時々 tokídokì

occult [əkʌlt] *n:* **the occult** 超自然 chôshizen, オカルト okárùto

occupant [ɑːk'jəpənt] *n:* (long-term: of house etc) 居住者 kyojúshà; (of office etc) テナント tenánto; (temporary: of car, room etc) 中にいる人 nakà ni irù hitó

occupation [ɑːkjəpeí'ʃən] *n* (job) 職業 shokúgyò; (pastime) 趣味 shumì; (of building, country etc) 占領 senryô

occupational hazard [ɑːkjəpeí'ʃənəl-] *n* 職業上の危険 shokúgyòjô no kikén

occupier [ɑːk'jəpaiəːr] *n* 居住者 kyojúshà

occupy [ɑːk'jəpi] *vt* (inhabit: house) ...に住む ...ni sumù; (take: place etc) ...に居る ...ni irù; (take over: building, country etc) 占領する senryô suru; (take up: time) ...が掛る ...ga kakárù; (: attention) 奪う ubáù; (: space) 取る torù

to occupy oneself in doing ...に専念する ...ni sénnen suru

occur [əkəːr'] *vi* (event: take place) 起る okórù; (phenomenon: exist) 存在する sonzai suru

to occur to someone ...の頭に浮ぶ ...no atáma ni ukábu

occurrence [əkəːr'əns] *n* (event) 出来事 dekígoto; (existence) 存在 sonzai

ocean [ou'ʃən] *n* 海 umì

Indian Ocean インド洋 indóyō ¶ *see also* Atlantic; Pacific

ocean-going [ou'ʃəngouiŋ] *adj* 外洋の gaíyò no

ocher [ou'kəːr] (*BRIT* **ochre**) *adj* (color) 黄土色の ôdòiro no, オークルの ôkùru no

o'clock [əklɑːk'] *adv: it is 5 o'clock* 5時です goʹjì desu

OCR [ousiɑːr'] *n abbr* (COMPUT: = *optical character recognition*) 光学読取り kôgakuyomítorí (: = *optical character reader*) 光学読取り装置 kôgakuyomísòchì

octagonal [ɑːktæg'ənəl] *adj* 八角形の hákkùkukèi no

octave [ɑːk'tiv] *n* (MUS) オクターブ okútàbu

October [ɑːktou'bəːr] *n* 10月 jûgatsu

octopus [ɑːk'təpəs] *n* タコ takò

odd [ɑːd] *adj* (strange: person, behavior, expression) 変な heñ na, 妙な myô na; (uneven: number) 奇数の kísû no; (not paired: sock, glove, shoe etc) 片方の katáhò no

60-odd 60幾つ rokújû ikutsu

at odd times 時々 tokídokì

to be the odd one out 例外である refgai de aru

oddity [ɑːd'iti:] *n* (person) 変り者 kawárimono; (thing) 変った物 kawatta mono

odd-job man [ɑːdʒɑːb'-] *n* 便利屋 beñriya

odd jobs *npl* 雑用 zatsúyò

oddly [ɑːd'li:] *adv* (strangely: behave, dress) 変な風に heñ na fû ni ¶ *see also* enough

oddments [ɑːd'mənts] *npl* (COMM) 残り物 nokórimono

odds [ɑːdz] *npl* (in betting) かけ率 kakéritsu, オッズ ozzù

it makes no odds 構いません kamáimasen

at odds 仲たがいして nakátagaishite

odds and ends *npl* 半端物 hañpamono

ode [oud] *n* しょう歌 shôkà, オード ôdo

odious [ou'di:əs] *adj* 不快な fukái na

odometer [oudɑːm'itəːr] *n* 走行距離計 sôkôkyorikeí

odor [ou'dəːr] (*BRIT* **odour**) *n* (smell) におい nióì; (: unpleasant) 悪臭 akúshû

of [ʌv] *prep* **1** (gen) ...の ...nò

the history of France フランスの歴史 furánsu nò rekíshi

a friend of ours 私たちの友達 watákushitàchì no árù tomódachi

a boy of 10 10才の少年 jússài no shônen

that was kind of you ご親切にどうもgo-shíñsetsu ni dômo

a man of great ability 才能抜群の人 saínô batsugùn no hitó

the city of New York ニューヨーク市 nyúyōkushi

south of Glasgow グラスゴーの南 gurásugō no minámi

2 (expressing quantity, amount, dates etc): *a kilo of flour* 小麦粉1キロ komúgiko ichíkiro

how much of this do you need? これはどのぐらい要りますか koré wà dono gúrai irimasú ka

there are 3 of them (people) 3人いました sańnin imáshita; (objects) 3個ありました sańko arimáshita

3 of us went 私たちの内から3人行きました watakushitáchi no uchí kara sańnin ikímashìta

the number of road accidents is increasing 交通事故の数が増えています kòtsūjikò no kázu ga fúète imásu

a cup of tea お茶1杯 o-chá ippai

a vase of flowers 花瓶に生けた花 kabín nì ĭkèta haná

the 5th of July 7月5日 shichĭgatsu itsúka

the winter of 1987 1987年の冬 señkyùhyakuhachĭjūnanáneñ no fuyú

3 (from, out of): a bracelet of solid gold 純金の腕輪 juńkin no udéwa

a statue of marble 大理石の彫像 dariseki no chōzō

made of wood 木製の mokúsei no

KEYWORD

off [ɔːf] *adv* 1 (referring to distance, time) 離れて hanárète

it's a long way off あれは遠い aré wà tōi

the game is 3 days off 試合は3日先で shiái wà mikká saki desù

2 (departure) 出掛けて dekákete

to go off to Paris/Italy パリ（イタリア）へ出掛ける párī(itária) e dekákerù

I must be off そろそろ出掛けます sorōsoro dekákemasù

3 (removal) 外して hazúshite

to take off one's hat/coat/clothes 帽子（コート、服）を脱ぐ bōshi(kòto, fukú)wo nūgú

the button came off ボタンが取れた botán gà tórèta

10% off (COMM) 10パーセント引き juppásentobiki

4 (not at work: on holiday) 休暇中で kyūkachū dè; (: due to sickness) 欠勤して kekkin shitè

I'm off on Fridays 私の休みは金曜日です watákushi nò yasúmi wa kiń-yōbi desu

he was off on Friday (on holiday) 金曜日には彼は休みでした kiń-yōbi ni wa kárè wa yasúmi deshìta; (sick etc) 金曜日には彼は欠勤しました kiń-yōbi ni wa kárè wa kékkin shimashìta

to have a day off (from work) 1日の休みを取る ichínichi nò yasúmi wò tórù

to be off sick 病欠する byōketsu suru

◆*adj* 1 (not turned on: machine, engine, water, gas etc) 止めてある tomête arù; (: tap) 締めてある shiméte arù; (: light) 消してある keshíte arù

2 (cancelled: meeting, match, agreement) 取消された toríkesareta

3 (BRIT: not fresh: milk, cheese, meat etc) 悪くなった wárùku natta

4: *on the off chance* (just in case) ...の場合に備えて ...no baái ni sonaète

to have an off day (not as good as usual) 厄日である yakúbi de árù

◆*prep* 1 (indicating motion, removal etc) ...から...を離して

to fall off a cliff 崖から落ちる gakè kará ochírù

the button came off my coat コートのボタンが取れた kōto no botán gà tórèta

to take a picture off the wall 壁に掛けてある絵を降ろす kabé nì kákète aru é wò orósù

2 (distant from) ...から離れて ...kárà hanárète

it's just off the M1 国道M1を降りて直ぐの所にあります kokúdo emúwañ wo ōrìte súgù no tokórò ni arímasu

it's 5 km off the main road 幹線道路から5キロの所にあります kansendōro

kara gókku no tokorō ni arímasu
an island off the coast 沖合の島 okí-ai no shíma
to be off meat (no longer eat it) 肉をやめている nikú wo yaméte irú; (no longer like it) 肉が嫌いになっている nikú ga kirái ni nátte irú

---

offal [ɔːf'əl] n (CULIN) もつ mótsu

off-color [ɔːf'kʌl'əːr] (BRIT **off-colour**) adj (ill) 病気の byóki no

offend [əfend'] vt (upset: person) 怒らせ る okóraseru

offender [əfen'dəːr] n (criminal) 犯罪者 hañzaisha, 犯人 hañnin, 犯人 … hañ

offense [əfens'] (BRIT **offence**) n (crime) 犯罪 hañzai
to take offense at …に怒る …ni okóru

offensive [əfen'siv] adj (remark, gesture, behavior) 侮辱的な bujókuteki na; (smell etc) いやな iyá na; (weapon) 攻撃用の kógekiyō no
♦n (MIL) 攻撃 kógeki

offer [ɔːf'əːr] n (proposal: to help etc) 申 出 móshide; (: to buy) 申込み móshikomi
♦vt (advice, help, information) …すると 申出る …surú to móshideru; (opportunity, service, product) 提供する teíkyō suru
on offer (BRIT: COMM) 値下げ品で neságehin de

offering [ɔːf'əːriŋ] n (of a company: product) 売物 urímono; (REL) 供物 sonáemono

off-hand [ɔːf'hænd'] adj (behavior etc) いい加減な iíkagen na
♦adv 即座に sokúza ni

office [ɔːf'is] n (place) 事務所 jimúsho, オ フィス ofisu; (room) 事務室 jimúshitsu; (position) 職務 shokúmu
doctor's office (US) 診察室 iín
to take office 職に就く shokú ni tsuku

office automation n オフィスオートメ ーション ofisu ōtómēshon

office building (BRIT **office block**) n オフィスビル ofisubīru

office hours npl (COMM) 業務時間 gyōmujikan; (US: MED) 診察時間 shiñ-

satsujikan

officer [ɔːf'isəːr] n (MIL etc) 将校 shōkō; (also: **police officer**) 警官 kefkan; (of organization) 役員 yakúin

office worker n 事務員 jimúin

official [əfiʃ'əl] adj (authorized) 公認の kōnin no; (visit, invitation, letter etc) 公 式の kōshiki no
♦n (in government) 役人 yakúnin; (in trade union etc) 役員 yakúin
official residence 官邸 kañtei

officialdom [əfiʃ'əldəm] (pej) n 官僚の世 界 kañryō no sekái

officiate [əfiʃ'iːeit] vi 司会をする shikái su-ru

officious [əfiʃ'əs] adj (person, behavior) 差出がましい sashídegamashíi

offing [ɔːf'iŋ] n: *in the offing* (fig: imminent) 差迫って sashísematte

off-licence [ɔːf'laisəns] (BRIT) n (shop selling alcohol) 酒屋 sakáya

off-line [ɔːf'lain'] adj (COMPUT) オフラ インの ofúrain no
♦adv オフラインで ofúrain de

off-peak [ɔːf'piːk'] adj (heating) オフピ ークの ofúpīku no; (train, ticket) 混んで いない時の koñde inai tokí no

off-putting [ɔːf'putiŋ] (BRIT) adj (person, remark etc) 気を悪くさせる kí wo warúku saseru

off-season [ɔːf'siːzən] adj (holiday, ticket) オフシーズンの ofúshizun no
♦adv (travel, book etc) オフシーズンに ofúshizun ni

offset [ɔːfset'] (pt, pp **offset**) vt (counteract) 補う ogínau

offshoot [ɔːf'ʃuːt] n (fig) 副産物 fukúsañbutsu

offshore [ɔːf'ʃɔːr'] adj (breeze) 陸からの rikú kara no; (oilrig, fishing) 沖合の okí-ai no

offside [ɔːf'said'] adj (SPORT) オフサイ ドの ofúsaido no; (AUT: with right-hand drive) 右の migí no; (: with left-hand drive) 左の hidári no

offspring [ɔːf'spriŋ] n inv 子孫 shison

offstage [ɔːf'steidʒ'] adv 舞台裏に[で] butáiura ni(de)

off-the-rack [ɔːfˈðəræk] (BRIT **off-the-peg**) adj 合わせ出来合いのdekfai no, 既製のkisei no

off-white [ɔːfˈwait] adj (grayish white) 灰色がかった白のhaiirogakatta shirō no; (yellowish white) 黄色がかった白のkiirogakatta shirō no

often [ɔːfˈən] adv (frequently) よく yokū, しょっちゅう shotchū, 度々 tabītabi
how often do you go? どのぐらい行きますか donō gurai ikimasu ká

ogle [ˈougəl] vt 色目で見る irōme de mírú

oh [ou] excl ああ à

oil [ɔil] n 油 abúra, オイル ōiru, ofrū; (CULIN) サラダ油 sarádàyu; (petroleum) 石油 sekfyu; (crude) 原油 geñyu; (for heating) 石油 sekfyu, 灯油 tōyu
♦vt (lubricate: engine, gun, machine) ...に油を差す ...ni abúra wo sásù

oilcan [ɔilˈkæn] n 油差し abúrasashi

oilfield [ɔilˈfiːld] n 油田 yudén

oil filter n (AUT) オイルフィルター oirufirutā

oil painting n 油絵 abúrae

oil refinery [-riːfainˈəriː] n 精油所 sefyujo

oil rig n 石油掘削装置 sekfyu kùssakusōchi

oilskins [ɔilˈskinz] npl 防水服 bōsuifuku

oil tanker n (ship) オイルタンカー ofrutañkā; (truck) タンクローリー tañkurōrī

oil well n 油井 yusêi

oily [ɔilˈiː] adj (rag) 油染みた abúrajimitã; (substance) 油の様な abúra no yō na; (food) 脂っこい abúrakkoi

ointment [ɔintˈmənt] n 軟こう nañkō

O.K., okay [ouˈkei] (inf) excl (agreement: alright) よろしい yoróshii, オーケー ōkē; (: don't fuss) 分かったよ wakáttà yo
♦adj (average: film, book, meal etc) まあまあの mā̀mā no
♦vt (approve) 承認する shōnin suru

old [ould] adj (aged: person) 年寄りの toshíyori no; (: thing) 古い furúī; (former: school, home etc) 元の motō no, 前の maê no

how old are you? お幾つですか o-fkutsu desu ká
he's 10 years old 彼は10才です karè wa jussái desu

older brother (one's own) 兄 ani; (of person spoken to) お兄さん o-nfisan; (of third party) 兄さん nfisan

old age n 老齢 rōrei

old-age pensioner [ould'eidʒ-] (BRIT) n 年金で生活する老人 nefikin dè sefkatsu surù rōjin, 年金暮しの人 nefkingurāshi no hitó

old-fashioned [ould'fæʃ'ənd] adj (style, design) 時代遅れの jidáiokūre no, 古くさい furúkusai; (person, values) 保守的な hoshūteki na

olive [ɑːlˈiv] n (fruit) オリーブ oríbū; (also: **olive tree**) オリーブの木 oríbū no ki
♦adj (also: **olive-green**) オリーブ色の oríbūiro no

olive oil n オリーブ油 oríbūyu

Olympic [ouˈlimpik] adj 五輪の gorín no, オリンピックの oríñpikku no

Olympic Games npl: **the Olympic Games** 五輪 gorín, オリンピック oríñpikku
♦**the Olympics** 五輪 gorín, オリンピック oríñpikku

omelet(te) [ɑːmˈlit] n オムレツ omúretsu

omen [ouˈmən] n (sign) 兆し kizáshi, 前触れ maébure

ominous [ɑːmˈənəs] adj (worrying) 不気味な bukími na

omission [oumiʃˈən] n 省略 shōryaku

omit [oumit'] vt (deliberately) 省略する shōryaku suru; (by mistake) うっかりして抜かす ukkárī shite nukásu

---

KEYWORD

on [ɑːn] prep 1 (indicating position) ...の上に(で) ...(no uê) ni(de)
on the wall 壁にある kabé ni áru
it's on the table テーブルの上にあります tēburu no uê nì arímasù
on the left 左に hidári nì
the house is on the main road 家は幹線道路に面しています iè wa kañsendōro

ni méń shite imásu

2 (indicating means, method, condition etc) ...で...de

on foot (go, be) 歩いて arúite

on the train/plane (go) 電車(飛行機)で deńsha(hikóki)de; (be) 電車(飛行機)に乗って deńsha(hikóki)ni notté

on the telephone/radio/television 電話(ラジオ, テレビ)で deńwa(rájio, térèbi)de

she's on the telephone 彼女は電話に出ています[電話中です] kánojo wa deńwa ni détè imasu(deńwachū désu)

I heard it on the radio/saw him on television 私はラジオで聞いた[テレビで彼を見ました] watákushi wā rájio de kikímashìta(térèbi de kárè wo mimáshita)

to be on drugs 麻薬をやっているmayáku wo yatté irú

to be on holiday 休暇中である kyúkachū de arú

to be away on business 商用で出掛けている shōyō dè dekákete irú

3 (referring to time) ...に ...ni

on Friday 金曜日に kiń-yóbi ni

on Fridays 金曜日に kiń-yóbi ni, 毎週金曜日に mafshū kiń-yóbi ni, 金曜日毎に kiń-yóbi gótò ni

on June 20th 6月20日に rokúgatsu hatsúka ni

on Friday, June 20th 6月20日金曜日に rokúgatsu hatsúka-bi kiń-yóbi ni

a week on Friday 来週の金曜日に rafshū no kiń-yóbi ni

on arrival he went straight to his hotel 到着すると彼はホテルへ行きました tōchaku suru tò kárè wa massúgù ni hóteru e ikímashìta

on seeing these これを見ると koré wo mírù to

4 (about, concerning) ...について ...ni tsúite, ...に関して ...ni kán shite

information on train services 列車に関する情報 ressha ni kań surù jōhō

a book on physics 物理の本 bútsùri no hóñ

◆adv 1 (referring to dress) 身につけて

mi nī tsukéte

to have one's coat on コートを着ている kôto wo kité irú

what's she got on? 彼女は何を着ていますか kánojo wa nánì wo kité imasù ka

she put her boots/gloves/hat on 彼女はブーツを履いた(手袋をはめた, 帽子をかぶった) kánojo wa bútsu wo haíta(tebúkuro wo haméta, bōshi wo kabútta)

2 (referring to covering): **screw the lid on tightly** ふたをしっかり締めて下さい futá wo shikkárì shiméte kudásaì

3 (further, continuously) 続けて tsuzúkete

to walk/drive/go 歩き(車に乗り, 車を走り)続ける arúkì(kuruma dè hashíri, ikí)tsuzukeru

to read on 読み続ける yomítsuzukeru

◆adj 1 (functioning, in operation: machine) 動いている ugóite irú; (: radio, TV, light) ついている tsuíte irú; (: faucet) 水が出ている mizú ga détè irú; (: brakes) かかっている kakátte irú; (: meeting) 続いている tsuzúite irú

is the meeting still on? (in progress) まだ会議中ですか mádà kaígichū desù ká; (not cancelled) 会議は正常に行なわれるんですか kaígi wa yotéi dòri ni yarún desù ká

there's a good film on at the cinema 映画館で今いい映画をやっています efga-kàn de imá ìi efga wò yatté imasù

2: **that's not on!** (inf: of behavior) それはいけません soré wa ikémaseñ

once [WʌNS] adv (on one occasion) 一度 ichído, 一回 ikkái; (formerly) 前は maè wa, かつて katsúte

◆conj (immediately afterwards) ...した後 ...shitá àto, ...してから ...shité kara

once he had left/it was done 彼が出て[事が済んで]から kare ga detè[kotó ga súnde]kara

at once (immediately) 直ちに tadáchi ni, 直ぐに súgù ni; (simultaneously) 同時に dōji ni

once a week 週一回 shū ikkái

once more もう一度 mô ichído
once and for all ついに断然 danzen
once upon a time 昔々 mukashi muka-shi

oncoming [ɑnˈkʌmɪŋ] *adj* (approaching: traffic etc) 向ってくる mukátte kurù

KEYWORD

one [wʌn] *num* 一（の）ichî (no), 1つ（の）hitótsū (no)

one hundred and fifty 150 hyakūgojū

I asked for two coffees, not one 注文したのは1つ、2つのコーヒーです chûmon shita no wà hitótsu jánakute futátsu désu

one day there was a sudden knock at the door ある日突然だれかがドアをノックしている right音 ある時 right hi totsúzen dáreka ga dóå wo nókkú shité iru

one by one 1つずつ hitótsu zùtsu

♦*adj* 1 (sole) ただ一つの tádá hitótsu no, 唯一の yúítsu no

it's the one book which interests me 私が興味を感じる唯一の本です watákushi ga kyómi wo kanjíru yúítsu no hóñ desu

that is my one worry 私が心配しているのはそれだけです watákushi ga shìñpai shite iru nò wa soré dake dèsu

the one man who ... ...する唯一の人 ...suru yúítsu no hitó

2 (same) 同じ onáji

they came in the one car 彼らは皆同じ車で来ました kárèra wa mínå onáji kurúma de kimáshìta

they all belong to the one family 彼らは皆身内です kárèra wa mínå miúchi desu

♦*pron* 1 物 monó

this one これ koré

that one それ、あれ aré

I've already got one/a red one 私は既に1つ（赤いの）を持っています watákushi wa sudé ni hitótsu (akái no wo) mótté imasu

2: *one another* お互いに o-tágai ni

do you two ever see one another? お二人は付合っていますか o-fútàri wa tsu-

kfatté imasu ká

the boys didn't dare look at one another 少年たちはあえて顔を合せる事ができなかった shônentàchi wa áète ka-ô wò awáseru kotò ga dekínakattà

3 (impersonal): *one never knows* どうなるか分かりません dó narù ka wakà-rimaseñ né

to cut one's finger 指を切る yubí wo kírù

one needs to eat 人は食べる必要がある hitó wà tabérù hitsúyò ga arù

one-day excursion [wʌnˈdeɪ-] (*US*) *n* (day return) 日帰り往復券 higáeri ôfuku-ken

one-man [wʌnˈmæn] *adj* (business) 1人だけの hitóri dake no, ワンマンの waň-man no

one-man band *n* ワンマンバンド waň-manbando

one-off [wʌnˈɔːf] (*BRIT*: *inf*) *n* 一つだけの物 hitótsu dake no mono

KEYWORD

oneself [wʌnˈself] *pron* (reflexive) 自分自身を jibúnjishìn wo; (after prep) 自分自身に jibúnjishìn ni; (alone: often after prep) 自分一人で jibún hitòri de; (emphatic) 自分で jibún de

to hurt oneself けがする kegá surù

to keep something for oneself 自分のために...を取って置く jibún no tamè ni ...wô tóttè oku

to talk to oneself 独り言を言う hitóri-gotò wo iú

one-sided [wʌnˈsaɪdɪd] *adj* (argument) 一方的な ippóteki na

one-to-one [wʌnˈtəwʌn] *adj* (relationship) 一対一の ittáìchi no

one-upmanship [wʌnʌpˈmænʃɪp] *n* 自分の方が一枚上だと見せ付ける事 jibún no hô ga ichímài ue da to misétsukerù kotó

one-way [wʌnˈweɪ] *adj* (street, traffic) 一方通行の ippótsúkò no

ongoing [ɑnˈɡəʊɪŋ] *adj* (project, situation etc) 進行中の shiňkôchu no

onion [ʌnʔjən] *n* タマネギ tamánegì

on-line [ɔːnʔlaɪn] *adj* (COMPUT) オンラインの oṉráiṉ no
♦*adv* (COMPUT) オンラインで oṉráiṉ de

onlooker [ɑːnʔlukəːr] *n* 見物人 keṉbutsunìn

only [ounʔliː] *adv* ...だけ ...dake
♦*adj* (sole, single) ただ一つの〔一人〕の tadá hitótsu(hitórì) no
♦*conj* (but) しかし shikáshì
an only child 一人っ子 hitórìkkò
not only ... but also ...ばかりでなく ...も ...bakári ni naku ...mo

onset [ɑːnʔset] *n* (beginning: of war, winter, illness) 始まり hajímarì, 始め hajíme

onshore [ɑːnʔʃɔːr] *adj* (wind) 海からの umí kara no

onslaught [ɑːnʔslɔːt] *n* 攻撃 kốgeki

onto [ɑːnʔtuː] *prep* = on to

onus [ounəs] *n* 責任 sekíniṉ

onward(s) [ɑːnʔwəːrd(z)] *adv* (forward: move, progress) 先へ sakí e
from that time onward(s) それ以後 soré igo

onyx [ɑːnʔiks] *n* オニキス oníkisu

ooze [uːz] *vi* (mud, water, slime) にじみでる nijímiderù

opal [oupəl] *n* オパール opáru

opaque [oupeik] *adj* (substance) 不透明な futómeì na

OPEC [ouʔpek] *n abbr* (= *Organization of Petroleum-Exporting Countries*) 石油輸出国機構 sekíyu yushutsukoku kíkò

open [ouʔpən] *adj* (not shut: window, door, mouth etc) 開いた aíta; (: shop, museum etc) 営業中の eígyòchū no, 開いている aíte irù; (unobstructed: road) 開通している kaítsū shite irù; (: view) 開けた hirákèta; (not enclosed: land) 囲いのない kakóì no naì; (fig: frank: person, manner, face) 率直な sótchoku na; (unrestricted: meeting, debate, championship) 公開の kốkai no
♦*vt* 開ける akérù, 開く hiráku
♦*vi* (flower, eyes, door, shop) 開く akú, 開く hiráku; (book, debate etc: commence) 始まる hajímaru

in the open (air) 野外に yagái ni
an open car オープンカー ốpùnkā

opening [ouʔpəniŋ] *adj* (commencing: speech, remarks etc) 開会の kaíkai no, 冒頭の bốtō no
♦*n* (gap, hole) 穴 aná; (start: of play, book etc) 始め hajíme, 冒頭 bốtō; (opportunity) 機会 kíkài, チャンス chaṉsu

openly [ouʔpənliː] *adv* (speak, act) 公然と kốzen ni; (cry) 人目をはばからず hitóme wo habákarazu

open-minded [ouʔpənmaiṉʔdid] *adj* 偏見のない heṉkèn no naì

open-necked [ouʔpənnekt] *adj* (shirt) 開きの kaíkin no

open on to *vt fus* (subj: room, door) ...に面している ...ni méṉ shite irù

open-plan [ouʔpəṉplæṉ] *adj* 間仕切りのない majíkiri no naì

open up *vt* (building, room: unlock) 開ける akérù; (blocked road) ...の障害物を取除く ...no shồgaibutsu wo torínozokù
♦*vi* (COMM: shop, business) 開く akú

opera [ɑːpʔrə] *n* 歌劇 kagéki, オペラ opéra

opera singer *n* オペラ歌手 opérakashu

operate [ɑːpʔəreit] *vt* (machine) 操作する sốsa suru; (vehicle) 運転する uṉteṉ suru
♦*vi* (machine) 動く ugókù; (vehicle) 走る hashirù, 動く ugókù; (company, organization) 営業する eígyō suru
to operate on someone (for) (MED) ...に（...の）手術をする ...ni （...no） shujútsu wo suru

operatic [ɑːpəræʔtik] *adj* 歌劇の kagéki no, オペラの opéra no

operating [ɑːpʔəreitiŋ] *adj*: *operating table* 手術台 shujútsudai
operating theater 手術室 shujútsushitsu

operation [ɑːpəreiʔʃən] *n* (of machine etc) 操作 sốsa; (of vehicle) 運転 uṉteṉ; (MIL, COMM etc) 作戦 sakúseṉ; (MED) 手術 shujútsu
to be in operation (law, regulation) 実施されている jisshí sarete iru
to have an operation (MED) 手術を受

けるshujutsu wo ukéru

operational [ɔːpəˈreɪʃənəl] *adj* (working: machine, vehicle etc) 使用可能な shíyōkanō na

operative [ˈɔːpərətɪv] *adj* (law, measure, system) 実施されている jisshí sarete iru

operator [ˈɔːpəreɪtər] *n* (TEL) 交換手 kōkanshu; (of machine) 技師 gishí

ophthalmic [ɔːfˈθælmɪk] *adj* 眼科の gań ka no

opinion [əˈpɪnjən] *n* (point of view, belief) 意見 ikén

in my opinion 私の意見では watákushi no ikén de wa

opinionated [əˈpɪnjəneɪtɪd] (*pej*) *adj* 独善的な dokúzenteki na

opinion poll *n* 世論調査 yorónchōsa

opium [ˈoʊpiːəm] *n* あへん ahén

opponent [əˈpoʊnənt] *n* (person not in favor) 反対者 hañtaisha; (MIL) 敵 tekí; (SPORT) 相手 aíte

opportunism [ɔːpəˈtjuːˌnɪzəm] (*pej*) *n* 日和見主義 hiyórimishugí

opportunist [ɔːpəˈtjuːˈnɪst] (*pej*) *n* 日和見主義者 hiyórimishugisha

opportunity [ɔːpəˈtjuːˈniːtiː] *n* 機会 kikái, チャンス chańsu

to take the opportunity of doing ...する折角の機会を利用して...suru sekkáku no kikái wo riyō shite ...suru

oppose [əˈpoʊz] *vt* (object to: wish, opinion, plan) ...に反対する ...ni hañtai suru

to be opposed to something ...に反対である ...ni hañtai de aru

as opposed to ...ではなくて ...de wa nakutè

opposing [əˈpoʊzɪŋ] *adj* (side, ideas) 反対の hañtai no; (team) 相手の aíte no

opposite [ˈɔːpəzɪt] *adj* (house) 向かい側の mukáigawa no; (end, direction, side) 反対の hañtai no; (point of view, effect) 逆の gyakú no

♦*adv* (live, stand, work, sit) 向い側に(で) mukáigawa ni(de)

♦*prep* (in front of) ...の向い側に(で) ...no mukáigawa ni(de)

♦*n: the opposite* (say, think, do etc) 逆 gyakú

the opposite sex 異性 iséi

opposition [ɔːpəˈzɪʃən] *n* (resistance) 反対 hañtai; (those against) 反対勢力 hañtaiseiryokù; (POL) 野党 yatō

oppress [əˈpres] *vt* 抑圧する yokúatsu suru

oppression [əˈpreʃən] *n* 抑圧 yokúatsu

oppressive [əˈpresɪv] *adj* (political regime) 抑圧的な yokúatsuteki na; (weather, heat) 蒸し暑い mushíatsuì

opt [ɔːpt] *vi*: *to opt for* ...を選ぶ ...wo erábù

to opt to do ...する事にする ...surú koto ni suru

optical [ˈɔːptɪkəl] *adj* (instrument, device etc) 光学の kōgaku no

optical illusion *n* 目の錯覚 mé no sakkáku

optician [ɔːpˈtɪʃən] *n* 眼鏡屋 megáneya

optimism [ˈɔːptɪmɪzəm] *n* 楽観 rakkán, 楽天主義 rakútenshugî

optimist [ˈɔːptɪmɪst] *n* 楽天家 rakútenka

optimistic [ɔːptɪˈmɪstɪk] *adj* 楽観的な rakkánteki na

optimum [ˈɔːptɪməm] *adj* (conditions, number, size) 最良の saíryō no, 最善の saízen no

option [ˈɔːpʃən] *n* (choice) 選択 señtaku, オプション opúshon

optional [ˈɔːpʃənəl] *adj* (not obligatory) 自由選択の jiyúsentakuno

opt out *vi*: *to opt out of* ...から手を引く ...kara te wò hiku

opulent [ˈɔːpjələnt] *adj* (very wealthy: person, society etc) 大金持の ōganêmochi no

or [ɔːr] *conj* (linking alternatives: up or down, in or out) それとも sorétomò, または matá wa; (otherwise) でないと de naî to, さもないと sa mô naì to; (with negative): *he hasn't seen or heard anything* 彼は何一つ見ても聞いてもいない karè wa nanî hitótsu mitè mo kiîte mo inai

or else (otherwise) でないと de naî to

oracle [ɔːˈrəkəl] n 予言者 yogénsha

oral [ɔːrəl] adj (spoken: test, report) 口頭の kōtō no; (MED: vaccine, medicine) 経口の keíkō no
♦n (spoken examination) 口頭試問 kōtōshimon

orange [ɔːˈrɪndʒ] n (fruit) オレンジ orénji
♦adj (color) だいだい色の daídaiiro no, オレンジ色の orénjiiro no

orator [ɔːˈreɪtər] n 雄弁家 yūbenka

orbit [ɔːˈbɪt] n (SPACE) 軌道 kidō
♦vt (circle: earth, moon etc) ...の周囲を軌道を描いて回る ...no shū wo kidō wo egaite mawaru

orchard [ɔːˈtʃɑːrd] n 果樹園 kajúen

orchestra [ɔːˈkɪstrə] n (MUS) 楽団 gakúdan, オーケストラ ōkesútora; (US: THEATER: seating) 舞台前の特等席 buốtaímae no tokútōseki

orchestrate [ɔːˈkɪstreit] vt (stage-manage) 指揮する shíki suru

orchid [ɔːˈkɪd] n ラン rañ

ordain [ɔːˈdein'] vt (REL) 聖職に任命する sefshoku ni ninímei suru

ordeal [ɔːdiːl'] n 試練 shíren

order [ɔːrˈdər] n (command) 命令 meírei; (COMM: from shop, company etc: also in restaurant) 注文 chúmon; (sequence) 順序 juñjo; (good order) 秩序 chitsújo; (law and order) 治安 chíán
♦vt (command) 命ずる meízuru; (COMM: from shop, company etc: also in restaurant) 注文する chúmon suru; (also: put in order) 整理する seíri suru

in order (gen) 整理されて seíri sarete; (of document) 規定通りで kiteídōri de

in (working) order 整備されて seíbi sarete

in order to do/that ...するために ...surú tame ni

on order (COMM) 発注してあって haíchū shite atte

out of order (not in correct order) 順番が乱れて juñban ga midárete; (not working) 故障して koshō shíte

to order someone to do something ...に...する様に命令する ...ni ...suru yō ni meírei suru

order form n 注文用紙 chúmon yōshi

orderly [ɔːrˈdərli] n (MIL) 当番兵 tōbanhei; (MED) 雑役夫 zatsúekifu
♦adj (well-organized: room) 整とんされた sefton sareta; (: person, system etc) 規則正しい kisókutadashii

ordinary [ɔːrˈdəneri] adj (everyday, usual) 普通の futsū no; (pej: mediocre) 平凡な heíbon na

out of the ordinary (exceptional) 変った kawátta

Ordnance Survey [ɔːrdˈnəns-] (BRIT) n 英国政府陸地測量局 efkokuseífu rikúchi sokuryōkyoku

ore [ɔːr] n 鉱石 kōseki

organ [ɔːrˈgən] n (ANAT) 器官 kíkan; (MUS) オルガン orúgan

organic [ɔːrgenˈik] adj (food, farming etc) 有機の yūki no

organism [ɔːrˈgənizəm] n 有機体 yūkítai, 生物 seíbutsu

organist [ɔːrˈgənist] n オルガン奏者 orúgansōsha, オルガニスト orúganisuto

organization [ɔːrgənizeiˈʃən] n (business, club, society) 組織 soshíki, 機構 kíkō, オーガニゼーション ōganizéshon

organize [ɔːrˈgənaiz] vt (arrange: activity, event) 企画する kikáku suru

organizer [ɔːrˈgənaizər] n (of conference, party etc) 主催者 shusaísha

orgasm [ɔːrˈgæzəm] n オルガズム orúgazumō

orgy [ɔːrˈdʒi] n 乱交パーティ rañkōpāti

Orient [ɔːriːˈənt] n: *the Orient* 東洋 tōyō

oriental [ɔːriːenˈtəl] adj 東洋の tōyō no

orientate [ɔːriːenˈteit] vt: *to orientate oneself* (in place) 自分の居場所を確認する jíbun no ibásho wo kakúnin suru; (in situation) 環境になれる kañkyō ni naréru

origin [ɔːrˈidʒin] n (beginning, source) 起源 kigén; (of person) 生れ umare

original [ərˈidʒənəl] adj (first: idea, occupation) 最初の saísho no; (genuine: work of art, document etc) 本物の hoñmono no; (fig: imaginative: thinker, writer, artist) 独創的な dokúsōteki na

♦n (genuine work of art, document) 本物 hōnmono

originality [əridʒænælˈitiː] n (imagination: of artist, writer etc) 独創性 dokusōsei

originally [əridʒˈæneit] adv (at first) 最初は sashō wa, 当初 tōsho

originate [əridʒˈæneit] vi: to originate from (person, idea, custom etc) ...から始まる ...kara hajimaru

to originate in ...で始まる ...de hajimaru

Orkneys [ɔːrkˈniːz] npl: the Orkneys (also: the Orkney Islands) オークニー諸島 ōkūnīshotō

ornament [ɔːrˈnəmənt] n (gen) 飾り kazāri, (being worn) 装身具 sōshingu

ornamental [ɔːrnəmenˈtəl] adj (decorative: garden, pond) 装飾的な sōshokuteki na

ornate [ɔːrneitˈ] adj (highly decorative: design, style) 凝った kottá

ornithology [ɔːrnəθˈɑːldʒiː] n 鳥類学 chōruigaku

orphan [ɔːrˈfən] n 孤児 kojí

orphanage [ɔːrˈfənidʒ] n 孤児院 kojín

orthodox [ɔːrˈθədɑːks] adj (REL: also fig) 正統派の seítōha no

orthodoxy [ɔːrˈθədɑːksiː] n (traditional beliefs) 正統思想 seítōshisō

orthopedic [ɔːrθəpiːˈdik] (BRIT **orthopaedic**) adj 整形外科の sefkeigeka no

oscillate [ɑːsˈəleit] vi (ELEC) 発振する hasshín suru; (PHYSICS) 振動する shindō suru; (fig: mood, person, attitude) 頻繁に変る hínpan ni kawáru

ostensibly [ɑːstenˈsəbliː] adv 表面上 hyōmenjō

ostentatious [ɑːstenteiˈʃəs] adj (showy: building, car etc) 派手な hadé na; (: person) 万事に派手な banji ni hadé na

osteopath [ɑːstiːəpæθ] n 整骨療法医 sefkotsuryōhōi

ostracize [ɑːsˈtrəsaiz] vt のけ者にする nokémono ni suru

ostrich [ɑːsˈtrit] n ダチョウ dachō

other [ʌðˈəːr] adj (that which has not

been mentioned: person, thing) 外の hoká no; (second of 2 things) もう一つの mō hitotsu no

♦pron: the other (one) 外の hoká no mono

♦adv: other than ...を除いて ...wo nozőite

others (other people) 他人 tanín

the other day (recently) 先日 señjitsu, この間 konó aida

otherwise [ʌðˈəːrwaiz] adv (in a different way) 違った方り方で chígatta yarikata de; (apart from that) それを除けば soré wo nozőkeba

♦conj (if not) そうでないと sō de nai to

otter [ɑːtˈəːr] n カワウソ kawáuso

ouch [autʃ] excl 痛い itá!

ought [ɔːt] (pt **ought**) aux vb: she ought to do it 彼女はそれをやるべきです ka-nōjo wa soré wo yarubeki desu

this ought to have been corrected これは直すべきだった koré wa naősubeki datta

he ought to win (probability) 彼は勝つはずです karē wa katsú hazu desu

ounce [auns] n (unit of weight) オンス oñsu

our [auˈəːr] adj 私たちの watákushitachi no ¶ see also **my**

ours [auˈəːr] pron 私たちの物 watákushitachi no mono ¶ see also **mine**

ourselves [auˈəːrselvˈz] pron 私たち自身 watákushitachi jishín ¶ see also **oneself**

oust [aust] vt (forcibly remove: government, MP etc) 追放する tsufhō suru

KEYWORD

out [aut] adv 1 (not in) 外に(で, へ) sótō ni (de, e)

they're out in the garden 彼らは庭にいます kárèra wa niwá ni imasū

(to stand) out in the rain/snow 雨(雪)の中に立っている ámè(yukī)no fúrū nákà ni tátte irū

it's cold out here/out in the desert 外(砂漠)は寒い sótō(sabáku)wa samúi

out here/there ここ(あそこ)だ・外の方に kokó(asőko)dà・sótō no hő ni

to go/come etc out 出て行く（来る）déte iku/kuru)

(to speak) out loud 大きな声で言う ōkina koè de iú

2 (not at home, absent) 不在で fuzái de, 留守で rúsū de

Mr Green is out at the moment グリーンさんはただ今留守ですが gurīn san wa tadáīma rúsū desu ga

to have a day/night out 1日（1晩）外出して遊ぶ ichínichí(hitóbán)gaishutsu shite asóbú

3 (indicating distance): *the boat was 10 km out* 船は10キロ沖にあった fúne wa jukkíró okí ni attá

3 days out from Plymouth プリマスを出港して3日めの purímàsu wo shukkō shite mikká no tokoró

4 (SPORT) アウトで áuto de

the ball is/has gone out ボールはアウトだ（出た）bōru wa áuto da(détà)

out! (TENNIS etc) アウト áuto

◆*adj* **1**: *to be out* (person: unconscious) 気絶（失神）している kizétsu(shisshín) shite irú; (: SPORT) アウトである áuto de árú; (out of fashion: style) 流行遅れである ryúkōokūre de árú, 廃れている sutárete irú; (: singer) 人気がなくなった nínki ga nakúnattá

2 (have appeared: flowers): *to be out* 咲いている saíte irú; (: news) 報道されている hōdō sarete irú; (: secret) ばれた bárèta, 発覚した hakkáku shita

3 (extinguished: fire, light, gas) 消えた kiéta

before the week was out (finished) その週が終らない内に sonó shū ga owáranai uchi nì

4: *to be out to do something* (intend) …しようとしている …shiyó to shité irú

to be out in one's calculations (wrong) 計算が間違っている kefsan gà machígatte irú

---

out-and-out [aut'əndaut'] *adj* (liar, thief etc) 全くの mattáku no, 根っからの nekkára no

outback [aut'bæk] *n* (in Australia) 奥地 okúchi

outboard [aut'bɔːrd] *adj*: *outboard motor* アウトボードエンジン áutobōdo-enjin

outbreak [aut'breik] *n* (of war, disease, violence etc) 勃発 boppátsu

outburst [aut'bərst] *n* (sudden expression of anger etc) 爆発 bakúhatsu

outcast [aut'kæst] *n* 除け者 nokémono

outcome [aut'kʌm] *n* (result) 結果 kekká

outcrop [aut'krɑːp] *n* (of rock) 露頭 rotó

outcry [aut'krai] *n* 反発 hañpatsu

outdated [autdei'tid] *adj* (old-fashioned) 時代遅れの jidáiokūre no

outdo [autduː'] (*pt* **outdid** *pp* **outdone**) *vt* しのぐ shinógu

outdoor [aut'dɔːr] *adj* (open-air: activities, games etc) 野外の yagái no, 屋外の okúgai no; (clothes) 野外用の yagáiyō no

outdoors [autdɔːrz'] *adv* (play, stay, sleep: in the open air) 野外に（で）yagái ni(de)

outer [aut'əːr] *adj* (exterior: door, wrapping, wall etc) 外側の sotógawa no

outer space 宇宙空間 uchúkūkan

outfit [aut'fit] *n* (set of clothes) 衣装 i-shō

outgoing [aut'gouiŋ] *adj* (extrovert) 外向性の gafkōsei no; (retiring: president, mayor etc) 退職する tafjin suru

outgoings [aut'gouiŋz] (BRIT) *npl* 出費 shuppí

outgrow [autgrou'] (*pt* **outgrew** *pp* **outgrown**) *vt* (one's clothes) 大きくなって …が着られなくなる ōkiku natte …ga kirárenaku naru

outhouse [aut'haus] *n* 納屋 nayá; (US) 屋外便所 okúgaibenjo

outing [au'tiŋ] *n* (excursion: family outing, school outing) 遠足 eñsoku

outlandish [autlæn'diʃ] *adj* (strange: looks, behavior, clothes) 奇妙な kimyō na

outlaw [aut'lɔː] *n* 無法者 muhómono

◆*vt* (person, activity, organization) 禁止する kifshi suru

outlay [aut'lei] *n* (expenditure) 出費

shuppī

outlet [aut'let] n (hole, pipe) 排水口 haisuikō; (US: ELEC) コンセント koñsento; (COMM: also: retail outlet) 販売店 hañbaiten

outline [aut'lain] n (shape: of object, person etc) 輪郭 riñkaku, アウトライン aūtorain; (brief explanation: of plan) あらまし aramashi, アウトライン aūtorain; (rough sketch) 略図 ryakúzu
♦vt (fig: theory, plan etc) ...の あらましを説明する ...no aramashi wo setsūmei suru

outlive [aut'liv'] vt (survive: person) ...より長生きする ...yórì naga-ikī suru; (: war, era) 生き延びる ikínobiru

outlook [aut'luk] n (view, attitude) 見方 mikáta; (fig: prospects) 見通し mitōshi; (: for weather) 予報 yohō

outlying [aut'laiin] adj (away from main cities: area, town etc) 中心部を離れた chūshinbu no hanáreta

outmoded [autmou'did] adj (oldfashioned: custom, theory) 時代遅れの jidáiokūre no

outnumber [autnʌm'bəɪ] vt ...より多い ...yórì ōi

KEYWORD

out of prep 1 (outside, beyond) ...の外へ (に、で) ...no sótò e (ni, de)
to go out of the house 家から外へ出る ié kará sótò e dérù
to look out of the window 窓から外を見る mádò kara sótò wo mírù
to be out of danger (safe) 危険がなくなった kikéñ ga nakúnattà
2 (cause, motive) ...に駆られて、...ni karárete
out of curiosity/fear/greed 好奇心 (恐怖、欲しさ)に駆られて kókìshiñ (kyōfu, hoshī-yoku)ni karárete
3 (origin) ...から ...kara
to drink something out of a cup コップから...を飲む káppù kara ...wo nómù
to copy something out of a book 本から...を写す hóñ kara ...wò utsúsù
4 (from among) ...の中から ...no nákà

kara, ...の内 ...no uchí
1 out of every 3 smokers 喫煙者3人に1人 kitsúeñsha safníñ ni hítorì
out of 100 cars sold, only one had any faults 売れた100台の車の内、1台だけに欠陥があった uréta hyakúdai no kurūma no uchi, íchìdai dake ni kekkán ga atta
5 (without) ...が切れて、...ga kírète, ...がなくなって ...ga nakúnatté
to be out of milk/sugar/gas (US)/**petrol** (BRIT) etc ミルク(砂糖、ガソリン)が切れている mírùku(satō, gasórin)ga kírète iru

out-of-date [autəvdeit'] adj (passport) 期限の切れた kigéñ no kíréta; (clothes etc) 時代遅れの jidáiokūre no

out-of-the-way [autəvðəwei'] adj (place) へんぴな hénpì na

outpatient [aut'peiʃənt] n (MED) 外来患者 gaíraikañja

outpost [aut'poust] n (MIL, COMM) 前しょう zeñshō; (COMM) 前進基地 zeñshinkichi

output [aut'put] n (production: of factory, mine etc) 生産高 sefsañdaka; (: of writer) 作品数 sakúhiñsū; (COMPUT) 出力 shutsūryoku, アウトプット aūtoputto

outrage [aut'reidʒ] n (action: scandalous) 不法行為 fuhōkōī; (: violent) 暴力行為 bóryokukōī; (anger) 激怒 gekído
♦vt (shock, anger) 激怒させる gekído saseru

outrageous [autrei'dʒəs] adj 非難すべき hinánsubeki

outright [adv autrait'/adj aut'rait] adv (absolutely: win) 圧倒的に attőteki ni; (at once: kill) 即座に sokúza ni; (openly: ask, deny, refuse) はっきりと hakkírì to
♦adj (absolute: winner, victory) 圧倒的な attőteki na; (open: refusal, denial, hostility) 明白な meñkaku na

outset [aut'set] n (start) 始め hajíme

outside [aut'said'] n (exterior: of container, building) 外側 sotőgawa
♦adj (exterior) 外側の sotőgawa no
♦adv (away from the inside: to be, go,

wait) 外に(で) sotó ni(de)
♦prep (not inside) ...の外に(で)...no sotó
ni(de); (not included in) ...の外に ...no
hoká ni; (beyond) ...を越えて ...wo koéte
at the outside (fig) せいぜい seízei

outside lane n (AUT) 追越し車線 oíko-
shíshaseń

outside line n (TEL) 外線 gaísen

outsider [autsaɪ'dər] n (stranger) 部外者
bugáisha

outside-left'-right [aut'saɪdleft'/raɪt']
n (SOCCER) レフト(ライト)ウイング re-
fúto(raíto)uíngu

outsize [aut'saɪz] adj (clothes) キングサ
イズの kíngusaízu no

outskirts [aut'skərts] npl (of city,
town) 外れ haźure

outspoken [aut'spou'kən] adj (statement, opponent, reply) 遠慮のない eńryo
no nai

outstanding [autstæn'dɪŋ] adj (exceptional) 並外れた namíhazureta, 優れた
sugúreta; (remaining: debt, work etc) 残
っている nokótte iru

outstay [autsteɪ'] vt: to outstay one's
welcome 長居して嫌われる nagái shite
kiráwareru

outstretched [autstretʃt'] adj (hand) 伸
ばした nobáshita; (arms) 広げた hirógе-
tá

outstrip [autstrɪp'] vt (competitors,
demand) 追抜く oínuku

out-tray [aut'treɪ] n 送信のトレー sōshin
no torè

outward [aut'wərd] adj (sign, appearances) 外部の gaíbu no; (journey) 行きの
ikí no

outwardly [aut'wərdli:] adv 外部的に
gaíbuteki ni

outweigh [autweɪ'] vt ...より重要である
...yóri jūyō de aru

outwit [autwɪt'] vt ...の裏をかく ...no urá
wo kaku

oval [ou'vəl] adj (table, mirror, face) だ
円形の daénkei no
♦n だ円形 daénkei

ovary [ou'vəri:] n 卵巣 rańsō

ovation [ouveɪ'ʃən] n 大喝さい dafkassai

oven [ʌv'ən] n (CULIN) 天火 teńpi, オー
ブン óbun (TECH) 炉 ro

ovenproof [ʌv'ənpruf] adj (dish etc) オ
ーブン用の óbun yō no

KEYWORD

over [ou'vər] adv 1 (across: walk, jump,
fly etc) を越えて ...wo koéte
*to cross over to the other side of the
road* 道路を横断する dòro wo ódan suru
here/there ここ(あそこ)に(で)
kokó(asóko) ni(de)
to ask someone over to one's house)
...を家に招く ...wo ié ní manékú

2 (indicating movement from upright:
fall, knock, turn, bend etc) 下へ shitá è,
地面へ jímén e

3 (excessively: clever, rich, fat etc) 余り
amári, 過度に kádò ni
she's not over intelligent, is she? 彼
女はあまり頭が良くないね kánòjo wa
amári atáma ga yókūnai ne

4 (remaining: money, food etc) 余って
amátte, 残って nokótte
there are 3 over 3個残っている sáñ-
ko ga nokótte irù
is there any cake (left) over? ケーキ
が残っていませんか kèki ga nokótte i-
masen ká

5: *all over* (everywhere) 至る所に(で)
itáru tokoro ni(de)、どこもかしこも dókò mo káshikò mo

over and over (again) (repeatedly) 何
度(何回, 何返)も nàndo(náñkai, náñ-
ben) mo

♦adj (finished): *to be over* (game, life,
relationship etc) 終りである owári de
arù

♦prep 1 (on top of) ...の上に(で)...no ué
ni(de); (above) ...の上方に(で)...no jóhō
ni(de)
to spread a sheet over something ...の
上にシーツを掛ける ...no ué ní shìtsu wo
kakèrù

there's a canopy over the bed ベッド
の上に天蓋がある béddò no ué ní teń-
gai ga arù

2 (on the other side of) ...の向こう側に

(で) ...no mukōgawa nī(dè)

the pub over the road 道路の向こう側
にあるパブ dốrỏ no mukōgawa ni arù
pábù

he jumped over the wall 彼は塀を飛
越えた kárè wa heí wò tobíkoèta

3 (more than) 以上 ijō

over 200 people came 200人以上の人
が来ました nihyákunīn íjỏ no hitó gà
kimáshità

over and above ...の外に ...no hóka ni,
...に加えて ...ni kuwáetè

*this order is over and above what
we have already ordered* この注文は
これまでの追加の注文に加えて konó chū-
mon wa koré madè no chūmon e ni
tsúfka desù

4 (during) ...の間 ...no aída

over the last few years 過去数年の間
kákỏ sūnèn no aída

over the winter 冬の間 fuyú nò aída

let's discuss it over dinner 夕食をし
ながら話し合いましょう yūshoku wò
shinágàra hanáshiaimashỏ

overall [adj, n ou'və:rɔːl adv ouvə:rɔ́ːl]
adj (length, study etc) 全体の zeńtai no;
(general: study, survey) 全面的な zeńmenteki na

◆adv (view, survey etc) 全面的に zeńmenteki ni; (measure, paint) 全体に zeńtai ni

◆n (BRIT: woman's, child's, painter's)
上っ張り uwáppari

overalls [ou'və:rɔːlz] npl オーバーオール
ốbăōrù

overawe [ouvə:rɔ́ː] vt 威圧する iátsu suru

overbalance [ouvə:rbǽl'əns] vi バラン
スを失う baráñsu wo ushínau

overbearing [ouvə:rbɛ́ːr'iŋ] adj (person,
behavior, manner) 横暴な ốbō na

overboard [ou'və:rbɔːrd] adv (NAUT):

to fall overboard 船から水に落ちる funè kara mízù ni ochíru

overbook [ou'və:rbuk] vt 予約を取り過
ぎる yoyáku wo torísugiru

overcast [ouvə:rkǽst] adj (day, sky) 曇
った kumóttà

overcharge [ou'və:rtʃɑːrdʒ] vt ...に不当
な金額を請求する ...ni futō na kiñgaku
wo sefkyū suru

overcoat [ou'və:rkout] n オーバーコー
ト ốbăkòto, オーバー ốbā

overcome [ouvə:rkʌm'] (pt overcame pp
overcome) vt (defeat: opponent, enemy)
...に勝つ ...ni katsù; (fig: difficulty, problem) 克服する kokúfuku suru

overcrowded [ouvə:rkrau'did] adj
(room, prison) 超満員の chốman-in no;
(city) 過密な kamítsu na

overdo [ouvə:rduː'] (pt overdid pp over-
done) vt (exaggerate: concern, interest)
誇張する kochō suru; (overcook) 焼き過
ぎる yakísugiru

to overdo it (work etc) やり過ぎる yarí-
sugirù

overdose [ou'və:rdous] n (MED: dangerous dose) 危険量 kikéñryò; (: fatal dose)
致死量 chíshìryō

overdraft [ou'və:rdræft] n 当座借越 tố-
zakarikoshi

overdrawn [ouvə:rdrɔːn'] adj (account)
借越した karíkoshi shita

overdue [ouvə:rduː'] adj (late: person,
bus, train) 遅れている okúrete iru;
(change, reform etc) 待望の taíbō no

overestimate [ouvə:res'təmeit] vt (cost,
importance, time) 高く見積りすぎる ta-
káku mitsúmorisugirò; (person's ability,
skill etc) 買いかぶる kaíkaburu

overexcited [ouvə:riksai'tid] adj 過度に
興奮した kadò ni kốfun shita

overflow [vb ouvə:rflou' n ou'və:rflou]
vi (river) はん濫する haríran suru; (sink,
vase etc) あふれる afúreru

◆n (also: overflow pipe) 放出パイプ hố-
shutsupaipu

overgrown [ouvə:rgroun'] adj (garden)
草がぼうぼうと生えた kusa ga bốbō ni
haèta

overhaul [vb ouvə:rhɔːl' n ou'və:rhɔːl]
vt (engine, equipment etc) 分解検査する
buñkaikensa suru, オーバーホールする
ốbăhoru suru

◆n オーバーホール ốbăhòru

overhead [adv ouvə:rhed'   adj, n

ou'vərhed] adv (above) 頭上に〔で〕zujō
ni [de]; (in the sky) 上空に〔で〕jōkū ni
[de]
♦adj (lighting) 上からの ué kara no;
(cables, railway) 高架の kōka no
♦n (US) = overheads

overheads [ou'vərhedz] npl (expenses)
経費 keíhi

overhear [ouvərhiər'] (pt, pp over-
heard) vt 耳にする mimí ni suru

overheat [ouvərhiːt'] vi (engine) 過熱す
る kanétsu suru, オーバーヒートする ō-
bāhīto suru

overjoyed [ouvərdʒɔid'] adj 大喜びした
ōyōrokobi shita

overkill [ou'vərkil] n やり過ぎ yarísugi

overland [ou'vərlænd] adj (journey) 陸
路の rikúro no
♦adv (travel) 陸路で rikúro de

overlap [ouvərlæp'] vi (edges) 部分的に
重なる bubúnteki ni kasánaru, オーバー
ラップする ōbārappu suru; (fig: ideas,
activities etc) 部分的に重複する bubúnteki ni chōfuku suru, オーバーラップす
る ōbārappu suru

overleaf [ou'vərliːf] adv ページの裏に
pḗji no urá ni

overload [ou'vərloud] vt (vehicle) ...に積
み過ぎる ...ni tsumísugiru; (ELEC) ...に負
荷を掛け過ぎる ...ni fuká wo kakésugi-
ru; (fig: with, problems etc) ...に負
担を掛け過ぎる ...ni fután wo kakésugi-
ru

overlook [ou'vərluk] vt (have view
over) 見下ろす mióorosu; (miss: by mistake) 見落す mióotosu; (excuse, forgive)
見逃す minógasu

overnight [adv ouvərnait' adj ou'vər-
nait] adv (during the whole night) 一晩中
hitóbanjū; (fig: suddenly) いつの間にか
itsú no ma ni ka
♦adj (bag, clothes) 1泊用の ippákuyō no
to stay overnight 一泊する ippáku suru

overpass [ou'vərpæs] n 陸橋 ríkkyō

overpower [ouvərpau'ər] vt (person) 腕
力で抑え込む wańryoku de' osáekomù;
(subj: emotion, anger etc) 圧倒する attó

suru

overpowering [ouvərpau'əriŋ] adj
(heat, stench) 圧倒する様な attó suru yō
na

overrate [ouvərreit'] vt (person, film,
book) 高く評価し過ぎる takáku hyōka
shisúgiru

override [ouvərraid'] (pt overrode pp
overridden) vt (order) 無効にする mukō-
ni suru; (objection) 無視する mushí suru

overriding [ouvərraid'iŋ] adj (importance) 最大の saídai no; (factor, consideration) 優先的な yūsénteki na

overrule [ouvərruːl'] vt (decision, claim,
person) 無効にする mukō ni suru; (person) ...の提案を退ける ...no teían wo shí-
rízokerù

overrun [ouvərran'] (pt overran pp
overrun) vt (country) 侵略する shińrya-
ku suru; (time limit) 越える koéru

overseas [adv ouvərsiːz' adj ou'vər-
siːz] adv (live, travel, work: abroad) 海外
に〔で〕kaígai ni [de]
♦adj (market, trade) 海外の kaígai no;
(student, visitor) 外国人の gaíkokujīn no

overshadow [ouvərʃæd'ou] vt (throw
shadow over: place, building etc) ...の上
にそびえる ...no ué ni sobíerô; (fig) ...の
影を薄くさせる ...no kagé wo usúku saseru

overshoot [ouvərʃuːt'] (pt, pp overshot)
vt (subj: plane, train, car etc) ...に止らず
に行き過ぎる ...ni tomárazu ni ikísugirù

oversight [ou'vərsait] n 手落ち teóchi

oversleep [ouvərsliːp'] (pt, pp overslept)
vi 寝過ごす nesúgosu, 寝坊する nebō su-
ru

overstate [ouvərsteit'] vt (exaggerate:
case, problem, importance) 誇張する kochō suru

overstep [ouvərstep'] vt: to overstep
the mark (go too far) 行き過ぎをやる
ikísugi wo yaru

overt [ouvərt'] adj あからさまな akára-
sama na

overtake [ouvərteik'] (pt overtook pp
overtaken) vt (AUT) 追越す oíkosu

overthrow [ouvərθrou'] vt (govern-

**ment, leader) 倒す taósu

overtime [ouˈvəːrtaim] n 残業 zańgyō

overtone [ouˈvəːrtoun] n (fig) 含み fukúmi

overture [ouˈvəːrtʃəːr] n (MUS) 序曲 jokyōku; (fig) 申出 mōshide

overturn [ouvəːrˈtəːrn] vt (car, chair) 引っ繰り返す hikkúrikaèsu; (fig: decision, plan, ruling) 翻す hirúgaèsu; (: government, system) 倒す taósu

♦vi (car, train, boat etc) 転覆する teńpuku suru

overweight [ouˈvəːrˈweit] adj (person) 太り過ぎの futórisugi na

overwhelm [ouvəːrˈwelm] vt 圧倒する attō suru

overwhelming [ouvəːrˈwelmiŋ] adj (victory, heat, feeling) 圧倒的な attōteki na

overwork [ouˈvəːrˈwəːrk] n 働き過ぎ határakisugi, 過労 karō

overwrought [ouvəːrˈrɔːt] adj 神経が高ぶった shińkei ga tákabuttà

owe [ou] vt: **to owe someone something, to owe something to someone** (money) …に借りている …ni …wo karîte iru, …に…を払う義務がある …ni …wo haráû gimû ga aru; (fig: gratitude, respect, loyalty) …にしなければならない …ni …shinákereba naranaî; (: life, talent, good looks etc) …のおかげである …wa …no okáge de aru

owing to [ouˈiŋ tuː] prep (because of) …のために …no tamé nî

owl [aul] n フクロウ fukúrò, ミミズク mimîzuku

own [oun] vt (possess: house, land, car etc) 所有する shoyū́ suru, 保有する hoyū́ suru

♦adj (house, work, style etc) 自分の jibún no, 自分自身の jubúnjishin no

a room of my own 自分の部屋 jibún no heyá

to get one's own back (take revenge) 復しゅうする fukúshū suru

on one's own (alone) 自分で jibún de, 自分の力で jibún no chíkára de

owner [ouˈnəːr] n (gen) 所有者 shoyū́sha, 持主 mochînushi, オーナー ōnà; (of shop

主人 shujín, 経営者 kéieìsha; (of pet) 飼主 kaînushi

ownership [ouˈnəːrʃip] n (possession) 所有 shoyū́

own up vi (admit: guilt, error) …を認める …wo mitómeru

ox [ɑːks] (pl **oxen**) n ウシ ushî ◇通常去勢した牡ウシを指す tsūjō kyoséi shita oûshi wo sasu

oxtail [ɑːksˈteil] n: **oxtail soup** オックステールスープ okkúsutērùsūpu

oxygen [ɑːkˈsidʒən] n 酸素 sańso

oxygen mask/tent n 酸素マスク（テント）sańsomasukù(teńto)

oyster [ɔisˈtəːr] n カキ kaki

oz. abbr = **ounce(s)**

ozone [ouˈzoun] n オゾン ozōn

ozone layer n オゾン層 ozōnsō

P

p [piː] abbr = **penny; pence**

P.A. [piːˈei] n abbr = **personal assistant; public address system**

p.a. abbr = **per annum**

pa [pɑː] (inf) n 父 ch**i**chan tōchan, パパ pápà

pace [peis] n (step) 1歩 íppò; (distance) 歩幅 hohâba; (speed) 早さ hâyàsa, 速度 sôkûdo, ペース pêsu

♦vi: **to pace up and down** (walk around angrily or impatiently) うろうろ歩く úrôùro suru

to keep pace with (person) …と足並をそろえる …to ashînami wo soróerù

pacemaker [peisˈmeikəːr] n (MED) ペースメーカー pêsumēkà; (SPORT: also: **pacesetter**) ペースメーカー pêsumēkà

Pacific [pəsifˈik] n: **the Pacific (Ocean)** 太平洋 tafheíyō

pacifist [pæsˈəfist] n 平和主義者 hefwashugisha

pacify [pæsˈəfai] vt (soothe: person) なだめる nadámerù; (: fears) 鎮める shizúmerù

pack [pæk] n (packet) 包み tsutsúmi; (US: of cigarettes) 1箱 hitóhako; (group:

of hounds) 群れ muré; (: of people) グループ gúrūpu; (pack) リュックサック ryukkúsakkú; (of cards) 1組 hitókùmi

♦*vt* (fill: box, container, suitcase etc) ...に詰込む ...ni tsumékòmu; (cram: people, objects): **to pack into** ...を...に詰込む tu ...wo ...ni tsumékòmu

to pack (one's bags) 荷造りをする nizúkùri wo suru

to pack someone off ...を追出す ...wo oídasù

pack it in! (*inf*: stop it!) やめなさい yaménasái!

package [pæk'idʒ] *n* (parcel) 小包 kozútsumi; (*also*: **package deal**) 一括取引 ikkátsutoríhìki

package holiday *n* = **package tour**

package tour *n* パッケージツアー pakkéjitsuà, パックツアー pakkútsuà

packed lunch [pækt-] *n* 弁当 beńtō

packet [pæk'it] *n* (box) 1箱 hitóhàko; (bag) 1袋 hitófùkuro

packing [pæk'iŋ] *n* (act) 詰込み事 tsumékòmu kotó; (material: paper, plastic etc) 包装 hósō

packing case *n* 木箱 kíbàko

pact [pækt] *n* 協定 kyótèi

pad [pæd] *n* (block of paper) 一つづり hitótsuzùri; (to prevent friction, damage) こん包材 końpòzai; (in shoulders of dress, jacket etc) パッド páddò; (*inf*: home) 住い súmài

♦*vt* (SEWING: cushion, soft toy etc) ...に詰物をする ...ni tsumémòno wo suru

padding [pæd'iŋ] *n* (material) 詰物 tsumémòno

paddle [pæd'əl] *n* (oar) かい kái, パドル pádòru; (*US*: for table tennis) ラケット rakéttò

♦*vt* (boat, canoe etc) こぐ kógù

♦*vi* (with feet) 水の中を歩く mizú no nakà wo arúkù

paddle steamer *n* (on river) 外輪船 gafrinsen

paddling pool [pæd'liŋ-] (*BRIT*) *n* (children's) 子供用プール kodómoyò pūru

paddock [pæd'ək] *n* (for horse: small field) 放牧場 hóbokujò; (: at race course)

パドック pádòkku

paddy field [pæd'i:-] *n* 水田 sufden, 田んぼ tańbo

padlock [pæd'lɑk] *n* (on door, bicycle etc) 錠 (前) jṑmae)

paediatrics [pi:di:æt'riks] (*BRIT*) *n* = **pediatrics**

pagan [pei'gən] *adj* (gods, festival, worship) 異教の ikyó no ◊キリスト教、ユダヤ教、イスラム教以外の宗教をさけすんで言う語 kirfsutokyò, yudáyakyò, isúramukyò igài no shúkyò wo sagésuñde iú go

♦*n* (worshipper of pagan gods) 異教徒 ikyóto

page [peidʒ] *n* (of book, magazine, newspaper) ページ pēji; (*also*: **page boy**) 花嫁付添いの少年 hanáyòmetsukisoi no shṑnen

♦*vt* (in hotel etc) ボーイ bòi

pageant [pædʒ'ənt] *n* (historical procession, show) ページェント pèjento

pageantry [pædʒ'əntri:] *n* 見世物 misémono

paid [peid] *pt*, *pp* of **pay**

♦*adj* (work) 有料の yūryó no; (staff, official) 有給の yūkyū no; (gunman, killer) 雇われた yatówareta

a paid holiday 有給休暇 yūkyūkyùka

to put paid to (*BRIT*: end, destroy) ...を台無しにする ...wo dafnashì ni surú

pail [peil] *n* (for milk, water etc) バケツ bakétsu

pain [pein] *n* (unpleasant physical sensation) 痛み itámi; (: mental) 苦痛 kutsū; (*fig*: unhappiness) 苦しみ kurúshimi, 心痛 shińtsū

to be in pain (person, animal) 痛み苦痛を感じている kutsū wò kańjite irú, 苦しんでいる kurúshìnde irú

to take pains to do something (make an effort) 苦心して ...する kushín shite ...surú

pained [peind] *adj* (expression) 怒った okótta

painful [pein'fəl] *adj* (back, wound, fracture etc) 痛い itái, 痛む itámù; (upsetting, unpleasant: sight etc) 痛々しい itáitashii; (memory) 不快な fukái na; (decision) 苦しい kurúshìi; (laborious: task, progress etc) 骨の折れる honé no oréru

painfully [pein'fəli:] *adv* (fig: very) 痛い程 itáihodo

painkiller [pein'kilər] *n* (aspirin, paracetamol etc) 鎮痛剤 chíntsūzai

painless [pein'lis] *adj* (operation, childbirth) 無痛の mutsū no

painstaking [peinz'teikiŋ] *adj* (work) 骨折れの honéore no; (person) 勤勉な kíñben na

paint [peint] *n* (decorator's: for walls, doors etc) 塗料 toryō, ペンキ peńki, ペイント peńto; (artist's: oil paint, watercolor paint etc) 絵の具 e no gú
♦*vt* (wall, door, house etc) ...にペンキを塗る ...ni mizúiro no nuru; (picture, portrait) 描く kákù
  to paint the door blue ドアに水色のペンキを塗る dóa ni mizúiro no peńki wo nurú

paintbrush [peint'brʌʃ] *n* (decorator's) 刷毛 hake, ブラシ búrāshi; (artist's) 絵筆 éfude

painter [pein'tər] *n* (artist) 画家 gakā; (decorator) ペンキ屋 peńkiya

painting [pein'tiŋ] *n* (activity: decorating) ペンキ塗り peńkinūri; (: art) 絵描き ekáki; (picture) 絵画 kálga
  an oil painting 油絵 abúraè

paintwork [peint'wərk] *n* (painted parts) 塗装の部分 tosō no bubûn

pair [peːr] *n* (of shoes, gloves etc) 対 tsúi
  a pair of scissors はさみ hasámi
  a pair of trousers ズボン zubóñ

pajamas [pədʒɑːm'əz] (*US*) *npl* パジャマ pájàma

Pakistan [pæk'istæn] *n* パキスタン pakísùtan

Pakistani [pæk'əstæn'i:] *adj* パキスタンの pakísùtan no
♦*n* パキスタン人 pakísutanjìn

pal [pæl] (*inf*) *n* (friend) 友達 tomódachi

palace [pæl'is] *n* (residence of monarch) 宮殿 kyūdeñ; (: of president etc) 官邸 kańtei; (: of Japanese emperor) 皇居 kōkyo, 御所 góshò

palatable [pæl'ətəbəl] *adj* (food, drink)

おいしい ofshìi

palate [pæl'it] *n* 口がい kōgai

palatial [pəlei'ʃəl] *adj* (surroundings, residence) 豪華な gōka na

palaver [pəlæv'əːr] *n* (*US*) 話し合い hanáshiai; (*BRIT*: *inf*: fuss) 大騒ぎ ōsawāgi

pale [peil] *adj* (whitish: color) 白っぽい shiróppoi; (: face) 青白い aōjirol, 青ざめた ぉ aōzametá; (: light) 薄明い usúgurai
♦*n*: *beyond the pale* (unacceptable) 容認できない yōnin dekinái

Palestine [pæl'istain] *n* パレスチナ parésùchina

Palestinian [pæləstin'i:ən] *adj* パレスチナの parésùchina no
♦*n* パレスチナ人 parésuchinajìn

palette [pæl'it] *n* (ART: paint mixing board) パレット parétto

palings [pei'liŋz] *npl* (fence) さく sakû

pall [pɔːl] *n*: *a pall of smoke* 一面の煙 ichímen no kemuri
♦*vi* ...が詰まらなくなる ...ga tsumáranakù naru, ...に飽きる ...ni akíru

pallet [pæl'it] *n* (for goods) パレット parétto

pallid [pæl'id] *adj* (person, complexion) 青白い aōjirol

pallor [pæl'əːr] *n* そう白 sōhaku

palm [pɑːm] *n* (also: **palm tree**) ヤシ yáshì; (of hand) 手のひら tenóhira
♦*vt*: *to palm something off on someone* (*inf*) ...をつかませる ...ni ...wo tsukámaserù

Palm Sunday *n* 枝の主日 edá no shujítsu

palpable [pæl'pəbəl] *adj* (obvious: lie, difference etc) 明白な mefhaku na

palpitations [pælpitei'ʃənz] *npl* (MED) 動き dóki

paltry [pɔːl'triː] *adj* (amount: tiny, insignificant) ささいな sásāi na

pamper [pæm'pəːr] *vt* (cosset: person, animal) 甘やかす amáyakasù

pamphlet [pæm'flit] *n* (political, literary etc) 小冊子 shōsasshì, パンフレット páñfuretto

pan [pæn] *n* (CULIN: *also*: **saucepan**) 片

手なべ katátenabè; (: also: **frying pan**) フライパン furáipan

panacea [pænəsi:'ə] n 万能薬 bafìnōyàku

panache [pənæʃ'] n 気取り kídori

Panama [pæn'əmɑ:] n パナマ pánama

Panama Canal n: **the Panama Canal** パナマ運河 pánama uñga

pancake [pæn'keik] n パンケーキ pañkēki, ホットケーキ hottókèki

pancreas [pæn'kri:əs] n すい臓 suízō

panda [pæn'də] n (ZOOL) ジャイアントパンダ jafàntopàñda

panda car (BRIT) n (police car) パトカー patōkā

pandemonium [pændəmoun'iəm] n (noisy confusion) 大混乱, dafkoñran

pander [pæn'də:r] vi: **to pander to** (person, whim, desire etc) ...に迎合する ...ni geígō suru

pane [pein] n (of glass) 窓ガラス madōgarāsu

panel [pæn'əl] n (oblong piece of wood, metal, plastic etc) 羽目板 haméita, パネル páneru; (group of judges, experts etc) ...の一団 ...no ichídan, パネル páneru

paneling [pæn'əliŋ] (BRIT **panelling**) n 羽目板張り haméita ◇総称 sōshō

pang [pæŋ] n: **a pang of regret** 悔恨の情 kaíkon no jō **hunger pangs** (physical pain) 激しい空腹感 hagéshiì kufúkukan

panic [pæn'ik] n (uncontrollable terror, anxiety) パニック páníkku ◆vi (person) うろたえる urótaerù; (crowd) パニック状態になる pañíkkujōtai ni nárù

panicky [pæn'iki:] adj (person) うろたえる urótaerù

panic-stricken [pæn'ikstrikən] adj (person, face) パニックに陥った pánìkku ni ochítta

panorama [pænəræm'ə] n (view) 全景 zefíkei, パノラマ pánórama

pansy [pæn'zi:] n (BOT) サンシキスミレ sañshikisumîre, パンジー pañjî; (inf: pej) 弱虫 yowámūshi

pant [pænt] vi (gasp: person, animal) あえぐ aégù

panther [pæn'θə:r] n ヒョウ hyō

panties [pæn'ti:z] npl パンティー pañtī

pantomime [pæn'təmaim] (BRIT) n クリスマスミュージカル kurísumasu myūjikaru

pantry [pæn'tri:] n 食料室 shokúryōshìtsu, パントリー pántorī

pants [pænts] npl (BRIT: underwear: woman's) パンティー pañtī; (: man's) パンツ pañtsu; (US: trousers) ズボン zubóñ

panty hose [pæn'ti: houz] n パンティーストッキング pañtīsutokkīñgu

papal [pei'pəl] adj ローマ法王の rōmahōō no

paper [pei'pə:r] n (gen) 紙 kamí; (also: newspaper) 新聞 shiñbun; (exam) 試験 shikéñ; (academic essay) 論文 roñbun, ペーパー pēpà; (also: **wallpaper**) 壁紙 kabégami
◆adj (made from paper: hat, plane etc) 紙の kamí no
◆vt (room: with wallpaper) ...に壁紙を張る ...ni kabégami wō hárù

paperback [pei'pə:rbæk] n ペーパーバック pépàbakku

paper bag n 紙袋 kamíbukùro

paper clip n クリップ kuríppù

paper hankie n ティッシュ tísshù

papers [pei'pə:rz] npl (documents) 書類 shōrùi; (also: **identity papers**) 身分証明書 mibúnshōmeishò

paperweight [pei'pə:rweit] n 文鎮 buñchin

paperwork [pei'pə:rwə:rk] n (in office: dealing with letters, reports etc) 机上の事務 kijō no jimū, ペーパーワーク pépàwāku

papier-mâché [pei'pə:rməʃei'] n 張り子 haríko

paprika [pɑ:pri:'kə] n パプリカ papúrìka

par [pɑ:r] n (equality of value) 同等 dōtō; (GOLF) 基準打数 kijúndasù, パー pā
to be on a par with (be equal with) ...と同等である ...to dōtō de arù

parable [pær'əbəl] n たとえ話 tatóebanàshi

parachute [pær'əʃut] n 落下傘 rakkásàn, パラシュート páráshūto

parade [pəreid'] *n* (public procession) パレード parêdo
♦*vt* (show off: wealth, knowledge etc) 見せびらかす misébirakasù
♦*vi* (MIL) 行進する kōshin suru

paradise [pær'ədais] *n* (REL: heaven, nirvana etc: *also fig*) 天国 têngoku, 極楽 gokúraku

paradox [pær'ədɑks] *n* (thing, statement) 逆説 gyakúsetsu

paradoxically [pærədɑk'sikli:] *adv* 逆説的に言えば gyakúsetsuteki ni iêba

paraffin [pær'əfin] (*BRIT*) *n* (*also*: **paraffin oil**) 灯油 tōyu

paragon [pær'əgɑn] *n* (of honesty, virtue etc) 模範 mohán, かがみ kagámi

paragraph [pær'əgræf] *n* 段落 dañrakù, パラグラフ parágurafu

Paraguay [pær'əgwei] *n* パラグアイ parágùai

parallel [pær'əlel] *adj* (lines, walls, streets etc) 平行の heſkō no; (*fig*: similar) 似た nitá
♦*n* (line) 平行線 heſkōsen; (surface) 平行面 heſkōmen; (GEO) 緯度線 idōsèn; (*fig*: similarity) 似た所 nitá tokoro

paralysis [pəræl'isis] *n* (MED) 麻ひ máhì

paralyze [pær'əlaiz] *vt* (MED) 麻ひさせる máhì sasérù; (*fig*: organization, production etc) 麻ひ状態にする maſhìjōtai ni suru

parameters [pəræm'itəːz] *npl* (*fig*) 限定要素 geñteiyōso

paramilitary [pærəmil'iteː ri:] *adj* (organization, operations) 準軍事的な juñgunjiteki na

paramount [pær'əmaunt] *adj*: **of paramount importance** 極めて重要な kiwámète jūyō na

paranoia [pærənɔi'ə] *n* 被害妄想 higáimōsō

paranoid [pær'ənɔid] *adj* (person, feeling) 被害妄想の higáimōsō no

parapet [pær'əpit] *n* 欄干 rañkan

paraphernalia [pærəfəːrneil'jə] *n* (gear) 道具 dōgu

paraphrase [pær'əfreiz] *vt* (poem, arti-

cle etc) やさしく言替える yasáshikù if-kaerù

paraplegic [pærəpliː'dʒik] *n* 下半身麻ひ患者 kahánshinmahi kañja

parasite [pær'əsait] *n* (insect: *also fig*: person) 寄生虫 kiséichù; (plant) 寄生植物 kiséishokùbutsu

parasol [pær'əsɔːl] *n* 日傘 higasa, パラソル parásoru

paratrooper [pær'ətruːpəːr] *n* (MIL) 落下傘兵 rakkásanhei

parcel [pɑːr'səl] *n* (package) 小包 kozútsumi
♦*vt* (object, purchases: *also*: **parcel up**) 小包にする kozútsùmi ni suru

parch [pɑːrtʃ] *vt* (land) 干上がらす hiágarasu; (crops) からからに枯らす karákara ni karasù

parched [pɑːrtʃt] *adj* (person) のどがからからの nódò ga karákara no

parchment [pɑːrtʃ'mənt] *n* (animal skin) 羊皮紙 yōhishì; (thick paper) 硫酸紙 ryūsanshì

pardon [pɑːr'dən] *n* (LAW) 赦免 shamén
♦*vt* (forgive: person, sin, error etc) 許す yurúsù

pardon me!, I beg your pardon! (I'm sorry) 済みません sumímasen, 失礼しました shitsúrèi shimashita, ごめんなさい gomén nasaì

(I beg your) pardon?, pardon me? (what did you say?) もう一度言って下さい もう ichido ittê kudásaì

parent [per'ənt] *n* (mother or father) 親 oyá; (mother) 母親 haháoya; (father) 父親 chichíoya

parental [pəren'təl] *adj* (love, control, guidance etc) 親の oyá no

parenthesis [pəren'θəsis] (*pl* **parentheses**) *n* 括弧 kákkò

parents [per'ənts] *npl* (mother and father) 両親 ryōshin

Paris [par'is] *n* パリ parî

parish [pær'iʃ] *n* (REL) 教区 kyōkù; (*BRIT*: civil) 行政教区 gyōseikyōku

Parisian [pəriː'ʒən] *adj* パリの parî no
♦*n* パリっ子 parîkko

parity [pær'itiː] *n* (equality: of pay, conditions etc) 平等 byōdō

park [pɑːrk] *n* (public) 公園 kōen
♦*vt* (AUT) 駐車させる chūsha saserù
♦*vi* (AUT) 駐車する chūsha suru

parka [pɑːrkə] *n* パーカ pāka, アノラック anórakkū

parking [pɑːrkiŋ] *n* 駐車 chūsha
「no parking」駐車禁止 chūshakinshi

parking lot (*US*) *n* 駐車場 chūshajō

parking meter *n* パーキングメーター pākingumētā

parking ticket (*fine*) 駐車違反切符 chūshaihan kippū

parlance [pɑːrləns] *n* 用語 yōgo

parliament [pɑːrləmənt] (*BRIT*) *n* (institution) 議会 gīkai

parliamentary [pɑːrləmén'tɑːriː] *adj* (business, behavior etc) 議会の gīkai no

parlor [pɑːrlər] (*BRIT* **parlour**) *n* (in house) 居間 imá, 応接間 ōsetsuma

parochial [pərouːkiːəl] (*pej*) *adj* (person, attitude) 偏狭な heñkyō na

parody [pær'ədiː] *n* (THEATER, LITERATURE, MUS) パロディー párōdī

parole [pəroul'] *n*: **on parole** (LAW) 仮釈放で karíshakuhō de

paroxysm [pær'əksizəm] *n* (of rage, jealousy, laughter) 爆発 bakúhatsu

parquet [pɑːrkeiː'] *n*: *parquet floor(ing)* 寄せ木張りの床 yoségibari nō yuká

parrot [pær'ət] *n* オウム ōmu

parry [pær'iː] *vt* (blow) かわす kawásu

parsimonious [pɑːrsəmou'niːəs] *adj* けちな kechí na

parsley [pɑːrz'liː] *n* パセリ pāseri

parsnip [pɑːrs'nip] *n* 白にんじん shironinjin, パースニップ pāsunippú

parson [pɑːr'sən] *n* (REL) 牧師 bōkushi

part [pɑːrt] *n* (section, piece) 部分 bubun; (of machine, vehicle) 部品 buhíñ; (THEATER, CINEMA etc: role) 役 yakú; (PRESS, RADIO, TV: of serial) 第...部 dai...bu; (*US*: in hair) 分け目 wakéme
♦*adv* = **partly**
♦*vt* (separate: people, objects, hair) 分ける wakérù

♦*vi* (people: leave each other) 別れる wākarerù; (crowd) 道を開ける michí wo akerù

to take part in (participate in) ...に参加する ...ni sañka suru

to take something in good part ... を怒らない ...wo okóranaì

to take someone's part (support) ...の肩を持つ ...no kátá wo mótsù

for my part 私としては watákushi to-shite wa

for the most part (usually, generally) ほとんど hotóñdo wa

part exchange *n*: *in part exchange* (*BRIT*: COMM) 下取りで shitádòri de

partial [pɑːr'ʃəl] *adj* (not complete: victory, support, solution) 部分的な bubúnteki na

to be partial to (like: person, food, drink etc) ...が大好きである ...ga daísuki de arù

participant [pɑːrtis'əpənt] *n* (in competition, debate, campaign etc) 参加者 sañkasha

participate [pɑːrtis'əpeit] *vi*: *to participate in* (competition, debate, campaign etc) ...に参加する ...ni sañka suru

participation [pɑːrtisəpei'ʃən] *n* (in competition, debate, campaign etc) 参加 sañka

participle [pɑːr'tisipəl] *n* (LING) 分詞 bûñshi

particle [pɑːr'tikəl] *n* (tiny piece: gen) 粒子 ryūshi; (: of dust) 一片 ippéñ; (of metal) 砕片 saíhen; (of food) 粒 tsûbù

particular [pɑːrtik'jələːr] *adj* (distinct from others: person, time, place etc) 特定の tokútei no, (special) 特別な tokúbetsu na; (fussy, demanding) やかましい yakámashìi

in particular 特に tókù ni

particularly [pɑːrtik'jələːliː] *adv* 特に tókù ni

particulars [pɑːrtik'jələːrz] *npl* (facts) 詳細 shōsai; (personal details) 経歴 keíreki

parting [pɑːr'tiŋ] *n* (action) 分ける事 wakérù kotó; (farewell) 別れ wakáre;

(*BRIT:* hair) 分け目 wakéme
◆*n* (words, opinions etc) 別れの wakáre no

partisan [pɑːrˈtizən] *adj* (politics, views) 党派心の tôhashìn no
◆*n* (supporter) 支援者 shíensha; (fighter) パルチザン parúchizàn

partition [pɑːrˈtiʃən] *n* (wall, screen) 間仕切り majíkiri; (POL: of country) 分割 bunkatsu

partly [pɑːrˈtliː] *adv* (to some extent) 幾分か ikúbun ka

partner [pɑːrˈtnəːr] *n* (wife, husband) 配偶者 hafgûsha; (girlfriend, boyfriend) 交際の相手 kôsai nò afte; (COMM) 共同経営者 kyôdōkeieisha; (SPORT) パートナー pâtonā; (at dance) 相手 afte

partnership [pɑːrˈtnəːrʃip] *n* (COMM) 共同経営事業 kyôdōkeieijigyô; (POL etc) 協力 kyôryoku

partridge [pɑːrˈtridʒ] *n* ウズラ uzúra

part-time [pɑːrˈtaim] *adj* (work, staff) 非常勤の hijôkin no, パートタイムの pâtotaìmu no
◆*adv* (work, study) パートタイムで pâtotaìmu de

part with *vt fus* (money, possessions) ...を手放す ...wo tebánasù

party [pɑːrˈtiː] *n* (POL) 党 tô; (celebration, social event) パーティ pâti; (group of people) 一行 ikkô, パーティ pâti; (LAW) 当事者 tôjisha; (individual) 人 hitô
◆*cpd* (POL) 党の tô no

party dress *n* パーティドレス pâtidoresu

party line *n* (TEL) 共同線 kyôdōsen

pass [pæs] *vt* (spend: time) 過ごす sugôsù; (hand over: salt, glass, newspaper etc) 渡す watásù; (go past: place) 通り過ぎる tôrisugirù; (overtake: car, person etc) 追越す oíkosù; (exam) ...に合格する ...ni gôkaku suru; (approve: law, proposal) 可決する kakétsu suru
◆*vi* (go past) 通る tôru; (in exam) 合格する gôkaku suru, パスする pásu suru
◆*n* (permit) 許可証 kyokáshò; (membership card) 会員証 kaíinshò; (in mountains) 峠 tôge; (SPORT) パス pásu;

(SCOL: *also:* **pass mark**) *to get a pass in* ...で及第する ...de kyúdai suru, ...でパスする ...de pásu suru
to pass something through something ...を...に通す ...wo ...ni tôsu
to make a pass at someone (inf) ...にモーションを掛ける ...ni môshon wo kakérù

pass away *vi* (die) 死ぬ shinú

passbook [pæsˈbuk] *n* 銀行通帳 giñkōtsūchō

pass by *vi* (go past) ...のそばを通る ...no sôba wo tôru
◆*vt* (ignore) 無視する múshi suru

passenger [pæsˈindʒəːr] *n* (in car, boat, plane etc) 乗客 jôkyaku

passer-by [pæsəːrbaiˈ] *n* 通行人 tsúkōnin

pass for *vt fus* ...で通る ...de tôru

passing [pæsˈiŋ] *adj* (fleeting: moment, glimpse, thought etc) 束の間の tsuká no ma no
in passing (incidentally) ついでに tsufjte ni

passing place *n* (AUT) 待避所 taíhijo

passion [pæˈʃən] *n* (love: for person) 情欲 jôyoku; (fig: for cars, football, politics etc) 熱狂 nekkyô, マニア mánia

passionate [pæˈʃənit] *adj* (affair, embrace, person etc) 情熱的な jônetsuteki na

passive [pæsˈiv] *adj* (person, resistance) 消極的な shôkyokuteki na; (LING) 受動態の judôtai no, 受身の ukémi no

pass on *vt* (news, object) 伝える tsutáerù; (illness) 移す utsúsu

pass out *vi* (faint) 気絶する kizétsu suru

Passover [pæsˈouvəːr] *n* 過越し祭 sugíkōshisai

passport [pæsˈpɔːrt] *n* (official document) 旅券 ryokén、パスポート pasúpòto

passport control *n* 出入国管理所 shutsúnyūkoku kańrijo

pass up *vt* 逃す nogásù

password [pæs'wə:rd] *n* (secret word, phrase) 合言葉 aíkotòba、パスワード pasúwàdo

past [pæst] *prep* (drive, walk, run: in front of) …を過ぎて wo tórisugìte; (: beyond: also in time: later than) …を過ぎて …wo sugíte

◆*adj* (previous: government, monarch etc) 過去の kákò no; (: week, month etc) この前の konó maè no、先…se中…

◆*n* (period and events prior to the present: also of person) 過去 kákò

he's past forty (older than) 彼は40才を過ぎている kárè wa yońjussaì wo sugíte irù

ten/quarter past eight 8時10分〔15分〕過ぎ hachíjì juppún〔jūgòfun〕sugí

for the past few/3 days ここ数日〔3日〕の間 konó sūjitsu(mikkà) no aída

pasta [pɑs'tə] *n* パスタ pásùta

paste [peist] *n* (wet mixture) 練り物 nérimòno; (glue) のり norí; (CULIN: fish, meat, tomato etc paste) ペースト pésùto

◆*vt* (stick: paper, label, poster etc) 張る harú

pastel [pæstel'] *adj* (color) パステルの pásùteru no

pasteurized [pæs'tʃəraizd] *adj* (milk, cream) 低温殺菌された te仕onsakkîn sáreta

pastille [pæsti:l'] *n* (sweet) ドロップ dóròppu

pastime [pæs'taim] *n* (hobby) 趣味 shúmì

pastoral [pæs'tə:rəl] *adj* (REL: duties, activities) 牧師としての bókùshi toshite no

pastry [peis'tri:] *n* (dough) 生地 kíjì; (cake) 洋菓子 yōgàshi、ケーキ kèki

pasture [pæs'tʃə:r] *n* (grassland) 牧場 bokújō

pasty [*n* pæs'ti: *adj* peis'ti:] *n* (meat and vegetable pie) ミートパイ mítòpài

◆*adj* (complexion, face) 青ざめた aóza-

metå

patch [pætʃ] *n* (with hand: dog, someone's back etc) 軽くたたく karúku tatákù

patch [pætʃ] *n* (piece of material) 継ぎ tsugí; (also: **eye patch**) 眼帯 gańtaì; (area: damp, bald, black etc) …部 ichíbù; (repair: on tire etc) 継ぎはぎ tsugíhàgi

◆*vt* (clothes) …に継ぎを当てる …ni tsugí wo ateru

to go through a bad patch 不運の時期に合う fúùn no jíkì ni áù

patch up *vt* (mend temporarily) 応急的に直す ōkyúteki ni naosù; (quarrel) …をやめて仲直りする …wo yaméte nakánaori surù

patchwork [pætʃ'wə:rk] *n* (SEWING) パッチワーク patchíwàku

patchy [pætʃ'i:] *adj* (uneven: color) むらの多い múrà no ōì; (incomplete: information, knowledge etc) 不完全な fukánzen na

pâté [pɑ:tei'] *n* パテ pátè ◇肉、魚などを香辛料とすり合せて蒸焼きにして冷ました肉、sakana nadò wo kōshińryō to surfawasete mushfyaki ni shité samáshita mono

patent [pæt'ənt] *n* (COMM) 特許 tókkyo

◆*vt* (COMM) …の特許を取る …no tókkyo wo tórù

◆*adj* (obvious) 明白な meñaku na

patent leather *n*: **patent leather shoes** エナメル靴 enámerugùtsu

paternal [pətə:r'nəl] *adj* (love, duty) 父親の chichíoya no; (grandmother etc) 父方の chichígàta no

paternity [pətə:r'niti:] *n* 父親である事 chichíoya de arù koto

path [pæθ] *n* (trail, track) 小道 kómìchi; (concrete path, gravel path etc) 道 michí; (of planet, missile) 軌道 kidō

pathetic [pəθet'ik] *adj* (pitiful: sight, cries) 哀れな áwàre na; (very bad) 哀れな程悪い áwàre na hodò warúi

pathological [pæθəlɑːdʒ'ikəl] *adj* (liar, hatred) 病的な byōteki na; (of pathology: work) 病理の byōri no

pathology [pəθɑːl'ədʒiː] *n* (medical field) 病理学 byōrigàku

pathos [peiˈθɔːs] n 悲哀 hiái

pathway [pǽθwei] n (path) 歩道 hódō

patience [péiˈʃəns] n (personal quality) 忍耐 nńtai; (BRIT: CARDS) 一人トランプ hitóritoránpu

patient [péiˈʃənt] n (MED) 患者 kañja
♦adj (person) 忍耐強い nińtaizuyoi

patio [pǽtːiːou] n テラス tērāsu

patriot [péiˈtriːət] n 愛国者 afkokushá

patriotic [peitriːaˈtik] adj (person) 愛国心の強い afkokushín no tsuyói; (song, speech etc) 愛国の afkoku no

patriotism [péiˈtriːətizəm] n 愛国心 afkokushín

patrol [pətrouˈl] n (MIL, POLICE) 巡回 juñkai, パトロール patórōru
♦vt (MIL, POLICE: city, streets etc) 巡回する juñkai suru, パトロールする patórōru suru

patrol car (POLICE) n パトカー patókā

patrolman [pətroulˈmən] (pl patrolmen: US) n (POLICE) 巡査 juñsa

patron [péiˈtrən] n (customer, client) 客 kyakú; (benefactor: of charity) 後援者 kōéñsha

patron of the arts 芸術のパトロン geíjutsu no pátóron

patronage [péiˈtrənidʒ] n (of artist, charity etc) 後援 kōen

patronize [péiˈtrənaiz] vt (pej: look down on) 尊大にあしらう soñdai nì ashíraù; (artist, writer, musician) 後援する kōen suru; (shop, club, firm) ひいきにする hifki ni surù

patron saint n (REL) 守護聖人 shugóseijìn

patter [pǽtˈəːr] n (sound: of feet) ぱたぱたという音 pátapata to iù oto; (of rain) パラパラという音 párápara to iū otò; (sales talk) 売込み口上 urîkomikōjō
♦vi (footsteps) ぱたぱたと歩く pátapata to arúkù; (rain) ぱらぱらと降る párápara to fúrù

pattern [pǽtˈəːrn] n (design) 模様 moyó; (SEWING) 型紙 katágami, パターン patán

paunch [pɔːntʃ] n 太鼓腹 taíkobara

pauper [pɔːˈpəːr] n 貧乏人 bińbōnin

pause [pɔːz] n (temporary halt) 休止 kyúshi, ポーズ pōzu
♦vi (stop temporarily) 休止する kyúshi suru; (: while speaking) 間を置く má wò okú

pave [peiv] vt (street, yard etc) 舗装する hosō suru

to pave the way for (fig) ...を可能にする ...wo kanō ni surù

pavement [peivˈmənt] n (US) 路面 romén; (BRIT) 歩道 hódō

pavilion [pəvilˈjən] n (BRIT: SPORT) 選手更衣所 señshukōíjō

paving [peivˈiŋ] n (material) 舗装材 hosōzai

paving stone n 敷石 shikíshi

paw [pɔː] n (of animal) 足 ashí

pawn [pɔːn] n (CHESS) ポーン pòn; (fig) 操り人形 ayátsuriniñgyò
♦vt 質に入れる shichí ni irerù

pawnbroker [pɔːnˈbroukəːr] n 質屋 shichíya

pawnshop [pɔːnˈʃɑːp] n 質屋 shichíya

pay [pei] n (wage, salary etc) 給料 kyúryō
♦vt (sum of money, debt, bill, wage) 払う haráù
♦vi (be profitable) 利益になる rîeki ni nárù

to pay attention (to) (...に) 注意する (...ni) chūi surù

to pay someone a visit ...を訪問する ...wo hōmon suru

to pay one's respects to someone ...にあいさつする ...ni áisatsu wo suru

payable [peiˈəbəl] adj (sum of money) 支払うべき shiháraubeki

payable to bearer (check) 持参人払いの jisánninbaraì no

pay back vt (money) 返す kaésù; (person) ...に仕返しをする ...ni shikáeshi wo suru

payday [peiˈdei] n 給料日 kyúryòbi

payee [peiː] n (of check, postal order) 受取人 ukétorinin

pay envelope (US) n 給料袋 kyúryòbukúro

pay for vt fus (purchases) ...の代金を払う ...no daikin wo haraū, (fig) 償う tsugunaū

pay in vt (money, check etc) 預け入れる azukeirerū, 入金する nyūkin suru

payment [pei'mənt] n (act) 支払い shiharai; (amount of money) 支払い金額 shiharaikingaku

a monthly payment 月賦 géppu

pay off vt (debt) 返済する heńsai suru; (person: with bribe etc) 買収する baíshū suru

♦vi (scheme, decision) 成功する sefkō suru

pay packet (BRIT) n = **pay envelope**

pay phone n 公衆電話 kōshūdeńwa

payroll [pei'roul] n 従業員名簿 jūgyōin-meibo

pay slip n 給料明細書 kyūryōmeisaisho

pay up vi 支払う shiharaū

PC [pi:si:'] n abbr = **personal computer**; (BRIT: = police constable) 巡査 juńsa

p.c. abbr = **per cent**

pea [pi:] n エンドウマメ eńdōmame

peace [pi:s] n (not war) 平和 heíwa; (calm: of place, surroundings) 静けさ shizukèsa; (: personal) 心の平和 kokórô no heíwa

peaceful [pi:s'fəl] adj (calm: place, time) 静寂な seíjaku na; (: person) 穏和なo-fiwa na

peach [pi:tʃ] n モモ momó

peacock [pi:'kɑ:k] n クジャク kujáku

peak [pi:k] n (of mountain: top) 頂上 chōjō; (of cap) つば tsubá; (fig: physical, intellectual etc) 頂点 chōten, ピーク pīku

peak hours npl ピーク時 pīku-jì

peak period n ピーク時 pīkuji

peal [pi:l] n (of bells) 鳴음 rafshō

peal of laughter 大きな笑い声 ōkina waráigoè

peanut [pi:'nʌt] n 落花生 rakkáseì, ピーナッツ pínattsu

peanut butter n ピーナッツバター pínattsubatà

pear [pe:r] n セイヨウナシ seíyōnashì

pearl [pə:rl] n 真珠 shińju, パール pāru

peasant [pez'ənt] n 百姓 hyakúshò, 農夫 nōfu

peat [pi:t] n 泥炭 deftan

pebble [peb'əl] n 小石 koíshi

peck [pek] vt (also: **peck at**: subj: bird) つつく tsutsúkù

♦n (of bird) つつく事 tsutsúkù kotò; (kiss) 軽いキス kárûi kísù

pecking order [pek'iŋ-] n (fig: hierarchy) 序列 jorétsu

peckish [pek'iʃ] (BRIT: inf) adj (hungry): *to be peckish* おなかがすいた onáka ga suíta

peculiar [pikju:l'jə:r] adj (strange: person, taste, shape etc) 変った kawátta; (belonging exclusively): *peculiar to* 独特な dokútoku na

peculiarity [pikju:li:ær'iti:] n (strange habit, characteristic) 癖 kusé; (distinctive feature: of person, place etc) 特徴 tokúchō

pedal [ped'əl] n (on bicycle, car, machine) ペダル pédàru

♦vi (on bicycle) こぐ kógù

pedantic [pədæn'tik] adj げん学的な geńgakuteki na

peddler [ped'lə:r] n (also: **drug peddler**) 麻薬の売人 mayáku no baínin

pedestal [ped'istəl] n 台座 daíza

pedestrian [pədes'tri:ən] n 歩行者 hokōshà

♦adj 歩行者の hokōshà no

pedestrian crossing (BRIT) n 横断歩道 ōdanhodō

pediatrics [pi:di:æt'riks] (BRIT **paediatrics**) n (hospital department) 小児科 shōnika; (subject) 小児科学 shōnikagaku

pedigree [ped'əgri:] n (of animal) 血統 kettō; (fig: background) 経歴 keíreki

♦cpd (animal) 血統の juńketsu no

pee [pi:] (inf) vi おしっこする o-shíkkò suru

peek [pi:k] vi のぞく nozóku

peel [pi:l] n (of orange, apple, potato) 皮 kawá

♦vt (vegetables, fruit) ...の皮をむく ...no kawá wo muku

♦vi (paint, wallpaper) はげる hagérù; (skin) むける mukérù

peep [pi:p] n (look) のぞき見 nozókimi; (sound) 鳴き声 nakígoè
♦vi (look) のぞく nozóku

peephole [pi:p'houl] n のぞき穴 nozókiàna

peep out vi (be visible) のぞく nozóku

peer [pi:r] vi: **to peer at** ...をじっと見る ...wo jíttò mírù
♦n (noble) 貴族 kízoku; (equal) 同等の人 dôtō nò hitó; (contemporary) 同輩 dôhai

peerage [pi'ridʒ] n (rank) 貴族の地位 kízoku no chíi

peeved [pi:vd] adj (annoyed) 怒った okóttà

peevish [pi'viʃ] adj (bad-tempered) 機嫌の悪い kigén nò warúi

peg [peg] n (hook, knob: for coat etc) フック fúkkù; (BRIT: also: clothes peg) 洗濯ばさみ seńtakubasàmi

pejorative [pidʒɔːr'ativ] adj (word, expression) 軽べつ的な keíbetsuteki na

Peking [pi:kiŋ'] n 北京 pékìn

Peking(e)ese [pi:kəni:z'] n (dog) ペキニーズ pekínīzu

pelican [pel'ikən] n (ZOOL) ペリカン períkàn

pelican crossing (BRIT) n (AUT) 押しボタン式信号 oshíbotanshìki shiñgō

pellet [pel'it] n (of paper, mud etc) 丸めた球 marúmeta tamá; (also: **shotgun pellet**) 散弾銃の弾 sańdanjū no tamá

pelt [pelt] vt: **to pelt someone with something** ...に...を浴びせ掛ける ...ni ...wo abísekakerù
♦vi (rain) 激しく降る hagéshikù fúrù; (inf: run) 駆ける kakérù
♦n (animal skin) 毛皮 kegáwa

pelvis [pel'vis] n 骨盤 kotsúbàn

pen [pen] n (for writing: fountain pen, ballpoint pen) ペン péñ; (: felt-tip pen etc) サインペン saínpen; (enclosure: for sheep, pigs etc) 囲い sakói

penal [pi:'nəl] adj (colony, institution) 刑罰の kefbatsu no; (system, code, reform) 刑法の kefhō no

penalize [pi:'nəlaiz] vt (punish) 罰する bassúrù; (: SPORT) ...にペナルティーを科する ...ni peńarutī wo kasúrù

penalty [pen'əlti:] n (punishment) 刑罰 bátsù; (fine) 罰金 bakkín; (SPORT) ペナルティー peńarutī

penalty (kick) n (RUGBY, SOCCER) ペナルティーキック peńarutī kikkù

penance [pen'əns] n 償い tsugúnai

pence [pens] pl of **penny**

pencil [pen'səl] n (for writing, drawing) 鉛筆 eñpìtsu

pencil case n 筆入れ fudére

pencil sharpener n 鉛筆削り eńpitsu-kezùri, シャープナー shápunà

pendant [pen'dənt] n ペンダント péndànto

pending [pen'diŋ] prep ...を待つ間 ...wo mátsù aída
♦adj (business) 未決の mikétsu no; (law-suit) 審理中の shińrichū no; (exam) 差迫った sashísemattà

pendulum [pen'dʒələm] n (of clock) 振子 furśko

penetrate [pen'itreit] vt (subj: person: enemy territory) ...に侵入する ...ni shińnyū suru; (forest etc) ...に入り込む ...ni hafrikomù; (: water etc) 染込む shimíkomù; (: light) 通る tôru

penetrating [pen'itreitiŋ] adj (sound, glance, mind, observation) 鋭い surúdoi

penetration [penitrei'ʃən] n (action) 入り込む事 hafrikomù kotó

penfriend [pen'frend] (BRIT) n = **pen pal**

penguin [pen'gwin] n ペンギン péñgin

penicillin [penisil'in] n ペニシリン peníshirin

peninsula [pənin'sələ] n 半島 hańtō

penis [pi:'nis] n 陰茎 ińkei, ペニス pénìs

penitent [pen'itənt] adj (person: very sorry) 後悔している kôkai shite irú

penitentiary [peniten'tʃəːri:] (US) n 刑務所 kefmushò

pen name n ペンネーム peńnèmu

penniless [pen'i:lis] adj (person) 一文無しの ichímoñnashi no

penny [pen'i:] (pl **pennies** or BRIT **pence**) n (US) ペニ péni, セント séñto;

(BRIT: after 1971: = one hundredth of a pound) ペニ pénī

pen pal n ペンパル pénparu、ペンフレンド penfureńdo

pension [pen'ʃən] n (state benefit) 年金 neńkin; (company pension etc) 恩給 ońkyū

pensioner [pen'ʃənəːr] n (BRIT) n (old-age pensioner) 年金で生活する老人 neńkin de séfkatsu surù rōjìn, 年金暮らしの人 neńkingurāshi no hitó

pension fund n 年金基金 neńkinkikìn

pensive [pen'siv] adj (person, expression etc) 考え込んだ kańgaekoñda

pentagon [pen'təgɑn] n: the Pentagon (US: POL) 国防総省 kokúbōsōshò、ペンタゴン peńtágon

Pentecost [pen'təkɔst] n 聖霊降臨祭 seíreikōrìnsai

penthouse [pent'haus] n (flat) 屋上階 okújōkai

pent-up [pent'ʌp'] adj (feelings) たまった tamátta

penultimate [pinʌl'təmit] adj 最後から2番目の sáîgo kara nibánme no

people [pi:'pəl] npl (persons) 人々 hitóbìto; (inhabitants) 住民 jūmin; (citizens) 市民 shimín; (POL): the people 国民 kokúmin

♦n (nation) 国民 kokúmin; (race) 民族 mínzoku

several people came 数人来ました súnin kimashìta

people say that ... だと言われている ...da to iwárete irù、...だそうだ ...da sō da

pep [pep] (inf) n (energy, vigor) 元気 geńki

pepper [pep'əːr] n (spice) こしょう koshō; (hot pepper) トウガラシ tōgarashi; (sweet pepper) ピーマン pìman

♦vt (fig): to pepper with ... を振掛ける ...wo furíkakerù

peppermint [pep'əːrmint] n (sweet) ハッカあめ hakkáame

peptalk [pep'tɔk] (inf) n (encouraging talk) 激励演説 gekíreieñzetsù

pep up vt (enliven) 活気付ける kakkízukerù

per [pəːr] prep (of amounts, prices etc: for each) ...につき ...ni tsukí

per day/person 1日(1人)につき... ichínichi(hitórì)ni tsukí

per annum 1年につき... ichínèn ni tsukí

per capita [-kæp'itə] adj (income) 一人当たりの hitórí atarí no

♦adv 一人当たり hitórí atarí

perceive [pəːrsiːv'] vt (sound) 聞く kikù; (light) 見る mirù; (difference) 認識する niñshiki suru; (notice) ...に気が付く ...ni ki gá tsukù; (realize, understand) 分かる wakárù

per cent n パーセント páseńto

percentage [pəːrsen'tidʒ] n (amount) 割合 waríai、率 rítsù

perception [pəːrsep'ʃən] n (insight) 洞察力 dōsatsuryòku; (opinion, understanding) 理解 rikái; (faculty) 知覚 chikáku

perceptive [pəːrsep'tiv] adj (person) 洞察力のある dōsatsuryòku no arù、鋭敏な efbìn na; (analysis, assessment) 鋭い surúdoī

perch [pəːrtʃ] n (for bird) 止り木 tomárigì; (fish) パーチ páchi〈スズキに似た淡水魚 suzúki ni nità tańsuigyò

♦vi: to perch (on) (bird) ...に止る ...ni tómarù; (person) ...に腰掛ける ...ni koshíkakerù

percolator [pəːr'kəleitəːr] n (also: coffee percolator) パーコレーター pākorētā

percussion [pəːrkʌʃ'ən] n 打楽器 dagákkì

♦adj (section) 総称 sōshō

peremptory [pəːremp'təːri] (pej) adj (person) 横柄な ōhei na; (order, instruction) 断固たる dańkotarù

perennial [pəren'iːəl] adj (flower, plant) 多年生の tanéñsei no; (fig: problem, feature etc) ありがちな arígachi na

perfect [adj, n pəːr'fikt vb pəːrfekt'] adj (without fault: person, weather, behavior etc) 完璧な kańpeki na; (utter: nonsense, stranger etc) 全くの mattáku no

♦n (also: perfect tense) 完了形 kańryōkei

♦*vt* (technique) 仕上げる shiágerù

perfection [pərfɛkˈʃən] *n* (faultlessness) 完璧さ kańpekisa

perfectionist [pərfɛkˈʃənist] *n* 完璧主義者 kańpekishugìshà

perfectly [pəːrˈfiktli] *adv* (emphatic) 全く mattàku; (faultlessly: function, do etc) 完璧に kańpeki ni; (completely: understand etc) 完全に kańzen ni

perforate [pəːrˈfəreit] *vt* ...に穴を開ける ...ni anà wo akérù

perforations [pəːrfəreiˈʃənz] *npl* (series of small holes) ミシン目 mishíñme

perform [pərfɔːrm'] *vt* (carry out: task, operation, ceremony etc) 行う okónaù, する surú; (piece of music) 演奏する eñsō suru; (play etc) 上演する jōen suru
♦*vi* (well, badly) する surú, やる yarú

performance [pərfɔːrˈməns] *n* (of actor) 演技 eñgi; (of dancer) 踊り odóri; (of musician) 演奏 eñsō; (of singer) 歌い方 utáikata; (of play, show) 上演 jōen; (of car, engine) 性能 seínō; (of athlete, company, economy) 成績 seíseki

performer [pərfɔːrˈmər] *n* (actor, dancer, singer etc) 芸能人 geínōjìn

perfume [pərˈfjuːm'] *n* (cologne, toilet water, essence) 香水 kōsui; (pleasant smell: of flowers etc) 香り kaórì

perfunctory [pərfʌŋkˈtəːri:] *adj* (kiss, remark etc) いい加減な ifkagen na

perhaps [pərhæpsˈ] *adv* (maybe) たぶん ...だろう ...daròう

peril [per'əl] *n* (great danger) 危険 kikén

perimeter [pərimˈitəːr] *n* 周辺 shūhen

period [pi:r'i:əd] *n* (length of time) 期間 kikàn; (SCOL) 時限 jigén; (full stop) 終止符 shūshìfu, ピリオド pírìodo; (MED) 月経 gekkéi, メンス méñsu, 生理 seíri
♦*adj* (costume, furniture) 時代の jidái no

periodic(al) [pi:ri:ɑːdˈik(əl)] *adj* (event, occurrence) 周期的な shūkiteki na, 定期的な tefkiteki na

periodical [pi:ri:ɑːdˈikəl] *n* (magazine) 雑誌 zasshí

periodically [pi:ri:ɑːdˈikli:] *adv* 定期的に tefkiteki ni

peripheral [pərifˈəːrəl] *adj* 二次的な nijí-

teki na; (on the edge: also COMPUT) 周辺の shūhen no

♦*n* (COMPUT) 周辺機器 shūhenkikì

periphery [pərifˈəːri:] *n* (edge) 周辺 shūhen

periscope [per'iskoup] *n* 潜望鏡 señbōkyō

perish [per'iʃ] *vi* (die) 死ぬ shinú; (die out) 滅びる horóbirù; (rubber, leather etc) 腐る kusárù

perishable [per'iʃəbəl] *adj* (food) いたみやすい itámiyasuì

perjury [pəːrˈdʒəːri:] *n* (LAW) 偽証 gishō

perk [pəːrk] (*inf*) *n* (extra) 役得 yakútoku

perk up *vi* (cheer up) 元気を出す geńki wo dásù

perky [pəːrˈki:] *adj* (cheerful) 朗らかな hogáraka na

perm [pəːrm] *n* (for hair) パーマ pāma

permanent [pəːrˈmənənt] *adj* 永久的な efkyūteki na

permeate [pəːrˈmi:eit] *vi* (pass through) 浸透する shiñtō suru; (*fig*: spread) 広まる hirógarù
♦*vt* (subj: liquid) ...に染込む ...ni shimíkomù; (: idea) ...に広まる ...ni hirómarù

permissible [pərmisˈəbəl] *adj* (action, behavior) 許される yurúsarerù

permission [pərmiʃˈən] *n* (consent, authorization) 許可 kyóka

permissive [pərmisˈiv] *adj* (person, behavior, society) 甘い amáì

permit [*n* pəːrˈmit *vb* pərmitˈ] *n* (official authorization) 許可証 kyokáshō
♦*vt* (allow) 許可する kyóka suru; (make possible) 可能にする kanō ni surú

permutation [pəːrmjəteiˈʃən] *n* 置換える kikáe

pernicious [pərniʃˈəs] *adj* (very harmful: attitude, influence etc) 有害な yúgai na; (MED) 悪性の akúsei no

perpendicular [pəːrpəndikˈjələːr] *adj* (line, surface) 垂直の suíchoku no; (cliff, slope) 険しい kewáshiì

perpetrate [pəːrˈpitreit] *vt* (commit: crime) 犯す okásù

perpetual [pərpetʃˈuːəl] *adj* (constant:

motion, darkness) 永久の　eikyū no; (: noise, questions) 年がら年中の nefigaranefijū no

perpetuate [pərrpetʃ'ueit] vt (situation, custom, belief etc) 永続きさせる eízoku saserū

perplex [pərrpleks'] vt (person) まごつかせる magótsukaserū

persecute [pə:'səkju:t] vt (harass, oppress: minorities etc) 迫害する hakúgai suru

persecution [pə:rsəkju:'ʃən] n (of minorities etc) 迫害 hakúgai

perseverance [pə:rsəvi:r'əns] n 根気 kóñki

persevere [pə:rsəvi:r'] vi 辛抱強く続ける shifibōzuyokū tsuzukérū

Persian [pə:r'ʒən] adj ペルシアの perúshiawan
♦n ペルシア人 perúshiajīn
the (Persian) Gulf ペルシア湾 perúshiawan

persist [pə:rsist'] vi: *to persist (in doing something)* (…を) 続ける (…wo shi)tsuzukérū

persistence [pə:rsis'təns] n (determination) 根気強さ koñkizuyōsa

persistent [pə:rsis'tənt] adj (noise, smell, cough etc) いつまでも続く ítsumademo tsuzukú; (person: determined) 根気強い koñkizuyoī

person [pə:r'sən] n 人 hitó
in person (appear, sing, recite etc) 本人が hoñnin ga

personal [pə:r'sənəl] adj (belongings, phone etc) 個人の kójin no; (opinion, life, habits etc) 個人的な kojínteki na; (in person: visit) 本人自身の hoñninjishin no

personal assistant n 秘書 hishó

personal call n (TEL) 私用の電話 shiyō no deñwa

personal column n 私信欄 shishínran

personal computer n パーソナルコンピュータ pásonarukoñpyūta, パソコン pasókoñ

personality [pə:rsənæl'iti:] n (character) 人格 jiñkaku; (famous person) 有名人 yūmeijin

personally [pə:r'sənəli:] adv (for my own part) 個人的には kojínteki ni wà; (in person) 本人が hoñnin ga
to take something personally …を個人攻撃と受止める …wo kojínkōgeki to ukétomerū

personal organizer n 予定帳 yotéichō

personify [pə:rsɑn'əfai] vt (evil) …の権化である …no goñge de árū; (good) …の化身である …no késhin de árū

personnel [pə:rsənel'] n (staff) 職員 shokúin 〈総称 sōshō

perspective [pə:rspek'tiv] n (ARCHIT, ART) 遠近法 eñkinhō; (way of thinking) 見方 mikáta
to get something into perspective (fig) 事情をある …を見る jijō wò kañgaetè …wo mírū

Perspex [pə:rs'peks] ® n アクリル akúriru

perspiration [pə:rspərei'ʃən] n 汗 ásè

persuade [pə:rsweid'] vt: *to persuade someone to do something* …する様に …を説き伏せる …surú yō ni …wo tokífusserū

persuasion [pə:rswei'ʒən] n (act) 説得 settóku; (creed) 信条 shiñjō

persuasive [pə:rswei'siv] adj (person, argument) 説得力のある settókuryoku no árū

pertaining [pə:rtein'iŋ]: *pertaining to* prep (relating to) …に関する …ni kañ suru

pertinent [pə:r'tənənt] adj (answer, remark) 適切な tekísetsu na

perturb [pə:rtə:rb'] vt (person) 不安にする fuán ni surū

Peru [pə:ru:'] n ペルー pérū

peruse [pə:ru:z'] vt (newspaper, documents etc) …に目を通す …ni mé wo tōsū

Peruvian [pə:ru:'vi:ən] adj ペルーの perú no
♦n ペルー人 perújin

pervade [pə:rveid'] vt (subj: smell, feeling) …に充満する …ni jūman suru

perverse [pə:rvə:rs'] adj (contrary: behavior) 天のじゃくの amá no jāku no

perversion [pə:rvə:r'ʒən] n (sexual) 変態

hentai; (of truth) 曲解 kyokkai; (of justice) 悪用 akúyō

pervert [n pɑːrˈvəːrt vb pəːrˈvəːrt] n (sexual pervert) 変態 heñtai

♦vt (person, mind) 堕落させる daˈraku saseru; (truth, someone's words) 曲解する kyokkái suru

pessimism [pesˈəmizəm] n 悲観主義 hikáñshùgi, ペシミズム peshímizùmu

pessimist [pesˈəmist] n 悲観主義者 hikánshugisha, ペシミスト peshímisùto

pessimistic [pesəmisˈtik] adj (person) 悲観的な hikáñteki na, ペシミスティックな peshímisutìkkù na

pest [pest] n (insect) 害虫 gaíchū; (fig: nuisance) うるさいやつ urúsai yatsù

pester [pesˈtəːr] vt (bother) 悩ませる naˈyámaseru

pesticide [pesˈtisaid] n 殺虫剤 satchúzài

pet [pet] n (domestic animal) 愛がん動物 aígandòbutsu, ペット péttò

♦cpd (theory, hate etc) 十八番の ohákonoの

♦vt (stroke: person, animal) 愛する aíbu suru

♦vi (inf: sexually) ペッティングする pettíñgu suru

teacher's pet (favorite) 先生のお気に入り señsei nò o-kí ni irì

petal [petˈəl] n 花びら hanábira

peter [piːˈtəːr]: *peter out* vi (road, stream etc) だんだんなくなる dañdañ nakúnarù; (conversation, meeting) しりすぼまりに終る shirísubomarì ni owárù

petite [pətiːtˈ] adj (referring to woman: small) 小柄な kogára na

petition [pətiʃˈən] n (signed document) 陳情書 chiñjòshò; (LAW) 請願 seígan

petrified [petˈrəfaid] adj (fig: terrified) 恐怖に駆られた kyófu ni karáreta

petrol [petˈrəl] (BRIT) n (fuel) ガソリン gasórin

two/four-star petrol レギュラー（ハイオク）ガソリン regyúra(haíoku)gasórin

petrol can n ガソリン缶 gasóriñkan

petroleum [pətrouˈliːəm] n 石油 sekíyu

petrol pump (BRIT) n (in garage) ガソリンポンプ gasóriñpòñpu

petrol station (BRIT) n ガソリンスタンド gasórinsutàñdo

petrol tank (BRIT) n ガソリンタンク gasórintàñku

petticoat [petˈiːkout] n (underskirt) ペチコート péchikòto

petty [petˈiː] adj (small, unimportant) ささいな sásai na; (small-minded) 狭量な kyóryō na

petty cash n (in office) 小口現金 kogúchigeñkin

petty officer n (in navy) 下士官 kashíkan

petulant [petʃˈələnt] adj せっかちな sekkáchi na

pew [pjuː] n (in church) 長いす nagáisu

pewter [pjuːˈtəːr] n 白ろう shíróme

phallic [fælˈik] adj (object, symbol) 陰茎状の iñkeíjō no

phantom [fænˈtəm] n (ghost) お化け o-báke

pharmaceutical [fɑːrməsuːˈtikəl] adj 製薬の seíyaku no

pharmacist [fɑːrˈməsist] n 薬剤師 yakúzaishì

pharmacy [fɑːrˈməsiː] n 薬局 yakkyókù

phase [feiz] n (stage) 段階 dañkai

♦vt: *to phase something in/out* ...を段階的に取入れる（なくす）...wo dañkaiteki ni toríreru (nakúsu)

Ph.D. [piːˈeitʃˈdiːˈ] abbr = Doctor of Philosophy

pheasant [fezˈənt] n キジ kijî

phenomena [finɑːmˈənə] npl of phenomenon

phenomenal [finɑːmˈənəl] adj 驚異的な kyóíteki na

phenomenon [finɑːmˈənɑːn] (pl phenomena) n 現象 geñshō

philanthropist [filænˈθrəpist] n 慈善家 jizéñka

Philippines [filˈipiːnz] npl: *the Philippines* フィリピン firípin

philosopher [filɑsˈəfəːr] n (scholar) 哲学者 tetsúgakushà

philosophical [filəsɑˈfikəl] adj (ideas, conversation etc) 哲学的な tetsúgakuteki na; (fig: calm, resigned) 冷静な reísei na

philosophy [fɪlɑsˈəfiː] n (SCOL) 哲学 tetsūgaku; (set of ideas: of philosopher) ...の哲学 ...no tetsūgaku; (theory: of any person) 考え方 kañgaekata, 思想 shisō

phlegm [flem] n (substance) たん tan

phlegmatic [flegmætˈik] adj (person) のろまな noróma na

phobia [foubˈiːə] n (irrational fear: of insects, flying, water etc) 恐怖症 kyōfushō

phone [foun] n (system) 電話 deñwa; (apparatus) 電話器 deñwakì
♦vt ...に電話を掛ける ...ni deñwa wò kakérù
to be on the phone (BRIT: possess a phone) 電話を持っている deñwa wò motté irù; (: be calling) 電話中である deñwachū de arù

phone back vt ...に電話を掛け直す ...ni deñwa wò kakénaosù
♦vi 電話を掛け直す deñwa wò kakénaosù

phone book n (directory) 電話帳 deñwachō

phone booth n 電話ボックス deñwabokkùsu

phone box (BRIT) n 電話ボックス deñwabokkùsu

phone call n 電話 deñwa

phone-in [founˈin] (BRIT) n (RADIO, TV) 視聴者が電話で参加する番組 shichōsha ga deñwa de sañka surù bañgumi

phonetics [fənetˈiks] n 音声学 oñseigaku

phone up vt ...に電話を掛ける ...ni deñwa wò kakérù
♦vi 電話を掛ける deñwa wò kakérù

phoney [founˈiː] adj (false: address) うその ùsó no; (: accent) 偽の nisé no; (person) 信用できない shiñ-yō dekinai

phonograph [founˈəgræf] (US) n 蓄音機 chikúonkì

phosphorus [fɑsˈfərəs] n りん ríñ

photo [foutˈou] n (photograph) 写真 shashín

photocopier [foutˈəkɑːpiːəːr] n (machine)

写真複写機 shashínfukushakì, コピー機 kopíkì

photocopy [foutˈəkɑːpiː] n コピー kópì
♦vt (picture, document etc) ...のコピーを取る ...no kópì wo tórù

photogenic [foutədʒenˈik] adj (person) 写真写りの良い shashín-utsurì no yôi

photograph [foutˈəgræf] n 写真 shashín
♦vt (person, object, place etc) 撮影する satsúei suru

photographer [fətɑgˈrəfəːr] n カメラマン kameramàn

photographic [foutəgræfˈik] adj (equipment etc) 写真の shashín no

photography [fətɑgˈrəfiː] n (art, subject) 写真撮影 shashínsatsùei

phrase [freiz] n (group of words, expression) 言い方 iíkatà; (LING) 句 kú
♦vt (express) 表現する hyōgen suru

phrase book n (foreign language aid) 表現集 hyōgenshū

physical [fizˈikəl] adj (of the body: needs, punishment, exercise etc) 肉体的の nikútaitekì na; (geography, properties) 物理的な butsúriteki na; (world, universe, object) 自然の shizén no; (sciences) 物理学の butsúrigaku no

physical education n 体育 taíiku

physically [fizˈikliː] adv (fit, attractive) 肉体的に nikútaiteki ni

physician [fiziˈən] n (doctor) 医者 ishá

physicist [fizˈəsist] n 物理学者 butsúrigakushà

physics [fizˈiks] n 物理学 butsúrigaku

physiology [fiziːɑlˈədʒiː] n (science) 生理学 seírigaku; (functioning: of animal, plant) 生理 seíri

physiotherapy [fiziːouθeːrˈəpiː] n (MED) 物理療法 butsúriryōhō

physique [fizìːk] n (build: of person) 体格 taíkaku

pianist [piːˈænist] n (MUS) ピアニスト piánisùto

piano [piːænˈou] n (MUS) ピアノ piáno

piccolo [pikˈəlou] n (MUS) ピッコロ pikkóro

pick [pik] n (tool: also: pick-axe) つるはし tsurúhàshi

♦*vt* (select) 選ぶ erábù; (gather: fruit, flowers) 摘む tsúmù; (remove, take) 取る tórù; (lock) こじ開ける kojfakerù

take your pick (choose) 選ぶ erábù

the pick of (best) ...からえり抜かれた物 ...kara erfnukareta mònò

to pick one's nose/teeth 鼻[歯]をほじる haná[há]wò hojírù

to pick a quarrel (with someone) (...に) けんかを売る (...ni) kénka wò urú

pick at *vt fus* (food) ちびちび食べる chíbìchibi tabérù

picket [pik'it] *n* (in strike) ピケ piké

♦*vt* (factory, workplace etc) ...にピケを張る ...ni piké wò hárù

pickle [pik'əl] *n* (*also*: **pickles**: as condiment) ピクルス pfkurusu; (*fig*: mess) 苦境 kukyō

♦*vt* (in vinegar) 酢漬けにする suzúke ni suru; (: in salt water) 塩漬けにする shfozuke ni surù

pick on *vt fus* (person: criticize) 非難する hínàn suru; (: treat badly) いじめる ijímerù

pick out *vt* (distinguish) 識別する shikfbetsu suru; (choose from a group) 選び出す erábìdasù, ピックアップする pikkúappù suru

pickpocket [pik'pɑːkit] *n* すり súrì

pick up *vi* (improve: health, economy, trade) 良くなる yóku naru

♦*vt* (object: from floor) 拾う hiróu; (POLICE: arrest) 逮捕する tahò suru; (collect: person, parcel etc) 引取る hikítorù; (AUT: passenger) 乗せる noséru; (person: for sexual encounter) 引っ掛ける hikkákerù; (learn: language, skill etc) 覚える obóerù; (RADIO) 受信する jushfn suru

to pick up speed 加速する kasóku suru

to pick oneself up (after falling etc) 起き上がる okfagarù

pickup [pik'ʌp] *n* (small truck) ピックアップ pikkúappù

picnic [pik'nik] *n* (outdoor meal) ピクニック pikunikku

picture [pik'tʃər] *n* (painting, drawing, print) 絵 é; (photograph) 写真 shashín;

(TV) 画像 gazō; (film) 映画 éfga; (*fig*: description) 描写 byōsha; (: situation) 事態 jítai

picture book *n* 絵本 ehőn

pictures [pik'tʃərz] (*BRIT*) *npl*: **the pictures** (cinema) 映画 éfga

picturesque [piktʃəresk'] *adj* (place, building) 風情のある fúzèi no árù

pie [pai] *n* (CULIN: vegetable, meat, fruit) パイ paí

piece [piːs] *n* (bit or part of larger thing) かけら kákèra, (portion: of cake, chocolate, bread etc) 一切れ hitókìre; (length: of string, ribbon) 一本 íppòn; (item): **a piece of clothing/furniture/advice** 1つ hitótsù

to piece together (information) 総合する sōgō suru; (parts of a whole) 組合せる tsugfawaserù

to take to pieces (dismantle) 分解する bufkai suru

piecemeal [piːs'miːl] *adv* (irregularly) 少しずつ sukóshizutsù

piecework [piːs'wəːrk] *n* 出来高払いの仕事 dekfdakabarài no shigőto

pie chart *n* 円形グラフ efikeiguráfu

pier [piːr] *n* 桟橋 safibashi

pierce [piːrs] *vt* (puncture: surface, material, skin etc) 貫通する kaftsū suru

piercing [piːr'siŋ] *adj* (*fig*: cry) 甲高い kaftdakaî; (: eyes, stare) 鋭い surúdoì; (wind) 刺す様な sásù yō na

piety [pai'əti:] *n* (REL) 信心 shifjìn

pig [pig] *n* (ZOOL) ブタ butá; (*pej*: unkind person) 畜生 chikúshò; (: greedy person) 欲張り yokúbarì

pigeon [pidʒ'ən] *n* (bird) ハト hátò

pigeonhole [pidʒ'ənhoul] *n* (for letters, messages) 小仕切り kojfkiri

piggy bank [pig'iː-] *n* (money box) 貯金箱 chokfnbako

pigheaded [pig'hedid'] (*pej*) *adj* (stubborn) 頑固な gafiko na

piglet [pig'lit] *n* 子ブタ kobúta

pigment [pig'mənt] *n* 色素 shfkìso

pigskin [pig'skin] *n* ブタのなめし革 butá no naméshigawa

pigsty [pig'stai] *n* (on farm) ブタ小屋 butágoya

pigtail [pig'teil] *n* (plait) お下げ o-ságe

pike [paik] *n* (fish) カワカマス kawákamàsu, パイク páiku

pilchard [pil'tʃərd] *n* (fish) イワシ iwáshi

pile [pail] *n* (heap, stack) 山 yamá; (of carpet, cloth) 毛足 keáshi, パイル páiru
♦*vt* (*also*: **pile up**: objects) 積上げる tsumíagerù
♦*vi* (*also*: **pile up**: objects) 積重なる tsumíkasanarù; (problems, work) たまる tamárù

pile into *vt fus* (car) ...に乗り込む ...ni noríkomù

piles [pailz] *npl* (MED) じ pji

pile-up [pail'ʌp] *n* (AUT) 衝突事故 shótotsujìko

pilfering [pil'fərŋ] *n* (petty thieving) くすねる事 kusúnerù kotó

pilgrim [pil'grim] *n* (REL) 巡礼者 junréisha

pilgrimage [pil'grəmidʒ] *n* (REL) 巡礼 junrei

pill [pil] *n* (MED: tablet) 錠剤 jōzai
the pill (contraceptive pill) 経口避妊薬 kefkóhinìñ-yaku, ピル píru

pillage [pil'idʒ] *vt* (loot: house, town etc) 略奪する ryakúdatsu suru

pillar [pil'ər] *n* (ARCHIT) 柱 hashíra

pillar box [BRIT] *n* (MAIL) ポスト pósuto

pillion [pil'jən] *n*: *to ride pillion* (on motorcycle) 後ろに相乗りする ushíro ni aínori suru

pillory [pil'əːri] *vt* (criticize strongly) 非難する hínan suru

pillow [pil'ou] *n* (cushion: for head) まくら mákūra

pillowcase [pil'oukeis] *n* (cover: for pillow) 枕カバー makúrakabà, ピロケース pirókèsu

pilot [pai'lət] *n* (AVIAT) 操縦士 sōjūshi, パイロット páirotto
♦*cpd* (scheme, study etc) 試験的な shikén-teki na
♦*vt* (aircraft) 操縦する sōjū suru

pilot light *n* (on cooker, boiler, fire) 口火 kuchíbi

pimp [pimp] *n* ポン引き poñbiki, ひも himó

pimple [pim'pəl] *n* にきび nfkíbi

pin [pin] *n* (metal: for attaching, fastening) ピン píñ
♦*vt* (fasten with pin) ピンで止める píñ de tomérù

pins and needles (in arms, legs etc) しびれが刺す shibíre gà kirérù kotó

to pin someone down (*fig*) ...に約束させる ...ni yakúsoku saserù, ...に言質を刺す ...ni kugí wò sásù

to pin something on someone (*fig*) ...に ...のぬれぎぬを着せる ...ni ...no nuréginù wo kiserù

pinafore [pin'əfɔːr] *n* (*also*: **pinafore dress**) エプロンドレス epúrondorèsu

pinball [pin'bɔːl] *n* (game) スマートボール sumátobòru; (machine) スマートボール機 sumátobòruki

pincers [pin'sərz] *npl* (TECH) やっとこ yattóko, ペンチ péñchi; (of crab, lobster etc) はさみ hasámi

pinch [pintʃ] *n* (small amount: of salt etc) 一つまみ hitótsumàmi
♦*vt* (person: with finger and thumb) つねる tsunérù; (*inf*: steal) くすねる kusúnerù

at a pinch 緊急の場合 kíñkyū nò baái

pincushion [pin'kuʃən] *n* (SEWING) 針刺し harísashì

pine [pain] *n* (*also*: **pine tree**) マツ mátsù; (wood) マツ材 matsúzài
♦*vi*: *to pine for* (person, place) 思い焦がれる omóikogarerù

pine away *vi* (gradually die) 衰弱して死ぬ suíjaku shite shinú

pineapple [pain'æpəl] *n* (fruit) パイナップル paínappùru

ping [piŋ] *n* (noise) ちゅーんという音 pyūn to iú otò

ping-pong [piŋ'pɔːŋ] ® *n* (sport) 卓球 takkyū, ピンポン píñpon

pink [piŋk] *adj* ピンク色の piñkuiro no
♦*n* (color) ピンク色 piñkuiro; (BOT) ナデシコ nadéshìko

pinnacle [pín'əkəl] n (of building, mountain) 天辺 teppén; (fig) 頂点 chóteñ

pinpoint [pín'pɔint] vt (discover) 発見する hakkén suru; (explain) 説明する setsúmei suru; (position of something) 正確に示す sefkaku ni shimésu

pint [paint] n (US: = 473 cc; BRIT: = 568 cc) パイント paíñto

a pint of beer, (BRIT: inf) a pint ビールパイント bíru ichípaíñto

pin-up [pín'ʌp] n (picture) ピンナップ写真(絵) píñnappushashíñ(e)

pioneer [paiəni:r'] n (initiator: of scheme, science, method) 先駆者 sefkushà, パイオニア paíonìa; (early settler) 開拓者 kaftakushà

pious [pái'əs] adj (person) 信心深い shíñjiñbukaì

pip [pip] n (seed of fruit) 種 tané; (BRIT: time signal on radio) 時報 jihó

pipe [paip] n (gen, also for smoking) パイプ páipu; (also: water pipe) 水道管 suídōkan; (also: gas pipe) ガス管 gasúkan

♦vt (water, gas, oil) パイプで運ぶ páipu de hakóbu

pipes [paips] npl (also: bagpipes) バグパイプ bagúpaìpu

pipe cleaner n パイプクリーナー paípukurìnā

pipe down (inf) vi (be quiet) 黙る damárù

pipe dream n (hope, plan) 夢想 musó

pipeline [paip'lain] n (for oil, gas) パイプライン paípuraìn

piper [pai'pər] n (bagpipe player) バグパイプ奏者 bagúpaìpu sòsha

piping [pai'piŋ] adv: piping hot (water, food, coffee) うんと熱い úñto atsúì

piquant [pi:'kɑnt] adj (food: spicy) ぴりっとした piríttò shitá; (fig: interesting, exciting) 興味深い kyómibukaì

pique [pi:k] n 立腹 rippúkù

pirate [pai'rit] n (sailor) 海賊 kafzoku

♦vt (book, video tape, cassette etc) ...の海賊版を作る ...no kafzokubañ wo tsukúrù

pirate radio (BRIT) n 海賊放送 kafzokuhōsō

pirouette [piruɛt'] n つま先旋回 tsumásakiseñkai

Pisces [pai'si:z] n (ASTROLOGY) 魚座 uóza

piss [pis] (inf!) vi (urinate) おしっこする oshíkko suru

pissed [pist] (inf!) adj (US) 怒った okótta; (BRIT: drunk) 酔っ払った yoppárattà

pistol [pís'təl] n けん銃 keñjū, ピストル písùtoru

piston [pís'tən] n ピストン pfsùton

pit [pit] n (hole in ground) 穴 aná; (in surface of something) くぼみ kubómi; (also: coal pit) 炭坑 tañkō; (quarry) 採石場 saísekijō

♦vt: to pit one's wits against someone ...と知恵比べをする ...to chiékurabe wo suru

♦n (fall forwards) つんのめる tsunńomerù

pitch [pits] n (BRIT: SPORT: ground) グラウンド guráuñdo; (MUS) 調子 chóshi, ピッチ pítchi; (fig: level, degree) 度合 dóai; (tar) ピッチ pítchi

♦vt (throw) 投げる nagérù

♦vt (fall forwards) つんのめる tsunńomerù

to pitch a tent (erect) テントを張る téñto wo hárù

pitch-black [pits'blæk'] adj (night, place) 真っ暗な makkúra na

pitched battle [pits't-] n (violent fight) 激戦 gekísen

pitchfork [pits'fɔːrk] n ホーク hóku

piteous [pit'i:əs] adj (sight, sound etc) 悲壮な hisán na

pitfall [pit'fɔːl] n (difficulty, danger) 落し穴 otóshiàna, 危険 kikén

pith [piθ] n (of orange, lemon etc) わた watá

pithy [piθ'i:] adj (comment, saying etc) 中身の濃い nakámì no kói

pitiful [pit'ifəl] adj (touching: appearance, sight) 哀れな awáre na

pitiless [pit'ilis] adj (person) 冷酷な reíkoku na

pits [pits] npl (AUT) ピット pitto

pittance [pit'əns] n (very small income) スズメの涙 suzúme no namída

pity [pit'i:] *n* (compassion) 哀れみ awáre-mi

♦*vt* 哀れむ awáremù

what a pity! (expressing disappointment) 残念だ zańnen da

pivot [piv'ət] *n* (TECH) 旋回軸 señkaijiku, ピボット pfbòtto; (*fig*) 中心 chúshin

pizza [pi:t'sə] *n* ピッツァ pfttsà, ピザ pfzà

placard [plæk'ɑːrd] *n* (sign: in public place) 看板 kańban; (: in march etc) プラカード purákàdo

placate [plei'keit] *vt* (person, anger) な だめる nadámerù

place [pleis] *n* (in general: point, building, area) 所 tokórò, 場所 bashó; (position: of object) 位置 íchi; (seat) 席 sékì; (job, post etc) 職 shokú, ポスト pósùto; (home): *at/to his place* 彼の家で(へ) kárè no ié de(e); (role: in society, system etc) 役割 yakúwarì

♦*vt* (put: object) 置く okú; (identify: person) 思い出す omóidasù

to take place (happen) 起る okórù

out of place (not suitable) 場違いの ba-chígài no

in the first place (first of all) まず第一 に mázù daíchi nì

to change places with someone …と交代する …to kótai suru

to be placed (in race, exam) 入賞する nyúshō suru

place of birth *n* 出生地 shusséichi

placenta [pləsen'tə] *n* 胎盤 taíban

placid [plæs'id] *adj* (person) 穏和な oñwa na

plagiarism [plei'dʒərizəm] *n* ひょう窃 hyósetsu, 盗作 tósaku

plague [pleig] *n* (MED) 伝染病 deñsenbyō; (*fig*: of locusts etc) 異常発生 ijóhassèi

♦*vt* (*fig*: subj: problems, difficulties) 悩ます nayámasù

plaice [pleis] *n inv* (fish) カレイ kárèi

plaid [plæd] *n* (cloth) チェックの生地 chékkù no kíjì

plain [plein] *adj* (unpatterned) 無地の mújì no; (simple: dress, food) 質素な shfs-

só na; (clear, easily understood) 明白な mefhaku na; (not beautiful) 不器量な bukfryō na

♦*adv* (wrong, stupid etc) 全く mattáku

♦*n* (area of land) 平原 hefgen

plain chocolate *n* ブラックチョコレート burákku chokorèto

plain-clothes [plein'klouz] *adj* (police officer) 私服の shifúku no

plainly [plein'li:] *adv* (obviously) 明白に mefhaku ni; (hear, see, smell: easily) は っきりと hakkfrì to; (state: clearly) ぎっ くばらんに zákkùbaran ni

plaintiff [plein'tif] *n* (LAW) 原告 geńkoku

plaintive [plein'tiv] *adj* (cry, voice) 哀れ っぽい awárepoì

plait [plæt] *n* (of hair) お下げ o-ságe; (of rope, leather) 編みひも状の物 amíhimojò no monó

plan [plæn] *n* (scheme, project) 計画 kefkaku, プラン puráǹ; (drawing) 図面 zúmèn; (schedule) 予定表 yotéihyó

♦*vt* (work out in advance: crime, holiday, future etc) 計画する kefkaku suru

♦*vi* (think ahead) 計画する kefkaku suru

to plan to do …しようと計画する …shíyó suru

plane [plein] *n* (AVIAT) 飛行機 hfkòki; (MATH) 面 meǹ; (*fig*: level) 段階 dańkai; (tool) かんな kanna; (*also*: **plane tree**) スズカケノキ suzúkake no ki, プラタナス purátanàsu

planet [plæn'it] *n* 惑星 wakúsei

plank [plæŋk] *n* (of wood) 板 fta

planner [plæn'əːr] *n* (*gen*) 計画をする人 kefkaku wo suru hitò; (*also*: **town planner**) 都市計画担当者 toshfkeikaku tantóshà; (of TV program, project) 計画者 kefkakushà

planning [plæn'iŋ] *n* (of future, project, event etc) 計画 kefkaku; (*also*: **town planning**) 都市計画 toshfkeikaku

family planning 家族計画 kazókukefkaku

planning permission *n* 建築許可 keń-chikukyòka

plant [plænt] *n* (BOT) 植物 shokúbùtsu;

(machinery) 設備 sétsubi; (factory) プラント puránto
♦vt (seed, plant, sapling) 植える uéru; (field, garden) ...に植える ...ni uéru; (secretly: microphone, bomb, incriminating evidence etc) 仕掛ける shikákerù

plantation [plæntéiʃən] n (of tea, rubber, sugar etc) 農園 nóen; (area planted out with trees) 植林地 shokúrinchi

plaque [plæk] n (commemorative plaque: on building etc) 銘板 meíban; (on teeth) 歯こう shíkō

plasma [plæz'mə] n 血清 kesséi

plaster [plæs'tər] n (for walls) しっくい shikkúi; (also: plaster of Paris) 石こう sekkō; (BRIT: also: sticking plaster) ばんそうこう bańsōkō
♦vt (wall, ceiling) ...にしっくいを塗る ...ni shikkúi wo nurú; (cover): to plaster with ...に...をべったり塗る ...ni ...wo bettárì harú

plastered [plæs'tərd] (inf) adj 酔っ払った yoppáratta

plasterer [plæs'tərər] n (of walls, ceilings) 左官屋 sakáñ-ya

plastic [plæs'tik] n 合成樹脂 góseijushi, プラスチック purásuchikkù
♦adj (made of plastic: bucket, chair, cup etc) プラスチック製の purásuchikkusei no

plastic bag n ポリ袋 porífukuro

Plasticine [plæs'tisin]® n 合成粘土 góseineñdo

plastic surgery n 整形手術 sefkeishujùtsu

plate [pleit] n (dish) 皿 sará; (plateful: of food, biscuits etc) 一皿 hitósara; (in book: picture, photograph) 1ページ大の挿絵 ichípejidai no sashíe, プレート puréto; (dental plate) 入れ歯 iréba

gold/silver plate 貴金属の食器類 kikínzoku no shokkírùi

plateau [plætou'] (pl plateaus or plateaux) n (GEO) 高原 kógen

plate glass n (for window, door) 板ガラス itágarasu

platform [plæt'fɔrm] n (at meeting, for band) 演壇 eńdan; (raised structure: for

landing, loading etc) 台 dái; (RAIL: platform) ホーム hōmu; (BRIT: of bus) 踏段 fumídan, ステップ sutéppù; (POL) 綱領 kōryō

platinum [plæt'ənəm] n 白金 hakkín, プラチナ puráchina

platitude [plæt'ətud] n 決り文句 kimárimoñku

platonic [plətɑn'ik] adj 純粋に精神的な juñsui ni sefshinteki na, プラトニックな puratonikkù na

platoon [plətun'] n 小隊 shōtai

platter [plæt'ər] n 盛皿 morízara

plausible [plɔ:'zəbəl] adj (theory, excuse, statement) もっともらしい mottómorashiì; (person) 口先のうまい kuchísaki nò umáì

play [plei] n (THEATER, RADIO, TV) 劇 gékì
♦vt (subj: children: game) ...して 遊ぶ ...shite asóbù; (football, tennis, chess) やる yarú; (compete against) ...と試合をする ...to shiái wò suru; (part, role: in play, film etc) 演ずる efizurù, ...に ふんする ...ni fuñsurù; (instrument, tune) 演奏する efisō suru; (listen to: tape, record) 聞く kikú
♦vi (children: on beach, swings etc) 遊ぶ asóbù; (MUS: orchestra, band) 演奏する efisō suru; (: record, tape, radio) かかる kakárù

to play safe 大事を取る dáijì wò tórù

playboy [plei'bɔi] n プレーボーイ puréboi

play down vt 軽く扱う karúku atsukaù

player [plei'ər] n (SPORT) 選手 señshu, プレーヤー puréyà; (MUS) 奏者 sōsha; (THEATER) 役者 yakúsha

playful [plei'fəl] adj (person, animal) 遊び好きの asóbizukì no

playground [plei'graund] n (in park) 遊び場 asóbibà; (in school) 校庭 kótei, 運動場 uñdójō

playgroup [plei'gru:p] (BRIT) n 保育園 hoíkuèn

playing card [plei'iŋ-] n トランプ toráñpu

playing field n グラウンド guráuñdo

playmate [plei'meit] n 遊び友達 asóbitòmòdachi

play-off [plei'ɔːf] n (SPORT) 優勝決定戦 yúshōkettēsen, プレーオフ purêofu

playpen [plei'pen] n ベビーサークル bebísākuru

plaything [plei'θiŋ] n おもちゃ omóchà

playtime [plei'taim] n (SCOL) 休み時間 yasúmijikàn

play up vi (cause trouble: machine) 調子が悪くなる chôshi gà wárùku naru; (: children) 行儀を悪くする gyógi wò wárùku suru

playwright [plei'rait] n 劇作家 gekísakka

plc [piːelsiː'] abbr (= public limited company) 有限株式会社 yúgen kabushikigaishà

plea [pliː] n (request) 懇願 kóngan; (LAW) 申し立て mōshítate

plead [pliːd] vt (LAW) 申立てる mōshítateru; (give as excuse: ignorance, ill health etc) ...だと言い訳する ...dá tò iíwake surù

♦vi (LAW) 申立てる mōshítateru; (beg):
to plead with someone ...に懇願する ...ni kóngan suru

pleasant [plez'ənt] adj (agreeable, nice: weather, chat, smile etc) 気持の良い kimóchi no yoì; (agreeable: person) 愛想の良い aíso no yoì

pleasantries [plez'əntriːz] npl: **to exchange pleasantries** あいさつを交わす aísatsu wo kawásù

please [pliːz] excl (polite request) どうぞ dōzo, どうか dōka; (polite acceptance):
yes, please ええ, 有難う eé, arígatō; (to attract someone's attention) 済みません sumímasèn

♦vt (give pleasure or satisfaction to) 喜ばす yorókobasu

♦vi (give pleasure, satisfaction) 人を喜ばす hitó wò yorókobasù; (think fit): **do as you please** お好きな様にして下さい o-súki na yō ni shité kudasaì

please yourself! (inf) ご勝手に go-kátte nì

pleased [pliːzd] adj (happy, satisfied):
pleased (with) (...で) 満足している

(...de) mañzoku shite irù

pleased to meet you 初めまして hajímemashīte

pleasing [pliː'ziŋ] adj (remark etc) 愉快な yúkai na, うれしい uréshīi; (picture) 楽しい tanóshiì; (person) 愛敬のある afkyō no arù

pleasure [pleʒ'əːr] n (happiness, satisfaction) 快楽 káiraku; (activity of enjoying oneself, enjoyable experience) 楽しみ tanóshimì

it's a pleasure どういたしまして dō itáshimashitè

pleasure boat n 遊覧船 yûransen

pleat [pliːt] n ひだ hídà, プリーツ purítsù

pledge [pledʒ] n (promise) 約束 yakúsoku

♦vt (promise: money, support, help) 約束する yakúsoku suru

plentiful [plen'tifəl] adj (food, supply, amount) 豊富な hófù na

plenty [plen'tiː] n: **plenty of** (much, many) 沢山の takúsan no; (sufficient) 十分な jûbun na

pleurisy [pluːr'isiː] n ろく膜炎 rokúmakuèn

pliable [plai'əbəl] adj (material) しなやかな shináyàka na; (fig: person) 素直な súnào na

pliant [plai'ənt] adj = **pliable**

pliers [plai'əːrz] npl ペンチ péñchi

plight [plait] n (of person, country) 苦境 kukyô

plimsolls [plim'sɑːlz] (BRIT) npl 運動靴 uñdōgutsu, スニーカー suníkā

plinth [plinθ] n 台座 dáiza

plod [plɑːd] vi (walk) とぼとぼ歩く tóbòtobo arúku; (fig) 何とかやる nán to ka yarú

plonk [plɑːŋk] (inf) n (BRIT: wine) 安ワイン yasúwaìn

♦vt: **to plonk something down** たたきつける様に...を置く tatákitsukerù yō ni ...wo óku

plot [plɑːt] n (secret plan) 陰謀 iñbō; (of story, play, film) 筋 sújì, プロット puróttò; (of land) 区画 kukáku

♦vt (sb's downfall etc) たくらむ takúramù; (AVIAT, NAUT: position on chart) 地図に書き込む chízu ni kakíkomù; (MATH: point on graph) グラフに点を うつ gúrafu ni ten wo útsù

♦vi (conspire) 陰謀を企てる iñbó wò kuwádateru

plotter [plɑːtʼər] n (instrument) 製図道具 sefzudōgu

plough [plau] (US also: **plow**) n (AGR) すき sukí

♦vt (earth) 耕す tagáyasù

to plough money into (company, project etc) ...に金をつぎ込む ...ni kané wò tsugíkomù

ploughman's lunch [plauˈmənz-] (BRIT) n 軽食 kefshoku (パブのランチで、パン、チーズ、ピクルスからなる pábù no ráñchi de, páñ, chízu, pfkùrusu kara nárù

plough through vt fus (crowd) ...をかき分けて歩く ...wo kakíwakete arúkù

plow [plau] (US) = **plough**

ploy [plɔi] n 策略 sakúryaku

pluck [plʌk] n (of fruit, flower, leaf) 摘む tsúmù; (musical instrument) つま弾く tsumábikù; (bird) ...の羽をむしる ...no hané wo mushírù; (remove hairs from: eyebrow) ...の毛を抜く ...no kè wò nukú

♦n (courage) 勇気 yúki

to pluck up courage 勇気を出す yúki wo dásù

plug [plʌg] n (ELEC) 差し込み sashíkomi, プラグ púràgu; (stopper: in sink, bath) 栓 séñ; (AUT: also: **spark(ing) plug**) スパークプラグ supákupùràgu

♦vt (hole) ふさぐ fuságù; (inf: advertise) 宣伝する señden suru

plug in vt (ELEC) ...のプラグを差し込む ...no púràgu wo sashíkomù

plum [plʌm] n (fruit) プラム púràmu

♦cpd (inf): **plum job** (持)けを咥える職 amái shirú wo suérù shokú

plumage [pluˈmidʒ] n 羽 hané ⊘ 鳥の体を覆う羽の総称 torf no karáda wo ṓù hané no sōshó

plumb [plʌm] vt: **to plumb the depths** (fig) (of unpleasant emotion) 辛酸をなめ尽す shiñsan nò naḿetsukusù; (of un-

pleasant expression) ...を極端に表現する ...wo kyokútan nì hyṓgen suru

plumber [plʌmˈər] n 配管工 hafkankō

plumbing [plʌmˈiŋ] n (piping) 水道設備 sufdōsetsubì; (trade, work) 配管業 hafkangyō

plume [pluːm] n (of bird) 羽 hané; (on helmet, horse's head) 前立 maédate

plummet [plʌmˈit] vi: **to plummet (down)** (bird, aircraft) 真っ直ぐに落下する massúgù nì rakká suru; (price, amount, rate) 暴落する bóraku suru

plump [plʌmp] adj (person) ぽっちゃりした potchárì shita

♦vi: **to plump for** (inf: choose) 選ぶ erábù

plump up vt (cushion, pillow) 膨らませる fukúramaserù

plunder [plʌnˈdaːr] n (activity) 略奪 ryakúdatsu; (stolen things) 分捕り品 buñdorihiñ

♦vt (steal from: city, tomb) 略奪する ryakúdatsu suru

plunge [plʌndʒ] n (dive: of bird, person) 飛込み tobíkomi; (fig: of prices, rates etc) 暴落 bóraku

♦vt (hand, knife) 突っ込む tsukkómù

♦vi (fall: person, thing) 落ちる ochírù; (dive: bird, person) 飛び込む tobíkomù; (fig: prices, rates etc) 暴落する bóraku suru

to take the plunge 冒険する bóken suru

plunger [plʌnˈdʒəːr] n (for sink) プランジャー puráñjà ⊘ 吸い棒の付いたゴムカップ nagáî bṑ no tsuità gomúkappù

plunging [plʌnˈdʒiŋ] adj (neckline) 切込みの深い kirfkomi nò fukái

pluperfect [pluːpəːrˈfikt] n 過去完了形 kakókanryōkei

plural [plurˈəl] adj 複数の fukúsū no

♦n 複数形 fukúsūkei

plus [plʌs] n (also: **plus sign**) 加符号 kafúgō, プラス púràsu

♦prep (MATH) ...に ...を加算して ...ni ...wo kasán shite, ...を足して ...wo tashíte; (in addition to) ...に加えて ...ni kuwáete

2 plus 2 is 4 2足す2は4 ní tasú ní wà yón

ten/twenty plus (more than) 10(20)以上 jū(nijū)ijō

plush [plʌʃ] *adj* (car, hotel etc) 豪華な gōka na

plutonium [plu:'tou'ni:əm] *n* プルトニウム purátōnīumu

ply [plai] *vt* (a trade) 営む itónamù
♦*vi* (ship) 往復する ōfuku suru
♦*n* (of wool, rope) 太さ futósa
to ply someone with drink ...に強引に酒を勧める ...ni gōín ni saké wo susúmerù

plywood [plai'wud] *n* ベニヤ板 beníyaità

P.M. [pi:'em'] *abbr* = **Prime Minister**

p.m. [pi:'em'] *adv abbr* (= *post meridiem*) 午後 gógò

pneumatic [nu:mæt'ik] *adj* (air-filled) 空気で膨らませた kūki de fukúramasetà; (powered by air) 空気... kūki...

pneumatic drill *n* 空気ドリル kūkídorìru

pneumonia [nu:moun'jə] *n* 肺炎 hafen

poach [poutʃ] *vt* (steal: fish) 密漁する mitsúryō suru; (: animals, birds) 密猟する mitsúryō suru; (cook: egg) 落し卵にする otóshitamagò ni suru, ポーチドエッグにする pōchítoeggù ni suru; (: fish) 煮る nirú
♦*vi* (steal: fish) 密漁する mitsúryō suru; (: animals, birds) 密猟する mitsúryō suru

poached [poutʃt] *adj:* **poached egg** 蒸し卵 múshitamagò, ポーチドエッグ pōchítoeggù

poacher [pou'tʃəːr] *n* (of fish) 密漁者 mitsúryōshà; (of animals, birds) 密猟者 mitsúryōshà

P.O. Box [pi:'ou-] *n abbr* = **Post Office Box**

pocket [pɑːk'it] *n* (on jacket, trousers, suitcase, car door etc) ポケット pokéttò; (fig: small area) 孤立地帯 korítsuchitài
♦*vt* (put in one's pocket) ポケットに入れる pokéttò ni irérù; (steal) くすねる kusúnerù
to be out of pocket (BRIT) 損する sốn suru

pocketbook [pɑːk'itbuk] (US) *n* (wallet) 財布 sáĭfu; (handbag) ハンドバッグ hañdobaggù

pocket calculator *n* 電卓 deñtaku

pocket knife *n* ポケットナイフ pokéttonaìfu

pocket money *n* 小遣い kózùkai

pod [pɑːd] *n* さや saya

podgy [pɑːdʒ'i] *adj* 小太りの kobútòri no

podiatrist [pədai'ətrist] (US) *n* 足治療医 ashíchiryòi

poem [pou'əm] *n* 詩 shi

poet [pou'it] *n* 詩人 shijín

poetic [pouet'ik] *adj* (relating to poetry) 詩の shi no; (like poetry) 詩的な shitéki na

poet laureate *n* 桂冠詩人 keikanshijìn

poetry [pou'itri] *n* (LITERATURE) 詩歌 shíìka

poignant [pɔin'jənt] *adj* (emotion, look, grief etc) 痛ましい itámashiì

point [pɔint] *n* (gen) 点 teñ, ポイント poínto; (sharp end: of needle, knife etc) せん teñ, 先 señtan; (purpose) 目的 mokúteki; (significant part) 要点 yōteñ; (detail, aspect, quality) 特徴 tokúchò; (particular place or position) 地点 chiteñ; (moment) 時点 jíteñ; (stage in development) 段階 dañkaì; (score: in competition, game, sport) 得点 tokúteñ, 点 teñ; (BRIT: ELEC: socket) コンセント kóñsento; (also: **decimal point**) 小数点 shōsūteñ; (in numbers): **2 point 3 (2.3)** 2点3 ní teñ sañ
♦*vt* (show, mark) 指す sásù; (gun etc): **to point something at someone** ...に...を向ける ...wo ...wo mukérù
♦*vi:* **to point at** (with finger, stick etc) ...を指す ...wo sásù

to be on the point of doing something ...をする所である ...wo suru tokorò de árù

to make a point of doing 努めて...する tsutómete ...surù

to get/miss the point 相手が言わんとする事が分る(分らない) áite ga iwáñ to suru kotò ga wakárù(wakáranaì)

to come to the point 要点を言う yōteñ

wǒ iú

there's no point (in doing) (...するの
は) 無意味です ...surú no wà) mufmi dà

point-blank [pɔint'blæŋk'] *adv* (say,
ask) ずばり zubári; (refuse) きっぱり kippári;
(*also*: **at point-blank range**) 至近距
離で shikínkyorí de

pointed [pɔin'tid] *adj* (stick, pencil, chin,
nose etc) とがった togátta; (*fig*: remark)
辛らつな shiríratsu na

pointedly [pɔin'tidli:] *adv* (reply etc) 意
味深長に ímishínchō ni

pointer [pɔin'tə:r] *n* (on chart, machine)
針 hári; (*fig*: piece of information or
advice) ヒント hínto

pointless [pɔint'lis] *adj* (useless, senseless) 無意味な mufmi na

point of view *n* (opinion) 観点 kañten

point out *vt* (in debate etc) ...を指摘する
...wo shitéki suru

points [pɔints] *npl* (AUT) ポイント poñto;
(RAIL) 転てつ機 teñtetsukī, ポイント
poñto

point to *vt fus* (*fig*) ...を指摘する ...wo
shitéki suru

poise [pɔiz] *n* (composure) 落ち着き ochítsuki

poison [pɔi'zən] *n* (harmful substance)
毒 dokú
♦ *vt* (person, animal: kill with poison) 毒
殺する dokúsatsu suru; (: give poison to)
...に毒を飲ませる ...ni dokú wo nomáserū

poisonous [pɔi'zənəs] *adj* 有毒な yúdoku
na, 毒の dokú no

poke [pouk] *vt* (jab with finger, stick etc)
つつく tsutsúkū; (put: **to poke something in(to)**) ...の中へ...を突っ込む no
nákā e ...wo tsukkómū

poke about *vi* (search) 物色する busshóku suru

poker [pou'kə:r] *n* (metal bar) 火かき棒
hikákibō; (CARDS) ポーカー pókā

poky [pou'ki:] *adj* (room, house) 狭苦し
い semákurushíi

Poland [pou'lənd] *n* ポーランド pōrando

polar [pou'lə:r] *adj* (GEO, ELEC) 極地の
kyókuchi no

polar bear *n* 北極グマ hokkyókugúma

polarize [pou'lə:raiz] *vt* 分裂させる buñretsu saserú

Pole [poul] *n* ポーランド人 pōrandojín

pole [poul] *n* (post, stick) 棒 bō, さお sáo;
(GEO, ELEC) 極 kyóku

flag pole 旗ざお hatázao

telegraph/telephone pole 電柱 deñchū

pole bean (US) *n* (runner bean) インゲ
ン豆 iñgen

pole vault *n* 棒高飛び bótakátobi

police [pəli:s'] *n* (organization) 警察 keñsatsu; (members) 警官 kefkan
♦ *vt* (street, area, town) ...の治安を維持す
る ...no chiáñ wð jíjí suru

police car *n* パトカー patókā

policeman [pəli:s'mən] (*pl* **policemen**) *n*
警官 kefkan

police state *n* (POL) 警察国家 kefsatsukokkā

police station *n* 警察署 kefsatsusho

policewoman [pəli:s'wumən] (*pl* **policewomen**) *n* 婦人警官 fujíñkeíkan, 婦警 fukéi

policy [pɑl'isi:] *n* (POL, ECON: set of
ideas, plans) 政策 sefsaku; (*also*: **insurance policy**) 保険証券 hokéñshōken

polio [pou'li:ou] *n* 小児麻ひ shónímahí,
ポリオ pórīo

Polish [pou'liʃ] *adj* ポーランドの pōrando no; (LING) ポーランド語の pōrando
go no
♦ *n* (LING) ポーランド語 pōrandogo

polish [pɑl'iʃ] *n* (*also*: **shoe polish**) 靴墨
kutsúzûmi; (for furniture, floors etc) 光
沢剤 kōtakuzái; (shine: on shoes, floors,
furniture etc) 光沢 kōtaku; (*fig*: refinement) 洗練 señren
♦ *vt* (put polish on, make shiny) 磨く
migákū

polish off *vt* (work) 仕上げる shiágerū;
(food) 平らげる tafragerū

polished [pɑl'iʃt] *adj* (*fig*: person, style)
洗練された señren sareta

polite [pəlait'] *adj* (person: well-
mannered) 礼儀正しい refgítadashíi;
(socially superior: company, society) 上
流の jōryū no

politeness [pəlaɪt'nɪs] n 礼儀正しさ reigitadashisa

political [pəlɪt'ɪkəl] adj (relating to politics) 政治の seiji no; (person) 政治に関心ある seiji ni kanshin arū

politically [pəlɪt'ɪkli] adv 政治的に seijiteki ni

politician [pɑːlɪtɪʃ'ən] n 政治家 seijika

politics [pɑːl'ɪtɪks] n (activity) 政治 seiji; (subject) 政治学 seijigaku
♦npl (beliefs, opinions) 政治的思想 seijitekishisō

poll [poul] n (also: **opinion poll**) 世論調査 yoronchōsa; (political election) 選挙 sénkyo
♦vt (in opinion poll) ...の意見を聞く ...no íken wo kikú; (number of votes) 獲得する kakútoku suru

pollen [pɑːl'ən] n 花粉 kafún

polling day [pou'lɪŋ-] (BRIT) n 投票日 tōhyōbi

polling station (BRIT) n 投票所 tōhyōjo

pollute [pəluːt'] vt (air, water, land) 汚染する osén suru

pollution [pəluːʃ'ən] n (process) 汚染 osén; (substances) 汚染物質 osénbusshítsu

polo [pou'lou] n (sport) ポロ pórō

polo-necked [pou'lounekt] adj (sweater) とっくりえりの tokkúrierí no

poltergeist [poul'tə:rgaɪst] n ラップ 騒霊 kefsōrei, ポルターガイスト portágaisuto

polyester [pɑːlɪes'tə:r] n ポリエステル poriésuteru

polyethylene [pɑːliːeθ'əliːn] (US) n ポリエチレン porichiren

polystyrene [pɑːlɪstaɪ'riːn] n ポリスチレン porísuchiren

polytechnic [pɑːlɪtek'nɪk] n 科学技術専門学校 kagákugijutsu senmongakkō ◊ 英国では大学レベルの高等教育機関で英国 de wā daígakurebéru no kōtōkyōiku ku kikán

polythene [pɑːl'əθiːn] (BRIT) n = **polyethylene**

pomegranate [pɑːm'əgrænit] n ザクロ zákūro

pomp [pɑːmp] n 華やかさ hanáyakasa

pompom [pɑːm'pɑːm] n ポ...

pompon [pɑːm'pɑːn] n = **pon**

pompous [pɑːm'pəs] (pej) adj ...; piece of writing) もったい振った buttá

pond [pɑːnd] n (natural, artificial) 池

ponder [pɑːn'də:r] vi 熟考する jukkō suru

ponderous [pɑːn'də:rəs] adj (large and heavy) 大きくて重い ōkikute omói; (speech, writing) 重苦しい omókurushii

pong [pɑːŋ] (BRIT: inf) n 悪臭 akúshū

pontificate [pɑːntɪf'ɪkeɪt] vi (fig): **to pontificate (about)** (...について) もったい振って話す ...ni tsūtte mottáibutté hanásū

pontoon [pɑːntuːn'] n (platform) ポンツーン pofitsūn; (for seaplane etc) フロート fúroto

pony [pou'niː] n ポニー pónī

ponytail [pou'niːteɪl] n (person's hairstyle) ポニーテール ponīteru

pony trekking [-trek'ɪŋ] n 乗馬旅行 jōbaryokō

poodle [puː'dəl] n プードル púdoru

pool [puːl] n (also: **pool of water**) 水たまり mizútamari; (pond) 池; (also: **swimming pool**) プール pūru; (fig: of light, liquid) たまり tamári; (SPORT) 玉突 tamátsuki, ビリヤード biríyādo
♦vt (money, knowledge, resources) 出し合う dashfaū, プールする pūru suru
typing pool タイピストのプール taípisūto no pūru

pools [puːlz] npl (football pools) トトカルチョ totókarúcho

poor [puːr] adj (not rich: person, place, country) 貧しい mazúshiī, 貧乏な bínbō na; (bad) 粗末な somátsu na
♦npl: **the poor** 貧乏人 bínbōnin ◊総称 sōshō

poor in (resources etc) ...が不足している ...ga fusóku shite irú

poorly [puːr'liː] adj (ill) 病気の byōki no
♦adv (badly: designed) 粗末に somátsu ni; (paid, furnished) 不十分に fujúbun ni

pop [pɑːp] n (MUS) ポップス póppùsu;

iñryō, ソー
ちゃんと
という音

り. nōō

poplar [pɑ:pˈlər] n ポプラ pópura

poplin [pɑ:pˈlin] n ポプリン pópurin

pop out vi 飛出る tobídérù

popper [pɑ:pˈər] (BRIT) n (for fastening) スナップ sunáppù

poppy [pɑ:pˈi:] n ケシ keshí

Popsicle [pɑ:pˈsikəl] (R) (US) n (ice lolly) アイスキャンディー aísukyàndī

pop star n ポップスター poppusutā

populace [pɑ:pˈjələs] n 大衆 taíshū

popular [pɑ:pˈjələr] adj (well-liked: person, place, thing) 人気のある nínki no arù; (of ordinary people: idea, belief) 一般の ippán no, 流行の ryūkō no; (nonacademic) 一般向けの ippánmuke no; (POL) 国民の kokúmin no

popularity [pɑ:pjəlærˈiti:] n (of person, thing, activity) 人気 nínki

popularize [pɑ:pˈjələraiz] vt (sport, music, fashion) 普及させる fukyū saserù; (science, ideas) 分かりやすくする wakáriyasukù suru

population [pɑ:pjəleiˈʃən] n (inhabitants: of country, area) 住民 jūmin; (number of inhabitants) 人口 jínkō

populous [pɑ:pˈjələs] adj (country, city, area) 人口の多い jínkō no ōi

pop up vi 現れる aráwarerù

porcelain [pɔ:rˈsəlin] n 磁器 jíki

porch [pɔ:rtʃ] n (ARCHIT: entrance) 玄関 genkan; (US) ベランダ beránda

porcupine [pɔ:rˈkjəpain] n ヤマアラシ yamáarashì

pore [pɔ:r] n (ANAT) 毛穴 keána; (BOT) 気孔 kikó; (GEO) 小穴 koána
♦vi: **to pore over** (book, article etc) 熟読する jukúdoku suru

pork [pɔ:rk] n 豚肉 bútaniku

pornographic [pɔ:rnəgræfˈik] adj (film, book, magazine) わいせつな waísetsu na, ポルノの poruno no

pornography [pɔ:rnɑːˈgrəfi:] n (films, books, magazines) ポルノ pórùno

porous [pɔ:rˈəs] adj (soil, rock, clay etc) 小穴の多い koána nò ōī

porpoise [pɔ:rˈpəs] n イルカ irúka

porridge [pɔ:rˈidʒ] n オートミール ōtomīru

port [pɔ:rt] n (harbor) 港 mínato; (NAUT: left side) 左げん sagén; (wine) ポートワイン pōtowain
port of call 寄港地 kikóchi

portable [pɔ:rˈtəbəl] adj (television, typewriter, telephone etc) 携帯用の keítai yō no, ポータブルの pōtaburu no

porter [pɔ:rˈtər] n (for luggage) 赤帽 akábō, ポーター pōtā; (doorkeeper) 門番 moñban

portfolio [pɔ:rtfouˈli:ou] n (case) かばん kabán; (POL) 大臣の職 daíjin no shokú; (FINANCE) ポートフォリオ pōtoforio; (of artist) 代表作品集 daíhyōsakuhìnshū

porthole [pɔ:rtˈhoul] n げん窓 geñsō

portion [pɔ:rˈʃən] n (part) 部分 búbun; (helping of food) 一人前 ichíninmae

portly [pɔ:rtˈli:] adj (man) 太った futótta

portrait [pɔ:rˈtrit] n (picture) 肖像 shōzō, ポートレート pōtorēto

portray [pɔ:rtreiˈ] vt (subj: artist) 描く egákù; (: actor) 演じる eñjirù

portrayal [pɔ:rtreiˈəl] n (artist's: also representation in book, film etc) 描写 byōsha; (actor's) 演技 eñgi

Portugal [pɔ:rˈtʃəgəl] n ポルトガル pórùtogaru

Portuguese [pɔ:rtʃəgi:ˈz] adj ポルトガルの porútogaru no; (LING) ポルトガル語の porútogarugò no
♦n inv ポルトガル人 porútogarujìn; (LING) ポルトガル語 porútogarugò

pose [pouz] n (posture) ポーズ pōzu
♦vi (pretend): **to pose as** ...を装う ...wo yosōoù, ...の名をかたる ...no nå wò katárù
♦vt (question) 持出す mochídasù; (prob-

lem, danger) ...である ...de árú

to pose for (painting etc) ...のためにポーズを取る ...no tamé nǐ pózu wo tórù

posh [pɑːʃ] *adj* (painting etc) ...高級なkókyū na; (upper class: person, behavior) 上流階級の jōryūkàikyū no

position [pəzíʃən] *n* (place: of house, thing, person) 位置 íchì; (of person's body) 姿勢 shìséi; (social status) 地位 chíi; (job) 職 shokū; (in race, competition) 第...位 dái ...i; (attitude) 態度 táìdo; (situation) 立場 tachíba
 ◆*vt* (person, thing) を置く óků

positive [pɑ́zitiv] *adj* (certain) 確かなtáshíka na; (hopeful, confident) 確信している kakúshìn shite irú; (definite: decision, action, policy) 積極的なsekkyòkuteki na

posse [pɑ́ːsiː] (*US*) *n* 捜索隊 sōsakutai

possess [pəzés] *vt* (have, own: car, watch, radio etc) 所有する shoyū suru, 保有する hoyū suru; (quality, ability) ...がある ...ga árù, ...を持っている ...wo móttè irú; (subj: feeling, belief) 支配する shíhaì suru

possession [pəzéʃən] *n* (state of possessing) 所有 shoyū
 to take possession of 占領する senryō suru

possessions [pəzéʃənz] *npl* (belongings) 持物 mochímòno

possessive [pəzésiv] *adj* (of another person) ...の愛情を独占したがる ...no aíjō wò dokúsen shitagarù; (of things) 他人に使わせたがらない tanín nǐ tsukáwasetagaranài; (LING) 所有を表す shoyū wo aráwasù

possibility [pɑːsəbílʲitìː] *n* (chance) 可能性 kanōsei; (possible event) 可能な事 kanō na kotð

possible [pɑ́ːsəbəl] *adj* (which can be done) 可能な kanō na; (event, reaction) 有り得る arúrù; (candidate, successor) 成り得る narúrù
 it's possible (may be true) そうかも知れない sṑ ka mo shirénaì
 as fast as possible できるだけ早く de-

kíru dakè hayákù

possibly [pɑ́ːsəblìː] *adv* (perhaps) あるいは arúìwa; (expressing surprise, shock, puzzlement) ...としか思えない ...ga kañgaerarenàì; (emphasizing someone's efforts) できる限り dekíru kagírì
 I cannot possibly come どう合っても私は行かれません dōttè mo watákushi wà ikáremaseñ

post [poust] *n* (*BRIT*: service, system) 郵便 yūbín; (: letters) 郵便物 (bútsu); (: delivery) 配達 haftatsu ◇1回分の配達郵便を指す ikkáibun no haftatsu-yūbin wo sásù; (pole) 柱 hashíra; (job, situation) 職務 shokūmù; (MIL) 持場 mochíba
 ◆*vt* (*BRIT*: send by post) 郵送する yūsō suru; (: put in mailbox) 投かんする tōkan suru; (: appoint): **to post someone to** ...を...へ配置する ...wo ...e haíchi suru

postage [poustidʒ] *n* (charge) 郵便料金 yūbin ryōkin

postage stamp *n* (郵便)切手 (yūbin) kitté

postal [poustəl] *adj* (charges, service, strike) 郵便の yūbin no

postal order *n* 郵便為替 yūbin kawàse

postbox [poustbɑ̀ks] (*BRIT*) *n* (郵便)ポスト (yūbin) pósùto

postcard [poustkɑ̀rd] *n* (郵便)葉書 (yūbin) hagáki

postcode [poustkoud] (*BRIT*) *n* 郵便番号 yūbin bañgō

postdate [poustdeit] *vt* (check) ...に先の日付を付ける ...ni sakí nò hízukè wò tsukérù

poster [poustər] *n* ポスター pósùtā

poste restante [poust restánt] (*BRIT*) *n* 局留め kyokúdome

posterity [pɑːstérʲitìː] *n* 後世 kōsei

postgraduate [poustgrǽdʒùit] *n* 大学院生 dafgakuíñsei

posthumous [pɑ́ːstʃəməs] *adj* (award, publication) 死後の shígð no

postman [poustmən] (*pl* **postmen**) *n* 郵便屋 yūbin-ya

postmark [poustmɑ̀rk] *n* 消印 keshíin

post-mortem [poustmɔ́rtəm] *n* 司法解剖 shihōkaibō, 検死解剖 keñshikaibō

post office n (building) 郵便局 yúbínkyoku; (organization): *the Post Office* 郵政省 yúseíshóō

Post Office Box n 私書箱 shishóbáka

postpone [poust'poun'] vt 延期する eñki suru

postscript [poust'skript] n 追伸 tsuíshin

posture [pɑːs'tʃəːr] n (position of body) 姿勢 shiséi; (fig) 態度 táīdo

postwar [poust'wɔːr'] adj (building, period, politics) 戦後の señgo no

posy [pou'ziː] n 花束 hanátaba ◊小さい花束を指す chiísaí hanátaba wo sásū

pot [pɑːt] n (for cooking) なべ nábe; (also: **teapot**) ティーポット tíīpottó; (also: **coffeepot**) コーヒーポット kóhīpottó; (tea/coffee in pot) ティー[コーヒー]ポット一杯 tíī[kóhī] pottó íppaí; (bowl, container: for paint etc) つぼ tsubó; (flowerpot) 植木鉢 ueki-bāchi; (inf: marijuana) マリファナ marffāna

◆vt (plant) 鉢に植える hachí ni uérū

to go to pot (inf: work, performance) 駄目になる damé ni narū

potato [pəteí'tou] (pl **potatoes**) n ジャガイモ jagáimo

potato peeler [-piː'ləːr] n 皮むき器 kawámukíkí

potent [pout'ənt] adj (powerful: weapon, argument, drink) 強力な kyóryoku na; (man) 性的能力のある seftekiñóryoku no árū

potential [pəten'tʃəl] adj (candidate) 成り得る narfurú; (sales, success) 可能な kanō na; (danger etc) 将来の señzai suru

◆n (talents, abilities) 潜在能力 señzaiñóryoku; (promise, possibilities) 将来性 shóraisei

potentially [pəten'tʃəliː] adv 潜在的に señzaiteki ni

pothole [pɑːt'houl] n (in road) 穴ぼこ anábōko; (BRIT: underground) 洞くつ dókutsu

potholing [pɑːt'houliŋ] (BRIT) n: *to go potholing* 洞くつを探検する dókutsu wǒ tañken suru

potion [pou'ʃən] n (of medicine, poison etc) 水薬 mizúgusúri

potluck [pɑːt'lʌk] n: *to take potluck* 有り合せの物で間に合せる arfawase no monô de ma nf awaserú

potted [pɑːt'id] adj (food) つぼ詰めの tsubózume no; (plant) 鉢植えの hachfue no; (abbreviated: account, biography etc) 要約した yǒyaku shita

potter [pɑːt'əːr] n (pottery maker) 陶芸家 tóngeika

◆vi: *to potter around/about in the garden* (BRIT) ぶらぶらと庭いじりをする búrabura to niwáijíri wo suru

pottery [pɑːt'əːriː] n (pots, dishes etc) 陶器 tǒki; (factory, workshop) 陶器製造所 tókisseizójo

potty [pɑːt'iː] adj (inf: mad) 狂った kurúttá

◆n (for child) おまる o-máru

pouch [pautʃ] n (for tobacco, coins etc) 小袋 kobúkuro; (ZOOL) 袋 fukúro

poultry [poul'triː] n (live chickens, ducks etc) 家きん kakfn; (meat from chickens etc) 鳥肉 torfniku

pounce [pauns] vi: *to pounce on* (animal, person) ...に襲い掛る ...ni osóikakarú; (fig: mistake, idea etc) 攻撃する kǒgeki suru

pound [paund] n (unit of weight) ポンド póñdo; (BRIT: unit of money) ポンド póñdo

◆vt (beat: table, wall etc) 強くたたく tsúyóku tatákú; (crush: grain, spice etc) 砕く kudákú

◆vi (heart) どきどきする dókídoki suru

pound sterling n ポンド póñdo

pour [pɔːr] vt (tea, wine, cereal etc) つぐ tsugú

◆vi (water, blood, sweat etc) 流れ出る nagáredérù

to pour someone a drink ...に酒をついでやる ...ni saké wǒ tsufde yarú

pour away/off vt 流して捨てる nagáshite suterú

pour in vi (people) ぞろぞろと入って来る zórózoro to hafte kurú; (information) 続々と入る zókúzoku to háīru

pouring [pɔːr'iŋ] adj: *pouring rain* 土砂

降りの雨 dosháburi no amè

pour out vi (people) ぞろぞろと出て来る zòrózoro to deté kurù

♦vt (tea, wine etc) つぐ tsugú; (fig: thoughts, feelings, etc) せきを切った様に吐き出す sékì wo kittá yṑ nì hakídasù

pout [paut] vi 膨れっ面をする fukúrettsura wò suru

poverty [pɑːvˈəːrti] n 貧乏 bínbō

poverty-stricken [pɑːvˈəːrtistrikən] adj (people, town, country) 非常に貧しい hijō nì mazúshiì

powder [pauˈdəːr] n (tiny particles of solid substance) 粉 koná; (face powder) おしろい oshíroi, パウダー páudā

♦vt: **to powder one's face** 顔におしろいをつける kaó nì oshíroì wò tsukérù

powder compact n コンパクト kõñpakuto

powdered milk [pauˈdəːrd-] n 粉ミルク konámirùku

powder puff n パフ páfù

powder room n 化粧室 keshóshitsu

power [pauˈəːr] n (control: over people, activities) 権力 kéñryoku; (ability, opportunity) 能力 nōryoku; (legal right) 権力 kéñri; (of explosion, engine) 威力 íryòku; (electricity) 電力 déñryoku

to be in power (POL etc) 権力を握っている kéñryoku wo nigítte irù

power cut (BRIT) n 停電 teíden

powered [pauˈəːrd] adj: **powered by** ...で動く ...de ugókù

power failure n 停電 teíden

powerful [pauˈəːrfəl] adj (person, organization) 有力な yūryoku na; (body) 力強い chikárazuyòi; (blow, kick etc) 強力な kyóryoku na; (engine) 馬力の強い baríki no tsuyóì; (speech, piece of writing) 力強い chikárazuyòi

powerless [pauˈəːrlis] adj (without control or influence) 無力な múryòku na

powerless to do ...する力がない ...súrù chikára ga naì

power point (BRIT) n コンセント kõñsento

power station n 発電所 hatsúdensho

p.p. [piːˈpiː] abbr (= per procurationem):

p.p. J. Smith J.Smithの代理として jē sumísù no dáiri tòshité; (= pages) ページ pēji

PR [piːˈɑːr] abbr = **public relations**

practicable [prækˈtikəbəl] adj (scheme, task, idea) 実用的な jitsúyōteki na

practical [prækˈtikəl] adj (not theoretical: difficulties, experience etc) 実際の jissái no; (person: sensible) 現実的な geñjitsuteki na; (: good with hands) 器用な kíyō na; (ideas, methods) 現実的な geñjitsuteki na; (clothes, things: sensible) 実用的な jitsúyōteki na

practicality [præktikælˈitiː] n (no pl) 現実主義 geñjitsushùgi; (of situation etc) 現実 geñjitsu

practical joke n 悪ふざけ warúfuzàke

practically [prækˈtikliː] adv (almost) ほとんど hotóñdo

practice [prækˈtis] n (habit) 習慣 shū́kan; (of profession) 業務 gyṓmu; (REL) おきてを行う事 ōkíte wo mamórù kotó; (exercise, training) 練習 reñshū; (MED, LAW: business) 開業 kaígyō

♦vt (train at: musical instrument, sport etc) 練習する reñshū suru; (carry out: custom, craft etc) 行う okónaù; (religion) ...のおきてを守る ...no ōkíte wo mamorù; (profession) ...に従事する ...ni jū́ji suru

♦vi (train) 練習する reñshū suru; (lawyer, doctor etc) ...の業務をする ...no gyṓmu wo suru

in practice (in reality) 実際には jissái ni wà

out of practice 腕が鈍っている udé gà nibútte irù

practicing [prækˈtisiŋ] (BRIT **practising**) adj (Christian etc) おきてを守っている okíte wò mamótte irù; (doctor, lawyer) 業務をしている gyṓmu wo shité irù

practise [prækˈtis] vt, vi (BRIT) = **practice**

practitioner [præktiʃˈənəːr] n (MED): **medical practitioner** 医者 ishá

pragmatic [prægmætˈik] adj (person, reason etc) 現実的な geñjitsuteki na

prairie [preˈriː] n 草原 sōgen

praise [preiz] *n* (expression of approval, admiration) 賞賛 shōsan
♦*vt* (express approval, admiration: of person, thing, action etc) ほめる homéru

praiseworthy [preiz'wə:rði:] *adj* (person, act etc) ほめるべき homérubeki

pram [præm] (*BRIT*) *n* 乳 母 車 ubágurúma

prance [præns] *vi* (person) 威張って歩く ibátte arúku; (horse) 躍る様に歩く odóru yō ni arúkú

prank [præŋk] *n* いたずら itázura

prawn [prɔ:n] *n* エビ ebí

pray [prei] *vi* (REL) 祈る inórù; (*fig*) 祈る inórù, 願う negáō

prayer [prer] *n* (REL: activity, words) 祈り ínóri

preach [pri:tʃ] *vi* (REL) 説教する sékkyō suru; (*pej*: moralize) お説教する o-sékkyō suru
♦*vt* (peace, doctrine etc) 説く tókù
to preach a sermon 説教する sékkyō suru

preacher [pri:'tʃə:r] *n* (REL) 説教者 sekkyōsha

preamble [pri:'æmbəl] *n* (to spoken words) 前置き maéokì; (to written words) 前書 maégaki

precarious [prikær'i:əs] *adj* (dangerous: position, situation) 不安定な fuántei na; (*fig*) 危険な kikén na

precaution [prikɔ:'ʃən] *n* 用心 yōjin

precede [prisi:d'] *vt* (event, period of time) …の前に起る …no máè ni okórù; (person) …の前を歩く …no máè wo arúkù; (sentence, paragraph, chapter) …の前にある …no máè ni árù

precedence [pres'idəns] *n* (priority) 優先 yūsen

precedent [pres'idənt] *n* (action, official decision) 判例 hañrei; (something that has happened before) 先例 señrei

preceding [prisi:'diŋ] *adj* (chapter, programme, day) 前の máè no

precept [pri:'sept] *n* おきて okíte

precinct [pri:'siŋkt] *n* (*US*: part of city) 管区 káñku

pedestrian precinct (*BRIT*) *n* 歩行者天

国 hokōshateñgoku

shopping precinct (*BRIT*) ショッピングセンター shóppìngu señtà ◇車が閉出される kurúma ga shimédasarerù

precincts [pri:'siŋkts] *npl* (of a large building) 構内 kōnai

precious [preʃ'əs] *adj* (commodity: valuable, useful) 貴重な kichō na; (object, material) 高価な kōka na

precious stone *n* 宝石 hōseki

precipice [pres'əpis] *n* 断崖 dañgai

precipitate [prisip'iteit] *vt* (hasten) 早める hayámerù

precise [prisais'] *adj* (exact: time, nature etc) 正確な séikaku na; (detailed: instructions, plans etc) 細かい komákài

precisely [prisais'li:] *adv* (accurately) 正確に sekáku ni; (exactly) その通り sonó tòri

precision [prisiʒ'ən] *n* 正確さ sefkakusa

preclude [priklu:d'] *vt* (action, event) 不可能にする fukánō ni surù

precocious [prikou'ʃəs] *adj* (child, talent) 早熟な sōjuku na

preconceived [pri:kənsi:vd'] *adj*: *preconceived idea* 先入観 señnyūkan

precondition [pri:kəndiʃ'ən] *n* 前提条件 zeñteijōken

precursor [prikər'sər] *n* (person) 先駆者 señkushá; (thing) 前触れ maébure

predator [pred'ətər] *n* 捕食者 hoshókusha

predecessor [pred'isesər] *n* (person) 前任者 zeñniñsha

predestination [pri:destinei'ʃən] *n* 予定説 yoténsetsu

predicament [pridik'əmənt] *n* 苦境 kukyō

predict [pridikt'] *vt* 予言する yogén suru

predictable [pridikt'əbəl] *adj* (event, behavior etc) 予知できる yóchì dekírù

prediction [pridik'ʃən] *n* 予言 yogén

predominantly [pridam'ənntli:] *adv* 圧倒的に attőteki ni

predominate [pridam'əneit] *vi* (person, thing) …が圧倒的である …ga attőteki de arù; (feature, quality) 目立つ medátsù

pre-eminent [priæm'ənənt] *adj* (person,

thing) 優れた sugúretà

pre-empt [pri:ˈempt] vt (decision, action, statement) 先取りする sakídori suru

preen [pri:n] vt: **to preen itself** (bird) 羽 繕いをする hazúkûroi wo suru
to preen oneself 得意がる tokúîgaru

prefab [pri:ˈfæb] n プレハブ住宅 puréhabujûtaku

prefabricated [pri:fæbˈrikeitid] adj (buildings) プレハブの puréhabu no

preface [pref'is] n (in book) 前書 máegaki

prefect [pri:ˈfekt] n (BRIT) (in school) 監督生 kaftokusèi

prefer [prifəːr'] vt (like better: person, thing, activity) ...の方を好む ...no hō wo konômù
to prefer doing/to do ...する方が好き である ...suru hō gá sukí de arù

preferable [pref'ərəbəl] adj ...が望ましい ...ga nozômashiî

preferably [pref'ərːəbli:] adv できれば dekîrèba

preference [pref'ərəns] n (liking) 好み konômi
to give preference to ...を優先的に扱う ...wo yûsenteki ni atsûkaù

preferential [prefərenˈʃəl] adj: **preferential treatment** 優先的な取扱い yûsenteki ná toriatsûkai

prefix [pri:ˈfiks] n 接頭辞 settôji

pregnancy [preg'nənsi:] n (of woman, female animal) 妊娠 nifshin

pregnant [preg'nənt] adj (woman, female animal) 妊娠している nifshin shite irù

prehistoric [pri:histɔːrˈik] adj (person, dwelling, monster etc) 有史以前の yûshiizèn no

prejudice [predʒ'ədis] n (unreasonable dislike) 偏見 henkèn; (bias in favor) ひいき hîki

prejudiced [predʒ'ədist] adj (person: prejudiced against) ...に対して偏見のある ...ni táishite henkèn no arù; (: prejudiced in favor) ...をひいきにした ...wo hîki ni shitá

preliminary [prilim'əneːriː] adj (action,

discussion) 予備的な yobîteki na

prelude [prel'uːd] n (preliminary event) 前兆 zeñchô; (MUS) 序曲 jókyoku

premarital [pri:mærˈitəl] adj 婚前の koñzen no

premature [pri:mətʃuːr'] adj (earlier than expected: baby) 早産の sòzan no; (death, arrival) 早過ぎた hayásugita; (too early: action, event etc) 時期尚早の jíkíshòsô no
premature aging 早老 sòrô

premeditated [primed'əteitid] adj 計画 的な kefkakuteki na

premier [primjiːr'] adj (best) 最良の safryô no
♦n (POL) 総理大臣 sôridaïjin, 首相 shushô

première [primjiːr'] n (of film) 初公開 hatsúkôkai; (of play) 初演 shoén

premise [prem'is] n 前提 zefītei

premises [prem'isiz] npl (of business, institution) 構内 kônai
on the premises 構内で kônai de

premium [pri:mi:əm] n (COMM: extra sum of money) 割増金 warfmashikin; (INSURANCE: sum paid for insurance) 掛金 kakékìn
to be at a premium (expensive) 高価である kôka de arù; (hard to get) 手に入りにくい té ni hafrinikûi

premium bond (BRIT) n 割増金付き債 券 warfmashikíntsukisaìken ◇抽選によ る賞金が付く chûsen ni yorù shôkin ga tsuků

premonition [premənij'ən] n 予感 yokán

preoccupation [pri:ɑːkjəpeiˈʃən] n (obsession) 専念さえ専 señnen surú kotô; (worry) 気がかり事 kigákàri na kotô

preoccupied [pri:ɑːkˈjəpaid] adj (person) 上の空になった uwánosorà ni nátta

prep [prep] n (SCOL: study) 勉強 beñkyô

prepaid [pri:pedˈ] adj (paid in advance) 支払い済みの shiháraizumi no

preparation [prepəreiˈʃən] n (activity) 準備 jûñbi; (food) 料理 ryôri; (medicine) 薬品 yakúhin; (cosmetic) 化粧品 keshôhin

preparations [prepəreiˈʃənz] npl (arrangements) 準備 jûñbi

preparatory [pripær'ətɔ:ri:] *adj* (report) 予備の yóbi no; (training) 準備の júnbi no

preparatory school *n* (US) 予備校 yobíkō; (BRIT) 私立小学校 shiritsú shōgakkō

prepare [pripeə'r] *vt* (make ready: plan, speech, room etc) 準備する júnbi suru; (CULIN) 調理する chōri suru

♦*vi*: **to prepare for** (event, action) の準備をする ...no júnbi wo suru

prepared (to: willing) ...する用意がある ...surú yōi ga árù

prepared for (ready) ...の用意ができている ...no yōi ga dékite irū

preponderance [pripɑn'dɑːrəns] *n* (of people, things) 大多数 daítasū

preposition [prepəzíʃ'ən] *n* 前置詞 zénchishi

preposterous [pripɑs'tɑːrəs] *adj* (suggestion, idea, situation) 途方もない tohō-monaí

prep school *n* = preparatory school

prerequisite [prirek'wizit] *n* 必要条件 hitsúyōjōken

prerogative [priərɑg'ətiv] *n* (of person, group) 特権 tokkén

Presbyterian [prezbitiːr'iːən] *adj* 長老派の chōrōha no

♦*n* 長老派の信者 chōrōha no shínja

preschool [pri:'sku:l'] *adj* (age, child, education) 就学前の shūgakumae no

prescribe [priskraib'] *vt* (MED: medicine) 処方する shohō suru; (treatment) 命ずる mefzurū

prescription [priskrip'ʃən] *n* (MED: slip of paper) 処方せん shohōsen; (: medicine) 処方薬 shohōyáku

presence [prez'əns] *n* (state of being somewhere) ...に居る事 ...ni irú kotō; (fig: strong personal quality) 風さい fūsai; (spirit, invisible influence) 霊 reí

in someone's presence ...の居る前で ...no irú maè de

presence of mind *n* 機転 kitén

present [*adj, n, prep'ənt vb* prizent'] *adj* (current: person, thing) 現在の genzái no; (in attendance) 出席している shussé-

ki shite irū

♦*n* (actuality): **the present** 現在 genzai; (gift) 贈り物 okúrimono, プレゼント purézènto

♦*vt* (give: prize, award etc) 贈る okúrù; (cause, provide: difficulty, threat etc) ...に なる atáerù; (information) 与える atáerù; (describe: person, thing) 描写する byōsha suru; (RADIO, TV) 提供する tefkyō suru; (formally introduce: person) 紹介する shōkai suru

to give someone a present ...にプレゼントを上げる ...ni purézènto wo agérù

at present 今の所 imá no tokoro

presentable [prizen'təbəl] *adj* (person) 人前に出られる hitómae nì derárerù

presentation [prezəntei'ʃən] *n* (of plan, proposal, report etc) 提出 tefshutsu; (appearance) 体裁 tefsai; (formal ceremony) 贈呈式 zōteishíki

present-day [prez'əntdei'] *adj* 現代の géndai no

presenter [prizen'tə:r] *n* (RADIO, TV) 司会者 shikáisha

presently [prez'əntli:] *adv* (soon) 間もなく mamónàku; (now) 現在 genzai

preservation [prezərvei'ʃən] *n* (act of preserving) 保存 hozón; (state of being preserved) 保存状態 hozónjōtai

preservative [prizə:r'vətiv] *n* (for food, wood, metal etc) 保存剤 hozónzài

preserve [prizə:rv'] *vt* (maintain: situation, condition) 維持する ījì suru; (: building, manuscript) 保存する hozón suru; (food) 保存する hozón suru

♦*n* (often pl: jam, marmalade) ジャム jámù

preside [prizaid'] *vi*: **to preside (over)** (meeting, event etc) (...の) 議長をする (...no) gichō wo suru

presidency [prez'idənsi:] *n* (POL: post) 大統領職 daftōryōshòku; (: time in office) 大統領の任期 daftōryō no nínki

president [prez'idənt] *n* (POL) 大統領 daftōryō; (of organization) ...長 ...chō

presidential [prezidən'tʃəl] *adj* 大統領の daftōryō no

press [pres] *n*: **the Press** (newspapers)

報道機関 hōdōkikan; (journalists) 報道陣 hōdōjin; (printing press) 印刷機 ínsatsuki; (of switch, button, bell) 押す事 osú kotō

♦vt (hold one thing against another) 押付ける oshítsukerù; (button, switch, bell etc) 押す osú; (iron: clothes) ...にアイロンを掛ける ...ni aíron wò kakérù; (put pressure on: person) せき立てる sekítaterù; (insist): to press something on someone ...に...を押付ける ...ni ...wo oshítsukerù

♦vi (squeeze) 押える osáerù; (pressurize): to press for (improvement, change etc) ...のために働く ...no tamé ni határakù; (forcibly) 強要する kyōyō suru
we are pressed for time/money 時間 [金]が足りない jíkan[kané] ga tarínai

press agency n 通信社 tsúshínsha

press conference n 記者会見 kishákaíken

pressing [pres'iŋ] adj (engagement, decision etc) 緊急の kínkyū no

press on vi (despite problems etc) ひるまずに続ける hirúmazù ni tsuzúkerù

press stud (BRIT) n スナップ sunáppù

press-up [pres'ap] (BRIT) n 腕立て伏せ udétatefùse

pressure [preʃ'əːr] n (physical force: also fig) 圧力 atsúryòku; (also: air pressure) 気圧 kiátsu; (also: water pressure) 水圧 sufatsu; (also: oil pressure) 油圧 yuátsu; (stress) 圧迫 appáku, プレッシャー puréssha
to put pressure on someone (to do) (...する様に) ...に圧力を掛ける ...surú yō ni) ...ni atsúryòku wo kakérù

pressure cooker n 圧力ガマ atsúryokugāma

pressure gauge n 圧力計 atsúryokukei

pressure group n (POL) 圧力団体 atsúryokudañtai, プレッシャーグループ purésshāgùrùpu

pressurized [preʃ'əraizd] adj (cabin, container, spacesuit) 気圧を一定に保った kiátsu wò ittéi ni tamotta

prestige [prestiːʒ'] n 名声 mefsei

prestigious [prestidʒ'əs] adj 著名な cho-

méi na

presumably [prizuːm'əbli] adv たぶん tábùn, おそらく osórakù

presume [prizuːm'] vt: to presume (that) (suppose) (...だと) 推定する (...dá tò) suítei suru

presumption [prizʌmp'ʃən] n (supposition) 推定 suítei

presumptuous [prizʌmp'tʃuːəs] adj せん越な señ-etsu na

presuppose [priːsəpouz'] vt ...を前提とする ...wo zeñtei tò suru

pretence [pritens'] (US also: pretense) n (false appearance) 見せ掛け misékake
under false pretences うそを言ってúsò wo itté

pretend [pritend'] vt (feign) ...の振りをする ...no furí wò suru
♦vi (feign) 見せ掛ける misékakerù
to pretend to do ...する振りをする ...suru furí wò suru

pretense [pritens'] (US) n = pretence

pretentious [priten'tʃəs] adj (claiming importance, significance: person, play, film etc) うぬぼれた unúboreta

pretext [priː'tekst] n 口実 kōjitsu

pretty [prit'iː] adj (person, thing) きれいな kírèi na
♦adv (quite) かなり kánàri

prevail [priveil'] vi (be current: custom, belief) はやる hayárù; (gain acceptance, influence: proposal, principle) 勝つ kátsu

prevailing [privei'liŋ] adj (wind) 卓越風 takúetsufù; (dominant: fashion, attitude etc) 一般の ippán no

prevalent [prev'ələnt] adj (common) 一般的な ippánteki na

prevent [privent'] vt: to prevent someone from doing something ...が...をするのを妨げる ...ga ...wo suru nò wo samátagerù
to prevent something from happening ...が起るのを防ぐ ...ga ...wo fuségù

preventative [priven'tativ] adj = preventive

prevention [priven'tʃən] n 予防 yobō

preventive [priven'tiv] *adj* (measures, medicine) 予防の yobô no

preview [pri:'vju:] *n* (of film) 試写会 shishákai; (of exhibition etc) 招待展示内覧 shôtaitenjinaíran

previous [pri:'vi:əs] *adj* (earlier: event, thing, period of time) 前の mâe no

previously [pri:'vi:əsli] *adv* 前に mâe ni

pre-war [pri:'wɔːr] *adj* 戦前の señzen no

prey [prei] *n* 獲物 emôno

♦*vi*: **to prey on** (animal: feed on) ...を捕食する ...wo hoshôku suru

it was preying on his mind 彼はそれを気にしていた kâre wa soré wo kí ni shite itâ

price [prais] *n* (amount of money) 値段 nedán; (fig) 代償 dafshô

♦*vt* (goods) ...に値段を付ける ...ni nedán wo tsukérù

priceless [prais'lis] *adj* 非常に貴重な hijô ni kichô na

price list *n* 値段表 nedánhyô

prick [prik] *n* (short, sharp pain) ちくっとする痛み chikúttò suru itámi

♦*vt* (make hole in) 鋭い物で刺す surúdoi monó dè sásù; (cause pain) ちくっと刺す chikúttò sásù

to prick up one's ears (listen eagerly) 耳を澄まして聞く mimí wò sumáshite kikù

prickle [prik'əl] *n* (of plant) とげ togé; (sensation) ちくちくする痛み chíkùchikù suru itámi

prickly [prik'li:] *adj* (plant) とげだらけの togédarake no; (fabric) ちくちくする chíkùchikù suru

prickly heat *n* あせも asêmo

pride [praid] *n* (satisfaction) 誇り hokóri; (dignity, self-respect) 自尊心 jisónshin, プライド puráido; (*pej*: feeling of superiority) 高慢 kôman

♦*vt*: **to pride oneself on** ...を誇りびてる ...wo hokôri o bǔ

priest [pri:st] *n* (Christian: Catholic, Anglican etc) 司祭 shísai; (non-Christian) 僧侶 sôryo

priestess [pri:s'tis] *n* (non-Christian) みこ mfkò

priesthood [pri:st'hud] *n* (position) 司祭職 shísaishoku

prig [prig] *n* 気取り屋 kidóriya

prim [prim] (*pej*) *adj* (formal, correct) 堅苦しい katákurushiî; (easily shocked) 上品ぶった jôhinbutta

primarily [praimer'i:li] *adv* (above all) 主に ômò ni

primary [prai'me:ri:] *adj* (first in importance) 主要な shuyô na

♦*n* (*US*: election) 予備選挙 yobfseñkyo

primary school *n* 小学校 shôgakkô

primate [prai'meit] *n* (*ZOOL*) 霊長類 reíchôrui

prime [praim] *adj* (most important) 最も重要な mottômò jûyô na; (best quality) 最上の saijô no

♦*n* (of person's life) 盛り sakári

♦*vt* (wood) ...に下塗りをする ...ni shitánuri wò suru; (*fig*: person) ...に教え込む ...ni oshîekomû

prime example (typical) 典型的な例 teñkeiteki nà reî

Prime Minister *n* 総理大臣 sôridaijin, 首相 shushô

primeval [praimi:'vəl] *adj* (existing since long ago): *primeval forest* 原生林 geñseirin; (feelings, tribe) 原始的な geñshiteki na

primitive [prim'ətiv] *adj* 原始的な geñshiteki na

primrose [prim'rouz] *n* ツキミソウ tsukímisô

primus (stove) [prai'məs-] (*BRIT*) *n* 石油こんろ sekíyukoñro

prince [prins] *n* (king etc) 王子 ôji; (son of Japanese emperor) 親王 shifnô

princess [prin'sis] *n* (daughter of king etc) 王女 ôjo; (daughter of Japanese emperor) 内親王 nafshinnô

principal [prin'səpəl] *adj* (most important: reason, character, aim etc) 主要な shuyô na

♦*n* (of school) 校長 kôchô; (of college) 学長 gakúchô

principle [prin'səpəl] *n* (moral belief) 信念 shifnen; (general rule) 原則 geñsoku; (scientific law) 法則 hôsoku

in principle (theoretically) 原則として gensoku tōshité

on principle (morally) 主義として shugí tōshité

print [print] n (letters and numbers on page) 印刷文字 insatsumojī; (ART) 版画 hafiga; (PHOT) 陽画 yōga, プリント purínto; (footprint) 足跡 ashfatð; (fingerprint) 指紋 shimón

♦vt (produce: book, newspaper, leaflet) 印刷する insatsu suru; (publish: story, article etc) 記載する kisái suru; (cloth) …に...を染する ...ni nassén suru; (write in capitals) 活字体で書く katsújitai de káku

out of print 絶版で zeppán de

printed matter [prin'tid-] n 印刷物 insatsubútsu

printer [prin'tə:r] n (person, firm) 印刷屋 insatsuyà; (machine) 印刷機 insatsukī

printing [prin'tin] n (act, art) 印刷 insatsu

printout [print'aut] n (COMPUT) プリントアウト purīntoàuto

prior [prai'ə:r] adj (previous: knowledge, warning, consent etc) 事前の jízén no; (more important: claim, duty) より重要な yorí júyō na

prior to …の前に …no máe ni

priority [praiɔ:r'iti:] n (most urgent task) 優先課題 yūsenkadài; (most important thing, task) 最重要課題 saíjūyōkadài

to have priority (over) (…に) 優先する (…ni) yūsen suru

prise [praiz] vt: **to prise open** こじ開けする kojíakerù

prism [priz'əm] n プリズム purízumu

prison [priz'ən] n (building) 刑務所 kefmusho

♦cpd (life) 刑務所の kefmusho no

prisoner [priz'ənə:r] n (in prison) 囚人 shújin; (captured person) 捕虜 hóryò

prisoner of war n 戦争捕虜 seńsōhòryò

pristine [pris'ti:n] adj (condition: new) 真新しい maátarashiì; (: like new) 新品 同様の shińpindòyō no

privacy [prai'vəsi:] n プライバシー puráìbashì

private [prai'vit] adj (not public: property, club etc) 私有の shíyū no; (: not state-owned: industry, service) 民間の mińkan no; (discussion, sitting etc) 非公開の hikókai no; (personal: activities, belongings) 個人の kójin no; (: thoughts, plans) 心の中の kokóro no naka no; (quiet: place) 奥まった okúmattà; (: person) 内気な uchíki na; (confidential) 内密の naímitsu no; (intimate) 部外者立入禁止の bugáìsha tachírikinshi no

♦n (MIL) 兵卒 heísotsu

「**private**」(on envelope) 親展 shińten; (on door) 部外者立入禁止 bugáìsha tachírikinshi

in private 内密に naímitsu ni

private enterprise n (not state owned) 民間企業 mińkan kigyò; (owned by individual) 個人企業 kójin kigyò

private eye n 私立探偵 shirítsutàntei

private property n 私有地 shíyūchi

private school n (fee-paying) 私立学校 shirítsugakkò

privatize [prai'vətaiz] vt (government-owned company etc) 民間に払い下げる mińkan ni haráì sagerù

privet [priv'it] n イボタノキ ibótanoki

privilege [priv'əlidʒ] n (advantage) 特権 tokkén; (opportunity) 光栄な機会 kóei na kikai

privileged [priv'əlidʒd] adj (having advantages) 特権のある tokkén no arù; (having special opportunity) 光栄な機会を待った kóei na kikai o...

privy [priv'i:] adj: **to be privy to** 内々に 関知している naítai ni kánchi shité irù

prize [praiz] n (reward) 賞 shō

♦adj (first class, top) 最優秀の teńkeiteki na

♦vt 重宝する chóhō suru

prize-giving [praiz'givin] n 表彰式 hyóshōshìki

prizewinner [praiz'winə:r] n 受賞者 jushóshà

pro [prou] n (SPORT) 職業選手 shokúgyōsenshu, プロ púrò

◆*prep* (in favor of): に賛成して ...ni sansei shite

the pros and cons 賛否両論 sánpiryóron

probability [prɒbəˈbilɪti] *n* (likelihood): *probability of that* ...の (...が起こる) 公算 ...no (...ga okóru) kōsan

in all probability たいてい taítei

probable [ˈprɒbəbl] *adj* (likely to happen) 起こりそうな okórisō na; (likely to be true) ありそうな arísō na

probably [ˈprɒbəbli] *adv* たぶん tábun, おそらく osóràku

probation [prəˈbeiʃən] *n*: *on probation* (LAW) 保護観察で hogókañsatsu de; (employee) 見習いで minárai de

probe [prəub] *n* (MED) ゾンデ zốnde; (SPACE) 探査衛星 tañsaeiséi, (enquiry) 調査 chōsa

◆*vt* (investigate) 調査する chōsa suru; (poke) つついて探る tsutsúite sagúru

problem [ˈprɒbləm] *n* 問題 mońdai

problematic(al) [prɒbləˈmætik(əl)] *adj* 問題になる mońdai ni narú

procedure [prəˈsiːdʒər] *n* (way of doing something) やり方 yaríkata; (ADMIN, LAW) 手続 tetsúzuki

proceed [prəˈsiːd] *vi* (do afterwards): *to proceed to do something* ...をし始める ...wo shihájimerù; (continue): *to proceed (with)* (...を) 続ける (...wo) tsuzúkerù; (activity, event, process: carry on) 続ける tsuzúkerù; (person: go) 行く ikú

proceedings [prəˈsiːdɪŋz] *npl* (organized events) 行事 gyōji; (LAW) 訴訟手続き soshótetsuzuki

proceeds [ˈprəusiːdz] *npl* 収益 shúeki

process [ˈprɒses] *n* (series of actions): *also* BIOL, CHEM) 過程 katéi, プロセス purósèsu

◆*vt* (raw materials, food) 加工する kakō suru; (information) 処理する shórì suru

processing [ˈprɒsesiŋ] *n* (PHOT) 現像 geñzō

procession [prəˈseʃən] *n* 行列 gyōretsu

proclaim [prəˈkleim] *vt* (announce) 宣言する señgen suru

proclamation [prɒkləˈmeiʃən] *n* 宣言 señgen

procrastinate [prəˈkræstəneit] *vi* 先に延ばす sakí ni nobásù

procreation [prəukriˈeiʃən] *n* 生殖 sefshoku

procure [prəˈkjuər] *vt* 調達する chōtatsu suru

prod [prɒd] *vt* (push: with finger, stick, knife etc) つつく tsutsúkù

◆*n* (with finger, stick, knife etc) 一突き hitótsuki

prodigal [ˈprɒdɪgəl] *adj*: *prodigal son/daughter* 放とう息子 (娘) hōtómusùko (musúme)

prodigious [prəˈdɪdʒəs] *adj* 巨大な kyódai na

prodigy [ˈprɒdɪdʒi] *n* 天才 teñsai

produce [*n* ˈprɒdjuːs *vb* prəˈdjuːs] *n* (AGR) 農産物 nōsanbūtsu

◆*vt* (cause: effect, result etc) 起す okósù; (make, create: object) 作る tsukúrù; (BIOL: fruit, seeds) つける tsukérù, ...には...がある ...nf wa ...ga nárù; (: young) 産む umú; (CHEM) 作り出す tsukúridasù; (fig: evidence, argument) 示す shimésù; (: bring or take out) 取り出す torídasù; (play, film, program) 製作する sefsaku suru

producer [prəˈdjuːsər] *n* (of film, play, program, record) 製作者 sefsakushā, プロデューサー purōdyūsà; (country: of food, material) 生産国 sefsankōku; (company: of food, material) 生産会社 sefsangaìsha

product [ˈprɒdʌkt] *n* (thing) 産物 sañbutsu; (result) 結果 kekká

production [prəˈdʌkʃən] *n* (process of manufacturing, growing) 生産 sefsan; (amount of goods manufactured, grown) 生産高 sefsandaka; (THEATER) 上演 jōen

electricity production 発電 hatsúden

production line *n* 工程ライン kōteirañ, ライン ráin

productive [prəˈdʌktiv] *adj* (person, thing: *also fig*) 生産的な sefsanteki na

productivity [prɒdʌkˈtiviti] *n* 生産能

力 seísannōryoku

profane [prəˈfeɪn] *adj* (secular, lay) 世俗的な sezókuteki na; (language etc) 下品な gehín na

profess [prəˈfes] *vt* (claim) 主張する shuchō suru; (express: feeling, opinion) 明言する meígen suru

profession [prəˈfeʃən] *n* (job requiring special training) 知的職業 chítékíshokúgyō; (people) 同業者仲間 dōgyōshanakama

professional [prəˈfeʃənəl] *adj* (skill, organization, activity) 専門職の seǐmonshoku no; (not amateur: photographer, musician etc) プロの púro no; (highly trained) 専門家の seǐmonka no; (of a high standard) 本職らしい hoǹshokurashī
◆*n* (doctor, lawyer, teacher etc) 知的職業者 chítékíshokúgyōsha; (SPORT) プロ púrò; (skilled person) 玄人 kúrōto

professor [prəˈfesər] *n* (US) 教師 kyóshi, 先生 señsei; (BRIT) 教授 kyóju

proficiency [prəˈfiʃənsiː] *n* 熟練 jukúren

proficient [prəˈfiʃənt] *adj* 熟練した jukúren shita

profile [ˈprouˌfaɪl] *n* (of person's face) 横顔 yokógaō; (fig: article) 経歴 keíreki

profit [ˈprɑːfit] *n* (COMM) 利益 rḗki
◆*vi*: **to profit by/from** (fig) ...のためになる ...ga tamé ni nárù

profitability [prɑːfitəˈbiləˌtiː] *n* (ECON) 収益性 shūekisei

profitable [ˈprɑːfitəbəl] *adj* (ECON) 利益になる rḗki ni nárù

profound [prəˈfaʊnd] *adj* (great: shock, effect) 強い tsuyóī; (intellectual: idea, work) 深遠な shiń-en na

profusely [prəˈfjuːsliː] *adv* (bleed) 多量に taryó ni; (thank) 重ね重ね kasánegasàne

profusion [prəˈfjuːʒən] *n* 大量 tairyó

prognoses [prɑːgˈnoʊsiːz] *npl* of **prognosis**

prognosis [prɑːgˈnoʊsəs] (*pl* **prognoses**) *n* (forecast) 予想 yosó; (of illness) 予後 yógò

program [ˈprouˌgræm] (BRIT **programme**) *n* (of actions, events) 計画 keí-

kaku; (RADIO, TV) 番組 bañgumi; (leaflet) プログラム puróguràmu; (COMPUT) プログラム puróguràmu
◆*vt* (machine, system) ...にプログラムを入れる ...ni puróguràmu wo irérù

programming [prouˈgræmɪŋ] (BRIT **programming**) *n* (COMPUT) プログラム作成 puróguràmu sakúsèi, プログラミング puróguraǹṁgu

programmer [prouˈgræmər] *n* (COMPUT) プログラマー puróguràmā

progress [*n* ˈprɑːgres *vb* prəˈgres'] *n* (process of getting nearer to objective) 前進 zeǹshin; (changes, advances in society) 進歩 shíṅpo; (development) 発展 hattén
◆*vi* (become more advanced, skilled) 進歩する shíṅpo suru; (become higher in rank) 昇進する shōshin suru; (continue) 続く tsuzúkù

in progress (meeting, battle, match) 進行中で shiǹkōchū de

progression [prəˈgreʃən] *n* (gradual development) 進展 shiǹten; (series) 連続 reǹzoku

progressive [prəˈgresiv] *adj* (person) 進歩的な shiǹpoteki na; (change) 段階的な dańkaiteki na

prohibit [prouˈhibit] *vt* (forbid, make illegal) 禁じる kiǹjirù

prohibition [prouəˈbiʃən] *n* (law, rule) 禁制 kiǹsoku; (forbidding: of strikes, alcohol etc) 禁止 kiǹshi; (US): **Prohibition** 禁酒法時代 kiǹshuhōjidai

prohibitive [prouˈhibitiv] *adj* (cost etc) 法外な hōgai na, 手が出ない様な té ga dénài yō na

project [*n* ˈprɑːdʒekt *vb* prədʒekt'] *n* (large-scale plan, scheme) 計画 keíkaku; (SCOL) 研究テーマ keǹkyūtēma
◆*vt* (plan) 計画する keíkaku suru; (estimate: figure, amount) 見積る mitsúmorù; (light) 投射する tōsha suru; (film, picture) 映写する eísha suru
◆*vi* (stick out) 突出る tsukíderù

projectile [prəˈdʒektʌl] *n* 弾丸 dañgan

projection [prəˈdʒekʃən] *n* (estimate) 見積り mitsúmori; (overhang) 突起 tokkf;

(CINEMA)映写 efsha

projector [prədzek'tər] n 映写機 efsha-ki

proletarian [prouliter'i:ən] adj 無産階級の músankaíkyū no, プロレタリアの puróretaria no

proletariat [prouliter'i:ət] n 無産階級 músankaíkyū, プロレタリア puróretaria

proliferate [prouláf'əreit] vi 急増する kyūzo suru

prolific [proulíf'ik] adj (artist, composer, writer) 多作の tasáku no

prologue [prou'lɔ:g] n (of play) 序幕 jomáku, プロローグ purórōgu; (of book) 序言 jogén

prolong [prəlɔ:ŋ'] vt (life, meeting, holiday) 引延ばす hikínobasū, 延長する eñchō suru

prom [prɑ:m] n abbr = promenade; (US: ball) 学生舞踏会 gakúseibutōkai

promenade [prɑ:məneid'] n (by sea) 海岸の遊歩道 kaígan nò yūhodō

promenade concert (BRIT) n 立見席のある音楽会 tachímiseki no árù oñgakukai

prominence [prɑ:m'ənəns] n (importance) 重要性 jūyōsei

prominent [prɑ:m'ənənt] adj (important) 重要な jūyō na; (very noticeable) 目立つ medátsū

promiscuous [prəmis'kjuəs] adj (person) 相手構わずにセックスをする aíte kamawazů ni sékkůsu wo suru

promise [prɑ:m'is] n (vow) 約束 yakúsoku; (talent) 才能 saínō; (hope) 見込み mikómi

◆vi (vow) 約束する yakúsoku suru

◆vt: **to promise someone something, promise something to someone** ...に...を約束する ...ni ...wo yakúsoku suru

to promise (someone) to do something/that (...に) ...すると約束する (...ni) ...surů tò yakúsoku suru

promising [prɑ:m'isiŋ] adj (person, thing) 有望な yūbō na

promote [prəmout'] vt (employee) 昇進させる shōshin saserů; (product, pop star) 宣伝する señden suru; (ideas) 促進

する sokúshin suru

promoter [prəmou'tər] n (of event) 興業主 kōgyōshù, プロモーター purőmōtà; (of cause, idea) 推進者 sufshinsha

promotion [prəmou'ʃən] n (at work) 昇進 shōshin; (of product, event, idea) 宣伝 señden

prompt [prɑ:mpt] adj (rapid: reaction, response etc) 早速の jiñsoku na

◆adv (exactly) 丁度 chōdo

◆n (COMPUT) プロンプト puróňputo

◆vt (cause) ...の原因となる ...no geñ-in tò narů; (when talking) ...に水を向ける ...ni mizú wò mukérů

to prompt someone to do something ...が...をするきっ掛けとなる ...ga ...wo suru kikkáke to narů

promptly [prɑ:mpt'li:] adv (immediately) 直ちに tádachi ni; (exactly) 丁度 chōdo

prone [proun] adj (lying face down) うつ伏せの utsúbuse no

prone to (inclined to) ...しがちな ...shigáchi na

prong [prɔ:ŋ] n (of fork) 歯 há

pronoun [prou'naun] n 代名詞 daímeishi

pronounce [prənauns'] vt (word) 発音する hatsúon suru; (declare) 宣言する señgen suru; (give verdict, opinion) 言渡す iíwatasů

pronounced [prənaunst'] adj (marked) 著しい ichíjirushii

pronunciation [prənʌnsi:ei'ʃən] n 発音 hatsúon

proof [pru:f] n (evidence) 証拠 shōko; (TYP) 校正刷り kōseizurì, ゲラ gerá

◆adj: **proof against** ...に耐えられる ...ni taérarerů

prop [prɑ:p] n (stick, support: also fig) 支え sasáe

◆vt (also: **prop up**) 支える sasáerů; (lean): **to prop something against** ...を...に立掛ける ...wo ...ni tatékakerů

propaganda [prɑ:pəgæn'də] n 宣伝 señden, プロパガンダ purópaganda

propagate [prɑ:p'əgeit] vt (idea, information) 普及させる fukyů saserů

propel [prəpel'] vt (vehicle, boat,

machine 推進する suíshin suru; (fig: person) 駆立てる karítaterů

propeller [prə'pel'ər] n プロペラ purőpe-rá

propensity [prəpen'siti:] n 傾向 keíkō

proper [prɑːp'ər] adj (real, authentic) ちゃんとした chánto shita; (correct) 正しい tadáshiī; (suitable) 適当な tekítō na; (socially acceptable) 社会の通念にかなった shákāi no tsûnen ni kanáttá; (referring to place): the village proper 村そのもの murá sono monő

properly [prɑːp'ərli:] adv (adequately: eat, study) 充分に jūbun ni; (decently: behave) 正しく tadáshiku

proper noun n 固有名詞 koyúmeîshi

property [prɑːp'ərti:] n (possessions) 財産 zâisan; (building and that is land) 物件 bukkén; (land owned) 所有地 shoyúchi; (quality: of substance, material etc) 特性 tokúsei

property owner n 地主 jinúshi

prophecy [prɑːf'isi:] n 予言 yogén

prophesy [prɑːf'isai] vt (predict) 予言する yogén suru

prophet [prɑːf'it] n (REL) 予言者 yogénsha

prophetic [prəfet'ik] adj (statement, words) 予言的な yogénteki na

proportion [prəpɔːr'ʃən] n (part: of group, amount) 割合 warîai; (number: of people, things) 数 kâzū; (ratio) 率 rîtsû

proportional [prəpɔːr'ʃənəl] adj: **proportional (to)** (...)に比例する (...)ni hiréi suru

proportional representation n 比例代表制 hiréidaihyōsei

proportionate [prəpɔːr'ʃənit] adj: **proportionate (to)** (...)に比例する (...)ni hiréi suru

proposal [prəpou'zəl] n (plan) 提案 teían; **a proposal of marriage** 結婚の申込み kekkón nò mőshikomi, プロポーズ purőpőzu

propose [prəpouz'] vt (plan, idea) 提案する teían suru; (motion) 提出する teíshutsu suru; (toast) 音頭を取る ... no ôndo wo tôrů

♦vi (offer marriage) 結婚を申込む kekkón wð mőshikomů, プロポーズする purőpőzu suru

to propose to do ... ...するつもりでいる ...suru tsumôri de irû

proposition [prɑːpəziʃ'ən] n (statement) 主張 shuchő; (offer) 提案 teían

proprietor [prəprai'ətər] n (of hotel, shop, newspaper etc) 持主 mochínūshi, オーナー őnā

propriety [prəprai'əti:] n (seemliness) 礼儀正しさ reígitadashīsa

pro rata [-rɑːʹtə] adv 比例して hiréi-shi-te

prosaic [prouzei'ik] adj (person, piece of writing) 散文的な sañbunteki na

prose [prouz] n (not poetry) 散文 sañbun

prosecute [prɑːs'əkjuːt] vt (LAW) 訴追する sotsúi suru

prosecution [prɑːsəkjuː'ʃən] n (action) 訴追 sotsúi; (accusing side) 検察側 keńsatsugawa

prosecutor [prɑːs'əkjuːtər] n (also: **public prosecutor**) 検察官 keńsatsukàn

prospect [prɑːs'pekt] n (possibility) 可能性 kanősei; (outlook) 見込み mikőmi
♦vi: **to prospect (for)** (gold etc) (...を) 探鉱する (...wo) tañkő suru

prospecting [prɑːs'pektiŋ] n (for gold, oil etc) 探鉱 tañkő

prospective [prəspek'tiv] adj (son-in-law, customer, candidate etc) ...になろうとしている ...ni narő tő shité irû

prospects [prɑːs'pekts] npl (for work etc) 見込み mikőmi

prospectus [prəspek'təs] n (of college, school, company) 要綱 yőkō

prosper [prɑːs'pər] vi (person, business, city etc) 繁栄する hañ-ei suru

prosperity [prɑːsper'iti:] n 繁栄 hañ-ei

prosperous [prɑːs'pərəs] adj (person, city etc) 裕福な yûfuku na; (business, city etc) 繁盛している hañjő shite irû

prostitute [prɑːs'tituːt] n (female) 売春婦 baíshunfu; (male) 男娼 dañshő

prostrate [prɑːs'treit] adj (face down) うつ伏せの utsúbuse no

protagonist [proutæg'ənist] n (supporter) 支援者 shiénsha; (leading participant: in event, movement) リーダー格の人 rídakaku nò hitó; (THEATER) 主役 shuyáku; (in story etc) 主人公 shujínkô

protect [prə'tekt'] vt (person, thing) 守る mamórù, 保護する hôgò suru

protection [prətek'ʃən] n 保護 hôgò

protective [prətek'tiv] adj (clothing, layer, etc) 防護の bôgo no; (gesture) 防衛の bôei no; (person) 保護的な hogóteki na

protégé [prou'təʒei] n 偉い人のひいきを受ける人 erǎi hitó nò hîfki wò ukérù hitó

protein [prou'ti:n] n たんぱく質 tañpakukushîtsu

protest [n prou'test vb prətest'] n (strong expression of disapproval, opposition) 抗議 kôgi
◆vi: to protest about/against/at ...に抗議する ...ni kôgi suru
◆vt (insist): to protest (that) (...だと) 主張する (...dá tò) shúchô suru

Protestant [prɑt'istənt] adj 新教の shiñkyô no, プロテスタントの purótesùtanto no
◆n 新教徒 shiñkyôto, プロテスタント教徒 purótesùtanto kyôto

protester [prətes'tər] n 抗議者 kôgisha

protocol [prou'təkɑl] n 外交儀礼 gafkôgirèi

prototype [prou'tətaip] n 原型 geñkei

protracted [prətræk'tid] adj (absence, meeting etc) 長引いた nagábiità

protrude [proutruːd'] vi (rock, ledge, teeth etc) 突き出る tsukíderù

proud [praud] adj (pleased): **proud of** ...を誇りとする ...wo hokóri tò suru; (dignified) プライドのある puráido no arú; (arrogant) 尊大な soñdai na

prove [pruːv] vt (verify) 立証する risshô suru
◆vi: to prove (to be) correct etc 結局 ...が正しいと判明する kekkyóku ...ga tadáshiì to hañmei suru
to prove oneself 自分の才能を立証する jibún nò saínô wò risshô suru

proverb [prɑːv'ərb] n ことわざ kotówaza

proverbial [prəvər'bi:əl] adj ことわざの kotówaza no

provide [prəvaid'] vt (give) 与える atáerù; (make available) 供給する kyôkyû suru
to provide someone with something ...に...を供給する ...ni ...wo kyôkyô suru

provided (that) [prəvai'did-] conj ...という条件で ...to iú jôken de

provide for vt fus (person) ...の面倒を見る ...no meñdô wò mfrù
◆vt (future event) ...に備える ...ni sonáerù

Providence [prɑv'idəns] n 摂理 sétsùri

providing [prəvai'diŋ] conj: **providing (that)** ...という条件で ...to iú jôken de

province [prɑv'ins] n (of country) 州 kén; (fig) 管轄 kañkatsu

provincial [prəvin'tʃəl] adj (town, newspaper etc) 地方の chihô no; (pej) 田舎じみた inákajimità

provision [prəviʒ'ən] n (supplying) 供給 kyôkyû; (of contract, agreement) 規定 kitéi

provisional [prəviʒ'ənəl] adj (government, agreement, arrangement etc) 暫定的な zañteiteki na

provisions [prəviʒ'ənz] npl (food) 食料 shokúryô

proviso [prəvai'zou] n 規定 kitéi

provocation [prɑvəkei'ʃən] n 挑発 chôhatsu

provocative [prəvɑk'ətiv] adj (remark, article, gesture) 挑発的な chôhatsuteki na; (sexually stimulating) 扇情的な señjôteki na

provoke [prəvouk'] vt (annoy: person) 怒らせる okóraserù; (cause: fight, argument etc) 引起こす hikíokosù

prow [prau] n へさき hesáki, 船首 señshu

prowess [prau'is] n (outstanding ability) 手腕 shûwan

prowl [praul] vi (also: **prowl about**, **prowl around**) うろつく urótsukû
◆n: **on the prowl** あさり歩いて asár- ruité

prowler [prau'lər] n うろつく人 urótsuku hitô

proximity [prɔːksim'iti:] *n* 近さ chikása

proxy [prɔːk'si:] *n*: **by proxy** 代理を通じて daîri wo tsújíte

prude [pruːd] *n* 上品ぶる人 jōhínburu hitó

prudence [pruː'dəns] *n* (care, sense) 慎重さ shínchōsa

prudent [pruː'dənt] *adj* (careful, sensible) 慎重な shíchō na

prune [pruːn] *n* 干しプラム hoshípuràmu
♦*vt* (bush, plant, tree) 剪定する sefitei suru

pry [prai] *vi*: **to pry (into)** (...を) せん索する (...wo) sefisaku suru

PS [piːes'] *abbr* = **postscript**

psalm [sɑːm] *n* 詩編 shíhén

pseudo- [suː'dou] *prefix* 偽... nisé...

pseudonym [suː'dənim] *n* 筆名 hitsúmei, ペンネーム peñnēmu

psyche [sai'ki:] *n* 精神 seíshin

psychiatric [saikiæt'rik] *adj* (hospital, problem, treatment) 精神科の seíshinka no

psychiatrist [sikai'ətrist] *n* 精神科医 seíshinka-ì

psychiatry [sikai'ətri:] *n* 精神医学 seíshin-ígàku

psychic [sai'kik] *adj* (person: also: **psychical**) 霊媒の reíbai no; (of the mind) 精神の seíshin no

psychoanalysis [saikouænæl'isis] *n* 精神分析 seíshinbuñseki

psychoanalyst [saikouæn'əlist] *n* 精神分析医 seíshinbuñseki-ì

psychoanalyze [saikouæn'əlaiz] *vt* ...の精神分析をする ...no seíshinbuñseki wo suru

psychological [saikəlɑːdʒ'ikəl] *adj* (related to the mind: difference, problem etc) 精神的な seíshinteki na; (related to psychology: test, treatment etc) 心理の shíríteki na

psychologist [saikɑːl'ədʒist] *n* 心理学者 shíríɡakùsha

psychology [saikɑːl'ədʒi:] *n* (study) 心理学 shíríɡakù; (mind) 心理 shíríri

psychopath [sai'kəpæθ] *n* 精神病質者 seíshinbyōshitsushà

psychosomatic [saikousoumæt'ik] *adj* 精神身体の seíshinshíntai no

psychotic [saikɑːt'ik] *adj* 精神病の seíshinbyō no

PTO [pi:ti:'ou'] *abbr* (= *please turn over*) 裏面に続く rímen ni tsuzukú

pub [pʌb] *n abbr* (= *public house*) 酒場 sakába, パブ pábù

puberty [pjuː'bəːrti:] *n* 思春期 shishúñki

pubic [pjuː'bik] *adj*: **pubic hair** 陰毛 ínmō

public [pʌb'lik] *adj* (of people: support, opinion, interest) 国民の kokúmin no; (for people: building, service) 公共の kōkyō no; (for people to see: statement, action etc) 公の ōyake no
♦*n*: **the public** (all people of country, community) 公衆 kōshū; (particular set of people) ...層 ...sō; (fans, supporters) 支持者 shíjíshà

in public 公に ōyake ni, 人前で hitómaè de

to make public 公表する kōyō suru

public address system *n* 場内放送 (装置) jōnaíhōsō(sòchi)

publican [pʌb'likən] *n* パブの亭主 pábù no teíshu

publication [pʌblikei'ʃən] *n* (act) 出版 shuppáñ; (book, magazine) 出版物 shuppáñbutsu

public company *n* 株式会社 kabúshikiɡaìsha

public convenience (*BRIT*) *n* 公衆便所 kōshūbeñjo

public holiday *n* 休日 kyūjitsu

public house (*BRIT*) *n* 酒場 sakába, パブ pábù

publicity [pʌblis'əti:] *n* (information) 宣伝 señden; (attention) 広く知られる事 hfróku shirárerù kotó

publicize [pʌb'lisaiz] *vt* (fact, event) 報道する hōdō suru

publicly [pʌb'likli:] *adv* 公に ōyake ni, 人前で hitómaè de

public opinion *n* 世論 yóròn

public relations *n* 広報活動 kōhōkatsudō, ピーアール píaru

public school *n* (*US*) 公立学校 kōritsugakkō; (BRIT) 私立学校 shiritsugakkō

public-spirited [pʌb'lik'spir'itid] *adj* 公共心のある kōkyōshin nò áru

public transport *n* 公共輸送機関 kōkyōyusōkikan

publish [pʌb'liʃ] *vt* (book, magazine) 出版する shuppan suru; (newspaper) 発行する hakkō suru; (letter etc: in newspaper) 記載する kisái suru; (subj: person: article, story) 発表する happyō suru

publisher [pʌb'liʃər] *n* (person) 発行者 hakkōsha; (company) 出版社 shuppánsha

publishing [pʌb'liʃiŋ] *n* (profession) 出版業 shuppangyō

puce [pjuːs] *adj* 暗かっ色の añkasshoku no

pucker [pʌk'əːr] *vt* (part of face) ...をしかめる ...wo shikámerù; (fabric etc) ...にしわを寄せる ...ni shiwá wò yosérù

pudding [pud'iŋ] *n* (cooked sweet food) プディング púdiñgu; (BRIT: dessert) デザート dezáto

black pudding ブラッドソーセージ buráddosōsēji

puddle [pʌd'əl] *n* (also: **a puddle of water**) 水溜まり mizutamarì; (of blood etc) 溜まり tamari

puff [pʌf] *n* (of cigarette, pipe) 一服 ippóku; (gasp) あえぎ aégi; (of air, smoke) 一吹き hitófukì

♦*vt*: **to puff one's pipe** パイプをふかす páipu wo fukásu

♦*vi* (breathe loudly) あえぐ aégu

puffed [pʌft] (*inf*) *adj* (out of breath) 息を切らせた ikí wo kirásetà

puff out *vt* (fill with air: one's chest, cheeks) 膨らます fukúramasù

puff pastry *n* パイ皮 paíkawa

puffy [pʌf'iː] *adj* (eye) はれぼったい harébottaì; (face) むくんだ mukúnda

pull [pul] *n* (tug): **to give something a pull** ...を引っ張る ...wo hippárù

♦*vt* (*gen*) 引く hikú; (tug: rope, hair etc) 引っ張る hippárù

♦*vi* (tug) 引く hikú, 引っ張る hippárù

to pull to pieces 引裂く hikísakù

to pull one's punches 手加減する teká-

gen suru

to pull one's weight 仲間同様に働く nakámadōyō ni határakù

to pull oneself together 落着きを取り戻す ochítsukì wò torímodosù

to pull someone's leg (*fig*) ...をからかう ...wo karákaù

pull apart *vt* (break) ばらばらにする barábara nì suru

pull down *vt* (building) 取壊す toríkowasù

pulley [pul'iː] *n* 滑車 kasshá

pull in *vi* (AUT: at the curb) ...に停車する ...ni tefsha suru; (RAIL) 到着する tōchaku suru

pull off *vt* (take off: clothes etc) 脱ぐ nǔgū; (*fig*: difficult thing) ...に成功する ...ni sefkō suru

pull out *vi* (AUT: from curb) 発進する hasshín suru; (RAIL) 出発する shuppátsu suru

♦*vt* (extract) 取出す torídasù

pull over *vi* (AUT) 道路わきに寄せて停車する dōrowaki nì yosete tefsha suru

pullover [pul'ouvər] *n* セーター sētā

pull through *vi* (MED) 治る naóru

pull up *vi* (AUT, RAIL: stop) 停車する tefsha suru

♦*vt* (raise: object, clothing) 引上げる hikágerù; (uproot) 引抜く hikínukù

pulp [pʌlp] *n* (of fruit) 果肉 kaníku

pulpit [pul'pit] *n* 説教壇 sekkyōdaň

pulsate [pʌl'seit] *vi* 脈動する myakudō suru

pulse [pʌls] *n* (ANAT) 脈拍 myakúhaku; (rhythm) 鼓動 kodō; (BOT) 豆類 mamérùi

pulverize [pʌl'vəːraiz] *vt* (crush to a powder) 砕く kudákù; (*fig*: destroy) 破壊する hakái suru

puma [pju'mə] *n* ピューマ pyūma

pummel [pʌm'əl] *vt* 続け様にげんこつで打つ tsuzúkezama nì geñkotsu de utsù

pump [pʌmp] *n* (for water, air, petrol) ポンプ póňpu; (shoe) パンプス páňpusu

♦*vt* (force: in certain direction: liquid, gas) ポンプで送る póňpu de okúrù; (obtain supply of: oil, water, gas) ポンプで

で汲む pônpu de kúmù

pumpkin [pʌmpˈkin] n カボチャ kabóchà

pump up vt (inflate) ポンプで膨らます pônpu de fukúramasù

pun [pʌn] n しゃれ sharé

punch [pʌntʃ] n (blow) げんこつで打つ事 geńkotsu dè útsù kotó, パンチ pánchì; (tool: for making holes) パンチ pánchì; (drink) ポンチ pónchì

♦vt (hit): **to punch someone/something** げんこつで...を打つ geńkotsu de ...wo útsù

punchline [pʌntʃˈlain] n 落ち ochí

punch-up [pʌntʃˈʌp] n (BRIT: inf) けんか keńka

punctual [pʌŋkˈtʃuːəl] adj 時間を厳守する jíkàn wo geńshu suru

punctuation [pʌŋktʃuːeiˈʃən] n 句読法 kutóhō

puncture [pʌŋkˈtʃər] n パンク páǹku

♦vt ...に穴を開ける ...ní aná wò akéru

pundit [pʌnˈdit] n 物知り monóshirì

pungent [pʌnˈdʒənt] adj (smell, taste) 刺激的な shigékitekì na

punish [pʌnˈiʃ] vt (person, crime) 罰する bassúru

punishment [pʌnˈiʃmənt] n (act) 罰する事 bassúru kotó; (way of punishing) 罰 bátsù

punk [pʌŋk] n (also: **punk rock**) パンクロック pańkurokkù; (also: **punk rocker**) パンクロッカー pańkurokkà; (US: inf: hoodlum) ちんぴら chińpira

punt [pʌnt] n (boat) ポート bōto ◇底が平らでさおで川底を突いて進める舟を指す sokó ga taíra de sáò de kawázoko wo tsuíte susúmeru mono wò sásù

punter [pʌnˈtər] n (BRIT: gambler) ばくち打ち bakúchìuchi; (inf: client, customer) 客 kyakú

puny [pjuːˈniː] adj (person, effort) ちっぽけな chippóke na

pup [pʌp] n (young dog) 子イヌ koínu

pupil [pjuːˈpəl] n (SCOL) 生徒 seítò; (of eye) 瞳孔 dōkō

puppet [pʌpˈit] n (doll) 操り人形 ayátsuriningyō; (fig: person) かいらい kaírai

puppy [pʌpˈiː] n 子イヌ koínu

purchase [pərˈtʃis] n (act of buying) 購入 kōnyū; (item bought) 買い物 kaímono

♦vt (buy: house, book, car etc) 買う kaú

purchaser [pərˈtʃisər] n 買い手 kaíte

pure [pjuːr] adj (not mixed with anything: silk, gold etc) 純粋な juńsui na; (clean, healthy: water, air etc) 清潔な seíketsu na; (fig: woman, girl) 純潔な juńketsu na; (complete, total: chance, bliss) 全くの mattáku no

purée [pjureiˈ] n (of tomatoes, potatoes, apples etc) ピューレ pyúrè

purely [pjuːrˈliː] adv 単にtáǹ ni

purgatory [pərˈgətɔːriː] n (REL) れん獄 reńgoku; (fig) 地獄 jigóku

purge [pərdʒ] n (POL) 粛正 shukúsei, パージ pāji

♦vt (organization) 粛正する shukúsei suru, パージする pāji suru

purify [pjuːrˈəfai] vt (air, water etc) 浄化する jōka suru

purist [pjuːrˈist] n 純正主義者 juńseishugìshà

puritan [pjuːrˈitən] n 禁欲主義者 kiń-yokushugìsha

purity [pjuːrˈitiː] n (of silk, gold etc) 純粋さ juńsuisa; (of water, air etc) 清潔さ seíketsu; (fig: of woman, girl) 純潔 juńketsu

purple [pərˈpəl] adj 紫色の murásakiiro no

purport [pərˈpɔːrt] vi: **to purport to be/do** ...である(...ができる)と主張する ...de árù(...ga dekírù)to shuchō suru

purpose [pərˈpəs] n (reason) 目的 mokúteki; (objective: of person) 目標 mokúhyō

on purpose 意図的に itóteki ni, わざと wázà to

purposeful [pərˈpəsfəl] adj (person, look, gesture) 果敢な kakán na

purr [pər] vi (cat) ごろごろとのどを鳴らす gorógoro to nódò wo narásù

purse [pərs] n (for money) 財布 saífu; (US: handbag) ハンドバッグ hańdobaggù

♦vt (lips) すぼめる subómerù

purser [pəːrsəːr] *n* (NAUT) 事務長 jimúchō, パーサー pāsā

pursue [pəːrsúː] *vt* (follow: person, thing) 追う oú, 追跡する tsufseki suru; (*fig*: activity, interest) 追う okonaú; (: plan) 実行する jikkō suru; (: aim, result) 追い求める ofmotomerú

pursuer [pəːrsúːəːr] *n* 追跡者 tsufsekísha

pursuit [pəːrsúːt] *n* (chase: of person, thing) 追跡 tsufseki; (*fig*: of happiness, pleasure etc) 追求 tsufkyū; (pastime) 趣味 shúmí

pus [pʌs] *n* うみ umí

push [puʃ] *n* 押す事 osú kotó
♦*vt* (press, shove) 押す osú; (promote) 宣伝する sefden suru
♦*vi* (press, shove) 押す osú; (*fig*: demand urgently): **to push for** 要求する yōkyū suru

push aside *vt* 押しのける oshfnokerú

pushchair [puʃ'tʃeːr] *n* バリ型ベビーカー isúgata bebíka

pusher [puʃ'əːr] *n* (drug pusher) 売人 bafnin

push off *(inf) vi: push off!* 消えうせろ kiéuserò

push on *vi* (continue) 続ける tsuzūkerù

pushover [puʃ'ouvəːr] *(inf) n: it's a pushover* 朝飯前だ asámeshìmaè da

push through *vi* (crowd etc) ...を押し分けて進む ...wo oshfwaketè susumù
♦*vt* (measure, scheme etc) 押し通す oshftōsu

push up *vt* total, prices 押し上げる oshfagerù

push-up [puʃ'ʌp] *(US) n* (press-up) 腕立て伏せ udétatefùse

pushy [puʃ'iː] *(pej) adj* 押しの強い oshf no tsuyoï

puss [pus] *(inf) n* ネコちゃん nékochàn

pussy(cat) [pus'i(:kæt)] *(inf) n* ネコちゃん nékochàn

put [put] *(pt, pp* **put)** *vt* (place: thing) 置く okú; (: person: in institution etc) 入れる irérù; (express: idea, remark etc) 表現する hyōgen suru; (present: case, view) 説明する setsúmei suru; (ask: question) する súrù; (place: person: in state, situa-

tion) 追い込む ofkomù, 置く okú; (estimate) 推定する suftei suru; (write: type: word, sentence etc) 書く kákù

put about/around *vt* (rumor) 広める hirómerù

put across *vt* (ideas etc) 分からせる wakáraserù

put away *vt* (store) 仕舞っておく shimátte okù

put back *vt* (replace) 戻す modósù; (postpone) 延期する efki suru; (delay) 遅らせる okúraserù

put by *vt* (money, supplies etc) 蓄えておく takúwaete okù

put down *vt* (on floor, table) 下ろす orósù; (in writing) 書く kákù; (riot, rebellion) 鎮圧する chiń-atsu suru; (kill: animal) 安楽死させる afrakushì saserù; (attribute): **to put something down to** ...を...のせいにする ...wo ...no seí ni surù

put forward *vt* (ideas, proposal) 提案する tefan suru

put in *vt* (application, complaint) 提出する tefshutsu suru; (time, effort) つぎ込む tsugfkomù

put off *vt* (delay) 延期する efki suru; (discourage) いやにさせる iyá ni saserù

put on *vt* (shirt, blouse, dress etc) 着る kírù; (hat etc) かぶる kabúrù; (shoes, pants, skirt etc) はく hakú; (gloves etc) はめる hamérù; (make-up, ointment etc) つける tsukérù; (light etc) つける tsukérù; (play etc) 上演する jōen suru; (brake) かける kakérù; (record, tape, video) かける kakérù; (kettle, dinner etc) 火にかける hí ni kakérù; (assume: look, behavior etc) 装う yosóoù; (gain): **to put on weight** 太る futórù

put out *vt* (fire, candle, cigarette, light) 消す kesú; (take out: rubbish, cat etc) 出す dásù; (one's hand) 伸ばす nobásù; (inf: person): **to be put out** 怒っている okótte irù

putrid [puː'trid] *adj* 腐った kusátta

putt [pʌt] *n* (GOLF) パット pátto

put through *vt* (TEL: person, call) つなぐ tsunágù; (plan, programme) 成功させる sefkō saserù

putting green [pʌt'iŋ-] n (GOLF: smooth area around hole) グリーン gurín; (: for practice) パット練習場 páttōreñshūjō

putty [pʌt'i:] n パテ páte

put up vt (build) 建てる tatérù; (raise: umbrella) 広げる hírógerù; (: tent) 張る hárù; (: hood) かぶる kabúrù; (poster, sign etc) 張る harù; (increase: price, cost) 上げる agérù; (accommodate) 泊める tomérù

put-up [put'ʌp]: **put-up job** (BRIT) n 八百長 yaóchō

put up with vt fus 我慢する gámàn suru

puzzle [pʌz'əl] n (question, game) なぞなぞ nazónazo; (toy) パズル pázùru; (mystery) なぞ nazó

♦vt 当惑させる tōwaku saserù

♦vi: **to puzzle over something** …を思案する …wo shíàn suru

puzzling [pʌz'liŋ] adj (thing, action) 訳の分からない wákè no wakáranai

pyjamas [pədʒɑːm'əz] (BRIT) npl = **pajamas**

pylon [pai'lɑːn] n (for electric cables) 鉄塔 tettó

pyramid [pir'əmid] n (ARCHIT) ピラミッド pirámiddò; (shape, object, pile) ピラミッド状の物 pirámiddòjō no monó

Pyrenees [pir'əni:z] npl: **the Pyrenees** ピレネー山脈 pírènē sáñmyaku

python [pai'θɑːn] n ニシキヘビ nishíkihebì

Q

quack [kwæk] n (of duck) がーがー gāgā; (pej: doctor) やぶ医者 yabúisha

quad [kwɑːd] abbr = **quadrangle**; **quadruplet**

quadrangle [kwɑːd'ræŋgəl] n (courtyard) 中庭 nakániwa

quadruple [kwɑːdruː'pəl] vt (increase fourfold) 4倍にする yońbai ni suru

♦vi 4倍になる yońbai ni naru

quadruplets [kwɑːdrʌ'plits] npl 四つ子 yotsúgo

quagmire [kwæg'maiəːr] n (bog) 湿地 shitchí; (muddy place) ぬかるみ nukárumi

quail [kweil] n (bird) ウズラ uzúra

♦vi: **to quail at/before** (anger, prospect) …の前でおじけづく …no maè de ojíkezùku

quaint [kweint] adj (house, village) 古風で面白い kofū de omóshiroì; (ideas, customs) 奇妙な kimyō na

quake [kweik] vi (with fear) 震える furúerù

♦n abbr = **earthquake**

Quaker [kwei'kəːr] n クエーカー教徒 kuēkākyōto

qualification [kwɑːləfəkei'ʃən] n (often pl: training, degree, diploma) 資格 shikáku; (skill, quality) 能力 nōryòku; (reservation, modification) 限定 geñtei, 条件 jōken

qualified [kwɑːl'əfaid] adj (trained) 資格のある shikáku no arù; (fit, competent): **qualified to** …をする能力がある shíkàku nōryòku ga arù; (limited) 条件付きの jōkentsuki no

qualify [kwɑːl'əfai] vt (make competent) …に資格を与える …ni shikáku wo ataérù; (modify) 限定する geñtei suru

♦vi (pass examination(s)): **to qualify (as)** …の資格を取る …no shikáku wo torù; (be eligible): **to qualify (for)** (…の) 資格がある (…no) shíkàku ga arù; (in competition): **to qualify (for)** (…に進む) 資格を得る (…ni susúmu) shíkàku wo erù

quality [kwɑːl'iti:] n (standard: of work, product) 品質 hiñshitsu; (characteristic: of person) 性質 sefshitsu; (: of wood, stone etc) 特徴 tokúchō

qualm [kwɑːm] n (doubt) 疑問 gimón **qualms of conscience** 良心のかぎ ryōshin nō kashǎku

quandary [kwɑːn'dri:] n: **to be in a quandary** 途方に暮れる tohō ni kuréru

quantity [kwɑːn'titi:] n (amount: of uncountable thing) 量 ryō; (: of countable things) 数 kazù

quantity surveyor n 積算士 sekīsan-shi ◊工事などの費用を見積もり計算する人 kōji nadŏ no híyŏ wo mitsúmori dè kefsan suru hitŏ

quarantine [kwɔːrˈɒntiːn] n (isolation) 隔離 kákûri

quarrel [kwɔrˈəl] n (argument) けんか keñka
◊vi: to quarrel (with) (...と) けんかする (...to) keñka suru

quarrelsome [kwɔrˈəlsəm] adj けんかっ早い kéñkappayaf

quarry [kwɔrˈiː] n (for stone) 石切り場 ishíkiriba, 採石場 safsekijŏ; (animal) 獲物 emóno

quart [kwɔːrt] n クォート kwŏto

quarter [kwɔːrtˈəːr] n (fourth part) 4分の1 yoñbun no ichi; (US: coin) 25セント玉 nijūgoseñtodamā; (year) 四半期 shihâñki; (district) 地区 chíkû
◊vt (divide by four) 4等分する yoñtŏbun suru; (MIL: lodge) 宿泊させる shukúha-ku saseru

a quarter of an hour 15分 jūgófun

quarter final n 準々決勝 juñjunkesshŏ

quarterly [kwɔːrtˈəːrliː] adj (meeting, payment) 年4回の nēn-yoñkai no
◊adv (meet, pay) 年4回に nēn-yoñkai ni

quarters [kwɔːrtˈəːrz] npl (barracks) 兵舎 hefsha; (living quarters) 宿舎 shúkusha

quartet(te) [kwɔːrtetˈ] n (group: of instrumentalists) 四重奏団 shijūsŏdan, カルテット karûtetto; (: of singers) 四重唱団 shijūshŏdan, カルテット karûtetto; (piece of music) 四重奏曲 shijūsŏkyokû

quartz [kwɔːrts] n 水晶 suíshŏ

quash [kwɑʃ] vt (verdict, judgement) 破棄する hakî suru

quasi- [kweiˈzai] prefix 疑似... gijf...

quaver [kweiˈvəːr] n (BRIT: MUS) 八分音符 hachfbûon ofpu
◊vi (voice) 震える furúeru

quay [kiː] n (also: quayside) 岸壁 gañpeki

queasy [kwiːˈziː] adj (nauseous) 吐気がする hakíkê ga suru

queen [kwiːn] n (monarch) 女王 joŏ; (king's wife) 王妃 ŏhî; (ZOOL: also:

queen bee 女王バチ joŏbachi; (CARDS, CHESS) クイーン kuîñ

queen mother n 皇太后 kŏtaigŏ

queer [kwiːr] adj (odd) 変な heñ na
◊n (inf: homosexual) ホモ homŏ

quell [kwel] vt (of opposition) 鎮める shizû-meru; (unease, fears) なだめる nadâme-ru, 静める shizûmeru

quench [kwentʃ] vt: to quench one's thirst のどの乾きをいやす nodŏ no ka-wâkî wo iyâsu

querulous [kwerˈələs] adj (person, voice) 愚痴っぽい guchîppôi

query [kwiˈriː] n (question) 質問 shitsû-mon
◊vt (question) ...に聞く ...ni kikû, ...に質問する ...ni shitsûmon suru

quest [kwest] n 探求 tañkyû

question [kwesˈtʃən] n (query) 質問 shitsûmon; (doubt) 疑問 gimón; (issue) 問題 moñdai; (in test: problem) 問 tof
◊vt (ask) ...に聞く ...ni kikû, ...に質問する ...ni shitsûmon suru; (interrogate) 尋問する jiñmon suru; (doubt) ...に疑問を投げ掛ける ...ni gimón wo nagêkakeru

beyond question 疑いもなく utágai mo naku

out of the question 全く不可能で mattâku fukânŏ de

questionable [kwesˈtʃənəbəl] adj (doubt-ful) 疑わしい utâgawashiî

question mark n 疑問符 gimóñfu

questionnaire [kwestʃənˈeːr] n 調査票 chŏsahyŏ, アンケート añkêto

queue [kjuː] (BRIT) n 列 retsú
◊vi (also: queue up) 列を作る retsú wo tsukûru

quibble [kwibˈəl] vi 詰まらない議論をする tsumárañai girôn wo suru

quiche [kiːʃ] n キッシュ kisshû ◊パイの一種 paf no isshû

quick [kwik] adj (fast: person, movement, action etc) 早い hayâī; (agile) 素早い subâyai; (: mind) 理解の早い rikâi no hayâī; (brief: look, visit) 短い mijfkaī, ちょっとした chottŏ shita
◊n: cut to the quick (fig) ...の感情を害する ...no kañjŏ wo gaf súru

be quick! 急いで isólde

quicken [kwik'ən] vt (pace, step) 早める hayámeru
◆vi (pace, step) 早くなる hayáku naru

quickly [kwik'li:] adv 早く hayáku

quicksand [kwik'sænd] n 流±砂 ryúdosha, クイックサンド kuíkkûsando

quick-witted [kwik'wit'id] adj (alert) 機敏な kibín na

quid [kwid] (BRIT: inf) n inv ポンド póndo

quiet [kwai'it] adj (not loud or noisy) 静かな shízùka na; (silent) 何も言わない naní mo iwánai; (peaceful place) 平和な heíwa na; (calm: person) もの静かな monóshizuka na; (without fuss etc: ceremony) 簡単な kańtan na
◆n (peacefulness) 静けさ shízùkesa; (silence) 静かにする事 shízùka ni suru koto
◆vi (US: also: **quiet down**) (grow calm) 落着く ochítsuku; (grow silent) 静かになる shízùka ni naru
◆vt (person, animal) 落着かせる ochítsukaserú

quieten [kwai'itən] (BRIT) = **quiet** vi, vt

quietly [kwai'itli:] adv (speak, play) 静かに shízùka ni; (silently) 黙って damátte

quietness [kwai'itnis] n (peacefulness) 静けさ shízùkesa; (silence) 静かにする事 shízùka ni suru koto

quilt [kwilt] n (covering) ベッドカバー beddókabá; (also: **continental quilt**) 掛布団 kakébuton, キルト kirúto

quin [kwin] n abbr = **quintuplet**

quinine [kwai'nain] n キニーネ kiníne

quintet(te) [kwintet'] n (group) 五重奏団 gojúsōdan, クインテット kuíntetto; (piece of music) 五重奏曲 gojúsōkyoku

quintuplets [kwintʌp'lits] npl 五つ子 itsútsugo

quip [kwip] n 警句 kefku

quirk [kwə:rk] n (unusual characteristic) 癖 kusé; (accident of fate, nature) 気まぐれ kímágure

quit [kwit] (pt, pp **quit** or **quitted**) vt (smoking, grumbling) やめる yamérù;

(job) 辞める yamérù; (premises) ...から出ていく ...kara détè iku
◆vi (give up) やめる yamérù; (resign) 辞める yamérù

quite [kwait] adv (rather) かなり kánàri; (entirely) 全く mattáku, 完全に kañzen ni; (following a negative: almost): *that's not quite big enough* それはちょっと小さい sorê wa chottó chiísai
I saw quite a few of them 私はそれらをかなり沢山見ました watákushi wa sorêra wo kánàri takúsan mimashita
(that so!) 全くその通り mattáku sonó tōri

quits [kwits] adj (with) (...と) おあいこである (...to) o-áiko de aru
let's call it quits (call it even) おあいこにしましょう o-áiko ni shimáshō, (stop working etc) やめましょう yamé-mashō

quiver [kwiv'ə:r] vi (tremble) 震える furúerù

quiz [kwiz] n (game) クイズ kuízu; (US: short test) 小テスト shótesutò
◆vt (question) 尋問する jiñmon suru

quizzical [kwiz'ikəl] adj (look, smile) なぞめいた nazómeita

quorum [kwɔ:r'əm] n (of members) 定足数 teísokusū

quota [kwou'tə] n 割当数(量) warfatesú (ryō)

quotation [kwoutei'ʃən] n (from book, play etc) 引用文 iñ-yōbun; (estimate) 見積り mítsūmori

quotation marks npl 引用符 iñyófu

quote [kwout] n (from book, play etc) 引用文 iñ-yōbun; (estimate) 見積り mítsūmori
◆vt (sentence, proverb etc) 引用する iñ-yō suru; (figure, example) 引合いに出す hikíai ni dasù; (price) 見積る mítsumorù
◆vi: *to quote from* (book, play etc) ...から引用する ...kara iñ-yō suru

quotes [kwouts] npl (quotation marks) 引用符 iñ-yófu

quotient [kwou'ʃənt] n (factor) 指数 shísū

R

rabbi [ræbˈai] (*BRIT*) *n* ラビ rábì ◇ユダヤ教の聖職者 yudáyakyō nò sefshokushà

rabbit [ræbˈit] *n* ウサギ usági

rabbit hutch *n* ウサギ小屋 uságigoyà

rabble [ræbˈəl] (*pej*) *n* 群衆 gunshū

rabies [reiˈbiːz] *n* 恐水病 kyōkeubyō

RAC [ɑːreisiːˈ] (*BRIT*) *n abbr* [= *Royal Automobile Club*] 英国自動車連盟 efkoku jidōsha reñmei

raccoon [rækuːnˈ] *n* アライグマ aráigùma

race [reis] *n* (*species*) 人種 jiñshu; (*competition: for speed*) 競走 kyōsō, レース rēsù; (: *for power, control*) 競争 kyōsō; (*public gambling event: on*: **horse race**) 競馬 kebba; (: *also*: **bicycle race**) 競輪 kefrin; (: *also*: **motorboat race**) 競艇 kyōtei
♦*vt* (*horse*) 競馬に出場させる kefba nī shutsʊ̄jō saserʊ̀; (*compete against: person*)...と競走する ...to kyōsō suru
♦*vi* (*compete: for speed*) 競走する kyōsō suru; (: *for power, control*) 競争する kyōsō suru; (*hurry*) 急いで行く isóide ikù; (*pulse*) どきどきする dókìdoki suru; (*engine*) 空回りする karámawarì suru

race car (*US*) *n* レーシングカー rēshingukà

race car driver (*US*) *n* レーサー rēsà

racecourse [reisˈkɔːrs] *n* 競馬場 kefbajō

racehorse [reisˈhɔːrs] *n* 競走馬 kyōsōba

racetrack [reisˈtræk] *n* (*for people*) トラック torákkù; (*for cars*) サーキット sắkitto

racial [reiˈʃəl] *adj* 人種の jiñshu no, 人種... jiñshu...

racing [reiˈsiŋ] *n* (*horses*) 競馬 kefba; (*bicycles*) 競輪 kefrin; (*motorboats*) 競艇 kyōtei; (*cars*) 自動車レース jidōsharèsu; (*motorcycles*) オートレース ōtorèsu

racing car (*BRIT*) *n* = **race car**

racing driver (*BRIT*) *n* = **race car driver**

racism [reiˈsizəm] *n* 人種差別 jiñshusabetsu

racist [reiˈsist] *adj* (*statement, policy*) 人種差別的な jiñshusabetsuteki na
♦*n* 人種差別主義者 jiñshusabetsushugishà

rack [ræk] *n* (*also*: **luggage rack**) 網棚 amídana; (*shelf*) 棚 taná; (*also*: **roof rack**) ルーフラック rūfurakkù; (*dish rack*) 水切りかご mizékirikago
♦*vt*: **racked by** (*pain, anxiety*)...でもだえ苦しんで ...de modáekurushiñde
to rack one's brains 知恵を絞る chié wo shibórù

racket [rækˈit] *n* (*for tennis, squash etc*) ラケット rakéttò; (*noise*) 騒音 sōon; (*swindle*) 詐欺 sági

racoon [rækuːnˈ] *n* = **raccoon**

racquet [rækˈit] *n* (*for tennis, squash etc*) ラケット rakéttò

racy [reiˈsiː] *adj* きびきびした kíbìkibi shita

radar [reiˈdɑːr] *n* レーダー rēda

radiance [reiˈdiːəns] *n* (*glow*) 光 hikári

radiant [reiˈdiːənt] *adj* (*happy, joyful*) 輝く kagáyakù

radiate [reiˈdiːeit] *vt* (*heat*) 放射する hōsha suru; (*emotion*)...で輝く ...de kagáyakù
♦*vi* (*lines*) 放射状に広がる hōshajō nī hirógarù

radiation [reidiːeiˈʃən] *n* (*radioactive*) 放射能 hōshanō; (*from sun etc*) 放射 hōsha

radiator [reiˈdiːeitəːr] *n* ラジエーター rajfetā

radical [rædˈikəl] *adj* (*change etc*) 抜本的な bappónteki na; (*person*) 過激な kagéki na; (*organization*) 過激派の kagékiha no, 過激派... kagékiha...

radii [reiˈdiːai] *npl of* **radius**

radio [reiˈdiːou] *n* (*broadcasting*) ラジオ放送 rajfohōsō; (*device: for receiving broadcasts*) ラジオ rájìo; (: *for transmitting and receiving signals*) 無線通信機 muséntsūshinki
♦*vt* (*person*)...と無線で通信する ...to tsūshin suru
on the radio ラジオで rájìo de

radioactive [reidiːəuˈæk'tiv] adj 放射性の hōshasei no

radiography [reidiˈɔgˈrafi:] n レントゲン撮影 rentogensatsuěi

radiology [reidiˈɔlˈədʒi:] n 放射線医学 hōshasen-igāku

radio station n ラジオ放送局 rajfo hōsōkyōku

radiotherapy [reidiːouˈθerˈəpiː] n 放射線療法 hōshasenryōhō

radish [ræd'iʃ] n はつかだいこん hatsukadaīkon

radius [reidiˈəs] (pl radii) n (of circle) 半径 hańkeī; (from point) 半径内の範囲 hańkeinai no hán-i

RAF [ɑːreief] n abbr = **Royal Air Force**

raffle [ræf'əl] n 宝くじ takarakúji ◇当る と金ではなく賞品をもらえる物を指す a-tárū to kanē de wa nakū shōhin wo moráerū monó wo sásū

raft [ræft] n (craft) いかだ ikáda; (also: life raft) 救命いかだ kyūmei ikáda

rafter [ræf'tɑːr] n はり harí

rag [ræg] n (piece of cloth) ぞうきん zōkin; (torn cloth) ぼろ bōrō; (pej: newspaper) 三流紙 safryūshi; (BRIT: UNIVERSITY: for charity) 慈善募金運動 jizénbokin-uńdō

rag-and-bone man [ræɡənboun'-] (BRIT) n = **ragman**

rag doll n 縫いぐるみ人形 nuíguruminíngyō

rage [reidʒ] n (fury) 憤怒 fóndo
♦vi (person) 怒り狂う ikárikuruū; (storm) 荒れ狂う arékuruū; (debate) 荒れる arérū
it's all the rage (very fashionable) 大流行している dairyūkō shite irū

ragged [ræg'id] adj (edge) ぎざぎざの gizágiza no; (clothes) ぼろぼろの boróboro no; (appearance) ぞろぞろの fuzórobo no

ragman [ræg'mæn] (pl ragmen) n くず屋 kuzúya

rags [ræɡz] npl (torn clothes) ぼろぼろの衣服 boróboro no ifuku

raid [reid] n (MIL) 襲撃 shūgeki; (criminal) 不法侵入 fuhōshinnyū; (by police) 手

入れ tefre
♦vt (MIL) 襲撃する shūgeki suru; (criminally) ...に不法侵入する ...ni fuhōshinnyū suru; (subj: police) 手入れをする tefre suru

rail [reil] n 手すり tesúri
by rail (by train) 列車で ressha de

railing(s) [rei'liŋ(z)] n(pl) (fence) さく sakú

railroad [reil'roud] (US) n (track) 線路 sēnro; (company) 鉄道 tetsúdō

railroader [reil'roud-] (US) n 鉄道員 tetsúdōīn

railroad line (US) n 鉄道線 tetsúdōsen

railroad station (US) n 駅 éki

rails [reilz] npl (for train) レール rēru

railway [reil'wei] (BRIT) n = **railroad etc**

railwayman [reil'weiman] (BRIT: pl railwaymen) n = **railroader**

rain [rein] n 雨 ámē
♦vi 雨が降る ámē ga fúrū
in the rain 雨の中で ámē no nákā de
it's raining 雨が降っている ámē ga futté irū

rainbow [rein'bou] n にじ nijf

raincoat [rein'kout] n レーンコート réhkōto

raindrop [rein'drɑːp] n 雨の一滴 ámē no ittéki

rainfall [rein'fɔːl] n 降雨量 kōuryō

rainy [rei'ni:] adj 雨模様の amémoyō no

raise [reiz] n (payrise) 賃上げ chín-age
♦vt (lift) 持ち上げる mochíageru; (increase: salary) 上げる agérū; (: production) 増やす fuyásū; (: improve; morale) 高める takámerū; (: standards) 引上げる hikfagérū; (produce: doubts, question) 引起こす hikfokosū; (rear: cattle) 飼育する shiíku suru; (: family) 育てる sodáterū; (cultivate: crop) 栽培する saíbai suru; (get together: army, funds, loan) 集める atsúmerū
to raise one's voice 声を大きくする kóē wo ōkiku suru

raisin [rei'zin] n 干しぶどう hoshíbudō, レーズン rēzun

rake [reik] n (tool) レーキ rēki
♦vt (garden) レーキで...の土をならす rē-

ki de ...no tsuchí wò narásù; (leaves) か
き集める kakfigsumerù; (with machine
gun) 掃射する sósha suru

rally [ˈrælɪ] n (POL etc) 集会 shūkai;
(AUT) ラリー rarī; (TENNIS etc) ラリ
ー rārī
♦vt (support) 集める atsúmerù
♦vi (sick person, Stock Exchange) 持直
す mochínaosù

rally round vt fus (fig: give support to)
...の支援に駆け付ける ...no shién ni kaké-
tsukerù

RAM [ræm] n abbr = (**random access
memory**) ラム rámù

ram [ræm] n (ZOOL) 雄ヒツジ osúhitsùji
♦vt (crash into) ...に激突する ...ni gekítto-
tsu suru; (push: bolt, fist etc) 押込む oshíkomù

ramble [ˈræmbəl] n (walk) ハイキング
háikingu
♦vi (walk) ハイキングする háikingu suru; (talk: also: **ramble on**) だらだらしゃ
べる dárädara shaberù

rambler [ˈræmblər] n (walker) ハイカー
háikä; (BOT) ツルバラ tsurúbara

rambling [ˈræmblɪŋ] adj (speech) 取留め
のない torítome no naì; (house) だだっ広
い dadáppiroì; (BOT) つる性の tsurúsei
no

ramp [ræmp] n 傾斜路 kefsharo
on/off ramp (US: AUT) 入口(出口)ラ
ンプ iríguchi(degúchi)ranpu

rampage [ˈræmpeɪdʒ] n: **to be on the
rampage** 暴れ回っている abáremawat-
te irú
♦vi: **they went rampaging through
the town** 彼らは町で暴れ回った kárèra
wa machíjù abáremawattà

rampant [ˈræmpənt] adj (crime) はびこ
る habíkorù; (disease) まん延する mañ-en
suru

rampart [ˈræmpɑːrt] n (fortification) 城
壁 jōheki

ramshackle [ˈræmʃækəl] adj (house,
car, table) がたがたの gatágata no

ran [ræn] pt of **run**

ranch [ræntʃ] n 牧場 bokújō

rancher [ˈræntʃər] n 牧場主 bokújōshu

rancid [ˈrænsɪd] adj (butter, bacon etc)
悪くなった wárùku natta

rancor [ˈræŋkər] (BRIT **rancour**) n 恨
み urámi

random [ˈrændəm] adj (arrangement,
selection) 手当り次第の teátarishidaì no;
(COMPUT, MATH) 無作為の musákuì
no
♦n: **at random** 手当り次第に teátarishi-
dài ni

random access n (COMPUT) ランダム
アクセス rañdamuákùsesu

randy [ˈrændɪ] (inf) adj セックスをした
がっている sékkùsu wo shitágatte irú

range [reɪndʒ] n (also: **mountain range**)
山脈 safimyaku; (of missile) 射程距離
shatékiyorì; (of voice) 声域 sefíki;
(series: of proposals, offers, products) 一
連の... ichíren no ...; (MIL: also: **shooting range**) 射撃場 shagékìjō; (also:
kitchen range) レンジ rénji
♦vt (place) 歩き回る arúkimawarù;
(arrange) 並べる naráberù
♦vi: **to range over** (extend) ...にわたる
...ni watárù
to range from ... to ... ...から...までに
わたる ...kárà ...mádè ni watárù

ranger [ˈreɪndʒər] n 森林警備隊員 shiń-
rinkeibitaìn, レンジャー rénjā

rank [ræŋk] n (row) 列 rétsù; (MIL) 階級
kafkyū; (status) 地位 chíi; (BRIT: also:
taxi rank) タクシー乗場 takúshìnorìba
♦vi: **to rank among** ...のうちに数えられ
る ...no uchí ni kazőerarerù
♦adj (stinking) 臭い kusáì
the rank and file (fig: ordinary members) 一般の人 ippáñ no hitó, 一般人 ip-
páñjìn

rankle [ˈræŋkəl] vi (insult) わだかまる
wadákamarù

ransack [ˈrænsæk] vt (search) 物色する
busshóku suru; (plunder) 略奪する ryakúdatsu suru

ransom [ˈrænsəm] n (money) 身代金 mi-
nóshirokìñ
to hold to ransom (fig: nation, company, individual) ...に圧力を掛ける ...ni

atsúryòku wo kakérù

rant [rænt] *vi* (rave) わめく wamékù

rap [ræp] *vt* (on door, table) たたく tatákù

rape [reip] *n* (of woman) 強かん gókan; (BOT) アブラナ abúrànà
♦*vt* (woman) 強かんする gókan suru

rape(seed) oil [reip'(si:d)-] *n* ナタネ油 natáneabùra

rapid [ræp'id] *adj* (growth, development, change) 急速な kyúsoku na

rapidity [rəpid'iti:] *n* (speed) 速さ háyàsa

rapidly [ræp'idli:] *adv* (grow, develop, change) 急速に kyúsoku ni

rapids [ræp'idz] *npl* (GEO) 早瀬 hayáse

rapist [rei'pist] *n* 強かん者 gókansha

rapport [ræpɔːr'] *n* (delight) 親和 shiñwakánkei

rapture [ræp'tʃəːr] *n* (delight) 歓喜 kánki

rapturous [ræp'tʃəːrəs] *adj* (applause) 熱狂的な nekkyóteki na

rare [reːr] *adj* (uncommon) まれな marê na; (unusual) 珍しい mezúrashiì; (CULIN: steak) レアの reâ no

rarely [reːr'li:] *adv* (seldom) めったに ...ない méttà ni ...naì

raring [reːr'iŋ] *adj*: **raring to go** (*inf*: keen) 意気込んでいる ikígonde irù

rarity [reːr'iti:] *n* (exception) 希有な物 kéù na monô; (scarcity) 希少性 kishôsei

rascal [ræs'kəl] *n* (rogue) ごろつき gorótsuki; (mischievous child) いたずらっ子 itázurakkò

rash [ræʃ] *adj* (person) 向こう見ずの mukómìzu no; (promise, act) 軽率な keísotsu na
♦*n* (MED) 発しん hasshín; (spate: of events, robberies) 多発 tahátsu

rasher [ræʃ'əːr] *n* (of bacon) 一切れ hitókìre

raspberry [ræz'beːri:] *n* キイチゴ kíìchigo

rasping [ræs'piŋ] *adj*: **a rasping noise** きしむ音 kishímù otó

rat [ræt] *n* ネズミ nezúmi

rate [reit] *n* (speed) 速度 sókùdo; (of change, inflation) 進行度 shiñkôdo;

(ratio: *also of interest*) 率 rítsù; (price: at hotel etc) 料金 ryôkin
♦*vt* (value, estimate) 評価する hyôka suru

to rate someone/something as ... は ...と評価する ...wo ...to hyôka suru

rateable value [rei'tabəl-] (*BRIT*) *n* 課税評価額 kazéi hyôkagaku

ratepayer [reit'peiəːr] (*BRIT*) *n* 納税者 nôzeisha ◊固定資産税の納税者について言う kotéishisañzei no nôzeisha ni tsuíte iú

rates [reits] *npl* (*BRIT*: property tax) 固定資産税 kotéishisañzei; (fees) 料金 ryôkin

rather [ræð'əːr] *adv* (quite, somewhat) かなり kánàri; (to some extent) 少しsukóshì; (more accurately) 正確に言えば sefkaku ni iêba

it's rather expensive (quite) かなり値段が高い kánàri nedán ga takáì; (too much) 値段過ぎる nedán ga takásugirù

there's rather a lot かなり沢山ある kánàri takúsan arû

I would rather go どちらかというと行きたいと思う dóchìra ka to iú tò ikítaì to omôu

ratify [ræt'əfai] *vt* (agreement, treaty) 批准する hijún suru

rating [rei'tiŋ] *n* (assessment) 評価 hyôka; (score) 評点 hyôten; (NAUT: *BRIT*: sailor) 兵曹卒 kafgunheísotsu

ratings [rei'tiŋz] *npl* (RADIO, TV) 視聴率 shichôrìtsu

ratio [rei'ʃou] *n* 率 rítsù
in the ratio of 100 to 1 100に1つという割合で hyakú ni hitotsù to iu warfai de

ration [ræʃ'ən] *n* (allowance: of food, petrol etc) 配給分 hafkyúbun
♦*vt* (food, petrol etc) 配給する hafkyú surun

rational [ræʃ'ənəl] *adj* (solution, reasoning) 合理的な gôriteki na; (person) 訳の分かる wákè no wakárù

rationale [ræʃənæl'] *n* 根拠 kónkyo

rationalize [ræʃ'ənəlaiz] *vt* (justify) 正当化する seftôka suru

rationally [ˈræʃʲnəliː] adv (sensibly) 合理的に gōriteki ni

rationing [ˈræʃʲnɪŋ] n (of food, petrol etc) 配給 haikyū

rations [ˈræʃʲanz] npl (MIL) 兵糧 hyōrō

rat race n 競争の世界 kyōsō nō sékai

rattle [ˈrætʲəl] n (of door, window) がたがたという音 gátàgata to iú oto; (of train, car, engine etc) ごう音 gōon; (of coins) じゃらじゃらという音 járàjara to iú oto; (of chain) がらがらという音 gáràgara to iú oto; (object: for baby) がらがら garágara
♦vi (small objects) がらがら鳴る gáràgara-ra narú; (car, bus): **to rattle along** がたがた走る gatagata hashírù
♦vt (unnerve) どぎまぎさせる dógìmagi sasérù

rattlesnake [ˈrætʲəlsneik] n ガラガラヘビ garágarahebì

raucous [ˈrɔːkas] adj しゃがれ声の sha-gáregoè no

ravage [ˈrævidʒ] vt (damage) 荒す arásù

ravages [ˈrævidʒiz] npl (of time, weather) 荒廃 kōhai

rave [reiv] vi (in anger) わめく wamékù; (with enthusiasm) ...をべたほめする ...wo betábðme suru; (MED) うわごとを言う uwágoto wò iú

raven [ˈreivan] n ワタリガラス watáriga-rāsu

ravenous [ˈrævanas] adj 猛烈におなかがすいた mōretsu ní onáka ga suíta

ravine [ravˈiːn] n 渓谷 keíkoku

raving [ˈreiviŋ] adj: **raving lunatic** どう気違い dokíchìgai

ravishing [ˈrævɪʃiŋ] adj (beautiful) 悩殺する nōsatsu suru

raw [rɔː] adj (uncooked) 生の namá no; (not processed: cotton, sugar etc) 原料のままの genryō no mamá no; (sore) 赤むけした akámuke shità; (inexperienced) 青二才の aónisai no; (weather, day) 肌寒い hadázamùi

raw deal (inf) n ひどい仕打ち hidói shíùchi

raw material n (coal, oil, gas etc) 原料 geñryō

ray [rei] n (also: **ray of light**) 光線 kōsen; (also: **ray of heat**) 熱線 nessén
the rays of the sun 太陽の光線 táiyō nō kōsen
a ray of hope 希望のひらめき kibō nō hirámeki

rayon [ˈreian] n レーヨン rēyon

raze [reiz] vt 根こそぎ破壊する nekósògi hakái suru

razor [ˈreizər] n (open razor) かみそり kamísori; (safety razor) 安全かみそり añ-zenkamisòri; (electric razor) 電気かみそり deñkikamisòri

razor blade n かみそりの刃 kamísori no há

Rd n abbr = **road**

re [rei] prep (with regard to) ...に関して ...ni kañ shite

reach [riːtʃ] n (range: of arm) 手が届く範囲 té gà todókù hâñ-i; (scope: of imagination) 範囲 hâñ-i; (stretch: of river etc) 区域 kūiki
♦vt (arrive at: place) ...に到着する ...ni tōchaku suru; (: conclusion, agreement, decision, end) ...に達する ...ni tassúrù; (be able to touch) ...に手が届く té gà todókù; (by telephone) ...に連絡する ...ni reñraku suru
♦vi (stretch out one's arm) 手を伸ばす té wò nobásù
within reach 手の届く所に té nò todókù tokórò ni
out of reach 手の届かない所に té nò todókanaì tokórò ni
within reach of the shops/station 商店街(駅)の近くに shōteñgai(ékì)no chikákù ni
"keep out of the reach of children" 子供の手が届かない所に保管して下さい kodómo no té gà todókanaì tokórò ni hokán shite kudásaì

reach out vt (hand) 伸ばす nobásù
♦vi 手を伸ばす té wò nobásù
to reach out for something ...を取ろうとして手を伸ばす ...wo toró tò shite té wò nobásù

react [riˈækt] vi (CHEM): **to react (with)** (...と)反応する (...to) hañnō suru; (MED): *to react (to)* (...に対して) 副作用が起る (...ni tāīshīte fukūsayō ga okórū; (respond): *to react (to)* (...に) 反応する (...ni hañnō suru; (rebel): *to react (against)* (...に) 反発する (...ni hañpatsu suru

reaction [riːækˈʃən] *n* (response): *reaction (to)* (...に対する) 反応 (...ni tāīsūrū) hañnō; (rebellion): *reaction (against)* (...に対する) 反発 (...ni tāīsūrū) hañpatsu; (belief in conservatism): 反動 hañdō; (CHEM) 反応 hañnō; (MED): 副作用 fukūsayō

reactionary [riːækˈʃəneːriː] *adj* (forces, attitude): 反動的な hañdōteki na

reactions [riːækˈʃənz] *npl* (reflexes): 反応 hañnō

reactor [riːækˈtər] *n (also:* **nuclear reactor**) 原子炉 geñshīrō

read [riːd] *(pt, pp* **read**) *vt* (person, child) ...を読む ...wo yómū; (piece of writing, letter etc) ...と書いてある ...to kāīte ārū; (mood, thoughts) 読取る yomītórū; (meter, thermometer etc) 読む yómū; (study: at university) 学ぶ manábū

readable [riːdˈəbəl] *adj* (writing) 読める yomérū; (book, author etc) 読ませる yomáserū

reader [riːdˈər] *n* (of book, newspaper etc) 読者 dókūsha; (book) リーダー rídā; (*BRIT*: at university) 助教授 jokyṓju
    an avid reader 読書家 dokūshíka

readership [riːdˈərːʃīp] *n* (of newspaper etc) 読者層 dokūshasṓ

readily [redˈəliː] *adv* (willingly) 快く kokóroyokū; (easily) たやすく tayásukū; (quickly) 直ぐに súgū ni

readiness [redˈiːnis] *n* (preparedness) 用意ができている事 yṓī ga dekīte iru koto; (willingness) ...する意志 ...suru ishi
    in readiness (prepared) 用意ができて yṓī ga dekíte

reading [riːdˈin] *n* (of books, newspapers etc) 読書 dokūsho; (in church, as entertainment) 朗読 rṓdoku; (on meter, thermometer etc) 記録 kiroku

readjust [riːədʒʌst] *vt* (alter: position,

knob, mirror etc) 調節する chōsetsu suru
    vi (adapt): *to readjust (to)* (...に) 慣れる (...ni) nareru

read out *vt* 朗読する rṓdoku suru

ready [redˈiː] *adj* (prepared) 用意ができている yṓī ga dekīte iru; (willing): ...する意志がある ...surū ishi ga ārū; (available) 用意されている yṓī sarēte irū
    n: at the ready (MIL) 銃を構えて jū wo kamáete
    to get ready
    vi 支度する shitáku suru
    vt 準備する júñbi suru

ready-made [redˈiːmeid] *adj* 既製の kiséi no

ready money *n* 現金 geñkin

ready reckoner [-rekˈənər] *n* 計算表 kefsañhyṓ

ready-to-wear [redˈiːtəweːr] *adj* 既製の kiséi no

reaffirm [riːəfərːm] *vt* 再び言明する futátabi geñmei suru

real [riːl] *adj* (actual, true: reason, interest, result etc) 本当の hoñtō no; (not artificial: leather, gold etc) 本物の hoñmono no; (not imaginary: life, feeling) 実際の jissāi no; (for emphasis): *a real idiot/miracle* 正真正銘のばか (奇跡) shóshin-shṓmei no bāka (kiséki)
    in real terms 事実上 jijītsu wa

real estate *n* 不動産 fudṓsan

realism [riːˈəlizəm] *n* (practicality) 現実主義 geñjitsushugī; (ART) リアリズム ríárízūmu

realist [riːˈəlist] *n* 現実的な人 geñjitsuteki-ki na hitō

realistic [riːəlisˈtik] *adj* (practical) 現実的な geñjitsuteki na; (true to life) 写実的な shajītsuteki na

reality [riːælˈiːtiː] *n* (actuality, truth) 事実 jijītsu
    in reality 事実は jijītsu wa

realization [riːələzeiˈʃən] *n* (understanding: of situation) 気付き jikkañ; (fulfillment: of dreams, hopes) 実現 jitsūgen; (of asset) 現金化 geñkinka

realize [riːˈəlaiz] *vt* (understand) 気付き

る jikkán suru; (fulfil: a dream, hope, project etc) 実現する jitsúgen suru; (COMM: asset) 現金に替える genkíñ ni kaérù

really [ri:'əli:] *adv* (for emphasis) 実に jitsū ni, とても totémo; (actually): *what really happened* 実際に起った事は jissái nì okótta kotò wa

really? (indicating interest) そうですか so desu ka; (expressing surprise) 本当ですか hoñtō desu ka

really! (indicating annoyance) うんも う! úñ mo!

realm [relm] *n* (of monarch) 王国 ōkoku; (*fig*: area of activity or study) 分野 búñ-ya

realtor [ri:'əltɔːr] (*US*) *n* 不動産業者 fudōsangyōsha

reap [ri:p] *vt* (crop) ...の刈入れをする ...no karfire wò suru; (*fig*: benefits, rewards) 収穫する shūkaku suru

reappear [ri:əpi:r'] *vi* 再び現れる futátabi arawarerū

rear [ri:r] *adj* (back) 後ろの ushfro no
◆*n* (back) 後ろ ushfro
◆*vt* (cattle) 飼育する shifku suru; (family) 育てる sodáteru
◆*vi* (also: **rear up**: animal) 後足で立ち上 る atóashi de tachágarù

rearguard [ri:r'gɑ:rd] *n* (MIL) 後衛 kōei

rearmament [ri:rɑ:'mənt] *n* 再軍備 saígunbi

rearrange [ri:əreindʒ'] *vt* 並べ直す narábenaosù

rear-view mirror [ri:r'vju:-] *n* (AUT) バックミラー bakkūmirá

reason [ri:'zən] *n* (cause) 理由 riyū; (ability to think) 理性 riséi
◆*vi: to reason with someone* ...の説得に当る ...no settóku ni atárù

it stands to reason that ...という事は当然である ...to iú kotò wa tōzen de arù

reasonable [ri:'zənəbl] *adj* (sensible) 訳の分かる wákè no wakárù; (: number, amount) 程々の hodóhodo no; (: quality) まあまあの mâmâ no; (: price) 妥当な datō na

reasonably [ri:'zənəbli:] *adv* (sensibly)

常識的に jōshikiteki ni; (fairly) 程々に hodóhodo ni

reasoned [ri:'zənd] *adj* (argument) 筋の通った sújì no tótta

reasoning [ri:'zəniŋ] *n* (process) 推理 sufri

reassurance [ri:əʃu:r'əns] *n* 安と áñdo

reassure [ri:əʃu:r'] *vt* (comfort) 安心させる afshiñ saserù

to reassure someone of ...に...だと安心させる ...ni ...dá tò afshiñ saserù

reassuring [ri:əʃu:r'iŋ] *adj* (smile, manner) 安心させる afshiñ saserù

rebate [ri:'beit] *n* (on tax etc) リベート ribétò

rebel [*n* reb'əl *vb* ribel'] *n* (against political system) 反逆者 hañgyakushá; (against society, parents etc) 反抗分子 hañkōbuñshi
◆*vi* (against political system) 反乱を起す hañran wò okósù; (against society, parents etc) 反抗する hañkō suru

rebellion [ribel'jən] *n* (against political system) 反乱 hañran; (against society, parents etc) 反抗 hañkō

rebellious [ribel'jəs] *adj* (subject) 反逆者の hañgyakushá no; (child, behavior) 反抗的な hañkōteki na

rebirth [ri:bə:rθ'] *n* 復活 fukkátsu

rebound [*vb* ri:baund' *n* ri:'baund] *vi* (ball) 跳ね返る hanékaerù
◆*n: on the rebound* (ball) 跳ね返った所を hanékaettà tokóro wò; (*fig*: person) ...した反動で ...shftá hañdō de

rebuff [ribʌf'] *n* 拒絶 kyozétsu

rebuild [ri:bild'] (*pt, pp* **rebuilt**) *vt* (town, building etc) 建直す taténaosù; (economy, confidence) 立直す taténaosù

rebuke [ribju:k'] *vt* しかる shikárù

rebut [ribʌt'] *vt* しりぞける shirízokerù

recalcitrant [rikæl'sitrənt] *adj* (child, behavior) 反抗的な hañkōteki na

recall [rikɔ:l'] *vt* (remember) 思い出すおもídasù; (parliament, ambassador etc) 呼戻す yobímodosù
◆*n* (ability to remember) 記憶 kióku; (of ambassador etc) 召還 shōkan

recant [rikænt'] *vi* 自説を取消す jisétsu

wò torískesù

recap [riːˈkæp] vt (summarize) 要約する yōyaku suru

♦vi ...を要約する ...wo yōyaku suru

recapitulate [riːkæpitʃˈuːleit] vt, vi = recap

recapture [riːˈkæptʃəːr] vt (town, territory etc) 奪還する dakkán suru; (atmosphere, mood etc) 取り戻す torímodosù

rec'd abbr = **received**

recede [risid] vi (tide) ひく hikú; (lights etc) 遠のく tónokù; (memory) 薄らぐ úsúragù; (hair) はげる hagérù

receding [risiˈdiŋ] adj (hair) はげつつある hagétsutsu arù; (chin) 無いに等しい náī ni hitóshiì

receipt [risiːt] n (document) 領収書 ryōshūsho; (from cash register) レシート reshíto; (act of receiving) 受取る事 ukétorù kotó

receipts [risiːts] npl (COMM) 収入 shūnyū

receive [risiv] vt (get: money, letter etc) 受け取る ukétorù; (criticism, acclaim) 受ける ukérù; (visitor, guest) 迎える mukáerù

to receive an injury けがする kegá surù

receiver [risiˈvəːr] n (TEL) 受話器 juwáki; (RADIO, TV) 受信機 jushínki; (of stolen goods) 故買屋 kobáiya; (COMM) 管財人 kanzáinīn

recent [riˈsant] adj (event, times) 最近の saíkin no; (period) 近ごろの chikágōro no

recently [riˈsantliː] adv 近ごろ chikágōro

receptacle [risepˈtəkəl] n 容器 yṓkì

reception [risepˈʃən] n (in hotel, office, hospital etc) 受付 ukétsuke; (party) レセプション résepùshon; (welcome) 歓迎 kangéi; (RADIO, TV) 受信 jushín

reception desk n 受付 ukétsuke, フロント furóntò

receptionist [risepˈʃənist] n 受付係 ukétsukegakàri

receptive [riseptˈiv] adj (person, attitude) 前向きの maémuki no

recess [riˈses] n (in room) 壁のくぼみ

kabé nò kubómi; (secret place) 奥深い所 okúfukaî tokórò; (POL etc: holiday) 休暇期間 kyūkeijìkan

recession [riseˈʃən] n 景気後退 keíkikōtai

recharge [riːtʃɑːrdʒ] vt (battery) 充電する jūden suru

recipe [resˈəpi] n (CULIN) 調理法 chōrihō; (fig: for success) 秘けつ hikétsu; (: for disaster) やり方 yaríkata

recipient [risipˈiənt] n (of letter, payment etc) 受取人 ukétorinīn

reciprocal [risipˈrəkəl] adj (arrangement, agreement) 相互の sōgo no

recital [risaiˈtəl] n (concert) リサイタル risáïtaru

recite [risaiˈt] vt (poem) 暗唱する añshō suru

reckless [rekˈlis] adj (driving, driver) 無謀な mubō na; (spending) 無茶な múcha na

recklessly [rekˈlisliː] adv (drive) 無謀に mubō ni; (spend) むやみに múyàmi ni

reckon [rekˈən] vt (calculate) 計算する kefsan suru; (think): I reckon that ...だと思う ...dá tò omóu

reckoning [rekˈəniŋ] n (calculation) 計算 keísan

reckon on vt fus (expect) 当てにする a-té ni suru

reclaim [rikleim] vt (demand back) ...の返還を要求する ...no heñkan wò yōkyū suru; (land) 埋め立てる umétaterù; (: by draining) 干拓する kañtaku suru; (waste materials) 再生する saísei suru

reclamation [rekləmeiˈʃən] n (of land: by filling in) 埋め立て umétate; (: by draining) 干拓 kañtaku

recline [riklaiˈn] vi (sit or lie back) もたれる motárerù

reclining [riklaiˈniŋ] adj: reclining seat リクライニングシート rikúraïningushīto

recluse [rekˈluːs] n 隠とん者 iñtonsha

recognition [rekəgniˈʃən] n (of person, place) 認識 nifshìki; (of problem, fact) 意識 fshìki; (of achievement) 認める事

mitōmeru kotō

transformed beyond recognition 見分けが付かない程変化した miwake ga tsukanai hodo hēnka shita

recognizable [rekəgnaɪ'zəbəl] *adj*: **recognizable (by)** (...で) 見分けが付く (...de) miwake ga tsuku

recognize [rek'əgnaiz] *vt* (person, place, attitude, signature) ...だと分かる ...da to wakarū; (problem, need) 意識する fshīki suru; (qualification, achievement) 認める mitōmerū; (government) 承認する shōnin suru

to recognize by/as ...で(として)分かる ...de (toshitē) wakarū

recoil [rikɔɪl'] *vi* (person): **to recoil from doing something** ...するのをいやがる ...surū no wo iyágarū

♦*n* (of gun) 反動 hańdō

recollect [rekəlekt'] *vt* (remember) 思い出す omóidasū

recollection [rekəlek'ʃən] *n* (memory) 思い出 omóide; (remembering) 思い出す事 omóidasu kotō

recommend [rekəmend'] *vt* (book, shop, person) 推薦する sufsen suru; (course of action) 勧める susúmerū

recommendation [rekəmendei'ʃən] *n* (of book, shop, person) 推薦 sufsen; (of course of action) 勧告 kańkoku

recompense [rek'əmpens] *n* (reward) 報酬 hōshū

reconcile [rek'ənsail] *vt* (two people) 仲直りさせる nakánaori saserū; (two facts, beliefs) 調和させる chōwa saserū

to reconcile oneself to something (unpleasant situation, misery etc) ...だとあきらめる ...dá tō akframerū

reconciliation [rekənsiliːei'ʃən] *n* (of people etc) 和解 wakái; (of facts etc) 調和 chōwa

recondition [riːkəndi'ʃən] *vt* (machine) 修理する shūri suru

reconnaissance [rikɑːn'isəns] *n* (MIL) 偵察 tefsatsu

reconnoiter [riːkənɔi'tɜːr] (*BRIT* **reconnoitre**) *vt* (MIL: enemy territory) 偵察する tefsatsu suru

reconsider [riːkənsid'ɜːr] *vt* (decision, opinion etc) 考え直す kańgaenaosū

reconstruct [riːkənstrʌkt'] *vt* (building) 建直す taténaosū; (event, system) 練り直す nerínaosū; (event, crime) 再現する saígen suru

reconstruction [riːkənstrʌk'ʃən] *n* (of building, country) 再建 saíken; (of crime) 再現 saígen

record [*n* rek'ɜːrd *vb* rekɜːrd'] *n* (gen) 記録 kiróku; (MUS: disk) レコード rekōdò; (history: of person, company) 履歴 riréki; (*also*: **criminal record**) 前科 zénka

♦*vt* (write down) 記録する kiróku suru; (temperature, time etc) 表示する hyōji suru; (MUS: song etc) 録音する rokúon suru

in record time 記録的な速さで kiróku-teki hayása de

off the record *adj* (remark) オフレコの ofúreko no

♦*adv* (speak) オフレコで ofúreko de

record card *n* (in file) ファイルカード faírukādo

recorded delivery [rikɔːr'did-] (*BRIT*) *n* (MAIL) 簡易書留 kań-i kakītome

reorder [rikɔːr'dɜːr] *n* (MUS: instrument) リコーダー rikōdà

record holder *n* (SPORT) 記録保持者 kiróku hojishá

recording [rikɔːr'diŋ] *n* 録音 rokúon

record player *n* レコードプレーヤー rekōdopurēyà

recount [rikaunt'] *vt* (story, event etc) 述べる nobērù

re-count [*n* riː'kaunt *vb* riːkaunt'] *n* (POL: of votes) 数え直し kazōenaoshi

♦*vt* (votes etc) 数え直す kazōenaosū

recoup [rikuːp'] *vt*: **to recoup one's losses** 損失を取戻す sofshitsu wð torímodosū

recourse [riː'kɔːrs] *n*: **to have recourse to something** ...wo mochfirū

recover [rikʌv'ɜːr] *vt* (get back: stolen goods, lost items, financial loss) 取戻す torímodosū

♦*vi*: **to recover (from)** (illness) (...から)

治る (...ga) naórù; (operation, shock, experience) (...から) 立直る (...karâ) tachínaorû

recovery [rikʌv'əri] n (from illness, operation: in economy etc) 回復 kaffuku; (of stolen, lost items) 取戻し torímodoshi

re-create [ri:kri:eit'] vt 再現する saîgen suru

recreation [rekri:ei'ʃən] n (play, leisure activities) 娯楽 goráku

recreational [rekri:ei'ʃənəl] adj 娯楽の goráku no

recrimination [rikrimənei'ʃən] n 責合い seméai

recruit [rikru:t'] n (MIL) 新兵 shiñpei; (in company, organization) 新入社(会)員 shiñnyūsha(kai)ìn

◆vt 募集する boshū suru

recruitment [rikru:t'mənt] n 募集 boshū

rectangle [rek'tæŋgəl] n 長方形 chôhôkei

rectangular [rektæŋ'gjələr] adj (shape, object etc) 長方形の chôhôkei no

rectify [rek'təfai] vt (correct) 正す tadásù

rector [rek'tər] n (REL) 主任司祭 shuníñshisài

rectory [rek'təri] n (house) 司祭館 shisáikan

recuperate [riku:'pəreit] vi (recover: from illness etc) 回復する kaffuku suru

recur [rikə:r'] vi (error, event) 繰返される kurîkaesarerù; (illness, pain) 再発する saîhatsu suru

recurrence [rikə:r'əns] n (of error, event) 繰返し kurîkaeshi; (of illness, pain) 再発 saîhatsu

recurrent [rikə:r'ənt] adj 頻繁に起る hiñpan nì okórù

red [red] n (color) 赤 ákà; (pej: POL) 過激派 kagékiha

◆adj 赤い akáì

to be in the red (bank account, business) 赤字になっている akáji nì natté irù

red carpet treatment n 盛大な歓迎式 seídai nà kañgeishìkī

Red Cross n 赤十字 sekíjūji

redcurrant [red'kʌr'ənt] n アカフサスグリ akáfusasugùri

redden [red'ən] vt (turn red) 赤くする a-kákù suru

◆vi (blush) 赤面する sekímen suru

reddish [red'iʃ] adj 赤っぽい akáppòi

redeem [ridi:m'] vt (fig: situation, reputation) 救う sukúù; (something in pawn, loan) 請出す ukédasû; (REL: rescue) 救う sukúù

redeeming [ridi:'miŋ] adj: **redeeming feature** 欠点を補う取柄 ketten wò ogínaû torê

redeploy [ri:diplɔi'] vt (resources) 配置し直す haíchi shinaosù

red-haired [red'he:rd] adj 赤毛の akáge no

red-handed [red'hæn'did] adj: **to be caught red-handed** 現行犯で捕まる geñkôhan de tsukámarû

redhead [red'hed] n 赤毛の人 akáge no hitô

red herring n (fig) 本論から注意をそらす物 hoñron karà chūî wo soràsû monò

red-hot [red'hɑːt'] adj (metal) 真っ赤に焼けた makká nì yakéta

redirect [ri:dərekt'] vt (mail) 転送する teñsō suru

red light n: **to go through a red light** (AUT) 信号無視をする shiñgōmushi wo suru

red-light district [red'lait-] n 赤線地区 akásenchìkū

redo [ri:du:'] (pt **redid** pp **redone**) vt やり直す yarínaosù

redolent [red'ələnt] adj: **redolent of** (smell: also fig) ...臭い ...kusáì

redouble [ri:dʌb'əl] vt: **to redouble one's efforts** 一層努力する issô doryòku suru

redress [ridres'] n (compensation) 賠償 baíshō

◆vt (error, wrong) 償う tsugúnaû

Red Sea n: **the Red Sea** 紅海 kôkai

redskin [red'skin] n (pej) インディアン ñdian

red tape n (fig) 形式的な手続き keshíkiteki tetsuzúki

reduce [ridu:s'] *vt* (decrease: spending, numbers etc) 減らす herásù

to reduce someone to (begging, stealing) ...を余儀なくさせる ...wo yogínaku saserú

to reduce someone to tears 泣かせる nakáserù

to reduce someone to silence 黙らせる damáraserù

「*a reduce speed now*」(AUT) 徐行 jokō

at a reduced price (goods) 割引で warſbiki de

reduction [ridʌk'ʃən] *n* (in price) 値下げ neságe; (in numbers etc) 減少 geñshō

redundancy [ridʌn'dənsi:] *n* (dismissal) 解雇 káiko; (unemployment) 失業 shitsúgyō

redundant [ridʌn'dənt] *adj* (worker) 失業中の shitsúgyōchū no; (detail, object) 余計な yokéi na

to be made redundant 解雇される káiko sarérù

reed [ri:d] *n* (BOT) アシ ashí; (MUS: of clarinet etc) リード rído

reef [ri:f] *n* (at sea) 暗礁 añshō

reek [ri:k] *vi: to reek (of)* (...の) においがぷんぷんする (...no) nióì ga púñpun suru

reel [ri:l] *n* (of thread, string) 巻き makí; (of film, tape: also on fishing-rod) リール rīru; (dance) リール rīru

♦*vi* (sway) よろめく yorómekù

reel in *vt* (fish, line) 手繰り寄せる tagúriyoserù

ref [ref] (*inf*) *n abbr* = **referee**

refectory [rifek'tə:ri] *n* 食堂 shokúdō

refer [rifə:r'] *vt* (person, patient): *to refer someone to* ...を...に回す ...wo ...ni mawásù; (matter, problem): *to refer something to* ...を...に委託する ...wo ...ni itáku suru

♦*vi: to refer to* (allude to) ...に言及する ...ni geñkyū suru; (consult) ...を参照する ...wo sañshō suru

referee [refəri:'] *n* (SPORT) 審判員 shiñpañ-in, レフェリー réferi; (BRIT: for job application) 身元保証人 mimótohoshōnìn

♦*vt* (football match etc) ...のレフェリーをやる ...no réferi wo yárù

reference [ref'ə:rəns] *n* (mention) 言及 geñkyū; (in book, paper) 引用文献 iñ-yōbuñken; (for job application: letter) 推薦状 suíseñjō

with reference to (COMM: in letter) ...に関しては ...ni kañshite wa

reference book *n* 参考書 sañkōsho

reference number *n* 整理番号 sefríbañgō

referenda [refəren'də] *npl of* **referendum**

referendum [refəren'dəm] (*pl* **referenda**) *n* 住民投票 jūmíntōhyō

refill [*vb* ri:fil' *n* ri:'fil] *vt* (glass etc) ...にもう一杯つぐ ...ni mō ippaí tsugú; (pen etc) ...に...を詰替える ...ni ...wo tsumékaerù

♦*n* (of drink etc) お代り o-káwari (for pen etc) スペアー supéà

refine [rifain'] *vt* (sugar, oil) 精製する seísei suru; (theory, idea) 洗練する señren suru

refined [rifaind'] *adj* (person, taste) 洗練された señren sareta

refinement [rifain'mənt] *n* (of person) 優雅さ yūgasa; (of system) 精度 seído

reflect [riflekt'] *vt* (light, image) 反射する hañsha suru; (situation, attitude) 反映する hañ-ei suru

♦*vi* (think) じっくり考える jikkúrì kañgaerù

it reflects badly/well on him それは彼の悪い(いい)所を物語っている soré wa kárè no warúi (íi) tokoró wo monógatatte irú

reflection [riflek'ʃən] *n* (of light, heat) 反射 hañsha; (image) 影 kágè; (of situation, attitude) 反映する物 hañ-ei suru jukkō; (criticism) 非難 hínàn; (thought) 熟考 jukkō

on reflection よく考えると yōkù kañgaerù to

reflector [riflek'tə:r] *n* 反射器 hañshakì

reflex [ri:'fleks] *adj* (action, gesture) 反射的な hañshateki na

♦*n* (PHYSIOLOGY, PSYCH) 反射 hañsha

reflexive [rɪflek'sɪv] *adj* (LING) 再帰的の saɪki no

reform [rɪfɔːrm'] *n* (of sinner, character) 改心 kaɪshin; (of law, system) 改革 kaɪkaku

♦*vt* (sinner) 改心させる kaɪshin saserú; (law, system) 改革する kaɪkaku suru

Reformation [refərmeɪ'ʃən] *n* : *the Reformation* 宗教改革 shúkyòkaɪkaku

reformatory [rɪfɔːr'mətɔːriː] *n* (*US*) n 感化院 kaɪkaɪn

refrain [rɪfreɪn'] *vi: to refrain from doing* ...をしない様にする ...wo shináɪ yṓ ni suru

♦*n* (of song) 繰返し kurïkaeshi, リフレイン rïfúreɪn

refresh [rɪfreʃ'] *vt* (subj: sleep, drink) 元気付ける geñkízukerú

to refresh someone's memory ...に思い出させる ...ni omóɪdasaserú

refresher course [rɪfreʃ'əːr-] (*BRIT*) *n* 研修会 keñshūkaɪ

refreshing [rɪfreʃ'ɪŋ] *adj* (drink) 冷たくておいしい tsumétakùte oɪshíɪ; (sleep) 気分をさわやかにする kíbùn wo sawáyàka ni suru

refreshments [rɪfreʃ'mənts] *npl* (food and drink) 軽食 keɪshoku

refrigeration [rɪfrɪdʒəreɪ'ʃən] *n* (of food) 冷蔵 reɪzō

refrigerator [rɪfrɪdʒ'əːreɪtəːr] *n* 冷蔵庫 reɪzōko

refuel [riːfjuː'əl] *vi* 燃料を補給する neñryō wo hokyū suru

refuge [ref'juːdʒ] *n* (shelter) 避難場所 hɪnáñbasho

to take refuge in ...に避難する ...ni hɪnán suru

refugee [refjudʒiː'] *n* 難民 nañmin

refund [*n* riːfʌnd *vb* rɪfʌnd'] *n* 払い戻し haráɪmodoshi

♦*vt* (money) 払い戻す haráɪmodosū

refurbish [riːfəːr'bɪʃ] *vt* (shop, theater) 改装する kaɪsō suru

refusal [rɪfjuː'zəl] *n* 断り kotówari, 拒否 kyóhɪ

first refusal (option) オプション権 o-

púshoñken

refuse [*n* rɪfjuːz' *vt* (request, offer, gift) 断る kotówarū; (invitation) 辞退する jɪtáɪ suru; (permission, consent) 拒む kobámù

♦*vi* (say no) 断る kotówarū; (horse) 飛越を拒否する hɪétsu wò kyóhɪ suru

to refuse to do something ...するのを拒む ...surú no wo kobámù

refuse² [ref'juːs] *n* (rubbish) ごみ gomí

refuse collection *n* ごみ収集 gomíshūshū

refute [rɪfjuːt'] *vt* (argument) 論破する roñpa suru

regain [rɪgeɪn'] *vt* (power, position) 取戻す torímodosū

regal [riː'gəl] *adj* 堂々とした dṓdō to shíta

regalia [rɪgeɪ'liːə] *n* (costume) 正装 seɪsō

regard [rɪgɑːrd'] *n* (gaze) 視線 shɪsen; (attention, concern) 関心 kañshin; (esteem) 尊敬 soñkeɪ

♦*vt* (consider) 見なす mɪnásù

to give one's regards to ...から...によろしく伝える ...kará ...nɪ yoróshikù tsutáerù

with kindest regards 敬具 keɪgu

regarding, as regards, with regard to (with reference to, concerning) ...に関して ...ni kañshité

regardless [rɪgɑːrd'lɪs] *adv* (carry on, continue) 構わずに kamáwazù ni

regardless of (danger, consequences) ...を顧みず ...wo kaérìmizù

regatta [rɪgɑːt'ə] *n* ヨット（ボート）競技会 yottó (bṓto) kyógìkaɪ

regenerate [rɪdʒen'əːreɪt] *vt* (inner cities, arts) よみがえらせる yomígaeràserú

regent [riː'dʒənt] *n* 摂政 sesshō

regime [reɪʒiːm'] *n* (system of government) 政治体制 seɪjìtaɪseɪ

regiment [redʒ'əmənt] *n* (MIL) 連隊 reñtaɪ

regimental [redʒəmen'təl] *adj* 連隊の reñtaɪ no

region [riː'dʒən] *n* (area: of land) 地区 chíkù; (: of body) ...部 ...bù; (administra-

tive division of country) 行政区 győsei-
ku

in the region of (fig: approximately)
約 yákū

regional [riːdʒənəl] adj (organization,
wine, geography) 地方の jimōto no; (provincial) 地方の chihō no

register [redʒˈistər] n (list: of births,
marriages, deaths, voters) 登録簿 tóro-
kūbo; (SCOL: of attendance) 出席簿
shussekibō n (MUS: of voice) 声域 sefiki;
(: of instrument) 音域 oñ-iki

♦vt (birth, death, marriage) 届ける todō-
kederū; (car) 登録する tóroku suru; (MAIL:
letter) 書留にする kakftome nī
suru; (subj: meter, gauge) 示す shimésū

♦vi (at hotel) チェックインする chekkūñn
suru; (for work) 名前を登録する namáe
wo tóroku suru; (as student) 入学の手続き
をする nyūgakutesuzuki wō suru;
(make impression) ぴんと来る piñ tō kú-
rū

registered [redʒˈistərd] adj (MAIL: letter, parcel) 書留の kakftome no

registered trademark n 登録商標 tó-
rokushōhyō

registrar [redʒˈistrɑːr] n (official) 戸籍
係 kosékigakàri; (in college, university)
教務係 kyōmugakàri; (BRIT: in hospital) 医療史員 iμrūríñ

registration [redʒˈistreiʃən] n (gen) 登録
tóroku; (of birth, death) 届出 todōkede;
(AUT: also: **registration number**) ナン
バー nánbā

registry [redʒˈistri] n 登記所 tókisho

registry office (BRIT) n 戸籍登記所
kosékitōksho

to get married in a registry office 戸
籍登記所で結婚する kosékitōksho dè
kekkón suru

regret [rigret] n (sorrow) 悔み kuyámi
♦vt (decision, action) 後悔する kōkai suru; (loss, death) 悔む kuyámū; (inability
to do something) 残念に思う zafínen nī
omóū; (inconvenience) 済まないと思う
sumánai to omóū

regretfully [rigret'fəli:] adv (sadly) 残念
ながら zafínen nàgara

regrettable [rigret'əbəl] adj (unfortunate: mistake, incident) あいにくの afni-
ku no

regular [reg'jələr] adj (even: breathing,
pulse etc) 規則的な kisōkuteki na;
(evenly-spaced: intervals, meetings etc)
定期的な tefkiteki na; (symmetrical: features, shape etc) 対称的な tafshōteki na;
(frequent: raids, exercise etc) 頻繁な hífn-
pan na; (usual: time, doctor, customer
etc) 通常の tsújō no; (soldier) 正規の sefki no; (LING) 規則変化の kisōkuheñka
no

♦n (client etc) 常連 jōren

regularity [regjəlærˈiti] n (frequency)
高頻度 kōhíñdo

regularly [reg'jələrliː] adv (at evenly-
spaced intervals) 規則的に kisōkuteki
ni; (symmetrically: shaped etc) 対称的に
tafshōteki ni; (often) 頻繁に híñpan ni

regulate [reg'jəleit] vt (conduct, expenditure) 規制する kiséi suru; (traffic, speed)
調整する chōsei suru; (machine, oven) 調
節する chōsetsu suru

regulation [regjəleiʃən] n (of conduct,
expenditure) 規制 kiséi; (of traffic,
speed) 調整 chōsei; (of machine, oven) 調
節 chōsetsu; (rule) 規則 kisoku

rehabilitation [riːhəbilæteiʃən] n (of
criminal, addict) 社会復帰 shakáifukkī,
リハビリテーション rihābiritēshon

rehearsal [rihɑːrˈsəl] n リハーサル rihāsāru

rehearse [rihɑːrs] vt (play, dance,
speech etc) ...のリハーサルをする
rihāsāru wo suru

reign [rein] n (of monarch) 治世 chiséi;
(fig: of terror etc) 支配 shíhai

♦vi (monarch) 君臨する kuñrin suru;
(fig: violence, fear etc) はびこる habíko-
rū; (: peace, order etc) 行渡る ikíwatarū

reimburse [riːimbəːrs] vt (pay back)
...に弁償する ...ni beñshō suru

rein [rein] n (for horse) 手綱 tazúna

reincarnation [riːinkɑːrneiʃən] n
(belief) 輪廻 ríñne

reindeer [rein'diːr] n inv トナカイ toná-
kai

reinforce [riːinfɔːrs] *vt* (strengthen: object) 補強する hokyō suru; (: situation) 強化する kyōka suru; (support: idea, statement) 裏付けする urázukerù

reinforced concrete [riːinfɔːrst'-] *n* 鉄筋コンクリート tekkín konkurīto

reinforcement [riːinfɔːrs'mənt] *n* (strengthening) 補強 hokyō

reinforcements [riːinfɔːrs'mənts] *npl* (MIL) 援軍 eñgun

reinstate [riːinsteit'] *vt* (worker) 復職させる fukúshoku saserù; (tax, law, text) 元通りにする motódōri ni surú

reiterate [riːit'əreit] *vt* (repeat) 繰返す kuríkaesù

reject [*n* riː'dʒekt *vb* ridʒekt'] *n* (COMM) 傷物 kizúmono

♦*vt* (plan, proposal etc) 退ける shiŕizokerù; (offer of help etc) 拒否する kotówarù; (belief, political system) 拒絶する kyozétsu suru; (candidate) 不採用にする fusáiyō ni suru; (coin) 受付けない ukétsukenai; (goods, fruit etc) 傷物として処分する kizúmono toshitè shóbun suru

rejection [ridʒek'ʃən] *n* (of plan, proposal, offer of help etc) 拒否 kyóhi; (of belief etc) 拒絶 kyozétsu; (of candidate) 不採用 fusáiyō

rejoice [ridʒɔis'] *vi*: **to rejoice at/over** ...を喜ぶ ...wo yorókobù

rejuvenate [ridʒuː'vəneit] *vt* (person) 若返らせる wakágaeraserù

relapse [rilæps'] *n* (MED) 再発 saíhatsu

relate [rileit'] *vt* (tell) 話す hanásù; (connect) 結び付ける musúbitsukerù

♦*vi*: **to relate to** (person, subject, thing) ...に関係がある ...ni kañkei ga arù

related [rilei'tid] *adj* (person) 血縁がある ketsúen ga arù; (animal, language) 近縁の kiń-en no

related to ...に関係がある ...ni kañkei ga arù

relating [rilei'tiŋ]: **relating to** *prep* ...に関する ...ni kañ suru

relation [rilei'ʃən] *n* (member of family) 親せき shiñseki; (connection) 関係 kañkei

relations [rilei'ʃənz] *npl* (dealings) 関係

kañkei; (relatives) 親せき shiñseki

relationship [rilei'ʃənʃip] *n* (between two people, countries, things) 関係 kañkei; (: family relationship) 親族関係 shifízokukañkei

relative [rel'ətiv] *n* (member of family) 親類 shiŕrui, 親せき shiñseki

♦*adj* (comparative) 相対的な sōtaitekí na; (connected) *relative to* ...に関する ...ni kañ suru

relatively [rel'ətivli] *adv* (comparatively) 比較的 hikákuteki na

relax [rilæks'] *vi* (person: unwind) くつろぐ kutsúrogù; (muscle) 緩む yurúmù

♦*vt* (one's grip) 緩める yurúmerù; (mind, person) くつろがせる kutsúrogaserù; (rule, control etc) 緩める yurúmerù

relaxation [riːlækseiʃən] *n* (rest) 休み yasúmi; (of muscle, grip) 緩み yurúmi; (of rule, control etc) 緩和 kañwa; (recreation) 娯楽 goráku

relaxed [rilækst'] *adj* (person) 落着いた ochítsuità; (discussion, atmosphere) くつろいだ kutsúroĺda

relaxing [rilæks'iŋ] *adj* (holiday, afternoon) くつろげる kutsúrogerù

relay [riː'lei] *n* (race) リレー rírē

♦*vt* (message, question) 伝える tsutáerù; (programme, signal) 中継する chúkei suru

release [riliːs'] *n* (from prison) 釈放 shakúhō; (from obligation) 免除 méñjo; (of gas, water etc) 放出 hōshutsu; (of film) 封切 fukíri; (of book, record) 発売 hatsúbai

♦*vt* (prisoner: from prison) 釈放する shakúhō suru; (: from captivity) 解放する kaíhō suru; (gas: etc) 放出する hōshutsu suru; (free: from wreckage etc) 救出する kyúshutsu suru; (TECH: catch, spring etc) がす hazúsù; (book, record) 発売する hatsúbai suru; (film) 公開する kōkai suru; (report, news) 公表する kōhyō suru

relegate [rel'əgeit] *vt* (downgrade) 格下げする kakúsage suru; (BRIT: SPORT): *to be relegated* 格下げされる kakúsage sarerù

relent [rilent'] *vi* (give in) ...の態度が軟化

する ...no táldo ga nánika suru

relentless [rilent'lis] *adj* (unceasing) 絶間ない taémanaì; (determined) 執念深い shūneñbukai

relevance [rel'əvəns] *n* (of remarks, information) 意義 gígì; (of question etc) 関連 kañren

relevant [rel'əvənt] *adj* (fact, information, question) 意義ある ígì árù
relevant to (situation, problem etc) ...に関連のある ...ni kañren no arù

reliability [rilaiəbil'əti:] *n* (of person, machine) 信頼性 shiñraisei; (of information) 信びょう性 shiñpyōsei

reliable [rilai'əbəl] *adj* (person, firm) 信頼できる shiñrai dekirù; (method, machine) 信頼性のある shiñraisei no arù; (news, information) 信用できる shiñyō dekirù

reliably [rilai'əbli:] *adv*: *to be reliably informed that ...* 確かな情報筋による と... táshìka na jōhōsújì ni yorú tò ...

reliance [rilai'əns] *n*: *reliance (on)* (...への) 依存 (...é nò) izón

relic [rel'ik] *n* (REL) 聖遺物 sefbùtsu; (of the past) 遺物 ibùtsu

relief [rili:f'] *n* (from pain, anxiety etc) 緩和 kañwa; (help, supplies) 救援物資 kyūeñbusshì; (ART) 浮彫 ukfbori, レリーフ rerífò; (GEO) 際立つ事 kiwádatsu kotò

relieve [rili:v'] *vt* (pain, fear, worry) 緩和する kañwa suru; (patient) 安心させる añshin saserù; (bring help to: victims, refugees etc) ...に救援物資を届ける ...ni kyūeñbusshì wo todókerù; (take over from: colleague, guard) ...と 交替する ...to kōtai suru
to relieve someone of something (load) ...の ...を 持って上げる ...no ...wo móttè agérù; (duties, post) ...を解任する ...wo kaínin suru
to relieve oneself 小便する shōben suru

religion [rilidʒ'ən] *n* 宗教 shūkyō

religious [rilidʒ'əs] *adj* (activities, faith) 宗教の shūkyō no; (person) 信心深い shíñjiñbukai

relinquish [rilɪŋ'kwiʃ] *vt* (authority) ...から手を引く ...kara té wò hikú; (plan, habit) やめる yamérù

relish [rel'iʃ] *n* (CULIN) レリッシュ rerísshù; (enjoyment) 楽しみ tanóshimi
♦*vt* (enjoy: food, competition) 楽しむ tanóshimu
to relish the thought/idea/prospect of something/doing something ...を (...する の を)心待ちに待つ ...wo (...surú nò wo) kokóromachi nì mátsù

relocate [ri:lou'keit] *vt* 移動させる idō saserù
♦*vi* 移動する idō suru

reluctance [rilʌk'təns] *n* (unwillingness) 気が進まない事 kí gà susúmanaì kotò

reluctant [rilʌk'tənt] *adj* (unwilling) 気が進まない kí gà susúmanaì

reluctantly [rilʌk'təntli:] *adv* (unwillingly) いやいやながら iyáiyanagàra

rely [rilai'] *fus* (be dependent on) ...に頼る ...ni tayórù; (trust) ...を信用する ...wo shiñ-yō suru

remain [rimein'] *vi* (survive, be left) 残る nokórù; (continue to be) 相変らず...であ る afkawarazù ...de árù; (stay) とどまる todómarù

remainder [rimein'də:r] *n* (rest) 残り no-kōri

remaining [rimei'niŋ] *adj* 残りの nokóri no

remains [rimeinz'] *npl* (of meal) 食べ残り tabénokorì; (of building) 廃墟 hálkyo; (corpse) 遺体 itái

remand [rimænd'] *n*: *on remand* 拘置中 で kōchìchū de
♦*vt*: *to be remanded in custody* 拘置 される kōchi sarerù

remand home (*BRIT*) *n* 少年院 shōnen-in

remark [rimɑ:rk'] *n* (comment) 発言 ha-tsúgen
♦*vt* (comment) 言う iú

remarkable [rimɑ:r'kəbəl] *adj* (outstanding) 著しい ichíjirushiì

remarry [ri:mær'i:] *vi* 再婚する safkon suru

remedial [rimi:'di:əl] *adj* (tuition, clas-

ses) 補修の hoshū no; (exercise) 矯正の
kyōsei no

remedy [rem'idi:] *n* (cure) 治療法 chiryōhō
♦*vt* (correct) 直す naōsū

remember [rimem'bər] *vt* (call back to
mind) 思い出す omoidasū; (bear in mind)
忘れない様にする wasūrenai yō ni suru;
(send greetings): **remember me to him**
彼によろしくお伝え下さい kárè ni yo-
roshikū o-tsútae kudasái

remembrance [rimem'brəns] *n* (memory: of dead person) 思い出 omóide;
(souvenir: of place, event) 記念品 kinénhin

remind [rimaind'] *vt*: **to remind someone to do something** ...するのを忘れな
い様に...に注意する...surū no wò wasūrenai yō ni ...ni chūi suru
to remind someone of something ...に
...を思い出させる ...ni ...wo omóidasasē-
ru
she reminds me of her mother 彼女を
見ると彼女の母親を思い出す kánòjo wo
mírù to kánòjo no haháoya wo omóidasū

reminder [rimaind'ər] *n* (souvenir) 記念
品 kinénhin; (letter) 督促状 obōgekaki

reminisce [reminis'] *vi* (about the past)
追憶する tsufoku suru

reminiscent [reminis'ant] *adj*: **to be
reminiscent of something** ...を思い出
させる ...wo omóidasaserū

remiss [rimis'] *adj* (careless) 不注意な fuchūi na
it was remiss of him 彼は不注意だっ
た kárè wa fuchūi dátta

remission [rimij'ən] *n* (of debt) 免除 mén-
jo; (of prison sentence) 減刑 genkéi; (of
illness) 緩解 kańkai; (REL: of sins) 許し
yurúshi

remit [rimit'] *vt* (send: money) 送金する
sōkin suru

remittance [rimit'əns] *n* (payment) 送金
sōkin

remnant [rem'nənt] *n* (small part
remaining) 残り nokóri; (of cloth) 切れ端
kiréhashi

remnants [rem'nənts] *npl* (COMM) 端切
れ hagíre

remorse [rimɔ:rs'] *n* (guilt) 後悔 kōkai

remorseful [rimɔ:rs'fəl] *adj* (guilty) 後悔
している kōkai shite irū

remorseless [rimɔ:rs'lis] *adj* (*fig*: noise,
pain) 絶間ない taémanai

remote [rimout'] *adj* (distant: place,
time) 遠い tōi; (person) よそよそしい yo-
sóyososhìi; (slight: possibility, chance)
かすかな kásùka na

remote control *n* 遠隔操作 eńkakusō-
sa, リモートコントロール rimōtokonto-
rōru

remotely [rimout'li:] *adv* (distantly) 遠く
に tōku ni; (slightly) かすかに kásùka ni

remould [ri:'mould] (*BRIT*) (tire) 再生
タイヤ saíseitaiya

removable [rimu:'vəbəl] *adj* (detachable) 取外しのできる toríhazushi no dekírù

removal [rimu:'vəl] *n* (taking away) 取
除く事 torínozoku kotō; (of stain) 消し
取る事 keshítoru kotō; (*BRIT*: from
house) 引っ越し hikkóshi; (from office:
dismissal) 免職 meńshoku; (MED) 切除
sétsùjo

removal van (*BRIT*) *n* 引っ越しトラッ
ク hikkóshi torakkù

remove [rimu:v'] *vt* (*gen*) 取除く toríno-
zokū; (clothing) 脱ぐ núgū; (bandage etc)
外す hazúsū; (stain) 消し取る keshítoru;
(employee) 解雇する káīko suru; (MED:
lung, kidney, appendix etc) 切除する se-
tsùjo suru

removers [rimu:'vərz] (*BRIT*) *npl*
(company) 引っ越し屋 hikkóshiya

remuneration [rimju:nərei'ʃən] *n* (payment) 報酬 hōshū

Renaissance [ren'isɑ:ns] *n*: **the Renaissance** ルネッサンス runéssànsu

render [ren'dər] *vt* (give: thanks, service) する surū; (make) させる saserū

rendering [ren'dəriŋ] *n* (MUS: instrumental) 演奏 eńsō; (: song) 歌い方 utáikata

rendez-vous [rɑ:n'deivu:] *n* (meeting) 待
ち合せ machíawase; (place) 待ち合せの

場所 machíawase nò báshò

renegade [ren'əgeid] *n* 裏切者 urágiri-mono

renew [rinu:'] *vt* (resume) 再び始める futátabi hajimerú; (loan, contract etc) 更新する kōshin suru; (negotiations) 再開する safkai suru; (acquaintance, relationship) よみがえらせる yomfgaeraserù

renewal [rinu:'əl] *n* (resumption) 再開 safkai; (of license, contract etc) 更新 kōshin

renounce [rinauns'] *vt* (belief, course of action) 捨てる sutérù; (claim, right, peerage) 放棄する hōki suru

renovate [ren'əveit] *vt* (building, machine) 改造する kaízō suru

renovation [renəvei'ʃən] *n* 改造 kaízō

renown [rinaun'] *n* (fame) 名声 meísei

renowned [rinaund'] *adj* (famous) 有名な yūmei na

rent [rent] *n* (for house) 家賃 yáchìn
♦*vt* (take for rent: house) 賃借する chínshaku suru; (: television, car) レンタルで借りる réntaru de karírù; (*also*: **rent out**: house) 賃貸する chíntai suru; (: television, car) 貸出す kashídasù

rental [ren'təl] *n* (for television, car) レンタル réntaru

renunciation [rinʌnsi:ei'ʃən] *n* 放棄 hōki

reorganize [ri:ɔːr'gənaiz] *vt* 再編成する safhensei suru

rep [rep] *n abbr* (COMM) = **representative**; (THEATER) = **repertory**

repair [ripeːr'] *n* (of clothes, shoes) 修繕 shúzen; (of car, road, building etc) 修理 shúri
♦*vt* (clothes, shoes) 修繕する shúzen suru; (car, engine, road, building) 修理する shúri suru

in good/bad repair 整備が行届いている(いない) seíbi ga ikítodoite iru (inái)

repair kit *n* 修理キット shúrikittò

repatriate [ri:pei'trieit] *vt* (refugee, soldier) 送還する sōkan suru

repay [ripei'] (*pt, pp* **repaid**) *vt* (money, debt, loan) 返済する hefsai suru; (person) ...に借金を返済する ...ni shakkín wo

hefisaí suru; (sb's efforts) ...に答える ...ni kotáerù; (favor) ...の恩返しをする ...no ongaeshi wo suru

repayment [ripei'mənt] *n* (amount of money) 返済金 hefsaikìn; (of debt, loan etc) 返済 hefsai

repeal [ripi:l'] *n* (of law) 廃止 haíshi
♦*vt* (law) 廃止 haíshi

repeat [ripi:t'] *n* (RADIO, TV) 再放送 saíhōsō
♦*vt* (say/do again) 繰返す kurfkaesù; (RADIO, TV) 再放送する saíhōsō surù
♦*vi* 繰返す kurfkaesù

repeatedly [ripi:t'idli:] *adv* (again and again) 三度 saísan

repel [ripel'] *vt* (drive away: enemy, attack) 撃退する gekítai suru; (disgust: subj: appearance, smell) ...に不快な感じを与える ...ni fukái na kafji wo atáerù

repellent [ripel'ənt] *adj* いやな iyá nà
♦*n*: **insect repellent** 虫よけ mushíyoke

repent [ripent'] *vi*: **to repent (of)** (sin, mistake) (...を) 後悔する (...wo) kōkai suru

repentance [ripen'təns] *n* 後悔 kōkai

repercussions [ri:pəːrkʌʃ'ənz] *npl* 反響 hañkyō

repertoire [rep'əːrtwaːr] *n* レパートリー repátòrì

repertory [rep'əːrtɔːri:] *n* (*also*: **repertory theater**) レパートリー演劇 repátòriefgeki

repetition [repitiʃ'ən] *n* (repeat) 繰返し kurfkaeshi

repetitive [ripet'ətiv] *adj* (movement, work) 単純 反復 の tañjunhañpuku no; (speech) くどい kudóì; (noise) 反復される hañpuku sarerù

replace [ripleis'] *vt* (put back) 元に戻す mótò ni modósù; (take the place of) ...に代る ...ni kawárù

replacement [ripleis'mənt] *n* (substitution) 置き換え okíkae; (substitute) 代りの物 kawári no monò

replay [ripleis'] *n* (of match) 再試合 saíshiai; (of tape, film) 再生 saísei

replenish [riplen'iʃ] *vt* (glass) ...にもう一

杯つぐ ...ni mó ippái tsugú; (stock etc) 補充する hojū suru

replete [ripli:t'] *adj* (well-fed) 満腹の mañpuku no

replica [rep'ləkə] *n* (copy) 複製 fukúsei, レプリカ repúrika

reply [riplai'] *n* (answer) 答え kotáè
♦*vi* (to question, letter) 答える kotáèrú

reply coupon *n* 返信券 heñshiñken ◇切手と交換できる券 kitté tò kòkan dekirù kèñ

report [ripɔ:rt'] *n* (account) 報告書 hòkokushò; (PRESS, TV etc) 報道 hódò; (BRIT: also: **school report**) レポート repòtò; (of gun) 銃声 jùsei
♦*vt* (give an account of: event, meeting) 報告する hòkoku suru; (PRESS, TV etc) 報道する hódò suru; (theft, accident, death) 届け出る todókèderù
♦*vi* (make a report) 報告する hòkoku suru; (present oneself): **to report (to someone)** (...ni) 出頭する (...ni) shuttó suru; (be responsible to): **to report to someone** ...が直属の上司である ...ga chokúzoku nò jòshi de arù

report card (*US, SCOTTISH*) *n* 通知表 tsùchihyò

reportedly [ripɔ:rt'idli:] *adv* うわさによると uwása ni yoru tò

reporter [ripɔ:r'tər] *n* (PRESS, TV etc) 記者 kishà

repose [ripouz'] *n*: **in repose** (face, mouth) 平気で heñjo de

reprehensible [reprihen'səbəl] *adj* (behavior) 不届きな futódòki na

represent [reprizent'] *vt* (person, nation) 代表する dañhyò suru; (belief) ...の典型的な例である ...no teñkeiteki na rèi de arù; (symbolize: idea, emotion) ...のシンボルである ...no shìñboru de arù; (constitute) ...である ...de arù; (describe): **to represent something as** ...として描写する ...wo ...toshite byòsha suru; (COMM) ...のセールスマンである ...no sèrusumàn de arù

representation [reprizentei'ʃən] *n* (state of being represented) 代表を立てている事 daìhyò wò tàtète irù kotò; (pic-

ture) 絵 è; (statue) 彫像 chòzò; (petition) 陳情 chiñjò

representations [reprizentei'ʃənz] *npl* (protest) 抗議 kògi

representative [reprizen'tətiv] *n* (of person, nation) 代表者 daìhyòsha; (of view, belief) 典型 teñkei; (COMM) セールスマン sèrusumàn; (*US*: POL) 下院議員 kaìngiñ
♦*adj* (group, survey, cross-section) 代表的な daìhyòteki na

repress [ripres'] *vt* (people, revolt) 抑圧する yokúatsu suru; (feeling, impulse) 抑制する yokúsei suru

repression [repreʃ'ən] *n* (of people, country) 抑圧 yokúatsu; (of feelings) 抑制 yokúsei

repressive [ripres'iv] *adj* (society, measures) 抑圧的な yokúatsuteki na

reprieve [ripri:v'] *n* (LAW) 執行延期 shikkòeñki ◇特に死刑について言う tòkù ni shikéi ni tsuìte iú; (*fig*: delay) 延期 eñki

reprimand [rep'rəmænd] *n* (official rebuke) 懲戒 chòkai
♦*vt* 懲戒する chòkai suru

reprint [*n* ri:'print *vb* ri:print'] *n* 復刻版 fukkòkuban
♦*vt* 復刻する fukkòku suru

reprisal [riprai'zəl] *n* 報復 hòfuku

reprisals [riprai'zəlz] *npl* (acts of revenge) 報復行為 hòfukukòi

reproach [riproutʃ'] *n* (rebuke) 非難 hínàn
♦*vt*: **to reproach someone for something** ...の...を非難する ...no'...wo hínàn suru

reproachful [riprout'fəl] *adj* (look, remark) 非難めいた hinánmeita

reproduce [ri:prədu:s'] *vt* (copy: document etc) 複製する fukúsei suru; (sound) 再生する saísei suru
♦*vi* (mankind, animal, plant) 繁殖する hañshoku suru

reproduction [ri:prədʌk'ʃən] *n* (copy: of document, report etc) 複写 fukúsha; (of sound) 再生 saísei; (of painting, furniture) 複製品 fukúseìhin; (of mankind, animal etc) 繁殖 hańshoku

reproductive [riːprədʌk'tiv] *adj* (system, process) 繁殖の hańshoku no

reproof [ripruːf'] *n* しっ責 shisséki

reprove [ripruːv'] *vt: to reprove someone for something* ...の事で...をしっ責する ...no koto dé ...wo shisséki suru

reptile [rep'tail] *n* は虫類 hachūrùi

republic [ripʌb'lik] *n* 共和国 kyówakòku

republican [ripʌb'likən] *adj* (system, government etc) 共和国の kyówakòku no; *(US: POL): Republican* 共和党の kyówatō no

repudiate [ripjuː'diːeit] *vt* (accusation, violence) 否定する hitéi suru

repugnant [ripʌg'nənt] *adj* 不愉快な fuyúkai na

repulse [ripʌls'] *vt* (enemy, attack) 撃退する gekítai suru

repulsive [ripʌl'siv] *adj* (sight, idea) 不愉快な fuyúkai na

reputable [rep'jətəbəl] *adj* 評判の良い hyóban no yoi

reputation [repjətei'ʃən] *n* 評判 hyóban

reputed [ripjuː'tid] *adj* (supposed) ...とされる ...to saréru

reputedly [ripjuː'tidli] *adv* (supposedly) 人の言うには hitó nò iú ni wà

request [rikwest'] *n* (polite demand) 願い negái; (formal demand) 要望 yóbō; (RADIO, TV) リクエスト rikúesùto
  ♦*vt: to request something of/from someone* (politely) ...に...をお願いする ...ni ...wo o-négai suru; (formally) ...に...を要望する ...ni ...wo yóbō suru; (RADIO, TV) リクエストする rikúesùto suru

request stop (*BRIT*) *n* 随時停留所 zuíjiteiryùjo (乗降客がいる時だけバスが留る停留所 jōkōkyaku ga irú toki dake básu ga tomárù teíryùjo)

requiem [rek'wiːəm] *n* (REL) 死者のためのミサ曲 ...no tamé nò misá kyòku; (MUS) 鎮魂曲 chiñkoñkyòku, レクイエム rekúiemu

require [rikwaiəːr'] *vt* (need) ...が必要である ...ga hitsúyō de arù; (order): *to*

require someone to do something ...に...する事を要求する ...ni ...surú kotò wo yókyū suru

requirement [rikwaiəːr'mənt] *n* (need) 必要条件 hitsúyōjōkèn; (want) 要求 yókyū

requisite [rek'wizit] *n* (requirement) 必要条件 hitsúyōjōkèn
  ♦*adj* (required) 必要な hitsúyō na

requisition [rekwizíʃ'ən] *n: requisition (for)* (demand) ...の) 請求 (...no) seíkyū
  ♦*vt* (MIL) 徴発する chōhatsu suru

resale [riːˈseil] *n* 転売 teñbai

rescind [risind'] *vt* (law) 廃止する haíshi suru; (contract, order etc) 破棄する hákì suru

rescue [res'kjuː] *n* (help) 救援 kyūen; (from drowning, accident) 人命救助 jíñmeikyùjo
  ♦*vt: to rescue (from)* (person, animal) (...から) 救う (...kará) sukúū; (company) 救済する kyūsai suru

rescue party *n* 救援隊 kyūentai, レスキュー隊 resúkyòtai

rescuer [res'kjuːəːr] *n* 救助者 kyūjoshà

research [risəːrtʃ'] *n* 研究 keñkyū
  ♦*vt* (story, subject) 研究する keñkyū suru; (person) ...について情報を集める ...ni tsúìte jōhō wo atsúmerù

researcher [risəːr'tʃəːr] *n* 研究者 keñkyūsha

resemblance [rizem'bləns] *n* (likeness) 似ている事 nité irù kotò

resemble [rizem'bəl] *vt* ...に似ている ...ni nité irú

resent [rizent'] *vt* ...に対して腹を立てる ...ni táìshite harâ wò tatérù

resentful [rizent'fəl] *adj* 怒っているらしい... kótte irù

resentment [rizent'mənt] *n* 恨み urámì

reservation [rezəːrvei'ʃən] *n* (booking) 予約 yoyáku; (doubt) 疑い utágai; (for tribe) 居留地 kyoryúchì

reserve [rizəːrv'] *n* (store) 備蓄 bichíku, 蓄え takéwae; (SPORT) 補欠 hokétsu; (game reserve) 保護区 hogōkù; (restraint) 遠慮 eñryo

◆*vt* (keep) 取って置く tóttè oku; (seats, table etc) 予約する yoyáku suru

in reserve 蓄えてあって takúwaete attě

reserved [rizə:rvd'] *adj* (restrained) 遠慮深い eñryobúkai

reserves [rizə:rvz'] *npl* (MIL) 予備軍 yobígùn

reservoir [rez'ə:rvwɑ:r] *n* (of water) 貯水池 chosúichí

reshuffle [ri:ʃʌf'əl] *n*: *Cabinet reshuffle* (POL) 内閣改造 naíkakukaìzò

reside [rizaid'] *vi* (person: live) 住む súmù

residence [rez'idəns] *n* (formal: home) 住い sumái; (length of stay) 滞在 taízai

residence permit (*BRIT*) *n* 在留許可 zaíryūkyokà

resident [rez'idənt] *n* (of country, town) 住民 jūmin; (in hotel) 泊り客 tomárikyakù

◆*adj* (population) 現住の geñjū no; (doctor) レジデントの réjidento no

residential [rezidentʃəl] *adj* (area) 住宅の jūtaku no; (course) 寄宿の sumíkomi no; (college) 全寮制の zeñryōsei no

residue [rez'idu:] *n* (remaining part) 残留物 zañryūbùtsu

resign [rizain'] *vt* (one's post) 辞任する jinín suru

vi (from post) 辞任する jinín suru

to resign oneself to (situation, fact) あきらめて...を認める akírametě...wo mitómerù

resignation [rezigneiʃən] *n* (post) 辞任 jinín; (state of mind) あきらめ akírame

resigned [rizaind'] *adj* (to situation etc) あきらめている akírameté irù

resilience [rizil'jəns] *n* (of material) 弾力 dañryokù; (of person) 回復力 kaffukuryòku

resilient [rizil'jənt] *adj* (material) 弾力のある dañryoku no arù; (person) 立直りの速い tachínaori nò hayáì

resin [rez'in] *n* 樹脂 jushí

resist [rizist'] *vt* 抵抗する tefkō suru

resistance [rizis'təns] *n* (*gen*) 抵抗 tefkō; (to illness, infection) 抵抗力 tefkōryoku

resolute [rez'əlu:t] *adj* (person) 意志の強い ishí no tsuyóì; (refusal) 断固とした dáñko to shitá

resolution [rezalu:'ʃən] *n* (decision) 決心 kesshíñ; (determination) 決意 ketsúi; (of problem, difficulty) 解決 kaíketsu

resolve [rizɑ:lv'] *n* (determination) 決意 ketsúi

◆*vt* (problem, difficulty) 解決する kaíketsu suru

◆*vi*: *to resolve to do* ...しようと決心する ...shiyō to kesshíñ suru

resolved [rizɑ:lvd'] *adj* (determined) 決心している kesshíñ shité irù

resonant [rez'ənənt] *adj* 朗朗たる rôrô taru

resort [rizɔ:rt'] *n* (town) リゾート rizótò; (recourse) 利用 riyó

◆*vi*: *to resort to* ...を利用する ...wo riyó suru

in the last resort 結局 kekkyókù

resound [rizaund'] *vi*: *to resound (with)* (...の音が...中に) 鳴り響く (...no otō ga ...jū ni) narfhibikù

resounding [rizaun'diŋ] *adj* (noise) 響き渡る hibíkiwatarù; (fig: success) 完全な kañzen na

resource [ri:'sɔ:rs] *n* (raw material) 資源 shígeñ

resourceful [risɔ:rs'fəl] *adj* (quickwitted) やり手の yaríte no

resources [ri:'sɔ:rsiz] *npl* (coal, iron, oil etc) 天然資源 tefnenshigèn; (money) 財産 zaísan

respect [rispekt'] *n* (consideration, esteem) 尊敬 soñkei

◆*vt* 尊敬する soñkei suru

with respect to ...に関して ...ni káñ shite

in this respect この点では konó ten de wà

respectability [rispektəbil'əti:] *n* 名声 meísei

respectable [rispek'təbəl] *adj* (morally correct) 道理にかなった dóri ni kanáttà; (large: amount) かなりの káñari no; (passable) まあまあの mámà no

respectful [rispekt'fəl] *adj* (person, behavior) 礼儀正しい refgitadashìì kốrỏ wo ochĩtsukaserú

respective [rispek'tiv] *adj* (separate) それぞれのソれぞれの soréễồre no

respectively [rispek'tivli] *adv* それぞれ soréễồre

respects [rispekts'] *npl* (greetings) あいさつ áisatsu

respiration [respərei'ʃən] *n see* **artificial respiration**

respite [res'pit] *n* (rest) 休息 kyúsoku

resplendent [risplen'dənt] *adj* 華やかな hanáyàka na

respond [rispɑnd'] *vi* (answer) 答える kotáerů; (react: to pressure, criticism) 反応する hañnó suru

response [rispɑns'] *n* (answer) 答え kotáẽ; (reaction) 反応 hañnó

responsibility [rispɑːnsəbil'əti:] *n* (liability) 責任 sekínin; (duty) 義務 gímù

responsible [rispɑn'səbəl] *adj* (liable): **responsible (for)** (...の) 責任がある (...no) sekínin gà árù; (character, person) 責任感のある sekínìnkan no arù; (job) 責任の重い sekínin nò omói

responsive [rispɑn'siv] *adj* (child, gesture) 敏感な bíñkan na; (to demand, treatment) よく応じる yókù ójirù

rest [rest] *n* (relaxation) 休み yasúmi; (pause) 休止 kyúshi; (remainder) 残り nokóri; (object: to support something) 台 dái; (MUS) 休止符 kyúshifù
♦*vi* (relax) 休む yasúmù; (stop) 休止する kyúshi suru: **to rest on** (idea) ...に基づく ...ni motózukù; (weight, object) ...に置かれている ...ni okárete irû
♦*vt* (head, eyes, muscles) 休ませる yasúmaserù; (lean): **to rest something on/against** ...を...に掛ける(寄り掛ける) ...wo ...ni okú (yorīkakerù)
the rest of them (people) 残りの人たち nokóri nò hitótàchi; (objects) 残りの物 nokóri no monð
it rests with him to ... ...するのは彼の責任だ ...surú no wà kárè no sekínin dá

restaurant [res'tərənt] *n* レストラン rěsùtoran

restaurant car (*BRIT*) *n* 食堂車 sho-kúdòsha

restful [rest'fəl] *adj* 心を落着かせる ko-

rest home *n* 養老院 yốrôīn

restitution [restitu:'ʃən] *n*: **to make restitution to someone for something** (compensate) ...に対して...の弁償をする ...ni táìshite ...no beñshó wo surú

restive [res'tiv] *adj* (person, crew) 反抗的な hañkốteki na; (horse) 言う事を聞かない li kotð wò kikánaì

restless [rest'lis] *adj* (person, audience) 落着かない ochítsukanaì

restoration [restərei'ʃən] *n* (of building etc) 修復 shúfuku; (of law and order, faith, health) 回復 kaffuku; (of something stolen) 返還 heñkan; (to power, former state) 復旧 fukkyů

restore [ristɔːr'] *vt* (building) 修復する shúfuku suru; (law and order, faith, health) 回復する kaffuku suru; (something stolen) 返す káèsu; (to power, former state) 元に戻す mótò ni modósù

restrain [ristrein'] *vt* (feeling, growth, inflation) 抑制する yokúsei suru; (person): **to restrain (from doing)** (...しない様に) 抑える (...shináì yð ni) osáerù

restrained [ristreind'] *adj* (style, person) 控え目な hikáeme na

restraint [ristreint'] *n* (restriction) 抑制 yokúsei; (moderation) 程々 hodóhodo; (of style) 控え目な調子 hikáeme nà chốshi

restrict [ristrikt'] *vt* (limit: growth, numbers etc) 制限する seígen suru; (: vision) 邪魔する jámà suru; (confine: people, animals) ...の動きを制限する ...no ugóki wò seígen suru; (: activities, membership) 制限する seígen suru

restriction [ristrik'ʃən] *n* (gen) 制限 seígen; (or vision) 妨げ samátagè; (limitation): **restriction (on)** (...の) 制限 (...no) seígen

restrictive [ristrik'tiv] *adj* (environment) 束縛的な sokúbakutèki na; (clothing) きつい kitsúì

restrictive practices *npl* (INDUSTRY) 制限的慣行 seígentekikañkố

rest room (*US*) *n* お手洗い o-téaraì

restructure [riːstrʌk'tʃəːr] *vt* (business,

economy) 再編成する sañheñsei suru

result [rɪzʌlt] *n* (of event, action) 結果 kekkà; (of match) スコア sukôa; (of exam, competition) 成績 sefseki
♦*vi*: **to result in** ...に終る ...ni owárù **as a result of** ...の結果 ...no kekkà

resume [rɪzuːm] *vt* (work, journey) 続ける tsuzúkerù
♦*vi* (start again) また始まる matá hájimarù

résumé [rezʲuːmei] *n* (summary) 要約 yôyaku; (US: curriculum vitae) 履歴書 rirékishò

resumption [rɪzʌmpʲən] *n* (of work, activity) 再開 saîkai

resurgence [rɪsəːrdʒəns] *n* 復活 fukkátsu

resurrection [rezərekʲən] *n* (of hopes, fears) よみがえる事 yomígaeraserù kotô; (REL): **the Resurrection** キリストの復活 kirísuto no fukkátsu

resuscitate [rɪsʌsʲəteit] *vt* (MED) 生させる soséi saserù

resuscitation [rɪsʌsʲəteiʲən] *n* 生 soséi

retail [riːteil] *adj* (trade, department, shop, goods) 小売の koúri no
♦*adv* 小売で koúri de

retailer [riːteilər] *n* (trader) 小売業者 koúrigyòsha

retail price *n* 小売価格 koúrikakàku

retain [rɪtein] *vt* (keep) 保つ tamótsù

retainer [rɪteinər] *n* (fee) 依頼料 iráiryō

retaliate [rɪtæliːeit] *vi*: **to retaliate (against)** (attack, ill-treatment) (...に対して) 報復する (...ni táìshite) hôfuku suru

retaliation [rɪtæliːeiʲən] *n* 報復 hôfuku

retarded [rɪtaːrdid] *adj* (child) 知恵遅れの chiéokùre no; (development, growth) 遅れた okúreta

retch [retʃ] *vi* むかつく mukátsukù

retentive [rɪtentiv] *adj* (memory) すぐれた sugúretà

reticent [retisənt] *adj* 無口な mùkùchi na

retina [retʲənə] *n* (ANAT) 網膜 mômaku

retire [rɪtaiər] *vi* (give up work: gen) 引

退する iñtai suru; (: at a certain age) 定年退職する teñnentaíshoku suru; (withdraw) 引き下がる hikísagarù; (go to bed) 寝る nérù

retired [rɪtaiərd] *adj* (person: gen) 引退した iñtai shita; (: at a certain age) 定年退職した teñnentaíshoku shita

retirement [rɪtaiərmənt] *n* (giving up work: gen) 隠退 iñtai; (: at a certain age) 定年退職 teñnentaíshoku

retiring [rɪtaiəriŋ] *adj* (leaving) 退職する taîshoku suru; (shy) 内気な uchíki na

retort [rɪtɔːrt] *vi* しっぺ返しをする shippégaèshi wo suru

retrace [riːtreis] *vt*: **to retrace one's steps** 来た道を戻る kitá michì wo modórù

retract [rɪtrækt] *vt* (statement, offer) 撤回する tekkái suru; (claws, aerial etc) 引っ込める hikkómerù

retrain [riːtrein] *vt* 再訓練する saîkuñren suru

retraining [riːtreiniŋ] *n* 再訓練 saîkuñren

retread [riːtred] *n* (tire) 再生タイヤ saîseitaìya

retreat [rɪtriːt] *n* (place) 隠れ家 kakúregà; (withdrawal) 避難 hínàn; (MIL) 退却 tafkyaku
♦*vi* (from danger, enemy) 避難する hínàn suru; (MIL) 退却する tafkyaku suru

retribution [retrəbjuːʲən] *n* 天罰 teñbatsu

retrieval [rɪtriːvəl] *n* (of object) 回収 kaíshū; (of situation) 繕う事 tsukúrou kotô; (of honor) ばん回 bañkai; (of error) 償い tsugúnaì; (loss) 取返し toríkaeshi

retrieve [rɪtriːv] *vt* (object) 回収する kaíshū suru; (situation) 繕う tsukúroù; (honor) ばん回する bañkai suru; (error) 償う tsugúnaù; (loss) 取返す toríkaesù

retriever [rɪtriːvər] *n* (dog) リトリーバ犬 rítoríbakèn

retrograde [retrəgreid] *adj* 後戻りの atómodòri no

retrospect [retrəspekt] *n*: **in retrospect** 振返ってみると furíkaette miru tô

retrospective [retrəspekʲtiv] *adj* (exhibition) 回顧的な kafkoteki na; (feeling, opinion) 過去にさかのぼる kâkó ni sakánoború; (law, tax) に及する sokyū suru

return [ritə:rn'] *n* (going or coming back) 帰り kaéri; (of something stolen, borrowed etc) 返還 henkan; (FINANCE: from land, shares, investment) 利回り rímáwari

◆*cpd* (journey) 帰りの kaéri no; (BRIT: ticket) 往復の ōfuku no; (match) 雪辱の setsújoku no

◆*vi* (person etc: come or go back) 帰る kaérù; (feelings, symptoms etc) 戻る modórù; (regain): **to return to** (consciousness) ...を回復する ...wo kaífuku suru; (power) ...に返り咲く ...ni kaérizakù

◆*vt* (favor, love etc) 返す kaésù; (something borrowed, stolen etc) 返却する henkyaku suru; (LAW: verdict) ...を言渡す ...to tôshin suru; (POL: candidate) 選出する seňshutsu suru; (ball) 返す kaésù

in return (for) (...の) ...(no) o-káeshi ni

by return of post 折返し郵便で orfkaeshiyūbin de

many happy returns (of the day)! お誕生日おめでとう o-tánjōbi omédetō

returns [ritə:rnz'] *npl* (COMM) 利益 rfeki

reunion [ri:jun'jən] *n* (of family) 集い tsudói; (of school, class etc) 同窓会 dōsōkai; (of two people) 再会 safkai

reunite [ri:ju:nait'] *vt* (bring or come together again) 元のさやに収めさせる mótò no sáyà ni osámesaserù; (reconcile) 和解させる wakái saserù

rev [rev] *n abbr* (AUT: = *revolution*) 回転 kaften

◆*vt* (also: **rev up**: engine) ふかす fukásù

revamp [ri:væmp'] *vt* (organization, company, system) 改革する kaíkaku suru

reveal [rivi:l'] *vt* (make known) 明らかにする akfraka ni suru; (make visible) 現す aráwasù

revealing [rivi:l'iŋ] *adj* (action, statement) 手の内を見せるような té nò uchf wò misérù; (dress) 肌をあらわにする hádà

wo arawa ni suru

reveille [rev'əli:] *n* (MIL) 起床らっぱ kishō rappá

revel [rev'əl] *vi: to revel in something/ in doing something* (enjoy) ...を(...する のを)楽しむ ...wo (...surú no wo) tanóshimù

revelation [revəlei'ʃən] *n* (fact, experience) 意外な新知識 igái nà shínchishiki

revelry [rev'əlri:] *n* どんちゃん騒ぎ dońchan sawági

revenge [rivendʒ'] *n* (for injury, insult) 復しゅう fukúshū

to take revenge on (enemy) ...に復しゅうする ...ni fukúshū surù

revenue [rev'ənu:] *n* (income: of individual, company, government) 収入 shūnyū

reverberate [rivə:r'bəreit] *vi* (sound, thunder etc: *also fig*) 響く hibfkù

reverberation [rivə:rbərei'ʃən] *n* (of sound, etc: *also fig*) 響き hibfki

revere [rivi:r'] *vt* 敬愛する kefai suru

reverence [rev'ərəns] *n* 敬愛 kefai

Reverend [rev'ərənd] *adj* (in titles) ...師 ...shi ◇聖職者の名前に付ける敬称 sefshokushá no namáè ni tsukérù keíshō

reversal [rivə:r'səl] *n* (of order) 反転 haňten; (of direction) 逆戻り gyakúmodòri; (of decision, policy) 逆転 gyakúten; (of roles) 入れ替り irékawari

reverse [rivə:rs'] *n* (opposite) 反対 haňtai; (back) 裏 urá; (AUT: *also:* **reverse gear**) バック bákkù; (setback, defeat) 失敗 shíppaí

◆*adj* (opposite: order, direction, process) 反対の haňtai no, 逆の gyakú no; (: side) 裏の urá no

◆*vt* (order, position, direction) 逆にする gyakú ni suru; (process, policy, decision) 引っ繰り返す hikkúrikaèsu; (roles) 入れ替える irékaerù; (car) バックさせる bákkù saserù

◆*vi* (BRIT: AUT) バックする bákkù suru

reverse-charge call [rivə:rs'tʃɑ:rdʒ-] (BRIT) *n* 受信人払い電話 jushfnninbarai deñwa

reversing lights [rivə:r'siŋ-] (BRIT)

npl (AUT) バックライト bakkúraito

revert [rivə:rt'] *vi*: *to revert to* (former state) ...に戻る ...ni modórù; (LAW: money, property) ...に帰属する ...ni kizó-ku surù

review [rivju:'] *n* (magazine) 評論雑誌 hyōronzasshì; (MIL) 閲兵 eppéi; (of book, film etc) 批評 hihyó; (examination: of situation, policy etc) 再検討 saf-kentō

♦*vt* (MIL) 閲兵する eppéi suru; (book, film etc) の批評を書く ...no hihyō wð kákù; (situation, policy etc) 再検討する safkentō suru

reviewer [rivju:'ər] *n* (of book, film etc) 批評者 hihyōshà

revile [rivail'] *vt* (insult) 侮辱する bujóku suru

revise [rivaiz'] *vt* (manuscript) 修正する shúsei suru; (opinion, price, procedure) 変える kaérù

♦*vi* (BRIT: study) 試験勉強する shikén-benkyō suru

revision [riviʒ'ən] *n* (amendment) 修正 shúsei; (for exam) 試験勉強 shikénbenkyō

revitalize [ri:vai'təlaiz] *vt* ...に新しい活力を与える ...ni atárashiì katsúryðku wo atáerù

revival [rivai'vəl] *n* (recovery) 回復 kaffuku; (of interest, faith) 復活 fukkátsu; (THEATER) リバイバル ríbaibaru

revive [rivaiv'] *vt* (person) の意識を回復させる ...no íshìki wo kaffuku saserù; (economy, industry) 復興させる fukkō saserù; (custom, hope, courage) 復活させる fukkátsu saserù; (play) 再上演する sa-fjōen suru

♦*vi* (person: from faint) 意識を取戻す fshìki wo torímodosù; (: from ill-health) 元気になる génki ni nárù; (activity, economy etc) 回復する kaffuku suru; (faith, interest etc) 復活する fukkátsu suru

revoke [rivouk'] *vt* 取消す toríkesù

revolt [rivoult'] *n* (rebellion) 反逆 hańgyaku

♦*vi* (rebel) 反逆する haňgyaku suru

♦*vt* (disgust) むかつかせる mukátsuka-serù

revolting [rivoul'tiŋ] *adj* (disgusting) むかつかせる mukátsukaserù

revolution [revəlu:'ʃən] *n* (POL) 革命 ka-kúmei; (rotation: of wheel, earth etc: *also* AUT) 回転 kaften

revolutionary [revəlu:'ʃəneri:] *adj* (method, idea) 革命的な kakúmeiteki na; (leader, army) 革命の kakúmei no

♦*n* (POL: person) 革命家 kakúmeika

revolutionize [revəlu:'ʃənaiz] *vt* (industry, society etc) ...に大変革をもたらす ...ni dañhenkaku wð motárasù

revolve [rivɑːlv'] *vi* (turn: earth, wheel etc) 回転する kaften suru; (life, discussion): *to revolve (a)round* ...を中心に展開する ...wo chúshin ni teñkai suru

revolver [rivɑːl'vər] *n* けん銃 keñjū, リボルバー ríbòrubā ◇回転式の物を指す kaftenshìki no monó wð sásu

revolving [rivɑːl'viŋ] *adj* (chair etc) 回転の kaftenshìki no

revolving door *n* 回転ドア kaften doà

revue [rivju:'] *n* (THEATER) レビュー rébyū

revulsion [rivʌl'ʃən] *n* (disgust) 嫌悪 kén-o

reward [riwɔːrd'] *n* (for service, merit, work) 褒美 hóbì; (money for capture of criminal, information etc) 賞金 shōkín

♦*vt*: *to reward (for)* ...のため(に) ...に褒美を与える (... no tamé nì) hóbì wð ataerù

rewarding [riwɔːrd'iŋ] *adj* (fig: worthwhile) やりがいのある yarígai no arù

rewind [ri:waind'] (*pt*, *pp* **rewound**) *vt* (tape, cassette) 巻戻す makímodosù

rewire [ri:waiər'] *vt* (house) ...の電気配線を直す ...no deñki haĭsen wo shináo-sù

rewrite [ri:rait'] (*pt* **rewrote**, *pp* **rewritten**) *vt* 書き直す kakínaosù

rhapsody [ræp'sədi:] *n* (MUS) 狂詩曲 kyōshikyòku, ラプソディー rápùsodī

rhetorical [ritɔːr'ikəl] *adj* (question, speech) 修辞的な shújiteki na

rheumatic [ruːmæt'ik] *adj* リューマチの ryūmachi no

rheumatism [ruːˈmətizəm] n リューマチ ryūmachi

Rhine [rain] n: *the Rhine* ライン川 raingawa

rhinoceros [rainɔsˈɑːrəs] n サイ sái

rhododendron [roudədenˈdrən] n シャクナゲ shakúnage

Rhone [roun] n: *the Rhone* ローヌ川 rōnūgawa

rhubarb [ruːˈbɑːrb] n ルバーブ rúbābu

rhyme [raim] n (of two words) 韻 ín; (verse) 詩 shi; (technique) 韻を踏む事 ín wò fumú kotó

rhythm [riˈðəm] n リズム rízumu

rhythmic(al) [riˈðmik(əl)] adj リズミカルな rízumikàru na

rib [rib] n (ANAT) ろっ骨 rokkótsu
♦vt (tease) からかう karákaù

ribbon [ribˈən] n リボン ríbòn
   in ribbons (torn) ずたずたになって zutázuta ni natté

rice [rais] n (grain) 米 komé; (cooked) 御飯 góhan

rice pudding n ライスプディング raísu pudíngu ◊御飯にミルク、卵、砂糖などを加えたデザート góhan ni mírùku, tamágo, satő nadò wo kuwáetà dezátð

rich [ritʃ] adj (person, country) 金持の kanémochi no; (clothes, jewels) 高価な kökà na; (soil) 肥えた koétà, 肥よくな híyòku na; (food, diet) 濃厚な nókò na; (color, voice, life) 豊かな yútàka na; (abundant): *rich in* (minerals, resources etc) ...に富んだ ...ni tóndà
♦npl: *the rich* 金持 kanémochi ◊総称 sőshő

riches [ritʃˈiz] npl (wealth) 富 tómi

richly [ritʃˈli:] adv (dressed, decorated) 豪華に gőka ni; (rewarded, deserved, earned) 十分に jůbuň ni

rickets [rikˈits] n くる病 kurúbyð

rickety [rikˈəti:] adj (shaky) がたがたのgatágatà no

rickshaw [rikˈʃɔ:] n 人力車 jinrikishà

ricochet [rikəjeˈ] vi (bullet, stone) 跳ね飛ぶ hanétobù

rid [rid] (pt, pp rid) vt: *to rid someone of something* ...の...を取除く ...no ...wo torínozokù
   to get rid of (something no longer required) 捨てる sutérù; (something unpleasant or annoying) ...を取除く ...wo torínozokù

ridden [ridˈən] pp of ride

riddle [ridˈəl] n (conundrum) なぞなぞ nazónazò; (mystery) なぞ nazó
♦vt: *to be riddled with* ...だらけである ...dárake de árù

ride [raid] n (in car, on bicycle, horse) 乗る事 norú kotó; (distance covered) 道の行 michínori
♦vb (pt rode, pp ridden)
♦vi (as sport) 乗馬をする jőba wo suru; (go somewhere: on horse, bicycle, bus) 乗って行く notté ikù
♦vt (a horse, bicycle, motorcycle) ...に乗る norú kotó; (distance) 行く ikú
   to take someone for a ride (fig: deceive) ...にいんちきを掛ける petén ni kakérù
   to ride a bicycle 自転車に乗る jiténsha ni norú
   to ride at anchor (NAUT) 停泊する teíhaku suru

rider [raiˈdər] n (on horse) 乗り手 noríte; (on bicycle, motorcycle) 乗る人 norú hitð, ライダー ráìda

ridge [ridʒ] n (of hill) 尾根 ðnè; (of roof) 天辺 teppén; (wrinkle) うねり ùné

ridicule [ridˈəkjuːl] n あざける azákeru
♦vt あざける azákerù

ridiculous [ridikˈjələs] adj (foolish) ばかげた bakágetà

riding [raiˈdiŋ] n (sport, activity) 乗馬 jőba

riding school n 乗馬学校 jőbagakkő

rife [raif] adj: *to be rife* (bribery, corruption, superstition) 流行る habíkorù
♦vt nazó
   to be rife with (rumors, fears) ...がはびこっている ...ga habíkotte irù

riffraff [rifˈræf] n (rabble) ろくでなしの連中 rokúdenashì nò reńchū

rifle [raiˈfəl] n (gun) ライフル ráìfuru
♦vt (steal from: wallet, pocket etc) ...の中身を盗み取る ...no nákàmi wo nusúmitorù

rifle range n (for sport) 射撃場 shagékijð; (at fair) 射的 shatéki

rifle through vt fus (papers) ...をかき回して探す ...wo kakímawashíte sagásù

rift [rift] n (split: in ground) 亀裂 kirétsu; (: in clouds) 切れ間 kiréma; (fig: disagreement) 仲たがい nakátagaì

rig [rig] n (also: **oil rig**) 油井掘削装置 yuséi kussakú sóchi

♦vt (election, game etc) 不正操作する fuséisòsa suru

rigging [rig'iŋ] n (NAUT) 索具 sakúgu

right [rait] adj (correct: answer, solution, size etc) 正しい tadáshiì; (suitable: person, clothes, time) 適当な tekítō na; (: decision etc) 適切な tekísetsu na; (morally good) 正当な séitō na; (fair, just) 公正な kōsei na; (not left) 右の migí no

♦n (what is morally right) 正義 séigi; (entitlement) 権利 kénri; (not left) 右 migí

♦adv (correctly) answer etc) 正しく tadáshìku; (properly, fairly: treat etc) 公正に kōsei ni; (not on the left) 右に migí ni; (directly, exactly: **right now** 今すぐ íma súgù

♦vt (put right way up: ship, car etc) 起す okósù; (correct: fault, situation, wrong) 正す tadásù

♦excl では正しい dé wà

to be right (person) ...の言う事が合っている ...no iú kotó ga attè irù; (answer) 正解である séikai de arù; (clock, reading etc) 合っている attè irù

by rights 当然 tōzen

on the right 右に migí ni

to be in the right ...の方が正しい ...no hō gà tadáshiî

right away すぐに súgù ni

right in the middle 丁度真ん中に chōdo mannàka ni

right angle n (MATH) 直角 chokkáku

righteous [rai'tʃəs] adj (person) 有徳な yūtoku na; (anger) 当然な tōzen na

rightful [rait'fəl] adj (heir, owner) 合法の gōhō no; (place, share) 正当な séitō na

right-handed [rait'hændid] adj (person) 右利きの migíkikì no

right-hand man [rait'hænd'-] n 右腕 migífude

right-hand side n 右側 migígawa

rightly [rait'li:] adv (with reason) 当然 tōzen

right of way n (on path etc) 通行権 tsūkōken; (AUT) 先行権 senkōken

right-wing [rait'wiŋ] adj (POL) 右翼の úyòku no

rigid [ridʒ'id] adj (structure, back etc) 曲らない magáranaì; (attitude, views etc) 厳格な geníkaku na; (principle, control etc) 厳格な geníkaku na

rigmarole [rig'mərool] n (procedure) 手続 tetsúzùki

rigor [rig'ər] (BRIT **rigour**) n (strictness) 厳格さ geníkakusa; (severity): **rigors of life/winter** 生活(冬)の厳しさ sefkatsu(fuyú)nò kibíshisa

rigorous [rig'ərəs] adj (control, test) 厳密な genímitsu na; (training) 厳しい kibíshiì

rig out (BRIT) vt: **to rig out as** ...の仮装をする ...no kasō wò suru

to rig out in ...を着る ...wo kirù

rig up vt 作り上げる tsukúriageru

rile [rail] vt (annoy) ...を怒らせる ...wo okóraserù

rim [rim] n (of glass, dish) 縁 fuchí; (of spectacles) フレーム fúrèmù; (of wheel) リム rímù

rind [raind] n (of bacon, fruit, cheese) 皮 kawá

ring [riŋ] n (of metal, light, smoke) 輪 wá; (for finger) 指輪 yubíwà; (of spies, drug-dealers etc) 組織 sóshiki; (for boxing, of circus) リング ríngu; (bullring) 闘牛場 tōgyūjō; (sound of bell) ベルの音 bérù no otó

♦vb (pt **rang**, pp **rung**)

♦vi (person: by telephone) 電話を掛ける deñwa wo kakérù; (telephone, bell, doorbell) 鳴る narú; (also: **ring out**: voice, words) 鳴り響く narfhibìku

♦vt (BRIT: TEL) ...に電話を掛ける ...ni deñwa wò kakérù; (bell etc) 鳴らす narásù

a ring of people 車座になった人々 kurúmaza ni nattá hitóbìto

a ring of stones 環状に並んだ石 kañjō

ni naránda ishí

to give someone a ring (BRIT: TEL)
...に電話を掛ける ...ni denwa wò kakérù
my ears are ringing 耳鳴りがする mimínari ga surù

ring back (BRIT) vt (TEL) ...に電話を掛け直す ...ni denwa wò kakénaosù
◆vi (TEL) 電話を掛け直す denwa wò kakénaosù

ringing [riŋ'iŋ] n (of telephone, bell) 鳴る音 narú otò; (in ears) 耳鳴り mimínari

ringing tone n (TEL) ダイヤルトーン dafyarutōn

ringleader [riŋ'li:dəːr] n (of gang) 主犯 shúhàn

ringlets [riŋ'lits] npl (of hair) 巻毛 makíge

ring off (BRIT) vi (TEL) 電話を切る denwa wò kírù

ring road (BRIT) n 環状線 kanjōsen

ring up (BRIT) vt (TEL) ...に電話を掛ける ...ni denwa wò kakérù

rink [riŋk] n (also: **ice rink**) スケートリンク sukétoriǹku

rinse [rins] n (of dishes, hands) すすぎ susúgi; (of hair) リンスする事 rínsu suru kotò; (dye: for hair) リンス rínsu
◆vt (dishes, hands etc) すすぐ susúgù; (hair etc) リンスする rínsu suru; (also: **rinse out**: clothes) すすぐ susúgù; (: mouth) すすぐ yusúgù

riot [rai'ət] n (disturbance) 騒動 sódò
◆vi (crowd, protestors etc) 暴動を起す bódò wo okósù

a riot of colors 色取り取り irótoridòri
to run riot (children, football fans etc) 大暴れをする óaباre wo suru

riotous [rai'ətəs] adj (mob, assembly etc) 暴動的な bódòteki na; (behavior, living) 遊とな分まい yútồzanzai; (party) どんちゃん騒ぎの donchan sawàgi no

rip [rip] n (tear) 破れ目 yabúremè
◆vt (paper, cloth) 破る yabúrù
◆vi (paper, cloth) 破れる yabúrerù

ripcord [rip'kɔːrd] n (on parachute) 引き綱 hikízùna

ripe [raip] adj (fruit, grain, cheese) 熟した jukú shità

ripen [rai'pən] vt (subj: sun) 熟させる jukú saserù
◆vi (fruit, crop) 熟する jukú suru

ripple [rip'əl] n (of water) 波 さ ざ波 sazánami; (of laughter, applause) ざわめき zawámeki
◆vi (water) さざ波が立つ sazánami gà tátsù

rise [raiz] n (slope) 上り坂 nobórizaka; (hill) 丘 oká; (increase: in wages: BRIT) 賃上げ chín-age; (: in prices, temperature) 上昇 jōshō; (fig: to power etc) 出世 shussé
◆vi (pt rose, pp risen) (prices, numbers) 上がる agárù; (waters) 水かさが増す mizúkasa gà masù; (sun, moon) 昇る nobórù; (person: from bed etc) 起きる okírù; (sound, voice) 大きくなる ōkiku nárù; (also: **rise up**: tower, building) そびえる sobíerù; (: rebel) 立ち上がる tachíagarù; (in rank) 昇進する shōshin suru

to give rise to ...を起す ...wo okósù
to rise to the occasion 腕前を見せる udémae wo miséru

risen [riz'ən] pp of **rise**

rising [rai'ziŋ] adj (increasing: number, prices) 上がる agárù; (tide) 満ちる michíru; (sun, moon) 昇る nobórù

risk [risk] n (danger) 危険 kikén; (INSURANCE) リスク rísùku
◆vt (endanger) 危険にさらす kikén nì sarásù; (chance) ...の危険を冒す ...no kinén wò okásù

to take/run the risk of doing ...する危険を冒す ...surú kikén wò okásù

at risk 危険にさらされて kikén nì sarasárete

at one's own risk 自分の責任で jibún no sekínin de

risky [ris'ki:] adj (dangerous) 危険な kikén na

risqué [riskei'] adj (joke) わいせつがかった waísetsugakàttà

rissole [ris'əl] n (of meat, fish etc) メンチカツ mefíchikatsu

rite [rait] n 儀式 gíshìki

last rites (REL) 終油の秘蹟 shúyu nò hiséki

ritual [ritʃʊəl] adj (law, dance) 儀式的な gishíkiteki na
♦n 儀式 gíshìkì

rival [raivəl] n ライバル ráìbaru
♦adj ライバルの ráìbaru no
♦vt (match) ...に匹敵する ...ni hittéki suru

rivalry [raivəlri] n (competition) 競争 kyósṓ

river [rivəːr] n 川 kawá
♦cpd (port, traffic) 川の kawá no
up/down river 川上(下)へ kawákami (shimo) e

riverbank [rivəːrbæŋk] n 川岸 kawágìshì

riverbed [rivəːrbed] n 河原 kawára

rivet [rivit] n (bolt) リベット ríbètto
♦vt (fig): **to rivet one's eyes/attention on** ...に注目する ...ni chúmòku suru

Riviera [riviːerə] n: **the (French) Riviera** リビエラ ribíèra
the Italian Riviera イタリアのリビエラ itária nò ribíèra

road [roud] n (gen) 道 michí, 道路 dṓro
♦cpd (accident, sense) 交通の kốtsū no
major/minor road 優先(非優先)道路 yū́sen(hiyū́sen)dṓro

roadblock [roudblɑːk] n 検問所 keńmonjo

roadhog [roudhɑːg] n マナーの悪いドライバー mánā no warúi doráibā

road map n 道路地図 dṓrochízù

road safety n 交通安全 kṓtsū́ańzen

roadside [roudsaid] n 道路脇 dṓrowàkì

roadsign [roudsain] n 道路標識 dṓrohyṓshìki

road user n ドライバー doráibā

roadway [roudwei] n 車道 shádō

roadworks [roudwəːrks] npl 道路工事 dṓrokṓji

roadworthy [roudwəːrði] adj (car) 整備状態のいい sefbíjotai no fi

roam [roum] vi (wander) さまよう samáyoù

roar [rɔːr] n (of animal) ほえ声 hoégoè; (of crowd) どよめき doyómekì; (of vehicle, storm) とどろき todóroki
♦vi (animal) ほえる hoérù; (person) どな

る donárù; (crowd) どよめく doyómekù; (engine, wind etc) とどろく todórokù
a roar of laughter 大笑い ṓwarài
to roar with laughter 大笑いする ṓwarài suru

roast [roust] n (of meat) ロースト rṓsuto
♦vt (meat, potatoes) オーブンで焼く ṓbun de yakú; (coffee) いる írù

roast beef n ローストビーフ rṓsutobìfu

rob [rɑːb] vt (person, house, bank) ...から盗む ...kara nusúmù
to rob someone of something ...から...を 盗む ...kará ...wo nusúmù; (fig: deprive) 奪う ubáù

robber [rɑːbəːr] n 泥棒 doróbō

robbery [rɑːbəːri] n (theft) 盗み nusúmi

robe [roub] n (for ceremony etc) ローブ rṓbu; (also: **bath robe**) バスローブ basúrōbu; (US) ひざ掛け hizákake

robin [rɑːbin] n コマドリ komádòri

robot [roubɑt] n ロボット robóttò

robust [roubʌst] adj (person) たくましい takúmashiì; (economy) 健全な kefzen na; (appetite) おう盛な ṓsei na

rock [rɑːk] n (substance) 岩石 gañseki; (boulder) 岩 iwá; (US: small stone, pebble) 小石 koíshi; (BRIT: sweet) 氷砂糖 kṓrizatō
♦vt (swing gently: cradle) 優しく揺する yasáshìku yusurù; (: child) あやす ayásù; (shake: subj: explosion, waves etc) 激しく揺さぶる hagéshìku yusuburù
♦vi (object)揺れる yurérù; (person) 震える furúerù
on the rocks (drink) オンザロックで oñzarokkù de; (marriage etc) 危ぶまれて ayábumarete

rock and roll n ロックンロール rokkúnrōru

rock-bottom [rɑːkbɑtəm] adj (fig: lowest point) 最低の saítei no

rockery [rɑːkəːri] n (in garden) 庭石 niwá-ishi (=築石 sōshō

rocket [rɑːkit] n (space rocket) ロケット rokéttò; (missile) ロケット弾 rokéttodaň; (firework) ロケット花火 rokétto hanábí

rocking chair [rɑːkˈiŋ-] n 揺りいすyu-rîisu

rocking horse n 揺り木馬yurîmokúba

rocky [rɑːkˈi] adj (covered with rocks) 岩だらけの iwádarake no; (unsteady: table) 不安定な fuántei na; (unstable: business, marriage) 危ぶまれている ayábumarete irú

rod [rɑːd] n (pole) さお saó; (also: **fishing rod**) 釣ざお tsurízao

rode [roud] pt of **ride**

rodent [rou'dənt] n げっ歯類 gesshírúi

rodeo [rou'diːou] n ロデオ ródèo

roe [rou] n (species: also: **roe deer**) ノロジカ norójìka; (of fish) 卵 tamágò

  hard roe 腹子 harákò

  soft roe 白子 shiráků

rogue [roug] n 野郎 yaró

role [roul] n 役 yakú

roll [roul] n (of paper, cloth etc) 巻き makí; (of banknotes) 札束 satsútàbà; (also: **bread roll**) ロールパン rôrupàñ; (register, list) 名簿 meíbo; (sound: of drums etc) とどろき todôroki

  ♦vt (ball, stone etc) 転がす korógasù; (also: **roll up**: string) 巻く makú; (: sleeves) まくる makúrù; (cigarette) 巻く makú; (eyes) 白黒させる shírókuro sasérù; (also: **roll out**: pastry) 延ばす nobású; (flatten: lawn, road, surface) ならす narásù

  ♦vi (ball, stone etc) 転がる korógarù; (drum) 鳴り響く naríhibikù; (vehicle: also: **roll along**) 走る hashírù; (ship) 揺れる yurérù

roll about/around vi 転がる korógarù

roll by vi (time) 過ぎる sugírù

roll call n 点呼 teñko

roller [rou'ləːr] n (gen) ローラー rôrà; (for hair) カーラー kára

roller coaster [-kous'təːr] n ジェットコースター jettôkōsutà

roller skates npl ローラースケート rôrasukèto

roll in vi (mail, cash) 大量に入る taíryō ni hafrù

rolling [rou'liŋ] adj (landscape) うねりのある unéri no áì

多い unéri no ôì

rolling pin n めん棒 méñbō

rolling stock n (RAIL) 車両 sharyô ◇総称 sôshò

roll over vi 寝返りを打つ negáeri wò útsù

roll up vi (inf: arrive) やって来る yatté kurù

  ♦vt (carpet, newspaper, umbrella etc) 巻く makú

ROM [rɑːm] n abbr (COMPUT: = read only memory) ロム rômù

Roman [rou'mən] adj ローマの rôma no

Roman Catholic adj ローマカトリックの rômakatorikku no

  ♦n ローマカトリック信者 rômakatorikku shíñja

romance [roumæns'] n (love affair) 恋愛 reń-ai; (charm) ロマンス rômàñsu; (novel) 恋愛小説 reń-ai shôsetsu

Romania [roumeí'niːə] n = **Rumania**

Roman numeral n ローマ数字 rômasûji

romantic [roumæn'tik] adj ロマンチックな románchikkù na

Rome [roum] n ローマ rôma

romp [rɑːmp] n 騒々しい遊び sôzòshiî asòbi

  ♦vi (also: **romp about**: children, dogs etc) はしゃぎ回る hashágimawarù

rompers [rɑːm'pəːrz] npl ロンパース rofpāsu

roof [ruːf] (pl **roofs**) n 屋根 yáné, ルーフ rûfu

  ♦vt (house, building etc) 屋根を付ける yáné wo tsukérù

  the roof of one's mouth 口がい kôgai

roofing [ruː'fiŋ] n 屋根ふき材 yanéfukizài

roof rack n (AUT) ルーフラック rûfurakkù

rook [ruk] n (bird) ミヤマガラス miyámagaràsu; (CHESS) ルック rúkkù

room [ruːm] n (in house, hotel etc) 部屋 heyá; (space) 空間 kûkan, 場所 bashó; (scope: for improvement, change etc) 余地 yôchì

「rooms for rent」, 「rooms to let」 貸間

あり kashíma arí

single/double room シングル(ダブル)部屋 shínguru(dabúru)beyà

rooming house [ru:'mɪŋ-] (US) n 下宿屋 geshúkuya

roommate [ru:m'meit] n ルームメート rúmumèto ◇寄宿舎などで同室に泊まる人 kishúkusha nàdò de dōshitsu ni tomárù hitō

rooms [ru:mz] npl (lodging) 下宿 geshúku

room service n (in hotel) ルームサービス rūmusābisu

roomy [ru:'mi:] adj (building, car) 広々とした hirōbìro to shitá; (garment) ゆったりした yuttári shità

roost [ru:st] vi (birds) ねぐらにつく negúra ni tsukū

rooster [ru:s'tər] n オンドリ oñdòri

root [ru:t] n (BOT) 根 né; (MATH) 根 kóñ; (of problem, belief) 根源 koñgen
♦vi (plant) 根を下ろす né wò orósù; (belief) 定着する teíchaku suru
  the root of a hair 毛根 mōkòn
  the root of a tooth 歯根 shíkòn

root about vi (fig: search) かき回す kakímawasù

root for vt fus (support) ...を応援する ...wo óeñ surù

root out vt (find) 捜し出す sagáshidasù

roots [ru:ts] npl (family origins) ルーツ rūtsu

rope [roup] n (thick string) ロープ rōpu; (NAUT) 綱 tsunā; (for climbing) ザイル zāiru
♦vt (tie) 縛る shibárù; (climbers: also: **rope together**) ザイルでつなぐ zāiru de tsunágù; (an area: also: **rope off**) 縄で仕切る nawá dè shikírù
  to know the ropes (fig: know how to do something) こつが分かっている kotsú gà wakátte irù

rope in vt (fig: person) 誘い込む sasóikomù

rope ladder n 縄ばしご nawábashigo

rosary [rou'zəːri:] n ロザリオ rozárìo

rose [rouz] pt of **rise**
♦n (single flower) バラ bará; (shrub) バ

ラの木 bará nò kf; (on watering can) 散水口 hasósuiku

rosé [rouzei'] n ロゼワイン rozéwàin

rosebud [rouz'bʌd] n バラのつぼみ bará nò tsubómi

rosebush [rouz'buʃ] n バラの木 bará no kí

rosemary [rouz'meːriː] n ローズマリー rózumarì

rosette [rouzet'] n ロゼット rozéttò

roster [rɑs'təːr] n: **duty roster** 勤務当番表 kíñmutōbañhyō

rostrum [rɑs'trəm] n 演壇 eñdan

rosy [rou'zi:] adj (color) バラ色の bará-iro no; (face, cheeks) 血色のいい kesshóku no ì; (situation) 明るい akárùi
  a rosy future 明るい見通し akáruì mitōshi

rot [rɑt] n (decay) 腐敗 fuhái; (fig: pej: rubbish) でたらめ detárame
♦vt (cause to decay: teeth, wood, fruit etc) 腐らす kusárasù
♦vi (decay: teeth, wood, fruit etc) 腐る kusárù

rota [rou'tə] (BRIT) n 勤務当番表 kíñmutōbañhyō

rotary [rou'təːriː] adj 回転式の kaíteñshiki no

rotate [rou'teit] vt (revolve) 回転させる kaíteñ saserù; (change round: jobs) 交替でやる kōtai de yarū
♦vi (revolve) 回転する kaíteñ suru

rotating [rou'teitiŋ] adj (movement) 回転する kaíteñ suru

rotation [routei'ʃən] n (revolving) 回転 kaíteñ; (changing round: jobs) 交替 kōtai; (of crops) 輪作 riñsaku

rote [rout] n: **by rote** 暗記で añki de

rotor [rou'təːr] n (also: **rotor blade**) 回転翼 kaíteñyoku, ローター rōtā

rotten [rɑt'ən] adj (decayed: fruit, meat, wood, eggs etc) 腐った kusátta; (fig: person) いやな iyá na; (inf: bad) ひどい hidói
  a rotten tooth 虫歯 mushíba
  to feel rotten (ill) 気分が悪い kíbùn ga warúi

rotund [routʌnd'] adj (person) 丸々と太

った marumāru to futóttā

rouble [ruːˈbəl] n = **ruble**

rouge [ruːʒ] n ほお紅 hôbeni

rough [rʌf] adj (skin, surface, cloth) 粗い arái; (terrain, road) 凸凹の dekóboko no; (voice) しゃがれた shagáretá; (person, manner: violent) 荒っぽい aráppoi; (: brusque) ぶっきらぼうな bukkírabô na; (treatment) 荒い arái; (weather, sea) 荒れた aréta; (town, area) 治安の悪い chiánno warúi; (plan, sketch) 大まかな ōmaka na; (guess) 大よその ōyoso no

♦n (GOLF): **in the rough** ラフに ráfū ni

to rough it 原始的な生活をする genshīteki na seíkatsu wo suru

to sleep rough (BRIT) 野宿する nójūku suru

roughage [rʌˈfidʒ] n 繊維 sén-i

rough-and-ready [rʌfˈænredˈiː] adj 原始的な genshīteki na

roughcast [rʌfˈkæst] n (for wall) 小石を混ぜたしっくい koíshi wo mazétá shikkúí

rough copy n 下書き shitágakí

rough draft n 素案 soán

roughly [rʌfˈliː] adv (handle) 荒っぽく aráppokū; (make) 大まかに ōmaka ni; (speak) ぶっきらぼうに bukkírabô ni; (approximately) 大よそ ōyoso

roughness [rʌfˈnis] n (of surface) 荒い arása; (of manner) がさつさ gasátsusa

roulette [ruːlˈet] n ルーレット rūretto

Roumania [ruːmeíˈniːə] n = **Rumania**

round [raund] adj 丸い marúi; (figures, sum) 概数の gaísū no

♦n (BRIT: of toast) 一切 hitókire; (of policeman, milkman, doctor) 巡回 junkai; (game of cards) 一勝負 hitóshôbu; (: in competition) 一試合 hitóshiái; (of ammunition) 一発 ippátsu; (BOXING) ラウンド ráundo; (also: **round of golf**) ラウンド ráundo; (of talks) 一連 ichíren

♦vt (corner) 回る mawárù

♦prep (surrounding) ...の回りに ...no mawári ni: **to run round his neck/the table** 首/机の回りに kubí[ié]no mawári ni; (in a circular movement): **to move round the room** 部屋の中を一回りする heyá no nakà wo hitómawari

suru: **to sail round the world** 世界一周の航海をする sékaíisshū nō kōkai wo suru; (in various directions): **to move round a room/house** 部屋[家]の中を動き回る heyá [ié]no nakà wo ugókimawarū; (approximately): **round about 300** 大よそ300 ōyoso sańbyaku

♦adv: **all round** 回りに mawári ni

a round of golf ゴルフのワンラウンド gōrufu no wańraundo

the long way round 遠回り tōmawari

all the year round 一年中 ichínenjū

it's just round the corner (fig) 直ぐそこまで来ている súgū sokó madè kité irū

round the clock 24時間 nijū-yo jíkan

to go round to someone's (house) ...のうちに行く ...no uchí ni ikú

to go round the back 裏に回る urá ni mawárù

to go round a house ある家を訪ねる árū ié wò tazúnerū

enough to go round みんなに足りる程 mińna ni tarírù hodó

a round of applause 拍手 hákūshu

a round of drinks/sandwiches みんなに一回の飲み物(サンドウィッチ)をおごる事 mińna ní hitótori nò nomímóno (sańdouicchī)wo ogórù kotó

roundabout [raundˈəbaut] n (BRIT) (AUT) ロータリー rōtarí; (at fair) メリーゴーラウンド merígôraundo

♦adj (route) 遠回りの tōmawàri no; (means) 遠回しの tōmawashi no

rounders [raunˈdəːrz] npl (game) ラウンダーズ raúndàzu (野球に似た英国のゲーム yakyū ni nitá eńkoku no gēmu

roundly [raundˈliː] adv (fig: criticize) 厳しく kibíshikù

round off vt (speech etc) 終える oérù

round-shouldered [raundˈʃouldəːrd] adj ねこ背の nekóze no

round trip n 往復旅行 ōfukuryokō

round up vt (cattle, people) 駆集める karításumerù; (figure) 概数にする gaísū ni suru

roundup [raundˈʌp] n (of cattle, people) まとめ matóme; (of animals) 駆集 karításume; (of criminals) 一斉逮捕

isséitalho

rouse [rauz] *vt* (wake up) 起き okósù; (stir up) 引起す hikfokosù

rousing [rau'ziŋ] *adj* (cheer, welcome) 熱狂的な nekkyóteki na

rout [raut] *n* (MIL) 敗走 haísō
♦*vt* (defeat) 敗走させる haísō saserù

route [ru:t] *n* (way) ルート rûto; (of bus, train) 路線 rosén; (of shipping) 航路 kồro; (of procession) 通り道 tórimichi

route map (*BRIT*) *n* (for journey) 道路地図 dồrochizù

routine [ru:tin'] *adj* (work) 日常の nichíjō no; (procedure) お決りの o-kímari no
♦*n* (habits) 習慣 shūkan; (drudgery) 反復作業 hañpukusagyò; (THEATRE) お決りの演技 o-kímari no éñgi

rove [rouv] *vt* (area, streets) はいかいする haíkai suru

row[1] [rou] *n* (line of people, things) 列 rétsù; (KNITTING) 段 dáñ; (in boat) こぐ事 kogú kotó
♦*vi* (in boat) こぐ kogú
♦*vt* (boat) こぐ kogú
in a row (*fig*) 一列に ichíretsu ni

row[2] [rau] *n* (racket) 騒ぎ sáwàgi; (noisy quarrel) 口論 kóron; (dispute) 論争 roñsō; (*BRIT inf*: scolding): *to give someone a row* ...に大目玉を食らわす ...ni ómedàma wo kuráwasù
♦*vi* (argue) 口論する kóron suru

rowboat [rou'bout] (*US*) *n* ボート bôto

rowdy [rau'di:] *adj* (person: noisy) 騒がしい sawágashii; (occasion) 騒々しい sōzōshiì

rowing [rou'iŋ] *n* (sport) ボートレース bôtorēsu

rowing boat (*BRIT*) *n* = **rowboat**

royal [roi'əl] *adj* 国王(女王)の kokúō(jóṓ) no

Royal Air Force (*BRIT*) *n* 英国空軍 eíkokukūgùn

royalty [roi'əlti:] *n* (royal persons) 王族 ōzoku; (payment to author) 印税 iñzei

rpm [ɑ:rpi:em'] *abbr* (= *revolutions per minute*) 毎分回転数 maífunkaiteñsū

RSVP [ɑ:resvi:pi:'] *abbr* (= *répondez s'il vous plaît*) 御返事を願う go-hénji wò kóù

Rt Hon. (*BRIT*) *abbr* (= *Right Hon-*

ourable) 閣下 kákkà

rub [rʌb] *vt* こする kosúrù
♦*n: to give something a rub* こする kosúrù
to rub one's hands (together) もみ手をする momíte wò suru
to rub someone the wrong way (*US*) *or to rub someone up the wrong way* (*BRIT*) 怒らせる okóraserù

rubber [rʌb'əːr] *n* (substance) ゴム gómù; (*BRIT*: eraser) 消しゴム keshígomu

rubber band *n* 輪ゴム wagómu

rubber plant *n* ゴムの木 gómù no ki

rubbery [rʌb'əːri:] *adj* (material, substance) ゴムの様な gómù no yō na; (meat, food) 固い katáì

rubbish [rʌb'iʃ] *n* (waste material) ごみ gomí; (junk) 廃品 haíhin; (*fig. pej*: nonsense) ナンセンス nâñsensu

rubbish bin (*BRIT*) *n* ごみ箱 gomíbako

rubbish dump *n* ごみ捨て場 gomísuteba

rubble [rʌb'əl] *n* (debris) がれき garéki; (CONSTR) バラス bárasu

ruble [ru:'bəl] (*BRIT* **rouble**) *n* (currency) ルーブル rûburu

rub off *vi* (paint) こすり取る kosúritorù

rub off on *vt fus* ...に移る ...ni utsúrù

rub out *vt* (erase) 消す késù

ruby [ru:'bi:] *n* ルビー rûbī

rucksack [rʌk'sæk] *n* リュックサック ryukkúsakkù

rudder [rʌd'əːr] *n* (of ship) かじ kajî; (of plane) 方向かじ hókōda

ruddy [rʌd'i:] *adj* (face, complexion) 血色の良い kesshóku no yoì; (*BRIT: inf*: damned) くそったれの kusóttarè no

rude [ru:d] *adj* (impolite: person, manners, word) 無礼な buréi na; (shocking: word, behavior) 下品な gehín na

rudeness [ru:d'nis] *n* (impoliteness) 無礼 buréi

rudimentary [ru:dəmen'tɑ:ri:] *adj* (equipment, knowledge) 原始的な geñshiteki na

rudiments [ru:'dəmənts] *npl* (basics) 基本 kihóñ

rueful [ru:'fəl] *adj* 悲しい kanáshiì

ruffian [rʌfiːən] n ごろつき gorótsuki

ruffle [rʌfəl] vt (hair) 乱す midásù; (clothes) しわくちゃにさせる shiwákucha ni suru; (fig: person) 怒らせる okóraserù

rug [rʌɡ] n (on floor) じゅうたん jūtan; (BRIT: blanket) ひざ掛け hizákake

rugby [rʌɡbi] n (also: **rugby football**) ラグビー rágùbī

rugged [rʌɡid] adj (landscape) 岩だらけの iwádarake no; (features) ごつい gótsùi; (character) 無愛想な buáiso na

rugger [rʌɡər] (BRIT: inf) n ラグビー rágùbī

ruin [ruːin] n (destruction: of building) 破壊 hakái; (: of hopes, plans) 挫折 zasétsu; (downfall) 失墜 shittsúi; (bankruptcy) 破産 hasán; (remains: of building) 廃虚 haíkyo

♦vt (destroy: building) 破壊する hakái suru; (: hopes, plans, health) 壊す kowásù; (: future) 台無しにする dafnashi ni suru; (: plans) 失墜させる shittsúi sasérù; (: financially) 破産に追込む hasán ni oikomù

ruinous [ruːinəs] adj (expense, interest) 破滅的な hamétsuteki na

ruins [ruːinz] npl (of building, castle etc) 廃虚 haíkyo

rule [ruːl] n (norm, regulation) 規則 kísòku; (government) 君臨 kunírin; (ruler) 物差し monósashi

♦vt (country, person) 支配する shíhài suru

♦vi (leader, monarch etc) 君臨する kunírin suru; (LAW) 裁定する saítei suru

as a rule 普通は futsū wà

ruled [ruːld] adj (paper) けい線 keíshin のある jogái suru

rule out vt (idea, possibility etc) 除外する jogái suru

ruler [ruːlər] n (sovereign) 元首 génshu; (for measuring) 物差し monósashi

ruling [ruːliŋ] adj 支配する shíhài suru

♦n (LAW) 決定 kettéi

ruling party 与党 yótō

ruling class n 支配階級 shiháikaîkyù

rum [rʌm] n ラム酒 ramúshu

Rumania [ruːmeiˈniːə] n ルーマニア rúmania

Rumanian [ruːmeiˈniːən] adj ルーマニアの rúmania no; (LING) ルーマニア語の rúmaniago no

♦n (person) ルーマニア人 rúmaniajîn; (LING) ルーマニア語 rúmaniago

rumble [rʌmbəl] n ごう音 gôon, とどろき todóroki

♦vi (make rumbling noise: heavy truck) ごう音を響かせて走る gôon wò hibíkasète hashírù; (: stomach) 鳴る narú; (: pipes) ゴボゴボいう góbògobo iû; (: thunder) とどろく todóroku

rummage [rʌmidʒ] vi (search) 引っかき回して捜す hikkákimawashite sagásù

rumor [ruːmər] (BRIT **rumour**) n うわさ uwása

♦vt: it is rumored that ... ...だとうわさされている ...dà tò uwá sarete irú

rump [rʌmp] n (of animal) しり shirí; (of group, political party) 残党 zantō

rump steak n ランプステーキ rañpusutēki

rumpus [rʌmpəs] n 騒ぎ sawági

run [rʌn] n (fast pace) 駆け足 kakéashi; (for exercise) ジョギング jógîngu; (in car) ドライブ dóraibu; (distance traveled) 行程 kôtei; (journey) 区間 kukán; (series) 継続 kefzoku; (SKI) ゲレンデ gerénde; (CRICKET, BASEBALL) 得点 tokúten; (THEATER) 上演期間 jôenkikan; (in tights, stockings) ほころび hokórobi

♦vb (pt **ran**, pp **run**)

♦vt (race, distance) 走る hashírù; (operate: business, hotel) 経営する keíei suru; (: competition, course) 行う okónaù; (: house) ...の切盛りをする ...no kírmòri wò suru; (COMPUT) 走らせる hashíraserù; (pass: hand) 通す tôsu; (water) 出す dasù; (bath) ...に水を張る ...ni mizú wò hárù; (PRESS: feature) 載せる nosérù

♦vi (move quickly) 走る hashírù; (flee) 逃げる nigérù; (work: machine) 作動する sadó suru; (bus, train: operate) 動く ugókù; (: travel) 走る hashírù; (continue: play) 上演される jôen sarerù; (: contract) 継続する kefzoku suru; (flow: river, liquid) 流れる nagárerù; (colors) 走る ochirù; (washing) 色落ちする iróochi suru; (in election) 立候補する rikkōho suru; (nose) 鼻水が出る hanámizu ga derù

there was a run on ... (meat, tickets) 人々は...を買いに殺到した hitóbito wa ...wo kaí ni sattó shita

in the long run 行く行く (は) yukú-yuku (wà)

on the run 逃亡中で tōbōchū de

I'll run you to the station 駅まで車で送ろう ékí made kurúma dè okúrō

to run a risk 危険を冒す kikén wò okásù

run about/around vi (children) はしゃぎ回る hashágimawarù

run across vt fus (find) 偶然に見付ける gūzen ni mitsúkerù

run away vi (from home, situation) 逃げる nigérù

runaway [rʌnˈəwei] adj (horse, truck) 暴走の bōsō no; (person) 逃走中の tōsōchū no

run down vt (production, factory) の規模を縮小する ...no kíbò wo shukúshō suru; (AUT: person) ひく hikú; (criticize) kenásù

to be run down (person: tired) へとへとになっている hetóheto ni natté irù

rung [rʌŋ] pp of ring
♦n (of ladder) 一段 ichídàn

run in (BRIT) vt (car) のならし運転をする ...no naráshiunten wo suru

run into vt fus (meet: person, trouble) ...に出会う ...ni deáù; (collide with) ...にぶつかる ...ni butsúkarù

runner [rʌnˈəːr] n (in race: person) 競走の選手 kyōsō nò senshu, ランナー rấnnā; (: horse) 競走馬 kyōsōba; (on sledge) 滑り木 subérigi, ランナー rấnnā; (for drawer etc) レール rếru

runner bean (BRIT) n サヤインゲン sayáingèn

runner-up [rʌnəːrʌp] n 第2位入賞者 daí ni-i nyūshōsha

running [rʌnˈiŋ] n (sport) ジョギング jogíngu; (of business, organization) 経営 keíei
♦adj (water) 水道の sufdō no

to be in/out of the running for something ...の候補者である(でなくなっている)...no kōhosha de árù (de nakúnatte ir)

6 days running 連続6日間 reńzoku muikakàn

running commentary n 生中継 namá-chūkei

running costs npl (of car, machine etc) 維持費 ijíhi

runny [rʌnˈi] adj (honey, egg) 緩い yurúi; (nose) 垂れる tarérù; (eyes) 目やにの出る meyáni no dérù

run off vt (water) ...から流れ落ちる ...kara nagáreochirù; (copies) 印刷する ińsatsu suru
♦vi (person, animal) 逃げる nigérù

run-of-the-mill [rʌnəvðəmil] adj (ordinary) ごく普通の gokú futsū no

run out vi (person) 走って出る hashítte derù; (liquid) 流れ出る nagáredérù; (lease, passport) 切れる kirérù; (money) なくなる nakúnarù

run out of vt fus (money, time, ideas) ...がなくなる ...ga nakúnarù

run over vt (AUT) ひく hikú
♦vt fus (revise) おさらいをする o-sárai suru

runt [rʌnt] n (animal) 未熟児 mijúkujì; (pej: person) どちび dochíbi

run through vt fus (instructions) ...に目を通す ...ni mé wo tōsù; (rehearse, practice: play) 一通り練習する hitótōri reńshū suru

run up vt (debt) ...がかさむ ...ga kasámù

to run up against (difficulties) ...にぶつかる ...ni butsúkarù

run-up [rʌnˈʌp] n (BRIT): **run-up to** (election etc) ...への準備期間 ...é no jūbikikàn

runway [rʌnˈwei] n (AVIAT) 滑走路 kassōro

rupee [ruːˈpiː] n (currency) ルピー rúpī

rupture [rʌpˈtʃəːr] n (MED) ヘルニア herúnia

rural [ruːrˈəl] adj (area) 田舎の ináka no; (economy) 地方の chihō no

ruse [ruːz] n 策略 sakúryaku

rush [rʌʃ] *n* (hurry) 大急ぎ ōisogi; (COMM: sudden demand) 急激な需要 kyūgeki nà juyō; (of water, current) 奔流 hoñryū; (of feeling, emotion) 高まり takámari; (BOT) イグサ igúsa

♦*vt* (hurry) 急がせる isógaserú

♦*vi* (person) 急ぐ isógù; (air, water) 速く流れる háyaku nagárerù

rush hour *n* ラッシュアワー rasshúawā

rusk [rʌsk] *n* (biscuit) ラスク rásúkù

Russia [rʌʃə] *n* ロシア róshìa

Russian [rʌʃ'ən] *adj* ロシアの róshìa no; (LING) ロシア語の roshfagò no

♦*n* (person) ロシア人 roshíajìn; (LING) ロシア語 roshfagò

rust [rʌst] *n* さび sabí

♦*vi* (iron, metal etc) さびる sabírù

rustic [rʌs'tik] *adj* (style, furniture) 田舎風の ináka fū no

rustle [rʌs'əl] *vi* (leaves) かさかさいう kásàkasa iú

♦*vt* (paper) かさかさ動かす kásàkasa ugókasù; (US: cattle) 盗む nusúmù

rustproof [rʌst'pru:f] *adj* (car, machine) さびない sabínai

rusty [rʌs'ti:] *adj* (car) さびた sábìta; (fig: skill) ...の勘が鈍くなった ...no kañ gà nibúku natta

ruthless [ru:θ'lis] *adj* (person) 血も涙もない chf mo namfda mò naf; (action) 残酷な zañkoku na

rye [rai] *n* (cereal) ライ麦 raímugì

rye bread *n* ライパン raípàñ

S

Sabbath [sæb'əθ] *n* (Jewish) 土曜日 doyōbì; (Christian) 日曜日 nichíyòbi

sabbatical [səbæt'ikəl] *n* (*also*: **sabbatical year**): 一年間 7年置きに大学教授などに与えられる1年間の長期有給休暇 nánánèñ okf nì dafgakukyōju nádò nì atáerarerù ichfnèn no chōkyū-

kyūkyūka

sabotage [sæb'əta:ʒ] *n* 破壊工作 hakáikōsaku

♦*vt* (machine, building) 破壊する hakáisurù; (plan, meeting) 妨害する bōgai suru

saccharin(e) [sæk'ərin] *n* サッカリン sakkárīn

sachet [sæʃei'] *n* (of shampoo, sugar, etc) 小袋 kobúkùro ◇一回分ずつのシャンプー、砂糖などを入れた小さな包 ikkáibun zutsu no sháñpū, satō nádò wo iréta chíìsana tsutsúmì

sack [sæk] *n* (bag: for flour, coal, grain, etc) 袋 fukúro

♦*vt* (dismiss) 首にする kubf ni surù; (plunder) 略奪する ryakúdatsu suru

to get the sack 首になる kubf ni narù

sacking [sæk'iŋ] *n* (dismissal) 解雇 kákò; (material) ズック zúkkò

sacrament [sæk'rəmənt] *n* (ceremony: Protestant) 聖礼典 sefreitèñ; (: Catholic) 秘跡 hiséki

sacred [sei'krid] *adj* (of religion: music, history, writings) 宗教の shūkyō no; (holy: animal, building, memory) 神聖な shiñsei na

sacrifice [sæk'rəfais] *n* (offering of someone/something) 犠牲 giséi; (thing/person offered) いけにえ ikénie

♦*vt* (animal) 殺す korósu; (fig: human lives, health, career) 犠牲にする giséi ni surù

sacrilege [sæk'rəlidʒ] *n* 冒とく bōtoku

sacrosanct [sæk'rousæŋkt] *adj* (*also fig*) 神聖な shiñsei na

sad [sæd] *adj* (unhappy: person, day, story, news) 悲しい kanáshiì; (: look) 悲しそうな kanáshisō na; (deplorable: state of affairs) 嘆かわしい nagékawashì

saddle [sæd'əl] *n* (for horse) くら kurá; (of bicycle) サドル sadóru

♦*vt* (horse) ...にくらを付ける ...ni kurá wò tsukérù

to be saddled with (*inf* ...) の重荷を負わされる ...no omóni wò owásarerù

saddlebag [sæd'əlbæg] *n* (on bicycle) サ

ドルバッグ sadórubaggù

sadism [sei'dizəm] *n* サディズム sadízumu

sadistic [sədis'tik] *adj* サディスティック na sadísutikkù na

sadly [sæd'li:] *adv* (unhappily) 悲しそう に kanáshisō ni; (unfortunately) 残念ながら zaññennagara; (seriously): mistaken, neglected ひどく hídòku

sadly lacking (in) 残念ながら (...が) ない zaññennagara (...ga) náì

sadness [sæd'nis] *n* 悲しみ kanáshimi

sae [eseii'] *abbr* (= *stamped addressed envelope*) 返信用封筒 heñshin-yō fútò ◊ 宛先を書き、切手を張った物をさします atésaki wò kákì, kitté wò hattá mono wò sásù

safari [səfɑ:'ri:] *n* サファリ sáfàri

safe [seif] *adj* (out of danger) 安全な場所 にいる(ある) añzen na bashò ni irú (árù); (not dangerous, sure: place) 安全な añzen na; (unharmed: return, journey) 無事な bují na; (without risk: bet, subject, appointment) 安全な añzen na, 信頼できる añshin dekírù; (: seat in parliament) 落選する恐れのない rakúsen surù osore nò náì

♦*n* (for valuables, money) 金庫 kíñko

safe from (attack) ...される心配のない場所にいる(ある) ...saréru shiñpai no náì báshò ni irú (árù)

safe and sound (return, sleep, etc) 無事で bují de

(just) to be on the safe side 念のために neñ no tame ni

safe-conduct [seif'kɑːn'dʌkt] *n* (right to pass) 通行許可 tsúkōkyokà

safe-deposit [seif'dipɑːzit] *n* (vault) 貸金庫 kashíkiñkoshìtsu; (*also*: **safe deposit box**) 貸金庫 kashíkiñko

safeguard [seif'gɑːrd] *n* 保護手段 hogóshudàn

♦*vt* 保護する hógò surù

safekeeping [seifki:'piŋ] *n* 保管 hokán

safely [seif'li:] *adv* (without risk: assume, say) 安心して añshin shite; (without mishap: drive) 安全に añzen ni; (arrive) 無事に bují ni

safety [seif'ti:] *n* 安全 añzen

safety belt *n* 安全ベルト añzenberùto, シートベルト shítoberùto

safety pin *n* 安全ピン añzenpin

safety valve *n* 安全弁 añzenben

saffron [sæf'rən] *n* (powder) サフラン sáfùran

sag [sæg] *vi* (breasts, hem) 垂れ下がる tarésagarù; (roof) 凹む kubómu

saga [sæg'ə] *n* (long story, *also fig*) 長編物語 chōhenmonogatàri

sage [seidʒ] *n* (herb) セージ sèji; (wise man) 賢人 keñjin

Sagittarius [sædʒiter:'i:əs] *n* (sign of Zodiac) 射手座 itéza

Sahara [səher'ə] *n*: *the Sahara (Desert)* サハラ砂漠 sahára sabàku

said [sed] *pt, pp of* **say**

sail [seil] *n* (on ship) 帆 hó; (trip): *to go for a sail* ヨットに乗る yóttò ni noru

♦*vt* (boat) 操縦する sōjū suru

♦*vi* (travel: ship) 航海する kōkai suru; (SPORT) ヨットに乗る yóttò ni norú; (begin voyage: ship) 出航する shukkō suru; (: passenger) 船で出発する fúnè de shuppátsu suru

they sailed into Copenhagen 彼らはコペンハーゲンに入港した kárèra wa kopénhàgen ni nyūkō shitá

sailboat [seil'bout] (US) *n* ヨット yóttò

sailing [sei'liŋ] *n* (SPORT) ヨット遊び yottóasòbi

to go sailing ヨットに乗る yóttò ni norú, ヨット遊びをする yottóasòbi wo suru

sailing boat *n* ヨット yóttò

sailing ship *n* 帆船 hañsen

sailor [sei'lə:r] *n* (seaman) 船乗り funánòri

sail through *vt fus* (fig: exams, interview etc)...に楽々と合格する ...ni rakúraku to gōkaku suru

saint [seint] *n* (*also fig*) 聖人 seíjin

saintly [seint'li:] *adj* (person, life, expression) 聖人の様な seíjin no yō nà

sake [seik] *n*: *for the sake of someone/something* ...のために、...の tamé ni

salad [sæl'əd] *n* サラダ sáràda

salad bowl *n* サラダボール sarádabòru

salad cream (BRIT) n マヨネーズ mayónēzu

salad dressing n サラダドレッシング saráddadoresshíngu

salami [səlɑ:'mi:] n サラミ sárámi

salary [sæl'əri:] n 給料 kyúryō

sale [seil] n (act of selling: commercial goods etc) 販売 hańbai; (: house, land etc) 売却 baíkyaku; (at reduced prices) 安売り yasúuri, セール sếru; (auction) 競売 kyóbai

'for sale' 売物 urímono

on sale 発売中 hatsúbaíchū

on sale or return (goods) 委託販売で itákubańbai de

saleroom [seil'ru:m] BRIT n = sales-room

sales [seilz] npl (total amount sold) 売上 uríage

sales clerk (BRIT **sales assistant**) n 店員 teñ-in

salesman [seilz'mən] (pl **salesmen**) n (in shop) 男子店員 dańshiteñ-in; (representative) セールスマン sérusumàn

salesroom [seilz'ru:m] (US) n 競売場 kyóbaijō

saleswoman [seilz'wumən] (pl **saleswomen**) n 女子店員 joshíteñ-in

salient [sei'li:ənt] adj (features, points) 重要な jūyō na

saliva [səlai'və] n だ液 daéki

sallow [sæl'ou] adj (complexion) 血色の悪い kesshóku nò warúi

salmon [sæm'ən] n inv サケ sáke

salon [səlɑn'] n (hairdressing salon, beauty salon) 美容院 bíyoin

saloon [səlu:n'] n (US) bar) 酒場 sakába, (BRIT: AUT) セダン sédan; (ship's lounge) 広間 híroma

salt [sɔ:lt] n 塩 shió
◆vt (preserve: fish, beef etc) 塩漬けにする shiózukè ni suru; (put salt on) ...に塩を掛ける ...ni shió wò kakérû

salt cellar n 塩入れ shió-ire

saltwater [sɔ:lt'wɔ:tər] adj (fish, plant) 海水の kaísui no

salty [sɔ:l'ti:] adj しょっぱい shoppái

salutary [sæl'jəteri:] adj (lesson,

reminder) ためになる tamé ni narú

salute [səlu:t'] n (MIL) 敬礼 kefrei; (with guns) 礼砲 refhō; (gen: greeting) あいさつ aísatsu
◆vt (MIL) ...に敬礼する ...ni kefrei suru; (fig) ...に敬意を現す ...ni kếli wo aráwasū

salvage [sæl'vidʒ] n (action: gen) 救助作業 kyújo sagyō; (: of shipwreck) 海難救助作業 kaínan kyújo sagyō; (things saved) サルベージ sárubēji, 救助された物 kyújo sareta monó
◆vt (also fig) 救助する kyújo suru; (fig: situation etc) 取繕う shúshū suru

salvation [sælvei'ʃən] n (REL) 霊魂の救い refkon no sukúi; (economic etc) 救済 kyúsai

Salvation Army n 救世軍 kyúseigùn

salvo [sæl'vou] n (in battle) 一斉射撃 isséishagèki; (ceremonial) 一斉祝砲 isséishukùhō

same [seim] adj 同じ onáji
◆pron: *the same* 同じ物 onáji monò
the same book as ...と同じ本 ...to onáji hoñ
at the same time (at the same moment) 同時に dóji ni; (yet) とはいえ it wā ie
all/just the same それにしても soré ni shite mo
to do the same (as someone) (...と) 同じ事をする (...to) onáji koto wo suru
the same to you! お前もだ omáe mo da ◆侮辱を返す時に言う bujóku wo kaésu toki ni iú

sample [sæm'pəl] n (MED: blood/urine sample) 検体 kefitai, サンプル sáñpuru; (of work, merchandise) 見本 mihón, サンプル sáñpuru
◆vt (food) 試食する shishóku suru; (drink) 試飲する shíin suru

sanatoria [sænətɔ:'ri:ə] npl of **sanatorium**

sanatorium [sænətɔ:'ri:əm] (pl **sanatoria**) n = **sanitarium**

sanctify [sæŋk'təfai] vt 神聖にする shiñsei ni suru

sanctimonious [sæŋktəmou'ni:əs] adj

sanction [sæŋk'ʃən] n (approval) 承認 or 是認 osōnín or 是認 osōmítsūki, 認可 nínka
♦vt (give approval to) 認可する nínka suru

sanctions [sæŋk'ʃənz] npl (severe measures) 制裁処置 sefsaíshochì

sanctity [sæŋk'titi] n 神聖さ shínseisa

sanctuary [sæŋk'tʃueri:] n (also: **bird sanctuary**) 鳥類保護区 chōruíhogokū, サンクチュアリ safíkuchūari; (place of refuge) 避難所 hinánjo; (REL: in church) 内陣 naíjin

sand [sænd] n (material, fine grains) 砂 sunā; (beach: also: **sands**) 砂浜 sunáhama
♦vt (piece of furniture: also: **sand down**) 紙やすりで磨く kamíyasùri de migáku

sandal [sænd'əl] n (shoe) サンダル sandaru

sandbox [sænd'baːks] US n (for children) 砂場 sunába

sandcastle [sænd'kæsal] n 砂の城 sunā no shírō

sand dune n 砂丘 sakyū

sandpaper [sænd'peipər] n 紙やすり kamíyasùri, サンドペーパー sandópepà

sandpit [sænd'pit] (BRIT) n = **sandbox**

sandstone [sænd'stoun] n 砂岩 sagán

sandwich [sænd'witʃ] n サンドイッチ safídoitchì
♦vt: **sandwiched between** ...の間に挟まれて ...no aída ni hasámaréte
cheese/ham sandwich チーズ(ハム)サンドイッチ chízū (hámù) safídoitchì

sandwich course (BRIT) n サンドイッチコース safídotchikōsu ◇勉強と現場実習を交互に行う benkyō to genbajisshū wo kōgō ni okónaū katéi

sandy [sænd'iː] adj (beach) 砂の sunā no; (color) 砂色の suná-iro no

sane [sein] adj (person) 正気の shōki no; (sensible: action, system) 合理的な gōriteki na

sang [sæŋ] pt of **sing**

sanitarium [sæniteːr'iːəm] (US) n 療養所 ryōyōjo, サナトリウム sanátoriùmu

sanitary [sæn'iteri:] adj (system, arrangements, inspector) 衛生の efsei no; (clean) 衛生的な efseiteki na

sanitary napkin (BRIT **sanitary towel**) n 生理用ナプキン sefriyō napūkin

sanitation [sæniteiʃən] n (in house) 衛生設備 efseísetsūbi; (in town) 下水道設備 gesúídosetsūbi

sanitation department (US) n 清掃局 sefsókyòku

sanity [sæn'iti] n (quality of being sane: of person) 正気 shōki; (common sense: of situation etc) 合理性 gōrisei

sank [sæŋk] pt of **sink**

Santa Claus [sæn'tə klɔːz] n サンタクロース safitakurōsu

sap [sæp] n (of plants) 樹液 juéki
♦vt (strength, confidence) 失わせていく ushínawasete ikū

sapling [sæp'liŋ] n 苗木 naégi

sapphire [sæf'aiər] n サファイア safáfa

sarcasm [sɑːr'kæzəm] n 皮肉 hínìku

sarcastic [sɑːrkæs'tik] adj (person) いやみな (iyámizòki na; (remark, smile) 皮肉な hínìku na

sardine [sɑːrdiːn'] n イワシ iwáshi

Sardinia [sɑːrdin'iːə] n サルディニア島 sardūiniatō

sardonic [sɑːrdɑːn'ik] adj (smile) あざける様な azákeru yōna

sari [sɑː'riː] n サリー sárī

sash [sæʃ] n (Western) サッシュ sásshū; (Japanese) 帯 óbì

sat [sæt] pt, pp of **sit**

Satan [sei'tən] n 大魔王 daímaò, サタン sátàn

satchel [sætʃ'əl] n (child's) かばん kabán

satellite [sæt'əlait] n (body in space) 衛星 éisei; (communications satellite) 通信衛星 tsūshin-eisei

satellite dish n パラボラアンテナ parábora antena

satin [sæt'ən] n サテン sátèn
♦adj サテンの sátèn no

satire [sæt'aiər] n (form of humor) 風刺 fūshi; (novel) 風刺小説 fūshíshōsetsu; (play) 風刺劇 fūshígekì

satirical [sətir'ikəl] adj (remarks, drawings etc) 風刺の fúshi no

satisfaction [sætisfæk'ʃən] n (pleasure) 満足 mánzoku; (refund, apology etc) 謝罪 shazái

satisfactory [sætisfæk'tə:ri:] adj (patient's condition) 良い yói; (results, progress) 満足な mánzoku na

satisfy [sæt'isfai] vt (please) 満足させる mánzoku saserú; (meet: needs, demand) …に応じる ...ni ójirù; (convince) 納得させる nattóku saserú

satisfying [sæt'isfaiiŋ] adj (meal, job, feeling) 満足な mánzoku na

saturate [sætʃ'əreit] vt: **to saturate (with)** (also fig) (...で)一杯にする (...de) ippái ni surù

saturation [sætʃərei'ʃən] n (also fig) 飽和状態 hōwajōtai

Saturday [sæt'ə:rdei] n 土曜日 doyóbǐ

sauce [sɔːs] n (sweet, savory) ソース sósu

saucepan [sɔːs'pæn] n ソースパン sōsupaǹ

saucer [sɔː'sə:r] n 受皿 ukézàra, ソーサー sōsā

saucy [sɔːs'iː] adj (cheeky) ずうずうしい zūzūshiì

Saudi [sau'di:] n: **Saudi Arabia** サウジアラビア saúijiarābia

Saudi (Arabian) adj サウジアラビアの saújiarábia no

sauna [sɔː'nə] n サウナ sáuna

saunter [sɔːn'tə:r] vi のんびりと歩く noñbiri to árukù

sausage [sɔː'sidʒ] n ソーセージ sōséjiì

sausage roll n ソーセージパン sōséjìpaǹ

sauté [sɔːtei'] adj: **sauté potatoes** フライポテト furáipotèto

savage [sæv'idʒ] adj (cruel, fierce: dog) どうもうな dōmō na; (: attack) 残忍な zañnin na; (primitive: tribe) 未開な mikái na

♦n 野蛮人 yabáñjin

savagery [sæv'idʒri:] n 残忍さ zañninsa

save [seiv] vt (rescue: someone's life, marriage) 救う sukúù; (economize on: money, time) 節約する setsúyaku suru; (put by: receipts etc) 取って置く tóttè oku; (: money) 蓄える takúwaerù;

(COMPUT) 格納する kakúnō suru, セーブする sébu suru; (avoid: work, trouble) 省く habúkù; (keep: seat) 確保する kákùho suru; (SPORT: shot, ball) セーブする sébu suru

♦vi (also: **save up**) 貯金をする chokíñ suru

♦n (SPORT) セーブ sébu

♦prep (except) (...を)除いて (...wo) nozóìte

saving [sei'viŋ] n (on price etc) 節約 setsúyaku

♦adj: **the saving grace of something** …の唯一の長所 ...no yuíitsu no chōshò

savings [sei'viŋz] npl (money) 貯金 chokíñ

savings account n 普通預金口座 futsúyokiñkòza

savings bank n 普通銀行 futsúgiñkò

savior [seiv'jə:r] (BRIT **saviour**) n (gen) 救い主 sukúinùshi; (REL) 救世主 kyúseishu

savor [sei'və:r] (BRIT **savour**) vt (food, drink, experience) 味わう ajíwaù

savory [sei'və:ri:] (BRIT **savoury**) adj (dish: not sweet: spicy) ぴりっとした pirírtto shita; (: salt-flavored) 塩味の shióaji no

saw [sɔː] n (tool) のこぎり nokógìri

♦vt (pt **sawed**, pp **sawed** or **sawn**) のこぎりで切る nokógìri de kírù

♦pt of **see**

sawdust [sɔː'dʌst] n のこくず nokókuzù

sawed-off [sɔːd'ɔːf] n (US): **sawed-off shotgun** 短身散弾銃 tañshin sandañjū ◊ のこぎりで銃身を短くした散弾銃 nokógìri de jūshin wo mijſkaku kittá sañdañjū

sawmill [sɔː'mil] n 製材所 seízaisho

sawn-off [sɔːn'ɔːf] adj (BRIT) = **sawed-off**

saxophone [sæk'səfoun] n サキソフォーン sakísofòn

say [sei] n: **to have one's say** 意見を言う íken wo iú

♦vt (pt, pp **said**) 言う iú

to have a/some say in something …についてある程度の発言権がある ...ni tsúìte árù teídò no hatsúgeñken ga árù

to say yes/no 承知する〔しない〕shōchi suru (shinai)

could you say that again? もう一度言ってくれませんか mō ichidó ittè kuremasèn ka

that is to say つまり tsūmāri

that goes without saying それは言うまでもない soré wà iú made mo naí

saying [sei'iŋ] *n* (proverb) ことわざ kotówaza; (words of wisdom) 賢言 kakúgen; (often repeated phrase) 愛用の言葉 aíyō no kotoba

scab [skæb] *n* (on wound) かさぶた kasábuta; (pej: strike-breaker) スト破り sutó-yabùri

scaffold [skæf'əld] *n* (for execution) 死刑台 shikéidai; (for building etc) = **scaffolding**

scaffolding [skæf'əldiŋ] *n* 足場 ashíba

scald [skɔːld] *n* やけど yakédo ◊ (熱湯や蒸気などによるやけどを指す nettō ya jṓki nado ni yórù yakédo wò sásù

♦ *vt* (burn: skin) やけどさせる yakédo saserù

scale [skeil] *n* (gen: set of numbers) 目盛 memóri; (of salaries, fees etc) 表 hyṓ; (of fish) うろこ uróko; (MUS) 音階 ońkai; (of map, model) 縮小率 shukúshōrìtsu; (size, extent) 規模 kíbo

♦ *vt* (mountain, tree) 登る noborù

on a large scale 大規模で daíkibò de

scale of charges 料金の表 ryōkín no hyṓ

scale down *vt* 縮小する shukúshō suru

scales [skeilz] *npl* (for weighing) 量り hakári

scallop [skɑːl'əp] *n* (ZOOL) ホタテガイ hotátegài; (SEWING) スカラップ sukáruppù

scalp [skælp] *n* 頭の皮膚 atáma no hifù, 頭皮 tṓhi

♦ *vt* ...の頭皮をはぐ ...no tṓhi wo hágù

scalpel [skæl'pəl] *n* メス mésu

scamper [skæm'pəːr] *n*: **to scamper away/off** (child, animal) ばたばた走って行く pátapata hashítte ikú

scampi [skæm'piː] *npl* エビフライ ebífuraì

scan [skæn] *vt* (examine: horizon) 見渡す

miwátasu; (glance at quickly: newspaper) ...にきっと目を通す ...ni sáttō mé wò tṓsù; (TV, RADAR) 走査する sṓsa suru

♦ *n* (MED) スキャン sukyán

scandal [skæn'dəl] *n* (shocking event) 醜聞 shūbun, スキャンダル sukyándaru; (defamatory: reports, rumors) 陰口 kagéguchi; (gossip) うわさ uwása; (*fig*: disgrace) 恥ずべき事 hajíbekì koto

scandalize [skæn'dəlaiz] *vt* 憤慨させる fuńgai saserù

scandalous [skæn'dələs] *adj* (disgraceful, shocking: behavior etc) 破廉恥な harénchi na

Scandinavian [skændənei'viːən] *adj* スカンディナビアの sukándinabìa no

scant [skænt] *adj* (attention) 不十分な fujúbùn na

scanty [skæn'tiː] *adj* (meal) ささやかな sasáyàka na; (underwear) 極めて小さい kiwámète chísaì

scapegoat [skeip'gout] *n* 身代り migáwari

scar [skɑːr] *n* (on skin: *also fig*) 傷跡 kizúato

♦ *vt* (*also fig*) 傷跡を残す kizúato wò nokósù

scarce [skeːrs] *adj* (rare, not plentiful) 少ない sukúnaì

to make oneself scarce (inf) 消えうせる kiéuserù

scarcely [skeːrs'liː] *adv* (hardly) ほとんど...ない hotóndo ...naí; (with numbers: barely) わずかに wázùka ni

scarcity [skeːr'siti:] *n* (shortage) 不足 fusóku

scare [skeːr] *n* (fright) 恐怖 kyṓfu; (public fear) 恐慌 kyṓkō

♦ *vt* (frighten) 怖がらす kowágarasù

bomb scare 爆弾騒ぎ bakúdan sawàgi

to scare someone stiff ...に怖い思いをさせる ...ni kowái omoì wo saserù

scarecrow [skeːr'krou] *n* かかし kakáshi

scared [skeːrd] *adj*: **to be scared** 怖がる kowágarù

scare off/away *vt* おどかして追い払う odókashite oiharaū

scarf [skɑːrf] (*pl* **scarfs** *or* **scarves**) *n* (long) マフラー máfūrā; (square) スカーフ sukáfū

scarlet [skɑːrlit] *adj* (color) 火色 hífiro

scarlet fever *n* しょう紅熱 shókōnetsu

scarves [skɑːrvz] *npl of* **scarf**

scary [skeːriː] (*inf*) *adj* 怖い kowáī

scathing [skeíðiŋ] *adj* (comments, attack) 辛らつな shiratsu na

scatter [skætˈər] *vt* (spread: seeds, papers) まき散らす makíchirasū; (put to flight: flock of birds, crowd of people) 追散らす oíchirasū

♦*vi* (crowd) 散る chírū

scatterbrained [skætˈərbreind] (*inf*) *adj* (forgetful) おつむの弱い o-tsúmū no yowáī

scavenger [skævˈindʒər] *n* (person) くず拾い kuzúhiroi

scenario [sineːrˈiːou] *n* (THEATER, CINEMA) 脚本 kyakúhon, シナリオ shinárìo; (*fig*) 筋書 sujígakì

scene [siːn] *n* (THEATER, *fig*) 場な ba, シーン shín; (of crime, accident) 現場 génba; (sight, view) 景色 késhìki; (fuss) 騒ぎ sáwàgi

scenery [siːnəriː] *n* (THEATER) 大道具 ốdôgu; (landscape) 景色 késhìki

scenic [siːnik] *adj* (picturesque) 景色の美しい késhìki no utsúkushiī

scent [sent] *n* (pleasant smell) 香り kaóri; (track) 通った後のにおい tótta átò no nióī; (*fig*) 手がかり tegákàri; (liquid perfume) 香水 kósui

scepter [septˈər] (*BRIT* **sceptre**) *n* しゃく sháku

sceptic [skepˈtik] (*BRIT*) *n* = **skeptic** *etc*

schedule [skedʒˈuːl] *n* (of trains, buses) 時間割 jikánwari; (list of events and times) 時刻表 jikókuhyò; (list of prices, details etc) 表 hyố

♦*vt* (timetable, visit) 予定する yotéi suru

on schedule (trains, buses) 定刻通りに teñkokúdôri ni; (project etc) 予定通りに yotéidôri ni

to be ahead of schedule 予定時間より

早い yotéijikàn yórī hayáī

to be behind schedule 予定時間に遅れる yotéijikàn ni okúrerū

scheduled flight [skedʒˈuːld-] *n* 定期便 tefkíbin

schematic [skiːmætˈik] *adj* (diagram etc) 模式的な moshíkiteki na

scheme [skiːm] *n* (personal plan, idea) もくろみ mokúromi; (dishonest plan, plot) 陰謀 ífibô; (formal plan: pension plan etc) 計画 kefkaku, 案 áñ; (arrangement) 配置 háīchi

♦*vi* (intrigue) たくらむ takúramù

scheming [skiːmˈiŋ] *adj* 腹黒い haráguroì

♦*n* たくらむ事 takúramù kotó

schism [sizˈəm] *n* 分裂 buñretsu

schizophrenic [skitsəfrenˈik] *adj* 精神分裂症の sefshinbunretsushô no

scholar [skɑlˈər] *n* (pupil) 学習者 gakúshûsha; (learned person) 学者 gakúsha

scholarly [skɑlˈərliː] *adj* (text, approach) 学問的な gakúmonteki na; (person) 博学的な hakúgakuteki na

scholarship [skɑlˈərʃip] *n* (academic knowledge) 学問 gakúmon; (grant) 奨学金 shôgakukìn

school [skuːl] *n* (place where children learn: *gen*) 学校 gakkô; (*also:* **elementary school**) 小学校 shôgakkô; (*also:* **secondary school:** lower) 中学校 chúgakkô; (: higher) 高(等学)校 kố(tôgak)kô; (*US:* university) 大学 daígaku

♦*cpd* 学校の gakkô no

school age *n* 学齢 gakúrei

schoolbook [skuːlˈbuk] *n* 教科書 kyôkashò

schoolboy [skuːlˈboi] *n* 男子生徒 dañshíseìto

schoolchildren [skuːlˈtʃildrən] *npl* 生徒 seìto

schooldays [skuːlˈdeiz] *npl* 学校時代 gakkójìdai

schoolgirl [skuːlˈgərl] *n* 女子生徒 joshíseìto

schooling [skuːlˈiŋ] *n* (education at school) 学校教育 gakkôkyòiku

schoolmaster [skuːlˈmæstər] *n* 教師

kyōshi, 教員 kyōin, 先生 sensei ◇男子教員 danshikyōin

schoolmistress [sku:l'mistris] n 教師 kyōshi, 教員 kyōin, 先生 sensei ◇女子教員 joshīkyōin

schoolteacher [sku:l'ti:tʃəːr] n 教師 kyōshi, 教員 kyōin, 先生 sensei ◇男女を問わず使う dānjo wo tōwázu tsukáū

schooner [sku:'nəːr] n (ship) 帆船 hańsen

sciatica [saiæt'ikə] n 座骨神経痛 zakótsushinkeítsū

science [sai'əns] n (study of natural things) 科学 kágaku; (branch of such knowledge) ...学 ...gaku

science fiction n 空想科学物語 kūsōkagakumonogátàri, SF esuefu

scientific [saiəntif'ik] adj (research, instruments) 科学の kágaku no

scientist [sai'əntist] n 科学者 kagakúshà

scintillating [sin'təleitiŋ] adj (fig: conversation, wit, smile) 輝く様な kagáyakū yō na

scissors [siz'əːrz] npl (also: **a pair of scissors**) はさみ hasámi

scoff [skɑ:f] vt (BRIT: inf: eat) がつがつ食う gátsugatsu kū

◆vi: **to scoff (at)** (mock) ...をあざける ...wo azákerū

scold [skould] vt しかる shikárū

scone [skoun] n スコーン sukón ◇小さなホットケーキの一種 chīsa na hottókèki no fsshū

scoop [sku:p] n (measuring scoop: for flour etc) スコップ sukóppů; (for ice cream) サーバー sábà; (PRESS) スクープ sukúpů

scoop out vt すくい出す sukúidasū

scoop up vt すくい上げる sukúiagerū

scooter [sku:'təːr] n (also: **motor scooter**) スクーター sukútà; (toy) スクーター sukútà ◇片足を乗せて走る遊び道具 katáashi wo nosete hashfrū asóbidògu

scope [skoup] n (opportunity) 機会 kikái; (range: of plan, undertaking) 範囲 hán-i; (: of person) 能力 nōryòku

scorch [skɔ:rtʃ] vt (clothes) 焦がす kogásù; (earth, grass) 枯らす karásù

score [skɔ:r] n (total number of points etc) 得点 tokúteñ, スコア sukóà; (MUS) 楽譜 gakúfu; (twenty) 20 nījū

◆vt (goal, point, mark) 取る tórù; (achieve: success) 収める osámerù

◆vi (in game) 得点する tokúteñ suru; (FOOTBALL etc) トライする toráì suru; (keep score) 得点を記録する tokúteñ wo kirőkū suru

scores of (very many) 多数の tasū no

on that score その点に関して sonó teñ ni kańshite

to score 6 out of 10 10回中6回成功する jukkáìchū rokkáì sefkō suru

scoreboard [skɔːr'bɔːrd] n スコアボード sukóabōdo

score out vt 線を引いて消す señ wo hifte kesū

scorn [skɔːrn] n 軽べつ keíbetsu

◆vt 軽べつする keíbetsu suru

scornful [skɔːrn'fəl] adj (laugh, disregard) 軽べつの keíbetsuteki na

Scorpio [skɔːr'pi:ou] n (sign of Zodiac) さそり座 sasórizà

scorpion [skɔːr'pi:ən] n サソリ sasóri

Scot [skɑːt] n スコットランド人 sukóttorandojīn

Scotch [skɑːtʃ] n (whisky) スコッチ sukótchī

scotch [skɑːtʃ] vt (end: rumor) 言い止める keshftomerū; (plan, idea) 没にする botsū ni suru

scot-free [skɑːtfri:'] adv: **to get off scot-free** (unpunished) 何の罰も受けない naň no bátsū mo ukénaī

Scotland [skɑːt'lənd] n スコットランド sukóttorando

Scots [skɑːts] adj (accent, people) スコットランドの sukóttorando no

Scotsman [skɑːts'mən] (pl **Scotsmen**) n スコットランドの男性 sukóttorando no dansei

Scotswoman [skɑːts'wumən] (pl **Scotswomen**) n スコットランドの女性 sukóttorando no josei

Scottish [skɑːt'iʃ] adj (history, clans, people) スコットランドの sukóttorando no

scoundrel [skaun'drəl] n 悪党 akútō

scour [skaur] vt (search: countryside etc) くまなく捜し回る kumánāku sagáshimawarù

scourge [skɔːrdʒ] n (cause of trouble: also fig) 悩みの種 nayámi no tané

scout [skaut] n (MIL) 斥候 sekkō; (also: **boy scout**) ボーイスカウト bōisukautò
girl scout (US) ガールスカウト gārusukautò

scout around vi 捜し回る sagáshimawarù

scowl [skaul] vi 顔をしかめる kaó wo shikámerù
to scowl at someone しかめっつらをして … を にらむ shikámettsura wò shité …wo nirámù

scrabble [skræb'əl] vi (claw): **to scrabble (at)** (…を)引っかく (…wo) hikkákù; (also: **scrabble around**: search) 手探りで探す teságuri de sagású
♦n: Scrabble Ⓡ (game) 単語作りゲーム tañgozukurigēmu

scraggy [skræg'i:] adj (animal, body, neck etc) やせこけた yasékoketà

scram [skræm] (inf) vi (get away fast) うせる userú

scramble [skræm'bəl] n (difficult climb) よじ上り yojínobori; (struggle, rush) 奪い合い ubáiai
♦vi: to scramble out/through 慌てて出る(通る) awátete derù (tōru)
to scramble for …の奪い合いをする …no ubái wo surù

scrambled eggs [skræm'bəld-] npl いり卵 iritamagò, スクランブルエッグ sukúranburu eggù

scrap [skræp] n (bit: of paper, material etc) 切れ端 kiréhashi; (of information) 少し sukóshi; (fig: of truth) 欠けら kakéra; (fight) けんか keñka; (also: **scrap iron**) くず鉄 kuzútetsu
♦vt (discard: machines etc) くず鉄にする kuzútetsu ni surù; (fig: plans etc) 捨てる sutérù
♦vi (fight) けんかする keñka surù

scrapbook [skræp'buk] n スクラップブック sukúrappubukkù

scrap dealer n くず鉄屋 kuzútetsuyà

scrape [skreip] n (fig: difficult situation) 窮地 kyūchì
♦vt (scrape off: potato skin etc) むく mukú; (scrape against: hand, car) こする kosúrù
♦vi: to scrape through (exam etc) …をどうにか切抜ける …wo dō ni ka kirínukerù

scrape together vt (money) かき集める kakíatsumerù

scrap heap n (fig): **on the scrap heap** 捨てられて sutérarete

scrap merchant n (BRIT) = **scrap dealer**

scrap paper n 古い紙 furúi kamí, 古紙 kóshì, ほご紙 hogógami

scrappy [skræp'i:] adj (piece of work) 雑な zatsú na

scraps [skræps] npl (leftovers: food, material etc) くず kuzú

scratch [skrætʃ] n (cut: on body, furniture: also from claw) かき傷 kakíkizu
♦cpd: scratch team 寄集めチーム yoseátsumechīmu
♦vt (rub: one's nose etc) かく kákù; (damage: paint, car) 傷付ける kizútsukerù; (with claw, nail) ひっかく hikkákù
♦vi (rub one's body) …をかく …wo kákù
to start from scratch 何もない所から始める naní mo naí tokóro kara hajímerù
to be up to scratch …は線をいっている …fi séñ wo itté irù

scrawl [skrɔːl] n なぐり書き nagúrigaki
♦vi なぐり書きする nagúrigaki suru

scrawny [skrɔː'ni:] adj (person, neck) やせこけた yasékoketà

scream [skriːm] n 悲鳴 himéi
♦vi 悲鳴を上げる himéi wo agérù

scree [skriː] n 岩くず iwákuzu (小岩石から落ちてたい積した岩くずで覆う山腹を指す kuzúreochità tafséki shità iwákuzu wo ōu)

screech [skriːtʃ] vi (person) 金切り声を出す kanákirigoè wo dásù; (bird) きーきー声で鳴く kīkīgoè de nakú; (tires, brakes) きーきーと鳴る kīkī to nárù

screen [skriːn] n (CINEMA) スクリーン

sukúrīn; (TV, COMPUT) ブラウン管 bu-
ráunkan; (movable barrier) ついたて
tsuftate; (fig: cover) 幕 makú

♦vt (protect, conceal) 覆い隠す ōikaku-
sū; (from the wind etc) ...の...によけになる
...no...yoké ni narú; (film) 映写する efsha
suru; (television programme) 放映する hóei
suru; (candidates etc) 審査する shífusa
suru

screening [skri:'niŋ] n (MED) 健康診断
keñkōshiñdan

screenplay [skri:n'plei] n 映画脚本 efga-
kyakúhòn

screw [skru:] n (for fixing something) ね
じ néjī

♦vt (fasten) ねじで留める neji de tomérù

screwdriver [skru:'draivər] n ねじ回し
nejīmawashī

screw up vt (paper etc) くしゃくしゃに
する kushākūsha ni suru

to screw up one's eyes 目を細める mé
wò hosómerù

scribble [skrib'əl] n 走り書き hashírigaki

♦vt (write carelessly: note etc) 走り書き
する hashírigaki suru

♦vi (make meaningless marks) 落書する
rakúgaki suru

script [skript] n (CINEMA etc) 脚本
kyakúhon, スクリプト sukūrīpùto; (system of writing) 文字 mójì

scripture(s) [skrip'tʃər(z)] n(pl) (holy
writing(s) of a religion) 聖典 seiten

scroll [skroul] n (official paper) 巻物 ma-
kímono

scrounge [skraundʒ] vt (inf): to
scrounge something off/from someone ...に...をねだる ...ni...wo nedárù

♦n: on the scrounge たかって takátte

scrub [skrʌb] n (land) 低木地帯 tefbokú-
chìtai

♦vt (rub hard: floor, hands, pan, washing) ごしごし洗う góshìgoshi aráù; (inf:
reject: idea) 取り止めする torfyamerù

scruff [skrʌf] n: by the scruff of the
neck 首筋をつかんで kubfsuji wò tsukáñ-
de

scruffy [skrʌf'i:] adj (person, object,

appearance) 薄汚い usúgitanaì

scrum(mage) [skrʌm'(idʒ)] n (RUGBY)
スクラム sukūrāmu

scruple [skru:'pəl] n (gen pl) 良心のとが
め ryōshìn no togáme

scrupulous [skru:'pjələs] adj (painstaking: care, attention) 細心の safshìn
no; (fair-minded: honesty) 公正な kōsei
na

scrutinize [skru:'tənaiz] vt (examine
closely) 詳しく調べる kuwáshikù shiráberù

scrutiny [skru:'təni:] n (close examination) 吟味 gíñmi

to keep someone under scrutiny ...を
監視する ...wo kañshi suru

scuff [skʌf] vt (shoes, floor) すり減らす
surfherasù

scuffle [skʌf'əl] n (fight) 乱闘 rañtō

sculptor [skʌlp'tər] n 彫刻家 chōkoku-
ka

sculpture [skʌlp'tʃər] n 彫刻 chōkoku

scum [skʌm] n (on liquid) 汚い泡 kitánaì
awà; (pej: people) 人間のくず nifgen no
kúzù

scupper [skʌp'ər] n (BRIT: inf) (plan,
idea) 邪魔して失敗させる jamá shité
shippái saserù

scurrilous [skʌr'ələs] adj 口汚い kuchf-
gitanaì

scurry [skə:r'i:] vi ちょこちょこ走る chókòchoko hashíru

scurry off vi ちょこちょこ走って行く
chókòchoko hashítte ikú

scuttle [skʌt'əl] n (also: coal scuttle) 石
炭入れ sekítan-ire

♦vt (ship) 沈没させる chíñbotsu saserù

♦vi (scamper): to scuttle away/off ち
ょこちょこ走って行く chókòchoko ha-
shítte ikú

scythe [saið] n 大がま ōgamà ◇柄も刃も
長いかま é mò hâ mò nagáì kamà

sea [si:] n 海 úmì; (fig: very many) 多数
tasú; (: very much) 多量 taryō

♦cpd (breeze, bird, air etc) 海の úmì no

by sea (travel) 船路で kāiro de

on the sea (boat) 海上で kafjō de;
(town) 海辺の umîbe no

out to/at sea 沖に okí ni

to be all at sea (fig) 頭が混乱している atáma gà końran shite irù

a sea of faces (fig) 顔の海 kaó nò úmì

seaboard [si:'bɔːrd] *n* 海岸 kaígan

seafood [si:'fuːd] *n* 魚介類 gyokáirùi, シーフード shífödo ◊ 料理に使う魚介類を指す ryőri ni tsukáù gyokáirùi wo sásù

seafront [si:'frʌnt] *n* 海岸 kaígan ◊ 海辺の町などの海沿いの部分を指す umíbe nò machí nadð no umízoi no bubún wo sásù

sea-going [si:'gouŋ] *adj* (ship) 遠洋航海用の eń-yōkōkaiyð no

seagull [si:'gʌl] *n* カモメ kamóme

seal [si:l] *n* (animal) アザラシ azárashi ◊ セイウチを除いて全てのひれ足類を含む sefuchí wo nozóïte súbète no hiréashirùi wo fúkumù; (official stamp) 印章 ińshō; (closure) 封印 füin

♦*vt* (close: envelope) ...の封をする ...no fū wō suru; (: opening) 封じる füjirù

sea level *n* 海面 kaímen

sea lion *n* トド tódð

seal off *vt* (place) 封鎖する fūsa suru

seam [si:m] *n* (line of stitches) 縫目 nuíme; (where edges meet) 継目 tsugíme, 合せ目 awásème; (of coal etc) 薄層 hakúsō

seaman [si:'mən] (*pl* **seamen**) *n* 船乗り funánòri

seamy [si:'mi:] *adj*: *the seamy side of* ...の汚い裏面 ...no kitánaí rímèn, ...の恥部 ...no chíbù

seance [sei'ɑːns] *n* 降霊会 kōreíkai

seaplane [si:'plein] *n* 水上飛行機 suíjōhikòki

seaport [si:'pɔːrt] *n* 港町 minátomàchi

search [sɜːrtʃ] *n* (hunt: for person, thing) 捜索 sōsaku; (COMPUT) 探索 tańsaku, 検索 keńsaku; (inspection: of someone's home) 家宅捜査 katákusòsa

♦*vt* (look in: place) ...の中を捜す ...no náka wo sagásù; (examine: memory) 捜す sagásù; (person) ...の身体検査をする ...no shińtaikeñsa wo suru

♦*vi*: *to search for* ...を捜す ...wo sagásù

in search of ...を求めて ...wo motómète

searching [sɜːr'tʃiŋ] *adj* (question, look) 鋭い surúdoì

searchlight [sɜːrtʃ'lait] *n* サーチライト sáchiràito

search party *n* 捜索隊 sōsakutai

search through *vt fus* ...の中をくまなく捜す ...no náka wo kumánàku sagásù

search warrant *n* 捜査令状 sōsareijð

seashore [si:'ʃɔːr] *n* 海岸 kaígan

seasick [si:'sik] *adj* 船酔いになった funáyòi ni náttà

seaside [si:'said] *n* 海辺 umíbe

seaside resort *n* 海辺の行楽地 umíbe nð kōrakuchì

season [si:'zən] *n* (of year) 季節 kisétsù; (time of year for something: football season etc) シーズン shízun; (series: of films etc) シリーズ shírìzu

♦*vt* (food) ...に味を付ける ...ni ajf wð tsukérù

in season (fruit, vegetables) しゅんで shúñ de

out of season (fruit, vegetables) 季節外れて kisétsuhàzure de

seasonal [si:'zənəl] *adj* (work) 季節的な kisétsuteki na

seasoned [si:'zənd] *adj* (fig: traveler) 経験豊かな keñken yutåka na

seasoning [si:'zəniŋ] *n* 調味料 chōmiryò, 薬味 yakúmi

season ticket *n* (RAIL) 定期券 teíkiken; (THEATER) シーズン入場券 shízun nyūjōken

seat [si:t] *n* (chair) いす isú; (in vehicle, theater: place) 席 sékì; (PARLIAMENT) 議席 giséki; (buttocks: also of trousers) しり shírí

♦*vt* (place: guests etc) 座らせる suwáraserù; (subj: table, theater: have room for) ...人分の席がある ...nińbun no sékì ga árð

to be seated 座る suwárù

seat belt *n* シートベルト shítoberùto

sea water *n* 海水 kaísui

seaweed [si:'wiːd] *n* 海草 kaísō

seaworthy [si:'wəːrði] *adj* (ship) 航海に耐えられる kōkai nì taérarerù

sec. *abbr* = **second(s)**

secluded [siklu:'did] *adj* (place) 人里離れた hitózato hanaretà; (life) 隠とんの iñtoñ no ton no

seclusion [siklu:'ʒən] n 隔離 kákùri

second [sek'ənd] adj (after first) 第二
(の) dâi nf (no)

♦adv (come, be placed: in race etc) 二番
に nîbàn ni; (when listing) 第二に dâi nf ni
no

♦n (unit of time) 秒 byô; (AUT: also:
second gear) セカンド sekándo;
(COMM: imperfect) 二流品 niryúhìn;
(BRIT: SCOL: degree) 2級優等卒業資格
nfkyû yûtô sotsugyô gakùi ¶ see also
first

♦vt (motion) ...に支持を表明する ...ni shî-
jì wo hyômeì suru; (BRIT: worker) 派遣
する hakén suru

secondary [sek'ənderi:] adj (less important) 二次的な nijíteki na

secondary school n 中等高等学校 chú-
tôkôtôgakkô

second-class [sek'əndklæs] adj (hotel,
novel, work) 二流の niryû no; (tickets,
transport) 2等の nitô no

♦adv (travel) 2等で nitô de

secondhand [sek'əndhænd] adj (clothing, car) 中古の chûko no

second hand n (on clock) 秒針 byôshìn

secondly [sek'əndli:] adv 2番目に nibánme ni

secondment [sek'əndmənt] (BRIT) n 派
遣 hakén

second-rate [sek'əndreit'] adj (film etc)
二流の niryû no

second thoughts npl ためらい taméraì
on second thought (US) or **thoughts**
(BRIT) 気が変って ki ga kawátte

secrecy [si:'krisi:] n 秘密 himfitsu
to swear someone to secrecy ...に秘密を誓わせる ...ni himítsu wò chikáwaserù

secret [si:'krit] adj (plan, passage, agent)
秘密の himîtsu no; (admirer, drinker) ひ
そかな hisôka na

♦n 秘密 himîtsu
in secret 内密に naímitsu ni

secretarial [sekriter:i:al] adj (work,
course, staff, studies) 秘書の hishò no

secretariat [sekriter:i:ət] n 事務局 ji-
múkyòku

secretary [sek'riteri:] n (COMM) 秘書
hishô; (of club) 書記 shokí

  Secretary of State (for) (BRIT:
POL) (...)大臣 (...)dâijìn

secretion [sikri:'ʃən] n (substance) 分泌
物 buñpitsubûtsu

secretive [si:'kritiv] adj 秘密主義の hi-
mîtsushûgì no

secretly [si:'kritli:] adv (tell, marry) 内密
に naímitsu ni

sect [sekt] n 宗派 shúha

sectarian [sekter:i:an] adj (riots etc) 宗
派間の shúhakàn no

section [sek'ʃən] n (part) 部分 bûbùn;
(department) ...部 ...bù; (of document) 章
shô; (of opinion) 一部 ichîbù; (cross-
section) 断面図 dañmeñzù

sector [sek'tər] n (part) 部門 bûmòn;
(MIL) 戦闘地区 señtôchìku

secular [sek'jələ:r] adj (music, society
etc) 世俗の sezôku no; (priest) 教区の
kyôku no

secure [sikju:r'] adj (safe: person) 安全な
場所にいる   añzen na bashô ni irû;
(: money) 安全な場所にある añzen na
bashô ni ârù; (: building) 防犯対策完備の
bôhantaisakukañbi no; (firmly fixed,
strong: rope, shelf) 固定された kotéi sa-
retâ

♦vt (fix: rope, shelf etc) 固定する kotéi
suru; (get: job, contract etc) 確保する
kákùho suru

security [sikju:'riti:] n (protection) 警備
kêibì; (for one's future) 保証 hoshô;
(FINANCE) 担保 tâñpo

sedan [sidæn'] (US) n (AUT) セダン sê-
dàn

sedate [sideit'] adj (person, pace) 落着い
た ochítsuità

♦vt (MED: with injection) ...に鎮静剤を
注射する ...ni chiñseizâi wo chûsha suru;
(: with pills etc) ...に鎮静剤を飲ませる
...ni chiñseizâi wo nomáserù

sedation [sidei'ʃən] n (MED): *under
sedation* 薬で鎮静されて kusúri dè chiñ-
sei saretê

sedative [sed'ətiv] n 鎮静剤 chiñseizâi

sedentary [sed'ənte:ri:] adj (occupation,

work) 座ってする suwátte surù

sediment [sed'əmənt] *n* (in bottle) おり orí; (in lake etc) 底のたい積物 sokó nò tafsekíbutsu

seduce [sidus'] *vt* (entice: *gen*) 魅了する miryó suru, たらし込む taráshikomù; (: sexually) 誘惑する yûwaku suru, たらし込む taráshikomù

seduction [sidʌk'ʃən] *n* (attraction) 魅 惑 miwáku; (act of seducing) 誘惑 yûwaku

seductive [sidʌk'tiv] *adj* (look, voice, *also fig* offer) 誘惑的な yûwakuteki na

see [si:] (*pt* saw, *pp* seen) *vt* (*gen*) 見る mírù; (accompany): *to see someone to the door* ...を戸口まで送る ...wo tógõchi mádè okúrù; (understand) 分かる wakárù
♦*vi* (*gen*) 見える miérù; (find out) 調べる shiráberù
♦*n* (REL) 教区 kyókù
to see that someone does something ...が...する様に気を付ける ...ga...surú yõ ni kí wo tsukérù
see you soon! またね matá né

see about *vt fus* ...の問題を調べて片付ける ...no mondai wo shirábete katazùkeru

seed [si:d] *n* (of plant, fruit) 種 tánè; (sperm) 精液 sefeki; (*fig*: *gen pl*) 種 tánè; (TENNIS) シード shído
to go to seed (plant) 種ができる tánè ga dekírù; (*fig*) 衰える otóroerù

seedling [si:d'liŋ] *n* 苗 nâê

seedy [si:'di:] *adj* (shabby: person, place) 見すぼらしい misúborashiì

seeing [si:'iŋ] *conj*: *seeing (that)* ...だから ...dákàra

seek [si:k] (*pt*, *pp* sought) *vt* (truth, shelter, advice, post) 求める motómerù

seem [si:m] *vi* ...に見える ...ni miérù
there seems to be ... ...がある様です ...ga árù yõ desù

seemingly [si:'miŋli:] *adv* ...らしく ...rashīkù

seen [si:n] *pp of* see

see off *vt* ...を見送る ...wo miókurù

seep [si:p] *vi* (liquid, gas) 染み透る shimítõru

seesaw [si:'sɔ:] *n* シーソー shísõ

seethe [si:ð] *vi* (place: with people/things) 騒然としている sōzen to shité irù
to seethe with anger 怒りで煮え繰り返る ikári dè niékurikaèru

see through *vt* 最後までやり通す sáigo made yaríõsu
♦*vt fus* 見抜く minúkù

see-through [si:'θru:] *adj* (blouse etc) すけすけの sukésukerukkû no

see to *vt fus* ...の世話をする ...no sewá wð suru

segment [seg'mənt] *n* (part: *gen*) 一部 ichíbù; (of orange) みかんの房 mikán nò fusá

segregate [seg'rəgeit] *vt* 分ける wakérù

seismic [saiz'mik] *adj* (activity) 地震の jishín no

seize [si:z] *vt* (grasp) つかむ tsukámù; (take possession of: power, control, territory) 奪う ubáù; (: hostage) 捕まえる tsukámaerù; (opportunity) 捕える toráeru

seize up *vi* (TECH: engine) 焼け付く yakétsukù

seize (up)on *vt fus* ...に飛び付く ...ni tobítsukù

seizure [si:'ʒər] *n* (MED) 発作 hossá; (LAW) 没収 bosshú; (: of power) 強奪 gódatsu

seldom [sel'dəm] *adv* めったに...ない méttà ni...nâî

select [silekt'] *adj* (school, group, area) 一流の ichíryà no
♦*vt* (choose) 選ぶ erábù

selection [silek'ʃən] *n* (being chosen) 選ばれる事 erábareru kotõ; (COMM: range available) 選択 sefitaku

selective [silek'tiv] *adj* (careful in choosing) 選択的な sefitakuteki na; (not general: strike etc) 限られた範囲の kagírareta hán-i no

self [self] (*pl* selves) *n*: *the self* 自我 jígà
♦*prefix* 自分で(の)... jibún de (no) ...

self-assured [self'əʃurd'] *adj* 自信のある jishín no arù

self-catering [self'kei'təriŋ] *adj* (BRIT: holiday, apartment) 自炊の jisúi no

self-centered [self'sen'tərd] (BRIT **self-centred**) *adj* 自己中心の jikóchúshinno

self-colored [self'kʌl'ərd] (BRIT **self-coloured**) adj (of one color) 単色の tañshoku no

self-confidence [self'kɑːn'fidəns] n 自信 jishiñ

self-conscious [self'kɑːn'tʃəs] adj (nervous) 照れる terérù

self-contained [self'kənteind'] (BRIT) adj (flat) 設備完備の setsúbikañbi no

self-control [self'kəntroul'] n 自制 jiséi

self-defense [self'difens'] (BRIT **self-defence**) n 自己防衛 jikóbòei
in self-defense 自己防衛で jikóbòei de

self-discipline [self'dis'əplin] n 気力 kíryòku

self-employed [self'imploid'] adj 自営業の jíéigyò no

self-evident [self'ev'idənt] adj 自明の jiméi no

self-governing [self'gʌv'ərniŋ] adj 独立の dokúritsu no

self-indulgent [self'indʌl'dʒənt] adj 勝手気ままな kattékimama na

self-interest [self'in'trist] n 自己利益 jikórièki

selfish [sel'fiʃ] adj 身勝手な migátte na

selfishness [sel'fiʃnis] n 利己主義 ríkóshùgi

selfless [self'lis] adj 献身的な keńshintekì na

self-made [self'meid'] adj: *self-made man* 自力でたたき上げた人 jírîki dè tatákiageta hitò

self-pity [self'pit'i:] n 自己れんびん jikórèñbin

self-portrait [self'pɔːr'trit] n 自画像 jigázò

self-possessed [self'pəzest'] adj 落着いた ochítsuità

self-preservation [self'prezəːrvei'ʃən] n 本能的自衛 hoñnótekijièi

self-respect [self'rispekt'] n 自尊心 jisóñshin

self-righteous [self'rai'tʃəs] adj 独善的な dokúzeñtekì na

self-sacrifice [self'sæk'rəfais] n 献身 keńshin

self-satisfied [self'sæt'isfaid] adj 自己満足の jikómañzòku no

self-service [self'səːr'vis] adj (shop, restaurant, service station) セルフサービスの serúfusàbisu no

self-sufficient [self'səfiʃ'ənt] adj (farm, country) 自給自足の jikyújisòku no; (person) 独立独歩の dokúritsudoppò no

self-taught [self'tɔːt'] adj 独学の dokúgaku no

sell [sel] (pt, pp **sold**) vt (gen) 売る urú; (fig: idea) 売込む urîkomù
♦vi (goods) 売れる uréru
to sell at/for $10 値段は10ドルである nedáñ wà 10 dórù de árù

sell-by date [sel'bai-] (BRIT) n 賞味期限 shōmikigèn

seller [sel'əːr] n 売手 uríte

selling price [sel'iŋ-] n 値段 nedáñ

sell off vt うり払らう uríharaù

sell out vi (use up stock): *to sell out (of something)* (...が)売切れる (...ga) uríkirerù
the tickets are sold out 切符は売切れだ kippú wà uríkire da

sellotape [sel'əteip]® (BRIT) n セロテープ serótèpu

selves [selvz] n pl of **self**

semaphore [sem'əfɔːr] n 手旗 tebáta

semblance [sem'bləns] n 外観 gaíkan

semen [siː'mən] n 精液 sefeki

semester [simes'təːr] (US) n 学期 gakkí

semi... [sem'i:] prefix 半分の...hañbùn no

semicircle [sem'isəːrkəl] n 半円形 hañeñkei

semicolon [sem'ikoulən] n セミコロン semíkoròn

semiconductor [semi:kəndʌk'təːr] n 半導体 hañdōtai

semidetached (house) [semi:ditætʃt'] (BRIT) n 二戸建て住宅 nikódate jūtaku

semifinal [semi:fai'nəl] n 準決勝 juñkesshō

seminar [sem'ənaːr] n セミナー semínā

seminary [sem'əneːriː] n (REL) 神学校 shiñgakkō

semiskilled [semi:skild'] adj (work,

worker) 半熟練の haňjukuren no

senate [sen'it] *n* 上院 jōin

senator [sen'ətər] *n* 上院議員 jōingíin

send [send] (*pt, pp* **sent**) *vt* (dispatch) 送る okúrù; (transmit: signal) 送信する sōshin suru

send away *vt* (letter, goods) 送る okúrù; (unwelcome visitor) あしらう oɦaraú

send away for *vt fus* 郵便で注文する yūbin dè chūmon suru

send back *vt* 送り返す okúrikaesù

sender [send'ər] *n* 差出人, sashídashinīn

send for *vt fus* (thing) 取寄せる toríyoseru; (person) 呼寄せる yobíyoserù

send off *vt* (goods) 送る okúrù; (BRIT: SPORT: player) 退場させる taíjō saserù

send-off [send'ɔːf] *n: a good send-off* 素晴らしい送別 subárashíì sõbetsu

send out *vt* (invitation) 送る okúrù; (signal) 発信する hasshín suru

send up *vt* (price, blood pressure) 上昇させる jōshō saserù; (astronaut) 打上げる uchfagerù; (BRIT: parody) 風刺する fūshi suru

senile [siː'nail] *adj* 老いぼれた oíboretà, ぼけた bóketa の rōjinsei no

senior [siːn'jər] *adj* (older) 年上の toshíue no; (on staff: position, officer) 幹部の kánbu no; (of higher rank: partner) 上級 の jōkyū no

senior citizen *n* 老人 rōjin, 高齢者 kṓreishà

seniority [siːnjɔːr'itiː] *n* (in service) 年功 neńkō

sensation [sensei'ʃən] *n* (feeling) 感覚 kaňkaku; (great success) 大成功 daíseikō

sensational [sensei'ʃənəl] *adj* (wonderful) 素晴らしい subárashíì; (causing much interest: headlines) 扇情的な señjōteki na; (: result) センセーショナルな seńsēshonaru na

sense [sens] *n* (physical) 感覚 kaňkaku; (feeling: of guilt, shame etc) 感じ kaňji; (good sense) 常識 jōshiki; (meaning: of word, phrase etc) 意味 ímì

◆*vt* (become aware of) 感じる kaňjirù

it makes sense (can be understood) 意味が分かる ímì ga wakáru; (is sensible) 賢明だ keńmei dà

sense of humor ユーモアを解する心 yūmóa wo káí surú kokórò, ユーモアのセンス yūmóa no séňsu

senseless [sens'lis] *adj* (pointless: murder) 無意味な muími na; (unconscious) 気絶した kizétsu shità

sensible [sen'səbəl] *adj* (person) 利口な rikō na; (reasonable: price, advice) 合理的な gōriteki na; (: decision, suggestion) 賢明な keńmei na

sensitive [sen'sətiv] *adj* (understanding) 理解のある ríkai no árù; (nerve, skin) 敏感な bíňkan na; (instrument) 高感度の kōkando no; (fig: touchy: person) 怒りっぽい okóríppòi; (: issue) 際どい kiwádoì

sensitivity [sensətiv'əti:] *n* (understanding) 理解 ríkai; (responsiveness: to touch etc) 敏感さ bíňkansa; (: of instrument) 感度 kaňdo; (touchiness: of person) 怒りっぽさ okóríppòsa; (delicate nature: of issue etc) 際どさ kiwádosà

sensual [sen'ʃuːal] *adj* (of the senses: rhythm etc) 官能的な kaňnōteki na; (relating to sexual pleasures) 肉感的な nikkáňteki na

sensuous [sen'ʃuːəs] *adj* (lips, material etc) 官能的な kaňnōteki na

sent [sent] *pt, pp of* **send**

sentence [sen'təns] *n* (LING) 文 búň; (LAW) 宣告 seňkoku

◆*vt: to sentence someone to death/to 5 years in prison* ...に死刑(懲役5年)の判決を言渡す ...ni shikéi〔chōeki gonén〕no haňketsu wo iíwatasù

sentiment [sen'təmənt] *n* (tender feelings) 感情 kaňjō; (opinion, *also* pl) 意見 íkeň

sentimental [sentəmen'təl] *adj* (song) 感傷的な kańshōteki na, センチメンタルな seńchimeñtaru na; (person) 情にもろい jō ní morói

sentry [sen'triː] *n* 番兵 baňpei

separate [adj, n sep'rit vb sep'əreit] *adj* (distinct: piles, occasions, ways, rooms) 別々の betsúbetsu no

♦vt (split up: people, things) 分ける wakérù; (make a distinction between: twins) 見分ける miwákerù; (: ideas etc) 区別する kubétsu suru

♦vi (split up, move apart) 分かれる wakárerù

separately [sep'ritli:] adv 別々に betsúbetsu ni

separates [sep'rits] npl (clothes) セパレーツ sepáretsu

separation [separei'ʃən] n (being apart) 分離 bunri; (time spent apart) 別れ別れになっている期間 wakárewakare ni natté irú kikán; (LAW) 別居 bekkyó

September [septəm'bəːr] n 9月 kúgatsu

septic [sep'tik] adj (wound, finger etc) 感染した kañsen shita

septic tank n 浄化槽 jókasò

sequel [si:'kwəl] n (follow-up) 後日談 gojítsudàn; (of film, story) 続編 zokúhen

sequence [si:'kwins] n (ordered chain) 連続 reñzoku; (also: **dance sequence**, **film sequence**) 一場面 ichíbamèn, シークエンス shíkueñsu

sequin [si:'kwin] n シークイン shíkuiñ, スパンコール supáñkōru

serene [sərin'] adj (smile, expression etc) 穏やか odáyàka na

serenity [sərɛni'ti:] n 穏やかさ odáyàkasa

sergeant [saːr'dʒənt] n (MIL etc) 軍曹 guñsò; (POLICE) 巡査部長 juñsabùchò

serial [si'ri:əl] n (in newspaper, magazine) 連載物 reñsai suru; (on radio, TV) 連続物として放送する reñzokumono toshité hōsō suru

serial number n 製造番号 sefzóbañgō

series [si'ri:z] n inv (group) 一連 ichíren; (of books, TV programs) シリーズ shirízù

serious [si'ri:əs] adj (person, manner) 真剣な shiñken na; (important: matter) 大きな dafji na; (grave: illness, condition) 重い omóì

seriously [si'ri:əsli:] adv (talk, take) 真剣に shiñken ni; (hurt) ひどく hídòku

seriousness [si'ri:əsni:s] n (of person,

manner) 真剣さ shiñkensa; (importance) 重大さ jūdaisa; (gravity) 重々しさ omósa

sermon [səːr'mən] n (also fig) 説教 sekkyó

serrated [sereit'id] adj (edge, knife's) こぎり状の nokógirijo no

serum [si'rəm] n 血清 kessé

servant [səːr'vənt] n (gen) 使い meshítsukái; (fig) 人に仕える物 hitó ni tsukáerù monó

serve [səːrv] vt (gen: company, country) 仕える tsukáerù; (in shop: goods) 売る urú; (: customer) ...の用をきく...no yó wò ukáw.; (subj: train) ...の足になる ...no ashí ni narù; (apprenticeship) 務める tsutómerù

♦vi (at table) 給仕する kyújì suru; (TENNIS) サーブをする sábu suru; (be useful): *to serve as/for ...*として役に立つ ...to shité yakú ni tatsú

♦n (TENNIS) サーブ sábu

to serve to do ...をするのに役に立つ ...wo surú no ni yakú ni tatsú

it serves him right 自業自得だ jigójitòku da

to serve a prison term 服役する fukúeki suru

serve out/up vt (food) 出す dásù

service [səːr'vis] n (gen: help) 役に立つ事 yakú ni tatsú kotó; (in hotel) サービス sábisu; (REL) 式 shikf; (AUT) 整備 sefbi; (TENNIS) サーブ sábu; (plates, dishes etc) 一そろい hitósoròi; (also: **train service**) 鉄道の便 tetsúdō nò bên; (also: **plane service**) 空の便 sóra no bên

♦vt (car, washing machine) 整備する sefbi suru

military/national service 兵役 hefeki

to be of service to someone ...に役に立つ ...ni yakú ni tatsú

serviceable [səːr'visəbəl] adj 役に立つ yakú ni tatsú

service area n (on motorway) サービスエリア sábisu erìa

service charge (BRIT) n サービス料 sábisuryō

serviceman [səːr'vismæn] (pl **servicemen**) n (MIL) 軍人 guñjin

Services [sɜːˈviːsiz] *npl*: *the Services* (army, navy etc) 軍隊 gúntai

service station *n* ガソリンスタンド gasōrinsutáñdo; (*BRIT*: on motorway) サービスエリア sábisu erìa

serviette [sɜːrviˈet] (*BRIT*) *n* 紙ナプキン kamínapùkin

servile [sɜːˈvail] *adj* (person, obedience) おもねる様な omónerù yō na

session [seʃˈən] *n* (period of activity: recording/drinking session ...する事を集まる事...surú tamé nì atsúmarù kotò

to be in session (court) 開廷中である kaíteichū de arù; (Parliament etc) 開会中である kaíkaichū de arù

set [set] *n* (collection of things) …そろい hitósoroì, 一式 isshíki, セット séttò; (radio set) ラジオ rájìo; (TV set) テレビ térèbi; (TENNIS) セット séttò; (group of people) 連中 reńchū; (MATH) セット séttò; (CINEMA, THEATER) 舞台装置 butáisochì, セット séttò; (HAIRDRESSING) セット séttò

♦*adj* (fixed: rules, routine) 決りのkimárì no; (ready) 用意ができた yōì ga dekíta

♦*vb* (*pt*, *pp* **set**)

♦*vt* (place) 置く ókù; (fix, establish: time, price, rules etc) 決める kimérù; (: record) 作る tsukúrù; (adjust: alarm, watch) セットする séttò suru; (impose: task) 命ずる meízurù; (: exam) 作る tsukúrù

♦*vi* (sun) 沈む shizúmù; (jam, jelly, concrete) 固まる katámarù; (broken bone) 治る naórù

to set the table 食卓の用意をする shokútaku nò yōì wó suru

to be set on doing something ...をすると決めている dōshite mo ...wo surú tò kimetè iru

to set to music ...に曲を付ける ...ni kyokú wò tsukérù

to set on fire ...に火を付ける ...ni hí wò tsukérù

to set free 放してやる hanáshite yarù, 自由にする jiyū ni surù

...wo hajímesaserù

to set sail 出航する shukkō suru

set about *vt fus* (task) 始める hajímerù

set aside *vt* (money etc) 取って置く tótte oku; (time) 空けておく akétè okù

set back *vt* (cost): *to set someone back $5* 5ドル払わなければならない go dórù haráwanakerèba naránaì; (in time): *to set someone back (by)* ...を (...) 遅らせる ...wo (...) okúraserù

setback [setˈbæk] *n* (hitch) 苦難 kúnàn

set menu *n* 定食メニュー teíshokumenyū

set off *vi* 出発する shuppátsu suru

♦*vt* (bomb) 爆発させる bakúhatsu saserù; (alarm) 鳴らす narásù; (chain of events) ...の引金となる ...no hikígane to narù; (show up well: jewels) 引立たせる hikítataserù

set out *vi* (depart) 出発する shuppátsu suru

♦*vt* (arrange: goods etc) 並べて置く narábete okù; (state: arguments) 述べる nobérù

to set out to do something ...をするつもりである ...wo surú tsumorì de arù

settee [setˈiː] *n* ソファー sófā

setting [setˈiŋ] *n* (background) 背景 haíkei; (position: of controls) セット séttò; (of jewel) はめ込み台 hamékomidaì

the setting of the sun 日没 nichíbotsu

settle [setˈəl] *vt* (argument, matter) ...に決着を付ける ...ni ketcháku wò tsukérù; (accounts) 清算する sefsan suru; (MED: calm: person) 静める shizúmerù

♦*vi* (also: **settle down**) 一カ所に落着く ikkásho nì ochítsukù; (bird) 降りる orírù; (dust etc) つく tsukú; (calm down: children) 静まる shizúmarù

to settle for something ...で我慢する ...de gámàn suru

to settle on something ...に決める ...ni kimérù

settle in *vi* 新しい所に落着く atárashiì tokórò nì ochítsukù

settle up *vi*: *to settle up with someone* ...に借金を返す ...ni shakkíñ wo káèsu

settlement [set'əlmənt] n (payment) 清算 seisan; (agreement) 和解 wakái; (village etc) 集落 shūraku

settler [set'lər] n 入植者 nyūshokusha

set up vt (organization) 設立する setsúritsu suru

setup [set'ʌp] n (organization) 機構 kikō; (situation) 様子 yōsu, 状況 jōkyō

seven [sev'ən] num 七(の) nánā (no), 七つ(の) nanátsù (no)

seventeen [sev'əntiːn'] num 十七(の) jūnanā (no)

seventh [sev'ənθ] num 第七(の) dái nanà (no)

seventy [sev'əntiː] num 七十(の) nanájù (no)

sever [sev'ər] vt (artery, pipe) 切断する setsūdan suru; (relations) 切る kírù, 断つ tátsù

several [sev'ə:rəl] adj (things) 幾つかの fkūtsu ka no; (people) 幾人かの fkūnin ka no

♦pron 幾つかの fkūtsu ka

   several of us 私たちの中から幾人か watákushitàchi no nákā kara fkūnin ka

severance [sev'ə:rəns] n (of relations) 断交 dańkō

severance pay n 退職金 tafshokukìn

severe [sivir'] adj (serious: pain) 激しい hageshiì; (: damage) 大きな ōki na; (: shortage) 深刻な shińkoku na; (hard: winter, climate) 厳しい kibíshiì; (stern) 厳格な gefkaku na; (plain: dress) 簡素な kańso na

severity [siver'iti:] n (seriousness: of pain) 激しさ hageshìsa; (: of damage) 大きさ ōkìsa; (: of shortage) 深刻さ shińkokusa; (bitterness: of winter, climate) 厳しさ kibíshiì; (sternness) 厳格さ gefkakusa; (plainness: of dress) 簡素さ kańsosa

sew [sou] (pt **sewed**, pp **sewn**) vt 縫う nūù

sewage [suː'idʒ] n (waste) 汚水 osúì

sewer [suː'ər] n 下水道 gesúidō

sewing [sou'iŋ] n (activity) 裁縫 safhō; (items being sewn) 縫物 nufmono

sewing machine n ミシン míshìn

sewn [soun] pp of **sew**

sew up vt (item of clothing) 縫い合せる nuíawaserù

sex [seks] n (gender) 性別 sefbetsu; (lovemaking) セックス sékkùsu

   to have sex with someone …とセックスをする …to sékkùsu wo suru

sexist [seks'ist] adj 性差別の sefsabetsu no

sextet [sekstet'] n (group) セクステット sekúsutettò

sexual [sek'ʃuːəl] adj (of the sexes: reproduction) 有性の yūsei no; (: equality) 男女の dáñjo no; (of sex: attraction) 性的な sefteki na; (: relationship) 肉体の nikūtai no

sexy [sek'siː] adj (pictures, underwear etc) セクシーな sékūshiì na

shabby [ʃæb'iː] adj (person, clothes) 見すぼらしい misúboràshiì; (trick, treatment) 卑劣な hirétsu na

shack [ʃæk] n バラック barákkū

shackles [ʃæk'əlz] npl (on foot) 足かせ ashfkasè; (on hands) 手かせ tékàse; (fig) 束縛 sokúbaku

shade [ʃeid] n (shelter) 日陰 hikáge; (also: **lampshade**) ランプのかさ rańpu no kásā; (of colour) 色合 iróaì; (small quantity): **a shade too large** ちょっと大き過ぎる chottó ōkisugirù

♦vt (shelter) …の日よけにする …no hiyókè ni surù; (eyes) …に手をかざす …ni té wò kazásù

   in the shade 日陰に hikáge ni

   a shade more もうちょっと mō chottò

shadow [ʃæd'ou] n 影 kágè

♦vt (follow) 尾行する bikō suru

shadow cabinet (BRIT) n (POL) 影の内閣 kágè no náìkaku

shadowy [ʃæd'ouiː] adj (in shadow) 影の多い kágè no ōi; (dim: figure, shape) 影の様な kágè no yō na

shady [ʃei'diː] adj (place) 日陰のある hikáge no arù; (trees) 日よけになる hiyóke ni narù; (fig: dishonest: person, deal) いかがわしい ikágawashiì

shaft [ʃæft] n (of arrow) 矢柄 yagára; (of spear) 柄 e; (AUT, TECH) 回転軸 kaftenjiku, シャフト sháfùto; (of mine) 縦坑 tatékō; (of elevator) 通路 tsūro

a shaft of light 一条の光 ichijō no hikarî

shaggy [ʃægˈiː] *adj* (appearance, beard, dog) ぼさぼさの bosábosa na

shake [ʃeik] (*pt* **shook**, *pp* **shaken**) *vt* (gen) 揺する yusûburu; (bottle) 振る fúru; (cocktail) シェイクする shefkû suru; (building) 揺らがす yurûgasō; (weaken: beliefs, resolve) ぐらつかせる gurátsukaserō; (upset, surprise) ...にショックを与える ...ni shókkū wo atáerū

♦*vi* (tremble) 震える furúerū

to shake one's head (in refusal, dismay) 頭を振る atáma wo fúrū

to shake hands with someone ...と握手をする ...to ákushu wo suru

shaken [ʃeiˈkən] *pp of* **shake**

shake off *vt* 振り落す furîotosū; (*fig:* pursuer) まく makû

shake up *vt* (lit: ingredients) よく振る yókū furu; (*fig:* organization) 一新する isshîn suru

shaky [ʃeiˈkiː] *adj* (hand, voice) 震える furúerū; (table, building) ぐらぐらする gurágura suru

shall [ʃæl] *aux vb*: *I shall go* 行きます ikímasū

shall I open the door? ドアを開けましょうか dóa wo akémashō ka

I'll get some, shall I? 少し取ってきましょうか sukóshi totté kimashō ka

shallow [ʃælˈou] *adj* (water, box, breathing) 浅い asáî; (*fig:* ideas etc) 浅薄な senpaku na

sham [ʃæm] *n* いんちき ínchiki

♦*vt* ...の振りをする ...no furî wó suru

shambles [ʃæmˈbəlz] *n* 大混乱, dafkonfran

shame [ʃeim] *n* (embarrassment) 恥 hajî; (disgrace) 不面目 fuménboku

♦*vt* 辱める hazúkashimerū

it is a shame that ... ...であるのは残念だ ...de árū no wa zafnen da

it is a shame to do ... ...するのはもったいない ...surū no wa mottáinai

what a shame! 残念だ! zafnen da

shamefaced [ʃeimˈfeist] *adj* 恥ずかしそうな hazúkashisō na

shameful [ʃeimˈfəl] *adj* (disgraceful) 恥ずべき hazúbekī

shameless [ʃeimˈlis] *adj* (liar, deception) 恥知らずの hajîshirazū no

shampoo [ʃæmpuːˈ] *n* シャンプー sháňpu

♦*vt* シャンプーする sháňpu suru

shampoo and set シャンプーとセット sháňpu tó séttō

shamrock [ʃæmˈrɑːk] *n* ツメクサ tsumékusa, クローバー kurôbā

shandy [ʃænˈdiː] *n* シャンディー sháňdī ◇ビールをレモネードで割った飲物 bíru wo remónēdo de wattá nomimono

shan't [ʃænt] = **shall not**

shanty town [ʃænˈtiː-] *n* バラック集落 barákkushūraku

shape [ʃeip] *n* (form, outline) 形 katáchi

♦*vt* (fashion, form) 形作る katáchizukurū; (someone's ideas, life) 方向付ける hōkōzukerū

to take shape (painting) 段々格好がつく dańdañ kakkō ga tsukū; (plan) 具体化してくる gutáika shite kurū

-shaped [ʃeipt] *suffix*: *heart-shaped* ハート形の hátōgata no

shapeless [ʃeipˈlis] *adj* 不格好な bukákkō na

shapely [ʃeipˈliː] *adj* (woman, legs) 美しい utsûkushiî

share [ʃeːr] *n* (part received) 分け前 wakémae; (part contributed) 持分 mochíbun, 負担分 futáňbun; (COMM) 株 kabû

♦*vt* (books, toys, room) 共用する kyôyō suru; (cost) 分担する buntâň suru; (one's lunch) 分けてやる wakéte yarū; (have in common: features, qualities etc) ...の点で似ている ...no téň de nité irū

shareholder [ʃeːrˈhouldəːr] *n* 株主 kabûnūshi

share out *vi* 分配する buňpai suru

shark [ʃɑːrk] *n* サメ samé

sharp [ʃɑːrp] *adj* (razor, knife) よく切れる yókū kirérū; (point, teeth) 鋭い surûdoi; (nose, chin) とがった togátta; (outline) くっきりした kukkíri shitá; (pain)

鋭い surudói; (cold) 身を切る様な mí wò kírù yō na; (taste) ピッ taste) 酸味のきいた shitá wò sásù yō na; (MUS) ピッチが高過ぎる pítchī ga takásugírù; (contrast) 鮮やかな azáyaka na; (increase) 急な kyū́ na; (voice) 甲高い kandakaí; (person: quick-witted) 抜け目の ない nukéme no naí; (dishonest: practice etc) 不正な fuséi na

♦n (MUS) えい音記号efonkigō, シャープ shāpù

♦adv (precisely): **at 2 o'clock sharp** 2 時きっかりに nijī kikkárí ni

sharpen [ʃɑːr'pən] *vt* (stick etc) とがらせ togáraserù; (pencil) 削る kezúrù; (fig: appetite) そそる sosórù

sharpener [ʃɑːr'pənər] *n* (*also*: **pencil sharpener**) 鉛筆削り efpitsukezúri

sharp-eyed [ʃɑːrp'aid'] *adj* 目の鋭い mé nò surodoí

sharply [ʃɑːrp'liː] *adv* (turn, stop) 急に kyū́ ni; (stand out) くっきりと kukkírī to; (contrast) 強く tsuyóku; (criticize, retort) 辛らつに shifíratsu ni

shatter [ʃæt'əːr] *vt* (break) 割る warú,木っ端みじんにする kóppàmijin ni suru; (fig: ruin) 台無しにする daínashi ni suru; (: upset) がっくりさせる gakkúrī sasérù

♦vi (break) 割れる warérù

shave [ʃeiv] *vt* (person, face, legs etc) そ る sórù

♦vi ひげをそる higé wò sórù

♦n: **to have a shave** (at barber's) ひげ をそってもらう higé wò sóttè moráù; (oneself) ひげをそる higé wò sórù

shaver [ʃei'vəːr] *n* (*also*: **electric shaver**) 電気かみそり defikikamísori

shaving [ʃei'viŋ] *n* (action) ひげをそる事 higé wò sórù kotó

shaving brush *n* シェービングブラシ shébingubúrashi

shaving cream, shaving foam *n* シェービングクリーム shébingukurímu

shavings [ʃei'viŋz] *npl* (of wood etc) か んなくず kafinakuzú

shawl [ʃɔːl] *n* 肩掛 katákàke, ショール shórù

she [ʃiː] *pron* 彼女は(が) kánòjo wa (ga)

sheaf [ʃiːf] *n* (*npl* **sheaves**) *n* (of corn, papers)

束 tábà

shear [ʃiːr] *vt* (*pt* **sheared**, *pp* **shorn**) (sheep)...の毛を刈る...no ké wò karú

shear off *vi* 折れる orérù

shears [ʃiːrz] *npl* (for hedge) はさみ ha-sámi

sheath [ʃiːθ] *n* (of knife) さや sáyà; (contraceptive) コンドーム kofídòmu, スキン sukíñ

sheaves [ʃiːvz] *npl of* **sheaf**

she-cat [ʃiː'kæt] *n* 雌ネコ mesúneko

shed [ʃed] *n* 小屋 koyá

♦vt (*pt, pp* **shed**) (leaves, tears, hair etc) 落 す otósù; (skin) 脱皮する dappí suru; (tears) 流す nagásù

to shed blood 人を殺す hitó wò korósù

to shed a load (subj: truck etc) 荷崩れ を起す nikázure wò okósù

she'd [ʃiːd] = **she had; she would**

sheen [ʃiːn] *n* つや tsuyá

sheep [ʃiːp] *n inv* ヒツジ hitsúji

sheepdog [ʃiːp'dɔːg] *n* 牧用犬 bokúyōken

sheepish [ʃiː'piʃ] *adj* 恥ずかしそうな ha-zúkashisō na

sheepskin [ʃiːp'skin] *n* ヒツジの毛皮 hi-tsúji nò kegáwa, シープスキン shípusu-kiñ

sheer [ʃiːr] *adj* (utter) 全くの mattáku no; (steep) 垂直の suíchoku no; (almost transparent) ごく薄手の gokú usúde no

♦adv (straight up: rise) 垂直に suíchoku ni

sheet [ʃiːt] *n* (on bed) シーツ shítsù; (of paper, glass, metal) 一枚 ichímaî

a sheet of ice アイスバーン aísubàn

sheik(h) [ʃiːk] *n* 首長 shuchō

shelf [ʃelf] (*pl* **shelves**) *n* 棚 taná

shell [ʃel] *n* (on beach) 貝殻 kaígara; (of egg, nut etc) 殻 kará; (explosive) 弾丸 dañgan; (of building) 外壁 sotókabe

♦vt (peas) むく múkù; (MIL: fire on) 砲撃する hōgeki suru

she'll [ʃiːl] = **she will; she shall**

shellfish [ʃel'fiʃ] *n inv* (crab) カニ kanî; (prawn, shrimp etc) エビ ebî; (lobster) ロブスター róbùsutā; (scallop, clam etc) 貝 kaí ◇料理用語として殻のある海の生物を指す ryōriyōgo toshite kará no arú umí no séíbutsu wo sású

shelter [ʃel'tər] n (building) シェルター shérùtā; (protection: for hiding) 隠れ場所 kakúrebashò; (: from rain) 雨宿りの場所 amáyàdori no bashó

♦vt (protect) 守る mamórù; (give lodging to: homeless, refugees) ...に避難の場所を提供する ...ni hínàn no bashó wò tefkyō suru; (: wanted man) かくまう kakúmau

♦vi (from rain etc) 雨宿りをする amáyàdori wo suru; (from danger) 避難する hínàn suru; (hide) 隠れる kakúrerù

sheltered [ʃel'tərd] adj (life) 世間の荒波から守られた sékèn no aránami karà mamórareta; (spot) 雨風を避けられる ámèkaze wo sakérarerù

sheltered housing 老人・身障者用住宅 rōjíñ, shíñshōshayō jūtáku

shelve [ʃelv] vt (fig: plan) 棚上げにする tanà-age ni surú

shelves [ʃelvz] npl of shelf

shepherd [ʃep'ərd] n ヒツジ飼い hitsújikài

♦vt (guide) 案内する añnai suru

shepherd's pie (BRIT) n シェパードパイ shepádopaì ◊ひき肉にマッシュポテトを乗せて焼いた料理 hikíniku ni masshúpotètò wo nosète yaità ryōri

sheriff [ʃer'if] (US) n 保安官 hoáñkan

sherry [ʃer'i:] n シェリー酒 sherfshù

she's [ʃiːz] = she is; she has

Shetland [ʃet'lənd] n (also: the Shetlands, the Shetland Isles) シェットランド諸島 shéttorando shotó

shield [ʃiːld] n (MIL) 盾 táte; (SPORT: trophy) 盾形トロフィー tatégata toròfī; (protection) ...よけ ...yóke

♦vt: to shield (from) ...の(...)よけになる ...no (...) yóke ni narú

shift [ʃift] n (change) 変更 heñkō; (work-period) 交替 kótai; (group of workers) 交替組 kótaigúmi

♦vt (move) ...の位置を変える ...no íchi wo kaérù; (remove: stain) 抜く nukú

♦vi (move: wind, person) 変る kawárù

shiftless [ʃift'lis] adj ろくでなしの rokúdenashi no

shift work n 交替でする作業 kótai de suru sagyō

shifty [ʃif'tiː] adj (person, eyes) うさん臭い usáñkusaì

shilling [ʃil'iŋ] (BRIT) n シリング shírìñgu ◊かつての英国の硬貨でポンドの1/20 kátsute no efkoku no kóka de póñdo no nijúbùn no ichi

shilly-shally [ʃil'iːʃæliː] vi ぐずぐずする gúzùguzu suru

shimmer [ʃim'ər] vi ちらちら光る chíràchira hikárù

shin [ʃin] n 向こうずね mukózune

shine [ʃain] n つや tsuyá

♦vb (pt, pp shone)

♦vi (sun) 照る térù; (torch, light, eyes) 光る hikárù; (fig: person) 優れる sugúrerù

♦vt (glasses) ふく fukú; (shoes) 磨く migákù

to shine a torch on something ...を懐中電燈で照す ...wo kaíchūdeñtō de terásù

shingle [ʃiŋ'gəl] n (on beach) 砂利 jarí

shingles [ʃiŋ'gəlz] n (MED) 帯状ヘルペス tajóheruþēsu

shiny [ʃai'niː] adj (coin) ぴかぴかの pikápika no; (shoes, hair, lipstick) つやつやの tsuyátsuya no

ship [ʃip] n 船 fúne

♦vt (transport by ship) 船で運ぶ fúne de hakóbù; (send: goods) 輸送する yusó suru

shipbuilding [ʃip'bildiŋ] n 造船 zósen

shipment [ʃip'mənt] n (goods) 輸送貨物 yusókamòtsu

shipper [ʃip'ər] n 送り主 okúrinùshi

shipping [ʃip'iŋ] n (transport of cargo) 運送 uñsō; (ships collectively) 船舶 séñpaku

shipshape [ʃip'ʃeip] adj きちんとした kichíñto shita

shipwreck [ʃip'rek] n (event) 難破 náñpa; (ship) 難破船 nañpaseñ

♦vt: to be shipwrecked 難破する náñpa suru

shipyard [ʃip'jɑːrd] n 造船所 zóseñjo

shire [ʃaiər] (BRIT) n 郡 gúñ

shirk [ʃərk] vt (work, obligations) 怠る

okótarù

shirt [ʃəːt] n (man's) ワイシャツ waíshatsu; (woman's) シャツブラウス shatsúburaùsu

in (one's) shirt sleeves 上着を脱いで
uwági wò nùide

shit [ʃit] (*inf!*) *excl* くそっ kusót!

shiver [ʃiv'əːr] n (act of shivering) 身震い
mibúruì

♦*vi* 震える furúerù

shoal [ʃoul] n (of fish) 群れ muré; (*fig*:
also: **shoals**) 大勢 ózeì

shock [ʃɑːk] n (start, impact) 衝撃 shógeki; (ELEC) 感電 kańden; (emotional) 打
撃 dagéki, ショック shókkù; (MED) ショ
ック shókkù

♦*vt* (upset, offend) ...にショックを与える
...ni shókkù wo atáerù

shock absorber n 緩衝器 kańshōkì

shocking [ʃɑk'iŋ] *adj* (awful: standards,
accident) ひどい hidóì; (outrageous:
play, book) 衝撃的な shógekiteki na

shod [ʃɑd] *pt, pp of* **shoe**

shoddy [ʃɑd'iː] *adj* (goods, workmanship) 粗雑な sozátsu na

shoe [ʃuː] n (for person) 靴 kutsú; (for
horse) てい鉄 teítetsu

♦*vt* (*pt, pp* **shod**) (horse) ...にてい鉄を付
ける ...ni teítetsu wo tsukérù

shoebrush [ʃuː'brʌʃ] n 靴ブラシ kutsúburàshi

shoelace [ʃuː'leis] n 靴ひも kutsúhìmo

shoe polish n 靴墨 kutsúmigàki

shoeshop [ʃuː'ʃɑp] n 靴屋 kutsúyà

shoestring [ʃuː'striŋ] n (*fig*: **on a shoestring** わずかの金で wázùka no kané de

shone [ʃoun] *pt, pp of* **shine**

shoo [ʃuː] *excl* しっ shit; (動物を追い払う
時に言う言葉 dóbutsu wò ofharaù toki ni
iú kotoba

shook [ʃuk] *pt of* **shake**

shoot [ʃuːt] n (on branch, seedling) 若枝
wakáeda

♦*vb* (*pt, pp* **shot**)

♦*vt* (gun) 撃つ útsù; (arrow) 射る írù;
(kill: bird, robber etc) 撃ち殺す uchíkorosù; (wound) 撃つ sogéki suru;
(execute) 銃殺する jùsatsu suru; (film) 撮

影する satsúei suru; *to shoot (at)* (...を
目掛けて)撃つ(射る)(...wo megákete)
útsù (írù); (SOCCER) シュートする shù-
to suru

♦*vi* (with gun/bow): *to shoot (at)* (...を
目掛けて)撃つ(射る)(...wo megákete
útsù (írù)

shoot down *vt* (plane) 撃ち落とす uchíotosù

shoot in/out *vi* (rush) 飛び込む(飛び出す)
tobíkomù (tobídasù)

shooting [ʃuː'tiŋ] n (shots) 発砲事件 happójikèn; (HUNTING) 狩猟 shuryó

shooting star n 流れ星 nagárebòshi

shoot up *vi* (*fig*) 急上昇する kyùjòshō
suru

shop [ʃɑp] n (selling goods) 店 misé;
(*also*: **workshop**) 作業場 sagyóba

♦*vi* (*also*: **go shopping**) 買物する kaímono suru

shop assistant (*BRIT*) n 店員 teń-in

shop floor (*BRIT*) n 労働側 ródōgawa

shopkeeper [ʃɑp'kiːpəːr] n 店主 teńshu

shoplifting [ʃɑp'liftiŋ] n 万引 mańbìki

shopper [ʃɑp'əːr] n (person) 客 kyakú

shopping [ʃɑp'iŋ] n (goods) 買物 kaímono

shopping bag n ショッピングバッグ
shoppíngubaggù

shopping center (*BRIT* **shopping centre**) n ショッピングセンター shoppíngusentā

shop-soiled [ʃɑp'sɔild] *adj* (goods) 棚ざ
らしの tanázarashi no

shop steward (*BRIT*) n (INDUSTRY)
職場代表 shokúbadaihyò

shop window n ショーウインドー shòuindò

shore [ʃɔːr] n 岸 kishí

♦*vt*: *to shore up* 補強する hokyó suru

on shore 陸に riku no

shorn [ʃɔːrn] *pp of* **shear**

short [ʃɔːrt] *adj* (in length) 短い mijíkaì;
(person: not tall) 背の低い sé nò hikúì;
(curt) ぶっきらぼうな bukkírabò na; (insufficient) 不足している fusóku shite irù

to be short of something ...が不足して
いる ...ga fusóku shite irù

in short 要するに yō surù ni

short of doing ... ...をしなければ ...wo shinákereba

it is short for それは...の短縮形です soré wà ... no tańshukukei desu

to cut short (speech, visit) 予定より短くする yotéi yorì mijíkakù suru

everything short of ... ...を除いて何でも ...wo nozóite nâñ de mo

to fall short of ... ...に達しない ...ni tasshínai

to run short of ... ...が足りなくなる ...ga tarínakunarù

to stop short (while walking etc) 急に立ち止まる kyū́ ni tachídomarù; (when doing something) 急にやめる kyū́ ni yamérù

to stop short of ... ...まではしない ...mádè wa shinâî

shortage [ʃɔːrtidʒ] n: *a shortage of ...* ...不足 ...busóku

shortbread [ʃɔːrtbred] n ショートブレッド shótòbureddò 小麦粉, バター, 砂糖で作った菓子 komúgiko, bátà, satô dè tsukúttà kashí

short-change [ʃɔːrtʃeindʒ] vt ...に釣銭を少なく渡す ...ni tsurísen wò sukúnakù watásù

short-circuit [ʃɔːrtsəːrkit] n (ELEC) ショート shótò

shortcoming [ʃɔːrtkʌmiŋ] n 欠点 kettéñ

short(crust) pastry [ʃɔːrt(krʌst)-] (BRIT) n パイ生地 páikijĩ

shortcut [ʃɔːrtkʌt] n 近道 chikámichi

shorten [ʃɔːrtən] vt (clothes, visit) 短くする mijíkakù suru

shortfall [ʃɔːrtfɔːl] n 不足 fusóku

shorthand [ʃɔːrthænd] n 速記 sokkí

shorthand typist (BRIT) n 速記もできるタイピスト sokkí mo dekírù taípisùto

shortlist [ʃɔːrtlist] (BRIT) n (for job) 予備審査の合格者リスト yobíshiñsa no gókakushà risúto

short-lived [ʃɔːrtlivd] adj つかの間の tsuká no ma no

shortly [ʃɔːrtli] adv 間もなく ma mò nâku

shorts [ʃɔːrts] npl: *(a pair of) shorts* (short trousers) 半ズボン hañzúboñ; (men's underwear) パンツ páñtsu

short-sighted [ʃɔːrtsaitid] (BRIT) adj 近眼の kiñgan no; (fig) 先見の明のない señken no mêî no nâi

short-staffed [ʃɔːrtstæft] adj: *to be short-staffed* 人手不足である hitódebùsoku de aru

short story n 短編小説 tañpeñshōsetsu

short-tempered [ʃɔːrttempəːrd] adj 短気な tâñki na

short-term [ʃɔːrttəːrm] adj (effect, borrowing) 短期の tâñki no

shortwave [ʃɔːrtweiv] n (RADIO) 短波 tấñpa

shot [ʃɑt] pt, pp of shoot
♦n (of gun) 発砲 happṓ; (try, also SOCCER etc) シュート shūto; (injection) 注射 chūsha; (PHOT) ショット shóttò

a good/poor shot (person) 射撃のうまい[下手な]人 shagéki no umaí [hetà na] hitó

like a shot (without any delay) 鉄砲玉の様に teppódama no yṓ ni

shotgun [ʃɑtgʌn] n 散弾銃 sañdañjū́

should [ʃud] aux vb: *I should go now* もうおいとましなくては mô o-ftoma shinakute wà

he should be there now 彼は今あそこにいるはずです kárè wa ímà asóko ni irú hazù desu

I should go if I were you 私だったら、行きますね watákushi dattàra, ikímasù yó

I should like to ... ...をしたいと思います が ...wo shitái tò omóimasù ga

shoulder [ʃouldəːr] n (ANAT) 肩 kátà
♦vt (fig: responsibility, blame) 負う óù

shoulder bag n ショルダーバッグ shórudàbaggù

shoulder blade n 肩甲骨 keñkókotsu

shoulder strap n ショルダーストラップ shórudàsutorappù

shouldn't [ʃudʲnt] = should not

shout [ʃaut] n 叫び声 sakébigòe
♦vt 大声で言う ṓgoè de iú
♦vi (also: shout out) 叫ぶ sakébù

shout down vt (speaker) どなって黙らせる dónàtte damáraserù

shouting [ˈʃautɪŋ] *n* 叫び声 sakébigoè

shove [ʃʌv] *vt* 押す osú; (*inf*: put): **to shove something in** ...を ...に 押し込む ...wo ...ni oshíkomù

shovel [ˈʃʌvəl] *n* (*gen*) スコップ sukóppù, シャベル shábèru; (mechanical) パワーシャベル pawáshabèru
♦*vt* (snow) かく kákù; (coal, earth) すくう sukúù

shove off *vi*: **shove off!** (*inf*) うせろ userő

show [ʃou] *n* (demonstration: of emotion) 表現 hyőgen; (semblance) 見せ掛け misékake; (exhibition: flower show etc) 展示会 tenjíkai, ショー shò; (THEATER, TV) ショー shò
♦*vb* (*pt* showed, *pp* shown)
♦*vt* (indicate) 表して示せる shiméseru, 見せる misérù; (exhibit) 展示する tenjí suru; (courage etc) 示せる shimésu; (illustrate, depict) 描写する byósha suru; (film: in movie theater) 上映する jóei suru; (program, film: on television) 放送する hósō suru
♦*vi* (be evident) 見える miérù; (: appear) 現れる aráwarerù

for show 格好だけの kakkő dake no
on show (exhibits etc) 展示中 tenjíchù

show business *n* 芸能界 geínōkai

showdown [ˈʃoudaun] *n* 対決 taíketsu

shower [ˈʃauˈər] *n* (of rain) にわか雨 niwákaamè; (of stones etc) ...の雨 ...no amè; (for bathing in) シャワー sháwà
♦*vi* 降ってくる futté kurù
♦*vt*: **to shower someone with** ...の上に ...を降らす ...no uè ni...wo furásù
to have a shower シャワーを浴びる sháwà wo abírù

showerproof [ˈʃauˈərpruːf] *adj* 防水の bősui no ◇わか雨程度なら耐えられるが強い雨には濡れてしまうコートなどについて言う kańtanà téido nara tae̋rareru ga tsuyői amè ni wa nuréteshimaù kőto ni tsűìte iú

show in *vt* (person) 中へ案内する nákà e añnai suru

showing [ˈʃouˈɪŋ] *n* (of film) 上映 jóei

show jumping [-ˈdʒʌmˈpɪŋ] *n* (of horses) 障害飛越 shőgaihiètsu

shown [ʃoun] *pp* of show

show off *vi* (*pej*) 気取る kidőru
♦*vt* (display) 見せびらかす misébirakasù

show-off [ˈʃouːɔːf] (*inf*) *n* (person) 自慢屋 jimán-ya

show out *vt* (person) 出口へ案内する déguchi e añnai suru

showpiece [ˈʃouˈpiːs] *n* (of exhibition etc) 立派な見本 rippá na mihőn

showroom [ˈʃouˈruːm] *n* ショールーム shőrumu

show up *vi* (stand out) 目立つ medátsù; (*inf*: turn up) 現れる aráwarerù
♦*vt* (uncover: imperfections etc) 暴露する bákùro suru

shrank [ʃræŋk] *pt* of shrink

shrapnel [ˈʃræpnəl] *n* 弾丸の破片 dañgan nő hahén

shred [ʃred] *n* (*gen pl*) 切れ端 kiréhashi
♦*vt* (paper) ずたずたにする zutázuta ni suru; (CULIN) 刻む kizámù

shredder [ˈʃredˈər] *n* (vegetable shredder) 削り器 kezúrikì; (document shredder) シュレッダー shuréddà

shrewd [ʃruːd] *adj* (businessman) 抜け目のない nukéme no naì; (assessment) 賢明な keńmei na

shriek [ʃriːk] *n* 金切り声 kanákirigoè
♦*vi* 金切り声を出す kanákirigoè wo dásù

shrill [ʃril] *adj* (cry, voice) 甲高い kañdakaì

shrimp [ʃrimp] *n* (shellfish) えび ebí

shrine [ʃrain] *n* (place of worship) 礼拝堂 reíhaidō; (for relics) 聖遺物container sefíbutsuyőki; (*fig*: building) 殿堂 deńdō; (: place) 聖地 seíchi

shrink [ʃriŋk] (*pt* shrank, *pp* shrunk) *vi* (cloth) 縮む chijîmù; (be reduced: profits, audiences) 減る herú; (move: *also*: **shrink away**) 縮こまって逃げる chijíkomattè nigérù
♦*vt* (cloth) 縮める chijímerù
♦*n* (*inf*: *pej*: psychiatrist) 精神科医 seíshinka-ì
to shrink from (doing) something ...を(するの)をいやがる ...wo (surú no wò) iyágarù

shrinkage [ʃrɪŋkɪdʒ] n 縮まる分 chijímarū bún

shrinkwrap [ʃrɪŋkræp] vt ラップで包む ráppū de tsutsúmū

shrivel [ʃrɪvəl] (also: **shrivel up**) vt しわさせる shíóresaserú

♦vi しおれる shíórerū

shroud [ʃraud] n 覆い ói

♦vt: **shrouded in mystery** なぞに包まれて nazó ni tsutsúmarete

Shrove Tuesday [ʃrouv-] n 謝肉祭の火曜日 shaníkusái no kayóbi

shrub [ʃrʌb] n 低木 teíboku

shrubbery [ʃrʌbˈəːri] n 植込み uékemi

shrug [ʃrʌg] n 肩をすくめる事 kátà wo sukúmerū kotó

♦vt, vi: **to shrug (one's shoulders)** 肩をすくめる kátà wo sukúmerū

shrug off vt (criticism) 受流す ukénagasū; (illness) 無視する mushí surú

shrunk [ʃrʌŋk] pp of **shrink**

shudder [ʃʌdˈəːr] n 身震い mibúrùi

♦vi (person: with fear, revulsion) 身震いする mibúrùi suru

shuffle [ʃʌfˈəl] n (cards) 混ぜる mazérū

♦vi (walk) 足を引きずって歩く ashí wò hikízùtte arukú

to shuffle (one's feet) (while standing, sitting) 足をもそもぞ動かす ashí wò mózòmozo ugókasū

shun [ʃʌn] vt (publicity, neighbors etc) 避ける sakérū

shunt [ʃʌnt] vt (train) 分岐線に入れる buńkisen ni irérū; (object) 動かす ugókasū

shut [ʃʌt] (pt, pp **shut**) vt (door) 閉める shímérū; (shop) しまう shimáū; (mouth, eyes) 閉じる tojírū

♦vi (door, eyes, shop) 閉まる shimárū

shut down vt (for a time) 休業させる kyúgyð saserú; (forever) 閉鎖する heísa suru

♦vi (for a time) 休業する kyúgyõ surú; (forever) 閉鎖になる heísa ni narú

shut off vt (supply etc) 遮断する shadán suru

shutter [ʃʌtˈəːr] n (on window: also PHOT) シャッター sháttà

shuttle [ʃʌtˈəl] n (plane etc) シャトル

shátòru; (also: **space shuttle**) スペースシャトル spésu shátòru; (also: **shuttle service**) 折り返し運転 orfkaeshi uñten

shuttlecock [ʃʌtˈəlkɑːk] n シャトルコック shátòrukokkù

shut up vi (inf: keep quiet) 黙る damárū

♦vt (close) しまう shimaū; (silence) 黙らせる damáraserū

shy [ʃai] adj (timid: animal) 臆病な okúbyõ na; (reserved) 内気な uchíki na

shyness [ʃaiˈnis] n (timidity: of animal) 臆病 okúbyõ; (reservedness) 内気 uchíki

Siamese [saiamiːz] adj: **Siamese cat** シャムネコ shamúneko

Siberia [saibiˈriːə] n シベリア shibéria

sibling [sibˈliŋ] n 兄弟 kyódai〈男兄弟にも女兄弟 (姉妹) にも使う otókokyódai ni mo oñnakyódai (shímai) ni mo tsukáũ

sic [sik] adv 原文通り geñbun dóri

sick [sik] adj (ill) 病気の byóki no; (nauseated) むかついた mukátsuita; (humor) 病的な byóteki na; (vomiting): **to be sick** 吐く hákū

to feel sick むかつく mukátsukū

to be sick of (fig) ...にうんざりしている ...ni uñzari shite iru

sick bay n (on ship) 医務室 imúshitsu

sicken [sikˈən] vt むかつかせる mukátsukaserū

sickening [sikˈəniŋ] adj (fig) 不快な fukái na

sickle [sikˈəl] n かま kámà

sick leave n 病気休暇 byókikyùka

sickly [sikˈliː] adj (child, plant) 病気がちな byókigachi na; (causing nausea: smell) むかつかせる mukátsukaserū

sickness [sikˈnis] n (illness) 病気 byóki; (vomiting) おうと óto

sick pay n 病気手当 byókiteate

side [said] n (of object) 横 yokó; (of body) 脇腹 wakíbara; (of lake) 岸 kishí; (aspect) 面 men; (team) 側 gawá

♦adj (door, entrance) 横の yokó no

♦vi: **to side with someone** ...の肩を持つ ...no kátà wo mótsū

the side of the road 路肩 rokáta

the side of a hill 山腹 sañpuku

by the side of ...の横に ...no yokó ni

side by side 横に並んで yokō ni narande

from side to side 左右に sáyū ni

from all sides 四方八方から shihóhap-
pō kara

to take sides (with) (...に)味方する
(...ni) mikáta suru

sideboard [said'bɔːrd] *n* 食器戸棚 shok-
kídodāna, サイドボード saídobòdo

sideboards [said'bɔːrdz] *(BRIT) npl* =
sideburns

sideburns [said'bəːrnz] *npl* もみあげ mo-
míage

side drum *n* (MUS) 小太鼓 kodáiko

side effect *n* (MED, *fig*) 副作用 fukúsa-
yō

sidelight [said'lait] *n* (AUT) 車幅灯 sha-
fúkutō

sideline [said'lain] *n* (SPORT) サイドラ
イン saídorain; (*fig*: supplementary job)
副業 fukúgyō

sidelong [said'lɔːŋ] *adj: to give some-
one/something a sidelong glance* ...を
横目で見る ...wo yokóme de mírù

sidesaddle [said'sædəl] *adv: to ride
sidesaddle* 馬に横乗りする umá ní yo-
kónori surù

side show *n* (stall at fair, circus) 見世物
屋台 misémonoyātai

sidestep [said'step] *vt* (*fig*) 避けて通る
sakétetòru

side street *n* わき道 wakímichi

sidetrack [said'træk] *vt* (*fig*)...の話を脱
線させる ...no hanáshi wò dassén saserù

sidewalk [said'wɔːk] *(US)* n 歩道 hodō

sideways [said'weiz] *adv* (go in) 横向き
に yokómuki ni; (lean) 横へ hokó e

siding [sai'diŋ] *n* (RAIL) 側線 sokúsen

sidle [sai'dəl] *vi: to sidle up (to)* (...に)
こっそり近寄る (...ni) kossóri chikáyorù

siege [siːdʒ] *n* (*gen*, MIL) 包囲 hôi

siesta [siːes'tə] *n* 昼寝 hírùne

sieve [siv] *n* ふるい furúi

♦*vt* ふるう furúù

sift [sift] *vt* (*fig: also:* **sift through**: information) ふるい分ける furúiwakerù;
(sieve) ふるう furúù

sigh [sai] *n* ため息 taméiki

vi ため息をつく taméiki wo tsukú

sight [sait] *n* (faculty) 視覚 shikáku;
(spectacle) 光景 kōkei; (on gun) 照準器
shójunki

♦*vt* 見掛ける mikákerù

in sight 見える所に miérù tokórò ni

on sight (shoot) 見付け次第 mitsúkeshi-
dài

out of sight 見えない所に miénai tokórò ni

sightseeing [sait'siːiŋ] *n* 名所見物 mef-
shokéñbutsu

to go sightseeing 名所見物に行く mef-
shokéñbutsu ni ikú

sign [sain] *n* (with hand) 合図 aízu; (indication: of present condition) しるし shírúshi; (: of future condition) 兆し kizáshi; (notice) 看板 kañban; (written) 張紙
harígami

♦*vt* (document) ...に署名(サイン)する
...ni shoméi (sáIn) suru; (player) 雇う
yatóù

to sign something over to someone
...を...に譲渡する ...wo...ni jốtò suru

signal [sig'nəl] *n* (*gen*) 信号 shiñgō;
(equipment on highway, railway) 信号機
shiñgōki

♦*vi* (make signs: *also* AUT) 合図をする
aízu wo suru

♦*vt* (person) ...に合図をする ...ni aízu wo
suru; (message) ...する様に合図をする
...suru yō ni aizu wo suru

signalman [sig'nəlmən] (*pl* **signalmen**)
n (RAIL) 信号手 shiñgōshu

signature [sig'nətʃər] *n* 署名 shoméi, サ
イン sáIn

signature tune *n* テーマ音楽 têmaoñ-
gaku

signet ring [sig'nit-] *n* 印鑑 指輪 iñshō-
yubiwa

significance [signif'əkəns] *n* (importance) 重要性 jūyōsei

significant [signif'ikənt] *adj* (full of
meaning: look, smile) 意味深い imíbuka-
i; (important: amount, discovery) 重要な
jūyō na

signify [sig'nəfai] *vt* 意味する ímì suru

sign language *n* 手話 shúwa

sign on vi (MIL) 入隊する nyūtai surù; (BRIT: as unemployed) 失業手当を請求する shitsùgyōteàte wo sefkyû suru; (for course) 受講手続をする jukōtetsuzùki wo suru
♦vt (MIL: recruits) 入隊させる nyūtai saserù; (employee) 雇う yatóū

signpost [sain'poust] n 案内標識 annai-hyōshikì

sign up vi (MIL) 入隊する nyūtai surù; (for course) 受講手続をする jukōtetsuzù-ki wo suru

silence [sai'ləns] n (of person) 沈黙 chínmoku; (of place) 静けさ shizúkesà
♦vt (person, opposition) 黙らせる damáraserù

silencer [sai'lənsər] n (on gun) 消音器 shóonki, サイレンサー safrehsà; (BRIT: AUT) 消音器 shóonki, マフラー mafúrà

silent [sai'lənt] adj (person) 黙っている damátte irù; (place) しんとした shíñto shitá; (machine) 音のない otó no naí; (film) 無声の muséi no
to remain silent 黙っている damátte irù

silent prayer 黙とう mokútō

silent partner n (COMM) 出資者 shusshìsha ◇資本金の一部を出すが、業務に直接関与しない社員について言う shihónkin no ichíbu wo dásù ga, gyómū ni chokúsetsu kañyo shináì shá-īn ni tsuite iú

silhouette [siluet'] n シルエット shírùetto

silicon chip [sil'ikən-] n シリコンチップ shírìkonchippù

silk [silk] n 絹 kínù
♦adj (scarf, shirt) 絹の kínù no

silky [sil'ki:] adj (material, skin) 絹の様な kínù no yō na

silly [sil'i:] adj (person, idea) ばかな bákà na

silo [sai'lou] n (on farm, for missile) サイロ saírò

silt [silt] n (in harbor, river etc) 沈泥 chíndei

silver [sil'vər] n (metal) 銀 gíñ; (coins) 硬貨 kókà; (items made of silver) 銀製品

gíñseihin

silver paper (BRIT) n 銀紙 gíngami

silver-plated [sil'və:rplei'tid] adj 銀めっきの gifmekkî no

silversmith [sil'və:rsmiθ] n 銀細工師 gíñzaikūshi

silvery [sil'və:ri:] adj (like silver) 銀の様な gíñ no yō na

similar [sim'ələr] adj: **similar (to)** (...に)似た (...ni) nitá

similarity [siməlær'iti:] n 似ている事 nité irū kotó

similarly [sim'ələrli:] adv 同じ様に onáji yồ ni

simile [sim'əli:] n 例え tatóe

simmer [sim'ə:r] vi (CULIN) ぐつぐつ煮える gútsùgutsu niérù

simpering [sim'pə:riŋ] adj (person) ばかみたいな作り笑いをする bákàmitai na tsukūriwarài wo surū
a simpering smile ばかみたいな作り笑い bákàmitai na tsukūriwarài

simple [sim'pəl] adj (easy) 簡単な kañtan na; (plain: dress, life) 素朴な sobókù na, シンプルな shíñpuru na; (foolish) ばかな bákà na; (COMM: interest) 単純な tañjun na

simplicity [simplis'əti:] n (ease) 簡単さ kañtansa; (plainness) 素朴さ sobókùsa; (foolishness) 白痴 hakuchi

simplify [sim'pləfai] vt 簡単にする kañtan ni surù

simply [sim'pli:] adv (in a simple way: live) 素朴に sobókù ni; (talk) 平易に héii ni; (just, merely) 単に táñ ni

simulate [sim'jəleit] vt (enthusiasm, innocence) 装う yosóoū

simulated [sim'jəleitid] adj (hair, fur) 偽の nisé no, 人工の jinkō no; (nuclear explosion) 模擬の mógì no

simultaneous [saiməltei'ni:əs] adj (translation, broadcast) 同時の dójì no

simultaneously [saiməltei'nəsli:] adv 同時に dójì ni

sin [sin] n 罪 tsúmì
♦vi 罪を犯す tsúmì wo okásù

since [sins] *adv* それ以来 soré irái
♦*prep* ...以来 ...írai
♦*conj* (time) ...して以来 ...shíté irái; (because) ...ので ...nódè
since then, *ever since* それ以来 soré irái

sincere [sinsi:r'] *adj* 誠実な seíjitsu na

sincerely [sinsi:r'li:] *adv*: *yours sincerely* (in letters) 敬具 kéīgu

sincerity [sinser'iti:] *n* 誠実さ seíjitsusa

sinew [sin'ju:] *n* (of body) 筋肉 kínniku, けん, 筋 sújī

sinful [sin'fəl] *adj* (thought, person) 罪深い tsumíbukaì

sing [siŋ] (*pt* **sang**, *pp* **sung**) *vt* 歌う utáū
♦*vi* (*gen*) 歌う utáū; (bird) 鳴く nakú

Singapore [siŋ'gəpɔːr] *n* シンガポール shíngapōru

singe [sindʒ] *vt* 焦がす kogásū

singer [siŋ'əːr] *n* 歌手 káshū

singing [siŋ'iŋ] *n* (noise: of people) 歌声 utágoè; (: of birds) 鳴き声 nakígoè; (art) 声楽 seígaku

single [siŋ'gəl] *adj* (individual) 一つ一つの hitótsuhitotsu no; (unmarried) 独身の dokúshin no; (not double) 一つだけの hitótsu dake nò
♦*n* (*BRIT*: *also*: **single ticket**) 片道乗車券 katámichijōshakèn; (record) シングル盤 shínguruban

single-breasted [siŋ'gəlbres'tid] *adj* (jacket, suit) シングルの shínguru no

single file *n*: *in single file* 一列縦隊で ichíretsujūtai de

single-handed [siŋ'gəlhæn'did] *adv* (sail, build something) 一人で hitórī de

single-minded [siŋ'gəlmain'did] *adj* 一つだけの目的を追う hitótsu dake nò mokúteki wò oú

single out *vt* (choose) 選び出す erábidasū; (distinguish) 区別する kubétsu suru

single room *n* シングル部屋 shínguru-beya

singles [siŋ'gəlz] *n* (TENNIS) シングルス shíngurusu

singly [siŋ'gli:] *adv* (alone, one by one: people) 一人ずつ hitórī zutsu; (: things) 一つずつ hitótsu zutsu

singular [siŋ'gjələːr] *adj* (odd: occurrence) 変った kawátta; (outstanding: beauty) 著しい ichíjirushiì; (LING) 単数の tansū no
♦*n* (LING) 単数形 tansūkeī

sinister [sin'istəːr] *adj* 怪しげな ayáshigè na

sink [siŋk] *n* 流し nagashí
♦*vb* (*pt* **sank**, *pp* **sunk**)
♦*vt* (ship) 沈没させる chínbotsu saserū; (well, foundations) 掘る hórū
♦*vi* (ship) 沈没する chínbotsu suru; (heart, spirits) しょげる shogérū, がっかりする gakkárī suru; (ground) 沈下する chínka suru; (*also*: **sink back**, **sink down**: into chair) 身を沈める mì wo shízumerū; (: to one's knees etc) 沈み込む shágamikomū; (: head etc) うなだれる unádarerū
to sink something into (teeth, claws etc) ...に...を食込ませる ...ni...wo kuíkomaserū

sink in *vi* (*fig*: words) 理解される ríkai sarérū, 身にしみる mí nī shimírū

sinner [sin'əːr] *n* 罪人 tsumíbito

sinus [sai'nəs] *n* (ANAT) 副鼻こう fukúbikō

sip [sip] *n* 一口 hitókuchi
♦*vt* ちびりちびり飲む chibírichibiri nómū

siphon [sai'fən] *n* サイホン sáihon

siphon off *vt* (liquid) サイホンで汲み出す sáihon de kumídasū; (money etc) ほかへ回す hoká e mawásū

sir [səːr] *n* (*gen*) 男性に対する丁寧な呼び掛け。日本語では表現しない dañsei ni taì surú teíneì na yobíkake. nihóngo de wa hyógen shinaì
Sir John Smith ジョン・スミス卿 jóñ súmisukyō
yes sir はい haí

siren [sai'rən] *n* サイレン sáīren

sirloin [səːr'lɔin] *n* (*also*: **sirloin steak**) サーロインステーキ sároinsutēki

sissy [sis'i:] *n* (*inf*) 弱虫 yowámushi

sister [sis'təːr] *n* (relation: gen) 女きょうだい ofinakyōdai, 姉妹 shímaì; (*also*: **older sister**) 姉 ané, 姉さん nēsan; (*also*:

younger sister 妹 imōto; (nun) 修道女 shūdōjo; (BRIT: nurse) 婦長 fuchō

sister-in-law [sis'tərinlɔ:] n (pl **sisters-in-law**) n (older) 義理の姉 giri nò ané; (younger) 義理の妹 giri nò imōto

sit [sit] (pt, pp **sat**) vi (also: **sit down**) 座る suwáru, 腰掛ける koshíkakerù; (be sitting) 座っている suwátte irù, 腰掛けている koshíkakete irù; (assembly) 会期中である kaíkichū de arù; (for painter) モデルになる mōderu ni narū

♦vt (exam) 受ける ukérù

sitcom [sit'kɑm] n abbr (= situation comedy) 連続放送コメディー reńzoku hōsōkomedi

sit down vi 座る suwárù, 腰掛ける koshíkakerù

site [sait] n (place) 場所 bashò; (also: **building site**) 用地 yōchī

♦vt (factory, cruise missiles) 置く ókù

sit-in [sit'in] n (demonstration) 座り込み suwárikomi

sit in on vt fus (meeting) 傍聴する bóchō suru

sitting [sit'iŋ] n (of assembly etc) 開会 kaíkai; (in canteen) 食事の時間 shokúji nò jikan

we have two sittings for lunch 昼食は 2代で出されます chūshoku wà nikódai de dasáremasù

sitting room n 居間 imá

situated [sitʃ'ueitid] adj ...にある ...ni árù

situation [sitʃuei'ʃən] n (state) 状況 jōkyō; (job) 職 shokú; (location) 立地条件 ritchíjōken

「situations vacant」 (BRIT) 求人 kyūjin ←新聞などの求人欄のタイトル shifūbun nadò no kyūjinrán no taítoru

sit up vi (after lying) 上体を起す jōtai wò okósu; (straight) きちんと座る kichíñto suwárù; (not go to bed) 起きている ókíte irú

six [siks] num 六 (の) rokú (no), 六つ (の) múttsu (no)

sixteen [siks'ti:n'] num 十六 (の) jūroku (no)

sixth [siksθ] num 第六(の) dáï roku (no)

sixty [siks'ti:] num 六十 (の) rokújù (no)

size [saiz] n (gen) 大きさ ōkisa; (extent: of project etc) 規模 kíbò; (of clothing, shoes) サイズ saízu; (glue) サイズ saízu ◇ 紙のにじみ止め kamí nò nijímidome

sizeable [sai'zəbəl] adj (crowd, income etc) かなり大きい kánàri ōkii

size up vt (person, situation) 判断する hafídan suru

sizzle [siz'əl] vi (sausages etc) じゅうじ ゅうと音を立てる jū jū to otó wò tatérù

skate [skeit] n (ice skate) スケート sukḗto; (roller skate) ローラースケート rōrā-sukḗto; (fish) エイ éì

♦vi スケートをする sukḗto wo suru

skateboard [skeit'bɔrd] n スケートボー ド sukḗtobōdo

skater [skei'tər] n スケートをする人 sukḗto wo suru hito, スケーター sukḗta

skating [skei'tiŋ] n (SPORT) スケート sukḗto

skating rink n スケートリンク sukḗto-rińku

skeleton [skel'itən] n (bones) がい骨 gáí-kotsu; (TECH: framework) 骨組 honé-gumi; (outline) 骨子 kósshi

skeleton staff n 最小限度の人員 saíshōgendo no jín-in

skeptic [skep'tik] (US) n 疑い深い人 utá-gaibukaí hitò

skeptical [skep'tikəl] (US) adj 疑っている utagátte irù, 信用しない shiñ-yō shinai

skepticism [skep'tisizəm] (US) n 疑問 gímon

sketch [sketʃ] n (drawing) スケッチ su-kḗtchi; (outline) 骨子 kósshi; (THEA-TER, TV) 寸劇 suńgeki, スキット sukítto

♦vt スケッチする sukḗtchi suru; (also: **sketch out**: ideas) ...のあらましを言う ...no arámashi wò iú

sketchbook [sketʃ'buk] n スケッチブッ ク sukḗtchibukkù

sketchy [sketʃ'i:] adj (coverage, notes etc) 大雑把な ōzappà na

skewer [skju:'ər] n くし kushí

ski [skiː] n スキー sukí
♦vi スキーをする sukí wo surú

ski boot n スキー靴 sukígútsu

skid [skid] n (gen, AUT) スリップ suríppù
♦vi (gen, AUT) スリップする suríppù suru

skier [skiːˈəːr] n スキーヤー sukíyā

skiing [skiːˈiŋ] n スキー sukíː

ski jump n スキージャンプ sukíjànpu

skilful [skilˈfəl] (BRIT) adj = skillful

ski lift n スキーリフト sukírifùto

skill [skil] n (ability, dexterity) 熟練 jukúren; (work requiring training: computer skill etc) 技能 gíjùtsu

skilled [skild] adj (able) 上手な jōzu na; (worker) 熟練の jukúren no

skillful [skilˈfəl] (BRIT: skilful) adj 上手な jōzu na

skim [skim] vt (milk) …の上澄みをすくい取る ...no uwázumi wò sukúitorù; (glide over) …すれすれに飛ぶ ...surésure nì tobú
♦vi: to skim through (book) …をざっと読む ...wo zátto yómù

skimmed milk [skimd-] n 脱脂乳 dasshínyū

skimp [skimp] vt (also: skimp on: work) いいかげんにする ikágen ni surú; (: cloth etc) けちる kechírù

skimpy [skimˈpiː] adj (meager: meal) 少な過ぎる sukúnasugirù; (too small: skirt) 短過ぎる mijíkasugirù

skin [skin] n (gen: of person, animal) 皮膚 hífù; (: of fruit) 皮 kawá; (complexion) 顔の肌 kaó nò hádà
♦vt (fruit etc) …の皮をむく ...no kawá wò múkù; (animal) …の皮を剥ぐ ...no kawá wò hágù

skin-deep [skinˈdiːp] adj (superficial) 表面だけの hyōmeñ daké no

skin-diving [skinˈdaiviŋ] n スキンダイビング sukíndaìbingu

skinny [skinˈiː] adj (person) やせた yaséta

skintight [skinˈtait] adj (jeans etc) 体にぴったりの karáda nì pittárì no

skip [skip] n (movement) スキップ sukíppù; (BRIT: container) ごみ箱 gomíbako
♦vi (jump) スキップする sukíppù suru; (with rope) 縄跳びする nawátobì suru
♦vt (pass over: boring parts) とばす tobásù; (miss: lunch) 抜く nukú; (: lecture) すっぽかす suppókasù

ski pants npl スキーズボン sukízubòn

ski pole n スキーストック sukísutokkù

skipper [skipˈəːr] n (NAUT) 船長 señchō; (SPORT) 主将 shushō, キャプテン kyáputen

skipping rope [skipˈiŋ-] n 縄跳びの縄 nawátobì nò nawá

skirmish [skəːrˈmiʃ] n (also MIL) こぜりあい kozérìai

skirt [skəːrt] n スカート sukátò
♦vt (fig: go round) 避けて通る sákète tōrù

skirting board [skəːrˈtiŋ-] (BRIT) n 幅木 habákì

ski slope n ゲレンデ geréñde

ski suit n スキー服 sukífùku

skit [skit] n スキット sukíttò

skittle [skitˈəl] n スキットルのピン sukíttòru no pín

skittles [skitˈəlz] n (game) スキットルsukíttòru ◇9本のピンを木のボールで倒すボーリングに似た遊び kyūhòn no píñ wo kí no bòru de taosu bōriñgu ni nita asobì

skive [skaiv] (BRIT: inf) vi サボる sabórù

skulk [skʌlk] vi うろつく urótsukù

skull [skʌl] n (ANAT) 頭がい骨 zugáikotsu

skunk [skʌŋk] n スカンク sukáñku

sky [skai] n 空 sórà

skylight [skaiˈlait] n 天窓 teñmado

skyscraper [skaiˈskreipəːr] n 摩天楼 matéñrō

slab [slæb] n (stone) 石板 sekíbañ; (of cake, cheese) 厚い一切れ atsúi hitokìre

slack [slæk] adj (loose: rope, trousers etc) たるんでいる tarúñde irú; (slow: period) 忙しくない isógashikunaì; (careless: security, discipline) いい加減な ifkagen na

slacken [slækˈən] (also: slacken off) vi

(demand) 減る herú; (speed) 落ちる ochírù
♦vt (trousers) 緩める yurúmeru; (speed) 緩めるyurúmerù, 落とすotósù

slacks [slæks] npl ズボン zubón, スラックス surákkùsu

slag heap [slæg-] n ぼた山 botáyama

slag off [BRIT: inf] vt (criticize) …の悪口を言う …no warúgùchi wo iú

slain [slein] pp of slay

slalom [slɑːˈlʌm] n 回転競技 kaítenkyōgi, スラローム surárōmu

slam [slæm] vt (door) ばたんと閉める batán to shimérù; (throw) 投げつける nagétsukerù; (criticize) 非難する hínàn suru
♦vi (door) ばたんと閉まる batán to shimárù

slander [slænˈdəːr] n 中傷 chūshō

slang [slæŋ] n (informal language) 俗語 zokúgo, スラング suráŋgu; (jargon: prison slang etc) 符丁 fuchō

slant [slænt] n (sloping: position) 傾斜 keísha; (fig: approach) 見方 mikáta

slanted [slænˈtid] adj (roof) 傾斜のある keísha no arú; (eyes) 吊り上った tsurfagattá

slanting [slænˈtiŋ] adj = slanted

slap [slæp] n (hit) 平手打ち hiráteuchi, びんた bínta
♦vt (child, face) びしゃりと打つ pishárì to útsù
♦adv (directly) まともに matómo ni
to slap something on something (paint etc) …に…を塗りつける …wo …ni tsukéru nî nurítsukerù

slapdash [slæpˈdæʃ] adj (person, work) いい加減な ifkagen na

slapstick [slæpˈstik] n (comedy) どたばた喜劇 dotábata kigéki

slap-up [slæpˈʌp] adj: *a slap-up meal* [BRIT] 御馳走 gochísō

slash [slæʃ] vt (cut: upholstery, wrists etc) 切る kírù 特に長くて深い切傷を付けるという意味で tókù ni nágàkute fukáì kirfkizu wo tsukérù to iú imí de tsukáù; (fig: prices) 下げる sagérù

slat [slæt] n (of wood, plastic) 板 ítà 百葉箱に使われる様な薄くて細い板を指す

hyakúyōbàko ni tsukáwareru yō na usúkùte hosóì ítà wo sásù

slate [sleit] n (material) 粘板岩 nefibangan; (piece: for roof) スレート surétò
♦vt (criticize) けなす kenásù

slaughter [slɔːˈtəːr] n (of animals) と殺 tosátsu; (of people) 虐殺 gyakúsatsu
♦vt (animals) と殺する tosátsu suru; (people) 虐殺する gyakúsatsu suru

slaughterhouse [slɔːˈtəːrhaus] n と殺場 tosátsujō

Slav [slɑːv] adj スラブ民族の surábumìnzoku no

slave [sleiv] n 奴隷 doréi
♦vi (also: slave away) あくせく働く ákùseku határakù

slavery [sleiˈvəːri] n (system) 奴隷制度 doréiseìdo; (condition) 奴隷の身分 doréi no mfbùn

slavish [sleiˈviʃ] adj (obedience) 卑屈な hikútsu na; (copy) 盲目的な mốmokutekī na no mfbùn

slay [slei] (pt slew, pp slain) vt 殺す korósù

sleazy [sliːˈziː] adj (place) 薄汚い usúgitanaì

sledge [sledʒ] n そり sórì

sledgehammer [sledʒˈhæməːr] n 大づち ōzúchi

sleek [sliːk] adj (shiny, smooth: hair, fur etc) つやつやした tsuyátsuyà no; (car, boat etc) 優雅な yūga na

sleep [sliːp] n 眠り nemúri
♦vi (pt, pp slept) (gen) 眠る nemúrù, 寝る nerú; (spend night) 泊まる tomárù
to go to sleep (person) 眠る nemúrù, 寝る neru

sleep around vi 色々な人とセックスをする irōiro na hito tò sékkùsu wo suru

sleeper [sliːˈpəːr] [BRIT] n (RAIL: on track) まくら木 makúragì; (: train) 寝台列車 shíñdaìressha

sleep in vi (oversleep) 寝坊する nebō suru

sleeping bag [sliːˈpiŋ-] n 寝袋 nebúkùro

sleeping car n (RAIL) 寝台車 shíñdaìsha

sleeping partner [BRIT] n (COMM)

= silent partner

sleeping pill n 睡眠薬 suímiñ-yaku

sleepless [slip'lis] adj: *a sleepless night* 眠れない夜 nemúrenai yoru

sleepwalker [slip'wɔːkəːr] n 夢遊病者 muyúbyōshà

sleepy [sli:'pi:] adj (person) 眠い nemúi; (fig: village etc) ひっそりとした hissórì to shita

sleet [sli:t] n みぞれ mizóre

sleeve [sli:v] n (of jacket etc) そで sodé; (of record) ジャケット jákètto

sleeveless [sli:v'lis] adj (garment) そでなしの sodénashi no, スリーブレスの suríburèsu no

sleigh [slei] n そり sórì

sleight [slait] n: *sleight of hand* 奇術 kíjùtsu

slender [slen'dəːr] adj (slim: figure) ほっそりした hossórì shita, スリムな surímu na; (small: means, majority) わずかな wázùka na

slept [slept] pt, pp of **sleep**

slew [slu:] vi (BRIT) = slue
♦pt of **slay**

slice [slais] n (of meat, bread, lemon) スライス surátsu; (utensil: fish slice) フライ返し furáigaeshì; (: cake slice) ケーキサーバー kḗkisàbā
♦vt (bread, meat etc) スライスする surátsu suru

slick [slik] adj (skillful: performance) 鮮やかな azáyàka na; (clever: salesman, answer) 抜け目のない nukéme no naì
♦n (also: **oil slick**) 油膜 yumáku

slid [slid] pt, pp of **slide**

slide [slaid] n (downward movement) 下落 geráku; (in playground) 滑り台 subéridai; (PHOT) スライド surátdo; (BRIT: also: **hair slide**) 髪留 kamídòme, ヘアクリップ heákurìppu
♦vb (pt, pp **slid**)
♦vt 滑らせる subéraserù
♦vi (slip) 滑る subérù; (glide) 滑る様に動く subéru yò ni ugokù

slide rule n 計算尺 kefsanjaku

sliding [slai'diŋ] adj: **sliding door** 引戸 hikídð

sliding scale n スライド制 surátdosei

slight [slait] adj (slim: figure) やせ型の yaségata no; (frail) か弱い kayówaì; (small: increase, difference) わずかな wázùka na; (error, accent, pain etc) ちょっとした chóttð shita; (trivial) ささいな sásài na
♦n (insult) 侮辱 bujóku

not in the slightest 少しも...ない sukóshì mo ...naì

slightly [slait'li:] adv (a bit, rather) 少し sukóshì

slim [slim] adj (person, figure) ほっそりした hossórì shita; (chance) わずかな wázùka na
♦vi (lose weight) やせる yaserù

slime [slaim] n ぬるぬるした物 núrùnuru shita monð

slimming [slim'iŋ] n (losing weight) そう身 sōshin

slimy [slai'mi:] adj (pond) ぬるぬるした物に覆われた núrùnuru shita monō ni ōwáretà

sling [sliŋ] n (MED) 三角きん sañkakùkin; (for baby) 子守り帯 komóriobì; (weapon) 石投げ器 ishínagekì
♦vt (pt, pp **slung**) (throw) 投げる nagérù

slip [slip] n (while walking) 踏み し fumíhazushì; (of vehicle) スリップ suríppû; (mistake) 過ち ayámachì; (underskirt) スリップ suríppû; (also: **slip of paper**) 一枚の紙 ichímai no kamí or 一枚の用紙, 伝票などの様な小さい紙を指す tsújð memóyòshi, defpyō nadò no yō na chíìsaí kamí wo sásù

♦vt (slide) こっそり...にやる kossórì ...wo ...ni yarù

♦vi (slide) 滑る subérù; (lose balance) 踏み外す fumíhazusù; (decline) 悪くなる wárùku nárù; (move smoothly): **to slip into/out of** (room etc) そっと入る (出る) sóttò hàiru (detè iku)

to give someone the slip ...をまく ...wo makû

a slip of the tongue うっかり言ってしまう事 ukkárì itté shimaù kotó

to slip something on/off さっと...を着る(脱ぐ) sáttð ...wo kírù (nugu)

slip away vi (go) そっと立ち去る sóttò tachísaru

slip in vt (put) こっそり入れる kossórì i-rérù

♦vi (errors) いつの間にか入ってしまう í-tsú no ma ni ká haîtte shimaû

slip out vi (go out) そっと出て行く sóttò détè ikú

slipped disc [slipt-] n つい間板ヘルニア tsuîkañbanherunía

slipper [slip'ə:r] n (carpet slipper) スリッパ suríppà

slippery [slip'ə:ri:] adj (road) 滑りやすい subériyasuí; (fish etc) つかみにくい tsu-káminikuí

slip road (BRIT) n (on motorway: access road) 入路 nyúro; (: exit road) 出口 deguchi

slipshod [slip'ʃɑd] adj いい加減な ífkagen na

slip up vi (make mistake) 間違いをする machígai wò suru

slip-up [slip'ʌp] n (error) 間違い machí-gaì

slipway [slip'wei] n 造船台 zósendai

slit [slit] n (cut) スリット surítto; (opening) すき間 sukíma

♦vt (pt, pp slit) 切り開く kiríhirakû

slither [slið'ə:r] vi (person) 足を取られながら歩く ashí wò toráренagara arukû; (snake etc) はう haû

sliver [sliv'ə:r] n (of glass, wood) 破片 hahén; (of cheese etc) 一切れ hitókìre

slob [slɑb] (inf) n (man) だらしない野郎 daráshinaì yaró; (woman) だらしないおんな daráshinaì ámà

slog [slɑg] (BRIT) vi (work hard) あくせく働く ákùseku határakù

♦n: it was a hard slog 苦労した kuró shità

slogan [slou'gən] n スローガン surógàn

slop [slɑp] vi (also: slop over) こぼれる kobórerù

♦vt こぼす kobósù

slope [sloup] n (gentle hill) 坂道 sakámichi; (side of mountain) 山腹 sañpuku; (ski slope) ゲレンデ geréñde; (slant) 傾斜 keísha

♦vi: to slope down 下り坂になる kudárizaka ni narù

slope up vi 上り坂になる nobórizaka ni narù

sloping [slou'piŋ] adj (ground, roof) 傾斜になっている kefsha ni natte irù; (hand-writing) 斜めの nanáme no

sloppy [slɑp'i:] adj (work, appearance) だらしない daráshinaì

slot [slɑt] n (in machine) 投入口 tónyúguchi, スロット surótto

♦vt: to slot something into ... (のスロットなど) に ...を入れる ... (no surótto nado) ni ...wo irérù

sloth [slɔθ] n (laziness) 怠惰 táìda

slot machine n (BRIT: vending machine) 自動販売機 jidóhanbaikì; (for gambling) スロットマシーン suróttomashìn

slouch [slautʃ] vi (person) だらしない姿勢で…する daráshinaì shiséi de …suru

slovenly [slʌv'ənli:] adj (dirty: habits, conditions) 汚い kitánaì; (careless: piece of work) だらしない daráshinaì

slow [slou] adj (music, journey) ゆっくりした yukkúrì shita; (service) 遅い osóì, のろい noróì; (person: not clever) 物覚えの悪い monóoboè no warúì; (watch, clock): to be slow 遅れている okúrete irù

♦adv ゆっくりと yukkúrì to, 遅く osóku

♦vt (also: slow down, slow up: vehicle) …のスピードを落す …no supídò wo otósù; (: business etc) 低迷させる teímei saserù

♦vi (also: slow down, slow up: vehicle) スピードを落す supídò wo otósù; (: business etc) 下火になる shitábì ni narù

slow (road sign) 徐行 jokó

slowly [slou'li:] adv ゆっくりと yukkúrì to, 遅く osóku

slow motion n: in slow motion スローモーションで surómòshon de

sludge [slʌdʒ] n (mud) へどろ hedóro

slue [slu:] (US vi) vi スリップする suríppù suru

slug [slʌg] n (creature) なめくじ namékujì; (bullet) 弾丸 dañgan, 鉄砲玉 teppódama

sluggish [slʌɡ'iʃ] *adj* (stream, engine, person) 緩慢な kańman na; (COMM: trading) 不活発な fukáppatsu na

sluice [slu:s] *n* (*also*: **sluicegate**) 水門 suímon; (channel) 水路 súiro

slum [slʌm] *n* (house) 汚い家 kitánaí ié; (area) 貧民街 hínmingai, スラム súràmu

slump [slʌmp] *n* (economic) 不景気 fukéiki; (COMM) スランプ suráňpu
♦*vi* (fall: person) 崩れ落ちる kuzúreochirù; (: prices) 暴落する bóraku suru

slung [slʌŋ] *pt, pp of* **sling**

slur [slə:r] *n* (*fig*): **slur (on)** (...の) 悪口 (...no) warúkuchi
♦*vt* (words) 口ごもって言う kuchígomotte iú

slush [slʌʃ] *n* (melted snow) 溶けかかった雪 tokékakattá yuki

slush fund *n* 裏金用資金 uráganeyōshikiñ

slut [slʌt] (*inf!*) *n* ずべ公 bafta

sly [slai] *adj* (smile, expression, remark) 意味ありげな imárige na; (person: clever, wily) ずるい zurúi

smack [smæk] *n* (slap) 平手打ち hiráteuchi; (on face) びんた bíñta
♦*vt* (hit: *gen*) 平手で打つ hiráte de útsū; (: child) ぶつ bútsū; (: on face) ...にびんたを食らわす ...ni bíñta wo kurawásū
♦*vi*: **to smack of** (smell of) ...くさい ...kusái; (remind one of) ...を思わせる ...wo omówaserù

small [smɔ:l] *adj* (person, object) 小さい chiísaì; (child: young) 幼い osánaì; (quantity, amount) 少しの sukóshī no

small ads (*BRIT*) *npl* 分類広告 buñruikōkoku

small change *n* 小銭 kozéni

small fry *npl* (unimportant people) 下っ端 shitáppa

smallholder [smɔ:l'houldə:r] (*BRIT*) *n* 小自作農 shōjisakunō

small hours *npl*: **in the small hours** 深夜に shíñya ni

smallpox [smɔ:l'pɑ:ks] *n* 天然痘 teńnentō

small talk *n* 世間話 sekéňbanashi

smart [smɑ:rt] *adj* (neat, tidy) きちんとした kichíñ to shitá; (fashionable: clothes etc) しゃれた sharéta, いきな ikí na, スマートな sumátō na; (: house, restaurant) しゃれた sharéta, 高級な kōkyū na; (clever) 頭がいい atáma ga iì; (quick) 早い hayáì
♦*vi* しみる shimírù; (*fig*) 悔しがる kuyáshigarù

smarten up [smɑ:r'tən-] *vi* 身なりを直す mínàri wo naósu
♦*vt* きれいにする kírèi ni suru

smash [smæʃ] *n* (collision: *also*: **smash-up**) 衝突 shōtotsu; (smash hit) 大ヒット daíhittò
♦*vt* (break) めちゃめちゃに壊す mechámecha ni kowásù; (car etc) 衝突してめちゃめちゃにする shōtotsu shite mechámecha ni suru; (SPORT: record) 破る yabúrù
♦*vi* (break) めちゃめちゃに壊れる mechámecha ni kowárerù; (against wall etc) 激突する gekítotsu suru

smashing [smæʃ'iŋ] (*inf*) *adj* 素晴らしい subárashii

smattering [smæt'əːriŋ] *n*: **a smattering of** ...をほんの少し ...wo hoñno sukoshì

smear [smi:'əːr] *n* (trace) 染み shimf; (MED) スミア sumía
♦*vt* (spread) 塗る nurú; (make dirty) 汚す yogosù

smear campaign *n* 中傷作戦 chūshōsakuseñ

smell [smel] *n* (odor) におい nióì; (sense) 臭覚 kyúkaku
♦*vb* (*pt, pp* **smelt** *or* **smelled**)
♦*vt* (become aware of odor) ...のにおいがする ...no nioi ga suru; (sniff) かぐ kagú
♦*vi* (*pej*) におう nióù, 臭い kusáì; (food etc) ...においがする ...nioi ga suru
to smell of ...のにおいがする ...no nióì ga suru

smelly [smel'i:] *adj* (cheese, socks) 臭い kusáì

smile [smail] *n* ほほえみ hohóemi
♦*vi* ほほえむ hohóemù

smirk [smə:rk] *n* にやにや笑い niyániya warái

smithy [smiθ'i:] *n* 鍛冶屋の仕事場 kajíyà no shigótobà

smock [smɑk] *n* (*gen*) 上っ張り uwáppari; (children's) スモック sumókkù; (*US*: overall) 作業着 sagyógì

smog [smɑg] *n* スモッグ sumóggù

smoke [smouk] *n* 煙 kemúri
♦*vi* (person) タバコを吸う tabáko wò súù; (chimney) 煙を出す kemúri wò dásù
♦*vt* (cigarettes) 吸う súù

smoked [smoukt] *adj* (bacon etc) 薫製の kunśei no; (glass) いぶした ibúshita

smoker [smou'kə:r] *n* (person) タバコを吸う人 tabáko wò súù hito, 喫煙者 kitsúeñsha; (RAIL) 喫煙車 kitsúeñsha

smokescreen [smouk'skri:n] *n* (*also fig*) 煙幕 éñmaku

smoking [smou'kiŋ] *n* (act) 喫煙 kitsúen
no smoking (sign) 禁煙 kiñ-en

smoky [smou'ki:] *adj* (atmosphere, room) 煙い kemúi; (taste) 薫製の(様な) kunśei no (yó na)

smolder [smoul'də:r] (*US*) *vi* (fire: *also fig*: anger, hatred) くすぶる kusúburù

smooth [smuːð] *adj* (*gen*) 滑らかな naméràka na; (sauce) つぶつぶのない tsubútsubu no nai; (flat: sea) 穏やかな odáyàka na; (flavor, whisky) まろやかな maróyàka na; (movement) 滑らかな naméràka na; (*pej*: person) 口先のうまい kuchísaki nò umái
♦*vt* (*also*: **smooth out**) skirt, piece of paper etc) ...のしわを伸ばす ...no shiwá wò nobásù; (: creases) 伸ばす nobásù; (: difficulties) 取除く torínozokù

smother [smʌð'ə:r] *vt* (fire) ...にかぶせて消す ...ni ...wo kabúsete kesù; (suffocate: person) 窒息させる chissóku saserù; (repress: emotions) 抑える osáerù

smoulder [smoul'də:r] (*BRIT*) *vi* = **smolder**

smudge [smʌdʒ] *n* 汚れ yogóre
♦*vt* 汚す yogósù

smug [smʌg] *adj* 独り善がりの hitóriyogàri no

smuggle [smʌg'əl] *vt* (diamonds etc) 密

輸する mitsúyu suru; (refugees) 密入国さ せる mitsúnyūkoku saserù

smuggler [smʌg'lə:r] *n* 密輸者 mitsúyusha

smuggling [smʌg'liŋ] *n* (traffic) 密輸 mitsúyu

smutty [smʌt'i:] *adj* (*fig*: joke, book) わ いせつな waísetsu na

snack [snæk] *n* (light meal) 軽食 keíshoku; (food) スナック sunákkù

snack bar *n* スナックバー sunákkubà, スナック店 sunákkùten

snag [snæg] *n* 障害 shógai

snail [sneil] *n* カタツムリ katátsumùri

snake [sneik] *n* ヘビ hébì

snap [snæp] *n* (sound) ぱちっという音 pachíttò iú otò; (photograph) 写真 shashín
♦*adj* (decision etc) 衝動的な shódōteki na
♦*vt* (break) 折る órù; (fingers) 鳴らす narásù
♦*vi* (break) 折れる orérù; (*fig*: person: speak sharply) 辛らつな事を言う shiráratsu na kotò wo iú
to snap shut (trap, jaws etc) がちゃっと閉まる gacháttò shimárù

snap at *vt fus* (subj: dog) かみつこうとする kamítsukoù to suru

snap off *vt* (break) 折れる orérù ◇ 折れ て取れる state で折れ取られ baái ni tsukáð

snappy [snæp'i:] (*inf*) *adj* (answer, slogan) 威勢のいい iséi no íi
make it snappy (hurry up) 早くしなさ い háyàku shinásaì

snapshot [snæp'ʃɑt] *n* 写真 shashín

snap up *vt* (bargains) 先買う súgù kaú

snare [sne:r] *n* わな wánà

snarl [snɑ:rl] *vi* (animal) うなる unárù; (person) どなる donárù

snatch [snætʃ] *n* (small piece of: conversation, song etc) 断片 dañpeñ
♦*vt* (snatch away: handbag, child etc) ひ ったくる hittákurù; (*fig*: opportunity) 利 用する riyó suru; (: look, some sleep etc)

急いでやる isóide yarú

sneak [sniːk] (*pt, pp* **sneaked** *also US* **snuck**) *vi*: **to sneak in/out** こっそり入る [出る] kossóri háiru (deru)

♦*n* (*inf*) 告げ口するひと tsugéguchi suru hitó

to sneak up on someone ...に忍び寄る ...ni shinóbiyorú

sneakers [sniːˈkəːrz] *npl* 運動靴 uñdōgutsu, スニーカー suníkā

sneer [sniːr] *vi* (laugh nastily) 冷笑する refshō suru; (mock): **to sneer at** ...をあざわらう ...wo azáwaraú

sneeze [sniːz] *n* くしゃみ kushámi

♦*vi* くしゃみをする kushámi wo suru

sniff [snif] *n* (sound) 鼻をくんくん鳴らす音 haná wo kúñkun narásù otó; (smell: by dog, person) くんくんかぐ事 kúñkun kagú kotó

♦*vi* (person: when crying etc) 鼻をくんくん鳴らす haná wo kúñkun narásù

♦*vt* (*gen*) かぐ kagú; (glue, drugs) 鼻で吸う haná dè súù

snigger [snigˈəːr] *vi* くすくす笑う kúsùkusu waráù

snip [snip] *n* (cut) はさみで切る事 hasámi dè kírù kotó; (BRIT: *inf*: bargain) 掘出し物 horídashimonoù

♦*vt* (cut) はさみで切る hasámi dè kírù

sniper [snaiˈpəːr] *n* 狙撃兵 sogékìhei

snippet [snipˈit] *n* (of information, news) 断片 dañpen

snivelling [snivˈəliŋ] *adj* (whimpering) めそめそ泣く mésòmeso naku

snob [snɑːb] *n* 俗物 zokúbutsu

snobbery [snɑːbˈəːri] *n* 俗物根性 zokúbutsukoñjō

snobbish [snɑːbˈiʃ] *adj* 俗物的な zokúbutsuteki na

snooker [snukˈəːr] *n* ビリヤード birfyādo

snoop [snuːp] *vi*: **to snoop about** こっそりのぞき回る kossóri nozókimawarù

snooty [snuːˈtiː] *adj* (person, letter, reply) 傲慢な ōhèi na

snooze [snuːz] *n* 昼寝 hirúne

♦*vi* 昼寝する hirúne suru

snore [snɔːr] *n* いびき ibíki

♦*vi* いびきをかく ibíki wo kákù

snorkel [snɔːrˈkəl] *n* (for swimming) シュノーケル shunōkeru

snort [snɔːrt] *n* 鼻を鳴らす事 haná wo narásù koto

♦*vi* (animal, person) 鼻を鳴らす haná wo narásù

snout [snaut] *n* 鼻 haná

snow [snou] *n* 雪 yukí

♦*vi* 雪が降る yukí gà fúrù

snowball [snouˈbɔːl] *n* 雪のつぶて yukí nò tsubúte

♦*vi* (*fig*: problem, campaign) どんどん大きくなる dóñdon ōkìku nárù

snowbound [snouˈbaund] *adj* (people) 雪に閉じ込められた yukí ni tojíkomeraretà; (vehicle) 雪で立ち往生した yukí dè tachíōjō shita

snowdrift [snouˈdrift] *n* 雪の吹きだまり yukí nò fukídamarī

snowdrop [snouˈdrɑːp] *n* 雪の花 yukí no hanà

snowfall [snouˈfɔːl] *n* (amount) 降雪量 kōsetsuryō; (a fall of snow) 降雪 kōsetsu

snowflake [snouˈfleik] *n* 雪のひとひら yukí nò hitóhira

snowman [snouˈmæn] (*pl* **snowmen**) *n* 雪だるま yukídaruma

snowplow [snouˈplau] (BRIT **snowplough**) *n* 除雪車 josétsusha

snowshoe [snouˈʃuː] *n* かんじき kañjiki

snowstorm [snouˈstɔːrm] *n* 吹雪 fúbùki

snub [snʌb] *vt* (person) 冷たくあしらう haná dè ashfraù

♦*n* 侮辱 bujóku

snub-nosed [snʌbˈnouzd] *adj* 鼻先の反った hanásaki nò sottá

snuck [snʌk] (US) *pt, pp* of **sneak**

snuff [snʌf] *n* かぎタバコ kagítabako

snug [snʌg] *adj* (sheltered: person, place) こじんまりした kojíñmarī shita; (person) 心地好い kokóchiyoì; (well-fitting) ぴったりした pittári shita

snuggle [snʌgˈəl] *vi*: **to snuggle up to someone** ...に体を擦り付ける ...ni karáda wo surítsukerù

KEYWORD

so [sou] *adv* **1** (thus, likewise) そう só, そ
の通り sonó tōri

so saying he walked away そう言って
彼は歩き去った sō ittè kárè wa arúkisattà

while she was so doing, he ... 彼女が
それをやっている間彼は... kánòjo ga soré wò yattè iru aìda kárè wa...

if so だとすれば dá tò suréba

*do you enjoy soccer? if so, come to
the game* フットボールが好きですか、
だったら試合を見に来て下さい futtóbō-
ru ga sukí desù ká, dáttàra shiaí wo mí
ní kitè kudasaì

I didn't do it - you did so! やったの
は私じゃない—いや、お前だ! yattá no wà
watákushi ja naì—iya, omáe dà

so do I, so am I etc 私もそうです watákushi mò sō desù

I like swimming - so do I 私は水泳が
好きです—私もそうです watákushi wà
suíei ga sukí desù—watákushi mò sō
desù

I'm still at school - so am I 私はまだ
学生です—私もそうです watákushi wà
mádà gakúseì desù—watákushi mò só
desù

I've got work to do - so has Paul 私
には仕事がありますから—ポールもそう
ですよ watákushi ni wà shigóto ga arímasu karà—pōru mo só desù yó

it's 5'o'clock - so it is! 5時です—あっ、
そうですね gójì desu -át, sō desù né

I hope so そう希望します só da tò
omóimasu

I think so そうだと思います só da tò
omóimasu

so far これまで koré madè

how do you like the book so far? こ
れまでその本はどうでしたか koré madè
sonó hoñ wa dō deshìta ka

so far I haven't had any problems
ここまでは問題はありません kokó madè
wa mońdai wà arímaseñ

2 (in comparisons etc: to such a degree)
そんなに sofína nì

so quickly (that) (...がある程) 素早
く (...ga árù hodo) subáyakù, とても素早
く (...shità no dè ...)... totémo subáyakù
(...shità no dè ...)

so big (that) (...がある程) 大きな
(...ga árù hodo) ókina, とても大きい(の
で...) totémo ōkii (nó dè ...)

she's not so clever as her brother 彼
女は兄さん程利口ではない kánòjo wa
nífsañ hodo ríkò de wa naì

we were so worried 私たちはとても心
配していました watákushitàchi wa totémo shiñpaì shite imashìta yó

I wish you weren't so clumsy あなた
の不器用さはどうにかなりませんか a-
nátà no bukíyòsa wa dō ni ka narímaseñ
kà né

I'm so glad to see you あなたを見てほ
っとしました anátà wo mítè hóttò shimáshìta

3: so much *adv* そんなに沢山で sofína nì
takúsañ de

◆*adj* そんなに沢山の sofína nì takúsañ
de

I've got so much work 私は仕事が山程
あります watákushi wà shigóto ga yamá
hodò arímasù

I love you so much あなたを心から愛
しています anátà wo kokórò kara áì
shite imasu

so many そんなに沢山 (の) sofína nì
takúsañ (no)

there are so many things to do する事
が山程あります surú kotò ga yamá
hodò arímasù

there are so many people to meet 私
が会うべき人たちは余りにも大勢で
watákushi gà áùbeki hitótàchi wa amári ní mò ōzeì desù **4** (phrases): *10 or so*
10個ぐらい jùkkó gurai

so long! (*inf*: goodbye) じゃねじゃ ně, ま
たね matá ně

◆*conj* **1** (expressing purpose): *so as to
do* ...する様(ため)に ...surú yò(tamé)ni

we hurried so as not to be late 遅れ
ない様に急いで行きました okúrenai yò
ni isódè ikímashìta

so (that) ...する様(ため)に ...surú yò

(tame)ni

I brought it so (that) you could see it あなたに見せるために持ってきました anàta ni misérù tame ni motté kimashìta

2 (expressing result): ...の場合から……の で……の で……no dé ...

he didn't arrive so I left 結局彼は来なかったので私は帰りました kárè ga kónakatta nó de watákushi wà kaérimashìta

so I was right after all 結局私の言った通りでした kekkyókù watákushi nó ittá tòri deshita

so you see, I could have gone ですからね、行こうと思えば行けたんです desù kara né, ikố tò omóebà ikétan desù

---

soak [souk] *vt* (drench) ずぶぬれにする zubúnure ni suru; (steep in water) 水に漬ける mizú ni tsukérù

♦*vi* (dirty washing, dishes) 漬かる tsukárù

soak in *vi* (be absorbed) 染み込む shimíkomu

soak up *vt* (absorb) 吸収する kyúshū surù

soap [soup] *n* 石けん sekkén

soapflakes [soup'fleiks] *npl* フレーク石けん furékusekkén ◊(洗濯用の固形石けんをフレークにした物を指す sentakuyô no kokéisekkèn wo furékù ni shità monò wo sásù

soap opera *n* メロドラマ meródorama ◊(テレビやラジオの連続物を指す térèbi ya rájiò no renzokumonō wo sásù

soap powder *n* 粉石けん konásekkén

soapy [sou'pi:] *adj* (hands etc) 石けんのついた sekkén no tsuità

soapy water 石けん水 sekkénsui

soar [sɔːr] *vi* (on wings) 舞上がる mañagarù; (rocket) 空中に上がる kúchū ni agarù; (price, production, temperature) 急上昇する kyújōshō suru; (building etc) そびえたつ sobétatsù

sob [sɑːb] *n* しゃくり泣き shakúrinaki

♦*vi* 泣きじゃくる nakíjakurù

sober [sou'bəːr] *adj* (serious) まじめな majíme na; (dull: color, style) 地味なji-

mí na; (not drunk) しらふの shfráfu no

sober up *vt* ...の酔いを覚ます ...no yoí wò samásù

♦*vi* 酔いが覚める yoí gà samérù

so-called [sou'kɔːld'] *adj* (friend, expert) いわゆる iwáyurù ◊(多くの場合不信を軽べつなどを表す ōku no baí fushìn ya kefbetsu nadò wo aráwasù

soccer [sɑːk'əːr] *n* サッカー sákkā

sociable [sou'ʃəbəl] *adj* 愛想の良い aísō no yoí

social [sou'ʃəl] *adj* (gen: history, structure, background) 社会の shakái no; (leisure: event, visit) 社交的な shakóteki na; (sociable: animal) 社会性のある shakái-sei no arù

♦*n* (party) 懇親会 konshínkai

social club *n* 社交クラブ shakókuràbu

socialism [sou'ʃəlizəm] *n* 社会主義 sha-káishugì

socialist [sou'ʃəlist] *adj* 社会主義の sha-káishugì no

♦*n* 社会主義者 shakáishugìsha

socialize [sou'ʃəlaiz] *vi*: **to socialize (with)** (...と) 交際する (...to) kōsai surù

socially [sou'ʃəli:] *adv* (visit) 社交的に shakóteki ni; (acceptable) 社会的に sha-káiteki ni

social security (BRIT) *n* 社会保障 sha-káihoshō

social work *n* ソーシャルワーク sōsharuwākù

social worker *n* ソーシャルワーカー sōsharuwākā

society [səsai'əti:] *n* (people, their lifestyle) 社会 shakái; (club) 会 káì; (also: **high society**) 上流社会 jōryūshakai

sociologist [sousi:ɑːl'ədʒist] *n* 社会学者 shakáigakùsha

sociology [sousi:ɑːl'ədʒi:] *n* 社会学 sha-káigakù

sock [sɑːk] *n* 靴下 kutsúshita

socket [sɑːk'it] *n* (gen: cavity) 受け口 u-kégūchi; (ANAT: of eye) 眼 gáñka; (ELEC: for light bulb) ソケット sokéttò; (BRIT: ELEC: wall socket) コンセント kóñsento

sod [sɔd] *n* (of earth) 草の生えた土 kusá nò háḗta tsuchí; (*BRIT: inf!*) くそ kusó

soda [sou'də] *n* (CHEM) ナトリウム化合物 nátóriùmu kagóbutsu の一般にか性ソーダ, 重曹などを指す ippán nì kaséisóda, jūsó nadò wo sásù; (*also:* **soda water**) ソーダ水 sốdàsui; (*US: also:* **soda pop**) 清涼飲料 sefryóinryó

sodden [sɔd'ən] *adj* びしょぬれの bishónure no

sodium [sou'di:əm] *n* ナトリウム nátóriùmu

sofa [sou'fə] *n* ソファー sốfầ

soft [sɔft] *adj* (not hard) 柔らかい yawárakaì; (gentle, not loud: voice, music) 静かな shízùka na; (not bright: light, color) 柔らかな yawárakà na; (kind: heart, approach) 優しい yasáshiì

soft drink *n* 清涼飲料水 sefryóinryósui

soften [sɔf'ən] *vt* (gen: make soft) 柔らかくする yawárakaku suru; (effect, blow, expression) 和らげる yawáragerù
♦*vi* (gen: become soft) 柔らかくなる yawárakaku narù; (voice, expression) 優しくなる yasáshiku narù

softly [sɔft'li:] *adv* (gently) 優しく yasáshiku; (quietly) 静かに shízùka ni

softness [sɔft'nis] *n* (gen) 柔らかさ yawárakasa; (gentleness) 優しさ yasáshisa

soft spot *n*: **to have a soft spot for someone** ...が大好きである ...ga dáìsukì de árù

software [sɔft'we:r] *n* (COMPUT) ソフトウエア sofútoueà

soggy [sɑg'i:] *adj* (ground, sandwiches etc) ぐちゃぐちゃの guchágucha no

soil [sɔil] *n* (earth) 土 tsuchí, 土壌 dójò; (territory) 土地 tóchì
♦*vt* 汚す yogósù

solace [sɑl'is] *n* 慰め nagúsame

solar [sou'lər] *adj* (eclipse, power etc) 太陽の táiyò no

sold [sould] *pt, pp* of **sell**

solder [sɑd'ər] *vt* はんだ付けにする hañdazuke nì suru
♦*n* はんだ hañda

soldier [soul'dʒər] *n* (in army) 兵隊 heítai; (not a civilian) 軍人 guñjin

sold out *adj* (COMM: goods, tickets, concert etc) 売切れの urſkire de

sole [soul] *n* (of foot) 足の裏 ashí nò urá; (of shoe) 靴の底 kutsú nò sokó; (fish: *pl inv*) シタビラメ shitábìrame
♦*adj* (unique) 唯一の yuíitsu no

solely [soul'li:] *adv* ...だけ ...dáke

solemn [sɑl'əm] *adj* (person) 謹厳な kíñgen na; (music) 荘厳な sốgon na; (promise) 真剣な shíñken na

sole trader *n* (COMM) 自営業者 jiéigyōshà

solicit [səlis'it] *vt* (request) 求める motómerù
♦*vi* (prostitute) 客引きする kyakúbiki suru

solicitor [səlis'itər] *n* (*BRIT*) (for wills etc, in court) 弁護士 beñgoshì

solid [sɑl'id] *adj* (not hollow) 中空でない chū́kū de naì; (not liquid) 固形の kokéi no; (reliable: person, foundations etc) しっかりした shikkárì shita; (entire) まる...まる..; (pure: gold etc) 純粋の juñsui no
♦*n* (solid object) 固体 kotái

solidarity [sɑlidær'iti:] *n* 団結 dañketsu

solidify [səlid'əfai] *vi* (fat etc) 固まる katámarù

solids [sɑl'idz] *npl* (food) 固形食 kokéishòku

solitaire [sɑl'iter] *n* (gem) 一つはめの宝石 hitótsuhame nò hốsekì; (game) 一人遊び hitóriasobì

solitary [sɑl'iteri:] *adj* (person, animal, life) 単独の tañdoku no; (alone: walk) 一人だけでする hitórì dake dè suru; (isolated) 人気のない hitóke no naì; (single: person) 一人だけの hitórì dake no; (: animal, object) 一つだけの hitótsu dake nò

solitary confinement *n* 独房監禁 dokúbō kañkin

solo [sou'lou] *n* (piece of music, performance) 独奏 dokúsō
♦*adv* (fly) 単独で tañdoku de

soloist [sou'louist] *n* 独奏者 dokúsòsha

soluble [sɑl'jəbəl] *adj* (aspirin etc) 溶ける tokérù

solution [səluːʃən] *n* (of puzzle, problem, mystery: answer) 解決 kaiketsu; (liquid) 溶液 yōeki

solve [sɑːlv] *vt* (puzzle, problem, mystery) 解決する kaiketsu suru

solvent [sɑːlvənt] *adj* (COMM) 支払い能力のある shiharainíyoku no aru
♦*n* (CHEM) 溶剤 yōzai

somber [sɑːmbəːr] (*BRIT* **sombre**) *adj* (dark: color, place) 暗い kuráì; (serious: person, view) 陰気な ińki na

---

KEYWORD

some [sʌm] *adj* 1 (a certain amount or number of) 幾らかの fkúraka no, 幾つかの fkútsuka no, 少しの sukóshī no

some tea/water/biscuits お茶〔水, ビスケット〕o-chá(mizú, bisúkettò) ◊この用法では日本語で表現しない場合が多い konó yōhō de wa nihóngo de hyōgen shināī baáì gā ōì

some children came 何人かの子供が来た nánninka no kodómo ga kitá

there's some milk in the fridge 冷蔵庫にミルクがあります refzōko ni mírūku ga arímasu

he asked me some questions 彼は色々な事で質問した kárè wa iróiro na kotō wo kikímashìta

there were some people outside 数人の人が外に立っていた sūnìn no hitó gà sotó ni tatté ità

I've got some money, but not much 金はあるにはありますが，少しだけです kané wà árù ni wa arímasu gã, sukóshī dake désù

2 (certain: in contrasts) ある árù

some people say that ... ...と言っている人います ...tò ittê irú hitô gã imásù

some people hate fish, while others love it 魚の嫌いな人もいれば好きな人もいます sakána no kiráì na hitó mo iréba daísukì na hitó mo imásù

some films were excellent, but most were mediocre 大半は平凡な物だったが，すぐれた映画もあった taíhan wa heíbon na monó dattá gà, súgureta eìga mo attá

3 (unspecified) 何かの nánika no, だれかの dárèka no

some woman was asking for you だれか女の人があなたを訪ねていました dárèka ofina no hitó gà anátà wo tazúnete imashīta yó

he was looking for some book (or other) 彼は何かの本を探していました kárè wa nánìka no hôn wo sagáshìte imashíta

some day いつか ítsùka, そのうち sonó uchì

we'll meet again some day そのうちまた会うチャンスがあるでしょう sonó uchì mata mata chánsu ga árù deshō

shall we meet some day next week? 来週のいつかに会いましょうか raíshū nò ítsùka ni amashô ká

♦*pron* 1 (a certain number) 幾つか fkútsuka

I've got some (books etc) 私は幾つか持っています watákushi wà fkútsuka mótte imasu

some (of them) have been sold 数個は売れてしまいました sūkò wa uréte shimaimashìta

some went for a taxi and some walked タクシーを拾いに行った人, 残りの人は歩いた nấnninka wa tákùshī wo híròi ni itta gã, nokóri nò hitó wà arútta

2 (a certain amount) 幾らか ikúbun ká

I've got some (money, milk) 私は幾らか持っています watákushi wà ikúbun ká móttè imasu

some was left 少し残っていた sukóshī nokótte ità

could I have some of that cheese? そのチーズを少しもらっていいかしら sonó chízu wo sukóshī morátte ii kashlrà

I've read some of the book 本の一部を読みました sonó hoñ no ichíbù wo yomímashìta

♦*adv*: *some 10 people* 10人ぐらい jūnìn gurai

somebody [sʌmbɑːdiː] *pron* = someone

somehow [sʌmhau] *adv* (in some way)

何とかして nán to ka shite; (for some reason) どういう訳とか dó iu wáke ka

KEYWORD

someone [sʌmˈwʌn] *pron* だれか dáreka, 人 hitó
there's someone coming 人が来ます hitó ga kimásù
I saw someone in the garden だれか庭にいました dáreka niwá nì imáshìta

someplace [sʌmˈpleis] (*US*) *adv* = **somewhere**

somersault [sʌmˈəːrsɔːlt] *n* とんぼ返り toñbogaèri
♦*vi* (person, vehicle) とんぼ返りする toñbogaèri suru

KEYWORD

something [sʌmˈθiŋ] *pron* 何か nánìka
something nice 何かいい物 nánìka íi mono
something to do 何かする事 nánìka suru kotò
there's something wrong 何かおかしい nánìka okáshiì
would you like something to eat/drink? 何か食べませんか(飲みませんか) nánìka tabémaseñ(nomímaseñ) ká

sometime [sʌmˈtaim] *adv* (in future) いつか ítsùka; (in past): *sometime last month* 先月のいつか señgetsu no ítsùka

sometimes [sʌmˈtaimz] *adv* 時々 tokídokì

somewhat [sʌmˈwʌt] *adv* 少し sukóshì

KEYWORD

somewhere [sʌmˈwɛːr] *adv* (be) どこか に (で) dókòka ni(de); (go) どこかへ dókòka e
I must have lost it somewhere どこかに落した様です dókòka ni otóshìta yō desu
it's somewhere or other in Scotland スコットランドのどこかにあります sukóttoràndo no dókòka ni arímasù
somewhere else (be) どこか外の所に

(で) dókòka hoká no tokorò ní(de); (go) どこか外の所へ dókòka hoká no tokorò e

son [sʌn] *n* 息子 musúko

sonar [souˈnɑːr] *n* ソナー sónà

song [sɔːŋ] *n* (MUS) 歌 utá; (of bird) さえずり saézurì

sonic [sɑːnˈik] *adj*: *sonic boom* ソニックブーム soníkkubùmu

son-in-law [sʌnˈinlɔː] (*pl* **sons-in-law**) *n* 義理の息子 girí no musuko

sonnet [sɑːnˈit] *n* ソネット sonéttð

sonny [sʌnˈiː] (*inf*) *n* 坊や bôya

soon [suːn] *adv* (in a short time) もうすぐ mō súgù; (a short time after) 間もなく mamónàku; (early) 早く hayákù
soon afterwards それから間もなく soré karà mamónàku *see also* **as**

sooner [suːˈnɑːr] *adv* (time) もっと早く móttò hayáku; (preference): *I would sooner do that* 私はむしろあれをやりたい watákushi wà múshìro aré wò yarítai
sooner or later 遅かれ早かれ osókare hayákare

soot [sut] *n* すす susú

soothe [suːð] *vt* (calm: person, animal) 落着かせる ochítsukaserù; (reduce: pain) 和らげる yawáragerù

sophisticated [səfisˈtikeitid] *adj* (woman, lifestyle, audience) 世慣れた yonáretà; (machinery) 精巧な sefkō na; (arguments) 洗練された sefiren saréta

sophomore [sɑːfˈəmɔːr] (*US*) *n* 2 年生 nîñsei

soporific [sɑːpərifˈik] *adj* (speech) 眠気を催させる nemúke wò moyóosaserù; (drug) 睡眠の sufmin no

sopping [sɑːpˈiŋ] *adj*: *sopping (wet)* (hair, clothes etc) びしょぬれの bishónùre no

soppy [sɑːpˈiː] *adj* (*pej*) (sentimental) センチな señchi na

soprano [səprænˈou] *n* (singer) ソプラノ sopúrano

sorcerer [sɔːrˈsərər] *n* 魔法使い mahôtsukài

sordid [sɔːʳdid] adj (dirty: bed-sit etc) 汚らしい kitánarashiî; (wretched: story etc) 浅ましい asámashiî, えげつない egétsunaì

sore [sɔːʳ] adj (painful) 痛い itái
♦n (shallow) ただれ tadáre; (deep) かいよう kaíyō

sorely [sɔːʳliː] adv: **I am sorely tempted to** よほど...しようと思っている yohôdo ...shiyô to omôtte irû

sorrow [sɑːʳou] n (regret) 悲しみ kanáshimi

sorrowful [sɑːʳoufəl] adj (day, smile etc) 悲しい kanáshiî

sorrows [sɑːʳouz] npl (causes of grief) 不幸 fúkō

sorry [sɑːʳiː] adj (regretful) 残念な zañneñ na; (condition, excuse) 情けない nasákenaî

sorry! (apology) 済みません sumímaseñ
sorry? (pardon) はい? haî? ◇相手の言葉聞き取れなかった時に言う aîte no kotóba wo kikítorenakatta tokí ni iú

to feel sorry for someone ...に同情する ...ni dôjō suru

sort [sɔːʳt] n (type) 種類 shúrui
♦vt (also: **sort out**: papers, mail, belongings) より分ける yoríwakerù; (: problems) 解決する kaíketsu suru

sorting office [sɔːʳtiŋ-] n 郵便物振分け場 yúbinbutsufuriwakejō

SOS [esoues'] n エスオーエス esú ō esú

so-so [sou'sou'] adv (average) まあまあ maâmaà

soufflé [suːfleiʳ] n スフレ sufúre

sought [sɔːt] pt, pp of **seek**

soul [soul] n (spirit etc) 魂 támashiî; (person) 人 hitô

soul-destroying [soul'distrɔiŋ] adj (work) ぼけさせる様な bokésaseru yō na

soulful [soul'fəl] adj (eyes, music) 表情豊かな hyōjō yutâka na

sound [saund] adj (healthy) 健康な keñkō na; (safe, not damaged) 無傷の múkizu no; (secure: investment) 安全な añzen na; (reliable, thorough) 信頼できる shiñrai dekirù; (sensible: advice) 堅実な kefjitsu na

♦adv: **sound asleep** ぐっすり眠って gussúrí nemútte
♦n (noise) 音 otô; (volume on TV etc) 音声 oñsei; (GEO) 海峡 kafkyō
♦vt (alarm, horn) 鳴らす narásù
♦vi (alarm, horn) 鳴る narú; (fig: seem) ...の様である ...no yô de arû

to sound like ...の様に聞こえる ...no yô ni kikôerù

sound barrier n 音速障害 oñsokushōgai

sound effects npl 音響効果 oñkyōkōka

soundly [saund'liː] adv (sleep) ぐっすり gussúrí; (beat) 手ひどく tehídokû

sound out vt (person, opinion) 打診する dashín suru

soundproof [saund'pruːf] adj (room etc) 防音の bôon no

soundtrack [saund'træk] n (of film) サウンドトラック saúndotorakkû

soup [suːp] n スープ sûpu
in the soup (fig) 困って komátte

soup plate n スープ皿 sûpuzara

soupspoon [suːp'spuːn] n スープスプーン sûpusupûn

sour [sau'əʳ] adj (bitter) 酸っぱい suppáî; (milk) 酸っぱくなった suppákù nátta; (fig: bad-tempered) 機嫌の悪い kigén no waruî

it's sour grapes (fig) 負け惜しみだ makéoshimi da

source [sɔːʳs] n (also fig) 源 minámoto

south [sauθ] n 南 minámi
♦adj 南の minámi no
♦adv (movement) 南へ minámi e; (position) 南に minámi ni

South Africa n 南アフリカ minámi afúrika

South African adj 南アフリカの minámi afûrika no
♦n 南アフリカ人 minámi afurikajîn

South America n 南米 nañbei

South American adj 南米の nañbei nô
♦n 南米人 nañbeijiñ

south-east n 南東 nañtō

southerly [sʌð'əʳliː] adj (to/towards the south: aspect) 南への minámi e nò; (from the south: wind) 南からの minámi kara nō

southern [sʌð'ɔːrn] *adj* (in or from the south of region) 南 の mínami no; (to/towards the south) 南向きの mínamimuki no

the southern hemisphere 南半球 mínamihánkyū

South Pole *n* 南極 nañkyoku

southward(s) [sauθ'wɔːrd(z)] *adv* 南 へ mínami e

south-west [sauθwest'] *n* 南西 nañsei

souvenir [suːvəniːr'] *n* (memento) 記念品 kíneñhin

sovereign [sɑːv'rin] *n* (ruler) 君主 kúñshu

sovereignty [sɑːv'rɑːnti:] *n* 主権 shukéñ

soviet [souʲviːit] *adj* ソビエトの sobfetó no

the Soviet Union ソ連 sórèn

sow[1] [sau] *n* (pig) 牝豚 mesúbutà

sow[2] [sou] (*pt* **sowed**, *pp* **sown**) *vt* (*gen: seeds*) 蒔く mákû; (*fig: spread: suspicion etc*) 広める hírómerù

soy [sɔi] (*BRIT* **soya**) *n*: *soy bean* 大豆 dáîzu

soy sauce しょう油 shôyû

spa [spɑː] *n* (*also: spa town*) 鉱泉町 kôseñmachi; (*US: also: health spa*) ヘルスセンター herfususeñtā

space [speis] *n* (gap) すき間 sukíma, ギャップ gyáppù; (place) 空所 kúsho, 余白 yoháku; (room) 空間 kúkàn; (beyond Earth) 宇宙 空間 uchúkūkan, スペース supêsu; (interval, period) 間 má

◆*cpd* 宇宙... úchû...

◆*vt* (*also: space out*): text, visits, payments) 間隔を置く kañkaku wo okû

spacecraft [speis'kræft] *n* 宇宙船 uchúsen

spaceman [speis'mæn] (*pl* **spacemen**) *n* 宇宙飛行士 uchûhikôshi

spaceship [speis'ʃip] *n* = **spacecraft**

spacewoman [speis'wumən] (*pl* **spacewomen**) *n* 女性宇宙飛行士 joséi uchûhikôshi

spacing [speis'siŋ] *n* (between words) スペース supêsu

spacious [speiʲʃəs] *adj* (car, room etc) 広

い hírôi

spade [speid] *n* (tool) スコップ sukóppù; (child's) おもちゃのスコップ omóchà no sukóppù

spades [speidz] *npl* (CARDS: suit) スペード supêdo

spaghetti [spəget'iː] *n* スパゲッティ supágettî

Spain [spein] *n* スペイン supéîn

span [spæn] *n* (of bird, plane) 翼長 yokúchô; (of arch) スパン supáñ; (in time) 期間 kikáñ

◆*vt* (river) ...にまたがる ...ni matágarù; (*fig: time*) ...に渡る ...ni watárù

Spaniard [spæn'jɔːrd] *n* スペイン人 supéîñjîn

spaniel [spæn'jəl] *n* スパニエル supánièru

Spanish [spæn'iʃ] *adj* スペインの supéîn no; (LING) スペイン語の supéîngo no

◆*n* (LING) スペイン語 supéîngo

◆*npl: the Spanish* スペイン人 supéîñjîn

◇総称 sôshô

spank [spæŋk] *vt* (someone, someone's bottom) ...のしりをたたく ...no shirf wo tatákù

spanner [spæn'ɔːr] (*BRIT*) *n* スパナ supánà

spar [spɑːr] *n* (pole) マスト másùto

◆*vi* (BOXING) スパーリングする supárìngu suru

spare [speːr] *adj* (free) 空きの akí no; (surplus) 余った amáttà

◆*n* = **spare part**

◆*vt* (do without: trouble etc) ...なしで済ます ...náshî de sumásù; (make available) 与える atáerù; (refrain from hurting: person, city etc) ...を許してやる tasúkete yarù

to spare (surplus: time, money) 余った amáttà

spare part *n* 交換用部品 kôkan-yôbuhìn

spare time *n* 余暇 yôka

spare wheel *n* (AUT) スペアタイヤ spéataià

sparing [speːr'iŋ] *adj: to be sparing with* ...を倹約する ...wo keñ-yaku suru

sparingly [speːr'iŋliː] *adv* (use) 控え目に

hikáeme ni

spark [spɑːrk] n 火花 híbana, スパーク supákù; (fig: of wit etc) ひらめき hirámekì

spark(ing) plug [spɑːrk'(iŋ)-] n スパークプラグ supákupuràgu

sparkle [spɑːr'kəl] n きらめき kirámekì
♦vi (shine: diamonds, water) きらめく kirámekù

sparkling [spɑːr'kliŋ] adj (wine) 泡立つ awádatsù; (conversation, performance) きらめくような kirámeku yǒ na

sparrow [spær'ou] n スズメ suzúme

sparse [spɑːrs] adj (rainfall, hair, population) 少ない sukúnaì

spartan [spɑːr'tən] adj (fig) 簡素な kánso na

spasm [spæz'əm] n (MED) けいれん keíren

spasmodic [spæzmɑːd'ik] adj (fig: not continuous, irregular) 不規則な fukísoku na

spastic [spæs'tik] n 脳性麻痺患者 nóseimahikañja

spat [spæt] pt, pp of spit

spate [speit] n (fig): a spate of (letters, protests etc) 沢山の takúsañ no

spatter [spæt'əːr] vt (liquid, surface) ...にはねかす ...ni hanékasù

spatula [spætʃ'ələ] n (CULIN, MED) へら hérà

spawn [spɔːn] vi (fish etc) 産卵する sañran suru
♦n (frog spawn etc) 卵 tamágo

speak [spiːk] (pt spoke, pp spoken) vt (language) 話す hanásù; (truth) 言う iú
♦vi (use voice) 話す hanásù; (make a speech) 演説する eñzetsu suru
to speak to someone ...に話し掛ける ...ni hanáshikakerù
to speak to someone of/about something ...に...のことを話す ...ni ...no kotó wò hanásù
speak up! もっと大きな声で話しなさい móttò ǒkìna kóè de hanáshi nasaì

speaker [spiː'kəːr] n (in public) 演説者 eñzetsushà; (also: loudspeaker) スピーカー supíkà; (POL): the Speaker (US,

BRIT) 下院議長 ka-íngichò

spear [spiːr] n (weapon) やり yarí
♦vt 刺す sásù

spearhead [spiːr'hed] vt (attack etc) ...の先頭に立つ ...no señtō nī tátsù

spec [spek] (inf) n: on spec 山をかけて yamá wo kakète

special [speʃ'əl] adj 特別な tokúbetsu na
special delivery 速達 sokútatsu
special school (BRIT) 特殊学校 tokúshugakkǒ
special adviser 特別顧問 tokúbetsukomòn
special permission 特別許可 tokúbetsukyokà

specialist [speʃ'əlist] n (gen) 専門家 señmonka; (MED) 専門医 señmoñ-i

speciality [speʃiːæl'əti:] n = specialty

specialize [speʃ'əlaiz] vi: to specialize (in) (...を) 専門的にする (...wo) señmonteki ni yarú

specially [speʃ'əli:] adv (especially) 特に tókù ni; (on purpose) 特別に tokúbetsu ni

specialty [speʃ'əlti:] n (dish) 名物 mèfbutsu; (study) 専門 señmon

species [spiː'jiːz] n inv 種属 shú

specific [spisif'ik] adj (fixed) 特定の tokútei no; (exact) 正確な sefkaku na

specifically [spisif'ikli:] adv (especially) 特に tókù ni; (exactly) 明確な mefkaku ni

specification [spesəfəkei'ʃən] n (TECH) 仕様 shíyò; (requirement) 条件 jókeñ

specifications · [spesəfəkei'ʃənz] npl (TECH) 仕様 shíyò

specify [spes'əfai] vt (time, place, color etc) 指定する shitéi suru

specimen [spes'əmən] n (single example) 見本 mihón; (sample for testing, also MED) 標本 hyóhon

speck [spek] n (of dirt, dust etc) 粒 tsúbù

speckled [spek'əld] adj (hen, eggs) 点々模様の teñtéñmoyò no

specs [speks] (inf) npl 眼鏡 mégane

spectacle [spek'təkəl] n (scene) 光景 kǒkei; (grand event) スペクタクル supékùtakuru

spectacles [spek'tæklz] *npl* 眼 鏡 mégane

spectacular [spektæk'jəlɑ:r] *adj* (dramatic) 劇的な gekíteki na; (success) 目覚しい mezámashii

spectator [spek'teitər] *n* 観客 kańkyaku

specter [spek'tə:r] (*US*) *n* (ghost) 幽霊 yûrei

spectra [spek'trə] *npl of* spectrum

spectre [spek'tə:r] (*BRIT*) = specter

spectrum [spek'trəm] (*pl* **spectra**) *n* (color/radio wave spectrum) スペクトル supékutoru

speculate [spek'jəleit] *vi* (FINANCE) 投機をする tôki wo suru; (try to guess): **to speculate about** …についてあれこれと憶測する …ni tsúite arékore to okúsoku suru

speculation [spekjəlei'ʃən] *n* (FINANCE) 投機 tôki; (guesswork) 憶測 okúsoku

speech [spi:tʃ] *n* (faculty) 話す能力 hanásu nôryoku; (spoken language) 話し言葉 hanáshikotóba; (formal talk) 演説 eńzetsu, スピーチ supíchi; (THEATER) せりふ serífù

speechless [spi:tʃ'lis] *adj* (be, remain etc) 声も出ない kôe mo denái

speed [spi:d] *n* (rate, fast travel) 速度 sôkùdo, スピード supíido; (haste) 急ぎ isógi; (promptness) 素早さ subáyasa

at full/top speed 全速力で zeńsokuryòku de

speed boat *n* モーターボート môtàboto

speedily [spi:'dili:] *adv* 素早く subáyakù

speeding [spi:'diŋ] *n* (AUT) スピード違反 supíido-ihàn

speed limit *n* 速度制限 sokúdoseigen

speedometer [spidɑm'itə:r] *n* 速度計 sokúdokei

speed up *vi* (*also fig*) 速度を増す sôkùdo wo masú

◆*vt* (*also fig*) …の速度を増す …no sôkùdo wo masú, 速める hayámeru

speedway [spi:d'wei] *n* (sport) オートレース ôtoresu

speedy [spi:'di:] *adj* (fast: car) スピードの出る supíido no dérù; (prompt: reply,

recovery, settlement) 速い hayáì

spell [spel] *n* (*also*: **magic spell**) 魔法 mahô; (period of time) 期間 kikán

◆*vt* (*pt, pp* **spelled** *or* (*Brit*) **spelt**) (*also*: **spell out**) …のつづりを言う …no tsuzúri wo iú; (*fig*: advantages, difficulties) …の兆しである …no kizáshi de arù

to cast a spell on someone 彼に魔法を掛ける …ni mahô wo kakérù

he can't spell 彼はスペルが苦手だ kárè wa supéru ga nigáte dà

spellbound [spel'baund] *adj* (audience etc) 魅せられた miséraretà

spelling [spel'iŋ] *n* つづり tsuzúri, スペリング supéringu

spend [spend] (*pt, pp* **spent**) *vt* (money) 使う tsukáu; (time, life) 過ごす sugósu

spendthrift [spend'θrift] *n* 浪費家 rôhìka

spent [spent] *pt, pp of* spend

sperm [spə:rm] *n* 精子 sêìshi

sphere [sfi:r] *n* (round object) 球 kyû; (area) 範囲 hán-i

spherical [sfer'ikəl] *adj* (round) 丸い marúì

sphinx [sfiŋks] *n* スフィンクス suffíkusu

spice [spais] *n* 香辛料 kôshìnryo, スパイス supâìsu

◆*vt* (food) …にスパイスを入れる …ni supâìsu wo irérù

spick-and-span [spik'ænspæn] *adj* きちんとされている kichín to kiréi na

spicy [spai'si:] *adj* (food) スパイスの利いた supâìsu no kîtà

spider [spai'də:r] *n* クモ kúmò

spike [spaik] *n* (point) くい kuî; (BOT) 穂 hó

spill [spil] (*pt, pp* **spilt** *or* **spilled**) *vt* (liquid) こぼす kobôsù

◆*vi* (liquid) こぼれる kobôrerù

spill over *vi* (liquid: *also fig*) あふれる afúrerù

spin [spin] *n* (in car) ドライブ doráibu; (AVIAT) きりもみ kirímomi; (on ball) スピン supín

◆*vb* (*pt, pp* **spun**)

◆vt (wool etc) 紡ぐ tsumúgù; (ball, coin) 回転させる kaiten saserú

◆vi (make thread) 紡ぐ tsumúgù; (person, head) 目が回る mé gà mawárù

spinach [spin'itʃ] n (plant, food) ホウレンソウ hőrefisō

spinal [spai'nəl] adj (injury etc) 背骨の sebőne no

spinal cord n せき髄 sekízùi

spindly [spin'li:] adj (legs, trees etc) か細い kabósoi

spin-dryer [spindrai'əːr] (BRIT) n 脱水機 dassúikì

spine [spain] n (ANAT) 背骨 sebőne; (thorn: of plant, hedgehog etc) とげ togé

spineless [spain'lis] adj (fig) 意気地なしの ikújinàshi no

spinning [spin'iŋ] n (art) 紡績 bőseki

spinning top n こま kómà

spinning wheel n 紡ぎ車 tsumúgigurùma

spin-off [spin'ɔːf] n (fig: by-product) 副産物 fukúsañbutsu

spin out vt (talk, job, money, holiday) 引延ばす hikínobasù

spinster [spin'stəːr] n オールドミス őrudomisù

spiral [spai'rəl] n ら旋形 rasénkei

◆vi (fig: prices etc) うなぎ登りに上る unáginobòri ni nobórù

spiral staircase n ら旋階段 rasénkaidàn

spire [spai'əːr] n せん塔 sefitō

spirit [spir'it] n (soul) 魂 támàshii; (ghost) 幽霊 yűrei; (energy) 元気 géñki; (courage) 勇気 yűki; (frame of mind) 気分 kibùn; (sense) 精神 seíshiñ

in good spirits 気分上々で kíbun jōjō de

spirited [spir'itid] adj (performance, retort, defense) 精力的な seíryokuteki na

spirit level n 水準器 suíjuñki

spirits [spir'its] npl (drink) 蒸留酒 jōryūshu

spiritual [spir'itʃuəl] adj (of the spirit: home, welfare, needs) 精神的な seíshinteki na; (religious: affairs) 霊的な reíteki

na

◆n (also: **Negro spiritual**) 黒人霊歌 kokújinreìka

spit [spit] n (for roasting) 焼きぐし yakígushi; (saliva) つばき tsubáki

◆vi (pt, pp spat) (throw out saliva) つばを吐く tsubá wo hákù; (sound: fire, cooking) じゅうじゅういう jűjū iu; (rain) ぱらつく parátsukù

spite [spait] n 恨み urámi

◆vt (person) ...に意地悪をする ...ni ijíwarù wo suru

in spite of ...にもかかわらず ...ní mò kakáwarazù

spiteful [spait'fəl] adj (child, words etc) 意地悪な ijíwarù na

spittle [spit'əl] n つばき tsubáki

splash [splæʃ] n (sound) ざぶんという音 zabűñ to iú otò; (of color) 派手なはん点 hadé nà hafiten

◆vt 浴び掛ける hanékakerù

◆vi (also: **splash about**) ぴちゃぴちゃ水をはねる pichápcha mizú wò hanérù

spleen [spliːn] n (ANAT) ひ臓 hiző

splendid [splen'did] adj (excellent: idea, recovery) 素晴らしい subárashiì; (impressive: architecture, affair) 立派な rippá na

splendor [splen'dəːr] (BRIT **splendour**) n (impressiveness) 輝き kagáyakì

splendors [splen'dəːrz] npl (features) 特色 tokúshokù

splint [splint] n 副木 fukúboku

splinter [splin'təːr] n (of wood, glass) 破片 hahéñ; (in finger) とげ togé

◆vi (bone, wood, glass etc) 砕ける kudákerù

split [split] n (crack) 割れ目 waréme; (tear) 裂け目 sakéme; (fig: division) 分裂 bufíretsu; (: difference) 差異 sáì

◆vb (pt, pp split)

◆vt (divide) 割る warú, 裂く sakú; (party) 分裂させる bufíretsu saserú; (share equally: work) 手分けしてやる tewáke shite yarù; (: profits) 山分けする yamáwake suru

◆vi (divide) 割れる warérù

split up vi (couple) 別れる wakárerù;

splutter

splutter [splʌt'ər] *vi* (engine etc) ぱちぱ
ち音を立てる páchipachi otó wo tatérù;
(person) どもる domórù

spoil [spɔil] (*pt, pp* **spoilt** *or* **spoiled**) *vt*
(damage, mar) 台無しにする daínashi ni
surù; (child) 甘やかす amáyakasù

spoils [spɔilz] *npl* (loot: *also fig*) 分捕り
品 buńdorihin

spoilsport [spɔil'spɔːrt] *n* 座を白けさせ
る人ざ wo shirákesaserù hitó

spoke [spouk] *pt of* **speak**

◆*n* (of wheel) スポーク supókù

spoken [spou'kən] *pp of* **speak**

spokesman [spouks'mən] (*pl* **spokes-
men**) *n* スポークスマン supókusuman

spokeswoman [spouks'wumən] (*pl*
spokeswomen) *n* 女性報道官 joséi hōdō-
kan, 女性スポークスマン joséi supōkusu-
man

sponge [spʌndʒ] *n* (for washing with) ス
ポンジ supóñji; (*also:* **sponge cake**) スポ
ンジケーキ supóñjikèki

◆*vt* (wash) スポンジで洗う supóñji de a-
ráù

◆*vi*: **to sponge off/on someone** ...にた
かる ...ni takárù

sponge bag (*BRIT*) *n* 洗面バッグ señ-
menbaggù ◇洗面道具を入れて携帯する
バッグ señmendògu wo iréte keitai surù
baggù

sponsor [spʌn'sər] *n* (of player, event,
club, program) スポンサー supóñsa; (of
charitable event etc) 協賛者 kyōsañsha;
(for application) 保証人 hoshóñnin; (for
bill in parliament etc) 提出者 teíshutsu-
shà

◆*vt* (player, event, club, program etc)
...のスポンサーになる ...no supóñsa ni
nárù; (charitable event etc) ...の協賛者に
なる ...no kyōsañsha ni nárù; (applicant)
...の保証人になる ...no hoshóñnin ni nárù;
(proposal, bill etc) 提出する teíshutsu
surù

sponsorship [spʌn'sərʃip] *n* (financial
support) 金銭的援助 kiñsentekiènjo

spontaneous [spɑntei'niːəs] *adj* (un-
planned: gesture) 自発的な jihátsuteki
na

spooky [spuː'kiː] (*inf*) *adj* (place, atmosphere) お化けが出そうな o-bákè gà de-
sō nà

spool [spuːl] *n* (for thread) 糸巻 itómaki;
(for film, tape etc) リール rírù

spoon [spuːn] *n* さじ sajì, スプーン supúñ

spoon-feed [spuːn'fiːd] *vt* (baby, patient)
スプーンで食べさせる supúñ de tabésa-
serù; (*fig*: students etc) ...に一方的に教え
込む ...ni ippōteki nì oshíekomù

spoonful [spuːn'ful] *n* スプーン一杯分
supúñ ippáibùn

sporadic [spɔːræd'ik] *adj* (glimpses,
attacks etc) 散発的な sañpatsuteki na

sport [spɔːrt] *n* (game) スポーツ supótsu;
(person) 気さくな kisáku nà hitó

◆*vt* (wear) これみよがしに身に付ける
korémiyogàshi ni mi ni tsukérù

sporting [spɔːr'tiŋ] *adj* (event etc) スポ
ーツの supótsū no; (generous) 気前がい
い kimáe gà ǐ

to give someone a sporting chance
...にちゃんとしたチャンスを与える ...ni
chafitó shita cháñsu wo atáerù

sport jacket (*US*) *n* スポーツジャケッ
ト supōtsujakettò

sports car [spɔːrts-] *n* スポーツカーsu-
pótsukà

sports jacket (*BRIT*) *n* = **sport
jacket**

sportsman [spɔːrts'mən] (*pl* **sportsmen**)
n スポーツマン supótsumàn

sportsmanship [spɔːrts'mənʃip] *n* スポ
ーツマンシップ supótsumanshippù

sportswear [spɔːrts'weər] *n* スポーツウ
ェア supótsuueà

sportswoman [spɔːrts'wumən] (*pl*
sportswomen) *n* スポーツウーマン supó-
tsuùman

sporty [spɔːr'tiː] *adj* (good at sports) ス
ポーツ好きの supótsuzuki no

spot [spɑt] *n* (mark) 染み shimf; (on pattern, skin etc) はん点 hañten; (place) 場
所 bashó; (RADIO, TV) コーナー kōnà;
(small amount): **a spot of** 少しの sukóshī no

◆*vt* (notice: person, mistake etc) ...に気

が付く ...ni kf gà tsúkù

on the spot (in that place) 現場で genba ni; (immediately) その場で sonó ba de, 即座に sókùza ni; (in difficulty) まごまごして komáttè

spot check n 抜取り検査 nukftorikeñsa

spotless [spɑːtˈlis] adj (shirt, kitchen etc) 清潔な sefketsu na

spotlight [spɑːtˈlait] n スポットライト supóttoraito

spotted [spɑːtˈid] adj (pattern) はん点模様の hafteñmoyō no

spotty [spɑːtˈiː] adj (face, youth: with freckles) そばかすだらけの sóbàkasudaràke no; (: with pimples) にきびだらけの nikíbidaràke no

spouse [spaus] n (male/female) 配偶者 hafgúsha

spout [spaut] n (of jug) つぎ口 tsugfgùchi; (of pipe) 出口 dégùchi

♦vi (flames, water etc) 噴出す fukfdasù

sprain [sprein] n ねんざ nefza

♦vt: **to sprain one's ankle/wrist** 足首 [手首]をねんざする ashfkùbi(tékùbi)wo nefza suru

sprang [spræŋ] pt of **spring**

sprawl [sprɔːl] vi (person: lie) 寝そべる nesóberù; (: sit) だらしない格好で座る daráshìnai kakkō de suwárù; (place) 無秩序に広がる muchítsujò ni hirógarù

spray [sprei] n (small drops) 水煙 mizú-kemùri; (sea spray) しぶき shfbùki; (container: hair spray etc) スプレー supúrē; (garden spray) 噴霧器 fuñmukf; (of flowers) 小枝 koéda

♦vt (crops) 噴霧器で...に...を掛ける fuñmukí de ...ni ...wo kakérù; (crops) 消毒する shódoku suru

spread [spred] n (range, distribution) 広がり hirógari; (CULIN: for bread) スプレッド supúreddò; (inf: food) ごちそう gochísō

♦vb (pt, pp **spread**)

♦vt (lay out) 並べる naráberù; (butter) 塗る nurú; (wings, arms, sails) 広げる hirógerù; (workload, wealth) 分配する buñpai suru; (scatter) まく mákù

♦vi (disease, news) 広がる hirógarù;

(also: **spread out**: stain) 広がる hirógarù

spread-eagled [spredˈiːgəld] adj 大の字に寝た daf no jí ni netá

spread out vi (move apart) 散らばる chirábarù

spreadsheet [spredˈʃiːt] n (COMPUT) スプレッドシート supúreddoshīto

spree [spriː] n: **to go on a spree** ...にふける ...ni fukérù

sprightly [spraitˈliː] adj (old person) かくしゃくとした kakúshaku to shitá

spring [spriŋ] n (leap) 跳躍 chóyaku; (coiled metal) ばね báne; (season) 春 hárù; (of water) 泉 izúmi

♦vi (pt **sprang**, pp **sprung**) (leap) 跳ぶ tobú

in spring (season) 春に hárù ni

springboard [spriŋˈbɔːrd] n スプリングボード supúringubōdo

spring-cleaning [spriŋˈkliːˈniŋ] n 大掃除 ōsōji と春とは関係なく言う hárù to wa kañkeinakù iú

springtime [spriŋˈtaim] n 春 hárù

spring up vi (thing: appear) 現れる aráwarerù

sprinkle [spriŋˈkəl] vt (scatter: liquid) まく mákù; (: salt, sugar) 振り掛ける furfkakerù

to sprinkle water on, sprinkle with water ...に水をまく ...ni mizú wo mákù

sprinkler [spriŋˈklɔːr] n (for lawn, to put out fire) スプリンクラー supúrinkurā

sprint [sprint] n (race) 短距離競走 tañkyorikyōsō, スプリント supúriñto

♦vi (gen: run fast) 速く走る háyàku hashfrù; (SPORT) スプリントする supúriñto suru

sprinter [sprinˈtɔːr] n スプリンター supúriñtā

sprout [spraut] vi (plant, vegetable) 発芽する hatsúga suru

sprouts [sprauts] npl (also: **Brussels sprouts**) 芽キャベツ mekyábètsu

spruce [spruːs] n inv (BOT) トウヒ tőhì

♦adj (neat, smart) スマートな sumátò na

sprung [spraŋ] pp of **spring**

spry [sprai] adj (old person) かくしゃく

とした kakúshaku to shitá

spun [spʌn] *pt, pp of* **spin**

spur [spəːr] *n* 拍車 hakúsha; (*fig*) 刺激 shigéki

on the spur of the moment とっさに tossá ni

♦*vt* (*also:* **spur on**) 激励する gekírei suru

spurious [spjuːriːəs] *adj* (false: attraction) 見せ掛けの misékake no; (: argument) 間違った machígattá

spurn [spəːrn] *vt* (reject) はねつける hanétsukerú

spurt [spəːrt] *n* (of blood etc) 噴出 funshutsu; (of energy) 奮発 funpatsu

♦*vi* (blood, flame) 噴出す fukídasú

spy [spai] *n* スパイ supái

♦*vi*: **to spy on** こっそり見張る kossóri miháru

♦*vt* (see) 見付ける mitsúkerú

spying [spai'iŋ] *n* スパイ行為 supáikòi

sq. *abbr* = **square**

squabble [skwɑːb'əl] *vi* 口げんかする kuchígenka suru

squad [skwɑːd] *n* (MIL, POLICE) 班 hán; (SPORT) チーム chímu

squadron [skwɑːd'rən] *n* (MIL) 大隊 daítai

squalid [skwɑːl'id] *adj* (dirty, unpleasant: conditions) 汚らしい kitánarashíì; (sordid: story etc) えげつない egétsunaì

squall [skwɔːl] *n* (stormy wind) スコール sukóru

squalor [skwɑːl'əːr] *n* 汚い環境 kitánai kánkyō

squander [skwɑːn'dəːr] *vt* (money) 浪費 する rōhi suru; (chances) 逃す nogásù

square [skweːr] *n* (shape) 正方形 sefhōkei; (in town) 広場 híròba; (*inf*: person) 堅物 katábutsu

♦*adj* (in shape) 正方形の sefhōkei no; (*inf*: ideas, tastes) 古臭い furúkusaì

♦*vt* (arrange) …を…に一致させる …wo …ni itchí saserú; (MATH)2乗する nijō suru; (reconcile) …を…と調和させる …wo …to chōwa saserú

all square 貸し借りなし kashíkàri náshì

a square meal 十分な食事 júbùn na

shokúji

2 meters square 2メーター平方 ni métā hefhō

2 square meters 2平方メーター ni hefhō métā

squarely [skweːr'liː] *adv* (directly: fall, land etc) まともに matómo nì; (fully: confront) きっぱりと kippárì to

squash [skwɑːʃ] *n* (US: marrow etc) カボチャ kabócha; (BRIT: drink): **lemon/orange squash** レモン[オレンジ]スカッシュ remón[órènji]sukasshū; (SPORT) スカッシュ sukásshū

♦*vt* つぶす tsubúsu

squat [skwɑːt] *adj* ずんぐりした zuñgurí shita

♦*vi* (*also:* **squat down**) しゃがむ shagámu

squatter [skwɑːt'əːr] *n* 不法居住者 fuhōkyojūsha

squawk [skwɔːk] *vi* (bird) ぎゃーぎゃー 鳴く gyágyā nakú

squeak [skwiːk] *vi* (door etc) きしむ kishímù; (mouse) ちゅーちゅー鳴く chúchū nakú

squeal [skwiːl] *vi* (children) きゃーきゃー 言う kyákyā iú; (brakes etc) キーキー言う kíkī iú

squeamish [skwiː'miʃ] *adj* やたらに弱い yatára ... ni yowáì

squeeze [skwiːz] *n* (gen: of hand) 握り締め tsukámi; (ECON) 金融引締め kin-yūhíkishime

♦*vt* (gen) 絞る shibórù; (hand, arm) 握り締める nigríshimerù

squeeze out *vt* (juice etc) 絞り出す shibóridasú

squelch [skweltʃ] *vi* ぐちゃぐちゃ音を立てる gúchàgucha otó wò tatérù

squid [skwid] *n* イカ iká

squiggle [skwig'əl] *n* のたくった線 notákuttá sèn

squint [skwint] *vi* (have a squint) 斜視になる shashí de árù

♦*n* (MED) 斜視 shásht

squire [skwaiːr] *n* (BRIT) 大地主 ōjinúshi

squirm [skwəːrm] *vi* 身もだえする mimódåe suru

squirrel [skwəːˈrəl] n リス rfsù

squirt [skwəːrt] vi 噴出す fukídasù
♦vt 噴掛ける fukíkakerù

Sr abbr = senior

St abbr = saint; street

stab [stæb] n (with knife etc) ひと刺し hitósashi; (inf: try): **to have a stab at (doing) something** ...をやってみる ...wo yatté mirù
♦vt (person, body) 刺す sásù
a stab of pain 刺す様な痛み sásù yō na itámi

stability [stəbílːəti] n 安定 aftei

stabilize [steíˈblaiz] vt (prices) 安定させる aftei saserù
♦vi (prices, one's weight) 安定する aftei suru

stable [steíˈbəl] adj (prices, patient's condition) 安定した aftei shita; (marriage) 揺るぎない yurúgi naì
♦n (for horse) 馬小屋 umágoya

staccato [stəkɑːˈtou] adv スタッカート sutákkåto

stack [stæk] n (pile) ...の山 ...no yamá
♦vt (pile) 積む tsumú

stadium [steíˈdiːəm] n 競技場 kyógijò, スタジアム sutájiàmu

staff [stæf] n (work force) 職員 shokúin; (BRIT: SCOL) 教職員 kyóshokuìn
♦vt ...の職員として仕事をして働く ...no shokúin to shite határakù

stag [stæg] n 雄ジカ ójīka

stage [steidʒ] n (in theater etc) 舞台 bútài; (platform) 台 dáì; (profession): **the stage** 俳優業 haíyūgyō; (point, period) 段階 dańkai
♦vt (play) 上演する jóen suru; (demonstration) 行う okónaù
in stages 少しずつ sukóshì zutsù

stagecoach [steidʒˈkoutʃ] n 駅馬車 ekíbashà

stage manager n 舞台監督 butáikaǹtoku

stagger [stæɡˈəːr] vi よろめく yorómekù
♦vt (amaze) 仰天させる gyóten saserù; (hours, holidays) ずらす zurásù

staggering [stæɡˈəːriŋ] adj (amazing) 仰天させる gyóten saserù

stagnant [stæɡˈnənt] adj (water) よどんだ yodónda; (economy etc) 停滞した teítai shita

stagnate [stæɡˈneit] vi (economy, business, person) 停滞する teítai suru; (person) だれる darérù

stag party n スタッグパーティ sutágu-gupàti

staid [steid] adj (person, attitudes) 古めかしい furúmekashìi

stain [stein] n (mark) 染み shimf; (coloring) 着色剤 chakúshokuzaì, ステイン suteín
♦vt (mark) 汚す yogósù; (wood) ...にステインを塗る ...ni suteín wo nūrû

stained glass window [steind-] n ステンドグラスの窓 suténdogurāsu no mádò

stainless steel [steínlis-] n ステンレス suténresu

stain remover [-rimuːˈvəːr] n 染み抜き shímnuki

stair [steːr] n (step) 段 dáǹ, ステップ sutéppù

staircase [steːrˈkeis] n 階段 kaídan

stairs [steːrz] npl (flight of steps) 階段 kaídan

stairway [steːrˈwei] n = staircase

stake [steik] n (post) くい kúì; (COMM: interest) 利害関係 rigáikaǹkei; (BETTING: gen pl) 賞金 shókin
♦vt (money, life, reputation) かける kakérù
to stake a claim to ...に対する所有権を主張する ...ni taî suru shoyūken wò shuchō suru
to be at stake 危ぶまれる ayábumarerù

stalactite [stəlækˈtait] n しょう乳石 shōnyūseki

stalagmite [stəlæɡˈmait] n 石じゅん sekíjun

stale [steil] adj (bread) 固くなった katáku nattá; (food, air) 古くなった fúrùku natta; (air) よどんだ yodónda; (smell) か び臭い kabíkusaì; (beer) 気の抜けた kí nò nukétà

stalemate [steil'meit] *n* (CHESS) ステールメート sutērēmēto; (*fig*) 行き詰り ikízumari

stalk [stɔːk] *n* (of flower, fruit) 茎 kukí
♦*vt* (person, animal) ...に忍び寄る ...ni shinóbiyorù

stalk off *vi* 威張って行く ibátte ikú

stall [stɔːl] *n* (in market) 屋台 yátài; (in stable) 馬房 bábô
♦*vt* (AUT: engine, car) エンストを起す ensúto wò okósù; (*fig*: person) 引き止める hikítomerù; (: decision etc) 引延ばす hikínobasù
♦*vi* (AUT: engine, car) エンストを起す ensúto wò okósù; (*fig*) 時間稼ぎをする jikánkasegi wò suru

stallion [stæl'jən] *n* 種ウマ tanéûma

stalls [stɔːlz] *npl* (in cinema, theater) 特別席 tokúbetsusèki

stalwart [stɔːl'wərt] *adj* (worker, supporter, party member) 不動の fudô no

stamina [stæm'inə] *n* スタミナ sutámìna

stammer [stæm'əːr] *n* どもり dómòri
♦*vi* どもる dómòru

stamp [stæmp] *n* (postage stamp) 切手 kitté; (rubber stamp) スタンプ sutáñpu; (mark, *also fig*) 特徴 tokúchô
♦*vi* (*also*: stamp one's foot) 足を踏み鳴らす ashí wò fumínarasù
♦*vt* (letter) ...に切手を張る ...ni kitté wò harú; (mark) 特徴付ける tokúchōzukerù; (with rubber stamp) ...にスタンプを押す ...ni sutáñpu wo osú

stamp album *n* 切手帳 kittéchō

stamp collecting [-kəlek'tiŋ] *n* 切手収集 kittéshūshū

stampede [stæmpiːd'] *n* (of animal herd) 暴走 bôsô; (*fig*: of people) 殺到 sattó

stance [stæns] *n* (way of standing) 立っている姿勢 tatté irú shiséi; (*fig*) 姿勢 shiséi

stand [stænd] *n* (position) 構え kámàe; (for taxis) 乗場 noríba; (hall, music stand) 台 dái; (SPORT) スタンド sutáñdo; (stall) 屋台 yátài
♦*vb* (*pt, pp* **stood**)
♦*vi* (be upright) 立つ tátsù; (rise) 立ち上る tachíagarù; (remain: decision, offer) 有効である yûkō de arù; (in election etc) 立候補する rikkôho suru

♦*vt* (place: object) 立てる tatérù; (tolerate, withstand: person, thing) ...に耐える ...ni taérù; (treat, invite to) おごる ogórù
to make a stand (*fig*) 立場を執る tachíba wò tórù
to stand for parliament (*BRIT*) 議員選挙に出馬する gíiñsenkyo ni shutsúba suru

standard [stæn'dəːrd] *n* (level) 水準 suíjun; (norm, criterion) 基準 kijún; (flag) 旗 hatá
♦*adj* (normal: size etc) 標準の hyôjunteki na; (text) 権威のある kéñ-i no arú

standardize [stæn'dəːrdaiz] *vt* 規格化する kikákuka suru

standard lamp *n* フロアスタンド furóasutañdo

standard of living *n* 生活水準 seíkatsusuìjun

standards [stæn'dəːrdz] *npl* (morals) 道徳基準 dôtoku kijùn

stand by *vi* (be ready) 待機する tàiki suru
♦*vt fus* (opinion, decision) 守る mamórù; (person) ...の力になる ...no chíkàra ni narú

stand-by [stænd'bai] *n* (reserve) 非常用の物 hijôyô no monó
to be on stand-by 待機している tàiki shité irú

stand-by ticket *n* (AVIAT) キャンセル待ちの切符 kyañserumachi nò kippú

stand down *vi* (withdraw) 引下がる hikísagarù

stand for *vt fus* (signify) 意味する fmí suru; (represent) 代表する daíhyō suru; (tolerate) 容認する yônin suru

stand-in [stænd'in] *n* 代行 daíkō

stand in for *vt fus* (replace) ...の代役を務める ...no dafyaku wò tsutómerù

standing [stæn'diŋ] *adj* (on feet: ovation) 立ち上っている tachíagatte irú; (permanent: invitation) 持続の jízòku no, 継続の keízoku no

♦*n* (status) 地位 chíi

of many years' standing 数年前から続いている sūnen maè kara tsuzúíte irū

standing joke お決りの冗談 o-kímari nò jōdań

standing order (BRIT) *n* (at bank) 自動振替 jidòfurīkae ◇支払額が定額である場合に使う支払いdfralgaku ga tefgaku de arū bāaì ni tsukáū

standing room *n* 立見席 tachímisekì

stand-offish [stændɔf'iʃ] *adj* 無愛想な buàísō na

stand out *vi* (be prominent) 目立つ medátsu

standpoint [stænd'pɔint] *n* 観点 kańteń

standstill [stænd'stil] *n*: **at a stand-still** (also fig) 滞って todókōtte

to come to a standstill 止ってしまう tomátte shimaû

stand up *vi* (rise) 立ち上る tachíagarù

stand up for *vt fus* (defend) 守る mamórù

stand up to *vt fus* (withstand: also fig) ...に立向かう ...ni tachímukaù

stank [stæŋk] *pt of* **stink**

staple [stei'pəl] *n* (for papers) ホチキスの針 hóchīkisu no hárì

♦*adj* (food etc) 主要の shuyô no

♦*vt* (fasten) ホチキスで留める hóchīkisu de tomérù

stapler [stei'plə:r] *n* ホチキス hóchīkisu

star [stɑ:r] *n* (in sky) 星 hoshî; (celebrity) スター sutā

♦*vi*: **to star in** ...で主演する ...de shuèn suru

♦*vt* (THEATER, CINEMA) 主役とする shuyáku to surù

starboard [stɑ:r'bə:rd] *n* 右げん úgeñ

starch [stɑ:rtʃ] *n* (for shirts etc) のり noří; (CULIN) でんぷん defpun

stardom [stɑ:r'dəm] *n* スターの身分 sutā no míbuñ

stare [ste:r] *n* じろじろ見る事 jírðjiro mírū koto

♦*vi*: **to stare at** じろじろ見る jírðjiro mírū

starfish [stɑ:r'fiʃ] *n* ヒトデ hitode

stark [stɑ:rk] *adj* (bleak) 殺風景な sap-

pūkèi na

♦*adv*: **stark naked** 素っ裸の suppádàka no

starling [stɑ:r'liŋ] *n* ムクドリ mukúdòri

starry [stɑ:r'i:] *adj* (night, sky) 星がよく見える hoshî ga yókù míérù

starry-eyed [stɑ:r'iaid] *adj* (innocent) 天真らん漫な teńshinranman na

stars [stɑ:rz] *npl*: **the stars** (horoscope) 星占い hoshíuranaî

start [stɑ:rt] *n* (beginning) 初め hajíme; (departure) 出発 shuppátsu; (sudden movement) ぎくっとする事 gikúttō suru kotò; (advantage) リード rīdo

♦*vt* (begin) 始める hajímerù; (cause) 引起こす hikíokosù; (found: business etc) 創立する sóritsu suru; (engine) かける kakérù

♦*vi* (begin) 始まる hajímarù; (with fright) ぎくっとする gikúttō suru; (train etc) 出発する shuppátsu suru

to start doing/to do something ...を始める ...wo shiháfjimerù

starter [stɑ:r'tə:r] *n* (AUT) スターター sutātâ; (SPORT: official) スターター sutātâ; (BRIT: CULIN) 最初の料理 safsho no ryôri

starting point [stɑ:r'tiŋ-] *n* 出発点 shuppátsutèn

startle [stɑ:r'təl] *vt* 驚かす odórokasù

startling [stɑ:r'liŋ] *adj* (news etc) 驚く様な odóroku yó na

start off *vi* (begin) 始める hajímerù; (begin moving) 出発する shuppátsu suru

start up *vi* (business etc) 開業する kaígyō suru; (engine) かける kakérù; (car) 走り出す hashírídasù

♦*vt* (business etc) 創立する sóritsu suru; (engine) かける kakérù; (car) 走らせる hashíraserù

starvation [stɑ:rvei'ʃən] *n* 飢餓 kígà

starve [stɑ:rv] *vi* (inf: be very hungry) おなかがぺこぺこである onáka ga pekôpeko dè arù; (also: **starve to death**) 餓死する gáshi suru

♦*vt* (person, animal: not give food to) 飢えさせる uésaserù; (: to death) 餓死させる gáshi sasérù

state [steit] *n* (condition) 状態 jōtai; (government) 国 kuní

♦*vt* (say, declare) 明言する meígen suru

to be in a state 取乱している torímidashite irú

stately [steit'li:] *adj* (home, walk etc) 優雅な yūga na

statement [steit'mənt] *n* (declaration) 陳述 chínjutsu

States [steits] *npl*: **the States** 米国 beíkoku

statesman [steits'mən] (*pl* **statesmen**) *n* リーダー格の政治家 rídakaku nò sejíkka

static [stæt'ik] *n* (RADIO, TV) 雑音 zatsúon

♦*adj* (not moving) 静的な seíteki na

static electricity *n* 静電気 seídeñki

station [stei'ʃən] *n* (RAIL) 駅 ékì; (police station etc) 署 shó; (RADIO) 放送局 hōsōkyoku

♦*vt* (position: guards etc) 配置する háichi suru

stationary [stei'ʃəne:ri:] *adj* (vehicle) 動いていない ugóite inaí

stationer [stei'ʃənə:r] *n* 文房具屋 buñbōguya

stationer's (shop) [stei'ʃənə:rz-] *n* 文房具店 buñbōgutèn

stationery [stei'ʃəne:ri:] *n* 文房具 buñbōgu

stationmaster [stei'ʃənmæstə:r] *n* (RAIL) 駅長 ekíchō

station wagon (*US*) *n* ワゴン車 wagóñsha

statistic [stətis'tik] *n* 統計値 tōkeichì

statistical [stətis'tikəl] *adj* (evidence, techniques) 統計学の tōkeigakuteki na

statistics [stətis'tiks] *n* (science) 統計学 tōkeigaku

statue [stætʃ'u:] *n* 像 zō

stature [stætʃ'ə:r] *n* 身長 shíñchō

status [stei'təs] *n* (position) 身分 míbùn; (official classification) 資格 shikáku; (importance) 地位 chíi

the status quo 現状 geñjō

status symbol *n* ステータスシンボル sutétasushìñboru

statute [stætʃ'u:t] *n* 法律 hōritsu

statutory [stætʃ'u:tɔ:ri:] *adj* (powers, rights etc) 法定の hōtei no

staunch [stɔ:ntʃ] *adj* (ally) 忠実な chújìtsu na

stave off [steiv-] *vt* (attack, threat) 防ぐ fuségù

stay [stei] *n* (period of time) 滞在期間 taízaikikàn

♦*vi* (remain) 居残る inókorù; (with someone, as guest) 泊る tomárù; (in place: spend some time) とどまる todómarù

to stay put とどまる todómarù

to stay the night 泊る tomárù

stay behind *vi* 居残る inókorù

stay in *vi* (at home) 家にいる ié ni irú

staying power [stei'iŋ-] *n* 根気 koñki

stay on *vi* 残る nokórù

stay out *vi* (of house) 家に戻らない ié ni modóranaì

stay up *vi* (at night) 起きている ókìte irú

stead [sted] *n*: **in someone's stead** …の代りに …no kawári ni

to stand someone in good stead …の役に立つ …no yakú ni tatsù

steadfast [sted'fæst] *adj* 不動の fudō no

steadily [sted'ili:] *adv* (firmly) 着実に chakújitsu ni; (constantly) ずっと zuttó; (fixedly) じっと jittó; (walk) しっかりと shikkárì to

steady [sted'i:] *adj* (constant: job, boyfriend, speed) 決った kimátta, 変らない kawáranaì; (regular: rise in prices) 着実な chakújitsu na; (person, character) 着実な kenjitsu na; (firm: hand etc) 震えない furénaì; (calm: look, voice) 落着いた ochitsúita

♦*vt* (stabilize) 安定させる añtei saserù; (nerves) 静める shizúmerù

steak [steik] *n* (*also*: **beefsteak**) ステーキ bífusutèki; (beef, fish, pork etc) ステーキ sutéki

steal [sti:l] (*pt* **stole**, *pp* **stolen**) *vt* 盗む nusúmù

♦*vi* (thieve) 盗む nusúmù; (move secretly) こっそりと行く kossóri to ikú

stealth [stelθ] *n*: **by stealth** こっそりと kossōrî to

stealthy [stel'θi] *adj* (movements, actions) ひそやかな hisōka na

steam [sti:m] *n* (mist) 水蒸気 sujōki; (on window) 曇り kumōri
♦*vt* (CULIN) 蒸す músū
♦*vi* (give off steam) 湯気を立てる yujōki wo tatérū

steam engine *n* 蒸気機関 jōkikikan

steamer [sti:'mɑːr] *n* 汽船 kisén

steamroller [sti:m'roulɑːr] *n* ロードローラー rôdorōrā

steamship [sti:m'ʃip] *n* = steamer

steamy [sti:'mi:] *adj* (room) 湯気でもうもうの yúgē de mômô no; (window) 湯気で曇った yúgē de kumóttà; (heat, atmosphere) 蒸暑い mushíhatsuí

steel [sti:l] *n* 鋼鉄 kôtetsu
♦*adj* 鋼鉄の kôtetsu no

steelworks [sti:l'wɑːrks] *n* 製鋼所 sefkôjo

steep [sti:p] *adj* (stair, slope) 険しい kewâshii; (increase) 大幅の ôhaba na; (price) 高い takái
♦*vt* (fig: soak) 浸す hitásū

steeple [sti:'pəl] *n* 小尖塔 señtô

steeplechase [sti:'pəltʃeis] *n* 障害レース shôgairēsu

steer [stiːr] *vt* (vehicle) 運転する ufiten suru; (person) 導く michíbikū
♦*vi* (maneuver) 車を操る kurúma wò ayátsurū

steering [stiːr'iŋ] *n* (AUT) ステアリング sutéaringu

steering wheel *n* ハンドル handôru

stem [stem] *n* (of plant) 茎 kukí; (of glass) 足 ashî
♦*vt* (stop: blood, flow, advance) 止める tomérū

stem from *vt fus* (subj: condition, problem) ...に由来する ...ni yurái suru

stench [stentʃ] *n* 悪臭 akūshū

stencil [sten'səl] *n* (lettering) ステンシルで描いた文字 sutéñshiru de káita mójì; (pattern applied) ステンシル sutéñshiru
♦*vt* (letters, designs etc) ステンシルで書く sutéñshiru de kákū

stenographer [stənɑːɡ'rəfɑːr] *(US)* *n* 速記者 sokkíshà

step [step] *n* (footstep, *also fig*) 一歩 fppò; (sound) 足音 ashîoto; (of stairs) 段 dáň, ステップ sutéppù
♦*vi*: **to step forward** 前に出る maě ni dérū **to step back** 後ろに下がる ushíro ni sagárū

in/out of step (with) (...と) 歩調が合って［ずれて］(...to) hochô ga attè [zurète]

stepbrother [step'brʌðɑːr] *n* 異父［異母］兄弟 ffù[ibò]kyôdai

stepdaughter [step'dɔːtɑːr] *n* まま娘 mamámusume

step down *vi* (fig: resign) 辞任する jinîn suru

stepfather [step'fɑːðɑːr] *n* まま父 mamáchichi

stepladder [step'lædɑːr] *n* 脚立 kyatátsu

stepmother [step'mʌðɑːr] *n* まま母 mamáhaha

step on *vt fus* (something: walk on) 踏む fumú

stepping stone [step'iŋ-] *n* 飛石 tobîîshi

steps [steps] *(BRIT)* *npl* = stepladder

stepsister [step'sistɑːr] *n* 異父［異母］姉妹 ffù[ibò]shímai

stepson [step'sʌn] *n* まま息子 mamámusūko

step up *vt* (increase: efforts, pace etc) 増す masú

stereo [ster'i:ou] *n* (system) ステレオ sutéreo; (record player) レコードプレーヤー rekôdopurēyā
♦*adj* (*also*: **stereophonic**) ステレオの sutéreo no

stereotype [ster'i:ətaip] *n* 固定概念 kotéigaînen

sterile [ster'əl] *adj* (free from germs: bandage etc) 殺菌した sakkíñ shita; (barren: woman, female animal) 不妊の funîn no; (: man, male animal) 子供を作れない kodómo wo tsukūrenaì; (land) 不毛の fumô no

sterilize [ster'əlaiz] *vt* (thing, place) 殺菌する sakkíñ suru; (woman) ...に避妊手術をする ...ni hinînshujútsu wo suru

sterling [stəːˈlɪŋ] adj (silver) 純銀の juñgin no
♦n (ECON) 英国通貨 eíkokutsúka
one pound sterling 英貨1ポンド éika ichí poñdo

stern [stəːn] adj (father, warning etc) 厳しい kibíshfì
♦n (of boat) 船尾 séñbi

stethoscope [steˈθəskoup] n 聴診器 chóshiñki

stew [stuː] n シチュー shíchû
♦vt (meat, vegetables) 煮込む nikómù; (fruit) 煮る nirú

steward [stuːˈərd] n (on ship, plane, train) スチュワード suchúwàdo

stewardess [stuːˈərdis] n (especially on plane) スチュワーデス suchúwàdesu

stick [stik] n (gen: of wood) 棒 bô; (as weapon) こん棒 koñbô; (walking stick) つえ tsúè
♦vb (pt, pp stuck)
♦vt (with glue etc) 張る harú; (inf: put) 置く okú; (: tolerate) ...の最後まで我慢する ...no sáìgo made gámàn surù; (thrust): **to stick something into** ...の中へ...を突っ込む ...no nákà e ...wo tsukkómù
♦vi (become attached) くっつく kuttsúkù; (be immovable) 引っ掛かる hikkákarù; (in mind etc) 焼付く yakítsukù
a stick of dynamite ダイナマイト1本 dainamaíto ippon

sticker [stikˈər] n ステッカー sutékkà

sticking plaster [stikˈiŋ-] n ばんそうこう bañsôkô

stickler [stikˈlər] n: **to be a stickler for** ...に関してやかましい ...ni káñ shite yakámashíì

stick out vi (ears etc) 突出る tsukíderù

stick up vi (hair etc) 立つ tátsù

stick-up [stikˈʌp] (inf) n ピストル強盗 pisútoru gôtô

stick up for vt fus (person) ...の肩をもつ ...no kátà wo môtsù; (principle) 守る mamórù

sticky [stikˈiː] adj (messy: hands etc) べたべたしている betábeta shité irù; (label) 粘着の neñchaku no; (fig: situation) 厄介な yákkài na

stiff [stif] adj (hard, firm: brush) 堅い katáì; (hard: paste, egg-white) 固まった katámattà; (moving with difficulty: arms, legs, back) こわばった kowábattà; (: door, zip etc) 堅い katáì; (formal: manner, smile) 堅苦しい katágurushíì; (difficult: competition, sentence) 厳しい kibíshfì; (strong: drink, breeze) 強い tsuyóì; (high: price) 高い takáì
♦adv (bored, worried, scared) ひどく hídòku

stiffen [stifˈən] vi (body, muscles, joints) こわばる kowábarù

stiff neck n 首が回らない事 kubí gà mawáranaì kotó

stifle [staiˈfəl] vt (cry, yawn) 抑える osáerù; (opposition) 抑圧する yokúatsu suru

stifling [staiˈfliŋ] adj (heat) 息苦しい ikígurushfì

stigma [stigˈmə] n (fig: of divorce, failure, defeat etc) 汚名 oméi

stile [stail] n 踏段 fumídàn ◇ (牧場のさくの両側に設けられ、人間が越えられるが家畜が出られない様にした物) bokújō no sakú nò ryôgawa nì mōkérarè, niñgen gà koérarerù ga kachíkù ga derárenaì yô ni shitá monò

stiletto [stiletˈou] (BRIT) n (also: **stiletto heel**) ハイヒール hafhîru

still [stil] adj (person, water, air) 動かない ugókanaì; (place) 静寂な sefjaku na
♦adv (up to this time, yet) まだ mádà; (even) 更に sárà ni; (nonetheless) それにしても soré nì shite mó

stillborn [stilˈbɔːrn] adj 死産の shízàn no

still life n 静物画 seíbutsugà

stilt [stilt] n (pile) 脚柱 kyakúchû; (for walking on) 竹馬 takéuma

stilted [stilˈtid] adj (behavior, conversation) 堅苦しい katákurushfì

stimulant [stimˈjələnt] n 覚せい剤 kakúseizài

stimulate [stimˈjəleit] vt (person, demand) 刺激する shigéki suru

stimulating [stimˈjəleitiŋ] adj (conversation, person, experience) 刺激的な shigékiteki na

stimuli [stim'jəlai] *npl of* **stimulus**

stimulus [stim'jələs] (*pl* **stimuli**) *n* (encouragement, *also* MED) 刺激 shigéki

sting [stiŋ] *n* (wound) 虫刺され mushísasaré; (pain) 刺すような痛み sásù yō na itámi; (organ) 針 hárì
◆*vt* (*pt, pp* **stung**)
◆*vt* (insect, plant etc) 刺す sásù; (fig) 傷付ける kizútsukerù
◆*vi* (insect, plant etc) 刺す sásù; (eyes, ointment etc) しみる shimírù

stingy [stin'dʒi:] *adj* けちな kéchì na

stink [stiŋk] *n* (smell) 悪臭 akúshū
◆*vi* (*pt* **stank**, *pp* **stunk**) (smell) におう nióù

stinking [stiŋ'kiŋ] (*inf*) *adj* (*fig*) くそったれの kusóttare nò

stint [stint] *n* 仕事の期間 shigóto no kikàn
◆*vi*: **to stint on** (work, ingredients etc) ...をけちる ...wo kechírù

stipulate [stip'jəleit] *vt* ...の条件を付ける ...no jōken wo tsukérù

stir [stəːr] *n* (fig: agitation) 驚き sáwàgi
◆*vt* (tea etc) かき混ぜる kakímazerù; (fig: emotions) 刺激する shigéki suru
◆*vi* (move slightly) ちょっと動く chóttò ugókù

stirrup [stəːr'əp] *n* あぶみ abúmi

stir up *vt* (trouble) 引起こす hikíokosù

stitch [stitʃ] *n* (SEWING, MED) 一針 hitóhàri; (KNITTING) ステッチ sutétchī; (pain) わき腹のけいれん wakíbara nò kefren
◆*vt* (sew: gen, MED) 縫う núù

stoat [stout] *n* てん tèñ

stock [staːk] *n* (supply) 資源 shígèn; (COMM) 在庫品 zaíkohìn; (AGR) 家畜 kachíku; (CULIN) 煮出し汁 nidáshijirū, ストック sutókkù; (descent) 血統 kettō; (FINANCE: government stock etc) 株式 kabúshikìn
◆*adj* (fig: reply, excuse etc) お決りの o-kímàri no
◆*vt* (have in stock) 常備する jōbì suru

stocks and shares 債券 safken
in/out of stock 在庫がある(ない) zaf-

ko ga árù (nai)

to take stock of (fig) 検討する kefitō suru

stockbroker [staːk'broukəːr] *n* 株式仲買人 kabúshikinakagainìn

stock cube *n* 固形スープの素 kokéi sūpu no moto

stock exchange *n* 株式取引所 kabúshikitorihikijó

stocking [staːk'iŋ] *n* ストッキング sutókkìngu

stockist [staːk'ist] (BRIT) *n* 特約店 tokúyakutèn

stock market *n* 株式市場 kabúshikishijō

stock phrase *n* 決り文句 kimárimoñku

stockpile [staːk'pail] *n* 備蓄 bichíku
◆*vt* 貯蔵する chozō suru

stocktaking [staːk'teikiŋ] (BRIT) *n* (COMM) 棚卸し tanáoroshi

stock up with *vt* ...を仕入れる ...wo shiírérù

stocky [staːk'i:] *adj* (strong, short) がっしりした gasshírì shita; (short, stout) ずんぐりした zuñgurì shita

stodgy [staːdʒ'i:] *adj* (food) こってりした kottérì shita

stoical [stou'ikəl] *adj* 平然とした hefzen tò shita

stoke [stouk] *vt* (fire, furnace, boiler) ...に燃料をくべる ...ni neńryō wo kubérù

stole [stoul] *pt of* **steal**
◆*n* ストール sutōrù

stolen [stou'lən] *pp of* **steal**

stolid [staːl'id] *adj* (person, behavior) 表情の乏しい hyōjō no tobóshiì

stomach [stʌm'ək] *n* (ANAT) 胃 i; (belly) おなか onáka
◆*vt* (fig) 我慢する gámàn suru

stomachache [stʌm'əkeik] *n* 腹痛 fukútsū

stone [stoun] *n* (rock) 石 ishf; (pebble) 小石 koíshi; (gem) 宝石 hōseki; (in fruit) 種 tánè; (MED) 結石 kesséki; (BRIT: weight) ストーン sutōn ◇体重の単位, 約6.3 kg tafjū no tañì, yáku 6.3 kg
◆*adj* (pottery) ストーンウェアの sutōn-uèa no

♦vt (person) ...に石を投付ける ...ni ishí wo nagetsukerù; (fruit) ...の種を取る ...no tánè wo tórù

stone-cold [stoun'kould'] adj 冷え切った hiékitta

stone-deaf [stoun'def'] adj かなつんぼの kanátsunbo no

stonework [stoun'wə:rk] n (stones) 石造りの物 ishízukuri nò monó

stony [stou'ni:] adj (ground) 石だらけの ishídaràke no; (fig: glance, silence etc) 冷淡な reítan na

stood [stud] pt, pp of **stand**

stool [stu:l] n スツール sutsúrù

stoop [stu:p] vi (also: **stoop down**: bend) 腰をかがめる koshí wò kagámerù; (also: **have a stoop**) 腰が曲っている koshí gà magátte irù

(also: **full stop**) 止まる tomárù; (short stay) 立ち寄り tachíyori; (in punctuation: also: **full stop**) ピリオド píriòdo; (bus stop etc) 停留所 teíryūjo

♦vt (break off) 止める tomérù; (block: pay, check) ...の支払を停止させる ...no shiháraì wo teíshi saserù; (prevent: also: **put a stop to**) やめさせる yamésaserù

♦vi (halt: person) 立ち止る tachídomarù; (: watch, clock) 止まる tomárù; (end: rain, noise etc) やむ yamú

to stop doing something ...するのをやめる ...surú no wo yamérù

stop dead vi 急に止る kyū́ nì tomárù

stopgap [stɑp'gæp] n (person/thing) 間に合せの人(物) ma ní awase nò hitó (monó)

stop off vi 立寄る tachíyorù

stopover [stɑp'ouvə:r] n (gen) 立寄って泊る事 tachíyotte tomáru kotò; (AVIAT) 給油着陸 kyū́yuchakùriku

stoppage [stɑp'idʒ] n (strike) ストライキ sutóraìki; (blockage) 停止 teíshi

stopper [stɑp'ə:r] n 栓 seń

stop press n 最新ニュース saíshinnyùsu

stop up vi (hole) ふさぐ fuságù

stopwatch [stɑp'wɑtʃ] n ストップウオッチ sutóppuuotchì

storage [stɔ:r'idʒ] n 保管 hokán

storage heater n 蓄熱ヒーター chikú-

netsuhītà ◇深夜など電気需要の少ない時に熱を作って蓄え、昼間それを放射するヒーター shiń-ya nádò deńkijuyō no sukúnai tokí nets wo tsukúttè takúwaè, hirúma soré wo hōsha surù hītà

store [stɔ:r] n (stock) 蓄え takúwaè; (depot) 倉庫 sōko; (BRIT: large shop) デパート depā́tò; (US) 店 misé; (reserve) 備蓄 bichíku

♦vt (provisions, information etc) 蓄える takúwaerù

in store 未来に待構えて mírai ni machíkamaetè

storeroom [stɔ:r'ru:m] n 倉庫 sōko

stores [stɔ:rz] npl (provisions) 物資 bússhi

store up vt (nuts, sugar, memories etc) 蓄える takúwaerù

storey [stɔ:r'i:] (BRIT: floor) n = **story**

stork [stɔ:rk] n コウノトリ kōnotòri

storm [stɔ:rm] n (bad weather) 嵐 áràshi; (fig: of criticism, applause etc) 爆発 bakúhatsu

♦vi (fig: speak angrily) どなる donárù

♦vt (attack: place) 攻撃する kōgeki suru

stormy [stɔ:r'mi:] adj (weather) 荒れ模様の arémoyò no; (fig: debate, relations) 激しい hagéshiì

story [stɔ:r'i:] n (gen: also: **history**) 物語 monógatàri; (lie) うそ usó; (US) 階 kaì

storybook [stɔ:r'i:buk] n 童話の本 dṓwa nò hoń

stout [staut] adj (strong: branch etc) 丈夫な jōbu na; (fat) 太った futótta; (resolute: friend, supporter) 不動の fudō no

♦n (beer) スタウト sutáòto

stove [stouv] n (for cooking) レンジ réñji; (for heating) ストーブ sutōbù

stow [stou] vt (also: **stow away**) しまう shimáù

stowaway [stou'əwei] n 密航者 mikkṓsha

straddle [stræd'əl] vt (chair, fence etc: also fig) ...にまたがる ...ni matágarù

straggle [stræg'əl] vi (houses etc) 散在する sañzai suru; (people etc) 落ごする rakúgo suru

straggly [stræg'li:] adj (hair) ぼさぼさし

た bōsabosa shita

straight [streit] *adj* (line, road, back, hair) 真っ直ぐの massúgù no; (honest: answer) 正直な shōjiki na; (simple: choice, fight) 簡潔な kańketsu na
♦*adv* (directly) 真っ直ぐに massúgù ni; (drink) ストレートで sutórèto de
to put/get something straight (make clear) 明らかにする akírāka ni suru
straight away, straight off (at once) 直ちに tádàchi ni

straighten [strei'tən] *vt* (skirt, bed etc) 整える totónoerù

straighten out *vt* (fig: problem, situation) 解決する kaíketsu suru

straight-faced [streit'feist] *adj* まじめ な顔をした majíme nā kaó wo shitá

straightforward [streitfɔːr'wəːrd] *adj* (simple) 簡単な kańtan na; (honest) 正直な shōjiki na

strain [strein] *n* (pressure) 負担 fután; (TECH) ひずみ hizúmi; (MED: tension) 緊張 kińchō; (breed) 血統 kettō
♦*vt* (back etc) 痛める itámerù; (stretch: resources) ...に負担をかける ...ni fután wò kakérù; (CULIN: food) こす kosú
back strain (MED) ぎっくり腰 gikkúrigòshi

strained [streind] *adj* (back, muscle) 痛めた itámetà; (relations) 緊迫した kińpaku shità
a strained laugh 作り笑い tsukúriwarài

strainer [strei'nəːr] *n* (CULIN) こし器 koshíkì

strains [streinz] *npl* (MUS) 旋律 señritsu

strait [streit] *n* (GEO) 海峡 kaíkyō

strait-jacket [streit'dʒækit] *n* 拘束衣 kōsokui

strait-laced [streit'leist] *adj* しかつめらしい shikátsumerashiì

straits [streits] *npl: to be in dire straits* (fig) 困り果てている komárihatete irú

strand [strænd] *n* (of thread, hair, rope) 一本 íppon

stranded [stræn'did] *adj* (holiday-

makers) 足留めされた ashídome sareta

strange [streindʒ] *adj* (not known) 未知の michí no; (odd) 変な hén na

strangely [streindʒ'liː] *adv* (act, laugh) 変った風に kawátta fū ni *¶ see also* **enough**

stranger [strein'dʒəːr] *n* (unknown person) 知らない人 shiránai hitò; (from another area) よそ者 yosómono

strangle [stræŋ'gəl] *vt* (victim) 絞め殺す shimékorosù; (fig: economy) 圧迫する appáku suru

stranglehold [stræŋ'gəlhould] *n* (fig) 抑圧 yokúatsu

strap [stræp] *n* 肩ひも katáhimo, ストラップ sutórappù

strapping [stræp'iŋ] *adj* たくましい takúmashiì

strata [stræt'ə] *npl of* **stratum**

stratagem [stræt'ədʒəm] *n* 策略 sakúryàku

strategic [strəti:'dʒik] *adj* (positions, withdrawal, weapons etc) 戦略的な señryakuteki na

strategy [stræt'idʒiː] *n* (plan, *also* MIL) 作戦 sakúsen

stratum [strei'təm] (*pl* **strata**) *n* (*gen*) 層 sō; (in earth's surface) 地層 chisō; (in society) 階層 kaísō

straw [strɔː] *n* (dried stalks) わら wárà; (drinking straw) ストロー sutórō
that's the last straw! もう我慢できない mō gámàn dekínaì

strawberry [strɔː'beːriː] *n* イチゴ ichígo

stray [strei] *adj* (animal) のら... norá...; (bullet) 流れ... nagáre...; (scattered) 点在する teńzai suru
♦*vi* (children, animals) はぐれる hagúrerù; (thoughts) 横道にそれる yokómichi ni sorérù

streak [stri:k] *n* (stripe: *gen*) 筋 sújì
♦*vt* ...に筋を付ける ...ni sújì wo tsukérù
♦*vi: to streak past* 猛スピードで通り過ぎる mōsupído de tōrisugirù

stream [stri:m] *n* (small river) 小川 ogáwa; (of people, vehicles, smoke) 流れ nagáre; (of questions, insults etc) 連続 reńzoku

♦*vt* (SCOL: students) 能力別に分ける nō-ryokubétsu ni wakérù

♦*vi* (water, oil, blood) 流れる nagárerù

to stream in/out (people) 流れ込む(出る) nagárekomù(dérù)

streamer [stri:'mər] *n* 紙テープ kamítèpu

streamlined [stri:m'laind] *adj* 流線形の ryūsénkei no

street [stri:t] *n* 道 michí

streetcar [stri:t'kɑːr] *n* (US) 路面電車 roménéssha

street lamp *n* 街灯 gaftō

street plan *n* 市街地図 shigáíchizu

streetwise [stri:t'waiz] (*inf*) *adj* 裏町の悪知恵を持っている urámáchi no warújíe wo motté irù

strength [streŋθ] *n* (physical) 体力 tái-ryoku; (of girder, knot etc) 強さ tsúyōsa; (*fig*: power, number) 勢力 sefryoku

strengthen [streŋk'θən] *vt* (building, machine) 補強する hokyō surù; (*fig*: group, argument, relationship) 強くする tsúyōku surù

strenuous [stren'ju:əs] *adj* (energetic: exercise) 激しい hagéshìi; (: determined: efforts) 精力的な sefryokuteki na

stress [stres] *n* (force, pressure, also TECH) 圧力 atsúryoku; (mental strain) ストレス sutórèsu; (emphasis) 強調 kyō-chō

♦*vt* (point, importance etc) 強調する kyōchō surù; (syllable) ...にアクセントを置く ...ni ákùsento wo okú

stretch [stretʃ] *n* (area: of sand, water etc) 一帯 ittái

♦*vi* (area, animal) 背伸びする sénòbi surù; (extend): *to stretch to/as far as* ...まで続く ...mádè tsuzúkù

♦*vt* (pull) 伸ばす nobásù; (subj: job, task: make demands of) ...に努力を要求する ...ni dóryòku wo yōkyū surù

stretcher [stretʃ'ɑːr] *n* 担架 tánka

stretch out *vi* 体を伸ばす karáda wo nobásù

♦*vt* (arm etc) 伸ばす nobásù; (spread) 広げる hirógerù

strewn [stru:n] *adj*: *strewn with* ...が散

らばっている ...ga chírabatte irù

stricken [strik'ən] *adj* (person) 打ちひしがれた uchíhishigaretà; (city, industry etc) 災いに見舞われた wazáwai nì mimáwaretà

stricken with (arthritis, disease) ...にかかっている ...ni kákàtte irù

strict [strikt] *adj* (severe, firm: person, rule) 厳しい kibíshiì; (precise: meaning) 厳密な gefmitsu na

strictly [strikt'li:] *adv* (severely) 厳しく kibíshikù; (exactly) 厳密に gefmitsu ni

stridden [strid'ən] *pp of* **stride**

stride [straid] *n* (step) 大またの一歩 ō-màta no fppó

♦*vi* (*pt* **strode**, *pp* **stridden**) 大またに歩く ṑmàta ni arúkù

strident [straid'ənt] *adj* (voice, sound) 甲高い kaſdakaì

strife [straif] *n* 反目 hańmoku

strike [straik] *n* (of workers) ストライキ sutóraìki; (of oil etc) 発見 hakkén; (MIL: attack) 攻撃 kōgeki

♦*vb* (*pt*, *pp* **struck**)

♦*vt* (hit: person, thing) 打つ útsù; (*fig*: subj: idea, thought) ...の心に浮ぶ ...no kokórò ni ukábù; (oil etc) 発見する hak-kén surù; (bargain, deal) 決める kiméru

♦*vi* (go on strike) ストライキに入る sutóraìki ni háìru; (attack: soldiers) 攻撃する kōgeki surù; (: illness) 襲う osóù; (: disaster) 見舞う mimáù; (clock) 鳴る narú

on strike (workers) ストライキ中で sutóraìkichū de

to strike a match マッチを付ける mátchi wo tsukérù

strike down *vt* (kill) 殺す korósù; (harm) 痛める itámerù

striker [strai'kər] *n* (person on strike) ストライキ参加者 sutóraikisankashà; (SPORT) 攻撃選手 kōgekisénshu

strike up *vt* (MUS) 演奏し始める efsō shihajímerù; (conversation) 始める hají-merù; (friendship) 結ぶ musúbù

striking [strai'kiŋ] *adj* (noticeable) 目立つ medátsù; (attractive) 魅力的な miryó-kuteki na

string [strɪŋ] n (thin rope) ひも himó; (row: of beads etc) 数珠つなぎの物 juzú-tsunági no monó; (: of disasters etc) 一連 ichíren; (MUS) 弦 gén

♦vt (pt, pp **strung**): to **string together** つなぐ tsunágú

a **string of islands** 列島 rettó

to **pull strings** (fig) コネを利用する kónè no riyó suru

to **string out** 一列に並べる ichíretsu ni naráberu

string bean n さや豆 sayámame

string(ed) instrument [strɪŋ(d)-] n (MUS) 弦楽器 gefgakkí

stringent [strɪndʒənt] adj (rules, measures) 厳しい kibíshii

strings [strɪŋz] npl: the **strings** (MUS: section of orchestra) 弦楽器 gefgakkí

strip [strɪp] n (gen) 細長い切れ hosónagaí kiré; (: of land, water) 細長い一帯 hosónagaí ittái

♦vt (undress) 裸にする hadáka ni surú; (paint) はがす hagásù; (also: **strip down**: machine) 分解する bufíkai suru

♦vi (undress) 裸になる hadáka ni narú

strip cartoon n 四こま漫画 yofíkoma mañga

stripe [straɪp] n (gen) しま shima; (MIL, POLICE) そで章 sodéshò

striped [straɪpt] adj しま模様の shimá-moyó no

strip lighting n 蛍光灯 kefkótō

stripper [strɪpər] n ストリッパー sutó-rippà

striptease [strɪptiːz] n ストリップショー sutórippushō

strive [straɪv] (pt **strove**, pp **striven**) vi: to **strive for something/to do something** ...しようと努力する ...shiyó tò dóryòku suru

striven [strɪvən] pp of **strive**

strode [stroud] pt of **stride**

stroke [strouk] n (blow) 一撃 ichígeki; (SWIMMING) ストローク sutórōku; (MED) 脳卒中 nósotchū; (of paintbrush) 筆の運び fudé nò hakóbi

♦vt (caress) なでる nadérù

at a **stroke** 一気に ík̀kì ni

stroll [stroul] n 散歩 safpo

♦vi 散歩する safpo suru

stroller [stroulər] (US) n (pushchair) いす型ベビーカー isúgata bebíkā

strong [strɔŋ] adj (person, arms, grasp) 強い tsuyóì; (stick) 丈夫な jóbu na; (wind) 強い tsuyóì; (imagination) 想像力のある sózòryoku no árù; (personality) 気性の強い kishó no hagéshìi; (influence) 強い tsuyóì; (nerves) 頑丈な gañjō na; (smell) 強烈な kyóretsu na; (coffee) 濃い kóì; (taste) 際立った kiwádattà

they are 50 **strong** 50人いる gojúnin irú

stronghold [strɔŋhould] n とりで torfde; (fig) 根城 néjìro

strongly [strɔŋli] adv (solidly: construct) 頑丈に gañjō ni; (with force: push, defend) 激しく hageshikù; (deeply: feel, believe) 強く tsúyòku

strongroom [strɔŋruːm] n 金庫室 kiñkoshìtsu

strove [strouv] pt of **strive**

struck [strʌk] pt, pp of **strike**

structural [strʌktʃərəl] adj (damage, defect) 構造的な kózòteki na

structure [strʌktʃər] n (organization) 組織 sóshìki; (building) 構造物 kózóbùtsu

struggle [strʌgl] n 闘争 tósō

♦vi (try hard) 努力する dóryòku suru; (fight) 戦う tatákaù

strum [strʌm] vt (guitar) つま弾く tsu-mábìkú

strung [strʌŋ] pt, pp of **string**

strut [strʌt] n (wood, metal) 支柱 shichū

♦vi 威張って歩く ibátte arukù

stub [stʌb] n (of check, ticket etc) 控え hikáè; (of cigarette) 吸殻 suígara

♦vt: to **stub one's toe** つま先をぶつける tsumásakì wo butsúkerù

stubble [stʌbl] n (AGR) 切株 kiríkàbu; (on chin) 不精ひげ bushóhìge

stubborn [stʌbərn] adj (child, determination) 頑固な gáñko na

stub out vt (cigarette) もみ消す momíkesù

stuck [stʌk] pt, pp of **stick**

◆*adj* (jammed) 引っ掛かっている hikkákatte iru

stuck-up [stʌkˈʌp] (*inf*) *adj* 天ぐになっている tengu ni natté irú

stud [stʌd] *n* (on clothing etc) 飾りボタン kazáribotàn; (earring) 丸玉 marúdama (on sole of boot) スパイク supáikù; (*also*: **stud farm**) 馬の繁殖牧場 umá no hańshokubokujồ; (*also*: **stud horse**) 種馬 tanéuma

◆*vt* (*fig*): **studded with** ...をちりばめた ...wo chiríbametà

student [stuːˈdənt] *n* (at university) 学生 gakúsei; (at lower schools) 生徒 seíto

◆*adj* (nurse, life, union) 学生の gakúsei no

student driver (*US*) *n* 仮免許運転者 karímenkyo unteñsha

studies [stʌdˈiːz] *npl* (subjects studied) 勉強の科目 beńkyō no kamóku

studio [stuːˈdiːou] *n* (TV etc) スタジオ sutájìo; (sculptor's etc) アトリエ atórìè

studio apartment (*BRIT* **studio flat**) *n* ワンルームマンション wafifrūmu mańshon

studious [stuːˈdiːəs] *adj* (person) 勉強家の beńkyōka no; (careful: attention) 注意深い chúibukaì

studiously [stuːˈdiːəsliː] *adv* (carefully) 注意深く chúibukakù

study [stʌdˈiː] *n* (activity) 勉強 beńkyō; (room) 書斎 shosái

◆*vt* (learn about: subject) 勉強する beńkyō suru; (examine: face, evidence) 調べる shirábemenì

◆*vi* 勉強する beńkyō suru

stuff [stʌf] *n* (things) 物 monố, 事 kotố; (substance) 素質 soshítsu

◆*vt* (soft toy: *also* CULIN) ...に詰める ...ni tsumérù; (dead animals) はく製にする hakúsei ni surù; (*inf*: push: object) 差し込む sashíkomù

stuffing [stʌfˈiŋ] *n* (*gen*, CULIN) 詰め物 tsumémòno

stuffy [stʌfˈiː] *adj* (room) 空気の悪い kúki ni warúì; (person, ideas) 古臭い furúkusaì

stumble [stʌmˈbəl] *vi* つまづく tsumázu-kù

to **stumble across/on** (*fig*) ...に出くわす ...ni dekúwasù

stumbling block [stʌmˈbliŋ-] *n* 障害 shōgai

stump [stʌmp] *n* (of tree) 切株 kirfkàbu; (of limb) 断端 dańtan

◆*vt*: to be **stumped** まごつく magótsu-kù

stun [stʌn] *vt* (subj: news) あ然とさせる azen to saserú; (: blow on head) 気絶させる kizetsu saserú

stung [stʌŋ] *pt*, *pp* of **sting**

stunk [stʌŋk] *pp* of **stink**

stunning [stʌnˈiŋ] *adj* (*fig*: news, event) 仰天させる gyōten saserú; (: girl, dress) 美しい utsúkushiì

stunt [stʌnt] *n* (in film) スタント sutáñto; (: *also*: **publicity stunt**) 宣伝用のトリック señden-yò no toríkkù

stunted [stʌnˈtid] *adj* (trees, growth etc) 成長を阻害された seíchō wò sogái sare-tà

stuntman [stʌntˈmæn] (*pl* **stuntmen**) *n* スタントマン sutáñtoman

stupefy [stuːˈpəfai] *vt* (*fig*) あ然とさせる bōzen to saserú

stupendous [stuːpenˈdəs] *adj* 途方もない tohōmonaì

stupid [stuːˈpid] *adj* (person, question etc) ばかな báka na

stupidity [stuːpidˈitiː] *n* 愚かさ orókasa

stupor [stuːˈpər] *n* 前後不覚 zeñgofukákù

sturdy [stərˈdiː] *adj* (person, thing) がっちりした gatchírì shita

stutter [stʌtˈər] *n* どもり dómòri

◆*vi* どもる domórù

sty [stai] *n* (*also*: **pigsty**) 豚小屋 butágoya

stye [stai] *n* (MED) ものもらい monómoràì

style [stail] *n* (way, attitude) やり方 yaríkata; (elegance) 優雅さ yúgàsa; (design) スタイル sutáìru

stylish [staiˈliʃ] *adj* 優雅な yúgà na

stylus [staiˈləs] *n* (of record player) 針 harí

suave [swɑːv] *adj* 物腰の丁寧な monógoshi no teínei na

subconscious [sʌbkɒnˈtʃəs] *adj* (desire etc) 潜在意識の señzaiíshìki no

subcontract [sʌbkəntrǽkt] *vt* 下請に出す shitáuke ni dásù

subdivide [sʌbdiváid'] *vt* 小分けする kowáke suru

subdue [səbdjuː'] *vt* (rebels etc) 征服する seffuku suru; (passions) 抑制する yokúsei suru

subdued [səbdjuːd'] *adj* (light) 柔らかな yawárakà na; (person) 落込んだ ochíkoñda

subject [*n* sʌb'dʒikt *vb* səbjekt'] *n* (matter) 話題 wadái; (SCOL) 学科 gakká; (of kingdom) 臣民 shíñmiñ; (GRAMMAR) 主語 shúgò

    ♦t: to subject someone to something ...を...にさらす ...wo ...ni sarásù

    to be subject to (law) ...に服従しなければならない ...ni fukújúù shinakerèba naránaì; (heart attacks) ...が起りやすい ...ga okóriyasuì

    to be subject to tax 課税される kazéi sarerù

subjective [səbdʒek'tiv] *adj* 主観的な shukánteki na

subject matter *n* (content) 内容 naíyō

subjugate [sʌb'dʒəgeit] *vt* (people) 征服する seffuku suru

subjunctive [səbdʒʌŋk'tiv] *n* 仮定法 katéihō

sublet [sʌb'let] *vt* また貸しする matágashi suru

sublime [səblaim'] *adj* 素晴らしい subárashiì

submachine gun [sʌbməʃiːn'-] *n* 軽機関銃 keíkikañjū

submarine [sʌb'məriːn] *n* 潜水艦 señsuikan

submerge [səbmərdʒ'] *vt* 水中に沈める suíchū ni shizúmerù

    ♦vi (submarine, sea creature) 潜る mogúrù

submission [səbmiʃ'ən] *n* (state) 服従 fukújū; (claim) 申請書 shiñseisho; (of plan) 提出 teíshutsu

submissive [səbmis'iv] *adj* 従順な júbjun na

submit [səbmit'] *vt* (proposal, application etc) 提出する teíshutsu suru

    ♦vi: to submit to something ...に従う ...ni shitágaù

subnormal [sʌbnɔːr'məl] *adj* (below average: temperatures) 通常以下の tsújoikà no

subordinate [səbɔːr'dənit] *adj* 二次的な nijíteki na

    ♦n 部下 búkà

subpoena [səpiːˈnə] *n* (LAW) 召喚状 shókañjō

subscribe [səbskraib'] *vi: to subscribe to** (opinion) ...に同意する ...ni dóì suru; (fund) ...に寄付する ...ni kifú suru; (magazine etc) ...を購読する ...wo kódoku suru

subscriber [səbskraib'əːr] *n* (to periodical, telephone) 購読者 kódokushà; (to telephone) 加入者 kanyúshà

subscription [səbskrip'ʃən] *n* (to magazine etc) 購読契約 kódokukeíyàku

subsequent [sʌb'səkwənt] *adj* (following) その後の sonó atò no; (resulting) その結果として起る sonó kekkà toshite okórù

subsequently [sʌb'səkwəntli:] *adv* その後 sonó atò

subside [səbsaid'] *vi* (feeling) 収まる osámarù; (flood) ひく hikú; (wind) やむ yamú

subsidence [səbsaid'əns] *n* (in road etc) 陥没 kañbotsu

subsidiary [səbsid'i:ri:] *adj* (question, details) 二次的な nijíteki na

    ♦n (also: **subsidiary company**) 子会社 kogáisha

subsidize [sʌb'sidaiz] *vt* (education, industry etc) ...に補助金を与える ...ni hojókìn wo atáerù

subsidy [sʌb'sidi:] *n* 補助金 hojókìn

subsistence [səbsis'təns] *n* (ability to live) 最低限度の生活水準 saíteigeñdò no seíkatsusuìjun

subsistence allowance (*BRIT*) *n* (advance payment) 支度金 shitákukìn;

(for expenses etc) 特別手当 tokúbetsu teáte

substance [sʌbstəns] n (product, material) 物質 busshítsu

substantial [səbstæntʃəl] adj (solid) 頑丈な gajíjō na; (fig: reward, meal) 多い ōi

substantially [səbstæntʃəli] adv (by a large amount) 大いに ōi ni; (in essence) 本質的に honshítsuteki ni

substantiate [səbstæntʃieit] vt 裏付ける urázukerú

substitute [sʌbstitjut] n (person) 代人 dafnín; (thing) 代用品 dafyōhín
◆vt: **to substitute A for B** Bの代りにAを置く B nò kawári nì A wò okú

substitution [sʌbstitjuːʃən] n (act of substituting) 置換え okíkae; (SOCCER) 選手交代 seńshukōtai

subterfuge [sʌbtərfjuːdʒ] n 策略 sakúryàku

subterranean [sʌbtəreiniən] adj 地下の chíká no

subtitle [sʌbtaitəl] n 字幕スーパー jimákusūpà

subtle [sʌtəl] adj (slight: change) 微妙な bimyō na; (indirect: person) 腹芸のできる harágèi no umái

subtlety [sʌtəlti] n (small detail) 微妙な所 bimyō na tokórò; (art of being subtle) 腹芸 harágèi

subtotal [sʌbtoutəl] n 小計 shōkei

subtract [səbtrækt] vt ...から...を引く ...kárà ...wò hikú

subtraction [səbtrækʃən] n 引算 hikízàn

suburb [sʌbəːrb] n 市外周辺の自治体 toshíshūhen no jichítài

suburban [səbəːrbən] adj (train, lifestyle etc) 郊外の kōgai no

suburbia [səbəːrbiə] n 郊外 kōgai

suburbs [sʌbəːrbz] npl: **the suburbs** (area) 郊外 kōgai

subversive [səbvəːrsiv] adj (activities, literature) 破壊的な hakáiteki na

subway [sʌbwei] n (US: underground railway) 地下鉄 chikátetsu; (BRIT: underpass) 地下道 chikádō

succeed [səksiːd] vi (plan etc) 成功する

sefkō suru; (person: in career etc) 出生する shusshō suru
◆vt (in job) ...の後任になる ...no kōnin ni naru; (in order) ...の後に続く ...no átò ni tsuzúkú

to succeed in doing ...する事に成功する ...surú kotò ni sefkō suru

succeeding [səksiːdiŋ] adj (following) その後の sonó atò no

success [səkses] n (achievement) 成功 sefkō; (hit, also person) 大ヒット dashíttò

successful [səksesfəl] adj (venture) 成功した sefkō shita; (writer) 出生した shusshō shita

to be successful 成功する sefkō suru

to be successful in doing ...する事に成功する ...surú kotò ni sefkō suru

successfully [səksesfəli] adv (complete, do) うまく úmàku

succession [səkseʃən] n (series) 連続 refzoku; (to throne etc) 継承 kefshō

in succession 続けさまに tatétsuzuke ni

successive [səksesiv] adj 連続の refzoku no

successor [səksesəːr] n 後任 kōnin

succinct [səksiŋkt] adj 簡潔な kańketsu na

succulent [sʌkjələnt] adj 汁が多くておいしい shiru gà ōkūte oíshii

succumb [səkʌm] vi (to temptation) 負ける makérù; (to illness: become very ill) ...で倒れる ...de taôrerù; (: die) ...で死ぬ ...de shinú

such [sʌtʃ] adj (emphasizing similarity) その(その、あの)様な konó (sonó, anó) yō na; (of that kind): **such a book** そんな本 sofna hon; (so much): **such courage** そんな勇気 sofna yūki
◆adv こんな(そんな、あんな)に kofna (sofina, afina) na

such books そんな本 sofna hoñ

such a long trip あんなに長い旅行 afna nì nagái ryokō

such a lot of そんなに沢山の sofna nì takúsan no

such as (like) ...の様な ...no yō na

as such その物 sonó monò

such-and-such [sʌtʃ'ənsʌtʃ] *adj* しかじかの shikájìka no

suck [sʌk] *vt* (gen: ice-lolly etc) なめる namérù; (bottle, breast) 吸う sūū

sucker [sʌk'əːr] *n* (ZOOL) 吸盤 kyūban; (inf: easily cheated person) かも kámò

suction [sʌk'ʃən] *n* 吸引 kyūín

Sudan [suːdæn'] *n* スーダン sūdàn

sudden [sʌd'ən] *adj* (unexpected, rapid: increase, shower, change) 突然の totsúzen no

all of a sudden (unexpectedly) 突然 totsúzen

suddenly [sʌd'ənliː] *adv* (unexpectedly) 突然 totsúzen

suds [sʌdz] *npl* 石けんの泡 sekkén no awá

sue [suː] *vt* ...を相手取って訴訟を起す ...wo aítedottè soshō wò okósù

suede [sweid] *n* スエード suédò

suet [suː'it] *n* 脂肪 shibō ◇料理に使うウシやヒツジの堅い脂肪を指す ryōri ni tsukáù ushí yà hitsúji nò katái shibō wò sásù

Suez [suː'ez] *n*: **the Suez Canal** スエズ運河 suézu unga

suffer [sʌf'əːr] *vt* (undergo: hardship etc) 経験する keíken suru; (bear: pain, rudeness) 我慢する gámàn suru

♦*vi* (be harmed: person, results etc) 苦しむ kurúshimù; (results etc) 悪くなる wárùku narú

to suffer from (illness etc) ...の病気にかかっている ...no byōkī ni kakátte irù

sufferer [sʌf'əːrəːr] *n* (MED) 患者 kanja

suffering [sʌf'əːriŋ] *n* (hardship) 苦しみ kurúshimì

suffice [səfais'] *vi* 足りる tarírù

sufficient [səfiʃ'ənt] *adj* (convenient: time, moment) 都合がいい tsugō no iì; (appropriate: person, clothes etc) 適当な tekítō na

sufficiently [səfiʃ'əntliː] *adv* 十分に jūbūn ni

suffix [sʌf'iks] *n* 接尾辞 setsúbijì

suffocate [sʌf'əkeit] *vi* 窒息する chissóku suru

suffocation [sʌfəkei'ʃən] *n* 窒息 chissóku

suffrage [sʌf'ridʒ] *n* (right to vote) 参政権 sańseìken

suffused [səfjuːzd'] *adj*: **suffused with** (light, color, tears) ...で満たされた ...de mitásareta

sugar [ʃug'əːr] *n* 砂糖 satō

♦*vt* (tea etc) ...に砂糖を入れる ...ni satō wò irérù

sugar beet *n* サトウダイコン satódaìkon

sugar cane *n* サトウキビ satókìbi

suggest [səgdʒest'] *vt* (propose) 提案する teían suru; (indicate) 示唆する shísà suru

suggestion [səgdʒes'tʃən] *n* (proposal) 提案 teían; (indication) 示唆 shísà

suggestive [səgdʒes'tiv] *(pej) adj* (remarks, looks) 卑わいな hiwái na

suicide [suː'isaid] *n* (death, *also fig*) 自殺 jisátsu; (person) 自殺者 jisátsushà *§ see also commit*

suit [suːt] *n* (man's) 背広 sebfro; (woman's) スーツ sūtsu; (LAW) 訴訟 soshō; (CARDS) 組札 kumíffuda

♦*vt* (be convenient, appropriate) ...に都合がいい ...ni tsugō ga iì; (color, clothes) ...に似合う ...ni niáù; (adapt): **to suit something to** ...を...に合せる ...wo ...ni awáserù

well suited (well matched: couple) お似合いの o-niaí no

suitable [suː'təbəl] *adj* (convenient: time, moment) 都合のいい tsugō no iì; (appropriate: person, clothes etc) 適当な tekítō na

suitably [suː'təbliː] *adv* (dressed) 適当に tekítō ni; (impressed) 期待通りに kitái-dòri ni

suitcase [suːt'keis] *n* スーツケース sūtsukēsu

suite [swiːt] *n* (of rooms) スイートルーム suítoruìmu; (MUS) 組曲 kumíkyòku; (furniture): **bedroom** / **dining room suite** 寝室〔食堂〕用家具の一そろい shińshitsu(shokúdò)yò kágù no hitósòroi

suitor [suː'təːr] *n* 求婚者 kyūkònsha

sulfur [sʌl'fəːr] (*US*) *n* 硫黄 iō

sulk [sʌlk] *vi* すねる sunérù

sulky [sʌl'kiː] *adj* (child, silence) すねた sunéta

sullen [sʌl'ən] *adj* (person, silence) すねた sunéta

sulphur [sʌl'fəːr] n = sulfur
日光 nīkkô

sultan [sʌl'tən] n サルタン サ スラム教国の君主 isúramukyókoku no kúñshu

sultana [sʌltæn'ə] n (fruit) 白いレーズン shiróī rḗsuñ

sultry [sʌl'tri:] adj (weather) 蒸暑い mushfatsuī

sum [sʌm] n (calculation) 計算 kefsan; (amount) 金額 kīñgaku; (total) 合計 gôkei

summarize [sʌm'əːraiz] vt 要約する yôyaku suru

summary [sʌm'əːri:] n 要約 yôyaku

summer [sʌm'əːr] n 夏 natsú
◆adj (dress, school) 夏の natsú no
in summer 夏に natsú ni

summerhouse [sʌm'əːrhaus] n (in garden) 東屋 azúmaya

summertime [sʌm'əːrtaim] n (season) 夏 natsú

summer time n (by clock) サマータイム samátàimu

summer vacation (US) n 夏休み natsúyasùmi

summit [sʌm'it] n (of mountain) 頂上 chôjō; (also: **summit conference/meeting**) 首脳会議 shunôkalgi, サミット samíttð

summon [sʌm'ən] vt (person, police, help) 呼ぶ yobů; (to a meeting) 召集する shôshu suru; (LAW: witness) 召喚する shôkan suru

summons [sʌm'ənz] n (LAW) 召喚書 shôkanhsho; (fig) 呼出し yobídashì
◆vt (JUR) 召喚する shôkan suru

summon up vt (strength, energy, courage) 奮い起す furúiokosù

sump [sʌmp] (BRIT) n (AUT) オイルパン ofrupañ

sumptuous [sʌmp'tʃuːəs] adj 豪華な gôkā na

sum up vt (describe) 要約する yôyaku suru
◆vi (summarize) 要約する yôyaku suru

sun [sʌn] n (star) 太陽 tāiyō; (sunshine)

sunbathe [sʌn'beið] vi 日光浴する nikkôyòku suru

sunburn [sʌn'bəːrn] n (painful) 日焼け hiyáke

sunburnt [sʌn'bəːrnt] adj (tanned) 日に焼けた hi nf yaketà; (painfully) ひどく日焼した hfdòku hiyáke shita

Sunday [sʌn'dei] n 日曜日 nichfyôbi

Sunday school n 日曜学校 nichfyôgakkô

sundial [sʌn'dail] n 日時計 hidôkèi

sundown [sʌn'daun] n 日没 nichfbotsu

sundries [sʌn'dri:z] npl (miscellaneous items) その他 sonó tā

sundry [sʌn'dri:] adj (various) 色々な iróiro na
all and sundry だれもかも dâre mo kâ mo

sunflower [sʌn'flauəːr] n ヒマワリ himáwàri

sung [sʌŋ] pp of sing

sunglasses [sʌn'glæsiz] npl サングラス sañgurâsu

sunk [sʌŋk] pp of sink

sunlight [sʌn'lait] n 日光 nīkkô

sunlit [sʌn'lit] adj 日に照らされた hi nf terasaretà

sunny [sʌn'i:] adj (weather, day) 晴れた hâreta; (place) 日当りの良い hiátàri no yoì

sunrise [sʌn'raiz] n 日の出 hi nô de

sun roof n (AUT) サンルーフ safírùfu

sunset [sʌn'set] n 日没 nichfbotsu

sunshade [sʌn'ʃeid] n (over table) パラソル párâsoru

sunshine [sʌn'ʃain] n 日光 nīkkô

sunstroke [sʌn'strouk] n 日射病 nisshábyō

suntan [sʌn'tæn] n 日焼け hiyáke

suntan lotion n 日焼け止めローション hiyákedòme rôshon

suntan oil n サンタンオイル safítan oirû

super [suː'pəːr] (inf) adj 最高の safkô no

superannuation [suːpəːrænjuːei'ʃən] n 年金の掛金 neñkin nð kakékìn

superb [supəːrb'] adj 素晴らしい subárashiì

supercilious [su:pər'sil'i:əs] *adj* (disdainful, haughty) 横柄な ōhei na

superficial [su:pər'fiʃ'əl] *adj* (wound) 浅い asái; (knowledge) 表面的な hyōmenteki na; (shallow: person) 浅はかな asáhaka na

superfluous [su:pɔːr'flu:əs] *adj* 余計な yokéi na

superhuman [su:pər'hju:'mən] *adj* 超人的な chōjinteki na

superimpose [su:pərimpouz'] *vt* 重ね合せる kasáneawaseru

superintendent [su:pərinten'dənt] *n* (of place, activity) …長 …chō; (POLICE) 警視 kefshi

superior [səpiːr'iːər] *adj* (better) (より) すぐれた (yorí) sugúretá; (more senior) 上位の jōi no; (smug) 偉ぶった erábuttá

♦*n* 上司 jōshi

superiority [səpiːriːɔːr'itiː] *n* 優位性 yūīsei

superlative [səpɔːr'lətiv] *n* (LING) 最上級 saíjōkyū

superman [su:pər'mæn] (*pl* **supermen**) *n* 超人 chōjin

supermarket [su:'pərmɑːrkit] *n* スーパー sūpā

supernatural [su:pərnætʃ'ərəl] *adj* (creature, force etc) 超自然の chōshizen no

♦*n: the supernatural* 超自然の現象 chōshizen no geňshō

superpower [su:pərpau'ər] *n* (POL) 超大国 chōtaikoku

supersede [su:pərsiːd'] *vt* …に取って代る …ni tótté kawáru

supersonic [su:pərsɑːn'ik] *adj* (flight, aircraft) 超音速の chōonsoku no

superstar [su:'pərstɑːr] *n* (CINEMA, SPORT etc) スーパースター sūpāsutā

superstition [su:pərstiʃ'ən] *n* 迷信 meíshin

superstitious [su:pərstiʃ'əs] *adj* (person) 迷信深い meíshinbúkai; (practices) 迷信的 meíshinteki na

supertanker [su:'pərtæŋkɑːr] *n* スーパータンカー sūpātaňkā

supervise [su:'pərvaiz] *vt* (person, activ-

ity) 監督する kaňtoku suru

supervision [su:pərviʒ'ən] *n* 監督 kaňtoku

supervisor [su:'pərvaizɑːr] *n* (of workers, students) 監督 kaňtoku

supine [su:'pain] *adj* 仰向きの aómuki no

supper [sʌp'ɑːr] *n* (early evening) 夕食 yūshoku; (late evening) 夜食 yashóku

supplant [səplænt'] *vt* (person, thing) …に取って代る …ni tótté kawáru

supple [sʌp'əl] *adj* (person, body, leather etc) しなやかな shináyaka na

supplement [*n* sʌp'ləmənt *vb* sʌp'ləment'] *n* (additional amount, e.g. vitamin supplement) 補給品 hokyūhin; (of book) 補遺 hōi; (of newspaper, magazine) 付録 furóku

♦*vt* 補足する hosóku suru

supplementary [sʌpləmen'tɑːriː] *adj* (question) 補足的な hosókuteki na

supplementary benefit (BRIT) *n* 生活保護費 seíkatsuhogóhi

supplier [səplai'ɑːr] *n* (COMM: person, firm) 供給業者 kyōkyūgyōsha

supplies [səplaiz'] *npl* (food) 食料 shokúryō; (MIL) 軍需品 guňjuhín

supply [səplai'] *vt* (provide) 供給する kyōkyū suru; (equip): *to supply (with)* (…を) 支給する (…wo) shikyū suru

♦*n* (stock) 在庫品 zaíkohin; (supplying) 供給 kyōkyū

supply teacher (BRIT) *n* 代行教師 daíkōkyōshi

support [səpɔːrt'] *n* (moral, financial etc) 支援 shién; (TECH) 支え shichế

♦*vt* (morally: football team etc) 支援する shiền suru; (financially: family etc) 養う yashínaū; (TECH: hold up) 支える saếru; (sustain: theory etc) 裏付ける urázukerú

supporter [səpɔːr'tɑːr] *n* (POL etc) 支援者 shiénsha; (SPORT) ファン fáň

suppose [səpouz'] *vt* (think likely) …だと思う …dá tó omóu; (imagine) 想像する sōzō suru; (duty): *to be supposed to do something* …する事になっている …surú kotò ni natté irû

supposedly [səpou'zidliː] *adv* …だとされ

supposing [səpou'ziŋ] *conj* もし ... もーshī...

suppress [səpres'] *vt* (revolt) 鎮圧するchiñ-atsu suru; (information) 隠す kakúsū; (feelings, yawn) 抑える osáeruū

suppression [səpreʃ'ən] *n* (of revolt) 鎮圧 chiñ-atsu; (of information) 隠ぺい iñpei; (of feelings etc) 抑制 yokúsei

supremacy [səprem'əsi:] *n* 優越 yūetsu

supreme [səprim'] *adj* (in titles: court etc) 最高 の safkō no; (effort, achievement) 最上の saījō no

surcharge [səːr'tʃɑːrdʒ] *n* (extra cost) 追加料金 tsuīkaryōkin

sure [ʃuːr] *adj* (definite, convinced) 確信 している kakúshin shite iru; (aim, remedy) 確実な kakújitsu na; (friend) 頼りになる tāyōri ni nárū

  to make sure of something ... を確かめる ...wo tashfkamerū

  to make sure that ...だと確かめる ...dá tō tashfkamerū

  sure! (col) いいとも fi to mo

  sure enough 案の定 áñ no jō

sure-footed [ʃuːr'fut'id] *adj* 足のしっかりした ashf nō shikkárī shita

surely [ʃuːr'li:] *adv* (certainly: *US: also* sure) 確かに tāshfka ni

surety [ʃuːr'əti:] *n* (money) 担保 tāñpo

surf [səːrf] *n* 打寄せる波 uchfyoseru namī

surface [səːr'fis] *n* (of object) 表面 hyōmen; (of lake, pond) 水面 suímen

  ♦*adj* (road) 舗装する hosō suru

  ♦*vi* (fish, person in water: *also fig*) 浮上する fujō suru

surface mail *n* 普通郵便 futsúyūbin

surfboard [səːr'bɔːrd] *n* サーフボード sáfubōdo

surfeit [səːr'fit] *n*: *a surfeit of* ...の過剰 ...no kajō

surfing [səːr'fiŋ] *n* サーフィン sáfīn

surge [səːrdʒ] *n* (increase: *also fig*) 高まり takámarī

  ♦*vi* (water) 波打つ namfutsū; (people, vehicles) 突進する tosshín suru; (emotion) 高まる takámarū

surgeon [səːr'dʒən] *n* 外科医 gekáī

surgery [səːr'dʒəri:] *n* (treatment) 手術 shújiutsu; (BRIT: room) 診察室 shiñsatsushītsu; (: *also:* surgery hours) 診療時間 shiñryō jikan

surgical [səːr'dʒikəl] *adj* (instrument, mask etc) 外科用の gekáyō no; (treatment) 外科の gekáa no

surgical spirit (BRIT) *n* 消毒用アルコール shōdokuyō arūkōrū

surly [səːr'li:] *adj* 無愛想な buáīsō na

surmount [səːrmaunt'] *vt fig*: problem, difficulty) 乗越える norfkoerū

surname [səːr'neim] *n* 名字 myōjī

surpass [sərpæs'] *vt* (person, thing) しのぐ shinógū

surplus [səːr'pləs] *n* (extra, *also* COMM, ECON) 余剰分 yojōbūn

  ♦*adj* (stock, grain etc) 余剰の余剰の yojō no

surprise [sərpraiz'] *n* (unexpected) 思い掛け無い物 omóigakenai monó; (astonishment) 驚き odóroki

  ♦*vt* (astonish) 驚かす odórokasū; (catch unawares: army, thief) ...の不意を突く ...no fuf wo tsukú

surprising [sərprai'ziŋ] *adj* 驚くべきなodórokubéki

surprisingly [sərprai'ziŋli:] *adv* (extra, helpful) 驚く程 odóroku hodō

surrealist [sri:'əlist] *adj* (paintings etc) 超現実主義の chōgenjitsushūgi no

surrender [sren'dər] *n* 降伏 kófuku

  ♦*vi* (army, hijackers etc) 降伏する kófuku suru

surreptitious [sərəptiʃ'əs] *adj* ひそかな hisókà na

surrogate [səːr'əgit] *n* 代理の dafri no

surrogate mother *n* 代理母 dafrihahà

surround [səraund'] *vt* (subj: walls, hedge etc) 囲む kakómu; (MIL, POLICE etc) 包囲する hōi suru

surrounding [səraun'diŋ] *adj* (countryside) 周辺の shūi no

surroundings [səraun'diŋz] *npl* 周辺 shūhen

surveillance [sərvei'ləns] *n* 監視 kañshi

survey [*n* səːr'vei *vb* sərvei'] *n* (examination of land, house) 測量 sokúryō;

(investigation: of habits etc) 調査 chōsa
♦*t* (land, house etc) 測量する sokúryō suru; (look at: scene, work etc) 見渡す miwátasū

surveyor [sərvei'ər] *n* (of land, house) 測量技師 sokúryōgishi

survival [sərvai'vəl] *n* (continuation of life) 生存 sefzon; (relic) 遺物 ibútsu

survive [sərvaiv'] *vi* (person, thing) 助かる tasúkarù; (custom etc) 残る nokórù
♦*vt* (outlive: person) ...より長生きする ...yórì nagáikì suru

survivor [sərvai'vər] *n* (of illness, accident) 生存者 sefzonsha

susceptible [səsep'təbəl] *adj*: **susceptible (to)** (affected by: heat, injury) (...に) 弱い...ni yowáì; (influenced by: flattery, pressure) (...に) 影響されやすい ...ni efkyō sareyasuì

suspect [*adj, n* sʌs'pekt *vb* səspekt']
adj 怪しい ayáshiì
♦*n* 容疑者 yōgìshà
♦*vt* (person) ...が怪しいと思う ...ga ayáshiì to omóù; (think) ...ではないかと思う ...dè wà naì ka to omóù

suspend [səspend'] *vt* (hang) つるす tsurúsù; (delay, stop) 中止する chūshi suru; (from employment) 停職処分にする tefshokushobùn ni suru

suspended sentence *n*
(LAW) 執行猶予付きの判決 shikkōyúyòtsuki no hañketsu

suspender belt [səspen'dər-] *n* ガーターベルト gátàberuto

suspenders [səspen'dərz] *npl* (US) ズボンつり zubóntsuri; (BRIT) ガーターベルトのストッキング留め gátàberuto no sutókkingudòme

suspense [səspens'] *n* (uncertainty) 気掛り kigákarì; (in film etc) サスペンス sásùpensu

to keep someone in suspense はらはらさせる háràhara sasérù

suspension [səspen'ʃən] *n* (from job, team) 停職 tefshoku; (AUT) サスペンション sásùpeñshon; (of driver's license, payment) 停止 tefshi

suspension bridge *n* つり橋 tsurfbàshi

suspicion [səspiʃ'ən] *n* (distrust) 疑い utágaì; ((bad) feeling) 漠然とした感じ bakúzen to shitá kañji

suspicious [səspiʃ'əs] *adj* (suspecting: look) 疑い深い utágaibukaì; (causing suspicion: circumstances) 怪しげな ayáshìge na

sustain [səstein'] *vt* (continue: interest etc) 維持する ijì suru; (subj: food, drink) ...に力を付ける ...ni chikára wò tsukérù; (suffer: injury) 受ける ukérù

sustained [səsteind'] *adj* (effort, attack) 絶間ない taémanaì

sustenance [sʌs'tənəns] *n* 食物 shokúmòtsu

swab [swɑb] *n* (MED) 綿球 mefkyū

swagger [swæg'ər] *vi* 威張って歩く i-bátte arukù

swallow [swɑl'ou] *n* (bird) ツバメ tsubáme
♦*vt* (food, pills etc) 飲込む nomíkomù; (fig: story) 信じ込む shiñjikomù; (: insult) ...に黙って耐える ...ni damátte taérù; (one's pride, one's words) 抑える osáerù

swallow up *vt* (savings etc) 飲込む nomíkomù

swam [swæm] *pt of* swim

swamp [swɑmp] *n* 沼地 numáchi
♦*vt* (with water etc) 水没させる suíbotsu saserù; (fig: person) 圧倒する attō suru

swan [swɑn] *n* ハクチョウ hakúchō

swap [swɑp] *n* 交換 kōkan
♦*vt*: *to swap (for)* (exchange for) (...) と交換する (...to) kōkan suru; (replace with) (...と) 取替える (...to) torfkaerù

swarm [swɔrm] *n* (of bees) 群れ muré; (of people) 群衆 gufshū
♦*vi* (bees) 群れで巣別れする muré de suwákarè suru; (people) 群がる murágarù; (place): *to be swarming with* ...に...がうじゃうじゃいる ...ni ...ga ūjauja irú

swarthy [swɔr'ði] *adj* 浅黒い aságuroì

swastika [swɑs'tikə] *n* かぎ十字 kagíjūji

swat [swɑt] *vt* (insect) たたく tatákù

sway [swei] *vi* (person, tree) 揺れる yurérù

♦ *vt* (influence) 揺さぶる yusáburù

swear [swe'əɾ] (*pt* **swore**, *pp* **sworn**) *vi* (curse) 悪態をつく akútai wò tsukú

♦ *vt* (promise) 誓う chikáǔ

swearword [swe'ɾwəɾd] *n* 悪態 akútai

sweat [swet] *n* 汗 ásè

♦ *vi* 汗をかく ásè wo kákù

sweater [swet'əɾ] *n* セーター sétā

sweatshirt [swet'ʃəɾt] *n* トレーナー torénā

sweaty [swet'i:] *adj* (clothes, hands) 汗ばんだ asébañda

Swede [swi:d] *n* スウェーデン人 suéden-jìn

swede [swi:d] (*BRIT*) *n* スウェーデンカブ suédènkabu

Sweden [swi:d'ən] *n* スウェーデン suéden

Swedish [swi:'diʃ] *adj* スウェーデンのsuéden no; (LING) スウェーデン語の suédeńgo no

♦ *n* (LING) スウェーデン語 suédeńgo

sweep [swi:p] *n* (act of sweeping) 掃く事 hakú kotó; (*also*: **chimney sweep**) 煙突掃除夫 eñtotsusōjìfū

♦ *vb* (*pt*, *pp* **swept**)

♦ *vt* (brush) 掃く hákù; (with arm) 払う haráǔ; (subj: current) 流す nagásù

♦ *vi* (hand, arm) 振る furú; (wind) 吹きまくる fukímakurù

sweep away *vt* 取除く torínozokù

sweeping [swi:'piŋ] *adj* (gesture) 大振りな ōburi na; (generalized: statement) 十把一からげの jíppabhitókàrage no

sweep past *vi* (at great speed) 猛スピードで通り過ぎる mōsupídò de tōrisugirù; (majestically) 堂々と通り過ぎる dōdō tō tōrisugirù

sweep up *vi* 掃き取る hakítorù

sweet [swi:t] *n* (candy) あめ amé; (*BRIT*: pudding) デザート dezátò

♦ *adj* (not savory: taste) 甘い amáì; (fig: air, water, smell, sound) 快い kokóroyoì; (: kind) 親切な shíñsetsu na; (attractive: baby, kitten) かわいい kawáiì

sweetcorn [swi:t'kɔːɾn] *n* トウモロコシ tōmoròkoshi

sweeten [swi:t'ən] *vt* (add sugar to) 甘くする amáku surū; (soften: temper) なだめる nadámerù

sweetheart [swi:t'hɑːɾt] *n* (boyfriend/girlfriend) 恋人 koíbito

sweetness [swi:t'nis] *n* (amount of sugar) 甘さ amása; (fig: of air, water, smell, sound) 快さ kokóroyosà; (kindness) 親切さ shíñsetsu; (attractiveness: of baby, kitten) かわいさ kawáisà

sweetpea [swi:t'pi:] *n* スイートピー suítopī

swell [swel] *n* (of sea) うねり uneri

♦ *adj* (*US: inf:* excellent) 素晴らしい subárashiì

♦ *vi* (*pt* **swelled**, *pp* **swollen** *or* **swelled**) (increase: numbers) 増える fuérù; (get stronger: sound, feeling) 増す masú; (*also*: **swell up**: face, ankle etc) はれる harérù

swelling [swel'iŋ] *n* (MED) はれ haré

sweltering [swel'təriŋ] *adj* (heat, weather, day) うだる様な udáru yō na

swept [swept] *pt, pp of* **sweep**

swerve [swəːrv] *vi* (person, animal, vehicle) それる sorérù

swift [swift] *n* (bird) アマツバメ amátsubàme

♦ *adj* (happening quickly: recovery) じん速な jíñsoku na; (moving quickly: stream, glance) 早い hayáì

swiftly [swift'li:] *adv* (move, react, reply) 早く háyàku

swig [swig] (*inf*) *n* (drink) がぶ飲み gabúnomi

swill [swil] *vt* (*also*: **swill out**, **swill down**) がぶがぶ飲む gabúgabu nòmu

♦ *n* (for animals) 残飯 zañpan

swim [swim] *n*: **to go for a swim** 泳ぎに行く oyógi ni ikú

♦ *vb* (*pt* **swam**, *pp* **swum**)

♦ *vi* (person, animal, fish) 泳ぐ oyógù; (head, room) 回る mawárù

♦ *vt* (the Channel, a length) 泳いで渡る oyóide watárù

swimmer [swim'əɾ] *n* 泳ぐ人 oyógu hitò

swimming [swim'iŋ] *n* 水泳 suíei

swimming cap *n* 水泳用の帽子 suíeiyō no bōshi

swimming costume (BRIT) n 水着 mizúgi

swimming pool n 水泳プール suéipūru

swimming trunks npl 水泳パンツ suíeipantsu

swimsuit [swim'su:t] n 水着 mizúgi

swindle [swin'dəl] n 詐欺 sági
◆vt ぺてんにかける petén ní kakérù

swine [swain] (inf!) n 畜生 me chikúshò-me

swing [swiŋ] n (in playground) ぶらんこ búrànko; (: movement) 揺れ yuré; (change: in opinions etc) 変動 hefidō; (MUS: also rhythm) スイング suíngu
◆vb (pt, pp swung)
◆vt (arms, legs) 振る furú; (also: **swing round**: vehicle etc) 回す mawásù
◆vi (pendulum) 揺れる yurérù; (on a swing) ぶらんこに乗る búrànko ni norù; (also: **swing round**: person, animal) 振向く furímukù; (: vehicle etc) 向きを変える múkì wo kaérù
to be in full swing (party etc) たけなわである takénawa de árù

swing bridge n 旋回橋 seńkaikyō

swingeing [swin'dʒiŋ] (BRIT) adj (blow, attack) 激しい hagéshiì; (cuts) 法外な hōgai na

swinging door [swin'iŋ-] (BRIT **swing door**) n 自在ドア jizáidòa

swipe [swaip] vt (hit) たたく tatákù; (inf: steal) かっ払う kappáraù

swirl [swəːrl] vi (water, smoke, leaves) 渦巻く uzúmakù

swish [swiʃ] vt (tail etc) 音を立てて振る otó wò tátète furú
◆vi (clothes) 衣ずれの音を立てる kinúzure nō otó wò tatérù

Swiss [swis] adj スイスの suísu no
◆n inv スイス人 suísujìn

switch [switʃ] n (for light, radio etc) スイッチ suítchì; (change) 取替え toríkae
◆vt (change) 取替える toríkaerù

switchboard [switʃ'bɔːrd] n (TEL) 交換台 kōkandai

switch off vt (light, radio) 消す kesú; (engine, machine) 止める tomérù

switch on vt (light, radio, machine) つ

ける tsukérù; (engine) かける kakérù

Switzerland [swit'sərlənd] n スイス suísu

swivel [swiv'əl] vi (also: **swivel round**) 回る mawárù

swollen [swou'lən] pp of **swell**

swoon [swuːn] vi 気絶する kizétsu suru

swoop [swuːp] n (by police etc) 手入れ te-íre
◆vi (also: **swoop down**: bird, plane) 舞降りる maíoriru

swop [swɑːp] = **swap**

sword [sɔːrd] n 刀 katána

swordfish [sɔːrd'fiʃ] n メカジキ mekájiki

swore [swɔːr] pt of **swear**

sworn [swɔːrn] pp of **swear**
◆adj (statement, evidence) 宣誓付きの señseitsuki no; (enemy) 年来の neńrai no

swot [swɑːt] vi がり勉する garíben suru

swum [swʌm] pp of **swim**

swung [swʌŋ] pt, pp of **swing**

sycamore [sik'əmɔːr] n カエデ káede

syllable [sil'əbəl] n 音節 oñsetsu

syllabus [sil'əbəs] n (teaching, also 概要) kōgigaiyō

symbol [sim'bəl] n (sign, also MATH) 記号 kígō; (representation) 象徴 shōchō

symbolic(al) [simbɑːl'ik(əl)] adj 象徴的な shōchōteki na

symbolism [sim'bəlizəm] n 象徴の意味 shōchōteki imì

symbolize [sim'bəlaiz] vt 象徴する shōchō suru

symmetrical [simet'rikəl] adj 対称的な taíshōteki na

symmetry [sim'itri:] n 対称 taíshō

sympathetic [simpəθet'ik] adj (showing understanding) 同情的な dōjōteki na; (likeable: character) 人好きのする hitózuki no surù; (showing support): **sympathetic (towards)** ...に好意的である ...ni kōiteki de árù

sympathies [sim'pəθiːz] npl (support, tendencies) 支援 shién

sympathize [sim'pəθaiz] vi: **to sympathize with** (person) ...に同情する ...ni dōjō suru; (feelings, cause) ...に共感する ...ni kyōkan suru

sympathizer [sim'pəθaizər] *n* (POL) 支援者 shiénsha

sympathy [sim'pəθi] *n* (pity) 同情 dōjō

with our deepest sympathy 心からお悔みを申し上げます kokórō kara o-kúyami wò mōshiagemasù

in sympathy (workers: come out) 同情して dṓjō shite

symphony [sim'fəni] *n* 交響曲 kṓkyōkyoku

symposia [simpou'ziə] *npl of* **symposium**

symposium [simpou'ziəm] *n* (*pl* **symposiums** *or* **symposia**) *n* シンポジウム shiñpojìùmu

symptom [simp'təm] *n* (indicator: MED) 症状 shōjō; (: gen) しるし shírùshi

synagogue [sin'əgɑːg] *n* ユダヤ教会堂 yudáyakàidō

synchronize [siŋ'krənaiz] *vt* (watches, sound) 合せる awáserù

syncopated [siŋ'kəpeitid] *adj* (rhythm, beat) シンコペートした shiñkopḕto shita

syndicate [sin'dəkit] *n* (of people, businesses, newspapers) シンジケート shiñjikḕto

syndrome [sin'droum] *n* (*also* MED) 症候群 shōkōgun

synonym [sin'ənim] *n* 同意語 dṓigo

synopses [sinɑːp'siːz] *npl of* **synopsis**

synopsis [sinɑːp'sis] (*pl* **synopses**) *n* 概要 gaíyō

syntax [sin'tæks] *n* (LING) 統語法 tṓgohō, シンタックス shiñtakkùsu

syntheses [sin'θəsiːz] *npl of* **synthesis**

synthesis [sin'θəsis] (*pl* **syntheses**) *n* (of ideas, styles) 総合する sṓgō surù

synthetic [sinθet'ik] *adj* (man-made: materials) 合成の gṓsei no

syphilis [sif'əlis] *n* 梅毒 baídoku

syphon [sai'fən] *n* = **siphon**

Syria [sir'iːə] *n* シリア shírìa

Syrian [sir'iːən] *adj* シリアの shírìa no
◆*n* シリア人 shiríajìn

syringe [sərindʒ'] *n* 注射器 chūshakì

syrup [sir'əp] *n* シロップ shiróppù

system [sis'təm] *n* (organization) 組織 sōshìki; (POL): *the system* 体制 taísei;

(method) やり方 yaríkata; (the body) 身体 shiñtai

the digestive system (MED) 消化器系 shōkakìkei

the nervous system (MED) 神経系 shiñkeikei

systematic [sistəmæt'ik] *adj* (methodical) 組織的な soshíkiteki na

system disk (COMPUT) システムディスク shisútemu disùku

systems analyst [sis'təmz-] *n* システムアナリスト shisútemu anarisùto

T

ta [tɑː] (*BRIT*: *inf*) *excl* (thanks) どうも dṓmo

tab [tæb] *n* (on file etc) 耳 mimf; (on drinks can etc) プルタブ purútàbu, プルトップ purútoppù; (label: name tab) 名札 nafúda

to keep tabs on (*fig*) 監視する kañshi suru

tabby [tæb'iː] *n* (*also*: **tabby cat**) とら毛のネコ toráge nò nékò

table [tei'bəl] *n* (piece of furniture) テーブル tḕburu; (MATH, CHEM etc) 表 hyṓ
◆*vt* (*BRIT*: motion etc) 上程する jōtei suru; (*US*: put off: proposal etc) 棚上げにする taná-age ni surū

to lay/set the table 食卓に皿を並べる shokútakù nì sará wò naráberù

tablecloth [tei'bəlklɔːθ] *n* テーブルクロス tēburukuròsu

table d'hôte [tæb'əl dout'] *adj* (menu, meal) 定食の teíshoku no

table lamp *n* 電気スタンド deñki sutañdo

tablemat [tei'bəlmæt] *n* (for plate) テーブルマット tēburumattò; (for hot dish) なべ敷 nabéshikì

table of contents *n* 目次 mokúji

tablespoon [tei'bəlspuːn] *n* (type of spoon) テーブルスプーン tēburusupùn; (*also*: **tablespoonful** as measurement) 大さじ一杯 ōsaji ippaì

tablet [tæb'lit] *n* (MED) 錠剤 jōzai

a stone tablet 石板 sekíban

table tennis *n* 卓球 takkyū

table wine *n* テーブルワイン tēburuwaiñ

tabloid [tæb'loid] *n* (newspaper) タブロ イド新聞 tabúroido shínbuñ

taboo [təbu:'] *n* (religious, social) タブ ー tabū

◆*adj* (subject, place, name etc) タブーの tabū no

tabulate [tæb'jəleit] *vt* (data, figures) 表 にする hyō ni suru

tacit [tæs'it] *adj* (agreement, approval etc) 暗黙の añmoku no

taciturn [tæs'itərn] *adj* (person) 無口な múkuchi na

tack [tæk] *n* (nail) びょう byō; (*fig*) やり 方 yaríkata

◆*vt* (nail) びょうで留める byō de toméru; (stitch) 仮縫する karínui suru

◆*vi* (NAUT) 間切る magíru

tackle [tæk'əl] *n* (gear: fishing tackle etc) 道具 dōgu; (for lifting) ろくろ rókuro, 滑車 kássha; (FOOTBALL, RUGBY) タックル tákkuru

◆*vt* (deal with: difficulty) ...と取組む ...to toríkumu; (challenge: person) ...に掛合う ...ni kakéau; (grapple with: person, animal) ...と取組む ...to toríkumu; (FOOT-BALL, RUGBY) タックルする tákkuru suru

tacky [tæk'i:] *adj* (sticky) べたべたする bétabeta suru; (*pej*: of poor quality) 安っ ぽい yasúppoi

tact [tækt] *n* 如才なさ josáinasa

tactful [tækt'fəl] *adj* 如才ない josáinai

tactical [tæk'tikəl] *adj* (move, with-drawal, voting) 戦術的な señjútsuteki na

tactics [tæk'tiks] *n* 用兵学 yōheigaku

◆*npl* 駆け引き kakéhiki

tactless [tækt'lis] *adj* 気転の利かない ki-téñ no kikánai

tadpole [tæd'poul] *n* オタマジャクシ otá-majakùshi

taffy [tæf'i:] (*US*) *n* (toffee) タフィー tafī の一種 amé nò ísshu

tag [tæg] *n* (label) 札 fudá

tag along *vi* ついて行く tsúite ikú

tail [teil] *n* (of animal) しっぽ shíppò; (of plane) 尾部 bíbù; (of shirt, coat) すそ su-só

◆*vt* (follow: person, vehicle) 尾行する bi-kō suru

tail away/off *vi* (in size, quality etc) 次 第に減る shídai ni herú

tailback [teil'bæk] (*BRIT*) *n* (AUT) 交 通渋滞 kōtsūjūtai

tail end *n* 末端 mattáñ

tailgate [teil'geit] *n* (AUT: of hatch-back) 後尾ドア kōbidòa

tailor [tei'lər] *n* 仕立屋 shitáteya

tailoring [tei'ləriŋ] *n* (cut) 仕立て方 shi-tátekata; (craft) 仕立職 shitáteshòku

tailor-made [tei'lə:rmeid] *adj* (suit) あつ らえの atsúrae no; (*fig*: part in play, person for job) おあつらえ向きの o-átsu-raemuki no

tails [teilz] *npl* (formal suit) えん尾服 efi-bífuku

tailwind [teil'wind] *n* 追風 oíkaze

tainted [teint'id] *adj* (food, water, air) 汚 染された osén saretá; (*fig*: profits, reputation etc) 汚れた yogóreta

Taiwan [tai'wa:n'] *n* 台湾 taíwañ

take [teik] (*pt* **took**, *pp* **taken**) *vt* (photo, notes, holiday etc) を撮る tóru; (shower, walk, decision etc) する surú; (grab: someone's arm etc) 取る tóru; (gain: prize) 得る érù; (require: effort, courage, time) ...が必要である ...ga hitsúyō de arù; (tolerate: pain etc) 耐える taéru; (hold: passengers etc) 収容する shūyō suru; (accompany, bring, carry: person) 連れ て行く tsuréte ikú; (: thing) 持って行く motté ikú; (exam, test) 受ける ukéru

to take something from (drawer etc) ...を...から取出す ...wo ...kárà torídasù; (steal from: person) ...を...から盗む ...wo ...kárà nusúmù

I take it that ... ...だと思っていいです ね ...dá tò omótte iì desu né

take after *vt fus* (resemble) ...に似てい る ...ni nité irú

take apart *vt* 分解する buñkai suru

take away *vt* (remove) 下げる sagéru; (carry off) 持って行く motté ikú; (MATH) 引く hikú

takeaway [teɪˈkəwei] (*BRIT*) n = **take-out**

take back vt (return) 返す kaésù; (one's words) 取消す toríkesù

take down vt (dismantle: building) 解体する kaítai suru; (write down: letter etc) 書き取る kakítorù

take in vt (deceive) だます damásù; (understand) 理解する rìkái suru; (include) 含む fukúmù; (lodger) 泊める tomérù

take off vi (AVIAT) 離陸する rìríku suru; (go away) 行ってしまう itté shimaù
♦vt (remove) 取り外す hazúsù

takeoff [teɪkˈɔːf] n (AVIAT) 離陸 rírìku

take on vt (work) 引き受ける hikífukerù; (employee: hire) 雇う yatóù; (opponent) ...と戦う ...to tatákaù

take out vt (invite) 外食に連れて行く gaíshoku ni tsuréte ikù; (remove) 取出す torídasù

takeout [teɪkˈaʊt] (*US*) n (shop, restaurant) 持帰り料理店 mochíkaeriryōritèn; (food) 持帰り料理 mochíkaeriryòri

take over vt (business, country) 乗っ取る nottórù
♦vi: to take over from someone ...と交替する ...to kòtai suru

takeover [teɪkˈoʊvər] n (COMM) 乗っ取り nottóri

take to vt fus (person, thing, activity) 気に入る ki ní irù, 好きになる sukf ni narù; (engage in: hobby etc) やり出す yarídasù

take up vt (a dress) 短くする mijíkakù suru; (occupy: post, time, space) ...につく ...ni tsukù; (: time) ...がかかる ...ga kakárù; (engage in: hobby etc) やり出す yarídasù

to take someone up on something (offer, suggestion) ...に応じる ...ni ôjirù

takings [teɪkˈiŋz] npl 売上 urfage

talc [tælk] n (*also*: talcum powder) タルカムパウダー tarúkamupaùdā

tale [teɪl] n (story, account) 物語 monôgatàri

to tell tales (fig: to teacher, parents etc) 告げ口する tsugéguchi suru

talent [tælˈənt] n 才能 saínō

talented [tælˈəntid] adj 才能ある saínō arù

talk [tɔːk] n (a prepared speech) 演説 eñzetsu; (conversation) 話 hanáshi; (gossip) うわさ uwása
♦vi (speak) 話す hanásù; (give information) しゃべる shabérù

to talk about ...について話す ...ni tsùíte hanásù

to talk someone into doing something ...する様に ...を説得する ...surú yó ni ...wo settóku suru

to talk someone out of doing something ...しない様に ...を説得する ...shinái yô ni ...wo settóku suru

to talk shop 仕事の話をする shigóto nò hanáshi wo suru

talkative [tɔːˈkətiv] adj おしゃべりな o-sháberi na

talk over vt (problem etc) 話し合う hanáshiaù

talk show n おしゃべり番組 o-shábèri bañgumi

tall [tɔːl] adj (person) 背が高い sé ga takáì; (object) 高い takáì

to be 6 feet tall (person) 身長が6フィートである shinchō ga 6 fítò de arù

tall story n ほら話 horábanàshi

tally [tælˈi] n (of marks, amounts of money etc) 記録 kiróku
♦vi: to tally (with) (subj: figures, stories etc) ...と合う (...to) áù

talon [tælˈən] n かぎづめ kagízume

tambourine [tæmbəriːn] n タンバリン tañbarìn

tame [teɪm] adj (animal, bird) なれた nárèta; (fig: story, style) 平凡な heñbon na

tamper [tæmˈpər] vi: to tamper with something ...をいじる ...wo ijírù

tampon [tæmˈpɑːn] n タンポン tañpon

tan [tæn] n (*also*: suntan) 日焼け hiyáke
♦vi (person, skin) 日に焼ける hi ní yakerù
♦adj (color) 黄かっ色の ôkasshòku no

tandem [tænˈdəm] n: in tandem (together) 2人で futári dè

tang [tæŋ] *n* (smell) 鼻をつくようなにおい hanā wò tsukū nìòì; (taste) ぴりっとした味 pirītto shita ajī

tangent [tæn'dʒənt] *n* (MATH) 接線 sessén

to go off at a tangent (fig) わき道へそれる wakīmìchi e sorérù

tangerine [tændʒəri:n'] *n* ミカン mīkàn

tangible [tæn'dʒəbəl] *adj* (proof, benefits) 具体的な gutáìteki na

tangle [tæŋ'gəl] *n* もつれ motsúre

to get in(to) a tangle (also fig) もつれる motsúrerù

tank [tæŋk] *n* (also: *water tank*) 貯水タンク chosúìtañku; (for fish) 水槽 suísò; (MIL) 戦車 séñsha

tanker [tæŋ'kə:r] *n* (ship) タンカー tâñkā; (truck) タンクローリー tañkurôrī

tanned [tænd] *adj* (skin) 日に焼けた hi ní yakèta

tantalizing [tæn'təlaizɪŋ] *adj* (smell, possibility) 興味をそそる kyômi wò sosórù

tantamount [tæn'təmaunt] *adj*: *tantamount to* ...も同然である ...mo dôzen de arù

tantrum [tæn'trəm] *n* かんしゃく kañshaku

tap [tæp] *n* (on sink etc) 蛇口 jagùchi; (also: *gas tap*) ガスの元栓 gásù no motósen; (gentle blow) 軽くたたく事 karūkù tatakù kotò

◆*vt* (hit gently) 軽くたたく karūkù tatakù; (resources) 利用する riyô suru; (telephone) 盗聴する tôchō suru

on tap (fig: resources) いつでも利用できる ítsùdemo riyô dekirù

tap-dancing [tæp'dænsɪŋ] *n* タップダンス tappúdañsu

tape [teip] *n* (also: *magnetic tape*) 磁気テープ jikītèpu; (cassette) カセットテープ kasēttotèpu; (sticky tape) 粘着テープ neñchakutèpu; (for tying) ひも himō

◆*vt* (record: sound) 録音する rokûon suru; (: image) 録画する rokûga suru; (stick with tape) テープで張る tèpu de harù

tape deck *n* テープデッキ tèpudekkì

tape measure *n* メジャー mèjā

taper [tei'pə:r] *n* (candle) 細いろうそく hosôi rôsoku

◆*vi* (narrow) 細くなる hósòku narù

tape recorder *n* テープレコーダー tèpurekòdā

tapestry [tæp'istri:] *n* (object) タペストリー tapésutòrī; (art) ししゅう shishū

tar [tɑ:r] *n* コールタール kôrutāru

tarantula [təræn'tʃələ] *n* タランチュラ tarāñchura

target [tɑ:r'git] *n* (thing aimed at, also fig) 的 matò

tariff [tær'if] *n* (tax on goods) 関税 kañzei; (BRIT: in hotels, restaurants) 料金表 ryôkiñhyō

tarmac [tɑ:r'mæk] *n* (BRIT: on road) アスファルト asúfàruto; (AVIAT) エプロン épùron

tarnish [tɑ:r'niʃ] *vt* (metal) さびさせる sabísaserù; (fig: reputation etc) 汚す yogósù

tarpaulin [tɑːrpɔː'lin] *n* シート shìto

tarragon [tær'əgən] *n* タラゴン táràgon ◇香辛料の一種 kôshiñryò no isshù

tart [tɑ:rt] *n* (CULIN) タルト tárùto ◇菓子の一種 kashì no isshū; (BRIT: inf: prostitute) ばいた báìta

◆*adj* (flavor) 酸っぱい suppái

tartan [tɑ:r'tən] *n* タータンチェック tātáñchekkù

◆*adj* (rug, scarf etc) タータンチェックの tātáñchekkù no

tartar [tɑ:r'tə:r] *n* (on teeth) 歯石 shiséki

tartar(e) sauce [tɑ:r'tə:r-] *n* タルタルソース tarútarusòsu

tart up (BRIT) *vt* (inf: object) 派手にする hadè ni suru

to tart oneself up おめかしをする o-mékàshi wo suru

task [tæsk] *n* 仕事 shigòto

to take to task ...の責任を問う ...no sekínin wo tôù

task force *n* (MIL, POLICE) 機動部隊 kidôbùtai

Tasmania [tæzmei'ni:ə] *n* タスマニア tasúmania

tassel [tæs'əl] *n* 房 fusá

taste [teist] n (*also*: **sense of taste**) 味覚 mikáku; (flavor: *also*: **aftertaste**) 味; (sample) 一口 hitókùchì; (*fig*: glimpse, idea) 味わい ajíwaì
♦vt (get flavor of) 味わう ajíwaù; (test) 試食する shishóku suru
♦vi: **to taste of/like** (fish etc) ...の味がする ...no ajî ga surú
you can taste the garlic (in it) (含まれている) ニンニクの味がする (fukúmarete irú) nínniku nò ajî ga surú
in good/bad taste 趣味がいい(悪い)趣味 shúmì ga íi(warúì)

tasteful [teist'fəl] adj (furnishings) 趣味の良い shúmì no yóì

tasteless [teist'lis] adj (food) 味がない ajî ga naì; (remark, joke, furnishings) 趣味の悪い shúmì no warúì

tasty [teis'ti:] adj (food) 味がいい shúmì ga íi

tatters [tæt'ə:rz] npl: **in tatters** (clothes, papers etc) ずたずたになって zutázuta ni nattè

tattoo [tætu:'] n (on skin) 入れ墨 irézumi; (spectacle) パレード paréðð
♦vt (name, design) ...の入れ墨をする ...no irézumì wo suru

tatty [tæt'i:] (BRIT: inf) adj (inf) 薄汚い usúgitanaì

taught [tɔːt] pt, pp of **teach**

taunt [tɔːnt] n あざけり azákerì
♦vt あざける azákerù

Taurus [tɔːr'əs] n 牡牛座 oúshizà

taut [tɔːt] adj ぴんと張った píñ tò hattà

tavern [tæv'ə:rn] n (old) 酒場 sakába

tax [tæks] n 税金 zeíkin
♦vt (earnings, goods etc) ...に税金をかける ...ni zeíkìn wò kakérù; (*fig*: test: memory) 最大限に使う saídaìgen ni tsukáù; (patience) 試練にかける shíren ni kakérù

taxable [tæk'səbəl] adj (income) 課税される kazéi sarérù

taxation [tæksei'ʃən] n (system) 課税 kazéi; (money paid) 税金 zeíkin

tax avoidance [-əvɔid'əns] n 節税 setsúzei

tax disc (BRIT) n (AUT) 納税ステッカ ー nőzeisutekkå

tax evasion n 脱税 datsúzei

tax-free [tæks'fri:'] adj (goods, services) 免税の meñzei no

taxi [tæk'si:] n タクシー tákùshī
♦vi (AVIAT: plane) 滑走する kasső suru

taxi driver n タクシーの運転手 tákùshī no úñteñshu

taxi rank (BRIT) n = **taxi stand**

taxi stand n タクシー乗場 takúshīnoríba

tax payer [-pei'ə:r] n 納税者 nőzeìshà

tax relief n 減税 geñzei

tax return n 確定申告書 kakúteishìnkokushð

TB [ti:bi:'] n abbr = **tuberculosis**

tea [ti:] n (drink: Japanese) お茶 o-chá; (: English) 紅茶 kōchà; (BRIT: meal) お やつ o-yátsð
high tea (BRIT) 夕食 yúshoku ◊夕方早目に食べる食事 yúgata hayáme nì tabérù shokúji

tea bag n ティーバッグ tíbaggù

tea break (BRIT) n 休憩 kyúkei

teach [ti:tʃ] (pt, pp **taught**) vt (gen) 教える oshíerù; (be a teacher of) ...の教師をする ...(no)kyőshi wo suru
♦vi (be a teacher: in school etc) 教師をする kyőshì wò suru

teacher [ti:'tʃə:r] n 教師 kyőshi, 先生 señseí

teaching [ti:'tʃiŋ] n (work of teacher) 教職 kyőshoku

tea cosy n お茶帽子 o-chábōshi

tea cup n (Western) ティーカップ tíkappù; (Japanese) 湯飲み茶碗 yunőmijàwàn, 湯飲み yunőmi

teak [ti:k] n チーク chíku

tea leaves npl 茶殻 chagára

team [ti:m] n (of people: *gen*, SPORT) チ ーム chíìmu; (of animals) 一組 hitőkumi

teamwork [ti:m'wə:rk] n チームワーク chímuwàku

teapot [ti:'pɑːt] n きゅうす kyúsu

tear¹ [te:r] n (hole) 裂け目 sakéme
♦vt (pt **tore**, pp **torn**)
♦vi (rip) 破ける yabúkerù
♦vi (become torn) 破れる yabúrerù

tear² [ti:r] n (in eye) 涙 námìda
in tears 泣いている naíte irù

tear along vi (rush) 猛スピードで走って行く mōsupídò de hashítte ikú

tearful [tiːr'fəl] adj (family, face) 涙ぐんだ namídagunda

tear gas n 催涙ガス saíruigasù

tearoom [tiː'ruːm] n 喫茶店 kissáteñ

tear up vt (sheet of paper etc) ずたずたに破る zutázuta ni yabúrù

tease [tiːz] vt からかう karákaů

tea set n 茶器セット chakísettő

teaspoon [tiː'spuːn] n (type of spoon) ティースプーン tísupùñ; (also: **teaspoonful**: as measurement) 小さじ一杯 kosáji íppai

teat [tiːt] n (ANAT) 乳首 chikúbì; (also: **bottle teat**) ほ乳瓶の乳首 honyúbìn no chikúbì

teatime [tiː'taim] n おやつの時間 o-yátsù no jikán

tea towel (BRIT) n ふきん fukíñ

technical [tek'nikəl] adj (terms, advances) 技術の gíjùtsu no

technical college (BRIT) n 高等専門学校 kōtōsenmongakkō

technicality [teknikæl'iti:] n (point of law) 法律の専門的細目 hōritsu no señmonteki saímokù; (detail) 細かい事 komákaì kotó

technically [tek'nikli:] adv (strictly speaking) 正確に言えば sefkaku ni iébà; (regarding technique) 技術的に gíjùtsuteki ni

technician [teknij'ən] n 技術者 gíjùtsushà

technique [tekniːk'] n 技術 gíjùtsu

technological [teknəlɑːdʒ'ikəl] adj 技術的な gíjùtsuteki na

technology [teknɑːl'ədʒi:] n 科学技術 kagákugijùtsu

teddy (bear) [ted'i:-] n クマのぬいぐるみ kumá no nufgurumi

tedious [tiː'di:əs] adj (work, discussions etc) 退屈な tafkutsu na

tee [tiː] n (GOLF) ティー tī

teem [tiːm] vi: **to teem with** (visitors, tourists etc) ...がぞろぞろ来ている ...ga zóròzoro kité irù

it is teeming (with rain) 雨が激しく

降っている áme ga hageshíkù futté irù

teenage [tiːn'eidʒ] adj (children, fashions etc) ティーンエージャーの tín-ējà no

teenager [tiːn'eidʒəːr] n ティーンエージャー tín-ējà

teens [tiːnz] npl: **to be in one's teens** 年齢は10代である nefirei wà júdài de árù

tee-shirt [tiː'ʃəːrt] n = **T-shirt**

teeter [tiː'təːr] vi (also fig) ぐらつく gurátsukù

teeth [tiːθ] npl of **tooth**

teethe [tiːð] vi (baby) 歯が生える há gà haérù

teething ring [tiː'ðiŋ-] n おしゃぶり o-shábùri ◊リング状の物を指す riñgujō no monó wò sásù

teething troubles npl (fig) 初期の困難 shókì no kôñnan

teetotal [tiː'tout'əl] adj (person) 酒を飲まない saké wò nománaì

telecommunications [teləkəmju:-nikei'ʃənz] n 電気通信 deñkítsūshin

telegram [tel'əgræm] n 電報 deñpō

telegraph [tel'əgræf] n (system) 電信 defíshìn

telegraph pole n 電柱 deñchū

telepathic [teləpæθ'ik] adj テレパシーの terépàshii no

telepathy [teləp'əθi:] n テレパシー terépàshii

telephone [tel'əfoun] n 電話 deñwa
◆vt (person) ...に電話をかける ...ni deñwa wò kakérù; (message) 電話で伝える deñwa dè tsutáerù

on the telephone (talking) 電話中で deñwachū de; (possessing phone) 電話を持っている deñwa wò mótte irù

telephone booth n 電話ボックス deñwabokkùsu

telephone box (BRIT) n = **telephone booth**

telephone call n 電話 deñwa

telephone directory n 電話帳 deñwa-chō

telephone number n 電話番号 deñwa-bañgō

telephonist [teləfouni:st] (BRIT) n 電話交換手 deñwakōkañshu

telescope [tel'əskoup] n 望遠鏡 bôenkyō

telescopic [teliskɔp'ik] adj (lens) 望遠の bôen no; (collapsible: tripod, aerial) 入れ子式の irékoshiki no

television [tel'əviʒən] n (all senses) テレビ térebi

on television テレビで térebi de

television set n テレビ受像機 terébijuzōki

telex [tel'eks] n テレックス terékkūsu
♦vt (company) …にテレックスを送る …ni terékkūsu wo okúrū; (message) テレックスで送る terékkūsu de okúrū

tell [tel] (pt, pp told) vt (say) …に言う …ni iú; (relate: story) 述べる nobérù; (distinguish): to tell something from …から …を区別する …karà …wò kúbètsu suru
♦vi (talk): to tell (of) …について話す …ni tsúìte hánàsu; (have an effect) 効果的である kôkateki de arù

to tell someone to do something …に…する様に言う …ni …surú yò ni sú

teller [tel'ər] n (in bank) 出納係 suítōgakàri

telling [tel'iŋ] adj (remark, detail) 意味深い imbukai

tell off vt: to tell someone off しかる shikaru

telltale [tel'teil] adj (sign) 証拠の shôko no

telly [tel'i:] (BRIT: inf) n abbr = television

temerity [təmer'iti:] n ずうずうしさ zūzūshisà

temp [temp] n abbr (= temporary) 臨時職員 rínjishokuìn

temper [tem'pər] n (nature) 性質 sefshitsu; (mood) 機嫌 kigén; (fit of anger) かんしゃく kańshaku
♦vt (moderate) 和らげる yawáragerù

to be in a temper 怒っている okótte irù

to lose one's temper 怒る okórù

temperament [tem'pərəmənt] n (nature) 性質 sefshitsu

temperamental [tempə:rəmen'təl] adj (person, fig: car) 気まぐれな kimágùre na

temperate [tem'pə:rit] adj (climate, country) 温帯の oñdan na

temperate zone n 温帯 oñtai

temperature [tem'pərətʃə:r] n (of person, place) 温度 ôndo

to have/run a temperature 熱がある netsú ga arû

tempest [tem'pist] n 嵐 árashi

tempi [tem'piː] npl of tempo

temple [tem'pəl] n (building) 神殿 shiñden; (ANAT) こめかみ komékami

tempo [tem'pou] (pl tempos or tempi) n (MUS) テンポ téñpo; (fig: of life etc) ペース pêsu

temporarily [tempərer'rili:] adv 一時的に ichíjiteki ni

temporary [tem'pə:re:ri:] adj (passing) 一時的な ichíjiteki na; (worker, job) 臨時の rínji no

tempt [tempt] vt 誘惑する yúwaku suru

to tempt someone into doing something …する様に…を誘惑する …surú yò ni …wo yūwaku suru

temptation [tempteiʃən] n 誘惑 yūwaku

tempting [temp'tiŋ] adj (offer) 魅惑的な miwákuteki na; (food) おいしそうな ofshisô na

ten [ten] num 十（の）jū (no)

tenacity [tənæsʼitiː] n (of person, animal) 根気強さ koñkizúosa

tenancy [ten'ənsi:] n (possession of room, land etc) 賃借 chiñshaku; (period of possession) 賃借期間 chiñshakukikàn

tenant [ten'ənt] n (rent-payer) 店子 tanáko, テナント tenáñto

tend [tend] vt (crops, sick person) …の世話をする …no sewá wo suru
♦vi: to tend to do something …しがちである …shigáchi de arù

tendency [ten'dənsi:] n (of person, thing) 傾向 kefkô

tender [ten'dəːr] adj (person, heart, care) 優しい yasáshiì; (sore) 触ると痛い sawáru tò itái; (meat) 柔らかい yawárakaì; (age) 幼い osánaì
♦n (COMM: offer) 見積り mitsúmori; (money): legal tender 通貨 tsūka

♦*vt* (offer, resignation) 提出する teíshutsu suru

to tender an apology 陳謝する chínsha suru

tenderness [ten'dəːrnis] *n* (affection) 優しさ yasáshisà; (of meat) 柔らかさ yawárakasà

tendon [ten'dən] *n* けん kén

tenement [ten'əmənt] *n* 安アパート yasúapāto

tenet [ten'it] *n* 信条 shínjō

tennis [ten'is] *n* テニス ténisu

tennis ball *n* テニスボール ténisubōru

tennis court *n* テニスコート ténisukōto

tennis player *n* テニス選手 tenísuseñshu

tennis racket *n* テニスラケット tenísurakettò

tennis shoes *npl* テニスシューズ tenísushūzu

tenor [ten'əːr] *n* (MUS) テノール tenórù

tenpin bowling [ten'pin-] *n* ボウリング bóriñgu

tense [tens] *adj* (person, smile, muscle) 緊張した kiñchō shita; (period) 緊迫した kiñpaku shita

♦*n* (LING) 時制 jiséi

tension [ten'ʃən] *n* (nervousness) 緊張 kiñchō; (between ropes etc) 張力 chōryoku

tent [tent] *n* テント téñto

tentacle [ten'təkəl] *n* (of octopus etc) あし ashí

tentative [ten'tətiv] *adj* (person, step, smile) 自信のない jishín no naí; (conclusion, plans) 差し当っての sashíatattè no

tenterhooks [ten'təːrhuks] *npl*: *on tenterhooks* はらはらして hárahara shite

tenth [tenθ] *num* 第十（の） dáijū (no)

tent peg *n* テントのくい téñto no kuí

tent pole *n* テントの支柱 téñto no shichū

tenuous [ten'juːəs] *adj* (hold, links, connection etc) 弱い yowáì

tenure [ten'jəːr] *n* (of land, buildings etc) 保有権 hoyúkeñ; (of office) 在職期間 zaíshokukikàn

tepid [tep'id] *adj* (tea, pool etc) ぬるい nurúì

term [təːrm] *n* (word, expression) 用語 yōgo; (period in power etc) 期間 kikáñ; (SCOL) 学期 gakkí

♦*vt* (call) ...と言う ...to iú

in the short/long term 短（長）期間で taí(chō)kikàn de

terminal [təːr'mənəl] *adj* (disease, cancer, patient) 末期の mákki no

♦*n* (ELEC) 端子 táñshi; (COMPUT) 端末機 tañmatsukì; (*also:* **air terminal**) ターミナルビル tấminarubirù; (BRIT: *also:* **coach terminal**) バスターミナル basútāminaru

terminate [təːr'məneit] *vt* (discussion, contract, pregnancy) 終らせる owáraserù, 終える oérù; (contract) 破棄する hákì suru; (pregnancy) 中絶する chúzetsu suru

termini [təːr'mənìː] *npl of* **terminus**

terminology [təːrmənɑl'ədʒìː] *n* 用語 yōgo, 総称 sōshō

terminus [təːr'mənəs] (*pl* **-mini**) *n* (for buses, trains) ターミナル tấminaru

terms [təːrmz] *npl* (conditions: *also* COMM) 条件 jōken

to be on good terms with someone ...と仲がいい ...to náka ga íì

to come to terms with (problem) ...と折合いがつく ...to oríai ga tsukù

terrace [teːr'əs] *n* (BRIT: row of houses) 長屋 nagáyà; (patio) テラス tếrasu; (AGR) 段々畑 dañdañbatàke

terraced [teːr'əst] *adj* (house) 長屋の nagáyà no; (garden) ひな壇式の hinádañshiki no

terraces [teːr'əsiz] (BRIT) *npl* (SPORT): *the terraces* 立見席 tachímisèki

terracotta [teːrəkɑt'ə] *n* テラコッタ terákottà

terrain [tərein'] *n* 地面 jímen

terrible [teːr'əbəl] *adj* ひどい hídòi

terribly [teːr'əbliː] *adv* (very) とても totémo; (very badly) ひどく hídòku

terrier [teːr'iːəːr] *n* テリア téria

terrific [tərif'ik] *adj* (very great: thunderstorm, speed) 大変な taíheñ na; (wonderful: time, party) 素晴らしい subárashī!

terrify [teˈrifai] vt おびえさせる obfesaserū

territorial [teritɔːˈrːəl] adj (waters, boundaries, dispute) 領土の ryódò no

territory [teˈritɔːri] n (gen) 領土 ryódò; (fig) 縄張 nawábarì

terror [terˈər] n (great fear) 恐怖 kyófu

terrorism [terˈərizəm] n テロ térð

terrorist [terˈərist] n テロリスト teórisùto

terrorize [terˈəːraiz] vt おびえさせる o-bfesaserū

terse [tɑːrs] adj (style) 簡潔な kañketsu na; (reply) そっけない sokkénai つ言葉数が少なmな無愛想な返事などについて言う kotóbakazù ga sukúnakù buáisò na heñji nadð ni tsúīte iū

Terylene [terˈəliːn]® n テリレン térìren ◇人工繊維の一種 jiñkóseñ-i no ísshu

test [test] n (trial, check: also MED, CHEM) テスト tésùto; (of courage etc) 試練 shfren; (SCOL) テスト tésùto; (also: **driving test**) 運転免許の試験 uñtenmeñkyo no shikén

♦vt (gen) テストする tésùto suru

testament [tesˈtəmənt] n 証拠 shóko

the Old/New Testament 旧(新)約聖書 kyū(shiñ)yaku seishó

testicle [tesˈtikəl] n こう丸 kógan

testify [tesˈtəfai] vi (LAW) 証言する shógen suru

to testify to something ...が...だと証言する ...ga ...dá tð shógen suru

testimony [tesˈtəmouniː] n (LAW: statement) 証言 shógen; (clear proof) 証拠 shóko

test match n (CRICKET, RUGBY) 国際戦 kokúsaisen, 国際試合 kokúsaijiài

test pilot n テストパイロット tesútopairottò

test tube n 試験管 shikénkan

tetanus [tetˈənəs] n 破傷風, hashófù

tether [teðˈər] vt (animal) つなぐ tsunágù

♦n: *at the end of one's tether* 行き詰って ikízumattè

text [tekst] n 文書 búñsho

textbook [tekstˈbuk] n 教科書 kyókasho

textiles [teksˈtailz] npl (fabrics) 織物 orímòno; (textile industry) 織物業界 orímonogyókai

texture [teksˈtʃər] n (of cloth, skin, soil, silk) 手触り tezáwàri

Thailand [taiˈlænd] n タイ国 tâi

Thames [temz] n: *the Thames* テムズ川 témùzugawa

than [ðæn] conj (in comparisons) ...より (も) ...yórì(mo)

you have more than 10 あなたは10個以上持っています anátà wa jùkkò íjò móttè imasu

I have more than you/Paul 私はあなた(ポール)より沢山持っています watákushi wa anátà(pórù)yori takúsañ móttè imasu

I have more pens than pencils 私は鉛筆より沢山持っています watákushi wa éñpitsu yorì péñ wo takúsañ móttè imasu

she is older than you think 彼女はあなたが思っているより年ですよ kánòjo wa anátà ga omótte irù yórì toshí desù yó

more than once 数回 sûkài

thank [θæŋk] vt (person) ...に感謝する ...ni kánsha suru

thank you (very much) (大変) 有難うございました (taíhen) arígatò gozáimashìta

thank God! ああ良かった ā yókàtta

thankful [θæŋkˈfəl] adj: *thankful (for)* (...を) 有難く思っている ...(wo) arígatakù omótte irù

thankless [θæŋkˈlis] adj (task) 割の悪い warí no waruî

thanks [θæŋks] npl 感謝 kánsha

♦excl *thanks: many thanks, thanks a lot)* 有難う arígatò

Thanksgiving (Day) [θæŋksgivˈiŋ-] n 感謝祭 kánshasai

thanks to prep ...のおかげで ...no o-káge dè

KEYWORD

that [ðæt] (*demonstrative adj, pron: pl* **those**) *adj* (demonstrative) その sonó, あの anó

that man/woman/book その(あの)男性〔女性〕,本 sonó (anó) dañsei (jósei, hoñ)

leave those books on the table その本をテーブルの上に置いていって下さい sonó hoñ wo téburu no ué nï otte ittè kudásaï

that one それ soré, あれ aré

that one over there あそこにある物 asóko nï áru monó

I want this one, not that one 欲しいのはこれです, あれは要りません hoshíi no wa koré desù, aré wa irímaseñ

♦*pron* 1 (demonstrative) それ soré, あれ aré

who's/what's that? あれはだれですか (何ですか) aré wa dáre desu ká (náñ desu ká)

is that you? あなたですか anátá desu ká

I prefer this to that あれよりこちらの方が好きです aré yorï kochíra no hô ga sukí desù

will you eat all that? あれを全部食べるつもりですか aré wò zénbu tabérù tsumóri desù ká

that's my house 私の家はあれです watákushi no ié wà aré desù

that's what he said 彼はそう言いましたよ káre wa sô iímashïta yó

what happened after that? それからどうなりましたか soré kará dô narimashïta ká

that is (to say) つまり tsúmàri, すなわち sunáwàchi

2 (relative): *the book (that) I read* 私の読んだ本 watákushi no yóñda hóñ

the books that are in the library 図書館にある本 toshókàn nï árù hóñ

the man (that) I saw 私の見た男 watákushi no mítà otóko

all (that) I have 私の持っているだけ watákushi gà móttè irú dàke

the box (that) I put it in それを入れた箱 soré wò iréta hakó

the people (that) I spoke to 私が声を掛けた人々 watákushi gà kôe wo kákèta hitóbìto

3 (relative: of time): *the day (that) he came* 彼が来た日 kâre ga kitá hï

the evening/winter (that) he came to see us 彼が私たちの家に来た夜(冬) kâre ga watákushitàchi no ié nï kitá yorù〔fuyù〕

♦*conj* ...だと ...dá tò

he thought that I was ill 私が病気だと彼は思っていました watákushi gà byôkï dà tò kâre wa omôtte imashïta

she suggested that I phone you あなたに電話する様にと彼女は私に勧めました anátá nï deñwa suru yô nï tò kánojo wa watákushi nï susúmemashïta

♦*adv* (demonstrative) それ程 soré hodò, あれ程 aré hodò, そんなに soñna nï, あんなに añna nï

I can't work that much あんなに働けません afïna nï határakemaseñ

I didn't realize it was that bad 事態があれ程悪くなっているとは思っていませんでした jïtai gà aré hodò wárùku nattè irú to wa omôtte imaseñ deshïta

that high あんなに高い afïna nï takáï

the wall's about that high and that thick 壁はこれぐらい高くてこれぐらい厚い heí wà koré guràï tákàkute koré guràï atsúì

thatched [θætʃt] *adj* (roof, cottage) わらぶきの warábuki no

thaw [θɔ:] *n* 雪解けの陽気 yukídokè no yôkï

♦*vi* (ice) 溶ける tokérù, (food) 解凍される kaítò sarerù

♦*vt* (food: *also*: **thaw out**) 解凍する kaítò suru

KEYWORD

the [ðə] *def art* 1 (*gen*) その sonó ◇通常日本語では表現しない tsújō nïhóngo de wà hyógen shináì

the history of France フランスの歴史

furánsu nò rekfshi

the books/children are in the library 本(子供たち)は図書館にあります(います) hón(kodómotáchi)wa toshó-kàn ni arímasù(imásù)

she put it on the table/gave it to the postman 彼女はテーブルに置きました(郵便屋さんにあげました)kànōjo wa tèburu ni okímashīta(yūbin-yasan ni agémashīta)

he took it from the drawer 彼は引出しから取り出しました kàre wa hikídashi karà torídashimashīta

I haven't the time/money 私にはそれだけの時間(金)がありません watákushi ni wa sorè dakè no jikán(kanè)ga arímasèn

to play the piano/violin ピアノ(バイオリン)をひく piáno(baforin)no hikū

the age of the computer コンピュータの時代 kofipyūta no jídái

I'm going to the butcher's/the cinema 肉屋に(映画を見に)行って来ます nikūyà ni(efga wò mf nī)ittè kimasù

2 (+ adjective to form noun)

the rich and the poor 金持と貧乏人 kanémochī-to bifibónin

the wounded were taken to the hospital 負傷者は病院に運ばれた fushóshà wa byōín ni hakóbareta

to attempt the impossible 不可能な事をやろうとする fukánō na kotò wo yarō to surù

3 (in titles): **Elizabeth the First** エリザベス1世 erízabēsu fsséi

Peter the Great ピョートル大帝 pyótōru taftei

4 (in comparisons): **the more he works the more he earns** 彼は働けば働く程もうかる kàre wa határakèba határaku hodò mōkarù

the more I look at it the less I like it 見れば見る程いやになります mfreba mfru hodò iyá ni narimasù

---

theater [θi:'ətər] n (BRIT **theatre**) n (building with stage) 劇場 gekfjō;(art form) 演劇 efigeki;(also: lecture thea-

ter) 講義室 kōgishītsu;(MED: also: **operating theater**) 手術室 shujútsushītsu

theater-goer [θi:'ətərgouər] n 芝居好き shibáizùki

theatrical [θiæt'rikəl] adj (event, production) 演劇の efigeki no;(gestures) 芝居染みた shibáijimìta

theft [θeft] n 窃盗 settó

their [ðe:r] adj 彼らの kárera no § see also **my**

theirs [ðe:rz] pron 彼らの物 kárera no monó § see also **mine**

them [ðem] pron (direct) 彼らを kárera wo;(indirect) 彼らに kárera ni;(stressed, after prep) 彼ら kárera § see also **me**

theme [θi:m] n (main subject) 主題 shudái;テーマ tèma;(MUS) テーマ tèma

theme park n テーマ遊園地 tèmayūènchi

theme song n 主題歌 shídáika

themselves [ðəmselvz'] pl pron (reflexive) 彼ら自身を karéra jishìn wo;(after prep) 彼ら自身 karéra jishìn § see also **oneself**

then [ðen] adv (at that time) その時(に) sonó tokī(ni);(next, later, and so) それから soré karà

♦conj (therefore) だから dá kàra

♦adj: **the then president** 当時の大統領 tōjī no daftóryō

by then (past) その時 sonó tokī;(future) その時になったら sonó tokī ni nattárà

from then on その時から sonó tokī kara

theology [θi:a:l'ədʒi:] n 神学 shifigaku

theorem [θi:r'əm] n 定理 teíri

theoretical [θi:əret'ikəl] adj (biology, possibility) 理論的な rirónteki na

theorize [θi:'əraiz] vi 学説を立てる gakúsetsu wo tatérù

theory [θi:r'i:] n (all senses) 理論 rírôn

in theory 理論的には rirónteki ni wa

therapeutic(al) [θerəpju:'tik(əl)] adj 治療の chiryó no

therapist [θe:r'əpist] n セラピスト será-pisùto

therapy [θeːrˈəpi] *n* 治療 chiryō

KEYWORD

there [ðeːr] *adv* 1: **there is, there are** ...がある[いる] ...ga áru[irú]

there are 3 of them (things) 3つあります *or* míttsu arímasù; (people) 3人 います saɲˈiɲ imásù

there is no one here だれもいません dáre mo imáseɲ

there is no bread left パンがなくなりました páɲ ga nakúnarimashita

there has been an accident 事故があ りました jíkò ga arímashìta

there will be a meeting tomorrow 明 日会議があります asú káĩgi ga arímasù

2 (referring to place) そこに[で、へ] sokó ni[de, e], あそこに[で、へ] asokó ni [de, e]

where is the book? - it's there 本はど こにありますか-あそこにありますよ hóɲ wa dókò ni arímasù ká - asóko ni arímasù

put it down there そこに置いて下さい sokó ni ófte kudasaì

he went then on Friday 彼は金曜日 に行きました kárè wa kiɲ-yòbi ni ikímashìta

I want that book there そこの本が欲 しい sokó no hóɲ ga hoshíi

there he is! いました imáshìta

3: **there, there** (especially to child) よし よし yóshì yóshì

there, there, it's not your fault/don't cry よしよし、お前のせいじゃな いから[泣かないで] yóshì yóshì, omáe nò seí ja naì karà (nakánaìde)

thereabouts [ðeːrˈəbauts] *adv* (place) その こら辺 sokórahen; (amount) それぐらい soré gurai

thereafter [ðeːræfˈtəːr] *adv* それ以来 soré irài

thereby [ðeːrbaiˈ] *adv* それによって soré ni yotté

therefore [ðeːrˈfɔːr] *adv* だから dá kara

there's [ðeːrz] = there is; there has

thermal [θəːrˈməl] *adj* (underwear) 防 寒

用の bókan-yō no; (paper) 感熱の kafíne-tsu no; (printer) 熱式の netsúshìki no

thermal spring *n* 温泉 ofíseɲ

thermometer [θəːrmɑːmˈitəːr] *n* (for room/body temperature) 温度計 ofído-kèi

Thermos [θəːrˈməs] ® *n* (*also:* **Thermos flask**) 魔法瓶 mahōbiɲ

thermostat [θəːrˈməstæt] *n* サーモスタ ット sāmosutattò

thesaurus [θisɔːrˈəs] *n* シソーラス shisōrāsu

these [ðiːz] *pl adj* これらの korérà no
  ♦*pl pron* これらは[を] korérà wa[wo]

theses [θiːˈsiːz] *npl of* **thesis**

thesis [θiːˈsis] (*pl* **theses**) *n* (for doctor-ate etc) 論文 rofíbuɲ

they [ðei] *pl pron* 彼らは[が] kárèra wa [ga]

they say that ... (it is said that) ...と言 われている ...to iwárete irù

they'd [ðeid] = they had; they would

they'll [ðeil] = they shall, they will

they're [ðeːr] = they are

they've [ðeiv] = they have

thick [θik] *adj* (in shape: slice, jersey etc) 厚い atsúi; (line) 太い futói; (in consis-tency: sauce, mud, fog etc) 濃い kóì; (: forest) 深い fukáì; (stupid) 鈍い níbùi
  ♦*n*: **in the thick of the battle** 戦いの さなかに tatákai nò sánàka ni

it's 20 cm thick 厚さは20センチだ atsúsa wà nijússeɲchì da

thicken [θikˈən] *vi* (fog etc) 濃くなる kókù naru; (plot) 込入ってくる komfítte kurù
  ♦*vt* (sauce etc) 濃くする kókù suru

thickness [θikˈnis] *n* 厚み atsúmi

thickset [θikˈset] *adj* (person, body) が っちりした gatchírì shita

thickskinned [θikˈskind] *adj* (*fig*: per-son) 無神経な mushíɲkei na

thief [θiːf] (*pl* **thieves**) *n* 泥棒 doróbō

thieves [θiːvz] *npl of* **thief**

thigh [θai] *n* 太もも futómomo

thimble [θimˈbəl] *n* 指抜き yubínuki

thin [θiɲ] *adj* (*gen*) 薄い usúi; (line) 細い hosóì; (person, animal) やせた yasétà (crowd) まばらな mabára na

♦vt: to thin (down) (sauce, paint) 薄める usumerú

thing [θiŋ] n (gen) 物事 monógóto; (physical object) 物 monó; (matter) 事 kotó;

to have a thing about someone/something (mania) ...が大嫌いである ...ga dáíkirai de árù; (fascination) ...が大好きである ...ga dáísuki de árù

poor thing かわいそうに ni kawáisò

the best thing would be to ....するのが一番いいだろう ...surú no ga ichíban ii darō

how are things? どうですか dő desu ká

things [θiŋz] npl (belongings) 持物 mochímono

think [θiŋk] (pt, pp thought) vi (reflect) 考える kańgaerù; (believe) 思う omóù

♦vt (imagine) ...だと思う ...dá tò omóù

what did you think of them? 彼らの事をどう思いましたか kárèra no totě wo dó òmóimashtá ka

to think about something/someone ...について考える ...ni tsúìte kañgaerù

I'll think about it 考えておくね kafgaete okú né

to think of doing something ...しようと思う ...shiyô to omóù

I think so/not そうだ(違う)と思う sō dà (chigáù)to omóù

to think well of someone ...に対して好感を持つ ...ni táìshite kókan wò mótsù

think over vt (offer, suggestion) よく考える yókù kańgaerù

think tank n シンクタンク shíñkutañku

think up vt (plan, scheme, excuse) 考え出す kańgaedasù

thinly [θín'li:] adv (cut, spread) 薄く usúkù

third [θərd] num 第三(の) dái san (no)

♦n (fraction) 3分の1 sañbun no ichi; (AUT: also: third gear) サードギヤ sådogiya; (BRIT: SCOL: degree) 3級優等卒業学位 sańkyū itto sotsugyó gakúi

¶see also first

thirdly [θərd'li:] adv 第三に san ni

third party insurance (BRIT) n 損害倍償保険 sofgaibaishōhokén

third-rate [θərd'reit'] adj 三流の sañryū no

Third World n: the Third World 第三世界 dal san sekái

thirst [θərst] n 渇き kawáki

thirsty [θərs'ti:] adj (person, animal) のどが渇いた nódò ga kawáìta; (work) のどが渇く nódò ga kawákù

to be thirsty (person, animal) のどが渇いている nódò ga kawáìte irù

thirteen [θər'tin'] num 十三(の) jūsan (no)

thirty [θər'ti:] num 三十(の) sáñju (no)

this [ðis] (pl these) adj (demonstrative) この konó

this man/woman/book この男性〔女性, 本〕konó dansei(josei, hon)

these people/children/records この人たち〔子供たち, レコード〕konó hitótàchi(kodomótàchi, rekódo)

this one これ koré

it's not that picture but this one that I like 私が好きなのはあの絵ではなくて、この絵です watákushi gà sukí na no wa anó e de wa nakúte, konó e desù

♦pron (demonstrative) これ koré

what is this? これは何ですか koré wà nán desu ká

who is this? この方はどなたですか konó katà wa dónàta desu ká

I prefer this to that 私はあれよりこの方が好きです watákushi wà aré yorì konó hồ ga sukí desù

this is where I live 私の住いはここです watákushi no sumái wa kokó desù

this is what he said 彼はこう言いました kárè wa kố iimashtà

this is Mr Brown (in introductions/photo) こちらはブラウンさんです kochíra wà buráùnsan desu; (on telephone) こちらはブラウンですが kochíra wà burá-

ûn desu ga
♦*adv* (demonstrative): *this high/long*
高さ(長さ)はこれぐらいで tákasa(nágasa)wa korê gurâi de
it was about this big 大きさはこれぐ
らいでした ôkîsa wa korêgurâi deshita
the car is this long 車の長さはこれぐ
らいです kurûma no nagâsa wa korê
gurâi desu
*we can't stop now we've gone this
far* ここまで来たらやめられません kokô madê kitâra yameraremasên

thistle [θis'əl] *n* アザミ azámi

thong [θɔːŋ] *n* バンド bándo

thorn [θɔːrn] *n* とげ togé

thorny [θɔːr'niː] *adj* (plant, tree) とげの
多いとげ no ôi; (problem) 厄介な yákkâi
na

thorough [θəːr'ou] *adj* (search, wash) 徹
底的な tettéiteki na; (knowledge,
research) 深い fukâi; (person: methodical) きちょうめんな kichômen na

thoroughbred [θəːr'oubred] *n* サラブレッド
サラブレッド sarâbureddô

thoroughfare [θəːr'oufeːr] *n* 目抜き通
り menúkidôri
「no thoroughfare」通行禁止 tsûkôkinshi

thoroughly [θəːr'ouliː] *adv* (examine,
study, wash, search) 徹底的に tettéiteki
ni; (very) とても totêmo

those [ðouz] *adj* それらの sorêra no,
あれらの arêra no
♦*pl pron* それらを sorêra wo, あれらを
arêra wo

though [ðou] *conj* …にもかかわらず …ni
mô kakâwarazù
♦*adv* しかし shikâshî

thought [θɔːt] *pt, pp of* think
♦*n* (idea, reflection) 考え kańgaê; (opinion) 意見 îkén

thoughtful [θɔːt'fəl] *adj* (person: deep in
thought) 考え込んでいる kańgaekonde
irû; (: serious) 真剣な shinkên na; (considerate: person) 思いやりのある omôiyari no arû

thoughtless [θɔːt'lis] *adj* (inconsiderate:

behavior, words, person) 心ない kokôronaî

thousand [θau'zənd] *num* 千 (の) señ
(no)
two thousand 二千 (の) nisêñ (no)
thousands of 何千もの… nañzeñ mo
no …

thousandth [θau'zəndθ] *num* 第 千
(の) dâî señ (no)

thrash [θræʃ] *vt* (beat) たたく tatákû;
(defeat) …に neg负 …ni kañshô surú

thrash about/around *vi* のたうつ notáutsù

thrash out *vt* (problem) 討議する tôgi
suru

thread [θred] *n* (yarn) 糸 fitô; (of screw)
ねじ山 nejíyãma
♦*vt* (needle) …に糸を通す …ni fitô wo tôsû

threadbare [θred'beːr] *adj* (clothes, carpet) 擦り切れた surfkireta

threat [θret] *n* (also *fig*) 脅し odôshi;
(*fig*) 危険 kikén

threaten [θret'ən] *vi* (storm, danger) 迫
る semárù
♦*vt: to threaten someone with/to do
…で* (…すると言って)…を脅す …de (…surú tô ittê)…wô odôsù

three [θriː] *num* 三 (の) sañ (no)

three-dimensional [θriː'dimen'tʃənəl]
adj 立体の rittâi no

three-piece suit [θriː'piːs-] *n* 三つぞろ
い mitsúzorôi

three-piece suite *n* 応接三点セット ôsetsu santensettô

three-ply [θriː'plai] *adj* (wool) 三重織り
の sañjûori no

thresh [θreʃ] *vt* (AGR) 脱穀する dakkôku suru

threshold [θreʃ'ould] *n* 敷居 shikíi

threw [θruː] *pt of* throw

thrift [θrift] *n* 節約 setsúyaku

thrifty [θrif'tiː] *adj* 節約家の setsúyakukâ no

thrill [θril] *n* (excitement) スリル súrîru;
(shudder) ぞっとする事 zottô suru kotô
♦*vt* (person, audience) わくわくさせる
wákûwaku sasérû

to be thrilled (with gift etc) 大喜びである ōyorōkobi de árú

thriller [θrɪl'ər] n (novel, play, film) スリラー surfrā

thrilling [θrɪl'iŋ] adj (ride, performance, news etc) わくわくさせる wákuwaku sasérù

thrive [θraiv] vi (grow: plant) 生茂る ofshigerù; (: person, animal) よく育つ yókù sodátsù; (: business) 盛んになる sakán ni narù; (: do well): **to thrive on something** ...で栄える ...de saéerù

thriven [θraivən] pp of **thrive**

thriving [θraiv'iŋ] adj (business, community) 繁盛している háñjō shité irù

throat [θrout] n のど nódò

to have a sore throat のどが痛い nódò ga itáì

throb [θrɑb] n (of heart) 鼓動 kodō; (of wound) うずき uzúkì; (of engine) 振動 shifidō

◆vi (heart) どきどきする dókìdokì suru; (head, arm: with pain) ずきずきする zúkìzukì suru; (machine: vibrate) 振動する shifidō suru

throes [θrouz] npl: ***in the throes of*** (war, moving house etc) ...と取組んでいるさなかに ...to toríkunde irù sánàka ni

thrombosis [θrɑmbou'sis] n 血栓症 kessénshō

throne [θroun] n 王座 ōzá

throng [θrɔːŋ] n 群衆 guńshū

◆vt (streets etc) ...に殺到する ...ni sattō suru

throttle [θrɑːt'əl] n (AUT) スロットル suróttòru

◆vt (strangle) ...ののどを絞める ...no nódò wo shimérù

through [θruː] prep (space) ...を通って ...wo tōtte; (time) ...の間中 ...no aída jū; (by means of) ...を使って ...wo tsukátte; (owing to) ...が原因で ...ga geñ-in de

◆adj (ticket, train) 直通の chokútsū no

◆adv 通して tōshite

to put someone through to someone (TEL) ...を...につなぐ ...wo ...ni tsunágu

to be through (TEL) つながれる tsuná-

garerù; (relationship: finished) 終る owárù

「***no through road***」(BRIT) 行き止り ikídomarì

throughout [θruːaut'] prep (place) ...の至る所に ...no itárù tokoro ni; (time) ...の間中 ...no aída jū

◆adv 至る所に itárù tokoro ni

throve [θrouv] pt of **thrive**

throw [θrou] n (gen) 投げる事 nagérù kotô

◆vt (pt **threw**, pp **thrown**) (object) 投げる nagérù; (rider) 振り落す furítosù; (fig: person: confuse) 迷わせる mayówaserù

to throw a party パーティをやる pátī wo yárù

throw away vt (rubbish) 捨てる sutérù; (money) 浪費する róhí suru

throwaway [θrou'əwei] adj (tooth-brush) 使い捨ての tsukáìsute no; (line, remark) 軽で言い込まれた sutézerifúkimìta

throw-in [θrou'in] n (SPORT) スローイン suróín

throw off vt (get rid of: burden, habit) かなぐり捨てる kanágurisuterù; (cold) ...が治る ...ga naórù

throw out vt (rubbish, idea) 捨てる sutérù; (person) ほうり出す hōrídasù

throw up vi (vomit) 吐く hákù

thru [θruː] (US) = **through**

thrush [θrʌʃ] n (bird) つぐみ tsugûmi

thrust [θrʌst] n (TECH) 推進力 sufshiñryoku

◆vt (pt, pp **thrust**) (person, object) 強く押す tsuyôku osû

thud [θʌd] n ばたんという音 batáñ to iú otò

thug [θʌg] n (pej) ちんぴら chiñpira; (criminal) 犯罪者 hañzaîsha

thumb [θʌm] n (ANAT) 親指 oyáyubi

◆vt: ***to thumb a lift*** ヒッチハイクする hitchháìku suru

thumbtack [θʌm'tæk] (US) n 画びょう gabyō

thumb through vt fus (book) 拾い読みする hiróiyomi suru

thump [θʌmp] *n* (blow) 一撃 ichígeki; (sound) どしんという音 doshín to iú otó
♦*vt* (person, object) たたく tatákū
♦*vi* (heart etc) どきどきする dókìdoki suru

thunder [θʌn'dəːr] *n* 雷 kamínari
♦*vi* 雷が鳴る kamínari ga narú; (*fig*: train etc): **to thunder past** ごう音を立てて通り過ぎる góon wo tátète tōrisugírù

thunderbolt [θʌn'dəːrboult] *n* 落雷 rakúrai

thunderclap [θʌn'dəːrklæp] *n* 雷鳴 raímei

thunderstorm [θʌn'dəːrstɔːrm] *n* 雷雨 ráìu

thundery [θʌn'dəːri] *adj* (weather) 雷が鳴る kamínari ga narú

Thursday [θəːrz'dei] *n* 木曜日 mokúyōbi

thus [ðʌs] *adv* (in this way) こうして shíte; (consequently) 従って shitágattè

thwart [θwɔːrt] *vt* (person, plans) 邪魔する jamá suru

thyme [taim] *n* タイム táìmu

thyroid [θai'rɔid] *n* (*also*: **thyroid gland**) 甲状腺 kōjōsen

tiara [tiːer'ə] *n* ティアラ tíàra

Tibet [tibet'] *n* チベット chíbètto

tic [tik] *n* チック chíkkù

tick [tik] *n* (sound of clock) かちかち kachíkachi; (mark) 印 shírùshi; (ZOOL) だに danî; (*BRIT*: *inf*): **in a tick** すぐ mố sugù
♦*vi* (clock, watch) かちかちいう kachíkachi iú
♦*vt* (item on list) ...に印を付ける ...ni shírùshi wò tsukérù

ticket [tik'it] *n* (for public transport, theater etc) 切符 kippú; (in shop: on goods) 値札 nefúda; (for raffle, library etc) チケット chíkètto; (*also*: **parking ticket**) 駐車違反のチケット chūsha-ihán no chíkètto

ticket collector *n* 改札係 kaísatsugàkari

ticket office *n* (RAIL, theater etc) 切符売場 kippú urîba

tickle [tik'əl] *vt* (person, dog) くすぐる kusúguru
♦*vi* (feather etc) くすぐったい kusúguttai

ticklish [tik'liʃ] *adj* (person) くすぐったがる kusúguttagàru; (problem) 厄介な yákkài na

tick off *vt* (item on list) ...に印を付ける ...ni shírùshi wò tsukérù; (person) しかる shikárù

tick over *vi* (engine) アイドリングする afdorìngu suru; (*fig*: business) 低迷する teímei suru

tidal [taid'əl] *adj* (force) 潮の shió no; (estuary) 干満のある kafîman no arû

tidal wave *n* 津波 tsunámi

tidbit [tid'bit] (*US*) *n* (food) うまいもの 一口 umái monò hitókùchi; (news) 好奇心をあおり立てられる話 kōkishîn wo aórìtaterù uwásabanàshi

tiddlywinks [tid'liːwiŋks] *n* おはじき ohájìki

tide [taid] *n* (in sea) 潮 shió; (*fig*: of events, fashion, opinion) 動向 dōkō
high/low tide 満(干)潮 man(kán)chō

tide over *vt* (help out) ...の一時的な助けになる ...no ichíjiteki nà tasúke ni narú

tidy [tai'di] *adj* (room, dress, desk, work) きちんとした kichín to shita; (person) きれいな kiréi na
♦*vt* (*also*: **tidy up**: room, house etc) 片付ける katázukerù

tie [tai] *n* (string etc) ひも himó; (*BRIT*: *also*: **necktie**) ネクタイ nékùtai; (*fig*: link) 縁故 éñko; (SPORT: even score) 同点 dóten
♦*vt* (fasten: parcel) 縛る shibárù; (: shoelaces, ribbon) 結ぶ musúbù
♦*vi* (SPORT etc) 同点になる dóten nì narú
to tie in a bow ちょう結びにする chōmusùbi ni suru
to tie a knot in something ...に結び目を作る ...ni musùbime wò tsukúrù

tie down *vt* (*fig*: person: restrict) 束縛する sokúbaku suru; (: to date, price etc) 縛り付ける shibáritsukerù

tier [tiːr] *n* (of stadium etc) 列 rétsù; (of cake) 層 sō

tie up vt (parcel) ...にひもを掛ける ...ni himó wò kakérù; (dog, boat) つなぐ tsunagu; (prisoner) 縛る shibárù; (arrangements) 整える totónoerù
to be tied up (busy) 忙しい isógashíì

tiger [tai'gə:r] n トラ torá

tight [tait] adj (firm: grip) ぴんと張った pín tò hattá; (scarce: money) 少ない sukúnaì; (narrow: shoes, clothes) きつい kitsúi; (bend) 急な kyū́ na; (strict: security, budget, schedule) 厳しい kibíshíì; (inf: drunk) 酔っ払った yoppárattà
♦adv (hold, squeeze, shut) 堅く katákù

tighten [tait'ən] vt (rope, screw) 締める shimérù; (grip) 固くする katákù suru; (security) 厳しくする kibíshikù suru
♦vi (grip) 固くなる katákù narù; (rope) 締る shimárù

tightfisted [tait'fis'tid] adj けちな kéchi na

tightly [tait'li:] adv (grasp) 固く katákù

tightrope [tait'roup] n 綱渡りの綱 tsunáwatàri no tsuná

tights [taits] npl タイツ táitsu

tile [tail] n (on roof) かわら kawára; (on floor, wall) タイル táiru

tiled [taild] adj (roof) かわらぶきの kawárabuki no; (floor, wall) タイル張りの tafrúbari no

till [til] n (in shop etc) レジの引出し réjì no hikídashi
♦vt (land: cultivate) 耕す tagáyasù
♦prep, conj = until

tiller [til'ə:r] n (NAUT) だ柄 dahéi, チラ - chírà

tilt [tilt] vt 傾ける katámukerù
♦vi 傾く katámukù

timber [tim'bə:r] n (material) 材木 zaímoku; (trees) 材木用の木 zaímokuyṑ no kí

time [taim] n (gen) 時間 jfkàn; (epoch: often 時) 時代 jidái; (by clock) 時刻 jfkòku; (moment) 瞬間 shunkan; (occasion) 回 kái; (MUS) テンポ tênpo
♦vt (measure time of: race, boiling an egg etc) ...の時間を計る ...no jfkàn wo hakárù; (fix moment for: visit etc) ...の時期を選ぶ ...no jfkì wo erábù; (remark

etc) ...のタイミングを合せる ...no tafmìngu wo awáserù

a long time 長い間 nagái aidà

for the time being 取りあえず toríaezù

4 at a time 4つずつ yottsú zútsu

from time to time 時々 tokídoki

at times 時には tokí ni wà

in time (soon enough) 間に合って ma ní attè; (after some time) やがて yagáte; (MUS) ...のリズムに合せて ... no rízùmu ni awáserù

in a week's time 1週間で isshū́kàn de

in no time すぐに súgù ni

any time いつでも ítsù de mo

on time 間に合って ma ní attè

5 times 5 5かける5 gó kakérù gó

what time is it? 何時ですか nánji desu ka

to have a good time 楽しむ tanóshimù

time bomb n 時限爆弾 jigénbakùdan

time lag n 遅れ okúre

timeless [taim'lis] adj 普遍的な fuhénteki na

time limit n 期限 kígen

timely [taim'li:] adj (arrival, reminder) 時宜を得た jígì wo étà, 丁度いい時の chôdo ii tokí no, タイムリーな tâimurī na

time off n 休暇 kyūka

timer [tai'mə:r] n (time switch) タイムスイッチ tafmusuitchì; (in cooking) タイマー - tâimā

time scale (BRIT) n 期間 kíkàn

time-share [taim'ʃe:r] n リゾート施設の共同使用権 rizótoshisètsu no kyódōshiyóken

time switch n タイムスイッチ tafmusuitchì, タイマー taimā

timetable [taim'teibəl] n (RAIL etc) 時刻表 jikókuhyō; (SCOL etc) 時間割 jikánwari

time zone n 時間帯 jíkàntai

timid [tim'id] adj (shy) 気が小さい kí gà chíisaì; (easily frightened) 臆病な okúbyō na

timing [tai'miŋ] n (SPORT) タイミング tafmìngu

the timing of his resignation 彼の辞

退のタイミング kâre no jîtái no taímíngu

timpani [tim'pəni:] npl ティンパニー tînpanî

tin [tin] n (material) すず súzù; (also: **tin plate**) ブリキ buríkì; (container: biscuit etc) 箱 hakô; (: BRIT: can) 缶 kấñ

tinfoil [tin'fɔil] n ホイル hốîru

tinge [tindʒ] n (of color) 薄い色合 usûî iróaì; (of feeling) 気味 kimî
◆vt: **tinged with** (color) …の色合を帯びた …no iróaì wo óbìta; (feeling) …の気味を帯びた …no kimî wò óbìta

tingle [tin'gəl] vi (person, arms etc) ぴりぴりする bíríbiri suru

tinker [tiŋk'əːr] n: **to tinker with** vt fus いじくる ijîkurù

tinned [tind] (BRIT) adj (food, salmon, peas) 缶詰の kañzume no

tin opener [-ou'pənə] (BRIT) n 缶切り kañkiri

tinsel [tin'səl] n ティンセル tîñseru

tint [tint] n (color) 色合い iróaì; (for hair) 染毛剤 señmōzai
tinted [tin'tid] adj (hair) 染めた sómèta; (spectacles, glass) 色付きの irótsuki no

tiny [tai'ni:] adj 小さな chîìsa na

tip [tip] n (end: of paintbrush etc) 先端 señtan; (gratuity) チップ chíppù; (BRIT: for rubbish) ごみ捨て場 gomî suteba; (advice) 助言 jogêñ
◆vt (waiter) …にチップをあげる …ni chíppò wo agérù; (tilt) 傾ける katâmukerù; (overturn) 引っ繰り返す hikkúrikaesù; (empty: also: **tip out**) 空ける akérù

tip-off [tip'ɔːf] n (hint) 内報 naîhō

tipped [tipt] (BRIT) adj (cigarette) フィルター付きの fîrùtātsuki no

Tipp-Ex [tip'eks] ® (BRIT) n 修正ホワイト shûseipèñ ◇白い修正液の出るフェルトペン shirôì shûseiekì no derû ferútopèñ

tipsy [tip'si:] (inf) adj 酔っ払った yoppárattà

tiptoe [tip'tou] n: **on tiptoe** つま先立って tsumásakidattè

tiptop [tip'tɑːp] adj: **in tiptop condition** 状態が最高な jôtai gà saîkō dè

tire [taiəːr] n (BRIT **tyre**) タイヤ tâìya
◆vt (make tired) 疲れさせる tsukâresaserù
◆vi (become tired) 疲れる tsukârerù; (become wearied) うんざりする uñzari suru

tired [taiəːrd] adj (person, voice) 疲れた tsukâretà
to be tired of something …にうんざりしている …ni uñzari shité irù

tireless [taiəːr'lis] adj (worker) 疲れを知らない tsukâre wò shirânaì; (efforts) たゆまない tayúmanaì

tire pressure n タイヤの空気圧 tâìya no kûkìatsù

tiresome [taiəːr'səm] adj (person, thing) うんざりさせる uñzari saserù

tiring [taiəːr'iŋ] adj 疲れさせる tsukâresaserù

tissue [tiʃ'uː] n (ANAT, BIO) 組織 sôshìki; (paper handkerchief) ティッシュ tîsshùpèpā

tissue paper n ティッシュペーパー tissĥùpèpā

tit [tit] n (bird) シジュウカラ shijûkàra
to give tit for tat しっぺ返しをする shippégàeshi suru

titbit [tit'bit] = **tidbit**

titillate [tit'əleit] vt 刺激する shigéki suru ◇特に性的描写などについて言う tókù ni sêîtekì byôsha nádò ni tsûîte iú

title [tait'əl] n (of book, play etc) 題名 daîmeì; (personal rank etc) 肩書 katâgaki; (BOXING etc) タイトル taîtoru

title deed n (LAW) 権利証書 keñrishồsho

title role n 主役 shuyâku

titter [tit'əːr] vi くすくす笑う kusúkusu waráù

TM [ti:em'] abbr = **trademark**

---

to [tuː] prep 1 (direction) …へ …é
to go to France/London/school/the station フランス(ロンドン, 学校, 駅)へ行く furánsu(róñdon, gakkô, ékì)e ikù
to go to Claude's/the doctor's クロー

ドの家〔医者〕へ行く kurôdo no ié(ishá)e ikú

the road to Edinburgh エジンバラへの道 ejĭnbara é nò michí

to the left/right 左(右)へ hidári(mìgî)e

2 (as far as): ...まで ...mádé

from here to London ここからロンドンまで kokó kara rôndon madé

to count to 10 10まで数える jû kazóerù

from 40 to 50 people 40ないし50人の人 yônjû nàishí gojūnín no hitô

3 (with expressions of time): *a quarter to 5* 5時15分前 gójĭ jûgófùn máe

it's twenty to 3 3時20分前です sánji nijúppùn máe desu

4 (for, of) ...の ...no

the key to the front door 玄関のかぎ génkan no kagî

she is secretary to the director 彼女は所長の秘書です kânojo wa shochô nò hishô desû

a letter to his wife 妻への手紙 tsúma e no tegámì

5 (expressing indirect object): ...に ...ni

to give something to someone ...に...を与える ...ni ...wò atâerù

to talk to someone ...に話す ...ni hanâsù

I sold it to a friend 友達にそれを売り たのtomódachi nì sorê wò urímashĭta

to cause damage to something ...に損害を与える ...ni sõngai wò atâerù

to be a danger to someone/something ...を危険にさらす ...wò kikén ni sarásù

to carry out repairs to something ...を修理する ...wò shûrî suru

you've done something to your hair あなたは髪型を変えましたね anátā wa kamígata wò kaémashĭta ne

6 (in relation to): ...に対して ...ni tâĭshite

A is to B as C is to D A対Bの関係はC対Dの関係に等しい A tái B no kankéi wà C tái D no kankéi nì hitôshiî

3 goals to 2 スコア3対2 sukôa　wa sañ tái ní

30 miles to the gallon ガソリン1ガロンで30マイル走れる gasórin ichígarôn de sañjūmáĭru hashírerù

7 (purpose, result): *to come to someone's aid* ...を助けに来る ...wò tasúke nī kúrù

to sentence someone to death ...に死刑の宣告を下す ...ni shikéi nò señkoku wò kudásù

to my surprise 驚いた事に odôroita kotô ni

◆*with vb* **1** (simple infinitive): *to go/eat* 行く〔食べる〕事 ikû(tabérù)kotô

2 (following another verb): *to want to do* ...したい ...shitái

to try to do ...をしようとする ...wò shiyô tò suru

to start to do ...し始める ...wò shihájimerù

3 (with vb omitted): *I don't want to* それをしたくない sorê wò shitákùnai

you ought to あなたはそうすべきです anátā wa sô sùbeki desu

4 (purpose, result): ...するために ...surú tamè ni, ...する様に ...surú yô ni, ...に ...shî nî

I did it to help you あなたを助け様と思ってそれをしました anátā wo tasúkeyô to omôtte sorê wò shimáshĭta

he came to see you 彼はあなたに会いに来ました kârè wa anátā ni áĭ ni kimáshĭta

I went there to meet him 彼に会おうとしてあそこへ行きました kârè ni aô tò shite asôko e ikimashĭta

5 (equivalent to relative clause): *I have things to do* する事があります irôiro tò suru kotô ga arímasû

he has a lot to lose if ... ...が起これば、彼は大損をするだろう ...ga okôrebā, kârè wa ôzòn wo suru darô

the main thing is to try 一番大切なのは努力です ichíban taïsetsu ná no wa dóryòku desu

6 (after adjective etc): *ready to go* 行く準備ができた ikú juñbi ga dékĭta

too old/young to ... ...するのに年を取り過ぎている〔若過ぎる〕 ...surú no ni to-

shī wò torísugite irū (wakásugirū)
it's too heavy to lift 重くて持上げられ
ません omókute mochíagerareraerareemaseñ
♦*adv*: push/pull the door to ドアを閉
める dóawo shiméru ◊ぴったり閉めない
場合に使う pittárt shiménai baái ni tsukáū

toad [toud] *n* ヒキガエル hikígaeru

toadstool [toud'stu:l] *n* キノコ kínoko

toast [toust] *n* (CULIN) トースト tósuto;
(drink, speech) 乾杯 kañpai
♦*vt* (CULIN: bread etc) 焼く yákū;
(drink to) ...のために乾杯する ...no tamé
ni kañpai suru

toaster [tous'tər] *n* トースター tósutā

tobacco [təbæk'ou] *n* タバコ tabáko

tobacconist [təbæk'ənist] *n* タバコ売り
tabákouri

tobacconist's (shop) [təbæk'ənists-] *n*
タバコ屋 tabákoya

toboggan [təbɑg'ən] *n* (*also*: child's ト
ボガン tobógañ

today [tədei'] *adv* (*also fig*) 今日 kyó
(wà)
♦*n* 今日 kyó; (*fig*) 現在 geñzai

toddler [tɑd'lər] *n* 幼児 yóji

to-do [tədu:'] *n* (fuss) 騒ぎ sáwagi

toe [tou] *n* (of foot) 足指 ashíyùbi; (of
shoe, sock) つま先 tsumásaki
♦*vt*: to toe the line (*fig*) 服従する fukújū suru

toenail [tou'neil] *n* 足のつめ ashí no tsumé

toffee [tɔ:f'i:] *n* = taffy

toffee apple (*BRIT*) *n* タフィー衣のり
んご tafígoromo no ríñgo

toga [tou'gə] *n* トーガ tóga

together [tugeð'ər] *adv* (with each
other) 一緒に ísshò ni; (at same time) 同
時に dójì ni
together with ...と一緒に ...to ísshò ni

toil [tɔil] *n* 労苦 róku
♦*vi* 辛そうに働く ákùseku határakū

toilet [tɔi'lit] *n* (apparatus) 便器 bēñki,
トイレ tóire; (room with this apparatus)
便所 beñjo, お手洗い o-téarai, トイレ tóire

toilet bag (for woman) 化粧バッグ ke-
shóbaggù; (for man) 洗面バッグ señmen-
baggù

toilet paper *n* トイレットペーパー tofrettopépà

toiletries [tɔi'litri:z] *npl* 化粧品 keshóhìn

toilet roll *n* トイレットペーパーのロー
ル tofrettopépà no róru

toilet soap *n* 化粧石けん keshósekèn

toilet water *n* 化粧水 keshósùi

token [tou'kən] *n* (sign, souvenir) 印 shirúshi; (substitute coin) コイン kóñ
♦*adj* (strike, payment etc) 名目の mef-
moku no
book/record/gift token (*BRIT*) 商品
券 shóhìñken

Tokyo [tou'ki:jou] *n* 東京 tókyò

told [tould] *pt, pp of* **tell**

tolerable [tɑl'ərəbəl] *adj* (bearable) 我
慢できる gámàn dekírù; (fairly good) ま
あまあの mámà no

tolerance [tɑl'ərəns] *n* (patience) 寛容
kañ-yò; (TECH) 耐久力 taíkyùryoku

tolerant [tɑl'ərənt] *adj*: *tolerant (of)*
(...に) 耐えられる (...ni) taérarerù

tolerate [tɑl'əreit] *vt* (pain, noise, injustice) 我慢する gámàn suru

toll [toul] *n* (of casualties, deaths) 数 kázù; (tax, charge) 料金 ryókin
♦*vi* (bell) 鳴る narú

tomato [təmei'tou] (*pl* **tomatoes**) *n* トマ
ト tómàto

tomb [tum] *n* 墓 haká

tomboy [tɑm'bɔi] *n* お転婆 o-téñba

tombstone [tum'stoun] *n* 墓石 haká-ìshi

tomcat [tɑm'kæt] *n* 雄ネコ osúneko

tomorrow [təmɔr'ou] *adv* (*also fig*) 明
日 asú, あした ashíta
♦*n* 明日 asú, あした ashíta
the day after tomorrow あさって a-
sátte
tomorrow morning あしたの朝 ashíta
nò ása

ton [tʌn] *n* トン tóñ ◊*BRIT* = 1016 kg;
US = 907 kg
tons of (*inf*) ものすごく沢山の monósu-
gòku takúsan no

tone [toun] *n* (of voice) 調子 chóshi; (of

instrument) 音色 ne-íro; (of color; also: **tone in**) 色調 shíkíchō

♦*vi* (colors: *also*: **tone in**) 合う áù

tone-deaf [toun'def] *adj* 音痴の ôńchi no

tone down *vt* (color, criticism, demands) 和らげる yawáragerù; (sound) 小さくする chíísakù suru

tone up (muscles) 強くする tsúyòku suru

tongs [tɔːŋz] *npl* (*also*: **coal tongs**) 炭ばさみ sumíbasàmi; (curling tongs) 髪ごて kamígote

tongue [tʌŋ] *n* (ANAT) 舌 shitá; (CULIN) タン táñ; (language) 言語 gêñgo

tongue in cheek (speak, say) からかって karákàtte

tongue-tied [tʌŋ'taid] *adj* (fig) ものも言えない monó mò iénaî

tongue-twister [tʌŋ'twistəːr] *n* 早口言葉 hayákuchi kotòba

tonic [tɑːn'ik] *n* (MED, *also fig*) 強壮剤 kyōsōzai; (*also*: **tonic water**) トニックウオーター toníkkùuōtā

tonight [tənait'] *adv* (this evening) 今日の夕方 kyō nò yūgàta; (this night) 今夜 kóñ-ya

♦*n* (this evening) 今日の夕方 kyō nò yūgàta; (this night) 今夜 kóñ-ya

tonnage [tʌn'idʒ] *n* (NAUT) トン数 tońsù

tonsil [tɑːn'səl] *n* へんとうせん heńtòsen

tonsillitis [tɑːnsəlai'tis] *n* へんとうせん炎 heńtōsen-èn

too [tuː] *adv* (excessively) あまりに...過ぎる amári nì ...sugírù; (*also*) ...も (また) ...mo (matá)

too much adv あまり沢山で amári takùsañ de

♦*adj* あまり沢山の amári takùsañ no

too many adv あまり沢山の amári takùsañ no

♦*pron* あまり沢山 amári takùsañ

took [tuk] *pt* of **take**

tool [tuːl] *n* 道具 dōgù

tool box *n* 道具箱 dōgubàko

toot [tuːt] *n* (of horn) ぷーぷー pūpù, (of whistle) ぴーぴー pīpī

♦*vi* (with car-horn) クラクションを鳴らす kurákùshoñ wo narásù

tooth [tuːθ] *(pl* teeth*)* *n* (ANAT, TECH) 歯 há

toothache [tuːθ'eik] *n* 歯の痛み há nò itámì, 歯痛 shitsū

toothbrush [tuːθ'brʌʃ] *n* 歯ブラシ habúrashì

toothpaste [tuːθ'peist] *n* 歯磨き hamígakì

toothpick [tuːθ'pik] *n* つまようじ tsumáyòji

top [tɑːp] *n* (of mountain, tree, head, ladder) 天辺 teppèñ; (page) 頭 atáma; (of cupboard, table, box) ...の上 ...no uê; (of list etc) 筆頭 hittô; (lid: of box, jar, bottle) ふた futá; (blouse etc) トップ tôppù; (toy) こま kómà

♦*adj* (highest: shelf, step) 一番上の ichíbañ ue no; (: marks) 最高の saíkō no; (in rank: salesman etc) ぴかーの pikấ-ichì no

♦*vt* (be first in: poll, vote, list) ...の首位に立つ ...no shūî ni tátsù; (exceed: estimate etc) 越える koérù

on top of (above) ...の上に ...no uê ni; (in addition to) ...に加えて ...ni kuwáetè

from top to bottom 上から下まで uê kara shitá madè

top floor *n* 最上階 saíjōkai

top hat *n* シルクハット shirúkuhattò

top-heavy [tɑːp'hevi] *adj* (object) 不安定な fuáñtei na; (administration) 幹部の多過ぎる káñbu no ōsugìrù

topic [tɑːp'ik] *n* 話題 wadái

topical [tɑːp'ikəl] *adj* 時事問題の jíjímòñdai no

topless [tɑːp'lis] *adj* (bather, waitress, swimsuit) トップレスの tôppùresu no

top-level [tɑːp'lev'əl] *adj* (talks, decision) 首脳の shunō no

topmost [tɑːp'moust] *adj* (branch etc) 一番上の ichíbañ ue no

top off (US) *vt* = **top up**

topple [tɑːp'əl] *vt* (government, leader) 倒す taósù

♦*vi* (person, object) 倒れる taórerù

top-secret [tɑːp'si:'krit] *adj* 極秘の gokũhi no

topsy-turvy [tɑp'si:tɜːr'vi:] *adj* (world) はちゃめちゃの háchamecha no

♦*adv* (fall, land etc) 逆様に sakásama ni

top up *vt* (bottle etc) 一杯にする ippái ni surú

torch [tɔːrtʃ] *n* (with flame) たいまつ táimatsu; (BRIT: electric) 懐中電とう kaíchūdentố

tore [tɔːr] *pt of* tear

torment [*n* tɔːr'ment *vb* tɔːrment'] *n* 苦しみ kurúshimì

♦*vt* (subj: feelings, guilt etc) 苦しませる kurúshimaserù, 悩ませる nayámaserù; (fig: annoy: subj: person) いじめる ijímerù

torn [tɔːrn] *pp of* tear

tornado [tɔːrnei'dou] (*pl* tornadoes) *n* 竜巻 tatsúmaki

torpedo [tɔːrpiː'dou] (*pl* torpedoes) *n* 魚雷 gyorái

torrent [tɔːr'ənt] *n* (flood) 急流 kyűryũ; (fig) 奔流 hońryũ

torrential [tɔːren'tʃəl] *adj* (rain) 土砂降りの doshábùri no

torrid [tɔːr'id] *adj* (sun) しゃく熱の shakúnetsu no; (love affair) 情熱的な jônetsuteki na

torso [tɔːr'sou] *n* 胴 dố

tortoise [tɔːr'təs] *n* カメ kámè

tortoiseshell [tɔːr'təsʃel] *adj* べっ甲の bekkố no

tortuous [tɔːr'tʃuəs] *adj* (path) 曲りくねった magárikunettà; (argument) 回りくどい mawárikudoì; (mind) 邪悪な jaáku na

torture [tɔːr'tʃər] *n* 拷問 gốmon

♦*vt (also fig)* 拷問にかける gốmon ni kakérù

Tory [tɔːr'iː] (BRIT) *adj* 保守党の hoshútồ no

♦*n* 保守党員 hoshútồin

toss [tɔs] *vt* (throw) 投げる nagérù; (one's head) 振る furú

to toss a coin コインをトスする kốn wo tósù surú

to toss up for something コインをトスして…を決める kốn wo tósù shité …wò

kimérù

to toss and turn (in bed) ころり回る korógemawarù

tot [tɑt] *n* (BRIT: drink) おちょこ一杯 ochōkò íppai; (child) 小さい子供 chíísaì kodómo

total [tout'əl] *adj* (complete: number, workforce etc) 全体の zefitai no; (: failure, wreck etc) 完全な kańzen na

♦*n* 合計 gốkei

♦*vt* (add up: numbers, objects) 合計する gốkei suru; (add up to: X dollars/pounds) 合計は…になる gốkei wà …ni nárù

totalitarian [toutæliter'iːən] *adj* 全体主義の zeńtaishùgi no

totally [tou'təliː] *adv* (agree, write off, unprepared) 全く mattàku

totter [tɑt'əːr] *vi* (person) よろめく yorómekù

touch [tʌtʃ] *n* (sense of touch) 触覚 shokkáku; (contact) 触る事 sawárù kotó

♦*vt* (with hand, foot) …に触る …ni sawárù; (tamper with) いじる ijíru; (make contact with) …に接触する …ni sesshóku suru; (emotionally) 感動させる kańdố saserù

a touch of (fig: frost etc) 少しばかり sukóshi bakári

to get in touch with someone …に連絡する …ni reńraku suru

to lose touch (friends) …との連絡が途絶える …tò nố reńraku ga todáerù

touch-and-go [tʌtʃ'əngou'] *adj* 危ない abúnai

touchdown [tʌtʃ'daun] *n* (of rocket, plane: on land) 着陸 chakúriku; (: on water) 着水 chakúsui; (US FOOTBALL) タッチダウン tatchídaun

touched [tʌtʃt] *adj* (moved) 感動した kańdố shita

touching [tʌtʃ'iŋ] *adj* 感動的な kańdốteki na

touchline [tʌtʃ'lain] *n* (SPORT) サイドライン saídorain

touch on *vt fus* (topic) …に触れる …ni furérù

touch up *vt* (paint) 修正する shűsei suru

touchy [tʌtʃiː] *adj* (person) 気難しい ki-
múzukashii

tough [tʌf] *adj* (strong, hard-wearing:
material) 丈夫な jōbu na; (meat) 固い katái; (person: physically) 頑丈な gañjō na;
(: mentally) 神経が太い shiñkei ga futói;
(difficult: task, problem, way of life) 難
しい muzúkashíi; (firm: stance, negotiations, policies) 譲らない yuzúranáī

toughen [tʌfən] *vt* (someone's character) 強くする tsúyoku suru; (glass etc) 強
化する kyōka suru

toupée [tuːpeɪ] *n* かつら katsúra ◇男性
のはげを隠す小さな物 dañsei no
hagé wo kakúsū chíísa na monō wo sásu

tour [tuːər] *n* (journey) 旅行 ryokō; (also:
package tour) ツアー tsūā; (of town,
factory, museum) 見学 keñgaku; (by pop
group etc) 巡業 juñgyō

♦*vt* (country, city, factory etc) 観光旅行
する kañkōryokō; (city) 見物する
keñbutsu suru; (factory etc) 見学する ken-
gaku suru

tourism [tuːrizəm] *n* (business) 観光 kañkō

tourist [tuːrist] *n* 観光客 kañkōkyaku
♦*cpd* (attractions etc) 観光の kañkō no

tourist class (on ship, plane) ツーリスト
クラス tsūrisutokúrasu

tourist office *n* 観光案内所 kañkōan-
naisho

tournament [tuːrnəmənt] *n* トーナメン
ト tōnámento

tousled [tauzəld] *adj* (hair) 乱れた midáretà

tout [taut] *vi*: **to tout for business**
(business) 御用聞きする goyōkiki suru
♦*n* (also: **ticket tout**) だふ屋 dafúya

tow [tou] *vt* (vehicle, caravan, trailer) 引
く hikú, けん引する kefi-in suru
「**in** (US) **or** (BRIT) **on tow**」(AUT) け
ん引中 kefi-inchū

toward(s) [tɔːrd(z)] *prep* (direction) ...の
方へ ...no hō e; (attitude) ...に対して ...ni
táīshite; (purpose) ...に向かって ...ni mukátte; (in time) ...のちょっと前に ...no
chōttō máē ni

towel [tauəl] *n* (hand/bath towel) タオ

ル táoru

towelling [tauəlɪŋ] *n* (fabric) タオル地
taórujī

towel rack (BRIT: **towel rail**) *n* タオル
掛け taórukàke

tower [tauər] *n* 塔 tō

tower block (BRIT) *n* 高層ビル kōsōbi-
rù

towering [tauərɪŋ] *adj* (buildings,
trees, cliffs) 高くそびえる tákaku sobíerù; (figure) 体の大きな karáda nō ōkī na

town [taun] *n* 町 machí
to go to town 町に出掛ける machí ni
dekákerù; (fig: on something) 思い切り
やる omóīkiri yarú, 派手にやる hadé ni
yarú

town center *n* 町の中心部 machí nō
chūshñbu

town council *n* 町議会 chōgikài

town hall *n* 町役場 machíyakùba

town plan *n* 町の道路地図 machí nō dō-
rochizú

town planning *n* 開発計画 kaíhatsuke-
ikàku

towrope [touroup] *n* けん引用ロープ keñ-
in-yō rōpù

tow truck (US) *n* (breakdown lorry) レ
ッカー車 rekkāshà

toxic [tɑksik] *adj* (fumes, waste etc) 有
毒の yūdoku no

toy [tɔɪ] *n* おもちゃ omóchà

toyshop [tɔɪʃɑp] *n* おもちゃ屋 omóchá-
yà

toy with *vt fus* (object, food) いじくり
回す ijíkurimawasù; (idea) ...しようかな
と考えてみる ...shiyō ka na to kañgaete
mirú

trace [treis] *n* (sign) 跡 átð; (small
amount) 微量 biryō
♦*vt* (draw) トレースする torésù suru;
(follow) 追跡する tsuíseki suru; (locate)
見付ける mitsúkerù

tracing paper [treisiŋ-] *n* トレーシング
ペーパー torēshingupèpā

track [træk] *n* (mark) 跡 átð; (path: gen)
道 michí; (: of railway) 線路 señro; (: of
suspect, animal) 足跡 ashíatò; (RAIL) 線
路 señro; (on tape, record: also SPORT)

トラック torákkù
◆vt (follow: animal, person) 追跡する tsuiseki suru

to keep track of ...を監視する ...wo kafishi suru

track down vt (prey) 追跡める oftsume-rù; (something lost) 見付ける mitsúkerù

tracksuit [træk'su:t] n トレーニングウエア toréningu uéa

tract [trækt] n (GEO) 地帯 chítái; (pamphlet) 論文 rofibun

traction [træk'ʃən] n (power) けん引力 kefi-ifiryoku; (MED): **in traction** けん引療法中 kefi-inryóhōchū

tractor [træk'tər] n トラクター toráku-tā

trade [treid] n (activity) 貿易 bóeki; (skill) 技術 gíjutsu; (job) 職業 shokúgyō
◆vi (do business) 商売する shóbai suru
◆vt (exchange): **to trade something (for something)** (...と) ...を交換する (...to) ...wo kókan suru

trade fair n トレードフェアー toródo-feā

trade in vt (old car etc) 下取に出す shitádori nì dásù

trademark [treid'mɑːrk] n 商標 shóhyō

trade name n 商品名 shóhinmei

trader [trei'dər] n 貿易業者 bóekigyó-sha

tradesman [treidz'mən] (pl **tradesmen**) n 商人 shónin

trade union n 労働組合 ródōkumiai

trade unionist [-jun'jənist] n 労働組合員 ródōkumiaíin

tradition [tradiʃ'an] n 伝統 defitō

traditional [tradiʃ'ənəl] adj (dress, costume, meal) 伝統的な defitōteki na

traffic [træf'ik] n (movement: of people, vehicles) 往来 órai; (: of drugs etc) 売買 báibai; (air traffic, road traffic etc) 交通 kótsū
◆vi: **to traffic in** (liquor, drugs) 売買する báibai suru

traffic circle (US) n ロータリー rótarī

traffic jam n 交通渋滞 kótsūjūtai

traffic lights npl 信号(機) shifigó(kì)

traffic warden n 違反駐車取締官 ihán-

chūsha torîshimarikan

tragedy [trædʒ'idi:] n 悲劇 higéki

tragic [trædʒ'ik] adj (death, consequences) 悲劇的な higékiteki na; (play, novel etc) 悲劇的の higéki no

trail [treil] n (path) 小道 kómìchi; (track) 足跡 ashfató; (of smoke, dust) 尾 ó
◆vt (drag) 後に引く átò nì hikú; (follow: person, animal) 追跡する tsuíseki suru
◆vi (hang loosely) 後ろに垂れる ushfro nì tarérù; (in game, contest) 負けている makéte irú

trail behind vi (lag) 遅れる okúrerù

trailer [trei'lər] n (AUT) トレーラー to-rérā; (US: caravan) キャンピングカー kyañpiñgukā; (CINEMA) 予告編 yokó-kuheñ

train truck (US) n トレーラートラック toréràtorakkù

train [trein] n (RAIL) 列車 resshá; (underground train) 地下鉄 chikátetsu; (of dress) トレーン torén
◆vt (educate: mind) 教育する kyóiku suru; (teach skills to: apprentice, doctor, dog etc) 訓練する kufíren suru; (athlete) 鍛える kitáerù; (point: camera, hose, gun etc): **to train on** 向ける mukérù
◆vi (learn a skill) 訓練を受ける kufíren wò ukérù; (SPORT) トレーニングする toréniñgu suru

one's train of thought 考えの流れ kañgaé no nagaré

trained [treind] adj (worker, teacher) 技術が確かな gíjutsu ga táshíka na; (animal) 訓練された kufíren saretá

trainee [treini:'] n (apprentice: hairdresser etc) 見習 minárai; (teacher etc) 実習生 jisshūsei

trainer [trei'nər] n (SPORT: coach) コーチ kōchi; (: shoe) スニーカー sunīkà; (of animals) 調練師 kufíreñshi

training [trei'niŋ] n (for occupation) 訓練 kufíren; (SPORT) トレーニング toré-niñgu

in training トレーニング中 toréniñgu-chū

training college n (gen) 職業大学 sho-kúgyōdaigàku; (for teachers) 教育大学

kyőikudaigákú

training shoes *npl* スニーカー suníkǎ

traipse [treips] *vi* 足を棒にして歩き回る ashí wò bổ ni shité arúkimawarù

trait [treit] *n* 特徴 tokúchō

traitor [trei'tər] *n* 裏切者 urágirimono

tram [træm] (*BRIT*) *n* (*also*: **tramcar**) 路面電車 roméndensha

tramp [træmp] *n* (person) ルンペン rúnpen; (*inf*: *pej*: woman) 浮気女 uwákiồnna
♦*vi* どしんどしん歩く doshíndoshin arúkù

trample [træm'pəl] *vt*: **to trample (underfoot)** 踏み付ける fumítsukerù

trampoline [træmpəlin'] *n* トランポリン toránporin

trance [træns] *n* (gen) こん睡状態 kofísuijötai; (*fig*) ぼう然とした状態 bôzen to shitá jôtai

tranquil [træŋ'kwil] *adj* (place, old age) 平穏な heíon na; (sleep) 静かな shízuka na

tranquillity [træŋkwil'iti:] *n* 平静さ heíseisâ

tranquillizer [træŋ'kwəlaizə:r] *n* (*MED*) 鎮静剤 chínseîzai

transact [trænsækt'] *vt*: **to transact business** 取引する toríhiki suru

transaction [trænsæk'ʃən] *n* (piece of business) 取引 toríhiki

transatlantic [trænsətlæn'tik] *adj* (flight, phone-call etc) 英米間の ebeíkan no

transcend [trænsend'] *vt* 越える koérù

transcript [træn'skript] *n* (of tape recording etc) 記録文書 kiróku bufísho

transfer [træns'fə:r] *n* (moving: of employees etc) 異動 idố; (: of money) 振替 furíkaè; (POL: of power) 引継ぎ hikítsugi; (SPORT) トレード torêdò; (picture, design) 写し絵 utsúshiê
♦*vt* (move: employees etc) 転任させる tefínin saserù; (: money) 振替える furíkaerù; (: power) 譲る yuzúrù

to transfer the charges (*BRIT*: TEL) コレクトコールにする korékutokồru ni suru

transform [træn'sfɔːrm] *vt* 変化させる héňka saserù

transformation [trænsfɔːrmei"] *n* 変化 héňka

transfusion [trænsfju:'ʒən] *n* (*also*: **blood transfusion**) 輸血 yukétsu

transient [træn'ʃənt] *adj* 一時的な ichíjiteki na

transistor [trænzis'tə:r] *n* (ELEC) トランジスタ toránjisuta; (*also*: **transistor radio**) トランジスタラジオ toránjisuta rajîo

transit [træn'sit] *n*: **in transit** (people, things) 通過中の tsűkachū no

transition [trænzi'ʃən] *n* 移行 ikố

transitional [trænzi'ʃənəl] *adj* (period, stage) 移行の ikố no

transitive [træn'sətiv] *adj* (LING): **transitive verb** 他動詞 tadőshi

transit lounge *n* (at airport etc) トランジットラウンジ toránjitto raúnji

transitory [træn'sitɔːri:] *adj* つかの間の tsuká no ma nò

translate [trænz'leit] *vt* (word, book etc) 翻訳する hoń-yaku suru

translation [trænzlei'ʃən] *n* (act/result of translating) 訳 yakú

translator [trænslei'tə:r] *n* 訳者 yákùsha

transmission [trænsmi'ʃən] *n* (of information, disease) 伝達 defítatsu; (TV: broadcasting, program broadcast) 放送 hôsỗ; (AUT) トランスミッション toránsumisshồn

transmit [trænsmit'] *vt* (message, signal, disease) 伝達する defítatsu suru

transmitter [trænsmit'ə:r] *n* (piece of equipment) トランスミッタ toránsumittâ

transparency [trænspe:r'ənsi:] *n* (of glass etc) 透明度 tồmeîdo; (PHOT: slide) スライド suráldo

transparent [trænsper'ənt] *adj* (see-through) 透明の tồmei no

transpire [trænspaiə:r'] *vi* (turn out) 明らかになる akfräka ni nárù; (happen) 起る okórù

transplant [*vb* trænzplænt' *n* trænz'-plænt] *vt* (seedlings: *also*: MED: organ)

移植する ishóku suru
♦*n* (MED) 移植 ishóku

transport [*n* træns'pɔːrt *vb* træns-pɔːrt'] *n* (moving people, goods) 輸送 yusō; (*also*: **road/rail transport** *etc*) 輸送機関 yusōkikan; (car) 車 kurúma
♦*vt* (carry) 輸送する yusō suru

transportation [trænspəːrtei'ʃən] *n* (transport) 輸送 yusō; (means of transport) 輸送機関 yusōkikan

transport café (BRIT) *n* トラック運転手向きのレストラン torákkuunteñshu mukí no resútoran

transvestite [trænsves'tait] *n* 女装趣味の男性 jo**s**ō**s**hūmi no dañsei

trap [træp] *n* (snare, trick) わな wánà; (carriage) 軽馬車 kefbashà
♦*vt* (animal) わなで捕える wánà de toráerù; (person: trick) わなにかける wánà ni kakérù; (: confine: in bad marriage, burning building): **to be trapped** 逃げられなくなっている nigérarenakù natté irù

trap door *n* 落し戸 otóshidò

trapeze [træpiːz'] *n* 空中ぶらんこ kúchū-burañko

trappings [træp'iŋz] *npl* 飾り kazári

trash [træʃ] *n* (rubbish: *also pej*) ごみ gomí; (: nonsense) でたらめ detárame

trash can (*US*) *n* ごみ入れ gomírè

trauma [trɔː'mə] *n* 衝撃 shōgeki, ショック shōkkù

traumatic [trɔːmæt'ik] *adj* 衝撃的な shōgekiteki na

travel [træv'əl] *n* (traveling) 旅行 ryokō
♦*vi* (person) 旅行する ryokō suru; (news, sound) 伝わる tsutáwarù; (wine etc): **to travel well/badly** 運搬に耐えられる〔耐えられない〕uñpan ni taérarerù〔taérarenaì〕
♦*vt* (distance) 旅行する ryokō suru

travel agency *n* 旅行代理店 ryokódairiten

travel agent *n* 旅行業者 ryokógyōsha

traveler [træv'ələːr] (BRIT **traveller**) *n* 旅行者 ryokósha

traveler's check [træv'ələːrz-] (BRIT **traveller's cheque**) *n* トラベラーズチェ

ック toráberāzuchekkù

traveling [træv'əliŋ] (BRIT **travelling**) *n* 旅行 ryokō

travels [træv'əlz] *npl* (journeys) 旅行 ryokō

travel sickness *n* 乗物酔い norímono-yoì

travesty [træv'isti] *n* パロディー párodī

trawler [trɔː'ləːr] *n* トロール漁船 torōru-gyòsen

tray [trei] *n* (for carrying) お盆 o-bón; (on desk) デスクトレー desúkutorè

treacherous [tretʃ'əːrəs] *adj* (person, look) 裏切りの urágirimòno no; (ground, tide) 危険な kikén na

treachery [tretʃ'əːri] *n* 裏切り urágirì

treacle [triː'kəl] *n* 糖蜜 tōmitsu

tread [tred] *n* (step) 歩調 hochō; (sound) 足音 ashíotò; (of stair) 踏面 fumízura; (of tire) トレッド torēddò
♦*vi* (*pt* **trod**, *pp* **trodden**) 歩く arúkù

tread on *vt fus* 踏む fumú

treason [triː'zən] *n* 反逆罪 hañgyakuzài

treasure [treʒ'əːr] *n* (gold, jewels etc) 宝物 takáramono; (person) 重宝な人 chōhō nà hitò
♦*vt* (value: object) 重宝する chōhō suru; (: friendship) 大事にしている daijí ni shité irù; (: memory, thought) 心に銘記する kokórò ni méki suru

treasurer [treʒ'əːrəːr] *n* 会計 kaíkei

treasures [treʒ'əːrz] *npl* (art treasures etc) 貴重品 kichōhin

treasury [treʒ'əːri] *n*: (*US*) **the Treasury Department**, (BRIT) **the Treasury** 大蔵省 ōkurashō

treat [triːt] *n* (present) 贈物 okúrimono
♦*vt* (handle, regard: person, object) 扱う atsúkaù; (MED: patient, illness) 治療する chiryō suru; (TECH: coat) 処理する shórì suru

to treat someone to something …に…をおごる …ni …wo ogórù

treatment [triːt'mənt] *n* (attention, handling) 扱い方 atsúkaikata; (MED) 治療 chiryō

treaty [triː'tiː] *n* 協定 kyōtei

treble [treb'əl] *adj* 3倍の safbai no;

(MUS) 高音部の kôonbu no
♦vt 3倍にする sanbai ni suru
♦vi 3倍になる sanbai ni narù

treble clef n (MUS) 高音部記号 kôonbu-kigô

tree [tri:] n 木 kí

tree trunk n 木の幹 kí no míkì

trek [trek] n (long difficult journey: on foot) 徒歩旅行 tohóryokô; (: by car) 自動車長距離旅行 jidôsharyokô; (tiring walk) 苦しい遠のり kurúshiî michínori

trellis [trel'is] n (for climbing plants) 棚 tanâ

tremble [trem'bəl] vi (voice, body, trees: with fear, cold etc) 震える furúerû; (ground) 揺れる yurérû

tremendous [trimen'dəs] adj (enormous: amount etc) ばく大な bakúdai na; (excellent: success, holiday, view etc) 素晴らしい subárashiî

tremor [trem'əːr] n (trembling: of excitement, fear: in voice) 震え furúe; (also: **earth tremor**) 地震 jishîn

trench [trentʃ] n (channel) 溝 mizô; (for defense) ざんごう zangô

trend [trend] n (tendency) 傾向 kefkô; (of events) 動向 dôkô; (fashion) トレンド torêndo

trendy [tren'di:] adj (idea, person, clothes) トレンディな torêndi na

trepidation [trepidei'ʃən] n (apprehension) 不安 fuân

trespass [tres'pæs] vi: **to trespass on** (private property) ...に不法侵入する ...ni fuhôshinnyû suru
「**no trespassing**」立入禁止 tachfirikinshi

trestle [tres'əl] n (support for table etc) うま umâ

trial [trail] n (LAW) 裁判 saíban; (test: of machine etc) テスト tesúto
on trial (LAW) 裁判に掛けられて saíban ni kakérarete
by trial and error 試行錯誤で shikô-sakûgo de

trial period n テスト期間 tesúto kikan

trials [trailz] npl (unpleasant experiences) 試練 shfren

triangle [trai'æŋgəl] n (MATH) 三角 sánkaku; (MUS) トライアングル toráiánguru

triangular [traiæŋ'gjələːr] adj 三角形の sankákkêi no

tribal [trai'bəl] adj (warrior, warfare, dance) 種族の shûzôku no

tribe [traib] n 種族 shûzôku

tribesman [traibz'mən] (pl **tribesmen**) n 種族の男性 shûzôku no dansei

tribulations [tribjulei'ʃənz] npl 苦労 kúrô, 苦難 kúnân

tribunal [traibju:'nəl] n 審判委員会 shínpan iînkai

tributary [trib'jəteːriː] n 支流 shiryû

tribute [trib'ju:t] n (compliment) ほめの言葉 homê no kotôba
to pay tribute to ...をほめる...wô homêrû

trice [trais] n: **in a trice** あっという間に áttô iû ma ni

trick [trik] n (magic trick) 手品 téjîna; (prank, joke) いたずら itázura; (skill, knack) こつ kotsû; (CARDS) トリック torfkkû
♦vt (deceive) だます damásû
to play a trick on someone ...にいたずらをする ...ni itázura wô suru
that should do the trick これでいいはずだ koré de iî hazú da

trickery [trik'əːri:] n 計略 kefryaku

trickle [trik'əl] n (of water etc) 滴り shitátari
♦vi (water, rain etc) 滴る shitátaru

tricky [trik'i:] adj (job, problem, business) 厄介な yákkâi na

tricycle [trai'sikəl] n 三輪車 sanrinsha

trifle [trai'fəl] n (small detail) ささいな事 sásâi na kotô; (CULIN) トライフル toráifuru ◇カステラにゼリー、フルーツ、プリンなどをのせたデザート kasútera ni zêrî, furútsû, púrîn nádô wo nosétâ dezâto
♦adv: **a trifle long** ちょっと長い chóttô nagâi

trifling [trai'liŋ] adj (detail, matter) ささいな sásâi na

trigger [trig'əːr] n (of gun) 引金 hikígane

trigger off vt (reaction, riot) ...の引金
となる ...no hikígane tò náru

trigonometry [trigənɑːm'ətri:] n 三角法
sańkakuhō

trill [tril] vi (birds) さえずる saézurù

trim [trim] adj (house, garden) 手入れの
行届いた tefre nð ikítodoità; (figure) す
らっとした suráttð shitá

♦n (haircut etc) 刈る事 karú kotó; (on
car) 飾り kazári

♦vt (cut: hair, beard) 刈る karú; (decorate): **to trim (with)** (...で) 飾る (...de)
kazárù; (NAUT: a sail) 調節する chốse-
tsu suru

trimmings [trim'iŋz] npl (CULIN) お飾
りの付け合せ o-kħmári no tsukéawàse

trinket [triŋ'kit] n (ornament) 安い置物
yasúi okímono; (piece of jewellery) 安い
装身具 yasúi sōshíngu

trio [tri:'ou] n (gen) 三つ組 mitsúgumi;
(MUS) トリオ tório

trip [trip] n (journey) 旅行 ryokṓ; (outing) 遠足 eńsoku; (stumble) つまずき tsu-
mázuki

♦vi (stumble) つまずく tsumázukù; (go
lightly) 軽快に歩く kefkai nì árukù
on a trip 旅行中で ryokṓchū de

tripe [traip] n (CULIN) トライプ torái-
pu ○ウシ、ブタなどの胃の料理 ushí, bu-
tá nadò no i no ryṓri; (pej: rubbish) くだ
らない物 kudáranài monó ○特に人の発言
や文書について言う búnshō ni hitó nò ha-
tsúgen yà búnsho ni tsúlte iú

triple [trip'əl] adj (ice cream, somersault
etc) トリプルの torípüru no

triplets [trip'lits] npl 三つ子 mitsúgo

triplicate [trip'ləkit] n: **in triplicate** 三
通で sańtsū de

tripod [trai'pɑd] n 三脚 sańkyaku

trip up vi (stumble) つまずく tsumázu-
kù

♦vt (person) つまずかせる tsumázukase-
rù

trite [trait] adj 陳腐な chíñpu na

triumph [trai'əmf] n (satisfaction) 大満
足 daímanzoku; (great achievement) 輝
かしい勝利 kagáyakashìì shṓri

♦vi: **to triumph (over)** (...に) 打勝つ
(...ni) uchíkatsù

triumphant [traiʌm'fənt] adj (team,
wave, return) 意気揚々とした íkìyōyṓ to
shitá

trivia [triv'i:ə] npl 詰まらない事 tsumá-
ranai kotò

trivial [triv'i:əl] adj (unimportant) 詰ま
らない tsumáranaì; (commonplace) 平凡
な hefbon na

trod [trɑd] pt of tread

trodden [trɑd'ən] pp of tread

trolley [trɑl'i:] n (for luggage, shopping,
also in supermarkets) 手車 tegúruma;
(table on wheels) ワゴン wágon; (also:
trolley bus) トロリーバス toróribàsu

trombone [trɑmboun'] n トロンボーン
toróñbōn

troop [tru:p] n (of people, monkeys etc)
群れ muré

troop in/out vi ぞろぞろと入って来る
[出て行く] zórozoro to haítte kurù
(détè iku)

trooping the color [tru:p'iŋ-] (BRIT)
n (ceremony) 軍隊敬礼の分列行進 kuñki-
keīrei no bufretsu kṓshin

troops [tru:ps] npl (MIL) 兵隊 heítai

trophy [trou'fi:] n トロフィー toróñ

tropic [trɑp'ik] n 回帰線 kafkisen
the tropics 熱帯地方 nettái chihṓ

tropical [trɑp'ikəl] adj (rain forest etc)
熱帯(地方)の nettái(chihṓ) no

trot [trɑt] n (fast pace) 小走り kobáshiri; (of horse) 速足 hayáashi, トロット to-
róttō

♦vi (horse) トロットで駆ける toróttò de
kakérù; (person) 小走りで行く kobáshiri
de ikú
on the trot (BRIT: fig) 立続けに tatétsuzuke ni

trouble [trʌb'əl] n (difficulty) 困難 koń-
nan; (worry) 心配 shíñpai; (bother,
effort) 苦労 kúrō; (unrest) トラブル torá-
bùru; (MED): **heart etc trouble** ...病
...byṓ

♦vi (worry) ...に心配を掛ける ...ni shíñpai wð kakérù; (person: disturb) 面倒を
かける mefdō wo kakérù

◆vi: **to trouble to do something** わざわざ...する wázawaza ...suru

to be in trouble (gen) 困っている komátte irú; (ship, climber etc) 危険にあっている kikén ni atte irú

it's no trouble! 迷惑ではありませんから mêiwaku de wa arimáseñ kará

what's the trouble? (with broken television etc) どうなっていますか か natté imasû ká; (doctor to patient) いかがですか ikága desû ká

troubled [trʌb'əld] adj (person, country, life, era) 不安な fuáñ na

troublemaker [trʌb'əlmeikəːr] n トラブルを起す常習犯 torábūru wo okósū jōshūhan; (child) 問題児 mońdaiji

troubles [trʌb'əlz] npl (personal, POL etc) 問題 mońdai

troubleshooter [trʌb'əlʃuːtəːr] n (in conflict) 調停人 chōteinin

troublesome [trʌb'əlsəm] adj (child, cough etc) 厄介な yákkai na

trough [trɔːf] n (also: **drinking trough**) 水入れ mizúire; (feeding trough) えさ入れ esá-ire; (depression) 谷間 taníma

troupe [truːp] n (of actors, singers, dancers) 団 dáñ

trousers [trau'zəːrz] npl ズボン zubóñ
short trousers 半ズボン hañzubóñ

trousseau [truː'sou] (pl trousseaux or trousseaus) n 嫁入り道具 yomé-iri dōgu

trout [traut] n inv マス másu

trowel [trau'əl] n (garden tool) 移植ごて ishókugòte; (builder's tool) こて koté

truant [truː'ənt] (BRIT) n: **to play truant** 学校をサボる gakkō wo sabórù

truce [truːs] n 休戦 kyūsen

truck [trʌk] n (US) トラック torákkù; (RAIL) 台車 daíshà

truck driver n トラック運転手 torákku unténshu

truck farm (US) n 野菜農園 yasáiñen

trudge [trʌdʒ] vi (also: **trudge along**) とぼとぼ歩く tobótobo arúkù

true [truː] adj (real: motive) 本当の hoñtō no; (accurate: likeness) 正確な sefkaku na; (genuine: love) 本物の hoñmono no; (faithful: friend) 忠実な chūjitsu na

to come true (dreams, predictions) 実現する jitsúgen suru

truffle [trʌf'əl] n (fungus) トリュフ tóryùfu; (sweet) トラッフル toráffūru ◇菓子の一種 káshī no ísshū

truly [truː'liː] adv (really) 本当に hoñtō ni; (truthfully) 真実に shiñjitsu ni; (faithfully) **yours truly** (in letter) 敬具 kéïgu

trump [trʌmp] n (also: **trump card**: also fig) 切札 kirífūda

trumped-up [trʌmpt'ʌp'] adj (charge, pretext) でっち上げた detchfageta

trumpet [trʌm'pit] n トランペット toráñpetto

truncheon [trʌn'tʃən] n 警棒 keíbō

trundle [trʌn'dəl] vt (push chair etc) ごろごろ動かす gorógoro ugókasù
◆vi: **to trundle along** (vehicle) 重そうに動く omósō ni ugókù; (person) ゆっくり行く yukkúri ikú

trunk [trʌŋk] n (of tree, person) 幹 míkī; (of person) 胴体 dō; (of elephant) 鼻 haná; (case) トランク toráñku; (US: AUT) トランク toráñku

trunks [trʌŋks] npl (also: **swimming trunks**) 水泳パンツ sufei pañtsu

truss [trʌs] n (MED) ヘルニアバンド herúnia bañdo

truss (up) vt (CULIN) 縛る shibárù

trust [trʌst] n (faith) 信用 shiñ-yō; (responsibility) 責任 sekíniñ; (LAW) 信託 shiñtaku
◆vt (rely on, have faith in) 信用する shiñ-yō suru; (hope) きっと...だろうね kittó ...dárō né; (entrust) **to trust something to someone** を...に任せる ...wo ...ni makáserù

to take something on trust (advice, information) 証拠なしで...を信じる証拠 nashí de ...wo shiñjirù

trusted [trʌs'tid] adj (friend, servant) 信用された shiñ-yō sareta

trustee [trʌstiː'] n (LAW) 受託者 jutáku-shà; (of school etc) 理事 rîji

trustful/trusting [trʌst'fəl/'tiŋ] adj (person, nature, smile) 信用する shiñ-yō suru

trustworthy [trʌst'wəːrðiː] adj (person,

report) 信用できる shiñ-yō dekirú

truth [truːθ] n (true fact) 真実 shiñjitsu; (universal principle) 真理 shíñri

truthful [truːθfəl] adj (person, answer) 正直な shōjiki na

try [trai] n (attempt) 努力 dóryòku; (RUGBY) トライ toráì
♦vt (attempt) やってみる yatté mirú; (test: something new: also: **try out**) 試す tamésù; (LAW: person) 裁判にかける sáìban ni kakérù; (strain: patience) ぎりぎりまで追込む giriḡiri madé oíkomù
♦vi (make effort, attempt) 努力する dóryòku suru

to have a **try** やってみる yatté mirú

to **try** to do something (seek) …をしようとする …wo shiyó to surù

trying [traiˈŋ] adj (person) 気難しい kimúzukashiì; (experience) 苦しい kurúshiì

try on vt (dress, hat, shoes) 試着する shíchaku suru

tsar [zɑːr] n ロシア皇帝 roshía kôtei

T-shirt [tiːˈʃəːrt] n Tシャツ tíshatsu

T-square [tiːˈskwəːr] n T定規 tíjōgi

tub [tʌb] n (container: relatively small) たらい taráì; (: deeper) 大おけ ōke; (bath) 湯舟 yúbùne

tuba [tuːˈbə] n チューバ chūba

tubby [tʌbˈiː] adj 太った futóttà

tube [tuːb] n (pipe) 管 kúdà; (container, in tire) チューブ chūbu; (BRIT: underground) 地下鉄 chíkátetsu

tuberculosis [tubəːrkjəlouˈsis] n 結核 kekkáku

tube station (BRIT) n 地下鉄の駅 chíkátetsu no éki

tubular [tuːˈbjələːr] adj (furniture, metal) 管状の kañjō no; (furniture) チューブ型の paſpusei no

TUC [tiːjuːsiːˈ] n abbr (BRIT: = Trades Union Congress) 英国労働組合会議 eíkoku ródōkumiai kaígi

tuck [tʌk] vt (put) 押込む oshíkomù

tuck away vt (money) 仕舞い込む shímáikomù; (building): to be **tucked away** 隠れている kakúrete irú

tuck in vt (clothing) 押込む oshíkomù;

(child) 毛布にくるんで寝かせる mōfu ni kurúñde nekáserù
♦vi (eat) かぶりつく kabúritsukù

tuck shop (BRIT) n (school) 学校内でお菓子などを売る売店を指す gakkō-naì de o-káshi nadò wo urú baíten wò sásù

tuck up vt (invalid, child) 毛布にくるんで寝かせる mōfu ni kurúñde nekáserù

Tuesday [tuːzˈdei] n 火曜日 kayóbi

tuft [tʌft] n (of hair, grass etc) 一房 hitófùsa

tug [tʌg] n (ship) タグボート tagúbòto
♦vt 引っ張る hippárù

tug-of-war [tʌgˈɔvwɔːrˈ] n (SPORT) 綱引き tsunáhiki; (fig) 競り合い serʔaì ◇二者間の競り合いを指す nishákàn no serʔai wo sásù

tuition [tuiʃˈən] n (BRIT) 教授 kyōju; (: private tuition) 個人教授 kojíñkyōju; (US: school fees) 授業料 jugyōryō

tulip [tuːˈlip] n チューリップ chūrippu

tumble [tʌmˈbəl] n (fall) 転ぶ事 koróbu kotō
♦vi (fall: person) 転ぶ koróbù; (water) 落ちる ochírù

to **tumble** to something (inf) …に気が付く …ni ki gá tsukù

tumbledown [tʌmˈbəldaun] adj (building) 荒れ果てた aréhatetà

tumble dryer (BRIT) n 乾燥機 kaſsōki

tumbler [tʌmˈbləːr] n (glass) コップ kopʔpu

tummy [tʌmˈiː] n (inf) (belly, stomach) おなか onáka

tumor [tuːˈməːr] (BRIT **tumour**) n しゅよう shuyō

tumult [tuːˈmʌlt] n 大騒ぎ ōsawàgi

tumultuous [tuːmʌlˈtʃuːəs] adj (welcome, applause etc) にぎやかな nigíyàka na

tuna [tuːˈnə] n inv (also: **tuna fish**) マグロ maguro; (in can, sandwich) ツナ tsúnà

tune [tuːn] n (melody) 旋律 señritsu
♦vt (MUS) 調律する chōritsu suru; (RADIO, TV) 合せる awáserù; (AUT) チューンアップする chūn-appù suru

to be in/out of **tune** (instrument, singer)

調子が合って〔外れて〕いる chōshi gà atte〔hazúrete〕irū

to be in/out of tune with (*fig*) …と気が合っている〔いない〕…to ki ga atte irū (inái)

tuneful [tju:n'fəl] *adj* (music) 旋律のきれいな senritsu nò kírei na

tuner [tu:'nər] *n*: *piano tuner* 調律師 chōritsushì

tune in *vi* (RADIO, TV): *to tune in (to)* (…を) 聞く(…wo) kikú

tune up *vi* (musician, orchestra) 調子を合せる chōshi wò awáserū

tunic [tu:'nik] *n* チュニック chunîkkù

Tunisia [tu:ni:'ʒə] *n* チュニジア chunîjîa

tunnel [tʌn'əl] *n* (passage) トンネル tofinneru; (in mine) 坑道 kōdō

♦*vi* トンネルを掘る tofinneru wo hórū

turban [tər'bən] *n* ターバン tâbàn

turbine [tər'bain] *n* タービン tâbin

turbulence [tər'bjələns] *n* (AVIAT) 乱気流 rafikiryū

turbulent [tər'bjələnt] *adj* (water) 荒れ狂う arékuruū; (*fig*: career) 起伏の多い kífûku no ôi

tureen [təri:n'] *n* スープ鉢 sûpubàchi, チューリン chûrin

turf [tərf] *n* (grass) 芝生 shibáfu; (clod) 芝土 shibátsuchi

♦*vt* (area) 芝生を…で敷く shibáfu wo shíkū

turf out (*inf*) *vt* (person) 追出す ofdasu

turgid [tər'dʒid] *adj* (speech) 仰々しい gyōgyōshiī

Turk [tərk] *n* トルコ人 torúkojìn

Turkey [tər'ki:] *n* トルコ torûko

turkey [tər'ki:] *n* (bird, meat) 七面鳥 shichímenchò, ターキー tâkî

Turkish [tər'kiʃ] *adj* トルコの torûko no; (LING) トルコ語の torûkogo no

♦*n* (LING) トルコ語 torûkogo

Turkish bath *n* トルコ風呂 torúkoburò

turmoil [tər'mɔil] *n* 混乱 kofiran

in turmoil 混乱して kofiran shíte

turn [tərn] *n* (change) 変化 héñka; (in road) カーブ kâbu; (tendency: of mind, events) 傾向 kefkō; (performance: act) 出し物 dashímonò; (chance) 番 bán; (MED) 発作 hossá

♦*vt* (handle, key) 回す mawásù; (collar, page) めくる mekúrû; (steak) 裏返す urágaesù; (change): *to turn something into* …を…にする …wo …ni kaérù

♦*vi* (object) 回る mawárù; (person: look back) 振向く furímukù; (reverse direction: in car) Uターンする yútân suru; (: wind) 向きが変る mûkì ga kawárù; (milk) 悪くなる wárùku nárù; (become) なる nárù

a good turn 親切 shiñsetsu

it gave me quite a turn ああ、怖かった ā, kowákattà

"no left turn" (AUT) 左折禁止 sasétsukiñshi

it's your turn あなたの番です anáta nò bañ desu

in turn 次々と tsugítsugi tò

to take turns (at) 交替で (…を) する kōtai dè (…wo) suru

turn away *vi* 顔をそむける kaó wò somúkerù

♦*vt* (applicants) 門前払いする mofizenbarài suru

turn back *vi* 引返す hikíkaesù

♦*vt* (person, vehicle) 引返させる hikíkaesaserù; (clock) 遅らせる okúraserù

turn down *vt* (refuse: request) 断る kotôwarù; (reduce: heating) 弱くする yowâku suru; (fold: bedclothes) 折返す oríkaesù

turn in *vi* (*inf*: go to bed) 寝る nerú

♦*vt* (fold) 折込む oríkomû

turning [tər'niŋ] *n* (in road) 曲り角 magárikadò

turning point *n* (*fig*) 変り目 kawárimè

turnip [tər'nip] *n* カブ kábù

turn off *vi* (from road) 横道に入る yokómichi nì háīru

♦*vt* (light, radio etc) 消す kesū; (tap) …の水を止める …no mizú wò tomérù; (engine) 止める tomérù

turn on *vt* (light, radio etc) つける tsukérù; (tap) …の水を出す …no mizú wò dásù; (engine) かける kakérù

turn out *vt* (light, gas) 消す kesú; (produce) 作る tsukúrù

♦*vi* (voters) 出る dérù

to turn out to be (prove to be) 結局...であると分かる kekkyóku ...de áru to wakaru

turnout [tɜːrnaut] n (of voters etc) 人出 hitóde

turn over vi (person) 寝返りを打つ negáeri wò utsú
♦vt (object) 引っ繰り返す hikkúrikaesu; (page) めくる mekúru

turnover [tɜːrnouvər] n (COMM: amount of money) 売上高 uríagedàka; (: of goods) 回転率 kaítenřitsu; (: of staff) 異動率 idórìtsu

turnpike [tɜːrnpaik] n (US) n 有料道路 yūryōdōro

turn round vi (person) 振り向く furímukù; (vehicle) Uターンする yútàn suru; (rotate) 回転する kaíten suru

turnstile [tɜːrnstail] n ターンスタイル tánsutaìru

turntable [tɜːrnteibl] n (on record player) ターンテーブル tántèburu

turn up vi (person) 現れる aráwarerù; (lost object) 見付かる mitsúkarù
♦vt (collar) 立てる tatérù; (radio, stereo etc) ...のボリュームを上げる ...no voryúmu wò agérù; (heater) 強くする tsúyoku suru

turn-up [tɜːrnʌp] n (BRIT) n (on trousers) 折返し oríkaeshi

turpentine [tɜːrpəntain] n (also: turps) テレピン油 terébìn-yu

turquoise [tɜːrkɔiz] n (stone) トルコ石 torúkoìshi
♦adj (color) 青みどりの aőmidòri no

turret [tɜːrit] n (on building) 小塔 shótō; (on tank) 旋回砲塔 seňkaihōtō

turtle [tɜːrtl] n カメ kámè

turtleneck (sweater) [tɜːrtlnek-] n タートルネック tátorunekkù

tusk [tʌsk] n きば kíba

tussle [tʌsl] n (fight, scuffle) 取っ組み合い torýkumiài

tutor [tuːtər] n (SCOL) チューター chútā; (private tutor) 家庭教師 katéikyōshi

tutorial [tuːtɔːriəl] n (SCOL) 討論授業 tőronjugyō

tuxedo [tʌksiːdou] (US) n タキシード ta-

kfshído

TV [tiːviː] n abbr = television

twang [twæŋ] n (of instrument) ぴゅんという音 byún to iú otó; (of voice) 鼻声 hanágoè

tweed [twiːd] n ツイード tsuídò

tweezers [twiːzərz] npl ピンセット pínsetto

twelfth [twelfθ] num 第十二の dái jűni no

twelve [twelv] num 十二 (の) jűnî (no)
at twelve (o'clock) (midday) 正午 に shőgò ni; (midnight) 零時に reíji ni

twentieth [twentiːθ] num 第二十の dái nîjù no

twenty [twenti] num 二十 (の) níjù (no)

twice [twais] adv 2回 nikái
twice as much ...の二倍 ...no nibái

twiddle [twidl] vt いじくる ijíkurù
♦vi: *to twiddle (with) something* ...をいじくる ...wo ijíkurù
to twiddle one's thumbs (fig) 手をこまねくせ wo kománekù

twig [twig] n 小枝 koéda
♦vi (inf: realize) 気が付く ki gá tsukú

twilight [twailait] n 夕暮 yúgure

twin [twin] adj (sister, brother) 双子の futágo no; (towers, beds etc) 対の tsuí no, ツインの tsuíñ no
♦n 双子の一人 futágo nò hitórì
♦vt (towns etc) 姉妹都市にする shímáitoshì ni suru

twin-bedded room [twinbedid-] n ツインルーム tsuínrūmu

twine [twain] n ひも himó
♦vi (plant) 巻付く makítsukù

twinge [twindʒ] n (of pain) うずき uzúki; (of conscience) とがめ kasháku; (of regret) 苦しみ kurúshimì

twinkle [twinkl] vi (star, light, eyes) きらめく kirámekù

twirl [twɜːrl] vt くるくる回す kúrùkuru mawásù
♦vi くるくる回る kúrùkuru mawárù

twist [twist] n (action) ひねり hinéri; (in road, coil, flex) 曲り magári; (in story) ひねり hinéri

♦*vt* (turn) ひねる hinérù; (: injure: ankle etc) ねんざする nefiza suru; (weave) より合さる yoríawasarú; (roll around) 巻付ける makítsukerù; (fig: meaning, words) 曲げる magérù

♦*vi* (road, river) 曲りくねる magárikunerú

twit [twit] (*inf*) *n* ばか bákà

twitch [twitʃ] *n* (pull) ぐいと引く事 guí tò hikú kotò; (nervous) 引きつり hikítsuri

♦*vi* (muscle, body) 引きつる hikítsurù

two [tu:] *num* 二 (の) nf (no), 二つ (の) futátsù (no)

to put two and two together あれこれを統合してなぞを解く arékòre wo sồgô shité nazồ wò tókù

two-door [tu:'dɔːr] *adj* (AUT) ツードアの tsúdoà no

two-faced [tu:'feist] (*pej*) *adj* (person) 二枚舌の nimáìjita no

twofold [tu:'fould] *adv*: *to increase twofold* 倍になる bai ni narù

two-piece (suit) [tu:'pi:s-] *n* ツーピースの服 tsúpìsu no fuku

two-piece (swimsuit) *n* ツーピースの水着 tsúpìsu no mizúgi

twosome [tu:'səm] *n* (people) 二人組 futárigùmi

two-way [tu:'wei'] *adj*: *two-way traffic* 両方向交通 ryóhôkôkôtsú

tycoon [taikuːn'] *n*: *(business) tycoon* 大物実業家 ômonojitsugyóka

type [taip] *n* (category, model, example) 種類 shúrùi; (TYP) 活字 katsúji

♦*vt* (letter etc) タイプする táipu suru

type-cast [taip'kæst] *adj* (actor) はまり役の hamáriyaku no

typeface [taip'feis] *n* 書体 shótai

typescript [taip'skript] *n* タイプライターで打った原稿 taípuraìta de úttà geñkô

typewriter [taip'raitəːr] *n* タイプライター taípuraìta

typewritten [taip'ritən] *adj* タイプライターで打った taípuraìta de úttà

typhoid [tai'fɔid] *n* 腸チフス chôchífusu

typhoon [taifuːn'] *n* 台風 taffû

typical [tip'ikəl] *adj* 典型的な teñkeitéki

na

typify [tip'əfai] *vt* …の典型的な例である …no teñkeiteki nà réi de arù

typing [tai'piŋ] *n* タイプライターを打つ事 taípuraìta wo útsù kotò

typist [tai'pist] *n* タイピスト taípisùto

tyranny [tir'əni:] *n* 暴政 bôsei

tyrant [tai'rənt] *n* 暴君 bôkun

tyre [taiəːr'] (*BRIT*) *n* = tire

tzar [zɑːr] *n* = tsar

U

U-bend [ju:'bend] *n* (in pipe) トラップ toráppù

ubiquitous [ju:bik'witəs] *adj* いたる所にある itárù tokoro ni árù

udder [ʌd'əːr] *n* 乳房 chibúsa ◊ ウシ、ヤギなどに言う ushí, yagí nado ni tsuite iú

UFO [juːefou'] *n abbr* (= *unidentified flying object*) 未確認飛行物体 mikákunin hikôbuttai, ユーフォー yúfô

Uganda [juːgæn'də] *n* ウガンダ ugáñda

ugh [ʌ] *excl* おえっ oê

ugliness [ʌg'liːnis] *n* 醜さ miñkúsà

ugly [ʌg'liː] *adj* (person, dress etc) 醜い miñkúi; (dangerous: situation) 物騒な bussô nà

UK [ju:'kei'] *n abbr* = United Kingdom

ulcer [ʌl'səːr] *n* かいよう kaíyô

Ulster [ʌl'stəːr] *n* アルスター arúsutà

ulterior [ʌltiːr'iːəːr] *adj*: *ulterior motive* 下心 shitágokòro

ultimate [ʌl'təmit] *adj* (final: aim, destination, result) 最後の saígo no; (greatest: insult, deterrent, authority) 最大の saídai no

ultimately [ʌl'təmitliː] *adv* (in the end) やがて yagáte; (basically) 根本的に koñponteki ni

ultimatum [ʌltiːmei'təm] *n* 最後通ちょう saígotsúchô

ultrasound [ʌl'trəsaund] *n* (MED) 超音波 chôôñpa

ultraviolet [ʌltrəvai'əlit] *adj* (rays, light) 紫外線の shigáisen no

umbilical cord [ʌmbil'ikəl-] *n* へその緒 heso no o

umbrella [ʌmbrel'ə] *n* (for rain) 傘 kasà, 雨傘 amágasa; (for sun) 日傘 higása, パラソル parásoru

umpire [ʌm'paiər] *n* (TENNIS, CRICKET) 審判 shinpan, アンパイア añpaia
♦*vt* (game) ...のアンパイアをする ...no añpaia wo suru

umpteen [ʌmp'ti:n'] *adj* 沢山の uñto takusan no

umpteenth [ʌmp'ti:nθ'] *adj*: **for the umpteenth time** 何回目か分からないが nañkaime kà wakáranài ga

UN [ju:'en'] *n abbr* = **United Nations**

unable [ʌnei'bəl] *adj*: **to be unable to do something** ...する事ができない ...surú koto gà dekínai

unaccompanied [ʌnəkʌm'pənid] *adj* (child, woman) 同伴者のいない dòhañsha no inai; (luggage) 別送の bessō no; (song) 無伴奏の mubáñsō no

unaccountably [ʌnəkaʊnt'əbli:] *adv* 妙に mȳo ni

unaccustomed [ʌnəkʌs'təmd] *adj*: **to be unaccustomed to** (public speaking, Western culture etc) ...になれていない ...ni narète inai

unanimous [ju:næn'əməs] *adj* (vote) 満場一致の mañjòitchi no; (people) 全員同意の zeñ-indòi no

unanimously [ju:næn'əmsəli:] *adv* (vote) 満場一致で mañjòitchi de

unarmed [ʌnɑ:rmd'] *adj* 武器を持たない búkì wo motánaì, 丸腰の marúgoshi no
unarmed combat 武器を使わない武術 búkì wo tsukáwanaì bújùtsu

unashamed [ʌnəʃeimd'] *adj* (greed) 恥知らずの hajíshirãzu no; (pleasure) 悪びれない warábirénaì

unassuming [ʌnəsu:'miŋ] *adj* (person, manner) 気取らない kidòranai

unattached [ʌnətætʃt'] *adj* (person) 独身の dokúshin no; (part etc) 遊んでいる asónde iru

unattended [ʌnəten'did] *adj* (car, luggage, child) ほったらかしの hottárakashi no

unattractive [ʌnətræk'tiv] *adj* (person, character) いやな iyá na; (building, appearance, idea) 魅力のない miryóku no nai

unauthorized [ʌnɔ:θ'əraizd] *adj* (visit, use, version) 無許可の mukyókà no

unavoidable [ʌnəvɔi'dəbəl] *adj* (delay) 避けられない sakérarenài

unaware [ʌnəweːr'] *adj*: **to be unaware of** ...に気が付いていない ...ni ki gà tsuite inai

unawares [ʌnəweːrz'] *adv* (catch, take) 不意に fuí ni

unbalanced [ʌnbæl'ənst] *adj* (report) 偏った katáyottà; (mentally) 狂った kurútta

unbearable [ʌnbeːr'əbəl] *adj* (heat, pain) 耐えられない taérarenài; (person) 我慢できない程いやな gámàn dekínai hodo iyá na

unbeatable [ʌnbi:'təbəl] *adj* (team) 無敵の mutékì no; (quality) 最高の saíkō no; (price) 最高に安い saíkō ni yasúi

unbeknown(st) [ʌnbinoun(st)'] *adv*: **unbeknown(st) to me/Peter** 私(ピーター)に気付かれずに watákushi(pītā)ni kizúkarezù ni

unbelievable [ʌnbili:'vəbəl] *adj* 信じられない shiñjirarenài

unbend [ʌnbend'] (*pt, pp* **bent**) *vi* (relax) くつろぐ kutsúrogù
♦*vt* (wire) 真直ぐにする massúgù ni suru

unbiased [ʌnbai'əst] *adj* 公正な kōséi na

unborn [ʌnbɔ:rn'] *adj* (child, young) おなかの中の onáka no nakà no

unbreakable [ʌnbrei'kəbəl] *adj* (glassware, crockery etc) 割れない warénaì; (other objects) 壊れない kowárenaì

unbroken [ʌnbrou'kən] *adj* (seal) 開けてない akète nai; (silence, series) 続く tsuzúku; (record) 破られていない yabúrarete inai; (spirit) くじけない kujíkenài

unbutton [ʌnbʌt'ən] *vt* ...のボタンを外す ...no botàn wo hazúsu

uncalled-for [ʌnkɔ:ld'fɔ:r] *adj* (remark)

余計な yokéi na; (rudeness etc) いわれのない iwáre no nai

uncanny [ʌnˈkæniː] *adj* (silence, resemblance, knack) 不気味な bukími na

unceasing [ʌnˈsiːsiŋ] *adj* 引っ切り無しの hikkfrinashí no

unceremonious [ʌnserəmouˈniːəs] *adj* (abrupt, rude) ぶしつけな bushítsuke na

uncertain [ʌnˈsəːrtən] *adj* (hesitant: voice, steps) 自信のない jishín no nai; (unsure) 不確実な fukákūjitsu na

uncertainty [ʌnˈsəːrtəntiː] *n* (not knowing) 不確実さ fukákūjitsusa; (*also pl:* doubts) 疑問 gimón

unchanged [ʌntʃeindʒd'] *adj* (condition) 変っていない kawátte inai

unchecked [ʌntʃekt'] *adv* (grow, continue) 無制限に muséigen ni

uncivilized [ʌnsivˈilaizd] *adj* (*gen:* country, people) 未開の mikái no; (*fig:* behavior, hour etc) 野蛮な yabán na

uncle [ʌŋˈkəl] *n* おじ ojf

uncomfortable [ʌnkʌmfˈtəbəl] *adj* (physically, *also* furniture) 使い心地の悪い tsukáigokochi no warúi; (uneasy) 不安な fuán na; (unpleasant: situation, fact) 厄介な yakkái na

uncommon [ʌnkɑːmˈən] *adj* (rare, unusual) 珍しい mezúrashii

uncompromising [ʌnkɑːmˈprəmaiziŋ] *adj* (person, belief) 融通の利かない yūzū no kikánai

unconcerned [ʌnkənsəːrnd'] *adj* (indifferent) 関心がない kańshin ga nai; (not worried) 平気な hefki na

unconditional [ʌnkəndiʃˈənəl] *adj* 無条件の mujóken no

unconscious [ʌnkɑːnˈtʃəs] *adj* (in faint, *also* MED) 意識不明の ishíkifumei no; (unaware) *unconscious of* ...に気が付かない ...ni kf ga tsukanaí

♦*n: the unconscious* 潜在意識 señzaí-ishiki

unconsciously [ʌnkɑːnˈtʃəsliː] *adv* (unawares) 無意識に mushíkí ni

uncontrollable [ʌnkəntrouˈləbəl] *adj* (child, animal) 手に負えない te nf oénai; (temper) 抑制のきかない yokúsei no ki-

kánai; (laughter) やめられない yamérarenai

unconventional [ʌnkənvenˈtʃənəl] *adj* 型破りの katáyaburi no

uncouth [ʌnkuːθ'] *adj* 無様な buzáma na

uncover [ʌnkʌvˈəːr] *vt* (take lid, veil etc off) ...の覆いを取る ...no ōī wo torú; (plot, secret) 発見する hakkén suru

undecided [ʌndisaiˈdid] *adj* (person) 決定していない kettéi shite inai; (question) 未決定の mikettéi no

undeniable [ʌndinaiˈəbəl] *adj* (fact, evidence) 否定できない hitéi dekínai

under [ʌnˈdəːr] *prep* (beneath) ...の下に ...no shitá ni; (in age, price: less than) ...以下に ...iká ni; (according to: law, agreement etc) ...によって ...ni yotté; (someone's leadership) ...のもとに ...no motó ni

♦*adv* (go, fly etc) ...の下に〔で〕 ...no shitá ni〔de〕

under there あそこの下に〔で〕asóko no shitá ni〔de〕

under repair 修理中 shūríchū

under... *prefix* 下の... shitá no...

under-age [ʌndəːreidʒ'] *adj* (person, drinking) 未成年の misétnen no

undercarriage [ʌndəːrkæˈridʒ] (*BRIT*) *n* (AVIAT) 着陸装置 chakúrikusōchi

undercharge [ʌndəːrtʃɑːrdʒ'] *vt* ...から正当な料金を取らない ...kara séitō na ryō-kín wo toránái

underclothes [ʌndəːrklouz'] *npl* 下着 shitági

undercoat [ʌndəːrkout'] *n* (paint) 下塗り shitánuri

undercover [ʌndəːreidʒ'] *adj* (work, agent) 秘密の himftsu no

undercurrent [ʌndəːrkəːrənt] *n* (*fig:* of feeling) 底流 tefryū

undercut [ʌndəːrkʌt'] (*pt, pp* undercut) *vt* (person, prices) ...より低い値段で物を売る ...yorí hikúi nedán de monó wo urú

underdog [ʌnˈdəːrdɔːg] *n* 弱者 jakúsha

underdone [ʌndəːrdʌn'] (CULIN) 生焼けの namáyake no

underestimate [ʌndəːresˈtəmeit] *vt* (person, thing) 見くびる mikúbiru

underexposed [ˌʌndərɪkspouzd'] adj (PHOT) 露出不足の roshútsubusoku no

underfed [ʌndəːrfed'] adj (person, animal) 栄養不足の eíyōbusòku no

underfoot [ʌndəːrfut'] adv (crush, trample) 脚の下に(で) ashí no shitá ni(de)

undergo [ʌndəːrgou'] vt (pt **underwent** / pp **undergone**) vt (test, operation, treatment) 受ける ukérù

  to undergo change 変る kawáru

undergraduate [ʌndəːrgrædʒ'uɪt] n 学部の学生 gakúbu no gakúsei

underground [ʌndəːrgraund'] n (BRIT: railway) 地下鉄 chikátetsu; (POL) 地下組織 chikásoshìki

  ♦adj (car park) 地下の chiká no; (newspaper, activities) 潜りの mogúri no

  ♦adv (work) 潜りで mogúri de; (fig): *to go underground* 地下に潜る chiká ni mogúrù

undergrowth [ʌndəːrgrouθ'] n 下生え shitábae

underhand [ʌndəːrhænd'] adj (fig) ずるい zurúi

underhanded [ʌndəːrhæn'did] adj = **underhand**

underlie [ʌndəːrlaɪ'] (pt **underlay** / pp **underlain**) vt (fig: be basis of) ...の根底になっている ...no kóntei ni natté iru

underline [ʌndəːrlaɪn'] vt (subject) 下線を引く ...ni andáːrain wo hikú; (fig) 強調する kyóchō suru

underling [ʌndəːrlɪŋ] (pej) n 手下 teshíta

undermine [ʌndəːrmaɪn'] vt (confidence) 失わせる ushínawaseru; (authority) 弱める yowámerù

underneath [ʌndəːrniːθ'] adv ...の下に(で) shitá ni(de)

  ♦prep ...の下に(で) ...no shitá ni(de)

underpaid [ʌndəːrpeɪd'] adj 安給料の yasúkyūryō no

underpants [ʌndəːrpænts] npl パンツ pańtsu

underpass [ʌndəːrpæs] (BRIT) n 地下道 chikádō

underprivileged [ʌndəːrprɪv'əlidʒd] adj

(country, race, family) 恵まれない megúmarenai

underrate [ʌndəːreɪt'] vt (person, power etc) 見くびる mikúbirù; (size) 見誤る miáyamarù

undershirt [ʌndəːrʃəːrt] (US) n アンダーシャツ afidáshatsù

undershorts [ʌndəːrʃəːrts] (US) npl パンツ pańtsu

underside [ʌn'dəːrsaid] n (of object) 下側 shitágawa; (of animal) おなか onáka

underskirt [ʌndəːrskəːrt] (BRIT) n アンダースカート afidásukàto

understand [ʌndəːrstænd'] (pt, pp **understood**) vt 分かる wakárù, 理解する rikái suru

  ♦vi (believe): *I understand that* ...だそうですfa ...da sódesū ne, ...だと聞いていますが ...da tó kíite imasu ga

understandable [ʌndəːrstæn'dəbəl] adj (behavior, reaction, mistake) 理解できる rikái dekírù

understanding [ʌndəːrstæn'diŋ] adj (kind) 思いやりのある omóiyari no aru

  ♦n (gen) 理解 rikái; (agreement) 合意 gói

understatement [ʌndəːrsteit'mənt] n (of quality) 控え目な表現 hikáeme na hyōgen

  that's an understatement! それは控え目過ぎるよ sore wa hikáemesugírō yo

understood [ʌndəːrstud'] pt, pp of **understand**

  ♦adj (agreed) 合意された gói saretà; (implied) 暗黙の afmoku no

understudy [ʌn'dəːrstʌdi] n (actor, actress) 代役 dafyaku

undertake [ʌndəːrteik'] (pt **undertook** / pp **undertaken**) vt (task) 引受ける hikíkerù

  to undertake to do something ...する事を約束する ...surú koto wo yakúsoku suru

undertaker [ʌndəːrteikəːr] n 葬儀屋 sógiyà

undertaking [ʌndəːrteikiŋ] n (job) 事業 jigyó; (promise) 約束 yakúsoku

undertone [ʌndəːrtoun] n: *in an undertone* 小声 kogóe

underwater [ʌndə'wɔːt'əː] *adv* (use) 水中に(で) suíchū ni(de); (swim) 水中に 潜って suíchū ni mogútte
♦*adj* (exploration) 水中の sénsuiyō no; (camera etc) 潜水用の sénsuiyō no

underwear [ʌn'dəːrwəːr] *n* 下着 shítagi

underworld [ʌn'dəːrwəːrld] *n* (of crime) 暗黒街 ańkokugai

underwriter [ʌn'dəːraitəːr] *n* (INSURANCE) 保険業者 hokéngyōshā

undesirable [ʌndizaiəːr'əbəl] *adj* (person, thing) 好ましくない konómashiku-nai

undies [ʌn'diːz] (*inf*) *npl* 下着 shítagi ◊ 女性用と言う joséiyō wo sasú

undisputed [ʌndispju:'tid] *adj* (fact) 否定できない hítéi dekínai; (champion etc) 断トツの dañtotsu no

undo [ʌndu:'] (*pt* **undid** *pp* **undone**) *vt* (unfasten) 外す hazúsu; (spoil) 台無しにする dafnashi ni suru

undoing [ʌndu:'iŋ] *n* 破滅 hamétsu

undoubted [ʌndau'tid] *adj* 疑う余地のない utágau yochí no naí

undoubtedly [ʌndau'tidli:] *adv* 疑う余地なく utágau yochí naku

undress [ʌndres'] *vi* 服を脱ぐ fukú wo nugú

undue [ʌndu:'] *adj* (excessive) 余分な yobún na

undulating [ʌn'dʒəleitiŋ] *adj* (countryside, hills) 起伏の多い kifúku no ōĪ

unduly [ʌndu:li:] *adv* (excessively) 余分に yobún ni

unearth [ʌnəːrθ'] *vt* (skeleton etc) 発掘する hakkútsu suru; (*fig*: secrets etc) 発見する hakkén suru

unearthly [ʌnəːrθ'liː] *adj* (hour) とんでもない tofide mo naí

uneasy [ʌniː'ziː] *adj* (person: not comfortable) 窮屈な kyūkútsu na; (: worried: *also* feeling) 不安な fuán na; (peace, truce) 不安定な fuáñtei na

uneconomic [ʌniːkənəm'ik(əl)] *adj* 不経済な fukéizai na

uneducated [ʌned'ʒukeitid] *adj* (person) 教育のない kyōíku no nai

unemployed [ʌnemplɔid'] *adj* (worker) 失業中の shitsúgyōchū no
♦*npl*: **the unemployed** 失業者 shitsú-gyōsha ◊総称 sōshō

unemployment [ʌnemplɔi'mənt] *n* 失業 shitsúgyō

unending [ʌnen'diŋ] *adj* 果てし無い ha-téshi naí

unerring [ʌnəːr'iŋ] *adj* (instinct etc) 確実な kakújitsu na

uneven [ʌniː'vən] *adj* (not regular: teeth) 不ぞろいの fuzóroi no; (performance) むらのある murá no aru; (road etc) 凸凹のdekóboko no

unexpected [ʌnikspek'tid] *adj* (arrival) 不意の fuí no; (success etc) 思い掛けない omóigakenaĪ, 意外な igái na

unexpectedly [ʌnikspek'tidli:] *adv* (arrive) 不意に fuí ni; (succeed) 意外に igái ni

unfailing [ʌnfei'liŋ] *adj* (support, energy) 尽きる事のない tsukíru koto no naĪ

unfair [ʌnfeːr'] *adj*: **unfair (to)** (...に 対して) 不当な (...ni taíshite) futō na

unfaithful [ʌnfeiθ'fəl] *adj* (lover, spouse) 浮気な uwáki na

unfamiliar [ʌnfəmil'jəːr] *adj* (place, person, subject) 知らない shiránai
to be unfamiliar with ...を知らない ...wo shiránai

unfashionable [ʌnfæʃ'ənəbəl] *adj* (clothes, ideas, place) はやらない hayáranai

unfasten [ʌnfæs'ən] *vt* (undo) 外す hazúsu; (open) 開ける akéru

unfavorable [ʌnfeiʹvəːrəbəl] (*BRIT* **unfavourable**) *adj* (circumstances, weather) 良くない yokúnaī; (opinion, report) 批判的な hiháñteki na

unfeeling [ʌnfiː'liŋ] *adj* 冷たい tsumétai, 冷酷な refkoku na

unfinished [ʌnfin'iʃt] *adj* (incomplete) 未完成の mikáñsei no

unfit [ʌnfit'] *adj* (physically) 運動不足のufídōbusoku no; (incompetent): **unfit (for)** (...に) 不向きな (...ni) fumúki na
to be unfit for work 仕事に不向きである shigóto ni fumúki de aru

unfold [ʌnˈfould] *vt* (sheets, map) 広げる hirogeru

♦*vi* (situation) 展開する tenkai suru

unforeseen [ʌnfɔːrˈsiːn] *adj* (circumstances etc) 予期しなかった yokî shínákatta, 思い掛けない omóigakenai

unforgettable [ʌnfərˈgetəbəl] *adj* 忘れられない wasúrerarenai

unforgivable [ʌnfərˈgivəbəl] *adj* 許せない yurúsenai

unfortunate [ʌnˈfɔːrtʃənit] *adj* (poor) 哀れな awáre na; (event) 不幸な fukô na; (remark) まずい mazúi

unfortunately [ʌnfɔːrtʃəˈnitli:] *adv* 残念ながら zafínennagara

unfounded [ʌnˈfaundid] *adj* (criticism, fears) 根拠のない koñkyo no nái

unfriendly [ʌnˈfrendliː] *adj* (person, behavior, remark) 不親切な fushíñsetsu na

ungainly [ʌnˈgeinliː] *adj* ぎこちない gíkōchinai

ungodly [ʌnˈgɑːdliː] *adj* (hour) とんでもない tofídemonai

ungrateful [ʌnˈgreitfəl] *adj* (person) 恩知らずの ofíshíràzu no

unhappiness [ʌnˈhæpiːnis] *n* 不幸せ fushíawàse, 不幸 fukô

unhappy [ʌnˈhæpiː] *adj* (sad) 悲しい kanáshii; (unfortunate) 不幸な fukô na; (childhood) 恵まれない megúmarenai; (dissatisfied): **unhappy about/with** (arrangements etc) ...に不満がある ...ni fumáñ ga aru

unharmed [ʌnˈhɑːrmd] *adj* 無事な bují na

unhealthy [ʌnˈhelθiː] *adj* (person) 病弱な byójaku na; (place) 健康に悪い keñkôni warúî; (*fig*: interest) 不健全な fukéñzen na

unheard-of [ʌnˈhɜːrdʌv] *adj* (shocking) 前代未聞の zeñdaimimon no; (unknown) 知られていない shírárete inai

unhurt [ʌnˈhɜːrt] *adj* 無事な bují na

unidentified [ʌnaiˈdentəfaid] *adj* 未確定の mikákùtei no ¶ *see also* UFO

uniform [ˈjuːnəfɔːrm] *n* 制服 seffuku, ユニフォーム yunífōmù

♦*adj* (length, width etc) 一定の ittéi no

uniformity [juːnəfɔːrˈmitiː] *n* 均一性 kiñitsusei

unify [ˈjuːnəfai] *vt* 統一する tôitsu suru

unilateral [juːnəˈlætəːrəl] *adj* (disarmament etc) 一方的な ippôteki na

uninhabited [ʌninhæbˈitid] *adj* (island etc) 無人の mujín no; (house) 空き家になっている akíya ni natté iru

unintentional [ʌninˈtenʃənəl] *adj* 意図的でない itóteki de nái

union [ˈjuːnjən] *n* (joining) 合併 gappéi; (grouping) 連合 reñgô; (*also*: **trade union**) 組合 kumíai

♦*cpd* (activities, leader etc) 組合の kumíai no

Union Jack *n* 英国国旗 efkokukókki, ユニオンジャック yuníoñjakkù

unique [juːniːk'] *adj* 独特な dokútoku na, ユニークな yuníkû na

unisex [ˈjuːniseks] *adj* (clothes, hairdresser etc) ユニセックスの yunísekkùsu no

unison [ˈjuːnisən] *n*: **in unison** (say) 一同に ichídô ni; (sing) 同音で dôon de, ユニゾンで yunízon de

unit [ˈjuːnit] *n* (single whole, *also* measurement) 単位 tañ-i; (section: of furniture etc) ユニット yunítto; (: team, squad) 班 háñ

kitchen unit 台所用ユニット daídokoroyô yunítto

unite [juːnaitʹ] *vt* (join: *gen*) 一緒にする isshô ni suru, 一つにする hitótsû ni suru; (: country, party) 結束させる kessôku saseru

♦*vi* 一緒になる isshô ni naru, 一つになる hitótsû ni naru

united [juːnaitʹid] *adj* (*gen*) 一緒になった isshô ni natta, 一つになった hitótsû ni natta; (effort) 団結した dañketsu shita

United Kingdom *n* 英国 efkoku

United Nations (Organization) *n* 国連 kokúren

United States of America) *n* (アメリカ) 合衆国 (américa)gasshûkoku

unit trust (*BRIT*) *n* ユニット型投資信託 yuníttogata tôshishiñtaku

unity [juːnitiː] *n* 一致 itchí

universal [juːnəvəːrsəl] *adj* 普遍的な fuhénteki na

universe [juːnəvəːrs] *n* 宇宙 úchū

university [juːnəvəːrsitiː] *n* 大学 dáìgaku

unjust [ʌndʒʌst] *adj* 不当な futó na

unkempt [ʌnkempt] *adj* (appearance) だらしのない daráshi no naí; (hair, beard) もじゃもじゃの mojámoja na

unkind [ʌnkaind] *adj* (person, behavior, comment etc) 不親切な fushínsetsu na

unknown [ʌnnoun] *adj* 知られていない shirárete ináì

unlawful [ʌnlɔːfəl] *adj* (act, activity) 非合法な higóhō na

unleash [ʌnliːʃ] *vt* (fig: feeling, forces etc) 爆発させる bakúhatsu saseru

unless [ʌnles] *conj* ...しなければ(でなければ)...しなければ(でなければ) (denákereba)
unless he comes 彼が来なければ karè ga konákereba

unlike [ʌnlaik] *adj* (not alike) 似ていない nité inaí; (not like) 違った chigátta
◆*prep* (different from) ...と違って ...to chigátte

unlikely [ʌnlaikliː] *adj* (not likely) ありそうもない arísō mo naí; (unexpected: combination etc) 驚くべき odórokubeki

unlimited [ʌnlimitid] *adj* (travel, wine etc) 無制限の muséìgen no

unlisted [ʌnlistid] (*BRIT* **ex-directory**) *adj* (ex-directory) 電話帳に載っていない deñwachō ni notté inaí

unload [ʌnloud] *vt* (box, car etc) ...の積荷を降ろす ...no tsumíni wo orósù

unlock [ʌnlɑk] *vt* ...のかぎを開ける ...no kagí wo akérù

unlucky [ʌnlʌkiː] *adj* (person) 運の悪い uñ no warúì; (object, number) 縁起の悪い eñgi no warúì
to be unlucky (person) 運が悪い uñ ga warúì

unmarried [ʌnmæriːd] *adj* (person) 独身の dokúshin no; (mother) 未婚の mikón no

unmask [ʌnmæsk] *vt* (reveal: thief etc) ...の正体を暴く ...no shótaì wo abákù

unmistakable [ʌnmisteikəbəl] *adj* (voice, sound, person) 間違える様のない machígaeyō no naí

unmitigated [ʌnmitəgeitid] *adj* (disaster etc) 紛れもない magíre mò naí

unnatural [ʌnnætʃərəl] *adj* 不自然な fushízèn na

unnecessary [ʌnnesiseriː] *adj* 不必要な fuhítsuyō na

unnoticed [ʌnnoutist] *adj*: *(to go/pass) unnoticed* 気付かれない kizúkarenaí

UNO [uːnou] *n abbr* = **United Nations Organization**

unobtainable [ʌnəbteinəbəl] *adj* (item) 手に入らない te ni hafranái; (TEL): *this number is unobtainable* この電話番号は現在使用されていません koñó deñwabangō wa geñzai shiyō sarete imáseñ

unobtrusive [ʌnəbtruːsiv] *adj* (person) 遠慮がちな eñryogachi na; (thing) 目立たない medátanaí

unofficial [ʌnəfiʃəl] *adj* (news) 公表されていない kóhyō sarete inaí; (strike) 公認されていない kónin sarete inaí

unorthodox [ʌnɔːrθədɑks] *adj* (treatment) 通常でない tsújō de nai; (REL) 正統でない seftō de nai

unpack [ʌnpæk] *vi* 荷物の中身を出して片付ける nimótsu no nakámi wo dashíte katázukerù
◆*vt* (suitcase etc) ...の中身を出して片付ける ...no nakámi wo dashíte katázukerù

unpalatable [ʌnpælətəbəl] *adj* (meal) まずい mazúì; (truth) 不愉快な fuyúkai na

unparalleled [ʌnpærəleld] *adj* (unequalled) 前代未聞の zeñdaimìmon no

unpleasant [ʌnplezənt] *adj* (disagreeable: thing) いやな iyá na; (: person, manner) 不愉快な fuyúkai na

unplug [ʌnplʌg] *vt* (iron, TV etc) ...のプラグを抜く ...no puragu wo nukú

unpopular [ʌnpɑpjəlaːr] *adj* (person, decision etc) 不評の fuhyō no

unprecedented [ʌnpresidentid] *adj* 前代未聞の zeñdaimìmon no

unpredictable [ʌnpridiktəbəl] *adj*

(weather, reaction) 予測できない yosóku dekínai; (person): **he is unpredictable** 彼のする事は予測できない karè no suru koto wa yosóku dekínai

unprofessional [ʌnprəféʃˈənəl] adj (attitude, conduct) 職業倫理に反する shokúgyōrìnri ni hañ suru

unqualified [ʌnkwɔ́:ləfaid] adj (teacher, nurse etc) 資格のない shikáku no naì; (complete: disaster) 全くの mattáku no, 大...dal...; (: success) 完全な kañzen na, 大...dal...

unquestionably [ʌnkwésˈtʃənbli:] adv 疑いもなく utágai mò naku

unravel [ʌnrǽvəl] vt (ball of string) ほぐす hogúsù; (mystery) 解明する kaímei suru

unreal [ʌnri:ˈl] adj (not real) 偽の nisé no; (extraordinary) うその様な usó no yō na

unrealistic [ʌnri:əlisˈtik] adj (person, project) 非現実的な higéñjitsuteki na

unreasonable [ʌnri:ˈzənəbəl] adj (person, attitude) 不合理な fugóri na; (demand) 不当な futó na; (length of time) 非常識な hijōshiki na

unrelated [ʌnrilei'tid] adj (incident) 関係のない kañkei no naì, 無関係な mukáñkei na; (family) 親族でない shiñzoku de naì

unrelenting [ʌnrilen'tiŋ] adj 執念深い shúnenbukai

unreliable [ʌnrilaiˈəbəl] adj (person, firm) 信頼できない shiñrai dekinaì; (machine, watch, method) 当てにならない ate ni naranai

unremitting [ʌnrimit'iŋ] adj (efforts, attempts) 絶間ない taéma naì

unreservedly [ʌnrizəːrˈvidli:] adv 心から kokórò kara

unrest [ʌnrest'] n (social, political, industrial etc) 不安 fuáñ

unroll [ʌnroul'] vt 広げる hirógeru

unruly [ʌnru:ˈli:] adj (child, behavior) 素直でない sunáo de nai, 手に負えない te nì oénaì; (hair) もじゃもじゃの mojámoja no

unsafe [ʌnseif'] adj (in danger) 危険な

らされた kiñken ni sarásareta; (journey, machine, bridge etc) 危険な kikén na, 危ない abúnai

unsaid [ʌnsed'] adj: **to leave something unsaid** ...を言わないでおく ...wo iwánaide okù

unsatisfactory [ʌnsætisfæk'tə:ri:] adj (progress, work, results) 不満足な fumáñzoku na

unsavory [ʌnsei'və:ri:] adj (BRIT **unsavoury**) (person, place) いかがわしい ikágawashiì

unscathed [ʌnskeiðd'] adj 無傷の mukìzu no

unscrew [ʌnskru:'] vt (bottletop etc) ねじって開ける nejítte akérù; (sign, mirror etc) ...のねじを抜く ...no nejì wo nukú

unscrupulous [ʌnskru:ˈpjələs] adj (person, behavior) 悪徳... akútoku...

unsettled [ʌnset'əld] adj (person) 落付かない ochítsukanàì; (weather) 変りやすい kawáriyasui

unshaven [ʌnʃei'vən] adj 不精ひげのbushóhìge no

unsightly [ʌnsait'li:] adj (mark, building etc) 醜い miníkuì, 目障りな mezáwàri na

unskilled [ʌnskild'] adj (work, worker) 未熟練の mijúkuren no

unspeakable [ʌnspi:ˈkəbəl] adj (indescribable) 言語に絶する geñgo ni zéssuru, 想像を絶する sōzō wo zéssurù; (awful) ひどい hidóì

unstable [ʌnstei'bəl] adj (piece of furniture) ぐらぐらする gurágura suru; (government) 不安定な fuáñtei na; (mentally) 情緒不安定な jōchofuáñtei na

unsteady [ʌnsted'i:] adj (step, legs) ふらふらする furáfura suru; (hands, voice) 震える furúerù; (ladder) ぐらぐらする gurágura suru

unstuck [ʌnstʌk'] adj: **to come unstuck** (label etc) 取れてしまう torète shimaú; (fig: plan, idea etc) 失敗する shippái suru

unsuccessful [ʌnsəkses'fəl] adj (attempt) 失敗した shippái shita; (writer) 成功しない sefkō shinaì, 売れない urénaì; (proposal) 採用されなかった saíyō sarénakatta *to be unsuccessful* (in attempting something) 失敗する shippai suru; (application) 採用されない saiyō sarénai

unsuccessfully [ʌnsəkˈsesˈfəli] *adv* (try) 成功せずに seikō sezu ni

unsuitable [ʌnsuːˈtəbəl] *adj* (inconvenient: time, moment) 不適当な futékittō na; (inappropriate: clothes) 場違いの bachígai no; (: person) 不適切な futékittō na

unsure [ʌnʃuˈər] *adj* (uncertain) 不確実な fukákújitsu na
unsure about ...について確信できない ...ni tsuíte kakúshin dekinai
to be unsure of oneself 自信がない jishín ga nai

unsuspecting [ʌnsəspekˈtiŋ] *adj* 気付いていない kizúite inai

unsympathetic [ʌnsimpəθetˈik] *adj* (showing little understanding) 同情しない dōjō shinai; (unlikeable) いやな iyá na

untapped [ʌntæptˈ] *adj* (resources) 未開発の mikáihatsu no

unthinkable [ʌnθiŋkˈəbəl] *adj* 考えられない kangáerarenai

untidy [ʌntaiˈdiː] *adj* (room) 散らかった chírakatta; (person, appearance) だらしない daráshi nai

untie [ʌntaiˈ] *vt* (knot, parcel, ribbon) ほどく hodókú; (prisoner) ...の綱をほどく ...no nawá wo hodókú; (parcel, dog) ...の ひもをほどく ...no himó wo hodókú

until [ʌntilˈ] *prep* ...まで ...madé
♦*conj* ...するまで ...surú madé
until he comes 彼が来るまで karé ga kurú madé
until now 今まで imámadè
until then その時まで sonó toki madè

untimely [ʌntaimˈliː] *adj* (inopportune: moment, arrival) 時機の悪い jikí no warúi
an untimely death 早死に hayájini, 若死に wakájini

untold [ʌntouldˈ] *adj* (story) 明かされていない akásarete inai; (joy, suffering, wealth) 想像を絶する sōzō wo zessúru

untoward [ʌntɔːrdˈ] *adj* 困った komátta

unused [ʌnjuːzdˈ] *adj* (not used: clothes, portion etc) 未使用の mishíyō no

unusual [ʌnjuːˈʒuːəl] *adj* (strange) 変った kawátta; (rare) 珍しい mezúrashii; (exceptional, distinctive) 並外れた namfhazureta

unveil [ʌnveilˈ] *vt* (statue) ...の除幕式を 行う ...no jomákushìki wo okónau

unwanted [ʌnwɑːntidˈ] *adj* (clothing etc) 不要の fuyō no; (child, pregnancy) 望まれなかった nozőmarenakatta

unwavering [ʌnweiˈvəriŋ] *adj* (faith) 揺るぎ無い yurúginai; (gaze) じっとした jittő shita

unwelcome [ʌnwelˈkəm] *adj* (guest) 歓迎されない kangéisarenai; (news) 悪い warúi

unwell [ʌnwelˈ] *adj*: *to feel unwell* 気分が悪い kibún ga warúi
to be unwell 病気である byóki de aru

unwieldy [ʌnwiːlˈdiː] *adj* (object, system) 大きくて扱いにくい ōkíkute atsúkainikuī

unwilling [ʌnwilˈiŋ] *adj*: *to be unwilling to do something* ...するのをいやがっている ...surú no wo iyagatte iru

unwillingly [ʌnwilˈiŋli] *adv* いやがって iyágatte

unwind [ʌnwaindˈ] (*pt, pp* **unwound**) *vt* (undo) ほどく hodókú
♦*vi* (relax) くつろぐ kutsúrogù

unwise [ʌnwaizˈ] *adj* (person) 思慮の足りない shiryō no tarínai; (decision) 浅はかな asáhàka na

unwitting [ʌnwitˈiŋ] *adj* (victim, accomplice) 気付かない kizúkānai

unworkable [ʌnwɔːrˈkəbəl] *adj* (plan) 実行不可能な jikkőfukanō nà

unworthy [ʌnwɔːrˈðiː] *adj* ...の値打がない ...no neúchi ga naí

unwrap [ʌnræpˈ] *vt* 開ける akéru

unwritten [ʌnritˈən] *adj* (law) 慣習の kañshū no; (agreement) 口頭での kőtō de no

---
KEYWORD
---

up [ʌp] *prep*: *to go up something* ...を登る ...wo nobóru
to be up something ...の上に（登って）いる ...no ué ni nobotte iru

he went up the stairs/the hill 彼は階段(坂)を登った kare wa kaídan(saka) wo nobótta

the cat was up a tree ネコは木の上にいた nekó wa ki nò ué ni ita

we walked/climbed up the hill 私たちは丘を登った watákushitachi wa oká wo nobótta

they live further up the street 彼らはこの道をもう少し行った所に住んでいます karéra wa konó michi wo mó sukoshi ittá tokoro ni súñde imasu

go up that road and turn left この道を交差点まで行って左に曲って下さい konó michi wo kôsaten máde itte hidári ni magátte kudásaì

◆*adv* 1 (upwards, higher) 上に(で、へ) ué ni(de, e)

up in the sky/the mountains 空(山の上)に sorâ(yamá no ué)ni

put it a bit higher up もう少し高い所に置いて下さい mó sukoshì takáì tokoro ni oîte kudásaì

up there あの上に anó ue ni

what's the cat doing up there? ネコは何でああいう所にいるのかしら nekó wa nañde anó ue nì irú no kashira

up above 上の方に(で) ué no hó nì(de)

there's a village and above, a monastery 村があって、その上の丘に修道院がある murá ga atte, sonó ue no oká ni shûdòin ga aru

2: *to be up* (out of bed) 起きている okíte iru; (prices, level) 上がっている agátte iru; (building) 建ててある tatéte aru, 立っている tátte iru; (tent) 張ってある hatté aru

3: *up to* (as far as) ...まで ...made

I've read up to p. 60 私は60ページまで読みました watákushi wa rokújùpèji máde yomímashita

the water came up to his knees 水が彼のひざまできた mizu ga karè no hizà máde datta

up to now 今(これ)まで imà(koré)máde

I can spend up to $10 10ドルまで使えます jû dóǹru made tsukáemasu

4: *to be up to* (depending on) ...の責任である ...no sekíniñ de aru, ...次第である ...shídaì de aru

it's up to you あなた次第です anàta shídaì desu

it's not up to me to decide 決めるのは私の責任ではない kimèru no wa watákushi no sekíniñ de wa naì

5: *to be up to* (equal to) ...に合う ...ni aù

he's not up to it (job, task etc) 彼にはその仕事は無理です karè ni wa sonó shigoto wo murî desu

his work is not up to the required standard 彼の仕事は基準に合いません karè no shigòto wa kijûñ ni aimaseñ

6: *to be up to* (inf: be doing) やっている yatté iru

what is he up to? (showing disapproval, suspicion) あいつは何をやらかしているんだろうねえ àitsu wa nani wo yarákushireñ irûn darō né

◆*n: ups and downs* (in life, career) 浮き沈み ukíshizumi

we all have our ups and downs だれだっていい時と悪い時がありますよ darè datte iî toki to warúì toki ga arímasu yo

his life had its ups and downs, but he died happy 彼の人生には浮き沈みが多かったが、死ぬ時は幸せだった karè no jiñsei ni wa ukíshizumi ga ôkattà ga, shinú toki wa shiâwase datta

---

upbringing [ʌp'briŋiŋ] *n* 養育 yôiku

update [ʌpdeit'] *vt* (records, information) 更新する kôshin suru

upgrade [ʌp'greid'] *vt* (improve: house) 改装する kaíshiku suru; (job: make bigger) 格上げする kakûage suru; (employee) 昇格させる shôkaku saseru

upheaval [ʌphi:'vəl] *n* 変動 héndo

uphill [*adj* ʌp'hil' *adv* ʌp'hil'] *adj* (climb) 上りの nobóri no; (*fig*: task) 困難な koñnan na

◆*adv: to go uphill* 坂を上る sakà wo nobóru

uphold [ʌphould'] (*pt, pp* **upheld**) *vt* (law, principle, decision) 守る mamórù

upholstery [ʌphoul'stə:ri:] *n* いすに張っ

た生地 isū ni hattá kijí

upkeep [ʌp'kiːp] n (maintenance) 維持 ijí

upon [əpɔn'] prep ...の上に〔で〕...no ué ni 〔de〕

upper [ʌp'əːr] adj 上の方の ué no hó no
◆n (of shoe) 甲皮 kóhi

upper-class [ʌp'əːrklæs'] adj (families, accent) 上流の jóryū no

upper hand n: **to have the upper hand** 優勢である yúsei de aru

uppermost [ʌp'əːrmoust] adj 一番上の ichíban ué no
what was uppermost in my mind 私が真っ先に考えたのは watákushi ga massákí ni kañgáeta no wa

upright [ʌp'rait] adj (straight) 直立の chokúritsu no; (vertical) 垂直の chokúchoku no; (fig: honest) 正直な shójiki na

uprising [ʌp'raiziŋ] n 反乱 hañran

uproar [ʌp'rɔːr] n (protests, shouts) 大騒ぎ ōsawagi

uproot [ʌpruːt'] vt (tree) 根こそぎにする nekósogi ni suru; (fig: family) 故郷から追出す kokyō kara ofdasú

upset [n adj verb vb ʌpset'] (pt, pp upset) n (to plan etc) 失敗 shippái
◆vt (knock over: glass etc) 倒す taósú; (routine, plan) 台無しにする damnashi ni suru; (person: offend, make unhappy) 動転させる dōten ni saseru
◆adj (unhappy) 動転した dōten shita
to have an upset stomach 胃の具合が悪い i nó gúai ga warúí

upshot [ʌp'ʃɑt] n 結果 kekká

upside down [ʌp'said-] adv (hang, hold) 逆様に〔で〕 sakásama ni 〔de〕
to turn a place upside down (fig) 家中を引っかき回す iéjū wo hfkkakímawasu

upstairs [ʌp'steːrz'] adv (be) 2階 に〔で〕 nikái ni 〔de〕; (go) 2階へ nikái e
◆adj (window, room) 2階の nikái no
◆n 2階 nikái

upstart [ʌp'stɑːrt] n 横柄な奴 ōhei na yatsú

upstream [ʌp'striːm] adv 川上 に〔で、へ〕 kawákami ni 〔de, e〕, 上流に〔で、へ〕 jóryū ni 〔de, e〕

uptake [ʌp'teik] n: **to be quick/slow on**

the uptake 物分かりがいい〔悪い〕 monówakári ga íi 〔waruí〕

uptight [ʌp'tait'] adj ぴりぴりした píri-píri shita

up-to-date [ʌp'tədeit'] adj (most recent: information) 最新の saíshin no; (person) 最新の情報に通じている saíshin no jōhō ni tsūjíte irú

upturn [ʌp'təːrn] n (in luck) 好転 kóten; (COMM: in market) 上向き uwámuki

upward [ʌp'wəːrd] adj (movement, glance) 上への ué e no

upwards [ʌp'wəːrdz] adv (move, glance) 上の方へ ué no hó e; (more than): **upward(s) of** ...以上の ...ijō no

uranium [jurei'niːəm] n ウラン urán, ウラニウム uránìumù

urban [əːr'bən] adj 都会の tokái no

urbane [əːrbein'] adj 上品な jōhin na

urchin [əːr'tʃin] n (child) 童 gakí; (waif) 浮浪児 furōji

urge [əːrdʒ] n (need, desire) 衝動 shōdō
◆vt: **to urge someone to do something** ...する様に...を説得する ...surú yō ni ...wo settóku suru

urgency [əːr'dʒənsi] n (importance) 緊急性 kiñkyūsei; (of tone) 緊迫した調子 kiñpaku shita chōshi

urgent [əːr'dʒənt] adj (need, message) 緊急な kiñkyū na; (voice) 切迫した seppákú shita

urinal [jur'ənəl] n 小便器 shōbeñki

urinate [jur'əneit] vi 小便をする shōben suru

urine [jur'in] n 尿 nyó, 小便 shōben

urn [əːrn] n (container) 骨つぼ kotsútsubo; (also: **coffee/tea urn**) 大型コーヒー〔紅茶〕メーカー ōgátakōhī〔kōcha〕mēkà

Uruguay [jur'əgwei] n ウルグアイ urúguai

us [ʌs] pron 私たちを〔に〕 watákushitachi wo〔ni〕 see also **me**

USA [ju:'es'ei'] n abbr = United States of America

usage [juː'sidʒ] n (LING) 慣用 kañyō

use [n juːs vb juːz] n (using) 使用 shíyō; (usefulness, purpose) 役に立つ事 yakú ni tatsu koto 利益 ríeki

♦vt (object, tool, phrase etc) 使う tsukáu, 用いる mochíírú, 使用する shíyō suru

in use 使用中 shíyōchū

out of use 廃れて sutárete

to be of use 役に立つ yakú ni tatsu

it's no use (not useful) 使えません tsukáemasen; (pointless) 役に立ちません yakú ni tachimasen, 無意味です mumí desu

she used to do it 前は彼女はそれをする習慣でした maè wa kanòjo wa soré wo suru shûkan deshita

to be used to ...に慣れている ...ni naréte iru

used [juːzd] adj (object) 使われた tsukáwareta; (car) 中古の chūkō no

useful [juːsˈfəl] adj 役に立つ yakú ni tatsu, 有益な yúeki na, 便利な benʹrí na

usefulness [juːsˈfəlnis] n 実用性 jitsúyōsei

useless [juːsˈlis] adj (unusable) 使えない tsukáenai; (pointless) 役に立たない yakú ni tatanai; (person: hopeless) 能無しの nōnashi no, 役に立たない yakú ni tatanai

user [juːˈzəːr] n 使用者 shiyōsha

user-friendly [juːˈzəːrfrendˈliː] adj (computer) 使いやすい tsukáiyasuí, ユーザーフレンドリーな yúzāfurèndorí na

use up vt 全部使ってしまう zénbu tsukátte shimaû, 使い尽す tsukáitsukusù

usher [ʌˈʃəːr] n (at wedding) 案内係 afínaigakàri

usherette [ʌʃəretʹ] n (in cinema) 女性案内係 joséi afínaigakàri

USSR [juːesesaːrʹ] n: **the USSR** ソ連 sorèn

usual [juːˈʒuːəl] adj (time, place etc) いつもの itsúmo no

as usual いつもの様に itsúmo no yō ni

usually [juːˈʒuːəli:] adv 普通は futsū wa

usurp [juːsəːrpʹ] vt (title, position) 強奪する gōdatsu suru

utensil [juːtenʹsəl] n 用具 yōgu

kitchen utensils 台所用具 daídokoro yōgu

uterus [juːˈtəːrəs] n 子宮 shikyū

utility [juːtilʹiti:] n (usefulness) 有用性

yūyōsei, 実用性 jitsúyōsei; (also: **public utility**) 公益事業 kōekijigyō

utility room n 洗濯部屋 seńtakubeya

utilize [juːʹtəlaiz] vt (object) 利用する riyō suru, 使う tsukáu

utmost [ʌtʹmoust] adj 最大の saídai no

♦n: **to do one's utmost** 全力を尽す zeńryoku wo tsukusù

utter [ʌtʹəːr] adj (total: amazement, fool, waste, rubbish) 全くの mattáku no

♦vt (sounds) 出す dasú, 発する hassúru; (words) 口に出す kuchí ni dasù, 言う iû

utterance [ʌtʹəːrəns] n 発言 hatsúgen, 言葉 kotóba

utterly [ʌtʹəːrliː] adv 全く mattáku

U-turn [juːʹtəːrn] n Uターン yútāñ

V

v. abbr = **verse**; **versus**; **volt**; (= **vide**) ...を見よ ...wo mlyo

vacancy [veiʹkənsi:] n (BRIT: job) 欠員 ketsúin; (room) 空き部屋 akíbeya

vacant [veiʹkənt] adj (room, seat, toilet) 空いている aíte iru; (look, expression) うつろの utsúro no

vacant lot (US) n 空き地 akíchi

vacate [veiʹkeit] vt (house, one's seat) 空ける akéru; (job) 辞める yaméru

vacation [veikeiʹʃən] n (esp US: holiday) 休暇 kyúka; (SCOL) 夏休み natsúyasùmi

vaccinate [vækʹsəneit] vt: **to vaccinate someone (against something)** ...に (...の) 予防注射をする ...ni (...no) yobōchūsha wo suru

vaccine [væksiːnʹ] n ワクチン wakúchin

vacuum [vækʹjuːm] n (empty space) 真空 shifíkú

vacuum cleaner n (真空) 掃除機 (shifíkú)sōjikí

vacuum-packed [vækʹjuːmpækt] adj 真空パックの shifíkúpakkú no

vagabond [vægʹəband] n 浮浪者 furôshà, ルンペン ruñpen

vagina [vədʒaiʹnə] n ちつ chitsú

vagrant [veiʹgrənt] n 浮浪者 furôshà, ルンペン ruñpen

vague [veig] *adj* (blurred: memory, outline) ぼんやりとした bon'yari to shita; (uncertain: look, idea, instructions) 漠然とした bakúzen to shita; (person: not precise) 不正確な fuséikaku na; (: evasive) 曖昧ぎりない niékiranái

価値観 kachíkaň

vaguely [veig'li:] *adv* (not clearly) ぼんやりとして bon'yari to shite; (without certainty) 漠然と bakúzen to, 不正確に fuséikaku ni; (evasively) あいまいに af-mai ni

vain [vein] *adj* (conceited) うぬぼれた unúboreta; (useless: attempt, action) 無駄な mudá na

in vain 何のかいもなく nań no kaí mo nakú

valentine [væl'əntain] *n* (*also:* **valentine card**) バレンタインカード baréntaiňkàdo; (person) バレンタインデーの恋人 baréntaiňdē no kóibito

valet [væléi] *n* 召使い meshítsukai

valiant [væl'jənt] *adj* (attempt, effort) 勇敢な yūkan na

valid [væl'id] *adj* (ticket, document) 有効な yūkō na; (argument, reason) 妥当な datō na

validity [vəlid'iti:] *n* (of ticket, document) 有効性 yūkōsei; (of argument, reason) 妥当性 datōsei

valley [væl'i:] *n* 谷 (間) taní(ma)

valor [væl'ə:r] (*BRIT* **valour**) *n* 勇ましさ isámashisà

valuable [væl'ju:əbəl] *adj* (jewel etc) 高価な kōka na; (time, help, advice) 貴重な kichō na

valuables [væl'ju:əbəlz] *npl* (jewellery etc) 貴重品 kichōhìn

valuation [væljuei'ʃən] *n* (worth: of house etc) 価格 kakáku; (judgment of quality) 評価 hyōka

value [væl'ju:] *n* (financial worth) 価値 kachí, 価格 kakáku; (importance, usefulness) 価値 kachí
◆*vt* (fix price or worth of) …に値を付ける …ni ne wó tsukérù; (appreciate) 大切にする taísetsu ni suru, 重宝する chōhō suru

values [væl'ju:z] *npl* (principles, beliefs)

value added tax [-æd'id-] (*BRIT*) *n* 付加価値税 fukákachizèi

valued [væl'ju:d] *adj* (appreciated: customer, advice) 大切な taísetsu na

valve [vælv] *n* 弁 beň, バルブ barúbu

vampire [væm'paiə:r] *n* 吸血鬼 kyūketsùki

van [væn] *n* (AUT) バン baň

vandal [væn'dəl] *n* 心無い破壊者 kokóronaì hakáisha

vandalism [væn'dəlizəm] *n* 破壊行動 hakáikōdō

vandalize [væn'dəlaiz] *vt* 破壊する hakái suru

vanguard [væn'gɑːrd] *n* (*fig*): *in the vanguard of* …の先端に立って …no señtan ni tattè

vanilla [vənil'ə] *n* バニラ baníra

vanilla ice cream *n* バニラアイスクリーム baníra afsukurímu

vanish [væn'iʃ] *vi* (disappear suddenly) 見えなくなる miénàku narù, 消える kiéru

vanity [væn'iti:] *n* (of person: unreasonable pride) 虚栄心 kyóeishìn

vantage point [væn'tidʒ-] *n* (lookout place) 観察点 kafísatsuten; (viewpoint) 有利な立場 yūri na tachíba

vapor [vei'pə:r] (*BRIT* **vapour**) *n* (gas) 気体 kitái; (mist, steam) 蒸気 jōki

variable [ver'iːəbəl] *adj* (likely to change: mood, quality, weather) 変りやすい kawáriyasuì; (able to be changed: temperature, height, speed) 調節できる chōsetsu dekírù

variance [ver'iːəns] *n*: *to be at variance (with)* (people) (…と) 仲たがいしている (…to) nakátagaì shité irù; (facts) (…と) 矛盾している (…to) mujúň-shité iru

variation [veːriːei'ʃən] *n* (change in level, amount, quantity) 変化 heňka, 変動 heňdō; (different form of: plot, musical theme etc) 変形 heňkei

varicose [værʻəkous] *adj*: *varicose veins* 拡張蛇行静脈 kakúchōdakōjōmyakú

varied

venison

varied [veː'riːd] *adj* (diverse: opinions, reasons) 様々な sámāzama na; (full of changes: career) 多彩な tasái na

variety [vərai'əti] *n* (degree of choice, diversity) 変化 hénka, バラエティー baráeti; (varied collection, quantity) 様々な物 sámāzama na mono; (type) 種類 shurúi

variety show *n* バラエティーショー baráetishō

various [veː'riːəs] *adj* 色々な iróiro na

varnish [vɑːr'niʃ] *n* (product applied to surface) ニス nísu

◆*vt* (apply varnish to: wood, piece of furniture etc) ...にニスを塗る ...ni nísu wo nurú; (: nails) ...にマニキュアをする ...ni maníkyua wo suru

nail varnish マニキュア maníkyua

vary [veː'riː] *vt* (make changes to: routine, diet) 変える kaéru

◆*vi* (be different: sizes, colors) ...が色々ある ...ga iróiro aru; (become different): **to vary with** (weather, season etc) ...によって変る ...ni yótte kawáru

vase [veis] *n* 花瓶 kabín

Vaseline [væs'əlin] ® *n* ワセリン wasérin

vast [væst] *adj* (wide: area, knowledge) 広い hirói; (enormous: expense etc) ばく大な bakúdai na

VAT [væt] *n abbr* = **value added tax**

vat [væt] *n* 大おけ ōke

Vatican [væt'ikən] *n*: **the Vatican** (palace) バチカン宮殿 bachíkan kyūden; (authority) ローマ法王庁 rōma hōchō

vault [vɔːlt] *n* (of roof) 丸天井 marúteñjō; (tomb) 地下納骨堂 chikánōkotsudō; (in bank) 金庫室 kiñkoshitsú

◆*vt* (also: **vault over**) 飛越える tobíkoerù

vaunted [vɔːn'tid] *adj*: **much-vaunted** ご自慢の go-jíman no

VCR [viːsiːɑːr'] *n abbr* = **video cassette recorder**

VD [viːdiː'] *n abbr* = **venereal disease**

VDU [viːdiːjuː'] *n abbr* = **visual display unit**

veal [viːl] *n* 子ウシ肉 koúshiniku

veer [viːr] *vi* (vehicle, wind) 急に向きを変える kyū ni mukí wo kaéru

vegetable [vedʒ'təbəl] *n* (BOT) 植物 shokúbutsu; (edible plant) 野菜 yasái

◆*adj* (oil etc) 植物性の shokúbutsusei no

vegetarian [vedʒitər'iːən] *n* 菜食主義者 saíshokushugìsha

◆*adj* (diet etc) 菜食主義の saíshokushugi no

vegetate [vedʒ'iteit] *vi* 無為に暮す muí ni kurásu

vegetation [vedʒitei'ʃən] *n* (plants) 植物 shokúbutsu /総称 sōshō

vehement [viː'əmənt] *adj* (strong: attack, passions, denial) 猛烈な mōretsu na

vehicle [viː'ikəl] *n* (machine) 車 kurúma; (fig: means of expressing) 手段 shudán

veil [veil] *n* ベール bēru

veiled [veild] *adj* (fig: threat) 隠された kakúsareta

vein [vein] *n* (ANAT) 静脈 jōmyaku; (of ore etc) 脈 myaku

vein of a leaf 葉脈 yōmyaku

velocity [vəlɑːs'itiː] *n* 速度 sokúdo

velvet [vel'vit] *n* ビロード bíròdo, ベルベット berúbetto

◆*adj* ビロードの bíròdo no, ベルベットの berúbettō no

vendetta [vendet'ə] *n* 復しゅう fukúshū

vending machine [ven'diŋ-] *n* 自動販売機 jidóhanbaiki

vendor [ven'dər] *n* (of house, land) 売手 uríte; (of cigarettes, beer etc) 売子 uríko

veneer [viniːr'] *n* (on furniture) 化粧張り keshóbari; (fig: of person, place) 虚飾 kyoshóku

venereal [vəniːr'iːəl] *adj*: **venereal disease** 性病 seíbyō

Venetian blind [vəniː'ʃən-] *n* ベネシャンブラインド benéshanburaindò

Venezuela [venizwei'lə] *n* ベネズエラ benézuèra

vengeance [ven'dʒəns] *n* (revenge) 復しゅう fukúshū

with a vengeance (fig: to a greater extent) 驚く程 odórokù hodo

venison [ven'isən] *n* シカ肉 shikániku

venom [ven'əm] n (of snake, insect) 毒 dokú; (bitterness, anger) 悪意 ákui

venomous [ven'əməs] adj (poisonous: snake, insect) 毒... dokú...; (full of bitterness: look, stare) 敵意に満ちた tekíi ni michíta

vent [vent] n (also: **air vent**) 通気孔 tsúkikō; (in jacket) ベンツ béntsu
♦vt (fig: feelings, anger) ぶちまける buchímakeru

ventilate [ven'təleit] vt (room, building) 換気する kañki suru

ventilation [ventəlei'ʃən] n 換気 kañki

ventilator [ven'təleitər] n (TECH) 換気装置 kañkisōchi, ベンチレーター beńchirētā; (MED) 人工呼吸器 jiñkokyūkī, レスピレター resúpirētā

ventriloquist [ventril'əkwist] n 腹話術師 fukúwajútsushi

venture [ven'tʃər] n (risky undertaking) 冒険 bōken
♦vt (opinion) おずおず言う ozúozu iú
♦vi (dare to go) おずおず行く ozúozu ikú
business venture 投機 tōki

venue [ven'ju:] n (place fixed for something) 開催地 kafsaichi

veranda(h) [vəræn'də] n ベランダ beránda

verb [vəːrb] n 動詞 dōshi

verbal [vəːr'bəl] adj (spoken: skills etc) 言葉の kotóba no; (: translation etc) 口頭の kōtō no; (: of verb) 動詞の dōshi no

verbatim [vəːrbei'tim] adj 言葉通りの kotóbadōri no
♦adv 言葉通りに kotóbadōri ni

verbose [vəːrbous'] adj (person) 口数の多い kuchíkazu no ōi; (speech, report etc) 冗長な jōchō na

verdict [vəːr'dikt] n (LAW) 判決 hañketsu; (fig: opinion) 判断 hañdan

verge [vəːrdʒ] n (BRIT: of road) 路肩 rokáta
「**soft verges**」 (BRIT: AUT) 路肩軟弱 rokáta nanjaku
to be on the verge of doing something ...する所である ...surú tokoro dè arú

verge on vt fus ...同然である ...dōzen de arú

verify [ver'əfai] vt (confirm, check) 確認する kakúnin suru

veritable [ver'itəbəl] adj (reinforcer: = real) 全くの mattáku no

vermin [vəːr'min] npl (animals) 害獣 gaíjū; (fleas, lice etc) 害虫 gaíchū

vermouth [vəːrmuːθ'] n ベルモット berúmotto

vernacular [vəːrnæk'jələr] n (language) その土地の言葉 sonó tochi no kotóba

versatile [vəːr'sətail] adj (person) 多才の tasái no; (substance, machine, tool etc) 幅広い用途の多い tsukáimichi no ōi

verse [vəːrs] n (poetry) 詩 shi; (one part of a poem: also in bible) 節 setsú

versed [vəːrst] adj: **(well-)versed in** ...に詳しい ...ni kuwáshiī

version [vəːr'ʒən] n (form: of design, production) 型 katá; (: of book, play etc) ...版 ...bañ; (account: of events, accident etc) 説明 setsúmei

versus [vəːr'səs] prep ...対... ...tai ...

vertebra [vəːr'təbrə] (pl **vertebrae**) n せきつい sekítsui

vertebrae [vəːr'təbrei] npl of **vertebra**

vertebrate [vəːr'təbreit] n せきつい動物 sekítsuidōbutsu

vertical [vəːr'tikəl] adj 垂直の suíchoku no

vertigo [vəːr'təgou] n めまい memái

verve [vəːrv] n (vivacity) 気迫 kihákù

very [ver'i:] adv (+ adjective, adverb) とても totémo, 大変 taíhen, 非常に hijō ni
♦adj: **it's the very book he'd told me about** 彼が話した正にこれだ karè ga hanáshite ita no wà masá ni sonó hon dá
the very last 正に最後の masá ni saígo no
at the very least 少なくとも sukunákutomo
very much 大変 taíhen

vessel [ves'əl] n (NAUT) 船 fune; (container) 容器 yōki see **blood**

vest [vest] n (US: waistcoat) チョッキ chókki; (BRIT) アンダーシャツ añdashatsu

vested interests [ves'tid-] *npl* 自分の利益 jibún no ríeki, 私利 shirí

vestige [ves'tidʒ] *n* 残り nokóri

vet [vet] (*BRIT*) *n abbr* = **veterinary surgeon**

♦*vt* (examine: candidate) 調べる shirábe-rù

veteran [vet'əːran] *n* (of war) ...戦争で戦った人 ...sensō de tatákatta hitó; (of former soldier) 退役軍人 taíekigunjìn; (old hand) ベテラン betéran

veterinarian [vetəːrəneːr'iːən] (*US*) *n* 獣医 jūi

veterinary [vet'əːrineːriː] *adj* (practice, care etc) 獣医の jūi no

veterinary surgeon (*BRIT*) *n* = **vet-erinarian**

veto [viː'tou] (*pl* **vetoes**) *n* (right to forbid) 拒否権 kyohíken; (act of forbidding) 拒否権の行使 kyohíken no kōshī

♦*vt* ...に拒否権を行使する ...ni kyohíken wo kōshī suru

vex [veks] *vt* (irritate, upset) 怒らせる o-kóraserù

vexed [vekst] *adj* (question) 厄介な yak-kái na

via [vai'ə] *prep* (through, by way of) ...を経て ...wo hetè, ...経由 ...kéìyu

viable [vai'əbəl] *adj* (project) 実行可能な jikkōkanō na; (company) 存立できる sonritsu dekirù

viaduct [vai'ədʌkt] *n* 陸橋 rikkyō

vibrant [vai'brənt] *adj* (lively) 力強い chikárazuyoì; (bright) 生き生きした ikíkì shita; (full of emotion: voice) 感情のこもった kańjō no komóttà

vibrate [vai'breit] *vi* (house, machine etc) 振動する shindō suru

vibration [vaibrei'ʃən] *n* 振動 shindō

vicar [vik'əːr] *n* 主任司祭 shuninshisaì

vicarage [vik'əːridʒ] *n* 司祭館 shisáikaǹ

vicarious [vaikeːr'iːəs] *adj* (pleasure) 他人の身になって感じる tanín no mi ni nattè kańjirù

vice [vais] *n* (moral fault) 悪徳 akútoku; (TECH) 万力 mańriki

vice [vais] *prefix* 副... fukú...

vice-president [vais'prez'idənt] *n* (*US* POL) 副大統領 fukúdaitōryō

vice squad *n* 風俗犯罪取締班 fūzokuhaǹzai toríshimarihaǹ

vice versa [vais'vəːr'sə] *adv* 逆の場合も同じ gyakú no baaì mo onáji

vicinity [visin'əːtiː] *n* (area): **in the vicinity (of)** (...の) 近所に (...no) kíǹjo ni

vicious [viʃ'əs] *adj* (violent: attack, blow) 猛烈な mōretsu na; (cruel: words, look) 残酷な zańkoku na; (horse, dog) どう猛な dōmō na

vicious circle *n* 悪循環 akújuñkan

victim [vik'tim] *n* (person, animal, business) 犠牲者 giséìsha

victimize [vik'təmaiz] *vt* (strikers etc) 食い物にする kuímono ni suru

victor [vik'təːr] *n* 勝利者 shōríshà

Victorian [viktoːr'iːən] *adj* ヴィクトリア朝の bikútoriachō no

victorious [viktoːr'iːəs] *adj* (triumphant: team, shout) 勝ち誇る kachíhokorù

victory [vik'təːriː] *n* 勝利 shōrí

video [vid'iːou] *cpd* ビデオの bideo no

♦*n* (video film) ビデオ映画 bídèo éìga; (also: **video cassette**) ビデオカセット bídèokasettò; (also: **video cassette recorder**) ビデオテープレコーダー bídèo tépurekòdā, VTR buitiārù

video tape *n* ビデオテープ bídèotèpù

vie [vai] *vi*: **to vie (with someone)(for something)** (...のために)(...と) 競り合う ...no tamè ni (...to) seríaù

Vienna [viːen'ə] *n* ウィーン uíìn

Vietnam [viːetnɑːm'] *n* ベトナム betóna-mu

Vietnamese [viːetnəmiːz'] *adj* ベトナムの betónamu no; (LING) ベトナム語の betónamugò no

♦*n inv* (person) ベトナム人 betónamujìn; (LING) ベトナム語 betónamugò

view [vjuː] *n* (sight) 景色 keshíkì; (outlook) 見方 mikáta; (opinion) 意見 íkèn

♦*vt* (look at: *also fig*) 見る mirù

on view (in museum etc) 展示中 teńjichū

in full view (of) (...の) 見ている前で (...no) mitè irú maè de

in view of the weather こういう天気 だから kō fu teñki da karā

in view of the fact that ... だという事 を考えて ...da tō iu koto wo kañgaetè

in my view 私の考えでは watákushi no kañgae de wà

viewer [vju:ər] *n* (person) 見る人 mirû hito

viewfinder [vju:ˈfaindər] *n* ファインダ ー faîndà

viewpoint [vju:ˈpoint] *n* (attitude) 考え 方 kañgaekata, 見地 keñchi; (place) 観察 する地点 kañsatsu suru chíteñ

vigil [vidʒˈil] *n* 不寝番 fushíñbaan

vigilance [vidʒˈələns] *n* 用心 yōjiñ

vigilant [vidʒˈələnt] *adj* 用心する yōjiñ suru

vigor [vigˈər] (*BRIT* **vigour**) *n* (energy: of person, campaign) 力強さ chikárazuyosà

vigorous [vigˈərəs] *adj* (full of energy: person) 元気のいい geñki no iî; (action, campaign) 強力な kyōryoku na; (: plant) よく茂った yokú shigéttà

vile [vail] *adj* (evil: action) 下劣な gerétsu na; (: language) 下品な gehíñ na; (unpleasant: smell, weather, food, temper) ひどい hidôi

villa [vilˈə] *n* (country house) 別荘 bessō; (suburban house) 郊外の屋敷 kōgai no yashikí

village [vilˈidʒ] *n* 村 murá

villager [vilˈidʒər] *n* 村民 soñmíñ

villain [vilˈin] *n* (scoundrel) 悪党 akútō; (in novel) 悪役 akúyaku; (*BRIT*: criminal) 犯人 hañniñ

vindicate [vinˈdikeit] *vt* (person: free from blame) ...の正しさを立証する ...no tadashīsa wo risshōsuru; (action: justify) ...が正当である事を立証する ...ga seftō de arú koto wo risshō suru

vindictive [vindikˈtiv] *adj* (person) 執念 深い shūneñbukaî; (action etc) 復しゅう心による fukúshūshiñ ni yoru

vine [vain] *n* (climbing plant) ツル tsurù; (grapevine) ブドウの木 budō no ki

vinegar [vinˈəgər] *n* 酢 su

vineyard [vinˈjərd] *n* ブドウ園 budéñ

vintage [vinˈtidʒ] *n* (year) ブドウ収穫年 budō shūkakuneñ

♦*cpd* (classic: comedy, performance etc) 典型的な teñkeiteki na

vintage car *n* クラシックカー kurashîkku kā

vintage wine *n* 当り年のワイン atáridoshi no waîñ

vinyl [vaiˈnil] *n* ビニール biníròu

viola [vi:oˈlə] *n* (MUS) ビオラ bîòra

violate [vaiˈəleit] *vt* (agreement, peace) 破る yabúrû; (graveyard) 汚す kegasù

violation [vaialeiˈʃən] *n* (of agreement etc) 違反 iháñ

violence [vaiˈələns] *n* (brutality) 暴力 bōryòku; (strength) 乱暴 rañbō

violent [vaiˈələnt] *adj* (brutal: behavior) 暴力の bōryòku no,乱暴な rañbō na; (intense: debate, criticism) 猛烈な mōrétsu na

a violent death 変死 heñshí

violet [vaiˈəlit] *adj* 紫色の murásakiiro no

♦*n* (color) 紫 murasáki; (plant) スミレ sumíre

violin [vaiəlinˈ] *n* バイオリン baíoriñ

violinist [vaiəlinˈist] *n* バイオリン奏者 baíoriñsoñsha, バイオリニスト baíorinisuto

VIP [vi:aipi:ˈ] *n abbr* (= *very important person*) 要人 yōjiñ, 貴賓 kihíñ, ブイアイ ピー bufaipī, ビップ bippū

viper [vaiˈpər] *n* クサリヘビ kusáriheb̀i

virgin [vəːrˈdʒin] *n* (person) 処女 shojô, バージン bājiñ

♦*adj* (snow, forest etc) 処女... shojô...

virginity [vəːrdʒinˈəti:] *n* (of person) 処女 shojô

Virgo [vəːrˈgou] *n* (sign) 乙女座 otómeza

virile [vilˈəl] *adj* 男らしい otókorashiî

virility [vərilˈəti:] *n* (sexual power) 性的 能力 seftekinôryoku; (*fig*: masculine qualities) 男らしさ otókorashisà

virtually [vəːrˈtʃuːəliː] *adv* (almost) 事実 上 jijftsujō

virtue [vəːrˈtʃu:] *n* (moral correctness) 徳 tokū, 徳行 tokkō; (good quality) 美徳 bítoku; (advantage) 利点 riteñ, 長所 chōshō

by virtue of ...である事で ... de aru kótò de

virtuosi [vəːrtʃuːˈoːziː] *npl of* **virtuoso**

virtuoso [vəːrtʃuːˈouˈzou] (*pl* **virtuosos** *or* **virtuosi**) *n* 名人 meijín

virtuous [ˈvəːrtʃuəs] *adj* (displaying virtue) 良心的な ryōshínteki na, 高潔な kōkétsu na, 敬けんな kefken na

virulent [ˈvirjələnt] *adj* (disease) 悪性の akúsei no 危険な kiken na; (actions, feelings) 憎悪に満ちた zōō ni michìta

virus [ˈvaiˈrəs] *n* ウイルス uírusu

visa [ˈviːˈzə] *n* 査証 sashō, ビザ bìza

vis-à-vis [viːzɑːviːˈ] *prep* (compared to) ...と比べて ...to kurábete; (in regard to) ...に関して ...ni kañ shite

viscose [ˈvisˈkouz] *n* ビスコース人絹 bísukōsujínken, ビスコースレーヨン bísukōsúrēyòn

viscous [ˈvisˈkəs] *adj* ねばねばした nebáneba shita

visibility [vizabílˈiti:] *n* 視界 shikái

visible [ˈvizˈabəl] *adj* (able to be seen or recognized: *also fig*) 目に見える me ni mierú

vision [ˈviʒˈən] *n* (sight: ability) 視力 shiryòku; (: sense) 視覚 shikáku; (foresight) ビジョン bijòn; (in dream) 幻影 geñ-ei

visit [ˈvizˈit] *n* (to person, place) 訪問 hōmon

♦*vt* (person: *US also*: visit with) 訪問する hōmon suru, 訪ねる tazúnerù, ...の所へ遊びに行く ...no tokóro e asóbi ni ikú; (place) 訪問する hōmon suru, 訪ねる tazúneru

visiting hours [ˈvizˈitiŋ-] *npl* (in hospital etc) 面会時間 meñkaijikan

visitor [ˈvizˈitəːr] *n* (person visiting, invited) 客 kyakú; (tourist) 観光客 kañkōkyàku

visor [ˈvaiˈzəːr] *n* (of helmet etc) 面 meñ; (of cap etc) ひさし hísashi; (AUT: *also*: **sun visor**) 日よけ hiyóke

vista [ˈvisˈtə] *n* (view) 景色 keshíki

visual [ˈviʒˈuəl] *adj* (arts etc) 視覚の shikáku no

visual aid *n* 視覚教材 shikákukyōzai

visual display unit *n* モニター moníta, ディスプレー disúpurē

visualize [ˈviʒˈuəlaiz] *vt* (picture, imagine) 想像する sōzō suru

vital [ˈvaitˈəl] *adj* (essential, important, crucial) 重要な jūyō na; (full of life: person) 活発な kappátsu na; (necessary for life: organ) 生命に必要な seímei ni hitsúyō na

vitality [vaitǽlˈiti:] *n* (liveliness) 元気 genki

vitally [ˈvaitˈəli:] *adv*: *vitally important* 極めて重要な kiwámete jūyō na

vital statistics *npl* (of population) 人口動態統計 jiñkōdōtaitōkei; (*inf*: woman's measurements) スリーサイズ surísaizu

vitamin [ˈvaitˈəmin] *n* ビタミン bítamin

vivacious [viveiˈʃəs] *adj* にぎやかな nigíyàka na

vivid [ˈvivˈid] *adj* (clear: description, memory) 鮮明な señmei na; (bright: color, light) 鮮やかな azáyàka na; (imagination) はつらつとした hatsúratsu to shitá

vividly [ˈvivˈidliː] *adv* (describe) 目に見えるように me ni mierú yō ni; (remember) はっきりと hakkírì to

vivisection [vivisékʃən] *n* 生体解剖 seítaikaibō

V-neck [ˈviːˈnek] *n* (*also*: **V-neck jumper/pullover**) Vネックセーター buínekkusètā

vocabulary [voukǽbˈjələriː] *n* (words known) 語い goì

vocal [ˈvouˈkəl] *adj* (of the voice) 声の kóè no; (articulate) はっきり物を言う hakkírì monó wo iú

vocal c(h)ords *npl* 声帯 seítai

vocation [voukeiˈʃən] *n* (calling) 使命感 shiméikan; (chosen career) 職業 shokúgyō

vocational [voukeiˈʃənəl] *adj* (training etc) 職業の shokúgyō no

vociferous [vousifˈəːrəs] *adj* (protesters, demands) やかましい yakámashii, しつこい shitsúkoi

vodka [ˈvɑdˈkə] *n* ウオッカ uókkà

vogue [voug] *n* 流行 ryūkō

in vogue 流行して ryūkō shite

voice [vɔɪs] *n* (of person) 声 koè
♦*vt* (opinion) 表明する hyōmei suru

void [vɔɪd] *n* (emptiness) 空虚 kūkyò;
(hole) 穴 aná, 空間 kūkan
♦*adj* (invalid) 無効の mukō no; (empty):
void of ...が全くない ...ga mattakù naî

volatile [vɑ:ˈlətəl] *adj* (liable to change:
situation) 不安定な fuantei na; (: person)
気まぐれな kimágure na; (: liquid) 揮発
性の kihátsusei no

volcanic [vɑːlˈkænɪk] *adj* (eruption) 火山
の kazán no; (rock etc) 火山性の kazán-
sei no

volcano [vɑːlˈkeɪˈnou] (*pl* **volcanoes**) *n* 火
山 kazán

volition [vouliʃˈən] *n*: *of one's own*
volition 自発的に jihátsuteki ni, 自由意
志で jiyúishì de

volley [vɑːˈliː] *n* (of stones etc) 一斉に投
げられる ... isséi ni nagérareru ...; (of
questions etc) 連発 reņpatsu; (TENNIS
etc) ボレー borè
a volley of gunfire 一斉射撃 isséishagèki

volleyball [vɑːˈliːbɔːl] *n* バレーボール ba-
rébōrù

volt [voult] *n* ボルト borúto

voltage [voulˈtɪdʒ] *n* 電圧 deñ-atsu

voluble [vɑːˈljəbəl] *adj* (person) 口達者な
kuchídasshà na; (speech etc) 流ちょうな
ryūchō na

volume [vɑːˈljuːm] *n* (space) 容積 yōsèki;
(amount) 容量 yōryō; (book) 本 hoñ;
(sound level) 音量 oñryō, ボリューム bo-
ryūmu
Volume 2 第2巻 daínikan

voluminous [vəluˈmɪnəs] *adj* (clothes)
だぶだぶの dabúdabu no; (correspon-
dence, notes) 大量の taíryō no, 多数のta-
sū no

voluntarily [vɑːlənˈteˈriːliˌ] *adv* (willingly) 自発的に jihátsuteki ni, 自由意志で ji-
yúishì de

voluntary [vɑːˈlənteˌriː] *adj* (willing,
done willingly: exile, redundancy) 自発
的な jihátsuteki na, 自由意志による jiyúishì ni yoru; (unpaid: work, worker) 奉仕

の hōshf no a

volunteer [vɑːləntɪˈr] *n* (unpaid helper)
奉仕者 hōshísha, ボランティア boráñtia;
(to army etc) 志願者 shigáñsha
♦*vt* (information) 自発的に言う jihátsuteki ni iú, 提供する teíkyō suru
♦*vi* (for army etc) ...への入隊を志願する
...e no nyútai wo shigán suru
to volunteer to do ...しようと申出る
...shíyō to mōshíderu

voluptuous [vəlʌpˈtʃuˌəs] *adj* (movement, body, feeling) 官能的な kañnōteki-
na, 色っぽい iroppoi

vomit [vɑːmˈɪt] *n* 吐いた物 haíta monò,
反吐 hedð
♦*vt* 吐く hakū
♦*vi* 吐く hakū

vote [vout] *n* (method of choosing) 票決
hyōketsu; (indication of choice, ballot)
投票 tōhyō; (votes cast) 投票数 tōhyōsū;
(*also*: *right to vote* 投票権 tōhyōkèn
♦*vt* (elect): *to be voted chairman etc*
座長に選出される zachō ni señshutsu saréru; (propose): *to vote that* ...という事
を提案する ...to iú koto wo teían suru
♦*vi* (in election etc) 投票する tōhyō suru
vote of thanks 感謝決議 kañshaketsu-
gì

voter [vouˈtəɪr] *n* (person voting) 投票者
tōhyōshà, (person with right to vote) 有
権者 yūkeñsha

voting [vouˈtɪŋ] *n* 投票 tōhyō

vouch for [vautʃ-] *vt fus* (person, quality etc) 保証する hoshō suru

voucher [vauˈtʃəɪr] *n* (for meal: *also*:
luncheon voucher) 食券 shokkén; (with
petrol, cigarettes etc) クーポン kūpon;
(*also*: *gift voucher*) ギフト券 gifútokèn

vow [vau] *n* 誓い chíkài
♦*vt*: *to vow to do/that* ...する事 ...だと
いう事を誓う ...surú koto ...da to iú
koto) wo chikáu

vowel [vauˈəl] *n* 母音 boiñ

voyage [vɔɪˈɪdʒ] *n* (journey: by ship,
spacecraft) 旅行 ryokō, 旅行 ryokō

V-sign [viːˈsaɪn] (*BRIT*) *n* V サインの V
sain ①手の甲を相手に向けると軽べつの
サイン；手のひらを向けると勝利の意味

ン té no kō wo afte ni mukéru to keśbetsu no saīn; té ni hirā wo mukéru to shōrī no saīn

vulgar [vʌl'gər] *adj* (rude: remarks, gestures, graffiti) 下品な gehīn na; (in bad taste: decor, ornament) 野暮な yabō na

vulgarity [vʌlgær'iti:] *n* (rudeness) 下品 na言葉 gehīn na kotóba; (ostentation) 野暮ったい事 yabóttaī kotó

vulnerable [vʌl'nərəbəl] *adj* (person, position) やられやすい yaráreyasuī, 無防備な mubōbī na

vulture [vʌl'tʃər] *n* ハゲタカ hagétaka

W

wad [wɑːd] *n* (of cotton wool, paper) 塊 katámari; (of banknotes etc) 束 tabā

waddle [wɑːd'əl] *vi* (duck, baby) よちよち歩く yochíyochi arúkū; (fat person) よたよた歩く yotáyota arúkū

wade [weid] *vi*: **to wade through** (water) ...の中を歩いて通る ...no nakā wo arúite tōrū; (*fig*: a book) 苦労して読む kurō shité yomū

wafer [wei'fɑːr] *n* (biscuit) ウエハース uēhāsu

waffle [wɑːf'əl] *n* (CULIN) ワッフル waffúru; (empty talk) 下らない話 kudáranai hanáshi
♦*vi* (in speech, writing) 下らない話をする kudáranai hanáshi wo suru

waft [wæft] *vt* (sound, scent) 漂わせる tadáyowaseru
♦*vi* (sound, scent) 漂う tadáyou

wag [wæg] *vt* (tail, finger) 振る furù
♦*vi*: **the dog's tail was wagging** イヌ ははしっぽを振っていた inú no shíppo wo futtě itá

wage [weidʒ] *n* (*also*: **wages**) 賃金 chíngin, 給料 kyúryō
♦*vt*: **to wage war** 戦争をする señsō wo suru

wage earner [-əːr'nəːr] *n* 賃金労働者 chíngiñrōdōsha

wage packet *n* 給料袋 kyúryōbukūro

wager [wei'dʒəːr] *n* かけ kaké

waggle [wæg'əl] *vt* (hips) 振る furù; (eyebrows etc) ぴくぴくさせる pikúpiku saséru

wag(g)on [wæg'ən] *n* (*also*: **horse-drawn wag(g)on**) 荷馬車 nibāsha; (BRIT: RAIL) 貨車 kashā

wail [weil] *n* (of person) 泣き声 nakígoè; (of siren etc) うなり unárī
♦*vi* (person) 泣き声をあげる nakígoè wo agérù; (siren) うなる unárū

waist [weist] *n* (ANAT, *also* of clothing) ウエスト uésùto

waistcoat [weist'kout] (BRIT) *n* チョッキ chókki, ベスト besùto

waistline [weist'lain] *n* (of body) 胴回り dómawàri, ウエスト uésùto; (of garment) ウエストライン uésùtorain

wait [weit] *n* (interval) 待ち時間 machí jikan
♦*vi* 待つ matsù
to lie in wait for ...を待伏せする ...wo machíbuse suru
I can't wait to (*fig*) 早く...したい hayáku ...shitái
to wait for someone/something ...を待つ ...wo matsu

wait behind *vi* 居残って待つ inokotte matsu

waiter [wei'təːr] *n* (in restaurant etc) 給仕 kyúji, ウエーター uétā, ボーイ bōi

waiting [wei'tiŋ] *n*: **"no waiting"** (BRIT: AUT) 停車禁止 teíshä kifshi

waiting list *n* 順番待ちの名簿 juñbañmachi no meíbo

waiting room *n* (in surgery, railway station) 待合室 machíaishitsu

wait on *vt fus* (people in restaurant) ...に給仕する ...ni kyúji suru

waitress [wei'tris] *n* ウエートレス uétóresu

waive [weiv] *vt* (rule) 適用するのをやめる tekíyō suru no wò yaméru; (rights etc) 放棄する hōki suru

wake [weik] (*pt* **woke** *or* **waked**, *pp* **woken** *or* **waked**) *vt* (*also*: **wake up**) 起す okósū
♦*vi* (*also*: **wake up**) 目が覚める me gá samérù

♦*n* (for dead person) 通夜 tsuyǎ, tsúyǎ; (NAUT) 航跡 kōseki

waken [weɪˈkən] *vt, vi* = **wake**

Wales [weɪlz] *n* ウェールズ uērūzu

the Prince of Wales プリンスオブウェールズ purǐnsu obu uērūzu

walk [wɔːk] *n* (hike) ハイキング haɪ́kɪngu; (shorter) 散歩 sanpo; (gait) 歩 調 hochǒ; (in park, along coast etc) 散歩道 sanpomichi, 遊歩道 yūhodǒ

♦*vi* (go on foot) 歩く arúkù; (for pleasure, exercise) 散歩する sanpo suru

♦*vt* (distance) 歩く arúkù; (dog) 散歩に連れて行く sanpo ni tsurête ikú

10 minutes' walk from here ここから徒歩で10分の所に kokó karà tohó de juppún no tokórð ni

people from all walks of life あらゆる身分の人々 aráyurð mibûn no hitóbitð

walker [wɔːˈkər] *n* (person) ハイカー haɪ́kā

walkie-talkie [wɔːˈkiːtɔːˈkiː] *n* トランシーバー toránshībà

walking [wɔːˈkɪŋ] *n* ハイキング haɪ́kɪngu

walking shoes *npl* 散歩靴 sanpogutsu

walking stick *n* ステッキ sutékkì

walk out *vi* (audience: in protest) 途中で退出する totchū de detê ikú; (workers) ストライキをする sutóraĭki wo suru

walkout [wɔːˈkaut] *n* (of workers) ストライキ sutóraĭki

walk out on *vt fus* (family etc) 見捨てる misúterù

walkover [wɔːˈkouvər] *n* (*inf*) (competition, exam etc) 朝飯前 asámeshimaè

walkway [wɔːˈkweɪ] *n* 連絡通路 refírakutsùrð

wall [wɔːl] *n* (*gen*) 壁 kabě; (city wall etc) 城壁 jōheki

walled [wɔːld] *adj* (city) 城壁に囲まれた jōheki ni kakómaretà; (garden) 塀をめぐらした hei wo megúrashità

wallet [wɔːˈlit] *n* 札入れ satsúire, 財布 saffu

wallflower [wɔːlˈflauər] *n* ニオイアラセイトウ nióiarasèitō

to be a wallflower (*fig*) だれもダンスの相手になってくれない darê mo danšu

no aīte ni nattê kurénaì, 壁の花である kabê no hana de arû

wallop [wɔːˈləp] (*inf*) *vt* ぶん殴る bufínaguru

wallow [wɔːˈlou] *vi* (animal: in mud, water) ころげ回る korógemawarù; (person: in sentiment, guilt) ふける fukêrù

wallpaper [wɔːlˈpeɪpər] *n* 壁紙 kabégami

♦*vt* (room)…に壁紙を張る…ni kabéga-mi wo harú

wally [weɪˈliː] (*BRIT: inf*) *n* ばか bakǎ

walnut [wɔːlˈnʌt] *n* (nut) クルミ kurumi; (*also*: **walnut tree**) クルミの木 kurúmi no ki; (wood) クルミ材 kurúmizaì

walrus [wɔːlˈrəs] (*pl* **walrus** *or* **walruses**) *n* セイウチ sefuchi

waltz [wɔːlts] *n* (dance, MUS) 円舞曲 eñbukyòku, ワルツ warûtsu

♦*vi* (dancers) ワルツを踊る warûtsu wo odóru

wan [wɑːn] *adj* (person, complexion) 青白い aójiroi; (smile) 悲しげな kanáshige nà

wand [wɑːnd] *n* (*also*: **magic wand**) 魔法の棒 mahô no bô

wander [wɑːnˈdər] *vi* (person) ぶらぶら歩く buráburà arúkù; (attention) 散漫になる safíman ni narû; (mind, thoughts: here and there) さまよう samáyoù; (: to specific topic) 漂う tadáyoù

♦*vt* (the streets, the hills etc)…をぶらぶら歩く…wo buráburà arúkù

wane [weɪn] *vi* (moon) 欠ける kakêrù; (enthusiasm, influence etc) 衰える herú

wangle [wæŋˈgəl] (*inf*) *vt* うまい具合に獲得する umái guaì ni kakútoku suru

want [wɑːnt] *vt* (wish for) 望む nozómu, …が欲しい…ga hoshîì; (need, require) …が必要である…ga hitsúyō de arù

♦*n: for want of* …がないので…ga naì no de

to want to do…したい…shitáì

to want someone to do something…に…してもらいたい…ni …shité moraì-taì

wanted [wɑːntˈid] *adj* (criminal etc) 指名手配中の shiméiteháichū no

「**wanted**」(in advertisements) 求む mo-
tōmū

wanting [wɔ:ntiŋ] *adj*: **to be found
wanting** 期待を裏切る kitái wo urágirū

wanton [wɔntən] *adj* (gratuitous) 理由
のない riyū no nai; (promiscuous) 浮気な
uwáki na

wants [wɔnts] *npl* (needs) 必要とする物
hitsúyō to suru monō, ニーズ nízù

war [wɔ:r] *n* 戦争 seńsō
to make war (on) (*also fig*) …と戦う
...to tatákaū

ward [wɔ:rd] *n* (in hospital) 病棟 byótō;
(POL) 区 ku; (LAW: child: *also*: **ward of
court**) 被後見人 hikōkennin

warden [wɔ:rdən] *n* (of park, game
reserve, youth hostel) 管理人 kańrinīn;
(of prison etc) 所長 shochō; (BRIT: *also*:
traffic warden) 交通監視官 kōtsūkan-
shikań

warder [wɔ:rdər] *n* (BRIT) 看守 kań-
shu

ward off *vt* (attack, enemy) 食止める
kuftomeru; (danger, illness) 防ぐ fuségū

wardrobe [wɔ:rdroub] *n* (for clothes) 洋
服 だんす yōfukudańsu; (collection of
clothes) 衣装 ishō; (CINEMA, THEA-
TER) 衣装部屋 ishōbeya

warehouse [wer'haus] *n* 倉庫 sōko

wares [werz] *npl* 商品 shōhin, 売物 urímono

warfare [wɔ:r'fer] *n* 戦争 seńsō

warhead [wɔ:r'hed] *n* 弾頭 dańtō

warily [wer'ili:] *adv* 用心深く yōjinbu-
kakū

warlike [wɔ:r'laik] *adj* (nation) 好戦的な
kōsenteki na; (appearance) 武装した bu-
sōshita

warm [wɔ:rm] *adj* (meal, soup, day,
clothes etc) 暖かい atátakaī; (thanks) 心
からの kokóro kara no; (applause, welcome) 熱烈な netsúretsu na; (person,
heart) 優しい yasáshī, 温情のある ońjō
no arū
it's warm (just right) 暖かい atátakaī;
(too warm) 暑い atsúī
I'm warm 暑い atsúī
warm water ぬるま湯 murúmayū

warm-hearted [wɔ:rm'hɑ:r'tid] *adj* 心
の優しい kokóro no yasáshī

warmly [wɔ:rm'li:] *adv* (applaud, welcome) 熱烈に netsúretsu ni
to dress warmly 厚着する atsúgi suru

warmth [wɔ:rmθ] *n* (heat) 暖かさ atáta-
kasa; (friendliness) 温かみ atátakami

warm up *vi* (person, room, soup, etc)
暖まる atátamarū; (weather) 暖かくなる a-
tátakaku narū; (athlete) 準備運動をする
juńbiundō wo suru, ウォーミングアップ
する uōmínguappū suru
♦*vt* (hands etc) 暖める atátamerū;
(engine) 暖気運転する dańkiuńten suru

warn [wɔ:rn] *vt* (advise): **to warn someone of / that** ...にがあると(...だと)警
告する ...ni ...ga arū to (...da to) keǐkoku
suru
to warn someone not to do ...に...しな
いよう警告する ...ni ...shinái yō keǐkoku
suru

warning [wɔ:rniŋ] *n* 警告 keǐkoku

warning light *n* 警告灯 keǐkokutō

warning triangle (AUT) 停止表示板
tefshihyōjibañ

warp [wɔ:rp] *vi* (wood etc) ゆがむ yugámu
♦*vt* (*fig*: character) ゆがめる yugámeru

warrant [wɔ:r'ənt] *n* (voucher) 証明書
shōmeisho; (LAW: for arrest) 逮捕状 tal-
hojō; (: search warrant) 捜索令状 sōsa-
kureijō

warranty [wɔ:r'ənti:] *n* (guarantee) 保証
hoshō

warren [wɔ:r'ən] *n* (*also*: **rabbit warren**)
ウサギ小屋 uságigoya; (*fig*: of passages,
streets) 迷路 meíro

warrior [wɔ:r'i:ər] *n* 戦士 seńshi

Warsaw [wɔ:r'sɔ:] *n* ワルシャワ warú-
shawa

warship [wɔ:r'ʃip] *n* 軍艦 guńkan

wart [wɔ:rt] *n* いぼ ibō

wartime [wɔ:r'taim] *n*: **in wartime** 戦
時中 seńjichū

wary [wer'i:] *adj* 用心深い yōjinbukaī

was [wʌz] *pt* of **be**

wash [wɔʃ] *vt* (*gen*) 洗う aráū; (clothes
etc) 洗濯する seńtaku suru

♦*vi* (person) 手を洗う te wò aráu; (sea etc): **to wash over/against something** …に打吉せる ..ni uchíyoseru, …を洗う …wo aráu

♦*n* (clothes etc) 洗濯物 seńtakumono; (washing program) 洗い aráí; (of ship) 航跡の波 kōseki no namī

to have a wash 手を洗う te wò aráu

to give something a wash …を洗う …wo aráu

washable [wɔʃˈəbəl] *adj* 洗濯できる seńtaku dekirū

wash away *vi* (stain) 洗い落す araiotosu; (subj: flood, river etc) 流す nagasu

washbasin [wɔʃˈbeisin] (*US also:* washbowl) *n* 洗面器 seńmenki

washcloth [wɔʃˈklɔθ] (*US*) *n* (face cloth) フェースタオル fḗsutaorū

washer [wɔʃˈəːr] *n* (TECH: metal) 座金 zagáne, ワッシャー wasshā; (machine) 洗濯機 seńtakuki

washing [wɔʃˈiŋ] *n* (dirty, clean) 洗濯物 seńtakumono

washing machine *n* 洗濯機 seńtakuki

washing powder (*BRIT*) *n* 洗剤 seńzai

washing-up [wɔʃˈiŋʌp] (*BRIT*) *n* (action) 皿洗い saráarai; (dirty dishes) 汚れた皿 yogóreta sará

washing-up liquid (*BRIT*) *n* 台所用洗剤 daídokoroyō senzai

wash off *vi* (US) 手を洗う te wò aráu; (BRIT) 皿洗いをする saráarai wo suru

wash-out [wɔʃˈaut] (*inf*) *n* (failed event) 失敗 shippái

washroom [wɔʃˈruːm] (*US*) *n* お手洗い o-téarái

wash up *vi* (US) 手を洗う te wò aráu; (BRIT) 皿洗いをする saráarai wo suru

wasn't [wʌzˈənt] = **was not**

wasp [wɔsp] *n* アシナガバチ ashínagabáchi ◊スズメバチなど肉食性のハチの総称 suzúmebáchi nado nikúshokuseí no hachí no sōshō

wastage [weisˈtidʒ] *n* (amount wasted, loss) 浪費 rōhi

natural wastage 自然消耗 shizénshōmō

waste [weist] *n* (act of wasting): life, money, energy, time) 浪費 rōhi; (rubbish)

廃棄物 haíkibutsu; (*also:* **household waste**) ごみ gomí

♦*adj* (material) 廃棄の haíki no; (left over) 残りの nokórimono no; (land) 荒れた aréta

♦*vt* (time, life, money, energy) 浪費する rōhi suru; (opportunity) 失う ushínau, 逃す nogásū

to lay waste (destroy: area, town) 破壊する hakái suru

waste away *vi* 衰弱する suíjaku suru

waste disposal unit (*BRIT*) *n* ディスポーザー disúpozà

wasteful [weistˈfəl] *adj* (person) 無駄使いの多い mudázukai no ōi; (process) 不経済な fukéízai na

waste ground (*BRIT*) *n* 空き地 akíchi

wastepaper basket [weistˈpeipə:r-] *n* くずかご kuzúkàgo

waste pipe *n* 排水管 hafsuíkan

wastes [weists] *npl* (area of land) 荒れ野 aréno

watch [wɔtʃ] *n* (*also:* **wristwatch**) 腕時計 udédokéi; (act of watching) 見張り miharí; (vigilance) 警戒 kefkai; (group of guards: MIL, NAUT) 番兵 bańpeí; (NAUT: spell of duty) 当直 tōchoku, ワッチ watchí

♦*vt* (look at: people, objects, TV etc) 見る míru; (spy on, guard) 見張る miharu; (be careful of) …に気を付ける …ni ki wó tsukerú

♦*vi* (look) 見る míru; (keep guard) 見張る miharu

watchdog [wɔtʃˈdɔːɡ] *n* (dog) 番犬 bańken; (*fig*) 監視者 kańshisha, お目付け役 o-métsukeyaku

watchful [wɔtʃˈfəl] *adj* 注意深い chūíbukaì

watchmaker [wɔtʃˈmeikəːr] *n* 時計屋 tokéiya

watchman [wɔtʃˈmən] (*pl* **watchmen**) *n see* **night**

watch out *vi* 気を付ける ki wó tsukerú, 注意する chūí suru

watch out! 危ない! abúnai!

watch strap *n* 腕時計のバンド udédokèi no bańdo

water [wɔː'tər] *n* (cold) 水 mizû; (hot)
(お) 湯 (o)yú
♦*vt* (plant) ...に水をやる ...ni mizú wo
yarú
♦*vi* (eyes) 涙が出る namídà ga derú;
(mouth) よだれが出る yodáre ga derú
in British waters 英国領海に(で) eíkoku-
kuryōkai ni(de)
water cannon *n* 放水砲 hōsuíhō
water closet (*BRIT*) *n* トイレ tóire
watercolor [wɔː'tərkʌlər] *n* (picture)
水彩画 suísaiga
watercress [wɔː'tərkres] *n* クレソン ku-
réson
water down *vt* (milk etc) 水で薄める
mizú de usúmerù; (fig: story) 和らげる
yawáragerù
waterfall [wɔː'tərfɔːl] *n* 滝 takí
water heater *n* 湯沸器 yuwákashikì
watering can [wɔː'tərin-] *n* じょうろ
jōrò
water level *n* 水位 suíi
water lily *n* スイレン suíren
waterline [wɔː'tərlain] *n* (NAUT) 喫水
線 kíssuísen
waterlogged [wɔː'tərlɔːgd] *adj* (ground)
水浸しの mizúbitashi no
water main *n* 水道本管 suídōhonkàn
watermelon [wɔː'tərmelən] *n* スイカ
suíka
waterproof [wɔː'tərpruːf] *adj* (trousers,
jacket etc) 防水の bōsui no
watershed [wɔː'tərʃed] *n* (GEO: natural
boundary) 分水界 bunsuíkaì; (: high
ridge) 分水嶺 bunsuíreì; (fig) 分岐点 bunkíten
water-skiing [wɔː'tərskiːin] *n* 水上スキー
ー suíjōsukī
watertight [wɔː'tərtait] *adj* (seal) 水密
の suímitsu no
waterway [wɔː'tərwei] *n* 水路 suíro
waterworks [wɔː'tərwərks] *n* (building) 浄水場 jōsuijō
watery [wɔː'təri] *adj* (coffee) 水っぽい
mizúppoì; (eyes) 涙ぐんだ namídagundà
watt [wɑːt] *n* ワット wattò
wave [weiv] *n* (of hand) 一振り hitófuri;
(on water) 波 namí; (RADIO) 電波 deñ-

pa; (in hair) ウェーブ uēbù; (*fig*: surge) 高
まり takámari, 急増 kyūzō
♦*vi* (signal) 手を振る te wò furù;
(branches, grass) 揺れる yurérù; (flag) な
びく nabíkù
♦*vt* (hand, flag, handkerchief) 振る furù;
(gun, stick) 振回す furímawasù
wavelength [weiv'leŋkθ] *n* (RADIO) 波
長 hachō
on the same wavelength (*fig*) 気が合っ
て ki gà attè
waver [wei'vər] *vi* (voice) 震える furúerù; (love) 揺らぐ yurágu; (person) 動揺す
る dōyō suru
his gaze did not waver 彼は目を反ら
さなかった kárè wa mé wò soràsanakat-
tà
wavy [wei'viː] *adj* (line) くねくねした ku-
nékune shita; (hair) ウェーブのある uēbù
no aru
wax [wæks] *n* (polish, for skis) ワックス
wakkùsu; (*also*: **earwax**) 耳あか mimfa-
kà
♦*vt* (floor, car, skis) ...にワックスを掛け
る ...ni wakkùsu wo kakérù
♦*vi* (moon) 満ちる michírù
waxworks [wæks'wərks] *npl* (models)
ろう人形 rōniñgyô
♦*n* (place) ろう人形館 rōniñgyōkan
way [wei] *n* (route) ...へ行く道 ...e ikú
michî; (path) 道 michî; (access) 出入口
defríguchi (distance) 距離 kyórî; (direction) 方向 hōkō; (manner, method) 方法
hōhō; (habit) 習慣 shûkan
which way? - this way どちらへ? - こ
ちらへ dochîra è ? - kochîra e
on the way (en route) 途中で tochû de
to be on one's way 今向かっている imà
mukátte irù, 今進でいる imà suñde irù
to be in the way (*also fig*) 邪魔である
jamá de arù
*to go out of one's way to do some-
thing* わざわざ...する wazàwaza ...suru
under way (project etc) 進行中で shiñ-
kōchū de
to lose one's way 道に迷う michî ni
mayôû

in a way ある意味では arù imì de wa

in some ways ある面では arù men de wa

no way! (*inf*) 絶対に駄目だ zettái ni damé dà

by the way ... ところで tokóro dè

「*way in*」(BRIT) 入口 iríguchi

「*way out*」(BRIT) 出口 degúchi

the way back 帰路 kírò

「*give way*」(BRIT: AUT) 進路譲れ shíńro yuzúre

waylay [weileí'] (*pt, pp* **waylaid**) *vt* 待伏せする machíbuse suru

wayward [wei'wərd] *adj* (behavior, child) わがままな wagámàma na

W.C. [dʌb'əlju:si:'] (BRIT) n トイレ toíre

we [wi:] *pl pron* 私たちは(が) watákushitàchi wa(ga)

weak [wi:k] *adj* (*gen*) 弱い yowáì; (dollar, pound) 安い yasúì; (excuse) 下手な hetá nà; (argument) 説得力のない settókuryòku no naì; (tea) 薄い usúì

weaken [wi:'kən] *vi* (person, resolve) 弱る yowárù; (health) 衰える otóroerù; (influence, power) 劣る otórù

♦*vt* (person, government) 弱くする yowáku suru

weakling [wi:k'liŋ] *n* (physically) 虚弱児 kyojákujì; (morally) 骨無し honénashì

weakness [wi:k'nis] *n* (frailty) 弱さ yowása; (fault) 弱点 jakúteǹ

to have a weakness for ...に目がない ...ni me gà naì

wealth [welθ] *n* (money, resources) 富 tomí, 財産 zaísaǹ; (of: details, knowledge etc) 豊富さ hófu na

wealthy [wel'θi:] *adj* (person, family, country) 裕福な yúfùku na

wean [wi:n] *vt* (baby) 離乳させる rinyúu saséru

weapon [wep'ən] *n* 武器 bukí

wear [we:r] *n* (use) 使用 shiyó; (damage through use) 消耗 shómò; (clothing): *sportswear* スポーツウェア supótsùuea

♦*vb* (*pt* **wore**, *pp* **worn**)

♦*vt* (shirt, blouse, dress etc) 着る kirú; (hat etc) かぶる kabúrù; (shoes, pants, skirt etc) はく hakú; (gloves etc) はめる

haméru; (make-up) つける tsukérù; (damage: through use) 使い古す tsukáifurusù

♦*vi* (last) 使用に耐える shiyó ni taérù; (rub through etc: carpet, shoes, jeans) すり減る suríherù

babywear 幼児ウェア yójìuea

evening wear イブニングウェア ibúningu uea

wear and tear *n* 消耗 shómò

wear away *vt* すり減らす suríherasu

♦*vi* (inscription etc) すり減って消える suríhette kíeru

wear down *vt* (heels) すり減らす suríherasu; (person, strength) 弱くする yowáku suru, 弱らせる yowáraserù

wear off *vi* (pain etc) なくなる nakúnaru

wear out *vt* (shoes, clothing) 使い古す tsukáifurusù; (person) すっかり疲れさせる sukkárì tsukáresaséru; (strength) なくす nakúsu

weary [wi:'ri:] *adj* (tired) 疲れ果てた tsukárehatetà; (dispirited) がっかりした gakkárì shita

♦*vi: to weary of* ...に飽きる ...ni akírù

weasel [wi:'zəl] *n* イタチ itáchi

weather [weð'ər] *n* 天気 téñki, 天候 teñko

♦*vt* (storm, crisis) 乗切る noríkirù

under the weather (*fig*: ill) 気分が悪い kíbun ga warúì

weather-beaten [weð'ərbi:tən] *adj* (face, skin, building, stone) 風雪に鍛えられた fúsetsu ni kitáeraretà

weathercock [weð'ərkɑ:k] *n* 風見鶏 kazámidòri

weather forecast *n* 天気予報 teñkiyohò

weatherman [weð'ərmæn] (*pl* **weathermen**) *n* 天気予報係 teñkiyohōgakarì

weather vane [-vein] *n* = **weathercock**

weave [wi:v] (*pt* **wove**, *pp* **woven**) *vt* (cloth) 織る orù; (basket) 編む amù

weaver [wi:'vər] *n* 機織り職人 hatáorishokunin

weaving [wi:'viŋ] *n* (craft) 機織 hatáori

web [web] *n* (*also*: **spiderweb**) クモの巣 kumó no su; (on duck's foot) 水かき mizúkaki; (network, *also fig*) 網 amí

we'd [wiːd] = **we had; we would**

wed [wed] (*pt, pp* **wedded**) *vt* (marry) ...と結婚する ...to kekkón suru
♦*vi* 結婚する kekkón suru

wedding [wed'iŋ] *n* 結婚式 kekkónshiki
silver/golden wedding (anniversary) 銀〔金〕婚式 gín(kín)kónshiki

wedding day *n* (day of the wedding) 結婚の日 kekkón no hí; (*US*: anniversary) 結婚記念日 kekkónkinénbi

wedding dress *n* 花嫁衣装 hanáyome ishō, ウエディングドレス uédingudorèsu

wedding present *n* 結婚祝い kekkón iwaì

wedding ring *n* 結婚指輪 kekkón yubíwa

wedge [wedʒ] *n* (of wood etc) くさび kusábi; (of cake) 一切れ hitókire
♦*vt* (jam with a wedge) くさびで留める kusábi dè toméru; (pack tightly: of people, animals) 押込む oshíkomù

Wednesday [wenz'dei] *n* 水曜日 suíyōbi

wee [wiː] (*SCOTTISH*) *adj* (little) 小さい chíísaì

weed [wiːd] *n* 雑草 zassō
♦*vt* (garden) ...の草むしりをする ...no kusámushìri wo suru

weedkiller [wiːd'kiːlər] *n* 除草剤 josōzai

weedy [wiː'diː] *adj* (man) 柔そうな yawásō na

week [wiːk] *n* 週間 shūkan
a week today/on Friday 来週の今日〔金曜日〕rafshū no kyó(kín-yōbi)

weekday [wiːk'dei] *n* (*gen*, *COMM*) 平日 heijitsu, ウイークデイ uíkudeì

weekend [wiːk'end] *n* 週末 shūmatsu, ウイークエンド uíkuendò

weekly [wiːk'liː] *adv* (deliver etc) 毎週 maíshū
♦*adj* (newspaper) 週刊の shūkan no; (payment) 週払いの shūbarai no; (visit etc) 毎週の maíshū no
♦*n* (magazine) 週刊誌 shūkanshi; (newspaper) 週刊新聞 shūkanshínbun

weep [wiːp] (*pt, pp* **wept**) *vi* (person) 泣く naku

weeping willow [wiː'piŋ-] *n* シダレヤナギ shídáreyanàgi

weigh [wei] *vt* ...の重さを計る ...no sa wo hakáru
♦*vi* ...の重さは...である ...no omósa wa ...de arù
to weigh anchor いかりを揚げる ikári wo agéru

weigh down *vt* (person, pack animal etc) ...の重さで動きが遅くなる ...no omósa de ugóki ga osóku narù; (*fig*: with worry): *to be weighed down* ...で沈み込む ...de shizúmikomu

weight [weit] *n* (metal object) 重り omóri; (heaviness) 重さ omósa
to lose/put on weight 体重が減る〔増える〕taíjū ga herú(fueru)

weighting [wei'tiŋ] (*BRIT*) *n* (allowance) 地域手当 chííkiteàte

weightlifter [weit'liftər] *n* 重量挙げ選手 jūryōage señshu

weighty [wei'tiː] *adj* (heavy) 重い omói; (important: matters) 重大な jūdai na

weigh up *vt* (person, offer, risk) 評価する hyōka suru

weir [wir] *n* せき sekí

weird [wiːrd] *adj* 奇妙な kimyó na

welcome [wel'kəm] *adj* (visitor, suggestion, change) 歓迎すべき kangeisubeki; (news) うれしい ureshii
♦*n* 歓迎 kañgei
♦*vt* (visitor, delegation, suggestion, change) 歓迎する kañgei suru; (be glad of: news) うれしく思う ureshikú omoù
thank you - you're welcome! どうも有難う - どういたしまして dómo arígatō - dō itáshimashitè

weld [weld] *n* 溶接 yōsetsu
♦*vt* 溶接する yōsetsu suru

welfare [wel'fer] *n* (well-being) 幸福 kōfuku, 福祉 fukūshì; (social aid) 生活保護 seíkatsuhogō

welfare state *n* 福祉国家 fukúshikokkà

welfare work *n* 福祉事業 fukúshijigyō

well [wel] *n* (for water) 井戸 idò; (*also*: **oil well**) 油井 yuséi

♦adv (to a high standard, thoroughly; also for emphasis with adv, adj or prep phrase) よく yokù

♦adj: to be well (in good health) 元気である gefiki de árù

♦excl やあ、ねえ yā, nē

as well (in addition) も mo

as well as (in addition to) ...の外に ...no hokâ ni

well done! よくやった yokù yattá

get well soon! 早く治ります様に hayàku naôrimasu yō nì, お大事に o-dáiji ni

to do well (person) 順調である jufíchō de árù; (business) 繁盛する hañjō suru

we'll [wi:l] = we will; we shall

well-behaved [welbiheivd'] adj (child, dog) 行儀の良い gyōgi no yoî

well-being [wel'bi:'iŋ] n 幸福 kôfuku, 福祉 fukúshi

well-built [wel'bilt'] adj (person) 体格の良い tafkaku no yoî

well-deserved [wel'dizɑːrvd'] adj (success, prize) 努力相応の doryòkusôō no yoî

well-dressed [wel'drest'] adj 身なりの良い minàri no yoî

well-heeled [wel'hiːld'] (inf) adj (wealthy) 金持の kanêmochì no

wellingtons [wel'iŋtɑnz] npl (also: wellington boots) ゴム長靴 gomûnagagutsu

well-known [wel'noun'] adj (famous: person, place) 有名な yûmei na

well-mannered [wel'mæn'ərd] adj 礼儀正しい reîgitadashìî

well-meaning [wel'mi:'niŋ] adj (person) 善意の zeñ-i no; (offer etc) 善意に基づく zeñ-i ni motôzukû

well-off [wel'ɔːf'] adj (rich) 金持の kanê-mochì no

well-read [wel'red'] adj 博学の hakûga-ku no

well-to-do [wel'tədu:'] adj 金持の kanê-mochì no

well up vi (tears) こみ上げる komîageru

well-wisher [wel'wiʃər] n (friends, admirers) 支持者 shíjîsha, ファン faň

Welsh [welʃ] adj ウェールズの uêruzu no; (LING) ウェールズ語の uêruzugo no

♦n (LING) ウェールズ語 uêruzugo

Welsh npl: the Welsh ウェールズ人 uêruzujin

Welshman/woman [welʃ'mən/wumən] (pl Welshmen/women) n ウェールズ人の男性(女性) uêruzujin no dañsei(joséi)

Welsh rarebit [-rɛr'bit] n チーズトースト chîzûtôsùto

went [went] pt of go

wept [wept] pt, pp of weep

we're [wi:r] = we are

were [wəːr] pt of be

weren't [wəːr'ənt] = were not

west [west] n (direction) 西 nishî; (part of country) 西部 sefbu

♦adj (wing, coast, side) 西の nishî no, 西側の nishîgawa no

♦adv (to/towards the west) 西へ nishî e

west wind 西風 nishîkaze

West n: the West (POL: US plus western Europe) 西洋 sefyō

West Country: the West Country (BRIT) n 西部地方 sefbuchihô

westerly [wes'tərli:] adj (point) 西寄りの nishîyori no; (wind) 西からの nishî karà no

western [wes'tərn] adj (of the west) 西の nishî no; (POL: of the West) 西洋の sefyō no

♦n (CINEMA) 西部劇 sefbugeki

West Germany n 西ドイツ nishîdoitsu

West Indian n 西インド諸島の nishîndoshotô nô

♦n 西インド諸島の人 nishîndoshotô no hitó

West Indies [-in'di:z] npl 西インド諸島 nishîndoshotô

westward(s) [west'wɑːrd(z)] adv 西へ nishî e

wet [wet] adj (damp) 湿った shímetta; (wet through) ぬれた nurêta; (rainy: weather, day) 雨模様の amêmoyō no

♦n (BRIT: POL) 穏健派の人 oñkènha no hitó

to get wet (person, hair, clothes) ぬれる nurêru

「wet paint」ペンキ塗立て peñki nurîtate

to be a wet blanket (fig) 座を白けさせ

る za wò shirákesaseru

wet suit n ウェットスーツ uéttōsūtsu

we've [wiːv] = **we have**

whack [wæk] vt たたく tatákú

whale [weil] n (ZOOL) クジラ kujíra

wharf [wɔːrf] (pl **wharves**) n 岸壁 gañpeki

wharves [wɔːrvz] npl of **wharf**

KEYWORD

what [wɑt] adj 1 (in direct/indirect questions) 何の náñ no, 何...nánì...

what size is it? サイズは幾つですか sáìzu wa íkùtsu desu ká

what color is it? 何色ですか nánì iro desu ká

what shape is it? 形はどうなっていますか katáchi wà dō nattè imásù ká

what books do you need? どんな本がいりますか dóñna hoñ ga irímasù ká

he asked me what books I needed 彼は, にはどんな本があるかと彼は聞いています watákushi nì wà dôñna hòñ ga irú kà to kárè wa kíìte imáshità

2 (in exclamations) 何て...náñte...

what a mess! 何て有様だ náñte arísama dà

what a fool I am! 私は何てばかだ watákushi wa nâñte bákà da

◆pron 1 (interrogative) 何 náñ, 何 náñ

what are you doing? 何していますか náñ wo shité imasù ká

what is happening? どうなっていますか dō nattè imásù ká

what's in there? その中に何が入っていますかsonó nakà ni nánì ga háitte imasu ká

what is it? - it's a tool 何ですか-道具です náñ desu ká - dôgu desu

what are you talking about? 何の話ですか náñ no hanáshī desu ká

what is it called? これは何と言いますか kôrè wa náñ to iímasù ká

what about me? 私はどうすればいいんですか watákushi wa dō surébà iñ desu ká

what about doing ...? ...しませんか...shimáseñ ka

2 (relative): *is that what happened?* 事件は今話した通りですか jíkèn wa ímā hanáshita tòri desu ká

I saw what you did/was on the table あなたのした事[テーブルにあった物]を見ました anātā no shita kotō[tēbūru ni attá monō]wo mímashita

he asked me what she had said 彼は彼女の言った事を私に尋ねた kárè wa káñjo no ittá kotō wo watákushi nì tazúneta

tell me what you're thinking about 今何を考えているか教えて下さい ímā nánì wo kañgaete irù ká oshíete kudasai

what you say is wrong あなたの言っている事は間違っています anātā no itté irù kotō wà machígatte imàsù

◆excl (disbelieving) 何 náñ

what, no coffee! 何, コーヒーがないんだって? náñ, kôhī ga naîñ datté?

I've crashed the car - what! 車をぶつけてしまった-何? kúrùma wo butsúkete shimattā - nanî?

whatever [wʌtévˈəɾ] adj: *whatever book* どんな本でも dôñna hoñ de mo

◆pron: *do whatever is necessary/you want* 何でも必要な事をしなさい/する事をしなさい nañ de mo hitsúyō[suki]na koto wò shinásaì

whatever happens 何が起っても nanî ga okôtte mo

no reason whatever/whatsoever 全く理由がない mattáku riyū ga nai

nothing whatever 全く何もない mattáku nanî mo nai

whatsoever [watsouev'əɾ] adj = **whatever**

wheat [wiːt] n 小麦 komúgi

wheedle [wiːd'əl] vt: *to wheedle someone into doing something* ...を口車に乗せて...させる...wo kuchíguruma nì noséte ...sasérù

to wheedle something out of someone ...を口車に乗せて...を...からだまし取る kuchíguruma ni nosète ...wo ...kará damáshitorù

wheel [wiːl] n (of vehicle etc) 車 kurúma,

車輪 sharín, ホイール hoíru; (also: **steering wheel**) ハンドル handoru; (NAUT) だ舵 darín
♦vt (pram etc) 押す osú
♦vi (birds) 旋回する senkai suru; (also: **wheel round**: person) 急に向き直る kyū nī mukínaorū

wheelbarrow [wi:l'bærou] n 一輪車 i-chírínsha, ネコ車 nekóguruma

wheelchair [wi:l'tʃe:r] n 車いす kurúma-isū

wheel clamp n (AUT) ◇違反駐車の自動車車輪に付けて走れなくする金具 ihánchūsha no jidóshasharín nī tsukéte hashírenaku surú kanágu

wheeze [wiz] vi (person) ぜいぜい言う zeízei iū

KEYWORD

when [wen] adv いつ ítsū
when did it happen? いつ起ったんですか ítsū okóttań desu ká
I know when it happened いつ起ったかはちゃんと分かっています ítsū okótta kà wa chánto wakátte imásū
when are you going to Italy? イタリアにはいつ行きますか itária ni wa ítsū ikímasū ká
when will you be back? いつ帰って来ますか ítsū kaétte kimasū ká
♦conj 1 (at, during, after the time that) ...する時 ...surú tokī, ...すると ...surú tò, ...したら ...shitárá, ...してから ...shité kara
she was reading when I came in 私が部屋に入った時彼女は本を読んでいました watákushi ga heyá ni háītta tokī kánōjo wa hōń wo yōñde imáshita
when you've read it, tell me what you think これを読んだらご意見を聞かせて下さい kōré wo yóñdara go-ìkēn wo kikásete kudasaì
be careful when you cross the road 道路を横断する時には気を付けてね dóro wo ōdan surú tokī ni wa kī wo tsukéte né
that was when I needed you あなたにいて欲しかったのはその時ですよ aná-

tā ni ité hoshikattā no wa sonó tokī desu yó
2: (on, at which): *on the day when I met him* 彼に会った日は kárē ni áttà hī wà
one day when it was raining 雨が降っていたある日 ámē ga futté itá árū hī
3 (whereas): *you said I was wrong when in fact I was right* 私は間違っていると言いましたが、事実は間違っていませんでした watákushi gā machígatte irū to ímashita gà, jíjītsu wa machígatté imásen deshīta
why did you buy that when you can't afford it? 金の余裕がないのになぜあれを買ったんですか kané nò yoyū gà naī no nī náze aré wo kattàn desu ká

---

whenever [wenev'ə:r] adv いつでも ítsū dē ka
♦conj (any time) ...する time ...surú to ítsūmo...; (every time that) ...する度に ...surú tabí nì

where [we:r] adv (place, direction) どこ (に、で) dokó (ni, de)
♦conj ...の所に (で) ...no tokōro ni (de)
this is where ... これは...する所です kōré wa ...surū tokoro desu

whereabouts [we:r'əbauts] adv どの辺に donō hen ni
♦n: *nobody knows his whereabouts* 彼の居場所は不明が kárē no ibāsho wa fuméi da

whereas [we:ræz'] conj ...であるのに対して ...de arū no ni taìshite

whereby [we:rbai'] pron それによって soré ni yotté

whereupon [we:rəpɑ:n'] conj すると surú to

wherever [we:rev'ə:r] conj (no matter where) どこに (で)...しても dokó ni (de) ...shite mo; (not knowing where) どこに...か知らないが dokō ni ...ká shiranaì ga
♦adv (interrogative: surprise) 一体全体どこに (で) íttaí zentai dokó ni (de)

wherewithal [we:r'wiðɔ:l] n 金 kané

whet [wet] vt (appetite) そそる sosóru

whether [weð'ə:r] conj ...かどうか ...ka dō ká

I don't know whether to accept or not 引受けるべきかどうかは分からない hikifukerubeki kā dō ka wa wakāranāi
whether you go or not 行くにしても行かないにしても ikū nī shíté mō ikánai nī shité mō

it's doubtful whether he will come 彼はたぶん来ないだろう karè wa tabùn konāi darō

KEYWORD

which [witʃ] *adj* **1** (interrogative: direct, indirect) どの dónò, どちらの dóchīra no
which picture do you want? どちらの絵がいいですか dóchīra no é gà iī desu ká

which books are yours? あなたの本はどれとどれですか anáta no hón wa dòre to dòre desu ká
tell me which picture/books you want どの絵(本)が欲しいか言って下さい dónò é(hón)gā hoshíi ka iitté kudasāi
which one? どれ dòre

which one do you want? どれが欲しいんですか dòre ga hoshíiñ desu ká
which one of you did it? あなたたちのだれがやったんですか anáta tachi no dáre ga yattáñ desu ká

2: *in which case* その場合 sonó baāi
the train may be late, in which case don't wait up 列車が遅れるかもしれないが、その場合に寝て下さい rèssha ga okúreru ka mo shírénai ga, sonó baāi ni netè kudasāi
by which time その時 sonó tokī

we got there at 8 pm, by which time the cinema was full 映画館に着いたのは夜の8時でしたが、もう満席になっていました efgákañ ni tsúita no wa yòruno hachíji deshita ga, mō mañséki ni natté imashīta

♦*pron* **1** (interrogative) どれ dòre
which (of these) are yours? どれとどれがあなたの物ですか どれ どれ anáta no monó desū ká
which of you are coming? あなたたちのだれとだれが一緒に来てくれますか anátatachi no dáre to dáre ga ísshō ni

kité kuremasù この時 kono tokī
here are the books/files – tell me which you want 本(ファイル)はこれだけありますが、どれだけ欲しいのですか hón(fáiru)wa korê dake arímasu ga, dóre to dòre dake hoshīiñ desu ká
I don't mind which どれでもいいんです dòre de mo iíñ desu yó

2 (relative): *the apple which you ate/which is on the table* あなたの食べた〔テーブルにある〕りんご anáta no tábèta (tēburu ni árú)ríñgo
the meeting (which) we attended 私たちが出席した会議 watákushitàchi ga shusséki shità kāigi
the chair on which you are sitting あなたが座っているいす anáta ga suwátte irū ísú
the book of which you spoke あなたが話していた本 anáta ga hanáshite ità hóñ
he said he knew, which is true/I feared 彼は知っていると言ったが、その通りでした(私の心配していた通りでした) karè wa shitté irū to ittá gā, sonó tòri deshita(watákushi nò shíñpai shite ita tòri deshita)
after which その後 sonó atò

whichever [witʃevˈəːr] *adj*: *take whichever book you prefer* どれでもいいから好きな本を取って下さい dòre de mo iī kara sukí na hon wo tottè kudasāi
whichever book you take あなたがどの本を取っても anáta ga donò hon wo tottè mo

whiff [wif] *n* (of perfume, gasoline, smoke) ちょっと...のにおいがすること chottó ...no nióī ga suru koto

while [wail] *n* (period of time) 間 aída
♦*conj* (at the same time as) ...する間 ...surú aida; (as long as) ...する限りは ...surú kagīri wa; (although) ...するにもかかわらず ...surú nī mo kakáwarazu
for a while しばらくの間 shibárāku no aída

while away *vt* (time) つぶす tsubúsu

whim [wim] *n* 気まぐれ kimágure

whimper [wim'pər] n (cry, moan) 哀れ
っぽい泣き声 awáreppoì nakfgoè
♦vi (child, animal) 哀れっぽい泣き声を
出す awáreppoì nakfgoè wo dasù

whimsical [wim'zikəl] adj (person) 気ま
ぐれな kimágure na; (poem) 奇抜な kibátsu na; (look, smile) 変な heñ na

whine [wain] n (of pain) 哀れっぽい泣き
声 awáreppoì nakfgoè; (of engine, siren)
うなり unári
♦vi (person, animal) 哀れっぽい泣き声を
出す awáreppoì nakfgoè wo dasù; (engine,
siren) うなる unárù; (fig: complain) 愚痴
をこぼす guchí wo kobósù

whip [wip] n (lash, riding whip) むち mu-
chì; (POL) 院内幹事 iññaikañji
♦vt (person, animal) むちで打つ muchí de
utsù; (cream, eggs) 泡立てる awádaterù,
ホイップする hoíppù suru; (move quickly): **to whip something out/off** さっと
取出す (はずす, 脱ぐ) sattò torídasu
(hazúsu, nugú)

whipped cream [wipt-] n ホイップクリ
ーム hoíppukurímù

whip-round [wip'raund] (BRIT) n 募金
bokín

whirl [wəːrl] vt (arms, sword etc) 振回す
furímawasù
♦vi (dancers) ぐるぐる回る gurùguru
mawáru; (leaves, water etc) 渦巻く uzúmakù

whirlpool [wəːrl'puːl] n 渦巻 uzúmàki

whirlwind [wəːrl'wind] n 竜巻 tatsúmà-
ki

whir(r) [wəːr] vi (motor etc) うなり unári

whisk [wisk] n (CULIN) 泡立て器 awá-
datekì
♦vt (cream, eggs) 泡立てる awádaterù
to whisk someone away/off ...を素早
く連れ去る ...wo subáyakù tsurésarù

whiskers [wis'kəːrz] npl (of animal,
man) ひげ higé

whiskey [wis'kiː] (BRIT **whisky**) n ウイ
スキー uísukì

whisper [wis'pəːr] n (low voice) ささや
き sasáyaki
♦vi ささやく sasáyakù

♦vt ささやく sasáyakù

whist [wist] (BRIT) n ホイスト hoísuto

whistle [wis'əl] n (sound) 口笛 kuchíbue;
(object) 笛 fue
♦vi (person) 口笛を吹く kuchíbue wo fukù; (bird) ぴーぴーさえずる pípí saézurù;
(bullet) ひゅーとうなる hyú to unárù;
(kettle) ぴーと鳴る pyú to narú

white [wait] adj (color) 白い shiróì; (pale:
person, face) 青白い aójiroì; (with fear)
青ざめた aózametà
♦n (color) 白 shiró; (person) 白人 hakújin;
(of egg) 白身 shirómì

white coffee (BRIT) n ミルク入りコー
ヒー mírúku iri kòhì

white-collar worker [wait'kɑ:l'əːr-] n
サラリーマン sarárìmàn, ホワイトカラー
howáìtokarà

white elephant n (fig) 無用の長物 mu-
yò no chóbutsu

white lie n 方便のうそ hóben no usò

white paper n (POL) 白書 hakúsho

whitewash [wait'wɑ:ʃ] n (paint) のろ
の石灰, 白亜, のりと水に混ぜた塗料
sekkái, hakúa, norf wo mizú ni mazèta
toryò
♦vt (building) ...にのろを塗る ...ni norò
wo nurù; (fig: happening, career, reputation) ...の表面を繕う ...no hyómèn wo
tsukúroù

whiting [wai'tiŋ] n inv (fish) タラ tarà

Whitsun [wit'sən] n 聖霊降臨節 sefrei-
kòrìnsetsu

whittle [wit'əl] vt: **to whittle away,
whittle down** (costs: reduce) 減らす herásu

whiz(z) [wiz] vi: **to whizz past/by** (person, vehicle etc) ぴゅーんと通り過ぎる
byún to tòrisugirù

whiz(z) kid (inf) n 天才 teñsai

---

who [hu:] pron 1 (interrogative) だれ dárè, どなた dónàta
who is it?, who's there? だれですか
dárè desu ka
who are you looking for? だれを捜し
ているんですか dárè wo sagáshìte irùn

desu ká
I told her who I was 彼女に名乗りました kánôjo ni nanórimashtta
I told her who was coming to the party パーティの出席予定者を彼女に知らせました pâti no shussékiyotelsha wo kánôjo ni shírásemashtta
who did you see? だれを見ましたか dáre wo mímáshtta ká
2 (relative): *my cousin who lives in New York* ニューヨークに住んでいるいとこ nyûyôku ni súnde iru itôko
the man/woman who spoke to me 私に話しかけた男性/女性 watákushi ni hanáshikaketá danśei
those who can swim 泳げる人たち oyôgerû hitôtachi

whodunit [hu:dʌn'it] (inf) *n* 探偵小説 tanteishôsetsu

whole [houl] *adj* (entire) 全体 no zeñtai no; (not broken) 無傷の mukîzu no
♦*n* (entire unit) 全体 zeñtai; (all): *the whole of* 全体の zeñtai no
the whole of the town 町全体 machîzeñtai
on the whole, as a whole 全体として zeñtai toshite

whole food(s) [houl'fu:d(z)] *n(pl)* 無加工の食べ物 mukákô no tabêmonô

wholehearted [houl'hɑːr'tid] *adj* (agreement etc) 心からの kokôro kâra no

wholemeal [houl'mi:l] *adj* (bread, flour) 全粒の zeñryû no, 全麦の zeñbaku no

wholesale [houl'seil] *n* (business) 卸 orôshi, 卸売 orôshiuri
♦*adj* (price) 卸の orôshi no; (destruction) 大規模の dafkibô no
♦*adv* (buy, sell) 卸で orôshi dè

wholesaler [houl'seilɑːr] *n* 問屋 toñ-ya

wholesome [houl'sam] *adj* (food, climate) 健康に良い keñkô no ii genki
健全な keñzen na

wholewheat [houl'wi:t] *adj* = **wholemeal**

wholly [houl'li:] *adv* (completely) 完全に kafízen ni

whom [hu:m] *pron* **1** (interrogative) だれ を dáre wo, どなたを dónàta wo
whom did you see? だれを見ましたか dáre wo mímáshtta ká
to whom did you give it? だれに渡しましたか dáre ni watáshimashtta ká
tell me from whom you received it だれに[から]それをもらったかを教えて下さい dáre ni [kárà] soré wo morátta ká wo oshete kudasai
2 (relative): *the man whom I saw/to whom I spoke* 私が見た[話し掛けた]男性 watákushi ga mítà [hanáshikaketá] danśei
the lady with whom I was talking 私 と話していた女性 watákushi tò hanáshite ità jośei

whooping cough [wuː'piŋ-] *n* 百日ぜき hyakúnichizêki

whore [hɔːr] (inf: pej) *n* 売女 baíta

whose [huːz] *adj* **1** (possessive: interrogative) だれの dáre no, どなたの dónàta no
whose book is this? これはだれの本ですか koré wà dáre no hôñ desu ká
whose pencil have you taken? だれの鉛筆を持って来たのですか dáre no efipitsu wò motté kitâñ desu ká
whose daughter are you? あなたはどなたの娘さんですか anátà wa dónàta no musúme-sañ desu ká
I don't know whose it is だれの物か私に は分かりません dáre no monô kà watákushi ni wà wakárimaseñ
2 (possessive: relative): *the man whose son you rescued* あなたが助けた子供の父親 anátà ga tasúketa kodomô no chíchfoya
the girl whose sister you were speaking あなたと話していた女性の妹 anátà nó hanáshite ità jośei no imôtô
the woman whose car was stolen 車を盗まれた女性 kurúma wò nusúmareta

joséi

◆*pron* だれの物 dáre no monó、どなたの
物 dónata no monó

whose is this? これはだれのですか kó-
re wa dáre no desu ká

I know whose it is だれの物か知って
います dáre no monó ka shitté imasú

whose are these? これらはだれの物で
すか korérà wa dáre no monó desù ká

KEYWORD

why [wai] *adv* なぜ názè、どうして dōshí-
te

why is he always late? どうして彼は
いつも遅刻するのですか dōshitè kárè
wa ítsumo chikóku suru nò desu ká

why don't you come too? あなたも来
ませんか anátà mo kimásèn ká

I'm not coming - why not? 私は行き
ません-どうしてですか watákushi wà i-
kímasèn - dōshitè desu ká

fancy a drink? - why not? 一杯やろ
うか-いいね íppài yárò ká - íi né

why not do it now? 今すぐやりません
か íma súgù yarímasèn ka

◆*conj* なぜ názè、どうして dōshítè

I wonder why he said that どうして
そんな事を言ったのかしら dōshitè sofina
kotò wo ittá nò kashíra

the reason why 理由 riyū́

that's the not (the reason) why I'm here
私が来たのはそのためじゃありません
watákushi ga kitá no wà sonó tamè ja
arímasèñ

◆*excl* (expressing surprise, shock,
annoyance etc) 〈日本語では表現しない
場合が多い nihóngo de wa hyōgen shinaí
baái ga ōī

why, it's you! おや、あなたでしたか
oyá, anátà deshíta ka

*why, that's impossible/quite unac-
ceptable!* そんな事はできません〔認めら
れません〕sofina kotò wa dekímasèn
(mitómeraremasèñ)

*I don't understand - why, it's obvi-
ous!* 訳が分かりません-ばかでも分かる
事だよ wákè ga wakárimasèñ - báka de

mo wakárù kotò dà yó

whyever [waiev'əːr] *adv* 一体 なぜ ittai
názè

wicked [wik'id] *adj* (crime, man, witch)
極悪の gokúaku no; (smile) 意地悪そうな
ijíwarusō na

wickerwork [wik'əːrwəːrk] *adj* (basket,
chair etc) 籐細工の tōzáimi no、枝細工の
edázami no

◆*n* (objects) 籐細工品 tōzáimzaikuhin、
枝細小工品 edázamizaikuhin

wicket [wik'it] *n* (CRICKET: stumps) 三
柱門 safichūmòn、ウイケット ufkéttò; (:
grass area) ピッチ pítchì

◇2つのウイケット間のグランド fútàtsu
nò ufkettokàn no gurándo

wide [waid] *adj* (gen) 広い hirőí; (grin) 楽
しげな tanőshìge na

◆*adv*: *to open wide* (window etc) 大きく開
ける hiróku akéru

to shoot wide ねらいを外す neráì wo
hazúsu

wide-angle lens [waid'æŋ'gəl-] *n* 広角
レンズ kōkaku reñzu

wide-awake [waid'əweik'] *adj* すっかり
目が覚めた sukkárì me gà sámèta

widely [waid'liː] *adv* (gen) 広く hiróku;
(differing) 甚だしく hanáhadashìkù

widen [waid'ən] *vt* (road, river, experience) 広くする hiróku suru、広げる hiró-
geru

◆*vi* (road, river, gap) 広くなる hiróku
narú、広がる hirőgaru

wide open *adj* (window, eyes, mouth) 大
きく開けた ōkìku akéta

widespread [waidspred'] *adj* (belief etc)
はびこった habíkottà

widow [wid'ou] *n* 未亡人 mibṓjìn、後家
goké

widowed [wid'oud] *adj* (mother, father)
やもめになった yamóme ni nattá

widower [wid'ouəːr] *n* 男やもめ otőko-
yamòme

width [widθ] *n* (distance) 広さ hirōsa; (of
cloth) 幅 habá

wield [wiːld] *vt* (sword, power) 振るう furúu

wife [waif] (pl **wives**) n (gen) 妻 tsumá; (one's own) 家内 kánai; (someone else's) 奥さん okúsan

wig [wig] n カツラ katsúra

wiggle [wig'əl] vt (hips) くねらす kunérasù; (ears etc) ぴくぴく動かす pikúpiku ugokasù

wild [waild] adj (animal, plant) 野生の yaséi no; (rough: land) 荒れ果てた aréhatèta; (: weather, sea) 荒れ狂う arékuruù; (person, behavior, applause) 興奮した kốfun shita; (idea) 突飛な toppí na; (guess) 当てずっぽうの atézuppò no

wilderness [wil'dərnis] n 荒野 kōya, 原野 geń-ya, 未開地 mikáichi

wild-goose chase [waild'gus'-] n (fig) 無駄な捜索 mudá na sōsaku

wildlife [waild'laif] n (animals) 野生動物 yaséidōbutsu

wildly [waild'li:] adv (behave) 狂った様に kurútta yō ni; (applaud) 熱狂的に nekkyốteki ni; (hit) めくら滅法に mekúra-meppồ ni; (guess) 当てずっぽうに atézuppò ni; (happy) 最高に saíkō ni

wilds [waildz] npl 荒野 kōya, 原野 geń-ya, 未開地 mikáichi

wilful [wil'fəl] adj (obstinate: person, character) わがままな wagámama na; (deliberate: action, disregard etc) 故意の koí no

will [wil] (vt: pt, pp willed) aux vb 1 (forming future tense): **I will finish it tomorrow** 明日終ります ashíta owárimasù

I will have finished it by tomorrow 明日にでもなれば終るでしょう asú ni dè mo nárèba owáru dèshò

will you do it? - yes I will/no I won't やりますか、やります/いいえ、やりません yarímasù ká - háì, yarímasù(iíè, yarímaseñ)

when will you finish it? いつ終りますか ítsù owárimasù ká

2 (in conjectures, predictions): **he will/he'll be there by now** 彼はもう着いているでしょう kárè wa mō tsúite irú de-

shò

that will be the postman 郵便屋さんでしょう yūbínya-san dèshò

this medicine will help you この薬なら効くでしょう konó kusuri narà kikú deshò

this medicine won't help you この薬は何の役にも立ちません konó kusuri wà nañ no yakú nì mo tachímasen

3 (in commands, requests, offers): **will you be quiet!** 黙りなさい damárinasaì

will you come? 来てくれますか kitè kuremasù ká

will you help me? 手伝ってくれますか tetsúdattè kuremasù ká

will you have a cup of tea? お茶をいかがですかお茶をいかがですか o-chá wò ikága desù ká

I won't put up with it! 我慢できません gámàn dekímaseñ

♦vt: **to will someone to do something** 意志の力で…に…をさせようとする íshi no chikára dè …ni …wð saséyò tò suru

he willed himself to go on 彼は精神力だけで続けようとした kárè wa seishinryòku dake dè tsuzúkeyồ tò shita

♦n (volition) 意志 íshi; (testament) 遺言 yuígon

willful [wil'fəl] (US) adj = **wilful**

willing [wil'iŋ] adj (with goodwill) 進んで…する susúnde ...surù; (enthusiastic) 熱心な nesshìn na

he's willing to do it 彼はそれを引き受けてくれるそうです kárè wa soré wo hikíukète kureru sō dèsu

willingly [wil'iŋli:] adv 進んで susúnde

willingness [wil'iŋnis] n 好意 kôi

willow [wil'ou] n ヤナギ yanági

willpower [wil'pauə:r] n 精神力 seíshìnryòku

willy-nilly [wil'i:nil'i:] adv 否応なしに i-yáồ nashî ni

wilt [wilt] vi (flower, plant) 枯れる karéru

wily [wai'li:] adj (fox, move, person) ずる賢い zurúgashikoì

win [win] n (in sports etc) 勝利 shốrī, 勝ち kachí

♦vb (pt, pp won)
♦vt (game, competition) ...で 勝つ ...de katsù; (election) ...で当選する ...de tōsen suru; (obtain: prize, medal) もらう moráu, 受ける ukérù; (money) 当てる atérù; (support, popularity) 獲得する kakútoku suru
♦vi 勝つ katsù

wince [wins] vi 顔がこわばる kaő ga kowábaru

winch [wintʃ] n ウインチ uínchi

wind[1] [wind] n (air) 風 kazé; (MED) 呼吸 kokyū; (breath) 息 ikí
♦vt (take breath away from) ...の息を切らせる ...no ikī wo kiráserù

wind[2] [waind] (pt, pp **wound**) vt (roll: thread, rope) 巻く makú; (wrap: bandage) 巻付ける makítsukerù; (clock, toy) ...のぜんまいを巻く ...no zenmai wo makú
♦vi (road, river) 曲りくねる magárikunerù

windfall [wind'fɔ:l] n (money) 棚ぼた tanábota

winding [wain'diŋ] adj (road) 曲りくねった magárikunetta; (staircase) らせん状の rasénjō no

wind instrument n (MUS) 管楽器 kañgakki

windmill [wind'mil] n 風車 kazágurùma

window [win'dou] n 窓 mádò

window box n ウインドーボックス uíndōbokkūsu

window cleaner n (person) 窓ふき職人 madőfukishokúnin

window envelope n 窓付き封筒 madő-tsukifūtố

window ledge n 窓下枠 madőshitawàku

window pane n 窓ガラス madőgarásu

window-shopping [win'douʃɑ:piŋ] n ウインドーショッピング uíndōshoppiñgu

windowsill [win'dousil] n 窓下枠 madőshitawàku

windpipe [wind'paip] n 気管 kikán

windscreen [wind'skri:n] (BRIT) n = **windshield**

windshield [wind'ʃi:ld] (US) n フロント

ガラス furóntogarāsu, ウインドシールド uíndoshīrudo

windshield washer n ウインドシールドワッシャー uíndoshīrudowashā

windshield wiper [-waip'ər] n ワイパー waīpā

windswept [wind'swept] adj (place) 吹きさらしの fukísarashi no; (person) 風で髪が乱れた kamí ga midáreta

wind up vt (clock, toy) ...のぜんまいを巻く ...no zenmai wo makú; (debate) 終りにする owári ni suru

windy [win'di:] adj (weather, day) 風の強い kazé no tsuyoi
it's windy 風が強い kazé ga tsuyoi

wine [wain] n ブドウ酒 budőshu, ワイン waín

wine bar n ワインバー waínbā

wine cellar n ワインの地下貯蔵庫 waín no chikáchozōkò

wine glass n ワイングラス waíngurāsu

wine list n ワインリスト waínrisuto

wine merchant n ワイン商 waínshō

wine waiter n ソムリエ somúrie

wing [wiŋ] n (of bird, insect, plane) 羽根 hané, 翼 (tsubása; (of building) 翼 yokū; (BRIT: AUT) フェンダー feñdā

winger [wiŋ'ər] n (SPORT) ウイング uíñgu

wings [wiŋz] npl (THEATER) そで袖 sodé

wink [wiŋk] n (of eye) ウインク wíñku
♦vi (with eye) ウインクする uíñku suru; (light etc) 瞬く matátakù

winner [win'ər] n (of prize, race, competition) 勝者 shōshá

winning [win'iŋ] adj (team, competitor, entry) 勝った kattà; (shot, goal) 決勝の kesshő no; (smile) 愛敬たっぷりの aíkyotappūrī no

winnings [win'iŋz] npl 賞金 shōkin

win over vt (person: persuade) 味方にする mikáta ni suru

win round (BRIT) vt = **win over**

winter [win'tər] n (season) 冬 fuyú
in winter 冬には fuyú nī wa

winter sports npl ウインタースポーツ uíntāsupōtsù

wintry [win'tri:] adj (weather, day) 冬ら

しい fuyúrashiî

wipe [waip] *n*: *to give something a wipe* ...をふく ...wo fukú

♦*vt* (rub) ふく fukú; (erase: tape) 消す kesú

wipe off *vt* (remove) ふき取る fukítorû

wipe out *vt* (debt) 完済する kańsai suru; (memory) 忘れる wasúreru; (destroy: city, population) 滅ぼす messóbosū

wipe up *vt* (mess) ふき取る fukítorû

wire [wai'əːr] *n* (metal etc) 針金 harígane; (ELEC) 電線 deñseń; (telegram) 電報 deñpō

♦*vt* (house) ...の配線工事をする ...no háfseňkoĵi wo suru; (also: **wire up**: electrical fitting) 取付ける torítsukerū; (person: telegram) ...に電報を打つ ...ni deñpō wo utsú

wireless [wai'əːrlis] (BRIT) *n* ラジオ rajío

wiring [waiə'riŋ] *n* (ELEC) 配線 haíseñ

wiry [waiə'riː] *adj* (person) やせて強じんな yáse de kyōjin na; (hair) こわい kowáî

wisdom [wiz'dəm] *n* (of person) 知恵 chié; (of action, remark) 適切さ tekísetsusa

wisdom tooth *n* 親知らず oyáshirázu

wise [waiz] *adj* (person, action, remark) 賢い kashíkoî, 賢明な keńmei na

...wise *suffix*: *timewise/moneywise etc* 時間〔金銭〕的に jikán〔kíñseñ〕teki ni

wisecrack [waiz'kræk] *n* 皮肉な冗談 hiníku na jōdaň

wish [wiʃ] *n* (desire) 望み nozómi, 希望 kibō; (specific) 望みの物 nozómi no mono

♦*vt* (want) 望む nozómu, 希望する kibō suru

best wishes (for birthday, etc) おめでとう omédetō

with best wishes (in letter) 御体をお大事に o-kárada wo o-dáiji ni

to wish someone goodbye ...に別れのあいさつを言う ...ni wakáre no áisatsu wo iu, ...にさよならを言う ...ni sayónara wo iu

he wished me well 彼は「成功を祈る」と言いました karè wa 「sefkō wo inorū」to iimáshita

to wish to do ...したいと思う ...shitáî to omóu

to wish someone to do something ...に...してもらいたいと思う ...ni ...shíte moraitaí to omóu

to wish for ...が欲しいと思う ...ga hoshíî to omóu

wishful [wiʃ'fəl] *adj*: *it's wishful thinking* その考えは甘いsonó kangáe wa amáî, それは有り得ない事だ soré wa arénái kotó da

wishy-washy [wiʃ'iːwɑːʃiː] (*inf*) *adj* (color) 薄い usúi; (ideas, person) 迫力のない hakúryoku no naî

wisp [wisp] *n* (of grass, hair) 小さな束 chîsana tabá; (of smoke) 一筋 hitósûji

wistful [wist'fəl] *adj* (look, smile) 残念そうな zañneñsō na

wit [wit] *n* (wittiness) ユーモア yūmóa, ウィット uítto; (intelligence: *also*: **wits**) 知恵 chié; (person) ウィットのある人 uíttò no aru hito

witch [witʃ] *n* 魔女 majò

witchcraft [witʃ'kræft] *n* 魔術 majútsu

witch-hunt [witʃ'hʌnt] *n* (*fig*) 魔女狩り majôgari

KEYWORD

---

with [wiθ] *prep* **1** (accompanying, in the company of) ...と ...to, ...と一緒に ...to ísshò ni

I was with him 私は彼と一緒にいました watákushi wa kárè to ísshò ni imáshita

we stayed with friends 私たちは友達の家に泊りました watákushitáchi wa tomódachi nò ié ni tomárimashîta

we'll take the children with us 子供たちを一緒に連れて行きます kodómotáchi wo ísshò ni tsuréte ikimasù

mix the sugar with the eggs 砂糖を卵に混ぜて下さい satō wò tamágo nì mázete kudásaî

I'll be with you in a minute 直ぐ行きますからお待ち下さい súgù ikímasu karà o-máchi kudásaî

I'm with you (I understand) 分かります wakárimasù

to be with it (*inf*: up-to-date) 現代的である気だたいてき de あ る; (: alert) 抜け目がない nukéme ga nái

2 (descriptive): *a room with a view* 見晴らしのいい部屋 mihárashi nō íi heyá
the man with the grey hat/blue eyes 灰色の帽子をかぶった[青い目の]男 haíro no bóshi wò kabútta(aóí mè nò)otóko

3 (indicating manner, means, cause): *with tears in her eyes* 目に涙を浮かべながら mé ni námlda wo ukábènagara
to walk with a stick つえをついて歩く tsúè wo tsufte arúku
red with anger 怒りで顔を真っ赤にして íkari dè kaó wò makká ni shité
to shake with fear 恐怖で震える kyófu dè furúerù
to fill something with water ...を水で一杯にする ...wò mízu dè íppái ni suru
you can open the door with this key このかぎで ドアを開けられま す konó kagí dè dóà wo akéraremasù

ní(de)
♦*adv* (inside) 中の nakà no
within reach (of) (...に)手が届く所に(で) (...ni) té gà todókù tokoro ní(de)
within sight (of) (...が)見える所に (で) (...ga) miérù tokoro ní(de)
within the week 今週中に konshúchū ni
within a mile of ...の1マイル以内に ...no ichímairu inài ni

without [wiðaut'] *prep* ...なしで ...nashí de
without a coat コートなしで kōtō nashí de
without speaking 何も言わないで naní mo iwanàide
to go without something ...なしで済ます ...nashí de sumásù

withstand [wiðstænd'] (*pt, pp* **withstood**) *vt* (winds, attack, pressure) ...に耐える ...ni taérù

witness [wit'nis] *n* (person who sees) 目撃者 mokúgekisha; (person who countersigns document: *also* LAW) 証人 shōnin
♦*vt* (event) 見る miru, 目撃する mokúgeki suru; (document) 保証人として ...にサインする hoshónin toshite ...ni saín suru
to bear witness to (*fig*: offer proof of) ...を証明する ...wo shōmei suru

witness stand (*BRIT* **witness box**) *n* 証人席 shōnínseki

witticism [wit'əsizəm] *n* (remark) 冗談 jōdàn

witty [wit'i:] *adj* (person) ウイットのある uftto no arù; (remark etc) おどけた odóketa

wives [waivz] *npl of* **wife**

wizard [wiz'ərd] *n* 魔法使い mahōtsukāi

wk *abbr* = **week**

wobble [wɑːb'əl] *vi* (legs) よろめく yorómekù; (chair) ぐらぐらする gurágura suru; (jelly) ぷるぷるする purúpuru suru

woe [wou] *n* 悲しみ kānashimi

woke [wouk] *pt of* **wake**

woken [wou'kən] *pp of* **wake**

wolf [wulf] (*pl* **wolves**) *n* オオカミ ōkami

wolves [wulvz] *npl of* **wolf**

withdraw [wiðrɔː'] (*pt* **withdrew** *pp* **withdrawn**) *vt* (object) 取出す toridasu; (offer, remark) 取消す toríkesu, 撤回する tekkái suru
♦*vi* (troops) 撤退する tettái suru; (person) 下がる sagárù
to withdraw money (from the bank) 金を引出す kané wo hikidasù

withdrawal [wiðrɔː'əl] *n* (of offer, remark) 撤回 tekkái; (of troops) 撤退 tettái; (of services) 停止 teshí; (of participation) 取りやめる tom toryameru koto; (of money) 引出し hikfdashi

withdrawal symptoms *n* (MED) 禁断症状 kindanshñjō

withdrawn [wiðrɔːn'] *adj* (person) 引っ込みがちな hikkómigachi na

wither [wið'ər] *vi* (plant) 枯れる karérù

withhold [wiθhould'] (*pt, pp* **withheld**) *vt* (tax etc) 源泉徴収する gensenchōshū suru; (permission) 拒む kobámù; (information) 隠す kakúsù

within [wiðin'] *prep* (inside: referring to place, time, distance) ...以内に(で) ...inài

woman [wum'ən] (pl **women**) n 女 ofina, 女性 joséi

woman doctor n 女医 joí

womanly [wum'ənli:] adj (virtues etc) 女性らしい joséirashìi

womb [wu:m] n (ANAT) 子宮 shikyū

women [wim'ən] pl of **woman**

women's lib [wim'ənzlib'] (inf) n ウーマンリブ ūmanríbu

won [wʌn] pt, pp of **win**

wonder [wʌn'də:r] n (miracle) 不思議 fushígi; (feeling) 驚異 kyōi

◆vi: **to wonder whether/why** ...かしら (なぜ...かしら)と思う ...ka shira (nazè ...ka shira)to omōu

to wonder at (marvel at) ...に驚く ...ni odórokù

to wonder about ...の事を考える ...no kotó wò kangáeru

it's no wonder (that) ... (という事) は不思議ではない ... (to iú koto) wà fushígi de wà naì

wonderful [wʌn'də:rfəl] adj (excellent) 素晴らしい subárashiì; (miraculous) 不思議な fushígi na

wonderfully [wʌn'də:rfəli:] adv (excellently) 素晴らしく subárashikù; (miraculously) 不思議に fushígi ni

won't [wount] = **will not**

woo [wu:] vt (woman) ...に言い寄る ...ni iyóru; (audience etc) ...に取入る ...ni tofbfrù

wood [wud] n (timber) 木材 mokúzài, 木き; (forest) 森 morí, 林 hayáshi, 木立 kodáchi

wood carving n (act, object) 木彫 kibóri

wooded [wud'id] adj (slopes, area) 木の茂った kí nò shigéttà

wooden [wud'ən] adj (object) 木でできた kí de dekìta, 木製の mokúsei no; (house) 木造の mokúzō no; (fig: performance, actor) でくの坊の様な dekúnobō no yō nà

woodpecker [wud'pekə:r] n キツツキ kítsutsukì

woodwind [wud'wind] npl (MUS) 木管楽器 mokkángakkì

woodwork [wud'wə:rk] n (skill) 木material工芸 mokúzaikōgèi

woodworm [wud'wə:rm] n キクイムシ kikúimùshi

wool [wul] n (material, yarn) 毛糸 kefto, ウール ūrù

to pull the wool over someone's eyes (fig) ...をだます ...wo damásù

woolen [wul'ən] (BRIT **woollen**) adj (socks, hat etc) 毛糸の kefto no, ウールの ūrù no

the woolen industry 羊毛加工業界 yōmōkakògyōkài

woolens [wul'ənz] npl 毛糸衣類 keftoirùi

wooly [wul'i:] (BRIT **woolly**) adj (socks, hat etc) 毛糸の kefto no, ウールの ūrù no; (fig: ideas) 取留めのない toritome no nai; (person) 考え方のはっきりしない kañgaekatà no hakkírì shinai

word [wə:rd] n (unit of language: written, spoken) 語 go, 単語 tángo, 言葉 kotòba; (promise) 約束 yakúsoku; (news) 知らせ shiráse, ニュース nyūsu

◆vt (letter, message) ...の言回しを選ぶ ...no iímawashi wo erábù

in other words 言替えると ifkaerù to

to break/keep one's word 約束を破る (守る) yakúsoku wo yabúrù(mamórù)

to have words with someone ...と口げんかをする ...to kuchígeñka wo suru

wording [wə:r'diŋ] n (of message, contract etc) 言回し iímawashi

word processing n ワードプロセシング wādopurosèshìngu

word processor [-pra'sesə:r] n ワープロ wāpuro

wore [wə:r] pt of **wear**

work [wə:rk] n (gen) 仕事 shigóto; (job) 職,職業 shokúgyō; (ART, LITERATURE) 作品 sakúhin

◆vi (person: labor) 働く határakù; (mechanism) 動く ugókù; (be successful: medicine etc) 効く kikú

◆vt (clay, wood etc) 加工する kakō suru; (land) 耕す tagáyasù; (mine) 採掘する sakútsu suru; (machine) 動かす ugókasù; (cause: effect) もたらす motárasù; (: miracle) 行う okónau *to be out of work* 失業中である shitsū-gyōchū de arū

to work loose (part) 緩む yurúmù; (knot) 解ける tokérū

workable [wəːrkəbəl] *adj* (solution) 実行可能な jikkókanō na

workaholic [wəːrkəhɔ́ːlʼik] *n* 仕事中毒の人 shigótochūdòku no hito, ワーカホリック wākahorìkku

worker [wəːrkər] *n* 労働者 rōdōsha

workforce [wəːkfɔːrs] *n* 労働人口 rōdō-jinkō

working class [wəːrkiŋ-] *n* 労働者階級 rōdōshakaìkyū

working-class [wəːrkiŋklæs] *adj* 労働者階級の rōdōshakaìkyū no

working order *n*: *in working order* ちゃんと動く状態で chanto ugokù jōtai de

workman [wəːrkmən] (*pl* **workmen**) *n* 作業員 sagyōìn

workmanship [wəːrkmənʃip] *n* (skill) 腕前 udémae

work on *vt fus* (task) ...に取組む ...ni torìkumu; (person: influence) 説得する set-tóku suru; (principle) ...に基づく ...ni motózukù

work out *vi* (plans etc) うまくいく umáku iku

♦*vt* (problem) 解決する kaíketsu suru; (plan) 作る tsukúrù

it works out at $100 100ドルになる hyakúdorn ni narù

works [wəːrks] *n* (*BRIT*: factory) 工場 kōjō

♦*npl* (of clock, machine) 機構 kikō

worksheet [wəːrkʃiːt] *n* ワークシート wākushìtò

workshop [wəːrkʃap] *n* (at home, in factory) 作業場 sagyōjò; (practical session) ワークショップ wākushoppò

work station *n* ワークステーション wākusutēshòn

work-to-rule [wəːrktəruːl] (*BRIT*) *n* 順法闘争 junpótosō

work up *vt*: *to get worked up* 怒る okórù

world [wəːrld] *n* 世界 sekái

♦*cpd* (champion) 世界... sekái...; (power, war) 国際の... kokúsaiteki..., 国際... ko-kúsai...

to think the world of someone (*fig*: admire) ...を高く評価する ...wo takáku hyōka suru; (: love) ...が大好きである ...ga daísuki de arù

worldly [wəːrldliː] *adj* (not spiritual) 世俗的な sezókuteki na; (knowledgeable) 世才にたけた sesái ni takéta

worldwide [wəːrldwaid] *adj* 世界的な sekáiteki na

worm [wəːrm] *n* (*also*: **earthworm**) ミミズ mimízu

worn [wəːrn] *pp* of **wear**

♦*adj* (carpet) 使い古した tsukáifurushì-tà; (shoe) 履き古した hakífurushità

worn-out [wəːrnʼaut] *adj* (object) 使い古した tsukáifurushità; (person) へとへとに疲れた hetóheto ni tsukáreta

worried [wəːriːd] *adj* (anxious) 心配している shifńpai shite irù

worry [wəːriː] *n* (anxiety) 心配 shífnpai

♦*vt* (person) 心配させる shifńpai saserù

♦*vi* (person) 心配する shifńpai surù

worrying [wəːriiŋ] *adj* 心配な shífnpai na

worse [wəːrs] *adj* 更に悪い sarà ni warúi

♦*adv* 更に悪く sarà ni warúku

♦*n* 更に悪い事 sarà ni warúi koto

a change for the worse 悪化 akká

worsen [wəːrsən] *vt* 悪くする warúku suru

♦*vi* 悪くなる warúku naru

worse off *adj* (financially) 収入が減った shúnyū ga hettá; (*fig*): *you'll be worse off this way* そんな事は得策ではない sofina koto wa tokúsaku de wa naì

worship [wəːrʃip] *n* (act) 礼拝 reíhai

♦*vt* (god) 礼拝する reíhai suru; (person, thing) 崇拝する súhái suru

Your Worship (*BRIT*: to mayor, judge) 閣下 kakká

worst [wəːrst] *adj* 最悪の safáku no

♦*adv* 最もひどく mottómo hídòku

♦*n* 最悪 safáku

at worst 最悪の場合 safáku no baái

worth [wəːrθ] *n* (value) 価値 kachí

◆*adj*: **to be worth $100** 価格は100ドルである kakaku wa hyakūdoru de arū

it's worth it やる価値がある yarú kachī ga aru

to be worth one's while (to do) (...する事は) ...のためになる (...surú koto wa) ...no tamé ni naru

worthless [wərˈlis] *adj* (person, thing) 価値のない kachī no nai

worthwhile [wərθˈwaiˈ] *adj* (activity, cause) ためになる tamé ni naru

worthy [wərˈðiː] *adj* (person) 尊敬すべき soñkeisubeki; (motive) 良い yoí

worthy of ...にふさわしい ...ni fusawashíi

KEYWORD

would [wud] *aux vb* **1** (conditional tense): **if you asked him he would** 彼にお願いすればやってくれるでしょう kárè ni o-négai surèba yatté kureru deshō

if you had asked him he would have done it 彼に頼めばやってくれた事でしょう kárè ni tanómèba yatté kurètá kotó deshō

2 (in offers, invitations, requests): **would you like a biscuit?** ビスケットはいかがですか bisúkettò wa ikága desu ká

would you ask him to come in? 彼に入ってもらって下さい kárè ni háittè morátte kudasai

would you open the window please? 窓を開けてくれませんか mádò wo akéte kuremasù ká

3 (in indirect speech): **I said I would do it** 私はやってあげると約束しました watákushi wà agerú to yakúsoku shimashita

he asked me if I would go with him 一緒に行ってくれと彼に頼まれました isshó nǐ itté kurè ni kárè ni tanómaremareshìta

4 (emphatic): **it WOULD have to snow today!** 今日に限って雪が降るなんてなあ kyō nǐ kagíttè yukí gà fúrù nâñte nǎ

you WOULD say that, wouldn't you! あんたの言いそうな事だ áñta no ifsò na kotó dà

5 (insistence): **she wouldn't behave** あの子はどうしても言う事を聞いてくれない anó kò wa dō shite mò iú kotó wo kíkte kurenaí

6 (conjecture): **it would have been midnight** だとすれば夜中の12時という事になります dà tò surèbà yonáka nò júniji to iú kotó ni narímasù

it would seem so そうらしい sō rashíi né

7 (indicating habit): **he would go there on Mondays** 彼は毎週月曜にそこへ行く事にしていました kárè wa maíshū getsúyòbi ni sokó è ikú kotó ni shité imashìta

he would spend every day on the beach 彼は毎日浜でごろごろしていました kárè wa máinichi hamá dè górògoro shite imáshìta

---

would-be [wudˈbiː] *(pej) adj* ...志望の ...shibō no

wouldn't [wudˈənt] = **would not**

wound[1] [waund] *pt, pp of* **wind**

wound[2] [wuːnd] *n* 傷 kizú

◆*vt* ...に傷を負わせる ...ni kizú wo owáseru, 負傷させる fushō saserú

wove [wouv] *pt of* **weave**

woven [wouˈvən] *pp of* **weave**

wrangle [rӕŋˈgəl] *n* 口論 kóròn

wrap [rӕp] *n* (stole) 肩掛 katakake, ストール sutōrù; (cape) マント mañto, ケープ kēpū

◆*vt* (cover) 包む tsutsúmù; (pack: *also*: **wrap up**) こん包する koñpō suru; (wind: tape etc) 巻付ける makítsukerū

wrapper [rӕpˈəːr] *n* (on chocolate) 包み tsutsúmi; (*BRIT*: of book) カバー kabā

wrapping paper [rӕpˈiŋ-] *n* (brown) クラフト紙 kuráfùtoshi; (fancy) 包み紙 tsutsúmigami

wrath [rӕθ] *n* 怒り ikári

wreak [riːk] *vt* (havoc) もたらす motárasù

to wreak vengeance on ... に復しゅうす

る ...ni fukūshū suru

wreath [ri:θ] *n* (funeral wreath) 花輪 hanáwa

wreck [rek] *n* (vehicle) 残がい zañgai; (ship) 難破船 nañpasen; (*pej*: person) 変り果てた人 kawárihatetá hitó
♦*vt* (car etc) めちゃめちゃに壊す mechámecha ni kowásù; (*fig*: chances) 台無しにする dafnashi ni surú

wreckage [rek'idʒ] *n* (of car, plane, ship, building) 残がい zañgai

wren [ren] *n* (ZOOL) ミソサザイ misósazai

wrench [rentʃ] *n* (TECH: adjustable) スパナ supánà; (: fixed size) レンチ reñchi; (tug) ひねり hinéri; (*fig*) 心痛 shíñtsū
♦*vt* (twist) ひねる hinéru

to wrench something from someone ...から...をねじり取る ...kara ...wo nejíritorù

wrestle [res'əl] *vi*: *to wrestle (with someone)* (fight) (...と) 格闘する (...to) kakútō suru; (for sport) (...と) レスリングする (...to) resúriňgu suru

to wrestle with (*fig*) ...と取組む ...to toríkumu, ...と戦う ...to tatákau

wrestler [res'lər] *n* レスラー resúrā

wrestling [res'liŋ] *n* レスリング resúriňgu

wretched [retʃ'id] *adj* (poor, unhappy) 不幸な fukó na; (*inf*: very bad) どうしようもない dó shiyó mo naí

wriggle [rig'əl] *n* (*also*: **wriggle about**: person, fish, snake etc) うねうねする unéune suru

wring [riŋ] (*pt, pp* **wrung**) *vt* (wet clothes) 絞る shibóru; (hands) もむ momú; (bird's neck) ひねる hinéru; (*fig*): *to wring something out of someone* ...を吐かせる ...ni ...wo hákaserù

wrinkle [riŋ'kəl] *n* (on skin, paper etc) しわ shiwá
♦*vt* (nose, forehead etc) ...にしわを寄せる ...ni shiwá wo yoséru
♦*vi* (skin, paint etc) しわになる shiwá ni naru

wrist [rist] *n* 手首 tekúbi

wristwatch [rist'wɑ:tʃ] *n* 腕時計 udédokéi

writ [rit] *n* 令状 reijó

write [rait] (*pt* **wrote**, *pp* **written**) *vt* 書く kakú
♦*vi* 書く kakú

to write to someone ...に手紙を書く ...ni tegámi wo kakú

write down *vt* 書く kakú, 書留める ka-kftomeru

write off *vt* (debt) 帳消しにする chốkeshi ni suru; (plan, project) 取りやめる to-ríyameru

write-off [rait'ɔ:f] *n* 修理不可能な物 shurífukánō na monó

writer [rait'ə:r] *n* (author) 著者 chóshà; (professional) 作家 sakká; (person who writes) 書く人 kakú hitó

write up *vt* (report, minutes etc) 詳しく書く kuwáshikù kakú

writhe [raið] *vi* 身をもだえする mimódae suru

writing [rait'iŋ] *n* (words written) 文字 mojī, 文章 buñshō; (handwriting) 筆跡 hisséki; (of author) 作品 sakúhin, 作風 sakúfū; (activity) 書物 kakîmono

in writing 書面で shomén de

writing paper *n* 便せん bíñsen

written [rit'ən] *pp of* **write**

wrong [rɔ:ŋ] *adj* (bad) 良くない yokúnai; (incorrect: number, adds ess etc) 間違った machígatta; (not suitable) 不適当な futékitō na; (reverse: side of material) 裏側の urágawa no; (unfair) 不正な fuséi na
♦*adv* 間違って machígatte, 誤って ayámatte
♦*n* (injustice) 不正 fuséi
♦*vt* (treat unfairly) ...に悪い事をする ...ni warúi koto wo suru

you are wrong to do it それは不正な事です sore wa fuséi na koto desù

you are wrong about that, you've got it wrong それは違います soré wa chigáimasù

to be in the wrong 間違っている machígatté iru

what's wrong? どうしましたか dó shimáshita ká

to go wrong (person) 間違う machígaù; (plan) 失敗する shippái suru; (machine) 狂う kurúù

wrongful [rɔːŋ'fəl] *adj* (imprisonment, dismissal) 不当な futō na

wrongly [rɔːŋ'li:] *adv* 間違って machígattè

wrote [rəut] *pt of* **write**

wrought [rɔːt] *adj*: **wrought iron** 錬鉄 refítetsu

wrung [rʌŋ] *pt, pp of* **wring**

wry [rai] *adj* (smile, humor, expression) 皮肉っぽい hiníkuppoì

wt. *abbr* = **weight**

X

Xmas [eks'mis] *n abbr* = **Christmas**

X-ray [eks'rei] *n* (ray) エックス線 ekkúsusen; (photo) レントゲン写真 refítogeñshashin

◆*vt* ...のレントゲンを撮る ...no refítogeñ wo toru

xylophone [zai'ləfoun] *n* 木琴 mokkín

Y

yacht [jɑːt] *n* ヨット yottò

yachting [jɑːt'iŋ] *n* ヨット遊び yottóasobi

yachtsman [jɑːts'mən] (*pl* **yachtsmen**) *n* ヨット乗り yottónori

Yank [jæŋk] (*pej*) *n* ヤンキー yañkī

Yankee [jæŋ'ki:] (*pej*) *n* = **Yank**

yap [jæp] *vi* (dog) きゃんきゃんほえる kyañkyan hoèrù

yard [jɑːrd] *n* (of house etc) 庭 niwà; (measure) ヤード yádò

yardstick [jɑːrd'stik] *n* (*fig*) 尺度 shakúdò

yarn [jɑːrn] *n* (thread) 毛糸 keftò; (tale) ほら話 horábanashi

yawn [jɔːn] *n* あくび akúbi

◆*vi* あくびする akúbi suru

yawning [jɔːn'iŋ] *adj* (gap) 大きな ōkína

yd. *abbr* = **yard(s)**

yeah [je] (*inf*) *adv* はい haì

year [jiːr] *n* 年 neñ, toshí, 1年 ichíneñ

to be 8 years old 8才である hassái de aru

an eight-year-old child 8才の子供 hassái no kodőmo

◆*adv* 毎年 maínen, maftoshi

yearly [jiːr'li:] *adj* 毎年の maínen no, maftoshi no

◆*adv* 毎年 maínen, maftoshi

yearn [jərn] *vi*: **to yearn for something** ...を切に望む ...wo setsū ni nozőmu

to yearn to do ...をしたいと切に望む ...wo shitái to setsū ni nozőmu

yeast [jiːst] *n* 酵母 kőbò, イースト ísùto

yell [jel] *n* 叫び sakébi

◆*vi* 叫ぶ sakébù

yellow [jel'ou] *adj* 黄色い kiíroi

yelp [jelp] *n* (of animal) キャンと鳴く声 kyañ to nakú kové; (of person) 悲鳴 himéi

◆*vi* (animal) きゃんと鳴く kyañ to nakù; (person) 悲鳴を上げる himéi wò agérù

yeoman [jou'mən] (*pl* **yeomen**) *n*: **yeoman of the guard** 国王の親衛隊員 kokūō no shíñ-eitaiìñ

yes [jes] *adv* はい haì

◆*n* はいという返事 haì to iú heñji

to say/answer yes 承諾する shődaku suru

yesterday [jes'tərdei] *adv* 昨日 kinő, sakújìtsu

◆*n* 昨日 kinő, sakújìtsu

yesterday morning/evening 昨日の朝〔夕方〕kinő no asà〔yūgata〕

all day yesterday 昨日一日 kinő ichínichi

yet [jet] *adv* まだ madà; (already) もう mő

◆*conj* しかし ga shikàshì

it is not finished yet まだできていない madà dekíte inái

the best yet これまでの物で最も良い物 koré madè no mono dè mottőmo yoî mono

as yet まだ madà

yew [juː] *n* (tree) イチイ ichíi

Yiddish [jid'iʃ] *n* イディッシュ語 idisshugo

yield [jiːld] *n* (AGR) 収穫 shūkaku; (COMM) 収益 shūeki
♦*vt* (surrender: control, responsibility) 譲る yuzúru; (produce: results, profit) もたらす motárasu
♦*vi* (surrender) 譲る yuzúru; (US: AUT) 道を譲る michí wo yuzúru

YMCA [waieimsiːeɪ] *n abbr* (= *Young Men's Christian Association*) キリスト教青年会 kirísutokyósefnenkai, ワイエムシーエー wafemushíē

yog(h)ourt [jouˈgəːrt] *n* = **yog(h)ourt**

yog(h)urt [jouˈgəːrt] *n* ヨーグルト yōgúrùto

yoke [jouk] *n* (of oxen) くびき kubíki; (fig) 重荷 omóni

yolk [jouk] *n* 卵黄 rañ-ō, 黄身 kimí

KEYWORD

you [juː] *pron* **1** (subj: *sing*) あなたは[が] anáta wa[ga]; (: *pl*) あなたは[が] anátatáchi wa [ga]

you are very kind あなたはとても親切ですね anáta wa totémo shíñsetsu desu ne, ご親切に有難うございます go-shíñsetsu ni arígatō gozáimasu

you Japanese enjoy your food あなたち日本人は食べるのが好きですね anátatáchi nihóñjin wa tabéru no ga sukí desú ne

you and I will go あなたと私が行く事になっています anáta to watákushi ga ikú kotò ni natté imasu

2 (obj: direct, indirect: *sing*) あなたを[に] anáta wo[ni]; (: *pl*) あなたたちを[に] anátatáchi wo[ni]

I know you 私はあなたを知っています watákushi wa anáta wo shitté imasu

I gave it to you 私はそれをあなたに差し上げました watákushi wà soré wò anáta ni watáshimashita

3 (stressed): *I told YOU to do it* というのはあなたに言ったんですよと言ったのよ tò íд no wà anáta ni ittáñ desu yó

4 (after prep, in comparisons)

it's for you あなたのためです anáta no tamé desu

can I come with you? 一緒に行っていいですか isshō nǐ itté fi desu ka

she's younger than you 彼女はあなたより若いです kánòjo ga anáta yori wakái desu

5 (impersonal: one)

fresh air does you good 新鮮な空気は健康にいい shíñsen nà kūkì wa keñkō ni fi

you never know どうなるか分かりませんよ dō narù ka wakárimaseñ né

you can't do that! それはいけません soré wà ikémaseñ

---

you'd [juːd] = **you had; you would**

you'll [juːl] = **you will; you shall**

young [jʌŋ] *adj* (person, animal, plant) 若い wakái
♦*npl* (of animal) 子 ko; (people): *the young* 若者 wakámono

younger [jʌŋˈgəːr] *adj* (brother etc) 年下の toshíshita no

youngster [jʌŋˈstəːr] *n* 子供 kodómo

your [juːr] *adj* (singular) あなたの anáta no; (plural) あなたたちの anátatáchi no
¶ *see also* **may**

you're [juːr] = **you are**

yours [juːrz] *pron* (singular) あなたの物 anáta no mono; (plural) あなたたちの物 anátatáchi no mono ¶ *see also* **mine**; **faithfully**; **sincerely**

yourself [juːrself] *pron* あなた自身 anáta jishín ¶ *see also* **oneself**

yourselves [juːrselvz] *pl pron* あなたたち自身 anátatáchi jishín ¶ *see also* **oneself**

youth [juːθ] *n* (young days) 若い時分 wakái jibun; (young man: *pl* youths) 少年 shōnen

youth club *n* 青少年クラブ sefshōnen kurábu

youthful [juːˈfʃəl] *adj* (person) 若い wakái; (looks) 若々しい wakáwakashíi; (air, enthusiasm) 若者独特の wakámonodokútoku no

youth hostel *n* ユースホステル yūsúhosúteru

Youth Training (BRIT) *n* 職業訓練 shokúgyōkunreǹ ◇失業青少年のためのもの shitsǘgyōseishōnen no tamé no monǒ

you've [ju:v] = **you have**

Yugoslav [ju:'gousla:v] *adj* ユーゴスラビアの yūgosurabia no
♦*n* ユーゴスラビア人 yūgosurabiajin

Yugoslavia [ju:'gousla:'vi:ə] *n* ユーゴスラビア yūgosurabia

yuppie [jʌp'i:] (*inf*) *n* ヤッピー yappì
♦*adj* ヤッピーの yappì no

YWCA [waidabàlju:si:ei'] *n abbr* (= *Young Women's Christian Association*) キリスト教女子青年会 kirísutokyōjoshìseǐnenkai, ワイダブリューシーエー waidaburyūshìē

Z

Zambia [zæm'bi:ə] *n* ザンビア zaǹbia

zany [zei'ni:] *adj* (ideas, sense of humor) ばかげた bakágeta

zap [zæp] *vt* (COMPUT: delete) 削除する sakújo suru

zeal [zi:l] *n* (enthusiasm) 熱情 netsǔjō; (*also: religious zeal*) 狂信 kyōshìn

zealous [zel'əs] *adj* 熱狂的な nekkyōteki na

zebra [zi:'brə] *n* シマウマ shimáuma

zebra crossing (BRIT) *n* 横断歩道 ōdánhodō

zenith [zi:'niθ] *n* 頂点 chōten

zero [zi:'rou] *n* 零点 reǐten, ゼロ zèrò

zest [zest] *n* (for life) 意気 netsǔi; (of orange) 皮 kawá

zigzag [zig'zæg] *n* ジグザグ jigǔzagu
♦*vi* ジグザグに動く jigǔzagu ni ugókù

Zimbabwe [zimba:'bwei] *n* ジンバブウェ jinbabǔwe

zinc [ziŋk] *n* 亜鉛 aèn

zip [zip] *n* (*also: zip fastener*) = **zipper**
♦*vt* (*also: zip up*) = **zipper**

zip code (US) *n* 郵便番号 yūbinbaǹgō

zipper [zip'ə:r] (US) *n* チャック chakkǔ, ジッパー jippà, ファスナー fasǔnā
♦*vt* (*also: zipper up*) ...のチャックを締める ...no chakkǔ wo shimérù

zodiac [zou'di:æk] *n* 十二宮図 jūnfkyūzu

zombie [za:m'bi:] *n* (*fig*): *like a zombie* ロボットの様に(な) robóttò no yō ni (na)

zone [zoun] *n* (area, *also* MIL) 地帯 chítai

zoo [zu:] *n* 動物園 dóbutsùen

zoologist [zoua:l'ədʒist] *n* 動物学者 dóbutsugakùsha

zoology [zoua:l'ədʒi:] *n* 動物学 dóbutsugàku

zoom [zu:m] *vi*: *to zoom past* 猛スピードで通り過ぎる mōsupìdo de tōrísugirù

zoom lens *n* ズームレンズ zūmureǹzu

zucchini [zu:ki:'ni:] (US) *n inv* ズッキーニ zukkìnì